LE NORD AND PICARDY
Pages 192–205

CHAMPAGNE
Pages 206–217

ALSACE AND LORRAINE
Pages 218–233

Reims

NORTHEAST FRANCE

Stras...

Troyes

Dijon

RAL FRANCE
THE ALPS

Lyon

Grenoble

THE SOUTH OF FRANCE

THE MASSIF CENTRAL
Pages 352–371

BURGUNDY AND FRANCHE-COMTÉ
Pages 326–351

THE RHÔNE VALLEY AND FRENCH ALPS
Pages 372–391

LANGUEDOC-ROUSSILLON
Pages 476–497

PROVENCE AND THE CÔTE D'AZUR
Pages 498–531

Ajaccio

CORSICA
Pages 532–543

EYEWITNESS TRAVEL
FRANCE

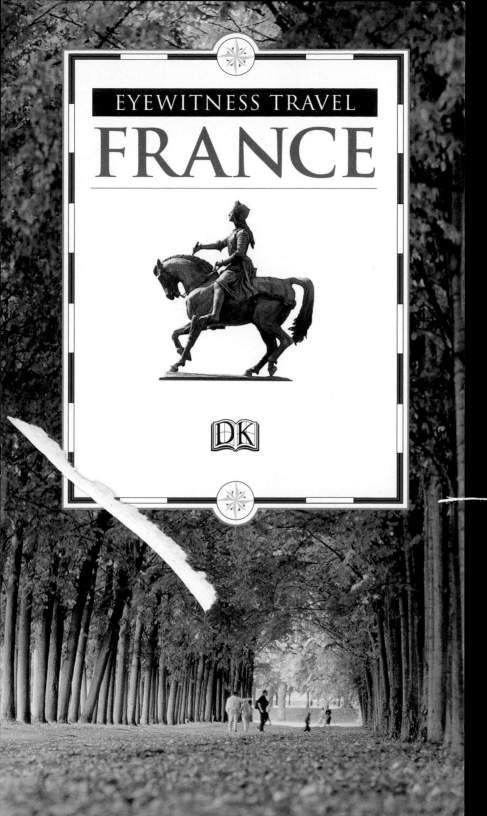

EYEWITNESS TRAVEL
FRANCE

DK

LONDON, NEW YORK,
MELBOURNE, MUNICH AND DELHI
www.dk.com

PROJECT EDITOR Rosemary Bailey
ART EDITOR Janis Utton
EDITORS Tanya Colbourne, Fiona Morgan,
Anna Streiffert, Celia Woolfrey
DESIGNERS Joy FitzSimmons, Erika Lang, Clare Sullivan
MAP CO-ORDINATORS Simon Farbrother, David Pugh
RESEARCHER Philippa Richmond

MAIN CONTRIBUTORS
John Ardagh, Rosemary Bailey, Judith Fayard, Lisa Gerard-Sharp, Colin
Jones, Alister Kershaw, Alec Lobrano, Anthony Roberts, Alan Tillier,
Nigel Tisdall

PHOTOGRAPHERS
Max Alexander, Neil Lukas, John Parker, Kim Sayer

ILLUSTRATORS
Stephen Conlin, John Lawrence, Maltings Partnership,
John Woodcock

Reproduced by Colourscan (Singapore)
Printed and bound by South China Printing Co. Ltd., China

First published in Great Britain in 1994
by Dorling Kindersley Limited
80 Strand, London WC2R 0RL

12 13 14 15 10 9 8 7 6 5 4 3 2

Reprinted with revisions 1994, 1995, 1996, 1997, 1998, 1999,
2000, 2001, 2002, 2003, 2004, 2005, 2006, 2007, 2008, 2009, 2010, 2012

Copyright 1994, 2012 © Dorling Kindersley Limited, London
A Penguin Company

A CIP CATALOGUE RECORD IS AVAILABLE FROM THE BRITISH LIBRARY.

ISBN: 978 1 4053 6868 1

FLOORS ARE REFERRED TO THROUGHOUT IN ACCORDANCE WITH FRENCH
USAGE; IE THE "FIRST FLOOR" IS THE FLOOR ABOVE GROUND LEVEL.

Front cover main image: Mont-St-Michel, Normandy

MIX
Paper from
responsible sources
FSC™ C018179
www.fsc.org

**The information in this DK Eyewitness
Travel Guide is checked regularly.**
Even though every effort has been made to ensure that this book is
as up-to-date as possible at the time of going to press. Some details,
however, such as telephone numbers, opening hours, prices, gallery
hanging arrangements and travel information are liable to change.
The publishers cannot accept responsibility for any consequences
arising from the use of this book, nor for any material on third-party
websites, and cannot guarantee that any website address in this book
will be a suitable source of travel information. We value the views
and suggestions of our readers very highly. Please write to: Publisher,
DK Eyewitness Travel Guides, Dorling Kindersley, 80 Strand, London
WC2R 0RL, Great Britain, or email: travelguides@dk.com.

◁ **Avenue of poplar trees, Parc de Marly, western outskirts of Paris**

CONTENTS

Bust of Charlemagne

INTRODUCING
FRANCE

PARIS AND ILE DE
FRANCE

The fishing village of St-Jean-de-Luz in the Pyrenees

Grape harvest in Alsace

Palais des Papes, Avignon

HOW TO USE THIS GUIDE

This guide helps you to get the most from your visit to France. It provides both expert recommendations and detailed practical information. *Introducing France* maps the country and sets it in its historical and cultural context. The 15 regional chapters, plus *Paris and Ile de France*, describe important sights, with maps, pictures and illustrations. Throughout, features cover topics from food and wine to culture and beaches. Restaurant and hotel recommendations can be found in *Travellers' Needs*. The *Survival Guide* has tips on everything from the French telephone system to transport.

PARIS AND ILE DE FRANCE

The centre of Paris has been divided into five sightseeing areas. Each has its own chapter, which opens with a list of the sights described. A further section covers Ile de France. All sights are numbered and plotted on an area map. The detailed information for each sight follows the map's numerical order, making sights easy to locate within the chapter.

Sights at a Glance lists the chapter's sights by category: Churches, Museums and Galleries; Historic Buildings, Squares and Gardens.

All pages relating to Paris and Ile de France have green thumb tabs.

A locator map shows where you are in relation to other areas of the city centre.

1 Area Map
For easy reference, the sights are numbered and located on a map. Sights in the city centre are also shown on the Paris Street Finder *on pages 156–69.*

2 Street-by-Street Map
This gives a bird's eye view of the key areas in each chapter.

A suggested route for a walk is shown in red.

Stars indicate the sights that no visitor should miss.

3 Detailed information
The sights in Paris and Ile de France are described individually. Addresses, telephone numbers, opening hours and information on admission charges and wheelchair access are also provided for each entry.

1 Introduction

The landscape, history and character of each region is described here, showing how the area has developed over the centuries and what it offers to the visitor today.

FRANCE AREA BY AREA

Apart from Paris and Ile de France, France has been divided into 15 regions, each of which has a separate chapter. The most interesting towns and places to visit have been numbered on a *Regional Map*.

Each area of France can be quickly identified by its colour coding, shown on the inside front cover.

2 Regional Map

This shows the road network and gives an illustrated overview of the whole region. All interesting places to visit are numbered and there are also useful tips on getting around the region by car and train.

3 Detailed information

All the important towns and other places to visit are described individually. They are listed in order, following the numbering on the Regional Map. Within each town or city, there is detailed information on important buildings and other sights.

Story boxes highlight noteworthy features of the top sights.

For all the top sights, a Visitor's Checklist provides the practical information you will need to plan your visit.

4 France's top sights

These are given two or more full pages. Historic buildings are dissected to reveal their interiors. The most interesting towns or city centres are shown in a bird's eye view, with sights picked out and described.

INTRODUCING FRANCE

DISCOVERING FRANCE

The chapters of this book have been divided into 16 colour-coded regions that reflect the diversity of France. These are based on the country's historical regions that were often defined by their geography and landscape as much as by

Gothic detail from Le Nord region

their influence and power.

Each has developed its own special flavour: its own architecture, cuisine, customs, music, dress, dialect and even language. The following pages give a taste of these areas and show you what there is to see and do.

Pyramide du Louvre in Paris, from across the fountain pools

PARIS AND THE ILE DE FRANCE

- **Fantastic art at the Louvre**
- **Café life *par excellence***
- **Captivating Versailles**

The pleasures of Paris can be picked off at leisure any time of the year. The **Louvre** *(see pp100–3)*, **Picasso Museum** *(see pp90–1)*, and **Pompidou Centre** *(see pp92–3)* may be on some people's ideal itinerary, while others may want to scale the **Eiffel Tower** *(see p113)* and shop

Les Deux Magots, one of Paris's most famous cafés

in the *grands boulevards*, or follow in the steps of the famous from **Montmartre** *(see pp132–3)* to the **Père Lachaise Cemetery** *(see p135)*. Whatever your fancy, there are cafés and brasseries to soak up the atmosphere, particularly on the **Left Bank** *(see pp116–127)* and in the **Marais** *(see pp80–93)*. For a day excursion, there are plenty of châteaux to visit, none more exalted than Louis XIV's fabulous palace at **Versailles** *(see pp168–71)*.

LE NORD AND PICARDY

- **Bustling Channel ports**
- **Lofty Gothic cathedrals**
- **Lille art collection**

The countryside north of Paris undulates towards Flanders and to the cliffs and sandy beaches around the Channel ports of **Dunkerque** *(see p197)*, **Calais** *(see pp196–7)* and **Boulogne-sur-**

Mer *(see p196)*. You can try your luck at the races, at **Chantilly** *(see pp204–5)* and **Le Touquet** *(see p196)*, or go to the lakes and woodland of the **Valley of the Somme** *(see p199)*, a name synonymous with the fatal trench warfare of World War I. High spots are the great Gothic cathedrals, such as **Amiens** *(see p200)*, the largest in France, and the city of **Lille** *(see p198)*, which has one of the best art galleries in the country.

CHAMPAGNE

- **Sparkling Champagne houses**
- **Royal Reims**
- **Gothic churches in Troyes**

Heidsieck Champagne label

Champagne means only one thing: fizzy white wine. Visit the producers' chalk caves in **Épernay** *(see p211)* and the premises of the *grandes marques* in **Reims** *(see pp210–1)*, where you will also find a great slice of French history in **Reims Cathedral** *(see p212)*. **Troyes** *(see pp216–7)*, the region's former capital, is a delightful town of many Gothic churches, while the castle keep at **Chaumont** *(see p217)* has echoes of its former residents, the Counts of Champagne. On the wild side is the **Vallée de la Meuse** *(see p214)* in the rocky Ardennes, while the region around **Lac du Der-Chantecog** *(see p215)* is known for its half-timbered churches.

ALSACE AND LORRAINE

• Alsace Wine Route
• Picturesque half-
 timbered towns
• Strasbourg, crossroads of
 Europe

Abutting Germany and
Switzerland, this is a
delightful, gentle rural area of
vineyards and orchards, and
pretty, half-timbered villages
and towns such as **Colmar**
(see p227), best seen along
the 180-km (110-mile) **Route
du Vin** *(see pp232–3)*. The
Vosges mountains *(see p225)*
attract skiers, and nearby is
the **Gérardmer lake** *(see
p225)* for summer water
sports. The region is full of
forts and castles, including
the romantic **Château du
Haut-Koenigsbourg** *(see
pp228–9)*. The main town is
Strasbourg *(see pp230–31)*.

Normandy's Mont-St-Michel, one of the most enchanting sights in France

The old town of Strasbourg, best
explored on its pretty waterways

NORMANDY

• D-Day beaches
• Cider and Calvados
• Magnificent Mont-St-
 Michel

Visit Claude Monet's garden
at **Giverny** *(see p266)* and see
the lily pond and bridge just
as he painted them.
Normandy's blustery skies
and billowing seas inspired
the Impressionists who
visited **Dieppe** *(see p263)*, **Le
Havre** *(see p262)* and pretty
Honfleur *(see p262)*, while
tout Paris used to decamp to

the resorts of **Cabourg** *(see
p255)*, **Deauville** *(see p255)*
and **Trouville** *(see p255)*.
Their beaches are known for
the World War II D-Day
landings. Normandy's
farmlands are renowned for
their cider, Calvados, butter
and cheese. Don't miss the
Abbaye de Mont-St-Michel
(see pp256–61) or **Rouen
Cathedral** *(see pp264–5)*.

BRITTANY

• Sandy beaches
• Mysterious Carnac
• Delightful fishing ports

In the far northwest, this
Celtic corner of France is a
land with a language and
culture of its own. Buffeted
by the Atlantic, its rocky
shores and sandy beaches,
peppered with picturesque
fishing ports, make it a
prime spot for family beach
vacations. Prehistory sighs in
the wind here, and
megalithic sites abound,
especially in the mysterious
rock formations at **Carnac**
(see p278).
 To steep yourself in Breton
culture, visit **Quimper** *(see
p274)*, eat crêpes, drink cider
and try to attend a *pardon*, a
feast of a local saint, when
traditional costumes are worn.
They take place between
March and October. Find out
about them at the **Musée de
Bretagne** *(see p285)* in the
region's capital, Rennes.

THE LOIRE VALLEY

• Fairytale Renaissance châ-
 teaux
• Chartres Cathedral
• Le Mans, motor racing

The fabulous châteaux of the
Loire capture all the elegance
and culture of France. Here
the French nobles lived out
the Renaissance in style.
Wines have made towns such
as **Saumur** *(see p292)* famous.
Historic centres include **Tours**
(see pp296–7) and **Chartres**
(see pp307–311), which has
stunning stained glass in its
magnificent cathedral windows, and **Orléans** *(see
pp312–3)*, saved from the
English by Joan of Arc, who
is celebrated in a 10-day
festival leading up to the
anniversary of the city's
liberation on 8 May. To the
north is **Le Mans** *(see p291)*,
another lovely old town, best
known for its motor racing
circuit. The 24-hour race is
held in June.

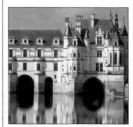

Château de Chenonceau in the
Loire Valley, across the River Cher

Côte de Nuits vineyard in Burgundy, part of the Côte d'Or region

BURGUNDY AND FRANCHE-COMTE

- Gastronomic paradise
- Impressive abbeys
- Fine trekking and skiing

Burgundy is corpulent France, conjuring up *boeuf bourguignon* and delicious wines that are among the most expensive in the world. The Dukes of Burgundy's legacy is splendid **Dijon** *(see pp340–2)*, but the true architectural gem is the **Hôtel-Dieu** in Beaune *(see pp346–7)*. The wealth of the Church is evident in harmonious Romanesque churches and abbeys, especially **Vézelay** *(see pp336–7)*. **The Franche-Comté's** *(see pp349–51)* lakes, mountains, woods and waterfalls are perfect for trekking, canoeing and skiing.

MASSIF CENTRAL

- Wild, beautiful landscapes
- Dramatic Gorges du Tarn
- Treasures of Ste-Foy

This is the place to go to enjoy the great outdoors. A plateau of extinct volcanoes, spas and lakes, the landscape reaches dramatic heights in the **Gorges du Tarn** *(see pp370–1)*. The **Cévennes** *(see p353)*, one of the least populated parts of the country, is known for its wild flowers and birds of prey. Remote villages and ancient churches top hills

and are tucked in valleys. The Abbaye de Ste-Foy in **Conques** *(see pp368–9)* has one of the most celebrated reliquaries in Christendom.

THE RHONE VALLEY AND FRENCH ALPS

- Lyon's enticing *bouchons*
- Grenoble and the ski slopes
- Elegant Evian-les-Bains

The south of France begins at **Lyon** *(see pp380–1)*, France's second largest city, where the River Saône joins the River Rhône and the Mediterranean starts to scent the air. The commercial and military capital of Roman Gaul is now a gastronomic capital known for its *bouchons* (bistros) and local wines from **Beaujolais** *(see p377)* as well as the Rhône. Natural attractions in the region include the dramatic, cave-pocked **Ardèche** *(see pp384–5)* and, to the east, **Grenoble** *(see pp388–9)* and the Alps where you'll find the elegant spa town of **Evian-les-Bains** *(see p391)* beside Lac Léman.

Wine from the Rhône Valley

POITOU AND AQUITAINE

- Marais Poitevin's canals
- Historic Poitiers
- Bordeaux wine châteaux

Set against a long coast of sandy beaches, this largely flat region runs from the port of **La Rochelle** *(see p416)* and

the popular holiday island of **Île d'Oléron** *(see p417)* to the Basque country. When La Rochelle is busy in summer, escape to the **Marais Poitevin** *(see pp408–9)*, a network of lily-blanketed canals teeming with wildlife. There are two historic centres – **Poitiers** *(see pp412–3)*, whose cathedral has the oldest carved choir stalls in France, and **Bordeaux** *(see pp420–3)*, beside the River Garonne. The latter has been long known as a wine port serving the magnificent surrounding châteaux estates.

PERIGORD, QUERCY AND GASCONY

- Sarlat Market
- Lascaux's famous caves
- Toulouse Space Park

Cut by the majestic Dordogne, Lot and Tarn rivers, this is bucolic, green France, where water activities help to beat the summer sun. Every town has a weekly market brimming with local produce, such as *foie gras* and **Agen** *(see p440)* prunes. Best known is the Wednesday market in **Sarlat-la-Caneda** *(see pp432–3)*, though stunning architecture makes it worth a visit any day of the week.

Rocamadour *(see pp436–7)* and **Moissac** *(see pp442–3)* are other architectural high points, while prehistoric man has left his mark in the famous **Lascaux caves** *(see pp402–3)*. **Toulouse** *(see pp446–7)* is the major town. Try its sausages and visit the hi-tech Space Park.

Sarlat Market, famous for *foie gras* and walnuts

THE PYRENEES

- Biarritz beaches
- Parc National des Pyrénées wildlife
- The shrine at Lourdes

The Pyrenees mountain range stretches from the Atlantic to the Mediterranean, forming a natural border with Spain. On the Atlantic coast is the **Basque country** *(see p449)* where **Bayonne** *(see p452)* is known for its ham and **Biarritz** *(see p452)*, a surfers' town, is renowned for its by-gone glories as the resort choice of kings. The **Parc National des Pyrénées** *(see pp460–1)* is at the heart of the mountains which are spectacular for walking and trekking. Skiers come in winter. **Lourdes** *(see pp458–9)* brings pilgrims all year round.

Flowers, butterflies, animals and birds brighten the Pyrenees trails

LANGUEDOC-ROUSSILLON

- Collioure, the artists' resort
- Carcassonne, fairytale walled town
- Pont du Gard, a Roman triumph

These are sunny, rolling lands of olives, vines, cypress trees and sunflowers, where old farm buildings have been baked by the sun. The Pyrenees reach the Mediterranean here, on the **Côte Vermeille** *(see p482)*, where the prettiest resort is **Collioure** *(see p483)*, long familiar to artists. To the

The fairytale sight of Carcassonne, restored in the 19th century

north is **Carcassonne** *(see pp488–9)*, a dreamy fortified town that has been perfectly restored. Romantics might also want to seek out **Montségur** *(see p463)*, the last stronghold of the persecuted Cathars. **Nîmes** *(see pp496–7)* was a major Roman city with a well-preserved amphitheatre and an astonishing aqueduct, the **Pont du Gard** *(see p495)*. It was the highest bridge the Romans ever built.

PROVENCE AND THE CÔTE D'AZUR

- The French Riviera
- Cannes' ritzy Film Festival
- Monte-Carlo Casino

St-Tropez *(see p516)*, **Nice** *(see pp526–7)*, **Menton** *(see p529)* – the French Riviera is the most fabulous waterfront

in the world. Admire top yachts in **Antibes** *(see p521)*, catch the rising stars at **Cannes' film festival** *(see p520)* and break the bank in **Monte-Carlo** *(see pp530–31)*. There is plenty to do all year round so it's best to avoid August when it can be incredibly busy. Away from the coast there are glorious ancient towns, from **Avignon** *(see p503)*, where popes built a palace, and **Aix** *(see p511)*, where good King Renée ruled, to Roman **Arles** *(see pp508–9)* and the cowboy country of the **Camargue** *(see pp510–11)*.

CORSICA

- Myrtle-scented maquis
- Beautiful sandy beaches
- Fortified towns

A mountainous island with coves and sandy beaches, Corsica is the place to hike, especially in spring, when the aromatic maquis puts on its best show. On the coast there are fortified towns such as **Bonifacio** *(see p543)* and **Porto** *(see p541)*, set in a magical bay. Napoleon Bonaparte was born in **Ajaccio** *(see p543)*. Find out about the island's history and customs in the Musée de la Corse in **Corte** *(see p540)*, which is a good base for exploring enchanting, remote Castagmiccia.

St-Tropez harbour, the most glamorous resort on the Provence coast

Putting France on the Map

France, one of the largest countries in Europe, has airline connections with most cities in the world. Paris is the major transport hub with two international airports; others include Bordeaux, Lille, Lyon, Nice and Toulouse. There are good, high-speed rail links with the rest of Europe, and a network of efficient motorways. A number of ferry routes cross the Mediterranean to Corsica and beyond. Cross-Channel ferries serve several ports, with the Channel Tunnel providing an alternative link by rail.

France, known as the "Hexagon" due to its six-sided shape, is bordered by six countries: Spain across the Pyrenees to the south; Italy and Switzerland beyond the Alps; Luxembourg and Belgium to the north; and Germany on the other side of the Rhine. The United Kingdom lies across the English Channel (La Manche).

KEY

- 🛳 Ferry service
- ✈ International airport
- Motorway
- Main road
- Railway line

0 kilometres   100

0 miles   100

Greater Paris

The capital of France, Paris is situated in Ile de France. Greater Paris has 11.8 million inhabitants, 2.2 million of whom live within the périphérique (ring road) in the Ville de Paris.

Regional France

France has a population of around 61 million, and
receives over 75 million visitors a year. It covers an
area of 543,965 sq km (210,025 sq miles). Paris is the
largest city, followed by Lyon, Marseille and the
conurbation of Lille-Lens-Valenciennes. The Loire,
Seine, Garonne and Rhône are the longest of France's
many rivers. This book divides the country into 15
regions, plus a separate
section for Paris and Ile de
France, although officially
France comprises 22 *régions*.

GETTING AROUND

In spite of its size, France is
relatively easy to travel around.
There is a well-organized rail
network, and travelling times
are considerably shortened
between towns with a high-
speed TGV link *(see p683)*.
Most motorways have expensive tolls but are fast and
efficient for longer distances.
City by-passes are usually free
and some longer sections of
motorway may also be free.
Smaller roads are usually
a more interesting way to
discover the country's varied
landscape *(pp686–8)* and
they are almost invariably well-
maintained and signposted.

KEY

▬▬	Motorway
▬▬	Major road
══	Minor road

0 kilometres   100

0 miles   100

Eyewitness France Regions
Each of the chapters in this guide has a colour code. The chapters are grouped into five sections – Northeast France, Western France, Central France and the Alps, Southwest France and the South of France – plus Paris and Ile de France.

KEY TO COLOUR-CODING

☐ Paris and Ile de France

Northeast France

☐ Le Nord and Picardy
☐ Champagne
☐ Alsace and Lorraine

Western France

☐ Normandy
☐ Brittany
☐ The Loire Valley

Central France and the Alps

☐ Burgundy and Franche-Comté
☐ Massif Central
☐ The Rhône Valley and French Alps

Southwest France

☐ Poitou and Aquitaine
☐ Périgord, Quercy and Gascony
☐ The Pyrenees

The South of France

☐ Languedoc-Roussillon
☐ Provence and the Côte d'Azur
☐ Corsica

CORSICA

Corsica
Situated 193 km (120 miles) from the Côte d'Azur, Corsica can be reached by ferry or air. Covering an area of 8,680 sq km (3,350 sq miles), it is the fourth-largest island in the Mediterranean.

A PORTRAIT OF FRANCE

The French are convinced that their way of life is best, and that their country is the most civilized on earth. Many millions of visitors agree with them. The food and wine are justly celebrated. French culture, literature, art, cinema, and architecture can be both profound and provocative. Whether cerebral, sensual, or sportive, France is a country where anyone might feel at home.

France's landscape ranges from mountain plateaux to lush farmland, traditional villages to chic boulevards. Its regional identities are equally diverse. The country belongs to both northern and southern Europe, and encompasses Brittany with its Celtic maritime heritage, the Mediterranean sunbelt, Germanic Alsace-Lorraine, and the hardy mountain regions of the Auvergne and the Pyrenees. Paris remains the linchpin, with its famously brusque citizens and intense tempo. Other cities range from the industrial conglomeration of Lille in the north, to Marseille, the biggest port on the Mediterranean. The differences

Marianne, symbol of France

between north and south, country and city are well-entrenched, indeed cherished. Advances such as the TGV (high-speed train), Internet and mobile phone technology have helped reduce distance (both physical and emotional) yet have simultaneously provoked an opposite reaction: as life in France becomes more city-based and industrialized, so the desire grows to safeguard the old, traditional ways and to value rural life.

The idea of life in the country – *douceur de vivre* (the Good Life), tables set in the sun for the wine and anecdotes to flow – is as seductive as ever for residents and visitors

Château de Saumur, one of the Loire's most romantic and complete castles

◁ Café life in L'Isle sur la Sorgue, one of the country's many pleasures alike. Nevertheless, the rural way of life has been changing. Whereas in 1945 one person in three worked in farming, today it is only one in 25. France's main exports used to be luxury goods such as perfumes and Cognac; today, they have been overtaken by cars, aircraft, nuclear power stations and telecom-munications equipment.

The popular scooter

People remain firmly committed to their roots, and often retain a place in

Chanel chic

the country for holidays or retirement. On average, more French people have second homes than any other nation-ality; and in many areas, such as Proven-ce, the dying villages have found a new life as chic summer residences for Parisians. Many artists and artisans now live and work in the country; and entrepreneurs have set up factory workshops there, more feasible in the age of the Internet.

The decline in the influence of the Catholic Church has resulted in social changes. Today only 9 per cent of people attend mass regularly. Many couples live togeth-er before marriage, and are allowed the same tax status as married couples. Abortion is now legal.

Feminism in France has quite a different look than in Anglo-Saxon countries. French feminists are unwilling to condemn frivolous sex-appeal. As EU citizens, women in France have legal equality with men, but French attitudes remain traditional. It may have seemed like a milestone in 1991, when Edith Cresson became France's first woman prime minister, but her unpopularity and the 1999 corruption case against her arguably held back women's equality in French politics. Ségolène Royal re-established a prominent political role for women when she won 47 per cent of the vote in the 2007 presidential elections, as did Martine Aubry in 2008, when she became head of the French Socialist party.

SOCIAL CUSTOMS AND POLITICS

French social life, except between close friends, has always been marked by formality – handshaking, the use of titles, the preference for the formal *vous* rather than the intimate *tu*. However, this is changing among the younger generation, who now call you

The May 1968 disturbances, a catalyst for profound change in France

Farming in Alsace-Lorraine

by your first name. Standards of dress have become much more informal too, though the French still dress well.

Formality lingers on, however, and France remains very legalistic – whether you are buying a house or exporting an antique. But the French are insouciant about their famous red tape. Rules and laws are there to be ingeniously evaded, twisted, or made more human. This sport of avoiding cumbersome bureaucracy has a name of its own, *le système D*, to be accompanied with a shrug and a smile.

Charles de Gaulle

Since the end of the Cold War, the sharp Left/Right divisions in French society have been replaced by pragmatic centrism. Over a period of 14 years, President François Mitterrand – elected in 1981 as the head of a Socialist Communist coalition – steadily moved towards a more central-focused political agenda. In 1995, he was replaced by Jacques Chirac who promised right-wing policies. He too moved to the centre. By the 2002 presidential elections, immigration and security fears, broken electoral promises and political corruption has caused widespread disenchantment and a swing to the Front National. The result was the elimination of Socialist Lionel Jospin in the first round and the election of Chirac by default in the second. Further electoral discontent was revealed by the rejection of the European Constitution in 2005.

In 2007, Chirac's Deputy Prime Minister, Nicolas Sarkozy, won the presidency by addressing public fears and promising an end to corruption. He has notably forged a closer relationship with the US, re-engaged France in the European Union and opened up his government to ministers from the Left. But Sarkozy's popularity waned in 2010, after his plans to raise the retirement age provoked strikes, and the deportation of gypsies drew criticism from other European states.

CULTURE AND THE ARTS

Culture is taken seriously in France, and writers, intellectuals, artists and fashion designers are held in high social esteem. As a result, the state finances

Designer Thierry Mugler at the Paris collections

a large network of provincial arts centres and has traditionally given subsidies that allow experimentation in art and design. The French remain justly proud of their own cinematic tradition and are determined to defend it against pressures from Hollywood. Other activities – from the music industry to the French language itself – are subject to the same protectionist attitudes.

Traditional Breton costumes, worn for festivals and *pardons*

Avant-garde art and literature and modern architecture all enjoy strong patronage in France. Some of the more exciting architectural projects range from the striking modern buildings in Paris – the Louvre pyramid and La Grande Arche at La Défense – to the post-modern housing developments of Nîmes, Montpellier, and Marseille in the south.

MODERN LIFE

While one half of the French were heralding the new millennium in true Gallic style, the other half were plunged into darkness caused by some of the worst storms ever to hit Europe. This is an extreme illustration of French ambivalence towards modernism. France's agro-business is one of the most advanced in the world, but the peasant farmer is deeply revered. France hankers after a leading role in the world, yet the country effectively closes down for the whole of August, when the French take to the roads and coastal resorts of France! However, two factors have forced a change of pace: the Internet, which France has embraced keenly, and the Euro, which, in one fell swoop, has swept away Europe's oldest decimalized currency, the Franc.

A view through the base of La Grande Arche, part of the huge business complex on the edge of Paris

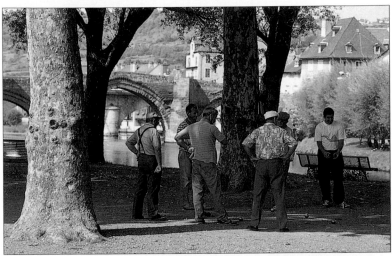

The traditional game of *boules or pétanque*, still extremely popular – especially in the south

The French are enthusiastic, discerning consumers. Even small towns have stylish clothes shops and street markets with the best of local produce. France also has Europe's largest hypermarkets, which have been steadily ousting the local grocery or corner shop. These are remarkably French in what they sell: a long delicatessen counter may display 100 or so

Southern produce: melons, peaches, and apricots

French cheeses and charcuterie, while the range of fresh vegetables and fruit is a tribute to their role in French cuisine.

However, modern pressures have been changing eating habits in a curious way. The French used to eat well daily as a matter of course. Today many are in a hurry, and for most weekly meals will eat simply – either a quick steak or pasta dish at home, or a snack in town (hence the wave of fast-food places that have sprung up, in defiance of French tradition).

But meals still remain an important part of French culture – not just for the food and wines, but also for the pleasure of lengthy meals and good conversation around a table of family or friends. They will reserve their gastronomy for the once-or-twice-a-week special occasion, or the big family Sunday lunch, an important French ritual. It is at these times that the French zest for life really comes into its own.

Remote farm – a nostalgic reminder of rural life

The Classic French Menu

The traditional French meal consists of at least three courses. *Les entrées* or *hors d'oeuvre* (starters or appetizers) include soups, egg dishes, salads or *charcuterie*, such as sliced sausage or hams. There may be a separate fish course before the main course. Otherwise, *les plats* (main courses) will be a choice of meat and fish dishes, often served with a sauce and accompanied by potatoes, rice or pasta and vegetables. The cheese course comes before the dessert. Desserts may include sorbets, fruit tarts and creamy or chocolate concoctions. A fixed-price menu is the cheapest option. For more information on French restaurants, see pp596–9.

Escargots à la Bourguignonne *In Bourgogne, snails are served in their shells with parsley and garlic butter.*

Moules marinières *In this classic dish, mussels are cooked in dry white wine with shallots and parsley.*

Fish soup

Endive salad with diced fried bacon

Goats cheese melted on toast with salad

Wild mushrooms sautéed with garlic and parsley

Sea bass grilled over fennel twigs, flamed in pastis

Scallops

Rabbit cooked "huntsman" style with mushrooms

Medallions of lamb

Steak with pepper sauce

Veal stew enriched with egg and cream

Breast of duck

Pork chops

Veal sweatbreads

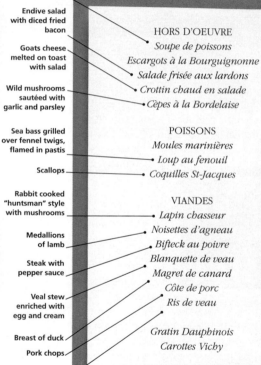

HORS D'OEUVRE
Soupe de poissons
Escargots à la Bourguignonne
Salade frisée aux lardons
Crottin chaud en salade
Cèpes à la Bordelaise

POISSONS
Moules marinières
Loup au fenouil
Coquilles St-Jacques

VIANDES
Lapin chasseur
Noisettes d'agneau
Bifteck au poivre
Blanquette de veau
Magret de canard
Côte de porc
Ris de veau

Gratin Dauphinois
Carottes Vichy

Gratin Dauphinois *Layers of potato are covered in cream, topped with Gruyère cheese and slowly baked.*

Carottes Vichy *Cooked in Vichy water with sugar, carrots take on a delicious, sweet glaze. They are served garnished with parsley.*

BREAKFAST

The French rarely eat cereal, eggs or meat for breakfast; assorted breads, spread with butter and jams, are their morning choice. These include *croissants* (flaky, buttery crescent-shaped pastries); a piece of *baguette* (the classic long thin loaf); *pain au chocolat* (an oblong of croissant dough rolled round a tablet of chocolate, then baked); and *brioche* (an airy, egg-enriched yeast bread or roll). They are accompanied by coffee or tea, or hot chocolate for children. Hotels will usually offer fresh fruit juice, too. The most common form of coffee at breakfast is *café au lait*, espresso served with warm milk.

Typical French breakfast selection

Menu à €20 — Fixed-price menu of the day

Céleri rémoulade — Grated celeriac in a piquant mayonnaise

Salade de pissenlits — Dandelion-leaf salad

Soupe à l'oignon — Dark, rich onion soup topped with bread and grilled cheese

Cuisses de grenouilles — Frogs' legs

Quenelles de brochet — Light, fluffy poached pike dumplings

Boeuf bourguignon

Andouillettes — Small tripe sausages, usually grilled

Coq au vin

Fromage ou dessert

Café

Boeuf Bourguignon *Beef is cooked in red Burgundy wine with bacon, baby onions and button mushrooms.*

Coq au vin *A male chicken is flamed in brandy, then stewed in wine with button mushrooms and onions.*

DESSERTS

Fromage

Tarte Tatin — Upside-down baked apple tart

Ile flottante — Meringues floating in a creamy sauce

Crêpes flambées — Sugared crêpes flamed in liqueur

Clafoutis — Baked fruit and batter dessert, often made with cherries

Crème caramel — Egg custard with a caramel sauce

Crème brulée

Fromage *Any good French restaurant will take pride in offering a good range of perfectly matured regional cheeses, including, as available, cows', ewes' and goats' milk, blue, soft and hard varieties.*

Crème Brulée *This rich, creamy custard is covered with brown sugar, grilled to form a crisp topping.*

The Wine of France

Picker's hod

Winemaking in France dates back to pre-Roman times, although it was the Romans who disseminated the culture of the vine and the practice of winemaking throughout the country. The range, quality and reputation of the fine wines of Bordeaux, Burgundy, the Rhône and Champagne in particular have made them rôle models the world over. France's everyday wines can be highly enjoyable too, with plenty of good value wines now emerging from the southern regions.

Traditional vineyard cultivation

WINE REGIONS

Each of the 10 principal wine-producing regions has its own identity, based on grape varieties, climate and *terroir* (soil). *Appellation contrôlée* laws guarantee a wine's origins and production methods.

KEY

- ☐ Bordeaux
- ■ Burgundy
- ☐ Champagne
- ☐ Alsace
- ☐ Loire
- ■ Provence
- ☐ Jura and Savoie
- ■ The Southwest
- ☐ Languedoc-Roussillon
- ■ Rhône

Map labels: Paris, Reims, Strasbourg, Nantes, Tours, Dijon, Clermont-Ferrand, Lyon, Bordeaux, Pau, Toulouse, Marseille, Perpignan. Rivers: Marne, Loire, Dordogne, Garonne, Rhône.

0 kilometres 150
0 miles 150

HOW TO READ A WINE LABEL

Even the simplest label will identify the wine and provide a key to its quality. It will bear the name of the wine and its producer, its vintage, if there is one, and whether it comes from a strictly defined area (*appellation contrôlée*), or is a more general IGP (*Indication Géographique Protégée*) wine or *vin de France*. It may also have a regional grading, as with the *crus classés* in Bordeaux. The shape and colour of the bottle is also a guide to the kind of wine it contains. Green glass is often used since this helps to protect the wine from light.

The property or producer

The vintage, from the French word *vendange*, or harvest

Pictures may be accurate or fanciful

CHÂTEAU MARGAUX
2008
GRAND VIN
PREMIER GRAND CRU CLASSÉ

Château-bottled, rather than a wine from a merchant or grower's co-operative

CHÂTEAU MARGAUX
PREMIER GRAND CRU CLASSÉ
MARGAUX
APPELLATION MARGAUX CONTRÔLÉE
2008
MIS EN BOUTEILLE AU CHÂTEAU

The wine's *appellation contrôlée*

Capacity of the bottle

HOW WINE IS MADE

Wine is the product of the juice of freshly picked grapes, after natural or cultured yeasts have converted the grape sugars into alcohol during the fermentation process. The yeasts, or lees, are normally filtered out before bottling.

WHITE WINE   RED WINE

Newly harvested grapes, *whether red or white, are first lightly crushed to bring the sugar-rich juices into contact with the yeasts in the grape skins' "bloom".*

Old wine press

Red wine *gets its backbone from tannins present in red grape skins. The stems also contain tannins, but of a harsher kind; most winemakers de- stem most or all of their red grapes before they are crushed.*

Tanks for maceration

Crusher and de-stemmer

For young *white wines and some reds (eg simple Beaujolais) that do not gain complexity from ageing, the crushed grape juice may be steeped, or macerated, with the grape skins for a few hours to add aroma and flavour.*

White wine *uses only free-run or lightly pressed juice for the freshest and fruitiest flavours. For red wine, the grapes are pressed thoroughly after fermen- tation, and this* vin de presse, *rich in tannins and other flav- our elements, can be blended back into the wine as needed.*

Press

Fermentation *is a natural process, but can be unpredictable; nowadays, many growers use cultured yeasts and hygienic, tempera- ture-controlled stainless-steel tanks to control fermentation and ensure consistent results.*

Early drinking wines *may be fil- tered straight into their bottles, but barrels are used to age many finer wines. The flavours imparted by the oak are an integral part of many wines' identities – for example, the tobaccoey,"wood-shavings" character of red Bordeaux.*

Fermentation vat

Oak casks

Different shades of glass identify the wine regions

Bottle shapes typical of red Bordeaux (left) and Burgundy

Artists in France

Artists have always been inspired by France, especially since landscape became a legitimate subject for art in the 19th century. Art and tourism have been closely linked for over a century, when the establishment of artists' colonies in the forest of Fontainebleau, Brittany, and the south of France did much to make these areas attractive to visitors. Today, one of the pleasures of touring the countryside is the recognition of landscapes made famous in paintings.

Follower of *the French Classical tradition of landscape painting, Jean-Baptiste-Camille Corot recorded* The Belfry of Douai *(1871).*

Le Nord a Picardy

Gustave Courbet, *socialist and leader of the Realist School of painting, captured this famous coastal town in* The Cliffs at Etretat after a Storm *(1869).*

Normandy

Paris and Ile France

Brittany

Loire Valley

Emile Bernard *was fascinated by the wild, almost primitive character of the Breton landscape and the individuality of its inhabitants. He was one of the community of artists based in Pont Aven. His* La Ronde Bretonne *(1892) portrays local Celtic customs.*

Poitou and Aquitaine

Neo-Impressionist *artist and exponent of Pointillism, Paul Signac indulged his love of maritime subjects on the coasts of France.* Entrance to the Port at La Rochelle *(1921) shows his use of myriad dots of colour to represent nature.*

Périgord, Quercy and Gascony

Pyrenees

Languedo Roussillo

Théodore Rousseau, *the leading light of the Barbizon School (see p181) of landscape painters, visited the Auvergne in 1830. It was here that he began to paint "en plein air" (in the open air). The results are seen in this sensitively observed scene,* Sunset, Auvergne *(c.1830).*

A few months *before his tragic death in July 1890, Vincent Van Gogh painted the* Church at Auvers. *He noted that the building "appears to have a violet-hued blue colour; pure cobalt".*

In his Eiffel Tower *(1926) Robert Delaunay investigated the abstract qualities of colour. His wife, artist Sonia Delaunay, said, "The Eiffel Tower and the Universe were one and the same to him".*

Alsace and Lorraine

Champagne

Scenes from *everyday life were realistically rendered by Gustave Courbet, as here in* Young Ladies of the Village Giving Alms to a Cow Girl in a Valley near Ornans *(1851–2).*

Burgundy and Franche-Comté

Maurice Utrillo *painted this village scene,* The Church of Saint Bernard in Summer *(1924), while staying at his mother's home. The sombre tone and emptiness reflect his unhappy life.*

The Massif Central

The Rhône Valley and French Alps

Provence and the Côte d'Azur

The French Riviera *attracted many artists (see pp472–3). Raoul Dufy particularly appreciated its pleasures, seen in this typical scene of blue skies and palm trees,* La Jetée Promenade à Nice *(1928).*

Landscape at Collioure *(1905) depicts the vivid colours of this little Catalan fishing village. It was here that Henri Matisse founded the art movement of the Fauves, or "Wild Beasts", who used exceptionally bright, expressive colours.*

0 kilometres	100	
0 miles		100

Writers in France

Writers and intellectuals traditionally enjoy
high prestige in France. One of the most
august of French institutions is the
Academie Française, whose 40 members,
most of them writers, have pronounced
on national events and, on occasion,
held public office.

Monument to Baudelaire

The work of many French novelists
is deeply rooted in their native area,
ranging from the Normandy of Gustave
Flaubert to Jean Giono's Provence. In addition to their
literary merit, these novels provide a unique guide to
France's regional identities.

Colette's house in Burgundy

THE NOVEL

The farmland of the Beauce, where Zola based his novel, La Terre

The first great French writer
was Rabelais, in the 16th
century, a boisterous, life-
affirming satirist *(see p295)*.
Many writers in the Age of
Enlightenment which followed
emphasized the tradition of
reason, clarity and objectivity

**Marcel Proust, author of
Remembrance of Things Past**

in their work. The 19th century was the golden age of
the French humanist novel,
producing Balzac, with his
vast fresco of contemporary
society; Stendhal, a critic of
the frailties of ambition in
Scarlet and Black; and Victor
Hugo, known for epics such
as *Les Misérables*. George
Sand broke ground with her
novels such as *The Devil's
Pool* which depicted peasant
life, albeit in an idealized
way. In the same century,
Flaubert produced his
masterwork *Madame Bovary*,
a study of provincialism and
misplaced romanticism. In
contrast, Zola wrote *Germinal*,
La Terre, and other studies
of lower-class life.

Marcel Proust combined a
poetic evocation of his boy-
hood with a portrait of high
society in his long novel,
Remembrance of Things Past.

Others have also written
poetically about their childhood, such as Alain-Fournier
in *Le Grand Meaulnes* and
Colette in *My Mother's House*.

A new kind of novel
emerged after World War I.
Jean Giono's *Joy of Man's
Desiring*, and François
Mauriac's masterly *Thérèse
Desqueyroux*, explored the
impact of landscape upon
human character. Mauriac,
and also George Bernanos in
his *Diary of a Country Priest*,
used lone spiritual struggle
as a theme. The free-thinker
André Gide was another
leading writer of the inter-
war years with his *Strait is
the Gate* and the autobio-
graphical *If it Die*.

In the 1960s Alain Robbe-
Grillet and others experi-
mented with the Nouveau
Roman, which subordinated
character and plot to detailed
physical description. Critics
held it in part responsible
for the recent decline of the
novel. Despite this, the 2008
Nobel Prize for literature was
awarded to Franco-Mauritian
Jean-Marie Gustave Le Clézio.

**Hugo's novel Les Misérables,
made into a musical in the 1980s**

THEATRE

The three classic playwrights of French literature, Racine, Molière, and Corneille, lived in the 17th century. Molière's comedies satirized the vanities and foibles of human nature. Corneille and Racine wrote noble verse tragedies. They were followed in the 18th century by Marivaux, writer of romantic comedies, and Beaumarchais whose *Barber of Seville* and *Marriage of Figaro* later became operas. Victor Hugo's dramas were the most vigorous product of the 19th century. The exceptional dramatists of the 20th century range from Jean Anouilh, author of urbane philosophical comedies, to Jean Genet, ex-convict critic of the establishment. In the 1960s, Eugene Ionesco from Romania and Samuel Beckett from Ireland were among the pioneers of a new genre, the "theatre of the absurd". Since then, no major playwrights have emerged but experimental work flourishes in state-subsidized theatre companies.

Molière, the 17th-century dramatist

POETRY

The greatest of early French poets was Ronsard, who wrote sonnets about nature and love in the 16th century. Lamartine, a major poet of the early 19th century, also took nature as one of his themes (his poem *Le Lac* laments a lost love). Later the same century, Baudelaire *(Les Fleurs du mal)* and Rimbaud *(Le Bateau Ivre)* were judged to be provocative in their day. Nobel prizewinner in 1904, Frédéric Mistral wrote in his native Provençal tongue. The greatest poet of the 20th century is considered to be Paul Valéry, whose work is profoundly philosophical.

PHILOSOPHY

France has produced a large number of major philosophers in the European humanist tradition. One of the first was

Novels by Albert Camus, who won the Nobel Prize in 1957

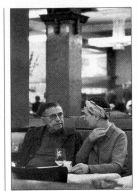
Sartre and de Beauvoir in La Coupole restaurant in Paris, 1969

Montaigne, in the 16th century, an inspired moralist. Then came Descartes, the master of logic, and Pascal. The 18th century produced Voltaire, the supreme liberal, and Rousseau, who preached the harmonizing influence of living close to nature.

In the 20th century, Sartre, de Beauvoir and Camus used the novel as a philosophical vehicle. Sartre led the existentialist movement in Paris in the early 1940s with his novel *Nausea* and his treatise *Being and Nothingness*. Camus' novel, *The Outsider,* was equally influential.

The 1970s and 1980s brought the structuralists, such as Foucault and Barthes, with their radical ideas. Poststructuralism took this rationalist approach into the 1990s, with Derrida, Kristeva, Deleuze and Lyotard. At the start of the 21st century, Badiou, known for his political ideas, is one of France's key philosophers.

FOREIGN WRITERS

Many foreign writers have visited and been inspired by France, from Petrarch in 14th-century Avignon to Goethe in Alsace in 1770–71. In the 20th century the Riviera attracted novelists Somerset Maugham, Katherine Mansfield, Ernest Hemingway and Graham Greene. In 1919 the American Sylvia Beach opened the first Shakespeare and Company bookshop in Paris, which became a cultural centre for expatriate writers. In 1922 she was the first to publish James Joyce's masterwork, *Ulysses*.

Hemingway with Sylvia Beach and friends, Paris 1923

Romanesque and Gothic Architecture in France

France is rich in medieval architecture, ranging from small Romanesque churches to great Gothic cathedrals. As the country emerged from the Dark Ages in the 11th century, there was a surge in Romanesque building, based on the Roman model of thick walls, round arches and heavy vaults. French architects improved this basic structure, leading to the flowering of Gothic in the 13th century. Pointed arches and flying buttresses were the key inventions that allowed for much taller buildings with larger windows.

LOCATOR MAP

① *Romanesque abbeys & churches*

⑬ *Gothic cathedrals*

ROMANESQUE FEATURES

The plan of Angoulême *shows the cross-shape and the rounded eastern apse typical of Romanesque architecture.*

A section of Le Puy *reveals a high barrel-vaulted nave with round arches and low side aisles. Light could enter through windows in the side aisles and the central lantern tower.*

The massive walls *of the nave bays of St-Etienne support a three-storey structure of arcades, a gallery and clerestory.*

GOTHIC FEATURES

The plan of Amiens *shows the nave and apse flanked by a continuous row of chapels.*

A section of Beauvais *shows how the nave could be raised to staggering heights thanks to exterior support from flying buttresses.*

Pointed arches *withstood greater stress, permitting larger windows as in the nave at Reims.*

WHERE TO FIND ROMANESQUE ARCHITECTURE

① St-Etienne, Caen *p254*
② Mont-St-Michel, Normandy *p258*
③ St-Pierre, Angoulême *p419*
④ Notre-Dame, Le Puy *p365*
⑤ St-Pierre, Moissac *pp442–3*
⑥ St-Sernin, Toulouse *pp446–7*
⑦ Ste-Foy, Conques *pp358–9*
⑧ Sacré-Coeur, Paray-le-Monial *p345*
⑨ St-Philibert, Tournus *p344*
⑩ St-Etienne, Nevers *p338*
⑪ Ste-Madeleine, Vézelay *pp336–7*
⑫ Marmoutier, Saverne *p233*

WHERE TO FIND GOTHIC ARCHITECTURE

⑬ Notre-Dame, Strasbourg *p231*
⑭ Notre-Dame, Reims *pp212–3*
⑮ Notre-Dame, Laon *p205*
⑯ Notre-Dame, Amiens *pp202–3*
⑰ St-Pierre, Beauvais *p200*
⑱ St-Denis, Ile-de-France *p172*
⑲ Sainte-Chapelle, Paris *pp84–5*
⑳ Notre-Dame, Paris *pp86–7*
㉑ Notre-Dame, Chartres *pp308–11*
㉒ St-Etienne, Bourges *p313*

TERMS USED IN THIS GUIDE

Basilica: Early church with two aisles and nave lit from above by clerestory windows.

Clerestory: A row of windows illuminating the nave from above the aisle roof.

 Rose: Circular window, often stained glass.

Buttress: Mass of masonry built to support a wall.

 Flying buttress: An arched support transmitting thrust of the weight downwards.

Portal: Monumental entrance to a building, often decorated.

Tympanum: Decorated space, often carved, over a door or window lintel.

Vault: Arched stone ceiling.

Transept: Two wings of a cruciform church at right angles to the nave.

Crossing: Centre of cruciform where transept crosses nave.

Lantern: Turret with windows to illuminate interior, often with cupola (domed ceiling).

Triforium: Middle storey between arcades and clerestory.

Apse: Termination of the church, often rounded.

Ambulatory: Aisle running round east end, passing behind the sanctuary.

Arcade: Set of arches and supporting columns.

Rib vault: Vault supported by projecting ribs of stone.

 Gargoyle: Carved grotesque figure, often a water spout.

Tracery: Ornamental carved stone pattern within Gothic window.

Flamboyant Gothic: Carved stone tracery resembling flames.

 Capital: Top of a column, usually carved.

The west façade of Marmoutier Abbey *with its towers, narrow windows and small portal give it a fortified appearance.*

The east end of Nevers *has a rounded apse surrounded by a semi-circular ambulatory and radiating chapels. The chapels were added to provide space for altars.*

The west façade of Laon *has decorative, sculpted portals and a rose window characteristic of Gothic style.*

The east end of Beauvais, *with its delicate buttresses topped by pinnacles, is the culmination of High Gothic.*

Rural Architecture

French farmhouses are entirely products of the soil, built of stone, clay or wood, depending on what materials are found locally. As the topography changes so does the architecture, from the steeply-sloped roofs covered in flat tiles in the north to the broad canal-tiled roofs of the south.

Despite this rich regional diversity, French farmhouses fall into three basic categories: the *maison bloc*, where house and outbuildings share the same roof; the high house, with living quarters upstairs and livestock or wine cellar below; and courtyard farmsteads, their buildings set around a central court.

Shuttered window in Alsace

Symmetrical façade

Wood from local forests

The chalet *is typical of the Jura, Alps and Vosges mountains. The* maison bloc *housed both family and livestock throughout the winter. Gaps between the gable planks allowed air to circulate around crops stored in the loft, and an earth ramp behind gave wagons access. Many lofts also had a threshing floor.*

Normandy wood structure

Flat-tiled roof

Half-timbered houses *are typical of Normandy, Alsace, Champagne, Picardy, the Landes and Basque country. The filling between the timbers was wattle and daub or in some cases brick, but it is the arrangement of the smaller posts, different in each region, that best expresses the local style.*

Dovecote with flat tiles

Raised stone foundations

Steps to front door

Animals or wine housed here

The high house *is most prominent in the southeast, and is normally built of stone with an exterior stone staircase and upstairs porch. Wine growers' barrels could be stored on the ground floor without hoisting, or livestock stabled there. High houses in the Lot Valley often boast a dovecote.*

The long house *is the oldest form of* maison bloc, *with family and livestock at opposite ends of the building – originally one room. In this Breton version, separate doorways lead to house and stable. A dividing wall only became common in the 19th century.*

Local stone

Slate roof

Entrance to lodging

Stable entrance

Dovecote with canal tiles

The word "mas" *generally refers to any Provençal farmhouse. In the Camargue and the Crau, it is a farmstead for large-scale sheep farming built in an "agglomerated" style: the outbuildings, although attached to one another, are of different heights. Often, a dovecote is included.*

Ochre and beige colours of the south

Rendered façade

Pebble and brick wall

Half-timber and brick

Compressed cob: *pisé*

Sun-dried adobe bricks

Pebbles in lime mortar

Brick, flint and chalk

WALLS

Limestone, granite, sandstone and pebbles were all used for building walls. But if no stone was available, clay was dug for infilling half-timbered houses, as wattle and daub. The alternative was to use a cob mixture *(pisé)*, pressed into blocks in a process called *banchange*. Adobe (sun-dried brick) was also used but fired brick was fairly rare as it was expensive to bake. However, brick was sometimes used as trim or combined with chalk or pebbles in a "composite" walling. Walls were generally rendered with mortar.

Flat terracotta tiles in colours of local sand

Pantiles, used in Flanders and Picardy

Canal clay tiles typical of the south

ROOFING

Two roof styles distinguish the north and south. Northern roofs are steeply pitched, so that any rainwater runs off easily. In the south, roofs are covered with canal clay tiles, and more gently sloped to prevent the tiles sliding off.

FRANCE THROUGH THE YEAR

The French, with their farming roots, are deeply aware of the changing seasons, and the mild climate means they can celebrate outdoors most of the year. History and tradition are honoured with *fêtes*, such as Bastille Day (14 July). For culture lovers, thousands of arts festivals are held throughout France, ranging from the huge Avignon Theatre Festival down to small village events. Large national sports events, such as the Tour de France cycle race, are a key feature in the calendar. Throughout the year, festivals take place celebrating every kind of food and wine. In high summer, the cities empty and French and foreign visitors flock to the beaches and countryside.

Formula One racing at the Monaco Grand Prix

SPRING

France's outdoor life resumes in spring, terrace-cafés filling up in the sunshine. Easter is a time of Catholic processions, and concerts of sacred music. The Cannes Film Festival in May is the best known of the season's many conventions and trade fairs.

MARCH

International Half Marathon beginning and ending at Château de Vincennes.
Tinta' Mars *(fortnight)*, Langres. Cabaret and musical evenings at various venues.
Grenoble Jazz Festival *(fortnight Mar)*. Jazz concerts.
Banlieues Blues Jazz Festival *(Mar)*, Saint-Denis. Jazz music.
Six Nations Rugby Tournament, Stade de France, Paris.

Rugby ball

Festival d'Amiens *(mid-Mar/early Apr)*. Celebrated jazz festival at various venues.
Europa Jazz Festival *(end Mar/early Apr)*, Le Mans. International jazz festival.

APRIL

Festival de Pâques *(Easter week)*, Deauville. Chamber music festival *(see p255)*.
Feria Pascale *(Easter week)*, Arles. Start of the bullfighting season *(see pp508–9)*.
Lourdes Pilgrimage *(Palm Sun to Oct, see p459)*.
Floréal Musical d'Epinal *(early Apr–mid-May)*, Epinal. Multi-genre music festival.

Bourges Spring Festival *(end Apr/early May, see p313)*. Modern music.
Joan of Arc Festival *(end Apr–early May)* Orléans. Pageant and cathedral service *(see p312)*.
Paris International Marathon from Place de la Concorde to Avenue Foch.

MAY

Spring asparagus

Asparagus harvest, notably in the Loire.
International Grand Prix de Monaco *(Ascension weekend, see p530)*.
La Bravade *(16–18 May)*, St-Tropez *(see p516)*.

La Bravade procession honoring Saint Torpes in St-Tropez

Cannes Film Festival *(second and third week).*
Gypsy Pilgrimage *(late May),* Stes-Maries-de-la-Mer *(see p510).*
Fête de la Transhumance *(end May).* Herds are taken up to summer pastures.
International Garden Festival *(May–mid-Oct),* Chaumont sur Loire.
Nîmes Feria *(Pentecost).* Bullfights and street music festival *(see p496).*
Grandes Eaux Musicales *(Apr–Oct: Sun; Jul–Sep: Sat–Sun),* Versailles. Classical music in

the grounds of the château.
Puy-du-Fou Pageant *(May–Sep).* Audio-guides and horse stunts evoke local life through the ages *(see p290).*

Traditional transhumance of animals to summer pastures

Football Cup Final *(second week),* Stade de France, Paris.
Le Printemps des Arts *(mid-May–Jun),* Nantes area. Baroque dance and music.

SUMMER

The French holiday season begins in mid-July, with the return to work and school *(la rentrée)* in early September. Beaches, marinas and camp sites are all full to bursting. Each village has its *fête* and there are festivals, sporting events and flea markets.

JUNE

French Tennis Open *(last wk May–first wk Jun),* Stade Roland Garros, Paris.
Strasbourg International Music Festival *(Jun–Jul).*
International Sailing Week *(early Jun),* La Rochelle.

The rose season in full bloom

Le Mans 24-Hour Automobile Race *(second or third w/e, see p291).*
Fête de la Musique *(21 Jun).* Music events all over France.
Fête de St-Jean *(24 Jun).* Music, bonfires and fireworks all over France.
Gay Pride March *(23 Jun).* The march engulfs Paris.
Tarasque Festival *(last w/e),* Tarascon *(see p507).*

JULY

Festival d'Art Lyrique *(Jun–Jul),* Aix-en-Provence *(see p511).*
Avignon Theatre Festival *(all month, see p503).*
Paris-Plage *(mid-Jul–mid-Aug).* Paris and other cities get an

Bullfighting in Mont-de-Marsan

annual temporary beach.
Tombées de la Nuit *(first week),* Rennes. Arts festival.
Troménie *(2nd Sun Jul),* Locronan. Procession of penitents *(see p273).*
Comminges Music Festival *(Jul–end Aug, see p462).*
Nice Jazz Festival *(late-Jul).*
Mont-de-Marsan Feria *(third w/e).* Bullfights and music *(see p425).*
International Jazz Festival *(second half),* Antibes and Juan-les-Pins *(see p521).*
Jazz Vienne *(first 2 weeks),* Vienne *(see p382).*
Fête de St-Louis *(around 25 Aug),* Sète *(see p492).*
Tour de France cycle race *(1st 3 weeks).* The grand finale takes place on the Champs-Elysées, Paris.
Francofolies *(mid-Jul).* Music festival at La Rochelle.

Cyclists in the final stage of the Tour de France cycle race

Holiday-makers on a crowded beach in Cannes on the Côte d'Azur

AUGUST

Pablo Casals Festival
(end Jul–mid-Aug),
Prades *(see p480)*.
**Les Rendezvous de
l'Erdre** *(last w/e)*,
Nantes. Jazz and river-
boats *(see p290)*.
Mimos *(first week)*,
Périgueux. World
famous international
mime festival.

Avignon Theatre
Festival performer

Fête du Jasmin *(first w/e)*,
Grasse *(see p517)*. Floats,
music, dancing in town.
Foire aux Sorciers
(first Sun), Bué
(nr Bourges).
Costumed witch and
wizard festival and
folk groups.
**Parade of Lavender
Floats** *(first or
second weekends)*,
Digne *(see p517)*.

Fête de la Véraison
(first or second w/e), medieval
celebration of thanksgiving
for the bounty of the fruit
harvest, Châteauneuf-du-
Pape *(see p502)*.
Interceltic Festival *(second
week)*, Lorient. Celtic arts
and music.
Feria – Bullfight *(mid-Aug)*,
Dax *(see p425)*.
**St-Jean-Pied-de-Port-Basque
Fête** *(mid-Aug, see p454)*.

AUTUMN

In wine regions, the grape
harvest is the occasion for
much gregarious jollity, and
every wine village has its
wine festival. When the new
wine is ready in November
there are more festivities. The
hunting season begins –
everywhere there is game
shooting. In the southwest,
migrating birds are trapped.

SEPTEMBER

**Deauville American film
Festival** *(first fortnight)*.
Picardy Cathedral Festival
(mid-Sep). Classical concerts
in the region's cathedrals.
"Musicades" *(first fortnight)*,
Lyon. Classical concerts.
Le Puy "Roi de l'Oiseau",
(second week). Renaissance-
style festival *(see p365)*.
Grape harvest, wine regions
throughout France.
Journées du Patrimoine,
(third w/e). Over 14,000 historical buildings can be visited, many not normally open.

Ceremony for the Induction of new Chevaliers at the Hospice de Beaune

OCTOBER

Dinard British film Festival
(first week, see p281).
Nuit Blanche *(first Sat)*,
Paris. Museums stay
open all night.
Prix de l'Arc de Triomphe
(first Sun), Horse racing
at Longchamp, Paris.
Espelette Pepper Festival
(last w/e, see p453).
**Festival de Lanvellec
and Trégor** *(mid-Oct)*,
Baroque music festival.

Classical cello

NOVEMBER

**Dijon International Food
and Wine Festival** *(first 2
weeks)*. Traditional
gastronomic fair.
Apple Festival *(mid-
Nov)*, Le Havre.
**Wine Auctions and
Les Trois Glorieuses**
(third w/e), Beaune
(see p346).
Truffle season *(until
Mar)*, Périgord, Quercy
and Provence.

WINTER

Christmas wreath

At Christmas, traditional nativity plays are held in churches and there are fairs and markets throughout France. In the Alps and the Pyrenees, and even the Vosges and Massif Central, the ski-slopes are crowded. In Flanders and Nice, carnivals take place before Lent.

DECEMBER

Critérium International de la Première Neige *(early Dec)*, Val d'Isère. First competition of the season.

JANUARY

Monte-Carlo Rally *(usually mid-Jan, see p530)*.
Limoux Carnival *(until Mar)*. Street festival held since the Middle Ages.
Fashion shows. Summer

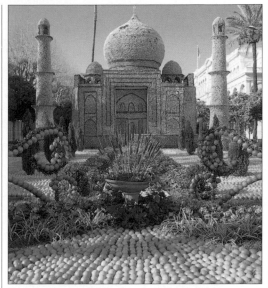

The Taj Mahal re-created at the Lemon Festival in Menton

collections, Paris.
Festival du Cirque *(end)*, Monaco. International event.
Festival de la Bande Dessinée *(last w/e)*. International strip cartoon festival, Angoulême.

FEBRUARY

Lemon Festival *(mid-Feb–Mar)*, Menton *(see p529)*.
Nice Carnival and the Battle of Flowers *(late Feb–early Mar, see p526)*.
Paris Carnaval, *(date varies, check)*, Quartier St-Fargeau.
Fête de Mimosa, *(3rd Sun)*, Bormes-les-Mimosas.

Downhill skier on the slopes in the French Alps

Celebrating the Nice Carnival and the Battle of Flowers

Bastille Day parade past the Arc de Triomphe

PUBLIC HOLIDAYS

New Year's Day (1 Jan)
Easter Sunday and Monday
Ascension Day (sixth Thursday after Easter)
Whit Monday (second Monday after Ascension)
Labour Day (1 May)
VE Day (8 May)
Bastille Day (14 Jul)
Assumption Day (15 Aug)
All Saints' Day (1 Nov)
Remembrance Day (11 Nov)
Christmas Day (25 Dec)

The Climate of France

Set on Europe's western edge, France has a varied, temperate climate. An Atlantic influence prevails in the north-west, with westerly sea winds bringing humidity and warm winters. The east experiences Continental temperature extremes with frosty, clear winters and often stormy summers. The south enjoys a Mediterranean climate with hot, dry summers and mild winters, punctuated by violent winds.

PARIS AND ILE DE FRANCE

°C				
	14.5	24	16	
	6.5	15	9.5	6.5
				2
	6 hrs	8 hrs	4.5 hrs	2 hrs
	50 mm	58 mm	55 mm	55 mm
month	Apr	Jul	Oct	Jan

- Average monthly maximum temperature
- Average monthly minimum temperature
- Average daily hours of sunshine
- Average monthly rainfall

NORMANDY

°C				
	13	21.5	16	
	5	12.5	8	7.5
				2
	5.5 hrs	7 hrs	4 hrs	2 hrs
	46 mm	48 mm	68 mm	64 mm
month	Apr	Jul	Oct	Jan

BRITTANY

°C				
	14.5	24	17	
	5.5	13	8.5	8
				2
	6 hrs	8 hrs	4.5 hrs	2 hrs
	44 mm	39 mm	62 mm	63 mm
month	Apr	Jul	Oct	Jan

LOIRE VALLEY

°C				
	15	24.5	17.5	
	6	14	9	8.5
				2.5
	6 hrs	8.5 hrs	4.5 hrs	2.5 hrs
	50 mm	46 mm	79 mm	87 mm
month	Apr	Jul	Oct	Jan

POITOU AND AQUITAINE

°C				
	16.5	26	19	
	6.5	14.5	9	9.5
				2.5
	6.5 hrs	9 hrs	5.5 hrs	2.5 hrs
	72 mm	47 mm	88 mm	100 mm
month	Apr	Jul	Oct	Jan

PYRENEES

°C				
	15	25	19	
	5	13.5	7.5	10
				0.5
	5 hrs	7.5 hrs	5.5 hrs	3.5 hrs
	98 mm	62 mm	78 mm	93 mm
month	Apr	Jul	Oct	Jan

PÉRIGORD, QUERCY AND GASCONY

°C				
	16.5	27	19	
	6	14.5	9	8.5
				2
	6 hrs	9 hrs	4.5 hrs	2.5 hrs
	60 mm	50 mm	57 mm	66 mm
month	Apr	Jul	Oct	Jan

Le Havre

PARI

Rennes

Nantes

Tours

Bordeaux

Montauban

Biarritz

THE HISTORY OF FRANCE

The only European country facing both the North Sea and the Mediterranean, France has been subject to a particularly rich variety of cultural influences. Though famous for the rootedness of its peasant population, it has also been a European melting pot, even before the arrival of the Celtic Gauls in the centuries before Christ, through to the Mediterranean immigrations of the 20th century.

Fleur-de-lys, the royal emblem

Roman conquest by Julius Caesar had an enduring impact, but from the 4th and 5th centuries AD, waves of Barbarian invaders destroyed much of the Roman legacy. The Germanic Franks provided political leadership in the following centuries, but when their line died out in the late 10th century, France was socially and politically fragmented.

THE FORMATION OF FRANCE

The Capetian dynasty gradually pieced France together over the Middle Ages, a period of great economic prosperity and cultural vitality. The Black Death and the Hundred Years' War brought setbacks, and the dynasty's power was seriously threatened by the rival Burgundian dukes. France recovered and despite the wars of religion

flourished during the Renaissance, followed by the grandeur of Louis XIV's reign. During the Enlightenment, in the 18th century, French culture was the envy of Europe.

The Revolution of 1789 ended the absolute monarchy and introduced major social and institutional reforms, many of which were endorsed and consolidated by Napoleon. Yet the Revolution also inaugurated the instability that remained a hallmark of French politics until de Gaulle and the 5th Republic: since 1789, France has known five republics, two empires and three brands of royal power, plus the Vichy government in World War II.

Modernization in the 19th and 20th centuries proved a slow process. Railways, the military service and radical educational reforms were crucial in forming a sense of French identity among the citizens.

Rivalry with Germany dominated French politics for most of the late 19th and early 20th century. The population losses in World War I were traumatic for France, while during 1940–44 the country was occupied by Germany. Yet since 1945, the two countries have proved the backbone of the developing European Union.

Inlaid marble table top showing the map of France in 1684

◁ *La République*, painted by Charles Landelle in 1848

Prehistoric France

The earliest traces of human life in France date back to around 2 million BC. From around 40,000 BC, *Homo sapiens* lived an itinerant existence as hunters and gatherers. Around 6000 BC, following the end of the Ice Age, a major shift in lifestyle occurred, as people settled down to herd animals and cultivate crops. The advent of metal-working allowed more effective tools and weapons to be developed. The Iron Age is associated particularly with the Celts, who arrived from the east during the first millennium BC. A more complex social hierarchy developed, consisting of warriors, farmers, artisans and druids (Celtic priests).

Bronze Age vase, Brittany

FRANCE IN 8000 BC
- ☐ *Former coastline*
- ☐ *Present-day land mass*

These carvings of horses' heads were found in the Pyrenees and date from around 9000 BC.

Carnac Stone Alignments *(4500–4000 BC)*
The purpose of the extensive networks of megaliths around Carnac (see p278) remains obscure. They possibly served in pagan rituals or as an astronomical calendar.

The mammoth, here carved from animal bone, was a thick-coated giant who died out after the end of the Ice Age.

Cro-Magnon Man
This skull, dating to c.25,000 BC, was discovered at Cro-Magnon in the Dordogne in 1868. In comparison with most of his predecessors, Cro-Magnon Man was tall, robust, and had a large head. He differed only marginally from us.

PREHISTORIC ART

The rich deposits of cave art in France have only been recognized as authentic for just over a century. They include wall paintings and daubings but also various engraved objects. Venus figurines, carved with flint tools, probably had ritual and religious rather than erotic purposes.

TIMELINE

Painting of bulls in Lascaux

2,000,000 BC	30,000	25,000	20,000
2,000,000 BC Early hominid societies	**30,000** Cro-Magnon Man		
	400,000 Discovery of fire by *Homo erectus*	**28,000** The first Venus sculptures, possibly representing fertility goddesses	*Primitive stone tool*

Doorway, Roquepertuse
Religion was an important part of Celtic life. The Celts made a cult of severed heads – presumably of their enemies – as seen in this sanctuary doorway dating from the 3rd century BC.

WHERE TO SEE PREHISTORIC FRANCE

The Lascaux cave paintings in Périgord *(see p434)* are among the best in the world. Further cave decoration is found around Les Eyzies *(pp434–5)*, at the Vallée des Merveilles near Tendes in the Alpes-Maritimes *(p529)* and in the Grotte du Pech Merle in the Lot Valley *(p438)*. The intriguing menhirs at Filitosa in Corsica *(pp542–3)* are about 4,000 years old.

The Lascaux *cave paintings, dating from 16,000–14,000 BC, include images of bulls and mammoths.*

The prehistoric hunter's quarry is here represented by a flock of chamois carved on a piece of bone.

This carved bone, found in Laugerie Basse in the Dordogne, shows a bison chased by a man with a spear.

Copper Axe *(c.2000 BC)*
Copper tools preceded the arrival of the stronger and more malleable bronze alloy. Iron was to prove the toughest and most useful metal of all.

Bronze Armor
Bronze and Iron Age people were highly warlike. The Celtic Gauls were feared even by Romans. Their protective armour, such as this breastplate dating from 750–475 BC, was light but reasonably effective.

This highly stylized female figure, a Venus figurine found in southwest France, was carved from mammoth tusk in around 20,000 BC.

15,000 Hunters live on wandering herds of mammoth, rhinoceros, and reindeer. Art includes the Lascaux caves and Val Camonica/Mont Bego engravings

7000–4500 Neolithic revolution: farming, megaliths, and menhir stone sculptures

600 Greek colony at Marseille. Mediterranean luxury goods exchanged for tin, copper, iron, and slaves. Early urban development

15,000	10,000	5,000

10,000 End of Ice Age. More regions become inhabitable

10,000–6000 Mammoth herds disappear and hunters must rely on animals of the forest, including wild boar and aurochs

1200–700 Arrival of the Celts during the Bronze and Iron Ages

500 Celtic nobles bury their dead with riches such as the Vix treasure *(see p334)*

Celtic helmet

Roman Gaul

The Romans had annexed the southern fringe of France by 125–121 BC. Julius Caesar brought the rest of Gaul under Roman control in the Gallic Wars (58–51 BC). The province of Gaul prospered: it developed good communications, a network of cities crammed with public buildings and leisure facilities such as baths

Roman mosaic from Vienne

and amphitheatres, while in the countryside large villas were established. By the 3rd century AD, however, barbarian raids from Germany were causing increasing havoc. From the 5th century barbarians began to settle throughout Gaul.

FRANCE IN 58 BC

☐ *Roman Gaul*

Emperor Augustus, who was considered a living God, was worshipped at this altar.

Roman Dolce Vita
The Romans brought material comfort and luxury, and wine-growing became widespread. This 19th-century painting by Couture conveys a contemporary view of Roman decadence.

Vercingetorix
The Celtic chieftain Vercingetorix was Julius Caesar's greatest military opponent. This bronze statue is at Alise-Sainte-Reine (see p334),the Gauls' final stand in 51 BC.

LA TURBIE
This impressive monument near Monaco was erected in 6 BC by the Roman Senate. It celebrates Augustus's victory over the Alpine tribes in 14–13 BC. Badly pillaged for its stone, restoration only began in the 1920's.

TIMELINE

125–121 BC Roman colonization of Southern Gaul

31 BC Frontiers of the Three Gauls (*Gallia Celtica, Gallia Aquitania* and *Gallia Belgica*) established by Augustus

Augustus

200 BC	100	0	AD 100

58–51 BC Julius Caesar's Gallic Wars result in establishment of Roman Gaul

Julius Caesar

16 BC Maison Carrée built in Nîmes *(see pp496–7)*

52–51 BC Vercingetorix revolt

AD 43 Lugdunum (Lyon) established as capital of the Three Gauls

Dancing Girl

Celtic art continued uninfluenced by Roman naturalistic ideals. This bronze statuette of a young woman dates from the 1st–2nd century AD.

A statue of Augustus was placed at the top of the original monument.

Enamelled Brooch

This decorative Gallo-Roman brooch dates from the second half of the 1st century BC.

WHERE TO SEE GALLO-ROMAN FRANCE

Gallo-Roman remains are to be found all over France, many of them in Provence. In addition to La Turbie *(see p529)* there is the Roman amphitheatre in Arles *(p485)* and the theatre and triumphal arch in Orange *(p502)*. Elsewhere, there are ruins at Autun in Burgundy *(p339)*, the Temple d'Auguste et Livie in Vienne *(p382)*, Les Arènes at Nîmes *(pp496–7)* and fragments of Vesunna in Périgueux *(p434)*.

Les Arènes in Nîmes, *built at the end of the 1st century AD, is still in use today.*

The Claudian Tables

In AD 48, Emperor Claudius persuaded the Senate to allow Gauls full Roman citizenship. The grateful Gauls recorded the event on stone tables found at Lyon.

The 44 tribes subjugated by Augustus are listed on an inscription, with a dedication to the emperor.

Emperor Augustus

Augustus, the first Roman Emperor (27 BC–AD 14), upheld the Pax Romana, an enforced peace which allowed the Gauls to concentrate on culture rather than war.

AD 177 First execution of Christian martyrs, Lyon. Sainte Blandine is thrown to the lions, who refuse to harm her

Sainte Blandine

360 Julian, prefect of Gaul, proclaimed Roman Emperor. Lutetia changes name to Paris

200	300	400

275 First Barbarian raids

313 Christianity officially recognized as religion under the rule of Constantine, the first Christian emperor

406 Barbarian invasion from the east. Settlement of the Franks and Germanic tribes

476 Overthrow of the last Roman emperor leads to end of the western Roman Empire

The Monastic Realm

9th-century gold chalice

The collapse of the Roman Empire led to a period of instability and invasions. Both the Frankish Merovingian dynasty (486–751) and the Carolingians (751–987) were unable to bring more than spasmodic periods of political calm. Throughout this turbulent period, the Church provided an element of continuity. As centres for Christian scholars and artists, the monasteries helped to restore the values of the ancient world. They also developed farming and viticulture and some became extremely powerful, dominating the country economically as well as spiritually.

FRANCE IN 751

☐ *Carolingian Empire*

Stable with lay brethren's quarters above

Charlemagne (742–814)
The greatest of Carolingian rulers, Charlemagne created an empire based on strictly autocratic rule. Powerful and charismatic, he could neither read nor write.

Bakery

The great infirmary hall could accommodate about 100 patients. It was flanked by the Lady Chapel.

Saint Benedict
Saint Benedict established the Benedictine rule: monks were to divide their time between work and prayer.

CLUNY MONASTERY

The Benedictine abbey of Cluny *(see p345)* was founded in 910 with the aim of major monastic reforms. This major religious centre, here shown as a reconstruction (after Conant), had great influence over hundreds of monasteries throughout Europe.

TIMELINE

481 Clovis the Frank becomes first Merovingian king

508 Paris made capital of the Frankish kingdom

c.590 Saint Colombanus introduces Irish monasticism to France

732 Battle of Poitiers: Charles Martel repulses Arab invasion

500	600	700

496 Conversion of Clovis, king of the Franks, to Christianity

629–37 Dagobert I, the last effective ruler of the Merovingian dynasty, brings temporary unity to the Frankish kingdom

Dagobert I

751 Pepin becomes first king of the Carolingian dynasty

Baptism of Clovis

The Frankish chieftain Clovis was the first barbarian ruler to convert to Christianity. He was baptized in Reims in 496.

The abbey church, begun in 1088, was the largest church in Europe before St Peter's was built in Rome in the 16th century.

Cemetery chapel

WHERE TO SEE MONASTIC FRANCE

The monastic realm has survived in austere Cistercian abbeys in Burgundy, such as Fontenay (see pp332–3). Little remains of Cluny, but some of the superb capitals can still be admired (p345). The best way to experience monastic France might be to retrace the steps of medieval pilgrims and visit the monastic centres on the route to Santiago de Compostela (pp400–01), such as Vézelay (pp336–7), Le Puy (pp364–5), Conques (pp368–9), Moissac (pp442–3) and St-Sernin in Toulouse (pp446–7).

Cluny capitals

Monastic Arts

In scriptoriums, talented artists dedicated their time to the meticulous art of illuminating and copying manuscripts for the libraries.

Monastic Labour

Monks of the Cistercian rule were renowned for their commitment to manual labour such as cultivating the land and producing wine and liqueurs.

Carolingian soldiers

987 Hugh Capet, first Capetian ruler

1096 First Crusade

1066 Conquest of England by the Normans

800	900	1000

843 Treaty of Verdun: division of the Carolingian Empire into three parts including West Francia

800 Coronation of Charlemagne as Holy Roman Emperor

910 Foundation of the Benedictine monastery of Cluny

1077 Bayeux tapestry

William the Conqueror's teering his ship on the Bayeux tapestry

Gothic France

The Gothic style, epitomized by soaring cathedrals *(see pp32–3)*, emerged in the 12th century at a time of growing prosperity and scholarship, crusades and an increasingly dominant monarchy. The rival French and Burgundian courts *(see p343)* became models of fashion and etiquette for all of Europe. *Chansons de gestes* (epic poems) performed by troubadours celebrated the code of chivalry.

Medieval knights in combat

FRANCE IN 1270

☐ *Royal territory*
▨ *Other fiefs*

Ciborium of Alpais

Alpais, a renowned 12th-century goldsmith in Limoges, made this superb ciborium used to hold wafers for the Holy Communion.

Winch to lift up stone sections

Courtly Love

According to the code of chivalry, knights dedicated their service to an ideal but unapproachable lady. Courtesy and romance were introduced in art and music.

The king supervised the building of the cathedral, accompanied by the architect.

Draper's Window

The textile trade benefited from the era of urban prosperity. This stained-glass window in a church in Semur-en-Auxois (see p335) shows wool washers at work.

TIMELINE

c.1100 First edition of the epic poem *Chanson de Roland*

1117 Secret marriage of the scholar Abelard and his student Héloïse. Her uncle, canon Filibert, does not approve and forces him to become a monk while she retires as a nun

1154 Angevin Empire created by Anglo-Norman dynasty starting with Henry Plantagenet, count of Anjou and king of England (as Henry II)

1100	1125	1150	1175

1115 Saint Bernard founds the Cistercian abbey at Clairvaux

1120 Rebuilding of the abbey of St-Denis; birth of the Gothic style

King Philip Augustus, who adopted the fleur-de-lys emblem

1180–1223 Reign of Philip Augustus

The Crusades

In an attempt to win back the Holy Land from the Turks, Philip Augustus set out on the Third Crusade (1189) alongside England's Richard the Lion-Heart and Holy Roman Emperor Frederick Barbarossa.

Lacelike sculpture adorned the façades of the Gothic cathedrals.

Stone masons cut stones on site.

ELEANOR OF AQUITAINE

Strong-willed and vivacious Eleanor, duchess of independent Aquitaine, contributed to the conflict between France and England. In 1137 she married the pious Louis VII of France. Returning from a Crusade, Louis found that their marriage had broken down. After the annulment in 1152, Eleanor married Henry of Anjou, taking her duchy with her. Two years later Henry successfully claimed the throne of England. Aquitaine came under English rule and thus the Angevin Empire began.

Eleanor of Aquitaine *and Henry II are buried in Fontevraud (p294).*

Holy Relic
Throughout the Middle Ages most churches could boast at least one saint's relic. The cult of relics brought pilgrims and more riches.

St Bernard *(1090–1153) Key figure of the Cistercian rule and counsellor to the pope, St Bernard preached rigorous simplicity of life.*

THE BUILDING OF A CATHEDRAL

In affluent, mercantile towns, skilled masons constructed towering Gothic cathedrals of revolutionary design, such as Chartres *(see pp308–11)* and Amiens *(pp202–3)*. With their improbable height and lightness they were a testimony to both faith and prosperity.

Louis IX on his death bed

1226 Louis IX crowned king

1270 Death of Louis IX at Tunis in the Eighth Crusade

1305 Papacy established in Avignon

1200	1225	1250	1275	1300

1214 Battle of Bouvines. Philip Augustus begins to drive the English out of France

1259 Normandy, Maine, Anjou, and Poitou acquired from England

1285 Philip the Fair crowned

1297 Louis IX is canonized, becoming Saint Louis

The Hundred Years' War

Public execution, in Froissart's 14th-century chronicle

The Hundred Years' War (1337–1453), pitting England against France for control of French land, had devastating effects. The damage of warfare was amplified by frequent famines and the ravages of bubonic plague in the wake of the Black Death in 1348. France came close to being permanently partitioned by the king of England and the duke of Burgundy. In 1429–30 the young Joan of Arc helped rally France's fortunes and within a generation the English had been driven out of France.

FRANCE IN 1429

☐ *France*

◼ *Anglo-Burgundy*

Angels with trumpets announce the Last Judgment.

Men of War

One of the reasons men enlisted as soldiers was hope for plunder. Both the French and English armies lived off the land, at the expense of the peasantry.

The elect, springing resurrected from their graves, are ushered into heaven.

The Black Death

The plague of 1348–52 caused 4–5 million deaths, about 25 per cent of the French population. For want of medicines people had to put their faith in prayers and holy processions.

TIMELINE

14th-century flame-thrower

1346 Battle of Crécy: French defeated by English

1356 French defeat at Battle of Poitiers

1328 Philip VI, first Valois monarch

1325

1350

1375

1337 Start of the Hundred Years' War

Plague victims

1348–52 The Black Death

1358 Bourgeois uprising in Paris led by Etienne Marcel. The Jacquerie peasant uprising in Northern France

Medieval Medicine

The state of the heavens was widely held to influence earthly conditions, such as health, and a diagnosis based on the zodiac was considered reliable. The standby cure for all sorts of ailments was blood letting.

English Longbow

The king's troops fought against England, but the individual French duchies supported whichever side seemed more favourable. In the confused battles, English bowmen excelled. Their longbows caused chaos among the hordes of mounted French cavalry.

Christ as Supreme Judge is flanked by angels bearing the instruments of the Passion.

Archangel Michael, resplendent with peacock wings, holds the judgment scales. The weight of sinners outbalances the elect.

John the Baptist is accompanied by the 12 apostles and the Virgin Mary, dressed in blue.

The damned, with hideously twisted faces, fall into Hell.

THE LAST JUDGMENT

With war, plague and famine as constant visitors, many people feared that the end of the world was nigh. Religious paintings, such as the great 15th-century altarscreen by Rogier van der Weyden in the Hôtel-Dieu in Beaune *(see pp346–7)*, reflected the moral fervour of the time.

Attack on Heresy

The general anxiety spilled over into anti-Semitic pogroms and attacks on alleged heretics, who were burned at the stake.

1415 Battle of Agincourt. French defeat by Henry V of England

1429 Intervention of Joan of Arc: Charles VII crowned king

1453 End of the Hundred Years' War. Only Calais remains in English hands

1400	1425	1450

1411 *Les Très Riches Heures du Duc du Berry* prayer book, by Paul and Jean de Limbourg *(see p204)*

1431 Joan of Arc burned at stake as witch by the English

1419 Charles VI of France makes Henry V of England his heir

Joan of Arc

Renaissance France

As a result of the French invasion of Italy in 1494, the ideals and aesthetic of the Italian Renaissance spread to France, reaching their height during the reign of François I. Known as a true Renaissance prince, he was skilled in letters and art as well as sports and war. He invited Italian artists, such as Leonardo and Cellini, to his court and enjoyed Rabelais' bawdy stories. Another highly influential Italian was Catherine de' Medici (1519–89). Widow of Henri II, she virtually ruled France through her sons, François II, Charles IX and Henri III. She was also one of the major players in the Wars of Religion (1562–93) between Catholics and Protestants, which divided the nobility and tore the country to pieces.

Masked lute-player

FRANCE IN 1527

☐ *Royal territory*

▨ *Other fiefs*

The corner towers are a Gothic feature transformed by Italian lightness of touch into pure decoration.

Galerie François I, Fontainebleau
The artists of the School of Fontaine-bleau blended late Italian Renaissance style with French elements.

Power Behind the Throne
Catherine de' Medici domi-nated French politics from 1559–89.

AZAY-LE-RIDEAU
One of the loveliest of the Loire châteaux, Azay was begun in 1518 *(see p296)*. Italian influences are visible and it is clear that this is a dwelling meant for pleasure rather than defence.

TIMELINE

1470 First printing presses established in France

Prototype tank by Leonardo da Vinci

1519 Leonardo da Vinci dies in the arms of François I at the French court in Amboise

1536 Calvin's *Institutes of the Christian Religion* leads to a new form of Protestantism

1470	1480	1490	1500	1510	1520	1530

1477 Final defeat of the Dukes of Burgundy, who sought to establish a middle kingdom between France and Germany

1494–1559 France and Austria fight over Italian territories in the Italian Wars

1515 Reign of François I begins

Golden coin showing the fleur-de-lys and the salamander of François I

Gold Pomander
Pomanders containing sweet-smelling herbs such as amber and cinnamon were carried in time of plague to ward off the bad air held responsible for contagion.

Ballroom with Flemish tapestries

The staircase was in the new Italian fashion with double flights of steps rather than a spiral.

WHERE TO SEE RENAISSANCE FRANCE

In Paris, many churches and the impressive place des Vosges *(see p91)* date from the Renaissance. There are countless 16th-century châteaux in the Loire and Burgundy. Among the finest are Chenonceau *(pp298–9)* and Tanlay *(p331)*. Salers *(p363)* is a virtually intact Renaissance town. The historic centre of Toulouse *(p446)* has many elegant Renaissance palaces.

This fireplace *stands in François I's room at Château de Chenonceau.*

François I and the Italian Influence
François I, here receiving Raphael's painting The Holy Family *in 1518, collected Italian art at Fontainebleau. Among the favoured painters were Michelangelo, Leonardo and Titian.*

The Red Room

New France
French expansion and quest for colonies started with Cartier's expedition to Canada in 1534 (see p282).

1559 Treaty of Cateau–Cambrésis ends the Italian Wars

1572 Massacre of Protestants on St Bartholomew's Eve in Paris

1589 Henry III murdered. The Huguenot Henry IV becomes first Bourbon king of France

1598 Edict of Nantes: tolerance for Protestantism

1608 Foundation of Quebec

1540	1550	1560	1570	1580	1590	1600

1539 Edict of Villers Cotterets makes French the official language of state

1562 Wars of Religion between Catholics and Protestants start

St Bartholomew's Eve Massacre

1593 Henry IV converts to Catholicism and ends the Wars of Religion

The Grand Siècle

Emblem of the Sun King

The end of the Religious Wars heralded a period of exceptional French influence and power. The cardinal ministers Richelieu and Mazarin paved the way for Louis XIV's absolute monarchy. Political development was matched by artistic styles of unprecedented brilliance: enormous Baroque edifices, the drama of Molière and Racine, and the music of Lully. Versailles *(see pp174–7)*, built under the supervision of Louis' capable finance minister Colbert, was the glory of Europe, but its cost and Louis XIV's endless wars proved expensive for the French state and led to widespread misery by the end of his reign.

FRANCE IN 1661

☐ *Royal territory*

■ *Avignon (papal enclave)*

Madame (married to Monsieur) as Flora

Molière *(1622–73)*
Actor-playwright Molière performed many plays for Louis XIV and his court, though some of his satires were banned. After his death, his company became the basis of the French state theatre, the Comédie Française.

Monsieur, the king's brother

Madame de Maintenon
In 1684, following the death of his first wife Marie-Thérèse, Louis secretly married his mistress Mme de Maintenon, then aged 49.

THE SUN KING AND HIS FAMILY

Claiming to be monarch by divine right, Louis XIV commanded court painter Jean Nocret to devise this allegorical scene in 1665. Surrounded by his family, the king appears as the sun god Apollo.

TIMELINE

1610–17 Marie de' Medici acts as Regent for Louis XIII	*Cardinal Richelieu* **1624** Cardinal Richelieu becomes principal minister	**1634** Foundation of the literary society Académie Française	**1642–3** Death of Louis XIII and Cardinal Richelieu. Accession of Louis XIV with Mazarin as principal minister
1610	**1620**	**1630**	**1640**	**1650**

1617 Louis XIII accedes at the age of 17

1631 Foundation of *La Gazette*, France's first newspaper

1637 Descartes' *Discourse on Method*

1635 Richelieu actively involves France in the Thirty Years' War

1648–52 The Fronde: French civil wars

Louis XIV's Book of Hours
After a lively and libertine youth, Louis became increasingly religious. His Book of Hours *(1688–93) is in Musée Condé (see p205).*

Royal Wedding
Louis XIII and Anne of Austria were married in 1615. After his death, Anne became regent for the young Louis XIV with Cardinal Mazarin as minister.

Baroque Figurine
The royal glory was reflected in the arts. This objet d'art *features a Christ in jasper on a pedestal decorated with gilded cherubs and rich enamelling.*

Louis XIV as Apollo

Anne of Austria as Cybele

The dauphin (the king's son)

Grande Mademoiselle, the king's cousin, as Diana

Queen Marie-Thérèse as Juno

WHERE TO SEE ARCHITECTURE OF THE GRAND SIÈCLE

Paris boasts many imposing Grand Siècle buildings, such as the Hôtel des Invalides *(see p114)*, the Dôme church *(p115)* and the Palais du Luxembourg *(pp126–7)*, but the Château de Versailles *(pp174–7)* is the ultimate example of the flamboyance of the period. Reminders of this glory include the sumptuous Palais Lascaris in Nice *(p528)* and the Corderie Royale in Rochefort *(p417)*. At the same time, military architect Vauban constructed mighty citadels, such as Neuf-Brisach *(see p226)*.

Versailles' *interior is a typical example of the gilded Baroque style.*

Playwright Jean Racine (1639–99)

1661 Death of Mazarin. Louis XIV becomes his own principal minister

1662 Colbert, finance minister, reforms finances and the economy

1680 Creation of the theatre Comédie Française

1685 Revocation of the Edict of Nantes of 1598: Protestantism banned

1682 Royal court moves to Versailles

1709 Last great famine in French history

1689 Major wars of Louis XIV begin

1686 Opening of the Café Procope (first coffee house in Paris)

1660	1670	1680	1690	1700

17th-century cannon

Enlightenment and Revolution

In the 18th century, Enlightenment philosophers such as Voltaire and Rousseau redefined man's place within a framework of natural principles, thus challenging the old aristocratic order. Their essays were read across Europe and even in the American colonies. But although France exported worldly items as well as ideas, the state's increasing debts brought social turmoil, triggering the 1789 Revolution. Under the motto "Liberty, Equality, Fraternity", the new Republic and its reforms had a far-reaching impact on the rest of Europe.

Plate of Louis XVI's execution

FRANCE IN 1789
☐ *Royal France*
■ *Avignon (papal enclave)*

Voltaire *(1694–1778)*
Voltaire, master of satire, wrote numerous essays and the novel Candide. *His fierce critiques sometimes forced him into exile abroad.*

National Assembly

Jacobin Club

The Guillotine
This infamous invention was introduced in 1792 as a humane alternative to other forms of capital punishment, which had usually involved torture.

Place de la Révolution
(see p98) is where Louis XVI's execution took place in 1793.

The Tuileries

Café Le Procope was the haunt of Voltaire and Rousseau.

Palais Royal
The private residence of the Duke of Orléans, the Palais Royal (see p99) became a centre of revolutionary agitation from 1789. It was also the site of several printing presses.

TIMELINE

1715 Death of Louis XIV, accession of Louis XV

Physician's protective costume worn during the plague

1743–64 Mme de Pompadour, Louis XV's favourite, uses her influence to support artists and philosophers during her time at court

1715	1725	1735	1745	1755

1720 Last outbreak of plague in France: population of Marseille decimated

1751 Publication of the first volume of Diderot's *Encyclopaedia*

1756–63 Seven Years' War: France loses Canada and other colonial possessions

Revolutionary Symbols
The motifs of the Revolution such as the blue, white and red of the tricolor even appeared on wallpaper in the 1790s.

Queen Marie-Antoinette
Marie-Antoinette's frivolous behaviour helped discredit the monarchy. She was held in the Conciergerie and brought to the guillotine in 1793.

The Marais, earlier an aristocratic area, fell into decay as a result of the Revolution.

Bastille

WHERE TO SEE 18TH-CENTURY FRANCE
The Palais de l'Elysée, built in 1718 (*see p108*), is an outstanding example of 18th-century Parisian architecture. Examples across France include the curious Saline Royale in Arc-et-Senans (*p350*), the Grand Théâtre in Bordeaux (*p422*) the elegant mansions in Condom (*p440*) and the merchants' houses in Ciboure (*p453*). The Château de Laàs in Sauveterre de Béarn is a feast of 18th-century art and furniture (*p454*).

The Grand Théâtre *in Bordeaux is an excellent example of elegant 18th-century architecture.*

REVOLUTIONARY PARIS
From 1789, Paris housed numerous political clubs, such as the left-wing Jacobins, and many revolutionary newspapers. The war tune *La Marseillaise*, introduced by volunteers from the south, was soon heard everywhere.

Revolutionary Calendar
A new calendar was introduced, the months named after seasonal events. This engraving shows Messidor, the month of harvest.

1768 Annexation of Corsica

1789 Storming of the Bastille, and establishment of constitutional monarchy: abolition of feudal laws

1783 First balloon ascent, by the Montgolfier brothers

Model of the Bastille

1765	1775	1785	1795

1774 Accession of Louis XVI

Electors' card for the Convention of 1792

1794 Overthrow of Robespierre and end of the Terror

1762 Rousseau's *Emile* and the *Social Contract*

1778–83 France aids the 13 colonies in the War of American Independence

1792 Overthrow of Louis XVI: establishment of First Republic

Napoleonic France

Two generations of Napoleons dominated France from 1800 to 1870. Napoleon Bonaparte took the title of Emperor Napoleon I. He extended his empire throughout most of western Europe, placing his brothers and sisters on the thrones of conquered countries. Defeated in 1814 and replaced by the restored Bourbon dynasty, followed by the 1830 Revolution and the so-called July Monarchy, the Napoleonic clan made a comeback after 1848. Napoleon I's nephew, Louis Napoleon, became President of the Second Republic, then made himself emperor as Napoleon III. During his reign Paris was modernized and the industrial transformation of France began.

Légion d'Honneur

EUROPE IN 1812

☐ Napoleonic rule
■ Dependent states

The Laurel, crown of the Roman emperors

Napoleon, as First Consul, is crowned by Chronos, the God of Time.

Musée du Louvre
The museum had opened in 1792, but it flourished during Napoleon's reign. He took a personal interest in both acquisitions and organization.

The revolutionary tricolor flag was kept throughout the empire.

Imperial Insignia
Napoleon I created a new titled aristocracy, who were allowed coats of arms. Only his, however, was permitted a crown. The eagle symbol was adopted in 1800, an evocation of Imperial Rome.

Légion d'Honneur medal

TIMELINE

Josephine's bed at Malmaison

1804 Napoleon crowned as Emperor. Napoleonic Civil Code established

1800 Establishment of the Bank of France

1809 Josephine and Napoleon divorce. She retains Château Malmaison *(see p173)*

1814 Defeat of Napoleon by the Allies (England, Russia, Austria and Prussia). Napoleon exiled to Elba

1800	1810	1820

1802 Treaty of Amiens brings temporary peace to Europe

1802 Establishment of the Légion d'Honneur

1806 Arc de Triomphe commissioned

1803 Resumption of wars to create the Napoleonic Empire

1815 The "Hundred Days": Napoleon returns from Elba, is defeated at Waterloo and exiled to St Helena

July Revolution
*Three days of street-fighting in
July 1830 ended unpopular
Bourbon rule.*

The Napoleons
*This imaginary group
portrait depicts
Napoleon I (seated), his
son "Napoleon II" – who
never ruled (right) –
Napoleon's nephew
Louis Napoleon
(Napoleon III) and the
latter's infant son.*

The Civil Code,
created by
Napoleon, is here
shown as a tablet.

Napoleon on Campaign
*A dashing general in the late 1790s,
Napoleon remained a remarkable mili-
tary commander throughout his reign.*

EMPIRE FASHION

Greek and Roman ideals were
evident in architecture, furniture,
design, and fashion. Women wore
light, Classical tunics, the most
daring with one shoulder or more
bare. David and Gérard were the
fashionable portraitists,
while Delacroix and
Géricault created many
Romantic masterpieces.

NAPOLEONIC GLORY
Though professing himself a true revolutionary, Napoleon developed a taste for
imperial pomp. However, he also achieved
some long-lasting reforms such as the Civil Code,
the new school system and the Bank of France.

Madame Récamier *held a popular
salon and was renowned for her beauty
and wit. David painted her in 1800.*

1832 Cholera
epidemics begin

1838 Daguerre
experiments with
photography

1851 Coup d'état by Louis
Napoleon

1848 Revolution of 1848: end of
July Monarchy and establishment
of the Second Republic

1852 Louis
Napoleon crowned
as Emperor
Napoleon III

1830	1840	1850	1860

1830 Revolution of 1830: Bourbon
Charles X replaced by the
July Monarchy of King
Louis-Philippe

1840 Large-scale railway
building

1853 Modernization of
Paris by Haussmann

1857 Baudelaire (*Les Fleurs
du Mal*) and Flaubert (*Mme
Bovary*) prosecuted for
public immorality

1859–60
Annexation
of Nice
and Savoy

*Train on the Paris –
St-Germain line*

The Belle Epoque

Art Nouveau vase by Lalique

The decades before World War I became the *Belle Epoque* for the French, remembered as a golden era forever past. Nevertheless this was a politically turbulent time, with working-class militancy, organized socialist movements, and the Dreyfus Affair polarizing the country between Left and anti-semitic Right. New inventions such as electricity and vaccination against disease made life easier at all social levels. The cultural scene thrived and took new forms with Impressionism and Art Nouveau, the realist novels of Gustave Flaubert and Emile Zola, cabaret and cancan and, in 1895, the birth of the cinema.

FRANCE IN 1871

☐ *Under Third Republic*

■ *Alsace and Lorraine*

Universal Exhibition

The 1889 Paris exhibition was attended by 3.2 million people. Engineer Eiffel's breathtaking iron structure dominated the exhibition and caused great controversy at the time.

Statue of Apollo by Aimé Millet

Stage

Copper-green roofed cupola

Backstage area

Peugeot Car *(1899)*
The car and bicycle brought new freedom, becoming a part of people's leisure time. Peugeot, Renault and Citroën were all founded before World War I.

The auditorium in gold and purple seated over 2,000 guests.

TIMELINE

Woman on the barricades in 1871

1865	1870	1875	1880	1885	1890

1869 Opening of the Suez Canal, built by Ferdinand de Lesseps

1871 The Paris Commune leads to the Third Republic

1880s Scramble for colonies in Africa and Asia begins

1889 Universal Exhibition in Paris; Eiffel Tower built

1870–71 Franco-Prussian War: defeat and overthrow of Napoleon III; France cedes Alsace and Lorraine to Germany

1874 Impressionist movement begins

1881–6 Reforms in education by Jules Ferry

1885 Pasteur produces vaccine for rabies, the first tested on a human

1890 Peugeot constructs one of the earliest automobiles

Poster Art
The poster was revolutionized by Art Nouveau, with designs by Alphonse Mucha particularly popular. This one from 1897 is for beer, the beverage of the lost Alsace and Lorraine, which became a "patriotic" drink.

WHERE TO SEE THE BELLE EPOQUE
Belle Epoque buildings include the Negresco Hotel, Nice *(see p526)*, the Grand Casino in Monte-Carlo *(p530)* and the Palais Hotel in Biarritz *(p452)*. The Musée d'Orsay in Paris *(pp120–21)* exhibits Art Nouveau objects and furniture.

Staircase at the Opera
The grand staircase had coloured marble columns and a frescoed ceiling. As this painting by Beroud from 1887 shows, it soon became a showcase for high society.

Guimard's *Metro entrance is a typical example of the elegant, swirling lines of Art Nouveau.*

Emperor's pavilion

Grand Foyer with balconies and lavishly decorated ceiling

Grand staircase

OPERA NATIONAL GARNIER
Founded by Napoleon III in 1862, the new opera was opened to great public acclaim in 1875 and became a focus of Belle Epoque social life. Designed by Charles Garnier, its extravagant exterior was matched by its sumptuous interior decor.

The Divine Sarah
Actress Sarah Bernhardt (1844–1923) worked in all theatrical genres, dominating the Paris stage.

1895 First public cinema by the Lumière brothers

Caricature of Zola

1894–1906 The alleged treason of Dreyfus sparks the Dreyfus Affair, involving the author Zola among others

1918 Germany asks for armistice to end war

1909 Blériot flies the Channel

1917 Mutinies in the army suppressed by Pétain

1916 Battle of Verdun

1895	1900	1905	1910	1915

1905 Official separation of church and state

1913 Publication of Proust's first volume of *Remembrance of Things Past*

1898 Marie and Pierre Curie discover radium

1914 World War I breaks out

1919 Treaty of Versailles

French recruit, 1916

Avant-Garde France

Despite the devastation wrought by two world wars, France retained its international renown as a centre for the avant garde. Paris in particular was a magnet for experimental writers, artists and musicians. The cafés were full of American authors and jazz musicians, French surrealists and film makers. The French Riviera also attracted colonies of artists and writers, from Matisse and Picasso to Hemingway and Scott Fitzgerald, along with the wealthy industrialists and aristocrats arriving in automobiles or the famous Train Bleu. And from 1936 paid holidays meant that the working classes could also enjoy the new fashion for sunbathing.

FRANCE IN 1919

☐ *French territory*

African Gods of Creation

Art Deco 1925
The International Exhibition in Paris in 1925 launched the Art Deco style: geometrical shapes and utilitarian designs, adapted for mass-production.

Dancers in heavy cardboard costumes

The Jazz Age
Paris welcomed American jazz musicians, such as Sidney Bechet in 1925 and Dizzy Gillespie (left), co-founder of Bebop in the 1940s.

Citroën Goddess *(1956)*
This elegant model became an icon of the new French consumerism evident in the 1950s and '60s.

The costumes and scenery by the Cubist Léger were striking and made to look partly mechanical.

TIMELINE

Air France aircraft, 1937

1920 French Communist Party founded. Publication of Tristan Tzara's Dadaist Manifesto

1928 Premiere of *Un Chien Andalou* by Luis Buñuel and Salvador Dalí

1933 Air France begins operation

1937 Premiere of *La Grande Illusion* by Jean Renoir

1920

1930

1924 Olympic Games in Paris. André Breton publishes the *Surrealist Manifesto*

Detail of poster for the 1924 Olympics

1929–39 The Depression

1936–38 The "Popular Front": radical social programme introduced, including paid holidays

1938 Munich Conference: height of appeasement

Coco Chanel (1883–1971)
*Chanel, here photographed by
Man Ray, revolutionized fashion
in the 1920s with her elegant
but comfortable clothes.*

Par Avion
*France pioneered the use of
airmail, starting in 1927.*

First
Man and
Woman

WORLD WAR II

Following the collapse of the
Third Republic in 1940, Paris
and the north and west parts of
France were occupied by the
Germans until the Liberation in
1944. Southeast France formed
the collaborationist Vichy state,
led by Marshal Pétain and
Pierre Laval. Meanwhile, the
Free French movement was
led by Charles de Gaulle, with
Jean Moulin coordinating the
operations of the many
different Resistance factions.

German soldiers *liked to pose
in front of the Eiffel Tower during
the occupation of Paris.*

Josephine Baker (1906–75)
*The music hall flourished in the
1920s with Mistinguett and Josephine
Baker as its undisputed queens.*

LA CREATION DU MONDE (1923)

The African theme
was based on text
by Blaise Cendrars.

Artistic experimentation thrived in the early
20th century. *La Création du Monde* by Les
Ballets Suédois had costumes by Léger and
music by Milhaud. Diaghilev's Ballets Russes
also competed for avant-garde artists like
Picabia, Cocteau, Satie and Sonia Delaunay.

1940 The Fall of France. Vichy government led by Pétain. De Gaulle fights on from London

1942 The whole of France controlled by Germany

1949 Establishment of NATO. Founding of the Council of Europe

1958 5th Republic begins under President de Gaulle

1956 Late in her career, Edith Piaf crowns her success at Carnegie Hall, New York

1940

1950

1944 D-Day: Allied landings in Normandy (June). Liberation of Paris (August)

1939 Declaration of World War II

1946 Sartre establishes *Les Temps Modernes*. First Cannes Film Festival

1945 End of the war. 4th Republic begins. Votes for women

1954 France withdraws from Indo-China after Battle of Dien Bien Phu. Start of Algerian insurrection

Modern France

After the 1950s, the traditional foundations of French society changed: the number of peasant farmers plummeted, old industries decayed, jobs in the service sector and high-technology industries grew dramatically, and the French came to enjoy the benefits of mass culture and widespread consumerism. High prestige projects, such as Concorde, TGV, La Défense and the Pompidou Centre, brought international acclaim. Efforts for European integration and the inauguration of the

Lemon squeezer by Philippe Starck

Channel Tunnel aim towards closer relations with France's neighbours.

FRANCE TODAY
☐ *France*
■ *European Union*

Pompidou Centre *(1977)*
The Pompidou Centre's controversial building changed the aspect of the historic quarter of Beaubourg. A major arts centre, it has revitalized the formerly rundown area (see pp92–3).

La Grande Arche was opened in 1989 to commemorate the bicentenary of the Revolution.

Shopping centre

New Wave Film
Directors like Godard and Truffaut launched a refreshing, personal style of films, such as Jules et Jim *(1961).*

LA DÉFENSE

The huge modernist business centre at La Défense *(see p130)*, on the edge of Paris, was developed in the 1960s and has become a prime site for the headquarters of major multinational companies.

TIMELINE

1960	1970	1980
1960 First French atomic bomb. Decolonization of black Africa	**1967** Common Agricultural Policy, subsidizing Europe's farmers	**1973** Extension of the Common Market (EU) from six to nine states	**1974** Giscard d'Estaing elected president	**1989** Bicentennial celebration of the French Revolution
			1980 Giverny, Monet's garden, opens to the public *(see p266)*	**1981** Socialist Mitterrand becomes president for 14 years
1962 Evian agreements lead to Algerian independence	**1963** First French nuclear power station	**1969** Pompidou replaces de Gaulle as president	**1976** Concorde's first commercial flight	**1977** Jacques Chirac first mayor of Paris since 1871. Opening of the Pompidou Centre	**1987** Mitterrand and Thatcher sign agreement for Channel Tunnel. Trial in Lyon of ex-SS Officer Klaus Barbie
	1968 May demonstrations				

François Mitterrand

EU Flag
France has been one of the leading forces in the European Union ever since the move toward closer European collaboration began in the 1950s.

TGV
The TGV (Train à Grande Vitesse) is one of the world's fastest trains (see pp682–3). It typifies the French government's commitment to high technology and improved communications.

The Areva (Fiat) Tower is one of Europe's tallest towers, at 178 m (584 ft).

Fashion by Lacroix
Despite less demand for haute couture, Paris is still a major fashion centre. The designs shown on the catwalk, here by Christian Lacroix, remain proof of the world-renowned skills of French designers.

Palais de la Défense was built first and houses the centre for industry.

MAY 1968

The events of May 1968 began as a political revolt by left-wing students against the Establishment and had a profound influence on French society. Around 9 million workers, and leading intellectuals like Jean-Paul Sartre, joined the rebellion, demanding better pay, better study conditions and the overhaul of traditional values and institutions.

Student riots *starting in Nanterre, just outside Paris, sparked widespread rioting and industrial unrest in France.*

1994 Channel Tunnel opens

2002 National Front defeat Socialists in 1st round of presidential campaign. France re-elects Jacques Chirac

Prince Albert II

2008 Jean-Marie Gustave Le Clézio wins the Nobel Prize for literature

2010 The head of France's King Henry IV is found after it was lost in 1793

90	2000		2010	2020

1991 Edith Cresson is first woman prime minister

2002 Euro replaces franc as legal tender

1996 Mitterrand dies after a long illness

2007 Centre-right Nicolas Sarkozy is elected president

2005 Prince Rainier III of Monaco dies and is succeeded by his only son, Prince Albert II

Kings and Emperors of France

Following the break-up of the Roman Empire, the Frankish king Clovis consolidated the Merovingian dynasty. It was followed by the Carolingians, and from the 10th century by Capetian rulers. The Capetians established royal power, which passed to the Valois branch in the 14th century, and then to the Bourbons in the late 16th century, following the Wars of Religion. The Revolution of 1789 seemed to end the Bourbon dynasty, but it made a brief come-back in 1814–30. The 19th century was dominated by the Bonapartes, Napoleon I and Napoleon III. Since the overthrow of Napoleon III in 1870, France has been a republic.

768–814 Charlemagne

743–751 Childéric III

716–721 Chilpéric II

695–711 Childebert II

566–584 Chilpéric I

558–562 Clothaire I

447–458 Merovich

458–482 Childéric I

674–691 Thierri III

655–668 Clothaire III

628–637 Dagobert I

954–986 Lothaire

898–929 Charles III, the Simple

884–888 Charles II, the Fat

879–882 Louis III

840–877 Charles I, the Bald

1137–80 Louis VII

987–996 Hugh Capet

1031–60 Henri I

1060–1108 Philippe I

400	500	600	700	800	900	1000	110
MEROVINGIAN DYNASTY				CAROLINGIAN DYNASTY		CAPETIAN DYNAST	
400	500	600	700	800	900	1000	110

751–768 Pépin the Short

721–737 Thierri IV

711–716 Dagobert III

691–695 Clovis III

668–674 Childéric II

637–655 Clovis II

584–628 Clothaire II

562–566 Caribert

511–558 Childebert I

996–1031 Robert II, the Pious

986–987 Louis V

936–954 Louis IV, the Foreigner

888–898 Odo, Count of Paris

882–884 Carloman

877–879 Louis II, the Stammerer

814–840 Louis I, the Pious

482–511 Clovis I

1108–37 Louis VI, the Fat

1515–47 François I

1226–70 Louis IX (St Louis)

1498–1515 Louis XII, Father of his People

1483–98 Charles VIII

1422–61 Charles VII, the Victorious

1270–85 Philippe III

1285–1314 Philippe IV, the Fair

1316–22 Philippe V

1328–50 Philippe VI

1774–92 Louis XVI

1547–59 Henri II

1559–60 François II

1610–43 Louis XIII

1643–1715 Louis XIV, the Sun King

1804–14 Napoleon I

1200	1300	1400	1500	1600	1700	1800
	VALOIS DYNASTY			BOURBON DYNASTY		
1200	1300	1400	1500	1600	1700	1800

1314–16 Louis X

1380–1422 Charles VI, the Fool

1560–74 Charles IX

1814–24 Louis XVIII

1574–89 Henri III

1824–30 Charles X

1364–80 Charles V, the Wise

1322–28 Charles IV, the Fair

1589–1610 Henri IV

1830–48 Louis-Philippe I

1852–70 Napoleon III

1350–64 Jean II, the Good

1223–6 Louis VIII

1180–1223 Philip Augustus

1461–83 Louis XI, the Spider

1715–74 Louis XV

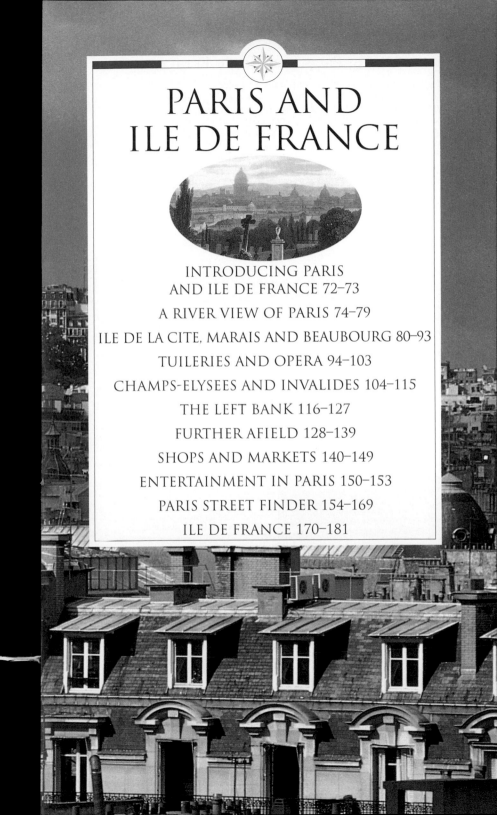

PARIS AND ILE DE FRANCE

Introducing Paris and Ile de France

The French capital is rich in museums, art galleries and monuments. The Louvre, Eiffel Tower and Pompidou Centre are among the most popular sights. Surrounding Paris, the Ile de France takes in 12,000 sq km (4,600 sq miles) of busy suburbs and commuter towns punctuated by châteaux, the most celebrated being Versailles. Further out, suburbia gives way to farmland, forests and the magnificent palace of Fontainebleau.

Arc de Triomphe

Opéra Garnie

CHAMPS-ELYSEES AND INVALIDES
Pages 104–15

Eiffel Tower

Musée d'Orsay

The Eiffel Tower, *designed for the Universal Exhibition of 1889, scandalized contemporary critics but is now the capital's most famous landmark (see p113).*

The Musée d'Orsay, *opened in 1986, was created from a late 19th-century railway terminus (see pp120–1). Its magnificent collection of 19th- and early 20th-century art (notably Impressionist art) includes Jean-Baptiste Carpeaux's* Four Quarters of the World *(1872).*

◁ **Rooftop view of Sacré-Coeur and the Butte Montmartre**

ILE DE FRANCE
Pages 170–81

0 kilometres 25

0 miles 25

TUILERIES AND OPERA
Pages 94–103

ILE DE LA CITE, MARAIS AND BEAUBOURG
Pages 80–93

the Louvre

Pompidou Centre

Notre-Dame

THE LEFT BANK
Pages 116–27

Musée de Cluny

0 kilometres 1

0 miles 0.5

The Pompidou Centre
(1977) is as famous for its novel inside-out design as it is for masterpieces by Picasso, Matisse and Miró (see pp92–3).

Notre-Dame, *a stunning example of Gothic architecture begun in 1163, took two centuries and armies of medieval workers to complete (see pp86–7). Architect Viollet-le-Duc designed the spire in the 19th century.*

A RIVER VIEW
OF PARIS

**Sculpture on the
Pont Alexandre III**

The remarkable French music-hall star Mistinguett described the Seine as a "pretty blonde with laughing eyes". The river most certainly has a beguiling quality, but the relationship that exists between it and the city of Paris is far more than one of flirtation.

No other European city defines itself by its river in the same way as Paris. The Seine is the essential point of reference to the city: distances are measured from it, street numbers determined by it, and it divides the capital into two distinct areas, the Right Bank on the north side of the river and the Left Bank on the south side. These are as well-defined as any of the official boundaries. The city is also divided historically: the east is linked to the city's ancient roots and the west to the 19th–20th centuries.

Practically every building of note in Paris is either along the river bank or within a stone's throw of it. The quays are lined by fine bourgeois apartments, magnificent townhouses, world-renowned museums and striking monuments.

Above all, the river is very much alive. For centuries fleets of small boats used it, but motorized land traffic stifled this once-bustling scene. Today, the river is busy with commercial barges and massive *bâteaux mouches* pleasure boats carrying sightseers up and down the river.

The Latin Quarter Quayside is on the left bank of the Seine. Associated with institutes of learning since the Middle Ages, it acquired its name from the early Latin-speaking students.

see pp76–7

CHAMPS-ELYSEES
AND INVALIDES

TUILERIES
AND
OPERA

see pp78–9

ILE DE LA CITE,
MARAIS AND
BEAUBOURG

CHAMPS-
ELYSEES
AND
INVALIDES

THE LEFT BANK

This map shows the sections of the river depicted on the following pages.

Les Bouquinistes, the bookstalls on the river banks, are treasure troves of second-hand books and prints, and perfect for an afternoon's browsing.

0 kilometres   2

0 miles   1

KEY

☐ Illustrated area

◁ Point Alexandre III, encrusted with exuberant statuary

From Pont de Grenelle to Pont de la Concorde

The grand monuments along this stretch of the river are remnants of the Napoleonic era and the Industrial Revolution. The elegance of the Eiffel Tower, the Petit Palais and the Grand Palais is matched by more recent buildings, such as the Palais de Chaillot and the Musée du Quai Branly.

Palais de Chaillot
Built for the 1937 Exhibition, the spectacular colonnaded wings house several museums and a theatre (p110).

The Palais de Tokyo
Bourdelle's statues adorn the façades (p110).

The Pont Bir-Hakeim has a dynamic statue by Wederkinch rising at its north end.

Bateaux Parisiens Tour Eiffel Vedettes de Paris Ile de France

Trocadéro M

Passerelle Debilly

Pont d'Iéna

Musée du Quai Branly

Maison de Radio France is an imposing circular building, inaugurated in 1963, which houses studios as well as a radio museum.

Passy M

Pont de Bir-Hakeim

Champ de Mars Tour Eiffel RER

Eiffel Tower
This is Paris's most identifiable landmark (p113).

Prés. Kennedy Radio France RER

Bir Hakeim M

The Statue of Liberty was given to the city in 1885. It faces west, towards the original Liberty in New York.

Pont de Grenelle

KEY

M	Metro station
RER	RER station
◻	Batobus stop
⛴	River trip boarding point

Grand Palais
Major exhibitions and a science museum are based here (p109).

Petit Palais
Now the Paris museum of fine arts, this was first designed as a companion to the Grand Palais (p108).

Champs-Elysées Clemenceau Ⓜ

Alma Ⓜ Marceau

Pont de l'Alma

Pont des Invalides

Pont Alexandre III

Pont de la Concorde

RER Pont de l'Alma

Invalides Ⓜ RER

Bateaux Mouches

La Tour Maubourg Ⓜ

The Zouave, a statue on the central pier, is a useful gauge for checking flood levels.

The Liberty Flame is a memorial to the fighters of the French Resistance during World War II.

The Assemblée Nationale Palais-Bourbon was originally built for Louis XIV's daughter. It has accommodated the lower house of the French Parliament since 1830.

Dôme Church
The majestic gilded dome (p115) is here seen from Pont Alexandre III. Napoleon's tomb is installed in the crypt.

Pont Alexandre III
Flamboyant statuary decorates Paris's most ornate bridge (p109).

From Pont de la Concorde to Pont de Sully

The historic heart of Paris lies on the banks and islands of the east river. At its centre is the Ile de la Cité, a natural stepping stone across the Seine and the cultural core of medieval Paris. Today it is still vital to Parisian life.

Jardin des Tuileries
These are laid out in the formal style (pp98–9).

Musée du Louvre
Before becoming the world's greatest museum and home to the Mona Lisa, *this was Europe's largest royal palace* (pp100–3).

Concorde M

Pont de la Concorde

Assemblée Nationale M

Passerelle Solférino

Musée d'Orsay RER

Pont Royal

Pont du Carrousel

Passerelle des Arts

Musée de l'Orangerie
An important collection of 19th-century paintings is on display here (p98).

Musée d'Orsay
This converted railway station houses Paris's outstanding collection of Impressionist art (pp120–21).

Bateaux Vedettes du Pont Neuf

BATOBUS CRUISES

The boarding points are: **Eiffel Tower. Map** 6 D3. M Bir Hakeim. **Champs-Elysées. Map** 7 A1. M Champs-Elysées-Clemenceau. **Musée d'Orsay. Map** 8 D2. M Assemblée Nationale. **Louvre. Map** 8 D2. M Palais Royal-Musée du Louvre. **Hôtel de Ville. Map** 9 B4. M Hôtel de Ville. **Notre-Dame. Map** 9 B4. M St-Michel. **St-Germain-des-Prés. Map** 8 E3. M St-Germain des Prés. **Jardin des Plantes. Map** 13 C1. M Jussieu. *Departures mid-Feb–mid-Mar, mid-Nov–mid-Dec: 10:30am– 4:30pm (to 5:30pm mid-Dec–early Jan); mid-Mar– May, Sep–11 Nov: 10am–7pm (to 9:30pm Jun– Aug); every 15–30 mins daily.* **www.batobus.com**

Passerelle des Arts This steel reconstruction of Paris's first cast-iron bridge (1804) was inaugurated in 1984.

Monnaie de Paris, the Mint, was built in 1778, and has an extensive coin and medallion collection in its old milling halls.

For hotels and restaurants in this region see pp550–5 and pp600–6

HOW TO TAKE A SEINE CRUISE

Bateaux Vedettes du Pont-Neuf Seine Cruise

Boarding point is: **Square du Vert-Galant** (Pont Neuf). **Map** 8 F3. **Tel** *01 46 33 98 38.* Pont Neuf. RER *Châtelet/St-Michel.* 🚌 *27, 58, 67, 70, 72, 74, 75.* **Departures** *15 Mar–31 Oct: 10:30am, 11:15am, noon, 1:30–10:30pm (every 30 mins) daily; Nov–14 Mar: 10:30am, 11:15am, noon, 2–6:30pm (every 45 mins), 8pm, 9pm, 10pm Mon–Thu; 10:30am, 11:15am, noon, 2–6:30pm, 8pm, 9–10pm (every 30 mins) Fri–Sun.* **Duration** *1 hr. Snacks available.* **www. vedettesdupontneuf.fr**

Bateaux Mouches Seine Cruise

Boarding point is: **Pont de l'Alma. Map** 6 F1. **Tel** *01 42 25 96 10.* 🚇 *Alma-Marceau.* RER *Pont de l'Alma.* 🚌 *28, 42, 63, 72, 80, 81, 92.* **Departures** *Apr–Sep: 10:15am–11pm daily (every 20–45 mins); Oct–Mar: 10:15am–9pm daily (every 30–60 min).* **Duration** *1hr 15 mins.* **Lunch cruise** *1pm Sat, Sun, bank hols (boarding 12:15pm).* **Dinner cruise** *boarding 7:30–8:30pm daily.* **Duration** *2 hr 15 mins. Jacket and tie.* **www. bateaux-mouches.fr**

Vedettes de Paris Ile de France Seine Cruise

Main boarding point is: **Port du Suffren. Map** 6 D3. **Tel** *01 44 18 19 50.* 🚇 *Trocadéro, Bir Hakeim.* RER *Champ-de-Mars–Tour Eiffel.* 🚌 *22, 30, 32, 42, 44, 63, 69, 72, 82, 87.* **Departures** *10:30am–10pm daily (11am–7:15pm Oct–Apr, until 9pm Sat–Sun) (every 20–45 mins).* **Duration** *1hr.* **Champagne cruise** *6pm Thu–Sat. Taste 3 champagnes on a 1-hr trip.* **Dinner cruise** *8pm Sat.* **Duration** *2 hrs 30 mins.* **www.vedettes deparis.com**

Bateaux Parisiens Tour Eiffel Seine Cruise

Boarding point is: **Pont d'Iéna** & **Quai de Montbello** (Apr–Nov). **Map** 6 D2. **Tel** *08 25 01 01 01.* 🚇 *Trocadéro, Bir Hakeim.* RER *Champ-de-Mars–Tour Eiffel.* 🚌 *42, 82.* **Departures** *Apr–Sep: 10am–10:30pm; Oct–Mar: 10:30am–10pm (every 30 mins).* **Lunch cruise** *daily 12:15pm.* **Duration** *2 hrs 15 mins.* **Dinner cruise** *daily, boarding 7:15–8:15pm.* **Duration** *3 hrs. Jacket and tie.* **www. bateauxparisiens.com**

Ile de la Cité

This tiny island on the Seine was first inhabited around 200 BC by a Celtic tribe known as the Parisii (pp82–3).

Conciergerie

During the Revolution this building, with its distinctive towers, became notorious as a prison (p83).

The Ile St-Louis has been a desirable address since the 17th century, when its elegant houses were built.

Pont Neuf 🚇

Neuf

🚇 Châtelet

Hotel de Ville 🚇

Pont au Change

Pont Notre-Dame

Cité 🚇

Pont d'Arcole

RER 🚇 St-Michel

Petit Pont

Pont au Double

Pont Louis-Philippe

Pont St-Louis

Pont de l'Archevêché

Pont Marie 🚇

Pont Marie

Sully Morland 🚇

Pont de la Tournelle

Pont de Sully

Notre-Dame

This towering cathedral surveys the river (pp86–7).

🚌 Bateaux Parisiens

ILE DE LA CITE, MARAIS AND BEAUBOURG

The Right Bank is dominated by the modernistic Forum des Halles and Pompidou Centre in the Beaubourg. These are Paris's most thriving public areas, with millions of tourists, shoppers and students flowing between them. Young people flock to Les Halles, shopping for the latest street fashions, but you should avoid the area at night. Renovations to improve Les Halles should be completed by 2017. All roads from here appear to lead to the Pompidou Centre, an avant-garde assembly of pipes, ducts and cables housing the Musée National d'Art Moderne. The smaller streets around the centre are full of art galleries housed in crooked, gabled

The crest of the city of Paris

buildings. The neighbouring Marais was abandoned by its royal residents during the 1789 Revolution, and it descended into architectural wasteland before being rescued in the 1960s. It has since become a very fashionable address, though small cafés, bakeries and artisans still survive in its streets.

Notre-Dame cathedral, the Palais de Justice, and Sainte-Chapelle continue to draw tourists to the Ile de la Cité, despite extensive redevelopment of the island in the last century. At the eastern end a bridge connects with the Ile St-Louis, a former swampy pastureland transformed into a residential area with pretty, tree-lined quays and mansions.

SIGHTS AT A GLANCE

Islands & Squares
Ile St-Louis ❼
Forum des Halles ⓭
Place des Vosges ⓳
Place de la Bastille ㉑

Churches
Sainte-Chapelle ❹
Notre-Dame pp86–7 ❻
St-Gervais–St-Protais ❾
St-Eustache ⓬

Historic Buildings
Conciergerie ❷
Palais de Justice ❸
Hôtel de Ville ❿
Tour St-Jacques ⓫

GETTING THERE
Metro stations include Châtelet, Hôtel-de-Ville and Cité. Buses 47 and 29 serve Beaubourg and the Marais respectively. Several bus routes cross Ile de la Cité and Ile St-Louis.

Museums and Galleries
Crypte Archéologique ❺
Hôtel de Sens ❽
Pompidou Centre pp92–3 ⓮
Musée d'Art et d'Histoire du Judaisme ⓯
Hôtel de Soubise ⓰
Musée Picasso ⓱
Musée Carnavalet ⓲
Maison de Victor Hugo ⓴

Bridges
Pont Neuf ❶

KEY

▪	Street by Street map *pp82–3*
▪	Street by Street map *pp88–9*
Ⓜ	Metro station
⊡	Batobus boarding point
RER	RER station

0 metres 500
0 yards 500

Street-by-Street: Ile de la Cité

The origins of Paris are on the Ile de la
Cité, the boat-shaped island on the Seine
first inhabited by Celtic tribes in the
3rd century BC. One tribe, the Parisii,
eventually gave its name to the city.
The island offered a convenient river
crossing on the route between northern
and southern Gaul and was easily
defended. In later centuries the settlement was expanded by the Romans, the
Franks and the Capetian kings to form
the nucleus of today's city.

★ Conciergerie
*This sinister-looking building was the country's
chief prison during the Revolution* ❷

Remains of the first buildings
can still be seen today in the
archaeological crypt of the
great medieval cathedral of
Notre-Dame. At the other
end of the island is Sainte-
Chapelle, another
Gothic masterpiece.

The Marché aux Fleurs et Oiseaux
in place Louis-Lépine is one of
the largest flower markets in
Paris, with birds for sale
on Sundays.

Metro Cité

To Pont Neuf

PONT AU CHANGE

QUAI DE LA CORSE

PONT NOTRE DAME

RUE DE LUTECE

M

QUAI DES ORFEVRES

BLVD DU PALAIS

RUE DE LA CITE

PONT ST MICHEL

QUAI DU MARCHE NEUF

PETIT PONT

PALAIS DU PARVIS NOTRE DAME

★ Sainte-Chapelle
*A jewel of Gothic
architecture, Sainte-
Chapelle is famous for its
magnificent stained-glass
windows* ❹

Palais de Justice
*With a history spanning
over 16 centuries, the old
palace is today a massive
complex of law courts* ❸

Point Zéro
marks the spot
from which all
road distances
are measured
in France.

PONT AU DOUBLE

To Latin Quarter

STAR SIGHTS

★ Notre-Dame

★ Sainte-Chapelle

★ Conciergerie

KEY

- - - Suggested route

CRYPTE
DU
PARVIS

Crypte Archéologique
*Deep under the square lie remnants
of houses dating back 2,000 years* ❺

For hotels and restaurants in this region see pp550–5 and pp600–6

Hôtel Dieu, the oldest hospital in Paris, was founded in AD 651 by St Landry, Bishop of Paris.

LOCATOR MAP
See Street Finder maps 8, 9

★ **Notre-Dame**
This cathedral, with its magnificent south-facing rose window and impressive array of gargoyles, is one of the finest examples of French Gothic architecture ❻

Square Jean XXIII, a formal garden with a Neo-Gothic fountain opened in 1844, is an ideal spot from which to view the east end of the cathedral.

0 metres   100
0 yards   100

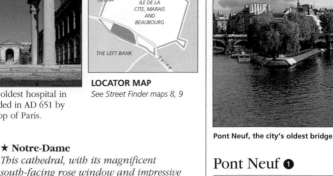

Pont Neuf, the city's oldest bridge

Pont Neuf ❶

75001. **Map** 8 F3. Ⓜ *Pont Neuf, Cité.*

Despite its name (New Bridge), this bridge is the oldest in Paris and has been immortalized by major literary and artistic figures. The first stone was laid by Henri III in 1578, but it was Henri IV (whose statue stands at the centre) who inaugurated it and gave it its name in 1607

Conciergerie ❷

2 bd du Palais 75001. **Map** 9 A3.
Tel 01 53 40 60 80. Ⓜ *Cité.*
⏰ *9:30am–6pm daily (9am–5pm Nov–Feb; last adm 30 mins before closing).* ⬤ *1 Jan, 1 May, 25 Dec.*
🎫 *Combined ticket with Sainte-Chapelle (see p84) available.* 📷 📹 *phone to check.* ♿

Forming part of the huge Palais de Justice, the historic Conciergerie served as a prison from 1391–1914. Henri IV's assassin, François Ravaillac, was imprisoned and tortured here in 1610.

During the Revolution the building was packed with over 4,000 prisoners. Its most celebrated inmate was Marie-Antoinette, who was held in a tiny cell until her execution in 1793. Others included Charlotte Corday, who stabbed Revolutionary leader Marat.

The Conciergerie has a superb four-aisled Gothic hall, where guards of the royal household once lived. Renovated during the 19th century, the building retains its 11th-century torture chamber and 14th-century clock tower.

A sculptured relief on the Palais de Justice

Palais de Justice ❸

4 bd du Palais (entrance at 8 bd du Palais) 75001. **Map** 9 A3. **Tel** 01 44 32 52 52. Ⓜ Cité. ☐ 9am–6pm Mon–Fri. ⬤ public hols & Aug recess.

This huge block of buildings making up the law courts of Paris stretches the entire width of the Ile de la Cité. It is a splendid sight with its Gothic towers lining the quays. The site has been occupied since Roman times when it was the governors' residence. It was the seat of royal power until Charles V moved the court to the Marais following a bloody revolt in 1358. In April 1793 the notorious Revolutionary Tribunal began dispensing justice from the Première Chambre Civile, or first civil chamber. Today the site embodies Napoleon's great legacy – the French judicial system.

Crypte Archéologique ❺

Parvis Notre-Dame–pl Jean-Paul II 75004. **Map** 9 A4. **Tel** 01 55 42 50 10. Ⓜ Cité. ☐ 10am–6pm Tue–Sun (last adm 30 mins before closing). ⬤ 1 Jan, 1 & 8 May, 1 & 11 Nov, 25 Dec. 🎦 📷 ♿

Situated beneath the *parvis* (main square) of Notre-Dame and stretching 120 m (393 ft) underground, the crypt was opened in 1980.

There are Gallo-Roman streets and houses with an underground heating system, sections of Lutetia's 3rd-century BC wall, and remains of the cathedral. Models explain the development of Paris from a settlement of the Parisii, the Celtic tribe who inhabited the island 2,000 years ago.

Notre-Dame ❻

See pp86–7.

Sainte-Chapelle ❹

6 bd du Palais 75001. **Map** 9 A3. 📞 01 53 40 60 80. Ⓜ Cité. ☐ Mar–Oct: 9:30am–6pm daily; Nov–Feb: 9am–5pm daily. ⬤ 1 Jan, 1 May, 25 Dec. 🎦 Combined ticket with Conciergerie (see p83) available. No sharp objects permitted. 📷 📹 ♿

Ethereal and magical, Sainte-Chapelle has been hailed as one of the greatest architectural masterpieces of the Western world. In the Middle Ages the devout likened this church to "a gateway to heaven". Today no visitor can fail to be transported by the blaze of light created by the 15 magnificent stained-glass windows, separated by pencil-like columns soaring 15 m (50 ft) to the star-studded roof. The windows portray more than 1,000 biblical scenes in a kaleidoscope of red, gold, green and blue. Starting from the left near the entrance and proceeding clockwise, you can trace the scriptures from Genesis through to the Crucifixion and the Apocalypse.

The chapel was completed in 1248 by Louis IX to house what was believed to be Christ's Crown of Thorns and fragments of the True Cross (now in the treasury at Notre-Dame). The king, who was canonized for his good works, purchased the relics from the Emperor of Constantinople, paying three times more for them than for the entire construction of Sainte-Chapelle.

The building actually consists of two separate chapels. The sombre lower chapel was used by servants and lower court officials, while the exquisite upper chapel, reached by means of a narrow spiral staircase, was reserved for the royal family and its courtiers. A discreetly placed window enabled the king to take part in the celebrations unobserved.

During the Revolution the building was badly damaged and became a warehouse. It was renovated a century later by architect Viollet-le-Duc.

Today, evening concerts of classical music are held regularly in the chapel, taking advantage of its superb acoustics.

The magnificent interior of Sainte-Chapelle

Île St-Louis ❼

75004. **Map** 9 B-C4-5. **M** *Pont Marie, Sully Morland.* **St-Louis-en-l'Île** *19 bis rue Saint-Louis en l'Île.* **Tel** *01 46 34 11 60.* ⬤ *9:30am–1pm, 2–7:30pm (7pm Sun, public hols).* **Concerts** www.saintlouisenlile.com

Across Pont St-Louis from Île de la Cité, smaller Île St-Louis is a little haven of quiet streets and riverside quays. There are luxurious restaurants and shops, including the famous ice-cream maker Berthillon. Almost everything on the Île was built in classical style in the 17th century. The church of **St-Louis-en-l'Île**, with its marble and gilt Baroque interior, was completed in 1726 from plans by royal architect Louis de Vau. Note the 1741 iron clock at the church entrance, the pierced iron spire, and a plaque given in 1926 by St Louis, Missouri. The church is also twinned with Carthage cathedral in Tunisia, where St Louis is buried.

The interior of St-Louis-en-l'Île

Hôtel de Sens ❽

1 rue du Figuier 75004. **Map** 9 C4. **Tel** *01 42 78 14 60.* **M** *Pont-Marie.* ⬤ *10am–7:30pm Wed, Thu (from 1pm Tue, Fri, Sat).* ⬤ *public hols.*

One of only a handful of medieval buildings still standing in Paris, the Hôtel de Sens is home to the Forney arts library. During the period of the Catholic League in the 16th century, it was turned into a fortified mansion and occupied by the Bourbons, the Guises and Cardinal de Pellevé.

St-Gervais–St-Protais ❾

Pl St-Gervais 75004. **Map** 9 B3. **Tel** *01 48 87 32 02.* **M** *Hôtel de Ville.* ⬤ *5:30am–9pm daily.* **Organ concerts**

Named after Gervase and Protase, two Roman soldiers martyred by the Emperor Nero, the origins of this magnificent church go back to the 6th century. It boasts the earliest Classical façade in Paris, dating from 1621, with a triple-tiered arrangement of Doric, Ionic and Corinthian columns.

Behind the façade lies a late Gothic church renowned for its association with religious music. François Couperin (1668–1733) composed his two masses for this church's organ.

UPPER CHAPEL WINDOWS

The spire rises 75 m (245 ft) into the air.

The stained-glass windows of the upper chapel constitute a vast illustrated Bible.

The upper chapel was reserved for the royal family and its entourage.

The Crown of Thorns adorns the chapel's pinnacle.

The Rose Window tells the biblical story of the Apocalypse in 86 panels of stained glass.

1 Genesis
2 Exodus
3 Numbers
4 Deuteronomy: Joshua
5 Judges
6 *left* Isaiah *right* Rod of Jesse
7 *left* St John the Evangelist *right* Childhood of Christ
8 Christ's Passion
9 *left* St John the Baptist *right* Story of Daniel
10 Ezekiel
11 *left* Jeremiah *right* Tobias
12 Judith and Job
13 Esther
14 Book of Kings
15 Story of the Relics
16 Rose Window: The Apocalypse

Main portals

The lower chapel was used by servants and commoners.

Notre-Dame ❻

No other building epitomizes the history of Paris more than Notre-Dame. Built on the site of a Roman temple, the cathedral was commissioned by Bishop de Sully in 1159. The first stone was laid in 1163, marking the start of two centuries of toil by armies of Gothic architects and medieval craftsmen. It has been witness to great events of French history ever since, including the coronations of Henry VI in 1422 and Napoleon Bonaparte in 1804. During the Revolution the building was desecrated and rechristened the Temple of Reason. Extensive renovations (including the addition of the spire and gargoyles) were carried out in the 19th century by architect Viollet-le-Duc.

★ **West Façade**
The beautifully proportioned west façade is a masterpiece of French Gothic architecture.

387 steps lead to the top of the south tower, where the famous Emmanuel bell is housed.

★ **Galerie des Chimères**
The cathedral's legendary gargoyles (chimères) gaze menacingly from the cathedral's ledge.

★ **West Rose Window**
This window depicts the Virgin in a medallion of rich reds and blues.

STAR FEATURES

★ West Façade and Portals

★ Flying Buttress

★ Rose Windows

★ Galerie des Chimères

The Kings' Gallery features 28 stone images of the kings of Judah.

Portal of the Virgin
The Virgin surrounded by saints and kings is a fine composition of 13th-century statues.

★ **Flying Buttresses**
*Jean Ravy's spectacular flying buttresses
at the east end of the cathedral have a
span of 15 m (50 ft).*

The spire, designed
by Viollet-le-Duc,
soars to a height of
96 m (315 ft).

View of Interior
*The view from the main
entrance takes in the high-
vaulted central nave,
choir and high
altar.*

The transept was built
at the start of Philippe-
Auguste's reign, in the
13th century.

The treasury houses the cathedral's
religious treasures, including ancient
manuscripts and reliquaries.

★ **South Rose Window**
*This south façade window, with
its central depiction of
Christ, is an impressive
13 m (43 ft) high.*

The "Mays" Paintings
*These religious paintings, by Charles
Le Brun and Le Sueur among others,
were presented by the Paris guilds
every 1 May from 1630 to 1707.*

Street-by-Street: The Marais

Once an area of marshland (*marais* means swamp), the Marais grew steadily in importance from the 14th century, by virtue of its proximity to the Louvre, the preferred residence of Charles V. Its heyday was in the 17th century, when it became a fashionable area for the monied classes, many of whose grand mansions (*hôtels*) have now been restored as museums. Once again fashionable, chic designer boutiques alternate with small restaurants and stores.

RUE BARBETTE

RUE DU PARC R

RUE ELZEVIR

RUE PAYENNE

RUE DES HOSPITALIÈRES ST GERVAIS

RUE DES

FRANCS

RUE DE

RUE DES ROSIERS

RUE MALHER

RUE PAVEE

To the Pompidou Centre

★ **Musée Picasso**
The palatial home of a 17th-century salt-tax collector houses the most extensive collection of Picassos in the world ⑰

Rue des Francs-Bourgeois, built in 1334, was named after the *francs* – almshouses for the poor at Nos. 34 and 36.

Musée Cognacq-Jay contains an exquisite collection of 18th-century paintings and furniture.

Hôtel de Lamoignon was built in 1584 and houses Paris's historical library.

Rue des Rosiers, heart of the city's oldest Jewish quarter, is lined with 18th-century houses, stores and cafés serving dishes such as hot pastrami and borscht.

KEY

– – – Suggested route

0 metres   100

0 yards   100

★ **Musée Carnavalet**
Occupying two large mansions, this museum covers the history of Paris from Prehistoric and Gallo-Roman times ⑱

★ **Place des Vosges**
*This enchanting square is
an oasis of peace and
tranquillity* ⓳

LOCATOR MAP
See Street Finder maps 9, 10

Maison de Victor Hugo
Author of Les Misérables, *Victor Hugo
lived at No. 6 place des Vosges, now
a museum of his life and work* ⓴

To Metro Sully
Morland

STAR SIGHTS

★ Musée Picasso

★ Musée Carnavalet

★ Place des Vosges

Hôtel de Sully, with its
orangerie and courtyard, is an
elegant Renaissance mansion.

Hôtel de Ville ⓾

Pl de l'Hôtel de Ville 75004.
Map 9 B3. **Tel** 01 42 76 40 40.
M *Hôtel-de-Ville*. ◯ *to groups:
phone to arrange (01 42 76 54 04).*
◉ *public hols, and for official
functions (phone to check).* ♿

Home of the city council, the
Hôtel de Ville is a 19th-
century reconstruction of the
17th-century town hall burned
down by insurgents of the
Paris Commune in 1871. It is
a highly ornate example of
Third Republic architecture,
with elaborate stonework,
turrets and statues overlooking
a pedestrianized square.

The 16th-century Tour St-Jacques

Tour St-Jacques ⓫

Square de la Tour St-Jacques 75004.
Map 9 A3. M *Châtelet.*
◯ *gardens only.*

This imposing late Gothic
tower, dating from 1523, is all
that remains of a medieval
church used as a rendezvous
by pilgrims setting out for
Compostela in Spain. The
building was destroyed by
revolutionaries in 1797.
 Earlier, Blaise Pascal, the
17th-century philosopher,
mathematician, physicist and
writer, used the tower for
barometric experiments. His
statue stands at the base of
the tower, which is now used
as a meteorological station.

St-Eustache ⑫

2 impasse St-Eustache 75001.
Map 9 A1. **Tel** 01 42 36 31 05.
Ⓜ Les Halles. Ⓡ Châtelet-Les-Halles.
◯ 9:30am–7pm Mon–Fri, 10am–
7pm Sat–Sun. ✝ 12:30pm Mon–Fri,
6pm Sat, 11am, 6pm Sun. **Concerts**
www.saint-eustache.org

With its Gothic plan and
Renaissance decoration, St-
Eustache is one of Paris's
most beautiful churches. Its
massive interior is modelled on
Notre-Dame, with five naves
and side and radial chapels.
The 105 years (1532–1637) it
took to complete the church
saw the flowering of the
Renaissance style, which is
evident in the magnificent
arches, pillars and columns.
    St-Eustache has hosted many
ceremonial events, including
the baptisms of Cardinal
Richelieu and Madame de
Pompadour, and the funerals
of fabulist La Fontaine, Colbert
(prime minister to Louis XIV),
17th-century dramatist Molière
and the revolutionary orator
Mirabeau. It was here that
Berlioz first performed his
Te Deum in 1855. Today
talented choir groups perform
regularly, and organ recitals
are often held here.

Forum des Halles ⑬

75001. **Map** 13 A2. Ⓜ Les Halles.
Ⓡ Châtelet-Les-Halles. **Le Forum des
Images**: 2 rue du Cinéma. ◯ 12:30–
11:30pm Tue–Fri, 2–11:30pm Sat, Sun.

Known simply as Les Halles
and built amid much controversy on the site of the famous
old fruit and vegetable market,
the complex occupies 7 ha
(750,000 sq ft), partly above
and partly below ground, and
has a reputation for being
unsafe, particularly at night.
The underground levels 2 and
3 are occupied by a varied
array of shops, from clothes
boutiques to megastores, as
well as two multi-screen
cinemas and a cinema resource
centre, **Le Forum des Images**.
Above ground there are well-
tended gardens, pergolas and
mini-pavilions. Extensive
renovations to improve the
area were due to start in 2006
but work is slow to commence.

**St-Eustache and sculptured head,
l'Ecoute, by Henri de Miller**

Pompidou Centre ⑭

See pp92–3.

Musée d'Art et d'Histoire du Judaïsme ⑮

Hôtel de St-Aignan, 71 rue du Temple
75003. **Map** 13 B2. **Tel** 01 53 01 86
60. Ⓜ Rambuteau. ◯ 11am–6pm
Mon–Fri, 10am–6pm Sun. ◯ Jewish
hols. 🖼 🔊 🖥 📷 www.mahj.org

This museum in a Marais
mansion, the elegant Hôtel de
St-Aignan, brings together
collections formerly scattered
around the city, and commemorates the culture of French
Jewry from medieval times to
the present. Visitors learn that
there has been a sizeable
Jewish community in
France since Roman
times, and some of the
world's greatest Jewish
scholars – Rashi, Rabenu
Tam, the Tosafists – were
French. Much exquisite
craftsmanship is dis-
played, with elaborate
silverware, Torah covers,
fabrics, and items of fine
Judaica and religious
objects for use both in
the synagogue and in the
home. There are also
photographs, paintings,
and cartoons and
historical documents,
including some on the
antisemitic Dreyfus Affair
more than a century ago.

Hôtel de Soubise ⑯

60 rue des Francs-Bourgeois 75003.
Map 9 C2. Ⓜ Rambuteau.
◯ 10am–12:30pm, 2–5:30pm Mon,
Wed–Fri; 2–5:30pm Sat & Sun.
◯ public hols.

This imposing mansion, built
from 1705 to 1709 for the
Princesse de Rohan, is one of
two main buildings housing the
national archives (the other
one being the Hôtel de Rohan).
It boasts a majestic courtyard
and 18th-century interior
decoration by some of the
best-known artists of the time.
    Notable items held here
include Natoire's *rocaille* work
in the Princess's bedchamber
and Napoleon's will. Unfortunately the interior is only
accessible by appointment to
historical researchers.

Musée Picasso ⑰

Hôtel Salé, 5 rue de Thorigny,
75003. **Map** 10 D2. ☎ 01 42 71
25 21. Ⓜ St-Sébastien Froissart.
◯ closed for renovation work until
2012. 🖼 📷 🔊 🖥 groups by
appointment only. 📷 🖥
www.musee-picasso.fr

On the death of the Spanish-
born artist Pablo Picasso
(1881–1973), who lived most
of his life in France, the
French State inherited one
quarter of his works in lieu of
death duties. In 1986, it used
them to create the Musée
Picasso in the beautifully

Woman Reading (1932) by
Pablo Picasso

restored Hôtel Salé, one of the loveliest buildings in the Marais. It was built in 1656 for Aubert de Fontenay, collector of the dreaded salt tax (*salé* means "salty").

Comprising over 200 paintings, 158 sculptures, 88 ceramic works and some 3,000 sketches and engravings, this unique collection shows the enormous range and variety of Picasso's work, including examples from his Blue, Pink and Cubist periods.

Highlights to look out for are his Blue period *Self-portrait*, painted at age 20; *Still Life with Caned Chair*, which introduced collage to Cubism; the Neo-Classical *Pipes of Pan*; and *The Crucifixion*.

The museum frequently loans canvases for special exhibitions elsewhere, so some works will be on show in other galleries. The museum closed in August 2009 for renovation work, which should be finished by late 2012.

A magnificent 17th-century ceiling painting by Charles Le Brun

Musée Carnavalet ⓲

23 rue de Sevigné 75003. **Map** 10 D3. **Tel** 01 44 59 58 58. Ⓜ St-Paul. ⏰ 10am–6pm Tue–Sun (rooms open in rotas: phone to check). ⬤ public hols. ⬤ ⬤ ring for times. ⬤ www.carnavalet.paris.fr

Devoted to the history of Paris since Prehistoric times, this vast museum is in two adjoining mansions. They include entire decorated rooms with gilded panelling, furniture and *objets d'art*; many works of art, such as paintings and sculptures of prominent

personalities; and engravings showing Paris being built.

The main building is the Hôtel Carnavalet, built as a town house in 1548 by Nicolas Dupuis. The literary hostess Madame de Sévigné lived here between 1677 and 1696, entertaining the intelligentsia of the day and writing her celebrated *Lettres*. Many of her possessions are in the first-floor exhibit covering the Louis XIV era.

The 17th-century Hôtel le Peletier, opened in 1989, features reconstructions of early 20th-century interiors and artifacts from the Revolution and Napoleonic era. The Orangery houses a department devoted to Prehistory and Gallo-Roman Paris. The collection includes pirogues discovered in 1992, during an archaeological dig in the Parc de Bercy, which unearthed a neolithic village.

Place des Vosges ⓳

75003, 75004. **Map** 10 D3. Ⓜ Bastille, St-Paul.

This perfectly symmetrical square, laid out in 1605 by Henri IV, is considered among the most beautiful in the world. Thirty-six houses, nine on each side, are built over arcades which today accommodate antiques shops and fashionable cafés. The square has been the scene of many historical events over the centuries, including a three-day tournament in celebration of the marriage of Louis XIII to Anne of Austria in 1615.

Maison de Victor Hugo ⓴

6 pl des Vosges 75004. **Map** 10 D4. **Tel** 01 42 72 10 16. Ⓜ Bastille. ⏰ 10am–6pm Tue–Sun. ⬤ public hols. ⬤ **Library** www.musee-hugo.paris.fr

The French poet, dramatist and novelist lived on the second floor of the former Hôtel de Rohan-Guéménée,

the largest house on the square, from 1832 to 1848. It was here that he wrote most of *Les Misérables*. On display are reconstructions of some of the rooms in which he lived, complete with his desk, furniture he made, his drawings and mementos from key periods of his life, from his childhood to his exile between 1852 and 1870. There are also regular temporary exhibitions.

Marble bust of Victor Hugo by Auguste Rodin

Place de la Bastille ㉑

75004. **Map** 10 E4. Ⓜ Bastille.

Nothing remains of the infamous prison stormed by the revolutionary mob on 14 July 1789, the event that sparked the French Revolution.

The 50-m (164-ft) Colonne de Juillet stands in the middle of the traffic-clogged square to honour the victims of the July Revolution of 1830. On the south side of the square (at 120 rue de Lyon) is the 2,700-seat **Opéra National Bastille**, completed in 1989, the bicentennial of the French Revolution.

The "genius of liberty" statue on top of the Colonne de Juillet

Pompidou Centre ⑭

The Pompidou is like a building turned inside out: escalators, lifts, air and water ducts and even the massive steel struts that make up the building's skeleton are all on the outside. This allowed the architects, Richard Rogers, Renzo Piano and Gianfranco Franchini, to create a flexible exhibition space. Among the artists featured in the museum are Matisse, Picasso, Miró and Pollock, representing such schools as Fauvism, Cubism and Surrealism. The Pompidou also keeps abreast of the Paris art scene with frequently changing temporary exhibitions. Outside in the Piazza, crowds gather to watch street performers.

KEY

☐ Exhibition space

■ Non-exhibition space

This riotous jumble of glass and steel, known as Beaubourg, is Paris's top tourist attraction, built in 1977 and drawing over 7 million visitors a year.

Mobile on Two Planes *(1955)*
20th-century American artist Alexander Calder introduced the mobile as an art form.

To the Atelier Brancusi ✎

GALLERY GUIDE

The permanent collections are on the fifth and fourth levels: works from 1905–60 are on the former, contemporary art on the latter. The first and sixth levels are for temporary exhibitions; the second and third house a library. The lower levels make up "The Forum", the focal public area, with a performance centre, a cinema, shops and a children's workshop.

Sorrow of the King *(1952)*
This collage was created by Matisse using gouache-painted paper cut-outs.

Portrait of the Journalist Sylvia von Harden *(1926) The surgical precision of Otto Dix's style makes this a harsh caricature.*

VISITORS' CHECKLIST

Centre d'Art et de Culture
Georges Pompidou, pl G
Pompidou, 75004. **Map** 9 B2. **Tel**
01 44 78 12 33. Ⓜ *Rambuteau,
Châtelet, Hôtel de Ville.* 🚌 *21,
29, 38, 47, 58, 69, 70, 72, 74,
75, 76, 81, 85, 96.* ℞℞ *Châtelet-
Les-Halles.* Ⓟ *Centre G
Pompidou.* ⬜ *MNAM & temp
exhibs: 11am–10pm Wed–Mon;
Atelier Brancusi: 2– 6pm
Wed–Mon; Library: noon–10pm
Mon, Wed–Fri, 11am–10pm w/e.*
🚫 ♿ ✍ 📷 🍴 🛍 🏪
www.cnac-gp.fr

Le Duo *(1937) Georges Braque, like Picasso, developed the Cubist technique of representing different views of a subject in a single picture.*

With the Black Arc *(1912) The transition to Abstraction, one of the major art forms of the 20th century, can be seen in the works of Wassily Kandinsky.*

Basin and
Sculpture Terrace

Stravinsky Fountain
This fountain, which was inaugurated in 1983, is in the place Igor Stravinsky near the Pompidou Centre. It was designed by sculptors Jean Tinguely and Niki de Saint Phalle, both of whom are represented in the Pompidou Centre.

BRANCUSI WORKSHOP

The Atelier Brancusi, on the rue Rambuteau side of the piazza, is a reconstruction of the workshop of the Romanian-born artist Constantin Brancusi (1876–1957), who lived and worked in Paris. He bequeathed his entire collection of works to the French state on condition that his workshop be rebuilt as it was. The collection includes over 200 sculptures and plinths, 1600 photographs, exhibited in rotation, and tools Brancusi used to create his works. Also featured are some of his more personal items such as documents, pieces of furniture and his book collection.

Interior of the Brancusi workshop, designed by Renzo Piano

TUILERIES AND OPERA

The 19th-century grandeur of Baron Haussmann's *grands boulevards* offsets the bustle of bankers, theatre-goers, sightseers and shoppers who frequent the area around the Opéra. A profusion of shops and department stores, ranging from the exclusively expensive to the popular, draws the crowds. Much of the area's older character is found in the early 19th-century shopping arcades, with elaborate steel and glass roofs. They are known as *galeries* or *passages*, and were restored to their former glory in the 1970s. Galerie Vivienne, which is the smartest, has an elaborate, patterned mosaic floor. The passage des Panoramas, passage Verdeau and tiny passage des Princes are more old-style Parisian. These streets abound with curious stores of all kinds, from

Lamppost of vestal virgin outside the Opéra

mouthwatering food shops, to antique book shops and stamp collectors.

The Tuileries area lies between the Opéra and the river, bounded by the vast place de la Concorde in the west and the Louvre to the east. The Louvre palace combines one of the world's greatest art collections with IM Pei's avant-garde glass pyramid. Elegant squares and formal gardens give the area its special character. Monuments to monarchy and the arts coexist with modern luxury at its most ostentatious. Place Vendôme, home to exquisite jewellery shops and the luxurious Ritz Hotel, is a heady mix of the wealthy and the chic. Parallel to the Jardin des Tuileries are two of Paris's foremost shopping streets, the rue de Rivoli and rue St-Honoré, full of expensive boutiques, bookshops and deluxe hotels.

SIGHTS AT A GLANCE

Museums and Galleries
Grévin ❸
Galerie Nationale du Jeu de Paume ❻
Musée de l'Orangerie ❽
Musée des Arts Décoratifs ⓫
Musée du Louvre pp100–3 ⓮

Squares, Parks and Gardens
Jardin des Tuileries ❾
Place Vendôme ❺
Place de la Concorde ❼

Monuments
Arc de Triomphe du Carrousel ⓬

Historic Buildings
Opéra de Paris Garnier ❷
Palais Royal ⓭

Churches
La Madeleine ❶
St-Roch ❿

Shops
Les Passages ❹

GETTING THERE
This area is well served by the metro system, with stations at Tuileries, Pyramides, Palais Royal, Madeleine and Opéra, among others. Bus route 72 passes along Rue de Rivoli and quai du Louvre, while routes 21, 27, 29 and 81 serve avenue de l'Opéra.

KEY

▓	Street-by-Street map *pp96–7*
Ⓜ	Metro station
🛈	Tourist information

0 metres   500
0 yards   500

◁ **View of the place de la Concorde and the Obelisk**

Street-by-Street: Opéra Quarter

It has been said that the whole world will pass you by if you sit for long enough at the Café de la Paix (opposite the Opéra National Garnier). During the day, the area is a centre of commerce, tourism and shopping, with mammoth department stores lining the *grands boulevards*. In the evening, the clubs and theatres attract a totally different crowd, and the cafés along boulevard des Capucines throb with life.

Statue by Gumery on the Opéra

★ **Opéra National de Paris Garnier**
Dating from 1875, the grandiose opera house has come to symbolize the opulence of the Second Empire ❷

STAR SIGHTS

- ★ La Madeleine
- ★ Opéra National de Paris Garnier

No. 26 place de la Madeleine is home to Fauchon, the most exclusive gourmet food shop in Paris.

RUE TRONCHET

RUE VIGNON

RUE GODOT DE MAUROY

RUE CAUMARTIN

RUE AUBER

RUE EDOUARD VI

PL DE MADELEINE

BLVD DES CAPUCINES

BLVD DE LA MADELEINE

Ⓜ

Metro Madeleine

★ **La Madeleine**
The original model of the Madeleine can be seen at the Musée Carnavalet (see p91) ❶

Boulevard des Capucines (No. 14) is where the Lumière brothers staged the first public screening of a movie on 28 December 1895.

LOCATOR MAP
See Street Finder maps 4, 7, 8

Musée de l'Opéra contains the scores of every ballet and opera performed at the Opéra, and memorabilia ranging from Nijinsky's dancing shoes to Pavlova's tiara.

PL DIAGHILEV

Metro Opéra

Place de l'Opéra was designed by Baron Haussmann and is one of Paris's busiest intersections.

Marochetti's *Mary Magdalene Ascending to Heaven* in La Madeleine

La Madeleine ❶

Pl de la Madeleine 75008. **Map** 3 C5.
Tel 01 44 51 69 00. **M** *Madeleine.*
◯ 9:30am–7pm daily. ✝ 12:30pm
Mon–Fri, 6:30pm Thu–Fri, 6pm Sat,
9:30am, 11am, 7pm Sun. 📷 🚻
Concerts

Modelled after a Greek temple, La Madeleine was begun in 1764 but not consecrated until 1845. Before that, there were proposals to turn it into a stock exchange, a bank or a theatre.

Corinthian columns encircle the building, supporting a sculptured frieze. Three ceiling domes crown the inside, which is richly decorated with sculptures, rose marble and gilt.

Opéra National de Paris Garnier ❷

Pl de l'Opéra 75009. **Map** 4 DF.
🛈 0892 89 90 90. **M** *Opéra.*
◯ 10am–4:30pm daily (until 5:30pm
Jun–Sep and 12:30pm on matinée
days). ● public hols. 📷 🎟
www.operadeparis.fr

Sometimes compared to a giant wedding cake, this lavish building was designed by Charles Garnier for Napoleon III in 1862. The Prussian War and the 1871 uprising delayed the opening until 1875.

The interior is famous for its Grand Staircase made of white Carrara marble, topped by a huge chandelier, as well as for its auditorium bedecked in red velvet and gold, with a false ceiling painted by Chagall

in 1964. Restored to its full glory, it is primarily used for dance, but shares operatic productions with the Opéra Bastille (see p153).

Grévin ❸

10 bd Montmartre 75009. **Map** 4
F4. *Tel* 01 47 70 85 05. **M** *Grands
Boulevards.* ◯ 10am–6:30pm Mon–
Fri (7pm Sat, Sun & school hols).
📷 🚻 www.grevin.com

Sign outside the Grévin

Founded in 1882, this is a Paris landmark, on a par with Madame Tussauds. The historical scenes include Louis XIV at Versailles and the arrest of Louis XVI. Notable figures from the worlds of art, politics, film and sport are also on display. On the first floor is a holography museum devoted to optical tricks. The museum also houses a 320-seat theatre.

Les Passages ❹

75002. **Map** 4 F5. **M** *Bourse.*

The early 19th-century glass-roofed shopping arcades (known as *galeries* or *passages*) are concentrated between boulevard Montmartre and rue St-Marc. They house an eclectic mixture of small stores selling anything from designer jewellery to rare books and art supplies. One of the most charming is the Galerie Vivienne (off the rue Vivienne or the rue des Petits Champs) with its mosaic floor and excellent tearoom.

Place Vendôme ❺

75001. **Map** 8 D1. Ⓜ *Tuileries.*

Perhaps the best example of 18th-century elegance in the city, the architect Jules Hardouin-Mansart's royal square was begun in 1698. The original plan was to house academies and embassies behind its arcaded façades, but instead bankers moved in and created sumptuous mansions for themselves. The square's most famous residents include Frédéric Chopin, who died here in 1849 at No. 12, and César Ritz, who established his famous hotel at No. 15 in 1898.

Monet's *Waterlilies (Nymphéas)* on display in the Musée de l'Orangerie

Galerie Nationale du Jeu de Paume ❻

Jardin des Tuileries, place de la Concorde 75008. **Map** 7 C1. **Tel** 01 47 03 12 50. Ⓜ *Concorde.* ◻ noon–9pm Tue, noon–7pm Wed–Fri, 10am–7pm Sat. ● 1 Jan, 1 May, 25 Dec. 🖼 ♿ 🎥 🛍 www.jeudepaume.org

The Jeu de Paume – literally "game of the palm" – was built as two royal tennis courts by Napoleon III in 1851 on the north side of the Tuileries gardens. The courts were later converted into an art gallery and exhibition space. The Jeu de Paume has rotating exhibitions of contemporary art and houses the Centre National de la Photographie. Its sister site is the Hôtel de Sully *(see p89)*.

Place de la Concorde ❼

75008. **Map** 7 C1. Ⓜ *Concorde.*

One of Europe's most magnificent and historic squares, covering over 8 ha (20 acres), the place de la Concorde was a swamp

The 3,200-year-old obelisk from Luxor

until the mid-18th century. It became the place Louis XV in 1775 when royal architect Jacques-Ange Gabriel was asked by the king to design a suitable setting for an equestrian statue of himself.

The monument, which lasted here less than 20 years, was replaced by the guillotine (the Black Widow, as it came to be known), and the square was renamed place de la Révolution. On 21 January 1793 Louis XVI was beheaded, followed by over 1,300 other victims including Marie Antoinette, Madame du Barry, Charlotte Corday (Marat's assassin) and revolutionary leaders Danton and Robespierre.

The blood-soaked square was optimistically renamed place de la Concorde after the Reign of Terror finally came to an end in 1794. A few decades later the 3,200-year-old Luxor obelisk was presented to King Louis-Philippe as a gift from the viceroy of Egypt (who also donated Cleopatra's Needle in London).

Flanking the rue Royale on the north side of the square are two of Gabriel's Neo-classical mansions, the Hôtel de la Marine and the exclusive Hôtel Crillon.

Musée de l'Orangerie ❽

Jardin des Tuileries, place de la Concorde 75001. **Map** 7 C1. **Tel** 01 44 77 80 07. Ⓜ *Concorde.* ◻ 9am–6pm Wed–Mon. ● 1 May, 25 Dec. 🖼 📷 ♿ 🎥 by appt. 🛍 www.musee-orangerie.fr

Paintings from Claude Monet's crowning work, representing part of his waterlily series, fill the two oval upper floor rooms. Known as the *Nymphéas*, most of the canvases were painted between 1899 and 1921.

This superb work is complemented by the Walter-Guillaume collection, including 27 Renoirs, notably *Young Girls at the Piano,* works by Soutine and 14 Cézannes, including *The Red Rock.* Picasso is represented by works including *The Female Bathers,* and Rousseau by 9 paintings, notably *The Wedding.* Other works are by Matisse, Derain, Utrillo and Modigliani.

Jardin des Tuileries ❾

75001. **Map** 8 D1. Ⓜ *Tuileries, Concorde.* ◻ Apr–May: 7am–9pm; Jun–Aug: 7am–11pm; Sep: 7am–9pm; Oct–Mar: 7:30am–7:30pm.

These Neo-Classical gardens once belonged to the Palais des Tuileries, which the

Communards razed to the ground in 1871. They were laid out in the 17th century by André Le Nôtre, who created the broad central avenue and geometric topiary. Ongoing restoration has created a new garden with lime and chestnut trees, and modern sculptures.

St-Roch ⑩

284 rue St-Honoré 75001. **Map** 8 E1. **Tel** 01 42 44 13 20. **M** *Tuileries.* 🚇 *8:30am–7pm daily.* 🔴 *non-religious public hols.* 🎵 **Concerts**

This huge church was designed by Jacques Lemercier, architect of the Louvre, and its foundation stone was laid by Louis XIV in 1653. It is a treasure house of religious art, much of it from now-vanished churches and monasteries, and contains the tombs of the playwright Pierre Corneille, the royal gardener André Le Nôtre and the philosopher Denis Diderot.

Vien's *St Denis Preaching to the Gauls* (1767) in St-Roch

Musée des Arts Décoratifs ⑪

Palais du Louvre, 107 rue de Rivoli 75001. **Map** 8 E2. **Tel** 01 44 55 57 50. **M** *Palais Royal, Tuileries.* 🚇 *11am–6pm Tue–Sun (until 9pm Thu).* **Library** 🔴 *public hols.* 📷 **www.lesartsdecoratifs.fr**

Occupying the northwest wing of the Palais du Louvre (along with the Musée de la Publicité and the Musée de la Mode et du Textile), this

The Buren Columns in the main courtyard of the Palais Royal

museum offers an eclectic mix of decorative art and domestic design from the Middle Ages to the present day. The Art Nouveau and Art Deco rooms include a reconstruction of the home of couturier Jeanne Lanvin. Other floors show Louis XIV, XV and XVI styles of decoration and furniture. Contemporary designers are also represented. The restaurant has breathtaking views over the Tuileries gardens.

Arc de Triomphe du Carrousel ⑫

Pl du Carrousel 75001. **Map** 8 E2. **M** *Palais Royal.*

This rose-marble arch was built by Napoleon to celebrate various military triumphs, notably the Battle of Austerlitz in 1805. The crowning statues, added in 1828, are copies of the famous Horses of St Mark's which Napoleon stole from Venice, which he was subsequently forced to return after his defeat at Waterloo in 1815.

Palais Royal ⑬

Pl du Palais Royal 75001. **Map** 8 E1. **M** *Palais Royal.* **Buildings** 🔴 *to the public.*

This former royal palace has had a turbulent history. It was built by Cardinal Richelieu in the early 17th century, passing to the Crown on his death and becoming the childhood home of Louis XIV. Under the 18th-century royal dukes of Orléans, it became the epicentre of brilliant gatherings, interspersed with periods of gambling and debauchery. It was from here that the clarion call to revolution roused the mobs to storm the Bastille on 14 July 1789.

Today the southern section of the building houses the Councils of State and the Ministry of Culture. Just west of the palace at 2 rue de Richelieu is the Comédie Française, established by Louis XIV in 1680. Luxury shops occupy the rear section of the palace, where artists such as Colette and Cocteau once lived.

The Arc de Triomphe du Carrousel crowned by Victory riding a chariot

Musée du Louvre 🄮

The Musée du Louvre, containing one of the most important art collections in the world, has a history dating back to medieval times. First built as a fortress in 1190 by King Philippe-Auguste to protect Paris against Viking raids, it lost its keep in the reign of François I, who replaced it with a Renaissance-style building. Thereafter, four centuries of kings and emperors improved and enlarged it. Visitors should request a schedule of room closures from the information point as not all rooms are open on any given day.

The Louvre's east façade, facing St-Germain l'Auxerrois

The Jardin du Carrousel was once the grand approach to the Tuileries Palace, which was set ablaze in 1871 by insurgents of the Paris Commune.

BUILDING THE LOUVRE

Over many centuries the Louvre was enlarged by a succession of French rulers, shown below with their dates.

MAJOR ALTERATIONS

- ▢ Reign of François I (1515–47)
- ▢ Catherine de' Medici (about 1560)
- ▢ Reign of Henri IV (1589–1610)
- ▢ Reign of Louis XIII (1610–43)
- ▢ Reign of Louis XIV (1643–1715)
- ▢ Reign of Napoleon I (1804–15)
- ▢ Reign of Napoleon III (1852–70)
- ▢ IM Pei (1989) (architect)

The Carrousel du Louvre underground visitors' complex (1993), with galleries, shops, lavatories, parking and an information desk, lies beneath the Arc de Triomphe du Carrousel.

Denon Wing

Pyramid entrance

The inverted glass pyramid brings light to the subterranean complex, echoing the museum's main entrance in the Cour Napoléon.

★ Arc de Triomphe du Carrousel

This triumphal arch was built to celebrate Napoleon's military victories in 1805.

STAR FEATURES

- ★ Perrault Colonnade
- ★ Medieval Moats
- ★ Arc de Triomphe du Carrousel

THE GLASS PYRAMID

Plans for the modernization and expansion of the Louvre were first conceived in 1981. They included the transfer of the Ministry of Finance from the Richelieu wing of the Louvre to new offices elsewhere, as well as a new main entrance designed by architect IM Pei in 1989. Made of metal and glass, the pyramid enables the visitor to see the buildings around the palace, while allowing light down into the underground visitors' reception area.

VISITORS' CHECKLIST

Map 12 E2. Automatic ticket booths at Carrousel du Louvre, 99 rue de Rivoli, 75001. [M] Palais Royal, Musée du Louvre. [bus] 21, 24, 27, 39, 48, 68, 69, 72, 81, 95. [RER] Châtelet-Les-Halles. [O] Louvre. [P] Carrousel du Louvre (entrance via av du Général Lemonnier); pl du Louvre, rue St-Honoré. [O] 9am–6pm Mon, Thu, Sat, & Sun, 9am–10pm Wed & Fri. History of the Louvre rooms open Sat, Sun only. [O] 1 Jan, 1 May, 25 Dec. [I] (free 1st Sun of each month and for under 18; reduced price for Nocturnals after 6pm). [&] partial 01 40 20 59 90. [camera] phone 01 40 20 52 09. [O] **Lectures, films, concerts** 01 40 20 55 55. [T][O][O] www.louvre.fr **Advance bookings**: www.ticketweb.com

Cour Marly is the glass-roofed courtyard that now houses the *Marly Horses (see p103).*

Richelieu Wing

Cour Puget

Hall Napoléon is situated under the pyramid.

Cour Khorsabad

Sully Wing

Cour Carrée

Cour Napoléon

★ **Perrault's Colonnade**
The east façade, with its majestic rows of columns, was built by Claude Perrault, who worked on the Louvre with Louis Le Vau in the mid-17th century.

The Salle des Caryatides is named after the four monumental statues created by Jean Goujon in 1550 to support the upper gallery. Built for Henri II, it is the oldest room in the palace.

The Louvre of Charles V
In about 1360, Charles V transformed Philippe-Auguste's old fortress, with its distinctive tower and keep, into a royal residence.

★ **Medieval Moats**
The base of the twin towers and the drawbridge support of Philippe-Auguste's fortress can be seen in the excavated area.

Exploring the Louvre's Collection

Owing to the vast size of the Louvre's collection, it is useful to set a few viewing priorities before starting. The collection of European paintings (1400–1848) is comprehensive, with over half the works by French artists. The extensively renovated departments of Oriental, Egyptian, Greek, Etruscan, and Roman antiquities feature numerous new acquisitions and rare treasures. The varied display of *objets d'art* includes furniture and jewellery.

Paintings after this date are housed in the Musée d'Orsay *(see pp120–21)*. Outstanding is Jean Fouquet's portrait of Charles VII (1450–55). The great 18th-century painter of melancholy, JA Watteau, is represented, as is JH Fragonard, master of the Rococo, whose delightfully frivolous subjects are evident in *The Bathers* from 1770.

The Raft of the Medusa (1819)
by Théodore Géricault

EUROPEAN PAINTING: 1200 TO 1848

Painting from northern Europe (Flemish, Dutch, German and English) is well covered. One of the earliest Flemish works is Jan van Eyck's *Madonna of the Chancellor Rolin* (about 1435), showing the Chancellor of Burgundy kneeling in prayer before the Virgin and Child. Hieronymus Bosch's *Ship of Fools* (1500) is a satirical account of the futility of human existence.

Mona Lisa (about 1504) by
Leonardo da Vinci

In the fine Dutch collection, Rembrandt's *Self-portrait*, his *Disciples at Emmaus* (1648) and *Bathsheba* (1654) are examples of the artist's genius.

The three major German painters of the 15th and 16th centuries are represented by important works. There is a youthful *Self-portrait* (1493) by Albrecht Dürer, a *Venus* (1529) by Lucas Cranach and a portrait of the great humanist scholar Erasmus by Hans Holbein.

The impressive collection of Italian paintings is arranged in chronological order from 1200 to 1800. The father figures of the early Renaissance, Cimabue and Giotto, are here, as is Fra Angelico, with his *Coronation of the Virgin* (1430–32), and Raphaël, with his stately portrait of Count Baldassare Castiglione (1514–15). Several paintings by Leonardo da Vinci are on display, for instance the *Virgin with the Infant Jesus and St Anne*, which is as enchanting as his *Mona Lisa*.

The Louvre's fine collection of French painting ranges from the 14th century to 1848.

EUROPEAN SCULPTURE: 1100 TO 1848

Early Flemish and German sculpture in the collection has many masterpieces such as Tilman Riemenschneider's *Virgin of the Annunciation* from the end of the 15th century and a life-size nude figure of the penitent Mary Magdalen by Gregor Erhart (early 16th century). An important work of Flemish sculpture is Adrian de Vries's long-limbed *Mercury and Psyche* from 1593, which was originally made for the court of Rudolph II in Prague.

The French section opens with early Romanesque works, such as the figure of Christ by a 12th-century Burgundian sculptor, and a head of St. Peter. With its eight black-hooded mourners, the late 15th-century tomb of Philippe Pot (a high-ranking official in Burgundy) is one of the more unusual pieces. Diane de Poitiers, Henri II's mistress, had a large figure of her namesake Diana, goddess of the hunt, installed in the courtyard of her castle west of Paris. It is now in the Louvre.

The tomb of Philippe Pot (late 15th century) by
Antoine le Moiturier

The celebrated *Marly Horses* (1745) by Guillaume Coustou

The works of French sculptor Pierre Puget (1620–94) have been assembled in the Cour Puget. They include a figure of Milo of Crotona, the Greek athlete who got his hands caught in the cleft of a tree stump and was eaten by a lion. The wild horses of Marly now stand in the Cour Marly, surrounded by other masterpieces of French sculpture, including Jean-Antoine Houdon's early 19th-century busts of famous men such as Diderot and Voltaire.

The collection of Italian sculpture includes such splendid exhibits as Michelangelo's *Slaves* and Benvenuto Cellini's Fontainebleau *Nymph*.

ORIENTAL, EGYPTIAN, GREEK, ETRUSCAN, AND ROMAN ANTIQUITIES

A substantial overhaul of the Louvre has boosted its collection of antiquities, which range from the Neolithic period to the fall of the Roman Empire. Among the exhibits are Greek and Roman glassware dating from the 6th century BC. Important works of Mesopotamian art include one of the world's oldest legal documents, a basalt block bearing the code of the Babylonian King Hammurabi, dating from about 1700 BC.

The warlike Assyrians are represented by delicate carvings and a spectacular reconstruction of part of Sargon II's (722–705 BC) palace with its

winged bulls. A fine example of Persian art is the enamelled brickwork depicting the king of Persia's personal guard of archers (5th century BC).

Most Egyptian art was made for the dead, who were provided with the things they needed for the after life. Examples include the life-like funeral portraits such as the *Squatting Scribe*, and several sculptures of married couples.

The departments of Greek, Roman and Etruscan antiquities contain a vast array of fragments, among them some exceptional pieces. There is a geometric head from the Cyclades (2700 BC) and an elegant swan-necked bowl hammered out of a gold sheet (2500 BC). The two most famous Greek marble statues, the *Winged Victory of Samothrace* and the *Venus de Milo*, both belong to the Hellenistic period (late 3rd to 2nd century BC), when more natural-looking human forms were produced.

The undisputed star of the Etruscan collection is the terracotta sarcophagus of a married couple who look as though they are attending an eternal banquet, while the highlight of the Roman section is a 2nd-century bronze head of the Emperor Hadrian.

***Squatting Scribe* (about 2500 BC), a life-like Egyptian funeral sculpture**

Venus de Milo (Greece, late 3rd–early 2nd century BC)

OBJETS D'ART

The catch-all term *objets d'art* (art objects) covers a vast range of items: jewellery, furniture, clocks, watches, sundials, tapestries, miniatures, silver and glassware, cutlery, Byzantine and Parisian carved ivory, Limoges enamels, porcelain, French and Italian stoneware, rugs, snuffboxes, scientific instruments, and armour. The Louvre has well over 8,000 pieces, from many ages and regions.

Many of these precious objects came from the Abbey of St-Denis, where the kings of France were crowned. The treasures include a serpentine stone plate from the 1st century AD with a 9th-century border of gold and precious stones, a porphyry vase which Suger, Abbot of St-Denis, had mounted in gold in the shape of an eagle, and the golden sceptre made for King Charles V in about 1380.

The French crown jewels include the coronation crowns of Louis XV and Napoleon, scepters, swords, and other accessories of the coronation ceremonies. On view also is the Regent, one of the purest diamonds in the world, which Louis XV wore at his coronation in 1722.

One whole room is taken up with a series of tapestries called the *Hunts of Maximilian,* originally executed for Emperor Charles V in 1530. The large collection of French furniture ranges from the 16th to the 19th centuries and is assembled by period, or in rooms devoted to donations by distinguished collectors. On display are pieces by exceptionally prominent furniture-makers such as André-Charles Boulle, cabinetmaker to Louis XIV, who worked in the Louvre in the late 17th to mid-18th centuries.

Gilded bronze statues by a number of sculptors, decorating the central square of the Palais de Chaillot

Argentine M

AVENUE FOCH

11

Victor Hugo M

AVENUE BUGEAUD

PLACE VICTOR HUGO

RUE COPERNI

AVENUE VICTOR HUGO

AVENUE RAYMOND

Bois

RUE DE POINCARE

AVENUE LONGCHA

AVENUE GEORGES MANDEL

10

AVEN

M Troca

13

JARDINS D TROCADER

12

RUE FRANKLIN

M Passy

CHAMPS-ELYSEES AND INVALIDES

The River Seine bisects this area, much of which is built on a monumental scale, from the imposing 18th-century buildings of Les Invalides to the Art Nouveau avenues surrounding the Eiffel Tower. Two of Paris's grandest avenues dominate the neighbourhood to the north of the Seine: the Champs-Elysées has many smart hotels and shops but today is more downmarket;

Ornate lamppost on Pont Alexandre III

while the more chic rue du Faubourg St-Honoré has the heavily guarded Palais de l'Elysée. The village of Chaillot was absorbed into the city in the 19th century, and many of its opulent Second Empire mansions are now embassies or company headquarters. Streets around the place du Trocadéro and Palais de Chaillot are packed full of museums and elegant cafés.

SIGHTS AT A GLANCE

Historic Buildings and Streets
Avenue des Champs-Elysées ❷
Palais de l'Elysée ❸
Les Egouts ⓮
No. 29 Avenue Rapp ⓱
Champ-de-Mars ⓲
Ecole Militaire ⓳
Hôtel des Invalides ㉑

Museums and Galleries
Petit Palais ❹
Grand Palais ❺
Musée d'Art Moderne de la
Ville de Paris ❼
Musée Galliera ❽

Musée National des Arts
Asiatiques Guimet ❾
Cité de l'Architecture
et du Patrimoine ❿
Musée Dapper ⓫
Palais de Chaillot ⓭
Musée du Quai Branly ⓯
Musée de l'Armée ㉒
Musée Rodin ㉕
Musée Maillol ㉗

Churches
St-Louis-des-Invalides ㉓
Dôme Church ㉔
Sainte-Clotilde ㉖

Monuments and Fountains
Arc de Triomphe ❶
Eiffel Tower p113 ⓰

Modern Architecture
UNESCO ⓴

Gardens
Jardins du Trocadéro ⓬

Bridges
Pont Alexandre III ❻

GETTING THERE
Metro stations in this area include Etoile, Trocadéro and Champs-Elysées. Bus routes 42 and 73 serve the Champs-Elysées; routes 82 and 69 serve avenue de Suffren and rue St-Dominique respectively.

KEY

▦	Street-by-Street map *pp106–7*
Ⓜ	Metro station
RER	RER station
⬚	Batobus boarding point
ℹ	Tourist information

0 metres 500
0 yards 500

Street by Street: Champs-Elysées

The formal gardens that line the Champs-Elysées from the place de la Concorde to the Rond-Point have changed little since they were laid out by the architect Jacques Hittorff in 1838. The gardens were used as the setting for the World Fair of 1855, which included the Palais de l'Industrie, Paris's response to London's Crystal Palace. The Palais was later replaced by the Grand Palais and the Petit Palais, which was created as a showpiece of the Third Republic for the Universal Exhibition of 1900. They sit on either side of an impressive vista that stretches from the place Clémenceau across the elegant curve of the Pont Alexandre III, with its four strong anchoring columns, to the Invalides.

Théâtre du Rond Point, an original Champs-Elysées building, presents the work of active authors.

Metro Franklin D Roosevelt

★ **Avenue des Champs-Elysées**
This was the setting for the victory parades following the two World Wars ❷

★ **Grand Palais**
Designed by Charles Girault, and built between 1897 and 1900, this elaborate exhibition hall with its splendid glass dome is frequently used for major exhibitions ❺

The Lasserre restaurant is decorated in the style of a luxury ocean liner dating from the 1930s.

Palais de la Découverte, a museum of scientific discovery, was originally opened in the Grand Palais for the World Fair of 1937.

STAR SIGHTS

★ Avenue des Champs-Elysées

★ Grand Palais

★ Petit Palais

KEY

– – – Suggested route

| 0 metres | 100 |
| 0 yards | 100 |

The Jardins des Champs-Elysées, with their fountains, flowerbeds and pleasure pavilions, have been a popular spot since the 19th century.

GABRIEL

AVE DE MARIGNY

AMPS

ELYSEES

CLEMENCEAU

PL

Metro
Champs-
Elysées-
Clémenceau

To place
de la
Concorde

★ **Petit Palais**
The art collections of the city of Paris are housed here. They contain 19th-century works from objets d'art to paintings by the Barbizon School ❹

CHURCHILL

WINSTON

AVE

PONT
ALEXANDRE III

To the Invalides

Pont Alexandre III
This ornate, single-span structure symbolizes the optimism of the Belle Epoque at the turn of the 20th century.

LOCATOR MAP
See Street Finder maps 2, 3, 6, 7

CHAMPS-
ELYSEES
AND
INVALIDES

SEINE

The east façade of the Arc de Triomphe

Arc de Triomphe ❶

Place Charles de Gaulle, 75008.
Map 2 D4. Ⓜ Charles de Gaulle-Etoile. **Tel** *01 55 37 73 77.* **Museum**
⬛ *Apr–Sep: 10am–11pm daily; Oct–Mar: 10am–10.30pm daily (last adm 30 mins earlier).* ⬛ *1 Jan, 1 May, 8 May, 14 Jul, 11 Nov, 25 Dec.*
📷 ♿ 🛍

After his greatest victory, the Battle of Austerlitz in 1805, Napoleon promised his men they would "go home beneath triumphal arches." The first stone of what was to become the world's most famous triumphal arch was laid the following year. But disruptions to architect Jean Chalgrin's plans and the demise of Napoleonic power delayed completion. Standing 50 m (164 ft) high, the Arc is encrusted with reliefs, shields, and sculptures. The viewing platform offers spendid views.

On 11 November 1920 the body of the Unknown Soldier was placed beneath the arch to commemorate the dead of World War I. The tomb's eternal flame is lit every evening.

High relief by JP Corot, celebrating the Triumph of Napoleon

BARON HAUSSMANN

A lawyer by training and civil servant by profession, Georges-Eugène Haussmann (1809–91) was appointed Prefect of the Seine in 1852 by Napoleon III. For 17 years Haussmann was responsible for the urban modernization of Paris. With a team of the best architects and engineers of the day, he demolished the crowded, insanitary streets of the medieval city and created a well-ventilated and ordered capital within a geometrical grid. The new scheme involved redesigning the area at one end of the Champs-Elysées and creating a star of 12 avenues, which were centred on the new Arc de Triomphe.

Arc de Triomphe

Two avenues forming a star (étoile)

Place de l'Etoile

Avenue des Champs-Elysées ❷

75008. **Map** 3 A5. **M** *Charles de Gaulle-Etoile, George V, Franklin D Roosevelt, Champs-Elysées -Clemenceau, Concorde.*

The majestic avenue "of the Elysian Fields" (the name refers to a mythical Greek heaven for heroes), first laid out in the 1660s by the landscape designer André Le Nôtre, forms a 3 km (2 mile) straight line from the huge place de la Concorde to the Arc de Triomphe. The 19th century saw it transformed from horseride into elegant boulevard. Today it's a crowded tourist trap with notorious traffic, but the Champs-Elysées keeps its style, its memories – and a special place in the French heart. National parades are held here, the finish of the annual Tour de France cycle race is always in the Champs-Elysées, and, above all, it is where Parisians instinctively go at times of great national celebration.

Palais de l'Elysée ❸

55 rue du Faubourg-St-Honoré 75008. **Map** 3 B5. **M** *St-Philippe-du-Roule.* ⬤ *to the public.*

Amid splendid gardens, the Elysée Palace was built in 1718 and has been the official residence of the President of the Republic since 1848. Several occupants left their mark. Louis XV's mistress, Madame de Pompadour, had the whole site enlarged. After the Revolution, it became a dance hall. In the 19th century, it was home to Napoleon's sister Caroline

Elysée guard

Murat, and his wife Empress Josephine. The President's Apartments are today on the first floor.

Petit Palais ❹

Av Winston Churchill 75008. **Map** 7 B1. **Tel** *01 53 43 40 00.* **M** *Champs-Elysées-Clemenceau.* ⬤ *10am–6pm Tue–Sun.* ⬤ *public hols.* 🈲 📷 *for exhibitions.* 📷 ♿ 🖥 www.petitpalais.paris.fr

Built for the Universal Exhibition in 1900 to stage a major display of French art, this jewel of a building was renovated in 2005 and houses the Musée des Beaux-Arts de la Ville de Paris. The architect, Charles Girault, arranged the

GRAND PALAIS

Exhibition space

Iron supports

Pont Alexandre III, built 1896–1900 for the Universal Exhibition

palace around a semi-circular courtyard and garden. Permanent exhibits, housed on the Champs-Elysées side, include the Dutuit Collection of medieval and Renaissance *objets d'art*, paintings and drawings; the Tuck Collection of 18th-century furniture and *objets d'art*; and the City of Paris collection, with work by Ingres, Delacroix and Courbet,

Entrance to the Petit Palais

and the landscape painters of the Barbizon School. Temporary exhibitions are housed in the Cours de la Reine wing.

Grand Palais ❺

Porte A, av Général Eisenhower 75008. **Map** 7 A1. **Tel** *01 44 13 17 17.* Ⓜ *Champs-Elysées-Clemenceau.* ◯ *for temporary exhibitions only; 10am–8pm Wed–Mon.* ◼ *1 May, 25 Dec.* ▨ ∅ ⬥ ⬭ ⬮ ⬜ ⬛
Palais de la Decouverte: av Franklin D. Roosevelt 75008. **Tel** *01 56 43 20 21.* Ⓜ *Franklin D. Roosevelt.* ◯ *9:30am–6pm Tue–Sat, 10am–7pm Sun & public hols.* ▨ ⬜ ⬛ www.grandpalais.fr

Built at the same time as the Petit Palais opposite, this huge, glass-roofed palace has a fine Classical façade adorned with statuary and Art Nouveau iron-work. Bronze flying horses and chariots stand at the four corners. The Great Hall and the glass cupola can be admired during the palace's superb exhibitions. On the west side of the building, with a separate entrance, the **Palais de la Découverte** is an imaginative child-oriented science museum.

Pont Alexandre III ❻

75008. **Map** 7 A1. Ⓜ *Champs-Elysées-Clemenceau.*

This is Paris's prettiest bridge, with exuberant Art Nouveau decoration of gilt and bronze lamps, cupids and cherubs, nymphs and winged horses at either end. It was built between 1896 and 1900 to commemorate the 1892 French-Russian alliance, and in time for the Universal Exhibition in 1900. Pont Alexandre III was named after Tsar Alexander III (father of Nicholas II), who laid the foundation stone in October 1896.

The style of the bridge reflects that of the Grand Palais, to which it leads on the Right Bank. The construction of the bridge is a marvel of 19th-century engineering. It consists of a 6-m- (18-ft-) high single-span steel arch across the Seine. The design was subject to strict controls that prevented the bridge from obscuring the view of the Champs-Elysées or the Invalides, so today you can still enjoy the magnificent views from here.

Great Hall

Glass cupola

Quadriga (chariot and four horses) by Récipon

Musée d'Art Moderne de la Ville de Paris **7**

Palais du Tokyo, 11 av du Président-Wilson 75016. **Map** 6 E1. **Tel** 01 53 67 40 00. M Iéna, Alma-Marceau. ◯ 10am–6pm Tue-Sun (until 10pm Thu for temporary exhibitions). ◯ 1 Jan, 25 Dec. 🖼 for temporary exhibitions. 🔊 🗂 🖬 🖸 www.mam.paris.fr

This museum covers trends in 20th-century art and is located in the east wing of the Palais de Tokyo. The Fauves and Cubists are well represented here. Highlights include Raoul Dufy's gigantic mural,
The Spirit of Electricity (created for the 1937 World Fair), and Matisse's *The Dance* (1932). There is also a collection of Art Deco furniture.

Musée Galliera **8**

10 ave Pierre 1er de Serbie 75116. **Map** 6 D1. **Tel** 01 56 52 86 00. M Iéna, Alma-Marceau. ◯ 10am–6pm daily & 2–6pm some public hols (check website). ◯ for renovation until spring 2012. 🖼 **Children's room.** www.galliera.paris.fr

Devoted to the evolution of fashion, this museum, also known as the Musée de la Mode et du Costume, is housed in the Renaissance-style
palace built for the Duchesse Maria de Ferrari Galliera in 1892. The collection includes more than 100,000 outfits and fashion accessories, from the 18th century to the present day. Donations have been made by such fashionable women as Baronne Hélène de Rothschild and Princess Grace of Monaco. Eminent couturiers such as Balmain and Balenciaga have donated their designs to the museum.

Often extremely fragile, the fashion exhibits are displayed in rotation, usually in two major exhibitions each year. These shows can highlight a particular couturier's career or explore a single theme.

Trocadéro fountains in front of the Palais de Chaillot

Musée Dapper **11**

35bis rue Paul-Valéry, 75016. **Map** 2 D5. **Tel** 01 45 00 91 75. M Victor-Hugo. ◯ 11am–7pm Wed–Mon. 🖼 www.dapper.com.fr

A world-class ethnographic research centre, this is one of France's premier showcases of African art and culture. Located in an attractive building with an "African" garden, it is a treasure house of colour and powerful, evocative work from the black nations. The focus is on pre-colonial folk arts, with sculpture, carvings and tribal work, but there is later art, too. The highlight is tribal masks, with a dazzling, extra-ordinary array of richly carved religious, ritual and funerary masks, as well as theatrical ones used for comic, magical or symbolic performances.

Jardins du Trocadéro **12**

75016. **Map** 6 D2. M Trocadéro. **Cinéaqua Tel** 01 40 69 23 23. ◯ 10am–8pm daily. ◯ 14 Jul. 🖼

These beautiful gardens cover 10 ha (25 acres). Their centrepiece is a long rectangular ornamental pool, bordered by stone and bronze-gilt statues, which looks spectacular at night when the fountains are illuminated. The statues include *Woman* by Georges Braque and *Horse* by Georges Lucien Guyot. On either side of the pool, the slopes of the Chaillot hill lead gently down to the Seine and the Pont d'Iéna. Cinéaqua, the hi-tech aquarium here, has over 25 sharks and a petting pool for children.

Palais de Chaillot **13**

Pl du Trocadéro 75016. **Map** 5 C2. M Trocadéro. **Théâtre National de Chaillot Tel** 01 53 65 30 00. **Musée de l'Homme Tel** 01 44 05 72 72. ◯ Wed–Mon. **Musée de la Marine Tel** 01 53 65 69 69. ◯ Wed–Mon. ◯ 1 Jan, 1 May, 25 Dec.

The Palais, with its huge, curved colonnaded wings each culminating in a vast pavillion, has three museums and a theatre. Designed in Neo-Classical style for the 1937 Paris Exhibition by Azéma, Louis-Auguste Boileau and Jacques Carlu, it is adorned with sculptures and bas-reliefs. On the walls of the pavillions are gold inscriptions which were written by the poet and essayist, Paul Valéry. The square *(parvis)* between the two pavillions has bronze

Musée National des Arts Asiatiques Guimet ⑨

6 pl d'Iéna 75016. **Map** 6 D1.
Tel 01 56 52 53 00. M Iéna.
◯ 10am–6pm Wed–Mon. 🖾 🗺 📷
♿ 🔲 Panthéon Bouddhique, 19 av
d'Iéna. **Tel** 01 40 73 88 00.
www.guimet.fr

One of the world's leading
museums of Asian art, the
Guimet has a fine collection
of Cambodian (Khmer) art.
It was set up in Lyon in 1889
by Emile Guimet, and later
moved to Paris. It includes
a comprehensive Asian
research centre.

Buddha head from Musée Guimet

Cité de l'Architecture et du Patrimoine ⑩

Palais de Chaillot, pl du Trocadéro
75016. **Map** 5 C2. **Tel** 01 58 51 52
00. M Trocadéro. ◯ 11am–7pm
Wed–Mon (until 9pm Thu). ● 1 Jan,
1 May, 25 Dec. 🖾 📷 🍴 🔲
www.citechaillot.fr

This museum charts French
architecture through the ages
and includes models of great
French cathedrals, such as
Chartres (see pp308–11).
There is also a reconstruction
of an apartment designed
by Le Corbusier.

PALAIS DE CHAILLOT

Place du Trocadéro

Musée de la Marine

Musée de l'Homme

PL J MARTI

AVE PAUL DOUMER

RUE FRANKLIN

Palais de Chaillot

Jardins du Trocadéro

BLVD DELESSERT

RUELLE NOIRE

PL DU TROCADÉRO

AVE DU PRÉSIDENT WILSON

AVE ALBERT DE MUN

AVE DES NATIONS UNIES

NEW YORK

Théâtre National de Chaillot

Cinéaqua

PL DE VARSOVIE

PONT D'IENA

AVE DE

AVE DES NATIONS UNIES

Cité de l'Architecture et du Patrimoine

Trocadéro Fountains

sculptures, ornamental pools
and fountains. Steps lead
down from the terrace to the
Théâtre National de Chaillot,
which has an experimental
approach to productions
covering all genres.
   The **Musée de l'Homme**,
in the west wing, stages

temporary exhibitions tracing
human evolution through a
series of anthropological
exhibits. The museum is
undergoing extensive
renovation. Next door is the

Musée de la Marine, devoted
to French naval history and
aspects of the modern-day
navy. The east wing contains
the **Cité de l'Architecture et
du Patrimoine** (see above).

Les Egouts ⑭

Opposite 93 quai d'Orsay 75007.
Map 6 F2. 01 53 68 27 81
(in English). M *Alma-Marceau.*
RER *Pont-de-l'Alma.* 11am–
4pm (5pm in summer) Sat–Wed.
last 3 wks Jan.

One of Baron Haussmann's
finest achievements, the majority of Paris's sewers (*égouts*)
date from the Second Empire.
If laid end to end the 2,400 km
(1,490 miles) of sewers would
stretch from Paris to Istanbul.
Tours of this popular attraction
have been limited to an area
around the quai d'Orsay
entrance and are on foot. Visitors
can discover the mysteries of
underground Paris in the
sewer museum. There are also
displays showing how the
machinery used in the sewers
has changed over the years.

Musée du Quai Branly ⑮

37 quai Branly 75007. **Map** 6 E2.
Tel 01 56 61 70 00. M *Alma-
Marceau.* RER *Pont-de-l'Alma.*
11am–7pm Tue, Wed, Sun,
·11am–9pm Thu, Fri, Sat. 1 May,
25 Dec. free 1st Sun of month &
for 18–25s after 6pm Sat.
**Exhibitions, theatre,
film, library.**
www.quaibranly.fr

Built to give the
arts of Africa,
Asia, Oceania and
the Americas a
platform as shining
as that for Western
art in the city, this
museum has a

**Aztec mask, Musée
du Quai Branly**

massive collection of
more than 300,000 objects.
It is particularly strong on
Africa, with stone, wooden
and ivory masks, as well as
ceremonial tools. The Jean
Nouvel-designed building,
which is raised on stilts, is a
worthwhile sight in itself,
while the ingenious use of
glass in its construction allows
the surrounding greenery to
act as a natural backdrop.

Eiffel Tower ⑯

See p113.

**Original Art Nouveau doorway at
No. 29 avenue Rapp**

No. 29 Avenue Rapp ⑰

75005. **Map** 6 E2. M *Alma-
Marceau.* RER *Pont-de-l'Alma.*

A prime example of Art
Nouveau architecture, No. 29
avenue Rapp won its designer,
Jules Lavirotte, first prize at
the Concours des Façades de
la Ville de Paris in 1901. Its
ceramics and brickwork are
decorated with animal and
flower motifs intermingling
with female figures. These
are superimposed on
a multi-coloured
sandstone base to
produce a façade
that is deliberately
erotic, and was
certainly subversive
in its day. Also
worth visiting
nearby is Lavirotte's
building, complete
with watchtower,
which can be found
in the square Rapp.

Champ-de-Mars ⑱

75007. **Map** 6 E3. M *Ecole-Militaire.*
RER *Champ-de-Mars–Tour-Eiffel.*

The vast gardens stretching
from the Eiffel Tower to the
Ecole Militaire (Military
School) were originally a
parade ground for young
officer cadets. The area has
since been used for horse-
racing, balloon ascents and
mass ceremonies to celebrate

the anniversary of the
Revolution on July 14th. The
first ceremony was held in
1790, in the presence of a
glum, captive, Louis XVI.
    Mammoth exhibitions were
held here in the late 19th
century, among them the
1889 World Fair for which the
Eiffel Tower was erected.

Ecole Militaire ⑲

1 pl Joffre 75007. **Map** 6 F4.
M *Ecole-Militaire.* **Visits** *by special
permission only – contact the
Commandant in writing.*

The Royal Military Academy
of Louis XV was founded in
1751 to educate 500 sons of
impoverished officers. Louis
XV and Madame de
Pompadour commissioned
architect Jacques-Ange
Gabriel to design a building
that would rival Louis XIV's
Hôtel des Invalides. Financing
the building became a
problem so a lottery was
authorized and a tax was
raised on playing-cards. One
of the main features is the
central pavilion – a magnificent example of the French
Classical style, with ten
Corinthian columns and a
quadrangular dome. Four
figures adorn the entablature
frieze, symbolizing France,
Victory, Force and Peace.
    An early cadet at the
academy was Napoleon,
whose passing-out report
stated that "he could go far if
the circumstances are right".

**A 1751 engraving showing the
planning of the Ecole Militaire**

Eiffel Tower ⑯

Eiffel Tower seen from the Trocadéro

Built for the Universal Exhibition of 1889, and to commemorate the centennial of the Revolution, the 324 m (1,063 ft) Eiffel Tower (Tour Eiffel) was meant to be a temporary addition to Paris's skyline. Designed by Gustave Eiffel, it was fiercely decried by 19th-century aesthetes. It stood as the world's tallest building until 1931, when New York's Empire State Building was completed.

VISITORS' CHECKLIST

Champ-de-Mars, 75007. **Map** 6
D3. **Tel** 08 92 70 12 39. M *Bir Hakeim.* 🚌 *42, 69, 72, 82, 87 to Champ-de-Mars.* RER *Champ-de-Mars.* 🅿️ *Tour Eiffel.* ⏰ *mid-Jun–Aug: 9am–12:45am; Sep–mid-Jun: 9:30am–11:45pm daily.* ♿
📷 🍴 🏛 ♿ www.tour-eiffel.fr

The third level, 276 m (905 ft) above the ground, can hold 400 people at a time.

★ **Viewing Gallery**
On a clear day it is possible to see for 72 km (45 miles), including a distant view of Chartres Cathedral.

DARING FEATS

The tower has always inspired crazy stunts. In 1912, Reichelt, a Parisian tailor, attempted to fly from the parapet with only a cape for wings. He plunged to his death in front of a large crowd.

Stuntman Reichelt

STAR FEATURES

★ Eiffel Bust

★ Viewing Gallery

The double-decker lifts have a limited capacity, and during the tourist season there can be long waits. Queuing for the lifts requires patience and a good head for heights.

Cineiffel
This small audio-visual museum shows historical film footage of the tower.

The second level is at 116 m (380 ft), separated from the first level by 359 steps or a few minutes in the lift.

Jules Verne restaurant is rated highly in Paris, offering not only superb food, but a breathtaking panoramic view.

★ **Eiffel Bust**
The achievement of Eiffel (1832–1923) was honoured by Antoine Bourdelle, who placed this bust under the tower in 1929.

The first level, 57 m (187 ft) high, can be reached by lift or by 345 steps.

LES INVALIDES

Musée de l'Armée   Hôtel des Invalides   Cour d'Honneur

Musée de l'Ordre   Dôme   St-Louis-des-   Musée des
de la Libération   Church   Invalides   Plans-Reliefs

Designed by Libéral Bruand, it was completed in 1676 by Jules Hardouin-Mansart. He later incorporated the Dôme Church, with its golden roof, which was built as Louis XIV's private chapel. Nearly 6,000 soldiers once lived here. Today there are fewer than 100.

The harmonious Classical façade is one of the most impressive sights in Paris. The building houses the Musée de l'Armée and the Musée de l'Ordre de la Libération. This was set up to honour feats of heroism during World War II under the leadership of Charles de Gaulle. The story is told using film, photographs and mementos. The Musée des Plans-Reliefs also houses a large collection of military models of French forts.

Musée de l'Armée ②

129 rue Grenelle 75007. **Map** 7 A3. **Tel** 08 10 11 33 99. M Varenne, Latour-Maubourg, Invalides. RER Invalides. ◯ 10am–6pm (7pm Tue, 5pm Oct–Mar) daily. ● 1st Mon of month, 1 Jan, 1 May, 1 Nov, 25 Dec. www.invalides.org

This is one of the most comprehensive museums of military history in the world. It is housed in two galleries, situated on either side of the magnificent courtyard of the Hôtel des Invalides and in the newly opened "Priests' Wing" with the World War II galleries.

A major exhibit recalls the victories and defeats of France through history, dedicated mainly to the Napoleonic era. The emperor's death mask and stuffed horse, Vizier, are on display. Other exhibits include François I's ivory hunting horns, Oriental arms from Japan, and a model of the 1944 Normandy landing.

UNESCO ②

7 pl de Fontenoy 75007. **Map** 6 F5. 01 45 68 10 60 (in English). M Ségur, Cambronne. ◯ for guided tours only (reservations essential): 3pm Mon (French), 3pm Wed (English). ● public hols. www.unesco.org

This is the headquarters of the United Nations Educational, Scientific and Cultural Organization (UNESCO). Its aim is to contribute to international peace through education, science and culture.

UNESCO is a treasure-trove of modern art, including an enormous mural by Picasso, ceramics by Joan Miró and sculptures by Henry Moore, and the calm Japanese garden by Noguchi. Exhibitions and films are also held here.

Hôtel des Invalides ②

75007. **Map** 7 A3. **Tel** 01 44 42 38 77. M Latour-Maubourg, Invalides, Varenne. ◯ 10am–6pm (5pm winter) daily. ● 1 Jan, 1 May, 1 Nov, 25 Dec. book ahead on 01 44 42 37 72. www.invalides.org

This imposing building, from which the area takes its name, was commissioned by Louis XIV in 1670 for his wounded and homeless veterans.

The façade of the Musée de l'Armée

For hotels and restaurants in this region see pp550–5 and pp600–6

Altar of St-Louis-des-Invalides with banners seized in battle

St-Louis-des-Invalides ㉓

Hôtel des Invalides 75007. **Map** 7 A3. **M** *Invalides, Latour-Maubourg, Varenne.* **Tel** 01 44 42 37 65. ☐ *10am–5:30pm (4:30pm winter) daily.* **www**.invalides.org

Also known as the "soldiers' church", this is the chapel of the Hôtel des Invalides. It was built from 1679 to 1708 by Jules Hardouin-Mansart, according to Bruand's design. The stark, Classical interior is well-proportioned, designed in the shape of a Greek cross.

There is a fine 17th-century organ on which the first performance of Berlioz's *Requiem* was given on 5 December 1837, with more than 200 musicians and choristers participating.

Dôme Church ㉔

Hôtel des Invalides, 129 rue de Grenelle, 75007. **Map** 7 A3. **Tel** 01 44 42 38 77. **M** *Latour-Maubourg, Varenne, Invalides.* **🚌** *82, 92 to Les Invalides.* **RER** *Invalides.* ☐ *Tour Eiffel.* ☐ *Apr–Sep: 10am–6pm daily (Jul & Aug: to 7pm); Oct–Mar: 10am–5pm.* ● *1st Mon of month, 1 Jan, 1 May, 17 Jun, 1 Nov, 25 Dec.* 🎫 ⊙ 🛗 *restr.* 🎫 🖥 🎧 **www**.invalides.org

Jules Hardouin-Mansart was asked in 1676 by the Sun King, Louis XIV, to build the Dôme Church to complement the existing buildings of the

Invalides military refuge, designed by Libéral Bruand. The Dôme was to be reserved for the exclusive use of the Sun King and as the location of royal tombs.

The resulting masterpiece is one of the greatest examples of 17th-century French architecture, the period known as the *grand siècle*. After Louis XIV's death, plans to bury the royal family in the church were abandoned.

The main attraction is the tomb of Napoleon; 20 years after his death on the island of St Helena, his body was returned to France and installed in this magnificent crypt, encased in six coffins in a vast red porphyry sarcophagus.

Dôme Church with cupola, first gilded in 1715

Musée Rodin ㉕

79 rue de Varenne 75007. **Map** 7 B3. **Tel** 01 44 18 61 10. **M** *Varenne.* ☐ *10am–5:45pm Tue–Sun.* ● *1 Jan, 1 May, 25 Dec.* 🎫 *free 1st Sun of month & for 18–25s after 6pm Sat.* 🛗 *restricted.* 🖥 🎧 **www**.musee-rodin.fr

Auguste Rodin (1840–1917), regarded as one of the greatest French sculptors, lived and worked in the Hôtel Biron, an elegant 18th-century mansion, from 1908 until his death. In return for a state-owned flat and studio, Rodin left his work to the nation, and it is now exhibited here.

Rodin's *The Thinker* in museum garden

Some of his most celebrated sculptures are on display in the garden: *The Burghers of Calais, The Thinker, The Gates of Hell (see p120)* and *Balzac*.

The indoor exhibits are arranged in chronological order, spanning the whole of Rodin's career. Highlights include *The Kiss* and *Eve*.

Sainte-Clotilde ㉖

23 bis rue Las Cases 75007. **Map** 7 B3. 🎫 *01 44 18 62 60.* **M** *Solférino, Varenne, Invalides.* ☐ *9am–7:30pm Mon–Fri, 10am–8pm Sat & Sun.* ● *non-religious public hols.* **Concerts**

Designed by the German-born architect Franz Christian Gau and built in 1846–56, this Neo-Gothic church was inspired by the 19th-century enthusiasm for the Middle Ages, popularized by such writers as Victor Hugo.

Inside are wall paintings by James Pradier and stained-glass windows with scenes relating to the patron saint of the church. The composer César Franck was organist here from 1858 to 1890.

Musée Maillol ㉗

61 rue de Grenelle 75007. **Map** 7 C4. **Tel** 01 42 22 59 58. **M** *Rue du Bac, Sèvres-Babylone.* ☐ *10:30am–7pm (9:30pm Fri).* ● *pub hols.* 🛗 🖥 🎧 **www**.museemaillol.com

This museum was created by Dina Vierny, muse to Aristide Maillol. His work is exhibited here in all its diverse forms: drawings, engravings, paintings, sculpture and decorative objects. The museum also plays host to two major temporary exhibitions a year. Allegorical figures of the city of Paris and the four seasons adorn Bouchardon's fountain outside.

THE LEFT BANK

The Left Bank has long been associated with poets, philosophers, artists and radical thinkers of all kinds. It still has its share of bohemian street life and pavement cafés, but the smart set has moved in, patronizing Yves St-Laurent and the exclusive interior design shops in rue Jacob.

The Latin Quarter is the ancient area lying between the Seine and Luxembourg Gardens, and is today filled with bookshops, art galleries and cafés. The boulevard St-Michel, bordering the Latin quarter and St-Germain-des-Prés, has slowly given way to commerce, and is full of

Clock in the Musée d'Orsay

fast-food outlets and cheap shops. The surrounding maze of narrow, cobbled streets has retained its character, with ethnic shop and avant-garde theatres dominated by the façade of the Sorbonne, France's first university, built in 1253. Many Parisians dream of living near the Luxembourg Gardens, a quiet area with charming old streets, gateways, and elaborate gardens full of paths, lawns and tree-lined avenues. Students come here to chat, and on warm days, old men still meet underneath the chestnut trees to play chess or the traditional French game of *boules*.

SIGHTS AT A GLANCE

Churches
St-Germain-des-Prés ❺
St-Séverin ❾
St-Julien-le-Pauvre ❿
St-Etienne-du-Mont ⓬
Panthéon ⓭

St-Sulpice ⓯
Val-de-Grâce ⓱

Museums and Galleries
Musée d'Orsay pp120–1 ❶
Musée Eugène Delacroix ❻
Musée de Cluny ❽

Fountains
Fontaine de l'Observatoire ⓰

Historic Buildings and Streets
Boulevard St-Germain ❷
Quai Voltaire ❸
Ecole Nationale Supérieure des Beaux Arts ❹
Rue de l'Odéon ❼
La Sorbonne ⓫
Palais du Luxembourg ⓮

GETTING THERE
This area is served by metro stations at St-Germain-des-Prés, St-Michel and St-Sulpice, among others, with RER stations at Musée d'Orsay and Luxembourg. Bus routes 63 and 87 serve boulevard St-Germain; route 38 serves boulevard St-Michel.

KEY
- ▮ Street-by-Street map *pp118–19*
- ▮ Street-by-Street map *pp124–5*
- ▮ Street-by-Street map *pp126–7*
- Ⓜ Metro station
- RER RER station
- ▣ Batobus boarding point

◁ **Jardin du Luxembourg with Panthéon**

Street-by-Street: St-Germain-des-Prés

Organ grinder in St-Germain

After World War II, St-Germain des-Prés became synonymous with intellectual life centred on bars and cafés. Philosophers, writers, actors and musicians mingled in the cellar nightspots and brasseries, where existentialist philosophy co-existed with American jazz. The area is now smarter than in the heyday of Jean-Paul Sartre and Simone de Beauvoir, the enigmatic singer Juliette Greco and the New Wave film-makers. However, the writers are still around, enjoying the pleasures of sitting in Les Deux Magots, Café de Flore and other haunts. The 17th-century buildings have survived, but signs of change are evident in the affluent shops dealing in antiques, books and fashion.

Les Deux Magots became a focus of bohemian and literary activity in the 1920s.

Café de Flore, the former favourite haunt of Jean-Paul Sartre, Simone de Beauvoir, and other French intellectuals, still has a classic Art Deco interior.

Brasserie Lipp, decorated with colourful ceramics, is a renowned brasserie frequented by politicians.

RUE DU DRAGON

RUE DU SABOT

RUE DE RENNES

RUE BONAPARTE

RUE DU FOUR

BLVD ST

RUE BONAPARTE

M

Metro St-Germain-des-Prés

★ **St-Germain-des-Prés**
The philosopher René Descartes is among the notables buried here in Paris's oldest church ❺

★ **Boulevard St-Germain**
Café terraces, boutiques, cinemas, restaurants and bookshops characterize the central section of the Left Bank's main street ❷

KEY

- - - Suggested route

LOCATOR MAP
See Street Finder maps 7, 8

★ **Musée Delacroix**
The home of the Romantic painter Eugène Delacroix (1798–1863) is now a museum devoted to his art ❻

Palais Abbatial was the residence of abbots from 1586 till the 1789 Revolution.

Rue de Buci was for centuries an important street and the site of some Real Tennis courts. It now holds a lively market.

RUE MAZARINE

RUE DE BUCI

GERMAIN

RUE DE SEINE

RUE DE L'ANCIENNE COMEDIE

RUE DE MONTFAUCON

RUE MABILLON

RUE FÉLIBIEN

M

Metro Odéon

M

CARREFOUR DE L'ODÉON

Metro Mabillon

| 0 metres | 100 |
| 0 yards | 100 |

Musée d'Orsay ❶

See pp120–1.

Boulevard St-Germain ❷

75006, 75007. **Map** 8 D4.
Ⓜ *Solférino, Rue du Bac, St-Germain-des-Prés, Mabillon, Odéon, Cluny-La Sorbonne, Maubert-Mutualité.*

The Left Bank's most celebrated thoroughfare curves across three districts from the Ile St-Louis to the Pont de la Concorde. The architecture is homogeneous because the boulevard was another of Baron Haussmann's bold strokes of urban planning, but it encompasses a wide range of different lifestyles from bohemian to bourgeois.
  Starting from the east, it passes Musée de Cluny and the Sorbonne. It is most lively from boulevard St-Michel to St-Germain-des-Prés, with its café culture.

Quai Voltaire ❸

75006, 75007. **Map** 8 D3.
Ⓜ *Rue du Bac.* Ⓡ *Museé d'Orsay.*

The quai Voltaire is now home to some of the most important antiques dealers in Paris. Many famous people have lived in the attractive 18th-century houses, among others Voltaire at No. 27 and Richard Wagner, Jean Sibelius and Oscar Wilde at No. 19.

Plaque marking the house in quai Voltaire where Voltaire died in 1778

Musée d'Orsay ●

In 1986, 47 years after it had closed as a mainline railroad station, Victor Laloux's turn-of-the-century building reopened as the Musée d'Orsay. Built as the Orléans railway terminus in the heart of Paris, it narrowly avoided demolition in the 1970s. In the conversion to a museum, much of the original architecture was retained.

The museum presents the rich diversity of visual arts from 1848 to 1914 and explains the social and technological context in which they were created. Exhibits include paintings, sculptures, furniture and decorative objects. The museum also has a programme of classical music concerts. Exhibits and access are subject to change due to major ongoing renovations.

Young Dancer of Fourteen (1881) by Edgar Degas

The Gates of Hell *(1880–1917)*
Rodin included figures that he had already created, such as The Thinker *and* The Kiss, *in this famous gateway.*

Dancing at the Moulin de la Galette *(1876)*
Renoir painted this picture outside to capture the light as it filtered through the trees.

The Dance *(1867–8)*
Carpeaux's dynamic sculpture caused a scandal when it was first unveiled in 1869.

KEY TO FLOORPLAN

▢ Architecture & Decorative Arts	▢ Naturalism and Symbolism
▢ Sculpture	▢ Art Nouveau
▢ Painting before 1870	▢ Temporary exhibitions
▢ Impressionism	▢ Non-exhibition space
▢ Neo-Impressionism	

Doctor Paul Gachet (1890)
This portrait by Van Gogh is one of three and was painted the same year the artist died.

GALLERY GUIDE
The ground floor has works from the mid- to late 19th century. The middle level features Art Nouveau decorative art and late-19th- to early-20th-century paintings and sculptures. The upper level is currently not open to the public.

Upper level

Middle level

Entrance

Ground floor

Shop entrance

VISITORS' CHECKLIST

Quai Anatole France 75007.
Map 8 D2. **Tel** 01 40 49 48 14.
Ⓜ Solférino. 🚌 24, 68, 69, 84 to quai A. France; 73 to rue de la Légion d'Honneur; 63, 83, 84, 94 to bd St-Germain. RER 🚤
Ⓟ Musée d'Orsay. P Quai A. France. 🕐 9:30am–6pm Tue–Sun (9:45pm Thu; last entry 1 hr before closing). 🔴 1 Jan, 1 May, 25 Dec.
🖼 ⓞ ♿ 🅿 🍴 🏛 **Concerts** phone 01 40 49 47 50.
www.musee-orsay.fr

EXPLORING THE MUSÉE D'ORSAY

Many of the paintings in the Musée d'Orsay came from the Louvre and the Impressionist collection once in the Jeu de Paume. Paintings from before 1870 are on the ground floor, presided over by Thomas Couture's massive *Romans of the Decadence*. Neo-Classical masterpieces, like Ingres's *La Source*, hang near Romantic works like Delacroix's turbulent *Tiger Hunt*. These exotic visions contrast with Realist works by artists like Courbet and early canvases by Degas and Manet, including the latter's famous *Olympia*.

The museum's central aisle overflows with sculpture, from Daumier's satirical busts of members of parliament to Carpeaux's exuberant *The Dance* and Rodin's *The Gates of Hell*. Decorative arts and architecture are on the middle level, where there is also a display of Art Nouveau – sinuous lines

Blue Waterlilies (1919)
by Claude Monet

characterize Lalique's jewellery and glassware and the designs of Hector Guimard, who produced the characteristic curvy entrances of the Paris metro.

Among the many highlights of the Impressionist rooms are Monet's *Rouen Cathedral* series *(see p267)* and Renoir's joyful *Moulin de la Galette*. The Post-Impressionist collection on the middle level includes the *Eglise d'Auvers* by Van Gogh, Seurat's pointillist compositions such as *Le Cirque*, Gauguin's highly coloured Symbolist works and Toulouse-Lautrec's depictions of Parisian nightlife. Among the highlights of the post-1900 display is Matisse's *Luxe, Calme et Volupté*. Some exhibits may be moved due to renovation work.

Le Déjeuner sur l'Herbe (1863) by Edouard Manet

The façade of the Ecole Nationale Supérieure des Beaux Arts

Ecole Nationale Supérieure des Beaux Arts ❹

14 rue Bonaparte 75006. **Map** 8 E3.
Tel 01 47 03 50 00. Ⓜ St-Germain-des-Prés. ◯ groups by appt only (01 47 03 50 00 to book). ▨ ▯
Library www.ensba.fr

The main French school of fine arts has an enviable position at the corner of the rue Bonaparte and the riverside quai Malaquais. It is housed in several buildings, the most imposing being the 19th-century Palais des Etudes. A host of budding French and foreign painters and architects have crossed the courtyard, which contains a 17th-century chapel, to learn in the ateliers of the school. Many American architects have studied here over the past century.

St-Germain-des-Prés ❺

3 pl St-Germain-des-Prés 75006.
Map 8 E4. **Tel** 01 55 42 81 33.
Ⓜ St-Germain-des-Prés. ◯ 8am–7pm daily. **Concerts** 8pm Tue, Thu.
www.eglise-sgp.org

This the oldest church in Paris, originating in 542 as a basilica to house holy relics. It became an immensely powerful Benedictine abbey, rebuilt in the 11th century, but most of it was destroyed by fire in 1794. Major restoration took place in the 19th century. One of the three original towers survives, housing one of the oldest belfries in France. The interior is an interesting mix of styles, with 6th-century marble columns, Gothic vaulting and Romanesque arches. Famous tombs include that of 17th-century philosopher René Descartes.

Musée Eugène Delacroix ❻

6 rue de Fürstenberg 75006.
Map 8 E4. **Tel** 01 44 41 86 50.
Ⓜ St-Germain-des-Prés. ◯ 9:30am–5pm Wed–Mon. ● 1 Jan, 1 May, 25 Dec. ▨ free 1st Sun of month & for 18–25s (EU residents). ▢ ▯
www.musee-delacroix.fr

The leading Romantic painter Eugène Delacroix lived and worked here from 1857 till his death in 1863. Here he painted *The Entombment of Christ* and *The Way to Calvary* (which hang in the museum). He also created murals for the Chapel of the Holy Angels in the nearby St-Sulpice church.
    The apartment and studio has a portrait of George Sand, and Delacroix self-portraits.

Jacob Wrestling with the Angel by Delacroix, in St-Sulpice (*see p127*)

Rue de l'Odéon ❼

75006. **Map** 8 F5. Ⓜ Odéon.

Opened in 1779 to improve access to the Odéon theatre, this was the first street in Paris to have pavements with gutters and it still has many 18th-century houses.
    Sylvia Beach's bookshop, the original Shakespeare & Company, stood at No. 12 from 1921 to 1940. It was a magnet for writers like James Joyce, Ezra Pound and Hemingway.

Musée de Cluny ❽

6 pl Paul-Painlevé. **Map** 9 A5.
Tel 01 53 73 78 16. Ⓜ St-Michel, Odéon, Cluny. ℝℰℝ St-Michel.
◯ 9:15am–5:45pm Wed–Mon.
● 1 Jan, 1 May, 25 Dec.
▨◉▯ **Concerts**.
www.musee-moyenage.fr

The museum (officially the Musée National du Moyen Age) is a unique combination

Stone heads of the Kings of Judah carved around 1220

St-Séverin ❾

1 rue-des-Prêtres-St-Séverin 75005.
Map 9 A4. **Tel** 01 42 34 93 50.
Ⓜ St-Michel. ◯ 11am–7:30pm Mon–Sat, 9am–8:30pm Sun. ▨

St-Séverin, one of the most beautiful churches in Paris, is named after a 6th-century hermit who lived in the area. It is a perfect example of the Flamboyant Gothic style. Finished in the early 16th century, it includes a remarkable double aisle encircling the chancel. In the garden stands the church's medieval gable-roofed charnel house.

Gargoyles adorning the gables of the Flamboyant Gothic St-Séverin

The School woodcarving (English, early 16th century)

The poetic elegance of a unicorn on the sixth tapestry

of Gallo-Roman ruins, incorporated into a medieval mansion (in newly created medieval gardens), and one of the world's finest collections of medieval art and crafts. Its name comes from Pierre de Chalus, Abbot of Cluny, who bought the ruins in 1330. The present building dates from 1485–98. Among the star exhibits are the

tapestries, remarkable for their quality, age and state of preservation. The highlight of the sculpture section is the Gallery of the Kings, while one of Cluny's most precious items, the Golden Rose of Basel from 1330, is found in the collection of jewellery and metalwork. Other treasures include stained glass, woodcarvings and books of hours.

St-Julien-le-Pauvre ⑩

1 rue St-Julien-le-Pauvre 75005. **Map** 9 A4. *Tel* 01 43 54 52 16. Ⓜ *St-Michel.* ⬤ *9:30am–1pm, 3–6:30pm daily.* ⬛ *10am, 11am, 6pm Sun.* **Concerts**

The church is one of the oldest in Paris, dating from between 1165 and 1220. The university held its official meetings in the church until 1524, when a student protest created so much damage that they were barred from the church by parliament. It has belonged to the Melchite sect of the Greek Orthodox Church since 1889 and is now the setting for classical and religious concerts.

La Sorbonne ⑪

47 rue des Ecoles 75005. **Map** 9 A5. *Tel* 01 40 46 22 11. Ⓜ *Cluny-La Sorbonne, Maubert-Mutualité.* 📷 *only by appt. Write to Service des Visites.* **www**.paris-sorbonne.fr

The Sorbonne, seat of the University of Paris until 1969, was established in 1253 by Robert de Sorbon, confessor to Louis IX, for 16 poor scholars to study theology. It went

on to become the centre of scholastic theology. In 1469, three printing machines were brought from Mainz, and the first printing house in France was founded. The college's opposition to liberal 18th-century philosophical ideas led to its suppression during the Revolution. It was re-established by Napoleon in 1806, and the 17th-century buildings replaced. In 1969, the Sorbonne split into 13 separate universities, but the building still holds some lectures.

St-Etienne-du-Mont ⑫

Pl Ste-Geneviève 75005. **Map** 13 A1. *Tel* 01 43 54 11 79. Ⓜ *Cardinal Lemoine.* ⬤ *8:45am–7:30pm Tue–Sun.* ⬤ *lunchtime Sat & Sun.* 📷 🚻

This remarkable church houses the shrine of Saint Geneviève, the legendary patron saint of Paris, and the remains of the great literary figures Racine and Pascal. Some parts of the building are Gothic, others Renaissance, including the eye-catching rood screen.

ST-ETIENNE-DU-MONT

16th-century belfry tower

Rood screen

Medieval window

Street by Street: Latin Quarter

Since the Middle Ages this riverside quarter has been dominated by the Sorbonne, and acquired its name from the early Latin-speaking students. It dates back to the Roman town across from the Ile de la Cité; at that time the rue St-Jacques was one of the main roads out of Paris. The area is generally associated with artists, intellectuals and a bohemian way of life; it also has a history of political unrest. In 1871, the place St-Michel became the centre of the Paris Commune, and in May 1968 it was a site of student uprisings. Today the eastern half has become sufficiently chic, however, to house members of the Establishment.

Latin jazz

★ St-Séverin
Begun in the 13th century, this church took 3 centuries to build and is a fine example of the Flamboyant Gothic style 9

Metro St-Michel

Saint-Michel Notre-Dame

Boulevard St-Michel, or Boul'Mich, as it is affectionately known by locals, is a lively mélange of cafés and book and clothes shops, with nightclubs and experimental cinemas nearby.

Metro Cluny La Sorbonne

0 metres   100
0 yards   100

★ Musée de Cluny
One of the finest collections of medieval art in the world is kept here in a superb late 15th-century building, incorporating the ruins of Gallo-Roman baths 8

KEY

– – – Suggested route

For hotels and restaurants in this region see pp550–5 and pp600–6

LOCATOR MAP
See Street Finder maps 8, 9, 12, 13

★ **St-Julien-le-Pauvre**
*Rebuilt in the 17th century,
this church was used to
store animal feed in
the Revolution* ⑩

Metro
Maubert
Mutualité

STAR SIGHTS

★ Musée de Cluny

★ St-Séverin

★ St-Julien-le-Pauvre

Panthéon ⑬

Pl du Panthéon 75005. **Map** 13 A1.
Tel 01 44 32 18 00. M Maubert-
Mutualité, Cardinal-Lemoine.
RER Luxembourg. ◻ Apr–Sep:
10am–6:30pm daily; Oct–Mar:
10am–6pm daily. ● 1 Jan, 1 May, 25
Dec. 🎫 📷 🔗 **http**://pantheon.
monuments-nationaux.fr

When Louis XV recovered
from illness in 1744, he was so
grateful that he conceived
a magnificent church to
honour Saint Geneviève, the
patron saint of Paris. The
French architect Jacques-
Germain Soufflot planned the
church in Neo-Classical
style. Work began in 1764
and was completed in 1790

The Panthéon Interior
*The interior has four
aisles arranged in the
shape of a Greek cross,
from the centre of which
the great dome rises.*

Entrance

under the control of
Guillaume Rondelet. But with
the Revolution underway, the
church was soon turned into
a pantheon – a monument
housing the tombs of France's
great heroes. Napoleon
returned it to the Church in
1806, but it was secularized
and then desecularized once
more before finally being
made a civic building in 1885.
  The façade, inspired by the
Rome Pantheon, has a pediment relief depicting the
mother country granting lau-
rels to her great men. Those
resting here include Voltaire,
Rousseau and Zola, and the
ashes of Pierre and Marie
Curie and André
Malraux.

**Iron-
Framed
Dome**
*The fresco
in the dome's
stone cupola represents
the* Glorification of Sainte
Geneviève, *commissioned
by Napoleon in 1811.*

The dome lantern

The dome
galleries

Crypt
*Under the building, the vast crypt
divides into galleries flanked by
Doric columns. Many French
notables rest here, including
Voltaire and Emile Zola.*

Street-by-Street: Luxembourg Quarter

Situated only a few steps from the bustle of St-Germain-des-Prés, this graceful and historic area offers a peaceful haven in the heart of a modern city. The Jardin du Luxembourg and Palais du Luxembourg dominate the surroundings. The gardens became fully open to the public in the 19th century under the ownership of the Comte de Provence (later to become Louis XVIII), when for a small fee visitors could come in and feast on fruit from the orchard. Today the gardens, palace and old houses on the streets to the north remain unspoilt and attract many visitors.

STAR SIGHTS

★ St-Sulpice

★ Palais du Luxembourg

To St-Germain-des-Prés

Place St-Sulpice, ringed by flowering chestnut trees, was begun in 1754.

★ St-Sulpice
This huge Classical church, by six different architects, took more than a century to build ⓯

RUE HENRI DE JOUVENEL

RUE FEROU

RUE SERVANDONI

RUE GARANCIERE

RUE DE TOURNON

Jardins du Luxembourg is a popular garden where people come to relax, sunbathe, sail boats in the pond or admire the many beautiful statues erected in the 19th century.

RUE DE VAUGIRARD

| 0 metres | | 100 |
| 0 yards | | 100 |

★ Palais du Luxembourg
First built as a royal residence, the palace has been used for various purposes from prison to Luftwaffe headquarters. This garden façade was added in 1841 ⓮

KEY

– – – Suggested route

LOCATOR MAP
See Street Finder maps 8, 12, 13

Fontaine de Médicis is a 17th-century fountain in the style of an Italian grotto. It is thought to have been designed by Salomon de Brosse.

Saint Geneviève, patron saint of Paris, whose prayers saved Paris from the Huns in AD 451, is honoured by this statue by Michel-Louis Victor in 1845.

Palais du Luxembourg ⑭

15 rue de Vaugirard 75006. **Map** 8 E5. **Tel** *01 44 54 19 49.* **M** *Odéon.* **RER** *Luxembourg.* 🛇 *groups: Mon, Fri, Sat (apply 3 months in advance); individuals: one Sat per month.* **Tel** *01 44 54 19 49.* 🖱 *www.senat.fr* **Museum** ⬜ *daily during exhibitions.* 📷 *www.museeduluxembourg.fr*

Now the home of the French Senate, this palace was built to remind Marie de' Médici, widow of Henri IV, of her native Florence. It was designed by Salomon de Brosse in the style of Florence's Pitti Palace. By the time it was finished (1631) she had been banished from Paris, but it remained a royal palace until the Revolution. In World War II it became the Luftwaffe head-quarters. The Musée du Luxembourg in the east gallery hosts world-class art exhibitions.

St-Sulpice ⑮

Pl St-Sulpice 75006. **Map** 8 E5. **Tel** *01 42 34 59 98.* **M** *St-Sulpice.* ⬜ *7:30am–7:30pm daily.* 📷 **Concerts**

This huge and imposing church was started in 1646 and took more than a century to finish. The result is a simple façade with two tiers of elegant columns and two mismatched towers at the ends. Large arched windows fill the vast interior with light.
   In the side chapel to the right are murals by Eugène Delacroix, including *Jacob Wrestling with the Angel (see p122)* and *Heliodorus Driven from the Temple.*

The Classical two-storey west front of St-Sulpice with its two towers

Carpeaux's fountain sculpture

Fontaine de l'Observatoire ⑯

Pl Ernest Denis, av de l'Observatoire 7500. **Map** 12 E2. **RER** *Port Royal.*

Situated at the southern tip of the Jardin du Luxem-bourg, this is one of the finest fountains in Paris. The central sculpture, by Jean-Baptiste Carpeaux, was erected in 1873. Made of bronze, it has four women holding aloft a globe representing four continents – the fifth, Oceania, was left out for reasons of symmetry. There are some subsidiary figures, including dolphins, horses and a turtle.

Val-de-Grâce ⑰

1 pl Alphonse-Laveran 75005. **Map** 12 F2. **Tel** *01 40 51 51 92.* **M** *Gobelins.* **RER** *Port Royal.* ⬜ *noon–6pm Tue–Sun.* 🛇 *Aug.* 📷 🚫 *except for nave.* ♿

This is one of the most beau-tiful churches in France, and forms part of a military hos-pital complex. Built for Anne of Austria (wife of Louis XIII) in gratitude for the birth of her son, young Louis XIV him-self laid the first stone in 1645.
   The church is noted for its dome. In the cupola is Pierre Mignard's enormous fresco, with over 200 triple-life-size figures. The six huge marble columns framing the altar are similar to St Peter's in Rome.

FURTHER AFIELD

Many of Paris's famous sights are slightly out of the city centre. Montmartre, long a mecca for artists and writers, still retains much of its bohemian atmosphere, and Montparnasse is full of bustling cafés and theatre crowds. The famous Cimetière du Père Lachaise numbers Chopin, Oscar Wilde and Jim Morrison among its dead and, along with the parks and gardens, provides a tranquil escape from sightseeing. Modern architecture can be seen at Fondation Le Corbusier and La Défense, and there is a huge selection of museums to visit. To the northeast, the science museum at La Villette provides an educational family day out.

SIGHTS AT A GLANCE

Museums and Galleries
Musée Marmottan
  Claude Monet ❺
Musée du Cristal de
  Baccarat ❻
Musée Gustave Moreau ❾
*Cité des Sciences et
  de l'Industrie pp136–7* ⓯
Cité Nationale de l'Histoire
  de l'Immigration ⓴
Musée National d'Histoire
  Naturelle ㉔

Churches and Mosques
St-Alexandre-Nevsky ❼
Sacré-Coeur ⓫
Mosquée de Paris ㉗

Parks and Gardens
Bois de Boulogne ❷
Parc Monceau ❽

Parc des Buttes-Chaumont ⓱
Parc Montsouris ㉓
Jardin des Plantes ㉕
Parc André Citroën ㉘

Cemeteries
Cimetière de Montmartre ⓭
Cimetière du Père Lachaise ⓲
Cimetière du Montparnasse ㉚

Historic Districts
Montmartre pp132–3 ❿
Canal St-Martin ⓰
Montparnasse ㉙

Historic Buildings and Streets
Rue La Fontaine ❹

Moulin Rouge ⓬
Château de Vincennes ㉑
Catacombes ㉛

Modern Architecture
La Défense ❶
Fondation Le Corbusier ❸
Bercy
Bibliothèque Nationale
  de France ㉒
Institut du Monde Arabe ㉖

Markets
Marché aux Puces
  de St-Ouen ⓮

KEY

Main sightseeing area
Major roads

0 kilometres   4

0 miles   2

FURTHER AFIELD

◁ The narrow rue St-Rustique winding up the hill to Sacré-Coeur

West of the City

La Défense ❶

La Grande Arche. **Tel** 01 49 07 27
55. RER La Défense. 🌐 for renovation; phone for information. 🎫 ♿
🚹 ♿ See **The History of France**
pp66–7. **www**.grandearche.com

This skyscraper business city
on the western edge of Paris
is the largest office development in Europe. La Grande
Arche is an enormous hollow
cube large enough to contain
Notre-Dame cathedral.
Designed by Danish architect
Otto von Spreckelsen in the
late 1980s, the arch houses a
gallery and a conference
centre, and has superb views.

La Grande Arche in La Défense

Bois de Boulogne ❷

75016. Ⓜ Porte Maillot, Porte
Dauphine, Porte d'Auteuil, Sablons.
🕐 24 hrs daily. 🎫 to specialist
gardens and museum. ♿

Located between the
western edges of Paris
and the River Seine, this
8.6 sq km (3.3 sq miles)
park offers a vast belt of
greenery for strolling,
cycling, riding, boating,
picnicking, or spending
a day at the races. The
Bois de Boulogne was
once part of the im-
mense Forêt du Rouvre.
In the mid-19th century
Napoleon III had the
Bois designed and
landscaped by Baron
Haussmann, along the
lines of Hyde Park in
London. Several self-
contained parks within
the forest include the

Jardin d'Acclimatation, a fun
park for children, Pré Catalan
and the Bagatelle gardens,
with architectural follies and
an 18th-century villa famous
for its rose garden. The villa
was built in just 64 days after
a bet between the Comte
d'Artois and Marie-Antoinette.
By day the Bois is busy
with families, joggers and
walkers, but after dark it is
notoriously seedy – and
best avoided.

Fondation Le Corbusier ❸

8–10 square du Docteur-Blanche
75016. **Tel** 01 42 88 41 53.
Ⓜ Jasmin. 🕐 1:30–6pm Mon,
10am–6pm Tue–Thu, 10am–5pm
Fri & Sat. 🌐 pub hols, Aug, 24 Dec–
2 Jan. 🎬 **Films, videos**.
www.fondationlecorbusier.fr

In a quiet corner of Auteuil
stand the villas La Roche and
Jeanneret, the first two Parisian
houses built by the influential
20th-century architect Charles-
Edouard Jeanneret, better
known as Le Corbusier. Built
at the start of the 1920s, they
demonstrate his revolutionary
use of white concrete in Cubist
forms. Rooms flow into each
other allowing maximum light
and volume, and the houses
stand on stilts with windows
along their entire length.
Villa La Roche was owned by
the art patron Raoul La Roche.
Today, the villas hold lectures
on Le Corbusier and his work.

**An Art Nouveau window in the
rue la Fontaine**

Rue la Fontaine ❹

75016. **Map** 5 A4. Ⓜ Michel-Ange-
Auteuil, Jasmin. RER Radio-France.

The rue la Fontaine and
surrounding streets act as a
showcase for some of the
most exciting early 20th-
century, low-cost architecture,
featuring sinuous decorative
detail. At No. 14 stands the
Castel Béranger, which firmly
established the reputation of
architect Hector Guimard. He
went on to design the city's
Art Nouveau metro entrances.

Musée Marmottan-Claude Monet ❺

2 rue Louis Boilly 75016. **Tel** 01 44 96
50 33. Ⓜ Muette. 🕐 11am–6pm
Wed–Sun (9pm Tue). 🌐 1 Jan,
1 May, 25 Dec. 🎫 ♿ 🛍
www.marmottan.com

The museum was
created in the 19th-
century mansion of the
famous art historian,
Paul Marmottan, in
1932. He bequeathed
his house, plus his
Renaissance, Consular
and First Empire paint-
ings and furniture, to
the Institut de France.
In 1966 the museum
acquired a fabulous
collection of work by
Impressionist painter
Claude Monet, the
bequest of his son,
Michel. Some of Monet's
most famous paintings
are here, including

A landscaped island in the Bois de Boulogne

Impression – Sunrise (hence the term "Impressionist"), a painting of Rouen Cathedral (see p267), and the Waterlilies series (see p98). Also here is the work painted at Giverny during the last years of Monet's life. This includes The Japanese Bridge and The Weeping Willow. The iridescent colours and daring brush-strokes make these some of the museum's most powerful works.

Part of Monet's personal art collection was passed on to the museum, including work by fellow Impressionists Camille Pissarro, Pierre-Auguste Renoir and Alfred Sisley. The museum also displays medieval illuminated manuscripts and 16th-century Burgundian tapestries. Piano and chamber music concerts are held on the third Tuesday of each month.

Musée du Cristal de Baccarat **6**

11 pl des Etats Unis 75016. *Tel* 01 40 22 11 00. **M** *Boissière.* ◻ *10am–6:30pm Mon, Wed–Sat (last adm 6pm).* ● *public hols.* 🎫 🎥 *by appt.* **www**.baccarat.fr

The Musée du Cristal, also known as the Galerie-Musée Baccarat, displays over 400 items made by the Baccarat company, which was founded in 1764 in Lorraine in eastern France. These include dinner services created for the royal and imperial courts of Europe and many of the best contemporary pieces produced in the workshops, such as fine vases, candelabras, decanters and perfume bottles, as well as watches and jewellery.

In the glassworks itself you can see some of the technical skills used to shape and decorate the crystal ware, such as fine cutting, wheel-engraving, gilding and enamelling.

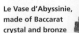

Le Vase d'Abyssinie, made of Baccarat crystal and bronze

Colonnade beside the *naumachia* basin in Parc Monceau

North of the City

St-Alexandre-Nevsky Cathedral

St-Alexandre-Nevsky **7**

12 rue Daru 75008. **Map** 2 F3. *Tel* 01 42 27 37 34. **M** *Courcelles, Ternes.* ◻ *3–5pm Tue & Fri, 10am–12:30pm, 3–6pm Sun.* 🎥 ✝ *6pm Sat, 10:30am Sun.*

This imposing Russian Orthodox cathedral with its five golden-copper domes signals the presence of a large Russian community in Paris. Designed by members of the St Petersburg Fine Arts Academy and financed jointly by Tsar Alexander II and the local Russian community, it was completed in 1861.

Inside, a wall of icons divides the church in two. The Greek-cross plan and the rich mosaics and frescoes decorating the interior are Neo-Byzantine, while the exterior and gilt domes are traditional Russian Orthodox.

Parc Monceau **8**

Bd de Courcelles 75017. **Map** 3 A3. *Tel* 01 42 27 08 64. **M** *Monceau.* ◻ *7am–8pm daily (10pm summer).* 🎥 *by appt.*

This green haven dates back to 1778 when the Duc de Chartres commissioned the painter-writer and amateur landscape designer Louis Carmontelle to create a magnificent garden. The result was an exotic landscape full of architectural follies in the English and German style.

In 1852 the garden became a chic public park. A few original features remain, among them the *naumachia* basin – an ornamental version of a Roman pool used for simulating naval battles.

Musée Gustave Moreau **9**

14 rue de la Rochefoucauld 75009. **Map** 4 E3. *Tel* 01 48 74 38 50. **M** *Trinité.* ◻ *10am–12:45pm, 2–5:15pm Wed–Mon.* ● *some public hols.* 🎫 🎥 🎥 **www**.musee-moreau.fr

The Symbolist painter Gustave Moreau (1826–98), known for his symbolic works depicting biblical and mythological fantasies, lived and worked in this handsome town house. *Jupiter and Semele*, one of the artist's outstanding works, is displayed here, along with other major paintings, and some of the collection's 7,000 drawings and 1,000 oils and watercolours.

Montmartre ⑩

The steep *butte* (hill) of Montmartre has been associated with artists for 200 years.

Théodore Géricault and Camille Corot came here at the start of the 19th century, and in the 20th century Maurice Utrillo immortalized the streets in his works. Today, street artists thrive predominantly on the tourist trade, but much of the area still preserves its rather louche, villagey prewar atmosphere. The name of the area is ascribed to martyrs who were tortured and killed in the area around AD 250, hence *mons martyrium*.

Streetside painter

Montmartre Vineyard

This is the last Parisian vineyard. The harvest is celebrated on the first Saturday in October.

Metro Lamarck Caulaincourt

Au Lapin Agile

"The Agile Rabbit", once a literary haunt, is now a nightclub.

A la Mère Catherine

This was a favourite restaurant of Russian cossacks. They would shout "Bistro!" (meaning "quick") – which gave the bistro its name.

Espace Montmartre Salvador Dalí

Some 330 works by the Surrealist painter and sculptor are on display here.

Place du Tertre

The tourist centre of Montmartre is full of portraitists. Artists first exhibited in the square in the 19th century.

KEY

– – – Suggested route

| 0 metres | 100 |
| 0 yards | 100 |

Musée de Montmartre
Changing, Montmarte-related exhibitions usually include works by artists who lived here, such as this Portrait of a Woman *(1918) by Amedeo Modigliani.*

LOCATOR MAP
See Street Finder maps 3, 4

Sacré-Coeur
This Neo-Romanesque church, started in the 1870s and completed in 1914, contains many treasures, such as this figure of the Virgin Mary and Child *(1896) by P Brunet* ⓫

St-Pierre de Montmartre
This is an early Parisian church with origins dating back to the 6th century.

The funiculaire, or cable railway, at the end of the rue Foyatier takes you to the foot of the basilica of the Sacré-Coeur. Metro tickets are valid for it.

Square Willette lies below the forecourt of the Sacré-Coeur. It is laid out on the side of the hill in a series of descending terraces with lawns, shrubs, trees and flowerbeds.

Musée de la Halle Saint Pierre
Exhibitions here showcase Outsider Art and Art Brut, such as this piece by S Feleggakis.

To metro Anvers

Sacré-Coeur ⓫

Parvis de Notre Dame 75018. **Map** 4
F1. **Tel** 01 53 41 89 00. Ⓜ Abbesses
(then funiculaire to steps of Sacré-
Coeur), Anvers. 🚌 30, 31, 80, 85.
Basilica ⬤ 6am–10:30pm daily.
Dome & crypt ⬤ 9am–6pm daily.
📷 ✞ 7am, 11:15am, 6:30pm,
10pm Mon–Thu, Sat; 3pm Fri; 11am,
6pm, 10pm Sun (Vespers 4pm).
www.sacre-coeur-montmartre.com

The Sacré-Coeur basilica,
dedicated to the Sacred Heart
of Christ and consecrated in
1919, was built as a result of a
private religious vow made at
the outbreak of the Franco-
Prussian war. Two Catholic
businessmen, Alexandre
Legentil and Hubert Rohault
de Fleury, promised to finance
the basilica should France be
spared from assault. Despite
the war and the Siege of
Paris, invasion was averted
and work began in 1875 to
Paul Abadie's designs. Never
considered very graceful, the
basilica is vast and impressive, and one of France's
most important Roman
Catholic buildings.

**The stained glass
gallery** affords a view
of the whole interior.

**The Great Mosaic of
Christ** (1912–22), by
Luc Olivier Merson,
dominates the
chancel vault.

The ovoid dome is
the second-highest
point in Paris, after
the Eiffel Tower.

Bronze doors
in the portico
show the Last
Supper and
other biblical
scenes.

The crypt vaults house a
chapel containing Alexandre
Legentil's heart in a stone urn.

Moulin Rouge ⓬

82 bd de Clichy 75018. **Map** 4 E1.
Tel 01 53 09 82 82. Ⓜ Blanche.
Shows at 9pm & 11pm daily; two
matinées per month at 1pm Sun.
📷 **www**.moulinrouge.com

Built in 1885, the Moulin Rouge
was turned into a dance hall
as early as 1900. Henri de
Toulouse-Lautrec immortalized
the wild and colourful cancan
shows here in his posters and
drawings of famous dancers
such as Jane Avril. The high-
kicking routines continue today
in glitzy, Las Vegas-style revues.

Cimetière de
Montmartre ⓭

20 av Rachel 75018. **Map** 4 D1.
Tel 01 53 42 36 30. Ⓜ Place de
Clichy. ⬤ 8:30am–5:30pm Mon–Sat,
9am–5:30pm Sun (6pm summer). ♿

This has been the resting
place for many luminaries of
the creative arts since the
beginning of the 19th century.

The composers Hector Berlioz
and Jacques Offenbach (who
wrote the famous cancan
tune), Russian dancer Vaslav
Nijinsky and film director
François Truffaut are just a
few of the famous people
who have been buried here
over the years.

There is also a Montmartre
cemetery near square Roland-
Dorgelès, known as the
St-Vincent cemetery. This is
where the French painter
Maurice Utrillo is buried.

**African stall in the Marché aux
Puces de St-Ouen**

Marché aux Puces
de St-Ouen ⓮

Rue des Rosiers, St-Ouen 93406.
Ⓜ Porte-de-Clignancourt. ⬤ 9am–
6pm Sat–Mon. See **Shops and
Markets** p142. **www**.les-puces.com

This is the oldest and largest
of the Paris flea markets,
covering 6 ha (15 acres)
near the Porte de Clignancourt.
In the 19th century, rag merchants and tramps would
gather outside the fortifications that marked the city
limits and offer their wares
for sale. Today the area is
divided into separate markets,
and is well-known for its
heavy Second Empire furniture and ornaments. Although
there are few bargains to be
had, this does not deter the
huge weekend crowds.

Cité des Sciences et
de l'Industrie ⓯

See pp136–7.

Canal St-Martin ⑯

Ⓜ *Jaurès, J Bonsergent, Goncourt.*

A walk along the quays on either side of the Canal St-Martin gives a glimpse of how this thriving, industrial, working-class area of the city looked at the end of the 19th century. The 5-km (3-mile) canal, opened in 1825, provided a shortcut for river traffic between loops of the Seine. A smattering of brick-and-iron factories and warehouses survive from this time along the quai de Jemmapes. Here, too, is the legendary Hôtel du Nord, from Marcel Carné's 1930s film of the same name. The canal itself is quietly busy with barges and anglers; around it are tree-lined quays with quirky shops and cafés, iron footbridges and public gardens. At Jaurès, it meets the Canal de l'Ourcq, which offers a pleasant stroll to Parc de la Villette *(see p136).*

Parc des Buttes-Chaumont ⑰

Place Armand Carrel 75019. *No phone.* Ⓜ *Botzaris, Buttes-Chaumont.* ◯ *May–Sep: 7am–10pm daily; Oct–Apr: 7am–9pm daily.*

For many this is the most pleasant park in Paris. Urban planner Baron Haussmann converted the hilly site from a rubbish dump and quarry with gallows at the foot, to English-style gardens in the 1860s. His colleague was landscape architect Adolphe Alphand, who was responsible for a vast 1860s programme to provide Haussmann's new pavement-lined Parisian avenues with benches, streetlights, kiosks and urinals *(see p108).*

Others involved in the creation of this highly praised park were the engineer Darcel and the landscape gardener Barillet-Deschamps. They created a lake, made an island with real and artificial rocks, gave it a Roman-style temple, and added a waterfall, streams and footbridges leading to the

Boats moored at Port de l'Arsenal

island. Today, in summer, visitors will also find boating facilities, donkey rides and beautiful lawns.

East of the City

Cimetière du Père Lachaise ⑱

16 rue du Repos 75020. *Tel 01 55 25 82 10.* Ⓜ *Père Lachaise, A Dumas.* 🚌 *60, 69, 102 to Pl Gambetta.* Ⓟ *Pl Gambetta.* ◯ *8am–5:30pm (6pm Apr–Nov; from 9am Sun & hols) daily.* 🖥 **www.pere-lachaise.com**

Paris's most prestigious cemetery is set on a wooded hill overlooking the city. The land was once owned by Père de la Chaise, Louis XIV's confessor, but it was bought by order of Napoleon in 1803. The cemetery became so popular that the boundaries were extended six times in the 19th century. Here are buried celebrities such as writer Honoré de Balzac and composer Frédéric Chopin, singer Jim Morrison and actors Yves Montand and Simone Signoret.

Bercy ⑲

75012. Ⓜ *Bercy, Cour St-Emilion.* 🚌 *24, 64, 87.* **Cinémathèque Française***: 51 rue de Bercy. Tel 01 71 19 32 00.* ◯ *noon–7pm Mon–Sat, 10am–8pm Sun.* ♿ *(phone 01 71 19 33 33).*

This former wine-trading quarter just east of the city centre, with its once-grim riverside warehouses and pavilions and slum housing, has been transformed into an ultra-modern district beside the Seine. A new automatic metro line (Line 14) links it to the heart of the city.

The centrepiece of this district is the Palais d'Omnisports de Paris-Bercy (POPB), which is the city centre's principal concert venue, as well as its premier sports stadium. The vast pyramidal structure, its sides clad with real lawns, has become a landmark for the eastern part of central Paris.

Other architecturally adventurous buildings dominate the skyline, notably Chemetov's Ministry of Finance building, and Frank Gehry's American Center, which houses the **Cinémathèque Française**, a cinema museum with film screenings, a library and retrospectives on directors.

At the foot of these structures, the 70-ha (173-acre) Parc de Bercy provides a welcome green space. Former wine stores and cellars along Cours St Emilion have been restored as restaurants, bars and shops. Some of the warehouses have been restructured as the Pavillons de Bercy, one of which contains the Musée des Arts Forains (Fairground Museum).

Bercy's striking American Center, designed by Frank Gehry

Cité des Sciences et de l'Industrie ⓯

This hugely popular science and technology museum occupies the largest of the old Villette slaughterhouses, which now form part of a massive urban park. Architect Adrien Fainsilber has created an imaginative interplay of light, vegetation and water in the high-tech, five-storey building, which soars 40 m (133 ft) high, stretching over 3 ha (7 acres). At the museum's heart is the Explora exhibit, a fascinating guide to the worlds of science and technology. Visitors can take part in computerized games on space, the earth and ocean, computers and sound. On other levels there are a children's science city, cinemas, a science newsroom, a library and shops.

Modern folly in the Parc de la Villette

Planetarium
In this 260-seat auditorium you can watch eclipses and fly over Martian landscapes, thanks to their 3-D video system.

Le Nautile
This full-scale model of the Nautile, France's technologically advanced exploration submarine, represents one of the most sophisticated machines in the world.

★ The Story of the Universe
An exploration of the birth of the universe, this exhibit takes you back 13.7 billion years to the creation of the first atom.

400-seat auditorium

Hemispheric screen

Main lobby

LA GÉODE
This giant entertainment sphere houses a huge hemispherical cinema screen, 1,000 sq m (11,000 sq ft), showing IMAX films on nature, travel, history and space.

The moat was designed by Fainsilber so that natural light could penetrate into the lower levels of the building.

The main hall is vast, with a soaring network of shafts, bridges, escalators and balconies, and has a cathedral-like atmosphere.

STAR EXHIBITS

★ Children's City

★ Story of the Universe

★ La Géode

Cupolas
The two glazed domes, 17 m (56 ft) in diameter, filter the flow of natural light into the main hall.

VISITORS' CHECKLIST

30 av Corentin-Cariou 75019.
📞 01 40 05 80 00. Ⓜ Porte de la Villette. 🚌 139, 150, 152, 249, 375, PC2. ☐ 10am–6pm Tue–Sat (7pm Sun). ⬜ ♿ 🅷
⬜ ⬜ 🎞 *Shows, films, videos, library, conference centre.* **www**.cite-sciences.fr

The greenhouse is a square hothouse, 32 m (105 ft) high and wide, linking the park to the building.

Mirage Aircraft
A full-size model of the French-built jet fighter is one of the exhibits illustrating advances in technology.

To La Géode

Walkways
The walkways cross the encircling moat to link the various floors of the museum to the Géode and the park.

★ **Children's City**
In this lively, extensive area children can experiment and play with machines that show how scientific principles work.

Bibliothèque Nationale de France

Cité Nationale de l'Histoire de l'Immigration ⑳

293 av Daumesnil 75012. *Tel 01 53 59 58 60.* Ⓜ *Porte Dorée.* ⬜ *10am–5:30pm Tue–Fri (7pm Sat & Sun).* ⬤ *1 May, 14 Jul, 25 Dec.* ⬛ 🔶 *restricted.* ⬛

Housed in the Palais de la Porte Dorée, this museum is devoted to immigration in France. The palace itself is an Art Deco building designed by architects Albert Laprade and Léon Jaussely for the city's grand colonial exhibition in 1931.

The cellar also contains tropical fish collections, along with tortoises and crocodiles.

Château de Vincennes ㉑

Av de Paris 94300 Vincennes. *Tel 01 48 08 31 20.* Ⓜ *Château de Vincennes.* ⬛ *Vincennes.* ⬜ *10am–5pm daily (6pm May–Aug).* ⬤ *1 Jan, 1 May, 1 & 11 Nov, 25 Dec.* ⬛ *Chapel & donjon* ⬛ ⬛ www.chateau-vincennes.fr

The Château de Vincennes was the permanent royal residence until the 17th century, before the court moved to Versailles. The donjon, the tallest fortified medieval building in Europe, the Gothic chapel, 17th-century pavilions and moat are all worth seeing.

Beyond lies the Bois de Vincennes. Once a royal hunting ground, it is now a landscaped forest with ornamental lakes and a racecourse.

Bibliothèque Nationale de France ㉒

Quai François-Mauriac 75013. *Tel 01 53 79 59 59.* Ⓜ *Bibliothèque François-Mitterrand.* ⬜ *10am–7pm Tue–Sat, 1–7pm Sun.* ⬤ *public hols, 2 wks mid-Sep.* ⬛ 🔶 ⬛ www.bnf.fr

These four great book-shaped towers house 10 million volumes. The libraries offer over 400,000 titles. Other resources include digitized illustrations, sound archives and CD-ROMs. There are also frequent temporary exhibitions.

South of the City

Parc Montsouris ㉓

Bd Jourdan 75014. *Tel 01 40 71 75 60.* Ⓜ *Pte d'Orléans.* ⬛ *Cité Universitaire.* ⬜ *8am–8:30pm (5:30pm winter) daily.* ⬛ 🔶

This English-style park, the second largest in Paris, was laid out by Adolphe Alphand from 1865–1878. Its restaurant, lawns and lake – home to a variety of birds – are popular with students and children.

Skull of the reptile dimetrodon

Musée National d'Histoire Naturelle ㉔

36 rue Geoffroy Saint-Hilaire 75006. **Map** 14 D1. *Tel 01 40 79 54 79.* Ⓜ *Jussieu, Austerlitz.* ⬜ *10am–6pm Wed–Mon.* ⬤ *1 May.* ⬛ 🔶 ⬛ ⬛ 🚫 *Library* www.mnhn.fr

The highlight of the museum is the Grande Galerie de l'Evolution. There are also four other departments: palaeontology, featuring skeletons, casts of various animals and an exhibition showing the evolution of the vertebrate skeleton; palaeo-botany, devoted to plant fossils; mineralogy, including gemstones; and entomology, with some of the oldest fossilized insects on earth. The bookstore is in the house that was occupied by the naturalist Buffon, from 1772 until his death in 1788.

Jardin des Plantes ㉕

57 rue Cuvier 75005. **Map** 13 C1. *Tel 01 40 79 56 01.* Ⓜ *Jussieu, Austerlitz.* ⬜ *8am–5:30pm daily.*

The botanical gardens were established in 1626 when Jean Hérouard and Guy de la Brosse, Louis XIII's physicians, obtained permission to found a royal medicinal herb garden. A school of botany, natural history and pharmacy followed and the garden opened to the public in 1640. One of the city's great parks, it contains a natural history museum, botanical school and zoo.

As well as beautiful vistas and walkways flanked by ancient statues, the park has an alpine garden with plants from Corsica, Morocco, the Alps and the Himalayas, and an unrivalled display of herbaceous and wild plants. The Cedar of Lebanon here, originally from Britain's Kew Gardens, was the first to be planted in France.

Rue Mouffetard, one of several markets near Jardin des Plantes

Institut du Monde Arabe 🕮

1 rue des Fossés St-Bernard,
Pl Mohammed V 75005. **Map** 9 C5.
Tel 01 40 51 38 38. Ⓜ *Jussieu,
Cardinal-Lemoine.* **Museum & temp
exhibs** ⬜ *10am–6pm Tue–Sun.*
Library ⬜ *1–8pm Tue–Sat.* 🎨 🖊
♿ 🖥 🍴 www.imarabe.org

This magnificent modern
building was designed by
French architect Jean Nouvel,
and cleverly combines high-
tech details with the spirit of
traditional Arab architecture.
   From the fourth to seventh
floors there is a comprehensive
display of Islamic art from the
9th to 19th centuries, including
glassware, ceramics and sculpture. The museum's highlight
is its collection of *astrolabes*,
the much-prized tool used by
ancient Arab astronomers.

Mosquée de Paris 🕮

2 pl du Puits de l'Ermite 75005.
Tel 01 45 35 97 33. Ⓜ *Place Monge.*
⬜ *9am–noon, 2–6pm Sat–Thu.*
⬛ *Muslim hols.* 🎨 🖊 🖥 🍴
Library www.mosquee-de-paris.org

Built in the 1920s in the
Hispano-Moorish style, these
buildings are the centre for
Paris's Muslim community.
Once used solely by scholars,
the mosque has expanded
over the years and now
houses some salubrious but
fun Turkish baths, a fine
restaurant and a beautiful
salon de thé.

Parc André Citroën 🕮

Quai André Citroën 75015. *Tel 01 40
71 75 60.* Ⓜ *Balard.* ⬜ *Mar–Oct:
9am–dusk (Nov–Feb: to 5pm) daily.* ♿

Designed by both landscapers
and architects, this park is a
fascinating blend of styles,
ranging from wildflower
meadow in the north to
sophisticated monochrome
mineral and sculpture gardens
in the southern section.
Modern water sculptures
dot the park.

Institut du Monde Arabe, covered with photosensitive lightscreens

Tour Montparnasse

Montparnasse 🕮

75014 & 75015. **Map** 11 & 12. Ⓜ
*Montparnasse, Vavin, Raspail, Edgar
Quinet.* **Tour Montparnasse** ⬜
*Apr–Sep: 9:30am–11:30pm; Oct–Mar:
9:30am–10:30pm (11pm Fri & Sat).*

The name Montparnasse was
first used ironically in the 17th
century, when arts students
performed their work on a
"mount" of rubble left over
from quarrying. In ancient
Greece, Mount Parnassus was
dedicated to poetry, music and
beauty. By the 19th century,
crowds were drawn to the
local cabarets and bars by
duty-free prices. The mixture
of art and high living was particularly potent in the 1920s
and 1930s when Hemingway,
Picasso, Cocteau, Giacometti,
Matisse and Modigliani were
"Montparnos", as the residents
were called. The modern
quartier is dominated by the
much-hated **Tour Montparnasse**,
although the view from the top
(the 56th floor) is spectacular.

Cimetière du Montparnasse 🕮

3 bd Edgar Quinet 75014. **Map** 12 D3.
Tel 01 44 10 86 50. Ⓜ *Edgar Quinet.*
⬜ *mid-Mar–Nov: 8am–6pm Mon–Fri,
8:30am–6pm Sat, 9am–6pm Sun;
Dec–mid-Mar: closes 5:30pm.*

Montparnasse cemetery
opened in 1824. Among
those buried here are
Serge Gainsbourg, Charles
Baudelaire, Jean-Paul Sartre
and Simone de Beauvoir,
and Guy de Maupassant.

Catacombes 🕮

1 av du Colonel Henri Rol-Tanguy
75014. **Map** 12 E3. *Tel 01 43 22
47 63.* Ⓜ *Denfert-Rochereau.* ⬜
10am–5pm Tue–Sun. ⬛ *public hols.*
🎨 🖊 www.catacombes-de-paris.fr

A long series of quarry
tunnels built in Roman times,
the catacombs are now lined
with ancient bones and
skulls. Thousands of rotting
corpses were transported
here in the 1780s to absorb
the excess from the insanitary
Les Halles cemetery.

Skulls and bones stored in the
catacombes

SHOPS AND MARKETS

For many people, Paris epitomizes luxury and good living. Exquisitely dressed men and women sip wine by the banks of the Seine against the backdrop of splendid French architecture, or shop from small specialist shops. The least expensive way of joining the chic set is to create French style with accessories or costume jewellery. Alternatively, try shopping in the January or July sales. If your budget allows, take the opportunity to buy world-famous Paris fashions, or feast on the wonderful gourmet delicacies, displayed with consummate artistry. Parisian shopping streets and markets are the ideal place to indulge in the French custom of strolling for the express purpose of seeing and being seen. For up-to-the-minute high fashion, the rue du Faubourg-St-Honoré is hard to beat, with its exquisite couture window displays. Browsing around the bookstalls along the Seine is another favourite French pastime. A survey of some of the best and most famous places to shop follows.

Shopping in avenue Montaigne

OPENING HOURS

Shops are usually open from 10am–7pm, Monday to Saturday, but hours can vary. Many department stores stay open late on Thursday, while boutiques may shut for an hour or two at midday. Markets and local neighbourhood shops usually close on Mondays. Some places shut for the summer, usually in August, but they may leave a note on the door suggesting an open equivalent nearby.

PAYMENT AND VAT

Cash is readily available from the ATMs in most banks, which accept both credit and bank debit cards. Visa and MasterCard are the most widely accepted credit cards.

A sales tax (TVA) from 5.5–19.6 per cent is imposed on most goods and services in EU countries. Non-EU residents shopping in France are entitled to a refund of this if they spend a minimum of 175€ in one shop in one day. You must have been resident in France for less than six months and either carry the goods with you out of the country within three months of purchase, or get the shop to forward them to you. Larger shops will generally supply a form (*bordereau de détaxe* or *bordereau de vente*) and help you to fill it in. When you leave France or the EU you present the form to Customs, who either permit you to be reimbursed straightaway, or forward

The Chanel logo, recognized worldwide

your claim to the place where you bought the merchandise; the shop eventually sends you a refund.

SALES

The best sales (*soldes*) are held in January and July, although you can sometimes find sale items before Christmas. If you see goods labelled *Stock*, it means that they are stock items, reduced for clearance. *Dégriffé* means designer labels, (with the label cut out) marked down, frequently from the previous year's collections. *Fripes* indicates that the clothes are second-hand.

THE CENTRE OF PARIS COUTURE

The couture houses are concentrated on the Right Bank, around rue du Faubourg-St-Honoré and avenue Montaigne.

DEPARTMENT STORES

Much of the pleasure of shopping in Paris is derived from going to the small specialist shops. But if time is short, try the *grands magasins* (department stores). Some still operate a ticket system for selling goods. The shop assistant writes up a ticket for goods from their own boutique which you take to one of the cashiers. You then return with your validated ticket to pick up your purchase. This can be time-consuming, so go early in the morning and don't shop on

The 1865 façade of Au Printemps department store

Kenzo designerwear in the place des Victoires

Saturdays, unless you enjoy a crush. The French do not pay much attention to queues so be assertive! One peculiarity of a visit is that the security guards may ask to inspect your bags as you leave. These are random checks and should not be taken as an implication of theft.

All department stores have places to eat, although the stores themselves tend to have different emphases. **Au Printemps** is noted for its exciting and innovative household goods section, vast cosmetic range and large menswear store. The clothes departments for women and children are well stocked. Fashion shows are held at 10am on Tuesdays (and each Friday from April to October: by invitation only). The lovely domed restaurant in the cupola often hosts chic after-hours parties, which are

private, but a visit to the restaurant during shopping hours is worthwhile.

BHV (Le Bazar de l'Hôtel de Ville) is a DIY enthusiast's paradise, and sells a host of other items, such as fashion decor. The Left Bank's **Le Bon Marché** was Paris's first department store and today is its chicest. The designer clothing sections are well-sourced, the high-end accessories are excellent and the own-brand linen has a good quality to price ratio. The prepared food sections serve restaurant-quality fare to take away.

Galeries Lafayette is perhaps the best-known department store and has a wide range of clothes available at all price levels. Its first-floor trends section plays host to lots of innovative designers. Galeries Lafayette Gourmet, the food court, sells a range of French and international delicacies. Across the road is the store's homeware

Cartier, one of the world's most exclusive stores

building, which stocks a good range of kitchenware.

Virgin Megastore is open until late and has an excellent record selection and an impressive book section. **FNAC** specializes in records, books (foreign editions can be found at Les Halles) and electronic equipment, while **FNAC Odéon** sells a wide range of the latest technological equipment.

ADDRESSES

Au Printemps
64 bd Haussmann 75009.
Map 4 D4. **Tel** 01 42 82 50 00.
www.printemps.com

BHV
55 rue de la Verrerie 75004.
Map 9 B3. **Tel** 01 42 74 90 00.
www.bhv.com

Le Bon Marché
24 rue de Sèvres 75007.
Map 7 C5. **Tel** 01 44 39 80 00.
www.lebonmarche.com

FNAC
Forum des Halles, 1 rue Pierre Lescot 75001. **Map** 9 A2.
Tel 0825 020 020.
www.fnac.com

FNAC Odéon
77–81 bd St-Germain 75006.
Map 9 A5. **Tel** 0825 020 020.

Galeries Lafayette
40 bd Haussmann 75009.
Map 4 E4. **Tel** 01 42 82 34 56.
www.galerieslafayette.com

Virgin Megastore
52–60 av des Champs-Elysées 75008. **Map** 2 F5. **Tel** 01 49 53 50 00. www.virginmegastore.fr

Clothes and Accessories

For many people Paris is synonymous with fashion, and Parisian style is the ultimate in chic. More than anywhere else in the world, women in Paris seem to be in tune with current trends and when a new season arrives appear, as one, to don the look. Though less trend-conscious generally, Parisian men are aware of style, and mix and match patterns and colours with *élan*. Finding the right clothes at the right price means knowing where to shop. For every luxury boutique on the avenue Montaigne, there are ten young designers' shops waiting to become the next Jean-Paul Gaultier – and hundreds more selling imitations.

HAUTE COUTURE

Paris is the home of *haute couture*. The original *couture* garments, as opposed to the imitations and adaptations, are one-off creations, designed by one of the nine *haute couture* houses listed with the Fédération Française de la Couture. The rules for being classified are fairly strict, and many of the top designers are not included. Astronomical prices put *haute couture* beyond the reach of all but a few immensely deep pockets, but it is still the lifeblood of the fashion industry providing inspiration for the mass market.

WOMEN'S CLOTHES

Most *couture* houses are found on or near the rue du Faubourg-St-Honoré and avenue Montaigne: **Christian Dior**, **Pierre Cardin**, **Chanel**, **Christian Lacroix**, **Versace**, **Givenchy**, **Nina Ricci**, **Georgio Armani** and **Yves Saint Laurent**.

Hermès has classic country chic. **MaxMara's** Italian elegance is popular in France, and no one can resist a **Giorgio Armani** suit. The legendary **Prada** store has stuck to the Right Bank, but many fashion houses prefer the Left Bank.

Many designers have a Left Bank branch in addition to their Right Bank bastions, and they all have ready-to-wear shops here. For sheer quality there's **Georges Rech**, and **Jil Sander** for exquisite tailoring. Try **Sonia Rykiel** for knitwear, and **Barbara Bui** for soft, feminine clothes. **Comptoir**

des Cotonniers has branches throughout Paris and stocks excellent basics, and **Vanessa Bruno** is extremely popular for feminine flair.

For ready-to-wear, head to place des Victoires. **Kenzo** is here (although its flagship store is located near the Pont Neuf), along with fellow Japanese designers **Comme des Garçons**, with its quirky fashion for both sexes. In nearby rue du Jour, find the timeless elegance of **Agnès B**.

The Marais is a haven for up-and-coming designers. One of the best streets is the rue des Rosiers, which includes the wonderful **L'Eclaireur**. **Anne Fontaine** is on the neighbouring rue des Francs-Bourgeois, and daring designer **Azzedine Alaïa's** is just around the corner.

The Bastille area has trendy boutiques, as well as established names, including **Jean-Paul Gaultier** and high-street stores like **Petit Bateau**. **Isabel Marant's** boutique is renowned for its originality.

Young designers' clothes are found at **Colette**, **Stella Cadente**, and **Zadig and Voltaire**.

CHILDREN'S CLOTHES

Lots of options for children exist in various styles and many price ranges. Many top designers of adult clothes also have boutiques for children. These include **Kenzo**, **Baby Dior**, **Agnès B**. Ready-to-wear shops such as **Jacadi** and **Du Pareil au Même** are serviceable and wide-ranging; and **Tartine et Chocolat's** best-selling garments are overalls.

Bonpoint stocks adorably chic clothing for mini-Parisians. **Petit Bateau** is coveted as much by grown-ups as it is by children. The inevitable has finally happened – children now have their own concept store in **Bonton**.

For little feet, **Froment-Leroyer** probably offers the best all-round classics.

MEN'S CLOTHES

Men don't have the luxury of *haute couture* dressing and their choice is limited to ready-to-wear. On the Right Bank, there's **Giorgio Armani**, **Pierre Cardin**, **Lanvin** (also good for accessories) and **Yves Saint Laurent**. On the Left Bank, **Michel Axel** and **Jean-Charles de Castelbajac** are known for their ties and **Francesco Smalto's** elegant creations are worn by some of the world's leading movie stars. Yohji Yamamoto's clothes in **Y3** are for those who are intent on making a serious fashion statement, while **Gianni Versace** is classic, suave, and Italian in style.

The ultimate in Parisian elegance for men, however, is a suit, custom-made shirt or silk tie from **Charvet**.

VINTAGE AND SECOND-HAND STORES

The vintage craze hit Paris some time back and there are some wonderful shops to plunder for a retro look. The best of the bunch is **Didier Ludot**, where an Aladdin's Cave of chic *haute couture* is elegantly displayed. The **Depôt-Vente de Buci-Bourbon** is another good place to bargain hunt. A cheaper option is to head for one of the second-hand consignment stores. Chic Parisians discard their outfits with the seasons so it is very easy to pick up some quality items, often in top condition, from places such as **Réciproque** in Passy or **Alternatives** in the Marais.

A cheaper option for sample pieces and sale stock can be found at **Le Mouton à Cinq Pattes**.

JEWELLERY

The *couture* houses probably stock some of the best jewellery and scarves. **Chanel's** jewels are classics and **Christian Lacroix**'s are fun. **Boutique YSL** is a great place for accessories.

Among the main expensive Paris jewellery outlets are **Boucheron**, **Mauboussin** and **Poiray**. They are for the serious jewellery buyer. Other top retailers include **Harry Winston** and **Cartier**. **Dinh Van** has some quirky pieces, whilst **Mikimoto** is a must for pearls and **H Stern** has some innovative designs using semi-precious and precious stones. For a range of more unusual jewellery

and accessories, try the **Swarovski Boutique**, which is owned by the Swarovksi crystal family.

SHOES AND BAGS

For both classic and wild footwear designs, you can't beat **Miu Miu**. **Rodolphe Ménudier** and **Christian Louboutin** are mainstays for sexy stilettos. **Carel** stocks smart basics and **Jonak** is a must for good imitations of designer footwear.

For ladies handbags, nothing beats **Chanel** or **Dior** at the top end of the scale, although **Goyard** comes close. Mid-range bags from **Furla** are a great compromise. Fabric bags from **Jamin Puech**

or **Vanessa Bruno** are a feature in every chic Parisian closet. For those with tighter purse strings, cheap, cheerful and stylish bags can be found at **Lollipops**.

LINGERIE

For modern lingerie go to **Fifi Chachnil**, whose shop is filled with colourful underwear. **La Boîte à Bas** sells fine French stockings, whereas **Princesse Tam Tam** offers quality items at reasonable prices, while divine designer underwear can be found at cult store **Sabbia Rosa**. The ultimate in Parisian lingerie can be bought off the peg or made to order at **Cadolle**, the store which invented the bra.

DIRECTORY

WOMEN'S CLOTHES

Agnès B.
2–3–6–19 rue du Jour 75001. **Map** 9 A1.
Tel 01 45 08 56 56.
One of several branches.

Anne Fontaine
12 rue des Francs-Bourgeois 75004.
Map 10 D3.
Tel 01 44 59 81 59.
One of several branches.

Azzedine Alaïa
7 rue de Moussy 75004.
Map 9 C3.
Tel 01 42 72 19 19.

Barbara Bui
23 rue Etienne-Marcel 75001. **Map** 9 A1.
Tel 01 40 26 43 65.
www.barbarabui.com
One of several branches.

Chanel
42 av Montaigne 75008.
Map 3 A5. *Tel 01 47 23 47 12.* **www**.chanel.com
One of several branches.

Christian Dior
30 av Montaigne 75008.
Map 6 F1. *Tel 01 40 73 73 73.* **www**.dior.com

Christian Lacroix
73 rue du Faubourg-St-Honoré 75008. **Map** 3 B5.
Tel 01 42 68 79 04.
www.christian-lacroix.fr

Colette
213 rue St-Honoré 75001.
Map 8 D1.
Tel 01 55 35 33 90.
www.colette.fr

Comme des Garçons
54 rue du Faubourg St-Honoré 75008. **Map** 2 E3.
Tel 01 53 30 27 27.

Comptoir des Cotonniers
12 pl St-Sulpice 75006.
Map 8 E4.
Tel 01 56 81 00 18.
One of several branches.

L'Eclaireur
40 rue de Sévigné 75003.
Map 10 D4.
Tel 01 48 87 10 22.

Georges Rech
54 rue Bonaparte 75006.
Map 8 E3.
Tel 01 43 26 84 11.
www.georges-rech.fr
One of several branches.

Giorgio Armani
18 av Montaigne 75008. **Map** 2 E3.
Tel 01 42 61 55 09.
www.giorgioarmani.com

Givenchy
3 av Georges V 75008.
Map 2 E5.
Tel 01 77 31 50 00.
www.givenchy.com

Hermès
24 rue du Faubourg-St-Honoré 75008. **Map** 3 C5. *Tel 01 40 17 47 17.*
www.hermes.com
One of several branches.

Isabel Marant
16 rue de Charonne 75011. **Map** 10 F4.
Tel 01 49 29 71 55.

Jean-Paul Gaultier
6 rue Vivienne 75002.
Map 8 F1.
Tel 01 42 86 05 05.
One of two branches.

Jil Sander
56 av Montaigne 75008.
Map 6 F1.
Tel 01 44 95 06 70.

Kenzo
3 pl des Victoires 75001.
Map 8 F1.
Tel 01 40 39 72 03.
One of several branches.

MaxMara
31 av Montaigne 75008.
Map 6 F1.
Tel 01 47 20 6113.
One of several branches.

Nina Ricci
39 av Montaigne 75008.
Map 6 F1.
Tel 01 40 88 67 60.
www.ninaricci.fr

Pierre Cardin
27 av de Marigny 75008.
Map 3 B5.

Tel 01 42 66 68 98.
www.pierrecardin.com
One of two branches.

Prada
10 av Montaigne 75008. **Map** 6 F1.
Tel 01 53 23 99 40.

Sonia Rykiel
175 bd St-Germain 75006. **Map** 8 D4.
Tel 01 49 54 60 60.
www.soniarykiel.com
One of several branches.

Stella Cadente
93 quai de Valmy 75010. **Map** 4 D4.
Tel 01 42 09 66 60.
www.stella-cadente.com

Vanessa Bruno
25 rue St-Sulpice 75006.
Map 8 E5.
Tel 01 43 54 41 04.

Versace
41 rue François 1er 75008.
Map 2 F5.
Tel 01 47 42 88 02.
www.versace.com

Yves Saint Laurent
38 rue du Faubourg-St-Honoré 75008. **Map** 3 C5.
Tel 01 42 65 74 59.
One of several branches.

Zadig & Voltaire
9 rue du 29 Juillet 75001.
Map 8 D1.
Tel 01 42 92 00 80.
One of several branches.

DIRECTORY

CHILDREN'S CLOTHES

Bonpoint
320 rue St-Honoré 75001.
Map 9 A2.
Tel 01 49 27 94 82.
www.bonpoint.com

Bonton
82 rue de Grenelle 75007.
Map 6 F3.
Tel 01 44 39 09 20.
www.bonton.fr

Du Pareil au Même
1 rue St-Denis 75001.
Map 9 B3.
Tel 01 42 36 07 57.
www.dpam.com

Froment-Leroyer
7 rue Vavin 75006.
Map 12 E1.
Tel 01 43 54 33 15.
www.froment-leroyer.fr

Jacadi
17 rue Tronchet 75008.
Map 3 C5.
Tel 01 42 65 84 98.
www.jacadi.fr

Petit Bateau
116 av des Champs
Elysées 75008. **Map** 2 E4.
Tel 01 40 74 02 03.
www.petit-bateau.fr

Tartine et Chocolat
84 rue du Faubourg-St-
Honoré 75008. **Map** 3 B5.
Tel 01 45 62 44 04.
www.tartine-et-chocolat.fr

MEN'S CLOTHES

Charvet
28 pl Vendôme
75001. **Map** 4 D5.
Tel 01 42 60 30 70.

Francesco Smalto
44 rue François 1er
75008. **Map** 2 F5.
Tel 01 47 20 96 04.
www.smalto.com

Gianni Versace
45 av Montaigne 75008.
Map 2 F5.
Tel 01 47 42 88 02.
www.versace.com

Giorgio Armani
(see p143).

**Jean-Charles de
Castelbajac**
61 rue des Saints Pères
75006. **Map** 8 D4. *Tel 09
64 48 48 54.* www.jc-de-
castelbajac.com

Kenzo
(see p143).

Lanvin
15 rue du Faubourg St-
Honoré 75008. **Map** 10
F4. *Tel 01 44 71 31 25.*
www.lanvin.com

Michel Axel
44 rue du Dragon 75006.
Map 8 E4.
Tel 01 42 84 13 86.

Pierre Cardin
(see p143).

Y3
47 rue Etienne
Marcel 75001.
Map 9 A1.
Tel 01 45 08 82 45.

Yves Saint Laurent
12 pl St-Sulpice 75006.
Map 8 D4.
Tel 01 43 26 84 40.

VINTAGE AND SECOND-HAND STORES

Alternatives
18 rue du Roi-de-Sicile
75004. **Map** 9 C3.
Tel 01 42 78 31 50.

**Depôt-Vente de
Buci-Bourbon**
6 rue de Bourbon-le-
Château 75006.
Map 8 E4.
Tel 01 46 34 45 05.

Didier Ludot
24 Galerie Mont-pensier
75001. **Map** 8 E1.
Tel 01 42 96 06 56.
www.didierludot.fr

**Le Mouton à
Cinq Pattes**
8 rue St-Placide 75006.
Map 8 D5.
Tel 01 45 48 86 26.
www.moutonacinq
pattes.com

Réciproque
95 rue de la Pompe
75016. **Map** 5 A1.
Tel 01 47 04 30 28.
www.reciproque.fr

JEWELLERY

Boucheron
26 pl Vendôme 75001.
Map 4 D5.
Tel 01 42 61 58 16.
www.boucheron.com

Cartier
13 rue de la Paix 75002.
Map 4 D5.
Tel 01 58 18 23 00.
www.cartier.fr

Dinh Van
16 rue de la Paix 75002.
Map 4 D5.
Tel 01 42 61 74 49.
www.dinhvan.com

H Stern
3 rue Castiglione 75001.
Map 8 D1.
Tel 01 42 60 22 27.
www.hstern.net

Harry Winston
29 av Montaigne 75008.
Map 6 F1.
Tel 01 47 20 03 09.
www.harrywinston.com

Mauboussin
20 pl Vendôme 75001.
Map 4 D5.
Tel 01 44 55 10 00.
www.mauboussin.com

Mikimoto
8 pl Vendôme 75001.
Map 4 D5.
Tel 01 42 60 33 55.
www.mikimoto.fr

Poiray
1 rue de la Paix 75002.
Map 4 D5.
Tel 01 42 61 70 58.
www.poiray.com

Swarovski Boutique
146 av des Champs
Elysées 75008. **Map** 2 E4.
Tel 01 45 61 13 80.
www.swarovski.com

SHOES AND BAGS

Carel
4 rue Tronchet 75008.
Map 4 D4.
Tel 01 42 66 21 58.
www.carel.fr

Christian Louboutin
38-40 rue de Grenelle
75007. **Map** 6 F3.
Tel 01 42 22 33 07.
www.christian
louboutin.com

Furla
8 rue de Sèvres 75006.
Map 7 C5.
Tel 01 40 49 06 44.
www.furla.com

Goyard
233 rue St-Honoré 75001.
Map 3 C5.
Tel 01 42 60 57 04.

Jamin Puech
26 rue Cambon 75001.
Map 4 D5.
Tel 01 40 20 40 28.

Jonak
70 rue de Rennes 75006.
Map 12 D1.
Tel 01 45 48 27 11.

Lollipops
60 rue Tiquetonne 75002.
Map 9 A1.
Tel 01 42 33 15 72.
www.lollipops.fr

Miu Miu
219 rue St-Honoré
75001. **Map** 8 D1.
Tel 01 58 62 53 20.
www.miumiu.com

Rodolphe Ménudier
14 rue de Castiglione
75001. **Map** 8 D1.
Tel 01 42 60 86 27.

Vanessa Bruno
25 rue St-Sulpice 75006.
Map 8 E5.
Tel 01 43 54 41 04.
www.vanessabruno.com

LINGERIE

La Boîte à Bas
27 rue Boissy-d'Anglas
75008. **Map** 3 C5.
Tel 01 42 66 26 85.

Cadolle
4 rue Cambon 75001.
Map 4 D5.
Tel 01 42 60 94 22.

Fifi Chachnil
231 rue St-Honoré
75001. **Map** 8 D1.
Tel 01 42 61 21 83.
www.fifichachnil.com

Princesse Tam Tam
52 bd St-Michel 75006.
Map 8 F5. *Tel 01 42
34 99 31.* www.
princessetamtam.com

Sabbia Rosa
73 rue des Sts-Pères
75006. **Map** 8 D4.
Tel 01 45 48 88 37.

Gifts and Souvenirs

Paris has a wealth of stylish gift options, from designer accessories to Eiffel Tower paperweights. Shops on the rue de Rivoli and around major tourist attractions offer a range of cheap holiday paraphernalia, or go to one of the souvenir stores such as **Les Drapeaux de France.**

PERFUME

Many shops advertise discounted perfume. They include **Eiffel Shopping** near the Eiffel Tower. The **Sephora** chain has a big selection, or try the department stores for a range of beauty brands which are hard to find elsewhere.

Parfums Caron has many scents created at the turn-of-the-19th century, which are unavailable elsewhere. Beautifully packaged perfumes made from natural essences are available from **Annick Goutal. Guerlain** has the ultimate in beauty care, while the elegant shops of **L'Artisan Parfumeur** specialize in exquisitely packaged scents evoking specific memories.

HOUSEHOLD GOODS

It is difficult to ignore some of the world's most elegant tableware. Luxury homeware stores line the rue Royale. **Lalique's** Art Nouveau and Art Deco glass sculptures are collected all over the world. Impeccable silverware comes from **Christofle**.

For significant savings on porcelain and crystal, try **Lumicristal**, which stocks Baccarat, Daum and Limoges crystal, or why not go to **Baccarat** itself.

La Chaise Longue has a selection of fun gift ideas to suit most tastes, and **BoConcept** has a wide range of contemporary goods to add a new lease of life to any home.

BOOKS

Some department stores have a books section, and there are several English-language bookshops such as **W H Smith** and **Brentano's**. The cosy **Shakespeare & Company** and **Red Wheelbarrow Bookstore** are good for convivial browsing among expats. French-language bookshops include **La Hune**, specializing in art, cinema, fashion and photography, and **Gilbert Joseph** for educational books.

SPECIALIST SHOPS

A La Civette is perhaps Paris's most beautiful tobacconists, stocking a vast range of cigars behind specially humidified store windows.

One of the world's most famous and delightful toystores is **Au Nain Bleu** while the name **Cassegrain** is synonymous with high-quality stationery and paper products.

DIRECTORY

SOUVENIR SHOPS

Les Drapeaux de France
1 pl Colette 75001.
Map 8 E1.
Tel 01 40 20 00 11.

PERFUME

Annick Goutal
16 rue de Bellechasse 75007.
Map 7 C3.
Tel 01 45 51 36 13.
www.annickgoutal.com

L'Artisan Parfumeur
24 bd Raspail 75007.
Map 12 D1.
Tel 01 42 22 23 32.
One of several branches.

Eiffel Shopping
9 av de Suffren 75007.
Map 6 D3.
Tel 01 45 66 55 30.

Guerlain
68 av des Champs-Elysées 75008. **Map** 2 F5.
Tel 01 45 62 52 57.
www.guerlain.com

Parfums Caron
34 av Montaigne 75008.
Map 6 F1.
Tel 01 47 23 40 82.
www.parfumscaron.com

Sephora
70 av des Champs-Elysées 75008. **Map** 7 B1.
Tel 01 53 93 22 50.
www.sephora.fr

HOUSEHOLD GOODS

Baccarat
11 pl de la Madeleine 75008. **Map** 3 C5.
Tel 01 42 65 36 26.

BoConcept
8 bd Sebastopol 75004.
Map 9 A3.
Tel 01 42 78 66 66.

La Chaise Longue
30 rue Croix-des-Petits-Champs 75001. **Map** 8 F1.
Tel 01 42 96 32 14.

Christofle
24 rue de la Paix 75002.
Map 4 D5.
Tel 01 42 65 62 43.
www.christofle.com

Lalique
11 rue Royale 75008.
Map 3 C5.
Tel 01 53 05 12 12.

Lumicristal
29 rue de Paradis 75010.
Tel 01 42 46 60 29.

BOOKS

Brentano's
37 av de l'Opéra 75002.
Map 4 E5.
Tel 01 42 60 87 37.
www.brentanos.fr

Gibert Joseph
26 bd St-Michel 75006.
Map 8 F5.
Tel 01 44 41 88 88.

La Hune
170 bd St-Germain 75006. **Map** 8 D4.
Tel 01 45 48 35 85.

Red Wheelbarrow Bookstore
22 rue St-Paul 75004.
Map 10 D4.
Tel 01 48 04 75 08.
www.theredwheel
barrow.com

Shakespeare & Company
37 rue de la Bûcherie 75005. **Map** 9 A4.
Tel 01 43 25 40 93.
www.shakespeare
andcompany.com

W H Smith
248 rue de Rivoli 75001.
Map 7 C1.
Tel 01 44 77 88 99.
www.whsmith.fr

SPECIALIST SHOPS

A La Civette
157 rue St-Honoré 75001. **Map** 8 F2.
Tel 01 42 96 04 99.

Au Nain Bleu
5 bd Malesherbes 75008.
Map 3 C5.
Tel 01 42 65 20 00.
www.aunainbleu.com

Cassegrain
422 rue St-Honoré 75008. **Map** 3 C5.
Tel 01 42 60 20 08.
www.cassegrain.fr.

Food and Drink

Paris is as famous for food as it is for fashion. Gastronomic treats include *foie gras*, cold meats from the *charcuterie*, cheese and wine. Certain streets are so overflowing with food shops that you can put together a picnic for 20 in no time: try the rue Montorgueil *(see Map 9 A1)*. The rue Rambuteau, running on either side of the Pompidou Centre, has a marvellous row of fishmongers and delicatessens.

BREAD AND CAKES

There is a vast range of breads and pastries in France's capital. The *baguette* is often translated as "French bread", a *bâtard* is similar but thicker, while a *ficelle* is thinner. A *fougasse* is a crusty, flat loaf often filled with onions, cheese, herbs or spices.

Croissants can be bought *ordinaire* or *au beurre* – the latter is flakier and more buttery. *Pain au chocolat* is a chocolate-filled pastry eaten for breakfast, and *chausson aux pommes* is filled with apples. There are also pear, plum and rhubarb variations. A *pain aux raisins* is a bread-like wheel filled with custard and raisins.

Poilâne sells perhaps the only bread in Paris known by the name of its baker (the late Lionel, brother of Max) and his hearty wholewheat loaves are tremendously popular.

Many think **Ganachaud** bakes the best bread in Paris. Thirty different kinds, including ingredients such as walnuts and fruit, are made in the old-fashioned ovens.

Les Panetons is a good chain bakery. Favourites here include five-grain bread, sesame rolls, and *mouchoir aux pommes*, a variation on the traditional *chausson*.

Many of the Jewish delicatessens have the best ryes and the only pumpernickels in town. One of the best is **Sacha Finkelsztajn**.

Le Moulin de la Vierge uses a wood fire to bake organic breads and rich pound cakes. **J L Poujauran** is known for his black-olive bread and nut-and-raisin wholegrain breads.

Pierre Hermé is to cakes what Chanel is to fashion, while **Ladurée**'s macaroons are legendary.

CHOCOLATE

Like all food in France, chocolate is to be savoured. **Christian Constant's** low-sugar creations are made with pure cocoa and are known to connoisseurs. **Dalloyau** makes all types of chocolate and is not too expensive (it is also known for its pâtisserie and cold meats). **Fauchon** is world famous for its luxury food products. Its chocolates are excellent, as is the pâtisserie. Robert Linxe at **La Maison du Chocolat** is constantly inventing fresh, rich chocolates with mouth-watering exotic ingredients. **Richart** boasts beautifully presented and hugely expensive chocolates, which are usually coated with dark chocolate or liqueur-filled.

CHARCUTERIE AND FOIE GRAS

Charcuteries often sell cheese, snails, truffles, smoked salmon, caviar and wine as well as cold meats. **Fauchon** has a good grocery, as does the department store **Le Bon Marché**. **Hédiard** is a luxury shop similar to Fauchon, and **Maison de la Truffe** sells *foie gras* and sausages as well as truffles. For Beluga caviar, Georgian tea and Russian vodka, go to **Petrossian**.

The Lyon and Auvergne regions of France are the best known for their *charcuterie*, and **Jean-Jacques Chrétienne** sells excellent examples. **Maison Pou** is a sparklingly clean and popular store selling *pâté en croute* (pâté baked in pastry), *boudins* (black and white puddings), Lyonnais sausages, ham and *foie gras*. Just off the Champs-Elysées, **Vignon** has superb *foie gras* and Lyonnais

sausages as well as popular prepared food.

Together with truffles and caviar, *foie gras* is the ultimate in gourmet food. Though most specialist food shops sell *foie gras*, you can be sure of quality at **Comtesse du Barry**, which has six outlets in Paris. **Divay** is relatively inexpensive and will ship overseas. **Labeyrie** has a range of beautifully packaged *foie gras* suitable for giving as presents.

CHEESE

Although camembert is undoubtedly a favourite, there is an overwhelming range of cheeses available and a friendly *fromager* will always help you choose. **Marie-Anne Cantin** is one of the leading figures in the fight to protect traditional production methods, and her fine cheeses are available from the store that she inherited from her father. Some say that **Alléosse** is the best cheese delicatessen in Paris – all the cheeses are made according to traditional methods. **Crèmerie Quatrehomme** sells farm-made cheeses, many of which are in danger of becoming extinct, these include a rare and delicious truffle Brie (when in season). **Le Jardin Fromager** is one of the best shops in Paris for all types of cheese – the *chèvre* (goat's cheese) is particularly good as are the *camemberts au lait cru* (cheese made with unpasteurized milk), which ooze over the plate. **Barthélémy** in the rue de Grenelle has a truly exceptional Roquefort. **Androuët** is a Parisian institution with several branches across the city. Try a pungent Munster or a really ripe Brie. A charming cheese shop, **La Fermette**, offers a dazzling array of dairy products, which the staff will encase in plastic for the journey home, imperative when bringing cheese through customs.

Well-heeled locals queue in the street to buy oozing *livarot* and sharp *chèvre* from **La Fromagerie d'Auteuil**.

WINE

The chain store which has practically cornered the everyday tippling market is **Nicolas** – there is a branch in every neighbourhood with a range of wines to suit all pockets. As a rule, the sales-people are knowledgeable and helpful. Try the charming **Legrand Filles et Fils** for a carefully chosen selection of high-end champagnes. **Caves Taillevent** on the rue du Faubourg-St-Honoré is worth a sightseeing tour. It is an enormous, overwhelming cellar with some of the most expensive wine.

Cave Péret on the rue Daguerre has a vast selection of wines and can offer personal advice to help you with your purchase. The beautiful **Ryst-Dupeyron**, in the St-Germain quarter, displays whiskies, wines, ports and Monsieur Ryst's own Armagnac. He will even personalize a bottle for that special occasion.

Other great wine stores include **Lavinia**, which is the largest in Europe, and, by contrast, **Renaud Michel** at Place de la Nation, whose small boutique is very well stocked and well connected. The staff in **Les Caves Augé** are also very knowledgeable and friendly.

DIRECTORY

BREAD AND CAKES

Ganachaud
226 rue des Pyrénées 75020.
Tel 01 43 58 42 62.

J L Poujauran
18 rue Jean-Nicot 75007.
Map 6 F2.
Tel 01 43 17 35 20.

Ladurée
75 av des Champs-Elysées 75008. **Map** 2 F5.
Tel 01 40 75 08 75.

**Le Moulin de
la Vierge**
105 rue Vercingétorix 75014. **Map** 11 A4.
Tel 01 45 43 09 84.

Les Panetons
113 rue Mouffetard 75005. **Map** 13 B2.
Tel 01 47 07 12 08.

Pierre Hermé
72 rue Bonaparte 75006.
Map 8 E4.
Tel 01 43 54 47 77.

Poilâne
8 rue du Cherche-Midi 75006. **Map** 8 D4.
Tel 01 45 48 42 59.
www.poilane.fr

Sacha Finkelsztajn
27 rue des Rosiers 75004.
Map 9 C3.
Tel 01 42 72 78 91.

CHOCOLATE

Christian Constant
37 rue d'Assas 75006.
Map 12 E1.
Tel 01 53 63 15 15.

Dalloyau
101 rue du Faubourg-St-Honoré 75008. **Map** 3 B5.
Tel 01 42 99 90 00.

Fauchon
26 pl de la Madeleine 75008. **Map** 3 C5.
Tel 01 70 39 38 00.

**La Maison du
Chocolat**
225 rue du Faubourg-St-Honoré 75008. **Map** 2 E3.
Tel 01 42 27 39 44.

Richart
258 bd St-Germain 75007. **Map** 7 C2.
Tel 01 45 55 66 00.

CHARCUTERIE
AND FOIE GRAS

Comtesse du Barry
1 rue de Sèvres 75006.
Map 8 D4.
Tel 01 45 48 32 04.

Divay
4 rue Bayen 75017.
Map 2 D2.
Tel 01 43 80 16 97.

Hédiard
21 pl de la Madeleine 75008. **Map** C5.
Tel 01 43 12 88 88.

**Jean-Jacques
Chrétienne**
58 rue des Martyrs 75009.
Map 4 F2.
Tel 01 48 78 96 45.

Labeyrie
11 rue d'Auteuil 75016.
Map 5 A5.
Tel 01 42 24 17 62.

Le Bon Marché
24 rue de Sèvres 75007.
Map 7 C5.
Tel 01 44 39 80 00.

Maison de la Truffe
19 pl de la Madeleine 75008. **Map** 3 C5.
Tel 01 42 65 53 22.

Maison Pou
16 av des Ternes 75017.
Map 2 D3.
Tel 01 43 80 19 24.

Petrossian
18 bd Latour-Maubourg 75007. **Map** 7 A2.
Tel 01 44 11 32 25.

Vignon
13 rue Clément-Marot 75008. **Map** 2 E5.
Tel 01 47 20 10 01.

CHEESE

Alléosse
13 rue Poncelet 75017.
Map 2 E3.
Tel 01 46 22 50 45.

Androuët
134 rue Mouffetard 75005.
Map 13 B1.
Tel 01 45 87 85 05.

Barthélémy
51 rue de Grenelle 75007.
Map 8 D4.
Tel 01 45 48 56 75.

**Crèmerie
Quatrehomme**
62 rue de Sèvres 75007.
Map 7 C5.
Tel 01 47 34 33 45.

La Fermette
86 rue Montorgueil 75002.
Map 9 A1.
Tel 01 42 36 70 96.

**La Fromagerie
d'Auteuil**
58 rue d'Auteuil 75016.
Map 5 A5.
Tel 01 45 25 07 10.

Le Jardin Fromager
53 rue Oberkampf 75011. **Map** 10 E1.
Tel 01 48 05 19 96.

Marie-Anne Cantin
12 rue du Champ-de-Mars 75007.
Map 6 F3.
Tel 01 45 50 43 94.

WINE

Cave Péret
6 rue Daguerre 75014.
Map 12 D4.
Tel 01 43 22 08 64.

Les Caves Augé
116 bd Haussman 75008.
Map 3 C4.
Tel 01 45 22 16 97.

Caves Taillevent
199 rue du Faubourg-St-Honoré 75008.
Map 2 F3.
Tel 01 45 61 14 09.

Lavinia
3–5 bd de la Madeleine 75008.
Map 4 D5.
Tel 01 42 97 20 20.

**Legrand Filles
et Fils**
1 rue de la Banque 75002.
Map 8 F1.
Tel 01 42 60 07 12.

Nicolas
35 bd Malesherbes 75008.
Map 3 C5.
Tel 01 42 65 00 85.

Renaud Michel
12 pl de la Nation 75012.
Tel 01 43 07 98 93.

Ryst-Dupeyron
79 rue du Bac 75007.
Map 8 D3.
Tel 01 45 48 80 93.

Arts and Antiques

In Paris you can either buy art and antiques from shops and galleries with established reputations, or from flea markets and avant-garde galleries. Many of the prestigious antiques shops and galleries are located around the rue du Faubourg-St-Honoré and are worth a visit even if you can't afford to buy. On the Left Bank is Le Carré Rive Gauche, an organization of 30 antiques dealers.

EXPORTING

Objets d'art over 50 years old, worth more than a given amount, will require a *Certificat pour un bien culturel* to be exported (provided by the vendor), plus a *licence d'exportation* for non-EU countries. Seek professional advice from the large antique shops. The **Centre des Renseignements des Douanes** has a booklet, *Bulletin Officiel des Douanes*, with all the details.

ANTIQUES

If you wish to buy antiques, you might like to stroll around the areas that boast the most galleries – in Le Carré Rive Gauche around quai Malaquais, try **L'Arc en Seine** and **Anne-Sophie Duval** for Art Nouveau and Art Deco. Rue Jacob is still one of the best places to seek beautiful objects, antique or modern. Close to the Louvre, the **Louvre des Antiquaires** comprises 250 shops selling mainly expensive, quality furniture. Many of the prestigious antiques stores are near rue du Faubourg-St-Honoré including **Didier Aaron**, expert on furniture from the 17th and 18th centuries. **Village St-Paul** is the most charming group of antiques shops and is also open on Sundays. In the south of the city, **Le Village Suisse** also groups many art and antiques dealers.

ART GALLERIES

Established art galleries are located on or around the avenue Montaigne. The **Louise Leiris** gallery was founded by D.H. Kahnweiler, the dealer who "discovered" both Georges Braque and Pablo Picasso. The gallery still shows Cubist masterpieces.

On the Left Bank **Galerie Maeght** has a tremendous stock of paintings at prices to suit most budgets; he also publishes fine art books.

Rue Louise-Weiss, known as Scène Est, has become the area for cutting-edge creativity and innovation. The **Air de Paris** gallery is popular.

In the Marais try **Yvon Lambert** and **Galerie du Jour Agnès B.**, in the Bastille, **Lavignes-Bastille** and **L et M Durand-Dessert**, also a fashionable place to buy catalogues on new artists, if not their works.

AUCTION HOUSES

The great Paris auction centre, in operation since 1858, is **Drouot-Richelieu**. Bidding can be intimidating since most of it is done by dealers. Beware of the auctioneer's high-speed patter. *La Gazette de L'Hôtel Drouot* tells you what auctions are coming up when. Drouot-Richelieu also has its own auction catalogue. The house only accepts cash and French cheques, but there is an exchange desk in-house. A 10–15 per cent commission to the house is charged, so remember to add it on to any price you hear. You may view from 11am–6pm on the day before the sale, and from 11am to noon on the morning of the sale.

DIRECTORY

EXPORTING

Centre des Renseignements des Douanes
Tel 08 11 20 44 44.
www.douane.gouv.fr

ANTIQUES

Anne-Sophie Duval
5 quai Malaquais 75006.
Map 8 E3.
Tel 01 43 54 51 16.
www.annesophieduval.com

L'Arc en Seine
31 rue de Seine 75006.
Map 8 E3.
Tel 01 43 29 11 02.

Didier Aaron
118 rue du Faubourg-St-Honoré 75008. Map 3 C5.
Tel 01 47 42 47 34.
www.didieraaron-cie.com

Louvre des Antiquaires
2 pl du Palais Royal 75001.
Map 8 E2.
Tel 01 42 97 27 27.

Village St-Paul
Between the quai des Célestins, the rue St-Paul and the rue Charlemagne 75004. Map 9 C4.

Le Village Suisse
78 av de Suffren 75015.
Map 6 E4.
www.levillagesuisse.com

ART GALLERIES

Air de Paris
32 rue Louise-Weiss 75013. Map 14 E4.
Tel 01 44 23 02 77.

Galerie du Jour Agnès B.
44 rue Quincampoix 75004. Map 9 B2.
Tel 01 44 54 55 90.

Galerie Maeght
42 rue du Bac 75007.
Map 8 D3.
Tel 01 45 48 45 15.

L et M Durand-Dessert
28 rue de Lappe 75011.
Map 10 F4.
Tel 01 48 06 92 23.

Lavignes-Bastille
27 rue de Charonne 75011. Map 10 F4.
Tel 01 47 00 88 18.

Louise Leiris
47 rue de Monceau 75008. Map 3 A3.
Tel 01 45 63 28 85.

Yvon Lambert
108 rue Vieille-du-Temple 75003. Map 10 D2.
Tel 01 42 71 09 33.

AUCTION HOUSES

Drouot-Richelieu
9 rue Drouot 75009.
Map 4 F4.
Tel 01 48 00 20 20.
www.drouot.fr

Markets

For eye-catching displays of wonderful food, or a lively shopping atmosphere, there is no better place than a Paris market. There are large covered food markets, markets where stalls change regularly, and permanent street markets. Some of the more famous markets, with approximate opening times, follow. While you are enjoying browsing round the stalls, remember to keep an eye on your money and be prepared to bargain.

FOOD MARKETS

The French still shop daily, hence food markets are always packed. Most fruit and vegetable markets are open from around 8am–1pm and from 4–7pm Tuesday to Saturday, and from 9am–1pm Sunday. Watch out for rotten goods – buy produce loose, not in boxes. A little language is useful for specifying *pas trop mûr* (not too ripe), or *pour manger ce soir* (to be eaten tonight).

FLEA MARKETS

It is often said that you can no longer find bargains at the Paris flea markets. Though this may be true, it is still worth going to one for the sheer fun of browsing. Whether you pick up any real bargains has as much to do with luck as with judgement. Often the sellers themselves have little or no idea of the true value of their goods – which can work either for or against you. The biggest and most famous market, incorporating several smaller ones, is the Marché aux Puces de St-Ouen. Keep an eye on your wallet, as pickpockets frequent these markets.

Marché d'Aligre

Pl d'Aligre 75012. **Map** 10 F5. Ⓜ *Ledru-Rollin*. ◯ *9am–1pm, 4–7:30pm Tue–Sat, 9am–1:30pm Sun.*

Reminiscent of a Moroccan bazaar, this must be the cheapest and liveliest market in the city. Here traders hawk ingredients such as North African olives, groundnuts and hot peppers, and there are even a few halal butchers. Stalls on the square sell mostly second-hand clothes and bric-à-brac. This is a less affluent area of town with few tourists and many Parisians.

Marché Enfant Rouges

39 rue de Bretagne 75003. **Map** 10 D2. Ⓜ *Temple, Filles-du-Calvaire*. ◯ *8:30am–1pm, 4–7pm Tue–Sat (8pm Fri & Sat), 8:30am–2pm Sun.*

This part-covered fruit and vegetable market dates from 1620. Famous for the freshness of its produce, on Sunday mornings street singers and accordionists help enliven the proceedings. There are also plenty of cheap eateries here.

Marché Raspail

75006. **Map** 8 D4. Ⓜ *Rennes*. ◯ *7am–2:30pm Tue & Fri, 9am–3pm Sun.*

Conveniently situated between Montparnasse and St-Germain, Raspail market sells fresh produce during the week and organic-only produce on Sundays.

Marché St-Germain

4–8 rue de Lobineau 75006. **Map** 8 E4. Ⓜ *Mabillon*. ◯ *10am–7:30pm Mon–Sat.*

St-Germain is one of the few covered markets left in Paris. Here you can buy Italian, Mexican, Greek, Asian and organic produce.

Rue Montorgueil

75001 & 75002. **Map** 9 A1. Ⓜ *Les Halles*. ◯ *9am–7pm daily (subject to change).*

The paved rue Montorgueil is what remains of the old Les Halles market. Here you can buy exotic fruit and vegetables like green bananas and yams, or sample offerings from the delicatessens. Expect high prices.

Rue Mouffetard

75005. **Map** 13 B2. Ⓜ *Pl Monge*. ◯ *8am–1pm Tue–Sun.*

This is one of the oldest market streets in Paris, and although it has become touristy it is still a charming winding street full of quality food. There is also a lively African market down the nearby side street of rue Daubenton.

Rue Poncelet

75017. **Map** 2 E3. Ⓜ *Ternes*. ◯ *8am–noon, 4–7:30pm Tue–Sat, 8am–12:30pm Sun.*

Situated away from the main tourist areas, this market street is worth visiting for its authentic French atmosphere. Choose from many bakeries, pâtisseries and *charcuteries*.

Marché de la Porte de Vanves

Av Georges-Lafenestre & av Marc-Sangnier 75014. Ⓜ *Porte-de-Vanves*. ◯ *7am–3 or 5pm Sat & Sun.*

Porte de Vanves is a small market selling good-quality bric-à-brac and junk as well as some second-hand furniture. It's best to get to the market early on Saturday morning for the best choice of wares. Artists exhibit nearby.

Marché aux Puces de Montreuil

Porte de Montreuil, 93 Montreuil 75020. Ⓜ *Porte-de-Montreuil*. ◯ *7am–7:30pm Sat–Mon.*

Go early to the Porte de Montreuil flea market, where you'll have a better chance of picking up a bargain. The substantial second-hand clothes section attracts many young people. Stalls sell everything from used bicycles to bric-à-brac and exotic spices.

Marché aux Puces de St-Ouen

(See p134.)

This is the most well known, the most crowded and the most expensive of all the flea markets. Here you'll find a range of markets, locals dealing from their car boots, and a number of large buildings packed with stalls. Some of them are very upmarket; others sell junk. A *Guide des Puces* (guide to the flea markets) can be obtained from the information kiosk in the Marché Biron on the rue des Rosiers.

Rue de Seine and Rue de Buci

75006. **Map** 8 E4. Ⓜ *Odéon*. ◯ *8am–1pm, 4–7pm Tue–Sat, 9am–1pm Sun.*

The stalls here are expensive and crowded but sell quality fruit and vegetables. There is also a large florist's and two excellent pâtisseries.

ENTERTAINMENT IN PARIS

Whether your preference is for classical drama, avant-garde theatre, ballet, opera or jazz, cinema or dancing the night away, Paris has it all. There is plenty of free entertainment too, from the street performers outside the Pompidou Centre to musicians busking all over town and in the metros.

Parisians themselves like nothing better than strolling along the boulevards or sitting at a pavement café nursing a drink as they watch the world go by. If, however, you're looking for the ultimate "Oh la-la!" experience, you can take in any of the celebrated nightclubs.

For fans of spectator sports there is tennis, the Tour de France or horse racing. Recreation centres and gyms cater to the more active. And for those disposed to more leisurely pursuits, there is always a quiet game of boules to be played in the park.

The glass façade of the Bastille Opéra

BOOKING TICKETS

Depending on the event, tickets can often be bought at the door, but for popular events it is wiser to purchase tickets in advance at the **FNAC** chains or **Virgin Megastore**. Theatre box offices open daily from about 11am–7pm. Most accept credit card bookings by telephone.

THEATRE

From the grandeur of the **Comédie Française** to slapstick farce and avant-garde drama, theatre is flourishing, both in Paris and in its suburbs. Founded in 1680 by royal decree, the Comédie Française is the bastion of French theatre, aiming to keep classical drama in the public eye and to perform works by the best modern playwrights. Formerly the second theatre of the Comédie Française, the **Odéon Théâtre de l'Europe** now specializes in plays from other countries, performed in their original language. In an underground auditorium in the Art Deco Palais de Chaillot, the **Théâtre National de Chaillot** is famed for staging some very lively productions of European classics. The **Théâtre National de la Colline** specializes in contemporary drama.

Among the most important of the serious independents is the **Comédie des Champs-Elysées**, while for over 100 years the **Palais Royal** has been known as the temple of risqué farce. The café theatres such as **Théâtre d'Edgar** and **Le Point Virgule** are always good venues for seeing the best of the emerging new talent.

In the summer, street theatre thrives in tourist areas such as the Pompidou Centre, Les Halles and St-Germain-des-Prés. Open-air performances of Shakespeare and classic French plays are given at the Shakespeare Garden in the Bois de Boulogne.

CLASSICAL MUSIC

Paris has many first-class venues with an excellent range of opera, classical and contemporary music productions. Opened in 1989, the stylish, 2,700-seat **Opéra National de Paris Bastille** stages classic and modern operas. The beautifully renovated **Opéra National Garnier** puts on mostly ballets.

The **Salle Pleyel** is Paris's principal concert hall, housing the Orchestre de Paris and Radio France's Philharmonic Orchestra. Both the **Théâtre des Champs-Elysées** and the **Théâtre du Châtelet** are recommended for their varied high-quality programmes. Venues for chamber music include the **Salle Gaveau** and the **Théâtre de la Ville**. The

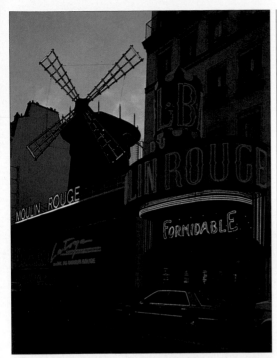

The famous silhouette of the Moulin Rouge nightclub

Cité de la **Musique** in the Parc de la Villette is one of Paris's most vibrant concert halls. The venue is renowned for its eclectic music programmes and workshops, while the museum charts the history of music and exhibits over 4,000 instruments.

DANCE

The French are very vocal in their appreciation or dislike of dance, and those who fail to please are subjected to boos, hisses and mass walk-outs in mid-performance.

The opulent **Opéra National Garnier** has space for 450 artists and is home to the Ballet de l'Opéra de Paris, which has earned a reputation as one of the best classical ballet companies in the world. Government support has helped the **Théâtre de la Ville** to become Paris's most important venue for modern dance, with subsidies keeping ticket costs relatively low.

The **Maison des Arts de Créteil** stages famous overseas companies, as well as its own much praised productions.

CLUBS AND CABARET

Music in Paris clubs tends to follow the trends set in the US and Britain. Only a few clubs such as **Balajo**, once frequented by Edith Piaf, and the ultra-hip **Showcase**, under the Alexandre III bridge, are genuinely up-to-the-minute with their music.

Showcase attracts a young crowd to its big-name DJ nights. **Le Baron** is a trendy nightspot, attracting people from the fashion world and from show business. For comedy in English, try **La Java**. The stage of this club, where Edith Piaf once performed, now showcases British and American comedians.

When it comes to picking a cabaret, the rule of thumb is simple: the better known places are best. The **Folies-Bergère** is the oldest music hall in Paris and probably the most famous in the world. It is closely rivalled by the **Lido** and the **Moulin Rouge**, birthplace of the cancan. **Paradis Latin** is the most "French" cabaret in the city. It shows variety acts whose sketches are enlivened by remarkable special effects and scenery.

ROCK, JAZZ AND WORLD MUSIC

The top international acts are usually to be found at the enormous arenas such as **Palais Omnisports Paris-Bercy** or the **Zénith**. For a more intimate atmosphere, the legendary **Olympia** has assigned seating and good acoustics. To hear indigenous rock groups like Les Negresses Vertes and Mano Negra go to **La Cigale** or **Elysée-Montmartre** in the Pigalle area.

Jazz-crazy Paris has innumerable packed clubs where the best talent in the world can be heard on any evening. All the great jazz musicians have performed at **New Morning**, which also hosts African, Brazilian and other sounds. For Dixieland go to **Le Petit Journal St-Michel**.

World music and jazz lovers alike can see top acts and dance until dawn at the excellent **Chapelle des Lombards**.

The spectacular façade of the Opéra National Garnier

CINEMA

Paris is the world's capital of film appreciation. It was the cradle of the cinematograph nearly 100 years ago. Then in the late 1950s and early 1960s the city nurtured that very Parisian vanguard movement, the New Wave, when film directors such as François Truffaut and Jean-Luc Godard revolutionized the way films were made and perceived.

There are now more than 370 screens within the city limits, distributed among over 100 cinemas. Most are concentrated in cinema belts, which enjoy the added appeal of nearby restaurants and shops. The Champs-Elysées has the densest cinema strip in town, where you can see the latest Hollywood smash or French *auteur* triumph, as well as some classic re-issues.

In the vicinity of the Opéra de Paris Garnier, the cinemas in the Grands Boulevards include two notable landmarks: the 2,800-seat **Le Grand Rex**, with its Baroque decor, and the **Max Linder Panorama**, which was completely refurbished in the 1980s. The place de Clichy is the last Parisian stronghold of Pathé, while the hub of Right Bank cinema is in the Forum des Halles mall. France's largest screen is at **La Géode**.

On the Left Bank, Odéon-St-Germain-des-Prés has taken over from the Latin Quarter as the city's heartland for art and repertory cinemas. The new, and huge, **MK2 Bibliothèque** points to the future with its collection of 14 screens, a bar, shops and exhibition space.

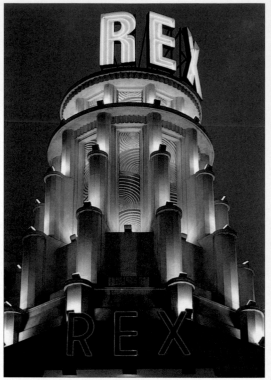

The dome of the 2,800-seat Le Grand Rex cinema

SPORT

Paris is host to some of the foremost sporting events in the world. City-wide frenzy sweeps Paris when the Tour de France bicycle race finishes there in July. From late May to mid-June Parisians live and breathe tennis during the **Roland Garros** national tennis championship. The Prix de l'Arc de Triomphe, held at the **Hippodrome de Longchamp** on the first Sunday in October, provides the opportunity to see the rich in all their finery as well as first-class flat racing.

The **Palais Omnisports Paris-Bercy** is the venue for a vast range of events, including the Paris tennis open, and rock concerts, as is the new **Stade de France** at St-Denis. **Parc des Princes** is home to Paris's top football team, Paris St-Germain.

THE CELEBRATED CAFES OF PARIS

One of the most enduring images of Paris is the Left Bank café scene where great artists, writers and eminent intellectuals consorted. Before World War I, hordes of Russian revolutionaries, including Lenin and Trotsky, whiled away their days in the Rotonde and the Dôme in Montparnasse. In the 1920s, Surrealists dominated café life. Later came the American writers led by Ernest Hemingway and Scott Fitzgerald, whose haunts included La Coupole. After World War II, Jean-Paul Sartre and other Existentialists shifted the cultural scene northwards to St-Germain.

Newspaper reading remains a typical café pastime

DIRECTORY

BOOKING TICKETS

FNAC
26–30 av des Ternes
75017. **Map** 2 D3.
Tel 0825 020 020. Forum
Les Halles, 1 rue Pierre
Lescot 75001. **Map** 9 A2.
Tel 0825 020 020.
www.fnac.com

Virgin Megastore
52–60 av des Champs-
Elysées 75008. **Map** 2 F5.
Tel 01 49 53 50 00.
www.virginmegastore.fr

THEATRE

Comédie des
Champs-Elysées
15 av Montaigne 75008.
Map 6 F1.
Tel 01 53 23 99 19.

Comédie Française
1 pl Colette 75001. **Map**
8 E1. *Tel* 0825 10 16 80.
www.comedie-francaise.fr

Odéon Théâtre
de l'Europe
Place de l'Odéon 75006.
Map 12 F5.
Tel 01 44 85 40 40.
www.theatre-odeon.fr

Palais Royal
38 rue Montpensier
75001. **Map** 8 E1.
Tel 01 42 97 40 00.

Le Point Virgule
7 rue Ste-Croix de la
Bretonnerie 75004. **Map**
9 C3. *Tel* 01 42 78 67 03.

Théâtre d'Edgar
58 bd Edgar-Quinet
75014. **Map** 12 D2.
Tel 01 42 79 97 97.

Théâtre National
de Chaillot
Pl du Trocadéro
75016. **Map** 5 C2.
Tel 01 53 65 30 00.
www.theatre-chaillot.fr

Théâtre National de
la Colline
15 rue Malte-Brun 75020.
Tel 01 44 62 52 52.
www.colline.fr

CLASSICAL MUSIC

Cité de la Musique
221 av Jean-Jaurès
75019.
Tel 01 44 84 44 84.
www.cite-musique.fr

Opéra National de
Paris Bastille
120 rue de Lyon 75012.
Map 10 E4.
Tel 08 92 89 90 90.
www.operadeparis.fr

Opéra National de
Paris Garnier
Pl de l'Opera 75009. **Map**
4 E5. *Tel* 08 92 89 90 90.

Salle Gaveau
45 rue la Boétie 75008.
Map 3 B4.
Tel 01 49 53 05 07.
www.sallegaveau.com

Salle Pleyel
252 rue du Faubourg St-
Honoré 75008. **Map** 2 E3.
Tel 01 42 56 13 13.
www.sallepleyel.fr

Théâtre des
Champs-Elysées
15 av Montaigne 75008.
Map 6 F1.
Tel 01 49 52 50 00.
www.theatredeschamps
elysees.fr

Théâtre du Châtelet
Pl du Châtelet 75001.
Map 9 A3.
Tel 01 40 28 28 40.
www.chatelet-theatre.
com

Théâtre de la Ville
2 pl du Châtelet 75004.
Map 9 A3.
Tel 01 42 74 22 77.
www.theatredelaville-
paris.com

DANCE

Maison des Arts de
Créteil
Pl Salvador Allende
94000 Créteil.
Tel 01 45 13 19 19.
www.maccreteil.com

Opéra Garnier
(See Classical Music.)

Théâtre de la Ville
(See Classical Music.)

CLUBS AND
CABARET

Balajo
9 rue de Lappe 75011.
Map 10 E4. *Tel* 09 54 94
54 09. **www**.balajo.fr

Le Baron
6 av Marceau 75008.
Map 6 E1.
Tel 01 47 20 04 01.

Folies-Bergère
32 rue Richer 75009.
Tel 08 92 68 16 50.
www.foliesbergere.com

La Java
105 rue du Faubourg-du-
Temple 75010.
Tel 01 42 02 20 52.

Lido
116 bis av des Champs-
Elysées 75008. **Map** 2 E4.
Tel 01 40 76 56 10.
www.lido.fr

La Machine du
Moulin Rouge
90 bd de Clichy 75018.
Map 4 D1.
Tel 01 56 55 52 04.

Moulin Rouge
82 bd de Clichy 75018.
Map 4 E1.
Tel 01 53 09 82 82.
www.moulinrouge.fr

Paradis Latin
28 rue du Cardinal-Lemoine
75008. **Map** 9 B5.
Tel 01 43 25 28 28.

Showcase
Porte des Champs-Elysées
75008. **Map** 7 A1.
Tel 01 45 61 25 43.
www.showcase.fr

ROCK, JAZZ AND
WORLD MUSIC

Chapelle des
Lombards
19 rue de Lappe 75011.
Map 10 F4.
Tel 01 43 57 24 24.

La Cigale
120 bd Rochechouart
75018. **Map** 4 F2.
Tel 01 49 25 89 99.

Elysée-Montmartre
72 bd Rochechouart
75018. **Map** 4 F2.
Tel 01 44 92 45 36.

New Morning
7–9 rue des Petites-
Ecuries 75010.
Tel 01 45 23 51 41.

Olympia
28 bd des Capucines
75009. **Map** 4 D5.
Tel 08 92 68 33 68.
www.olympiahall.com

Palais Omnisports
Paris-Bercy
8 bd de Bercy 75012.
Map 14 F2.
Tel 08 92 39 04 90.
www.bercy.fr

Le Petit Journal
St-Michel
71 bd St-Michel 75005.
Map 12 F1.
Tel 01 43 26 28 59.

Zénith
211 av de Jean-Jaurès
75019.
Tel 08 90 71 02 07.
www.zenith-paris.com

CINEMA

La Géode
26 av Corentin-Cariou
75019.
📞 08 92 68 45 40.
www.lageode.fr

Le Grand Rex
1 bd Poissonnière 75002.
📞 08 92 68 05 96.
www.legrandrex.com

Max Linder
Panorama
24 bd Poissonnière 75009.
📞 08 92 68 00 31.

MK2 Bibliothèque
128–162 av de France
75013.
📞 08 92 69 84 84.
www.mk2.com

SPORT

Hippodrome de
Longchamp
Route des Tribunes
75016.
Tel 01 44 30 75 00.

Palais Omnisports
Paris-Bercy
(See Rock section.)

Parc des Princes
24 rue du Commandant-
Guilbaud 75016.
Tel 3275.

Stade de France
La Plaine St-Denis 93210.
Tel 08 92 70 09 00.
www.stadedefrance.fr

Stade Roland
Garros
2 av Gordon-Bennett
75016.
Tel 01 47 43 48 00.
www.fft.fr/rolandgarros

PARIS STREET FINDER

The map references given with sights, shops and entertainment venues described in the Paris section of the guide refer to the maps on the following pages. Map references are also given for Paris hotels (*see pp550–5*) and restaurants (*pp600–6*), and for useful addresses in the *Travellers' Needs* and *Survival Guide* sections at the back of the book. The maps include not only the main sightseeing areas but also the most important districts for hotels, restaurants, shopping and entertainment venues. The key map below shows the area of Paris covered by the *Street Finder*, with the *arrondissement* numbers for the various districts. The symbols used for sights and other features on the *Street Finder* maps are listed opposite.

Paris is divided into 20 *arrondissements*, outlined in orange and numbered on this map.

KEY

- - Arrondissement boundary

HOW THE MAP REFERENCES WORK

The first figure tells you which *Street Finder* map to turn to.

Hôtel de Ville ❿

Pl de l'Hôtel-de-Ville 75004.
Map 9 B3. *Tel 01 42 76 40 40.*
Ⓜ *Hôtel-de-Ville.* ☐ to groups:
phone to arrange (01 42 76 54 04).
⬤ public hols and for official
functions (phone to check). ♿

The letter and number give the grid reference. Letters go across the map's top and bottom; figures on its sides.

The map continues on page 13 of the Street Finder.

KEY TO STREET FINDER

◼	Major sight
◼	Other sight
◻	Other building
Ⓜ	Metro station
RER	RER station
🚌	Main bus stop
⛴	River boat boarding point
P	Main car park
i	Tourist information
✚	Hospital with casualty unit
🛡	Police station
✝	Church
✡	Synagogue
⊠	Post office
⚏	Railway line
▬	Autoroute
—	Pedestrian street
«130	House number (main street)

SCALE OF MAP PAGES

0 metres	200	
		1:12,000
0 yards	200	

ILE DE FRANCE

S et at the heart of France, with Paris as its hub, Ile de France extends well beyond the densely populated suburbs of the city. Its rich countryside incorporates a historic royal region of monumental splendour central to *"la gloire de la France"*.

The region became a favourite with French royalty after François I transformed Fontainebleau into a Renaissance palace in 1528. Louis XIV kept the Ile de France as the political axis of the country when he started building Versailles in 1661. This Classical château created by the combined genius of Le Nôtre, Le Vau, Le Brun and Jules Hardouin-Mansart is France's most visited sight. It stands as a monument to the power of the Sun King and is still used for state occasions. Rambouillet, closely linked with Louis XVI, is now the summer residence of the French president, while Malmaison was the favourite home of Empress Josephine. To the north, the Château d'Ecouen offers a showcase of Renaissance life and to the south Vaux-le-Vicomte boasts some of the loveliest formal gardens in France.

Nourished by the Seine and Marne rivers, the Ile de France is a patchwork of chalky plains, wheatfields and forests. The serene, poplar-lined avenues and rustic charm of the region have been an inspiration to painters such as Corot, Rousseau, Pissarro and Cézanne.

SIGHTS AT A GLANCE

Châteaux and Museums
Château de Dampierre **8**
Château de Fontainebleau **13**
Château de Malmaison **5**
Château de Rambouillet **9**
Château de Sceaux **7**
Château de Vaux-le-Vicomte **11**
Château de Versailles **6**
Musée National de la
   Renaissance **2**

Towns
Provins **12**
St-Germain-en-Laye **4**

Abbeys and Churches
Abbaye de Royaumont **1**
Basilique St-Denis **3**

Theme Parks
Disneyland Resort Paris **10**

KEY
- Greater Paris
- Central Paris
- ✈ International airport
- Motorway
- Major road
- Minor road

0 kilometres   20
0 miles   10

ILE DE FRANCE

◁ **Magnificent formal gardens at the Château Vaux-le-Vicomte**

The vaulted Gothic refectory of Abbaye de Royaumont

Abbaye de Royaumont ❶

Fondation Royaumont, Asnières-sur-Oise, Val-d'Oise. **Tel** 01 30 35 59 70. ☐ daily. 🏃 🛦 📷 phone 01 30 35 59 00. 🎵 **Concerts.** www.royaumont.com

Set among woods "near water and far from mankind", 35 km (22 miles) north of Paris, Royaumont is the finest Cistercian abbey in the Ile de France. Chosen for its remoteness, the abbey's stark stonework and simplicity of line reflect the austere teachings of St Bernard. However, unlike his Burgundian abbeys, Royaumont was founded in 1228 by Louis IX and his mother, Blanche de Castille. "St Louis" showered the abbey with riches and chose it as a royal burial site.

The abbey retained its royal links until the Revolution, when much of it was destroyed. It was then a textiles mill and orphanage until its revival as a cultural centre. The original pillars still remain, along with a gravity-defying corner tower and the largest Cistercian cloisters in France, which enclose a charming Classical garden. The monastic quarters border one side of the cloisters.

The Château de Royaumont, erected as the abbot's palace on the eve of the Revolution, is set apart and resembles an Italianate villa. In the grounds are monks' workshops, woods, ponds and Cistercian canals.

In summer, concerts are held in the abbey on weekends (01 34 68 05 50 for details).

Musée National de la Renaissance ❷

Château d'Ecouen, Val-d'Oise. **Tel** 01 34 38 38 50. ☐ Wed–Mon. ● 1 Jan, 1 May, 25 Dec. **Park** ☐ Apr–Sep: 8am–7pm (Oct–Mar: 6pm); no animals 🏃 museum only. 🛦 📷 🍴 www.musee-renaissance.fr

This imposing moated château is curiously adrift, halfway between St-Denis and Royaumont. Now a Renaissance museum, Ecouen's magnificent quadrilateral exterior provides an authentic setting for an impressive collection of paintings, tapestries, coffers, carved doors and staircases salvaged from other 16th-century châteaux.

Ecouen was built in 1538 for Anne de Montmorency, adviser to François I and Commander-in-Chief of his armies. As the second most powerful person in the kingdom, he employed Ecole de Fontainebleau artists and craftsmen to adorn his palace. Their influence is apparent in the ravishing painted fireplaces, depicting biblical and Classical themes in mysterious landscapes. The most striking room is the chapel, containing a gallery and vaulted ceilings painted with the Montmorency coat of arms.

Upstairs is one of the finest series of 16th-century tapestries in France. Equally compelling are the princely apartments, the library of illuminated manuscripts, vivid ceramics from Lyon, Nevers, Venice and Faenza, and Iznik, and a display of early mathematical instruments. Recent acquisitions include 16th- and 17th-century engravings from France, Italy and Germany.

Basilique St-Denis ❸

1 rue de la Légion d'Honneur, St-Denis, Seine-St-Denis. **Tel** 01 48 09 83 54. 🅼 Line 13 Basilique de St-Denis. ☐ daily. ● 1 Jan, 1 May, 25 Dec. 🏃 🛦 📷 🕇 8:30am & 10am Sun.

According to legend, the decapitated St-Denis struggled here clutching his head, and an abbey was erected to commemorate the martyred bishop. Following the burial of Dagobert I in the basilica in 638, a royal link with St-Denis began, which was to span 12 centuries. Most French kings were entombed in St-Denis, and all the queens of France were crowned here.

The elegant, early Gothic basilica rests on Carolingian and Romanesque crypts. Of the medieval effigies, the most impressive are of Charles V (1364) and a 12th-century likeness in enamelled copper of Blanche de France with her

Statue of Louis XVI at St-Denis

The west wing of Musée National de la Renaissance

The Renaissance tomb of Louis XII and Anne de Bretagne in St-Denis

dog. The mask-like serenity of these effigies is in sharp contrast with the graphically realistic Renaissance portrayal of agony present in the grotesque mausoleum of Louis XII and Anne de Bretagne. Both are represented as naked figures, their faces eerily captured at the moment of death. Above the mausoleum, effigies of the finely dressed royal couple contemplate their own nakedness. As a reflection of humanity in the face of death, the tombs have few rivals.

St-Germain-en-Laye ➍

Yvelines. 🕴 42,200. 🚊 🚍
ℹ️ *Maison Claude Debussy, 38 rue au Pain.* **Tel** *01 34 51 05 12.*
🚌 *Tue–Wed, Fri–Sun.*

Dominating the Place Général de Gaulle in this chic suburb is the legendary Château de St-Germain, birthplace of Louis XIV. Louis VI built the original

stronghold in 1122 but only the keep and St-Louis chapel remain. Under François I and Henri II, the medieval upper tiers were demolished, leaving a moated pentagon. Henri IV built the pavilion and terraces that run down to the Seine, and Louis XIV had Le Nôtre landscape the gardens before leaving for Versailles in 1682.

Today the château houses the **Musée des Antiquités Nationales**, which exhibits archaeological finds from pre-history to the Middle Ages. Created by Napoleon III, the collection includes a 22,000-year-old carved female, a megalithic tomb, a bronze helmet from the 3rd century BC and Celtic jewellery. The finest treasure is the Gallo-Roman mosaic pavement.

🏛 **Musée des Antiquités Nationales**
Château de St-Germain-en-Laye.
Tel *01 39 10 13 00.* 🕐 *10am–5:15pm Wed–Mon.* ☒ 🎫 ♿ 🚻 **www**.
musee-antiquitesnationales.fr

Château de Malmaison ➎

Rueil-Malmaison, Hauts-de-Seine.
Tel *01 41 29 05 55.* 🕐 *Apr–Sep: 10am–5:45pm Wed–Mon (6:15pm Sat & Sun); Oct–Mar: 10am–5:15pm Wed–Mon (5:45pm Sat & Sun).*
🚫 *1 Jan, 25 Dec.* ☒ ♿ *restr.*
www.chateau-malmaison.fr

Situated 15 km (9 miles) west of Paris, this 17th-century estate is best known for its Napoleonic associations. Bought by Josephine as a retreat from the formality of the Emperor's residences at the Tuileries and Fontainebleau, it has charming rural grounds. While Josephine loved this country manor, Napoleon scorned its entrance as fit only for servants, and so he had a curious drawbridge built at the back of the château.

The finest rooms are the frescoed and vaulted library, the canopied campaign room and the sunny Salon de Musique. Napoleon's restrained, yellow canopied bedroom contrasts with the bedchamber Josephine died in, a magnificent indulgence bedecked in red. Many of the rooms overlook the romantic "English" gardens and the famous rose garden Josephine cultivated after her divorce.

Memorabilia abound, from imperial eagles to David's moody portrait of Napoleon, or Gérard's painting of the languid Josephine reclining on a chaise-longue.

Château Bois Préau, set in the wooded grounds, houses a museum dedicated to Napoleon's exile and death.

Empress Josephine's bed at Château de Malmaison

Château de Versailles ❻

The present palace, started by Louis XIV in 1668, grew around Louis XIII's original hunting lodge. Architect Louis Le Vau built the first section, which expanded into an enlarged courtyard. From 1678, Jules Hardouin-Mansart added north and south wings and the Hall of Mirrors. He also designed the chapel, completed in 1710. The Opera House (L'Opéra) was added by Louis XV in 1770. André Le Nôtre enlarged the gardens and broke the monotony of the symmetrical layout with expanses of water and creative use of uneven ground. Opposite the château is the Academie du Spectacle Equestre, where you can watch dressage shows.

Garden statue of a flautist

★ **Formal Gardens**
Geometric paths and shrubberies are features of the gardens.

The Orangery was built beneath the Parterre du Midi to house exotic plants in winter.

Fountain of Latona
Four marble basins rise to Balthazar Marsy's statue of the goddess Latona.

Water Parterre

★ **Château**
Under Louis XIV, Versailles became the centre of political power in France.

Dragon Fountain
The fountain's centrepiece is a winged monster.

The King's garden features a mirror pool in the 19th-century garden created by Louis XVIII.

Colonnade
Mansart designed this circle of marble arches in 1685.

VISITORS' CHECKLIST

Versailles, Yvelines. *Tel 01 30 83 78 00.* 🚌 *171 from Paris.* RER Versailles Rive Gauche. 🚉 Versailles Chantiers, Versailles Rive Droite. **Château** 🕐 9am–6:30pm (5:30pm Nov–Mar) Tue–Sun. 🔴 some public hols; phone to check. 📷 **Grand Trianon & Petit Trianon** 🕐 noon–7pm (5:30pm winter) daily (last adm: 30 mins before closing). 🔴 1 Jan, 1 May, 25 Dec. 📷 ♿ 📷 🔵 📷 📷 **Academie du Spectacle Equestre** 🕐 Thu, Sat, Sun. 📷 with Château ticket. 📷 Les Fêtes de Nuit (Aug–Sep); Les Grandes Eaux Nocturnes (Apr–Sep: Sat). www.chateauversailles.fr

The Grand Canal was the setting for Louis XIV's boating parties.

Fountain of Neptune
Groups of sculptures spray spectacular jets of water in Le Nôtre's 17th-century garden.

Petit Trianon
Built in 1762 as a retreat for Louis XV, this small château became a favourite with Marie-Antoinette.

★ **Grand Trianon**
Louis XIV built this small palace of stone and pink marble in 1687 to escape the rigours of court life, and to enjoy the company of Madame de Maintenon.

STAR FEATURES

★ Château

★ Formal Gardens

★ Grand Trianon

Inside the Château de Versailles

The sumptuous main apartments are on the first floor of this vast château complex. Around the Marble Courtyard are the private apartments of the king and queen. On the garden side are the state apartments where official court life took place. These were richly decorated by Charles Le Brun with marble, stone and wood carvings, murals, velvet, silver and gilded furniture. Beginning with the Salon d'Hercule, each state room is dedicated to an Olympian deity. The climax is the Hall of Mirrors, where 17 vast mirrors face tall arched windows. Not all rooms are open at the same time so check on arrival.

★ **Queen's Bedroom**
In this room the queens of France gave birth to the royal children in public view.

KEY TO FLOORPLAN

- ☐ South wing
- ☐ Coronation room
- ☐ Madame de Maintenon's apartments
- ☐ Queen's apartments and private suite
- ☐ State apartments
- ☐ King's apartments and private suite
- ☐ North wing
- ☐ Non-exhibition space

The Marble Courtyard is overlooked by a gilded balcony.

Entrance

The Salon du Sacre is adorned with huge paintings of Napoleon by Jacques-Louis David.

Entrance

★ **Salon de Vénus**
A statue of Louis XIV stands amid the rich marble decor of this room.

Stairs to ground floor reception area

★ **Chapelle Royale**
The chapel's first floor was reserved for the royal family and the ground floor for the court. The beautiful interior is decorated with Corinthian columns and white marble, gilding and Baroque murals.

STAR FEATURES

★ Chapelle

★ Salon de Vénus

★ Hall of Mirrors

★ Queen's Bedroom

★ Hall of Mirrors

Great state occasions were held in this room stretching 70 m (233 ft) along the west façade. Here in 1919 the Treaty of Versailles was ratified, ending World War I.

Oeil-de-Boeuf

The King's Bedroom is where Louis XIV died in 1715.

The Cabinet du Conseil was used by the king to receive his ministers and family.

Salon de la Guerre
The room's theme of war is reinforced by Antoine Coysevox's stuccoed relief of Louis XIV riding to victory.

Louis XVI's library features Neo-Classical panelling and the king's terrestrial globe.

Salon d'Apollon
Designed by Le Brun and dedicated to the god Apollo, this was Louis XIV's throne room. A copy of Hyacinthe Rigaud's famous portrait of the king (1701) hangs here.

Salon d'Hercule

TIMELINE

Louis XV

1650	1700	1750	1800	1850
1667 Grand Canal begun			**1793** Louis XVI and Marie-Antoinette executed	**1833** Louis-Philippe turns the château into a museum
1668 Construction of new château by Le Vau	**1722** 12 year-old Louis XV occupies Versailles			
1671 Interior decoration by Le Brun begun	**1715** Death of Louis XIV. Versailles abandoned by court		**1789** King and Queen forced to leave Versailles for Paris	**1919** Treaty of Versailles signed on 28 June
1661 Louis XIV enlarges château	**1682** Louis XIV and Marie-Thérèse move to Versailles		**1774** Louis XVI and Marie-Antoinette live at Versailles	

Château de Sceaux ❼

Sceaux, Hauts-de-Seine. **Tel** 01 41 87 29 50. ☐ Apr–Oct: 10am–6pm Wed–Mon (6:30pm Sun); Nov–Mar: 10am–5pm Wed–Mon. ⬤ public hols & lunchtimes. ♿ ✉ www.domaine-de-sceaux.fr

The Parc de Sceaux, bounded by elegant villas, is an appealing mixture of formal gardens, woods and water containing Classical gardens designed by Le Nôtre. The gardens use water to great effect, with tiered waterfalls and fountains presenting a moving staircase that cascades into an octagonal basin. This feeds into the Grand Canal and offers a poplar-lined view to the Pavillon de Hanovre. This elegant pavilion is one of several that adorn the park, which also contains Mansart's Classical Orangerie. Today it is the setting for exhibitions and music concerts.

Built for Colbert in 1670, the original château was demolished and rebuilt in Louis XIII style in 1856. The stylish fake contains the Musée de l'Ile de France, which celebrates the landscapes and châteaux of the region with paintings, furniture and sculpture.

Château de Dampierre ❽

Dampierre-en-Yvelines, Yvelines. **Tel** 01 30 52 53 24. ☐ Apr–mid-Oct: daily. ⬤ Sun lunch. ♿ ♿ restricted. ✉ 🍴 www.chateau-de-dampierre.fr

After Versailles and Rambouillet, Dampierre is the most celebrated château

southwest of Paris. Built in 1675 for the Duc de Chevreuse, the exterior of the château is a harmonious composition of rose-coloured brick and cool stone, designed by Hardouin-Mansart.

By contrast, the interior sumptuously evokes Versailles, particularly in the royal apartments and the Louis XIV dining room. The grandest room is the frescoed Salle des Fêtes, remodelled in the 19th century in triumphal Roman style. The rooms overlook gardens landscaped by Le Nôtre.

Château de Rambouillet

Château de Rambouillet ❾

Rambouillet, Yvelines. **Tel** 01 34 83 00 25. ☐ Wed–Mon. ⬤ 1 Jan, 1 May, 1 & 11 Nov, 25 Dec, when president in residence & lunchtimes. ♿ ✉ http://chateau-rambouillet.monuments-nationaux.fr

The château borders the deep Forêt de Rambouillet, once the favourite royal hunting ground. This ivy-covered red-brick château, flanked by five

stone towers, is curious rather than beautiful. Adopted as a feudal castle, country estate, royal palace and Imperial residence, it reflects a composite of French royal history. Since 1897, it has been the president's official summer residence.

Inside, oak-panelled rooms are adorned with Empire-style furnishings and Aubusson tapestries. The main façade overlooks Classical parterres. Nearby is the Queen's Dairy, given by Louis XVI to Marie-Antoinette so that she could play milkmaid.

Environs About 28 km (17 miles) north on the D11 is the **Château de Thoiry**, which has a safari park and an innovative play area for children.

Disneyland® Resort Paris ❿

Marne-la-Vallée, Seine-et-Marne. **Tel** 08 25 30 02 22. ☐ daily. [RER] Marne-la-Vallée-Chessy. 🚄 TGV from Lille or Lyon. ✈ from both airports. ♿ ♿ www.disneylandparis.com

Disneyland® Resort Paris covers 200 ha (500 acres), with 2 theme parks, seven hotels, facilities for shopping and dining and convention centres. Most interesting are the Parks – the first with its five themed Lands, offering magic dominated by Sleeping Beauty Castle, and Walt Disney Studios.

Minnie Mouse

Château de Vaux-le-Vicomte ⓫

Maincy, Seine-et-Marne. **Tel** 01 64 14 41 90. 🚌 shuttle from Melun railway station. ☐ mid-Mar–early Nov. ⬤ Wed (except Jul & Aug). ♿ 🍴 www.vaux-le-vicomte.com

Set north of Melun, not far from Fontainebleau, the château enjoys a peaceful rural

---

SÈVRES PORCELAIN

In 1756 Madame de Pompadour and Louis XV opened a porcelain factory near Versailles at Sèvres to supply the royal residences with tableware and *objets d'art*. Thus began the production of exquisite dinner services, statuettes, Etruscan-style vases, romantic cameos and porcelain paintings, depicting grand châteaux or mythological scenes. Sèvres porcelain is typified by its translucence, durability and narrow palette of colours.

Le Pugilat (1832), one of a pair of vases from Sèvres

ANDRE LE NÔTRE

As the greatest French landscape gardener, Le Nôtre (1613–1700) created masterpieces in château gardens all over France. His Classical vision shaped many in the Ile de France, such as those at Dampierre, Sceaux and Vaux-le-Vicomte. At Vaux he perfected the concept of the *jardin à la française*: avenues framed by statues and box hedges; water gardens with fountains and ornate pools; graceful terraces and geometrical parterres "embroidered" with motifs. His genius lay in architectural orchestration and a sense of symmetry, typified by the sweeping vistas of Versailles, his greatest triumph.

location. Nicolas Fouquet, a powerful court financier to Louis XIV, challenged the architect Le Vau and the decorator Le Brun to create the most sumptuous palace of the day. The result is one of the greatest 17th-century French châteaux. However, it also led to his downfall. Louis and his ministers were so enraged – because its luxury cast the royal palaces into the shade – that they arrested Fouquet.

The interior is a gilded banquet of frescoes, stucco, caryatids and giant busts. The Salon des Muses boasts Le Brun's magnificent frescoed ceiling of dancing nymphs and poetic sphinxes. La

Grande Chambre Carrée is decorated in Louis XIII style with panelled walls and an impressive triumphal frieze, evoking Rome. However, its many rooms feel intimate and the scale is not overwhelming.

Yet Vaux-le-Vicomte's continuing fame is due to André Le Nôtre's stunning gardens. The landscape designer's early training as a painter is evident in the magnificent succession of terraces, ornamental lakes and fountains, which descend to a formal canal. On Saturday evenings from May to October, the castle is lit with over 2,000 candles and classical music is played in the gardens.

Provins ⑫

Seine-et-Marne. 🏃 12,000. 🚇 🚉
ℹ️ Chemin de Villecran (01 64 60 26 26). 🚌 Sat. www.provins.net

As a Roman outpost, Provins commanded the border of Ile de France and Champagne. Today, it offers a coherent vision of the medieval world. Ville Haute, the upper town, is clustered within high 12th-century ramparts, complete with crenellations and defensive ditches. The ramparts to the west are the best preserved. Here, between the fortified gateways of Porte de Jouy and Porte St-Jean, the fortifications are dotted with square, round and rectangular towers.

The town is dominated by Tour César, a keep with four corner turrets and a pyramid shaped roof. The moat and fortifications were added by the English during the Hundred Years' War. A guard-room leads to a gallery and views over the place du Chatel, a busy square of medieval gabled houses, and over the wheatfields beyond.

Provins is proud of its crimson roses. Every June, a floral celebration is held in the riverside rose garden, marked by a medieval festival with falconry and jousting.

Château de Vaux-le-Vicomte seen across the gardens designed by Le Nôtre

Château de Fontainebleau ⓭

Ceiling detail from the Salle de Bal

Fontainebleau is not the product of a single vision but is a bewildering cluster of styles from different periods. Louis VII built an abbey here which was consecrated by Thomas Becket in 1169. A medieval tower survives but the present château harks back to François I.
Originally drawn by the local hunting, the Renaissance king created a decorative château modelled on Florentine and Roman styles.
Fontainebleau's abiding charm comes from its relative informality and spectacular forest setting. While impossible to cover in a day, the *grands appartements* provide a sumptuous introduction to this royal palace.

Ground floor

Jardin de Diane
Now more romantic than Classical, the garden features a bronze fountain of Diana as huntress.

★ Escalier du Fer-à-Cheval
This imposing horseshoe-shaped staircase by Jean Androuet du Cerceau, built in 1634, lies at the end of Cour du Cheval Blanc. Its ingenious design allowed carriages to pass beneath the two arches.

KEY TO FLOORPLAN

- Petits Appartements
- Galerie des Cerfs
- Musée Chinois
- Musée Napoléon
- Grands Appartements
- Salle Renaissance
- Appartements de Madame de Maintenon
- Grands Appartements des Souverains
- Escalier de la Reine/ Appartements des Chasses
- Chapelle de la Trinité
- Appartement Intérieur de l'Empereur

Cour du Cheval Blanc was once a simple enclosed courtyard. It was transformed by Napoleon I into the main approach to the château.

Museum entrance

Chapelle de la Sainte Trinité was designed by Henri II in 1550. The chapel acquired its vaulted and frescoed ceiling under Henri IV and was completed by Louis XIII.

STAR FEATURES

- ★ Escalier du Fer-à-Cheval
- ★ Salle de Bal
- ★ Galerie François I

Porte Dorée
Originally a feudal gate-house, this was transformed into the entrance pavillion to the forest by Gilles Le Breton for François I.

Cour Oval

First floor

VISITORS' CHECKLIST

Seine-et-Marne. **Tel** *01 60 71 50 70.* ◯ 9:30am–5pm (6pm Apr–Sep) Wed–Mon. 🖼 🔲 🎫 📷 **Gardens** ◯ 9am–5pm (6pm Mar–Apr & Oct, 7pm May–Sep). ⬤ 1 Jan, 1 May, 25 Dec. **www.**chateaudefontainebleau.fr

★ **Salle de Bal**
The Renaissance ballroom, de-signed by Primaticcio (1552), was finished under Henri II. His emblems adorn the walnut cof-fered ceiling, forming a pattern reflected in the parquet floor.

The Appartements de Napoléon I
house his grandiose throne in the Emperor's Salle du Trône, formerly the Chambre du Roi.

Cour de la Fontaine

The Jardin Anglais
is a romantic "English" garden, planted with cypress and plantain trees. It was re-designed in the 19th century by Maximilien-Joseph Hurtault.

★ **Galerie François I**
This gilded gallery is a tribute to the Italian artists in the Ecole de Fontainebleau. *Rosso Fiorentino's allegorical frescoes pay homage to the king's wish to create "a second Rome".*

THE BARBIZON SCHOOL
Artists have been drawn to the glades of Fontainebleau since the 1840s, when a group of landscape painters, determined to paint only from nature, formed around Théodore Rousseau and Millet. They settled in the nearby hamlet of Barbizon where the Auberge Ganne, a museum dedicated to the *Ecole de Barbizon*, is located.

Spring at Barbizon, painted by Jean-François Millet (1814–75)

NORTHEAST FRANCE

Introducing Northeast France

The rolling plains of Northern France run from the
English Channel to the wooded Ardennes hills and
the Vosges mountains of Alsace. Apart from sombre
battle memorials, the area has France's finest gothic
cathedrals – and a long tradition of brewing good
quality beers. There is fine wine, too, in Champagne
and Alsace. The old heavy industry has gone,
while Lille's growth as a transport
hub has brought new
prosperity. This map
shows some of the most
interesting sights.

Amiens cathedral *is renowned
for its fine wood carvings and
its nave, the highest in France*
(see pp202–3).

LE NORD AND PICARDY
(See pp192–205)

Amiens Cathedral

*Beauvais
Cathedral*

Château de Compiègne

*Reim
Cathe*

The pride of Beauvais *is its Gothic
cathedral and astronomical clock
(see p200) which escaped heavy
bombing during World War II.*

*Troyes
Cathedral*

Half-timbered houses *and
Renaissance mansions line the
streets and alleys of Troyes' Old
Town (see p216), rebuilt after the
great fire in 1524. Its cathedral has
remarkable stained-glass windows.*

The legacy of World War I *is strong in this area of former battlefields. The Douaumont Memorial outside Verdun (see pp190–91), with its 15,000 graves, is only one of many memorials and cemeteries here.*

Haut-Koenigsbourg, *a castle painstakingly rebuilt by Kaiser Wilhelm II when Alsace-Lorraine was under German rule, is one of Alsace's most popular attractions (see p228).*

Strasbourg, *seat of the Council of Europe, has a fine Gothic cathedral (see pp230–31) surrounded by delightful historic buildings.*

Douaumont Memorial

Porte Chaussée Verdun

Place Stanislas, Nancy

Strasbourg Cathedral

CHAMPAGNE
(See pp206–217)

ALSACE AND LORRAINE
(See pp218–33)

Haut-Koenigsbourg

0 kilometres   50

0 miles   50

The Flavours of Northeast France

The cuisine of northeast France is robust and warming, with rich beef stews, suckling pig, sausages and hams, dumplings and sauerkraut dishes, many of them closely related to German or Flemish staples. There is good fish from the Atlantic and from freshwater lakes and rivers. Vegetables and fruit are produced in abundance, and often served in a variety of savoury and sweet tarts, of which *quiche lorraine*, with bacon, eggs and cream, is the best known. Rich cakes are popular, especially *Kougelhopf*, a ring-shaped cake of raisins and almonds soaked in kirsch, and madeleine sponge cakes.

Leeks from a local market

The market gardens *(hortillons)* of Picardy are famous for their vegetables, often made into delicious soups. Leeks or chicory, braised or in gratins, accompany many dishes. Strong, washed-rind cheeses, such as Maroilles, are typical of the region.

Beer is often drunk with meals in the northeast, where traditional methods and small breweries thrive.

CHAMPAGNE

Champagne encompasses arable plains, wooded uplands as well as vineyards, and produces game, *charcuterie* and delicious freshwater fish. Nothing, however, can compete with its main claim to fame, Champagne itself, which is often used as a luxury cooking ingredient as well as, of course, being enjoyed in its own right.

Golden mirabelle plums alongside the more usual variety

LE NORD AND PICARDY

The northern coast offers a wide variety of fish dishes, the most popular being steamed mussels served with chips (fries). Herrings are pickled, soused, grilled or smoked and North Sea shrimps fried and eaten whole. Chicken may be cooked in beer, duck is made into pies and terrines, and eel served smoked as a starter.

Brioche   Ancienne   Madeleines   Boule de campagne
Siegle (rye)   Poïlane
Tarte d'abricots
Selection of typical regional breads and patisserie

REGIONAL DISHES AND SPECIALITIES

The classic dish of the region is *choucroute garni*, a platter of pickled cabbage, flavoured with juniper berries, and cooked with white wine, ham hock and smoked pork belly. Smoked Montbeliard and Strasbourg sausages are added towards the end of cooking. Sausages come in many variations, from *saucisses de Strasbourg* to *bratwurst*, made from
Beetroot   veal and pork, *lewerzurscht* (liver sausage), *andouillettes* (spicy chitterling sausages), *boudin noir* (black pudding of pork and pig's blood) and *boudin blanc* (white meat without blood). There are also smoked hams, cooked hams and many different terrines, such as *presskopf* (pig's brawn in jelly) and the jellied white meat terrine, *potjevleesch. Langue lucullus* is smoked ox tongue studded with *foie gras*, a speciality of Valenciennes.

Ficelle picardie *Pancakes are filled with mushrooms and ham in creme fraîche sauce, and baked with grated cheese.*

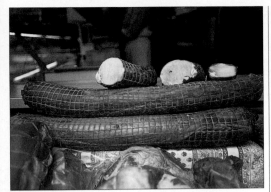
Display of traditional northern French charcuterie

Wild boar, deer, rabbit, hare, quail, partridge and woodcock are all found in the Ardennes, made into game pâtés and terrines as well as roasts and stews. The Ardennes is also noted for its fine quality smoked ham, while *jambon de Reims* is cooked ham with mustard, champagne and Reims vinegar. Troyes is famous for its *andouillettes*, usually served with onions or baked in a creamy mustard sauce. Fish come from the small lakes east of Troyes and trout are abundant in the clear streams of the Ardennes. The two best cheeses of Champagne are Chaource and Langres.

ALSACE AND LORRAINE

Rolling pastures, orchards, pine forests and rivers produce the ingredients of

Alsatian cooking. Meat is important, particularly pork, roasted or made into hams and sausages. In winter, game stews abound. There is a strong tradition of raising geese; after all, *foie gras* production originated in

Shopping at the fish market in the port of Boulogne

Strasbourg. The rivers are a good source of pike, trout, crayfish and carp, often cooked in beer and served on festive occasions. Locally grown vegetables include cabbage, potatoes and turnips, and fruit includes bilberries, quince, redcurrants and the golden mirabelle plums of Lorraine, the latter prized for both jam and *eau de vie* (fruit brandy). The best-known cheese is Munster, a soft cow's milk cheese.

The white wines of Alsace range from steely, bone-dry Riesling (the region's finest variety) to aromatic Muscat and Gerwurztraminer. For more on the wines of Alsace, see pp232–3.

ON THE MENU

Anguille au vert Eel baked with green herbs and potatoes.

Cassolette de petits gris Snails in champagne sauce.

Flamiche aux poireaux Leek tart.

Flammekueche Pizza style tart topped with bacon, creme fraîche and onions.

Marcassin à l'Ardennaise Wild boar with celeriac.

Potée champenoise Pork, ham, sausage, beans and vegetable stew.

Potée Lorraine Casserole of salt pork with vegetables.

Zewelwai A rich onion tart.

Truite à l'Ardennaise *Trout is stuffed with breadcrumbs and finely chopped Ardennes ham, then baked.*

Carbonnade de boeuf *Steak and caramelized onions are covered with beer and cooked for three hours.*

Babas au rhum *These are dry yeast cakes of raisins, eggs and butter, doused in rum and served with cream.*

France's Wine Regions: Champagne

Since its fabled "invention" by the monk Dom Pérignon in the 17th century, no other wine has rivalled champagne as the symbol of luxury and celebration. Only wines made in this region by the *Méthode Champenoise* can be called champagne *(see p210)*. Most champagne is non-vintage: the skill of the blenders, using reserves of older wines, creates consistency and excellence year on year. The "big names" *(grandes marques)*, command the prestige and

Giant carved barrel, Épernay

prices, but many small growers and cooperatives also produce excellent-value wines well worth seeking out.

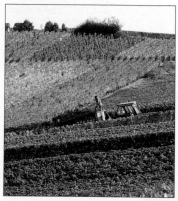

Grapes going for pressing, Montagne de Reims

WINE REGIONS

Champagne is a compact wine region, largely in the French *département* of the Marne. Certain areas within it are particularly identified with certain styles of wine. The Aube produces 25 per cent of all champagne as well as the exclusive Rosé des Riceys.

Soissons

D1

A4

Châte. Thierr

La Ferté-sous-Jouarre

N3

D407

Petit Morin

Grand Morin

KEY FACTS ABOUT CHAMPAGNE

Location and Climate
The cool, marginal climate creates the finesse that other sparkling wines strive for, but seldom achieve. Chalky soils and east- and north-facing aspects help produce the relatively high acidity champagne needs.

Grape Varieties
Three varieties are grown, red **Pinot Noir** and **Pinot Meunier**, and white **Chardonnay**. Most champagne is a blend of all three, though Blanc de Blancs is 100 per cent Chardonnay and Blanc de Noirs, although white, is made only from red grapes.

Good Producers
Grandes Marques: Bollinger, Gosset, Krug, Möet et Chandon, Joseph Perrier, Louis Roederer, Pol Roger, Billecart-Salmon, Veuve Clicquot, Taittinger, Ruinart, Laurent Perrier, Salon.
Négociants, cooperatives & growers: Boizel, M Arnould, Cattier, Bricout, Drappier, Ployez-Jacquemart, H Blin, Gimmonet, Andre Jacquart, Chartogne-Taillet, Vilmart, Alfred Gratien, Emile Hamm, B Paillard, P Gerbais.

Good Vintages
2005, 2003, 2000, 1998, 1996, 1990.

BOLLINGER
Spécial Cuvée
BRUT
Champagne ... *Ay-France*

From a name *famous even to non-wine lovers, this is in the classic* brut *(dry) style; only* brut non dosage *or* brut sauvage *is drier.*

Nogent-sur-Seine

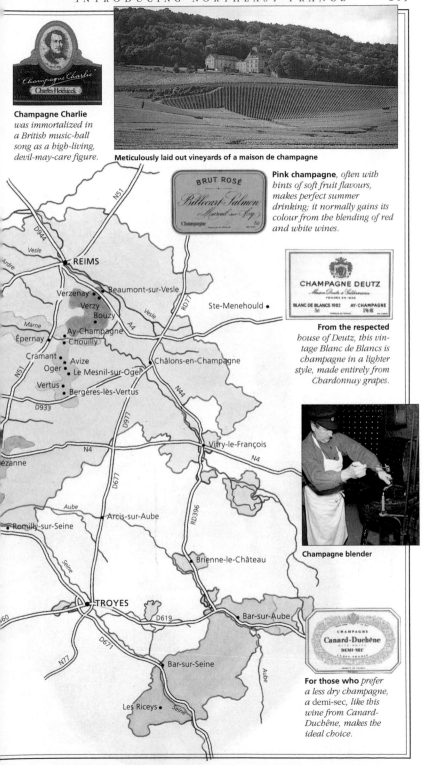

Champagne Charlie *was immortalized in a British music-hall song as a high-living, devil-may-care figure.*

Meticulously laid out vineyards of a maison de champagne

Pink champagne, *often with hints of soft fruit flavours, makes perfect summer drinking; it normally gains its colour from the blending of red and white wines.*

BRUT ROSÉ
Billecart-Salmon
Mareuil sur Aÿ
Champagne

CHAMPAGNE DEUTZ
Maison Deutz & Geldermann
FONDÉE EN 1838
BLANC DE BLANCS 1982   AŸ-CHAMPAGNE

From the respected *house of Deutz, this vintage Blanc de Blancs is champagne in a lighter style, made entirely from Chardonnay grapes.*

REIMS

Verzenay • Beaumont-sur-Vesle
Verzy
Bouzy
Ay-Champagne
Épernay • Chouilly
Cramant • Avize
Oger • Le Mesnil-sur-Oger
Vertus • Bergères-lès-Vertus

Ste-Menehould •

Châlons-en-Champagne

Vitry-le-François

Arcis-sur-Aube
• Romilly-sur-Seine

Brienne-le-Château

Champagne blender

TROYES

Bar-sur-Aube

Bar-sur-Seine

Les Riceys •

CHAMPAGNE
Canard-Duchêne
DEMI-SEC

For those who *prefer a less dry champagne, a demi-sec, like this wine from Canard-Duchêne, makes the ideal choice.*

The Battle of the Somme

The many cemeteries that cover the Somme region serve as a poignant reminder of the mass slaughter that took place on the Western Front in World War I (which ended with the Armistice on 11 November 1918). Between 1 July and 21 November 1916, the Allied forces lost more than 600,000 men and the Germans at least 465,000. The Battle of the Somme, a series of campaigns conducted by British and French armies against fortified positions held by the Germans, relieved the hard-pressed French at Verdun; but hopes of a breakthrough never materialized, and the Allies only managed to advance 16 km (10 miles).

British World War I soldier

Beaumont Hamel Memorial Park, a tribute to the Royal Newfoundland Regiment, has a huge bronze caribou.

Thiepval Memorial *was designed by Sir Edwin Lutyens. It dominates the landscape of Thiepval, one of the most hard-fought areas of the battle, appropriately chosen as a memorial to the 73,367 British soldiers with no known grave.*

Albert *was the site of heavy bombardment by German artillery in 1916. Today, the town is a convenient centre for visiting the battlefields. The Albert Basilique, with its leaning Virgin statue, was damaged but is now restored. It was a landmark for thousands of troops.*

Lochnager Mine Crater, formed by the largest of the British mines exploded on 1 July, 1916, lies on the ridge by La Boiselle.

The British Tank Memorial, *on the main road from Albert to Bapaume, commemorates the first use of tanks in warfare on 15 September, 1916. The attack was a limited success; the tanks of World War I were too few before 1918 to transform warfare dominated by artillery, machine guns and barbed wire.*

Propaganda in World War I *was employed by both sides to maintain support at home. This French postcard has a popular image for civilian consumption. It shows a dying soldier kissing the flag, under the tender gaze of a ministering nurse, affirming his faith in the cause with his last breath.*

Delville Wood South African Memorial and Museum show the importance of Commonwealth forces in the Somme.

VISITORS' CHECKLIST

D929, D938 from Albert.
🛈 *30 pl de la République, 80800 Corbie. Tel 03 22 96 95 76.*
www.*tourisme-albert.net* **Albert Basilique, Beaumont Hamel Memorial Park, Delville Wood, La Boiselle, Thiepval & Pozières memorials** ◯ *daily.* **Ulster Tower** ◯ *Feb–Mar: Tue–Sun; Apr–Nov: daily.* **South African Memorial,** *Delville Wood, Longueval. Tel 03 22 85 02 17.* ◯ *Feb–Nov: Tue–Sun.* ● *hols.*
Historial de Péronne
***Tel** 03 22 83 14 18.* ◯ *May–Sep: daily; Oct– Apr: Tue–Sun.* ● *mid-Dec–mid-Jan.* 🎫 ♿ ✔ ▢ 🛈
www.*historial.org*

Poppies were one of the few plants to grow on the battlefield. Ghengis Khan brought the first white poppy from China and, according to legend, it turned red after battle. Today poppies are a symbol of remembrance.

KEY

◼	Allied forces
◻	German forces
◻	Front Line before 1 July, 1916
◻	Front Line progress July–September 1916
◼	Front Line progress September–November 1916

0 kilometres   5

0 miles   5

The Front Line trenches *stretched from the North Sea to the Swiss frontier; only by keeping underground could men survive the terrible conditions. Trenches remain in a few areas, including the Beaumont Hamel Park.*

LE NORD
AND PICARDY

PAS DE CALAIS · NORD · SOMME · OISE · AISNE

*B*eneath the modern skin of France's northernmost region, the
sights and monuments bear witness to the triumphs and turbulence of its past: soaring Gothic cathedrals, stately châteaux
along the river Oise, and the battlefields and memorials of World War I.

The Channel ports of
Dunkerque, Calais and
Boulogne, and the refined
resort of Le Touquet, are the
focal points along a busy
coastline that stretches from
the Somme estuary to the
Belgian frontier. Boulogne has
a genuine maritime flavour, and the
white cliffs running from here to
Calais provide the most dramatic
scenery along the Côte d'Opale.

Flemish culture holds sway along
the border with Belgium: an unfamiliar France of windmills and canals
where the local taste is for beer, hot-
pots and festivals with gallivanting
giants. Lille is the dominant city here,
a sprawling modern metropolis with
a lively historic heart and an excellent
art museum. To the southwest, the
grace of Flemish architecture is handsomely displayed in the central
squares of Arras, the capital of Artois.

From here to the Somme
valley the legacy of World
War I, with its memorial
cemeteries and poppy-
strewn battlefields, makes
compelling viewing.

Cathedrals are the main
appeal of Picardy. In Amiens,
its capital, Cathédrale Notre-Dame is
a pinnacle of the Gothic style – its
magnificence echoed by the dizzying
achievements at Beauvais further
south. Splendid cathedrals at Noyon,
Senlis and the delightful hilltop town
of Laon chart the evolution of the
Gothic. Closer to Paris, two châteaux
command attention. Chantilly, the epicentre of French equestrianism, boasts
gardens by Le Nôtre and a 19th-century
château housing copious art treasures.
Compiègne, bordered by a large and
inviting forest, plays host to a lavish
royal palace favoured by French rulers
from Louis XV to Napoleon III.

Memorial cemetery in Vallée de la Somme, an area still haunted by the memory of World War I

◁ Catamarans on the busy beach of Le Touquet Paris-Plage

Exploring Le Nord and Picardy

As the gateway to England and Belgium, this northern corner of France is buzzing with business and industries, with the large, Euro-oriented city of Lille offering great culture as well as a new high-tech district. Yet peace and quiet is never far away. The coast between the historic port of Boulogne-sur-Mer and the Vallée de la Somme has a rich birdlife and is perfect for a relaxing seaside visit. Inland, the many Gothic cathedrals such as Amiens and Beauvais make an impressive tour, and the World War I battlefields and memorials provide an important insight into 20th-century history. Further south, the grand châteaux at Compiègne and Chantilly – which has the fascinating Musée Condé – are easily visited en route to or from Paris.

KEY

- Motorway
- Major road
- Secondary road
- Minor road
- Scenic route
- Main railway
- Minor railway
- International border
- Regional border

Lively outdoor café in the historic Grand' place in the heart of Arras

Channel Tunnel
Cap Blanc-Nez
Cap Griz Nez
DUNKERQUE ④ Malo-les-t
Gravelines
③ CALAIS
Bergues
Guînes
FLANDRE MARITIM'
⑥
Cassel
Wimereux
SAINT-OMER ⑤ Arques
BOULOGNE- La Coupole
SUR-MER ②
Hazebr
Desvres
Aire-sur-la
Samer
Fauquembergues
Béthun
LE TOUQUET ① Étaples
Bruay-la-Buissière
Montreuil-sur-Mer
Berck-sur-Mer
Hesdin
Fort-Mahon-Plage
Saint-Pol -sur-Ternoise
Tincq
Vron
Crécy-en- Frévent
NOR
Ponthieu
Le Crotoy
Nouvion
Douliens
La Pomn
Saint-Valéry- sur-Somme
Bernaville
Abbeville
VALLÉE DE
Ault
Fressenneville
LA SOMME
Dieppe
Plixecourt ⑨
N25
Albe
Gamaches
Airaines
Samara
Rouen
Picquigny
Corb
Hornoy
AMIENS ⑩
Aumale
Saint-Sauflieu
Poix-de- Picardie
Essertaux
Bouc
Grandvilliers
Breteuil
Marseille- en-Beauvaisis
Montd'
Crèvecœur -le-Grand
Wavignies
Songeons
Gournay-en-Bray
Saint-Just- en-Chaussée
BEAUVAIS ⑪
Bresles
Clermor
Noailles
Gisors
Mouy
Creil
SEN
Méru
CHANTILLY ⑯
PARC ASTERIX
Paris

0 kilometres   25

0 miles   25

For additional map symbols see back flap

SIGHTS AT A GLANCE

The meandering waters in the Vallée de la Somme

GETTING AROUND

The main entry point into the region is Calais (and the Channel Tunnel terminal 3 km/2 miles south). From here, autoroutes A16 and A26/A1, several major N and D roads, and mainline rail services run directly to Paris. In addition, TGVs serve Calais-Frethun, Lille and Paris. There is a dense road network throughout the region. With their many local bus and train connections, Lille and Amiens make good bases. The A26 (or *Autoroute des Anglais*) crosses the whole region from Calais to Troyes, via Arras and Laon, giving easy access to eastern Picardy. It's also a useful route if you're heading south and want to avoid Paris.

Poppies, the symbol of World War I battlefields, in the Vallée de la Somme

Le Touquet beach at low tide

Le Touquet ❶

Pas de Calais. 🏘 5,500. 🚆 🚌
ℹ️ *Palais de l'Europe (03 21 06 72 00).*
🛒 *Thu & Sat (Jun–mid-Sep: also Mon).*
www.letouquet.com

Properly known as Le
Touquet Paris-Plage, this
resort was created in the 19th
century and became fashionable with the rich and famous
between the two World Wars.

A vast pine forest, planted in
1855, spreads around the
town sheltering stately villas.
To the west, a grid of smart
hotels, holiday residences
and sophisticated shops and
restaurants borders a long,
sandy beach. A racecourse
and casino are complemented
by seaside amusements and
sports facilities, including two
excellent golf courses, horse-
riding and land yachting.

Further inland, the hilltop
town of **Montreuil** has lime-
washed 17th-century houses,
abundant restaurants and a
tree-shaded rampart walk.

Boulogne-sur-Mer ❷

Pas de Calais. 🏘 45,000. 🚆 🚌
ℹ️ *Parvis de Nausicaa (03 21 10 88
10).* 🛒 *Wed & Sat (pl Dalton), Sun (pl
Vignon).* **www.**tourisme-
boulognesurmer.com

An important fishing port
and busy marina, Boulogne
rewards its visitors well. Its
attractions come neatly boxed
in a walled Haute Ville, with
the Porte des Dunes opening
on to a 17th–19th-century

ensemble of Palais de Justice,
Bibliothèque and Hôtel de Ville
in **place de la Résistance**.

The 19th-century **Basilique
Notre-Dame** is capped by a
dome visible for miles. Inside,
a bejewelled wooden statue
represents Boulogne's
patroness, Notre-Dame de
Boulogne. She is wearing a
soleil, a head-dress also worn
by women during the *Grande
Procession* held annually in
her honour. Nearby, the powerful moated 13th-century
Château, built for the Counts
of Boulogne, is now a well-
organized historical museum.

In the centre of town, shops,
hotels and fish restaurants
line the quai Gambetta on the
east bank of the river Liane.
To the north lie Boulogne's
beach and **Nausicaa**, a vast,
spectacular and innovative
aquarium and Sea Centre.

North of the town, the
Colonne de la Grande Armée
was erected in 1841 as a monument to Napoleon I's planned
invasion of England in 1803–5.
From the top there is a panoramic view along the coast
towards Calais. This is the most
scenic stretch of the Côte
d'Opale (Opal Coast), with the

windblown headlands of **Cap
Gris-Nez** and **Cap Blanc-Nez**
offering breathtakingly extensive views across the Channel.

♟ **Château**
Rue de Bernet. **Tel** 03 21 10 02 20.
⭕ *Tue–Sun.* ⬤ *1 Jan, 1 May,
24 Dec–2 Jan.* 🈂️

🐟 **Nausicaa**
Bd Sainte-Beuve. **Tel** 03 21 30 99
99. ⭕ *daily.* ⬤ *3 wks Jan, 25 Dec.*
🈂️ ♿ **www.**nausicaa.fr

Calais ❸

Pas de Calais. 🏘 76,000. 🚆 🚌
🚢 ℹ️ *12 bd Clémenceau (03 21 96
62 40).* 🛒 *Wed, Thu & Sat.*
www.calais-cotedopale.com

Calais is a busy cross-Channel
port with a sandy beach to the
west. Clumsily rebuilt after
World War II, it seems to have
little to offer at first sight. Many
visitors never get closer than
the huge Cité Europe shopping
mall by the Eurotunnel exit.

The **Musée des Beaux Arts**,
however, has works by the
Dutch and Flemish Schools.
Also on show are studies for
Auguste Rodin's famous stat-
ue *The Burghers of Calais*

The windswept Cap Blanc-Nez on the Côte d'Opale

For hotels and restaurants in this region see pp556–8 and pp607–10

The Burghers of Calais by Auguste Rodin (1895)

(1895). The statue stands outside the Hôtel de Ville, and celebrates an event during Edward III's siege of Calais in 1347, when six burghers offered their lives to save the rest of the town.

The **Cité de la Dentelle et de la Mode** recalls the town's lace-making industry.

Musée de la Guerre, housed in a battle-scarred German blockhouse, offers a detailed account of local events during World War II.

🏛 **Musée des Beaux Arts**
25 rue Richelieu. *Tel* 03 21 46 48 40. ☐ Tue–Sat, Sun pm. 🈂 ♿

🏛 **Cité de la Dentelle**
Quai du Commerce. *Tel* 03 21 46 43 14. ☐ Wed–Sun. 🈂

🏛 **Musée de la Guerre**
Parc Saint Pierre. *Tel* 03 21 34 21 57. ☐ call for opening times. 🈂 ♿

Dunkerque ❹

Nord. 🏠 376,000. 🚇 🚌 ⛴
ℹ *Rue Amiral Ronarc'h (03 28 66 79 21).* 🏠 Wed, Sat.
www.ot-dunkerque.fr

Though a major industrial port, Dunkerque has much Flemish character. Start a tour from place du Minck, with its fresh fish stalls. Nearby **Musée Portuaire** celebrates the town's maritime history. In the old centre, a statue commemorates local hero Jean Bart, a 17th-century corsair, who lies in **Eglise St-Eloi**. Its belfry (1440) offers fine views.

Le Mémorial du Souvenir has an exhibition of the dramatic evacuation of 350,000 British and French troops in 1940. The **Lieu d'Art et d'Action Contemporaine (LAAC)** features ceramics and glassware.

🏛 **Musée Portuaire**
9 quai de la Citadelle. *Tel* 03 28 63 33 39. ☐ Wed–Mon. ● 1 Jan, 1 May, 25 Dec. 🈂 ♿

The port at Dunkerque

🏛 **Le Memorial du Souvenir**
32 Courtines du Bastion. *Tel* 03 28 66 79 21. ☐ Wed–Mon.
● 1 Jan, 1 Nov, 25 Dec. 🈂 🚻
♿ gr. fl. only.

🏛 **Lieu d'Art et d'Action Contemporaine**
Av des Bains. *Tel* 03 28 29 56 00.
☐ Tue–Sun. ● pub hols. 🈂 ♿

St-Omer ❺

Pas de Calais. 🏠 15,000. 🚇 🚌 ℹ 4 rue Lion d'Or (03 21 98 08 51). 🏠 Sat. www.tourisme-saintomer.com

Refined St-Omer seems untouched. Pilasters adorn the 17th- and 18th-century houses lining the cobbled streets, one of which, **Hôtel Sandelin**, is now a museum of fine and decorative arts. The cathedral has original 13th-century tiles and a huge organ. The **Bibliothèque Municipale** contains rare manuscripts from the Abbaye St-Bertin, a ruined 15th-century abbey east of town.

5 km (3 miles) from St-Omer, **La Coupole** is an informative WWII museum inside a converted bunker.

🏛 **Hôtel Sandelin**
14 rue Carnot. *Tel* 03 21 38 00 94. ☐ Wed–Sun. 🈂 ♿ gr. fl.

🏛 **Bibliothèque Municipale**
40 rue Gambetta. *Tel* 03 21 38 35 08. ☐ Tue–Sat. ● public hols.

🏛 **La Coupole**
Tel 03 21 12 27 27. ☐ daily.
● last week Dec–first week Jan.

CHANNEL CROSSINGS

Calais is only 36 km (22 miles) southeast of the English coast, and crossing the waters of the Channel – which the French know as La Manche (the Sleeve) – has inspired many intrepid exploits. The first crossing by balloon was in 1785 by Jean Pierre Blanchard; Captain M Webb made the first swim in 1875; and Louis Blériot's pioneering flight followed in 1909. Plans for an undersea tunnel, first laid as early as 1751, were finally achieved in 1994 with the opening of a railway link between Fréthun and Folkestone.

Children watching Louis Blériot taking off, 1909

Flandre Maritime ❻

Nord. 🏠 *5,000.* 🚊 *Lille.* 🚌 *Bergues.*
🚢 *Dunkerque.* 🛈 *Bergues, Le Beffroi,
pl Henri Billiaert (03 28 68 71 06).*

South of Dunkerque lies a flat, agricultural plain with narrow waterways and expansive skies – an archetypal Flemish landscape with canals, cyclists and ancient windmills. The **Noordmeulen**, built just north of Hondschoote in 1127, is thought to be the oldest windmill in Europe.

From Hondschoote the D3 follows the Canal de la Basse Colme west to Bergues, a fortified wool town with fine 16th–17th-century Flemish works in its **Musée Municipal**. Further south, the hilltop town of **Cassel** has a cobbled Grande place with 16th–18th-century buildings, and views across Flanders and Belgium from its Jardin Public.

🏛 **Musée Municipal**
1 rue du Mont de Piété, Bergues.
***Tel** 03 28 68 13 30.* ☐ *Thu–Mon.*
⬤ *Oct–Apr.* 📷

Lille ❼

Nord. 🏠 *232,000.* ✈ 🚊 🚌
🛈 *Palais Rihour (03 59 57 94 00).*
🗓 *daily.* **www**.lilletourism.com

Transformed in recent years, not least by the advent of Eurostar and its election as European City of Culture 2004,

Flower stalls in the arcades of the Vieille Bourse in Lille

Musicians in place du Général de Gaulle, in the heart of Vieux Lille

Lille has excellent shops and markets and a powerful sense of its historic Flemish identity – the Flemish name, Rijssel, is still used and some of the area's one million residents speak a Franco-Flemish patois. With heavy industry declining, the city has turned to high-tech. A modern commercial quarter, including the Euralille shopping complex, adjoins Lille Europe station, the TGV/Eurostar/Thalys rail interchange. The city's "metro" VAL, is a driverless automatic train.

The city's charm lies in its historic centre, Vieux Lille – a mass of cobbled squares and narrow streets that are packed with stylish shops, cafés and restaurants. Place du Général de Gaulle forms its hub, with façades including the 17th-century **Vieille Bourse** (Old Exchange). Adjacent stand the **Nouvelle Bourse** and the **Opéra**, both built in the early 20th century. The moated

five-point brick Citadel by Vauban is also worth a look.

🏛 **Musée de l'Hospice Comtesse**
32 rue de la Monnaie. ***Tel** 03 28 36 84 00.* ☐ *Wed–Sun, Mon pm.* 📷
A hospital was founded here in 1237. Now its 15th- and 17th-century buildings house exhibitions. The Sick Room has a barrel-vaulted ceiling, the Community Wing a Delft kitchen. There is a collection of ancient instruments.

🏛 **Palais des Beaux-Arts**
Pl de la République. ***Tel** 03 20 06 78 00.*
☐ *Wed–Sun, Mon pm.* 📷 🎫 ♿
One of the best art collections outside Paris, the museum is strong on Flemish works, including Rubens and Van Dyck. Other highlights are *Paradise and Hell* by Dirk Bouts, Van Goyen's *The Skaters*, Goya's *The Letter*, Delacroix's *Médée*, as well as works by Courbet and Impressionist paintings.

Arras ❽

Pas de Calais. 🏠 45,000. 🚇 🚉
ℹ️ Hôtel de Ville, pl des Héros
(03 21 51 26 95). 🛒 Wed, Sat.
www.ot-arras.fr

The centre of Arras, capital of the Artois region, is graced by two picturesque cobbled squares enclosed by 155 houses with 17th-century Flemish-style façades. A triumph of postwar reconstruction, each residence in the **Grand' place** and the smaller place des Héros has a slightly varying design, with some original shop signs still visible.

A monumental **Hôtel de Ville** rebuilt in the Flamboyant Gothic style stands at the west end of place des Héros – in the foyer are two giants, Colas Dédé and Jacqueline, who swagger round the town during local festivals. From the basement you can take a lift up to the belfry for superb views, or take a guided tour into the labyrinth of underground passages below Arras. These were cut in the limestone in the 10th century. They have often served as shelter; during World War I as a subterranean army camp.

The huge Abbaye St-Vaast includes an 18th–19th-century Neo-Classical cathedral and the **Musée des Beaux-Arts**. The museum contains some fine examples of medieval sculpture including

a pair of beautiful 13th-century angels. Among other exhibits are a local *arras* (hanging tapestry) and 19th-century works by the School of Arras, a group of realist landscape painters.

🏛 Hôtel de Ville
Pl des Héros. **Tel** 03 21 51 26 95. ⏰ Jul–Aug: daily. 📷 oblig for tunnels. 🎫

🏛 Musée des Beaux-Arts
22 rue Paul Doumer. **Tel** 03 21 71 26 43. ⏰ Wed–Mon. ● pub hols. 🎫

Vallée de la Somme ❾

Somme. 🚊 🚇 🚉 Amiens. ℹ️ 16 pl André Audinot, Péronne (03 22 84 42 38). **www**.somme-tourisme.com

The name of the Somme is synonymous with the slaughter and horror of trench warfare during World War I *(see pp190–91)*. Yet the Somme valley also means pretty countryside, a vast estuary wetland and abundant wildlife. Lakes and woods alongside provide enjoyable camping, walking and fishing.

Battlefields lie along the river and its tributaries north and northeast of Amiens, and extend north to Arras. Neat World War I Commonwealth cemeteries cover the area. The **Historial de la Grande Guerre** at Péronne gives a thoughtful introduction. Parc Mémorial Beaumont-Hamel,

Boating on the river Somme

near Albert, is a real battlefield being allowed to disappear in its own time. Travel to Vimy Ridge Canadian Memorial, near Arras, to see a bloodbath battle site preserved as it was, and to Notre-Dame de Lorette, the landmark French National Cemetery.

West of Amiens, **Samara** – Amiens' Gallo-Roman name – is France's largest archaeological park, with reconstructions of prehistoric dwellings, and exhibitions explaining early crafts like flint-cutting and corn-grinding. Further downstream, Eglise St-Vulfran at Abbeville is noted for its Flamboyant Gothic west front with beautifully carved 16th-century door panels.

St-Valéry-sur-Somme is a charming harbour resort with a historic upper town and a tree-lined promenade looking across the estuary. William departed for England from here in 1066. Birdwatchers should visit the Maison de l'Oiseau on the D3 nearby, or the Parc Ornithologique de Marquenterre on the far shore near delightful Le Crotoy. In summer, a little train links the two sides, passing through dunes and marshes.

🏛 Historial de la Grande Guerre
Château de Péronne. **Tel** 03 22 83 14 18. ⏰ Apr–Sep: daily; Oct–Mar: Tue–Sun. ● mid-Dec–mid-Jan. 🎫 🚻 📷 **www**.historial.org

🏛 Samara
La Chaussée-Tirancourt. **Tel** 03 22 51 82 83. ⏰ mid-Mar–mid-Nov: daily. 🎫 🚻 📷 **www**.samara.fr

Roadside shrine, Somme Valley

16th-century carvings on Eglise St-Vulfran in Abbeville, Somme Valley

Amiens ➓

Somme. ⓘ 130,000. � 🚍 ⓘ
6 bis rue Duvevel (03 22
71 60 50). 🖻 Wed & Sat.
www.amiens-tourisme.com

There is more to Amiens, the
capital of Picardy, than its
Cathédrale Notre-Dame (see
pp202–3). The picturesque
quarter of St-Leu is a pedestrianized area of low houses and
flower-lined canals with waterside restaurants, bars and
artisans' shops. Further east are
Les Hortillonnages, a colourful
patchwork of marshland
market gardens, once tended
by farmers using punts which
now ferry visitors around the
protected natural site.
    The **Musée de Picardie** has
many fine medieval and
19th-century sculptures and
16th–20th-century paintings,
including a remarkable set of
16th-century group portraits,
commissioned as offerings to
the cathedral. To the south is
the Cirque d'Hiver which Jules
Verne (1828–1905) inaugurated
in 1889. **Maison de Jules Verne**,
his renovated home, has over
700 objects spread over four
floors relating to the famous
author, who lived here from
1882 until 1900.

🏛 **Musée de Picardie**
48 rue de la République. **Tel** 03 22
97 14 00. ◯ Tue–Sun. ● 1 Jan,
1 May, 1 Nov, 11 Nov, 25 Dec. 🖾 🕭

🏛 **Maison de Jules Verne**
2 rue Charles Dubois. **Tel** 03 22 45
45 75. ◯ Easter–mid-Oct: daily;
mid-Oct–Easter: Wed–Mon. 🖾

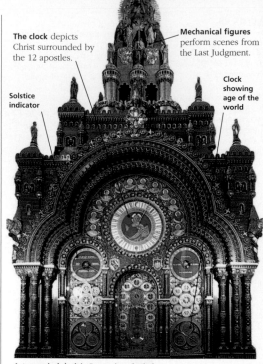

The clock depicts
Christ surrounded by
the 12 apostles.

**Solstice
indicator**

Mechanical figures
perform scenes from
the Last Judgment.

**Clock
showing
age of the
world**

Astronomical clock in Beauvais cathedral

Beauvais ➓➓

Oise. ⓘ 61,000. ✈ 🚍 🚍 ⓘ 1 rue
Beauregard (03 44 15 30 30). 🖻 Wed
& Sat. **www**.beauvaistourisme.fr

Heavily bombed in World
War II, Beauvais is now a
modern town with one
outstanding jewel. Though
never completed, **Cathédrale
St-Pierre** is a poignant, neck-
cracking finale to the vaulting
ambition that created the great

Gothic cathedrals. In 1227
work began on a building
designed to soar above all predecessors, but the roof of the
chancel caved in twice from
lack of support before its
completion in the early 14th
century. Delayed by wars and
inadequate funds, the transept
was not completed until 1550.
In 1573 its crossing collapsed
after a tower and spire were
added. What remains today is
nevertheless a masterpiece,
rising 48 m (157 ft) high.
In the transept much of the
original 16th-century stained
glass survives, while near the
north door is a 90,000-part
astronomical clock assembled
in the 1860s. What would
have been the nave is still
occupied by the remnants of
a 10th-century church known
as the Basse-Oeuvre.
    The former Bishop's Palace
is now home to the **Musée
Départemental de l'Oise**.
The collection includes
archaeological finds, medieval
sculpture, tapestries and local
ceramics. Beauvais has a long
tradition of tapestry manufacture, and examples from

VIOLLET-LE-DUC

The renowned architectural theorist Viollet-le-Duc (1814–79)
was the first to fully appreciate Gothic architecture. His
1854 dictionary of architecture celebrated medieval building
techniques, showing that the
arches and tracery of Gothic
cathedrals were solutions
to architectural problems,
not mere decoration. His
restoration work included
Château de Pierrefonds,
Notre-Dame in Paris
(see pp86–7) and Car-
cassonne (see pp488–9).

**Medieval architects, as
drawn by Viollet-le-Duc**

the French national collection are shown in the **Galerie Nationale de la Tapisserie.**

🏛 **Musée Départemental de l'Oise**
Ancien Palais Episcopal, 1 rue du Musée. *Tel 03 44 10 40 50.* ⭘ *Wed–Mon.* ⬤ *1 Jan, Easter, 1 May, 9 Jun, 1 Nov, 25 Dec.* 🖼

🏛 **Galerie Nationale de la Tapisserie**
22 rue St-Pierre. *Tel 03 44 15 39 10.* ⭘ *Tue–Sun.* 🖼 ⬤ *1 Jan, 1 May, 25 Dec.*

Noyon ⑫

Oise. 🏠 *15,200.* 🚉 🗩 *pl de l'Hôtel de Ville (03 44 44 21 88).* 🛒 *Wed & Sat, first Tue of each month.* **www**.noyon-tourisme.com

Noyon has long been a religious centre. The **Cathédrale de Notre-Dame**, dating from 1150, is the fifth to be built on this site and was completed by 1290. It provides a harmonious example of the transition from Romanesque to Gothic style.

A local history museum, the **Musée du Noyonnais**, occupies part of the former Bishop's Palace, and at the cathedral's east end is a rare half-timbered chapter library built in 1506.

Jean Calvin, the Protestant theologian and one of the leaders of the Reformation, was born here in 1509 and is commemorated in the small **Musée Jean Calvin.**

🏛 **Musée du Noyonnais**
Ancien Palais Episcopal, 7 rue de l'Evêché. *Tel 03 44 09 43 41.* ⭘ *Wed-Mon.* ⬤ *1 Jan, 11 Nov, 25 Dec.* 🖼

The rib-vaulted nave of Cathédrale de Notre-Dame, Noyon

Path through Forêt de Compiègne

Compiègne ⑬

Oise. 🏠 *70,000.* 🚉 🗩 🗩 *pl de l'Hôtel de Ville (03 44 40 01 00).* 🛒 *Wed & Sat.* **www**.compiegne-tourisme.fr

Compiegne is where Joan of Arc was captured by the Burgundians in 1430. A 16th-century Hôtel de Ville with a towering belfry rules over the centre, but the town is most famous for its royal **Château**.

Designed as a summer residence for Louis XV, the château was completed by Louis XVI, restored by Napoleon and later became a residence of Napoleon III and Empress Eugénie. Tours of the Imperial Apartments take in private chambers, such as the sumptuous bedrooms of Napoleon I and Marie-Louise.

Within the château, the Musée du Second Empire and Musée de l'Impératrice display furniture, memorabilia and portraits, while the Musée de la Voiture is an entertaining assembly of historic carriages, bicycles and early motor cars.

South and east of the town, the old hunting grounds of **Forêt de Compiègne** spread as far as Pierrefonds, with ample space for walks and picnics beneath its oaks and beeches. East of the D130, Les Beaux Monts provide majestic views back to the château.

The Clairière de l'Armistice, north of the N31, marks the spot where the armistice of World War I was signed on 11 November 1918. The small **Musée Wagon de l'Armistice** has a replica of the railway

carriage where the ceremony took place, which was used again in World War II by Hitler as a humiliating venue for the signing of the French surrender on 22 June 1940.

♣ **Château de Compiègne**
Pl du Général de Gaulle. *Tel 03 44 38 47 02.* ⭘ *Wed–Mon.* ⬤ *1 Jan, 1 May, 25 Dec.* 🖼 **www**.musee-chateau-compiegne.fr

🏛 **Musée Wagon de l'Armistice**
Clairière de l'Armistice (direc. Soissons). *Tel 03 44 85 14 18.* ⭘ *Wed–Mon.* ⬤ *1 Jan, Jan & Feb am, 25 Dec.* 🖼

Château de Pierrefonds

Château de Pierrefonds ⑭

Oise. *Tel 03 44 42 72 72.* ⭘ *daily.* ⬤ *Mon (5 Sep–Apr), 1 Jan, 1 May, 1 & 11 Nov, 25 Dec.* 🖼 🎬 **Concerts**

The immense Château de Pierrefonds dominates the small village below. A mighty castle was constructed here by Louis d'Orléans in the 14th century, but by 1813 it had become a picturesque ruin which Napoleon I purchased for less than 3,000 francs.

In 1857, Napoleon III commissioned the architect Viollet-le-Duc to restore it, and in 1884 Pierrefonds was reborn as a museum of fortification. The exterior, with its moat, drawbridge, towers and double sentry walks, is a diligent reconstruction of medieval military architecture. The interior, by contrast, is enlivened by the romantic fancies of Viollet-le-Duc and his patron. There are guided tours and a historical exhibition.

Amiens Cathedral

Work on France's largest cathedral started around 1220. It was built to house the head of St John the Baptist, brought back from the Crusades in 1206, which is still displayed here. Within 50 years, Notre-Dame was complete, a masterpiece of engineering – Gothic architecture carried to a bold extreme. Restored in the 1850s by Viollet-le-Duc *(see p200)*, and having miraculously survived two World Wars, the cathedral is famous for its statues and reliefs, which inspired John Ruskin's *The Bible of Amiens* in 1884. The annual *La Cathédrale en Couleurs* sound-and-light show recreates the original colours of the statuary around the west door.

★ **West Front**
The King's Gallery, a row of 22 colossal statues representing the kings of France, spans the west front. The statues are also thought to symbolize the Kings of Judah.

Weeping Angel
Sculpted by Nicolas Blasset in 1628, this sentimental statue in the ambulatory became a popular image during World War I.

St Firmin Portal is decorated with figures and scenes from the life of St Firmin, the martyr who brought Christianity to Picardy and became the first bishop of Amiens.

The Calendar shows signs from the Zodiac, with the corresponding monthly labours below. It depicts everyday life in the 13th century.

Central Portal
Scenes from the Last Judgment adorn the tympanum, with the Beau Dieu, *a statue of Christ, between the doors.*

STAR FEATURES

★ West Front

★ Nave

★ Choir Stalls

★ Choir Screens

Towers

Two towers of unequal height frame the west front. The south tower was completed in 1366; the north in 1402. The spire was replaced twice, in 1627 and 1887.

The Flamboyant tracery of the rose window was created in the 16th century.

VISITORS' CHECKLIST

Cathédrale Notre-Dame, pl Notre-Dame. **Tel** *03 22 71 60 50.*
◯ *Apr–Sep: 8:30am–6:15pm; Oct–Mar: 8:30am–5:15pm. Jun–Dec (nightly): La Cathédrale en Couleurs light show.*
● *1 Jan, last Sun Sep.* ✝ *9am daily (noon Wed); 9am, 10:15am, 11:30am, 6pm Sun.* ◙ ☑
www.amiens-cathedrale.fr

A double row comprising 22 elegant flying buttresses supports the construction.

★ Nave

Soaring 42 m (138 ft) high, with support from 126 slender pillars, the brightly illuminated interior of Notre-Dame is a hymn to the vertical.

★ Choir Stalls

The 110 oak choir stalls (1508–19) are delicately carved with over 4,000 biblical, mythical and real life figures.

The flooring was laid down in 1288 and reassembled in the late 19th century. The faithful followed its labyrinthine shape on their knees.

★ Choir Screens

Vivid scenes from the lives of St Firmin and St John, carved in the 15th–16th centuries, adorn the ambulatory.

Senlis **⓯**

Oise. 🚶 *17,000*. 🚉 🚌 **ℹ** *pl du Parvis
Notre-Dame (03 44 53 06 40).*
📅 *Tue & Fri.* **www.**senlis-tourisme.fr

Senlis, 10 km (6 miles) east
of Chantilly, is worth visiting
for its Gothic cathedral and
the well-preserved historic
streets that surround it.
Cathédrale Notre-Dame was
constructed during the 12th
century, and the sculpted
central doorway of its west
front, depicting the
Assumption of the Virgin,
influenced later cathedrals
such as Amiens *(see pp202–3).*
The south tower's spire dates
from the 13th century, while
the Flamboyant south transept,
built in the mid-16th century,
makes an ornate contrast with
the austerity of earlier years.
Opposite the west front, a
gateway leads to the ruins of
the Château Royal and its
gardens. Here the **Musée de
la Vénerie**, housed in a former
priory, celebrates hunting
through paintings, old
weapons and trophies.
   The **Musée d'Art** recalls the
town's Gallo-Roman past, and
also has an excellent collection
of early Gothic sculpture.

Les Très Riches Heures du Duc de Berry, on show in Chantilly

🏛 **Musée de la Vénerie**
Château Royal, pl du Parvis Notre-
Dame. **Tel** *03 44 32 00 81.* ⬜ *Mon,
Wed pm, Thu, Sun.* ⬛ *1 Jan, 1 May,
25 Dec.* 📷 🎫 *oblig.*

🏛 **Musée d'Art et
d'Archéologie**
Ancien Evêché, 2 pl Notre-Dame.
Tel *03 44 32 00 81.* ⬜ *Mon, Wed
pm, Thu, Sun.* ⬛ *1 Jan, 1 May,
25 Dec.* 📷

Chantilly **⓰**

Oise. 🚶 *11,200*. 🚉 🚌 **ℹ** *60 av
du Maréchal Joffre (03 44 67 37 37).*
📅 *Wed & Sat.*
www.chantilly-tourisme.com

The horse-racing capital of
France, Chantilly offers a
classy combination of château,
park and forest that has long
made it a popular excursion.
With origins in Gallo-Roman

times, the château of today
started to take shape in 1528,
when the famous Anne de
Montmorency, Constable of
France, had the old fortress
replaced and added the Petit
Château. During the time of
the Great Prince of Condé
(1621–86), renovation work
continued and Le Nôtre created
a park and fountains which
made even Louis XIV jealous.
Destroyed in the Revolution,

CHANTILLY HORSE RACING

Chantilly is the capital of thoroughbred racing in France, a
shrine to the long-standing love affair between the French
upper classes and the world of horses. It was the firm belief
of Prince Louis-Henri de Bourbon, creator of Chantilly's
monumental Grandes Ecuries, that he would one day be
reincarnated as a horse. Horse racing was introduced from
England around 1830 and soon became very popular. The
first official race meeting was held here in 1834 and today
around 3,000 horses are trained in the surrounding forests
and countryside. Every June, Chantilly becomes the focus of
the social and flat racing season when top riders and their
thoroughbreds compete for its two historic trophies, the Prix
du Jockey-Club and Prix de Diane-Hermès.

Prix Equipage de Hermès, one of many prestigious races at Chantilly

---

For hotels and restaurants in this region see pp556–8 and pp607–10

the Grand Château was again rebuilt and its receptions and hunting parties became crowded by the fashionable high society of the 1820s–30s. It was finally replaced by a Renaissance-style château in the late 19th century.

Today the Grand Château and the Petit Château form the **Musée Condé**, displaying art treasures collected by its last private owner, the Duke of Aumale. These include work by Raphael, Botticelli, Poussin and Ingres, and an entertaining gallery of 16th-century portraits by the Clouet brothers. Among the most precious items is the famous 15th-century illuminated manuscript *Les Très Riches Heures du Duc de Berry*, reproductions of which are on view. You can also tour the stately apartments, with decorative conceits ranging from frolicking monkeys to triumphant battles.

Asterix with friends, Parc Astérix

Both châteaux are somewhat upstaged by the magnificent stables (Grandes Ecuries), an equestrian palace designed by Jean Aubert in 1719 which could accommodate 240 horses and 500 dogs. It is occupied by the **Musée Vivant du Cheval**, presenting various breeds of horses and ponies, and riding displays.

🏛 **Musée Condé**
Château de Chantilly. *Tel 03 44 62 62 62.* ⬜ *Wed–Mon.* 🏷 🎥

🐎 **Musée Vivant du Cheval**
Grandes Ecuries du Prince de Condé, Chantilly. *Tel 03 44 27 31 80.*
⬜ *phone for information.* 🏷 ♿

Parc Astérix ⓱

Plailly. 📱 *08 26 30 10 40.* ⬜ *Jun–Aug daily & French schools hols (check).* 🏷 ♿ www.parcasterix.fr

Near Charles de Gaulle Airport a small fortified Gaulish village has its own customs controls, currency and radio station (Menhir FM). One of the

most popular theme parks in France, it is dedicated to Asterix the Gaul and all the other characters in Goscinny and Uderzo's famous cartoon strip: Getafix, Obelix, Cacofonix *et al*. The Romans are driven crazy as they try to subdue these larger than life Gauls, who dodge patrolling Roman centurions. Hilarious battles take place.

The Parc is as much about French history as about the cartoons. Via Antiqua and the Roman City are lighthearted but genuinely educational. Rue de Paris shows Paris through the centuries, including the construction of Notre-Dame cathedral. There are non-historical attractions too, like a dolphinarium and Zeus' Thunder high-speed roller-coaster. Check out the latest rides – there's usually something new every year.

Laon ⓲

Aisne. 🏠 *27,000.* ⬜ 🚌 *Hôtel-Dieu, pl du Parvis Gauthier de Montagne (03 23 20 28 62).*
🛒 *Wed–Thu & Sat.*
www.tourisme-paysdelaon.com

The capital of the Aisne *département*, Laon occupies a dramatic site on top of a

The pedestrianized rue Châtelaine, a main shopping street in Laon

Rose window in the 13th-century Cathédrale de Notre-Dame, Laon

long, narrow ridge surrounded by wide plains. The old town, on top of the mount, is best approached by Poma, an automated cable car that swings up from the railway station to the place du Général Leclerc.

The pedestrianized rue Châtelaine leads to Laon's splendid **Cathédrale de Notre-Dame**. Completed in 1235, the cathedral lost two of its original seven towers in the Revolution but remains an impressive monument to the early Gothic style.

Details include the deep porches of the west façade, the four-storey nave, and the carved Renaissance screens enclosing its side chapels. The immense 13th-century rose window in the apse represents the Glorification of the Church. Protruding from the cathedral's western towers are statues paying tribute to the oxen used to haul up stone for its construction.

The rest of medieval Laon rewards casual strolling: a promenade rings the 16th-century **Citadelle** further east, while to the south you can follow the ramparts past the Porte d'Ardon and Porte des Chenizelles to **Eglise St-Martin**, with views of the cathedral from rue Thibesard.

South of Laon is Chemin des Dames, named after Louis XV's daughters who used to take this route, but more often remembered as a World War I battlefield and lined with cemeteries and memorials.

CHAMPAGNE

MARNE · ARDENNES · AUBE · HAUTE-MARNE

*C*hampagne is a name of great resonance, conjuring up images of celebration and the world-famous cathedral at Reims. Yet beyond the glamour lies an unspoilt rural idyll of two strikingly contrasting landscapes: the rolling plains of Champagne, giving way to lakes and water meadows to the south, and the dense forests and hills of the Ardennes in the north.

The so-called "sacred triangle of Champagne", linking Épernay, Reims and Châlons-en-Champagne, is like a magnet for wine lovers. Here, the experience of drinking fine champagne is enhanced by gourmet meals of stuffed trout, Ardennes ham and the famous sausages called *andouillettes*.

The sign-posted *route touristique du champagne* wends its way through vineyards towards endless cereal plains stretching southwards to the "lake district", an area of oak forests, water meadows and streams.

On the border between France and Belgium lies the Ardennes, named after the Celtic word for deep forest. This wild border land of dramatic valleys, deciduous forests and hills is cut by the meanderings of the river Meuse. Border fortifications include the vast citadel of Sedan and the star-shaped town and fortress of Rocroi, as well as the Maginot Line outposts built before World War II. The Ardennes may offer appealing countryside but Champagne is culturally superior, with impressive towns that have painstakingly restored historic centres. It has some striking churches, from the Gothic majesty of Reims cathedral to the rustic charm of its typical half-timbered *champenoises* churches. These feature vivid stained-glass windows by the famous School of Troyes, whose subtle craftsmanship seems to typify the appeal of this quiet region.

Timber-framed *champenoise* church at Lac du Der-Chantecoq

◁ Cathédrale St-Etienne at Châlons-en-Champagne

Exploring Champagne

Champagne's fizz draws wine lovers to the sacred triangle between Reims, Épernay and Châlons-en-Champagne, but the region also attracts culture lovers to its great churches, notably Reims Cathedral. Reims abounds in gastronomic restaurants but Troyes, the former capital of Champagne, makes the most delightful base. Much of Champagne is flat or gently undulating, and the wild and wooded Ardennes to the north attracts walkers and nature-lovers. North of Reims, the Ardennes canal can be explored by barge or pleasure boat from Rethel; to the south, watersports are popular on the lakes to the east of Troyes.

Fishing by a canal in Montier-en-Der near Lac du Der-Chantecoq

GETTING AROUND

The region's main *autoroute* is the A26, which reaches Reims in under 3 hours from Calais, and also provides easy access to most of the region all the way down to Troyes and Langres (via the A5). The A4 motorway also links Reims to Paris and Alsace. Paris-Reims by the TGV high-speed train takes 45 minutes. Rail transport within the region is reasonably good, and so are the roads. To explore the wine-growing region, follow the signposted roads marked "Route de Champagne".

Windmill at Verzenay, Parc Naturel de la Montagne de Reims

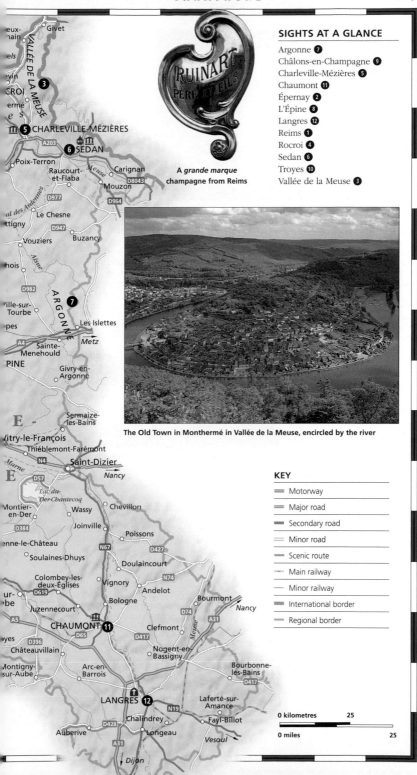

A *grande marque* champagne from Reims

SIGHTS AT A GLANCE

Argonne ⑦
Châlons-en-Champagne ⑨
Charleville-Mézières ⑤
Chaumont ⑪
Épernay ②
L'Épine ⑧
Langres ⑫
Reims ①
Rocroi ④
Sedan ⑥
Troyes ⑩
Vallée de la Meuse ③

The Old Town in Monthermé in Vallée de la Meuse, encircled by the river

KEY

━━ Motorway

━━ Major road

━━ Secondary road

═══ Minor road

━━ Scenic route

━━ Main railway

--- Minor railway

━━ International border

━━ Regional border

*Map labels:*

Givet
eux-nain
els
VALLÉE DE LA MEUSE
evin
③
CROI
erme
e s
⑤ CHARLEVILLE-MÉZIÈRES
A203
⑥ SEDAN
Poix-Terron
Raucourt-et-Flaba
Carignan
Meuse
Mouzon
D8043
D977
D964
al des Ardennes
ttigny
Le Chesne
D947
Vouziers
Buzancy
Aisne
hois
D982
A R G O N N E
⑦
ille-sur-Tourbe
Les Islettes
pes
A4
Sainte-Menehould
Metz
PINE
Givry-en-Argonne
E
Sermaize-les-Bains
Vitry-le-François
Thiéblemont-Farémont
Marne
N4
Saint-Dizier
D57
Nancy
E
Lac du Der-Chantecoq
Montier-en-Der
Wassy
Chevillon
D384
Joinville
Poissons
enne-le-Château
N67
D427
Soulaines-Dhuys
Doulaincourt
N74
Colombey-les-deux-Églises
Vignory
Andelot
ur-
D619
Bologne
Bourmont
be
Juzennecourt
D74
A31
Nancy
A5
CHAUMONT ⑪
Clefmont
Meuse
ayes
D65
D396
D417
Châteauvillain
Nogent-en-Bassigny
Montigny-sur-Aube
Arc-en-Barrois
Bourbonne-les-Bains
D417
LANGRES ⑫
Laferté-sur-Amance
N19
Chalindrey
Fayl-Billot
Auberive
D428
Longeau
Vesoul
A31
Dijon

0 kilometres 25

0 miles 25

Gilded reliquary (1896), with body of St Remi, in Basilique St-Remi, Reims

cellars and Baroque interior play their part as atmospheric film sets, notably for the film of Zola's *Germinal* (1992) and *Queen Margot* (1993). Highlights include the refectory's ceiling and the kitchen, the only room where fireplaces were permitted in an austere Jesuit establishment. A double spiral staircase leads to a Baroque library with yet another magnificent ceiling. Housed in the same building since 1979 is the **Planetarium**, with views of the sky from everywhere in the world.

Reims ❶

Marne. 🏠 *185,000.* ✈ 🚇 🚉
ℹ️ *2 rue Guillaume de Machault (08 92 70 13 51).* 🌙 *daily.*
www.reims-tourisme.com

Pronounced like the French word "prince" without the "p", Reims is home to some of the best known *grandes marques* in Champagne, and several are grouped around the Basilique St-Remi. But the city has another, much earlier, claim to fame: since the 11th century, all the kings of France have come to this "city of coronations" to be crowned in its remarkable Gothic **Cathédrale Notre-Dame** *(see pp212–13).*

Although World War II bombing destroyed much of Reims' architectural coherence, there are some remarkable monuments here. The **Cryptoportique**, part of the forum, and Porte Mars, a triumphal Augustan arch, recall the Roman past. In 1945, the German surrender was taken in the **Musée de la Reddition** in Eisenhower's French HQ during World War II.
Musée des Beaux-Arts houses a fine collection of 15th- and 16th-century canvases depicting biblical scenes, portraits by the Cranachs, *The Death of Marat* by David and more than 20 landscapes by Corot. Also here are the Barbizons, Impressionists and modern masters.

In 1996 Reims celebrated the 1,500-year anniversary of the baptism of Clovis, first King of the Franks, in its cathedral.

🏛 Ancien Collège des Jésuites & Planetarium

1 pl Museux. **Tel** *03 26 35 34 70.*
Collège 🖼 *(Planetarium).*
Founded in 1606, this college was a hospice until 1976. Nowadays its 300-year-old vines, Romanesque wine

Porte Mars, a reminder of Reims in Roman times

🏛 Basilique St-Remi

Pl St-Rémi. ⬜ *daily.* ♿
This Benedictine abbey church, the oldest church in Reims, began as a Carolingian basilica dedicated to Saint Rémi (440–533). Inside, an Early Gothic choir and radiating chapels

---

METHODE CHAMPENOISE

To produce its characteristic bubbles, champagne has to undergo a process of double fermentation.
First fermentation: The base wine, made from rather acidic grapes, is fermented at 20–22°C in either stainless steel tanks or, occasionally, in oak barrels. It is then siphoned off from the sediment and kept at colder temperatures to clear completely, before being drawn off and blended with wines from other areas and years (except in the case of vintage champagne). The wine is bottled and the *liqueur de tirage* (sugar, wine and yeast) is added.
Second fermentation: The bottles are stored for a year or more in cool, chalky cellars. The yeast converts the sugar to alcohol and carbon dioxide, which produces the sparkle, and the yeast cells die leaving a deposit. To remove this, the inverted bottles are turned and tapped daily *(remuage)* to shift the deposits into the neck of the bottle. Finally, the deposits are expelled by the process known as *dégorgement*, and a bit of sugar syrup *(liqueur d'expédition)* is added to adjust the sweetness before the final cork is inserted.

Champagne Mumm of Reims

---

can be seen, as well as sculpted Romanesque capitals in the north transept.

🏛 Musée St-Remi

53 rue Simon. **Tel** *03 26 85 00 01.* ⬛ *daily pm only.* ⬤ *1 Jan, 1 May, 14 Jul, 1 & 11 Nov, 25 Dec.* 📷

Set in the former abbey, the adjoining museum encloses the original Gothic chapterhouse within its cloistered 17th-century shell. On display are archaeological artifacts, 15th-century tapestries depicting the life of Saint Remi, and a collection of weapons dating from the 16th–19th centuries.

🏰 Fort de la Pompelle

8 km (5 miles) southeast of Reims. **Tel** *03 26 49 11 85.* ⬛ *Wed–Mon.* 📷 ♿

Built to protect Reims after the Franco-Prussian War, this fort houses a museum of German Imperial military headgear.

Épernay ❷

Marne. 🏠 *25,000.* 🚉 ℹ *7 av de Champagne (03 26 53 33 00).* 🛒 *Wed, Sat & Sun.* www.ot-epernay.fr

The sole reason for visiting Épernay is to burrow into the chalky *caves* and taste the champagne. This rather undistinguished town lives off the

Statue of Dom Perignon at Moët

fruits of its profitable champagne industry. As proof, the avenue de Champagne quarter abounds in mock-Renaissance mansions. **Moët & Chandon**, dating back to 1743, is the largest and slickest *maison*, the star of the Moët-Hennessy stable. Its cellars stretch some 28 km (18 miles) underground.

The group also owns other champagne houses, such as Mercier, Krug, Pommery, Veuve Clicquot and Canard Duchêne.

There is little to choose between a visit to the cellars of Moët & Chandon or **Mercier** – both are in Avenue de Champagne. Mercier has the distinction of displaying a giant tun (cask) created for the 1889 Paris Exhibition, and takes you through the *caves* in an electric train.

De Castellane offers a more personalized tour, accompanied by a heady *dégustation*.

🏰 Moët & Chandon

20 av de Champagne. **Tel** *03 26 51 20 20.* ⬛ *end Mar–mid-Nov: daily; mid-Nov–Dec, Feb–end Mar: Mon–Fri.* 📷 *only.* www.moet.com

🏰 Mercier

70 av de Champagne. **Tel** *03 26 51 22 22.* ⬛ *mid-Mar–Nov: daily; Dec–mid-Mar: Thu–Mon.* 📷 ♿ 🎦 *oblig.* www.champagnemercier.com

🏰 De Castellane

57 rue de Verdun. **Tel** *03 26 51 19 19.* ⬛ *daily (Jan–Mar: Sat & Sun only).* 📷 ♿ *restr.* 🎦 *oblig.* www.castellane.com

Dégorgement *is the final removal of the yeast deposits from the bottle. The neck of the bottle is plunged in freezing brine and the frozen block of sediment is then removed.*

Seductive marketing *of champagne since the 19th century has ensured its continuing success.*

The bubbles in champagne *are produced during the second fermentation. Champagnes, especially vintage ones, improve with ageing.*

Reims Cathedral

The magnificent Gothic Cathédrale Notre-Dame at Reims is noted for its harmony and monumentality. A cathedral has stood on this site since 401, but the present building was begun in 1211. Reims has been the backdrop for coronations from medieval times till 1825, when Charles X was crowned. The coronation of Charles VII here in 1429 was attended by Joan of Arc.

During the Revolution, the rood screen and windows were destroyed but the stonework survived. World War I damage was finally fully restored in 1996, to coincide with the 1,500th anniversary of the baptism of Clovis, King of the Franks, at Reims, which was considered the first coronation of a French king.

★ Great Rose Window
Best seen at sunset, the 13th-century window shows the Virgin surrounded by the apostles and angel musicians. It is set within a larger window, a feature common in 13th-century architecture.

The Nave
Compared with the nave at Chartres (see pp308–11), Reims is taller. Its elegant capitals are decorated with naturalistic floral motifs such as ivy and berries.

WEST FAÇADE

SOUTH FAÇADE

★ Smiling Angel
Rich in statuary, Reims is often called "the cathedral of angels." Situated above the left (north) portal, this enigmatic angel with unfurled wings is the most celebrated of the many that grace the building.

★ Gallery of the Kings
The harmonious west façade, decorated with over 2,300 statues, is the most notable feature at Reims. Fifty-six stone effigies of French kings form the Gallery of the Kings.

PALAIS DU TAU

The archbishop's palace adjoining the cathedral is named after its T-shaped design, based on early episcopal crosses. (Tau is Greek for T.) The palace, built in 1690 by Mansart and Robert de Cotte, encloses a Gothic Chapel and the 15th-century Salle du Tau, rooms associated with French coronations. On the eve of a coronation, the future king would spend the night in the palace. After being crowned in the cathedral, he held a magnificent banquet in the palace. The Salle du Tau, or banqueting hall, is the finest room in the palace, with a magnificent barrel-vaulted ceiling and walls hung with 15th-century

Arras tapestries. The palace now houses a museum of statuary and tapestries from the cathedral, including a 15th-century tapestry of the baptism of Clovis, the first Christian king.

Salle du Tau – the banqueting hall

Apse Gallery
The restored claire-voie (open work) gallery on the apse is crowned by statues of mythological beasts.

The radiating chapels of the apse are supported by flying buttresses and adorned with octagonal pinnacles.

South transept

APSE

The clerestory windows pioneered Gothic tracery by dividing the lights with slender bars of stone, creating a decorative, intersecting pattern.

Pinnacles on the flying buttresses shelter guardian angels, symbolic protectors of the cathedral.

STAR FEATURES

★ Gallery of the Kings

★ Smiling Angel

★ Great Rose Window

Chagall Window
The windows in the axial chapel were designed by the 20th-century artist Marc Chagall and made by local craftsmen. This one depicts the Crucifixion and the Sacrifice of Isaac.

The *sentier touristique*, a walk along the ramparts of Rocroi

Vallée de la Meuse ❸

Ardennes. 🏘 *8,900.* 🚆 *Revin.*
ℹ *65 quai Edgar Quinet, Revin (03 24 40 19 59).* www.meuselavallee.org

The Meuse meanders through the Ardennes among spectacular scenery of wild gorges, woods and warped rock formations of granite or schist.

Dramatically situated on a double meander of the Meuse, **Revin** is an unremarkable town in an exceptional site, with the Vieille Ville enfolded in the north bend. From the quay, you can see wooded **Mont Malgré Tout** and a route dotted with observation points and steep trails. Just south is **Dames de la Meuse**, a rocky outcrop over the river gorge.

Monthermé lies on two banks, with the Vieille Ville clustered on the charming left bank. The rocky gorges around **Roche à Sept Heures** on the far bank entice climbers and ramblers. The jagged crest of **Rocher des Quatre Fils d'Aymon** suggests the silhouette of four legendary local horsemen.

Rocroi ❹

Ardennes. 🏘 *2,430.* 🚆 🚆 *Revin.*
ℹ *14 pl d'Armes (03 24 54 20 06).*
🛒 *Tue & first Mon of month.*
www.otrocroi.com

Set on the Ardennes plateau, the star-shaped citadel of Rocroi was originally built under Henri II in 1555, and later made impregnable by Vauban in 1675 *(see p226).*

The main attraction is the walk along the ramparts from the southern gateway. The nature reserve at Rièzes is home to orchids and carnivorous plants.

Charleville-Mézières ❺

Ardennes. 🏘 *58,000.* 🚆 🚆
ℹ *4 pl Ducale (03 24 55 69 90).*
🛒 *Tue, Thu & Sat.*
www.charleville-tourisme.com

This riverside ford was originally two towns. The sombre medieval citadel of Mézières only merged with the neat Classical town of Charleville in 1966. Mézières has irregular slate-covered houses curving around a bend in the Meuse. Battered fortifications and gateways are visible from avenue de St-Julien. Tucked into the ramparts is the much remodelled Gothic **Notre-Dame de l'Espérance**.

The centrepiece of Charleville is **place Ducale**, a model of Louis XIII urban planning,

echoing place des Vosges in Paris *(see p91).* The poet Arthur Rimbaud was born nearby in 1854. His modest birthplace at No. 12 rue Bérégovoy is still there, along with his childhood home on the Meuse at 7 quai Arthur Rimbaud.

Just along the quayside is the Vieux Moulin, the town house whose view inspired *Le Bateau Ivre*, Rimbaud's greatest poem. Inside is the small **Musée Rimbaud**, with manuscripts and photographs by the poet.

🏛 **Musée Rimbaud**
Quai Arthur Rimbaud. **Tel** *03 24 32 44 65.* 🕐 *Tue–Sun.* 🕐 *1 Jan, 1 May, 25 Dec.* 🎫 *(free first Sun of month).*

Sedan ❻

Ardennes. 🏘 *20,000.* 🚆 🚆
ℹ *32 rue du Menil (03 24 27 73 73).* 🛒 *Wed & Sat.*
www.tourisme-sedan.com

Just to the east of Charleville is the **Château de Sedan**, the largest fortified castle in Europe. There has been a bastion on these slopes since the 11th century, but each Ardennes conflict has spelt a new tier of defences for Sedan.

In 1870, during the Franco-Prussian War, with 700 Prussian cannons turned on Sedan, Napoleon III surrendered and 83,000 French prisoners were deported to Prussia. In May 1940 after capturing Sedan, German forces reached the French coast a week later.

The seven-storeyed bastion contains sections dating from medieval times to the

The 19th-century poet Rimbaud, whose birthplace was Charleville

16th century. Highlights of any visit are the ramparts, the 16th-century fortifications and the magnificent 15th-century eaves in one tower. The **Musée du Château**, in the south wing, is rather jumbled, with a section on military campaigns.

The bastion is surrounded by 17th-century slate-roofed houses which hug the banks of the Meuse. These reflect the city's earlier prosperity as a Huguenot stronghold.

🏛 **Musée du Château**
1 pl du Château. **Tel** *03 24 27 73 73.* ⬜ *Jul & Aug: daily; Sep–mid-Mar: Tue–Sun.* 🎦 *Tue–Fri pms.*

Environs
Further south is **Fort de Villy-la-Ferté**, one of the few forts on the Maginot line to have been captured in devastating combat with the enemy in 1940.

Courtyard inside the heavily fortified Château de Sedan

Gargoyle on Basilique de Notre-Dame de l'Épine

Argonne ❼

Ardennes & Meuse. 🚆 *Châlons.* 🚌 *Ste-Menehould.* 🛈 *5 pl du Général Leclerc, Ste-Menehould (03 26 60 85 83).* **www**.argonne.fr

East of Reims, the Argonne is a compact region of picturesque valleys and forests, dotted with priories, trenches and war cemeteries.

As a wooded border between the rival bishoprics of Champagne and Lorraine, the Argonne was home to abbeys and priories. Now ruined, the Benedictine abbey of **Beaulieu-en-Argonne** boasts a 13th-century wine press and has forest views.

Just north is **Les Islettes**, known for its faïence pottery and tiles. The hilly terrain here was a battleground during the Franco-Prussian War and World War I. The disputed territory of **Butte de Vauquois**, north of Les Islettes, bears a war memorial.

L'Épine ❽

Marne. 🏘 *670.* 🚆 *Châlons.* 🚌 🛈 *Mairie (03 26 66 96 99).*

L'Épine is worth visiting if only for a glimpse of the **Basilique de Notre-Dame de l'Épine** surrounded by wheatfields. Designed on the scale of a cathedral, this 15th-century Flamboyant Gothic church has been a pilgrimage site since medieval times. Even French kings have come here to venerate a "miraculous" statue of the Virgin.

On the façade, three gabled portals are offset by floating tracery, a gauzy effect reminiscent of Reims cathedral. All around are gruesome gargoyles, symbolizing evil spirits and deadly sins, chased out by the holy presence within. Unfortunately, the most risqué sculptures were destroyed, judged obscene by 19th-century puritans. The subdued Gothic interior contains a 15th-century rood-screen and the venerated statue of the Virgin.

CHAMPAGNE TIMBER CHURCHES

Skirting Lac du Der-Chantecoq lies a region of woodland and water meadows, containing twelve Romanesque and Renaissance half-timbered churches with curious pointed gables and *caquetoirs*, rickety wooden porches. They have intimate and often beautifully carved interiors with stained-glass windows designed in the vivid colours of the School of Troyes. Rural roads link churches at Bailly-le-Franc, Chatillon-sur-Broué, Lentilles, Vignory, Outines, Chavanges and Montier-en-Der.

16th-century timber church in Lentilles

Châlons-en-Champagne **9**

Marne. ♦ 48,000. 🚊 🚌
ℹ 3 quai des Arts (03 26 65 17 89).
🛒 Wed, Fri am, Sat, Sun am.
www.chalons-tourisme.com

Encircled by the river Marne and minor canals, Châlons' sleepy bourgeois charm is made up of half-timbered houses and gardens mirrored in canals. Nearby are vineyards producing Blanc de Blancs.

From quai de Notre-Dame there are views of old bridges and the Romanesque towers of **Notre-Dame-en-Vaux**, a masterpiece of Romanesque-Gothic. Behind the church is a well-restored medieval quarter and the **Musée du Cloître**, containing the original Romanesque cloisters.

Cathédrale St-Etienne, by the canal, is a cool Gothic affair with a Baroque portal, Romanesque crypt and vivid medieval windows. Beyond is **Le Petit Jard**, riverside gardens overlooking the Château du Marché, and a turreted toll gate built by Henri IV. Excellent river tours of the city are available from the tourist office.

🏛 **Musée du Cloître de Notre-Dame-en-Vaux**
Rue Nicolas Durand. **Tel** 03 26 69 38 53. ⬜ Wed–Mon. ● 1 Jan, 1 May, 1 & 11 Nov, 25 Dec. 🎫 📷

Troyes **10**

Aube. ♦ 63,000. 🚊 🚌 **ℹ** 16 bd Carnot (03 25 82 62 70). 🛒 daily.
www.tourisme-troyes.com

Troyes is a delight, a city of magnificent Gothic churches and charming 16th-century courtyards, in a historical centre shaped like a champagne cork. The city is famous for its heritage of stained glass and sausages (andouillettes), its knitwear industry and factory shops.

The battered Flamboyant Gothic west front of the **Cathédrale St-Pierre-et-St-Paul** opens on to a splendid vaulted interior. The nave is bathed in mauvish-red rays

Statuary in Troyes' Cathédrale St-Pierre-et-St-Paul

from the 16th-century rose window, complemented by the discreet turquoise of the Tree of Jesse window and the intense blue of the medieval windows of the apse.

Nearby, **Eglise St-Nizier** glitters in the faded quarter behind the cathedral with its shimmering tiled Burgundian roof. Inside, it is lit by windows in a range of warm mauves and soothing blues.

The Gothic **Basilique St-Urbain** boasts grand flying buttresses and particularly fine 13th-century windows. **Eglise Ste-Madeleine** is noted for its elaborate 16th-century rood screen resembling lacey

Rue Larivey, a typical street with half-timbered houses, in Troyes

foliage, grapes and figs. Beyond is a wall of windows in browns, reds and blues. The ruelle des Chats, which is a quaint covered passageway, connects rue Charbonnet and rue Champeaux.

Set in one of the best-preserved quarters, **Eglise St-Pantaléon** faces a Renaissance mansion. A Gothic and Renaissance interior houses an imposing collection of 16th-century statuary and severe grisaille windows.

🏛 **Musée d'Art Moderne**
14 pl St-Pierre.
Tel 03 25 76 26 80. ⬜ Tue–Sun.
● public hols. 🎫 📷

Beside the cathedral, the former episcopal palace is now a museum of modern art, with a sculpture by Rodin and an especially fine collection of Fauvist paintings, as well as other modern art.

🏛 **Hôtel du Petit Louvre**
Rue de la Montée St-Pierre.
Courtyard only ⬜ daily.
Set off quai Dampierre, this well restored hôtel particulier boasts a fish-scale roof, medieval tower, Renaissance courtyard, staircase and well. The highlight is a façade adorned with quizzical multicoloured faces.

Environs

The city's green playground, **Lac et Forêt d'Orient**, is 25 km (15 miles) east of Troyes. The forest is dotted with marshes, nature reserves and smaller lakes. Lac d'Orient, the largest artificial lake in Europe, is popular for sailing, with water-skiing on Lac Amance, and fishing at Lac du Temple.

Chaumont **⑪**

Haute-Marne. 🏠 26,000. 🚉 ℹ️ 37 rue de Verdun (03 25 03 80 80). 🖐 Wed & Sat. www.tourisme-chaumont-champagne.com

As the former residence of the Counts of Champagne, this feudal town enjoyed great prestige in the 13th century. On the far side of a ravine, the old town is on a rocky spur, with the Palais de Justice and the medieval castle keep dominating.

The keep is a reminder that this quiet administrative centre had a formidable past. This impression is confirmed by the Renaissance town houses which are bulging with *tourelles d'escaliers*, turreted staircases.

Basilique St-Jean-Baptiste, a grey-stone Champenois church, is the most remarkable monument in Chaumont. The interior is enlivened by a spider's web of vaulting, a striking turreted staircase and Renaissance galleries. Near the entrance is a tiny chapel containing an unsettling *Mise au Tombeau* (1471), an intense multi-coloured stone group of 10 mourners gathered around Christ laid out on a shroud in his tomb. In the left transept is a bizarre but beguiling *Tree of Jesse*. On this ill-lit Renaissance stone relief, a family tree sprouts from the sleeping Jesus.

Environs

Twenty-three kilometres (14 miles) northwest of Chaumont, **Colombey-les-Deux-Eglises** will forever be associated with General Charles de Gaulle (1890–1970). The de Gaulles bought their home, **La Boisserie**, in 1933, but had to abandon it during the war,

Cathédrale St-Mammès in Langres

when it was badly damaged. After its restoration, de Gaulle would return to La Boisserie from Paris at weekends to write his memoirs. He died here on 9 November 1970. The house is now a museum.

In the village churchyard, the General lies in a simple tomb, but a giant granite cross of Lorraine, erected in 1972, dominates the skyline. At its foot is the **Mémorial**, a museum dedicated to de Gaulle's life.

🏛 **La Boisserie**
Colombey-les-Deux-Eglises. **Tel** 03 25 01 52 52. 🕐 mid-Apr–mid-Oct: daily; mid-Oct–mid-Apr: Wed–Mon. 🗭 ♿

🏛 **Mémorial Charles de Gaulle**
Tel 03 25 30 90 80. 🕐 May–Sep: daily; Oct–Apr: Wed–Mon. 🗭
www.memorial-charlesdegaulle.fr

Langres **⑫**

Haute-Marne. 🏠 9,000. 🚉 🚌 ℹ️ square Olivier Lahalle (03 25 87 67 67). 🖐 Fri. www.tourisme-langres.com

Set on a rocky spur, Langres lies beyond Chaumont, in the backwaters of southern Champagne. This ancient bishopric was one of the gateways to Burgundy and the birthplace of the encyclopedist, Denis Diderot (1713–84). Langres promotes itself as a land of springs, claiming that its proximity to the sources of the Seine and Marne grant it mystical powers.

Virtually the whole town is enclosed by medieval ramparts, Langres' undoubted attraction. A succession of towers and parapets provide glimpses of romantic town gates and sculpted Renaissance mansions, with panoramic views of the Marne valley, the Langres plateau, the Vosges and, on a clear day, even Mont Blanc.

Near Porte Henri IV is the much-remodelled **Cathédrale St-Mammès**. The gloomy vaulted interior, in Burgundian Romanesque style, is redeemed by the sculpted capitals in the apse, reputedly taken from a temple of Jupiter. The town's Musée d'Art et d'Histoire has some interesting collections.

Langres' lively summer season includes historical re-enactments, theatre and fireworks.

Memorial to General de Gaulle at Colombey-les-Deux-Eglises

ALSACE AND LORRAINE

MEURTHE-ET-MOSELLE · MEUSE · MOSELLE · BAS-RHIN
HAUT-RHIN · VOSGES

*A*s border regions, Alsace and Lorraine have been fought over for centuries by France, Austria and Germany, their beleaguered past recalled by many a military stronghold and cemetery. Today, the region presents only a peaceful aspect with pastel-painted villages, fortified towns and sleepy vineyards.

At the northeast frontier of France, bordered by the Rhine, Alsace forms a fertile watershed between the mountains of the Vosges and the Black Forest in Germany. Lorraine, with its rolling landscape on the other side of the mountains, is the poorer cousin but is more overtly French in character.

EMBATTLED TERRITORY

Caught in the wars between France and Germany, Alsace and part of Lorraine have changed nationality four times since 1871. Centuries of strife have made border citadels of Metz, Toul and Verdun in Lorraine, while Alsace abounds with castles, from the faithfully reconstructed Haut-Koenigsbourg to Saverne's ruined fortress, built to guard a strategic pass in the Vosges. However, the area has a strong identity of its own, taking pride in local costumes, traditions and dialects. In Alsace, Route des Vins vineyards nudge pretty villages in the Vosges foothills. Strasbourg, the capital, is a cosmopolitan city with a 16th-century centre, while Nancy, Lorraine's historical capital, represents elegant 18th-century architecture.

Much of the attraction of this region lies in its cuisine. Lorraine offers beer and quiche lorraine. In Alsace, cosy *winstubs*, or wine cellars, serve sauerkraut and flowery white wines, such as Riesling and Gewürztraminer. There are also fine restaurants here.

Villagers enjoying the view from their window in Hunspach, north of Strasbourg in the northern Vosges

◁ Half-timbered houses with flower-clad balconies along the Route du Vin in Alsace

Exploring Alsace and Lorraine

Visitors seeking art and architecture will be amply rewarded
by the charming medieval towns and excellent city
museums of the region. Undiscovered Lorraine is the place
to clamber over military citadels, walk in unspoiled
countryside and unwind at relaxing
spas. By contrast, Alsace offers
magnificent forests and rugged
mountain drives in the Vosges,
quaint villages and rich wines.
The Route des Vins *(see pp232–
3)* is one of the region's many
scenic routes. It is particularly
popular during the wine harvest festivities but is worth
visiting in any season.

SIGHTS AT A GLANCE

Betschdorf ⑱
Château du Haut-
  Koenigsbourg ⑬
Colmar ⑩
Eguisheim ⑨
Gérardmer ⑤
Guebwiller ⑦
Metz ③
Mulhouse ⑥
Nancy ④
Neuf-Brisach ⑧
Obernai ⑮
Ribeauvillé ⑫
Riquewihr ⑪
Saverne ⑰
Sélestat ⑭
Strasbourg ⑯
Toul ②
Verdun ①

Field of sunflowers just outside the village of Turckheim

0 kilometres   20

0 miles   10

The picturesque village of Riquewihr on the Route du Vin

GETTING AROUND
There are good roads and rail links between Strasbourg, Colmar, Metz and Nancy, and on to Switzerland and Germany. The main roads to and through the regions are the N4, A31, A35, A4 to Paris and N59, and the tunnel under the Vosges. The spectacular journey over the Vosges and along the Route des Vins is best made by car or on organized trips from Colmar or Strasbourg. The TGV link to the region from Paris takes 2 hours 20 minutes.

KEY

▬	Motorway
▬	Major road
▬	Secondary road
▬	Minor road
▬	Scenic route
—	Main railway
—	Minor railway
▬	International border
—	Regional border
△	Summit

The Ossuaire de Douaumont, a sentinel for the regiments of crosses on the battlefields of Verdun

Verdun ❶

Meuse. 🏘 *21,000.* 🚌 🚉
ℹ️ *pl de la Nation (03 29 86 14 18).*
🛒 *Fri.* **www**.verdun-tourisme.com

Verdun will be forever remembered for the horrors of the 1916–1917 Battle of Verdun, when about a million men died in almost a whole year of continuous bloodshed that is considered the worst single battle of the Great War. The Germans intended to strike a blow at French morale by destroying the forts of Douaumont and Vaux (which had been built to prevent a repeat of the humiliating French defeat of the Franco-Prussian War of 1870) and capture Verdun, France's northeastern stronghold. The French fought simply to prevent the town being taken. The stalemate and the killing continued here right up to the end of the war, and not until 1918 did the Germans draw back from their positions just 5 km (3 miles) from the town.

Several poignant museums, memorials, battle sites and cemeteries can be visited in the hills just outside Verdun on the north side. In this devastated region, nine villages were obliterated without trace. The **Musée-Memorial de Fleury** tells their story. Nearby, the **Ossuaire de Douaumont** contains the unidentified bones of over 130,000 French and German dead. One of the most striking monuments to the Battle of Verdun is Rodin's memorial in Verdun itself. It depicts the winged figure of Victory unable to soar triumphant because she has become caught in the remains of a dead soldier.

The town of Verdun was heavily fortified over the centuries. The crenellated **Porte Chaussée**, a medieval river gateway, still guards the eastern entrance to the town and is the most impressive of the remaining fortifications.

Although battered by war damage, the **Citadelle de Verdun** retains its 12th-century tower, the only relic from the original abbey that Vauban incorporated into his new military design. Now a war museum, the **Citadelle Souterraine**, it recreates Verdun's role in WWI. The citadel casemates come to life as grim trenches, and the presentation ends by showing how the "Unknown Soldier" was chosen for the symbolic tomb under the Arc de Triomphe in Paris *(see p107).*

The town centre is dominated by the cathedral, where Romanesque elements were rediscovered after the 1916 bombardments.

The 16th-century cloisters of Eglise St-Gengoult in Toul

🏛 **Citadelle Souterraine**
Ave du 5ième R.A.P. **Tel** *03 29 86 14 18.* ⏰ *daily.* ● *Jan & 25 Dec.*
🏷 🚫

Toul ❷

Meurthe-et-Moselle. 🏘 *16,500.*
🚌 🚉 ℹ️ *1 pl Charles de Gaulle (03 83 64 90 60).* 🛒 *Wed & Fri.*
www.lepredenancy.fr

Lying within dark forests west of Nancy, the octagonal fortress city of Toul is encircled by the Moselle and the Canal de la Marne. Along with Verdun and Metz, Toul was one of the 4th-century bishoprics. In the early 18th century, Vauban built the citadel, from which the ring of defensive waterways, the octagonal city ramparts and the **Porte de Metz** remain.

The **Cathédrale St-Etienne**, begun in the 13th century, took over 300 years to build. It suffered damage in World War II but the purity of the Champenois style has survived, notably in the arched, high-galleried interior. The imposing Flamboyant Gothic façade is flanked by octagonal towers. Rue du Général-Gengoult, behind the Gothic **Eglise St-Gengoult**, contains a clutch of sculpted Renaissance houses. North of the city the local "grey" Côtes de Toul wines are produced.

Environs
South of Toul, near the town of Neufchâteau, is the birthplace of Joan of Arc at **Domrémy-La-Pucelle**. Next door to the house where she

was born is an exhibition about her remarkable life.

The vast **Parc Régional de Lorraine** takes in red-tiled cottages, vineyards, forests, cropland, *chaumes* (high pastureland), marshes and lakes. Inns in the area are especially noted for their quiche lorraine and *potée lorraine*, a bacon casserole.

Jupiter Slaying a Monster on the Column of Merten in La Cour d'Or

Metz ❸

Moselle. 🏠 *125,000*. 🚄 🚌 🚗
ℹ️ *pl d'Armes (03 87 55 53 76).*
🗓️ *Sat.* www.tourisme.metz.fr

An austere yet appealing city, Metz sits at the confluence of the Moselle and the Seille. Twenty bridges criss-cross the rivers and canals, and there are pleasant walks along the banks. This Gallo-Roman city, now the capital of Lorraine, has always been a pawn in the game of border chess – annexed by Germany in 1871, regained by France in 1918.

Set on a hill above the Moselle, the **Cathédrale St-Etienne** overlooks the historic centre. Inside, there are stained-glass windows, including some by Chagall.

To the northwest of the cathedral, a narrow wooden bridge leads across to the island of Petit Saulcy, site of the oldest French theatre still in use. Located on the other side of the cathedral, the **Porte des Allemands**, spanning a river, more resembles a medieval castle because of its bridge, defensive towers and 13th-century gate with pepper-pot towers.

In the Vieille Ville, place St-Louis is a delightful square bordered by arcaded 14th-century mansions. **Eglise St-Pierre-aux-Nonnains** claims to be one of France's oldest churches. The external walls and façade date from Roman times, while much of the rest belongs to the 7th century. Nearby is the 13th-century **Chapelle des Templiers**, built by the Knights Templar.

🏛 Centre Pompidou Metz
1 parvis des Droits de l'Homme.
Tel 03 87 15 39 39. ◯ *Mon–Wed.*
● *1 May.* 🎫
This museum is an annex to the Pompidou Centre in Paris (*see pp92–3*). Modern European art is displayed inside an unusual hexagonal building.

🏛 Musée de la Cour d'Or
2 rue du Haut-Poirier. *Tel 03 87 20 13 20.* ◯ *Wed–Mon.* ● *pub hols.* 🎫
Also known as the Musée d'Art et d'Histoire, this is set in the Petits-Carmes, a deconsecrated 17th-century monastery incorporating Gallo-Roman baths and a medieval barn. On display are Merovingian stone carvings; Gothic painted ceilings and a variety of German, Flemish and French paintings.

WHITE STORKS
Until recently, the white stork, traditionally a symbol of good fortune in Alsace, was a frequent sight in northeast France. White storks spend the winter in Africa but migrate north to breed. However, the gradual draining of marshy ground, pesticides and electric cables have threatened their survival here. A programme to reintroduce them to the area has set up breeding centres, as at Molsheim and Turckheim, which means these striking birds can once again be seen in Alsace-Lorraine.

The 13th-century Chapelle des Templiers, with restored frescoes, in Metz

Place Stanislas in Nancy, with statue of Stanislas Leczinski, Duke of Lorraine and father-in-law of Louis XV

Nancy ❹

Meurthe-et-Moselle. 🏙 *108,000.*
✈ 🚉 🚌 *14 pl Stanislas
(03 83 35 22 41).* 🛍 *Tue–Sat.*
www.ot-nancy.fr

Lorraine's historic capital
backs on to the Canal du
Marne and the river Meurthe.
In the 18th century, Stanislas
Leczinski, Duke of Lorraine
(*see p302*), transformed the
city, making it a model of
18th-century town planning.

Nancy's second golden age
was the turn of this century,
when glassmaker Emile Gallé
founded the Ecole de Nancy,
a forerunner of the Art
Nouveau movement in France.

Nancy's principal and most
renowned landmark is **place
Stanislas**. Laid out in the 1750s,
this elegantly proportioned
square is enclosed by highly
ornate gilded wrought-iron
gates and railings, which have
been beautifully restored.
Lining the square are fine
hôtels particuliers (town
houses) and chic restaurants.

An Arc de Triomphe leads
to Place de la Carrière, a
gracious, tree-lined square. At
the far end, flanked by semi-
circular arcades, is the Gothic
Palais du Gouvernement.
Next door in the Parc de la

Pépinière is Rodin's statue of
Claude Lorrain, the landscape
painter, born near Nancy.

The Grande Rue provides a
glimpse of medieval Nancy.
Of the original fortifications
only the Porte de la Craffe
remains, which was used as a
prison after the Revolution.

🔒 Eglise et Couvent des Cordeliers et Musée Régional des Arts et Traditions Populaires

64 & 66 grande rue. **Tel** *03 83 32 18
74.* 🛍 *Tue–Sun.* 🔴 *1 Jan, Easter
Sun, 1 May, 14 Jul, 1 Nov, 25 Dec.* 📷
The Dukes of Lorraine are
buried in the crypt, and
the adjoining converted
monastery contains the Musée
Régional des Arts et Traditions
Populaires, covering folklore,
furniture, costumes and crafts.

🏛 Musée des Beaux-Arts

3 pl Stanislas. **Tel** *03 83 85 30 72.*
🛍 *Wed–Mon.* 🔴 *some public
hols.* 📷 ♿ 📷
Recent renovation and a modern extension have enabled
40 per cent more of the
museum's remarkable
collection of 14th- to 20th-
century European art to be
seen, including works by
Delacroix, Manet, Monet,
Utrillo and Modigliani. The
Daum glassware is stunning.

🏛 Musée Historique Lorraine

Palais Ducal, 64 grande rue.
Tel *03 83 32 18 74.* 🛍 *Tue–Sun.*
🔴 *1 Jan, 1 May, 14 Jul, 1 Nov,
25 Dec.* 📷
The Museum of the History of
Lorraine has a rich collection
of archaeological finds, sculptures and paintings, including
two by Georges de la Tour.

🏛 Musée de l'Ecole de Nancy

36–38 rue de Sergent Blandan.
Tel *03 83 40 14 86.* 🛍 *Wed–Sun.*
🔴 *1 Jan, 1 May, 14 July, 1 Nov,
25 Dec.* 📷 📷
Exhibits in reconstructed Art
Nouveau settings include
furniture, fabrics and
jewellery, as well as the
fanciful glassware of Emile
Gallé, founder of the Ecole
de Nancy.

Arc de Triomphe in place Stanislas,
leading to place de la Carrière

Vosges landscape seen from the Route des Crêtes

THE ROUTE DES CRÊTES

This strategic mountain road, 83 km
(50 miles) long, connects the Vosges valleys
from Col du Bonhomme to Cernay, east of
Thann, often through woodland. Hugging
the western side of the Vosges, the Route
des Crêtes was created during World War I to
prevent the Germans from observing French
troop movements. When not shrouded in
mist, there are breathtaking views over
Lorraine from its many "ridges" (*crêtes*).

Gérardmer ❺

Vosges. 🏚 *10,000.* 🚗 🚠
ℹ️ *4 pl des Déportés (03 29 27 27 27).* 🛒 *Thu & Sat.*
www.gerardmer.net

Nestling on the Lorraine side of the Vosges, on the shore of a magnificent lake stretching out before it, Gérardmer is a setting rather than a city. In November 1944, just before its liberation, Gérardmer was razed by the Nazi scorched-earth policy, but has since been reconstructed. Saw mills and wood-carving remain local trades, though tourism is fast replacing the textile industry.

Gérardmer is now a popular holiday resort. In winter, the steep slopes of the Vosges Cristallines around the town turn it into a ski resort, while the lake is used for watersports in summer. The town's attractions also include lakeside walks and boat trips, as well as Géromée cheese, similar to the more famous Munster, from just over the Alsatian border. Gérardmer also boasts the oldest tourist information office in the country, dating from 1875.

The scenic drives and mountain hikes in the Vosges attract adventurous visitors. Most leave the lakeside bowl to head for the Alsatian border and the magnificent **Route des Crêtes**, which can be joined at the mountain pass of Col de la Schlucht.

Recreating village crafts in Ecomusée d'Alsace in Ungersheim

Mulhouse ❻

Haut Rhin. 🏚 *115,000.* ✈️ 🚆 🚌
ℹ️ *9 av du Maréchal Foch (03 89 35 48 48).* 🛒 *Tue, Thu & Sat.*
www.tourisme-mulhouse.com

Close to the Swiss border, Mulhouse is an industrial city, which was badly damaged in World War II. However, there are technical museums and shopping galleries, as well as Alsatian taverns and Swiss wine bars. Most visitors use the city as a base for exploring the rolling hills of the Sundgau on the Swiss border.

Of the museums, **Musée de l'Impression sur Etoffes**, at 14 rue Jean-Jaques Henner, is devoted to textiles and fabric painting, while **Musée Français du Chemin de Fer**, at 2 rue Alfred Glehn, has a collection of steam and electric locomotives. A revamped **Musée National de l'Automobile**, at 192 avenue de Colmar, boasts over 100 Bugattis, a clutch of Mercedes and Ferraris, and Charlie Chaplin's Rolls Royce. In Place de la République is the **Musée Historique**, in the Renaissance former town hall.

Alsatian black pig in Ecomusée d'Alsace in Ungersheim

Environs
At Ungersheim, north of Mulhouse, the **Ecomusée d'Alsace** displays and preserves the region's rural heritage. The 12th-century fortified house from Mulhouse is a dramatic building, complete with Gothic garden. Farms are run along traditional lines, with livestock such as the Alsatian black pig. Rural crafts can be seen in their original settings.

🏛 **Ecomusée d'Alsace**
Chemin du Grosswald. **Tel** *03 89 74 44 65.* ◯ *Apr–Oct & Dec: daily.*
🅿️ ♿ 📷

The lake at Gérardmer, offering sporting and leisure activities

Guebwiller ❼

Haut Rhin. 🏙 12,000. 🚍
🛈 73 rue de la République
(03 89 76 10 63). 🛒 Tue & Fri.
www.tourisme-guebwiller.fr

Surrounded by vineyards and flower-filled valleys, Gueb-willer is known as "the gate-way to the valley of flowers". However, as an industrial town producing textiles and machine tools, it feels cut off from this rural setting. The *caves* and churches make it worth a visit.

Set on a pretty square, **Eglise Notre-Dame** combines Baroque theatricality with Neo-Classical elegance, while **Eglise des Dominicains** boasts Gothic frescoes and a fine rood screen. **Eglise St-Léger**, the richly decorated Romanesque church, is the most rewarding, especially the façade, triple porch and portal.

Eglise St-Léger in Guebwiller

Environs

The scenic Lauch valley, north-west of Guebwiller, is known as "Le Florival" because of its floral aspect. **Lautenbach** is used as a starting point for hikes through this recognized *zone de tranquillité*. The

village has a pink Roman-esque church, whose portal depicts human passion and the battle between Good and Evil. The square leads to the river, a small weir, *lavoir* (public washing place) and houses overhanging the water.

Neuf-Brisach ❽

Haut Rhin. 🏙 2,100. 🚍 🛈 Palais du Gouverneur, 6 pl d'Armes (03 89 72 56 66). 🛒 Sat. **www**.tourisme-rhin.com

Situated near the German border, this octagonal citadel is the military strategist Vauban's masterpiece. Built between 1698 and 1707, the citadel forms a typical star-shaped pattern, with symmetrical towers enclosing 48 equal squares. In the centre, from where straight streets radiate for ease of defence,

THE CITADEL OF NEUF-BRISACH

The outer ring of defences was built around two moats.

Porte de Bâle

Place d'Armes, once the parade ground, provided the innermost refuge.

Porte de Strasbourg was originally protected by a draw-bridge.

Bastion

The fortress is divided into 48 ilôts or squares.

The fortress walls are 9 m (30 ft) high and 4.5 m (14.5 ft) wide at their base.

The Porte de Belfort houses the Musée Vauban. A walk links Porte de Belfort with Porte de Colmar.

Porte de Colmar

The celebrated Issenheim altarpiece by Matthias Grünewald in Colmar

is the place d'Armes and the Eglise St-Louis, which was added in 1731–6. This was the usual homage to Louis XV, implying that the church was dedicated to the King, rather than the saint.

The Porte de Belfort houses the **Musée Vauban**, which includes a model of the town, showing the outlying defences, now concealed by woodland. They represent Vauban's barrier to the fortress and it is to his credit that the citadel was never taken.

🏛 **Musée Vauban**
Pl Porte de Belfort.
Tel 03 89 72 03 93.
🕓 *May–Oct: Wed–Mon; Nov–Apr: groups only, by appt.* 🔲 🔲

Eguisheim ⑨

Haut Rhin. 🏠 *1,600.* 🚉 🔲 ℹ️ *22a grand'rue (03 89 23 40 33).*
www.ot-eguisheim.fr

Eguisheim is a most exquisite small town, laid out within three concentric rings of 13th-century ramparts. The ensemble of austere fortifications and domestic elegance within makes for a surprisingly harmonious whole.

In the centre of town is the octagonal feudal **castle** of the Counts of Eguisheim. A Renaissance fountain in front has the statue of Bruno Eguisheim, born here in 1002. He became Pope Léon IX and was later canonized.

The Grand'Rue is lined with half-timbered houses, many showing their construction

date. Close to the castle is the **Marbacherhof**, a monastic tithe barn and cornhall. On a neighbouring square, the modern parish church retains the original Romanesque sculpted tympanum.

The rest of the town has its share of Hansel-and-Gretel atmosphere, while inviting courtyards offer tastings of *grands crus*. From rue de Hautvilliers, outside the ramparts, a marked path leads through scenic vineyards.

Colmar ⑩

Haut Rhin. 🏠 *68,000.* 🚉 🔲
ℹ️ *4 rue d'Unterlinden (03 89 20 68 92).* 🔲 *Mon, Wed, Thu & Sat.*
www.ot-colmar.fr

Colmar is the best preserved city in Alsace. As a trading post and river port, Colmar had its heyday in the 16th century, when wine merchants shipped their wine along the waterways running through

the picturesque canal quarter, now known as **Petite Venise**. "Little Venice" is best seen on a leisurely boat trip that takes you from the tanners' quarter to the Rue des Tanneurs. The adjoining Place de l'Alsacienne Douane is dominated by the **Koïfhüs**, a galleried customs house with a Burgundian tiled roof, overlooking half-timbered pastel houses which sport sculpted pillars.

Nearby, the place de la Cathédrale quarter is full of 16th-century houses. **Eglise St-Martin**, essentially Gothic, has a noted south portal. To the west, the place des Dominicains, with cafés, is dwarfed by the Gothic **Eglise Dominicaine**. Inside is *La Vierge au Buisson de Rose*s (1473), the red and gold "Virgin of the Rosebush" by Martin Schongauer, a renowned painter and native son of Colmar.

Place d'Unterlinden, the adjoining square, has the **Musée d'Unterlinden**. Set in a Dominican monastery, it displays early Rhenish paintings. The highlight is the Issenheim altarpiece. A masterpiece of emotional intensity, it is part of an early 16th-century Alsatian panel painting by Matthias Grünewald.

In the historic centre, the quaint rue des Têtes has the former wine exchange, a Renaissance town house known as the Maison des Têtes because of the grimacing heads on the gabled façade. And in rue Mercière, **Maison Pfister**, with its slender stair turret and galleried flower-decked façade, has come to typify the city.

Along the Quai de la Poissonerie in the Petite Venise area of Colmar

For hotels and restaurants in this region see pp561–2 and pp612–14

Riquewihr

Haut Rhin. 🚶 *1,300.* 🏠
ℹ️ *2 rue de 1ère Armée
(03 89 73 23 23).* 🗓️ *Fri.*
www.ribeauville-riquewihr.com

Vineyards run right up to the ramparts of Riquewihr, the prettiest village on the Route du Vin *(see pp232–3)*. Deeply pragmatic, Riquewihr winemakers plant roses at the end of each row of vines – both for their pretty effect and as early detectors of parasites. The village belonged to the Counts of Wurtemberg until the Revolution and has grown rich on wine, from Tokay and Pinot Gris to Gewürztraminer and Riesling. Virtually an open-air museum, Riquewihr abounds in cobbled alleys, geranium-clad balconies, galleried courtyards, romantic double ramparts and watchtowers.

From the Hôtel de Ville, the **rue du Général de Gaulle** climbs gently past medieval and Renaissance houses, half-timbered, stone-clad or corbelled. Oriel windows vie with sculpted portals and medieval sign boards. On the

right lies the idyllic **place des Trois Eglises**. A passageway leads through the ramparts to the vineyards on the hill. Further up lies the **Dolder**, a 13th-century belfry, followed by the **Tour des Voleurs** (both are museums, the latter with a medieval torture chamber), marking the second tier of ramparts. Beyond the gateway is the **Cour des Bergers**, gardens laid out around the 16th-century ramparts. Visitors outnumber the locals in summer or during the superb Christmas market.

The pretty – and popular – village of Riquewihr, set among vineyards

Ribeauvillé

Haut Rhin. 🚶 *5,000.* 🚉 🏠
ℹ️ *1 grand'rue (03 89 73 23 23).*
🗓️ *Sat.* www.ribeauville-riquewihr.com

Overlooked by three ruined castles, Ribeauvillé is stiflingly prettified, as may be expected from a favoured town on the Route du Vin. This status is partly due to healthy sales of the celebrated *grands crus* of Alsace, especially Riesling. There are ample opportunities for tastings, particularly near the park, in the lower part of town *(see pp232–3)*.

On the grand'rue (No. 14) is the **Pfifferhüs**, the minstrels' house. As locals declare, Ribeauvillé is the capital of the *kougelhopf*, the almond-flavoured Alsatian cake.

Tortuous alleys wind past steep-roofed artisans' and *vignerons'* houses in the upper part of the town. Beyond are Renaissance fountains, painted façades and **St Grégoire-le-Grand**, the Gothic parish church. A marked path, which begins in this part of town, leads into the vineyards.

Château du Haut-Koenigsbourg

Orschwiller. **Tel** *03 88 82 50 60.*
⏰ *daily.* ⏺️ *1 Jan, 1 May, 25 Dec.*
📷 ✔️ ♿ 🎁
www.haut-koenigsbourg.fr

Looming above the pretty village of St-Hippolyte, this castle is the most popular attraction in Alsace. In 1114, the Swabian Emperor, Frederick of Hohenstaufen, built the first Teutonic castle here, which was destroyed in 1462. Rebuilt and added to under the Habsburgs, it burned down in 1633. At the end of the 19th century, Kaiser Wilhelm II commissioned Berlin architect Bodo Ebhardt to restore the castle. The result of his painstaking work was a precise reconstruction of the original building.

With a drawbridge, fierce keep and rings of fortifications, this warm sandstone hybrid is

a sophisticated feudal château. The Cour d'Honneur is a breathtaking recreation, with a pointed corner turret and creaky arcaded galleries. Inside are gloomy "Gothic" chambers and "Renaissance" rooms. La Grande Salle is the most far-fetched, with a Neo-Gothic gallery and ornate panelling. From the

battlements, almost 750 m (2,500 ft) above the Alsace plain, stretches a Rhineland panorama, bordered by the Black Forest and the Alps. On the other side are views from the high Vosges to villages and vineyards below.

Upper garden

West bastion

West wing

Outer walls

Chapelle St-Sébastien outside Dambach-la-Ville, along the Route du Vin

Environs

Medieval **Dambach-la-Ville**, another pretty town, is linked to Andlau and red-tiled Itterswiller by a delightful rural road through vineyards.

Ebersmunster, a picturesque hamlet, has an onion-domed abbey church, whose Baroque interior is a sumptuous display of gilded stucco.

Obernai ⓯

Bas Rhin. 🏰 11,000. 🚇 🚌 ℹ️
pl du Beffroi (03 88 95 64 13).
🛒 Thu. www.obernai.fr

At the north end of the Route du Vin, Obernai retains a flavour of authentic Alsace: residents speak Alsatian, at festivities women wear traditional costume, and church services are well-attended in the cavernous Neo-Gothic **Eglise St-Pierre-et-St-Paul**. The place du Marché is well-preserved, and features the gabled **Halle aux Blés**, a 16th-century corn hall (now a restaurant) above a former butcher's shop, with a façade adorned with cows' and dragons' heads. Place de la Chapelle, the adjoining square, has a Renaissance fountain and the 16th-century **Hôtel de Ville** and the **Kapellturm**, the galleried Gothic belfry. Side streets have Renaissance and medieval timber-framed houses. A stroll past the cafés on rue du Marché ends in a pleasant park by the ramparts.

Sélestat ⓮

Bas Rhin. 🏰 17,000. 🚇 🚌 ℹ️
Commanderie Saint Jean, bd du Général Leclerc (03 88 58 87 20). 🛒 Tue, Sat. www.selestat-tourisme.com

During the Renaissance, Sélestat was the intellectual centre of Alsace, with a tradition of humanism fostered by Beatus Rhenanus, a friend of Erasmus. The **Bibliothèque Humaniste** has a collection of editions of some of the earliest printed books, including the first book to name America, in 1507. Nearby are the Cour des Prélats, a turreted ivy-covered mansion, and the Tour de l'Horloge, a clocktower. **Eglise Ste-Foy** is 12th-century, with an octagonal belltower. Opposite is **Eglise St-Georges**, glittering with green and red "Burgundian tiles".

🏛 Bibliothèque Humaniste
1 rue de la Bibliothèque. **Tel** 03 88 58 07 20. ⬜ Mon, Wed–Sat am; (Jul–Aug: Wed–Mon exc. Sun am). ⬤ public hols. 🎟 www.bibliotheque-humaniste.eu

Young *Alsaciens* in traditional costume

Environs
Odile, Alsace's seventh-century patron saint, was born in Obernai but she is venerated on **Mont Sainte-Odile**, to the west.

Molsheim, a former bishopric and fortified market town 10 km (6 miles) north, is noted for its Metzig, a Renaissance-style butchers' guildhall.

Le Mémorial de l'Alsace-Moselle at Schirmeck commemorates the 10,000 who died at the Struthof concentration camp across the valley.

North wing, with kitchens
South wing, with chapel
Entrance ramp to upper castle
Hostelry
Outer walls
Guardroom
Entrance
Well tower

Drawbridge within the walls of Château du Haut-Koenigsbourg

For hotels and restaurants in this region see pp561–2 and pp612–14

Strasbourg ⓰

Halfway between Paris and Prague, Strasbourg is not surprisingly often known as "the crossroads of Europe". The city wears its European cosmopolitanism with ease – after all, its famous cathedral has catered to both Catholic and Protestant congregations – and as one of the capitals of the European Union has sensibly located the futuristic European Parliament building some way from the historic centre. One of the ways to see this, along with the more traditional city sights, is to take a boat trip along the waterways encircling the Old Town. On the way you will take in the Ponts-Couverts, covered bridges linked by medieval watchtowers that provide an observation point for the four Ill canals, and the scenic Petite France, once the tanners' district, dotted with mills and criss-crossed by bridges.

Cathedral statue

Barge on the canal

The central portal of the west façade of the cathedral

🛉 Cathédrale Notre-Dame

A masterpiece of stone lacework, the sandstone cathedral "rises like a most sublime, wide-arching tree of God", as Goethe marvelled. Though construction began in the late 11th century (the choir is Romanesque, the nave is Gothic), it ended only in 1439, with the completion of the west façade, begun in 1277. The three portals are ornamented with statues. But the crowning glory is the rose window. The south portal leads to the Gothic Pillar of Angels (c. 1230), set beside the Astronomical Clock: mechanical figures appear accompanied by chimes at 12:31pm. There are wonderful views over the city from the viewing platform, and on some summer evenings there are organ concerts.

In place de la Cathédrale, Maison Kammerzell, now a popular restaurant, was once a rich merchant's mansion, its highly elaborate, carved façade dating from mid-15th–late-16th centuries.

🏛 Palais Rohan

2 pl du Château. **Tel** 03 88 80 50 50. ⬜ Wed–Mon. ⚫ 1 Jan, Good Fri, 1 May, 1 & 11 Nov, 25 Dec. 🖼 ♿ **www**.musee-strasbourg.org

Designed by the king's architect, Robert de Cotte, in 1730, this grand Classical palace was intended for the Prince-Bishops of Strasbourg. It houses three museums: the Musée des Beaux Arts; the Musée Archéologique; and the Musée des Arts Décoratifs, which contains the sumptuous State Apartments and one of the finest collections of ceramics in France.

The Alsace Route des Vins

Meandering over 180 km (110 miles) from Marlenheim to Thann, the picturesque wine route takes in historic towns with cobbled streets, medieval timber-framed houses and Renaissance fountains. Romantically appointed *winstubs,* or cellars, offer traditional *choucroute garnie* and flowery white Alsatian wines.

Alsatian wine master

Dedicated wine lovers could spend two or three days covering the route at leisure, or may want to make shorter trips in either direction to or from Colmar. For a refreshing contrast from the unremitting charm of the towns and villages, escape occasionally into *sentiers viticoles* – lovely paths through the vineyards themselves.

Harvesting grapes in Alsace

MARLENHEIM

A352

D422

Mont-Ste Odile

STRASBOURG →

Andlau

D35

Sélestat

Haut-Koenigsbourg

D1b

D10

N83

COLMAR

D85

A35

Rouffach

THANN

MULHOUSE

Molsheim ①
Renaissance buildings and Riesling vineyard vie for attention with Bugatti motor museum

Obernai ②
The galleried Kapellturm in the place du Marché dates from the 13th–16th centuries

Dambach-la-Ville ③
Vintner's carts now serve as decoration in this pretty medieval town renowned for its *grand cru* Frankstein.

Ribeauvillé ④
Famed for its Riesling, the town celebrates Pipers' Day, the first Sunday in September, with a fountain spouting free wine.

Riquewihr ⑤
A showcase of medieval and Renaissance houses, this is one of France's most visited towns.

Eguisheim ⑦
This ancient town ringed by medieval houses produces two *grands crus*, Eichberg (Oak Hill) and Pfersigberg (Peach Hill).

Guebwiller ⑧
Eglise St-Léger dates from the Middle Ages, when Guebwiller grew rich on wine. Today it is a busy textile town.

Turckheim ⑥
Ancient buildings encircle place Turenne in this Renaissance town famous for its Brand wine.

KEY

— Wine route

⚌ Other roads

0 kilometres   5

0 miles   5

late-harvested Alsatian classic

KEY FACTS

Location and climate
Protected by the Vosges, Alsace has a warm climate and France's lowest annual rainfall.

Grape varieties
Alsace wines are known simply by their grape variety. *Gewürztraminer*, with its exotic rose-petal character, is most typically Alsatian, although the *Riesling* is arguably the finest. *Muscat* is another aromatic variety. Spicy but less assertive than Gewürztraminer, *Pinot Gris* and the crisper, dry *Pinot Blanc* go well with food. *Pinot Noir* is the only red variety.

Lusciously rich, sweet, late-harvested wines are an Alsace speciality.

Best producers
Albert Boxler, Marcel Deiss, Rolly Gassmann, Beyer, Meyer-Fonne, Kuentz-Bas, Domaine Weinbach, Dopff & Irion, Olivier Zind-Humbrecht, Charles Schléret, Domaines Schlumberger, Domaine Ostertag, Domaine Trimbach, Hugel & Fils, Cave de Turckheim.

Good vintages
2008, 2004, 2001, 1998, 1996, 1995.

The 12th-century chapel of the Château du Haut-Barr, near Saverne

Saverne ⑰

Bas Rhin. 🏠 12,300. 🚉 🚌 ℹ️ 37 grand rue (03 88 91 80 47). 📅 Tue & Thu. **www**.ot-saverne.fr

Framed by hills, and situated on the river Zorn and the Marne-Rhine canal, Saverne is a pretty sight. The town was a fief of the prince-bishops of Strasbourg and its sandstone Château des Rohan was a favourite summer residence. Today, it houses the **Musée du Château des Rohan**, whose collection traces Saverne's past. On the far side of the château, the grand'rue is studded with restaurants and timber-framed Renaissance houses.

🏛 Musée du Château des Rohan
Château des Rohan. **Tel** 03 88 91 06 28. ☐ Jan–mid-Jun & mid-Sep–Dec: Mon–Fri pm, 10am–6pm Sat & Sun; mid-Jun–mid-Sep: 10am–6pm daily. ⬤ Tue. 🎫 ♿ restricted.

Environs
To the southwest, perched on a rocky spur, the ruined **Château du Haut-Barr** – the "Eye of Alsace" – once commanded the pass of Col de Saverne. In **Marmoutier**, 6 km (3.5 miles) south, is an abbey church with a Romanesque-Lombard façade and octagonal towers.

Betschdorf ⑱

Bas Rhin. 🏠 4,000. ℹ️ La Mairie (03 88 54 44 92). **www**.betschdorf.com

The vibrant village of Betschdorf borders the Forêt de Haguenau, 45 km (27 miles) north of Strasbourg. Many residents occupy timber-framed houses dating from the 18th century, when pottery made the village prosperous. Generations of potters have passed down the knowledge of the characteristic blue-grey glaze to their sons, while the women have been entrusted with decorating it in cobalt blue. A pottery museum, with a

Betschdorf pottery workshop attached, displays rural ceramics. Betschdorf is a good place to try *tartes flambées* – hot, crispy bases topped with cheese or fruit.

Environs
Another pottery village, **Soufflenheim**, lies 10 km (6 miles) southeast. Its earth-coloured pottery is usually painted with bold flowers. To the north, close to the German border, the picturesque town of **Wissembourg** has many half-timbered houses and the second-largest church in Alsace after Strasbourg Cathedral, Eglise St-Pierre et St-Paul.

WESTERN
FRANCE

Introducing Western France

The western regions of France have played very different historical roles, from the royal heartland of the Loire Valley to separatist Celtic Brittany. These are mainly rich farming regions, with fishing important along the coasts. Heavy industry and oil refineries are concentrated around Rouen and Le Havre. Visitors come for the wonderful beaches, quiet rural byways and the sumptuous Loire châteaux. This map shows some of the region's most celebrated sights.

The evocative silhouette of Mont-St-Michel *has welcomed pilgrims since the 11th century. Today nearly one million visitors a year walk across the causeway to the island abbey (see pp256–61).*

Guimiliau Parish Close

Mont-St-Michel

BRITTANY
(See pp268–85)

Carnac Megaliths

The megaliths of Carnac *are evidence of early settlers in Brittany. These ancient granite blocks, arranged in intriguing patterns, date back to 4000 BC and are thought to have had a religious or astronomical purpose (see p279).*

The Bayeux Tapestry (see pp252–3) *shows William the Conqueror's invasion of England from the French point of view. Among its 58 scenes, key events such as the Battle of Hastings in 1066 are depicted with great vigour and finesse. Here, two of William's messengers are shown hurrying to meet him.*

Château de Chambord *is the largest and most extravagant of the Loire châteaux* (see pp302–3). *François I transformed the original hunting lodge to a luxurious moated castle in 1519. Its splendour was completed by Louis XIV in 1685. Inside the 440 rooms are François' salamander emblem and 365 fireplaces, one for every day of the year.*

Rouen Cathedral

Bayeux Tapestry

NORMANDY
(See pp246–67)

Chartres Cathedral

Le Mans Cathedral

Château de Chambord

Château de Chenonceau

THE LOIRE VALLEY
(See pp286–313)

Château de Villandry

0 kilometres 50

0 miles 50

The Flavours of Western France

The Atlantic coast, the rich agricultural hinterland of dairy farms, orchards and vegetable fields, and the rivers of the Loire Valley combine to produce some of France's best loved food. Vegetables are grown in abundance in Brittany and the alluvial soils of the Loire, and the orchards of Normandy are bountiful. Fish from the windswept coast of Brittany or the channel ports of Normandy play a key role in the cuisine. Hearty meat dishes range from the celebrated duck of Rouen to the rabbit and game of the Sologne in the Loire. Fine cheeses are made here, and butter is the favoured cooking medium.

Normandy apples

Norman cheese-producer displaying his wares

NORMANDY

Normandy's lush green pastures, dotted with brown and white cows, and orchards heavy with apples, make it a great source of veal, milk, cheese, cream, butter, apples and pears. Duck is a speciality, as is *pre-salé* lamb from the salt-rich marshes around Mont-St-Michel. Many vegetables are grown

and wild mushrooms thrive in the damp meadows and woodlands in autumn. Fish is important, with catches of sole, plaice and mackerel, skate and herrings, and 80 per cent of France's scallops, plus a great variety of shellfish.

Camembert is Normandy's most famous cheese; others include Pont l'Evêque, the pungent-smelling Livarot, rich Brillat-Savarin and Petit-Suisse, a small, fresh white cheese eaten with sugar.

Apples symbolize Normandy above all, and cider is traditionally drunk with food while Calvados, the powerful apple brandy, is served with meals as *le trou normand*.

BRITTANY

Thousands of kilometres of coastline yield an abundance of fish and seafood. Oysters are highly prized, as are mussels, harvested both wild and cultivated. Other fish

Some of the favourite vegetables of western France (Artichokes, Asparagus, Shallots, Watercress, Broccoli, Radishes)

REGIONAL DISHES AND SPECIALITIES

Fish dominates the menus here, most spectacularly in the *plateau de fruits de mer*, featuring oysters, crabs, langoustines, prawns, shrimps, cockles and clams, piled on a bed of ice. Oysters are served simply with lemon or shallot vinegar, but can also come stuffed, gratinéed or wrapped in pastry. Fresh fish may be grilled, baked in sea salt (*sel de Guérande* is the best) braised in cider or served with *beurre blanc* ("white butter" sauce with shallots, wine vinegar and **Pears** cream). Lobster is often served *à l'Armoricaine*. *Cotriade*, the Breton fish stew, combines a selection of the catch of the day with onions and potatoes. *Moules marinières* (mussels steamed in white wine with shallots and butter) is the popular classic. As a change from fish, look for *gigot de sept heures* – lamb slowly pot-roasted for seven hours.

Homard à l'armoricaine
Lobster, served in a herby tomato and onion sauce, enriched with brandy.

Superb Breton oysters for sale at a regional fish market

caught include monkfish, tuna, sardines, scallops and lobster. Pig-rearing is important, so expect roast pork, smoked sausages, hams and *boudin noir* (black/blood pudding), delicious served with apples. A great delicacy is the *pre-salé* lamb from Ile de Ouessant, served with haricot beans. Artichokes are the symbol of Brittany, an indication of the importance of vegetables, especially winter produce like cauliflower, onions and potatoes.

Crêpes (pancakes), both sweet and savoury, are a key element of the Breton diet. They come as buckwheat *galettes* with savoury fillings such as ham, cheese, spinach or mushrooms, or as lacy light dessert versions with sweet fillings and known as *crêpes dentelles* (*dentelle* meaning "lace").

THE LOIRE VALLEY

This huge region takes pride in a truly diverse range of specialities. Grass-fed cattle are raised in Anjou, and sheep in the Berry region. Excellent free-range chick-

Cheese and charcuterie at Loches market in the Loire Valley

ens, *poulet fermier Loué*, are raised in Touraine and the Orléanais. The forests and lakes of the Sologne yield deer, wild boar, pheasant, partridge, hare and duck. Charcuterie includes *rillettes*, (shredded and potted pork), and ham from the Vendée. The Atlantic coast produces a variety of fish and the Loire itself is a source of pike, shad, tench, salmon, eels and lampreys. Mushrooms are cultivated in the limestone caves around Saumur, but of the many vegetables grown, best of all is Sologne asparagus. Superb goats' cheeses include St Maure de Touraine, ash-coated Valençay and the little Crottins de Chavignol.

ON THE MENU

Alose à l'oseille Shad in a sorrel sauce.

Côte de veau vallée d'Auge Veal in mushrooms, cream and cider or Calvados.

Far aux pruneaux Egg batter pudding baked with prunes.

Kig ha farz Meat and vegetable hotpot with buckwheat dumpling.

Marmite Dieppoise Assorted fish stewed in cider or white wine with cream.

Tergeule Creamy baked rice pudding with cinnamon.

Tripes à la Mode de Caen Tripe with calves' feet, onions or leeks, herbs and cider.

Sole Normande *Baked sole in sauce of egg and cream, garnished with mussels, oysters, mushrooms and prawns.*

Canard Rouennais *Duclair duck, part-roasted then finished in a rich sauce of duck liver and shallots.*

Tarte tatin *Caramelized upside-down apple tart, originally made at the Hotel Tatin in the Loire Valley.*

France's Wine Regions: the Loire

With a few exceptions, the Loire is a region of good rather than great wines. The fertile agricultural soils of the meandering flatlands of the "Garden of France" are fine for fruit and vegetables, less so for the production of great wines. The cool, northern, Atlantic-influenced climate nonetheless produces refreshing reds and summer rosés, both dry and lusciously sweet white

Cabernet Franc, red grape of the Loire

LOCATOR MAP

☐ Loire wine region

wines and attractively bracing sparkling wines. Dry white wines are very much in the majority here, and are usually intended for early consumption, so vintages in the Loire tend to matter less than in the classic red wine regions.

The sweet wine *of Quarts de Chaume, within the Coteaux du Layon appellation, is little-known outside France.*

Muscadet *with the words* sur lie *on the label has been aged on its "lees" (see page 27), giving the wine more flavour and interest.*

WINE REGIONS

The Loire, flowing for some 1,000 km (620 miles), links the major wine areas of the Loire Valley. From its source in the Ardèche, it flows north through the centre of France to the Sancerre and Pouilly Fumé vineyards, then west through Touraine and Anjou, finally reaching the coastal flats of the Pays Nantais, home of Muscadet.

Clos de l'Echo, Chinon, producer of fine, herbaceous red wine

KEY

☐ Pays Nantais

☐ Anjou-Saumur

☐ Haut-Poitou

☐ Touraine

☐ Central Vineyards

0 kilometres   15

0 miles   15

*is red wine has been
ade using grapes from
eilles vignes – the oldest
d the best vines on the
ower's property.*

Red wine vineyards at Bourgueil

Vouvray *makes
still and sparkling
white wine, the
latter often aged
in chalk caves
very like those
in Champagne.*

A classic wine *with a price to match,
Pouilly Fumé is revered for its
unique, smoky "gunflint" character.*

KEY FACTS ABOUT LOIRE WINES

Location and Climate
Fertile agricultural soils support
fruit, vegetables and cereals; the
poorer soils support grapes. The
climate is cool, influenced by the Atlantic,
giving the wines a refreshing acidity.

Grape Varieties
The **Melon de Bourgogne** makes
simple, dry white wines. The
Sauvignon makes gooseberryish,
flinty dry whites, finest in Sancerre and
Pouilly Fumé but also good in Touraine.
The **Chenin Blanc** makes dry and medium
Anjou, Savennières, Vouvray, Montlouis
and Saumur, sparkling Vouvray and Saumur,
and the famous sweet whites, Bonnezeaux,

Vouvray and Quarts de Chaume.
Summery reds are made from the
Gamay and the fruity,
herbaceous **Cabernet Franc**.

Good Producers
Muscadet: Sauvion, Guy Bossard,
Michel Bregeon. *Anjou, Savenn-
nières, Vouvray*: Richou, Ogereau,
Nicolas Joly, Huet, Domaine des
Aubuissières, Bourillon-Dorléans, Jacky
Blot, Domaine Gessey. *Touraine* (white):
Pibaleau. *Saumur-Champigny* (red):
Filliatreau, Chateâu du Hureau. *Chinon,
Bourgueil*: Couly-Dutheil, Yves Loiseau. *San-
cerre, Pouilly Fumé, Ménétou-Salon*: Francis
Cotat, Vacheron, Mellot, Vincent Pinard.

From Defence to Decoration

The great châteaux of the Loire Valley gradually evolved from purely defensive structures to decorative palaces. With the introduction of firearms, castles lost their defensive function and comfort and taste predominated. Defensive elements like towers, battlements, moats and gatehouses were retained largely as symbols of rank and ancestry. Renaissance additions, like galleries and dormer windows, added elegance.

Salamander emblem of François 1

Slate and stone walls

Angers (see p291), *a fortress built from 1230–40 by Louis IX, stands on a rocky hill in the town centre. In 1585, Henri III removed the pepper-pot shaped towers from 17 fortifications which were formerly 30 m (98 ft) high.*

Fortifications with pepper-pot towers removed

Circular tower, formerly defensive

Corbelled walkways, once useful in battle

Chaumont (see p306) *was rebuilt in 1445–1510 in Renaissance style by the Amboise family. Although it has a defensive appearance, with circular towers, corbelled walkways and a gatehouse, these features are mainly decorative. It was restored after c.1833.*

Decorated turret

Azay-le-Rideau (see p296), *regarded as one of the most elegant and well-designed Renaissance châteaux, was built by finance minister Gilles Berthelot (1518–1527) and his wife Philippa Lesbahy. It is a mixture of traditional turrets with Renaissance pilasters and pinnacles. Most dramatic is the interior staircase with its three storeys of twin bays and an intricately decorated pediment.*

Renaissance carved windows

Pilasters (columns)

Cylindrical tower

Dormer windows

Ussé (see p295) *was built in 1462 by Jean de Bueil as a fortress with parapets containing openings for missiles, battlements and gunloops. The Espinay family, chamberlains to both Louis XI and Charles VIII, bought the château and changed the walls overlooking the main court-yard to Renaissance style with dormer windows and pilasters. In the 17th century the north wing was demolished to create palatial terraces.*

Breton Traditions

Brittany was christened Breiz Izel (Little Britain) by the Welsh and Cornish migrants who fled here in the 5th and 6th centuries AD and imposed their customs, language and religion on the local Gauls. Brittany resisted Charlemagne, the Vikings, the Normans, English alliances and even French rule until 1532. Today, Breton is taught in some schools, and a busy calendar keeps Brittany in touch with its past and with other Celtic regions.

Bigouden lace headdresses

Breton music *has strong Celtic links. Instruments like the* biniou, *similar to the bagpipes, and the oboe-like* bombarde *are often heard at local festivals.*

A pardon *is an annual religious festival honouring a local saint. The name derives from the granting of indulgences to pardon the sins of the past year. Some* pardons, *like those at Ste-Anne d'Auray and Ste-Anne-la-Palud, still attract thousands of pilgrims who carry banners and holy relics through the streets. Most* pardons *take place between April and September.*

Lace *coiffe*   **Felt hat**   **Linen** *coiffe*   **Small headdress**

Wooden clogs

Embroidered apron

Baggy Breton trousers

Breton costumes, *still seen at pardons and weddings, varied as each area had distinctive headdresses or* coiffes. *Artists like Gauguin often painted the costumes. There are good museum collections in Quimper (see p274) and Pont l'Abbé in Pays Bigouden (see p273).*

Brittany's Coastal Wildlife

With its granite cliffs, sweeping bays, rias and deep estuaries, the Brittany coastline contains a wealth of varied wildlife habitats. Parts of the coast have a tidal range of more than 50 m (150 ft), the highest in France, and this great variation in sea level divides marine life into several distinct zones. Most of the region's famous shellfish, including mussels, clams, and oysters, live on the lower shore, either on rocks or in muddy sand where they are submerged for most of the day. Higher zones are the preserve of limpets and barnacles and several kinds of seaweed which can survive out of the water for long periods. Above the sea, towering cliffs offer a nursery for sea-birds and a foothold for many kinds of wild flowers.

Starfish

Cliffs at the Pointe du Raz, Brittany

The Ile de Bréhat at low tide

FEATURES OF THE COAST

This scene shows some of the wildlife habitats found on the Brittany coastline. When exploring the shore, make a note of the tide times, particularly if you plan to walk along the foot of the cliffs.

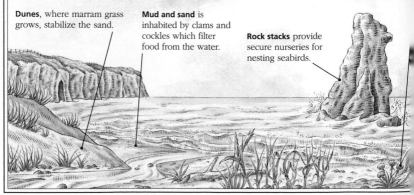

Salt-marsh flowers are at their best in late summer

Dunes, where marram grass grows, stabilize the sand.

Mud and sand is inhabited by clams and cockles which filter food from the water.

Rock stacks provide secure nurseries for nesting seabirds.

OYSTER BEDS

Like most marine molluscs, oysters begin their lives as tiny floating larvae. The first step in *ostréiculture*, or oyster cultivation, consists of providing the larvae with somewhere to settle, which is usually a stack of submerged tiles. The developing oysters are later transferred to beds and left to mature before being collected for the market.

Oyster beds at Cancale

Clifftop turf often contains a narrow band of wild flowers sandwiched between fields and the sea.

Rockpools are flooded twice daily by the tide. They are inhabited by fish, molluscs, sea anemones, and sponges.

COASTAL WILDLIFE

The structure of this shore determines the wildlife that lives on it. In a world beset by wind and waves, rocks provide solid anchorage for plants and a secure habitat for many small animals. Muddy sand is rich in nutrients, and has a greater abundance of life – although most of this is concealed beneath the surface.

Cliffs

The rock dove *is a cliff-dwelling ancestor of the well-known city pigeon.*

Thrift *is a common spring flower, found on exposed ledges near the sea.*

Rocks and Rockpools

Seaweed *of many different varieties is exposed each day by the falling tide.*

The limpet, *a slow-moving creature, scrapes tiny plants from the rock surface.*

The goby, *with its sharp eyesight, dashes for cover at the first sign of movement above.*

Crabs *live at many different water depths. Some species are extremely good swimmers.*

Mud and Sand

Cockles *live in large numbers just beneath the surface of muddy sand.*

The curlew *has a forceps-like curved beak for extracting shell-fish from mud and sand.*

NORMANDY

EURE · SEINE-MARITIME · MANCHE · CALVADOS · ORNE

The quintessential image of Normandy is of a lush, pastoral region of apple orchards and contented cows, cider and pungent cheeses – but the region also spans the windswept beaches of the Cotentin and the wooded banks of the Seine valley. Highlights include the great abbey churches of Caen, the mighty island of Mont-St-Michel and Monet's garden at Giverny.

Normandy gets its name from the Viking Norsemen who sailed up the river Seine in the 9th century. Pillagers turned settlers, they made their capital at Rouen – today a cultured cathedral city that commands the east of the region. Here the Seine meanders seaward past the ancient abbeys at Jumièges and St-Wandrille to a coast that became an open-air studio for Impressionist painters during the mid- and late 19th century.

North of Rouen are the chalky cliffs of the Côte d'Albâtre. The mood softens at the port of Honfleur and the elegant resorts of the Côte Fleurie to the west. Inland lies the Pays d'Auge, with its half-timbered manor houses and patch-eyed cows. The western half of Normandy is predominantly rural, a *bocage* countryside of small, high-hedged fields with windbreaks composed of beech trees.

The modern city of Caen is worth visiting for its two great 11th-century abbey churches built by William the Conqueror and his queen, Matilda. Close by in Bayeux, the story of William's invasion of England is told in detail by the town's famous tapestry. Memories of another invasion, the D-Day Landings of 1944, still linger along the Côte de Nacre and the Cotentin Peninsula. Thousands of Allied troops poured ashore on to these magnificent beaches in the closing stages of World War II. The Cotentin Peninsula is capped by the port of Cherbourg, still a strategic naval base. At its western foot stands one of France's greatest attractions: the monastery island of Mont-St-Michel.

Half-timbered manor house in the village of Beuvron-en-Auge, near Lisieux

◁ Rich pastures and brown and white Norman cattle, the traditional wealth of the province

Exploring Normandy

Normandy's rich historical sights and diverse landscape make it ideal for touring by car or bicycle.
Rewarding coastal drives and good beaches can be
found along the windswept Côte d'Albâtre and the
Cotentin Peninsula. Further south is one of France's
most celebrated sights, Mont-St-Michel. Inland,
follow the meanders of the Seine valley, passing cider
orchards and half-timbered houses along the way, to
visit historic Rouen and Monet's garden at Giverny.

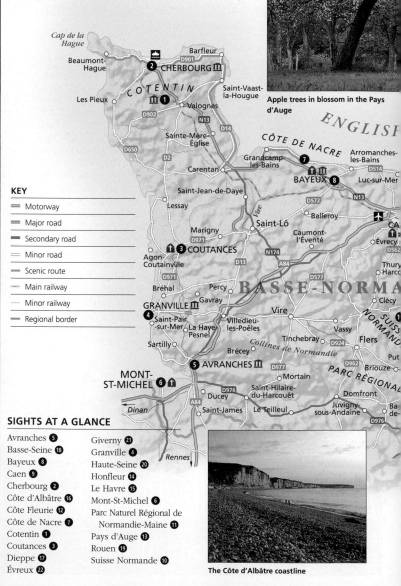

Apple trees in blossom in the Pays d'Auge

KEY

- ▬ Motorway
- ▬ Major road
- ▬ Secondary road
- ▬ Minor road
- ▬ Scenic route
- — Main railway
- — Minor railway
- ▬ Regional border

SIGHTS AT A GLANCE

The Côte d'Albâtre coastline

GETTING AROUND

Access to and through the region from Calais is quick and direct on the A16, which links up with the A28–A29 and A13 motorways to Paris, and runs west to Caen, and beyond on the A84. There are also main road and rail links to the cross-Channel ports of Dieppe, Le Havre, Caen (Ouistreham) and Cherbourg. Travel by public transport beyond these arteries is limited. The region is threaded with minor roads, particularly delightful in the Pays d'Auge and Cotentin Peninsula. The main airports are at Rouen, Le Havre and Caen.

The town of Les Andelys shrouded in mist

Rugged cliffs on the Cotentin Peninsula

Cotentin ❶

Manche. 🚹 � 🚐 🚢 *Cherbourg.*
🚹 *2 quai Alexandre III, Cherbourg
(02 33 93 52 02).* **www**.manche-
tourisme.com

Thrusting into the English
Channel, the Cotentin
Peninsula has a landscape
similar to Brittany's. Its long
sandy beaches have wild and
windblown headlands around
Cap de la Hague and Nez de
Jobourg. The latter is popular
among bird-watchers – gannets
and shearwaters fly by in large
numbers. Along the east coast
stretches Utah Beach, where
American troops landed as part
of the Allied invasion on
6 June 1944. Inland, Ste-Mère-
Eglise commemorates these
events with its **Musée Airborne**
(Airborne Troops Museum).
Just outside Ste-Mère-Eglise,
the **Ferme Musée du Cotentin**
has farm animals and activities,
which give an insight into
rural life in the early 1900s,
while further north, in the
market town of Valognes, the
**Musée Régional du Cidre et
du Calvados** celebrates the
thriving local talent for making
cider and Calvados.

Two fishing ports command
the Peninsula's northeast
corner: Barfleur and St-Vaast-la-
Hougue, the latter famous for
oysters and a base for boat
trips to the Ile de Tatihou. The
Val de Saire is ideal for a scenic
drive, with a view point at
La Pernelle the best place to
survey the coast. On the west
side of the Peninsula, warmed
by the Gulf Stream, the resort

of Barneville-Carteret offers
sandy beaches and summer
boat trips to the Channel
Islands. The low-lying, marshy
landscape east of Carentan
forms the heart of the Parc
Régional des Marais du
Potentin et du Bessin.

🏛 **Musée Airborne**
14 rue Eisenhower, Ste-Mère-Eglise.
Tel 02 33 41 41 35. ⬜ Feb–Nov:
daily & Christmas hols. ⬤ Dec–Jan.
📷 🚻 **www**.musee-airborne.com

🏛 **Ferme Musée du Cotentin**
Rte de Beauvais, Ste-Mère-Eglise.
Tel 02 33 95 40 20. ⬜ Jun–Sep:
daily; Feb sch hols–May & Nov sch
hols: daily pms. 📷

🏛 **Musée Régional du Cidre
et du Calvados**
Rue du Petit-Versailles, Valognes. *Tel*
02 33 40 22 73. ⬜ Apr–Sep: Wed–
Mon (Jul & Aug: daily). ⬤ Sun am. 📷

Cherbourg ❷

Manche. 🌅 44,100. 🚹 🚋 🚐
🚢 🚹 2 quai Alexandre III (02 33 93
52 02). ⬤ Tue, Thu & Sat.
www.otcherbourgcotentin.fr

Cherbourg has been a strategic
port and naval base since the
mid-19th century. The French
Navy still uses its harbours, as
do transatlantic ships and cross-
Channel ferries from England
and Ireland. For a good view
of the port, drive to the hilltop
Fort du Roule, which houses
the **Musée de la Libération**,
recalling the D-Day invasion
and the subsequent liberation
of Cherbourg. Most activity is
centred on the flower-filled
market square, place Général

de Gaulle, and along shopping
streets such as rue Tour-Carrée
and rue de la Paix. The fine art
in the **Musée Thomas-Henry**
includes 17th-century Flemish
works, and portraits by Jean
François Millet, born in
Gréville-Hague. **Parc Emmanuel
Liais** has small botanical gardens and a densely packed
Musée d'Histoire Naturelle.

The **Cité de la Mer**, a completely bilingual centre, has a
cylindrical deep-sea aquarium,
the world's largest visitable
submarine and other wonders.

🏛 **Musée de la Libération**
Fort du Roule. *Tel* 02 33 20 14 12.
⬜ May–Sep: Mon pm–Sat & Sun
pm; Oct– Apr: Wed–Sun pms.
⬤ pub hols. 📷 free Sun.

🏛 **Musée Thomas-Henry**
Rue Vastel. *Tel* 02 33 23 39 30.
⬜ May–Sep: Tue–Sat & Sun pm;
Oct–Apr: Tue–Sun pm.
⬤ public hols. 🚻

🏛 **La Cité de la Mer**
Gare Maritime Transatlantique. *Tel*
02 33 20 26 69. ⬜ Feb–Oct: daily;
Nov–Dec: Tue–Sun. ⬤ Jan, 25 Dec.
📷 🚻 🚹 **www**.citedelamer.com

Cherbourg town centre

Coutances ❸

Manche. 🌅 11,500. 🚋 🚐
🚹 pl Georges Leclerc (02 33 19 08
10). ⬤ Thu. **www**.coutances.fr

From Roman times until the
Revolution, the hill-top town
of Coutances was the capital
of the Cotentin. The slender
Cathédrale Notre-Dame, a fine
example of Norman Gothic
architecture, has a soaring
66 m (217 ft) lantern tower.
Founded in the 1040s by
Bishop Geoffroi de Montbray,
it was financed by the local
de Hauteville family using
monies gained in Sicily
where they had founded a
kingdom a few years earlier.
The town was badly damaged
during World War II but the

cathedral, the churches of St Nicholas and St Peter, and the beautiful public gardens with their rare plants, all survived.

The back of Coutances cathedral with its squat lantern tower

Granville ❹

Manche. 🏘 *13,500.* 🚆 🚌 ⛴
ℹ *4 cours Jonville (02 33 91 30 03).*
🗓 *Sat.* **www**.ville-granville.fr

Ramparts enclose the upper town of Granville, which sits on a spur overlooking the Baie du Mont-St-Michel. The walled town was developed from fortifications built by the English in 1439.

The **Musée de Vieux Granville**, in the town gate-house, recounts Granville's long-seafaring tradition. The chapel walls of the **Eglise de Notre-Dame** are lined with tributes from local fishermen to their patroness, Notre-Dame du Cap Lihou.

The lower town is an old-fashioned seaside resort with a casino, promenades and public gardens. From the port there are boat trips to the Iles Chausey, a scattering of low-lying granite islands.

Le Musée Christian Dior is housed in Les Rhumbs, the fashion designer's childhood home, surrounded by a beautiful cliff garden.

🏛 **Musée de Vieux Granville**
2 rue Le Carpentier.
Tel 02 33 50 44 10. ⏲ *Apr–Sep: Wed–Mon; Oct– Mar: Wed, Sat & Sun pms.* ⏺ *1 Nov, 22 Dec–Jan.* 🖼

🏛 **Musée Christian Dior**
Villa les Rhumbs. *Tel 02 33 61 48 21.* ⏲ *mid-May–Sep: daily; gardens open all year.* 🖼

D-DAY LANDINGS

In the early hours of 6 June 1944, Allied forces began landing on the shores of Normandy, the first step in a long-planned invasion of German-occupied France, known as Operation Overlord. Parachutists were dropped near Ste-Mère-Eglise and Pegasus Bridge, and sea-borne assaults were made along a string of code-named beaches. US troops landed on Utah and Omaha in the west, while British and Canadian troops, which included a contingent of Free French commandos, landed at Gold, Juno and Sword. Over 60 years on, the beaches are still referred to by their code names.

American troops coming ashore during the Allied invasion of France

Pegasus Bridge, where the first French house was liberated, is a natural starting point for a tour around the sights and memorials. Further west, evocative ruins of the artificial harbour towed across from England survive at Arromanches-les-Bains.

There are British, German and American war cemeteries at La Cambe, Ranville and St-Laurent-sur-Mer. War museums at Bayeux, Caen, St-Mère-Eglise and Cherbourg provide background on D-Day and the ensuing Battle for Normandy.

ALLIED LANDINGS ON 6 JUNE 1944   *LA MANCHE*

Cherbourg

Douve

Ste-Mère-Eglise

UTAH
St-Laurent-sur-Mer   OMAHA   GOLD   JUNO   SWORD

Carentan   La Cambe   Arromanches-les-Bains

Le Havre
Seine

Bayeux   Pegasus Bridge

Vire   Ranville

Caen

Orne

KEY
▬ American troops
▬ British troops
▬ Canadian troops
✝ War cemetery
☂ Parachute drop

0 kilometres   25
0 miles   25

By the end of D-Day, over 135,000 men had been brought ashore, with losses totalling around 10,000.

Avranches 🟤

Manche. 🏠 *9,500.* 🚊 🚌 ℹ️ *2 rue Général-de-Gaulle (02 33 58 00 22).* 📅 *Sat.* **www**.ot-avranches.com

Avranches has been a religious centre since the 6th century and is the final staging-post for visitors to the abbey on Mont-St-Michel. The origins of the famous abbey lie in a vision experienced by Aubert, the Bishop of Avranches. One night in 708 the Archangel Michael instructed him to build a church on the nearby island. Aubert's skull, with the finger-hole made in it by the angel, can be seen in the treasury of **St-Gervais** in Avranches. The best views of Mont-St-Michel are from the **Jardin des Plantes**, where spectacular light shows are held on summer evenings. After the Revolution, 203 illuminated manuscripts were rescued from Mont-St-Michel's abbey. These and many others are held in the **Musée des Manuscrits du Mont-St-Michel**. The **Musée d'Art et d'Histoire** details life in the Cotentin over the centuries, with a collection devoted to representations of Mont-St-Michel.

🏛 **Musée des Manuscrits du Mont-St-Michel**
Pl d'Estouteville. **Tel** *02 33 79 57 00.*
⏰ *Tue–Sun (Jul-Aug: daily).* ⬤ *Jan, 1 May, 1 Nov, 25 Dec.* 📷

🏛 **Musée d'Art et d'Histoire**
Place Jean de Saint-Avit. ⏰ *Jun–Sep: daily.* 📷

Remains of Mulberry Harbour from World War II off the Côte de Nacre

Mont-St-Michel 🟤

See pp256–9.

Côte de Nacre 🟤

Calvados. ✈️ *Caen.* 🚊 🚌 *Caen, Bayeux.* ⛴ *Caen-Ouistreham.* ℹ️ *pl St-Pierre, Caen (02 31 27 14 14).* 📅 *Fri, Sun.* **www**.tourisme.caen.fr

The stretch of coast between the mouths of the rivers Orne and Vire was dubbed the Côte de Nacre (Mother of Pearl Coast) in the 19th century. More recently it has become known as the site of the D-Day Landings when Allied troops poured ashore at the start of Operation Overlord *(see p251).* The associated cemeteries, memorials and museums, and the remnants of the Mulberry Harbour at Arromanches-les-Bains, provide focal points for a visit. However, the coastline is equally popular as a summer holiday destination, offering long, sandy beaches backed by seaside resorts such as Courseulles-sur-Mer and Luc-sur-Mer, which are more relaxed than the resorts of the Côte Fleurie further east.

Bayeux 🟤

Calvados. 🏠 *15,500.* 🚊 🚌 ℹ️ *Pont-St-Jean (02 31 51 28 28).* 📅 *Sat, Wed.* **www**.bessin-normandie.com

Bayeux was the first town to be liberated by the Allies in 1944 and fortunate to escape war damage. Today, an attractive nucleus of 15th–19th-century buildings remains around its central high streets,

BAYEUX TAPESTRY

A lively comic strip justifying William the Conqueror's invasion of England, this 70-m (230-ft) long embroidered hanging was commissioned by Bishop Odo of Bayeux. Offering insights into 11th-century life, and an action-packed account of Harold, King of England's defeat at the Battle of Hastings, the tapestry is valued as a work of art, an historical document, an early example of spin and an entertaining read.

Harold's retinue sets off for France to inform William that he will succeed to the English throne.

Trees with interlacing branches are sometimes used to divide the tapestry's 58 scenes.

rue St-Martin and rue St-Jean. The latter is lined with shops and cafés.

Above the town rise the spires and domed lantern tower of the Gothic **Cathédrale Notre-Dame**. Beneath its interior is an 11th-century crypt decorated with restored 15th-century frescoes of angels playing musical instruments. The original Romanesque church that stood here was consecrated in 1077, and it is likely that Bayeux's famous tapestry was commissioned for this occasion by one of its key characters, Bishop Odo.

The tapestry is displayed in a renovated seminary, **Centre Guillaume-le-Conquérant-Tapisserie de Bayeux**, which gives a detailed audio-visual explanation of events leading up to the Norman conquest. On the southwest side of the town, the restored **Musée Mémorial de la Bataille de Normandie** traces the events of the Battle of Normandy in World War II, with an excellent film compilation made from contemporary newsreels.

🏛 Centre Guillaume-le-Conquérant-Tapisserie
Rue de Nesmond. *Tel 02 31 51 25 50.* ◯ *daily.* ◯ *first wk Jan, 25–26 Dec.* 🖾 & **www**. tapisserie-bayeux.fr

🏛 Musée Mémorial de la Bataille de Normandie
Bd Fabian-Ware. *Tel 02 31 51 46 90.* ◯ *Mar–Dec: daily.* ◯ *1 Jan, 25–26 Dec.* 🖾 &

The Abbaye aux Hommes in Caen

Caen ❾

Calvados. 🏙 *117,200.* 👤 🚌 🚆 ⛴
🛈 pl St-Pierre *(02 31 27 14 14).*
📅 *Fri & Sun.* **www**.tourisme.caen.fr

In the mid-11th century Caen became the favoured residence of William the Conqueror and Queen Matilda, and despite the destruction of three-quarters of the city during World War II, much remains of their creation. The monarchs built two great abbeys and a castle on the north bank of the river Orne, bequeathing Caen a core of historic interest that justifies penetrating its industrial estates and postwar housing.

Much-loved by the citizens of Caen, the **Eglise St-Pierre** was built on the south side of the castle in the 13th–14th centuries, with an impressively ornate Renaissance east end added in the early 16th century. The frequently copied 14th-century belltower was destroyed in 1944 but has now been restored. To the east, rue du Vaugeux is the central street in Caen's small Vieux Quartier (Old Quarter). Now pedestrianized, the street still has some lovely half-timbered buildings. A walk west, along rue St-Pierre or boulevard du Maréchal Leclerc, leads to the city's main shopping district.

The English have a last meal on land before boarding with hunting dogs and falcons.

Wide moustaches distinguish the English characters from the clean-shaven Normans.

The coloured wool used to embroider the linen has faded little since the 11th century.

Latin inscriptions caption each main scene in the work and embody the heroic ideals shared by all the participants.

Borders provide wry comment through fables and asides.

CAEN CITY CENTRE

Abbaye aux Dames ⑥
Abbaye aux Hommes ①
Château Ducal ③
Eglise St-Etienne ②
Eglise St-Pierre ④
La Trinité ⑤

0 metres 250
0 yards 250

Key to Symbols *see back flap*

🔒 Abbaye-aux-Hommes

Esplanade Jean-Marie Louvel. *Tel 02
31 30 42 81.* ☐ *daily.* ● *1 Jan,
1 May, 25 Dec.* 🎟 & restr. 📷 oblig.
Work began on William's
Abbey for Men in 1063 and
was almost complete by his
death 20 years later. The abbey
church, **Eglise St-Etienne**,
is a masterpiece of Norman
Romanesque, with a severe,
unadorned west front crowned
with 13th-century spires. The
sparingly decorated nave was
roofed in the early 12th century with stone vaulting that
anticipates the Gothic style.

🔒 Abbaye-aux-Dames

Pl de la Reine Mathilde. *Tel 02 31
06 98 98.* ☐ *pms daily.* ● *1 Jan,
1 May, 25 Dec.* 📷 oblig. &
Like William's Abbaye-aux-
Hommes, Matilda's Abbey for
Women also has a Norman
Romanesque church, **La Trinité**,
flanked by 18th-century
buildings. Begun in 1060, it
was consecrated 6 years later.
Queen Matilda lies buried in
the choir under a slab of black
marble, and her beautifully
restored abbey, with its creamy
Caen stone, makes a serene,
dignified mausoleum.

🏛 Château Ducal

Esplanade du Château. **Musée des
Beaux Arts** *Tel 02 31 30 47 70.* ☐
Wed–Mon. **Musée de Normandie**
Tel 02 31 30 47 60. ☐ *Jun–Oct: daily:
Nov–May: Wed–Mon.* ● *1 Jan,
Easter, 1 May, Ascension, 1 Nov, 25
Dec (both museums).* 🎟 &
The ruins of Caen's castle, one
of the largest fortified enclos-
ures in Europe, offer spacious
lawns, museums and rampart
views. A fine art collection,
strong on 17th-century French
and Italian painting, is exhibited in the **Musée des Beaux
Arts**. The **Musée de Normandie**
recalls traditional life in the
region with utensils and displays on farming and lace.

🏛 Mémorial de Caen

Esplanade Dwight-Eisenhower.
Tel 02 31 06 06 45. ☐ *mid-Feb–Oct:
daily; Nov–mid-Feb: Tue–Sun.*
● *3 weeks in Jan, 25 Dec.* 🎟 &
www.memorial-caen.fr
Northwest of Caen, close to
the N13 ring-road (exit 7),
this museum is dedicated to
peace, placing D-Day into the
context of World War II using
a host of interactive and audio-
visual techniques, including
stunning compilations of
archive and fictional film.

A modern extension gives a
wider perspective on cultural,
religious, border and ecological
conflicts in the second half of
the 20th century.

Lush Orne valley in the Suisse Normande

For hotels and restaurants in this region see pp563–6 and pp614–18

Suisse Normande ⑩

Calvados & Orne. ✈ *Caen.* 🚌 🚆 *Caen, Argentan.* ℹ *2 pl St-Sauveur, Thury-Harcourt (02 31 79 70 45).* **www**.ot-suisse-normande.com

Though hardly like the mountains of Switzerland, the cliffs and valleys carved out by the river Orne as it winds north to Caen have become popular for walking, climbing, camping and river sports. The area is also ideal for a rural drive. Its highest and most impressive point is the Oëtre Rock, off the D329, where you can look down over the dramatic gorges created by the river Rouvre.

Parc Naturel Régional de Normandie-Maine ⑪

Orne & Manche. ✈ *Alençon.* 🚆 🚌 *Argentan.* ℹ *Carrouges (02 33 26 78 43).* **www**.parc-naturel-normandie-maine.fr

The southern fringes of central Normandy have been incorporated into France's largest regional park. Among the farmland and forests of oak and beech are several small towns. **Domfront** rests on a spur overlooking the river Varenne. The spa town **Bagnoles-de-l'Orne** offers a casino and sports facilities, while **Sées** has a Gothic cathedral. The **Maison du Parc** at Carrouges

Poster of Deauville, about 1930

has information on walks, cycling, and canoeing.

🌿 **Maison du Parc**
Carrouges. *Tel 02 33 81 13 33.* ⏰ *Jun–Sep: daily; Oct–May: Mon–Fri, Sat & Sun pms.* ⚫ *public hols.*

Environs
Just north of the park is the **Chateau d'O**, a Renaissance château with fine 17th-century frescoes. The **Haras du Pin** is France's national stud, called "a horses' Versailles" for its 17th-century architecture. Horse shows, dressage events and various tours take place throughout the year.

Côte Fleurie ⑫

Calvados. ✈ 🚌 🚆 *Deauville.* ℹ *pl de la Mairie, Deauville (02 31 14 40 00).* **www**.deauville.org

The Côte Fleurie (Flowery Coast) between Villerville and Cabourg has been planted with chic resorts which burst

into bloom every summer. **Trouville** was once a humble fishing village, but in the mid-19th century caught the attention of writers Gustave Flaubert and Alexandre Dumas. By the 1870s Trouville had acquired grand hotels, a railway station and pseudo-Swiss villas along the beachfront. It has, however, long been outclassed by its neighbour, **Deauville**, created by the Duc de Morny in the 1860s. This resort boasts a casino, racecourses, marinas and the famous beachside catwalk, Les Planches.

For something quieter, head west to smaller resorts such as Villers-sur-Mer or Houlgate. **Cabourg** further west is dominated by the turn-of-the-century Grand Hôtel *(see p551)* where novelist Marcel Proust spent many summers. Proust used the resort as a model for the fictional Balbec in his novel *Remembrance of Things Past*.

Pays d'Auge ⑬

Calvados. ✈ *Deauville.* 🚆 🚌 *Lisieux.* ℹ *11 rue d'Alençon, Lisieux (02 31 48 18 10).* **www**.lisieux-tourisme.com

Inland from the Côte Fleurie, the Pays d'Auge is classic Normandy countryside, lushly woven with fields, wooded valleys, cider orchards, dairy farms and manor houses. Its capital is **Lisieux**, a cathedral town devoted to Ste Thérèse of Lisieux, canonized in 1925, who attracts hundreds of thousands of pilgrims each year. Lisieux is an obvious base for exploring the region, but nearby market towns, such as St-Pierre-sur-Dives and Orbec, are smaller and more attractive.

The best way to enjoy the Pays d'Auge is to potter around its minor roads. Two tourist routes are devoted to cider and cheese, while picturesque manor houses, farmhouses and châteaux testify to the wealth of this fertile land. **St-Germain-de-Livet** can be visited, as can **Crèvecoeur-en-Auge**, and the half-timbered village of **Beuvron-en-Auge** is charming.

APPLES AND CIDER

Apple orchards are a familiar feature of the Normandy countryside, and their fruit a fundamental ingredient in the region's gastronomic repertoire. No self-respecting pâtisserie would be without its *tarte normande* (apple tart), and every country lane seems to sport an *Ici Vente Cidre* (cider sold here) sign. Much of the harvest forms the raw material for cider and Calvados, an apple brandy aged in oak barrels for at least two years. A local brew is also made from pears, and known as *poiré* (perry).

A crop ranging from sour cider apples to sweet eating varieties

Mont-St-Michel ⑥

Shrouded by mist, encircled by sea, soaring proudly above glistening sands – the silhouette of Mont-St-Michel is one of the most enchanting sights in France. Now linked to the mainland by a causeway, the island of Mont-Tombe (Tomb on the Hill) stands at the mouth of the river Couesnon, crowned by a fortified abbey that almost doubles its height. Lying strategically on the frontier between Normandy and Brittany, Mont-St-Michel grew from a humble 8th-century oratory to become a Benedictine monastery that had its greatest influence in the 12th and 13th centuries. Pilgrims known as *miquelots* journeyed from afar to honour the cult of St Michael, and the monastery was a renowned centre of medieval learning. Major engineering works to reverse the silting up of the sea around the island will be in place until 2015.

St Michael

The 10th-century abbey

The 11th-century abbey

The mid-18th-century abbey

St Aubert's Chapel
A small 15th-century chapel built on an outcrop of rock is dedicated to Aubert, the founder of Mont-St-Michel.

★ **Gabriel Tower**
Three floors of cannons point in all directions from this imposing 16th-century tower..

Entrance

TIMELINE

700	1000	1300	1600	1900
966 Benedictine abbey founded by Duke Richard I	**1211–28** Construction of La Merveille	**1434** Last assault by English forces. Ramparts surround the town	**1789** French Revolution: abbey becomes a political prison	**1874** Abbey declared a national monument
				1922 Services again held in abbey church
1017 Work on abbey church starts		**1516** Abbey falls into decline	**1877–9** Causeway built	**1895–7** Belfry, spire and statue of St Michael added
708 St Aubert builds an oratory on Mont-Tombe		**1067–70** Mont-St-Michel depicted in Bayeux Tapestry		**2007** Benedictine monks leave abbey; they are replaced by the Fraternité de Jérusalem

Bayeux Tapestry detail

VISITORS' CHECKLIST

to Pontorson, then bus.
bd de l'Avancée (02 33 60
14 30). **www**.ot-montsaint
michel.com **Abbey Tel** 02 33
89 80 00. May–Aug: 9am–
7pm; Sep–Apr: 9:30am–6pm.
Nocturnal visits in summer
(recommended). 1 Jan,
1 May, 25 Dec. 12:15pm
Tue–Sat, 11:30am Sun.
www.mont-saint-michel.
monuments-nationaux.fr

Tides of Mont-St-Michel
*Extremely strong tides in the Baie du Mont-
St-Michel act as a natural defence. They
rise and fall with the lunar calendar
and can reach speeds of
10 km/h (6 mph).*

★ Abbey
*Protected by high walls,
the abbey and its church
occupy an impregnable
position on the island.*

Gautier's Leap
*At the top of the Inner
Staircase, this terrace is
named after a prisoner
who leaped to his death.*

Eglise St-Pierre

Liberty Tower

King's Tower

The Arcade Tower provided
lodgings for the abbot's soldiers.

STAR FEATURES

★ Abbey

★ Ramparts

★ Grande Rue

★ Grande Rue
*Now crowded with
restaurants, the pilgrims'
route, followed since the 12th
century, climbs up past Eglise
St-Pierre to the abbey gates.*

The Abbey of Mont-St-Michel

The present buildings bear witness to the time when the abbey served both as a Benedictine monastery and, for 73 years after the Revolution, as a political prison. In 1017 work began on a Romanesque church at the island's highest point, building over its 10th-century predecessor, now the Chapel of Our Lady Underground. A monastery built on three levels, La Merveille (The Miracle) was added to the church's north side in the early 13th century.

Cross in the choir

★ Church
Four bays of the Romanesque nave survive. Three were pulled down in 1776, creating the West Terrace.

Refectory
The monks took their meals in this long, narrow room, which is flooded with light through tall windows.

★ La Merveille
The Miracle is a Gothic masterpiece – a three-storey monastic complex built in only 16 years.

Knights' Room
The rib vaults and finely decorated capitals are typically Gothic.

CHURCH LEVEL

MIDDLE LEVEL

LOWER LEVEL

Crypt of the Thirty Candles is one of two 11th-century crypts built to support the transepts of the main church.

★ Cloisters
The cloisters with their elegant columns in staggered rows are a beautiful example of early 13th-century Anglo-Norman style.

VISITING THE ABBEY

The three levels of the abbey reflect the monastic hierarchy. The monks lived at the highest level, in an enclosed world of church, cloister and refectory. The abbot entertained his noble guests on the middle level. Soldiers and pilgrims further down on the social scale were received at the lowest level. Guided tours begin at the West Terrace at the church level and end in the almonry, where alms were dispensed to the poor. The almonry is now a bookshop and souvenir hall.

CHURCH LEVEL

Cloister

Refectory

Abbey Church

West Terrace

Gautier's Leap

Great Inner Staircase

MIDDLE LEVEL

Knights' room

Guest room

Crypt of the Thirty Candles

Our Lady Underground

St Etienne's Chapel

St Martin's Crypt

Abbot's lodgings

Church Interior
A Flamboyant Gothic choir was built in 1446–1521, held up by crypts with massive supporting pillars.

LOWER LEVEL

Cellar

Almonry

Abbey gardens

Abbot's lodgings

Guard's room

St Martin's Crypt is an 11th-century barrel-vaulted chapel that preserves the austere forms of the original Romanesque abbey.

The abbot's lodgings were close to the abbey entrance, and he received prestigious visitors in the guest room. Poorer pilgrims were received in the almonry.

West Terrace
Guided tours start here, at the West Terrace. The Fraternité de Jérusalem, a small monastic community, lives in the abbey and welcomes visitors.

STAR FEATURES

★ Church

★ La Merveille

★ Cloisters

Mont-St-Michel by night ▷

Honfleur **⑭**

Calvados. 🏚 8,500. 🚉 Deauville.
ℹ️ quai Lepaulmier (02 31 89 23 30).
🛒 Wed, Sat; Thu, Sun: fish market
at harbour. www.ot-honfleur.fr

A major defensive port in the
15th century, Honfleur has
become one of Normandy's
most appealing harbours. At its
heart is the 17th-century **Vieux
Bassin** (Old Dock), with its
pretty tall houses (6–7 storeys).
Honfleur became a centre
of artistic activity in the 19th
century. Eugène Boudin, the
painter, was born here in 1824,
as was the composer Erik Satie
in 1866. Courbet, Sisley, Renoir,
Pissarro, and Cézanne all
visited Honfleur, often meeting
at the Ferme St-Siméon, now
a luxury hotel. Painters still
work from Honfleur's quayside,
and exhibit in the **Greniers à
Sel**, two salt warehouses built
in 1670. These lie to the east
of the Vieux Bassin in an area
known as l'Enclos, which made
up the fortified heart of the
town in the 13th-century.
The **Musée d'Ethnographie
et d'Art Populaire Normand**
displays mementos of Hon-
fleur's nautical past, with a
warren of Norman interiors
next door in the former prison.
Place Ste-Catherine has an
unusual 15th-century church
built by ship's carpenters. The
Musée Eugène-Boudin documents the artistic appeal of
Honfleur and the Seine estuary,
with works from Boudin to
Raoul Dufy. **Les Maisons Satie**
use extracts from Satie's
music to guide you round
reconstructions of the rooms.

🏧 Greniers à Sel
Rue de la Ville. ℹ️ 02 31 89 23 30.
⏰ for guided tours & exhibitions.
📷 obligatory, except during
summer exhibs. 🎟️ ♿

🏛 Musée d'Ethnographie et
d'Art Populaire Normand
Quai St Etienne. **Tel** 02 31 89 14 12.
⏰ mid-Feb–Mar, Oct–mid-Nov:
Tue–Fri (pms only), Sat, Sun; Apr–
Sep: Tue–Sun. ● 1 May. 🎟️ ♿

🏛 Musée Eugène-Boudin
Pl Erik Satie, rue de l'Homme
de Bois. **Tel** 02 31 89 54 00.
⏰ mid-Feb–mid-Mar & Oct–Dec:
Wed–Mon pms, Sat, Sun; mid-Mar–
Sep: Wed–Mon. ● 1 May, 14 Jul,
25 Dec. 🎟️ ♿

🏛 Les Maisons Satie
67 bd Charles V. **Tel** 02 31 89
11 11. ⏰ mid-Feb–Dec: Wed–Mon.
● public hols. 🎟️

Quai St-Etienne in Honfleur

Le Havre **⑮**

Seine-Maritime. 🏚 194,000. ✈️ 🚉
🚌 🚢 ℹ️ 186 bd Clemenceau
(02 32 74 04 04). 🛒 daily.
www.lehavretourisme.com

Strategically positioned on the
Seine estuary, Le Havre (The
Harbour) was created in 1517
by François I after the nearby
port of Harfleur silted up.

During World War II it was
virtually obliterated by Allied
bombing, but despite a vast
industrial zone which stands
beside the port, it still has
appeal. It is an important
yachting centre, and its beach
has two blue flags (very clean!).
Much of the city centre was
rebuilt in the 1950s–1960s by
August Perret, whose towering
Eglise St-Joseph (a UNESCO
World Heritage site) pierces
the skyline. On the seafront,
the **Musée Malraux** has works
by, amongst others, local
artist Raoul Dufy. France's
biggest skateboard park is
also on the seafront.

🏛 Musée Malraux
2 bd Clemenceau. **Tel** 02 35 19
62 62. ⏰ Wed–Mon. ● public
hols. 🎟️

Côte d'Albâtre **⑯**

Seine-Maritime. 🚉 🚌 🚢 ℹ️ quai
du Carénage, Dieppe (02 32 14 40 60).
www.dieppetourisme.com

The Alabaster Coast gets its
name from the chalky cliffs
and milky waters that
characterize the Normandy
coastline be-tween Le Havre
and Le Tréport. It is best
known for the **Falaise d'Aval**
west of Etretat, eroded into an
arch. The author Guy de Maupassant, born near Dieppe in
1850, compared these cliffs to
an elephant dipping its trunk
into the sea. From Etretat, a
chain of coastal roads runs
east across a switchback of
breezy headlands and
wooded valleys to Dieppe.
Fécamp is the only major
town along this route. Its
Benedictine abbey was once
an important pilgrimage centre
after a tree trunk said to contain drops of Christ's Blood
was washed ashore here in the
7th century. This is enshrined
in a reliquary at the entrance
to the Lady Chapel of the
abbey church, La Trinité.
The vast **Palais Bénédictine**
is a Neo-Gothic-and-
Renaissance homage to the
ego of Alexander Le Grand, a
local wine and spirits merchant
who rediscovered the monks'
recipe for Bénédictine, the
famous herbal liqueur. Built

Woman with Parasol (1880) by Boudin in the Musée Eugène-Boudin

The cliffs at Falaise d'Aval, famously likened to an elephant dipping its trunk into the sea

in 1882, it incorporates a distillery and an eccentric museum packed with curios. The adjacent halls provide an aromatic account and tastings of the 27 herbs and spices which make up the elixir.

🏛 Palais Bénédictine
110 rue Alexandre Le Grand, Fécamp. **Tel** 02 35 10 26 10. ◯ daily. ⬤ Jan, 1 May, 25 Dec. 🎫 🔲

View of Dieppe from the château and museum above the town

Dieppe ⑰

Seine-Maritime. 🔢 36,000. 🚉 🚌 🛳 🚹 Pont Jean Ango (02 32 14 40 60). ⬤ Tue, Thu & esp. Sat. **www.** dieppetourisme.com

Dieppe exploits a break in the chalky cliffs bordering the Pays de Caux, and has won historical prestige as a Channel fort, port and resort. Prosperity came during the 16th and 17th centuries, when local privateer Jehan Ango raided the Portuguese and English fleets, and a trading post called Petit Dieppe was founded on the West African coast. At that time, Dieppe's population was already 30,000, and included a 300-strong community of

craftsmen carving imported ivory. This maritime past is celebrated in **Le Château-Musée**, the 15th-century castle crowning the headland to the west of the seafront. Here you can see historical maps and model ships, a collection of Dieppe ivories, and paintings that evoke the town's development as a fashionable seaside resort during the 19th century. Dieppe had the nearest beach to Paris and it quickly responded to the developing passion for promenading, seawater cures and bathing.

Today Dieppe's broad seafront is given over to lawns, seaside amusements and car parks, and its liveliest streets surround the battle-scarred **Eglise St-Jacques** to the south. If the weather is poor, visit **L'Estran-La Cité de la Mer**, an exhibition centre with models on maritime themes.

🏛 Le Château-Musée
Tel 02 35 06 61 99. ◯ Jun–Sep: daily; Oct–May: Wed–Mon. ⬤ 1 Jan, 1 May, 1 Nov, 25 Dec. 🎫 🔲 www.mairie-dieppe.fr

🏛 L'Estran-La Cité de la Mer
37 rue de l'Asile Thomas. **Tel** 02 35 06 93 20. ◯ daily. ⬤ 1 Jan, 25 Dec. 🎫 ♿

Basse-Seine ⑱

Seine-Maritime & Eure. ✈ Le Havre, Rouen. 🚉 🚌 Yvetot. 🛳 Le Havre. 🚹 Yvetot (02 35 95 08 40).

Meandering seaward from Rouen to Le Havre, the river Seine is crossed by three spectacular road bridges: the Pont de Brotonne, the Pont de Tancarville and the Pont de

Normandie (completed in 1995, it links Le Havre and Honfleur). The grace and daring of these modern bridges echo the soaring aspirations of the abbeys founded on the river's banks in the 7th and 8th centuries. The abbeys now provide good stepping stones for a tour of the Lower Seine valley.

West of Rouen is the harmonious Eglise de St-Georges at **St-Martin-de-Boscherville** which until the Revolution was the church of a small walled abbey. Its 12th-century chapter house has remarkable biblical statues and carved capitals. From here the D67 runs south to the riverside village of La Bouille.

As you head northwest, an hourly car ferry at Mesnil-sous-Jumièges takes you over to the colossal ruins of the **Abbaye de Jumièges**. The abbey was founded in 654 and once housed 900 monks and 1,500 servants. The main abbey church dates from the 11th century; its consecration in 1067 was a major event, with William the Conqueror in attendance.

The D913 strikes through oak and beech woods in the Parc Régional de Brotonne to the 7th-century **Abbaye de St-Wandrille**. The Musée de la Marine de Seine at **Caudebec-en-Caux** gives an engrossing account of many aspects of life on this great river since the late 19th century.

Monk from Abbaye de St-Wandrille

Rouen ⑲

Founded at the lowest point where the Seine could be bridged, Rouen has prospered through maritime trade and industrialization to become a rich and cultured city. Despite the severe damage of World War II, the city boasts a wealth of historic sights on its right bank, all within walking distance of the central Cathédrale Notre-Dame, frequently painted by Monet. In turn a Celtic trading post, Roman garrison and Viking colony, Rouen became the capital of the Norman Duchy in 911. It was captured by Henry V in 1419 after a siege during the Hundred Years' War. In 1431 Joan of Arc was burned at the stake here in place du Vieux-Marché.

Rouen, a thriving port on the river Seine

| 0 metres | 250 |
| 0 yards | 250 |

(map of Rouen with streets and numbered sights, including Gare SNCF, Tour Jeanne d'Arc, Musée de la Céramique ④, Square Verdrel, Musée des Beaux-Arts ⑤, Musée le Secq des Tournelles ⑥, Église Ste-Jeanne d'Arc ①, Place du Vieux Marché, Palais de Justice ③, Gros Horloge ②, Place de la Cathédrale, Cathédrale Notre-Dame ⑦, Théâtre des Arts, etc.)

Exploring Rouen

From the cathedral, the rue du Gros Horloge runs west under the city's Great Clock, to the place du Vieux Marché and its post-war Eglise Ste-Jeanne-d'Arc. Rue aux Juifs leads past the 15th-century Gothic **Palais de Justice**, once Normandy's parliament, to the smart shops and cafés around rue des Carmes. Further east, between the St-Maclou and St-Ouen churches, are half-timbered houses in the rue Damiette and rue Eau de Robec. North, in place Général de Gaulle, is the 18th-century **Hôtel de Ville**.

⛪ Cathédrale Notre-Dame

This Gothic masterpiece is dominated by the famous west façade *(see p267)*, painted

Cathédrale Notre-Dame, Rouen

by Monet, which is framed by two unequal towers – the northern Tour St-Romain, and the later Tour du Beurre, supposedly paid for by a tax on butter consumption in Lent. Above the central lantern tower rises a Neo-Gothic spire, made from cast iron and erected in 1876. Recently restored, both the 14th-century northern Portail des Libraires and the 14th-century southern Portail de la Calende are worth seeing for their precise sculpting and delicate tracery. Many of the cathedral's riches are accessible by guided tour only, including the tomb of Richard the Lionheart, whose heart was buried here, and the rare 11th-century semi-circular hall crypt, rediscovered in 1934. The choir/chancel was badly hit by the 1999 storm.

⛪ Eglise St-Maclou

This Flamboyant Gothic church has an intensively

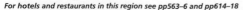

SIGHTS AT A GLANCE

timbers of its buildings, set around the quadrangle, are carved with a macabre array of grinning skulls, crossed bones, coffins and grave-diggers' implements.

🏛 Musée d'Histoire Naturelle

198 rue Beauvoisine. **Tel** 02 35 71 41 50. ◯ Tue–Sun pm. 🌐
The Musée d'Histoire Naturelle is the second largest museum of its kind in France, holding more than 800,000 objects.

🔒 Eglise St-Ouen

Once part of a formidable Benedictine abbey, St-Ouen is a solid Gothic church with a lofty, unadorned interior made all the more beautiful by its restored 14th-century stained glass. Behind the church there is a pleasant park which is ideal for picnics.

Jug from Musée de la Céramique

🏛 Musée des Beaux Arts

Square Verdrel. **Tel** 02 35 71 28 40. ◯ Wed–Mon. ● public hols except Easter & Whitsun. 🌐 ♿
The city's collection includes major art works: masterpieces by Caravaggio and Velázquez, and paintings by Normandy-born artists Théodore Géricault, Eugène Boudin and Raoul Dufy. Also on display is Monet's *Rouen Cathedral, The Portal, Grey Weather*.

🏛 Musée de la Céramique

Hôtel d'Hocqueville, 1 rue Faucon. **Tel** 02 35 07 31 74. ◯ Wed–Mon. ● public hols. 🌐

VISITORS' CHECKLIST

Seine Maritime. 👥 108,800.
✈ 11 km (7 miles) SE Rouen.
🚃 gare rive droite, pl Bernard Tissot (08 92 35 35 35). 🚌 25 rue des Charrettes (0825 076 027). 🛈 25 pl de la Cathédrale (02 32 08 32 40). 🗓 Tue–Sun.
🎉 Feast of Joan of Arc (late May).
www.rouenvalleedeseine.com

Exhibits of 1,000 pieces of Rouen faïence – colourful glazed earthenware – together with other pieces of French and foreign china are displayed in a 17th-century town house. The works trace the history of Rouen faïence to its zenith in the 18th century.

🏛 Musée Le Secq des Tournelles

Rue Jacques-Villon. **Tel** 02 35 88 42 92. ◯ Wed–Mon. ● public hols. 🌐 ♿ ground floor only.
Located in a 15th-century church, this wrought ironwork museum exhibits antique ironmongery ranging from keys to corkscrews and Gallo-Roman spoons to mighty tavern signs.

🏛 Musée Flaubert

51 rue de Lecat. **Tel** 02 35 15 59 95.
◯ Tue–Sat. ● public hols. 🌐
Flaubert's father was a surgeon at Rouen Hospital, and his family home combines memorabilia with an awesome – and occasionally gruesome – display of 17th–19th-century medical equipment.

GUSTAVE FLAUBERT

The novelist Gustave Flaubert (1821–80) was born and raised in Rouen, and the city provides the backdrop for some memorable scenes in his masterpiece, *Madame Bovary*. Published in 1857, this realistic study of a country doctor's wife driven to despair by her love affairs provoked a scandal that made Flaubert's name. His famous stuffed green parrot, which can be seen in the Musée Flaubert, was always perched on his writing desk.

Flaubert's stuffed parrot

---

decorated west façade with a five-bay porch and carved wooden doors depicting biblical scenes. Behind the church, its *aître*, or ossuary, is a rare surviving example of a medieval cemetery for the burial of plague victims. The

Château Gaillard and the village of Les Andelys, in a loop of the river Seine

Haute-Seine ⑳

Eure. 🚆 Rouen. 🚌 Vernon, Val de Reuil. 🚌 Gisors, Les Andelys. ℹ️ Les Andelys (02 32 54 41 93). http://office-tourisme.ville-andelys.fr

Southeast of Rouen, the river Seine follows a convoluted course, with most points of interest on its north bank. At the centre of the Forêt de Lyons, once the hunting ground for the Dukes of Normandy, is the country town of **Lyons-la-Forêt**, with half-timbered houses and an 18th-century covered market.

To the south the D313 follows the gracefully curving Seine to the town of **Les Andelys**. Above it tower the ruins of Château Gaillard which Richard the Lionheart, as King of England and Duke of Normandy, built in 1197 to defend Rouen from the French. They eventually took the castle in 1204.

Giverny ㉑

Eure. 🏘️ 600. ℹ️ 36 rue Carnot, Vernon (02 32 51 39 60). www.cape-tourisme.fr

In 1883 the Impressionist painter Claude Monet rented a house in the small village of Giverny, and worked here until his death. The house, known as the **Fondation Claude Monet**, and its garden are open to the public. The house is decorated in the colour schemes that Monet admired; the gardens are famous as the subject of some of the artist's studies. Only copies are on show, but there are outstanding original 19th- and 20th-century art works in the **Musée des Impressionnismes** nearby.

🏛 **Fondation Claude Monet**
Giverny, Gasny. **Tel** 02 32 51 28 21. ⬤ Apr–Oct: daily. 🅿️ www.fondation-monet.fr

🏛 **Musée des Impressionnismes**
99 rue Claude Monet, Giverny. **Tel** 02 32 51 94 65. ⬤ Apr–Oct. 🅿️ ♿

Évreux ㉒

1 Eure. 🏘️ 55,000. 🚆 🚌 ℹ️ 1ter pl du Général de Gaulle (02 32 24 04 43). 🛒 Wed & Sat. www.grandevreuxtourisme.fr

Though considerably damaged in the war, Évreux is a pleasant cathedral town set in wide, agricultural plains. At its heart, the **Cathédrale Notre-Dame** is renowned for its 14th–15th century stained glass. The building is predominantly Gothic, though Romanesque arches survive in the nave and Renaissance screens adorn its chapels. Next door, the former Bishop's Palace houses the **Musée de l'Ancien Evêché**, with Roman bronze statues of Jupiter and Apollo and fine 18th-century furniture and decorative art.

Monet's garden at Giverny, restored to its original profuse glory

Monet's Cathedral Series

In the 1890s Claude Monet made almost 30 paintings of Rouen's cathedral, several of which are now in the Musée d'Orsay in Paris *(see pp120–21)*. He studied the effects of changing light on its façades, and described both the surface detail and huge bulk, putting colour before contour. The archetypal Impressionist, Monet said he conceived this series when he watched the effects of light on a country church, "as the sun's rays slowly dissolved the mists … that wrapped the golden stone in an ideally vaporous envelope".

HARMONY IN BLUE AND GOLD *(1894)*
Monet selected a close vantage point for the series and was keen on this southwest view. The sun would cast afternoon shadows across the carved west front, accentuating the cavernous portals and the large rose window.

Monet's sketch, *one of many of Rouen, parallels the shimmering effect of the paintings.*

Harmony in Brown *(1894) is the only finished version of a frontal view of the west façade. Analysis has shown that it was begun as a southwest view like the others.*

Harmony in Blue *(1894), compared with Harmony in Blue and Gold, shows the stone of the west façade further softened by the diffuse light of a misty morning.*

The Portal, Grey Weather *(1894) was one of several canvases in the grey colour group which showed the cathedral façade in the soft light of an overcast day.*

BRITTANY

FINISTÈRE · CÔTES D'ARMOR · MORBIHAN · ILLE-ET-VILAINE

Jutting defiantly into the Atlantic, France's northwest corner has long been culturally and geographically distinct from the main bulk of the country. Known to the Celts as Armorica, the land of the sea, Brittany's past swirls with the legends of drowned cities and Arthurian forests. Prehistoric megaliths arise mysteriously from land and sea, and the medieval is never far from the modern.

A long, jagged coastline is the region's great attraction. Magnificent beaches line its northern shore, swept clean by huge tides and interspersed with well-established seaside resorts, seasoned fishing ports and abundant oysterbeds. The south coast is gentler, with wooded river valleys and a milder climate, while the west, being exposed to the Atlantic winds, has a drama that justifies the name Finistère – the End of the Earth.

Inland lies the Argoat – once the Land of the Forest, now a patchwork of undulating fields, woods, and rolling moorland. Parc Régional d'Armorique occupies much of central Finistère, and it is in western Brittany that Breton culture remains most evident. In Quimper, and in the Pays Bigouden, crêpes and cider, traditional costumes, and Celtic music are still a genuine part of the Breton lifestyle. Eastern Brittany has a more conventional appeal. Vannes, Dinan and Rennes, the Breton capital, have well-preserved medieval quarters where half-timbered buildings shelter inviting markets, shops, crêperies, and restaurants. The walled port of St-Malo on the Côte d'Emeraude recalls the region's maritime prowess, while the remarkably intact castles at Fougères and Vitré are reminders of the mighty border-fortresses that protected Brittany's eastern frontier before its final union with France in 1532.

Women dressed in traditional costume and *coiffe*, the typical Breton lace head-dress

◁ Characteristic pink granite cliffs on the Côte de Granit Rose, northern Brittany

Exploring Brittany

Ideal for a seaside holiday, Brittany offers enjoyable drives along the headlands and beaches of the northern Côte d'Emeraude and Côte de Granit Rose, while the south coast boasts wooded valleys and the prehistoric sites of Carnac and the Golfe du Morbihan. The parish closes *(see pp276–7)* provide an intriguing insight into Breton culture, as does the cathedral town of Quimper. Be sure to visit the regional capital, Rennes, and the great castle at Fougères, and in summer take a boat trip to one of Brittany's islands.

CÔTE DE GRANIT

Plougrescant
Perros-Guirec
Port-
Trebeurden
Lannion
TREG
Île de Batz
ROSCOFF
Plouescat
Plestin-les-
Goulven
Saint-Pol-
Grèves
Pontrie
de-Léon
Béga
Plouaret
Morlaix
Lesneven
Guinga
D10
Landivisiau
ST-THÉGONNEC
Belle-Isle-
Ploudalmézeau
LAMPAUL
en-Terre
D788
GUIMILIAU
GUIMILIAU
Plougonven
Bourbria
ÎLE
D68
Gouesnou
D787
D'OUESSANT
Landerneau
Sizun
D785
Saint-Renan
BREST
Monts d'Arrée
Callac
Le Conquet
Plougastel-
Huelgoat
Daoulas
D789
D18
Carhaix-Plouguer
Pointe St-Mathieu
D355
PARC NATUREL
RÉGIONAL D'ARMORIQUE
Rostre
Camaret-sur-Mer
D791
N164
Crozon
Châteauneuf-
D887
du-Faou
Montagnes Noires
Châteaulin
N165
Aulne
Gourin
POINTE
D15
DU RAZ
Pont-
LOCRONAN
D4
Île de Sein
Croix
DOUARNENEZ
Coray
Scaër
Audierne
D2
D784
Bub
QUIMPER
Bannalec
D769
Plouay
Plonéour-
Quimperlé
Lanvern
N785
CONCARNEAU
Fouesnant
D44
PAYS BIGOUDEN
PONT-
Hennebont
Pointe de la Torche
Pont-l'Abbé
AVEN
Laneste
Penmarc'h
Lesconil
LE POULDU
Lorient
Larmor-Plage
Be
Îles de Groix
CARN
PRESQU'ÎLE DE QUIBERO

SIGHTS AT A GLANCE

Quibe
Le Pa
BELLE ÎLE

KEY

▬	Motorway
▬	Major road
▬	Secondary road
▬	Minor road
▬	Scenic route
▬	Main railway
▬	Minor railway
▬	Regional border

For additional map symbols *see back flap*

Lighthouse on the Île de Bréhat, Côte de Granit Rose

GETTING AROUND
Expressways N12/N165
encircle Brittany, giving
easy access to coastal areas,
while the N12 and N24 give
direct access to Rennes,
Brittany's capital. Brittany
can be reached by air to
Brest, Nantes and Rennes
airports, by Channel ferries
to St Malo and Roscoff, by
autoroutes from Normandy,
the Loire, and A11 from
Paris, or by TGV direct
from Paris and Lille.

E DE BRÉHAT
de l'Arcouest
ol
uézec

CÔTE D'ÉMERAUDE   *Pointe du Grouin*

Saint-Quay-
Portrieux   Sables d'Or
n   Dinard **26**   **28** CANCALE
Le Val André   St-Cast-   **27**
Pordic   le-Guildo   SAINT-MALO   *Caen*
gat   Ploubalay   Dol-de-
Brieuc   Plancoët   Bretagne   Pontorson
        N12   Lamballe   N176   Louvigné-
                                                              du-Désert
                              29 DINAN   Antrain   Saint-Brice-en-Coglès
Ploeuc   Moncontour   Broons   D137   **30** COMBOURG
                                  Évran   **32** FOUGÈRES
        D700 Plouguenast   Tinténiac   Saint-Aubin-   N12
-de-   Rance   Bécherel   d'Aubigné   D178
agne   Merdrignac   Hédé D72   Saint-Aubin-
oudéac N164   FORÊT DE Montauban-de-Bretagne   du-Cormier
        La Chèze   PAIMPONT   Montfort- Liffré   VITRÉ
tivy   Rohan   Mauron   D773 sur-Meu **31**   Cesson-Sévigné D857 **33**
ETAGNE   **25**   RENNES N157   Château des
                          Paimpont Mordelles   Rochers-Sévigné
        JOSSELIN   D766   Plélan   Guichen D41 Châteaugiron *Le Mans*
        24 Ploërmel N24   Janzé
iné   Kerguéhennec   Guer   N137   La Guerche- D178
      Saint-Jean-   de-Bretagne
      Brévelay   N166 Malestroit   Vilaine   Martigné-Ferchaud
                              Pipriac   Bain-de-Bretagne
nd-o   Landes de Lanvaux D773 La Gacilly
mp   Elven   Oust   Vilaine
ray   Rochefort-en-Terre   Grand-Fougeray
                              Redon   *Nantes*
aquer **22** VANNES   Questembert
      23   N165
o   GOLFE DU   Muzillac   La Roche-
o   MORBIHAN   Bernard
                          Nantes

0 kilometres   25

0 miles   25

**Half-timbered houses in the medieval
part of Rennes**

Île d'Ouessant ❶

Finistère. ⚌ 930. ✈ Ouessant
(via Brest). 🚍 Brest, then boat.
🚍 Le Conquet, then boat. 🛈 pl de
l'Eglise, Lampaul (02 98 48 85 83).
www.ot-ouessant.fr

A well-known Breton proverb
declares "He who sees
Ouessant sees his own blood".
Also known as Ushant, the
island is notorious among
sailors for its fierce storms and
strong currents. However, this
westerly point of France has a
pleasant climate in summer
and, though often bleak and
stormy, can be surprisingly
mild in winter. Part of the Parc
Naturel Régional d'Armorique,
the windswept island supports
migrating birds and a small
seal population, which may
be observed from the Pern
and Pen-ar-Roc'h headlands.

Two museums shed light on
the island's defiant history,
dogged by shipwreck and
tragedy. At Niou Uhella, the
Ecomusée d'Ouessant has
furniture made from driftwood
and wrecks, often painted blue
and white in honour of the
Virgin Mary. Nearby at Phare
du Créac'h, the **Musée des
Phares et Balises** explains the
history of Brittany's many
lighthouses and their keepers.

🏛 **Ecomusée d'Ouessant**
Maison du Niou. **Tel** 02 98 48 86
37. ☐ Apr–Sep: daily; Oct–Mar:
Tue–Sun pm. 🔲 ♿

🏛 **Musée des Phares et Balises**
Pointe de Créac'h. **Tel** 02 98 48 80
70. ☐ Apr–Sep: daily; Oct–Mar:
Tue–Sun pm. 🔲

Brest ❷

Finistère. ⚌ 153,000. ✈ 🚍 🚍
🚢 to islands only. 🛈 place de la
Liberté (02 98 44 24 96). 🚩 daily.
www.brest-metropole-tourisme.fr

A natural harbour protected
by the Presqu'île de Crozon,
Brest is France's premier
Atlantic naval port with a rich
maritime history. Heavily
bombed during World War II,
it is now a modern commercial
city where cargo vessels,
yachts and fishing boats ply
the waters. The Cours Dajot
promenade has good views
of the Rade de Brest. The
Château houses a naval
museum with historic maps,
maritime paintings, model
ships, carved wooden figure-
heads and nautical instruments.

Across the Penfeld river –
reached by Europe's largest
lifting bridge, the Pont de
Recouvrance – is the 14th-
century **Tour de la Motte
Tanguy**. By the Port de
Plaisance, **Océanopolis** "sea
centre" has three vast pavilions simulating temperate,
tropical and polar ecosystems.

⚓ **Château de Brest**
Tel 02 98 22 12 39. ☐ Feb–Mar &
Oct–Dec: pm only daily; Apr–Sep:
daily. ☐ 1 May, 25 Dec. 🔲

🏯 **Tour de la Motte Tanguy**
Sq Pierre Peron.
Tel 02 98 00 88 60. ☐ Jun–Sep:
daily; Oct–May: Wed–Thu, Sat–Sun
pms. ☐ 1 Jan, 1 May, 25 Dec.

🐋 **Océanopolis**
Port de Plaisance du Moulin Blanc.
Tel 02 98 34 40 40. ☐ mid-Apr–
Sep: daily; Oct–mid-Apr: Tue–Sun.
☐ 2 wks Jan, 25 Dec. 🔲 ♿ 🛈
🍴 www.oceanopolis.com

Windswept moorlands near Ménez-Meur, Parc Régional d'Armorique

Traditional boatbuilding at Le Port
Musée, Douarnenez

Parc Naturel Régional d'Armorique ❸

Finistère. 🚶 Brest. 🚍 Chateaulin,
Landernau. 🚍 Le Faou, Huelgoat,
Carhaix. 🛈 Le Faou (02 98 81 90 08).

The Armorican Regional
Nature Park stretches west
from the moorlands of the
Monts d'Arrée to the Presqu'île
de Crozon and Ile d'Ouessant.
Within this protected area lies
a mixture of farmland, heaths,
remains of ancient oak forest
and wild, open spaces. The
park and its scenic coastline
is ideal for walking, riding
and touring by bicycle or car.

Huelgoat is a good starting
point for inland walks, while
Ménez-Hom (330 m/1,082 ft)
at the beginning of the Crozon
Peninsula, has excellent views.

The main information centre
for the park is at **Le Faou**.
Nearby at **Ménez-Meur** is a
wooded estate with wild and
farm animals, and a Breton
horse museum. Scattered
around the park are 16 small,
specialist museums, some
paying tribute to country
traditions like hunting, fishing
and tanning. The **Musée de
l'Ecole Rurale** at Trégarvan
recreates an early 20th-century
rural school, while other
museums cover subjects as
diverse as medieval monastic
life, rag-and-bone men and the
lifestyle of a Breton country
priest. Contemporary crafts and
art can be seen at the **Maison
des Artisans** in Brasparts.

Douarnenez ❹

Finistère. 👥 16,700. ✉
🏛 2 rue du Docteur Mével
(02 98 92 13 35). ✉ Mon–Sat.
www.douarnenez-tourisme.com

At the start of this century
Douarnenez used to be
France's leading sardine port;
today it is still devoted to
fishing, but is also a tourist
resort with beaches on both
sides of the Pouldavid estuary.

Nearby lies the tiny **Île
Tristan**, linked with the tragic
love story of Tristan and Iseult.
In the 16th century it was the
stronghold of a notorious
brigand, La Fontenelle.

The picturesque **Port du
Rosmeur** offers cafés, fish
restaurants and boat trips
around the bay, with a lively
early morning *criée* (fish
auction) held in the nearby
Nouveau Port. The Port-Rhu
has been turned into a floating
museum, **Le Port Musée**, with
over 100 boats and several
shipyards. Some of the larger
vessels can be visited.

🏛 **Le Port Musée**
Pl de l'Enfer. **Tel** 02 98 92 65 20.
⬜ Jul–Aug: daily; Sep–Jun: Wed–
Mon. 🎫 ♿ **www**.port-musee.org

Locronan's 15th-century Eglise
St-Ronan, seen from the churchyard

Locronan ❺

Finistère. 👥 1,000. 🏛 pl de la
Mairie (02 98 91 70 14).
www.locronan.org

During the 15th–17th
centuries Locronan grew
wealthy from the manufacture
of sail-cloth. After Louis XIV
ended the Breton monopoly
on this trade, the town
declined – leaving an elegant

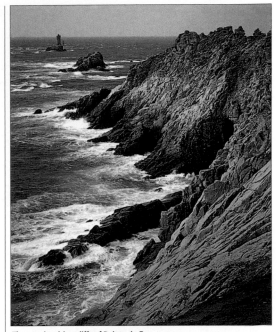

The awe-inspiring cliffs of Pointe du Raz

ensemble of Renaissance
buildings that attract many
visitors. In the town's central
cobbled square stands a late
15th-century church dedicated
to the Irish missionary St-
Ronan. Down Rue Moal is
the delightful **Chapelle Notre-
Dame-de-Bonne-Nouvelle**
with a calvary and a fountain.
Every July Locronan is the
scene of a *Troménie*, a
hilltop pilgrimage held in
honour of St Ronan. The more
elaborate *Grande Troménie*
takes place every 6 years.

Pointe du Raz ❻

Finistère. 🚉 Quimper. 🚌 Quimper,
then bus. 🏛 Audierne (02 98 70 12
20); Maison du Site (02 98 70 67 18).
www.pointeduraz.com

The dramatic Pointe du Raz,
almost 80 m (262 ft) high, is a
headland jutting into the
Atlantic at the tip of Cap
Sizun. The views of jagged
rocks and pounding seas are
breathtaking. Further west is
the flat Ile de Sein and
beyond that the lighthouse of
Ar Men. Despite being only
1.5 m (5 ft) above sea level,

Ile de Sein is nevertheless
home to 260 inhabitants, and
can be reached by boat from
Audierne in an hour.

Pays Bigouden ❼

Finistère. 🚌 Pont l'Abbé.
🏛 Pont l'Abbé (02 98 82 37 99).
www.ot-pontlabbe29.fr

Brittany's southwest tip is
known as the Pays Bigouden,
a windy peninsula with proud
and ancient traditions. The
region is famous for the
women's tall *coiffes* still worn
at festivals and *pardons* (see
p243), which can also be
seen at the **Musée Bigouden**.

Along the Baie d'Audierne
is a brooding landscape of
hamlets and isolated chapels
– the 15th-century calvary at
Notre-Dame-de-Tronoën is the
oldest in Brittany. There are
invigorating sea views from
Pointe de la Torche (a good
surfing spot) and from the
Eckmühl lighthouse.

🏛 **Musée Bigouden**
Le Château, Pont l'Abbé. **Tel** 02 98
66 00 40. ⬜ Apr–May: Tue–Sun
pms; Jun–Sep: daily. ● 1 May. 🎫

Quimper ❽

Finistère. 🏯 67,250. 🛬 🚆 🚌
ℹ️ pl de la Résistance (02 98 53 04
05). 🛒 Wed, Sat. **www**.quimper-
tourisme.com

The ancient capital of
Cornouaille, Quimper has a
distinctly Breton character.
Here you can find Breton
language books and music
on sale, buy a traditional
costume and tuck into some
of the best crêpes and cider
in Brittany. Quimper gets its
name from *kemper*, a Breton
word meaning the confluence
of two rivers, and the Steir
and Odet still flow through
this relaxed cathedral city.

West of the cathedral lies a
pedestrianized area known
as **Vieux Quimper**, full of
shops, crêperies and half-
timbered houses. Rue Kéréon
is the main thoroughfare, with
the place au Beurre and the
picturesque *hôtels particuliers*
(mansions) of rue des
Gentilshommes to the north.

Quimper has been pro-
ducing faïence, elegant hand-
painted pottery, since 1690.
The design often features
decorative flowers and
animals framed by blue and
yellow borders. Now mainly
decorative, faïence
is today exported to
collectors all over
the world. In the
southwest of the
city lies the
oldest factory,
**Faïenceries
HB-Henriot**,
which is open
to visitors all
year round.

🔒 Cathédrale
St-Corentin

Typical faïence plate
from Quimper

Quimper's cathedral
is dedicated to the city's
founder-bishop St Corentin.
Begun in 1240 – its colourfully painted interior now
restored – it is the earliest
Gothic building in Lower
Brittany, and was bizarrely
constructed with its choir at a
slight angle to the nave, perhaps to fit in with some since-
disappeared buildings. The
two spires of the west façade
were added in 1856. Between
them rides a statue of King

The Martyrdom of St Triphine (1910) by Sérusier, Pont-Aven School

Gradlon, the mythical founder
of the drowned city of Ys. After
this deluge he chose Quimper
as his new capital and St
Corentin as his spiritual guide.

🏛 Musée des Beaux-Arts

40 pl St-Corentin. **Tel** 02 98 95 45
20. 🔲 Jul–Aug: daily; Sep–Jun:
Wed–Mon. ⬤ most public hols;
Nov–Mar: Sun am. 🈂️ 🚻
www.musee-beauxarts.quimper.fr
Quimper's art museum is one
of the best in the region. The
collection is strong on late
19th- and early 20th-century
artists, and their work – such
as Jean-Eugène Buland's *Visite
à Ste-Marie de Bénodet*
– offers a valuable
insight into the
way visiting
painters
perpetuated a
romantic view
of Brittany.
Also on show
are works by
members of the
Pont-Aven School
and local artists
like J-J Lemordant
and Max Jacob.

🏛 Musée Départemental
Breton

1 rue de Roi-Gradlon. **Tel** 02 98 95
21 60. 🔲 Jun–Sep: daily; Oct–May:
Tue–Sat; Sun pm. 🈂️ 🚻
The 16th-century Bishop's
Palace has collections of
Breton costumes, furniture
and faïence, including
Cornouaille *coiffes*, ornately
carved box-beds and ward-
robes, and turn-of-the-century
tourist posters for Brittany.

Concarneau ❾

Finistère. 🏯 20,000. 🚌 ⛴ only
for islands. ℹ️ quai d'Aiguillon (02
98 97 01 44). 🛒 Mon & Fri.
www.tourismeconcarneau.fr

An important fishing port,
Concarneau's principal
attraction is its 14th-century
Ville Close (walled town),
built on an island in the harbour and encircled by massive
lichen-covered granite
ramparts. Access is by bridge
from place Jean Jaurès. Parts
of the ramparts can be toured,
and the narrow streets are full
of shops and restaurants. The
Musée de la Pêche, housed in
the port's ancient barracks,
explains the local techniques
and history of sea-fishing.

🏛 Musée de la Pêche

3 rue Vauban. **Tel** 02 98 97 10
20. 🔲 Feb–Sep: daily. ⬤ public
hols. 🈂️ 🚻

Fishing boats in Concarneau's busy
harbour

Pont-Aven ⑩

Finistère. 3,000.
5 pl de l'Hôtel de Ville
(02 98 06 04 70). Tue, Sat.
www.pontaven.com

Once a market town of
"14 mills and 15 houses",
Pont-Aven's picturesque
location in the wooded Aven
estuary made it attractive to
many late 19th-century artists.

In 1888 Paul Gauguin, along
with like-minded painters
Emile Bernard and Paul
Sérusier, developed a crude,
colourful style of painting
known as Synthetism.
Drawing inspiration from the
Breton landscape and its
people, the Ecole de Pont-
Aven (Pont-Aven School)
worked here and in nearby
Le Pouldu until 1896.

The town is devoted to art
and has 50 private galleries,
along with the informative
Musée de Pont-Aven which
documents the achievements
of the Pont-Aven School. The
surrounding woods proved
inspirational to many artists,
and offer pleasant walks –
one leads through the Bois
d'Amour to the **Chapelle de
Trémalo**, where the wooden
Christ in Gauguin's *Le Christ
Jaune* still hangs.

Musée de Pont-Aven
Pl de l'Hôtel de Ville. **Tel** 02 98 06 14
43. daily. early Jan–mid-Feb;
between exhibitions.

Notre-Dame-de-Kroaz-Baz, Roscoff

Le Pouldu ⑪

Finistère. 4,000. Pouldu
Plage, rue C. Filiger (02 98 39 93 42).

A quiet port at the mouth of
the river Laïta, Le Pouldu has
a small beach and good
walks. Its main attraction is
Maison Musée du Pouldu, a
reconstruction of the inn
where Paul Gauguin and other
artists stayed between 1889
and 1893. They covered every
inch of the dining room,
including the window-panes,
with self-portraits, caricatures
and still-lifes. These were
discovered in 1924 beneath
layers of wallpaper.

Maison Musée du Pouldu
10 rue des Grands Sables.
Tel 02 98 39 98 51. Apr–Oct
(phone for times). www.
museedupouldu.clohars-carnoet.fr

Roscoff ⑫

Finistère. 3,690.
Quai d'Auxerre (02 98 61 12 13).
Wed. www.roscoff-tourisme.com

Once a Corsairs' haunt, Roscoff
is a thriving Channel port and
seaside resort. Signs of its
wealthy seafaring past can be
found in the old port, along
rue Amiral Réveillère and in
place Lacaze-Duthiers. Here
the granite façades of the 16th-
and 17th-century shipowners'
mansions, and the weather-
beaten caravels and cannon
decorating the 16th-century
**Eglise Notre-Dame-de-Kroaz-
Baz**, testify to the days when
the privateers of Roscoff
were as notorious as those
of St-Malo *(see p282).*

The famous French onion
sellers (Johnnies) first crossed
the Channel in 1828, selling
their plaited onions door to
door. The **Maison des Johnnies**
tells their colourful history.
The **Thalado** is an informative
seaweed exhibition centre.
From the harbour you can take
a boat trip to the peaceful
Ile de Batz. Near Pointe de
Bloscon are tropical gardens.

Maison des Johnnies
48 rue Brizeux. **Tel** 02 98 61 25 48.
mid-Jun–mid-Sep: Mon, Tue, Thu
& Fri pm. Jan.

Thalado
5 rue Victor Hugo. daily.
Sep–mid-Jul: Sun.
www.pointeduraz.com

PAUL GAUGUIN IN BRITTANY

**Carving,
Chapelle
de Trémalo**

Paul Gauguin's (1848–1903)
story reads like a romantic
novel. At the age of 35 he left
his career as a stockbroker to
become a full-time painter.
From 1886 to 1894 he lived and
worked in Brittany, at Pont-Aven and Le
Pouldu, where he painted the landscape
and its people. He chose to concentrate
on the intense, almost "primitive" quality
of the Breton Catholic faith, attempting to
convey it in his work. This is evident in
Le Christ Jaune (Yellow Christ), inspired
by a woodcarving in the Trémalo chapel. In
Gauguin's painting, the Crucifixion is a reality
in the midst of the contemporary Breton
landscape, rather than a remote or symbolic
event. This theme recurs in many of his
paintings from the period, including *Jacob
Wrestling with the Angel* (1888).

Le Christ Jaune **(1889) by Paul Gauguin**

St-Thégonnec ⑬

Finistère. 🚇 ◯ *daily.* ♿

This is one of the most complete parish closes in Brittany. Passing through its triumphal archway, the ossuary is to the left. The calvary, directly ahead, was built in 1610 and perfectly illustrates the extraordinary skills Breton sculptors developed as they worked with the local granite. Among the many animated figures surrounding the central cross, a small niche contains a statue of St Thégonnec with a cart pulled by wolves.

Guimiliau ⑭

Finistére. ◯ *daily.* ♿

Almost 200 figures adorn Guimiliau's intensely decorated calvary (1581–88), many wearing 16th-century dress. Among them you can contemplate the legendary torment of Katell Gollet, a servant girl tortured by demons for stealing a consecrated wafer to please her lover. The church is dedicated to St Miliau and has a richly decorated south porch. The baptistry's elaborate carved oak canopy dates from 1675.

Font canopy from 1675, Guimiliau

Lampaul-Guimiliau ⑮

Finistère. ◯ *daily.* ♿

Entering through the monumental gate, the chapel and ossuary lie to the left, while the calvary is to the right. Here, however, it is the church that demands most attention. The interior is zealously painted and carved, including some naive scenes from the Passion depicted along the 16th-century rood-beam dividing the nave and choir.

Parish Closes

Reflecting the religious fervour of the Bretons, the Enclos Paroissiaux (parish closes) were built during the 15th–18th centuries. At that time Brittany had few urban centres but many wealthy rural settlements that profited from maritime trading and the manufacture of cloth. Grand religious monuments, some taking over 200 years to complete, were built by small villages inspired by spiritual zeal and the more earthly desire to rival their neighbours. Some of the finest parish closes lie in the Elorn valley, linked by a well-signposted Circuit des Enclos Paroissiaux.

The enclosure, *surrounded by a stone wall, is the hallowed area. By following the wall, visitors are drawn towards the triumphal arch, shown here in Pleyben.*

The small cemetery reflects the size of the community that built these great churches.

GUIMILIAU PARISH CLOSE

The three essential features of a parish close are a triumphal gateway marking the entry into the hallowed enclosure, a calvary depicting scenes from the Passion and Crucifixion, and an ossuary beside the church porch.

The calvary *is unique to Brittany, and may have been inspired by the crosses set on top of menhirs (see p279) by the early Christians. They provide a walk-around Bible lesson, often with the characters in 17th-century costumes as in this example from St-Thégonnec.*

Brittany's parish closes *are mostly in the Elorn Valley. As well as St-Thégonnec, Lampaul-Guimiliau and Guimiliau, other parish closes to visit include Bodilis, La Martyre, La Roche-Maurice, Ploudiry, Sizun and Commana. Further afield lie Plougastel-Daoulas and Pleyben, while Guébenno is in the Morbihan region.*
🛈 *rue de Kerven, Landivisiau (02 98 68 33 33).*

Church interiors *are usually adorned with depictions of local saints and scenes from their lives, along with ornately carved beams and furniture. This is the altarpiece in Guimiliau.*

In the ossuary bones exhumed from the cemetery would be stored. Built close to the church entrance, the ossuary was considered a bridge between the living and the dead.

Church

South Porch

Calvary

Funeral Chapel

Field of the Dead

Triumphal Arch

The triumphal arch *at St-Thégonnec, a monumental entrance, heralds the worshipper's arrival on sacred ground, like the right-eous entering heaven.*

Carvings in stone *were created as biblical cartoons to instruct and inspire visitors. Their clear message is now often obscured by weather and lichen, but this one in St-Thégonnec is well preserved.*

The chapel of Notre-Dame, perched on the cliffs above the beach of Port-Blanc, Côte de Granit Rose

Côte de Granit Rose ⑯

Côtes d'Armor. ☒ ☐ ☐ *Lannion.*
🛈 *Lannion (02 96 46 41 00).*
☐ *Thu.* **www**.ot-lannion.fr

The coast between Paimpol and Trébeurden is known as the Côte de Granit Rose due to its pink cliffs. These are best between Trégastel and Trébeurden; their granite is also used in neighbouring towns. The coast between Trébeurden and Perros-Guirec is one of Brittany's most popular family holiday areas.

Further east there are quieter beaches and coves, as at **Trévou-Tréguignec** and **Port-Blanc**. Beyond Tréguier, **Paimpol** is a working fishing port that once sent huge cod and whaling fleets to fish off Iceland and Newfoundland.

Tréguier ⑰

Côtes d'Armor. 🏘 *2,950.*
🛈 *13 pl de l'Eglise, Penvenan (02 96 92 81 09).* ☐ *Wed.*

Overlooking the estuary of the Jaundy and Guindy rivers, Tréguier stands apart from the resorts of the Côte de Granit Rose. It is a typically Breton market town, with one main attraction, the 14th–15th century **Cathédrale St-Tugdual**. It has three towers: one Gothic, one Romanesque and one 18th-century. The last, financed by Louis XVI with winnings from the Paris Lottery, has holes in the shapes of playing-card suits.

Environs
Chapelle St-Gonery in Plougrescant has a leaning lead spire and a 15th-century painted wooden ceiling.

Ile de Bréhat ⑱

Côtes d'Armor. 🏘 *420.* ☐ ☐
Paimpol, then bus to Pointe de l'Arc-ouest (Mon–Sat winter; daily summer), then boat. 🛈 *Paimpol (02 96 20 83 16).* **www**.paimpol-goelo.com

A 15-minute crossing from the Pointe de l'Arcouest, the Ile de Bréhat is actually 2 islands, joined by a bridge, which together are only 3.5 km (2.2 miles) long. With motorized traffic banned, and a climate mild enough for mimosa and a variety of fruit trees to flourish, it has a relaxing atmosphere. Bicycle hire and boat tours are available in the main town, **Port-Clos**, and you can walk to the island's highest point, the **Chapelle St-Michel**.

Chapelle St-Michel, a landmark on Ile de Bréhat

Carnac ⑲

Morbihan. 🏘 *4,600.* ☐
🛈 *74 avenue des Druides (02 97 52 13 52).* **www**.ot-carnac.fr

Carnac, a popular seaside resort, is also one of the world's great prehistoric sites, with almost 3,000 menhirs in parallel rows, and an excellent **Musée de Préhistoire**.

The 17th-century **Eglise St-Cornély** is dedicated to St Cornelius, patron saint of horned animals. His life is depicted on its ceiling.

🏛 **Maison des Megaliths**
Tel *02 97 52 29 81.* ☐ *daily.*
● *1 Jan, 1 May, 25 Dec.*
🌀 *summer only.* 🎫 *oblig. Apr–Sep.*

🏛 **Musée de Préhistoire**
10 pl de la Chapelle. **Tel** *02 97 52 22 04.* ☐ *Feb–Jun & Sep–Dec: Wed–Mon; Jul–Aug: daily.* ● *Jan, 1 May, 25 Dec.* 🌀 ♿

Presqu'île de Quiberon ⑳

Morbihan. 🏘 *5,200.* ☒ *Quiberon (via Lorient).* ☐ *Jul–Aug.* ☐ ☐ *Quiberon.*
🛈 *Quiberon (08 25 13 56 00).* ☐ *Sat, Wed (summer).* **www**.quiberon.com

Once an Island, the slender Quiberon peninsula has a bleak west coast with sea-punished cliffs, known as the Côte Sauvage. The east is more benign. At the peninsula's southern tip is the fishing port and resort of **Quiberon**, with a car ferry to Belle-Ile. In 1795 10,000 Royalist troops were massacred here in an ill-fated attempt to reverse the French Revolution.

Brittany's Prehistoric Monuments

At Carnac, thousands of ancient granite rocks were arranged in mysterious lines and patterns by Megalithic tribes as early as 4000 BC. Their original purpose remains obscure: the significance was probably religious, but the precise patterns also suggest an early astronomical calendar. Celts, Romans and Christians have since adapted them to their own beliefs.

The Gavrinis Tumulus, Golfe du Morbihan

MEGALITHS

There are many different formations of megaliths, all with a particular purpose. Words from the Breton language, such as *men* (stone), *dole* (table) and *hir* (long), are still used to describe them.

Menhirs, *the most common megaliths, are upright stones, standing alone or arranged in lines. Those in circles are known as cromlechs.*

Dolmen, *two upright stones roofed by a third, were used as a burial chamber, such as the Merchant's Table at Locmariaquer.*

Allée couverte, *upright stones placed in a row and roofed to form a covered alley, can be seen at Carnac.*

A tumulus *is a dolmen covered with stones and soil to form a burial mound.*

KEY

■	Megalithic sites
■	Alignments

0 kilometres 10
0 miles 5

Brittany's major megalithic sites

Alignment at Carnac

Menhirs of all shapes in a field near Carnac

Belle-Île-en-Mer ㉑

Morbihan. 🏠 5,200. ✈ Quiberon
(via Lorient). 🚢 from Quiberon.
ℹ quai Bonnelle, Le Palais (02 97 31
81 93). 🗓 daily. www.belle-ile.com

Brittany's largest island lies
14 km (9 miles) south of
Quiberon and can be reached
in 45 minutes by car ferry
from Quiberon. The coast has
cliffs and good beaches;
inland lie exposed highlands
intersected by sheltered
valleys. In the main town, Le
Palais, stands the **Citadelle
Vauban**, a 16th-century star-
shaped fortress, and there are
fine walks and views along
the southern Côte Sauvage.

Cloisters of St-Pierre in Vannes

Vannes ㉒

Morbihan. 🏠 58,000. 🚌 🚋 ℹ 1
quai Tabarly (08 25 13 56 10). 🗓 Wed
& Sat. www.tourisme-vannes.com

Standing at the head of the
Golfe du Morbihan, Vannes
was the capital of the Veneti,
a seafaring Armorican tribe
defeated by Caesar in 56 BC.
In the 9th century Nominoë,
the first Duke of Brittany,
made it his power base. The
city remained influential up
until the signing of the union
with France in 1532, when
Rennes became the Breton
capital. Today it is a busy
commercial city with a well-
preserved medieval quarter,
and a good base for exploring
the Golfe du Morbihan.

The impressive eastern walls
of old Vannes can be viewed
from the promenade de la
Garenne. Two of the city's
old gates survive at either
end: Porte-Prison in the north,

Breton seafarer, off Belle-Ile's coast

and the southern Porte-Poterne
with a row of 17th-century
wash houses close by.

Walking up from Porte
St-Vincent, you find the city's
old market squares, still in
use today. The **place des
Lices** was once the scene of
medieval tournaments and
the streets around the rue de
la Monnaie are full of well-
preserved 16th-century houses.

Begun in the 13th century,
Cathédrale St-Pierre has since
been drastically remodelled
and restored. The Chapel of
the Holy Sacrament houses
the revered tomb of Vincent
Ferrier, a Spanish saint who
died in Vannes in 1419.

Opposite the west front
of the cathedral, the old
covered market **La Cohue**
(meaning throng or hubbub)
was once the city's central
meeting place. Parts of the
building date from the
13th century, and a small
museum inside displays art
and artifacts relevant to the
history of the area.

Housed in the 15th-century
Château Gaillard, the **Musée**

d'Histoire is a rich assembly
of finds from Morbihan's
many prehistoric sites,
including jewellery, pottery
and weapons. There is also
a gallery of medieval and
Renaissance *objets d'art*.

> 🏛 **Musée d'Histoire**
> Château Gaillard, 2 rue Noé.
> **Tel** 02 97 01 63 00. ◯ Jun–Sep:
> daily. ◯ public hols. 🖼

Environs
To the south of the city the
Parc du Golfe is a beautiful
leisure park with many
amusements, a butterfly
conservatory, an automaton
museum and an aquarium
that boasts over 400 species
of fish. Northeast of Vannes,
off the N166, lie the romantic
ruins of the 15th-century
Tours d'Elven.

Golfe du Morbihan ㉓

Morbihan. ✈ Lorient. 🚌 🚋 🚢
Vannes. ℹ Vannes (08 25 13 56 10).
www.tourisme-vannes.com

Morbihan means "little sea"
in Breton, an apt description
for this landlocked expanse
of tidal water. Only con-
nected to the Atlantic by a
small channel between the
Locmariaquer and Rhuys
peninsulas, the gulf is dotted
with islands. Around 40 are
inhabited, with the **Ile d'Arz**
and the **Ile aux Moines** the
largest. These are served by
regular ferries from Conleau
and Port-Blanc respectively.

Around the gulf several small
harbours earn a living from
fishing, oyster cultivation and

The picturesque fishing port of Le Bono in Golfe du Morbihan

For hotels and restaurants in this region see pp566–8 and pp618–20

Young holidaymakers on the beach at Dinard, a classic seaside resort on the Emerald Coast

tourism. There is a wealth of megalithic sites, notably the island of **Gavrinis** where stone carvings have been excavated *(see p279)*. There are boat trips to Gavrinis from Larmor-Baden and around the gulf from Locmariaquer, Auray, Vannes and Port-Navalo.

The medieval Château de Josselin on the banks of the river Oust

Josselin ❷❹

Morbihan. 🏠 2,500. 🚌 ℹ️ 26 rue de Trente (02 97 22 36 43). 🗓 Sat. www.josselin-communaute.fr

Overlooking the river Oust, Josselin is dominated by a medieval **Château** owned by the de Rohan family since the end of the 15th century. Only four of its nine towers survive. The elaborate inner granite façade incorporates the letter "A" – a tribute to the much-loved Duchess Anne of Brittany (1477–1514), who presided over Brittany's "Golden Age". Tours are given of the 19th-century interior, and in the former stables there is a Musée des Poupées with 600 dolls. In the town, **Basilique Notre-**

Dame-du-Roncier contains the mausoleum of the castle's most famous owner and constable of France, Olivier de Clisson (1336–1407). West of Josselin at Kerguéhennec, the grounds of an 18th-century château have become a modern sculpture park.

🏰 **Château de Josselin**
Tel 02 97 22 36 45. ◯ Apr–Sep: daily (Apr–mid-Jul: pms only); Oct: Sat & Sun pms. 🔲 ♿
www.chateaujosselin.fr

Forêt de Paimpont ❷❺

Ille-et-Vilaine. 🛪 Rennes. 🚌 Monfort-sur-Meu. 🚍 Rennes. ℹ️ Montauban de Bretagne (02 99 06 86 07).

Also known as the Forêt de Brocéliande, this is a remnant of the dense primeval woods that once covered much of Armorica. It has long been associated with the legends of King Arthur, and visitors still

Legendary sorcerer Merlin and Viviane, the Lady of the Lake

search for the magical spring where the sorcerer Merlin first met the Lady of the Lake. The small village of **Paimpont** is a good base for exploring both the forest and its myths.

Côte d'Emeraude ❷❻

Ille et Vilaine & Côtes d'Armor. 🚹 ✈️ Dinard–St-Malo. 🚌 🚍 ⛴ ℹ️ Dinard (02 99 46 94 12). www.ot-dinard.com

Between Le Val-André and the Pointe du Grouin, near Cancale, sandy beaches, rocky headlands and classic seaside resorts stretch along Brittany's northern shore. Known as the Emerald Coast, its self-proclaimed Queen is the aristocratic resort of **Dinard**, "discovered" in the 1850s and still playing host to the international rich.

To its west are resorts like St-Jacut-de-la-Mer, St-Cast-le-Guildo, Sables d'Or-les-Pins and Erquy, all with tempting beaches. In the Baie de la Frênaye, the medieval **Fort La Latte** provides good views from high in its ancient watchtower, while the lighthouse that dominates **Cap Fréhel** nearby offers even more extensive panoramas.

East of Dinard, the D186 runs across the **Barrage de la Rance** to St-Malo. Built in 1966 it was the world's first dam to generate electricity by using tidal power. Beyond St-Malo, coves and beaches surround La Guimorais, while around the Pointe du Grouin the seas are often truly emerald.

SEAFARERS OF ST-MALO

St-Malo owes its wealth and reputation to the exploits of its mariners. In 1534 Jacques Cartier, born in nearby Rothéneuf, discovered the mouth of the St Lawrence river in Canada and claimed the territory for France. It was Breton sailors who voyaged to South America in 1698 to colonize the Iles Malouines, known today as Las Malvinas or the Falklands. By the 17th century St-Malo was the largest port in France and famous for its corsairs – privateers licensed by the king to prey on foreign ships. The most illustrious were the swashbuckling René Duguay-Trouin (1673–1736), who captured Rio de Janeiro from the Portuguese in 1711, and the intrepid Robert Surcouf (1773–1827), whose ships hounded vessels of the British East India Company. The riches won by trade and piracy enabled St-Malo's ship-owners to build great mansions known as *malouinières*.

Explorer Jacques Cartier (1491–1557)

St-Malo ㉗

Ille-et-Vilaine. 🏘 53,000. ✈ 🚉
🚌 ⛴ 🛈 *esplanade St-Vincent*
(08 25 13 52 00). 🛒 *Tue & Fri.*
www.saint-malo-tourisme.com

Once a fortified island, St-Malo stands in a commanding position at the mouth of the river Rance.

The city is named after Maclou, a Welsh monk who came here in the 6th century to spread the Christian message. During the 16th–19th centuries the port won prosperity and power through the exploits of its seafarers. St-Malo was heavily bombed in 1944 but has since been scrupulously restored and is now a major port and ferry terminal as well as a resort.

The old city is encircled by ramparts that provide fine views of St-Malo and its islands. Take the steps up by the **Porte St-Vincent** and walk clockwise, passing the 15th-century **Grande Porte**.

Within the city is a web of cobbled streets with tall 18th-century buildings housing shops, fish restaurants and crêperies. Rue Porcon-de-la-Barbinais leads to **Cathédrale St-Vincent**, with its sombre 12th-century nave contrasting with the stained glass of the chancel. On cour La Houssaye, the 15th-century Maison de la Duchesse Anne has been carefully restored.

St-Malo seen at low tide through the gate of Fort National

♠ Château de St-Malo

Pl Châteaubriand, near the Marina. **Tel** 02 99 40 71 57. 🕐 *Apr–Sep: daily; Oct–Mar: Tue–Sun.* 🔴 *1 Jan, 1 May, 1 & 11 Nov, 25 Dec.* 🌀
St-Malo's castle dates from the 14th–15th centuries. The great keep contains a museum of the city's history, including the adventures of its state-sponsored corsairs. From its watch towers there is an impressive view. Nearby, in the place Vauban, a tropical aquarium has been built into the ramparts, while on the edge of town, the Grand Aquarium has a shark tank and simulated submarine rides.

⚓ Fort National

🕐 *Jun–Sep: daily at low tide.* 🌀
Constructed in 1689 by Louis XIV's famous military architect, Vauban, this fort can be reached on foot at low tide

and offers good views of St-Malo and its ramparts. At low tide you can also walk out to **Petit Bé Fort** (open Easter–mid -Nov) and **Grand Bé**, where St-Malo-born writer François-René de Chateaubriand lies buried. From the top there are great views along the whole of Côte d'Emeraude (*see p281*).

⚓ Tour Solidor

St-Servan. **Tel** 02 99 40 71 58. 🕐 *Apr–Oct: daily; Nov–Mar: Tue–Sun.* 🔴 *1 Jan, 1 May, 1 & 11 Nov, 25 Dec.* 🌀
To the west of St-Malo in St-Servan, the three-towered Tour Solidor was built in 1382. Formerly a toll house, it was also a prison under the Revolution, and now houses an intriguing museum devoted to the ships and sailors that rounded Cape Horn, with ship models, logs and various nautical instruments.

Environs

When the tide is out, good beaches are revealed around St-Malo and in the nearby suburbs of St-Servan and Paramé. A passenger ferry runs to Dinard in summer (*see p281*) and the Channel Islands and there are boat trips up the Rance to Dinan, and out to the Iles Chausey, Ile de Cézembre and Cap Fréhel.

At Rothéneuf you can visit the **Manoir Limoëlou**, home of the navigator Jacques Cartier. Nearby, on the coast, Les Rochers Sculptés is a

Cancale oysters, prized for their taste since Roman times

beguiling array of granite faces and figures carved into the cliffs by a local priest, Abbé Fouré, at the end of the 19th century.

⊞ Manoir Limoëlou
Rue D Macdonald-Stuart, Limoëlou-Rothéneuf. *Tel 02 99 40 97 73.* ☐ Jul–Aug: daily. ● public hols. 🖼 🎥 oblig. ♿

Cancale ②⑧

Ille-et-Vilaine. 🏠 5,350. 🚃
🖪 44 rue du Port (02 99 89 63 72).
🚋 Sun. www.cancale-tourisme.fr

A small port with views across the Baie du Mont-St-Michel, Cancale is entirely devoted to the cultivation and consumption of oysters. Prized by the Romans, the acclaimed flavour of Cancale's oysters is said to derive from the strong tides that wash over them daily. You can survey the beds from a *sentier des douaniers* (coastguards' footpath, the GR34) running along the cliffs.

There are plenty of opportunities for sampling the local

speciality provided by a multitude of bars and restaurants along the busy quays of the Port de la Houle, where the fishing boats arrive at high tide. Devotees should pay a visit to the **Musée de l'Huître, du Coquillage et de la Mer.**

🏛 Musée de l'Huître, du Coquillage et de la Mer – La Ferme Marine
Aurore. *Tel 02 99 89 69 99.* ☐ mid-Feb–Jun & mid-Sep–Oct: Mon–Fri pms; Jul–mid-Sep: daily. 🖼 🎥

Dinan ②⑨

Côtes d'Armor. 🏠 10,000. 🚃 🚌
🖪 9 rue du Château (02 96 87 69 76).
🚋 Thu. www.dinan-tourisme.com

Set on a hill overlooking the wooded Rance valley, Dinan is a modern market town with a medieval heart. Surrounded by ramparts, the well-kept, half-timbered houses and cobbled streets of its Vieille Ville have an impressive, unforced unity best appreciated by climbing to the top of its 15th-century **Tour d'Horloge**, in rue de l'Horloge. Nearby, **Basilique St-Sauveur** contains the heart of Dinan's most famous son, the 14th-century warrior Bertrand du Guesclin.

Behind the church, Les Jardins Anglais offer good views of the river Rance and the viaduct spanning it. A couple of streets further north, the steep, geranium-decorated rue du Jerzual winds down through the 14th-century town gate to the port. Once a busy harbour from which

cloth was shipped, it is now a quiet backwater where you can take a pleasure cruise, or walk along a towpath to the restored 17th-century **Abbaye St-Magloire** at Léhon.

The **Musée du Château** houses a small museum of local history. Next to it is the 15th-century **Tour de Coëtquen**. From here are walks beside the ramparts along the promenade des Petits Fossés and the promenade des Grands Fossés.

⛪ Musée du Château
Château de la Duchesse Anne, rue du Château. *Tel 02 96 39 45 20.* ☐ daily (Oct–May: pms only). ● Jan, 1 week Feb, public hols. 🖼

Author and diplomat François-René de Chateaubriand (1768–1848)

Combourg ③⓪

Ille-et-Vilaine. 🏠 5,000. 🚃 🚌
🖪 23 pl Albert Parent (02 99 73 13 93). 🚋 Mon. www.combourg.org

A small, sleepy town beside a lake, Combourg is completely overshadowed by the great, haunting **Château de Combourg**. The buildings seen today date from the 14th and 15th centuries. In 1761 the château was bought by the Comte de Chateaubriand, and the melancholic childhood spent there by his son, the author and diplomat François-René de Chateaubriand (1768–1848), is candidly described in his entertaining chronicle, *Mémoires d'Outre-Tombe*.

Empty after the Revolution, the château was restored in the 19th century and is open for tours. One room has the belongings of François-René de Chateaubriand.

⛪ Château de Combourg
23 rue des Princes. *Tel 02 99 73 22 95.* ☐ Apr–Jun & Sep–Oct: Mon–Fri & Sun pm; Jul–Aug: daily. 🖼 🎥 www.combourg.net

View over Dinan and the Gothic bridge crossing the river Rance

RENNES CITY CENTRE

Cathédrale St-Pierre ②
Eglise St-Germain ⑧
Eglise St-Sauveur ③
Hôtel de Ville ④
Musée des Beaux Arts ⑨
Palais du Parlement
　de Bretagne ⑥
Parc du Thabor ⑦
Portes
　Mordelaises ①
Théâtre de
　Rennes ⑤

0 metres　　　250
0 yards　　　　250

Key to Symbols *see back flap*

Rennes ㉛

Ille-et-Vilaine. 🏠 214,800. ✈ 🚊 🚌 🚏
11 rue St-Yves (02 99 67 11 11). 🚐
Tue–Sat. **www**.tourisme-rennes.com

Founded by the Gauls and
colonized by the Romans,
Rennes is strategically located
where the Vilaine and Ille
rivers meet. After Brittany's
union with France in 1532, the
town became regional capital.
In 1720 a fire lasting for six
days devastated the city. Today
a small part of the medieval
city survives, together with
the neat grid of 18th-century

**The lively market at place des Lices
in the heart of Rennes**

buildings that arose from the
ashes. Around this historic
core are the tower blocks and
hi-tech factories of modern
Rennes – a confident provincial
capital with two universities
and a thriving cultural life.
　Wandering through the
streets that radiate from the
place des Lices and the place
Ste-Anne, it is easy to imagine
what Rennes was like before
the Great Fire. Now mostly
pedestrianized, this area has
become the city's youthful
heart with plenty of bars,
crêperies and designer shops.
At the western end of rue de
la Monnaie stands the 15th-
century **Portes Mordelaises**,
once part of the city's ramparts.
　Close by, **Cathédrale St-Pierre**
was completed in 1844, the
third on this site. Note the
carved 16th-century Flemish
altarpiece. Nearby is the
18th-century **Eglise St-Sauveur**.
Just south of the attractive rue
St-George, **Eglise St-Germain**
has a typically Breton belfry
and wooden vaulting. In the
place de la Mairie stands the
early 18th-century **Hôtel de
Ville** and the Neo-Classical
Théâtre de Rennes. The **Parc
du Thabor**, once part of a
Benedictine monastery,
is ideal for walks and picnics.

**Half-timbered houses lining the
narrow streets of old Rennes**

🏛 Palais du Parlement
de Bretagne

Pl du Parlement. ☐ *Tourist Office
for guided tours (02 99 67 11 66).*
www.tourisme-rennes.com
Rennes' Law Courts, built in
1618–55, were the seat of
the region's governing body
until the Revolution. Severely
damaged by fire during riots
over fish prices in 1994, the
major restoration work is
all but complete, including the
unique coffered ceiling and
gilded woodwork of the
Grande Chambre. Today,
the Salle des Pas Perdus, with
its vaulted ceilings, can again
be admired by the public.

🏛 Musée des Beaux Arts
20 quai Zola. **Tel** 02 23 62 17 45.
⬜ *Tue–Sun.* ⬤ *public hols.* ♿
www.mbar.org. **Musée Bretagne** 10
cours des Alliés. **Tel** 02 23 40 66 70.
⬜ *Tue–Sun pm only.* ⬤ *public hols.*
♿ ♿ **www**.musee-bretagne.fr

The **Musée des Beaux Arts**
has a wide-ranging collection
of art from the 14th century to
the present, including a room
of art on Breton themes. There
are paintings by Gauguin,
Bernard and other members of
the Pont-Aven School *(see p275)*,
and three works by Picasso,
including the lively *Baigneuse*
painted at Dinard in 1928.

Housed in the Rennes
cultural centre along with the
Science Museum and Plane-
tarium, the **Musée de Bretagne**
includes examples of traditional
Breton furniture and costume,
and displays on Brittany's prehistoric megaliths, the growth
of Rennes, rural crafts and the
fishing industry.

Environs
Just south of Rennes, the
Eco-musée du Pays de Rennes
traces the history of a local
farm since the 17th century.

Some 16 km (10 miles) to
the southeast of Rennes is
Châteaugiron, a charming
medieval village, with an
imposing castle and houses
preserving their wooden eaves.

🏛 Ecomusée du Pays de Rennes
Ferme de la Bintinais, rte de
Châtillon-sur-Seiche. **Tel** 02 99 51
38 15. ⬜ *Apr–Sep: Tue–Sun; Oct–*
Mar: Tue–Fri (Sat, Sun pm only).
⬤ *public hols.* ♿ ♿ **www**.
ecomusee-rennes-metropole.fr

⛫ Château de Châteaugiron
⬜ *mid-Jun–mid-Sep: daily;*
call 02 99 37 89 02. ♿

Fougères ❸❷

Ille-et-Vilaine. 🏠 23,000. 🚉
ℹ 2 rue Nationale (02 99 94 12 20).
🛍 *Sat.* **www**.ot-fougeres.fr

A fortress town close to the
Breton border, Fougères rests
on a hill overlooking the
Nançon river. In the valley
below, and still linked to the
Haute Ville by a curtain of
ancient ramparts, stands the
mighty 11th–15th century

The mighty fortifications of Château de Fougères

Château de Fougères. To
get a good overview of the
château, go to the gardens of
place aux Arbres behind the
16th-century **Eglise St-Léonard**.
From here you can descend
to the river and the medieval
houses around place du
Marchix. The Flamboyant
Gothic **Eglise St-Sulpice**, with
its 18th-century wood-panelled
interior and granite retables,
is well worth visiting.

A walk around the castle's
massive outer fortifications
reveals the ambitious scale
of its construction, with
13 towers and walls over 3 m
(10 ft) thick. You can still climb
the castle's ramparts to get a
feel of what it was like to live
within its staggered defences.
Much of the action in Balzac's
novel *Les Chouans* (1829)
takes place in and around
Fougères and its castle.

⛫ Château de Fougères
Pl Pierre-Simon. **Tel** 02 99 99 79
59. ⬜ *Feb–Dec: daily.* ♿
www.chateau-fougeres.com

Overhanging timber-frame houses
on rue Beaudrairie, Vitré

Vitré ❸❸

Ille-et-Vilaine. 🏠 16,000. 🚉 🚌
ℹ pl Général de Gaulle
(02 99 75 04 46). 🛍 *Mon & Sat.*
www.ot-vitre.fr

The fortified town of Vitré is
set high on a hill overlooking
the Vilaine valley. Its medieval
Château is complete with
pencil-point turrets and
picturesque 15th–16th century
buildings in attendance.
The castle was rebuilt in the
14th–15th centuries and
follows a triangular plan,
with some of its ramparts
walkable. There is a museum
in the Tour St-Laurent.

To the east, rue Beaudrairie
and rue d'Embas have overhanging timber-frame houses
with remarkable patterning.

The 15th–16th century
Cathédrale Notre-Dame, built
in Flamboyant Gothic style,
has a south façade with an
exterior stone pulpit. Further
along rue Notre-Dame, the
promenade du Val skirts
around the town's ramparts.

To the southeast of Vitré on
the D88, the **Château des**
Rochers-Sévigné was once the
home of Mme de Sévigné
(1626–96), famous letter-writer
and chronicler of life at the
court of Louis XIV. The park,
chapel and some of her
rooms are open to the public.

⛫ Château de Vitré
Tel 02 99 75 04 54. ⬜ *Apr–Sep:*
daily; Oct–Mar: Wed–Mon (closed
Sun am). ⬤ *1 Jan, Easter, 1 Nov,*
25 Dec. ♿

⛫ Château des Rochers-Sévigné
Tel 02 99 96 76 51. ⬜ *Apr–Sep:*
daily; Oct–Mar: Fri–Sun pms.
♿ ♿ *restricted.*

THE LOIRE VALLEY

INDRE · INDRE-ET-LOIRE · LOIR-ET-CHER · LOIRET · EURE-ET-LOIR
CHER · VENDEE · MAINE-ET-LOIRE · LOIRE-ATLANTIQUE · SARTHE

R enowned for its sumptuous châteaux, the glorious valley of the Loire, now classified a UNESCO World Heritage Site, is rich both in history and architecture. Like the river Loire, this vast region runs through the heart of French life. Its sophisticated cities, luxuriant landscape and magnificent food and wine add up to a bourgeois paradise.

The lush Loire Valley is supremely regal. Orléans was France's intellectual capital in the 13th century, attracting artists, poets and troubadours to the royal court. But the medieval court never stayed in one place for long, which led to the building of magnificent châteaux all along the Loire. Chambord and Chenonceau, the two greatest Renaissance châteaux, remain prestigious symbols of royal rule, resplendent amid vast hunting forests and waterways.

Due to its central location, culture and fine cuisine, Tours is the natural visitors' capital. Angers is a close second but more authentic are the historic towns of Saumur, Amboise, Blois and Beaugency, strung out like jewels along the river. This is the classic Loire Valley, a château trail which embraces the Renaissance gardens of Villandry and the fairytale turrets of Ussé. Venture northwards and the cathedral cities of Le Mans and Chartres reign supreme, their medieval centres bordered by Gallo-Roman walls. Nantes in the west is a breezy, forward-looking port and gateway to the Atlantic.

Southwards, the windswept Vendée is edged by a wild, sandy coastline that is perfect for windsurfers and nature lovers alike. Inland, the Loire's more peaceful tributaries and the watery Sologne beg to be explored. Also ripe for discovery are troglodyte caves, sleepy hamlets, and small Romanesque churches decorated with frescoes. Inviting inns offer game, fish and abundant fresh vegetables to be lingered over with a light white Vouvray wine or a fruity Bourgueil. Overindulgence is no sin in this rich region.

The river Loire at Montsoreau, southeast of Saumur

◁ The fairytale Château de Saumur towering above the town and the river Loire

Exploring the Loire Valley

The lush valley landscape, studded with France's greatest
châteaux, is the main attraction. Numerous river cruises are
available, while the sandy Atlantic coast offers beach holidays.
Peaceful country holidays can be had in the Vendée, and in the
Loir and Indre valleys. Wine tours focus on Bourgueil, Chinon,
Muscadet, Saumur and Vouvray vintages. The most charming bases
are Amboise, Blois, Beaugency and Saumur, but culture-lovers are
well-provided for throughout the region.

Countryside around Vouvray

**The 16th-century Château de
Villandry and its famous gardens**

KEY

— Motorway

— Major road

— Secondary road

— Minor road

— Scenic route

— Main railway

— Minor railway

— Regional border

△ Summit

SIGHTS AT A GLANCE

Abbaye Royale de
  Fontevraud **7**
Amboise **18**
Angers **3**
Azay-le-Rideau **11**
Beaugency **21**
Blois **20**
Bourges **27**
Chambord **19**
Chartres **24**
Chenonceau **17**
Chinon **8**
Langeais **10**

Le Mans **4**
Loches **15**
The Loir **23**
Montrésor **16**
Montreuil-Bellay **6**
Nantes **1**
Orléans **25**
St-Benoît-sur-Loire **26**
Saumur **5**
Tours **13**
Ussé **9**
The Vendée **2**
Vendôme **22**
Villandry **12**
Vouvray **14**

**A bridge over the Loire river
pictured at dawn**

GETTING AROUND

The region is well served by
transport links. Nantes and Tours
airports have international flights;
Tours airport also serves Marseille
and Figari (Corsica). Chartres,
Le Mans, Angers and Nantes are
reached from Paris by the A11,
and the A10 links Orléans, Blois
and Tours. The TGV train travels
from Paris to Le Mans (1 hr);
Tours (1 hr); Angers (90 mins);
and Nantes (2 hrs). There is also
TGV access from Lille (Eurostar
interchange). The smaller châteaux can be difficult to reach by
public transport, but there are
tours from major tourist centres.

Tomb of François II and his wife, Marguerite de Foix, in Cathédrale St-Pierre

Nantes ❶

Loire-Atlantique. 🔼 270,000. ✈
🚉 🚌 🅸 3 cours Olivier-de-Clisson
(08 92 46 40 44). ⛴ Tue–Sun.
www.nantes-tourisme.com

For centuries, Nantes disputed with Rennes the title of capital of Brittany. Yet links with the Plantagenets and Henri IV also bound it to the "royal" river Loire. Since the 1790s it has officially ceased to be part of Brittany, and, though still Breton at heart, it is today capital of the Pays de la Loire.

Visually, Nantes is a city of variety, with high-tech towers overlooking the port, canals and Art Nouveau squares. Chic bars and restaurants cram the medieval nucleus, bounded by place St-Croix and the château.

The **Cathédrale St-Pierre et St-Paul**, completed in 1893, is notable both for its sculpted Gothic portals and Renaissance tomb of François II, the last duke of Brittany.

More impressive is the **Château des Ducs de Bretagne**, where Anne of Brittany was born in 1477 and where the Edict of Nantes was signed by Henri IV in 1598, granting Protestants religious freedom. Following major restoration work the château now houses the lively, interactive **Musée d'Histoire**. It charts the history of Nantes through 32 rooms of exhibits, including Turner's painting of the Loire embankments in Nantes and a virtual visit of the city in 1757.

♣ Château des Ducs de Bretagne

Pl Marc Elder. **Tel** 08 11 46 46 44.
⏰ Jul–Aug: daily; Sep–Jun: Wed–Mon. ⏺ 1 Jan, 1 May, 1 Nov, 25 Dec. 🏷 ♿

Environs

From Nantes, boats cruise the Erdre and Sèvre Nantaise rivers, passing châteaux and vineyards. Some 30 km (20 miles) southeast of Nantes is **Clisson**, a town razed to the ground during the Vendée Uprising of 1793, and later rebuilt by sculptor François-Frédéric Lemot along Italian lines, with Neo-Classical villas and red-tiled roofs. On a spur overlooking the Sèvre Nantaise river is the ruined 13th-century **Château de Clisson**.

♣ Château de Clisson

Tel 02 40 54 02 22. ⏰ Wed–Mon (Oct–Apr: Wed–Mon pm only).
⏺ 1 May, Christmas hols. 🏷 🎫

The Vendée ❷

Vendée and Maine-et-Loire.
✈ Nantes. 🚉 🚌 La Roche-sur-Yon.
🅸 La Roche-sur-Yon (02 51 36 00 85).
www.vendee-tourisme.com

The counter-revolutionary movement which swept western France between 1793 and 1799 began as a series of uprisings in the Vendée, still an evocative name to the French. As a bastion of the *Ancien Régime*, the region rebelled against urban Republican values. But a violent massacre in 1793 left 80,000 royalists dead in one day as they tried to cross the Loire at St-Florent-le-Vieil. The Vendée farmers were staunch royalists, and, although they ultimately lost, the region remains coloured by conservatism and religious fervour to this day.

This local history is dramatically retraced at **Le Puy du Fou** in Les Epesses, south of Cholet, with its spectacular summer evening live show, 'Cinéscenie'. More sober accounts are given at Logis de La Chabotterie near St-Sulpice-de-Verdon, and the Musée du Textile in Cholet, whose flax and hemp textiles provided the royalist heroes with their kerchiefs: originally white, then blood-red.

The tranquil Vendée offers green tourism inland, in the *bocage vendéen*, a wooded backwater with paths and nature trails. The Atlantic coast between the Loire and La Rochelle has beaches, yet the only sizeable resort here is **Les Sables d'Olonne**, with boat trips to the salt-marshes, out to sea or to the nearby **Ile**

The harbour at Ile de Noirmoutier in the Vendée

d'Yeu. To the north, the marshy Ile de Noirmoutier is connected to the mainland at low tide via the Gois causeway.

Inland lies the remote **Marais Poitevin** *(see p408)*, its marshes home to bird sanctuaries and fine churches (Maillezais, Vix, Maillé) in hamlets bordered by canals. It is France's largest complex of man-made waterways, largely reclaimed for farming in the west, whilst further east is a nature lover's paradise. Coulon is the main centre for hiring punts.

The Apocalypse Tapestry in Angers

Angers ❸

Maine-et-Loire. 🏠 156,300.
✈ 🚆 🚌 🛈 7 pl Kennedy
(02 41 23 50 00). 🛒 Tue–Sun.
www.angersloiretourisme.com

Angers is the historic capital of Anjou, home of the Plantagenets and gateway to the Loire Valley. The town has a formidable 13th-century **Château** *(see p242)*. Inside is the longest (103m) and one of the finest medieval tapestries in the world. It tells the story of the Apocalypse, with battles between hydras and angels.

A short walk from the castle is the **Cathédrale St-Maurice**, noted for its façade and 13th-century stained-glass windows. Close by is Maison d'Adam, with carvings showing the tree of life. The nearby **Galerie David d'Angers**, housed in the glass-covered ruins of a 13th-century church, celebrates the sculptor born in Angers. Across the river Maine, the Hôpital St-Jean, a hospital for the poor from 1174 to 1854, houses the **Musée Jean Lurçat**. Its prize exhibit is the exquisite *Chant du Monde* tapestry, which was created by Lurçat in 1957. In the same building is **Le Musée de la Tapisserie Contemporaine**, with displays of ceramics and paintings.

♜ **Château d'Angers**
Tel 02 41 86 48 77. ⬜ daily.
⬤ 1 Jan, 1 May, 1 & 11 Nov, 25 Dec. 🌐 🎫

🏛 **Galerie David d'Angers**
33 bis rue Toussaint. *Tel* 02 41 05 38 90. ⬜ Jun–Sep: daily; Oct–May: Tue–Sun. ⬤ most public hols. 🌐

🏛 **Musée Jean Lurçat / Le Musée de la Tapisserie Contemporaine**
4 bd Arago. *Tel* 02 41 24 18 45.
⬜ Jun–Sep: daily; Oct–May: Tue–Sun. ⬤ most public hols. 🌐 ♿

Environs
Within a 20-km (13-mile) radius of Angers lie the Classical **Château de Serrant** and the moated **Château du Plessis-Bourré**, a decorative pleasure dome encased in a feudal shell. Follow the Loire east along the sandbanks and dykes, enjoying the fish restaurants en route.

♜ **Château de Serrant**
St-Georges-sur-Loire. *Tel* 02 41 39 13 01. ⬜ call or check website for opening schedules. 🌐 🎫 oblig. ⬜ **www**.chateau-serrant.net

♜ **Château du Plessis-Bourré**
Ecuillé. *Tel* 02 41 32 06 72.
⬜ Apr–Jun & Sep: Thu pm– Tue (Feb, Mar, Oct, Nov: Thu–Tue pms only); Jul– Aug: daily. 🌐 🎫 oblig. **www**.plessis-bourre.com

Le Mans ❹

Sarthe. 🏠 150,000. ✈ 🚆 🚌 🛈 rue de l'Etoile (02 43 28 17 22). 🛒 Tue–Sun. **www**.lemanstourisme.com

Ever since Monsieur Bollée became the first designer to place an engine under a car bonnet, Le Mans has been synonymous with the motor trade. Bollée's son created an embryonic Grand Prix, since when the event *(see p37)* and associated **Musée Automobile de**

Stained-glass Ascension window in the Cathédrale St-Julien, Le Mans

la Sarthe have remained star attractions. Cité Plantagenét, the ancient fortified centre, is surrounded by the greatest Roman walls in France, best seen from the quai Louis Blanc. Once insalubrious and abandoned, the area has been restored, and is now used for filming epics such as Cyrano de Bergerac, set amongst its Renaissance mansions, half-timbered houses, arcaded alleys and tiny courtyards. The crowning point is the Gothic **Cathédrale St-Julien**, borne aloft by flying buttresses, with its Romanesque portal rivalling that of Chartres. Inside, the Angevin nave opens into a Gothic choir, complemented by sculpted capitals and a 12th-century Ascension window.

🏛 **Musée Automobile de la Sarthe**
9 pl Luigi Chinetti. *Tel* 02 43 72 72 24. ⬜ daily (call for times). 🌐 ♿

Le Mans racetrack: a 1933 print from the French magazine *Illustration*

Saumur **⑤**

Maine-et-Loire. ∰ 32,000. 🚊 🚌 🛈
pl de la Bilange (02 41 40 20 60). 🕰 *Thu,
Sat.* www.saumur-tourisme.com

Saumur is celebrated for its
fairytale château, cavalry
school, mushrooms and
sparkling wines. Its stone
mansions recall the city's
17th-century heyday, when it
was a bastion of Protestantism
and vied with Angers as the
intellectual capital of Anjou.

High above both town and
river is the turreted **Château
de Saumur**. The present
structure was started
in the 14th-century
by Louis I of Anjou
and remodelled
later by his
grandson, King
René. Collections
include medieval
sculpture, and
equestrian exhibits.

The Military
Cavalry School,
established in
Saumur in 1814, led
to the creation of the **Musée
des Blindés**, which exhibits
150 different armoured vehicles,
and of the prestigious Cadre
Noir horse-riding formation.

The Château de Saumur and spire of St-Pierre seen from the Loire

Morning training sessions and
stable visits, along with
occasional evening performances, can be seen at the
Ecole Nationale d'Equitation.
The nearby subterranean
**Parc Pierre et
Lumière** (sculptures
in the tufa cave walls
of prominent local
tourist sites), is well
worth a visit; as is
Europe's largest
dolmen, with its
collection of pre-
historic implements,
in Bagneux.

Before you leave
the area, be sure to
sample the local
méthode champenoise sparkling
wine – the best in France outside Champagne – in one of
the many wine cellars or at
the Maison des Vins in town.

**King René's
coat of arms**

🏰 **Château de Saumur**
Tel 02 41 40 24 40. ● *for
renovation (phone for details).*

Ecole Nationale d'Equitation
St-Hilaire-St-Florent. *Tel 02 41 53 50
60.* ◯ *phone for details of
performance times.* ● *public hols.*
🔲 🔲 🔲 *oblig.* 🔲
www.cadrenoir.fr

Environs
The lovely **Eglise Notre-Dame**
at Cunault, an 11th-century
Romanesque priory church,
has a fine west door and
carved capitals, while an
amazing subterranean fort and
myriad caves and tunnels can
be seen at **Château de Brézé**.

Montreuil-Bellay **⑥**

Maine-et-Loire. ∰ 4,500. 🚊 🚌
🛈 *pl du Concorde (02 41 52 32 39).*
🕰 *Tue (& Sun, mid-Jun–mid-Sep).*
www.ville-montreuil-bellay.fr

Set on the river Thouet 17 km
(11 miles) south of Saumur,
Montreuil-Bellay is one of the
region's most gracious small
towns and is an ideal base for
touring Anjou. The towering
roofline of the Gothic collegiate
church overlooks walled mansions and surrounding vineyards
(wine-tasting recommended).
The **Chapelle St-Jean** was an
ancient hospice and pilgrimage centre.

The imposing **Château de
Montreuil-Bellay**, established
in 1025, is a veritable fortress
with its 13 interlocking towers,
barbican and ramparts.

A 15th-century house lies
beyond the fortified gateway,
complete with vaulted medieval
kitchen and an oratory decorated with 15th-century frescoes.

🏰 **Château de Montreuil-
Bellay**
Tel 02 41 52 33 06. ◯ *Apr–Oct:
Wed–Mon (Jul–Aug: daily).* 🔲 🔲

TROGLODYTE DWELLINGS
Some of the best troglodyte settlements in France have been
carved out of the soft limestone (tufa) of the Loire Valley, especially around Saumur, Vouvray and along the river Loir. The
caves, cut out of cliff-faces or dug underground, have been a
source of cheap, secure accommodation for centuries. Today
they are popular as *résidences secondaires*, or used for wine
storage and mushroom growing. Some are now restaurants or
hotels, and old quarries at Doué-la-Fontaine accommodate a
zoo and a 15th-century amphitheatre. At Rochemenier, near
Saumur, is a well-preserved troglodyte village museum. A
central pit is surrounded by a warren of caves, barns, wine
cellars, dwellings and even a simple underground chapel.

Heralded by chimney pots, the underground hamlet of
La Fosse was inhabited until the late 20th century by three
families, and is now a museum of family life underground.

A typical troglodyte dwelling

Court Life in the Renaissance

François I's reign, from 1515 to 1547, witnessed the apogee of the French Renaissance, characterized by an intense period of château-building and an interest in humanism and the arts. The itinerant court travelled between the pleasure palaces of Amboise, Blois and Chambord in the Loire. Days were devoted to hunting, falconry, *fêtes champêtres* (country festivals) or *jeu de paume*, a forerunner of tennis. Nights were given over to feasting, balls, poetry and romantic assignations.

Lute and mandolin *music were much in vogue, as were Italian recitals and masquerades. Musicians played at the twice-weekly balls, where the pavane and galliard were danced.*

The antics *of François I's fools, Triboulet and Caillette, amused the court. Yet they were often mistreated: courtiers regularly nailed Caillette's ears to a post for fun, daring him to remain silent.*

RENAISSANCE FEASTS

Dinner usually took place before 7pm to the accompaniment of Italian music. Humanist texts were read aloud and the king's fools amused the courtiers.

Courtiers used their own knives at dinner. Forks were still rare, although their use was spreading from Italy.

A typical royal dinner comprised smoked eel, salted ham, veal pâté, egg and saffron soups, roast game and boiled meats, as well as fish dishes in lemon or gooseberry sauce.

The cost of lavish damask, satin and silk costumes often sent courtiers into debt.

Diane de Poitiers *(1499–1566) became the mistress of the future Henri II when he was 12 years old. Two years later he married Catherine de' Medici, but Diane remained his favourite until his death.*

Artists symbolized love *in different ways during the Renaissance. Winged hearts charmingly perform the function here.*

The Grand Moûtier cloisters

Abbaye Royale de Fontevraud 🕖

Maine-et-Loire. 🚌 *from Saumur.*
Tel 02 41 51 73 52. ⏰ *Feb–mid-Apr:*
Tue–Sun; mid-Apr–Dec: daily.
🔴 *Jan, 25 Dec.* 📷
www.abbaye-fontevraud.com

The Abbaye Royale de Fontevraud is the largest and most remarkably intact medieval abbey in Europe. It was founded in the early 12th century by Robert d'Arbrissel, a visionary itinerant preacher who set up a Benedictine

TOUR EVRAUD

Pepperpot chimneys top the towers of the kitchen, restored in the 20th century.

Fireplace alcoves that look like side chapels housed the ovens.

THE PLANTAGENETS

The legendary counts of Anjou were named after the *genêt*, the sprig of broom Geoffrey Plantagenet wore in his cap. He married Matilda, daughter of England's Henry I. In 1154, when their son Henry – who had married Eleanor of Aquitaine *(see p51)* – acceded to the English throne, the Plantagenet dynasty of English kings was founded, fusing French and English destinies for 300 years.

Effigies of Henry II, Plantagenet king of England, and Eleanor of Aquitaine

community of monks, nuns, nobles, lepers and vagabonds. The radical founder entrusted the running of the abbey to an abbess, usually from a noble family, and the abbey became a favourite sanctuary for the female aristocracy, including Eleanor of Aquitaine.

From 1804 to 1963 the abbey was used as a prison, since when the buildings have been undergoing painstaking restoration by the French State. Wandering around the abbey buildings and gardens gives a fascinating insight into monastic life.

The focal point was the Romanesque abbey church, consecrated in 1119. It boasts beautifully carved capitals and an immense nave with four domes, one of the finest examples of a cupola nave in France. Inside are the painted effigies of the Plantagenets, dating from the early 13th century: Henry II of England, his redoubtable wife Queen Eleanor of Aquitaine, their crusading son Richard the Lion-Heart and Isabelle d'Angoulême, widow of his infamous brother, King John of England.

The abbey's nuns lived around the Renaissance **Grand Moûtier cloisters**, forming one of the largest nunneries in France, and the leper colony was housed in the **St-Lazare priory**, now the atmospheric abbey hotel *(see p555)*. The monastic quarters of **St Jean de l'Habit** no longer exist. Most impressive is the octagonal kitchen with its fireplaces and chimneys in the **Tour Evraud**, a rare example of secular Romanesque architecture.

The abbey, now an important arts centre, regularly hosts concerts and exhibitions.

Chinon 🕗

Indre-et-Loire. 🚶 *9,000.* 🚌 🚉
🛈 *pl Hofheim (02 47 93 17 85).*
🛒 *Thu.* **www**.chinon-valdeloire.com

The Château de Chinon is an important shrine in Joan of Arc country and, as such, wheedles money from all passing pilgrims. It was here in 1429 that the saint first recognized the disguised dauphin (later Charles VII),

and persuaded him to give her an army to drive the English out of France. Before that, Chinon was the Plantagenet kings' favourite castle. Although the **château** is now mostly in ruins, the ramparts are an impressive sight from the opposite bank of the Vienne river. The town's bijou centre is like a

Stallholder at Chinon's market

medieval film set. **Rue Voltaire,** lined with 15th- and 16th-century houses and once enclosed by the castle walls, represents a cross-section of Chinonais history. At No. 12 is the **Musée Animé du Vin**, where animated figures tell the story of wine-making. **No. 44** which houses the Musée d'Art et d'Histoire, is a

Vineyard in the Chinon wine region

stone mansion where, in 1199, Richard the Lion-Heart is said to have died. The grandest mansion is the **Palais du Gouverneur,** with its double staircase and loggia. More charming is the **Maison Rouge** in the Grand Carroi, studded with a red-brick herringbone pattern.

The 15th-century **Hostellerie Gargantua,** where Rabelais' lawyer father once practised, is now an agreeable inn *(see p569).*The great Renaissance writer lived nearby in the Rue de la Lamproie.

The 1900s market, with stallholders in period costume, folk dancing and music is a must (3rd Sat Aug).

🏛 **Musée Animé du Vin**
12 rue Voltaire. *Tel 02 47 93 25 63.* ◯ Easter–Sep: daily. 🈂 🎫

Environs
5 km (3 miles) southwest of Chinon is **La Devinière,** birthplace of François Rabelais, the 16th-century writer, priest, doctor and humanist scholar.

🏛 **La Devinière**
Seuilly. *Tel 02 47 95 91 18.* ◯ Wed–Mon. ⬤ 1 Jan, 25 Dec. 🈂 🎫

Château d'Ussé ❾

Indre-et-Loire. 🚉 *Chinon, then taxi.*
Tel 02 47 95 54 05. ◯ *mid-Feb–mid-Nov: daily.* 🈂 🎫
www.chateaudusse.fr

The fairytale Château d'Ussé enjoys a bucolic setting by the river Indre. Its romantic turrets, pointed towers and chimneys inspired Charles Perrault's *Sleeping Beauty.*

Constructed in the 15th century, the castle was gradually transformed into an aristocratic château, which is still privately owned *(see p242).* However, the sunless and musty interior is rather disappointing and the *Sleeping Beauty* tableaux are clumsily presented.

The château's delightful Renaissance chapel, framed by the oak forest of Chinon, has lost its Aubusson tapestries, but retains a lovely della Robbia terracotta *Virgin.*

Château de Langeais ❿

Indre-et-Loire. 🚉 *Langeais.*
Tel 02 47 96 72 60. ◯ *daily.*
⬤ *1 Jan, 25 Dec.* 🈂 🎫
www.chateau-de-langeais.com

Compared with neighbouring towns, Langeais is distinctly untouristy and has a welcoming, unpretentious feel. Its château is fiercely feudal, built strictly for defence with a drawbridge, portcullis and no concessions to the Renaissance. It was constructed by Louis XI in just four years, from 1465–9, with hardly an alteration since then. The ruins of an impressive keep, built by Foulques Nerra in AD 994, stand in the small château courtyard.

A *son et lumière* in the Salle de la Chapelle represents the marriage of Charles VIII and Anne of Brittany in 1491. Many of the rooms have intricate designs on the tiled floors, and all are hung with fine 15th- and 16th-century Flemish and Aubusson tapestries.

FRANÇOIS RABELAIS

Rabelais, born in 1494, was a priest, doctor, diplomat and humanist scholar noted for his wisdom and tolerance. He is best remembered for his many ribald satires (written as "medicine" for his patients), such as *Pantagruel* and *Gargantua,* set around his native Chinon.

Infant Pantagruel, depicted by Doré in 1854, was fed on the milk of 17,913 cows

Château d'Azay-le-Rideau ⓫

Indre-et-Loire. 🔲 🔲 *Azay-le-Rideau*. **Tel** *02 47 45 42 04*.
◯ *daily.* ● *1 Jan, 1 May, 25 Dec.* 🔲
🔲 **Son et Lumière:** *Jul–Aug.*

Balzac called Azay-le-Rideau "A multi-faceted diamond set in the Indre". It is the most beguiling and feminine of Loire châteaux, created in the early 16th century by Philippa Lesbahy, wife of François I's corrupt finance minister. Although Azay is superficially Gothic (*see pp54–55, 242*), it clearly shows the transition to the Renaissance: the turrets are purely decorative and the moats are picturesque pools. Azay was a pleasure palace, lived in during fine weather and deserted in winter.

The interior is equally delightful, an airy, creaking mansion smelling faintly of cedarwood and full of lovingly re-created domestic detail. The first floor is furnished in the Renaissance style, with a fine example of a portable Spanish cabinet and exquisite tapestries. The ground floor has 19th-century furniture, dating from the period of the château's restoration. The four-storey grand staircase is unusual for its time, being straight as opposed to spiral.

Wine-tasting opportunities in the village are a welcome reminder that vineyards are all around. Unlike most Loire villages, Azay is lively at night, thanks to the château's poetic *son et lumière*.

The Château de Villandry's *jardin d'ornement*

Château de Villandry ⓬

Indre-et-Loire. 🔲 *Tours, then taxi.*
Tel *02 47 50 02 09.* ◯ **Château:** *mid-Feb–mid-Nov & mid-Dec–early Jan: daily.* **Gardens:** *daily.* 🔲 🔲 🔲 *Mar–Oct.* www.chateauvillandry.com

Villandry was the last great Renaissance château built in the Loire Valley, a perfect example of 16th-century architecture. Its gardens were restored to their original splendour early in the last century by Dr Joachim Carvallo, whose grandson continues his work.

The result is a patchwork of sculpted shrubs and flowers on three levels: the kitchen garden (*jardin potager*), the ornamental garden (*jardin d'ornement*) and, on the highest level, the water garden (*jardin d'eau*). There are signs to explain the history and meaning behind each plant: the marrow, for instance, symbolized fertility; the cabbage, sexual and spiritual corruption. Plants were also prized for their medicinal properties: cabbage was thought to help cure hangovers, while pimento aided digestion.

The delicate roots of the 52 kms (32 miles) of box hedge that outline and highlight each section mean that the whole 4 ha (10 acres) of gardens must be hand-weeded.

A chocolatier in Tours

Tours ⓭

Indre-et-Loire. 🔲 *140,000.* 🔲 🔲
🔲 🔲 *78 rue Bernard Palissy (02 47 70 37 37).* 🔲 *Tue–Sun.*
www.ligeris.com

Tours is the most appealing of the major Loire cities, thanks to bourgeois prosperity, an intelligent restoration programme and its university population. It is built on the site of a Roman town, and was a centre of Christianity in the 4th century under St Martin, bishop of Tours. In 1461 Louis XI made the city the French capital. However, during Henri IV's reign the city lost favour with the monarchy and the capital left Tours for Paris.

Bombarded by the Prussians in 1870, and bombed in World War II, Tours suffered extensive damage. By 1960, the middle classes had abandoned the historic centre and it became a slum, full of

Château d'Azay-le-Rideau reflected in the river Indre

For hotels and restaurants in this region see pp568–72 and pp620–5

crumbling medieval masonry. Regeneration of the city has succeeded due to the popular policies of Jean Royer, mayor of Tours from 1958 to 1996.

The pedestrianized **place Plumereau** is Tours' most atmospheric quarter, set in the medieval heart of the city and full of cafés, boutiques and galleries. Streets such as rue Briçonnet reveal half-timbered façades, hidden courtyards and crooked towers. A gateway leads to place St-Pierre-le-Puellier, a square with sunken Gallo-Roman remains and a Romanesque church converted into a café. A few streets away in place de Châteauneuf lies the Romanesque **Tour Charlemagne**, all that remains of St Martin's first church. West of here is the highly yuppified artisans' quarter, centred on the rue du Petit St-Martin.

The **Cathédrale St-Gatien**, in the eastern sector of the city, was begun in the early 13th century and completed in the 16th. Its Flamboyant Gothic façade is blackened and crumbling but still truly impressive, as are the medieval stained-glass windows.

The **Musée des Beaux Arts**, set in the former archbishop's palace nearby, overlooks

Cathédrale St-Gatien in Tours

Classical gardens and a giant cedar of Lebanon. Its star exhibits are *Christ in the Garden of Olives* and *The Resurrection* by Mantegna, and a room devoted to the modern artist Olivier Debré.

Further west, is the **Eglise St-Julien**, whose Gothic monastic cells and chapter-house contain a small wine museum. Next door, the **Musée du Compagnonnage** displays hundreds of finely created works by master crafts-men of the guilds. Across the rue Nationale lies the town's

finest Renaissance building, the **Hôtel Goüin**, which houses regular art exhibitions.

Musée des Beaux Arts

18 pl François Sicard. **Tel** 02 47 05 68 73. ◯ Wed–Mon. ◯ 1 Jan, 1 May, 14 Jul, 1 & 11 Nov, 25 Dec.

Musée du Compagnonnage

8 rue Nationale. **Tel** 02 47 21 62 20. ◯ mid-Jun–mid-Sep: daily; mid-Sep–mid-Jun: Wed–Mon. ◯ 1 Jan, 1 May, 14 Jul, 1 & 11 Nov, 25 Dec.

Environs
Just outside Céré la Ronde, on the D764 from Montrichard to Loches, lies the 15th-century **Château de Montpoupon** and its excellent Musée du Veneur, which looks at the important role of horses in hunting.

Backgammon players in Tours' place Plumereau

TOURS TOWN CENTRE

Cathédrale St-Gatien ⑤
Château Royal ④
Eglise St-Julien ③
Hôtel Goüin ②
Musée des Beaux Arts ⑥
Tour Charlemagne ①

0 metres   100
0 yards   100

Key to Symbols *see back flap*

Château de Chenonceau ⑰

A romantic pleasure palace, Chenonceau was created from the Renaissance onwards by a series of aristocratic women. A magnificent avenue bordered by plane trees leads to symmetrical gardens and the serene vision that Flaubert praised as "floating on air and water". The château stretches across the river Cher with a 60-m (197-ft) gallery built over a series of arches, its elegant beauty reflected in the languid waters. The grandeur continues inside with splendidly furnished rooms, airy bedchambers and fine paintings and tapestries.

Turreted Pavilion
This was built between 1513 and 1521 by Catherine Briçonnet and her husband, Thomas Bohier, over the foundations of an old water mill.

Chapelle
The chapel has a vaulted ceiling and pilasters sculpted with acanthus leaves and cockleshells. The stained glass, destroyed by a bomb in 1944, was replaced in 1953.

Catherine de' Medici's Garden
Lavish court receptions and transvestite balls were held under Catherine's auspices.

TIMELINE

Catherine de' Medici

1533 Marriage of Catherine de' Medici (1519–89) to Henri II (1519–59). Chenonceau becomes a Loire royal palace

1559 On Henri's death, Catherine forces the disgraced Diane to accept the Château de Chaumont in exchange for Chenonceau

1789 Chenonceau is spared in the French Revolution thanks to Madame Dupin

1500	1600	1700	1800

1575 Louise de Lorraine (1554–1601) marries Henri III, Catherine's third and favourite son

1547 Henri II offers Chenonceau to Diane de Poitiers, his lifelong mistress

1513 Thomas Bohier acquires medieval Chenonceau. His wife, Catherine Briçonnet, rebuilds it in Renaissance style

1863 Madame Pelo restores the château its original st

1730–99 Madame Dupin, a "farmer-general's" wife, makes Chenonceau a salon for writers and philosophers

VISITORS' CHECKLIST

🅿 *Chenonceaux.* 🚍 *from Tours.*
Tel *02 47 23 90 07.* ⭕ *daily.*
🈂 📷 ♿ *gr. fl. only.* 🍴 🎫
🎵 🎼 *Classical music: Jun–Aug.*
www.chenonceau.com

Grande Galerie
The elegant gallery crowning the bridge is Florentine in style, created by Catherine de' Medici from 1570–76.

The Creation of Chenonceau

The women responsible for Chenonceau each left their mark. Catherine Briçonnet, wife of the first owner, built the turreted pavilion and one of the first straight staircases in France; Henri II's mistress, Diane de Poitiers, added the formal gardens and arched bridge over the river; Catherine de' Medici transformed the bridge into an Italian-style gallery (having evicted Diane following her husband's death in 1559); Louise de Lorraine, bereaved wife of Henri III, inherited the château in 1590 and painted the ceiling of her bedchamber black and white (the colour of royal mourning); Madame Dupin, a cultured 18th-century châtelaine, saved the château from destruction in the Revolution; and Madame Pelouze undertook a complete restoration in 1863.

Ground floor

First floor

CHÂTEAU GUIDE

The main living area was in the square-shaped turreted pavilion in the middle of the river Cher. Four principal rooms open off the Vestibule on the ground floor: the Salle des Gardes and the Chambre de Diane de Poitiers, both hung with 16th-century Flemish tapestries; the Chambre de François I, with a Van Loo painting; and the Salon Louis XIV. On the first floor, reached via the Italianate staircase, are other sumptuous apartments including the Chambre de Catherine de' Médicis and the Chambre de Vendôme.

1   Vestibule
2   Salle des Gardes
3   Chapelle
4   Terrasse
5   Librairie de Catherine de' Médicis
6   Cabinet Vert
7   Chambre de Diane de Poitiers
8   Grande Galerie
9   Chambre de François I
10 Salon Louis XIV
11 Chambre des Cinq Reines
12 Cabinet des Estampes
13 Chambre de Catherine de' Médicis
14 Chambre de Vendôme
15 Chambre de Gabrielle d'Estrées

1913 The château is bought by the Menier family, the *chocolatiers* who still own it today

1941 Chenonceau chapel is damaged in a bombing raid

Diane de Poitiers

Chambre de Catherine de' Médicis

Vouvray ⓮

Indre-et-Loire. 🏠 *3,500.*
ℹ️ *12 rue Rabelais (02 47 52 68 73).*
🚉 *Tue & Fri.* **www**.tourisme
vouvray-valdeloire.com

Just east of Tours is the
village of Vouvray, home of
the delicious white wine that
Renaissance author Rabelais
likened to taffeta.

The quality of Vouvray's
wines has not changed.
The star vineyard is **Huet**,
where, since 1990, grapes
have been grown according
to biodynamic methods:
manual weeding and natural
fertilizers. In the preface to
his novel *Quentin Durward*,
Sir Walter Scott sang the
praises of its dry white wines,
which are still matured in
chestnut barrels. Gaston Huet
also hit the headlines in 1990
with his protests against the
building of tracks for the TGV
train over Vouvray vineyards.
A compromise was eventually
reached and tunnels were
built under the hilly vineyards.

The **Chateau de Mont-
contour**, where monks
first planted vines in the
4th century, has its own
wine-making museum in the
impressive 10th-century cellars
hewn out of the tufa rock.

The medieval town of Loches

Huet
11–13 rue de la Croix-Buisée.
Tel *02 47 52 78 87.* ⏰ *Jul–Aug:
Mon–Sat for wine tastings; cellar
visits by reservation only.*
🔵 *public hols.*

♟️ **Château de Moncontour**
Route de Rochecorbon. ***Tel*** *02 47
52 60 77.* ⏰ *Easter–Sep: daily;
Oct–before Easter: Mon–Fri.* 📷
📷 *Visits can be followed by wine
tastings.* **www**.moncontour.com

Loches ⓯

Indre-et-Loire. 🏠 *7,000.* 🚉 🚌
ℹ️ *pl de la Marne (02 47 91 82 82).*
🚉 *Wed & Sat.* **www**.loches-
tourainecotesud.com

This unspoilt medieval town
is removed from the château
trail in the Indre valley. It is a
backwater of late Gothic
gateways and sculpted façades.
Its keep boasts the deepest
dungeons in the Loire. The
Logis Royal is associated with
Charles VII and his mistress
Agnès Sorel. It is also where
Joan of Arc pleaded with
Charles to go to Reims and be
crowned. Anne of Brittany's
chapel is decorated with
ermines, and contains an
effigy of Agnès Sorel.

♟️ **Logis Royal de Loches**
Tel *02 47 59 01 32.* ⏰ *daily.*
🔵 *1 Jan, 25 Dec.* 📷 📷

THE HEROINE OF FRANCE

Joan of Arc is the quintessential French national heroine, a
virginal warrior, a woman martyr, a French figurehead. Her
divinely led campaign to "drive the English out of France"
during the Hundred Years' War has inspired plays, poetry and
films from Voltaire to Cecil B de Mille. Responding to
heavenly voices, she appeared on the scene as champion of
the dauphin, the uncrowned Charles VII. He faced an Anglo-
Burgundian alliance which held most of northern France, and
had escaped to the royal châteaux on the Loire. Joan con-

vinced him of her mission,
mustered the French troops
and in May 1429 led them to
victory over the English at
Orléans. She then urged the
dithering Charles to go to
Reims to be crowned.
However, in 1430 she was
captured and handed over to
the English. Accused of
witchcraft, she was burnt at
the stake in Rouen in 1431
at the age of 19. Her legendary bravery and tragic
martyrdom led to her
canonization in 1920.

**Earliest known drawing of
Joan of Arc (1429)**

Portrait of Joan of Arc *in the
Maison Jeanne d'Arc in Orléans (see
p312). She saved the city from the
English on 8 May 1429, a date the
Orléannais still celebrate annually.*

Montrésor ⑯

Indre-et-Loire. 🏠 *400.* 🛈 *43 grande rue (02 47 92 70 71).* **www**.tourisme-valdindrois-montresor.com

Classed as one of "the most beautiful villages in France", Montrésor does not disappoint. Set on the river Indrois, it became a Polish enclave in the 1840s. In 1849 a Polish nobleman, Count Branicki, bought the 15th-century **Château**, built on the site of one of Foulques Nerra's 11th-century fortifications. It has

Farm building and poppy fields near the village of Montrésor

remained in the family ever since, its interior unchanged.

⛪ **Château de Montrésor**
Tel *02 47 92 60 04.* ◻ *Apr–11 Nov: daily; mid-Nov–Mar: Sat & Sun pm.* 🖾 ☑

Château de Chenonceau ⑰

See pp288–9.

Amboise ⑱

Indre-et-Loire. 🏠 *12,000.* 🚌 🚉 🛈 *quai du Général de Gaulle (02 47 57 09 28).* 🛒 *Fri & Sun am.* **www**.amboise-valdeloire.com

Few buildings are more historically important than the **Château d'Amboise.** Louis XI lived here; Charles VIII was born and died here; François I was brought up here, as were Catherine de' Medici's 10 children. The château was also the setting for the 1560 Amboise Conspiracy, an ill-fated Huguenot plot against François II. Visitors are shown the metal lace-work balcony which served as a gibbet for 12 of the 1,200 conspirators who were put to death. The **Tour des Minimes**, the château's original entrance, is

Amboise seen from the Loire

famous for its huge spiral ramp up which horsemen could ride to deliver provisions.

On the ramparts is the beautifully restored Gothic **Chapelle St-Hubert,** Leonardo da Vinci's burial place. Under the patronage of François I, the artist lived in the nearby manor house of **Clos-Lucé,** whose gardens exhibit models of Leonardo's inventions constructed from his sketches.

⛪ **Château d'Amboise**
Tel *02 47 57 00 98.* ◻ *daily.* ● *1 Jan, 25 Dec.* 🖾 ☑ **www**.chateau-amboise.com

🏛 **Clos-Lucé**
2 rue de Clos-Lucé. **Tel** *02 47 57 00 73.* ◻ *daily.* ● *1 Jan, 25 Dec.* 🖾 ♿ restricted. **www**.vinci-closluce.com

A romantic heroine, *Joan of Arc was a popular subject for artists. This painting of her is by François Léon Benouville (1821–59).*

Burnt at the stake – *a scene from* St Joan, *Otto Preminger's 1957 epic film, which starred Jean Seberg.*

Château de Chambord ⑲

Henry James once said, "Chambord is truly royal – royal in its great scale, its grand air, and its indifference to common considerations." The Loire's largest residence, brainchild of the extravagant François I, began as a hunting lodge in the Forêt de Boulogne. In 1519 this was razed and the creation of present-day Chambord began, to a design probably initiated by Leonardo da Vinci. By 1537 the towers, keep and terraces had been completed by 1,800 men and three master masons. At one point, François suggested diverting the Loire to flow in front of his château, but he settled for redirecting the nearby Cosson instead. His son Henry II continued his work, and Louis XIV completed the 440-roomed edifice in 1685.

The Château de Chambord with the river Cosson, a tributary of the Loire, in the foreground

The Salamander
François I chose the salamander as his enigmatic emblem. It appears over 800 times throughout the château.

The chapel was begun by François I shortly before his death in 1547. Henri II added the second storey and Louis XIV the roof.

★ **Roof Terraces**
This skyline of delicate cupolas has been likened to a miniature Oriental town. The roof terraces include a forest of elongated chimney pots, miniature spires, shell-shaped domes and richly sculpted gables.

The central keep (donjon), with its four circular towers, forms the nucleus of the château.

STAR FEATURES

★ Roof Terraces

★ Vaulted Guardrooms

★ Grand Staircase

TIMELINE

1519–47 The Count of Blois' hunting lodge demolished by François I and the château created

1547–59 Henri II adds the west wing and second storey of the chapel

1547 Death of François I

1669–85 Louis XIV completes the building, then abandons it

1670 Molière's *Le Bourgeois Gentilhomme* staged at Chambord

1725–33 Inhabited by Stanislas Leczinski, exiled king of Poland who was made duke of Lorraine

1748 The Maréchal de Saxe acquires Chambord. On his death two years later, the château yet again falls into decline

1840 Chambord declared a *Monument Historique*

1970s Chambord is restored and refurnished and the moats re-dug

Molière

1500	1600	1700	1800	1900

★ Vaulted Guardrooms

Arranged in the form of a Greek cross around the Grand Staircase, the vaulted guardrooms were once the setting for royal balls and plays. Their ceilings are decorated with François I's initials and salamander motif.

VISITORS' CHECKLIST

Blois, then taxi or bus.
Tel 02 54 50 40 00.
Jan–Mar: 10am–5pm daily;
Apr–Sep: 9am–6pm daily;
Oct–Dec: 10am–5pm daily.
1 Jan, 1 May, 25 Dec.
Son et Lumière
"Rêve de Lumières" (sound and light show) mid-Jul–mid-Aug: nightly. www.chambord.org

The lantern tower is 32 m (105 ft) high. Surmounting the terrace, it is supported by arched buttresses and crowned by a fleur-de-lys.

François I's Bedchamber is where the king, hurt by a failed romance, scratched a message on a pane of glass: " *Souvent femme varie, bien fol est qui s'y fie.*" (Every woman is fickle, he who trusts one is a fool.)

Cabinet de François I
The king's barrel-vaulted study (cabinet) in the outer north tower was turned into an oratory in the 18th century by Queen Catherine Opalinska, wife of Stanislas Leczinski (Louis XV's father-in-law).

★ Grand Staircase
This innovative double-helix staircase was supposedly designed by Leonardo da Vinci. It ensures that the person going up and the person going down cannot meet.

Louis XIV's Bedchamber
Louis XIV's bedchamber lies within the Sun King's state apartments, the grandest quarters in the château.

Blois's Cathédrale St-Louis and Hôtel de Ville seen from across the Loire

Blois ⑳

Loir-et-Cher. 👥 60,000. 🚋 🚌
ℹ️ 23 pl du château (02 54 90 41
41). 🛒 Fri (organic market), Sat.
www.bloispaysdechambord.com

Once a fief of the counts of
Blois, the town rose to
prominence as a royal domain
in the 15th century, retaining
its historic façades and refined
atmosphere to this day. Architectural interest abounds in
Vieux Blois, the hilly, partially
pedestrianized quarter enclosed
by the château, cathedral and
river. Four well-signposted
walking tours act as a gentle
introduction to the noble
mansions and romantic courtyards that grace the Loire's
most beguiling town.

Set back from the north bank
of the river, the **Château Royal
de Blois** was the principal
royal residence until Henri IV
moved the court to Paris in
1598 – Louis XIV's creation
of Versailles *(see pp174–7)*
was to mark the final eclipse
of Blois. The château's four
contrasting wings make a

harmonious whole. The Salle
des Etats Généraux, the only
part of the building surviving
from the 13th century, housed
the council and court, and is
the largest and best-preserved
Gothic hall in France. The
adjoining late 15th-century
Louis XII wing, which houses
the **Musée des Beaux Arts**,
infuses Gothic design with
Renaissance spirit, sealed with
the king's porcupine symbol.

The 16th-century François I
wing is a masterpiece of the
French Renaissance containing
a monumental spiral staircase
in an octagonal tower. By
contrast, the 17th-century
Gaston d'Orléans wing is a
model of Classical sobriety.

Blois is authentically
furnished and hung with
paintings interpreting its
troubled past. These
include a portrayal
of the murder
of the Duc de Guise in
1588. Suspected of
heading a Catholic
plot against
Henri III, he was
stabbed to death

King Louis XII's porcupine symbol

by guards in the king's
chamber. The most intriguing
room is Catherine de' Medici's
study where, of the 237 carved
wooden wall panels, four are
secret cabinets said to have

François I Staircase

*Built between 1515 and
1524, this octagonal
staircase is a master-
piece of the
early French
Renaissance.*

The gallery
provided an
ideal setting
for viewing
jousts and re-
ceptions held
in the inner
courtyard.

**François I's
salamander
motif** adorns
the openwork
balustrades.

The staircase
within the
tower slopes
appreciably
more steeply
than the
balustrades.

Louis XII wing of the Château Royal de Blois

stored her poisons. Dominating the eastern sector of the city, the **Cathédrale St-Louis** is a 17th-century reconstruction of a Gothic church that was almost completely destroyed by a hurricane in 1678. Behind the cathedral the former bishop's palace, built in 1700, is the **Hôtel de Ville** (town hall). The surrounding terraced gardens have lovely views over the city and river. Opposite the cathedral is the **Maison des Acrobates**, carved with characters from medieval farces including acrobats and jugglers.

Place Louis-XII, the market-place, is overlooked by splendid 17th-century façades. Rue Pierre de Blois, a quaint alley straddled by a Gothic passageway, winds downhill to the medieval Jewish ghetto. The rue des Juifs boasts several distinguished *hôtels particuliers* (mansions), including the galleried **Hôtel de Condé**, with its Renaissance archway and courtyard, and the **Hôtel Jassaud**, with magnificent 16th-century bas-reliefs above the main doorway. On the rue du Puits-Châtel, also rich in Renaissance mansions, is the galleried **Hôtel Sardini**.

Place Vauvert is the most charming square in Vieux Blois, with a fine example of a half-timbered house.

♣ Château Royal de Blois
Tel 02 54 90 33 33. ☐ Jan–Mar & Nov–Dec: 9am–12:30pm, 1:30–5:30pm daily; Apr–Jun & Sep: 9am–6:30pm daily; Jul–Aug: 9am–7pm daily; Oct: 9am–6pm daily. ● 1 Jan, 25 Dec. 🗭 🖪

Covered Gothic passageway in rue Pierre de Blois

The nave of the abbey church of Notre-Dame in Beaugency

Beaugency ㉑

Loiret. 🏠 7,500. ☐ ☐ ℹ 3 pl de Docteur-Hyvernaud (02 38 44 54 42). ☐ Sat. **www**.beaugency.fr

Beaugency has long been the eastern gateway to the Loire. This compact medieval town makes a peaceful base for exploring the Orléanais region. Exceptionally for the Loire, it is possible to walk along the river banks and stone *levées*. At quai de l'Abbaye there is a good view of the 11th-century bridge which, until modern times, was the only crossing point between Blois and Orléans. An obvious target for enemy attack, it was captured four times by the English during the Hundred Years' War before being re-taken by Joan of Arc in 1429.

The town centre is domin-ated by a ruined 11th-century watchtower. It stands on **place St-Firmin**, along with a 16th-century belltower (the church was destroyed in the Revolution) and a statue of Joan of Arc. Period houses line the square. Further down is the **Château Dunois**, built on the site of the feudal castle by one of Joan of Arc's *compag-non d'armes*. Its regional museum features an array of costumes, furniture and antique toys. Facing the Château Dunois is **Notre-Dame**, a Romanesque abbey church that witnessed the annulment of the marriage between Eleanor of Aquitaine and Louis VII in 1152, leaving Eleanor free to marry the future Henry II of England.

Nearby is the medieval clocktower in rue du Change and the Renaissance **Hôtel de Ville**, with its façade adorned with the town's arms. Equally charming is the nearby ancient mill district, around the rue du Pont and the rue du Rü, with its streams and riot of flowers.

♣ Château Dunois (Musée Daniel Vannier)
3 pl Dunois. **Tel** 02 38 44 54 42. ● phone for details. 🗭 🖪 oblig.

Châteaux Tour of the Sologne

The mysterious Sologne is a secretive landscape of woods and marshes edged by vineyards. Wine-lovers can indulge in tastings of Loire Valley wines accompanied, in season, by a dinner of succulent wild game from the region's forests, popular hunting grounds for centuries. The Sologne is a hunter's paradise and devotees of the sport can see today's hounds, as well as hunting trophies of the past.

This ambling rural route takes in some of the Loire's most varied châteaux. The five on this tour – for which a couple of days is required – represent a delightful encapsulation of regional architecture. All styles are here, from feudal might to Renaissance grace and Classical elegance. Several are inhabited but can still be visited.

Château de Beauregard ②
Beauregard was built around 1520 as a hunting lodge for François I. It contains a gallery with 327 portraits of royalty.

Château de Chaumont ①
Chaumont is a feudal castle with Renaissance embellishments and lofty views over the river Loire *(see p242)*.

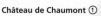

N152   ①   D751

← AMBOISE

D764

Pontlevoy

```
0 kilometres     5
0 miles          5
```

KEY

━━━ Tour route

═══ Other roads

Vendôme ㉒

Loir-et-Cher. 🏠 *18,500*. 🚆 🚌
ℹ️ *47 rue Poterie (02 54 77 05 07).*
🗓️ *Fri & Sun.* **www**.vendome.eu

Once an important stop for pilgrims en route to Compostela in Spain, Vendôme is still popular with modern pilgrims, thanks to the TGV rail service. Though a desirable address with Parisian commuters, the town still manages to retain its provincial charm. Vendôme's old stone buildings are encircled by the river Loir, its lush gardens and chic restaurants reflected in the water.

The town's greatest monument is the abbey church of **La Trinité**, founded in 1034. Its Romanesque belltower (all that remains of the original structure) is overshadowed by the church portal, a masterpiece of Flamboyant Gothic tracery. The interior is embellished with Romanesque capitals and 15th-century choir stalls.

Commanding a rocky spur high above the Loir is the ruined **château**, built by the counts of Vendôme in the 13th –14th centuries. Down below, rowing boats may be rented for gently exploring the meandering backwaters of the Loir, past a medieval *lavoir*, elegant buildings and a plane tree planted in 1759.

Vendôme's native son Rochambeau, hero of the American Revolution

The Loir ㉓

Loir-et-Cher. ✈️ Tours. 🚆 *Vendôme*.
🚌 *Montoire-sur-le-Loir.* ℹ️ *16 pl Clémenceau, Montoire-sur-le-Loir (02 54 85 23 30).*

Compared with the royal river Loire, the tranquil Loir to the north has a more rural charm. The stretch between Vendôme and Trôo is the most rewarding, offering troglodyte caves *(see p292)*, walking trails, wine-tasting, fishing and boat trips.

Les Roches-l'Evêque is a fortified village with cave dwellings visible in the cliff-face. Just downstream is **Lavardin**, with its Romanesque church, half-timbered houses, Gothic bridge and ruined château ringed by ramparts. In **Montoire-sur-le-Loir**, the Chapelle St-Gilles, a former leper colony, has Romanesque frescoes. **Trôo**, the next major village, is known for its Romanesque Eglise de St-Martin and a laby-

Château de Cheverny ③
Finished in 1634, this Classical château still belongs to a descendant of the original owner. His 70 hounds, used for stag-hunting, are fed at 5pm (summer) or 3pm (winter).

Château de Villesavin ④
This intriguing but dilapidated Renaissance château possesses an authentic dovecote, complete with revolving ladder and space for 3,000 birds.

Château du Moulin ⑤
The "pearl of the Sologne" (1490) was built by a knight of Charles VIII.

ROMORANTIN-LANTHENAY →

rinth of troglodyte dwellings. **St-Jacques-des-Guérets**, facing the village of Trôo, has a frescoed Romanesque chapel, as does **Poncé-sur-le-Loir**, farther downstream. On the slopes are vineyards producing Jasnières and Côteaux du Vendômois. Wine-tastings enliven sleepy **Poncé** and **La Chartre-sur-le-Loir**. The cliffs on the opposite bank are studded with caves, commonly used as wine cellars.

Northward, the **Forêt de Bercé** abounds with paths and streams, while to the west the small town of **Le Lude** sits on the south bank of the Loir, dominated by its romantic 15th-century château.

Some 20 km (12 miles) west of Le Lude lies the town of **La Flèche**, whose main attraction is the Prytanée Nationale Militaire, originally a Jesuit college founded by Henri IV in 1603. Philosopher René Descartes was one of the college's earliest and most illustrious pupils.

Chartres ㉔

Eure-et-Loir. 42,400. pl de la Cathédrale (02 37 18 26 26). Tue, Thu, Sat. www.chartres-tourisme.com

Chartres has the greatest Gothic cathedral in Europe (*see pp308–11*), and its churches should not be ignored. The Benedictine abbey church of **St-Pierre** has lovely medieval stained-glass windows, while **St-Aignan** abuts 9th-century ramparts. By the river is the Romanesque **Eglise de St-André**, a deconsecrated church used for art exhibitions and concerts. The **Musée des Beaux Arts**, in the former episcopal palace, offers a fine collection of 17th and 18th-century furniture, Renaissance enamels and paintings by Vlaminck.

As one of the first urban conservation sites in France, Chartres is a success story. Quirky half-timbered houses

One of the many washhouses along the Eure river

abound along such cobbled streets as the rue des Ecuyers. Steep staircases known as *tertres* lead down to the river Eure providing views of mills, humpback stone bridges, washhouses and the cathedral.

In the Grenier de Loens, next to the cathedral, is the Centre International du Vitrail. The building's 13th-century vaulted storerooms are also used for temporary exhibitions.

Musée des Beaux Arts
29 cloître Notre-Dame. **Tel** 02 37 90 45 80. Wed–Mon. Sun am, 1 Jan, 1 & 8 May, 1 & 11 Nov, 25 Dec.

Chartres Cathedral

According to art historian Emile Male, "Chartres is the mind of the Middle Ages manifest." Begun in 1020, the Romanesque cathedral was destroyed by fire in 1194. Only the north and south towers, south steeple, west portal and crypt remained; the sacred *Veil of the Virgin* relic was the sole treasure to survive. Peasant and lord alike helped to rebuild the church in just 25 years. Few alterations were made after 1250 and, fortunately, Chartres was unscathed by the Wars of Religion and the French Revolution. The result is a Gothic cathedral with a true "Bible in stone" reputation.

Part of the Vendôme Window

Elongated Statues
These statues on the Royal Portal represent Old Testament figures.

STAR FEATURES

★ Stained-Glass Windows

★ South Porch

★ Royal Portal

Gothic Nave
As wide as the Romanesque crypt below it, the nave reaches a lofty height of 37 m (121 ft).

The taller of the two spires dates from the start of the 16th century. Flamboyant Gothic in style, it contrasts sharply with the solemnity of its Romanesque counterpart.

★ Royal Portal
The central tympanum of the Royal Portal (1145–55) shows Christ in Majesty.

The lower half of the west front is a survivor of the original Romanesque church, the portal and the three windows dating from the mid-12th century.

Labyrinth

THE LABYRINTH

The 13th-century labyrinth, inlaid in the nave floor, was a feature of most medieval cathedrals. Pilgrims followed the tortuous route on their knees, echoing the way to Jerusalem and the complexity of life, in order to reach Christ. The journey – 262 m (851 ft) of broken concentric circles – took at least an hour.

VISITORS' CHECKLIST

Pl de la Cathédrale. *Tel* 02 37 21 75 02. ☐ 8:30am–6:45pm daily. ✝ 9am Tue & Fri; 11:45am & 6:15pm Mon –Sat (6pm Sat); 9:15am (in Latin), 9:15am & 11am Sun. ◻ ☐ ☐ ☐ ☐
http://cathedrale.chartres.free.fr

Our Lady of the Pillar
Carved from dark pear wood, this 16th-century replica of a 13th-century statue is a striking shrine which is often surrounded by candles.

Vaulted Ceiling
A network of ribs supports the vaulted ceiling.

★ **Stained-Glass Windows**
The windows cover a surface area of over 2,600 sq m (28,000 sq ft).

★ **South Porch**
Sculpture on the South Porch (1197–1209) reflects New Testament teaching.

The Crypt
This is the largest crypt in France, most of it dating from the early 11th century. It houses the Veil of the Virgin relic and comprises two galleries, a series of chapels and the 9th-century St Lubin's vault.

The Stained Glass of Chartres

Donated by royalty, aristocracy, priests and the merchant brotherhoods between 1210 and 1240, this glorious collection of stained glass is world-renowned. Around 176 windows illustrate biblical stories and daily life in the 13th century. During both World Wars the windows were dismantled piece by piece and removed for safety. There is an on-going programme, begun in the 1970s, to restore the windows in the cathedral.

Stained glass above the apse

Redemption Window
Six scenes illustrate Christ's Passion *and death on the Cross (c.1210).*

★ Tree of Jesse
This 12th-century stained glass shows Christ's genealogy. The tree rises up from Jesse, father of David, at the bottom, to Christ enthroned at the top.

★ West Rose Window
This window (1215), with Christ seated in the center, shows the Last Judgment.

KEY

1 Tree of Jesse	**12** Noah	**22** St Anthony and St Paul	**33** St Theodore and St Vincent
2 Incarnation	**13** St John the Evangelist	**23** Blue Virgin	**34** St Stephen
3 Passion and Resurrection	**14** Mary Magdalene	**24** Life of the Virgin	**35** St Cheron
4 North Rose Window	**15** Good Samaritan and Adam and Eve	**25** Zodiac Window	**36** St Thomas
5 West Rose Window	**16** Assumption	**26** St Martin	**37** Peace Window
6 South Rose Window	**17** Vendôme Chapel Windows	**27** St Thomas Becket	**38** Modern Window
7 Redemption Window	**18** Miracles of Mary	**28** St Margaret and St Catherine	**39** Prodigal Son
8 St. Nicholas	**19** St Apollinaris	**29** St Nicholas	**40** Ezekiel and David
9 Joseph	**20** Modern Window	**30** St Remy	**41** Aaron
10 St Eustache	**21** St Fulbert	**31** St James the Greater	**42** Annunciation-Visitation
11 St Lubin		**32** Charlemagne	**43** Isaiah and Moses
			44 Daniel and Jeremiah

North Rose Window
This depicts the Glorification of the Virgin, *surrounded by the kings of Judah and the prophets (c.1230).*

GUIDE TO READING THE WINDOWS

Each window is divided into panels, usually read from left to right, bottom to top (earth to heaven). The number of figures or abstract shapes used is thought to be symbolic: three stands for divinity, while the number four symbolizes the material world or the four elements.

Mary and Child in the sacred mandorla (c.1150)

Two angels doing homage before the celestial throne

Christ's triumphal entry into Jerusalem on Palm Sunday

Upper panels of the Incarnation Window

South Rose Window
This illustrates the Apocalypse, *with* Christ in Majesty *(c.1225).*

STAR WINDOWS

★ West Rose Window

★ Tree of Jesse

★ Blue Virgin Window

★ Blue Virgin Window
The window's bottom panel depicts the conversion of water into wine by Christ at The Marriage at Cana.

ORLEANS CITY CENTRE

Cathédrale Sainte-Croix ④
Hôtel Groslot ②
Maison de
  Jeanne d'Arc ①
Musée des
  Beaux Arts ③

0 metres   250
0 yards   250

Key to Symbols see back flap

Orléans' Cathédrale Sainte-Croix

Orléans ㉕

Loiret. 🏠 112,500. ✈ 🚂 🚌
ℹ 2 pl Etape (02 38 24 05 05).
🗓 Tue–Sun. **www**.tourisme-
orleans.com

Orléans' dazzling contemporary bridge symbolizes the
city's increasing importance
at the geographic heart of
both France and Europe. As
a tourist, however, one is
struck by the city's continued
attachment to its past, most
particularly to Joan of Arc. It

was from here that the Maid
of Orléans saved France from
the English in 1429 *(see p300)*.
Since her martyrdom at
Rouen in 1431, Joan remains
a presence in Orléans. Every
29 April and 1, 7–8 May
her liberation of the city is
reenacted in a pageant and
a blessing in the cathedral.

Orléans' historic centre was
badly damaged in World War
II, but much has been reconstructed, and a faded grandeur
lingers in Vieil Orléans, the
quarter bounded by the cathedral, the river Loire and the
place du Martroi. The latter, a
Classical but rather windswept
square, has an equestrian
statue of the city's heroine.
Nearby the half-timbered
Maison de Jeanne d'Arc was
rebuilt from period dwellings
in 1961 on the site where Joan
had lodgings in 1429.

From place du Martroi, the
rue d'Escures leads past
Renaissance mansions to the
cathedral. **Hôtel Groslot** is
the grandest, a 16th-century
red-brick mansion where
kings Charles IX, Henri III
and Henri IV all stayed. The
17-year-old François II died
here in 1560 after attending a
meeting of the Etats Généraux

with his child-bride, Mary,
later Queen of Scots. The
building served as Orléans'
town hall from 1790 to
1982, and the sumptuously
decorated interior, with its
Joan memorabilia, is still
used for marriages and
official ceremonies.

Virtually opposite the Hôtel
Groslot and alongside the
new town hall is the **Musée
des Beaux Arts**, displaying
European works of art from
the 16th to the 20th centuries.

The **Cathédrale Sainte-Croix**
nearby is an imposing edifice
begun in the late 13th century,
destroyed by the Huguenots
(Protestants) in 1568, and
then rebuilt in supposedly
Gothic style between the 17th
and 19th centuries.

🏛 **Hôtel Groslot**
Pl de l'Etape. **Tel** 02 38 79 22 30.
🗓 daily. ⬤ sporadically.

🏛 **Musée des Beaux Arts**
Pl Ste-Croix. **Tel** 02 38 79 21
55. 🗓 Tue–Sun. ⬤ 1 Jan,
1 May, 8 May, 1 & 11 Nov,
25 Dec. 🎟 free 1st Sun of
month. ♿

🏛 **Maison de Jeanne d'Arc**
3 pl du Général de Gaulle.
Tel 02 38 52 99 89. ⬤ phone for
further information.

Joan of Arc stained-glass window in Orléans' Cathédrale Sainte-Croix

St-Benoît-sur-Loire ㉖

Loiret. 🚶 *2,000.* 🚉 ℹ️ *44 rue Orléanaise (02 38 35 79 00).*
www.saint-benoit-sur-loire.fr

Situated along the river Loire between Orléans and Gien, St-Benoît-sur-Loire boasts one of the finest Romanesque abbey churches in France (1067–1108). It is all that survives of an important monastery founded in AD 650 and named after St Benedict, patron saint of Europe. His relics were brought from Italy at the end of the 7th century.

The church's belfry porch is graced with carved capitals depicting biblical scenes. The nave is tall and light, and the choir floor is an amazing patchwork of Italian marble. Daily services with Gregorian chant are open to the public.

Bourges ㉗

Cher. 🏛️ *80,000.* 🚉 🚌
ℹ️ *21 rue Victor Hugo (02 48 23 02 60).* 🕐 *Tue–Sun.*
www.bourgestourism.com

This Gallo-Roman city retains its original walls but is best known as the city of Jacques Coeur, financier and foreign minister to Charles VII. The greatest merchant of the Middle Ages and a self-made man *par excellence*, it was in his capacity as an arms dealer that he established a tradition maintained for four centuries, as Napoléon III had cannons manufactured here in 1862.

Built over part of the walls, the **Palais Jacques Coeur** is a Gothic gem and a lasting memorial to its first master. It was finished in 1453, and incorporates Coeur's two emblems, scallop shells and hearts, as well as his motto: *"A vaillan coeur, rien impossible"* – to the valiant heart, nothing is impossible. The obligatory tour reveals a barrel-vaulted gallery, a painted chapel and a chamber that had Turkish baths.

Bourges also flourishes as a university town and cultural mecca, renowned for its spring festival of music.

Rue Bourbonnoux leads to **St-Etienne**, the widest Gothic cathedral in France and the one most similar to Paris's Notre-Dame. The west façade has five sculpted portals, the

central one depicting an enthralling *Last Judgment*. In the choir are vivid 13th-century stained-glass windows presented by the guilds. The crypt holds the marble tomb of the 14th-century Duc de Berry, best

Statue of Jacques Coeur

known for commissioning the illuminated manuscript the *Très Riches Heures (see pp204–5).* From the top of the north tower stretch views of the beautifully restored medieval quarter and the marshes beyond. Beside the cathedral is a tithe barn and the remains of the Gallo-Roman ramparts.

The **Jardin des Prés Fichaux**, set along the river Yèvre, contains pools, and an open-air theatre.

To the north lie the **Marais de Bourges**, where gardeners transport their produce by boat.

Stained-glass window in the Cathédrale St-Etienne

🏛️ **Palais Jacques Coeur**
Rue Jacques Coeur. **Tel** *02 48 24 79 42.* 🕐 *daily.* ⬤ *1 Jan, 1 May, 1 & 11 Nov, 25 Dec.* ♿ 📷

Environs
About 35 km (22 miles) south of Bourges in the Berry region is the **Abbaye de Noirlac**. Founded in 1136, it is one of the best-preserved Cistercian abbeys in France.

Statue in the Jardin des Prés Fichaux

CENTRAL FRANCE AND THE ALPS

Introducing Central France and the Alps

The geological contrasts of this region reflect its enormous variety, from the industrial and gastronomic metropolis of Lyon to the largely agricultural landscape of Burgundy. The mountains of the Massif Central and the Alps attract visitors for winter sports, superb walking and other outdoor activities. The major sights of this richly rewarding area, both natural and architectural, are shown here.

Basilique Ste-Madeleine, *the famous pilgrimage church crowning the hill-top village of Vézelay, is a masterpiece of Burgundian Romanesque. It is renowned for its vividly decorated tympanum and capitals* (see pp336–7).

The Abbaye de Ste-Foy *in the village of Conques* (see pp366–7) *is one of the great pilgrimage churches of France, with a fabulous treasury of medieval and Renaissance gold reliquaries.*

THE MASSIF CENTRAL
(See pp352–71)

Abbaye de Ste-Foy, Conques

The Gorges du Tarn *have some of France's most spectacular natural scenery. The road which follows the plunging course of the river Tarn gives dramatic viewpoints along the canyon and across the limestone Causses* (see pp370–1).

The Abbaye de Fontenay, *founded by Saint Bernard in the early 12th century, is the oldest Cistercian monastery in France (see pp332–3). This well-preserved Romanesque abbey is a perfect testimony to the severe ideal of the Cistercian life.*

adeleine, zelay

Abbaye de Fontenay

Palais des Ducs, Dijon

Théâtre Romain, Autun

BURGUNDY
AND FRANCHE-COMTE
(See pp326–51)

*Brou Abbey Church,
Bourg-en-Bresse*

Mont Blanc

*Temple d'Auguste
et Livie, Vienne*

THE RHONE VALLEY
AND FRENCH ALPS
(See pp372–91)

*Palais Idéal du Facteur
Cheval, Hauterives*

Le Puy

Gorges du Tarn

0 kilometres	50
0 miles	50

The Flavours of Central France

The renowned gastronomic tradition of Lyon and the rich
wine and food of Burgundy combine to make central France
a gourmet paradise. The great chefs of the region have a
wide choice of excellent local produce: fine Bresse chicken,
Charolais beef and Morvan ham; wildfowl and frogs from the
marshes of the Dombe; fish from the Saône and the Rhône;
and fat snails called "oysters of Burgundy". Franche-Comté
and the Jura contribute smoked sausages, farmhouse cheeses,
walnut oil and fish from glacier-fed lakes. In the Massif Central,
sturdy regional fare features salted hams, pork, Cantal cheese,
the celebrated green lentils of Le Puy and wild mushrooms.

Chanterelle mushrooms

A mountain farmer shows off his
fine salt-cured ham

BURGUNDY AND FRANCHE-COMTE

Burgundy is one of France's
top wine regions so, not
surprisingly, wine plays a
major role in the cuisine,
such as in the signature dish,
boeuf bourguignon, made
from Charolais beef marinated and then stewed in
good red wine, with baby
onions, bacon and mush-
rooms added. Other specialities include *coq au vin* and
oeufs en meurette. Dijon's
famous mustard appears most
classically with steak and in
moutarde au lapin, rabbit in
a creamy mustard sauce. Burgundy and Franche-Comté
produce some of the most
celebrated French cheeses:
Epoisses, a cow's milk cheese
washed with *marc de Bourgogne*, Cîteaux, made by
monks, and the magnificent
Vacherin-Mont d'Or, a winter
treat to be scooped straight
from its wooden box. Black-
currants are widely grown
and contribute to many desserts as well as the famous
Kir: white wine with cassis
(blackcurrant liqueur).

THE MASSIF CENTRAL

The peasant cuisine of the
Auvergne is well known in
France due to the many
cafés run by Auvergnats in
Paris, where they serve local

Tomme de Savoie   Fourme d'Ambert   Raclette   Roquefort

St-Nectaire   Emmenthal   Reblochon

Mouthwatering array of classic French cheeses

REGIONAL DISHES AND SPECIALITIES

The cuisine of central France is rich with sauces
using wine, butter and cream, which
enhance almost every dish: snails in
butter and garlic; potatoes cooked
with cheese and cream; and beef,
lamb and chicken stewed slowly in
reduced wine sauces, often with
cream or butter added at the end of
cooking. Mushrooms are cooked in
cream sauces, and fish is often baked
in a creamy gratin. Most indulgent of
all is the Alpine fondue, where cheeses are melted,
together with Kirsch and wine, in a special earthenware
fondue pot. This is placed on a burner on the table, and
cubes of bread are speared onto special long forks and
dipped into the cheese. Traditionally, anyone who loses
their bread in the pot must kiss everyone else at the table.

String of onions

Oeufs en meurette *This Burgundian dish is eggs poached
in red wine with onions,
mushrooms and bacon.*

Traditional charcuterie on sale in a Lyon market

dishes like pork stuffed with cabbage, or *aligot*. Le Puy lentils, grown in the fertile volcanic soils of the Puy-en-Velay basin, combine well with sausages or *petit salé*, or are served cold as a salad. Good beef comes from the Salers cattle of the Auvergne or from the Limousin, where there is also plentiful game. Wild mushrooms are eagerly sought in season. Cheeses include Cantal, one of the country's oldest, and similar in flavour to Cheddar, and the famous blue Roquefort, ripened in the limestone caves of the Lozère.

THE RHONE VALLEY AND THE FRENCH ALPS

Lyon is famous for its traditional bistros, *bouchons*, where the cooks are often women, known as *mères*,

who dish up substantial fare like onion soup, lyonnais sausages and *charcuterie*. The markets of Lyon are equally famous, stocked with the region's wide range of fruit, particularly apricots, peaches and juicy berries.

Redcurrants and blackberries for sale by the punnet

Vegetables include onions, chard and cardoons, and the most northerly outpost of the olive is at Nyons. The Bresse region is famous for its high-quality chickens.

The Dombes lakes and the Alps are good sources of fish, such as perch, trout and lake salmon. Bony perch is most delicious eaten as *quenelles de brochet*, filleted fish blended, made into dumplings and baked in a creamy sauce. From the Alps comes a wide range of cheeses. As well as being delicious to eat fresh, they will often be found melted in *raclettes* or fondues, or layered with sliced potato to make an unctuous *gratin dauphinois*.

ON THE MENU

Chou farci Cabbage stuffed with pork and herbs.

Gigot Brayaude Leg of lamb baked over sliced potatoes and *lardons* of bacon.

Gougère Cheesy *choux* pastry baked in a ring-shape.

Jambon persillé Ham and parsley in aspic jelly.

Pochouse Freshwater fish (carp, pike, eel and trout) stewed in white wine.

Potée savoyarde Hotpot made with vegetables, chicken, ham and sausage.

Salade auvergnate Cubes of Auvergne ham, Cantal cheese and walnuts.

Petit salé *A speciality of the Auvergne region, salt pork is cooked in wine with tiny green Puy lentils.*

Aligot *Slivers of Cantal cheese are beaten into buttery, garlicky mashed potato until the mixture forms long strands.*

Clafoutis *This is usually made with black cherries, baked in batter and laced with Kirsch, a cherry liqueur.*

France's Wine Regions: Burgundy

Grape-picker's basket

Burgundy and its fine wines have inspired awe for centuries. The fame of the region's wines spread throughout Europe in the 14th century, under the Valois Dukes of Burgundy. The system of dividing wine areas into designated *appellations*, of which there are a bewildering number, came into effect in 1935. Even today, the classification system remains dauntingly complex. But despite its impenetrable image, this is unmissable territory for the "serious" wine lover, with its rich vinous history and tradition and dazzling *grands crus*.

LOCATOR MAP

☐ *Burgundy wine region*

Clos de Vougeot on the Côte de Nuits

WINE REGIONS
Between Chablis in the north and the Côte Chalonnaise and Mâconnais in the south is the Côte d'Or, incorporating Côte de Nuits and Côte de Beaune. The Beaujolais region *(see pp376–7)* lies below Mâcon.

PRINCIPAL WINE AREAS

KEY
- ☐ Chablis
- ☐ Côte de Nuits
- ☐ Côte de Beaune
- ☐ Côte Chalonnaise
- ☐ Mâconnais
- ☐ Beaujolais

0 kilometres 50
0 miles 50

KEY FACTS ABOUT BURGUNDY

Location and Climate
The continental climate (bleak winters and hot summers) can be very variable, making vintages a crucial quality factor. The best vineyards have chalky soil and face south or east.

Grape Varieties
Burgundy is at least relatively simple in its grape varieties. Red Burgundy is made from **Pinot Noir**, with its sweet flavours of raspberries, cherries and strawberries, while the **Gamay** makes red Mâcon and Beaujolais. **Chardonnay** is the principal white variety for Chablis and white Burgundy, though small amounts of **Aligoté** and **Pinot Blanc** are grown and the **Sauvignon** is a speciality of St Bris.

Good Producers
White Burgundy: Jean-Marie Raveneau, René Dauvissat, La Chablisienne, Comtes Lafon, Guy Roulot, Etienne Sauzet, Pierre Morey, Louis Carillon, Jean-Marc Boillot, André Ramonet, Hubert Lamy, Jean-Marie Guffens-Heynen, Olivier Merlin, Louis Latour, Louis Jadot, Olivier Leflaive.
Red Burgundy: Denis Bachelet, Daniel Rion, Domaine Dujac, Armand Rousseau, Joseph Roty, De Montille, Domaine de la Pousse d'Or, Domaine de l'Arlot, Jean-Jacques Confuron, Robert Chevillon, Georges Roumier, Leroy, Drouhin.

Good Vintages
(Reds) 2009, 2005, 2002, 1999.
(Whites) 2008, 2005, 2001, 1996.

DIJON

D108   D974   A31

Marsannay-la-Côte

So elaborate *are Burgundy's appellations that individual vineyards, like Clos la Roche, may have their own designation.*

CLOS LA ROCHE
1986
DOMAINE DUJAC

Fixin

Gevrey-Chambertin

D31   D974   A31   D31

Grand cru *vineyards are at the top of the quality pyramid; they also tend to occupy the upper slopes of the Côte d'Or.*

BOUCHARD PÈRE & FILS
RICHEBOURG
GRAND CRU
1985

D35   Morey-St-Denis
Chambolle-Musigny

Boise

Vougeot

Vosne-Romanée

D18

Vouge

0 kilometres   5
0 miles   5

Nuits-St-Georges   D8

Rhoin   A6   D974   A31   Meuzin

Pernand-Vergelesses   La Doix
Aloxe-Corton   Serrigny
Savigny-lès-Beaune

NUITS·S·GEORGES
SES GRANDS VINS
SON BEFFROI
SA CONFRERIE des CHEVALIERS du TASTEVIN

Chorey   A36

This "brotherhood" *of professionals distinguishes the area's best wines each year.*

BEAUNE   D973

Pommard   **KEY**

Volnay   D970   • Village *appellations*

Monthelie   ☐ Côte de Nuits-Villages

Auxey-Duresses   Meursault   A31   ☐ Hautes-Côtes de Nuits

Blagny   ☐ Hautes-Côtes de Beaune

St-Aubin   Puligny-Montrachet   ☐ Côte de Beaune-Villages

N6   Chassagne-Montrachet

Dheune

Vins de Bourgogne
Puligny-Montrachet
Champ-Canet

Dezize-les-Maranges
Santenay
Sampigny-les-Maranges   Chagny
Cheilly-les-Maranges   N6
Bouzeron

Burgundian villages *have often appropriated the name of their most famous vineyard: all the village wines of Puligny, for example, can benefit from the fame of Le Montrachet.*

THE CÔTE D'OR
The Côte de Nuits and Côte de Beaune, together forming the "golden" Côte d'Or *(see p344)*, meet at the historic town of Beaune, which hosts the most famous annual wine auction in the world *(see p346)*. "Hautes-Côtes" and "Villages" wines, from a different *terroir*, are less sought after than wines from the starry individual *appellations*.

Teams of grape-pickers at the vineyards of Nuits-St-Georges

The French Alps

In any season, the Alps are one of the most spectacular regions of France – a majestic mountain
range stretching south from Lake Geneva almost
to the Mediterranean, and climaxing in Europe's
loftiest peak, the 4,800-m (15,770-ft) Mont Blanc.
The area encompasses the old regions of Dauphiné
and Savoie, once remote and independent (Savoie
only became part of France in 1860). They have
prospered since alpine holidays and skiing became
popular over the last century, but are still very
conscious of their distinct identity.

Children in traditional Savoie costumes

The Alpine landscape in winter: chalets and skiers on the slopes at Courchevel

WINTER

The ski season usually starts
just before Christmas, and
finishes at the end of April.
Most resorts offer both cross-
country and downhill skiing,

A cable car at Courchevel, part of
Les Trois Vallées complex

with many pistes linking two
or more ski stations. The less
energetic can still enjoy the
landscape from some of
the highest cable cars
(téléphériques) in the world.

Of the 100 or more French
Alpine resorts, the most
popular include **Chamonix-
Mont Blanc**, the historic capital of Alpine skiing and site
of the first Winter Olympics
in 1924; **Megève**, which
boasts one of the best ski
schools in Europe; **Morzine**,
a year-round resort on the
Swiss border, overlooked by
the modern, car-free resort of
Avoriaz; modern **Albertville**,
site of the 1992 Winter
Olympics; **Les Trois Vallées**,
which include glamorous

A downhill skier at Val d'Isère

Courchevel and **Méribel**, and
the lesser-known **Val
Thorens/Les Ménuires**;
Tignes, a year-round resort;
Les Arcs and **La Plagne**,
both purpose-built; and
Val d'Isère, a favourite
among the rich and famous.

ALPINE FLOWERS

In spring and early summer the pastures of the French Alps are ablaze with flowers. These include blue and yellow gentians, bellflowers, lilies, saxifrages and a variety of orchids. Steep mountain meadows cannot be farmed intensively, and the absence of fertilizers and weed killers enables wild flowers to flourish.

Spring gentian (*Gentiana verna*)

Martagon lily (*Lilium martagon*)

The French Alps in spring: flower-filled meadows overlooked by brilliant white peaks

SPRING AND SUMMER

The Alpine summer season starts in late June, extending to early September – most resorts close in October and November

Bell-ringing dairy cows in an Alpine pasture

between the hiking and skiing seasons. After the spring thaw, flower-filled pastures, snow-fed mountain lakes and a huge number of marked trails make this area a hiker's paradise. In the Chamonix area alone there are over 310 km (195 miles) of hiking trails. The best known long-distance route is the **Tour du Mont Blanc**, a 10-day hike via France, Italy and Switzerland. The **GR5** traverses the entire Alps, passing through the **Parc National de la Vanoise** and **Parc Régional du Queyras** (*see p387*) to the south. *Téléphériques* give access to the higher trails, where the views are even more awesome. Be sure to bring plenty of warm,

waterproof clothing: the weather can change very quickly.

Many resorts are now concentrating on broadening their summer appeal – golf, tennis, mountain biking, horse-riding, paragliding, canoeing, white water rafting, glacier skiing and mountain climbing are all widely available.

Mountain climbers scaling the heights around Mont Blanc

Geology of the Massif Central

The Massif Central covers almost one-fifth of France and is over 250 million years old. Most of its peaks have been eroded to form a vast plateau split into deep valleys. The heart of the Massif consists of hard, igneous rocks like granite, with softer rocks such as limestone at its margins. Different rock types are reflected in the landscape and buildings; in the eroded Gorges du Tarn, the houses are built of russet-coloured limestone. Massive granite farmhouses are a feature of Limousin and Le Puy-en-Velay is distinguished by its giant basalt pillars.

LOCATOR MAP

Extent of the Massif Central

Basalt *is a dark, fine-grained rock formed by volcanic lava. A common building stone in the Auvergne, it is often cut into blocks and bonded with lighter-coloured mortar. In the medieval town of Salers (see p363), basalt was used for most of the buildings, including this one in the Grande Place.*

This granite portal *is found in the Romanesque church at Moutier d'Ahun (see p356). Granite underlies much of the Massif Central.*

Montluçon

Moutier d'Ahun ●

Limoges ●

Clermont Ferrand

Dordogne

● Salers

Schist tiling *is featured on these roofs at Argentat. Schist is a crystalline rock which splits readily into layers. It is particularly common on the edge of the Massif, and provides an effective roofing material.*

● Argentat

Gère

Lot

Limestone walls *can be seen on houses in Espalion (see p366). Of all the rocks in the Massif Central, it is among the most easily worked. It splits readily and is soft enough to be cut into blocks with a band saw. As with granite, its colour and consistency vary from area to area.*

Mill

Tarn

0 kilometres   50

0 miles   50

Crystallized lava, *like this dramatic curtain of columns at Prades, formed when liquid basalt seeped through the surrounding rock and solidified to form giant crystals.*

KEY

- Sedimentary rock
- Surface volcanic rock
- Granite
- Metamorphic rock

Nevers

Loire

Saône

Lyon •

St-Etienne

• Le-Puy-en-Velay

Rhône

Limestone plateaux (causses) *are typical of this region. Gorges, where rivers have cut through layers of this slightly soluble rock, run deep into the Massif Central.*

This mature landscape *at Mont Aigoual is the highest point in the Cévennes (see p367), dividing rivers flowing into the Atlantic and the Mediterranean. Its granite and schist rocks show erosion.*

RECOGNIZING ROCKS

Geologists divide rocks into three groups. Igneous rocks, like granite, are formed by volcanic activity and either extruded on to the surface or intrude into other rocks below ground. Sedimentary rocks are produced by sediment build-up. Metamorphic rocks have been transformed by heat or pressure.

SEDIMENTARY ROCK

Oolitic limestone *often contains fossils and small amounts of quartz.*

SURFACE VOLCANIC ROCK

Basalt, *which can form very thick sheets, is the most common lava rock.*

GRANITE

Pink granite, *a coarse-grained rock, is formed deep in the earth's crust.*

METAMORPHIC ROCK

Muscovite schist *is a medium-grained mud or clay-based rock.*

BURGUNDY
AND FRANCHE-COMTE

YONNE · NIEVRE · COTE D'OR · SAONE-ET-LOIRE
HAUTE-SAONE · DOUBS · JURA

*B*urgundy considers itself the heart of France, a prosperous
region with world-renowned wine, earthy but excellent
cuisine and magnificent architecture. Franche-Comté to the
east combines gentle farmland with lofty Alpine forests.

Under the dukes of Valois, Burgundy was France's most powerful rival, with territory extending well beyond its present boundaries. By the 16th century, however, the duchy was ruled by governors appointed by the French king, but it still managed to keep its privileges and traditions. Once a part of Burgundy, Franche-Comté – the Free County – struggled to remain independent of the French crown, and was a province of the Holy Roman Empire until annexed by Louis XIV in 1674.

Burgundy, now as in the past, is a wealthy region, a centre of medieval religious faith which produced Romanesque masterpieces at Vézelay, Fontenay, and Cluny. Dijon is a splendid city, filled with the great palaces of the old Burgundian nobility and a collection of great paintings and sculptures in the Musée des Beaux Arts. The vineyards of the Côte d'Or, the Côte de Beaune and Chablis yield some of the world's most venerated wines. Other richly varied landscapes – from the wild forests of the Morvan to the lush farmland of the Brionnais – produce snails, Bresse chickens and Charolais beef.

Franche-Comté has none of this opulence, though its capital, Besançon, is an elegant 17th-century city with a tradition of clockmaking. Topographically the Franche-Comté is divided into two, with gently-rolling farmland in the Saône valley and high Alpine scenery to the east. This forest country of Alpine torrents filled with trout is also the home of great cheeses, notably Vacherin and Comté, and of the characteristic yellow wine of Arbois.

The prehistoric site of the Roche de Solutré near Mâcon

◁ Vineyards at Santenay in the world-renowned Côte de Beaune district

Exploring Burgundy and Franche-Comté

Burgundy is arguably France's richest province – historically, culturally, gastronomically and economically. This lush kernel of a once great power possesses a concentration of unique Romanesque architecture in Fontenay and Vézelay, along with some of the world's most venerated wines. Dijon is a must for lovers of art, architecture, and food. Franche-Comté is better suited for outdoor holidays, such as trekking and canoeing in wild scenery and crystal-clear rivers.

Burgundian riverscape near Fontenay

Distinctive Burgundian glazed roof tiles, Hôtel Aubriot in Dijon

KEY

—	Motorway
—	Major road
—	Secondary road
═	Minor road
—	Scenic route
┄	Main railway
—	Minor railway
▬	International border
—	Regional border
△	Summit

0 kilometres 25

0 miles 25

SIGHTS AT A GLANCE

Wine harvest in Nuits-St-Georges, Côte d'Or

GETTING AROUND

Burgundy is well-served by the A6 autoroute from Paris to Lyon and Marseille, which is joined by the A31 from Nancy and Dijon (and the Channel ports via the A26), and the A36 from Besançon. An alternative route through the region from Dijon to Lyon is the A39. If you have time and a taste for quiet country roads, those in Burgundy and Franche-Comté are some of the most rewarding in France. The TGV links Dijon and Mâcon with Paris, Geneva, and Marseille. Dijon is a major rail hub and connects other towns in the region; its international airport serves most European destinations.

La Sainte Châsse, 11th-century reliquary in the Treasury in Sens

Sens **0**

Yonne. 🏠 30,000. 🚃 🚌
🛈 pl Jean-Jaurès (03 86 65 19 49).
🗓 Mon, Wed, Fri & Sat.
www.office-de-tourisme-sens.com

The little town of Sens, at the confluence of the rivers Yonne and Vanne, was important before Caesar came to Gaul. It was the Senones whose attempt to sack the Roman Capitol in 390 BC was thwarted by a flock of geese.

The **Cathédrale St-Etienne** is Sens' outstanding glory. Begun before 1140 it is the oldest of the great Gothic cathedrals and its noble simplicity influenced many other churches. Louis IX *(see p51)* did the town the honour of getting married here in 1234.

The exquisite stained-glass windows from the 12th–16th centuries show biblical scenes, including the Tree of Jesse, and a tribute to Thomas Becket who was exiled here. His liturgical robes are in the Treasury (part of the **Musées de Sens**), which has one of the finest collections in France, including a beautiful Byzantine reliquary.

🏛 **Les Musées de Sens**
Pl de la Cathédrale. **Tel** 03 86 64 46 22. ⬤ Jun–Sep: Wed–Mon; Oct–May: Wed, Sat, Sun (Mon, Thu, Fri pm only). 🖼 ♿ 🚻

La Puisaye-Forterre **2**

Yonne, Nièvre. 🚃 Auxerre, Clamecy, Bonny-sur-Loire, Cosne-Cours-sur-Loire. 🚌 St-Fargeau, St-Sauveur-en-Puisaye. 🛈 Charny (03 86 63 65 51).

The secret forest country of La Puisaye-Forterre was immortalized by Colette (1873–1954), who was born at **St-Sauveur** in "a house that smiled only on its garden side…". This 17th-century château now houses the **Musée Colette**.

The best way to explore the region is on foot or by bike around its watery woodlands, orchards and meadows. Alternatively, take a ride on the *Transpoyaudin*, a 27 km (17 mile) train ride from St-Sauveur to Villiers St-Benoît.

A hands-on visit can be made to **Château de Guédelon**, a 25-year project recreating a medieval castle, using only original building methods and materials found locally. Nearby is the genuine 13th-century **Château de Ratilly**, with pottery, art exhibitions, concerts and music workshops. More of this can be seen in **St-Amand**, the centre of Puisaye stoneware production, much of which was traditionally fired in the 18th-century horizontal kiln at Moutiers. Both the pottery and local frescoes

Colette in the 1880s at St-Sauveur

(see the churches at **Moutiers** and **La Ferté-Loupière**) made use of locally mined ochre, a major export in the 19th century. The pink brick **Château de St-Fargeau** housed the exiled Grande Mademoiselle *(p57)*.

🏛 **Musée Colette**
Château St-Sauveur-en-Puisaye.
Tel 03 86 45 61 95.
⬤ Apr–mid-Nov: Wed–Mon. 🖼

Auxerre **3**

Yonne. 🏠 40,000. 🚃 🛈 1–2 quai de la République (03 86 52 06 19).
🗓 Tue & Fri. www.ot-auxerre.fr

Beautifully sited overlooking the Yonne river, Auxerre justly prides itself on a fine collection of churches along with a charming pedestrianized main square, the place Charles-Surugue.

The Gothic **Cathédrale St-Etienne** took over three centuries to build and was completed in about 1560. It is famous for its intricate 13th-century stained glass. The choir with its slender columns and colonettes is the epitome of Gothic elegance, while the western portals are decorated with beautiful flamboyant sculpture which has been sadly mutilated by war and weather. The Romanesque crypt is adorned by unique 11th–13th-century frescoes, including one depicting Christ on a white horse. The badly pillaged treasury is less impressive, but still has an interesting collection of illuminated manuscripts.

Château de St-Fargeau in the Puisaye-Forterre region

St Germanus, mentor of St Patrick and bishop of Auxerre in the 5th century, was buried at the former abbey church of **St-Germain**. The abbey was founded by Queen Clothilde, wife of Clovis *(see pp48–9)*, the first Christian king of France, and is an important shrine. The crypt is partly Carolingian, with tombs and 11th–13th century frescoes. The former abbey houses the **Musée St-Germain** with local Gallo-Roman finds.

🏛 **Musée St-Germain**
2 pl St-Germain. *Tel 03 86 18 05 50.* ☐ *Apr–Sep: Wed–Sun; Oct–May: Wed–Fri am, Sat & Sun.* ⬤ *some public hols.* 🎟 🖼

Medieval fresco in Cathédrale St-Etienne at Auxerre

Chablis ❹

Yonne. 🏠 *2,700.* 🚌 🚹 *1 rue du Maréchal de Lattre de Tassigny (03 86 42 80 80).* 🐔 *Sun.* **www**.chablis.net

There can be no question that Chablis tastes best in Chablis. Although this is one of the

The intriguing spring of Fosse Dionne in Tonnerre

most famous wine villages on earth, its narrow stone streets still have an air of sleepy prosperity. February processions in nearby Fyé, attended by the wine brotherhood of Piliers Chablisiens, honour St Vincent, patron saint of wine-growers.

Tonnerre ❺

Yonne. 🏠 *6,200.* 🚌 🚍 🚹 *pl Marguerite de Bourgogne (03 86 55 14 48).* 🐔 *Sat & Wed.* **www**.tonnerre.fr

The mystical cloudy-green spring of **Fosse Dionne** is a good reason to visit the small town of Tonnerre. An astonishing volume of water bursts up from the ground into an 18th-century washing-place. Due to its depth and strong currents it has never been thoroughly explored and local legend has it that a serpent lives on undisturbed.

The **Hôtel-Dieu** is 150 years older than the Hôtel-Dieu in Beaune *(see p346–7).*

It was founded by Margaret of Burgundy in 1293 to care for the poor. In the Revolution it lost its tiling but the barrel-vaulted oak ceiling survived.

🏥 **Hôtel-Dieu & Musée**
Rue du Prieuré. *Tel 03 86 55 14 48.* ☐ *daily.* ⬤ *Oct–Mar: Wed, Sun & some public hols.* 🎟 ♿ 🖼

Château de Tanlay ❻

Tanlay. *Tel 03 86 75 70 61.* ☐ *Apr–mid-Nov: Wed–Mon.* 🎟 🖼 *oblig.*

The moated Château de Tanlay is a beautiful example of French Renaissance, built in the mid-16th century. There is a *trompe l'oeil* in the Grande Galerie and, in the corner tower, an intriguing School of Fontainebleau painted ceiling. Its antique divinities represent famous Protestants and Catholics in the 16th century, such as Diane de Poitiers as Venus.

The Renaissance façade and *cour d'honneur* of Château de Tanlay

Abbaye de Fontenay ❾

The tranquil Abbey of Fontenay is the oldest surviving Cistercian foundation in France and offers a rare insight into the Cistercian way of life. It represents the spirit of the order in the sublime gravity of its Romanesque church and its plain but elegant chapterhouse, in early Gothic style. The abbey was founded in 1118 by St Bernard. Situated deep in the forest, it offered the peace and seclusion the Cistercians sought. Supported by the local aristocracy, the abbey began to thrive and remained in use until the Revolution when it was sold and converted into a paper mill. In 1906 the abbey came under new ownership and was restored to its original appearance.

Dovecote
A magnificent circular dovecote, built in the 13th century, is situated next to the kennel where the precious hunting dogs of the dukes of Burgundy were guarded by servants.

The 17th-century abbot's lodgings were built when the abbots were appointed by royal favour.

The bakehouse is no longer intact but the 13th-century oven and chimney have survived.

The visitors' hostel is where weary wanderers and pilgrims were offered board and lodging by the monks.

★ Cloisters
For a 12th-century monk a walk through the cloisters was an opportunity for meditation and provided shelter from the weather.

Warming Room

In the forge monks produced their own tools and hardware.

Fontenay "Prison"
It may be that this 15th-century building was actually used to lock up not local miscreants but important abbey archives, in order to protect them against damage by rats.

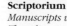

Scriptorium
Manuscripts were copied here. The adjacent Warming Room was used to warm chilled hands

★ Abbey Church
Rich decoration has no place in this church from the 1140s. But the severe architectural forms, the warm colour of the stone and the diffused light convey a grandeur of their own.

VISITORS' CHECKLIST

Marmagne. *Tel 03 80 92 15 00.*
⬚ Montbard. ◯ 10am–6pm
daily (mid-Nov–mid-Apr: 10am–
noon, 2–5pm). 🎫 ⬚ 📷
www.abbayedefontenay.com

Dormitory
Monks slept in long rows on straw mattresses in this large, unheated room. The timberwork roof is from the late 15th century.

STAR FEATURES

★ Abbey Church

★ Cloisters

The herb garden was skilfully cultivated by the monks in order to grow healing herbs for medicines and potions.

Infirmary

Chapterhouse
Once a day, monks and abbot assembled in this room to discuss matters concerning the community. It derives much of its charm from the elegant 12th-century piers and the rib-vaults.

ST BERNARD AND THE CISTERCIANS

In 1112 Bernard, a young Burgundian nobleman, joined the Cistercians. At the time the order was still obscure, founded 14 years earlier by a group of monks who wanted to turn their back on the elaborate lifestyle of Cluny *(see pp48–9)*, renounce the world, and espouse poverty and simplicity of life. During Bernard's lifetime the Cistercians became one of the largest and most famous orders of its time. Part of this success was clearly due to Bernard's powerful personality and his skills as a writer, theologian and statesman. He reinforced the poverty rule, rejecting all forms of embellishment. In 1174, only 21 years after his death, he was canonized.

The Virgin Protecting the Cistercian Order, by Jean Bellegambe

Château d'Ancy-le-Franc ❼

Ancy-le-Franc. **Tel** *03 86 75 14 63.*
◯ *mid-Mar–mid-Nov: Tue–Sun.*
🎨 🎫 *oblig.*
www.chateau-ancy.com

The Renaissance façade of
Château d'Ancy-le-Franc gives
an austere impression. Its inner
courtyard, however, has rich
ornamentation. The château
was built in the 1540s by the
Italian Sebastiano Serlio, for the
Duke of Clermont-Tonnerre.
Most of the interior decor-
ations were carried out by
Primaticcio and other members
of the Fontainebleau School
(*see pp180–81*). Diane de
Poitiers, the duke's sister-in-
law and mistress of Henry II,
is portrayed in the *Chambre
de Judith et Holophernes*.
    The château holds monthly
classical music concerts and
cookery workshops.

The vase of Vix in the Musée du
Châtillonnais, Châtillon-sur-Seine

Châtillon-sur-Seine ❽

Côte d'Or. 🏘 *5,837.* 🚌 🚮 🛈 *rue
du Bourg (03 80 91 13 19).* 🛍 *Sat.*
www.tourisme-chatillonnais.fr

World War II left Châtillon a
ruin, hence the town's largely
modern aspect. But the past
is still present in the **Musée du
Pays du Châtillonnais**, where
the Vix treasure is displayed.
In 1953, the tomb of a Gaulish
princess, from the 6th century
BC, was discovered near Vix
at Mont Lassois. The trove of
jewellery and artifacts of Greek
origin includes a stunning
bronze vase, 164 cm (66 in)
high and weighing 208 kg
(459 lb). Also of interest is the

The staid façade of Château d'Ancy-le-Franc

Romanesque **Eglise St-Vorles**
containing an *Entombment*
with Christ and mourners
splendidly sculpted (1527).
    At the nearby source of the
river Douix, which runs into
the Seine, is a beautiful grotto.

🏛 **Musée du Pays
du Châtillonnais**
Rue de la Libération. **Tel** *03 80 91
24 67.* ◯ *daily.* ● *1 Jan, 1 May,
25 Dec.* 🎨 🎫 **www**.musee-vix.fr

Abbaye de Fontenay ❾

See pp332–3.

Alise-Ste-Reine ❿

Côte d'Or. 🏘 *3,275.*
🛈 *pl Bingerbrück (03 80 96 89 13).*
www.alesia-tourisme.net

Mont Auxois, above the village
of Alise-Ste-Reine, was the site
of Caesar's final victory over
the heroic Gaulish chieftain

Vercingétorix in 52 BC after a
six-week siege (*see p46*). The
first excavations here were
undertaken in the mid-19th
century, and they uncovered
the vestiges of a thriving
Gallo-Roman town, with theatre, forum and well-laid-out
street plan. The **Musée Alésia**
houses artifacts, jewellery and
bronze figures from the site.
    Alise is dominated by Aimé
Millet's gigantic moustachioed
statue of Vercingétorix, which
was placed here in 1865 to
commemorate the first excavations. Cynics feel that it
bears a more than passing
resemblance to Napoleon III,
who sponsored the dig.

🏛 **Musée Alésia**
Rue de l'Hôpital. **Tel** *03 80 96 96 22.*
◯ *daily.* 🎨 **www**.alesia.com

Environs
In the vicinity lies **Château de
Bussy-Rabutin**. The spiteful
17th-century soldier and wit
Roger de Bussy-Rabutin
created its highly individualistic

Excavations at the Roman site near Alise-Ste-Reine

decor, while exiled from Louis XIV's court. One room is dedicated to portraits of his many mistresses, as well as a couple of imaginary ones.

♣ Château de Bussy-Rabutin
Bussy-le-Grand. *Tel* 03 80 96 00 03. ⬤ Tue–Sun. ⬤ 1 Jan, 1 & 11 Nov, 25 Dec. 🖼

Semur-en-Auxois ⓫

Côte d'Or. 🏠 5,000. 🖼 🛈 2 pl Gaveau (03 80 97 05 96). 🛒 Sun. **www**.ville-semur-en-auxois.fr

Approached from the west, Semur-en-Auxois comes as a surprise on an otherwise uneventful road. Its massive round bastions built in the 14th century (one of them with an unnerving gash in it) suddenly appear, towering over the Pont Joly and the peaceful river Armançon.

The **Eglise Notre-Dame** dates from the 13th and 14th centuries, and was modelled on the cathedral of Auxerre. The fragile high walls had to be restored in the 15th and 19th centuries. The church houses significant artworks, from the tympanum showing the legend of Doubting Thomas on the north doorway, to the 15th-century *Entombment* by Antoine le Moiturier. The stained glass presents the legend of Saint Barbara, and the work of different guilds such as butchers and drapers.

Environs
The village of Epoisses is the site of the moated **Château d'Epoisses**, its 11th–18th-century construction blending medieval towers with fine Renaissance details, and a huge 15th-century dovecote. Epoisses is also the home of one of Burgundy's most

Semur-en-Auxois by the river Armançon

revered cheeses, to be sampled at the local café or *fromagerie.*

♣ Château d'Epoisses
Epoisses. *Tel* 03 80 96 40 56. ⬤ Jul–Aug: Wed–Mon (grounds: all year). 🖼 📷 ♿ ground floor only.

Vézelay ⓬

See pp336–7.

Avallon ⓭

Yonne. 🏠 9,000. 🖼 🖼 🛈 6 rue Bocquillot (03 86 34 14 19). 🛒 Sat & Thu. **www**.avallonnais-tourisme.com

A fine old fortified town, Avallon is situated on a granite spur between two ravines by the river Cousin.

Avallon suffered in the wars of Saracens, Normans, English and French, which accounts for its defensive aspect. The town is quiet and rather beautiful, full of charming details. The main monument is the 12th-century Romanesque **Eglise St-Lazare**, with two carved doorways. The larger illustrates the signs of the zodiac, the labours of the month, and the horsemen of

Stained-glass window in Eglise Notre-Dame at Semur-en-Auxois

the Apocalypse. The nave is decorated with sophisticated acanthus capitals and polychrome statuary.

The **Musée de l'Avallonnais** features an intricate Venus mosaic from the 2nd century AD, and Georges Rouault's (1871–1958) series of Expressionist etchings, the *Miserere.*

🏛 Musée de l'Avallonnais
5 rue du College. *Tel* 03 86 34 03 19. ⬤ phone for information. 🖼 📷

Environs
To the southwest of Avallon is the 12th-century Château de Bazoches, given to Maréchal de Vauban by Louis XIV in 1675, and transformed by him into a military garrison.

Miserere by Georges Rouault in the Musée d'Avallonnais, Avallon

Vézelay ⑫

Decorated capital

The golden glow of the Basilique Ste-Madeleine crowning Vézelay's hill is visible from afar. Tourists follow in the footsteps of medieval pilgrims, ascending the narrow street up to the former abbey church. In the 12th century, at the height of its glory, the abbey claimed to house relics of Mary Magdalene and was also an important meeting point for pilgrims en route to Santiago de Compostela in Spain (see pp400–1). Today its attraction lies in the Romanesque church with its magnificent sculpture and Gothic choir.

View of Vézelay
The abbey dominates Vézelay's surroundings as it once dominated the religious and worldly affairs of the area.

Nave of Ste-Madeleine
The nave was rebuilt between 1120–35, using alternate dark and light stone in the transverse arches.

Tour St-Michel was built in 1150–1250. It derives its name from the statue of the archangel in the tower's southwest corner.

Nave of Ste-Madeleine

The façade dates from 1150 and has a large 13th-century window. It was about to collapse when Viollet-le-Duc was commissioned to restore it according to old plans in 1840.

The narthex used to be a gathering point for medieval processions.

★ Tympanum
This masterpiece of sculpture (1120–35) shows Christ on His throne, stretching out His hands from which rays of light descend on to the apostles.

STAR FEATURES

★ Tympanum

★ Capitals

Tour St-Antoine was built at the same time as the choir, in the late 12th century. Its counterpart on the north side was never finished.

The chapterhouse and cloister are the only parts remaining from the 12th-century monastic buildings. Viollet-le-Duc rebuilt part of the cloister and restored the rib-vaulted chapterhouse, once a graceful background for the monks' daily assemblies.

Crypt of Ste-Madeleine
The Romanesque crypt houses relics once thought to be Mary Magdalene's. The vault was rebuilt in 1165.

★ **Capitals**
The capitals in the nave and narthex are exquisitely carved, and give a vivid rendering of the stories of Classical antiquity and the Bible. The master who created them remains unknown.

Choir of Ste-Madeleine
The choir was rebuilt in the last quarter of the 12th century in the then modern Gothic style of the Ile de France.

Morvan, a region of rivers and forests, well-suited to fishing and other outdoor pursuits

Morvan ⓮

Yonne, Côte d'Or, Nièvre, Saône et Loire. 🚆 Dijon. 🚌 Autun, Mombard. 🚌 Château-Chinon, Saulieu, Avallon. 🅸 6 bd République, Château-Chinon (03 86 85 06 58); Maison du Parc, St-Brisson (03 86 78 79 57). **www**.parcdumorvan.org

Morvan is a Celtic word meaning Black Mountain, which is a good description of this area seen from afar. The immense, sparsely inhabited plateau of granite and woodland appears suddenly in the centre of the rich Burgundy hills and farmland. Stretching roughly north to south, it gains altitude as it proceeds southwards, reaching a culminating point of 901 m (2,928 ft) at **Haut-Folin**.

The Morvan's two sources of natural wealth are abundant water and dense forests of oak, beech and conifer. In the old days lumber used to be floated out of the area to Paris via a network of lakes and rivers. Today it travels by truck, and the Yonne, Cousin and Cure rivers are instead used for recreation and the production of electricity.

The Morvan has always been a poor, remote area. Each of its largest towns, Château-Chinon in the centre and Saulieu on the outskirts, has barely 3,000 inhabitants.

During World War II, the Morvan was a bastion of the French Resistance. Today a Regional Nature Park, its attraction is its wildness. Information on a wide variety of outdoor activities, including cycling, canoeing, skiing, and horse trekking, is available at the **Maison du Parc** at St-Brisson where there is also the very moving **Musée de la Resistance**. There are plenty of short walking trails, and two well-signed long-distance paths: the GR13 (Vézelay to Autun) and the Tour du Morvan par les Grands Lacs.

🏛 **Musée de la Résistance**
Maison du Parc, St-Brisson. **Tel** 03 86 78 72 99. ◯ Easter–mid-Nov: Wed–Mon (Jul & Aug: daily). 📷 ✔️ 🔂 ♿

Saulieu ⓯

Côte d'Or. 🏘 3,000. 🚆 🚌 🅸 24 rue d'Argentine (03 80 64 00 21). 🛒 Sat. **www**.saulieu.fr

On the edge of the Morvan, Saulieu has been a shrine of Burgundian cooking ever since the 17th century. The town was then a staging post on the Paris to Lyon coach road. Today the tradition is maintained by the famous chef Bernard Loiseau at the **Côte d'Or** restaurant *(see p598)*. Yet there is more to Saulieu than *ris de veau de lait braisé or poularde truffée à la vapeur.* The Romanesque **Basilique St-Andoche**, built in the early 12th century, has decorated capitals with representations of the Flight into Egypt and a comical version of the story of Balaam and his donkey waylaid by the Angel.

Nevers ⓰

Nièvre. 🏘 41,000. 🚆 🚌 🅸 Palais Ducal, rue Sabatier (03 86 68 46 00). 🛒 Sat. **www**.nevers-tourisme.com

Like all Burgundian towns fronting the Loire, Nevers should be approached from the west side of the river for a full appreciation of its noble site. Though lacking historical importance, the town has much to show. Considered to be the earliest of the Loire châteaux, the **Palais Ducal** has a long Renaissance façade framed by polygonal towers and a broad esplanade. The Romanesque 11th-century **Eglise St-Etienne** has graceful monolithic columns and a wreath of radiating chapels. In the crypt of the Gothic **Cathédrale St-Cyr** is a 16th-century sculpted *Entombment*, and the foundations of a 6th-century baptistry, discovered in 1944, after heavy bombing. The contemporary stained-glass windows are also noteworthy. The overlordship of Nevers passed to the Gonzaga family in the 16th century. They brought with them an Italian school of artists skilled in faïence-making and glass-blowing.

Nevers faïence vase

The industry has remained and the modern pottery is still traditionally decorated in blue, white, yellow and green, with its curious trademark, the little green arabesque knot, or *noeud vert*. The best place to view it is at the **Musée Municipal** and the best place to buy it is the 17th-century **Faïencerie Montagnon**.

🏛 **Musée Municipal Frédéric Blandin**
16 rue Saint-Geneste. **Tel** *03 86 68 44 60.* ◐ *for renovation until mid-2012; phone for details.*

Environs
Just south of Nevers, the 19th-century **Pont du Guetin** carries the Loire Canal majestically across the Allier river. The church at **St-Parize-le-Châtel** has a jolly Burgundian menagerie sculpted on the capitals of the crypt.

The *Temptation of Eve* in Autun

Autun ⑰

Saône-et-Loire. 🏠 *18,000.* 🚌
🚌 ℹ *13 rue Général Demetz (03 85 86 80 38).* 🛒 *Wed & Fri.*
www.autun-tourisme.com

Augustodunum, the town of Augustus, was founded in the late 1st century BC. It was a

The imposing Porte St-André in Autun, once part of the Roman wall

great centre of learning, with a population four times what it is today. Its theatre, built in the 1st century AD, could seat 20,000 people.

Today Autun is still a delight, deserving gastronomic as well as cultural investigation.

The magical **Cathédrale St-Lazare** was built in the 12th century. It is special because of its sculptures, most of them by the mysterious 12th-century artist Gislebertus. He sculpted both the capitals inside and the glorious Last Judgment tympanum over the main portal. This masterpiece, called a "Romanesque Cézanne" by André Malraux, escaped notice and was saved from destruction during the Revolution because it had been plastered over in the 18th century. Inside, some of the capitals can be seen close-up in a room in the tower. Look also for the

sculpture of Pierre Jeannin and his wife. Jeannin was the president of the Dijon parliament who prevented the Massacre of St Bartholomew *(see pp54–5)* spreading with the perceptive remark, "the commands of very angry monarchs should be obeyed very slowly".

The brilliant collection of medieval art at the **Musée Rolin** includes the bas relief *Temptation of Eve*, by Gislebertus. There is also the 15th-century painted stone Virgin of Autun, and the *Nativity of Cardinal Rolin* by the Master of Moulins, from about 1480.

The monumental **Porte St-André** and **Porte d'Arroux**, and the ruins of the **Théâtre Romain** and the **Temple de Janus**, are reminders of Autun's glorious Roman past.

🏛 **Musée Rolin**
3 rue des Bancs. **Tel** *03 85 52 09 76.* ◯ *Wed–Sat, Sun am.* ◐ *mid-Dec–mid-Feb, public hols.* 🌐 🎫

Remains of the Roman theatre at Autun, dating from the 1st century AD

Street by Street: Dijon ⓲

The centre of Dijon is noted for its architectural splendour – a legacy from the Dukes of Burgundy *(see p343)*. Wealthy parliament members also had elegant *hôtels particuliers* built in the 17th–18th centuries. The capital of Burgundy, Dijon today has a rich cultural life and a renowned university. The city's great art treasures are housed in the Palais des Ducs. Dijon is also famous for its mustard *(see p318)* and *pain d'épices* (gingerbread), a reminder of the town's position on the spice route. It became a major rail hub during the 19th century and now has a TGV link to Paris.

Hôtel de Vogüé
This elegant 17th-century mansion is decorated with Burgundian cabbages and fruit garlands by Hugues Sambin.

★ Notre-Dame
This magnificent 13th-century Gothic church has a façade with gargoyles, columns and the popular Jacquemart clock. The chouette (owl) is reputed to bring good luck when touched.

Musée des Beaux Arts
The collection of Flemish masters here includes this 14th-century triptych by Jacques de Baerze and Melchior Broederlam.

Place de la Libération was created by Mansart in the 17th century.

★ Palais des Ducs
The dukes of Burgundy held court here, but the building seen today was mainly built in the 17th century for the parliament. It now houses the Musée des Beaux Arts.

Rue Verrerie
This cobbled street in the old merchants' quarter is lined with medieval half-timbered houses. Some have fine wood-carvings, such as Nos. 8, 10 and 12.

VISITORS' CHECKLIST

Côte d'Or. 🏠 155,000. ✈ 5 km (3 miles) SSE Dijon. 🚌 🚕 cour de la Gare. 🚹 15 cour de la Gare & 11 rue des Forges (08 92 70 05 58). ⬛ Tue, Fri, Sat. 🎭 Florissimo (2015 next); Festival de Musique (Jun); Fêtes de la Vigne (Sep). **Hôtel de Vogüé** only inner courtyard open. **Musée Magnin** (03 80 67 11 10). ◯ Tue–Sun. ⬤ 1 Jan, 25 Dec. 🌐 www.visitdijon.com

★ St-Michel
Begun in the 15th century and completed in the 17th century, St-Michel's façade combines Flamboyant Gothic with Renaissance details. On the richly carved porch, angels and biblical motifs mingle with mythological themes.

Musée Magnin
A collection of French and foreign 16th–19th-century paintings are displayed among period furniture in this 17th-century mansion.

Eglise St-Etienne dates back to the 11th century but has been rebuilt many times. Its characteristic lantern was added in 1686.

STAR SIGHTS

★ Palais des Ducs

★ Notre-Dame

★ St-Michel

KEY

– – – Suggested route

0 metres   100

0 yards   100

Well of Moses by Claus Sluter, in the Chartreuse de Champmol

Exploring Dijon
The centre of Dijon is a warren of little streets that reward exploration. The rue des Forges, behind the Palais de Ducs, was the main street until the 18th century and is named after the jewellers and goldsmiths who had workshops there. Hôtel Chambellan at No. 34, is Flamboyant Gothic with a stone spiral staircase and wooden galleries. At No. 38 the Maison Maillard, built in 1560, has a stone façade decorated by Hugues Sambin.

Rue Chaudronnerie has a number of houses of note, especially the Maison des Cariatides at No. 28, with ten fine stone carved caryatids framing the windows. Place Darcy is lined with hotels and restaurants; the Jardin Darcy is delightful.

🏛 Musée des Beaux Arts
Palais des Etats de Bourgogne, Cour de Bar. *Tel* 03 80 74 52 70. ◯ Wed–Mon. ◉ 1 Jan, 1 & 8 May, 14 Jul, 1 & 11 Nov, 25 Dec. 🚻 limited. 📷
Dijon's prestigious art collection is housed in the former Palais des Ducs (see p340). The Salle des Gardes on the first floor is dominated by the giant mausoleums of the dukes, with tombs sculpted by Claus Sluter (c.1345–1405). Other exhibits include two gilded Flemish retables and a portrait of Philip the Good by Rogier van der Weyden.

The art collection has Dutch and Flemish masters and sculpture by Sluter and Rude. There are also Swiss and German primitives, 16th–18th century French paintings, and the Donation Granville of 19th- and 20th-century French art. Also note the ducal kitchens with 6 fireplaces, and the Tour Philippe le Bon, 46 m (150 ft) tall with a fine view of Burgundian tiled roof tops.

🛡 Cathédrale St-Bénigne
Pl Ste-Bénigne. *Tel* 03 80 30 39 33. ◯ daily. 📷 🚻
Little remains of the 11th-century Benedictine abbey first founded in honour of St Bénigne. Beneath the church is a Romanesque crypt with a fine rotunda ringed by three circles of columns.

🏛 Musée Archéologique
5 rue du Docteur Maret. *Tel* 03 80 30 88 54. ◯ Wed–Mon. ◉ most public hols.
The museum is housed in the old dormitory of the Benedictine abbey of St-Bénigne. The 11th-century chapterhouse, its stocky columns supporting a barrel-vaulted roof, houses a fine collection of Gallo-Roman sculpture. The ground floor, with its lovely fan vaulting, houses the famous head of Christ by Claus Sluter, originally from the Well of Moses.

⚜ Chartreuse de Champmol
1 bd Chanoine Kir. ◯ daily by appt (0892 70 05 58).
This was originally the site of a family necropolis built by Philip the Bold, destroyed during the Revolution. All that remains is a chapel doorway and the famous Well of Moses by Claus Sluter. It is now in the grounds of a psychiatric hospital east of Dijon railway station, not very easy to find but definitely worth the effort. Despite its name, it is not a well, but a monument, its lower part probably originally surrounded by water. Sluter is renowned for his deeply cut carving and here his work, depicting six prophets, is exquisitely lifelike.

The tomb of Philip the Bold by Claus Sluter, now in the Salle des Gardes of the Musée des Beaux Arts

The Golden Age of Burgundy

While the French Capetian dynasty fought in the Hundred Years' War *(see pp52–3)*, the dukes of Burgundy built up one of the most powerful states in Europe, which included Flanders and parts of Holland. From the time of Philip the Bold (1342–1404), the ducal court became a cultural force, supporting many of Europe's finest artists, such as painters Rogier Van der Weyden and the Van Eyck brothers and sculptor Claus Sluter. The duchy's dominions were, however, broken up after the death of Duke Charles the Bold in 1477.

The tomb of Philip the Bold *in Dijon was made by the Flemish sculptor Claus Sluter, who was among the most brilliant artists of the Burgundian golden age. The dramatic realism of the mourners is one of the most striking features of this spectacular tomb, begun while the duke was still alive.*

BURGUNDY IN 1477

■ *Extent of the duchy at its peak*

THE MARRIAGE OF PHILIP THE GOOD

Philip the Good, duke from 1419–67, married Isabella of Portugal in 1430. This 17th-century copy of a painting by Van Eyck shows the sumptuous wedding feast, when Philip also inaugurated the chivalric Order of the Golden Fleece.

The dukes surrounded themselves with luxury, including fine gold and silverware.

Isabella of Portugal

The Duchess of Bedford, Philip's sister

Greyhounds were popular hunting animals at the Burgundian court.

Philip the Good is dressed in white ceremonial finery.

Burgundian art, *such as this Franco-Flemish Book of Hours, reflected the Flemish origins of many of the dukes' favourite artists.*

Dijon's Palais des Ducs *was rebuilt in 1450 by Philip the Good to reflect the glory of the Burgundian court, a centre of art, chivalry and glorious feasts. Empty after Charles the Bold's death, it was reconstructed in the 17th century.*

Wine harvest in the vineyards of Nuits-St-Georges, part of the Côte d'Or district

Côte d'Or ⑲

Côte d'Or. ✈ Dijon. 🚉 🚌 Dijon,
Nuits-St-Georges, Beaune, Santenay.
🛈 Dijon (08 92 70 05 58).
www.cotedor-tourisme.com

In winemaking terms, the Côte d'Or includes the Côte de Beaune and the Côte de Nuits in a nearly unbroken line of vines from Dijon to Santenay. Squeezed in between the flat plain of the Saône to the southeast and a plateau of woodland to the northwest, this narrow escarpment is about 50 km (30 miles) long. The grapes of the great Burgundy vineyards grow in the golden reddish soil of the slope (hence the area's name).

The classification of the characteristics of the land is fabulously technical and elaborate, but for the layman a rough rule of thumb might be that 95 per cent of the best

Narrow street in Beaune's historic centre

vines are on the uphill side of the N74 thoroughfare (see pp320–21). The names on the signposts haunt the dreams of wine lovers the world over: Gevrey-Chambertin, Vougeot, Chambolle-Musigny, Vosne-Romanée, Nuits-St-Georges, Aloxe-Corton, Meursault, and Chassagne Montrachet.

Typical grape basket in the Musée du Vin de Bourgogne at Beaune

Beaune ⑳

Côte d'Or. 🏠 23,000. 🚉 🚌
🛈 6 bd Perpeuil (03 80 26 21 30).
🛍 Sat, Wed. 🎵 Baroque Music
(Jul). www.ot-beaune.fr

The old centre of Beaune, snug within its ramparts and encircling boulevards, is easy to explore on foot. Its indisputable treasure is the **Hôtel-Dieu** (see pp346–7). The Hôtel des Ducs de Bourgogne, built in the 14th–16th centuries, houses the **Musée du Vin de Bourgogne**. The building, with its flamboyant façade, is as interesting as its display of traditional winemaking equipment.

Farther to the north lies the **Collégiale Notre-Dame**, begun in the early 12th century. Inside this mainly Romanesque church hang five very fine 15th-century woollen and silk tapestries. With hints

of early Renaissance style, they delicately illustrate the life of the Virgin Mary in 19 scenes.

> 🏛 **Musée du Vin de Bourgogne**
> Rue d'Enfer. **Tel** 03 80 22 08 19.
> ◯ Apr–Nov: daily; Dec–Mar:
> Wed–Mon. ◯ 1 Jan, 25 Dec. 🔲

Tournus ㉑

Saône-et-Loire. 🏠 6,500. 🚉 🚌
🛈 pl de l'Abbaye (03 85 27 00 20).
🛍 Sat. www.tournugeois.fr

The Abbaye de St-Philibert is one of Burgundy's oldest and greatest Romanesque buildings. It was founded by a group of monks from Noirmoutier who had been driven from their island by invading Normans in the 9th century, who brought with them relics of their patron saint, Philibert (still in the choir). Rebuilt in the 10th–12th centuries, the well-fortified abbey church is

Dovecote in Cormatin château gardens, Mâconnais

Nave of St-Philibert in Tournus

made from lovely pale pink stone, with black and white vaulting inside.

The 17th-century Hôtel-Dieu has its original rooms intact with the furniture, equipment and pharmacy on display. It also houses the **Musée Greuze** dedicated to Tournus' most famous son, the artist Jean-Baptiste Greuze (1725–1805).

Environs

Southwest of Tournus lies the Mâconnais landscape of hills, vineyards, orchards, red-tiled farmhouses and Romanesque churches. **Brancion** is a pretty hill village, **Chapaize** has an 11th-century church and there is a sumptuous Renaissance château at **Cormatin**. The village of **Taizé** is the centre of a world-famous ecumenical community. To the north, **Chalon-sur-Saône** features the Musée Niepce, dedicated to the inventor of photography.

Cluny ㉒

Saône-et-Loire. ♟ 4,800. 🚌
ℹ 6 rue Mercière (03 85 59 05 34).
🛒 Sat. www.cluny-tourisme.com

The little town of Cluny is overshadowed by the ruins of its great abbey. The **Ancienne Abbaye de Cluny** was once the most powerful monastic foundation in Europe *(see pp48–9)*. The abbey was founded by William the Pious, Duke of Aquitaine in 910. Within 200 years, Cluny had become the head of a major reforming order with monasteries all over Europe. Its

abbots were considered as powerful as monarchs or popes, and four of them are venerated as saints. By the 14th century, however, the system was in decline. The abbey was closed in 1790 and the church was later dismantled.

The guided tour presents the abbey remains, notably the Clocher de l'Eau Bénite (Holy Water Belltower); **Musée d'Art**, housed in the former abbot's palace; and its figured capitals displayed in the 13th-century flour-store. In the town, don't miss the 12th-century **Eglise St-Marcel**.

Southwest of the town, the chapel in **Berzé-la-Ville** is decorated with superb 12th-century frescoes, similar to those once seen at Cluny.

ℹ **Ancienne Abbaye de Cluny**
Tel 03 85 59 15 93. ⬤ daily.
⬤ 1 Jan, 25 Dec. 📷 ✓

🏛 **Musée d'Art**
Palais Jean de Bourbon. **Tel** 03 85 59 15 93. ⬤ daily. ⬤ 1 Jan, 1 May, 1 & 11 Nov, 25 Dec. 📷 ♿

Paray-le-Monial ㉓

Saône-et-Loire. ♟ 10,000. 🚌 🚇
ℹ 25 av Jean-Paul II (03 85 81 10 92). 🛒 Fri. www.paraylemonial.fr

Dedicated to the cult of the Sacred Heart of Jesus, the **Basilique du Sacré-Coeur** has made Paray-le-Monial one of the most important sites of pilgrimage in modern France. Marguerite-Marie Alacoque, who was born here in 1647, had rather gory visions from which the cult later developed, sweeping across France in the 19th century. The church is a small version of the now lost abbey church of Cluny, with particularly harmonious and pure Romanesque architecture.

A visit to the **Musée de Paul Charnoz** provides an insight into industrial artistic tile production in the 19th and 20th centuries.

Situated on place Guignaud is the ornate **Maison Jayet**, dating from the 16th century, which houses the town hall.

Basilique du Sacré-Coeur at Paray-le-Monial

Hôtel-Dieu

Christ-de-Pitié

After the Hundred Years' War, many of Beaune's inhabitants suffered the effects of poverty and famine. To remedy this, the chancellor, Nicolas Rolin, and his wife founded a hospice here in 1443, which was inspired by the architecture of Northern French hospitals. The Rolins provided an annual grant and salt-works for income. Today the hospice is considered a medieval jewel, with its superb geometric, multi-coloured Burgundian roof tiles. It houses two religious masterpieces: the *Christ-de-Pitié* statue, carved from oak, and Rogier van der Weyden's *Last Judgment* polyptych.

★ Great Hall of the Poor
The hall, with its carved, painted roof, has 28 four-poster beds, each often used by two patients at a time. Meals were served at central tables.

Tribute to Rolin's Wife
A recurring motif features the entwined letters N and G, birds and stars, and the word "Seulle" referring to Rolin's wife Guigone, his "one and only".

Saint Hugues' Room contains a painting of the saint curing two children. Frescoes by Isaac Moillon show the miracles of Christ.

Entrance

Saint Anne's Room has a tableau of nuns working in what was once the linen room, and a colourful feast-day tapestry.

ANNUAL CHARITY WINE AUCTION

On the third Sunday in November, an annual charity auction in Beaune is the centrepiece of three days of festivities known as *Les Trois Glorieuses*. Saturday sees the banquet of the Confrérie des Chevaliers du Tastevin at the Château Clos de Vougeot. On Sunday the auction of wine from the 61 ha (151 acres) of vineyards, owned by nearby hospitals, takes place. Its prices are the benchmark for the entire vintage. On Monday at La Paulée de Meursault there is a party where growers bring along bottles of their best vintages to enjoy.

Wine sold at the famous auction

STAR FEATURES

★ Great Hall

★ Last Judgment Polyptych by Rogier van der Weyden

Kitchen
The centrepiece of the kitchen is a Gothic fireplace with a dual hearth and a mechanical spit, made in 1698, which is turned by a wooden "robot".

VISITORS' CHECKLIST

Rue de L'Hôtel-Dieu, Beaune. *Tel* *03 80 24 45 00.* ☐ *Apr–mid Nov: 9–6:30pm daily; mid-Nov–Mar: 9–11:30am, 2–5:30pm daily.* 🎫 📷 🐾 **Wine Auction** 3rd Sun Nov: Les Halles de Beaune *(03 80 24 45 00).* **www**.hospices-de-beaune.com

Cour d'Honneur
The buildings of Hôtel-Dieu are arranged around a splendid central courtyard. This is flanked by a wooden gallery, above which rise high dormer windows topped by weather vanes. The courtyard well is a fine example of Gothic wrought-iron work.

Glazed roof tiles, in a colourful geometric pattern, are the most dramatic feature of the Hôtel-Dieu.

Pharmacy
Such unusual potions as woodlouse powder, shrimps' eyes and vomit nut powder are stored in these earthenware pots. Nearby is a bronze mortar used to prepare the remedies.

St Louis' Room

★ Last Judgment Polyptych
The naked figures shown in Rogier van der Weyden's 15th-century polyptych were briefly given clothing in the 19th century. At the same time, the altarpiece was cut in half so that the outer and inner panels could be seen together.

Château de Pierreclos in the Mâconnais region

Brionnais ㉔

Saône-et-Loire. ✈ Mâcon.
🚃 Paray-le-Monial, Roanne.
🚌 Paray-le-Monial.
ℹ Marcigny (03 85 25 39 06).

The Brionnais is a
small and peaceful
rural district,
squeezed between
the river Loire and
the Beaujolais foot-
hills in the far south
of Burgundy.

Its agricultural staple
is the white Charolais
cow, which can be seen
grazing everywhere. For
a closer look at this
regional symbol, visit
the lively cattle-market
in **St-Christophe** on
Wednesday afternoons.

The area has an abundance
of Romanesque churches,
most of which are built of the
local ochre-coloured stone.
The 11th-century church of
Anzy-le-Duc has a majestic

Capital in St-
Julien-de-Jonzy

three-tiered polygonal tower
and exquisitely carved capitals.
Semur-en-Brionnais was the
birthplace of Cluny's famous
abbot St Hugues. Its church
is inspired by his great
monastery. The church at
St-Julien-de-Jonzy
has a very finely
carved tympanum.

A small town by
the river Genette,
La Clayette is
graced by a château
set in a lake. It is not
open to the public,
but has a vintage car
museum and in sum-
mer is the setting for a
son et lumière show.

Southeast of La
Clayette the lonely
Montagne de Dun
rises just over 700 m
(2,300 ft) and offers a panorama over the gentle, green
Brionnais hills. This is some of
the best picnic country in
Burgundy, full of sleepy
corners and quiet byways.

Mâcon ㉕

Saône-et-Loire. 🏠 36,000.
✈ 🚃 🚌 ℹ 1 pl Saint Pierre
(03 85 21 07 07). 🛒 Sat.
www.macon-tourism.com

At the frontier between
Burgundy and the south,
Mâcon is an industrial town
and wine centre on the Saône.

The lack of churches is due
to fervent anti-clericalism
during the Revolution, when
14 were destroyed. A 17th-
century convent has been
turned into the **Musée des
Ursulines**. Its collections
include French and Flemish
painting and an exhibition on
the prehistoric site of Solutré.
On the charming place aux
Herbes, where the market is
held, the **Maison de Bois** is a
15th-century wooden house
covered with bizarre carvings.

🏛 **Musée des Ursulines**
Allée de Matisco. **Tel** 03 85 39 90
38. ⏰ Tue–Sat & Sun pm. ● 1 Jan,
1 May, 14 Jul, 1 Nov, 25 Dec. 🌐

Environs
The great **Roche de Solutré**
rises dramatically above the
Pouilly-Fuissé vineyards in the
Mâconnais district (see p345).
Below the rock, finds from the
Stone Ages have established it
as a major archaeological site.

Mâconnais is also the land of
the Romantic poet Lamartine
(1790–1869). Born in Mâcon,
he spent his childhood at Milly
Lamartine and later lived at
Château de St-Point. **Château
de Pierreclos** is associated
with his epic poem *Jocelyn*.

Charolais cattle grazing on the gentle hills of the Brionnais

For hotels and restaurants in this region see pp572–5 and pp625–9

Franche-Comté

A region of woods and water, the Franche-Comté offers exceptional natural beauty combined with opportunities for canoeing, trekking and skiing. Apart from towns well worth visiting, this is a region to explore in the wild. Glorious scenery with grottoes and cascading waterfalls can be found all along the Vallée du Doubs. Further south are the spectacular sources of the rivers Lison and Loue. The Reculées is an area of extraordinary formations of ridges and waterfalls such as Baume-les-Messieurs. In Région des Lacs, the silent, peaceful lakes are surrounded by mountain peaks and virgin forests.

Cascades du Hérisson ㉖

Pays-des-Lacs. 🛈 Clairvaux-les-Lacs (03 84 25 27 47). 🗓 Wed.

The village of Doucier, at the foot of the Pic de l'Aigle, is the starting point for the valley of the river Hérisson, one of the finest natural settings in the Jura. Leave the car at the park by the Moulin Jacquand and walk up the trail through the woods to a spectacular waterfall, the 65-m (213-ft) Cascade de L'Éventail, and beyond to the equally impressive Cascade du Grand Saut. The walk, which takes about two hours there and back, is steep at times and can be slippery, so proper shoes are essential.

Arbois ㉗

Jura. 🏠 3,600. 🚉 🛈 17 rue de l'Hôtel de Ville (03 84 66 55 50). 🗓 Fri. www.arbois.com

The jolly wine town of Arbois lies on the vine-covered banks of the river Cuisance. It is famous for the sherry-like vin jaune (yellow wine) of the district. On the north side of

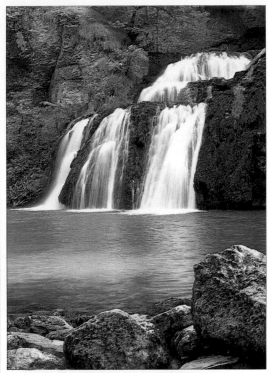

Nature at its purest at Source du Lison in the Franche-Comté

the town is **Maison de Pasteur**, the preserved house and laboratory of the great scientist Louis Pasteur (1822–95), the first to test vaccines on humans.

Environs
Southeast of Dole is the 18th-century **Château d'Arlay**, with immaculately kept gardens.

Dole ㉘

Jura. 🏠 28,000. 🚉 🚌 🛈 6 pl Grévy (03 84 72 11 22). 🗓 Tue, Thu & Sat. www.tourisme-paysdedole.fr

The busy town of Dole lies where the Doubs meets the Rhine-Rhône canal. The former capital of the Comté was always a symbol of the region's resistance to the French. The region had become used to relative independence, first under the Counts of Burgundy and then as part of the Holy Roman Empire. Though always French-speaking, its people did not appreciate the

idea of the French absolute monarchy and in 1636 endured a very long siege. The town finally submitted to Louis XIV, first in 1668, and again in 1674.

There is a charming historic quarter in the centre of town, full of winding alleys, houses dating back to the 15th century, and quiet inner courtyards. Place aux Fleurs offers an excellent view of this part of town and the mossy-roofed, 16th-century **Eglise Notre-Dame**.

Virgin and Child on the north portal of Eglise Notre-Dame, Dole

The Saline Royale at Arc-et-Senans

Arc-et-Senans ㉙

Doubs. 🏛 1,400. 🚊 🚌 *Ancienne Saline Royale (03 81 57 43 21).* **www**.ot-arcetsenans.fr

Designated a World Heritage Site since 1982, the Saline Royale (royal salt works) at Arc-et-Senans were designed by the great French architect Claude-Nicolas Ledoux (1736–1806). He envisaged a development built in concentric circles around the main buildings. However, the only ones to be completed (in 1775) were the buildings used for salt production. Nevertheless, these show the staggering scale of Ledoux's idea: salt water was to be piped from Salins-les-Bains nearby, and fuel to reduce it was to come from the Chaux forest. The enterprise, which was never a success, was closed down in 1895, but the buildings remain.

The **Musée Ledoux Lieu du Sel** displays intriguing models of the grand projects imagined by the visionary architect.

🏛 **Musée Ledoux Lieu du Sel**
Saline Royale. *Tel 03 81 54 45 45.* ⬤ daily. ⬤ 1 Jan, 25 Dec. 🎟 📷 🎧 ♿ gr. floor.

Champlitte ㉚

Haute Saône. 🏛 1,900. 🚊 🚌 *33B rue de la République (03 84 67 67 19).*

In the small town of Champlitte, the **Musée des Arts et Traditions Populaires** was created by a local shepherd who collected artifacts connected with disappearing local customs. One of the poignant displays housed in this Renaissance château recalls the emigration of 400 citizens to Mexico in the mid-19th century.

🏛 **Musée des Arts et Traditions Populaires**
Pl de l'Eglise. *Tel 03 84 67 82 00.* ⬤ Apr–Jun & Sep: Wed–Fri (Sat–Sun pms only); Jul–Aug: Mon–Fri (Sat–Sun pms only); Oct–Mar: Wed–Mon pm. ⬤ 1 Jan, 1 Nov, 25 Dec. 🎟 📷 🎧

Besançon ㉛

Doubs. 🏛 120,000. 🚊 🚌 🚌 *2 pl de la Première Armée Française (03 81 80 92 55).* 🛒 Tue–Sat & Sun am. **www**.besancon-tourisme.com

Besançon supplanted Dole as the capital of the Franche-Comté in the 17th century. It began as an ecclesiastical centre and is now an industrial one, specializing in precision engineering. The stately architecture of the old town, with its elegant wrought-iron work, is a 17th-century legacy.

Behind the fine Renaissance façade of the Palais Granvelle, in the grande rue, is the **Musée du Temps**, a fine collection of 'time-pieces' of all ages – a timely tribute to Besançon's renown as a clock and watch-making centre. An interactive exhibition on the third floor invites reflection on the relativity of the notion of time.

Further along the same street are the birthplaces of novelist Victor Hugo (1802–85) at No. 140 and the Lumière brothers (*see p63*) at place Victor Hugo. Behind **Porte Noire**, a Roman arch, is the 12th-century Cathédrale St-Jean. In its belltower is the **Horloge Astronomique** with its automatons that pop out on the hour.

The stunning **Musée des Beaux Arts et d'Archéologie** occupies the old corn market. Its collection includes works by Bellini, Cranach, Rubens, Fragonard, Boucher, Ingres, Goya, Matisse and Picasso.

Vauban's citadel overlooking the river Doubs has magnificent views and the intriguing **Musée Comtois**, with a collection of local artifacts, an insectarium and an aquarium.

🏛 **Musée du Temps**
Palais Granvelle, 96 grande rue. *Tel 03 81 87 81 50.* ⬤ Tue–Sun. ⬤ 1 Jan, 1 May, 1 Nov, 25 Dec. 🎟 📷 ♿

🎡 **Horloge Astronomique**
Rue de la Convention. *Tel 03 81 81 12 76.* ⬤ Apr–Sep: Wed–Mon; (Thu–Mon winter). ⬤ Jan, 1 May, 1 & 11 Nov, 25 Dec. 🎟 📷

🏛 **Musée des Beaux Arts et d'Archéologie**
1 pl de la Révolution. *Tel 03 81 87 80 49.* ⬤ Wed–Mon. 🎟 free Sun. 📷 ♿

🏛 **Musée Comtois**
La Citadelle, rue des Fusillés de la Résistance. *Tel 03 81 87 83 33.* ⬤ Apr–Oct: daily; Nov–Mar: Wed–Mon. ⬤ 1 Jan, 25 Dec. 🎟 📷 🎧 📷

The fantastic astronomical clock in Besançon, made in 1857–60

Ornans ㉜

Doubs. 🏛 4,300. 🚊 🚌 *7 rue Pierre Vernier (03 81 62 21 50).* 🛒 3rd Tue of month. **www**.valleedelaloue.com

The great Realist painter Gustave Courbet was born at Ornans in 1819. He painted the town in every possible

The striking Chapelle Notre-Dame-du-Haut by Le Corbusier at Ronchamp

light. His *Enterrement à Ornans* proved to be one of the most influential paintings of the 19th century. Courbet's work is displayed in three historic buildings, including his childhood home, which make up the **Musée Courbet.**

🏛 **Musée Courbet**
Pl Robert Fernier. *Tel 03 81 86 22 88.* ⬜ Wed–Mon. 🌙 1 Jan, 1 May, 1 Nov, 25 Dec. 📷 🔲 🔲 🔲
http://musee-courbet.doubs.fr

Environs
A canoeist's paradise, the **Vallée de la Loue** is the loveliest in the Jura. The D67 follows the river from Ornans eastwards to Ouhans, from where it is only a 15-minute walk to its magnificent source. Various belvederes offer splendid views over the area.

Southwest of Ornans, the spectacular **Source du Lison** (*see p349*) is a 20-minute walk from Nans-sous-Ste-Anne.

Belfort ❸

Territoire de Belfort. 🏠 52,000.
🚉 🚌 🚶 2 bis rue Clemenceau (03 84 55 90 90). 🛒 Wed–Sun.
www.ot-belfort.fr

The symbol of Belfort is an enormous pink sandstone lion. It was built (rather than carved) by Frédéric Bartholdi (1834–1904), whose other major undertaking was the Statue of Liberty.

Belfort's immensely strong **citadel**, designed by Vauban under Louis XIV, withstood three sieges, in 1814, 1815 and 1870. Today this remarkable array of fortifications provides an interesting walk and extensive views of the surroundings. The **Musée d'Art et d'Histoire** housed in some of the billets, displays models of the original fortifications as well as regional art and artifacts (closed Tuesday in winter).

Ronchamp ❹

Haute Saône. 🏠 3,000. 🚌
🚶 14 pl du 14 juillet (03 84 63 50 82). 🛒 Sat.
www.ot-ronchamp.fr

Le Corbusier's **Chapelle Notre-Dame-du-Haut** dominates this former miners' town. A sculpture rather than a building, its swelling concrete form was finalized in 1955. Inside, light, shape and space form a unity.

There is also a **Musée de la Mine** evoking the industry and the life of local miners.

Le Miroir d'Ornans in the Musée Courbet, Ornans

THE MASSIF CENTRAL

ALLIER · AVEYRON · CANTAL · CORRÈZE · CREUSE · HÂUTE-LOIRE
HAUTE-VIENNE · LOZÈRE · PUY DE DOME

The Massif Central is a region of strange, wild beauty – one of France's best-kept secrets. It is surprisingly little known beyond its sprinkling of spas and the major cities of Clermont-Ferrand, Vichy and Limoges. However, the new autoroutes through the heart of its uplands have started to open up this previously remote region.

The huge central plateau of ancient granite and crystalline rock that makes up the Massif Central embraces the dramatic landscapes of the Auvergne, Limousin, Aveyron and Lozère. Once a testing crossroads for pilgrims, and strung with giant volcanoes, it is a region of unsuspected richness, from the spectacular town of Le Puy-en-Velay, to the unique treasures at Conques.

With its crater lakes and hot springs, the Auvergne is the Massif Central's lush volcanic core, an outdoor paradise offering activities from hiking in summer to skiing in winter. It also has some of France's most beautiful Romanesque churches, medieval castles and Renaissance palaces. To the east are the mountain ranges of Forez, Livardois and Velay; to the west are the giant chains of extinct volcanoes, the Monts Dômes, Monts Dore and the Monts du Cantal. The Limousin, on the northwestern edge of the Massif Central, is gentler country with green pastures and blissfully empty roads.

The Aveyron spreads into the southwest from the Aubrac mountains, carrying with it the rivers Lot, Aveyron and Tarn through gorges and valleys with their cliff-hanging villages. To the east in the Lozère are the Grands Causses, the vast, isolated uplands of the Cévennes. These barren plateaux give farmers a poor living, but have been a favourite route with adventurous travellers across the centuries.

La Bourboule, a spa town in the Monts Dore

◁ The summit of Puy Mary, 1,787 m (5,863 ft), offering a superb view to walkers who attempt the ascent

Exploring the Massif Central

Nature is at its most magnificent in the volcanic mountain ranges and wild river gorges of the Massif Central. This is a vast and unspoiled territory which offers spectacular sightseeing and every imaginable outdoor activity, with rafting, paragliding, canoeing and hiking among the many choices. There are hundreds of churches, châteaux and museums to nourish lovers of history, architecture and art; and good, hearty regional cooking and wonderful local wines for lovers of good living.

| 0 kilometres | 25 |
| 0 miles | 25 |

KEY

═══	Motorway
═══	Major road
━━━	Secondary road
═══	Minor road
━━━	Scenic route
⌁	Main railway
───	Minor railway
━━━	Regional border
△	Summit

Limestone cliffs of the Gorges du Tarn

Map labels: Tours, Bonnat, Saint-Sulpice-les-Feuilles, Poitiers, La Souterraine, Creuse, Gouzón, Le Dorat, N145, Saint-Vaury, N145, Guéret, N147, Cartempe, Châteauponsac, Moûtier d'Ahun, Bellac, Laurière, D940, Ahun, Oradour-sur-Glane, Nantiat, Ambazac, Bourganeuf, Pontarion, AUBUSSON ②, Saint-Junien, N141, Aixe-sur-Vienne, LIMOGES ①, Saint-Léonard-de-Noblat, LIMOUS, D675, N21, Peyrat-le-Château, D982, Châlus, Pierre-Buffière, Eymoutiers, Plateau de Millevaches, D704, D12, D30, Saint-Yrieix-la-Perche, A20, Vézère, Meymac, D3, Treignac, D16, D1089, UZERCHE ⑭, Égletons, Vigeois, Corrèze, Objat, Tulle, D1089, Brive-la-Gaillarde, Saint-, Argentat, TURENNE ⑮, COLLONGES-LA-ROUGE ⑯, Toulouse, Saint-Mame-la-Salvet, N12, Maurs, Decazeville, Rign, Aveyr, Nauc, Toulous, Carcassonn

GETTING AROUND

There are good air and rail services connecting Paris with the major towns of Limoges, Clermont-Ferrand and Vichy. Many of the most interesting towns and sights are easily accessible only by car, and motorail from Calais to Brive is an effortless way of getting to the region with a car. Most minor roads are well kept, but slow going in the mountains. A few roads are vertiginous, especially the road to the summit of Puy Mary, which is utterly breath-taking. The A71/A75 (toll-free) through the Auvergne is a magnificent road.

For additional map symbols see back flap

Autumn view of the foothills of
Puy Mary in the Monts du Cantal

A Limoges enamel plaque, *The Bad Shepherd*

Limoges ❶

Haute-Vienne. 🏠 200,000. ✈ 🚊 🚌 🚶 12 bd de Fleurus (05 55 34 46 87). 🛒 daily.
www.limoges-tourisme.com

The capital of the Limousin has two hearts: the old Cité and the rival château, now the commercial centre of the modern city. The Cité was ravaged by the Black Prince during the Hundred Years' War and today it is a quiet place of half-timbered houses and narrow streets.

It was not until the 1770s that Limoges became synonymous with porcelain. The legendary local ware is on display at the superb **Musée National Adrien-Dubouché**. More than 10,000 exhibits trace the history of ceramics. The **Musée des Beaux Arts de Limoges** houses an Egyptian collection, archaeological artifacts tracing the history of Limoges, over 600 Limousin enamels and Impressionist paintings. This area was a centre of Resistance operations in World War II; the **Musée de la Résistance et**

de la **Déportation** has a collection of exhibits relating to Resistance acitivities.

🏛 **Musée National Adrien-Dubouché**
Pl Winston Churchill. **Tel** 05 55 33 08 50. ⬜ Wed–Mon. ⬤ 1 Jan, 1 May, 25 Dec. 🎫 🎧
www.musee-adriendebouche.fr

🏛 **Musée des Beaux Arts de Limoges**
1 pl de l'Evêché. **Tel** 05 55 45 98 10. ⬜ Wed–Mon. ⬤ 1 Jan, 1 May, 1 & 11 Nov, 25 Dec. www.museebal.fr

🏛 **Musée de la Résistance et de la Déportation**
Rue de la Règle, Jardin de L'Evêché. **Tel** 05 55 45 98 23. ⬜ Wed–Mon pm.

Environs
Resistance activity in the Limousin led to severe reprisals. On 10 June 1944 at the village of **Oradour-sur-Glane**, 25 km (16 miles) north-west of Limoges, SS troops burned alive the entire population. The ruins have been kept as a shrine, and a new village built nearby. St-Junien close by has been a glove-making town since the Middle Ages, and it still supplies today's designers with luxury leather items.

Aubusson ❷

Creuse. 🏠 5,000. 🚌 🚶 rue Vieille (05 55 66 32 12). 🛒 Sat. www.ot-aubusson.fr

Aubusson owes its renown to the exceptionally pure waters of the Creuse, perfect for making the delicately coloured dyes used for tapestries and rugs. Tapestry production was at its zenith in the 16th and 17th centuries, but by the end of the 18th century the Revolution and patterned wallpaper had swept away the clientele.

In the 1940s, Aubusson was revived, largely due to the artist Jean Lurçat, who persuaded other modern artists to design for tapestry. The **Musée Départemental de la Tapisserie** displays a permanent collection of these modern works. All 30 workshops welcome visitors – at the **Manufacture St Jean** you can watch tapestries and custom-made carpets being made by hand and restored.

🏛 **Musée Départemental de la Tapisserie**
Av des Lissiers. **Tel** 05 55 83 08 30. ⬜ Wed–Mon (Jul–Aug Tue pm). ⬤ 1 week Apr, 1 week Nov. 🎫 ♿

🏛 **Manufacture St Jean**
3 rue St Jean. **Tel** 05 55 66 10 08. ⬜ Mon–Fri. 🎫 🎧

Environs
A single street of 15th-century houses and a Roman bridge comprise **Moûtier-d'Ahun**,

Tapestry restoration at the Manufacture St Jean in Aubusson

Romanesque church at Moûtier-d'Ahun near Aubusson

tucked into the lush Creuse valley. Vestiges of a Benedictine abbey can still be detected in the half-Romanesque, half-Gothic church with its elaborate stone portal. The choir has wooden stalls, for which it is worth paying a visit to the church. They are masterpieces of late 17th-century carving with fantastical and intricately worked motifs of flora and fauna representing the many different facets of Good and Evil in figurative form. Today there is a garden where the nave once was.

Montluçon ❸

Allier. 🏠 45,000. 🚇 🚌
🛈 67 ter bd de Courtais
(04 70 05 11 44). 🛒 Tue, Thu–Sun.
www.montlucontourisme.com

Montluçon is the economic centre of the region, a small town with a medieval core. At its heart there is a Bourbon château, which now houses temporary exhibitions. **Jardin Wilson**, a pleasant *jardin à la française* in the medieval quarter, sits on the original ramparts of the town. Mostly destroyed in the 18th century, little remains of the ramparts now. The restored rose garden and spectacular flower beds are worth a visit. The 12th-century **Eglise de St-Pierre** is a surprise, with giant stone columns and a huge barrel-vaulted ceiling.

Moulins ❹

Allier. 🏠 23,000. 🚇 🚌 🛈 rue
François Péron (04 70 44 14 14). 🛒
Fri, Sun. www.moulins-tourisme.com

Capital of the Bourbonnais and seat of the Bourbon Dukes since the 10th century, Moulins flourished during the early Renaissance. Moulins' most celebrated sight is the Flamboyant Gothic **Cathédrale Notre-Dame**, where members of the Bourbon court appear amid the saints in the 15th- and 16th-century stained-glass windows. The treasury contains a luminous 15th-century Virgin and Child triptych by the "Master of Moulins". Benefactors Pierre II, Duke of Bourbon, and his wife Anne de Beaujeu, bedecked in embroidery and jewels, are shown being introduced to a less richly dressed Madonna.

The tower keep and the single remaining wing of the Bourbon **Vieux Château** house a superb collection of sculpture, painting and decorative art from the 12th to the 16th centuries. Housed in the former cavalry barracks is a magnificent collection of 10,000 theatrical costumes.

🏛 **Cathédrale Notre-Dame**
Pl de la Déportation. **Tel** 04 70 20 89 65. **Treasury** ☐ Tue–Sat.
● 25 Dec. 🗺 🛗

Stained-glass windows at the Cathédrale Notre-Dame in Moulins

Château de la Palice ❺

Allier. **Tel** *04 70 99 37 58.*
☐ *Easter–Oct: daily.* 🎫 📷

In the early 16th century, the Marshal of France, Jacques II de Chabannes, hired Florentine architects to reconstruct the feudal château-fort at Lapalisse, creating a refined Renaissance castle, which has been inhabited ever since by his descendants. The *salon doré* (gilded room) has a beamed ceiling panelled in gold, and two huge 15th-century Flemish tapestries showing the Crusader Knight Godefroy de Bouillon and Greek hero Hector, two of the nine classic braves of chivalric legend.

Environs

From Lapalisse, the D480 leads up through the beautiful Besbre valley past a handful of other small, well-preserved châteaux, including **Château de Thoury**.

🏯 **Château de Thoury**
Dompierre. **Tel** *04 70 42 00 41.*
Courtyard and exterior ☐ *Apr–May: Sat, Sun & public hols (pms only); Jun–Nov: Wed–Mon.*

Gilded ceiling, Château de la Palice

Vichy ❻

Allier. 👥 *27,000.* 🚉 🚌 🛈 *19 rue du Parc (04 70 98 71 94).* 🛍 *Wed.*
www.vichytourisme.com

This small city on the river Allier has long been known for its hot and cold springs, and reputed cures for rheumatism, arthritis and digestive complaints. The letter-writer Madame de Sévigné and the daughters of Louis XV visited in the late 17th and 18th centuries – the former compared the showers to "a rehearsal for Purgatory". The

Interior of the original Thermal Establishment building in Vichy

visits of Napoleon III in the 1860s put Vichy on the map and made taking the waters fashionable. The small town was spruced up and became a favourite among the French nobility and the world's wealthy middle classes. These days, the grand old Thermal Establishment, built in 1900, has been turned into shopping galleries. The modern baths are state-of-the-art and strictly

Vichy poster (about 1930–50) by Badia-Vilato

for medical purposes. A doctor's prescription and a reservation 30 days in advance are required for all treatments.

Vichy's fortunes changed for the better once again in the 1960s with the damming of the Allier, creating a huge lake in the middle of town, which rapidly became a thriving centre for watersports and international events. For a small fee, you can have a taste of sports from aikido to waterskiing or learn canoeing on the 3-km (2-mile) long artificial river.

The focal point of life in Vichy is the **Parc des Sources** in the centre of town, with its turn-of-the-century bandstand (afternoon concerts in season), Belle Epoque glass-roofed shopping galleries, and the Grand Casino and Opera House. Here there is gambling every afternoon and musical performances in the evenings, and an atmosphere of gaiety pervades. Also open to the public are the beautiful bronze taps of the **Source**

Célestin, in a riverside park containing vestiges of a convent bearing the same name. Only by making an effort to imagine the city in grainy black-and-white newsreel style is there the slightest reminder of the wartime Vichy government which was based in the town from 1940–44 *(see p65)*.

🌿 **Source Célestin**
Bd du Président Kennedy. ⬜ *daily.*
⬤ *Dec–Jan.* ♿

Thiers ❼

Puy de Dôme. 🏘 *13,500.* 🚉 🚌
ℹ *pl de Pirou (04 73 80 65 65).*
🏪 *Thu & Sat.* **www**.ville-thiers.fr

According to the writer La Bruyère, Thiers "seems painted on the slope of the hill", hanging dramatically as it does on a ravine over a sharp bend in the river Durolle. The city has been renowned for cutlery since the Middle Ages, when legend has it that Crusaders brought back techniques of metalwork from the Middle East. With grindstones powered by dozens of waterfalls on the opposite bank of the river, Thiers produced everything from table knives to guillotine blades, and cutlery remains its major industry today, much of it on display in the Cutlery Museum, the **Musée de la Coutellerie**.

The Old Town is filled with mysterious quarters like "the Corner of Chance" and "Hell's Hollow", honeycombed with tortuous streets and well-restored 14th–17th-century houses. Many have elaborately carved wooden façades, like the Maison du Pirou in place

The Virgin of Orcival, carried in procession above the village (1903)

Pirou. The view to the west from the rampart terrace, towards Monts Dômes and Monts Dore, is particularly splendid at sunset.

🏛 **Musée de la Coutellerie**
58 rue de la Coutellerie.
Tel 04 73 80 58 86. ⬜ *Jun–Sep: daily; Oct–May: Tue–Sun.* ⬤ *25 Jan, 1 May, 25 Dec.* 📷 🎫
www.musee-coutellerie-thiers.com

Issoire ❽

Puy de Dôme. 🏘 *15,000.* 🚉 🚌
ℹ *9 pl St-Paul (04 73 89 15 90).*
🏪 *Sat.* **www**.sejours-issoire.com

Most of old Issoire was destroyed in the 16th-century Wars of Religion. The present-day town has been an important industrial centre since the end of World War II.

Not only does Issoire have a thriving aeronautical tradition, it is also a mecca for glider pilots who come from miles around to take advantage of the strong local air currents.

Issoire's colourful 12th-century abbey church of **St-Austremoine** is one of the great Romanesque churches of the region. The capitals depict scenes from the *Life of Christ* (one of the Apostles at the Last Supper has fallen asleep at table), and imaginary demons and beasts. The 15th-century fresco of the *Last Judgment* shows Bosch-like figures of sinners being cast into the mouth of a dragon or carted off to hell. The nearby Tour de l'Horloge has scenes of Renaissance history.

Thiers from the south, spreading over the slopes above the river Durolle

St-Nectaire ⑨

Puy de Dôme. 🏘 *750.* 🚌
ℹ️ *Les Grands Thermes*
(04 73 88 50 86). 🟢 *Jul–Aug:*
Sun am. **www**.sancy.com

The Auvergne is noted for
Romanesque churches. The
Eglise St-Nectaire in the
upper village of St-Nectaire-le-Haut,
with its soaring, elegant
proportions, is one of the
most beautiful. The 103
stone capitals, 22 of them
polychrome, are vividly
carved, and the treasury
includes a gold bust of St
Baudime and a wooden
Notre-Dame-du-Mont-
Cornadore, both marvels of
12th-century workmanship.
The lower village, St-Nectaire-
le-Bas, has more than 40 hot
and cold springs.

Environs
The 12th-century citadel of
Château de Murol, partially in
ruins, offers costumed guides
demonstrating medieval life
and knightly pursuits. It is
wonderful for children.

🏰 **Château de Murol**
Murol. **Tel** *04 73 26 02 00.* 🟢 *Apr–*
Sep: daily; Oct–Mar: Sat & Sun. 📷
📷 📷 **www**.chateaudemurol.fr

Fontaine d'Amboise (1515) in Clermont-Ferrand

Clermont-Ferrand ⑩

Puy de Dôme. 🏘 *141,000.*
✈️ 🚉 🚌 ℹ️ *pl de la Victoire*
(04 73 98 65 00). 🟢 *Mon–Sat.*
www.clermont-fd.com

Clermont-Ferrand began as
two distinct – and rival – cities,
united only in 1630. Clermont
is a lively commercial centre
and student town, with thriving
cafés and restaurants. It was a
Celtic settlement before the
Roman era, had a cathedral as
early as the 5th century, and
by 1095 was significant enough
for the pope to announce the
First Crusade there. The Counts
of Auvergne, challenging the
episcopal power of Clermont,
made their base in what is now
old Montferrand, a short drive
from Clermont city centre.
Built on a bastide pattern, it is
a time warp of quiet streets
and Renaissance houses.

Clermont's more ancient
origins are well illustrated at
the **Musée Bargoin** with its
remarkable collections of
locally found Roman domestic
artifacts (closed Mondays).

Place St-Pierre is Clermont's
principal marketplace, with a
daily food market – especially
good on Saturdays. Nearby, the
pedestrianized rue du Port
leads steeply downhill from
the **Fontaine d'Amboise**
(1515) to the **Basilique Notre-
Dame-du-Port**. This is one of
the most important Roman-
esque churches in the region
and has benefitted from
extensive renovations. The
stone interior is beautifully
proportioned, with a magnificent raised choir and vivid
carved capitals – Charity
battles Avarice, in the form
of two knights.

The contrast with the black
lava **Cathédrale Notre-Dame-
de-l'Assomption** is startling,
from austere 12th-century
Romanesque to high-flying
13th-century Gothic.

Raised choir in the Basilique Notre-Dame-du-Port

For hotels and restaurants in this region see pp575–7 and pp629–31

CLERMONT CITY CENTRE

Basilique Notre-Dame-du-Port ③
Cathédrale Notre-Dame-de-l'Assomption ④
Fontaine d'Amboise ②
Place St-Pierre ①

0 metres   250
0 yards   250

Key to Symbols see back flap

The graceful lines of the interior are due to the strong local stone used for construction, allowing pillars to be thinner and the whole structure lighter. The dark volcanic rock provides a foil for the jewel-like 12th–15th-century stained-glass windows, which are believed to be from the same workshop as Sainte-Chapelle's in Paris (see p84).

The old section of Montferrand thrived from the 13th to the 17th centuries, and many fine houses – known as *hôtels particuliers* – built by prosperous merchants have survived. Some of the best of

Choir inside the Cathédrale Notre-Dame-de-l'Assomption

these, with Italianate loggias, mullioned windows and intriguing courtyards, line ancient **rue Kléber**. Between Clermont and old Montferrand lies a third mini-city, the headquarters and factories of the Michelin rubber-and-tyre company, founded here in 1830, which dominates the town.

Michelin man, c.1910

Environs

Once the rival of Clermont-Ferrand for supremacy in Auvergne, **Riom** is a sombre provincial town of black stone houses and lava fountains. The 14th-century château of Duke Jean de Berry was razed in the 19th century to build the Palais de Justice; all that remains is the delicate Sainte-Chapelle with its lovely 15th-century stained-glass windows.

Riom's greatest treasure is a graceful Madonna holding an infant with a small bird in his hand. The statue is housed in the Eglise de Notre-Dame-du-Marthuret, originally built in the 14th century, but much rearranged since then.

Orcival ⑪

Puy de Dôme. 🚏 300.
🛈 Le Bourg (04 73 65 89 77).
www.terresdomes-sancy.com

Crowded in summer, Orcival is nevertheless well worth visiting for its Romanesque church, the **Basilique d'Orcival**, which many would say is the best in the region. Completed at the beginning of the 12th century, and typically Auvergne Roman-esque in style, the apse is multi-tiered, and the side walls are supported by powerful buttresses and strong arches. Inside, the ornate silver and vermilion *Virgin and Child* (in the forward-facing position known as "in majesty") is enigmatic in its rigid, square chair. With an interior lit by 14 windows and a spacious crypt, the propor-tions of the building itself are the most graceful aspect.

Virgin and Child in the Basilique d'Orcival

Aerial view of Puy de Dôme in the Monts Dômes range

Monts Dômes ⓬

Puy de Dôme. 🎿 🚉 🚗 *Clermont-Ferrand.* 🛈 *Montlosier (04 73 65 64 00).* **www**.parc-volcans-auvergne.com

The youngest range of the Auvergne volcanoes at 4,000 years old, the Monts Dômes, or Chaîne des Puys, encompasses 112 extinct volcanoes aligned over a 30-km (19-mile) stretch just west of Clermont-Ferrand. At the centre, the **Puy de Dôme** towers above a high plateau. A road off the N922 spirals up the peak at a steady 12 per cent gradient, while the steeper Roman path is still used by hikers. For a less strenuous route, there is the mountain railway (phone 04 73 42 21 32 for details).

At the summit, half an hour further, are the vestiges of the Roman temple of Mercury and a meteorological/telecommunications tower. On a rare clear day, the view across the volcano will take away whatever breath you have left.

The volcanic Roche Tuilière below Col de Guéry in the Monts Dore

The controversial **Parc Européen du Volcanisme, Vulcania**, uses the latest technology to simulate volcanic activity in its 2 ha (5 acre) underground circuit.

In the southwest corner of the Monts Dômes region is the **Château de Cordès**, a small, privately owned 15th-century manor house with formal gardens designed by Le Nôtre (*see p179*).

🐞 **Vulcania**
D941B, Saint-Ours-les-Roches. **Tel** 0820 82 78 28. ☐ *mid-Mar–Aug: daily; Sep–mid-Nov: Wed–Sun.* 📷 ♿ 🏠 ☐ 📷 **Documentation centre** www.vulcania.com

♣ **Château de Cordès**
Orcival. **Tel** 04 73 65 81 34. ☐ *gardens only (phone 04 73 21 15 89 for times).* 📷 📷

Monts Dore ⓭

Puy de Dôme. 🎿 *Clermont-Ferrand.* 🚉 🚗 *Le Mont-Dore.* 🛈 *Montlosier, Aydat (04 73 65 64 00).*

Three giant volcanoes – the Puy de Sancy, the Banne d'Ordanche and the Puy de l'Aiguiller – and their secondary cones make up the Monts Dore: dark green, heavily wooded mountains laced with rivers and lakes and dotted with summer and winter resorts for skiing, hiking, paragliding, canoeing and sailing.

The 1,886-m (6,185-ft) **Puy de Sancy** is the highest point in Central France. It can be reached by taking a shuttle from the town of Le Mont-Dore to the cable car which goes up to the peak, followed by a long

hike across open terrain. From Le Mont-Dore, there is a scenic drive on the D36 which leads to the **Couze-Chambon valley**, a beautiful stretch of high moorland threaded with waterfalls.

The area has two popular spa towns, **La Bourboule**, for children's ailments, with its casino, and Le Mont-Dore, with its grandiose turn-of-the-century **Etablissement Thermal**.

Below the Col de Guéry on the D983, the eroded volcanic **Roche Sanadoire** and **Roche Tuilière** stand up like two gigantic gateposts. From their peaks are far-reaching views over the wooded Cirque de Chausse and beyond.

Church at La Bourboule in the Monts Dore

Uzerche ⓮

Corrèze. 🏚 *3,000.* 🚉 🚗 🛈 *pl de la Libération (05 55 73 15 71).* 🛒 *20th of the month.* **www**.pays-uzerche.fr

Uzerche is an impressive sight: grey slate roofs, turrets and belltowers rising from a hill above the Vézère river. This prosperous town never capitulated during the conflicts of the Middle Ages, and earlier withstood a seven-year siege by Moorish forces in 732: the townspeople sent a feast out to their enemy – in fact, the last of their supplies. The Moors, thinking such lavish offerings meant the city had stores to spare, gave up.

The Romanesque **Église St-Pierre** crests the hill above the town. Beyond Uzerche, the Vézère cuts through the green gorges of the Saillant.

CANTAL CHEESE

Transhumance is still practised in the Auvergne, with the local Salers cattle kept in barns in the valleys during winter and led up to mountain pastures for the summer. The robust grasses and flowers – gentian, myrtle, anemone – on which the cows graze produce a flavoursome milk that is the basis for the region's great cheese, Cantal. Curds were once turned and pressed through cheesecloth by hand, but now modern methods prevail. Cantal is the key ingredient in *aligot* – the potato-and-cheese purée flavoured with garlic that is one of the region's most famous dishes.

Salers cattle enjoying rich pastures

Turenne ⓯

Corrèze. 🖼 750. 🚉 🚌 🅸 *le Bourg* (05 55 24 00 00).

Turenne is one of the most appealing medieval towns in the Corrèze. Crescent-shaped and clustered on the cliffside, the town was the last independent feudal fiefdom in France, under the absolute rule of the La Tour d'Auvergne family until 1738. Henri de la Tour d'Auvergne, their most illustrious member, was a marshal of France under Louis XIV, and one of the greatest soldiers of modern times.

Now the sole remains of the **Château de Turenne** are the 13th-century Clock Tower and 11th-century Tower of Caesar, from which there is a quite stunning 360-degree view of the Cantal mountains across to the Dordogne valley. Not far away is the 16th-century collegiate church and the **Chapelle des Capucins** dating from the 18th century.

⛴ **Château de Turenne**
Tel 05 55 85 90 66. ⭘ Apr–Oct: daily; Nov–Mar: Sun pm. 🖼
www.chateau-turenne.com

Collonges-la-Rouge ⓰

Corrèze. 🖼 400. 🚉 *Brive, then bus to Collonges.* 🅸 *av de l'Auvitrie* (05 55 25 47 57).

There's something a little unsettling about Collonges' unique carmine sandstone architecture, quite beautiful in individual houses, though the overall effect is both austere and fairytale-like.

Founded in the 8th century, Collonges came under the rule of Turenne, whose burghers built the sturdy turreted houses in the surrounding vineyards. Look out for the communal bread oven in the marketplace, and the 11th-century church, later fortified with a tower keep. The church's unusual carved white limestone tympanum shows a man driving a bear, and other lively figures.

Salers ⓱

Cantal. 🖼 400. 🚌 *summer only.* 🅸 *pl Tyssandier d'Escous* (04 71 40 58 08). 🖼 Wed. **www**.salers-tourisme.fr

A handsome town of grey lava houses and 15th-century ramparts, Salers sits atop a steep escarpment at the edge of the Cantal mountains. It is one of few virtually intact Renaissance villages in the region. The church has an admirable polychrome *mise au tombeau* (entombment), dated 1495, and five 17th-century Aubusson tapestries.

From the fountain, streets lead up to the cliff edge, and allow views of the surrounding valleys, with the ever-present sound of cowbells in the distance. The town is very crowded in summer, but it makes a good starting point for excursions to the Puy Mary (*see p364*), the huge barrage at Bort-les-Orgues, the nearby Château de Val and the Cère valley to the south.

Medieval Château de Val at Bort-les-Orgues near Salers

Puy Mary peak in the volcanic Monts du Cantal

Monts du Cantal ⑱

Cantal. ✖ Aurillac. 🚌 🚉 Lioran.
🛈 Aurillac (04 71 48 46 58).
www.iaurillac.com

The Cantal mountains were
originally one enormous volcano – the oldest and the
largest in Europe, dating from
the Tertiary period. The highest peaks, the **Plomb du Cantal**
at 1,855 m (6,086 ft) and the
Puy Mary at 1,787 m (5,863
ft), are surrounded by crests
and deep river valleys.
Driving the narrow roads is
a thrill, compounded by the
views at every hairpin turn.
Between peaks and gorges,
rich mountain pastures provide
summer grazing for red-gold
Salers cows *(see p363)*. From
the **Pas de Peyrol**, the highest
road pass in the country at
1,589 m (5,191 ft), it's about a
25-minute journey on foot to
the summit of the Puy Mary.

Environs
One of the finest of the
Auvergne châteaux, **Château
d'Anjony** was built by Louis II
d'Anjony, a supporter of Joan
of Arc *(see pp300–1)*. Highlights are the 16th-century
frescoes: in the chapel, scenes
from the Life and Passion of
Christ, and upstairs in the
Salle des Preux (Knights'
Room), a dazzling series of
the nine heroes of chivalry. To
the south lies the small town of
Aurillac, a good base for
exploring the Cantal region.

🏰 **Château d'Anjony**
Tournemire. **Tel** 04 71 47 61 67.
⬜ Jul–Aug: daily; mid-Feb–mid-
Nov: daily pms. 📷 🎫 obligatory.

La Chaise-Dieu ⑲

Haute-Loire. 🏠 700. 🚌 🛈 pl de la
Mairie (04 71 00 01 16). 🛒 Thu.
www.la-chaise-dieu.info

Sombre and massive, midway
between Romanesque and
Gothic, the 14th-
century abbey
church of **St-
Robert** is the
prime reason to
visit the small
village of La
Chaise-Dieu. The
building is an
amalgam of styles;
the choir, however,
is sensational: 144
oak stalls carved
with figures of
Vice and Virtue.
Above them, en-
tirely covering the
walls, are some
of the loveliest
tapestries in
France. Made in Brussels and
Arras in the early 16th century
and depicting scenes from the
Old and New Testaments, they
are rich in colour and detail.

Statue of Notre-Dame-
de-France at Le Puy

On the outer walls of the choir
the 15th-century wall painting
of the *Danse Macabre* shows
Death in the form of skeletons
leading rich and poor alike to
their inevitable end. Beyond
the cloister is the Echo room,
in which two people whisper-
ing in opposite corners can
hear one another perfectly. A
Baroque Music Festival from
mid-August to September
makes the abbey crowded.

Le Puy-en-Velay ⑳

Haute-Loire. 🏠 20,500. ✖ 🚌 🚉
🛈 2 pl de Clauzel (04 71 09 38 41).
🛒 Sat. 🎪 Sep.
www.ot-lepuyenvelay.fr

Located in the bowl of a
volcanic cone, the town of
Le Puy teeters on a series of
rock outcrops and
giant basalt pillars.
The town has three
peaks, each
topped with a
landmark church
or statue. Seen
from afar, this is
one of the most
impressive sights
in France.
   Now a commer-
cial and tourist-
oriented town, Le
Puy's star attraction
is its medieval
Holy City. This
became a pilgrim-
age centre after the
Bishop of Le Puy,
Gotescalk, made one of the
first pilgrimages to Santiago
de Compostela in 962, and
built the **Chapelle St-Michel
d'Aiguilhe** on his return.

Detail of *Danse Macabre* at St-Robert, in La Chaise-Dieu

THE AUVERGNE'S BLACK MADONNAS

The cult of the Virgin Mary has always been strong in the Auvergne and this is reflected in the concentration of her statues in the region. Carved in dark walnut or cedar, now blackened with age, the Madonnas are believed to originate from the Byzantine influence of the Crusaders. Perhaps the most famous Madonna is the one in Le-Puy-en-Velay, a 17th-century copy of one which belonged to Louis IX in the Middle Ages.

Louis IX's Black Virgin

Pilgrims from eastern France and Germany assembled at the **Cathédrale de Notre-Dame** with its famous Black Madonna and "fever stone" – a Druid ceremonial stone with healing powers embedded in one of its walls – before setting off for Compostela.

Built on an early pagan site, the Cathédrale de Notre-Dame is a huge Romanesque structure. Multiform arches, carved palm and leaf designs and a chequerboard façade show the influences of Moorish Spain, and indicate the considerable cultural exchange that took place with southern France in the 11th and 12th centuries. In the transept are Romanesque frescoes, notably an 11th–12th-century St Michael; in the sacristy, the treasury includes the Bible of Theodolphus, a handwritten document from the era of Charlemagne. The cathedral is the centre of the Holy City complex that dominates the upper town, encompassing a baptistry, cloister, Prior's house and Penitents' chapel.

The colossal red statue of **Notre-Dame-de-France**, on the pinnacle of the Rocher Corneille, was erected in 1860, cast from 213 cannons captured at Sebastopol during the Crimean War. The statue is reached by a steep pathway, and can be climbed by an iron ladder on the inside.

The Chapelle St-Michel, like the cathedral, shows Moorish influences in the trefoil decoration and coloured mosaics on the rounded arch over the main entrance. It seems to grow out of a giant finger of lava rock and is reached by a steep climb. The church is thought to be located on the site of a Roman temple to Mercury, and its centre dates from the 10th century, although most of the building was constructed a century later. The floor has been constructed to follow the contours of the rock in places,

and the interior is ornamented with faded 10th-century murals and 20th-century stained-glass.

In the lower city, narrow streets of 15th- and 16th-century houses lead to the Vinay Garden and the **Musée Crozatier**, which has a collection of hand-made lace from the 16th century to the present. The museum also has a good collection of medieval *objets d'art* and 15th-century paintings. Once begun, renovation work will close the museum for several years, so call ahead.

In mid-September, Le Puy transforms itself into masked and costumed Renaissance carnival for the Bird King Festival, an ancient tradition celebrating the skill of the city's best archers *(see p38).*

Chapelle St-Michel d'Aiguilhe
Aiguilhe. *Tel* 04 71 09 50 03. mid-Feb–mid-Dec: daily; mid-Dec–mid-Feb: pms only. 1 Jan, 25 Dec.

Notre-Dame-de-France
Rocher Corneille. *Tel* 04 71 05 45 52. daily. mid-Nov–Jan (except Christmas hols).

Musée Crozatier
Jardin Henri Vinay. *Tel* 04 71 06 62 40. for renovations until 2014.

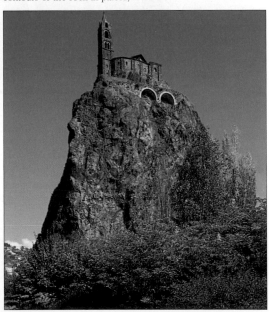

Chapelle St-Michel d'Aiguilhe, standing on a finger of lava rock

Ruins of the Castle of
Calmont d'Olt at Espalion in
the Lot Valley

Vallée du Lot ㉑

Aveyron. ✈ Aurillac, Rodez.
🚆 Rodez, Séverac-le-Château.
🚌 Espalion, Rodez. 🛈 Espalion (05
65 44 10 63). **www**.valleedulot.com

From Mende and the old river
port of La Canourgue all the
way to Conques, the river Lot
(or Olt in old usage) courses
through its fertile valley past
orchards, vineyards and pine
forests. **St Côme d'Olt**, near
the Aubrac mountains, is an
unspoiled, fortified village
whose 15th-century church is
surrounded by Medieval and
Renaissance houses. At
Espalion, the pastel
stone houses and a
turreted 16th-century
castle are reflected in
the river, which runs
beneath a 13th-
century arched stone
bridge. The town
has one of the best
markets in the
region on Friday
mornings. Just outside
town is the 11th-century
Perse Church, whose carved
capitals portray battling
knights and imaginary birds
sipping from a chalice.

Estaing was once the
fiefdom of one of the greatest
families of the Rouergue, dating back to the 13th-century.
The village nestles beneath its
massive château (open May–
Sep) on the river bank. The
road passes through the Lot
Gorge on the way to
Entraygues ("between
waters") where the old quarter and 13th-century Gothic
bridge are worth a visit.
Beyond Entraygues the river
widens to join the Garonne.

Conques ㉒

See pp368–9.

Rodez ㉓

Aveyron. 🏛 26,000. ✈ 🚆 🚌
🛈 pl Foch (05 65 75 76 77).
🗓 Wed, Sat. **www**.ot-rodez.fr

Like many medieval French
cities, Rodez was politically
divided: the shop-lined **place
du Bourg** on one side of town
and **place de la Cité**, near the
cathedral, on the other, reflect

Entombment in Rodez Cathedral

conflicting secular and ecclesiastical interests. Rodez's
commercial centre, the largest
in the region, is probably the
main attraction now, though
the 13th-century huge pink
stone **Cathédrale Notre-Dame**
is worth a look, with its
fortress-like west façade, and
its magnificent, ornate belltower. The 15th-century choir
stalls show a superb panoply
of creatures, including a
winged lion and one naughty
fellow exposing his derrière.

Environs
Southeast (45kms/28
miles) lies Saint Léons,
birthplace of Jean-
Henri Fabre, the
famous entomologist.
Here is **Micropolis**,
part interactive mus-
eum, part theme park,
dedicated to the glory
of insects (closed Nov–
mid-Feb). Watch the
breathtaking film of
the same name, if
nothing else.

ROBERT LOUIS STEVENSON

Robert Louis Stevenson (1850–94),
best known for his novels *Treasure
Island*, *Kidnapped* and *Dr Jekyll and
Mr Hyde,* was also an accomplished
travel writer. In 1878, he
set off across the remote Cévennes
mountain range with only a
small donkey, Modestine,
for company. His classic
account of this eventful
journey, *Travels with a
Donkey in the Cévennes*,
was published in the
following year.

Robert Louis Stevenson

Dramatic scenery in Corniche des Cévennes national park

Corniche des Cévennes ㉔

Lozère, Gard. ✈ *Nîmes.* ▤ *Alès.*
▤ *St-Jean-du-Gard.*
ℹ *St-Jean-du-Gard (04 66 85 32 11).*
www.cevennes-parcnational.fr

The dramatic Corniche road from Florac on the Tarn to St-Jean-du-Gard was cut in the early 18th century by the army of Louis XIV in pursuit of the Camisards, Protestant rebels who had no uniforms but fought in their ordinary shirts (*camiso* in the *langue d'oc*). The route of the D983 makes a spectacular drive. Fascination with the history of the Camisards was one of the reasons that Robert Louis Stevenson undertook his fabled trek in the Cévennes with Modestine, recounted in his *Travels with a Donkey.*

At St-Laurent-de-Trèves, where fossil remains suggest dinosaurs once roamed, there is a view of the Grands Causses and the peaks of Lozère and Aigoual. The Corniche ends in St-Jean-du-Gard, where the **Musée des Vallées Cévenoles**, depicting peasant life, is located in a former 17th-century inn.

🏛 Musée des Vallées Cévenoles

95 grand' rue, St-Jean-du-Gard.
Tel *04 66 85 10 48.* ◐ *Jul–Aug: 10am–7pm daily; Apr–Jun, Sep–Oct: 10am–noon, 2–7pm daily; Nov–Mar Tue, Thu, Sun pm.* ● *1 Jan, 25 Dec.*
▨ **www**.museedescevennes.com

Grands Causses ㉕

Aveyron. ✖ *Rodez-Marcillac.* ▤
▤ *Millau.* ℹ *Millau (05 65 60 02 42).*
▤ *Wed & Fri.* **www**.ot-millau.fr

The Causses are vast, arid limestone plateaux, alternating with green, fertile canyon valleys. The only sign of life at times is a bird of prey wheeling in the sky, or an isolated stone farm or shepherd's hut. The whole area makes for some desolate hiking for those who like solitude.

The four Grands Causses – Sauveterre, Méjean, Noir and Larzac – stretch out east of the city of Millau, which boasts the tallest vehicular bridge in the world. They extend from Mende in the north to the valley of the Vis river in the south.

Among the sights in the Causses are the *chaos* – bizarre rock formations reputed to resemble ruined cities, and named accordingly: there's the chaos of **Montpellier-le-Vieux**, **Nîmes-le-Vieux** and **Roquesaltes**. **Aven Armand** and the **Dargilan Grotto** are vast and deep natural underground grottoes.

A good place to head for in the Larzac Causse is the strange, rough-hewn stone village of **La Couvertoirade**, a fully-enclosed citadel of the Knights Templar in the 12th century. The unpaved streets and medieval houses are an austere reminder of the dark side of the Middle Ages. Entry to the village is free, with a fee for the tour of the ramparts.

The Causse du Larzac's best-known village is probably **Roquefort-sur-Soulzon**, a small grey town terraced on the side of a crumbled limestone outcrop. It has one main street and one major product, Roquefort cheese. This is made from unpasteurized sheep's milk, seeded with a distinctive blue mould grown on loaves of bread, and aged in the warren of damp caves above the town.

View over Méjean, one of the four plateaux of the Grands Causses

Conques 22

The village of Conques clusters around the splendid Abbaye de Ste-Foy, hemmed into a rugged site against the hillside. Sainte Foy was a young girl who became an early Christian martyr; her relics were first kept at a rival monastery in Agen. In the 9th century a monk from Conques stole the relics, thereby attracting pilgrims to this remote spot and firmly establishing Conques as a halt on the route to Santiago de Compostela *(see pp400–1)*.

View of the church from the village

The treasury holds the most important collection of medieval and Renaissance gold work in western Europe. Some of it was made in the abbey's own workshops as early as the 9th century. The Romanesque abbey church has beautiful stained-glass windows by Pierre Soulages (1994), and its tympanum is a triumph of medieval sculpture.

12th-century reliquary

The broad transepts were able to accommodate crowds of pilgrims.

Nave Interior
Pure and elegantly austere, the Romanesque interior dates from 1050–1135. The short nave soars to a height of 22 m (72 ft), with three tiers of arches topped by 250 decorative carved capitals.

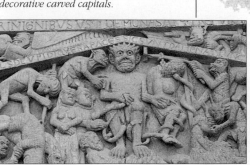

Tympanum
This sculpture from the early 12th century depicts the Last Judgment, *with the Devil in Hell (shown) in the lower part of the sculpture and Christ in Heaven in the tympanum's central position.*

CONQUES' TREASURES

The treasures date from the 9th to the 19th century, and are prized for both their beauty and their rarity. The gold-plated wood and silver reliquary of Ste Foy is studded with gems, rock crystal and even an *intaglio* of Roman Emperor Caracalla. The body is 9th century, but the face may be older, possibly 5th century. Other magnificent pieces include an "A"-shaped reliquary said to be a gift from Charlemagne; the small but exquisite Pépin's shrine from AD 1000; and a late 16th-century processional cross.

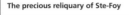

The precious reliquary of Ste-Foy

VISITORS' CHECKLIST

Aveyron. 🔼 1,600. 🚌 🚉 *from Rodez.* ℹ️ *Pl de l'Eglise (0820 820 803).* **Treasury/museum** ◯ *daily: Apr–Sep: 9:30am–12:30pm, 2–6:30pm; Oct–Mar: 10am–noon, 2–6pm.* ✝️ *8am Mon; 8am, 12:05pm Tue–Sat; 7:30am, 11am Sun.* 📷 ♿ *restr.* 🌐 www.conques.fr

Romanesque Chapels
The east end is three-tiered, topped by the blind arcades of the choir and a central bell-tower. Three chapels surround the eastern apse, built to accommodate extra altars for the celebration of mass.

Treasury
The precious contents of the treasury were hidden by the townspeople to prevent their destruc-tion during the French Revolution. Perhaps surpris-ingly, all were returned.

Entrance to Treasury

The Cloister consists of a reconstructed square: only two sections of the original early 12th-century arcades remain. However, 30 of the original carved capitals are displayed in the refectory and in the Musée Fau.

Gorges du Tarn ㉖

Near the beginning of its journey to meet the river Garonne, the Tarn flows through some of Europe's most spectacular gorges. For millions of years, the Tarn and its tributary the Jonte have eaten their way down through the limestone plateaux of the Cévennes, creating a sinuous forked canyon some 25 km (15 miles) long and nearly 400 m (1,300 ft) deep. The gorges are flanked by rocky bluffs and scaled by roads with dizzying bends and panoramic views, which are incredibly popular in the high season. The surrounding plateaux, or *causses*, are eerily different, forming an open, austere landscape, dry in summer and snow-clad in winter, where wandering sheep and isolated farms are sometimes the only signs of life.

Point Sublime
From 800 m (2,600 ft) up, there are stunning views of a major bend in the Tarn gorge, with the Causse Méjean visible in the distance.

Outdoor Activities
The Tarn and Jonte gorges are popular for canoeing and river-rafting. Although relatively placid in summer, melting snow can make the rivers hazardous in spring.

0 kilometres 5
0 miles 3

D46
D995
GORGES DU TARN
D907
D907
le Rozier
D996
GORGES DE LA JONTE
Tarn
D110
CAUSSE NOIR
N9
Millau

Pas de Souci
Just upriver from Les Vignes, Pas de Souci flanks a narrow point in the gorge as the Tarn makes its way northwards.

Chaos de Montpellier-le-Vieux
Situated on the flank of the Causse Noir off the D110 is a remarkable geological site – bizarre rock formations created by limestone erosion.

La Malène
An old crossing-point between the Causse de Sauveterre and the Causse Méjean, this village, with its 16th-century fortified manor, is a good starting point for boat trips.

CAUSSE DE SAUVETERRE
Ste-Enimie
Ispagnac
D907
Tarn
La Malène
CAUSSE MEJEAN
D985
en nd
D996
Jonte
e de gilan
D39
Meyrueis

Aven Armand Caves
On the Causse Méjean, many stalactites in the caves are tinted by minerals that are deposited by the slowly trickling water.

Causse Méjean
The high plateaux or causses are a botanist's paradise in spring and summer, with over 900 species of wild flowers, including orchids.

THE WILD CEVENNES

One of the least populated parts of France, this area is well known for its wild flowers and birds of prey, and griffon vultures were once common here. These giant but harmless scavengers nearly died out in the 20th century through being hunted, but now a reintroduction programme has led to growing numbers breeding in the Gorges de la Jonte.

Yellow wort
Kidney vetch
Green-winged orchid

Wild flowers *found in this thinly populated area include unusual alpine plants.*

The griffon vulture, *which now breeds in the region, has a wingspan of over 2.5 m (8 ft).*

THE RHONE VALLEY AND FRENCH ALPS

LOIRE · RHONE · AIN · ISEZERE · DROME
ARDECHE · HAUTE-SAVOIE · SAVOIE · HAUTES-ALPES

I *ts two most important geographical features, the Alps and the river Rhône, give this region both its name and its dramatic character. The east is dominated by majestic snowcapped peaks, while the Rhône provides a vital conduit between north and south.*

The Romans recognized this strategic route when they founded Lyon over 2,000 years ago. Today Lyon, with its great museums and fine Renaissance buildings, is the second city of France. It is one of the country's most vital commercial and cultural centres as well as the undisputed capital of French gastronomy. To the north lie the flat marshlands of the Dombes and the rich agricultural Bresse plain. Here, too, are the famous Beaujolais vineyards which, along with the Rhône vineyards, make the region such an important wine producer.

The French Alps are among the most popular year-round resort areas in the world, with internationally renowned ski stations such as Chamonix, Mégève and Courchevel, and historic cities like Chambéry, capital of Savoy before it joined France. Elegant spa towns line the shores of Lac Léman (Lake Geneva). Grenoble, a bustling university city and high-tech centre, is flanked by two of the most spectacular nature reserves in France, the Chartreuse and the Vercors.

To the south, orchards and fields of sunflowers give way to brilliant rows of lavender interspersed with vineyards and olive groves. Châteaux and ancient towns dot the landscape. Mountains and pretty, old-fashioned spa towns characterize the rugged Ardèche, and the deeply scoured gorges along the river Ardèche offer some of the wildest scenery in France.

The restored Ferme de la Forêt at St-Trivier-de-Courtes, north of Bourg-en-Bresse

◁ Annecy's medieval quarter

Exploring the Rhône Valley and French Alps

Lyon is the region's largest city, famed for its historic buildings and gastronomic tradition. Wine lovers can choose between the vineyards of the Beaujolais, Rhône Valley and Drôme region to the south. To the west, the Ardèche offers rugged wilderness, canoeing and climbing. Spa devotees from around the world flock to Évian-les-Bains and Aix-les-Bains, while the Alps are a favourite destination for sports enthusiasts (see pp322–3).

SIGHTS AT A GLANCE

Aix-les-Bains ㉒
Annecy ㉓
The Ardèche ⑪
Bourg-en-Bresse ①
Briançon ⑯
Chambéry ㉑
The Chartreuse ⑳
The Dombes ②
Grenoble ⑱
Grignan ⑭
Lac Léman ㉔
Le Bourg d'Oisans ⑰
Lyon ④
Montélimar ⑬
Nyons ⑮
Palais Idéal du Facteur Cheval ⑧
Pérouges ③
St-Étienne ⑦
St-Romain-le-Gal ⑥
Tournon-sur-Rhône ⑨
Valence ⑩
Vals-les-Bains ⑫
The Vercors ⑲
Vienne ⑤

The Pont des Amours in Annecy

KEY

═══ Motorway

═══ Major road

═══ Secondary road

═══ Minor road

─── Scenic route

═══ Main railway

─── Minor railway

─── International border

─── Regional border

△ Summit

Pont-en-Royans in the Vercors

GETTING AROUND

Lyon and Geneva are the main
transit hubs of the region. For
Lyon, change from Eurostar to
TGV at Lille. Apart from the
Alpine regions, local train and
bus services tend to be slow
and inconvenient. A car is
essential if you wish to get off
the most heavily travelled autoroutes – the most important
ones being the A7, linking
Lyon with Valence and the
south; and the A40 and
A43/A41, which run east to the
Alps. The three international
airports nearest the Alps are
Geneva-Cointrin in Switzerland,
St-Exupéry near Lyon and
Grenoble Isère. Note that high
Alpine passes can be closed
between November and June.

Farms around Le Poët Laval, near Montélimar

0 kilometres 25

0 miles 25

Bourg-en-Bresse ❶

Ain. 🏛 *43,000.* 🚋 🚌 ℹ️ *Centre Culturel Albert Camus, 6 av Alsace-Lorraine (04 74 22 49 40).* 🕎 *Wed & Sat.* www.bourgenbressetourisme.fr

Bourg-en-Bresse is a busy market town, with some beautifully restored half-timbered buildings. It is best known for its tasty *poulet de Bresse* (chickens raised in the flat agricultural region of Bresse and designated *appellation contrôlée, see p319*); and its abbey church of **Brou** on the southeast edge of town.

The latter, no longer a place of worship, has become one of the most visited sites in France. Flamboyant Gothic in style, it was built between 1505 and 1536 by Margaret of Austria after the death of her husband Philibert, Duke of Savoy, in 1504.

The couple's finely sculpted Carrara marble tombs can be seen in the choir, along with the tomb of Margaret of Bourbon, Philibert's mother, who died in 1483. Notice also the beautifully carved choir stalls, stained-glass windows, and rood screen with its elegant basket-handle arching.

The adjacent cloisters house a small museum with a good collection of 16th- and 17th-century Dutch and Flemish masters, as well as contemporary works by local artists.

Environs

About 24 km (15 miles) north of Bourg-en-Bresse at St-Trivier-de-Courtes, the restored **Ferme-Musée de la Forêt** offers a look at farm life in the region during the 17th century. The ancient house has what is known locally as a Saracen chimney, with a brick hood in the centre of the room, similar to constructions in Sicily and Portugal, and a collection of antique farm implements.

Bresse chickens

🏛 **Ferme-Musée de la Forêt**
Tel *04 74 30 71 89.* ⬜ *Apr–Jun & Oct: w/e & public hols; Jul–Sep: daily.* ⬤ *Mon am.* 📷 ♿

Tomb of Margaret of Austria in the abbey church of Brou at Bourg-en-Bresse

The Dombes ❷

Ain. 🛬 *Lyon.* 🚋 *Lyon, Villars les Dombes, Bourg-en-Bresse.* 🚌 *Villars-les-Dombes (from Bourg-en-Bresse).* ℹ️ *3 pl de Hôtel de Ville, Villars-les-Dombes (04 74 98 06 29).*

This flat, glacier-gouged plateau south of Bourg-en-Bresse is dotted with small hills, ponds and marshes, making it popular with anglers and bird-watchers.

In the middle of the area at **Villars-les-Dombes** is an ornithological park, the **Parc des Oiseaux**. Over 400 species of native and exotic birds live here, including tufted herons, vultures, pink flamingoes, emus and ostriches.

🦅 **Parc des Oiseaux**
Route Nationale 83, Villars-les-Dombes. **Tel** *04 74 98 05 54.* ⬜ *daily.* ⬤ *Dec–Feb.* 📷 ♿

Pérouges ❸

Ain. 🏛 *900.* 🚋 *Meximieux-Pérouges.* 🚌 ℹ️ *04 74 46 70 84.* www.perouges.org

Originally the home of immigrants from Perugia, Pérouges is a fortified hilltop village of medieval houses and cobblestone streets. In the 13th century it was a centre of linen-weaving, but with the mechanization of the industry in the 19th century, the local population fell from 1,500 to 90.

Restoration of its historic buildings and a new influx of craftsmen have breathed new life into Pérouges. Not surprisingly, the village has often been used as the setting for historical dramas such as *The Three Musketeers and Monsieur Vincent*. The village's main square, place de la Halle, is shaded by a huge lime tree planted in 1792 to honour the Revolution.

For hotels and restaurants in this region see pp577–80 and pp632–4

A Tour of Beaujolais

Beaujolais is an ideal area for wine tasting, offering delicious, affordable wine and glorious countryside. The south of the region produces most of the Beaujolais Nouveau, released fresh from the cellars on the third Thursday of November each year. In the north are the ten superior quality *cru* wines – St-Amour, Juliénas, Moulin-à-Vent, Chénas, Fleurie, Chiroubles, Morgon, Brouilly, Côte de Brouilly and Regnié – most of which can be visited in a day's drive. The distinctive *maisons du pays* have living quarters built over the wine cellar. Almost every village has its *cave* (wine cellar), offering tastings and a glimpse of the wine culture that dominates local life.

Côte de Brouilly

Juliénas ①
Famous for *coq au vin*, this village stores and sells wine in its church, at the Château du Bois de la Salle and at several private cellars.

Moulin-à-Vent ②
This 17th-century windmill has lovely views of the Saône valley. Tastings of the oldest *cru* in the region are held in the *caves* next door.

MACON →

Chénas

Romanèche-Thorins

Vineyard of Gamay grapes

Chiroubles ⑦
A bust in the village square honours Victor Pulliat, who saved the vines from the phylloxera blight in the 1880s by using American vine stocks.

Fleurie ③
The chapel of the Madonna (1875) stands guard over the vineyards, and village restaurants serve local *andouillettes au Fleurie*.

Villié-Morgon ④
Wine-tasting takes place in the cellars of the 18th-century Château Fontcrenne in the village centre.

Régnié-Durette

KEY

▬▬	Tour route
══	Other roads
☀	Viewpoint

0 kilometres 2
0 miles 1

Beaujeu ⑥
Once the ancient capital of the region, Beaujeu offers tastings in its 17th-century hospices. This Renaissance wooden building houses a shop, information centre and museum.

Cercié

Brouilly ⑤
The hill, with its tiny 19th-century chapel of Notre-Dame du Raisin, offers fine views and an annual Beaujolais wine festival.

VILLEFRANCHE-SUR-SAONE

Street-by-Street: Lyon ❹

On the west bank of the river Saône, the restored old
quarter of Vieux Lyon is an atmospheric warren of
cobbled streets, *traboules* (covered passageways),
Renaissance palaces, first-class restaurants, lively
bouchons (bistros) and bohemian shops. It is also
the site of the Roman city of Lugdunum, the
commercial and military capital of Gaul
founded by Julius Caesar in 44 BC.
Vestiges of this prosperous city can be
seen in the superb Gallo-Roman
museum at the top of Fourvière hill.
Two excavated Roman theatres still stage
performances from opera to rock concerts.
At the foot of the hill is the finest collection
of Renaissance mansions in France. The
spectacular Musée des Confluences makes an
exciting new addition to the city in 2013.

★ **Théâtres Romains**
*There are two Roman
amphitheatres here: the
Grand Théâtre, the oldest
theatre in France, built in
15 BC to seat 30,000
spectators and still used for
modern performances; and
the smaller Odéon, with its
geometric tiled flooring.*

★ **Musée de la Civilisation
Gallo-Romaine**
*This underground museum
contains a rich collection of
statues, mosaics, coins and
inscriptions evoking Lyon's
Roman past.*

Entrance
to funicular

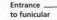

STAR SIGHTS

★ Théâtres Romains

★ Musée de la
   Civilisation
   Gallo-Romaine

★ Basilique Notre-Dame
   de Fourvière

Cathédrale St-Jean
*Begun in the late 12th century,
cathedral has a 14th-century astr
nomical clock that shows religi
feast days till the year 2019.*

★ **Basilique Notre-Dame de Fourvière**
This gaudy mock-Byzantine creation – a riot of turrets and crenellations, marble and mosaic – was built in the late 19th century and has become one of the symbols of Lyon.

Entrance to funicular

The Chemin du Rosaire is a beautiful path leading down from Notre-Dame de Fourvière, with spectacular views of the sprawling metropolis below.

The Tour Métallique was erected in 1893 and is now used as a television transmitter.

VISITORS' CHECKLIST

Rhône. 453,000. 25 km (16 miles) E Lyon. Perrache, Part-Dieu (SNCF 3635). Perrache (SNCF 3635). pl Bellecour (04 72 77 69 69). daily. Biennale Internationale d'Art Contemporain (Sep–Jan), Biennale Internationale de la Danse (Sep). **www**.lyon-france. com **Musée de la Civilisation Gallo-Romaine Tel** 04 72 38 49 30. Tue– Sun. **www**.musees-gallo-romains. com **Hôtel Gadagne Tel** 04 37 23 60 45. Wed–Sun.

Rue Juiverie boasts a number of splendid Renaissance mansions – look out for the Hôtel Patern at No. 4 and the Hôtel Bulliod at No. 8.

Rue St-Jean and rue du Boeuf are lined with Renaissance mansions, the former homes of bankers and silk merchants.

The 15th-century Hôtel Gadagne houses two museums: the **Musée Historique de Lyon** and the **Musée des Marionnettes du Monde**, which exhibits the famous Lyonnais puppets.

0 metres 100
0 yards 100

KEY

– – – Suggested route

Exploring Lyon

France's second city, dramatically sited on the banks of the Rhône and Saône rivers, has been a vital gateway between the north and south since ancient times. On arriving you immediately feel a *brin du sud*, or touch of the south. The crowds are not as quick-stepping as they are in Paris, and the sun is often shining here when it's rainy and cold in the north. Despite its importance as a banking, textile and pharmaceutical centre, most of the French immediately associate Lyon with their palates. The city is packed with restaurants, ranging from simple *bouchons* (bistros) to some of the most opulent tables in France.

The rue St-Jean in Vieux Lyon

The Presqu'île

The heart of Lyon is the Presqu'île, the narrow peninsula of land between the Saône and Rhône rivers, just north of their confluence. A pedestrianized shopping street, the rue de la République, links the twin poles of civic life: the vast **place Bellecour**, with its equestrian statue of Louis XIV in the middle, and the **place des Terreaux**. The latter is overlooked by Lyon's ornate 17th-century Hôtel de Ville (town hall) and the Palais St-Pierre, a former Benedictine convent and now the home of the **Musée des Beaux Arts**. In the middle of the square is a monumental 19th-century fountain by Bartholdi, sculptor of the Statue of Liberty.

Behind the town hall, architect Jean Nouvel's futuristic **Opéra de Lyon** – a black barrel vault of steel and glass encased in a Neo-Classical shell – was remodelled to a controversial design in 1993.

A few blocks to the south, the **Musée de l'Imprimerie** illustrates Lyon's contribution to the early days of printing in the late 15th century.

Two other museums worth visiting in the Presqu'île are the **Musée des Tissus**, which houses an extraordinary collection of silks and tapestries dating from early Christian times to the present day, and the **Musée des Arts Décoratifs**, which displays a range of tapestries, furniture, porcelain and *objets d'art*.

Nearby, the **Abbaye St-Martin d'Ainay** is an impressively restored Carolingian church dating from 1107.

LYON CITY CENTRE

Abbaye St-Martin d'Ainay ⑬
Amphithéâtre des Trois Gaules ①
Basilique Notre-Dame de Fourvière ⑨
Cathédrale St-Jean ⑫
Eglise St-Polycarpe ②
Hôtel Gadagne ⑦
Hôtel de Ville ④
Musée de la Civilisation Gallo-Romaine ⑩
Musée de l'Imprimerie et de la Banque ⑥
Musée des Arts Décoratifs ⑭
Musée des Beaux Arts ⑤
Musée Historique des Tissus ⑮
Opéra de Lyon ③
Théâtres Romains ⑪
Tour Métallique ⑧

0 metres   250
0 yards   250

KEY
Street-by-Street map *pp378–9*

Key to Symbols *see back flap*

Musée des Beaux Arts

Lyon's Musée des Beaux Arts showcases the country's largest and probably most important collection of art after the Louvre. The museum is housed in the 17th-century Palais St-Pierre, a former Benedictine convent for the daughters of the nobility. The Musée d'Art Contemporain, formerly located in the Palais St-Pierre, is now at 81 quai Charles de Gaulle, north of the Parc Tête d'Or. Housed in a building designed by Renzo Piano, it specializes in works dating from after the mid-20th century.

Food market on quai St-Antoine

La Croix-Rousse

This area north of Presqu'île became the centre of the city's silk-weaving industry in the 15th century. It is traced with covered passages known as *traboules*, used by weavers to transport their finished fabrics. To get a sense of them, enter at No. 6 place des Terreaux and continue till you reach the **Eglise St-Polycarpe**. From here, it is a short walk to the ruins of the **Amphithéâtre des Trois Gaules**, built in AD 19, and the **Maison des Canuts**, with its traditional silk loom.

La Part-Dieu

This modern business area on the east bank of the Rhône has a TGV station, a huge shopping complex and the **Auditorium Maurice-Ravel** for important cultural events.

🏛 **Musée de l'Imprimerie**
13 rue de la Poulaillerie.
Tel 04 78 37 65 98. ◯ Wed–Sun.
◯ public hols. 🖼 🎫

🏛 **Musée des Tissus**
34 rue de la Charité. *Tel* 04 78 38 42
00. ◯ Tue–Sun. ◯ public hols. 🖼

🏛 **Musée Arts Décoratifs**
30 rue de la Charité. *Tel* 04 78 38 42
00. ◯ Tue–Sun. ◯ public hols. 🖼

🏛 **Maison des Canuts**
10–12 rue d'Ivry. *Tel* 04 78 28 62
04. ◯ Mon–Sat. ◯ public hols.
🖼 ♿ 🎫

Environs

Bourgoin-Jallieu, southeast of Lyon, still prints silk for fashion houses, and has a fine textile collection in its museum.

ANTIQUITIES

Included in this wide-ranging collection on the first floor are Egyptian archaeological finds, Etruscan statuettes and 4,000-year-old Cypriot ceramics. Temporary exhibits, with a separate entrance on 16 rue Edouard Herriot, are also on the ground and first floors.

SCULPTURE AND OBJETS D'ART

Occupying the old chapel on the ground floor, the sculpture department includes works from the French Romanesque period and Italian Renaissance, as well as late 19th- and early 20th-century pieces. Represented are Rodin and Bourdelle (whose statues also appear in the courtyard), Maillol, Despiau and Pompon among others. The huge *objets d'art* collection, on the first floor, comprises medieval ivories, bronzes and ceramics, coins, medals, weapons, jewellery, furniture and tapestries.

Odalisque (1841) by James Pradier

PAINTINGS AND DRAWINGS

The museum's superb collection of paintings occupies the first and second floors. It covers all periods and includes works by Spanish and Dutch masters, the French schools of the 17th, 18th and 19th centuries, Impressionist

Fleurs des Champs (1845) by Louis Janmot of the Lyon School

and modern paintings, as well as works by the Lyon School, whose exquisite flower paintings were used as sources of inspiration by the designers of silk fabrics through the ages. On the first floor, the Cabinet d'Arts Graphiques has over 4,000 drawings and etchings by such artists as Delacroix, Poussin, Géricault, Degas and Rodin (by appointment only).

🏛 **Musée des Beaux Arts**
Palais St-Pierre, 20 pl des Terreaux.
Tel 04 72 10 17 40. ◯ Wed–Mon.
◯ public hols. 🖼 🎫 ♿

La Méduse (1923) by Alexeï von Jawlensky

Châtiment de Lycurgue in the Musée Archéologique, St-Romain-en-Gal

Vienne ❺

Isère. 🏠 30,000. 🚂 🚌 🛈 *cours Brillier (04 74 53 80 30).* 🛒 *Sat.* 🎵 *International Jazz Festival (end Jun–mid-Jul).* www.vienne-tourisme.com

No other city in the Rhône Valley offers such a concentration of architectural history as Vienne. Located in a natural basin of land between the river and the hills, this site was recognized for both its strategic and aesthetic advantages by the Romans, who vastly expanded an existing village when they invaded the area in the 1st century BC.

The centre of the Roman town was the **Temple d'Auguste et Livie** (10 BC) on place du Palais, a handsome structure supported by

Vienne's Temple d'Auguste et Livie (1st century BC)

Corinthian columns. Not far away off place de Miremont are the remains of the **Jardin Archéologique de Cybèle**, a temple dedicated to the goddess Cybèle.

The **Théâtre Romain**, at the foot of Mont Pipet off rue du Cirque, was one of the largest amphitheatres in Roman France, capable of seating over 13,000 spectators. It was restored in 1938, and is now used for a variety of events, including an international jazz festival. From the very top seats the view of the town and river is spectacular.

Other interesting Roman vestiges include a fragment of Roman road in the public gardens and, on the southern edge of town, the **Pyramide du Cirque**, a curious structure about 20 m (65 feet) high that was once the centrepiece of the chariot racetrack. The **Musée des Beaux Arts et d'Archéologie** also has a good collection of Gallo-Roman artifacts, as well as 18th-century French faïence. This museum may close when the city's museums are re-grouped so check before visiting.

The **Cathédrale de St-Maurice** is the city's most important medieval monument. It was built between the 12th and 16th century and represents an unusual hybrid of Romanesque and Gothic styles. The cathedral is being restored, so some areas

may be closed. Two of Vienne's earliest Christian churches are the 12th-century **Eglise St-André-le-Bas**, with richly carved capitals in its nave and cloister, and the **Eglise St-Pierre**, parts of which date from the 5th and 6th centuries. The latter houses the **Musée Lapidaire**, a museum of stone-carving, with bas-reliefs and statues from Gallo-Roman buildings.

🏛 **Musée des Beaux Arts et d'Archéologie**
Pl de Miremont. *Tel 04 74 85 50 42.* ⏰ *Apr–Oct: Tue–Sun; Nov–Mar: Tue–Fri & Sat–Sun pm.* 🚫 *1 Jan, 1 May, 1 & 11 Nov, 25 Dec.* 📷

🏛 **Musée Lapidaire**
Pl St-Pierre. *Tel 04 74 85 20 35.* ⏰ *Apr–Oct: Tue–Sun; Nov–Mar: Tue–Fri & Sat–Sun pm.* 🚫 *1 Jan, 1 May, 1 & 11 Nov, 25 Dec.* 📷 ♿ 📷 🎧

Vienne's Cathédrale de St-Maurice

St-Romain-en-Gal ❻

Rhône. 🏠 1,300. 🚂 *Vienne.* 🛈 *Vienne (04 74 53 80 30).*

In 1967, building work in this commercial town directly across the Rhône from Vienne revealed extensive remains of a significant Roman community dating from 100 BC to AD 300. It comprises the remnants of villas, public baths, shops and warehouses. Of particular interest is the House of the Ocean Gods, with a magnificent mosaic floor depicting the bearded Neptune and other ocean images.

Much of what has been unearthed during the ongoing excavations is housed in the **Musée Archéologique** adjoining the ruins. The impressive collection includes household objects, murals and mosaics. The star exhibit is the *Châtiment de Lycurgue*, a mosaic discovered in 1907.

⛫ Musée Archéologique
Tel 04 74 53 74 01. ⬤ Tue–Sun. ⬤ some publ hols. 🗺 🔲 🚻 restr. 🔲
ℹ️ www.musees-gallo-romains.com

St-Étienne ❼

Loire. 🏛 180,000. 🚐 🚌 🚗
ℹ️ 16 av de la Libération (04 77 49 39 00). 🚂 daily. www.tourisme-st-etienne.com

The dour industrial renown brought to this city by coal-mining and armaments is slowly being shaken off, with urban redevelopment well underway and an efficient tramway network. The downtown area around place des Peuple is lively. Nearby, Jean-Michel Wilmotte has overhauled the **Musée d'Art et d'Industrie**, which covers St-Étienne's industrial history, including the development of the revolutionary Jacquard loom, and world-class collections of cycles and ribbon-making machines.

To the north of the city, the **Musée d'Art Moderne** has a collection of 20th-century art, including works by Andy Warhol and Frank Stella.

Detail of the bizarre Palais Idéal du Facteur Cheval at Hauterives

⛫ Musée d'Art et d'Industrie
2 pl Louis Comte. *Tel* 04 77 49 73 00. ⬤ Wed–Mon. ⬤ some public hols. 🗺 🔲 🔲

⛫ Musée d'Art Moderne
La Terrasse. *Tel* 04 77 79 52 52.
⬤ Wed–Mon. ⬤ some public hols & when exhibitions change. 🗺 🔲
🔲 www.mam-st-etienne.fr

Palais Idéal du Facteur Cheval ❽

Hauterives, Drôme. 🚌 🚂 Romans-sur-Isère. *Tel* 04 75 68 81 19.
⬤ daily. ⬤ 1, 15–31 Jan, 25 Dec.
🗺 🔲 🚻 🔲 restricted.
www.facteurcheval.com

At Hauterives, 25 km (15 miles) north of Roman-sur-Isère on the D538, is one of the greatest follies of France, an eccentric "palace" made of stones and evoking Egyptian, Roman, Aztec and Siamese styles of architecture. It was built by a local postman, Ferdinand Cheval, who collected the stones during his daily rounds. His neighbours thought him mad, but the project attracted the admiring attention of Picasso, the surrealist André Breton and others.

The interior of the palace is inscribed with numerous mottos and exhortations by Cheval, the most poignant of which refers to his assiduous efforts to realize his lifelong fantasy: "1879–1912: 10,000 days, 93,000 hours, 33 years of toil".

THE RHÔNE'S BRIDGES

The Rhône has played a crucial role in French history, transporting armies and commercial traffic between the north and south. It has always been dangerous, a challenge to boatmen and builders for centuries. In 1825 the brilliant engineer, Marc Seguin, built the first suspension bridge using steel wire cables. This was followed by another 20 along the length of the Rhône, forever transforming communications between east and west.

Suspension bridge over the Rhône at Tournon-sur-Rhône

The town of Tournon-sur-Rhône

Tournon-sur-Rhône ❾

Ardèche. 🏛 *10,000.* 🚌
ℹ️ *Hôtel de la Tourette (04 75 08 10 23).* 🛒 *Wed & Sat.*
www.ville-tournon.com

Situated at the foot of impressive granite hills, Tournon is a lovely town with gracious tree-lined promenades and an imposing 11th–16th-century **château**. The latter houses a museum of local history, and has fine views of the town and river from its terraces.

The adjacent **Collégiale St-Julien**, with its square belltower and elaborate façade, is an interesting example of the Italian influence on architecture in the region during the 14th century. Inside is a powerful *Résurrection*, painted in 1576 by Capassin, a pupil of Raphael.

On quai Charles de Gaulle, the **Lycée Gabriel-Fauré** is the oldest secondary school in France, dating from 1536. Directly across the Rhône from Tournon, the village of **Tain l'Hermitage** is famous for its steep-climbing vineyards which produce both red and white Hermitage, the finest of all Rhône wines.

Environs

From Tournon's main square, the place Jean Jaurès, a narrow, twisting road signposted the **Route Panoramique** leads via the villages of Plats and St-Romain-de-Lerps to St-Péray. This route offers breathtaking views at every turn, and, at St-Romain, you are rewarded with a superb panorama extending over 13 *départements*.

Valence ❿

Drôme. 🏛 *67,000.* 🚇 🚌
ℹ️ *11 bd Bancel (08 92 70 70 99).* 🛒 *Thu & Sat.* 🎵 *Summer Music (Jul).* **www**.valencetourisme.com

Valence is a large, thriving market town set on the east bank of the Rhône and looking across to the cliffs of the Ardèche. Its principal sight is the Romanesque **Cathédrale St-Apollinaire** on place des Clercs, founded in 1095 and rebuilt in the 17th century.

Alongside the cathedral in the former bishop's palace, the small **Musée des Beaux Arts** contains a collection of late 18th-century chalk drawings of Rome by Hubert Robert.

A short walk from here are two Renaissance mansions. The **Maison des Têtes** at No. 57 Grande Rue was built in 1532 and is embellished with the sculpted heads of ancient Greeks including Aristotle, Homer and Hippocrates. On rue Pérollerie, the **Maison Dupré-Latour** has a finely sculptured porch and staircase.

The **Parc Jouvet**, south of avenue Gambetta, offers 6 ha (14 acres) of pools and gardens, with fine views across the river to the ruined **Château de Crussol**.

🏛 **Musée des Beaux Arts**
4 pl des Ormeaux.
Tel 04 75 79 20 80.
⬤ for restoration until 2013. 🏛

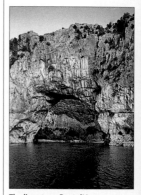

The limestone Pont d'Arc

The Ardèche ⓫

Ardèche. ✈ *Avignon.* 🚇 *Montélimar.* 🚌 *Montélimar, Vallon Pont d'Arc.* ℹ️ *Vallon Pont d'Arc (04 75 88 04 01).* **www**.vallon-pont-darc.com

Over the course of thousands of years, wind and water have endowed this south-central region of France

---

CÔTES DU RHÔNE

Rising in the Swiss Alps and travelling south to the Mediterranean, the mighty Rhône is the common thread that links the many vineyards of the Rhône Valley. A hierarchy of *appellations* divides into three levels of quality: at the base, the regional Côtes du Rhône provides the bulk of the Rhône's wines; next, Côtes du Rhône-Villages comprises a plethora of picturesque villages; and, at the top, there are 13 individual *appellations*. The most famous are the steep slopes of Hermitage and Côte Rôtie in the northern Rhône, and historic Châteauneuf-du-Pape (*see p503*) in the south. The lion's share of production is of red wine, which, based on the syrah grape, is often spicy, full-bodied and robust.

Harvest in a Côtes du Rhône vineyard

A farm near Le Poët Laval, east of Montélimar

Montélimar ⓮

Drôme. 🏘 33,000. 🚉 🚌
🛈 allées Provençales (04 75 01 00
20). 🚃 Wed–Sat. www.montelimar-
tourisme.com

Whether you choose to make
a detour to Montélimar will
largely depend on how sweet
a tooth you might have. The
main curiosity of this market
town is its medieval centre,
chock-full of shops selling
almond-studded nougat. This
splendid confection has been
made here since the start of
the 17th century, when the
almond tree was first introduced into France from Asia.

The **Château des Adhémar**,
a mélange of 12th-, 14th- and
16th-century architecture,
surveys the town from a tall
hill to the east.

♣ **Château des Adhémar**
Tel 04 75 00 62 30. ☐ *Apr–Oct:
daily; Nov–Mar: Wed–Mon (for exhibitions only).* ● *1 Jan, 25 Dec.* 🖼 ♿

Environs
The countryside east of
Montélimar is full of picturesque
medieval villages and scenic
routes. **La Bégude-de-Mazenc**
is a thriving little holiday
centre, with its fortified Old
Town perched on a hilltop.
Further east is **Le Poët Laval**,
a tiny medieval village of
set in the Alpine foothills.
Dieulefit, the capital of this
beautiful region, has several
small hotels and restaurants,
as well as facilities for tennis,
swimming and fishing. To
the south, the fortified village
of **Taulignan** is known for
its truffles.

Grignan ⓯

Drôme. 🏘 1,360. 🚉 🛈 pl du Jeu
de Ballon (04 75 46 56 75). 🚃 Tue.
www.tourisme-paysdegrignan.com

Attractively situated on a
rocky hill surrounded by fields
of lavender, this charming little
village owes its fame to
Madame de Sévigné (see p91),
who wrote many of her celebrated letters while staying at
the **Château de Grignan**.

Built during the 15th and
16th centuries, the château is
one of the finest Renaissance
structures in this part of France.
Its interior contains a good
collection of Louis XII furniture and Aubusson tapestries.

From the château's terrace,
a panoramic view extends as
far as the Vivarais mountains
in the Ardèche. Directly below
the terrace, the **Eglise de St-
Saveur** was built in the 1530s,
and contains the tomb of
Madame de Sévigné, who died
here in 1696 at the age of 69.

♣ **Château de Grignan**
Tel 04 75 91 83 55. ☐ *Apr–Oct:
daily; Nov–Mar: Wed–Mon.*
● *1 Jan, 25 Dec.* 🖼 🖼

Nyons ⓯

Drôme. 🏘 7,000. 🚉 🛈 pl de la
Libération (04 75 26 10 35). 🚃 Thu.
www.paysdenyons.com

As a major centre of olive
production, Nyons is synonymous with olives in France.
All manner of olive products
are on sale at the Thursday
morning market, from soap to
tapenade, the olive paste so
popular in the south.

The **Quartier des Forts** is
Nyons' oldest quarter, a warren
of narrow streets and stepped
alleyways, the most rewarding
of which is the covered rue
des Grands Forts. Spanning the
river Aygues is a graceful 13th-
century bridge; on its town side
are several old mills turned
into shops, where you can
see the enormous presses
once used to extract olive oil.
The **Musée de l'Olivier** further
explains the cultivation of the
olive tree and the myriad local
uses found for its fruit.

There is a fine view of the
area from the belvedere overlooking the town. Sheltered
by mountains, Nyons enjoys
an almost exotic climate, with
all the trees and plants of the
Riviera to be found here.

🏛 **Musée de l'Olivier**
Pl Olivier de Serres. *Tel 04 75 26
12 12.* ☐ *daily.* 🖼 *for guide.* 🖼
🖼 ♿

Environs
From Nyons, the D94 leads
west to **Suze-la-Rousse**, a
pleasant wine-producing village which, during the Middle
Ages, was the most important
town in the area. Today, it is
best known for its "university
of wine", one of the most respected centres of oenology in

The hilltop town of Grignan and its Renaissance château

Olive groves just outside Nyons

the world. It is housed in the 14th-century **Château de Suze-la-Rousse**, the hunting lodge of the princes of Orange. The interior courtyard is a masterpiece of Renaissance architecture and some rooms preserve original paint and stuccowork.

⚜ Château de Suze-la-Rousse
Tel 04 75 04 81 44. ☐ *Apr–Oct: daily; Nov–Mar: Wed–Mon.* ⚫ *1 Jan, 25 Dec.* 🖾 🗋 🗋

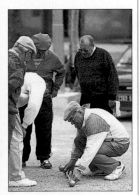

Playing *boules* in Nyons

Briançon ⓰

Hautes Alpes. 🏠 *12,000.* 🚉 🚌
🛈 *1 pl du Temple (04 92 21 08 50).*
🖾 *Wed.* 🎵 *Altitude Jazz Festival (early Feb).* **www**.ot-briancon.fr

Briançon – the highest town in Europe at 1,320 m (4,330 ft) – has been an important stronghold since pre-Roman times, guarding as it does the road to the Col de Montgen-

èvre, one of the oldest and most important passes into Italy. At the beginning of the 18th century, the town was fortified with ramparts and gates – still splendidly intact – by Louis XIV's military architect, Vauban. If driving, park at the Champs de Mars, and enter the pedestrianized Old Town via the **Porte de Pignerol**.

This leads to the **grande rue**, a steep, narrow street with a stream running down the middle, bordered by lovely period houses. The nearby **Eglise de Notre-Dame** dates from 1718, and was also built by Vauban with an eye to defence. To visit Vauban's **citadel**, stop by the tourist office, which organizes guided tours.

Briançon is a major sports centre, with skiing in winter; rafting, cycling and parapente in summer *(see pp660–61)*.

Environs
Just west of Briançon, the **Parc National des Ecrins** is the largest of the French national parks, offering lofty peaks and glaciers, and a magnificent variety of Alpine flowers.

The **Parc Régional du Queyras** is reached from Briançon over the rugged Col de l'Izoard. A wall of 3,000-m (9,850-ft) peaks separates this wild and beautiful national park from neighbouring Italy.

Le Bourg d'Oisans ⓱

Isère. 🏠 *3,000.* 🚉 *to Grenoble.*
🚌 *to Le Bourg d'Oisans.* 🛈 *quai Girard (04 76 80 03 25).* 🖾 *Sat.*
www.bourgdoisans.com

Le Bourg d'Oisans is an ideal base from which to explore the Romanche valley, providing numerous opportunities for sports such as cycling, rock-climbing and skiing, in the nearby resort of **L'Alpe d'Huez**.

Silver and other minerals have been mined here since the Middle Ages, and today the town has a scientific reputation as a centre for geology and mineralogy. Its **Musée des Minéraux et de la Faune des Alpes** is renowned for its collection of crystals and precious stones.

🏛 Musée des Minéraux et de la Faune des Alpes
Pl de l'Eglise. *Tel 04 76 80 27 54.* ☐ *2–6pm Wed–Mon (Jul–Aug: 11am–6pm).* ⚫ *1 Jan, Nov, 25 Dec.* 🖾

LIFE ON HIGH
The Alpine ibex is one of the rarest inhabitants of the French Alps, living high above the tree line for all but the coldest part of the year. Until the creation of the Parc National de la Vanoise *(see p323)*, this sure-footed climber had become almost extinct in France, but after rigorous conservation there are now about 500. Both males and females have horns; in the oldest males they can be almost 1 m (3 ft) long.

An ibex in the Parc National de la Vanoise

GRENOBLE TOWN CENTRE

Ancien Palais du Parlement du
  Dauphiné ③
Collégiale St-André ④
Fort de la Bastille ①
Musée Archéologique
  Grenoble
  Saint-Laurent ⑥
Musée
  Dauphinois ②
Musée de Grenoble ⑤

0 metres   250
0 yards   250

Key to Symbols see back flap

Hôtel Lesdiguières, Grenoble's
imposing former town hall

Grenoble ⑱

Isère. 🏠 165,000. ✈ 🚆 🚌
i 14 rue de la République
(04 76 42 41 41). 🗓 Tue–Sun.
www.grenoble-tourisme.com

Ancient capital of the
Dauphiné region and site of
the 1968 Winter Olympics,
Grenoble is a thriving city,
home to the science-oriented
University of Grenoble, and a
centre of chemical and electronics industries and nuclear
research. It is attractively situated at the confluence of the
Drac and Isère rivers, with the
Vercors and Chartreuse
massifs to the west and north.

A cable car starting at quai
Stéphane-Jay whisks you up
to the 19th-century **Fort de**

la Bastille, from where there
are superb views of the city
and surrounding mountains.
Paths lead down through the
Parc Guy Pape and Jardin
des Dauphins to the **Musée
Dauphinois**, a regional
museum in a 17th-century
convent devoted to local
history, arts and crafts.
Nearby, **Musée Archéologique
Saint-Laurent**, located
in a former church with a
6th-century crypt, exhibits
medieval artifacts and
decorative and religious art.

On the left bank of the Isère,
the focus of life is the pedestrian area around the place
Grenette. Nearby, the place
St-André is the heart of the
medieval city, overlooked by
Grenoble's oldest buildings,
including the 13th-century
Collégiale St-André and the
16th-century **Ancien Palais du
Parlement du Dauphiné**.

The **Musée de Grenoble**
exhibits include works by
Chagall, Picasso and Matisse.
The **Musée de l'Ancien Evêché**
recounts the history of Isère,
and includes a visit to the
4th-century baptistry. On rue
Hébert, the **Musée de la Résistance et de la Déportation** has
documents relating to the
French Resistance. Displays

of contemporary art can be
seen at **Le Magasin** (Centre
National d'Art Contemporain),
a renovated warehouse on
the cours Berriat. In the
Quartier Malherbe, **MC2**
(Maison de la Culture) hosts
concerts, dance and theatre.

🏛 **Musée Dauphinois**
30 rue Maurice Gignoux. **Tel** 04 57
58 89 01. 🗓 Wed–Mon. 🔴 1 Jan,
1 May, 25 Dec.

🏛 **Musée Archéologique
Grenoble Saint-Laurent**
Pl St-Laurent. **Tel** 04 76 44 78 68.
🗓 call for details. **www**.musee-
archeologique-grenoble.fr

Grenoble's gondola cable car

🏛 **Musée de Grenoble**
5 pl de Lavalette. **Tel** 04 76 63 44
44. ⭕ Wed–Mon. ⭕ 1 Jan, 1 May,
25 Dec. 🖼 ♿ 🚻 ⬛ ⬛

🏛 **Musée de l'Ancien Evêché**
2 rue Très Cloîtres. **Tel** 04 76 03 15
25. ⭕ daily. ⭕ Tue am. ♿

🏛 **Musée de la Résistance et
de la Déportation**
14 rue Hébert. **Tel** 04 76 42 38 53.
⭕ daily. ⭕ Tue am, 1 Jan, 1 May,
25 Dec. 🖼 ♿

🏛 **Le Magasin (CNAC)**
155 cours Berriat. **Tel** 04 76 21 95
84. ⭕ Tue–Sun pm only (during
exhibs). 🖼 ♿

🏛 **MC2**
4 rue Paul Claudel. **Tel** 04 76 00 79
00. ⭕ varies – phone to check. 🖼
♿ **www**.mc2grenoble.fr

The Vercors ⑲

Isère & Drôme. ✈ Grenoble. 🚉
Romans-sur-Isère, St-Marcellin, Grenoble. 🚌 Pont-en-Royans, Romans-
sur-Isère. 🛈 Pont-en-Royans (04 76
36 09 10). **www**.parc-du-vercors.fr

To the south and west of
Grenoble, the Vercors is one
of the most magnificent
regional parks in France – a
wilderness of pine forests,
mountains, waterfalls, caves
and deep, narrow gorges.

The D531 out of Grenoble
passes through **Villard-de-
Lans** – a good base for
excursions – and continues
west to the dark **Gorges de la
Bournes**. About 8 km (5 miles)
further west, the hamlet of
Pont-en-Royans is sited on a
limestone gorge, its stone
houses built into the rocks
overlooking the river Bourne.

South of Pont-en-Royans
along the D76, the **Route de
Combe-Laval** snakes along a
sheer cliff above the roaring
river. The **Grands Goulets**,
6.5 km (4 miles) to the east,
is a spectacularly deep,
narrow gorge overlooked by
sheer cliffs that virtually shut
out the sky above. The best-
known mountain in the park
is the **Mont Aiguille**, a soaring
outcrop of 2,086 m (6,844 ft).

The Vercors was a key base
for the French Resistance
during World War II. In July
1944 the Germans launched
an aerial attack on the region,
flattening several of its villages.
There are Resistance museums
at Vassieux and Grenoble.

Cows grazing in the Chartreuse

The Chartreuse ⑳

Isère & Savoie. ✈ Grenoble,
Chambéry. 🚉 Grenoble, Voiron.
🚌 St-Pierre-de-Chartreuse. 🛈 St-
Pierre-de-Chartreuse (04 76 88 64 00).

From Grenoble, the D512
leads north towards Chambéry
into the Chartreuse, a majestic
region of mountains and
forests where hydroelectricity
was invented in the late 19th
century. The **Monastère de la
Grande Chartreuse** is the main
local landmark, situated just
west of St-Pierre-de-Chartreuse
off the D520-B.

Founded by St Bruno in
1084, the monastery owes its
fame to the sticky green and
yellow Chartreuse liqueurs first
produced by the monks in
1605. The recipe, based on
a secret herbal elixir of 130
ingredients, is now produced
in the nearby town of Voiron.

The monastery itself is
inhabited by about 40 monks
who live in silence and seclusion. It is not open to visitors,
but there is a museum at the
entrance, the **Musée de la
Correrie**, which faithfully
depicts the daily routine of
the Carthusian monks.

🏛 **Musée de la Correrie**
St-Pierre-de-Chartreuse. **Tel** 04 76
88 60 45. ⭕ Apr–Nov: daily. 🖼

A farm in the pine-clad mountains of the Chartreuse

Chambéry ㉑

Savoie. 🏠 61,000. 🚆 🚌 🚗
🛈 5 bis pl Palais de Justice
(04 79 33 42 47). 🛒 Tue, Sat.
www.chambery-tourisme.com

Once the capital of Savoy,
this dignified city has aristocratic airs and a distinctly
Italianate feel. Its best-loved
monument is the splendidly
extravagant **Fontaine des
Eléphants** on rue de Boigne.
It was erected in 1838 to
honour the Comte de Boigne,
a native son who left to his
home town some of the
fortune he amassed in India.

The **Château des Ducs de
Savoie**, at the opposite end of
rue de Boigne, was built in the
14th century and is now mostly
occupied by the Préfecture.
Only parts of the building can
be visited, such as the late
Gothic Ste-Chapelle.

On the southeast edge of
town is the 17th-century
country house, **Les
Charmettes**, where
the philosopher
Rousseau lived with
his mistress Madame
de Warens. It is
worth a visit for its
gardens and museum
of memorabilia.

♣ **Les Charmettes**
892 chemin des
Charmettes. **Tel** 04 79
33 39 44. ⬤ Wed–Mon.
⬤ public hols. 🎫 📷

Roman statue in
the Temple of Diana

The Lac du Bourget at Aix-les-Bains

Aix-les-Bains ㉒

Savoie. 🏠 26,000. 🚆 🚌 🛈 pl
Maurice Mollard (04 79 88 68 00).
🛒 Wed & Sat am. 🎭 Festival
Musilac (Jul). www.aixlesbains.com

The great Romantic poet
Lamartine rhapsodized over
the beauty of Lac du Bourget,
site of the gracious spa
town of Aix-les-Bains.
The heart of the town
is the 19th-century
Thermes Nationaux,
thermal baths which
were first enjoyed by
the Romans over 2,000
years ago – in the base-
ment are the remains
of the original Roman
baths. The ruins are
closed to visitors due
to safety reasons,
but the Thermes

Nationaux spa is open all
year. Opposite the baths, the
2nd-century AD **Temple of
Diana** contains a collection
of Gallo-Roman artifacts.
The nearby **Musée Faure** has
some stunning Impressionist
paintings by Degas and
Sisley, Rodin sculptures and
Lamartine memorabilia.

♨ **Thermes Nationaux**
Pl Maurice Mollard. **Tel** 04 79 35 38
50. ⬤ Mon–Sat. 🎫 for treatment.
www.thermaix.com

🏛 **Musée Faure**
Villa des Chimères, 10 bd des Côtes.
Tel 04 79 61 06 57. ⬤ Wed–Mon
(mid-Nov–Feb: Wed–Sun). ⬤ 18
Dec–2 Jan, public hols. 🎫 ♿

Environs
Boats leave from Aix's Grand
Port and sail across Lac du
Bourget to the **Abbaye
d'Hautecombe**, a Benedictine
abbey containing the mausoleum of the Savoyard dynasty.

The small town of **Le Revard**,
just east of Aix on the D913,
has spectacular views of the
lake and Mont Blanc.

Annecy ㉓

Haute Savoie. 🏠 51,000. ✈ 🚌
🚆 🛈 1 rue Jean Jaurès (04 50 45
00 33). 🛒 Tue, Fri–Sun. 🎭 Fête du
Lac (firework display; 1st Sat Aug).
www.lac-annecy.com

Annecy is one of the most
charming towns in the Alps,
set at the northern tip of Lac

Annecy's 12th-century Palais de l'Isle, with the Thiou canal in the foreground

For hotels and restaurants in this region see pp577–80 and pp632–4

Cycling along the shores of Lac Léman (Lake Geneva)

d'Annecy and surrounded by snow-capped mountains. Its small medieval quarter is laced with canals, flower-covered bridges and arcaded streets. Strolling around is the main attraction here, though there are a couple of specific sights worth having a look at more closely: the formidable **Palais de l'Isle**, a 12th-century prison in the middle of the Thiou canal; and the turreted **Château d'Annecy**, set high on a hill above the town with impressive views of Vieil Annecy and the crystal-clear lake beyond.

The best spot for swimming and watersports is at the eastern end of the avenue d'Albigny near the Imperial Palace hotel, while boat trips leave from quai Napoléon III.

Environs

One of the best ways to enjoy the area's spectacular scenery is to take a boat from Annecy to **Talloires**, a tiny lakeside village celebrated for its hotels and restaurants. Facing Talloires across the lake is the 15th-century **Château de Duingt** (not open to visitors).

On the west bank of the lake, the Semnoz mountain and its summit, the **Crêt de Châtillon**, offer superb views of Mont Blanc and the Alps (*see pp322–3*).

Lac Léman ㉔

Haute Savoie & Switzerland. ⚑ Geneva. 🚊 🚌 Geneva, Thonon-les-Bains, Évian-les-Bains. ℹ Thonon-les-Bains (04 50 71 55 55). **www**.thononlesbains.com

The stirring scenery and gentle climate of the French shore of Lake Geneva (Lac Léman to the French) has made it a popular and fashionable resort area since the first spa buildings were erected at Évian-les-Bains in 1839.

Yvoire is a fine place to begin a visit to the area. This medieval port is guarded by a 14th-century castle, and its houses are bedecked with colourful flower boxes.

Further east along Lac Léman is **Thonon-les-Bains**, a prosperous, well-manicured little spa town perched on a cliff overlooking the lake. A funicular takes you down to Rives, the small harbour at the foot of the cliffs, where sailboats can be rented and excursion boats to the Swiss cities of Geneva and Lausanne call in. Just outside the town is the 15th-century **Château de Ripaille**, made famous by its one-time resident, Duke Amadeus VIII, who later became antipope (Felix V).

Though it has been modernized and acquired an international reputation for its eponymous spring water, **Évian-les-Bains** still exudes a polite *vie en rose* charm. The tree-lined lakefront promenade teems with leisurely strollers, while more energetic types can avail themselves of all kinds of sporting facilities including tennis, golf, riding, sailing and skiing in the winter. State-of-the-art spa treatments are available, and the exotic domed casino is busy at night, offering blackjack, roulette and baccarat among other games.

From Évian there are daily ferries across Lake Geneva to Lausanne in Switzerland, as well as coach excursions into the surrounding mountains.

Hôtel Royal in Évian-les-Bains (*see p578*)

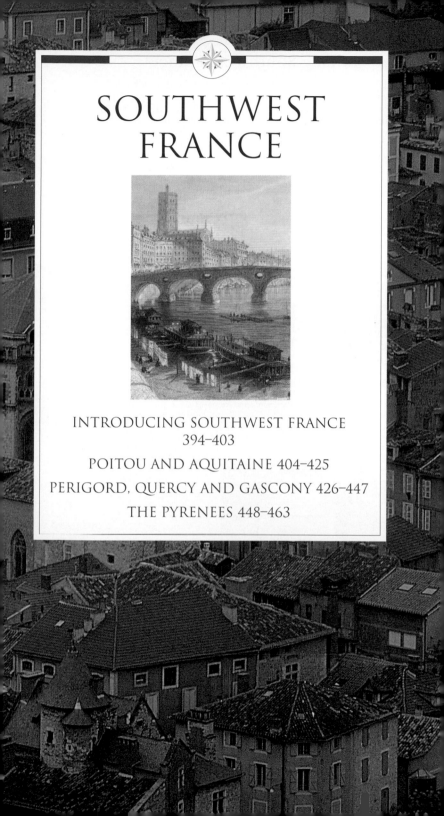

SOUTHWEST
FRANCE

Introducing Southwest France

The southwest is farming France, a green and peaceful land nurturing crops from sunflowers to *foie gras*. Other key country products include Landes forest timber, Bordeaux wines and Cognac. Major modern industries, including aerospace, are focused on the two chief cities, Bordeaux and Toulouse. Visitors are mainly drawn to the wide Atlantic beaches, the ski slopes of the Pyrenees and the rural calm of the Dordogne. The major sights of this favoured region are shown here and include some of France's most celebrated Romanesque buildings.

La Rochelle

Roman Ruins, Saintes

Grand Théâtre, Bor

La Rochelle's harbour *is today a haven for pleasure yachts as well as an important commercial port (see p416). Tour de la Chaîne and Tour St-Nicolas protect the entrance of the old port. The town's historic centre is filled with cobbled streets lined by merchants' houses.*

Bordeaux *is a town of grand buildings and monuments, including its theatre. The Monument aux Girondins, with its magnificent bronze statues and fountains, stands at the 18th-century Esplanade des Quinconces (see pp420–22).*

POITOU AND AQUITAINE
(See pp404–25)

THE PYRENEES
(See pp448–63)

0 kilometres   50

0 miles   50

Notre-Dame-la-Grande *is the queen among Poitiers' churches (see pp412–13) It has fine stained-glass windows and a splendid Romanesque façade, richly decorated in the Poitevin style.*

PERIGORD, QUERCY
AND GASCONY
(See pp426–47)

Rocamadour *is both a place of pilgrimage and a tourist sight, its chapels and shrines clinging to the edge of the rocky hillside (see pp436–7). Among its many venerated features is the statue of the Black Virgin and Child.*

Lascaux

Rocamadour

Moissac

Albi Cathedral

St-Sernin, Toulouse

Cirque de Gavarnie

Moissac Abbey *is the pre-eminent medieval monastery in southwest France (see pp442–3). Its tympanum, representing the Apocalypse, and the cloister capitals are outstanding examples of Romanesque sculpture.*

Notre-Dame-la-
Grande, Poitiers

The Flavours of Southwest France

"Great cooking and great wines make a paradise on earth," said Henri IV of his own region, Gascony. The southwest does indeed fulfil the requirements of the most demanding gourmet. The Atlantic coast supplies fine seafood; Bordeaux produces some of France's best wines to complement its rich cooking; geese and ducks provide the fat that is key to local cuisine; and regional produce includes delicacies such as *foie gras*, truffles and wild mushrooms. The Pyrenees offer beef and lamb grazed on mountain pastures, cheese and *charcuterie*, and the Basque country adds the spicy notes of red peppers and fine chocolate.

Espelette peppers

Walnuts, one of the southwest's most famous products

POITOU AND AQUITAINE

The coast is famous for its seafood, and is the most important oyster-producing region of France – the oysters of Marennes-Oleron are of especially high quality. The species of blue algae on which they feed give them a distinctive green colouring. Oysters are usually served simply with lemon or shallot

vinegar, but in Bordeaux they like to eat them with little sausages. Mussels are also raised here, and the sea yields a variety of fish. Eels, lamprey and sturgeon are caught in the Gironde estuary.

Poitou-Charentes is one of France's main goat-rearing areas, producing cheeses such as *chabichou de Poitou*, a small, soft, cylindrical cheese of distinct flavour.

PERIGORD, QUERCY AND GASCONY

High-quality ducks, geese and poultry form the basis of the cuisine of this region, and their fat is a key ingredient of many dishes from simple *pommes sarladaises* (potatoes cooked in goose fat) to *confit*, where entire duck legs are preserved in their own fat. The ultimate

Wild boar ham   Chorizo   Garlic saussicon   Truffle saussicon   Wild boar saussicon   Bayonne ham   Bilberry saussicon

Selection of traditional southwestern *charcuterie*

REGIONAL DISHES AND SPECIALITIES

Duck is one of the essential ingredients of southwestern cooking, and is served in a variety of ways. The *magret* is the breast – the best of all coming from a duck that has been bred for *foie gras*. Usually served pink *(rose)*, it may be served with a variety of sauces but is most perfectly complemented by the smoky flavour of local cèpe mushrooms in season. Duck

Pink garlic

confit is usually made with the legs, but gizzards are also preserved in this way. *Foie gras* is the most expensive (and controversial) product, resulting from the process of *gavage*, when the duck or goose is force-fed maize to enlarge and enrich its liver. *Foie gras* can be eaten freshly cooked, served with sauce or fruit, or preserved and served with toast or brioche, ideally accompanied by a sweet white wine such as Sauternes.

Omelette aux truffes *For this luxurious omelette the filling is local black truffles, with more sliced over the top.*

Fattened Toulouse geese, the source of *foie gras*

southwestern dish has to be *cassoulet*, a stew of duck or goose, sausages, pork and white beans topped with a crust of breadcrumbs; it arouses fierce competition among the dedicated chefs of the region.

Luxury ingredients enhance these basics: walnut oil is added to salads, and slivers of expensive truffles perfume sauces or omelettes. Wild mushrooms are eagerly sought in season, and are most delicious cooked simply with garlic, shallots and parsley. The region is one of the main producers of garlic, which appears studded into meat or served as whole baked heads. The finest fruits include *reines-claudes* (greengages) and the celebrated plums of Agen, which are dried as prunes or added to dishes of rabbit or hare.

THE PYRENEES

From the mountains pastures come beef and lamb of high quality, including Barèges mutton, as well as river trout, and an array of excellent *charcuterie*. Strong cheeses

Fishermen opening oysters at a local maritime festival

of goat's or ewe's milk are sometimes served with jam made from the black cherries of Itxassou. One of the most popular dishes is *garbure*, a hearty stew of cabbage, bacon and confit of duck or goose.

Basque cuisine has its own distinct identity, with the red Espelette pepper adding a touch of spice to chorizo, *piperade* or chipirones (baby squid cooked in their own ink). Succulent Bayonne ham is made from pigs that forage for acorns and chestnuts. Bayonne was also home to the first chocolatiers in France, 17th-century Jewish refugees from the Inquisition, and the town still makes top-quality dark, bitter chocolate.

ON THE MENU

Cagouilles à la charentaise Snails with sausage meat, herbs and wine.

Entrecôte à la bordelaise Steak in sauce of red wine, shallots and bone marrow.

Farçi poitevin Cabbage stuffed with bacon, pork and sorrel.

Gasconnade Leg of lamb with garlic and anchovy.

Mouclade Mussels in curry sauce, from the spice port of La Rochelle.

Salade landaise Salad of *foie gras*, gizzards and *confit*.

Ttoro Basque mixed fish and shellfish stew with potatoes, tomatoes and onions.

Cassoulet *This is a stew of white beans cooked with a variety of sausages and cuts of meat, such as pork or duck.*

Piperade *Eggs are added to a stew of peppers, onions, tomatoes and garlic, with Bayonne ham laid on top.*

Croustade *Thin pastry is layered with melted butter, and apples, perfumed with Armagnac and vanilla.*

France's Wine Regions: Bordeaux

Bordeaux is the world's largest fine wine region, and, for red wines, certainly the most familiar outside France. Following Henry II's marriage to Eleanor of Aquitaine, three centuries of courtly commerce with England ensured that claret was served at the finest foreign tables. In the 19th century, canny merchants capitalized on this fame and brought fantastic financial prosperity to the region, and with it, the famous 1855 Classification of the Médoc, a league table of châteaux that is still very much in force today.

Barrel-making

LOCATOR MAP

■ Bordeaux wine region

Picking red Merlot grapes at Château Palmer

Cos d'Estournel, *like all the châteaux included in the 1855 league of crus classés ("classed growths"), proudly proclaims the fact on its label.*

WINE REGIONS

The great wine-producing areas of Bordeaux straddle two great rivers; the land between the rivers ("Entre-Deux-Mers") produces lesser, mainly white wines. The rivers, and the river port of Bordeaux itself, have been crucial to the trade in Bordeaux wines; some of the prettiest châteaux line the river banks, enabling easy transportation.

Lac d'

KEY FACTS ABOUT BORDEAUX WINES

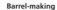 **Location and Climate**
Climatic conditions may vary not only from one year to another, but also within the region itself. The soils tend to be gravelly in the Médoc and Graves, and clayey on the right bank.

Grape Varieties
The five main red grape varieties are **Cabernet Franc**, **Cabernet Sauvignon**, **Merlot, Petit Verdot** and **Malbec**. Cabernet Sauvignon is the dominant grape on the west side of the Gironde, Merlot to the east. Most Bordeaux reds are, however, a blend of grapes. **Sauvignon Blanc** and **Sémillon** are grown and often blended for both dry and sweet whites.

 Good Producers
(reds) Latour, Margaux, Haut-Brion, Cos d'Estournel, Léoville Las Cases, Léoville Barton, Lascombes, Pichon Longueville, Pichon Lalande, Lynch-Bages, Palmer, Rausan-Ségla, Duhart Milon, d'Angludet, Léoville Poyferré, Branaire Ducru, Ducru Beaucaillou, Malescot St-Exupéry, Cantemerle, Phélan-Ségur, Chasse-Spleen, Poujeaux, Domaine de Chevalier, Pape Clément, Cheval Blanc, Canon, Pavie, l'Angelus, Troplong Mondot, La Conseillante, Lafleur, Trotanoy.

 Good Vintages
(reds) 2009, 2006, 2005, 2003, 2000, 1998, 1996.

Haut-Brion, *in the top division of Bordeaux's Classification, was and still is the single Graves château in this league of Médoc properties.*

Arcachon

Cap Ferret

Lac de Ca et de Sang

The famous legend *that guarantees château-bottling originated in Bordeaux, as a check to unscrupulous merchants.*

One of many wine-producing properties in the St-Emilion district

Entre-Deux-Mers, *largely undistinguished, has some good producers.*

St-Emilion *has its own crus classés league: Cheval Blanc shares top ranking.*

Verdon--Mer

Gironde

St-Christoly-Médoc

parre-Médoc   St-Estèphe

St-Seurin-de-Cadourne   Montendre

La Livenne

A10   N10

Pauillac

St-Julien-Beychevelle

Laurent-et-Benon   Blaye

Cussac-Fort-Médoc   Berson

Listrac-Médoc   Moulis-en-Médoc   Pugnac

Margaux   Bourg

stelnau-de-Médoc   Macau   Ambès

St-André-de-Cubzac

La Dordogne

D674

L'Isle   L'Isle   D6089

Pomerol

Libourne

St-Emilion

Castillon-la-Bataille

D936   Ste-Foy-la-Grande

D125

Blanquefort

25   Ambarès-et-Lagrave

St-Médard-en-Jalles   Vayres

Branne

Pujols

BORDEAUX

Martignas-sur-Jalle

St-Jean-d'Illac

L'Engranne

D106   Pessac

La Garonne

Créon

sin
rcachon   Cestas   Léognan   Targon

Castres-Gironde   Langoiran

66   A63

Podensac   Cadillac

Cérons   Loupiac

Barsac

Preignac   Ste-Croix-du-Mont

Landiras   St-Macaire   La Réole

Langon

Sauternes   A62

Le Dropt

Le Ciron

L'Eyre   Le Ballion

| 0 kilometres | 15 |
| 0 miles | 15 |

KEY

☐ Médoc	☐ Graves	☐ Sauternes
☐ Blaye	☐ Pessac-Léognan	☐ Libournais District
☐ Bourg	☐ Cérons	☐ Pomerol
☐ Entre-Deux-Mers	☐ Barsac	☐ St-Emilion

The Road to Compostela

Scallop symbol

Throughout the Middle Ages millions of Christians visited Santiago de Compostela in Spain to pay homage at the shrine of St James (Santiago). They travelled across France staying in monasteries or simple shelters and would return with a scallop shell, the symbol of St James, as a souvenir. Most pilgrims went in hope of redemption and were often on the road for years. In 1140, a monk called Picaud wrote one of the world's first travel guides about the pilgrimage. Today, travellers can follow the same routes, passing through ancient towns and villages with their magnificent shrines and churches.

Foreign pilgrims joined at ports such as St Malo.

The original cathedral *of Santiago de Compostela was built in 813 by Alfonso II over the tomb of St James. In 1075 construction started on the grandiose Romanesque church seen today which has, among other later additions, a resplendent 17th–18th-century Baroque façade.*

The routes converged on Santiago de Compostela.

Most pilgrims crossed the Pyrenees at Roncesvalles.

James the Greater, *an apostle, came to Spain to spread the Gospel, according to legend. On his return to Judaea, he was martyred by Herod. His remains were taken to Spain by boat and lay hidden for 800 years.*

The powerful Cluny monastery *in Burgundy (see pp48–9), and its affiliated monasteries, played an important role in promoting the pilgrimage. They built shelters and set up churches and shrines housing precious relics, to encourage the pilgrims on their way.*

THE PILGRIMS' WAY

Paris, Vézelay *(see pp336–7)*, Le Puy *(see p364)* and Arles are the rallying points for the four "official" routes across France. They cross the Pyrenees at Roncesvalles and Somport, and merge at Puente la Reina to form one route, culminating at the shrine on the Galician coast.

Conques purloined relics to boost its prestige.

Le Puy was a main rally- ing point for pilgrims.

WHAT TO SEE TODAY

Huge Romanesque churches, including Ste-Madeleine at Vézelay *(see p336)*, Ste-Foy at Conques *(pp368–9)* and St-Sernin at Toulouse *(p447)*, along with many small chapels, were built to accommodate large numbers of pilgrims.

Basilique Ste-Madeleine, Vézelay

The first recorded pilgrim *was the bishop of Le Puy in 951. But pilgrims have probably been coming to Santiago since 814, soon after the saint's tomb was found.*

The reliquary *of Ste-Foy, at Conques, is in one of many elaborate shrines on the way which drew crowds of pilgrims. A saint's relics were thought to have miraculous powers.*

The name *Santiago de Compostela is believed to originate from the Latin* Campus stellac *(field of stars). Legend has it that strange stars were seen hovering over a field in 814 and on 25 July, now the feast of Santiago, the saint's remains were found. Subsequent evidence showed that St James's remains were never in Compostela after all.*

Caves of the Southwest

Southwest France is well-known for its spectacular rock formations, created by the slow accumulation of dissolved mineral deposits. Caves and rock shelters exist throughout limestone country in France. But in the foothills of the Pyrenees and the Dordogne they also have something else to offer the visitor: a collection of extraordinary rock paintings, some dating back to the last Ice Age. These art forms were created when prehistoric peoples evolved and began engraving, painting and carving. This unique artistic tradition lasted for more than 25,000 years, reaching its zenith around 17,000 years ago. Some very fine examples of cave painting are still visible today.

Ancient cave paintings at Lascaux

CAVES OF THE DORDOGNE

There are many different cave systems to visit in or near the Dordogne valley. The entire Périgord region contains one of the densest concentrations of prehistoric sites anywhere in the world. In an uncertain climate, its rivers flanked by caves and rock shelters proved very attractive to prehistoric man.

CAVE FORMATION

Limestone is laid down in layers containing fissures that allow water to penetrate beneath the surface. Over thousands of years, the water slowly dissolves the rock, first forming potholes and then larger caverns. Stalactites develop where water drips from the cave roof; stalagmites grow upwards from the floor.

Grotte du Grand Roc in the Vézère valley, Périgord

Fissure | Limestone layers

Impermeable rock

1 Water percolates through fissures, slowly dissolving the surrounding rock.

Pothole

Fallen rocks | Chamber

2 The water produces potholes and loosens surrounding rocks, which gradually fall away.

Cavern formed by rockfall

Stalactites | Stalagmites

3 Dripping water containing dissolved limestone forms stalactites and stalagmites.

GOUFFRE DE PADIRAC

Chasm entrance · Lifts · Permeable limestone · Galerie de la Fontaine · Le Grand Cristal · Salle du Grand Dôme

Impermeable rock · Salle de la Fontaine · Rivière Plane (Smooth River) · Lac de la Pluie (Rain Lake) · Pas du Crocodile (Crocodile Track) · Lac des Grands Gours (Great Barrier Lake)

Underground river and chambers of the Gouffre de Padirac

Prehistoric caves at Les Eyzies

VISITING THE CAVES

Cougnac contains chasms ("gouffres") and galleries and its prehistoric paintings include human figures. Around **Les Eyzies** *(see pp434–5)* are the caves of **Les Combarelles**, and **Font de Gaume**, which have beautiful prehistoric paintings, drawings and engravings, as does **Rouffignac** in its network of caves. **Grand Roc** has chambers containing a profusion of stalactites and stalagmites. Northeast of Les Eyzies is the rock shelter of **L'Abri du Cap Blanc**, with its rare frieze of horses and bison dating from around 14,000 years ago.

On the south bank of the Dordogne, an underground river and lake with extraordinary rock formations can be seen at **Lacave**. The gigantic chasm and caverns at **Padirac** *(p438)* are even more spectacular. The caves at **Lascaux** with the finest prehistoric paintings have been closed but the exceptional replica at **Lascaux II** *(p434)* is well worth seeing. Further south, **Pech-Merle's** caverns *(p438)* have impressive rock formations. **Niaux**, in the foothills of the Pyrenees, can also be visited.

THE STORY OF CAVE ART

The first prehistoric cave paintings in Europe were discovered in northwest Spain in 1879. Since then, over 200 decorated caves and rock shelters have been found in Spain and France, mainly in the Dordogne region. A wide range of clues, from stone lamps to miraculously preserved footprints, has helped prehistorians to work out the techniques the cave artists used. But their motives are still not clear. Nearly all the paintings are of animals, with few humans, and many of them are in inaccessible underground chambers. The paintings undoubtedly had a symbolic or magical significance; a new theory suggests they were the work of shamans.

The techniques *used by Ice Age artists, who worked by lamplight, included cutting outlines into soft rock, using natural contours as part of the design. Black lines and shading were produced by charcoal, while colour washes were applied with mineral pigments such as kaolin and haematite. Hand silhouettes were made by sucking up diluted pigment and blowing it through a plant stem to form a fine spray. When the hand was removed from the rock, its eerie shape was left behind.*

Decorated stone lamp discovered in Lascaux cave

Kaolin

Charcoal

Haematite

The Great Bull from the Hall of Bulls frieze at Lascaux

POITOU AND AQUITAINE

DEUX-SEVRES · VIENNE · CHARENTE-MARITIME CHARENTE · GIRONDE · LANDES

*T*his vast area of southwest France spans a quarter of the country's windswept Atlantic coastline, a great expanse of fine sandy beaches. The region stretches from the marshes of the Marais Poitevin to the great pine forests of the Landes. Central to it is the celebrated wine region of Bordeaux and its great châteaux.

The turbulent history of Poitou and Aquitaine, fought over for centuries, has left a rich architectural and cultural heritage. The great arch and amphitheatre at Saintes bear witness to Roman influence in the area. In the Middle Ages, the pilgrimage route to Santiago de Compostela *(see pp400–1)* created an impressive legacy of Romanesque churches, such as those at Poitiers and Parthenay, as well as tiny chapels and glowing frescoes. The Hundred Years' War *(see pp52–3)* caused great upheaval but also resulted in the construction of mighty defence keeps by the English Plantagenet kings. As a result of the Wars of Religion *(see pp54–5)*, many towns, churches and châteaux were destroyed and had to be rebuilt.

Present-day Poitiers is a big, thriving commercial centre. To the west are the historic ports of La Rochelle and Rochefort. Further south, the wine-producing district of Bordeaux combines with Cognac, famous for its brandy, to supply an important part of the region's income. The city of Bordeaux is as prosperous today as in Roman times, combining a lively cultural scene with elegant 18th-century architecture. Its wines complement the region's cuisine: lampreys, mussels and oysters from the coast; and salty lamb and goat's cheeses from the inland pastures.

Shuttered houses in St-Martin-de-Ré, on Ile de Ré, off the coast of La Rochelle

◁ The seaside resort of Arcachon by the sandy dunes of the Bassin d'Arcachon

Exploring Poitou and Aquitaine

Blessed with a seemingly endless Atlantic coastline,
abundant navigable waterways, excellent ports and the
finest wine and brandy in the world, the region is ideal
for a relaxing holiday. Today most summer visitors head
straight for the beaches with their thundering waves, but
there is also a lush countryside inland with a lot to offer.
Fine medieval architecture can be seen along the pilgrim's
route to Santiago de Compostela *(see pp400–1)*, and
châteaux of all shapes and sizes characterize the wine
districts around Bordeaux. The only modern
city of major importance in the region,
Bordeaux is worth a visit for its
elegant 18th-century architecture
as well as for its rich cultural
life. The vast man-made
forest of Les Landes also adds
to this greatly undervalued
corner of France.

Beachlife in Bassin d'Arcachon on the Côte d'Argent

GETTING AROUND

The region's main motorway is the A10
connecting Paris and Poitiers with
Bordeaux and points east, such as
Toulouse, west to Rochefort and south
to Bayonne and Spain. This road carries
most of the area's heavy traffic, relieving
the excellent smaller roads. Bordeaux
can be reached by TGV direct from
Lille (Eurostar interchange), and the
Paris–Poitiers–Angoulême–Bordeaux
TGV line has halved rail travel times
(Paris–Bordeaux 3¼ hrs). Bordeaux,
Poitiers and La Rochelle have
international airports (direct flights
to UK), and Bordeaux also has coach
services to most European capitals.
Poitiers has buses to nearby towns.

Saumur

Argenton-
Château ⛪ THOU
Mauléon
N149   Ch
Bressuire   Airva
                                    D9
Moncoutant
                          PARTHENAY
Secondigny

Champdeniers   Sai
                              Mai
                              l'Éc
            D148
        ③ Coulon   NIORT ④
Marans MARAIS POITEVIN Celle
Île de Ré   N11   A10   B
Saint-Martin-de-Ré   ⛪ MEL
LA ROCHELLE ⑯   Surgères   D5
            Île
Saint-Denis- d'Aix POITOU-
d'Oléron   ROCHEFORT   ⑮ AUL
ÎLE-D'OLÉRON ⑱ ⑰
                          Saint-Jean
BROUAGE ⑲   d'Angély
Saint-Trojan   Marennes
La Tremblade Seudre SAINTES
Pointe   ㉒
de la Coubre Saujon N141 COGN
    ROYAN ⑳   Gémozac   ㉓
Pointe de Grave   Pons   Jar
Soulac-sur-Mer   ㉑
            TALMONT-
Montalivet- SUR-GIRONDE Barbezie
les-Bains D1215   D137
        Lesparre-   Mirambeau
Hourtin-Plage Médoc
        Hourtin PAUILLAC A10 N10
Lac d'Hourtin- ㉘
Carcans   Saint-Sav
                Blaye
        D101 Saint-André-
    Lacanau- de-Cubzac Cou
    Océan Lacanau D1215
        Blanquefort Libourne
    Mérignac   Cenon S
            ㉖ ÉMI
        D106 BORDEAUX
    Arès   Targon
BASSIN Parc Ornithologique
D'ARCACHON ㉚ du Teich A62 Ca
Arcachon D1010
    Gujan-   Langon
Dune du Pilat Mestras A63
Étang de Cazaux   Belin-Béliet D3
et Sanguinet Sanguinet
    Biscarrosse Moustey Saint
                Symphori
        AQUITAIN
    Labouheyre   Luxey
            Marqueze
Mimizan- Mimizan   A65
Plage   Sabres LANDES
    D38   Roqu
    Lévignacq   D932
Saint-Girons-Plage Morcenx N134
Étang de Léon Léon   ㉜ MONT-D
Vieux-Boucau- Tartas Midou MARSAN
les-Bains N10 Adour N124
    Soustons N124 Mugron Aire-sur-
Capbreton   Hagetmau l'Adour
    ㉝ DAX
Bayonne Pau
Biarritz

idun
Tours
ntour
Mirebeau
OSCOPE **7**
IERS **6**
8 NOUAILLÉ-MAUPERTUIS
Vivonne
Couhé
CHARROUX **14**
ARENTES
13 CONFOLENS
Saint-Claud
ANGOULÊME
Puymoyen   Marthon
Montmoreau
Verteillac
AUBETERRE-SUR-DRONNE
int-Aulaye
stérol
Sainte-Foy-la-Grande
Duras   Eymet
mande

Dangé
Châtellerault
Bonneuil-Matours **10**
CHAUVIGNY
9   **11** SAINT-SAVIN
12 MONTMORILLON
Lussac-les-Châteaux
Portes d'Enfer
L'Isle-Jourdain
Limoges
Champagne-Mouton
Chabanais
Chasseneuil
La Rochefoucauld
Nontron

One of the Ile de Ré's picturesque harbours

SIGHTS AT A GLANCE

Abbaye de Nouaillé-Maupertuis **8**
Angles-sur-l'Anglin **10**
Angoulême **24**
Aubeterre-sur-Dronne **25**
Aulnay **15**
Bassin d'Arcachon **30**
Bordeaux **26**
Brouage **19**
Charroux **14**
Chauvigny **9**
Cognac **23**
Confolens **13**
Dax **33**
Futuroscope **7**
Île d'Oléron **18**
La Côte d'Argent **29**

La Rochelle **16**
Les Landes **31**
Marais Poitevin **3**
Melle **5**
Mont-de-Marsan **32**
Montmorillon **12**
Niort **4**
Parthenay **2**
Pauillac **28**
Poitiers **6**
Rochefort **17**
Royan **20**
Saintes **22**
St-Émilion **27**
St-Savin **11**
Talmont-sur-Gironde **21**
Thouars **1**

0 kilometres   25
0 miles   25

KEY

Motorway
Major road
Secondary road
Minor road
Scenic route
Main railway
Minor railway
Regional border

Boats moored at Coulon in the Marais Poitevin

Rose window of St-Médard, Thouars

Thouars ❶

Deux-Sèvres. 🏛 *10,500.* �))) 🚍
🛈 *3 bis bd Pierre Curie (05 49 66
17 65).* 🛒 *Tue & Fri.*
www.tourisme-pays-thouarsais.fr

Thouars, on a rocky outcrop
surrounded by the river
Thouet, is on the border between Anjou and Poitou. There
are as many roofs of northern
slate as of southern red tiles.

In the centre stands **Eglise
St-Médard**. Its Romanesque
façade is a perfect example of
the Poitevin style that is typical
of the region *(see p412),*
although a splendid Gothic
rose window has been added.
Lined with half-timbered
medieval houses, the rue
du Château leads up to the
17th-century château which
dominates the town. It now
houses a school and is open to
the public during the summer.

East of Thouars lies the
moated **Château d'Oiron**,
which now hosts contemporary
art exhibitions. A masterpiece
of Renaissance architecture, it
was largely built from 1518–49.

🏛 **Château d'Oiron**
79100 Oiron. **Tel** *05 49 96 51 25.*
◻ *daily.* ● *some public hols.* 🎦

Parthenay ❷

Deux-Sèvres. 🏛 *11,000.* 🚍 🚍 🛈 *8
rue de la Vau-St-Jacques (05 49 94 90
05).* 🛒 *Wed.* **www**.cc-parthenay.fr

Parthenay is a classic, sleepy
provincial town, except on
Wednesday mornings, when
France's second biggest livestock market is held here. In
the Middle Ages, the town was
an important halt on the route
to Santiago de Compostela
(see pp400–1) and it is easy to
imagine the processions of
pilgrims in the medieval
quarter. Steep and cobbled,
rue de la Vau-St-Jacques
winds up to the 13th-century
ramparts, leading on from the
fortified Porte St-Jacques
which guards a 13th-century
bridge over the river Thouet.

West of Parthenay, the 12th-
century church of **St-Pierre de
Parthenay-le-Vieux** has a
splendid Poitevin façade,
featuring Samson and the Lion
and a cavalier with a falcon.

Marais Poitevin ❸

Charente-Maritime, Deux-Sèvres,
Vendée. ✈ *La Rochelle.* 🚍 *Niort, La
Rochelle.* 🚍 *Coulon, Arçais, Marans.*
🛈 *pl de la Coutume, Coulon
(05 49 35 81 04).*
www.parc-marais-poitevin.fr

The Poitevin marshes, which
have been slowly drained
with canals, dykes and sluices
for a thousand years, cover
about 800 sq km (309 sq miles)
between Niort and the sea.
The area is now a regional
park, divided into two parts.
To the north and south of the
Sèvre estuary is the Marais
Désséché (dry marsh), where
cereal and other crops are
grown. The huge swathe of
the Marais Mouillé (wet marsh)
is upstream towards Niort.

The wet marshes, known
as the Venise Verte (Green
Venice), are the most interesting. They are crisscrossed by
a labyrinth of weed-choked
canals, adorned with waterlilies,
and irises, shaded by poplars
and beeches, and support a
rich variety of birds and other
wildlife. The *maraîchins* who
live here stoutly maintain that
much of the huge, water-
logged forest is unexplored.
The picturesque whitewashed
villages hereabouts are all
built on higher ground, and
the customary means of transport is a flat-bottomed boat,
known as a *platte.*

Coulon, St-Hilaire-la-Palud,
La Garette and Arçais, as well
as Damvix and Maillezais in
the Vendée, are all convenient
starting points for boat trips

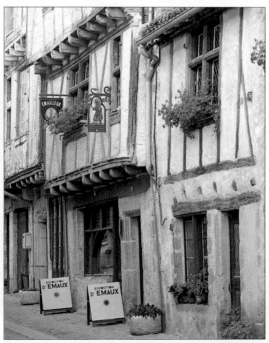

Medieval houses lining the cobbled rue de la Vau-St-Jacques in Parthenay

For hotels and restaurants in this region see pp580–2 and pp635–7

Flat-bottomed boats moored at Coulon in the Marais Poitevin

around the marshes. Boats can be rented with or without a guide. Make sure you bring plenty of insect repellent.

Coulon is the largest and best-equipped village, and a popular base for visiting the area. **La Maison du Marais Poitevin** presents an account of life in the marshes in times gone by, along with details of the wetlands' flora and fauna.

The Plantagenet donjon in Niort, now housing a local museum

Niort ❹

Deux-Sèvres. 👥 60,000. 🚇 🚌
ℹ️ pl de la Brèche (05 49 24 18 79).
🔄 Thu & Sat.
www.niortmaraispoitevin.com

Once a medieval port by the green waters of the Sèvre, Niort is now a prosperous industrial town specializing in machine tools, electronics, chemicals and insurance.

Its closeness to the marshes is evident in local specialities – eels, snails and angelica. This herb has been cultivated in the wetlands for centuries and is used for anything from liqueur to ice cream.

The town's immediate attraction is the huge 12th-century donjon overlooking the Vieux Pont. Built by Henry II and Richard the Lion-Heart, it played an important role during the Hundred Years' War and was later used as a prison. One prisoner was the father of Madame de Maintenon (see p56), who

spent her childhood in Niort. The donjon is now a museum of local arts and crafts, and archaeology. The **Musée d'Agesci** in avenue de Limoges exhibits ceramics, sculpture and paintings from the 16th to 20th centuries.

Environs
Halfway to Poitiers is the small town of **St-Maixent-L'Ecole**. A marvel of light and space, its abbey church is a Flamboyant Gothic recon-struction by François Le Duc (1670) of a building destroyed during the Wars of Religion. Further west, the **Tumulus de Bougon** consists of five tumuli (burial mounds), the oldest dating from 4500 BC.

Melle ❺

Deux-Sèvres. 👥 4,000. 🚌 ℹ️ rue
E Traver (05 49 29 15 10). 🔄 Fri.
www.ville-melle.fr

A Roman silver mine was the origin of Melle, which in the 9th century had the only mint in Aquitaine. Later its fame derived from the *baudet du Poitou*, an especially sturdy mule bred in the area. Now Melle is better known for its churches, of which the finest is **St-Hilaire**. It has a 12th-century Poitevin façade with an equestrian statue of the Emperor Constantine above the north door.

Environs
To the northwest, the abbey in **Celles-sur-Belle** has a great Moorish doorway which con-trasts strongly with the rest of the church, a 17th-century restoration in Gothic style.

Equestrian statue of Constantine on the façade of St-Hilaire, Melle

Canal in the Venise Verte region of the Marais Poitevin ▷

Poitiers ⑥

Three of the greatest battles in French history were fought around Poitiers, the most famous in 732 when Charles Martel halted the Arab invasion. After two periods of English rule *(see p51)* the town thrived during the reign of Jean de Berry (1369–1416), the great sponsor of the arts. Its university, founded in 1431, made Poitiers a major intellectual centre and saw Rabelais among its students. The Wars of Religion left Poitiers in chaos and not until the late 19th century did any major development take place. Today, however, the town is a modern and dynamic regional capital with a rich architectural heritage in its historic centre.

Fresco in Eglise St-Hilaire-le-Grand

⛪ Notre-Dame-la-Grande

Despite its name, Notre-Dame-la-Grande is not a large church. One of Poitiers' great pilgrim churches, it is most celebrated as a masterpiece of lively 12th-century Poitevin sculpture, notably its richly detailed façade. In the choir is a Romanesque fresco of Christ and the Virgin. Most of the chapels were added in the Renaissance.

⚖ Palais de Justice

Pl Alphonse Lepetit. *Tel* 05 49 50 22 00. ☐ *Mon–Fri.*
Behind the bland Renaissance façade is the 12th-century great hall of the palace of the Angevin kings, Henry II and Richard the Lion-Heart. This is thought to be the scene of Joan of Arc's examination by a council of theologians in 1429.

⛪ Cathédrale St-Pierre

The 13th-century carved choir stalls in St-Pierre are by far the oldest in France. Note the huge 12th-century east window showing the Crucifixion. The

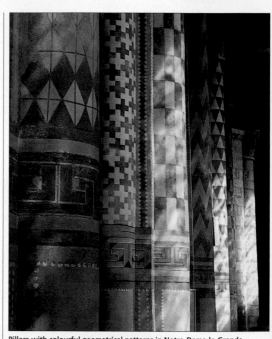

Pillars with colourful geometrical patterns in Notre-Dame-la-Grande

NOTRE-DAME-LA-GRANDE

Triangular gable

Cone-shaped pinnacles

Christ in Majesty is shown in the centre of the gable, surrounded by symbols of the evangelists.

Blind arcading is a distinctive feature of the Poitevin façade.

The portals on the Poitevin façade are deep and richly sculpted, often showing a pronounced Moorish influence.

The 12 apostles are represented by statues in the arcatures, together with the first bishop St Hilaire and his disciple St Martin.

tiny figures of the cathedral's patrons (Henry II and Eleanor of Aquitaine) are crouched at the foot of the window. Its organ (1787–91), made by François-Henri Cliquot, is one of the most prestigious and beautiful in Europe.

🏛 Espace Mendès France
1 pl de la Cathédrale. *Tel* 05 49 50 33 08. ◯ daily. ● Jun–Aug: Sun; some public holidays. 🈂
This museum contains a state-of-the-art planetarium, with laser shows to help explain the mysteries of the universe, plus events and exhibitions.

🛉 Eglise St-Hilaire-le-Grand
Fires and reconstructions have made St-Hilaire a mosaic of different styles. With its origins in the 6th century, the church still displays an 11th-century belltower and a 12th-century nave.

🛉 Baptistère St-Jean
Rue Jean Jaurès.
◯ Wed–Mon. 🈂
The polygonal 4th-century Baptistère St-Jean is one of the oldest Christian buildings in France. Many of the earliest converts were baptized here. Now a museum, it contains Romanesque frescoes of Christ

and Emperor Constantine, and some Merovingian sarcophagi.

🏛 Musée Sainte-Croix
3 bis rue Jean Jaurès. *Tel* 05 49 41 07 53. ◯ Tue–Sun pm. ● some public hols. 🈂
Musée Sainte-Croix exhibits prehistoric, Gallo-Roman and medieval archaeology, and a wide range of paintings and 19th-century sculpture. Five bronzes by Camille Claudel are on show, including *La Valse*. There is also a large collection of contemporary art.

🏛 Médiathèque François Mitterrand
4 rue de l'Université. *Tel* 05 49 52 31 51. ◯ Tue–Sat. ● public hols.
This modern building, in the historic quarter, is home to the **Maison du Moyen Age**, which displays a collection of medieval manuscripts, maps and engravings.

VISITORS' CHECKLIST

Vienne. 🏙 92,000. ✈ 5 km (3 miles) W Poitiers. 🚉 🚌 🚏 45 pl Charles de Gaulle (05 49 41 21 24). 🚋 Sat, Tue & Thu. 🎦 Les Expressifs (Oct). **www**.ot-poitiers.fr

One of Futuroscope's most popular attractions: the large-screen cinema

Futuroscope 🟦

Jaunay-Clan. 🚉 *Tel* 05 49 49 11 12. ◯ daily. ● Jan–early Feb. 🈂 🍴 🏠 **www**.futuroscope.com

Futuroscope is a fantastic theme park 7 km (4.5 miles) north of Poitiers, exploring visual technology in a futuristic environment. Attractions evolve yearly and include simulators, 3D and 360° screens and the "magic carpet" cinema, with one of its screens on the floor, creating the sensation of "flying". The cinema has the biggest screen in Europe.

POITIERS CITY CENTRE

Baptistère St-Jean ⑤
Cathédrale St-Pierre ③
Eglise St-Hilaire-le-Grand ⑦
Espace Mendès France ④
Musée Sainte-Croix ⑥
Notre-Dame-la-Grande ①
Palais de Justice ②

0 metres 250
0 yards 250

Key to Symbols see back flap

The castle ruins of Angles-sur-l'Anglin with the old watermill in the foreground

Abbaye de Nouaillé-Maupertuis **8**

Nouaillé-Maupertuis. **Tel** 05 49 55 35 69. **Church** ⬜ 9am–6pm (7pm in summer). 🚻 limited. 🎦 summer only.

On the banks of the river Miosson lies the Abbaye de Nouaillé-Maupertuis. First mentioned in 780, the abbey became independent in 808 and followed the Benedictine rule. Apart from the beauty of the site, it is also worth visiting the church, built in the 11th–12th centuries and reconstructed several times. Behind the altar is the 10th-century sarcophagus of St-Junien, with three great heraldic eagles carved on the front.

More interesting is the nearby battlefield, scene of the great English victory at Poitiers by the Black Prince in 1356. The view has altered little since the 14th century. Drive down the small road to La Cardinerie (to the right off the D142), which leads to the river crossing at Gué de l'Omme, the epicentre of the battle. There is a monument halfway up the hill where the heaviest fighting took place and where the French king Jean le Bon was captured. He had put up a heroic resistance with nothing but his battle-axe, and his small son Philippe to tell him where the next English knight was coming from.

Chauvigny **9**

Vienne. 🚶 7,000. 🚉 🛈 5 rue St-Pierre (05 49 46 39 01). 🛒 Tue, Thu, Sat. **www**.chauvigny.fr

Chauvigny, on its steep promontory overlooking the broad river Vienne, displays the ruins of no fewer than four fortified medieval castles. Stone from the local quarry was so plentiful that nobody ever bothered to demolish earlier castles for building material.

Nevertheless, the best thing in this town is the 11th–12th-century **Eglise St-Pierre**, whose decorated capitals are a real treasure – particularly those in the choir stalls. The carvings represent biblical scenes along with monsters, sphinxes and sirens. Look for

Monster capitals in Eglise St-Pierre in Chauvigny

the one which says *Gofridus me fecit* (Gofridus made me), with wonderfully natural scenes of the Epiphany.

Environs
Nearby is the lovely **Château de Touffou**, a Renaissance dream on the banks of the Vienne, with terraces and hanging gardens. Just north of it is the sleepy village of **Bonneuil-Matours**, with fine choir stalls in its Romanesque church.

🏰 **Château de Touffou**
Bonnes. **Tel** 05 49 56 08 48. ⬜ May–mid-Jun: Sat, Sun & public hols; mid-Jun–mid-Sep: Wed–Mon. 🦽

Angles-sur-l'Anglin **10**

Vienne. 🚶 400. 🛈 2 rue du Four Banal (05 49 48 86 87). 🛒 Sat & Sun. **www**.anglessuranglin.com

The village of Angles lies in an extremely beautiful riverside setting, dominated by its castle ruins. Adding to the charm is an old watermill by the slow-running river Anglin, graced by waterlilies and swaying reeds. Try to avoid visiting in summer, as the narrow streets become too crowded for comfort.

Angles is also famous for its tradition of fine needlework, the *jours d'Angles*, which is determinedly maintained by the local women today (their workshops can be visited).

St-Savin ⓫

Vienne. 🏘 *1,000.* 🚉 🚌 *20 pl de la Libération (05 49 84 30 00).* 🚌 *Fri.* www.abbaye-saint-savin.fr

The glory of St-Savin is its 11th-century abbey church with its slender Gothic spire and huge nave.

The abbey had enormous influence until the Hundred Years' War, when it was burnt down. It was later pillaged several times during the Wars of Religion. Despite restoration work by monks in the 17th century and again in the 19th century, the church appears quite untouched.

Its interior contains the most magnificent series of 12th-century Romanesque frescoes in Europe. These wallpaintings were among the very first in France to be classified as a *Monument Historique* in 1836. Some of the frescoes were restored in 1967–74 and have been protected by UNESCO since 1983. A full-scale replica of the St-Savin murals can be seen at the Palais de Chaillot in Paris (*see pp110–11*). The abbey-museum explains the historical context and techniques of these murals.

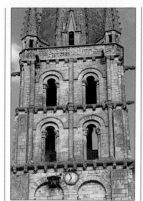

Belltower of St-Savin

Montmorillon ⓬

Vienne. 🏘 *7,000.* 🚉 🚌 *2 pl du Maréchal Leclerc (05 49 91 11 96).* 🚌 *Wed.* www.tourisme-montmorillon.fr

Montmorillon, built on the river Gartempe, has its origins in the 11th century. Like most towns in the region, it had a difficult time during the Hundred Years' War and the Wars of Religion. Some buildings survived, such as **Eglise Notre-Dame**, which has beautiful frescoes in its

12th-century crypt (contact tourist office for key). They include scenes from the life of St Catherine of Alexandria.

Environs

Half an hour's walk from the Pont de Chez Ragon, south of Montmorillon, is the **Portes d'Enfer**, a dramatically shaped rock above the sudden rapids of the Gartempe.

Confolens ⓭

Charente. 🏘 *3,000.* 🚉 🚌 *rue Fontaine des Jardins (05 45 84 14 08).* 🚌 *Wed & Sat.* www.mairieconfolens.com

On the border with Limousin, Confolens was once an important frontier town but now suffers from rural exodus. Efforts to prevent the town's isolation include the annual international folklore festival. Every August the town is transformed by a mix of music, costumes and crafts from all over the world.

Of historical interest is the medieval bridge across the Vienne, heavily restored in the early 18th century.

Charroux ⓮

Vienne. 🏘 *1,200.* 🚌 *2 route de Chatain (05 49 87 60 12).* 🚌 *Thu.* www.charroux-en-poitou.com

The 8th-century **Abbaye St-Sauveur** in Charroux was once one of the richest abbeys in the region. Today it is a ruin open to the sky (phone the tourist office to arrange a visit).

Its chief contribution to history was made in the 10th century, when the Council of Charroux declared the "Truce of God", the earliest-known attempt to regulate war in the manner of the Geneva convention. Rules included: "Christian soldiers may not plunder churches, strike priests or steal peasants' livestock while campaigning."

The huge tower marking the centre of the church, and some superb sculpture from the original abbey portal in the small museum here, give an idea of its original splendour.

ST-SAVIN WALL PAINTINGS

The frescoes of St-Savin represent Old Testament history from the Creation to the Ten Commandments. The sequence starts to the left of the entrance with the Creation of the stars and of Eve. It continues with scenes from Noah's Ark to the Tower of Babel, the story of Joseph and the parting of the Red Sea. It is believed that all the frescoes were created by the same group of artists, due to the similarity in style. Their harmonious colours – red and yellow ochre, green, black and white – have been softened by time.

Noah's Ark, from a 12th-century wall painting in St-Savin

Aulnay ⑮

Charente-Maritime. 🏠 1,500. ℹ 290
av de l'Eglise (05 46 33 14 44). 🏪
Thu & Sun. **www**.aulnaytourisme.com

Perhaps the most unusual fact
about the lovely 12th-century
Eglise St-Pierre at Aulnay is
that it was all built at once;
there is no ill-fitting apse or
transept added to an original
nave. Surrounded by nothing
but cypresses, it has remained
the same since the time of the
great pilgrimages.

The church is covered in
glorious sculpture, particularly
the outside of the south
transept. It is a rare example
of a complete Romanesque
façade, with rank on rank of
raucous monsters and graceful
human figures. Look for the
donkey with a harp. Inside
the church there is a pillar
decorated with elephants,
inscribed "Here be Elephants".

Façade of Eglise St-Pierre at Aulnay

La Rochelle ⑯

Charente-Maritime. 🏠 80,000. ✈
🚉 🚌 ℹ 2 quai Georges Simenon,
Le Gabut (05 46 41 14 68). 🏪 daily.
www.larochelle-tourisme.com

La Rochelle, a commercial
centre and busy port since
the 11th century, has suffered
much from a distressing tendency to back the wrong side
– the English and the Calvin-
ists, for example. This led to
the ruthless siege of the city
by Cardinal Richelieu in 1628,
during which 23,000 people
starved to death. The walls

Tour St-Nicolas in La Rochelle

were destroyed and the city's
privileges withdrawn. The
glory of La Rochelle is the old
harbour surrounded by stately
buildings. The harbour is now
the biggest yachting centre on
France's Atlantic coast. On
either side of its entrance are
Tour de la Chaîne and **Tour
St-Nicolas**. A huge chain used
to be strung between them to
ward off attack from the sea.

La Rochelle is easy to
explore on foot, though its
cobbled streets and arcades
can be congested in high
summer. To get an overview,
climb the 15th-century **Tour
de la Lanterne**. Its inner walls
were covered in graffiti by
prisoners, mostly mariners, in
the 17th–19th centuries. Ships
are the most common motif.

The study of the 18th-century
scientist Clément Lafaille is
preserved in the renovated
Muséum d'Histoire Naturelle,
complete with shell collection
and display cabinets. There are
also stuffed animals and
African masks. The town's
relation to the New World is
treated in the **Musée du
Nouveau Monde**. Emigration,
commerce and the slave trade
are explained through old
maps, paintings and artifacts.

The richly decorated 16th-
century courtyard façade of
the **Hôtel de Ville** is worth a
visit, as is the delightful
collection of perfume bottles
in the **Musée du Flacon à
Parfum** in the parfumerie at
No. 33 rue du Temple.

Next to the Vieux Port is the
huge **Aquarium**. Transparent
tunnels lead through tanks
with different marine biotopes,
including sharks and turtles.

🎪 **Tour de la Lanterne**
Rue des Murs, Le Port.
Tel 05 46 41 56 04. ◯ daily.
● 1 Jan, 1 May, 1 & 11 Nov,
25 Dec. 🏷

🏛 **Muséum d'Histoire
Naturelle**
28 rue Albert Premier. **Tel** 05 46 41
18 25. ◯ Tue–Sun. 🏷 ♿

🏛 **Musée du Nouveau
Monde**
10 rue Fleuriau. **Tel** 05 46 41 46 50.
◯ Wed–Mon. ● Sat am (Oct–
Mar), Sun am, 1 Jan, 1 May, 14 Jul,
1 & 11 Nov, 25 Dec. 🏷

🐟 **Aquarium**
Bassin des Grands Yachts, quai
Louis Prunier. **Tel** 05 46 34 00 00.
◯ daily. 🏷 ♿ ▢ ▢ ◗
www.aquarium-larochelle.com

Environs
Ile de Ré, also known as the
white island, is a long stretch
of chalky cliffs and dunes,
with a rich birdlife. Since 1988
it has been connected to the
mainland by a 3-km (2-mile)
long bridge. Head for **Ars-en-
Ré** or the island's main town,
St-Martin-de-Ré. There are
plenty of seafood restaurants
serving locally grown oysters.

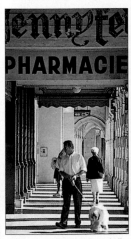

Arcade in rue du Palais, La Rochelle

Rochefort ⑰

Charente-Maritime. 🏠 27,000. 🚉
🚌 ℹ av Sadi-Carnot (05 46 99 08
60). 🏪 Tue, Thu & Sat.
www.rochefort-ocean.com

The historic rival of La
Rochelle, Rochefort was
purpose-built by Colbert

Phare des Baleines on the eastern point of the Ile de Ré, opposite La Rochelle

(see pp56–7) in the 17th century to be the greatest shipyard in France, producing over 300 sailing vessels per year.

This maritime heritage can be traced in the beautifully restored **Corderie Royale** from 1670. The building houses an exhibition on ropemaking. The **Musée de la Marine** displays models of the ships built in the arsenal.

Rochefort is also famous as the birthplace of the writer Pierre Loti (1850–1923). The author's extravagant **Maison de Pierre Loti** is filled with lush souvenirs in an oriental decor.

Outside the town is **Pont Transbordeur**, France's last transporter bridge, built in 1897 to connect Rochefort with southern points.

🏛 La Corderie Royale
Centre International de la Mer, rue Audebert. *Tel* 05 46 87 01 90. ◯ *daily.* ● *1, 7–25 Jan, 25 Dec.* 🖼 ⚙ 🛈 www.corderie-royale.com

🏛 Musée de la Marine
Pl de la Galissonnière. *Tel* 05 46 99 86 57. ◯ *daily.* ● *Jan, 1 May, 25 Dec.* 🖼 🛈 www.musee-marine.fr

🏛 Maison de Pierre Loti
141 rue Pierre Loti. *Tel* 05 46 99 16 88. ◯ *Wed–Mon.* ● *Jan, 1 & 11 Nov, 25 Dec.* 🖼 🛈 *only.*

🏛 Pont Transbordeur
3 av Maurice Chupin, Parc des Fourriers. *Tel* 05 46 83 30 86. ◯ *Apr–Sep: daily; Oct, Feb–Mar: Wed–Sun.* www.pont-transbordeur.fr

Environs
Ile d'Aix is served by a ferry from Fouras on the mainland. Napoleon was briefly kept here before being exiled to St

Helena. There are Napoleonic mementos in the **Musée Napoléonien**. The camel he rode in the Egyptian campaign is in the **Musée Africain**.

🏛 Musée Napoléonien
30 rue Napoléon. *Tel* 05 46 84 66 40. ◯ *Wed–Mon.* ● *1 May.* 🖼

🏛 Musée Africain
Rue Napoléon. *Tel* 05 46 84 66 40. ◯ *Wed–Mon.* ● *1 May.* 🖼 ⚙

Napoleon, who was detained at Ile d'Aix in 1814

Île d'Oléron ⑱

Charente-Maritime. ✈ *La Rochelle.* 🚊 *Rochefort, La Rochelle, Saintes then bus.* 🚌 *from La Rochelle (in summer).* 🛈 *Bourcefranc (05 46 85 65 23).* www.ile-oleron-marennes.com

Accessible from the mainland by bridge, Oleron is the second largest French island after Corsica, and a very popular holiday resort. Its south coast, the **Côte Sauvage**, is all dunes and pine forest, with excellent beaches at Vert Bois and Grande Plage, near the fishing port of La Cotinière. The north is used for farming and fishing.

The train from **St-Trojan** makes an interesting excursion through dunes and woodlands to the Pointe de Maumusson (Easter–October).

Brouage ⑲

Charente-Maritime. 🏠 *580.* 🛈 *2 rue de Québec (05 46 85 19 16).*

Cardinal Richelieu's fortress at Brouage, his base during the Siege of La Rochelle (1627–8), once overlooked a thriving harbour, but its wealth and population declined in the 18th century as the ocean receded. In 1659, Marie Mancini was sent into exile here by her uncle, Cardinal Mazarin, who did not approve of her liaison with Louis XIV. The king never forgot the beautiful Marie. Even on his way back from his wedding, he stayed alone at Brouage in the room once occupied by his first great love. Today the **ramparts** make a peaceful place to stroll and admire the view.

Environs
There are two reasons to go to **Marennes**, southwest of Brouage: the famous green-tinged oysters and the view from the steeple of Eglise St-Pierre-de-Sales. Nearby is the 18th-century **Château de la Gataudière** with an exhibition of horsedrawn vehicles.

One of Royan's five popular beaches

Royan

Charente-Maritime. 🚶 20,000.
🚆 🚌 ⛴ to Verdon only. 🛈 1 bd
de la Grandière (05 46 23 00 00).
⛴ Tue–Sun; daily in summer.
www.royan-tourisme.com

Badly damaged by Allied
bombing in World War II,
Royan is now thoroughly
modern and different in tone
from the rest of the towns
on this weather-beaten coast.
With five beaches of fine
sand, here called *conches*, it
becomes a heavily populated
resort in the summer months.

Built between 1955 and
1958, **Eglise Notre-Dame** is a
remarkable early example of
reinforced concrete architecture. Its interior is flooded
with colour and light by the
stained-glass windows.

The outstanding Renaissance
Phare de Cordouan, visible in
the distance from the coast,
offers a change from all the
modern architecture. Various
lighthouses have been erected
on the site since the 11th
century. The present one was

finished in 1611, with a chapel
inside. The construction was
later reinforced and heightened. Since 1789, nothing
has changed but the lighting
method. Boat trips in summer
ferry visitors to Phare de
Cordouan from Royan harbour.

Talmont-sur-Gironde

Charente-Maritime. 🚶 79.
🛈 rue de l'Église (05 46 90 16 25).

The tiny Romanesque **Eglise
Ste-Radegonde** is perched on
a spit of land overlooking the
Gironde. Built in 1094, the
church's apse was designed to
resemble the prow of a ship –
which is apt, since the nave
has already fallen into the
estuary. A 15th-century façade
closes off what's left. Inside
are richly decorated capitals,
including a tableau of St
George and the Dragon.

Talmont is a jewel of a
village, packed full of little
white houses and colourful
hollyhocks in summer.

Saintes

Charente-Maritime. 🚶 28,000. 🚆
🚌 🛈 Place Bassompierre (05 46 74
23 82). ⛴ Tue–Sun. **www**.
ot-saintes.fr

Capital of the Saintonge
region, Saintes has an extra-
ordinarily rich architectural
heritage. For centuries it
boasted the only bridge over
the lower Charente, well used
by pilgrims on their way to
Santiago de Compostela.
The Roman bridge no longer
exists but you can still admire
the magnificent **Arch of
Germanicus** (AD 19) which
used to mark its entrance.

On the same side of the
river is the beautiful **Abbaye
aux Dames**. Consecrated in
1047, it was modernized in
the 12th century. During the
17th–18th centuries noble
ladies were educated here.
Look for the decorated portal
and the vigorous 12th-century
head of Christ in the apse.

On the left bank is the 1st-
century Roman **amphitheatre**.
Further away lies the rather
unknown gem, **Eglise St-
Eutrope**. In the 15th century,
this church had the misfortune
to effect a miraculous cure of
the dropsy on Louis XI. In a
paroxysm of gratitude, he did
his best to wreck it with ill-
considered Gothic additions.
Luckily, its rare Romanesque
capitals have survived.

Arch of Germanicus in Saintes

Cognac

Charente. 🚶 20,000. 🚆 🚌 🛈 16
rue du 14 Juillet (05 45 82 10 71). ⛴
Tue–Sun. **www**.tourism-cognac.com

Wherever you spot the black
lichen stains from alcohol
evaporation on the exterior of
the buildings in this river

Necropolis in the monolithic Eglise St-Jean in Aubeterre-sur-Dronne

port, you may be sure that you are looking at a storehouse of cognac.

All the great cognac houses do tours – a good one is chez **Cognac Otard**, situated in the 15th– 16th-century château where François I was born. The distillery was established in 1795 by a Scot named Otard, who demolished an old chapel in the process. Luckily much of the Renaissance architecture was saved and can be seen during the tour, which includes a cognac-tasting.

Cognac in traditional snifter

The basic material for cognac is local white wine low in alcohol, which is then distilled. The resultant pale spirit is aged in oak barrels for 4–40 years before being bottled. The skill lies in the blending – therefore the only guide to quality is the name and the duration of ageing.

🏭 **Cognac Otard**
Château de Cognac, 127 bd Den-fert-Rochereau. **Tel** 05 45 36 88 86. ⬤ Apr–Oct: daily; Nov–Dec: by appt. ⬤ 1 May & public hols in winter. 🔲 ✓ obligatory. **www**.otard.com

Angoulême ㉔

Charente. 🔼 46,000. 🚉 🚌
🛈 7 bis rue du Chat (05 45 95 16 84). ⬤ daily.
www.angouleme-tourisme.com

The celebrated 12th-century **Cathédrale St-Pierre**, which dominates this industrial centre, is the fourth to be

built on the site. One of its most interesting features is the Romanesque frieze on the façade. Some restoration work was carried out by the 19th-century architect Abadie. In his eagerness to wipe out all details added after the 12th century, he destroyed a 6th-century crypt.

Unfortunately, he was also let loose on the old château, transforming it into a Neo-Gothic **Hôtel de Ville** (town hall). However, the 15th-century tower where Marguerite d'Angoulême was born in 1492 still stands. A statue of her can be seen in the garden. Sister of François I, she spoke six languages, had a major role in foreign policy and wrote a popular work, *Heptaméron*. The ramparts offer a bracing walk with views over the Charente Valley. A vintage car race takes place there in mid-September.

Angoulême has become the capital of comic book art *(band dessinée)*, hosting the prestigious Festival de la Bande Dessinée (Jan/Feb). The **Cité Internationale de la Bande-Dessinée et de l'Image** has a reference collection of French print and film cartoons dating back to 1946. From here, a footbridge leads to the Musée de la Bande Dessinée, where the history, techniques and aesthetics of the art form are explained.

🏛 **Cité Internationale de la Bande-Dessinée et de l'Image**
121 rue de Bordeaux. **Tel** 05 45 38 65 65. ⬤ Tue–Sun (w/e pms only). ⬤ Jan, public hols. 🔲 ♿ 🔲 🔲
Cinema www.cnbdi.fr

Aubeterre-sur-Dronne ㉕

Charente. 🔼 430. 🚌 🛈 8 pl du Champ de Foine (05 45 98 57 18). ⬤ Sun. **http://**aubeterresurdronne.com

The chief ornament of this pretty white village is the staggering monolithic **Eglise St-Jean**. Dug out of the white chalky cliff that gave the village its name (Alba Terra – White Earth), some parts of it date back to the 6th century. Between the Revolution and 1860, it served as the village's cemetery. It contains an early Christian baptismal font and an octagonal reliquary.

The Romanesque Eglise St-Jacques is also of note for its fine sculpted façade.

Detail from the Romanesque façade of Cathédrale St-Pierre in Angoulême

Street-by-Street: Bordeaux ㉖

Built on a curve of the river Garonne,
Bordeaux has been a major port since pre-
Roman times and for centuries a crossroads
of European trade. Today Bordeaux shows
little visible evidence of the Romans,
Franks, English or the Wars of Religion that
have marked its past. This forward-looking
town, the seventh largest in France, is an
industrial and maritime sprawl surrounding
a noble 18th-century centre.

Along the waterfront of this wealthy wine
metropolis is a long sweep of elegant
Classical façades, first built to mask the
medieval slums behind. Adding to the
magnificence are the Esplanade des
Quinconces, the Grand Théâtre
and the place de la Bourse.

Eglise Notre-
Dame, built
1684–1707

★ Grand Théâtre
*Built in 1773–80, the theatre
is a masterpiece of the
Classical style, crowned by
nine statues of the muses.*

STAR SIGHTS

★ Grand Théâtre

★ Esplanade des
  Quinconces

★ Place de la Bourse

KEY

— — — Suggested route

| 0 metres | 100 |
| 0 yards | 100 |

The quais, lined with graceful
façades, make a beautiful
walk along the Garonne.

★ Place de la Bourse
*This elegant and harmonious
square is flanked by two
majestic 18th-century
buildings, Palais de la Bourse
and Hôtel des Douanes.*

★ Esplanade des Quinconces
Replacing the 15th-century Château de Trompette, this vast space of tree-lined esplanades with statues and fountains was created in 1827–58.

VISITORS' CHECKLIST

Gironde. 240,000. ✈ 10 km (6 miles) W Bordeaux. 🚉 Gare St-Jean, rue Ch Domerq. 🚌 Allée de Chartres. 🛈 12 cours du 30 Juillet (05 56 00 66 00). 🛒 daily. 🍷 Fête le Vin (late Jun, even yrs); Fête le Fleuve (late Jun, odd yrs). **www**.bordeaux-tourisme.com

Quartier des Chartrons, the old merchants' quarter, has fine 18th-century buildings.

The Monument aux Girondins is a richly adorned monument (1804–1902). It commemorates the Girondists sent to the guillotine by Robespierre during the Terror (1793–5).

COURS DE TOURNON
RUE BOUDET
COURS DE GOURGUE
EMICYCLE DES QUINCONCES
COURS DU MARECHAL FOCH
ALLEE DE CHARTRES
RUE VAUBAN
ESPLANADE DES QUINCONCES
ALLEE DE BRISTOL
RUE FERRERE
RUE FOY
DE MUNICH
QUAI LOUIS XVIII

Terraces provide good views over the river.

CAPC Musée d'Art Contemporain
This museum of contemporary art and cultural centre is in an early 19th-century warehouse.

Loading wine barrels in 19th-century Bordeaux

THE BORDEAUX WINE TRADE

After Marseille, Bordeaux is the oldest trading port in France. From Roman times the export of wine was the basis for a modest prosperity, but under English rule (1154–1453, *see pp50–53*), the merchants began making immense fortunes from their monopoly of wine sales to England. After the discovery of the New World, Bordeaux took advantage of its Atlantic position to diversify and extend its wine market. Today the Bordeaux region produces over 60 million cases of wine per year.

GRAND THÉÂTRE DE BORDEAUX

Statues of the muses   Grand staircase

Concert hall

The façade's 12
Corinthian columns

Auditorium with panelling
and gilded columns

Stage

Exploring Bordeaux

Much of central Bordeaux is grand streets and 18th-century mansions. A triangle made by cours Clemenceau, cours de l'Intendance and allées de Tourny has chic boutiques and cafés. Cathédrale St-André is another focal point, with good museums nearby. Both the *quais* and the Chartrons district around the Jardin Public are worth exploring.

🎭 Grand Théâtre

Place de la Comédie. *Tel 05 56 00 85 95.* ◯ *by appointment only.* 🖼
Built by the architect Victor Louis, the 18th-century Grand Théâtre is one of the finest Classical constructions of its type in France. The auditorium is renowned for its extraordinary acoustics. The spectacular main staircase was later imitated by Garnier for the Paris Opéra *(see p97)*.

⛪ Eglise St-Seurin

This church is somewhat chaotic with a patchwork of styles ranging from the 11th to the 18th century. Most interesting are the 6th-century Gallo-Roman sarcophagi in the crypt, and a fine 14th-century bishop's throne.

⛪ Basilique St-Michel

It took 200 years to build the massive Basilique St-Michel, begun in 1350. This triple-naved edifice has a remarkable statue of St Ursula with her flock of penitents. Its freestanding belfry, built in 1472–92, is the tallest in southern France (114 m).

🏛 Musée des Beaux-Arts

20 cours d'Albret. *Tel 05 56 10 20 56.* ◯ *Wed–Mon.* ◯ *public hols.* 🖼 ♿
Housed in two wings of the Hôtel de Ville, the excellent collection of paintings here ranges from the Renaissance to our time. Masterpieces include works by Titian, Veronese, Rubens, Delacroix, Corot, Renoir, Matisse and Boudin.

🏛 Musée des Arts Décoratifs

39 rue Bouffard. *Tel 05 56 10 14 00.* ◯ *Wed–Mon.* ◯ *public hols.* 🖼 ▢
If you're interested in elegant furnishings and fine porcelain, stop off at this exceptional collection, housed in the suitably refined 18th-century Hôtel de Lalande.

🏛 Musée d'Aquitaine

20 cours Pasteur. *Tel 05 56 01 51 00.* ◯ *Tue–Sun.* ◯ *public hols.* ♿
This important museum traces life in the region from pre-historic times to the present, through artifacts, furniture and viticulture tools. Among its

Calm street in Bordeaux by the Porte de la Grosse Cloche

more spectacular exhibits are the Tayac treasure from the 2nd century BC, and the Garonne treasure, a hoard of over 4,000 Roman coins.

⛪ Cathédrale St-André

The nave of this gigantic church was begun in the 11th century and modified 200 years later. The Gothic choir and transepts were added in the 14th and 15th centuries. The excellent medieval sculptures on the Porte Royale include scenes from the Last Judgement.

🏛 CAPC Musée d'Art Contemporain

Entrepôt Lainé, 7 rue Ferrère. *Tel 05 56 00 81 50.* ◯ *Tue–Sun.* ◯ *public hols.* 🖼 ♿ ▢ ▢
This superbly converted 19th-century warehouse merits a visit, whatever you make of its high-profile temporary exhibitions and permanent collection of contemporary art.

St-Émilion ㉗

Gironde. 🏘 *2,100.* 🚆 🚌 ℹ *pl des Créneaux (05 57 55 28 28).* 🅿 *Sun.*
www.saint-emilion-tourisme.com

This charming village in the middle of the red wine district to which it gives its name, dates back to an 8th-century hermit, Émilion, who dug out a cave for himself in the rock. A monastery followed, and by the Middle Ages St-Émilion had become a small town. Today medieval houses still line the narrow streets, and parts of the 12th-century ramparts remain. The interior of the church dug out of the chalky cliff by followers of Saint Émilion after his death is somewhat ruined by concrete columns put up to prevent its collapse.

Famous châteaux in the district include the elegant **Figeac, Cheval Blanc** and **Ausone,** all of them St-Émilion Premiers Grands Crus Classés.

Vineyard close to Margaux in the Médoc region west of Bordeaux

Pauillac ㉘

Gironde. 🏠 5,400. 🚊 🚌 ℹ La Verrerie (05 56 59 03 08). 🛒 Sat. **www**.pauillac-medoc.com

One of the most famous areas in the Médoc wine region *(see pp398–9)* is the commune of Pauillac. Three of its châteaux are Médoc Premiers Grands Crus Classés.

The **Château Mouton-Rothschild** uses leading artists to create its wine labels and has a small museum of paintings on wine themes from all over the world. The **Château Lafite-Rothschild** is of medieval origin and the **Château Latour** is recognizable by its distinctive stone turret. They can be visited by appointment

(contact the tourist office). The town of Pauillac is situated on the west bank of the Gironde. In the 19th century it was the bustling arrival point for transatlantic steamships, but now the sleepy port is mostly used by pleasure boats. There are picturesque river views from the quais and plenty of cafés serving the local wine.

BORDEAUX WINE CHÂTEAUX

The château is at the heart of the quality system in Bordeaux, the world's largest fine wine region. A château includes a vineyard and a building which can range from the most basic to the grandest, historic as well as modern. But the château is also the symbol of a tradition and the philosophy that a wine's quality and character spring from the soil. Some châteaux welcome visitors for wine tasting as well as buying. Every major wine town has a Maison du Vin, which can provide information on visits to a château.

Latour *in Pauillac is famous for its powerful wines and the medieval stone turret that appears on its label.*

Cheval Blanc, *a great château in the St-Émilion area, boasts a rich, spicy Premier Grand Cru.*

Margaux, *built in 1802, produces a classic Margaux Premier Cru of the same elegant proportions as its Palladian façade.*

Palmer, *dating from 1856, is Neo-Renaissance in style and produces a very fine Margaux Troisième Cru.*

Gruaud-Larose *is a cream-coloured château with a Classical façade, distinguished by its full-bodied St-Julien Deuxième Cru Classé.*

Vieux Château Certan *is Belgian-owned and one of the great historic properties of Pomerol. Its wines are consistently in the first rank in the district, challenged only by Pétrus.*

The immense Dune du Pilat, stretching almost 3 km (2 miles) south of the inlet to Bassin d'Arcachon

La Côte d'Argent ㉙

Gironde, Landes. ✈ *Bordeaux, Biarritz.* 🚊 *Soulac-sur-Mer, Arcachon, Labenne, Dax.* 🚌 *Lacanau, Arcachon, Mimizan.* ℹ *Lacanau (05 56 03 21 01), Mimizan-Plage (05 58 09 11 20), Capbreton (05 58 72 12 11).*

The long stretch of coast between Pointe de Grave on the Gironde estuary and Bayonne *(see p452)* is called La Côte d'Argent – the Silver Coast. It is virtually one vast beach of shifting sand dunes. Treeplanting has now slowed down their progress.

The coast is dotted with seaside resorts like **Soulac-sur-Mer** in the north, followed by the big **Lacanau-Océan** and **Mimizan-Plage**. Down in the south is **Hossegor** with its salty lake, and **Capbreton**. Modern holiday resorts have been integrated with the old.

Inland are lakes popular for fishing and boating. They are connected to each other and the ocean by lively water currents, such as the **Courant d'Huchet** from Etang de Léon. Boat trips are available.

Bassin d'Arcachon ㉚

Gironde. 🏘 *12,000.* 🚢 *to Cap Ferret.* 🚌 🚊 ℹ *espl Georges Pompidou (05 57 52 97 97).* 🗓 *daily.* **www.**arcachon.com

In the middle of the Côte d'Argent the straight coastline suddenly forms a lagoon. Famous for its natural beauty,

fine beaches and oysters, the Bassin d'Arcachon is a protected area, perfect for holidaymakers, sailing enthusiasts and oyster-eaters.

The basin is dotted with smaller amorphous resorts, beaches and fishing/oyster villages, all worth exploring.

Cap Ferret, the northern headland that protects the basin from stiff Atlantic winds, is a preserve of the wealthy, whose luxurious villas stand among the pines. Look for the small road under the trees from Lège, which leads to the wild, magnificent beach of Grand-Crohot.

Between Cap Ferret and Arcachon, near Gujan-Mestras, the **Parc Ornitho-logique du Teich** provides care and shelter for damaged birds and endangered species. For the bird watcher, there are two fascinating walks, each carefully marked: an introductory one, and another of greater length. Both

provide concealed observation points from which people can watch the wild fowl without disturbing them.

Arcachon was created as a seaside resort in 1845. Its popularity grew and in the late 19th and early 20th centuries the elegant villas in Ville d'Hiver were built. The livelier Ville d'Eté, facing the lagoon, has a casino and sports facilities.

The immense **Dune du Pilat** is the largest sand dune in Europe. It is nearly 3 km (2 miles) long, 104 m (340 ft) high and 500 m (1,625 ft) wide. Aside from the view, the dune is a great vantage point in autumn for viewing flocks of migratory birds as they pass overhead on their way to the sanctuary at Le Teich.

🍴 **Parc Ornithologique du Teich**
Le Teich. *Tel 05 56 22 80 93.* 🗓 *daily.* 📷 ♿ 🛍 🍴 **www.** parc-ornithologique-du-teich.com

Parc Ornithologique du Teich, a bird sanctuary in Bassin d'Arcachon

LANDES FOREST

The vast, totally artificial 19th-century forest of Les Landes was an ambitious project to make use of an area of sand and marshes. Pines and grasses were planted to anchor the coastal dunes, and inland dunes were stabilized with a mixture of pines, reeds and broom. In 1855 the land was drained, and is now covered with pine groves and undergrowth, preserving a delicate ecological balance.

Pine trees in the Landes forest

Les Landes ❶

Gironde, Landes. ✈ Bordeaux, Biarritz. 🚉 Morcenx, Dax, Mont-de-Marsan. 🚌 Mont-de-Marsan. ℹ Mont-de-Marsan (05 58 05 87 37).

Almost entirely covered by an immense pine forest, the Landes area extends over the two *départements* of Gironde and Landes. The soil here is uniformly sandy. Until a century ago the whole region became a swamp in winter, because of a layer of tufa (porous rock) just under the surface which retained water from the brackish lakes. Any settlement or agriculture close to the sea was impossible due to the constantly shifting dunes. Furthermore, the mouth of the Adour river kept moving from Capbreton to Vieux-Boucau and back, a distance of 32 km (20 miles).

The Adour was fixed near Bayonne by a canal in the 16th century. This was the start of the slow conquest of the Landes. The planting of pine trees ultimately wiped out the migrant shepherds and their flocks. Today the inner Landes is still very under-populated, but wealthy from its pinewood and pine derivatives. The coastal strip has a large influx of holidaymakers.

In 1970, part of the forest was made into a nature park. At **Marqueze**, in the **Écomusée de la Grande Lande**, a typical 19th-century *airial* (clearing) has been restored. It commemorates the vanished world of Les Landes before the draining of the marshes, when shepherds still used stilts to get about. There are traditional *auberges landaises*, wooden houses with sloping roofs, as well as henhouses built on stilts because of the foxes. In **Luxey** a museum recalls old techniques of tapping and distillation of resin.

Levignacq, near the coast, is a perfect Landais village with a remarkable 14th-century fortified church full of charming native frescoes.

Mont-de-Marsan ❷

Landes. 🏠 32,000. 🚉 🚌 ℹ 6 pl du Général Leclerc (05 58 05 87 37). 🛒 Tue & Sat. www.tourisme-montdemarsan.fr

A bullfighting mecca, Mont-de-Marsan attracts all the great bullfighters of France and Spain in summer. A less bloodthirsty local variant of the sport is the *course landaise*, in which the object is to vault over the horns and back of a charging cow.

The administrative capital of the Landes is also known for its hippodrome and the production of poultry and *foie gras*.

Sculpture from the first half of the 20th century can be seen at **Musée Despiau-Wlérick**.

Dax ❸

Landes. 🏠 21,500. 🚉 🚌 ℹ 11 cours Foch (05 58 56 86 86). 🛒 Sat, Sun am. www.dax-tourisme.com

The thermal spa of Dax is second only to Aix-les-Bains (*see p390*) in importance. Its hot springs, with a constant temperature of 64° C (147° F) and tonic mud from the Adour, have been soothing aches and pains since the time of Emperor Augustus.

Apart from the 13th-century doorway of the otherwise 17th-century **Cathédrale Notre-Dame**, there isn't much of architectural interest in this warm, peaceful town. But the promenade along the river Adour is charming and the bullring is world-renowned.

La Force (1937) by Raoul Lamourdieu, in the bullfighting capital of Mont-de-Marsan

PERIGORD, QUERCY AND GASCONY

DORDOGNE · LOT · TARN · HAUTE GARONNE
LOT-ET-GARONNE · TARN-ET-GARONNE · GERS

*S*outhwest France is an archaeologist's heaven, for the region has been continuously inhabited by mankind for tens of thousands of years, longer than any other area in Europe. The landscape of these historic regions seems to have an ancient familiarity, derived from centuries of people living in harmony with the land.

The great cave sites around Les Eyzies and Lascaux harbour the earliest evidence we possess of primitive art. The castles, bastides *(see p445)* and churches that grace the countryside from Périgueux to the Pyrenees, from the Bay of Biscay to Toulouse and beyond to the Mediterranean, belong to a far more recent past. From the coming of Christianity until the late 18th century, this lovely region was the battlefield for a string of conflicts. The English fought and lost the Hundred Years' War for Aquitaine (1345–1453); this was followed by intermittent Wars of Religion, in which Catholics fought Huguenots (French Protestants) in a series of massacres and guerilla wars *(see pp52–3)*.

Today nothing is left of these old struggles but crumbling ramparts, keeps and bastides, which are part of the region's cultural and artistic heritage, attracting thousands of visitors every year. Yet it is as well to remember that all the great sights here, from the abbey church at Moissac, whose 12th-century portal is a masterpiece of Romanesque art, to the awesome clifftop site of Rocamadour, have suffered at one time or another from the attacks of marauding soldiers.

Over the last fifty years, the rural southwest has gone through a radical demographic shift. There has been a continual decline in the old peasant way of life with fewer and fewer people cultivating the land. A steady migration by the young to the cities has been matched by an influx of downsizers and commuters looking for a more relaxed way of life.

Périgord geese, reared for the area's celebrated *foie gras*

◁ La Roque-Gageac in the Dordogne Valley

Exploring Périgord, Quercy and Gascony

The market towns of Périgueux, Cahors and Albi make good bases for exploring the region, and are quieter alternatives to Toulouse – the only major urban centre. Elsewhere, the green hills and sleepy villages of Gascony and Périgord (also known as the Dordogne) are mainly for those who appreciate the slow pace of life in the countryside. But if you want more than peace and good food, this region offers some of France's finest medieval architecture, and Europe's most important prehistoric caves, notably Lascaux.

The medieval hilltop town of Cordes

GETTING AROUND

The west–east Autoroute des Deux Mers (A62-A61) is the main road through the region, linking Bordeaux, the Atlantic coast and the Mediterranean. The A20 from Montauban to Limoges provides access to the Dordogne and Quercy. Buses and mainline railways, including a Bordeaux–Marseille TGV, pass along the same two axes. They meet at Toulouse, where an international airport has daily flights to and from most European destinations.

KEY

═══	Motorway
═══	Major road
───	Secondary road
═══	Minor road
───	Scenic route
┈┈┈	Main railway
───	Minor railway
───	Regional border

Bourdeilles on the river Dronne

St-Jean-de-Côle ①

Dordogne. 🏠 *350.* 🚏 *pl du Château
(05 53 62 14 15).* 🎦 *Floralies (Apr–
May).* www.ville-saint-jean-de-cole.fr

St-Jean-de-Côle's medieval,
humpbacked bridge gives the
best view of this lovely
Dordogne village set in hilly
countryside. Stone and half-
timbered houses, roofed with
the distinctive red-brown tiles
of the region, cram the
narrow streets around the
main square. Here stand a
covered market place, château
and 12th-century church.
    The cupola of the church
used to be the largest in the
region – too large, it seems,
for it fell down twice in the
18th and 19th centuries. The
second time it happened
the builders gave up, and
there has been a plank ceiling
ever since.

**Main square in the lovely village of
St-Jean-de-Côle**

Hautefort ②

Tel 05 53 50 40 27. Château
⭘ *Apr– Sep: daily (Feb, Mar & early
Nov: Sat, Sun & hols, pm only; Oct:
daily, pm only).* ⚫ *mid-Nov–Feb.*
📷 🎟 *oblig.* ♿ *limited.*
www.chateau-hautefort.com

Hautefort clings to the sides
of a steep hill topped by a
massive 17th-century château,
one of the finest in southwest
France. Partially fortified and
built as a pleasure palace in
honour of King Louis XIII's
secret love, the Marquis de
Hautefort's sister Marie, the
castle sits among French gardens on terraces with superb
views of the rolling countryside
of northeast Périgord. In the
village, the hospice, of a
similar date, has a museum
of early medical implements.

Brantôme Abbey, with belfry

Brantôme ③

Dordogne. 🏠 *2,200.* 🚇 🚏 *inside
the abbey (05 53 05 80 52).* 🛒 *Fri.*
www.ville-brantome.fr

Surrounded by the river
Dronne, Brantôme is often
called the Venice of the
Périgord Vert. Its medieval
abbey and 11th-century belfry
(reputedly the oldest in
France), together with the
verdant rockface behind,
provide a dramatic backdrop
for this picturesque town.
    Pierre de Bourdeille, the poet
(1540–1614), was appointed
abbot here in his youth. His
lovers allegedly included Mary,
Queen of Scots. After a crip-
pling fall, Bourdeille retired
here in 1569 to write his racy
memoirs. It is possible to wander the stone staircases and
cloisters, and through the main
courtyard to the intriguing
troglodyte dwellings in the
cliff behind. In one is a huge
crucifixion scene cut into the
stone during the 16th century.

Just 12 km (7 miles) northeast
lies the Renaissance **Château
de Puyguilhem** and **Grotte de
Villars**. Discovered in 1953,
these caves lead to several
different levels. Apart from
spectacular rock formations,
there are some marvellous
1,700-year-old cave paintings.

🏰 **Château de Puyguilhem**
Villars. *Tel 05 53 54 82 18.* ⭘ *Apr–
Sep: daily; Oct–Mar: Wed–Sun.*
⚫ *1 Jan, 1 May, 1 &11 Nov, 25 Dec.*
📷 ♿ **http://**puyguilhem.
monuments-nationaux.fr

🦇 **Grotte de Villars**
Villars. *Tel 05 53 54 82 36.*
⭘ *Apr–Oct: daily.* 📷 🎟 *oblig.*
www.grotte-villars.com

Bourdeilles ④

Dordogne. 🏠 *800.* 🚏 *63 place
Tilleuls (05 53 03 42 96).*

This small town has everything – a Gothic bridge with
cutwater piers spanning the
Dronne, a mill and a medieval
château. The 16th-century
additions to the castle were
designed in a hurry by the
châtelaine Jacquette de Mont-
bron, when expecting Queen
Catherine de' Medici to visit.
When the royal visit was called
off, so were the building
works. The highlight is the
gilded salon, decorated in the
1560s by Ambroise le Noble,
of the Fontainebleau School.

🏰 **Château de Bourdeilles**
Tel 05 53 03 73 36. ⭘ *Feb–Mar &
Nov–mid-Dec: Mon, Wed, Thu &
Sun; Jul–Aug: daily; Sep–Oct & late
Dec: Wed–Mon.* ⚫ *Jan.* 📷 🎟
www.bourdeilles.com

The impressive Château de Bourdeilles towering above the town

For hotels and restaurants in this region see pp582–5 and pp637–40

century, when architect Paul
Abadie added the fancy domes
and cones. He later used
St-Front as inspiration for the
Sacré-Coeur in Paris (see p134).

Other gems of medieval
and Renaissance architecture
include **Maison Estignard**,
at No. 3 rue Limogeanne,
with its unusual corkscrew
staircase, and houses along
rue Aubergerie and rue de
la Constitution.

Also in the cathedral quarter
is the **Musée d'Art et d'Archéologie du Périgord**, one of the
most comprehensive prehistory
museums in France, with
remnants of burials dating
back 70,000 years. Beautiful
Roman glass, mosaics, earthenware and other artifacts from
Vesunna are in the Gallo-
Roman museum.

🏛 **Musée d'Art et
d'Archéologie du Périgord**
22 cours Tourny. **Tel** 05 53 06 40 70.
⬜ Wed–Mon. ⬤ public hols. 🈲

St-Amand-de-Coly ❻

Dordogne. **Tel** Maison du Patrimoine
(05 53 51 04 56, summer only); La
Mairie (05 53 51 47 85). ⬜ daily.
www.saint-amand-de-coly.org

This abbey church is an
outstanding example of
fortress architecture, built in
the 12th–13th centuries by
Augustinian monks to protect
their monastery. There are two
lines of defence: a high stone
rampart and, behind it, the
arched tower of the church
itself. The tower looks more
like a castle keep, and was
once pierced by arrow slits.

Inside, the church is beautifully simple, with pure lines,
a flat ribbed vault, 12th-
century cupola, a soaring
nave and a stone floor
sloping up to the altar. Yet
even this interior was arranged
for defence, with a gallery
from which enemies within
the building could be attacked.

St-Amand was damaged
during the Hundred Years'
War. In 1575, it survived a
siege by Huguenot cavalry
and a 6-day bombardment by
cannon. Religious life here
ended after the Revolution.

Cathédrale St-Front in Périgueux, restored in the 19th century

Périgueux ❺

Dordogne. 🏠 31,000. ✈ 🚆 🚌
🛈 26 pl Francheville (05 53 53 10
63). ⬤ daily. www.tourisme-
perigueux.fr

The ancient and truly gastronomic city of Périgueux, like
its neighbours Bergerac and
Riberac, should be visited on
market day, when stalls in the
lively squares in the medieval
part of town offer the pick
of local specialities, including truffles (Nov–Mar),
charcuterie and the
succulent pies called
pâtés de Périgueux.

Périgueux, now
the busy regional
capital, has long
been the crossroads
of Périgord. The
earliest part remain-
ing today is the quarter
known as **La Cité**,
once the important
Gallo-Roman settle-
ment of Vesunna. La
Domus de Vesonne, a
Gallo-Roman museum,
has just opened on site.
From Roman times to
the Middle Ages, this

was the focus of Périgueux.
Most of the fabric of Vesunna
was pulled down in the 3rd
century, but some vestiges of
a temple, a huge arena and a
sumptuous villa remain. The
Eglise St-Etienne nearby dates
back to the 12th century.

Walking up the hill from
La Cité to the city's dazzling
white cathedral you pass
through bustling streets and
squares, each with its market
activity. This is the medieval
quarter of **Le Puy St-
Front**, which began
to flourish as pilgrims
on their way to Santiago
de Compostela (see
p400) visited the
cathedral. As they
brought prestige and
wealth to the quarter,
it gradually eclipsed
La Cité.

At the top stands the
imposing **Cathédrale
St-Front**, the largest in
southwestern France.
The Romanesque con-
struction was heavily
restored in the 19th

**19th-century stained glass
in Cathédrale St-Front**

Sarlat ⑪

Sculptures of geese in Sarlat

Sarlat-la-Canéda possesses the highest concentration of medieval, Renaissance and 17th-century façades of any town in France. Its prosperity was a reflection of the privileged status it was granted in return for loyalty to the French crown during the Hundred Years' War. Behind the nondescript rue de la République are narrow lanes and archways, and ancient, ochre-coloured stone town houses rich in ornamental detail. Protected by law since 1962, Sarlat's buildings now form an open-air museum. The town is also famous for one of the best markets in France.

Place de la Liberté
The Renaissance heart of Sarlat is no[w] lined with luxury shops and cafés.

Rue des Consuls contains 15th-, 16th- and 17th-century mansions, built for the town's middle-class merchants, magistrates and church officials.

Rue Jean-Jacques Rousseau was the main street until rue de la République (known as "La Traverse") was built in the 19th century.

Walnuts, a key Périgord crop

SARLAT MARKET

Every Wednesday, the great Sarlat food market is held in place de la Liberté, and every Saturday there is a full-scale fair which attracts locals from all around. Sarlat lies at the heart of the nation's *foie gras* and walnut trades. These typical Périgord products absorb much of the town's attention and supply a good proportion of its revenue, as they did during Sarlat's heyday in the 14th and 15th centuries. Other local specialities are black truffles dug up in the woods in January, and wild mushrooms. Seek out, too, the cheeses of every shape, age and hue, and the huge range of pork delicacies available, which may be potted, fresh, smoked, dried, salted, fried, baked or boiled.

Bulbs of pink garlic

Town walls

KEY

– – – Suggested route

| 0 metres | 50 |
| 0 yards | 50 |

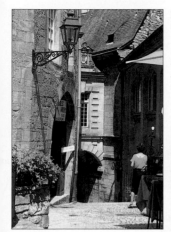

Rue de la Salamandre

This lane was named after the salamander emblem of King François I, seen on many of the town's 16th-century houses.

VISITORS' CHECKLIST

Dordogne. 10,500.
av de la Gare.
3 rue Tourny (05 53 31 45 45). Wed & Sat.
Theatre (Jul–Aug); Film (Nov).
www.sarlat-tourisme.com

Lanterne des Morts (Lantern of the Dead)

The conical tower in the cemetery was built to commemorate St Bernard's sermons in Sarlat in August 1147.

Cathédrale St-Sacerdos

Built largely in the 16th and 17th centuries, the cathedral is remarkable for its magnificent 18th-century organ.

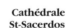

The Chapelle des Pénitents Bleus, built in pure Romanesque style, is the last vestige of the 12th-century abbey.

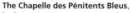

The former Bishop's Palace, with remains of a 16th-century loggia and a Renaissance interior, is now a tourist office which puts on excellent summer exhibitions.

Cour des Fontaines

A pure spring here attracted the monks who founded Sarlat's first abbey in the 9th century.

Painting of a bull from the original cave at Lascaux

Lascaux II **7**

Montignac. **Tel** 05 53 05 65 65.
◯ Feb–mid-Nov: daily; mid-Nov–Feb:
Tue–Sun; times vary – phone to
check. ◉ Jan, 25 Dec. 🎫 🎦
www.lascaux.culture.fr

Lascaux is the most famous
of the prehistoric sites
clustered around the junction
of the rivers Vézère and Beune
(see pp402–3). Four boys
came across the caves and
their astonishing palaeolithic
paintings in 1940, and the
importance of their discovery
was swiftly recognized.
   Lascaux has been closed to
the public since 1963 because
of deterioration, but an exact
copy has been created a few
minutes' walk down the hillside, using the same materials.
The replica is beautiful and
should not be spurned: high-
antlered elk, bison, bulls and
plump horses cover the walls,
surrounded by arrows and
geometric symbols thought to
have had ritual significance.

Bergerac **8**

Dordogne. 🏘 26,000. ✈ 🚆 🚌
🛈 97 rue Neuve d'Argenson (05 53
57 03 11). 🗓 Wed & Sat.
www.bergerac-tourisme.com

This small port, a tobacco
farming and commercial
centre, spreads itself over
both sides of the Dordogne.
Chief attractions are its extraordinary **Musée du Tabac**
(tobacco museum), and its
food and wine which are
invariably excellent. Bergerac's

most celebrated wine is Monbazillac, a sweet white wine,
often drunk on ceremonial
occasions. On show in the
small, lively museum are
some Native American pipes.

🏛 Musée du Tabac
Maison Peyrarède, pl du Feu.
Tel 05 53 63 04 13. ◯ Tue–Sun.
◉ Sun ams (Oct–Mar: Sun all day),
public hols. 🎫 ♿

Les Eyzies **9**

Dordogne. 🏘 900. 🚆 🛈 19 av
de la Préhistoire (05 53 06 97 05).
🗓 Mon (Apr–Oct).
www.tourisme-vezere.com

Four major prehistoric sites
and a group of smaller caves
cluster around the unassuming village of Les Eyzies.
Head first for the **Musée
National de Préhistoire**, in a
new building at the foot of a
16th-century castle over-
looking the village. The
timelines and other exhibits
are useful for putting the vast
warren of prehistoric painting
and sculpture into context.
   The **Grotte de Font de
Gaume** is the logical first stop
after the museum at Les
Eyzies. This cave, discovered
in 1901, contains probably
the finest prehistoric paintings
still on public view in France.
   Close by is the **Grotte des
Combarelles**, with engravings
of bison, reindeer, magic
symbols and human figures.

Les Eyzies, a centre for the area's concentration of prehistoric caves

Further on, you reach the rock shelter of **Abri du Cap Blanc**, discovered in 1909, with a rare, life-size frieze of horses and bison sculpted in the rock.

On the other side of Les Eyzies is the cave system at **Rouffignac**, a favourite place for excursions since the 15th century. There are 8 km (5 miles) of caves here, 2.5 km (1.5 miles) of which are served by electric train. The paintings include drawings of mammoths, and a frieze of two bison challenging each other to combat.

Tickets for all the caves sell out fast, especially in summer, so arrive early. Some must be booked 2 weeks ahead.

View of Domme from the medieval gateway of Porte de la Combe

Musée National de Préhistoire

🏛 **Musée National de Préhistoire**
Tel 05 53 06 45 45. ◻ *Jul & Aug: daily; Sep–Jun: Wed–Mon.*
◉ *1 Jan, 25 Dec.* 🎫 ♿ 🛍 📷

📸 **Grotte de Font de Gaume**
Tel 05 53 06 86 00. ◻ *Sun–Fri by appt; book 2 months ahead.*
◉ *some public hols.*

📸 **Grotte des Combarelles**
Tel 05 53 06 86 00. ◻ *Sun–Fri (book fortnight ahead).* ◉ *some public hols.* 🎫

📸 **Abri du Cap Blanc**
Marquay, Les Eyzies. *Tel* 05 53 06 86 00. ◻ *Apr–Oct: daily.* ◉ *some public hols.* 🎫 ♿

📸 **Grotte de Rouffignac**
Tel 05 53 05 41 71. ◻ *Apr–Oct: daily.* 🎫 ♿

Dordogne Valley ⑩

Dordogne. ✈ *Bergerac.* 🚉 *Bergerac, Le Buisson de Cadouin.* 🚌 *Beynac.* ℹ *Le Buisson de Cadouin (05 53 22 06 09).*

Probably no river in France crosses so varied a landscape and such different geological formations as the Dordogne. Starting in deep granite gorges in the Massif Central, it continues through fertile lowlands, then enters the limestone Causse country around Souillac. By the time the Dordogne has wound down to the Garonne, it is almost 3 km (2 miles) wide.

Don't be put off by the valley's touristy image. It is a beautiful area for wandering. Several villages make good stopping-off points, such as Limeuil, Beynac and La Roque-Gageac from where *gabarres* (river boats) ferry visitors (Easter–Oct).

Perched high above the river, southwest of Sarlat, is the 17th-century **Château de Marqueyssac**. Its topiary park offers panoramic views from Domme to Beynac, and of the Château de Castelnaud on the opposite river bank.

Sarlat ⑪

See pp432–3.

Domme ⑫

Dordogne. 🏘 *1,030.*
ℹ *pl de la Halle (05 53 31 71 00).*
🛒 *Thu.* **www**.ot-domme.com

Henry Miller wrote: "Just to glimpse the black, mysterious river at Domme from the beautiful bluff…is something to be grateful for all one's life." Domme itself is a neat bastide *(see p445)* of golden stone, with medieval gateways still standing. People come here to admire the view, which takes in the Dordogne valley from Beynac in the west to Montfort in the east, and wander the maze of old streets inside the walls. There is also a large cavern under the 17th-century covered market where the inhabitants hid at perilous moments during the Hundred Years' War and the 16th-century Wars of Religion. Despite a seemingly impregnable position, 30 intrepid Huguenots managed to capture Domme by scaling the cliffs under cover of night and opening the gates.

A *cingle* (loop) of the river Dordogne, seen from the town of Domme

Rocamadour ⓭

Rocamadour became one of the most famous centres of pilgrimage following a spate of miracles heralded, it is claimed, by the bell above the Black Virgin and Child in the Chapel of Notre-Dame. This was followed by the discovery in 1166 of an ancient grave and sepulchre containing an undecayed body, said to be that of the early Christian hermit St Amadour. Although the town suffered with the decline of pilgrimages in the 17th and 18th centuries, it was heavily restored in the 19th century. Still a holy shrine, as well as a popular tourist destination, Rocamadour's site on a rocky plateau above the Alzou valley is phenomenal. The best views are to be had from the ramparts of the château, reached from the hamlet of L'Hospitalet.

Black Virgin and Child

The Château stands on the site of a fort which protected the sanctuary from the west.

St Michael's Chapel contains well-preserved 12th-century frescoes.

General View
Rocamadour is at its most breathtaking in the sunlight of early morning: the cluster of medieval houses, towers and battlements seems to sprout from the base of the cliff.

The Tomb of St Amadour once held the body of the hermit called *roc amator* (lover of rock), from whom the town took its name.

Grand Stairway
Pilgrims would climb this broad flight of steps on their knees as they said their rosaries. The stairway leads to a square on the next level, around which the main pilgrim chapels are grouped.

The Chapel of St John the Baptist faces the fine Gothic portal of the Basilica of St-Sauveur.

The Basilica of St-Sauveur, a late 12th-century sanctuary, backs on to the bare rock face.

St Anne's Chapel dates from the 13th century, and contains a 17th-century gilded altar screen.

Ramparts

Cross of Jerusalem

Stations of the Cross
Pilgrims encounter the Cross of Jerusalem and 14 stations marking Jesus's journey to the Cross on their way up the hillside to the château.

Chapel of St Blaise (13th century)

Rocamadour Town
Now a pedestrian precinct, its main street is lined with souvenir shops to tempt the throngs of pilgrims.

Chapel of Notre-Dame (Miracles)
St Amadour's body was found in the cliff, near the Black Virgin Chapel. A statue of the Black Virgin, the supreme object of veneration, stands on the altar.

Gouffre de Padirac ⑭

Lot. **Tel** 05 65 33 64 56.
⬜ Apr–Oct: daily. 🎟 🔲
www.gouffre-de-padirac.com

Formed by the collapse of a cave, this huge crater measures 35 m (115 ft) wide and 103 m (337 ft) deep. The underground river and stunning succession of galleries *(see p403)* were discovered in 1889. The immense Salle du Grand Dôme chamber dwarfs the tallest of cathedrals. Take a jacket; the cave is 13° C (55° F).

Autoire ⑮

Lot. 🏛 370. 🚩 Saint Céré
(05 65 38 11 85).
www.tourisme-saint-cere.com

This is one of the loveliest places in Quercy, the fertile area east of Périgord. There are no grand monuments or dramatic history, just an unspoiled site at the mouth of the Autoire gorge. The **Château de Limarque** on the main square, and the **Château de Busqueille** overlooking it, are both built in characteristic Quercy style, with turrets and towers. Elsewhere, elaborate dovecotes stand in fields or are attached to houses.

Outside Autoire, past a 30-m (100-ft) waterfall, a path climbs to a rock amphitheatre giving panoramic views of the region.

The picturesque village of Autoire, seen from across the gorge

Cahors ⑯

Lot. 🏛 21,200. 🚉 🚌
🚩 pl François Mitterrand (05 65 53 20 65). 🛒 Wed & Sat am.
www.tourisme-cahors.com

The capital of the Lot *département*, Cahors is renowned for its dark, heady wine, which was produced as far back as Roman times. It is also famous for being the birthplace of the statesman Léon Gambetta (1838–82), who led France to recovery after the war with Prussia in 1870. The main street of Cahors – like many towns in France – is named after him.

Cathédrale de St-Etienne, entrenched behind the narrow streets of Cahors' Old Town, dates back to 1119. It has some fine medieval details: don't miss the lively figures of the Romanesque north door and tympanum, which depict the Ascension, or the huge cupola above the nave (said

A Tour of Two Rivers

Flanked by spectacular limestone cliffs, the beautiful Lot and Célé valleys feature ancient medieval villages and castles, narrow gorges and rushing waterfalls along lazy stretches of river. An unhurried tour of both valleys, around 160 km (100 miles), is best spread over 2 days, to savour the gastronomic delights as well as the superb views.

From Cahors, the route follows the Lot, then meanders slowly up the peaceful and picturesque Célé valley to reach Figeac, a handsome town full of charming shops, cafés and restaurants. The return route is via the busier Lot Valley, which has more sights including the spectacular village of St-Cirq-Lapopie (allow time to park above or below the village and enter on foot).

Grotte de Pech-Merle ①
This 25,000-year-old prehistoric site outside Cabrerets has huge chambers painted with mammoths, horses, bison and human figures.

CAHORS

Vers

Cabrerets ①

Bouziès

Lot

D653   D662

⑥

St-Cirq-Lapopie ⑥
Perched high above the Lot, one of France's prettiest villages has a 15th-century church and timber-framed houses built into the cliffs.

to be the largest in France). They are covered in 14th-century frescoes depicting the stoning of St Stephen (St-Étienne). The Renaissance cloisters are decorated with some intricate, though damaged, carvings.

Also worth seeking out in the cathedral quarter is the ornate 16th-century **Maison de Roaldès**, its north façade decorated with tree, sun and rose of Quercy motifs. It was here that Henri of Navarre (who later became King Henri IV) stayed for one night in 1580 after besieging and capturing Cahors.

The town's landmark monument is the **Pont Valentré**, a fortified bridge with seven pointed arches and three towers that spans the river. It was built between 1308 and 1360, and has withstood many attacks since then. It is claimed that the bridge is one of the most photographed monuments in the whole of

The fortified Pont Valentré spanning the river Lot at Cahors

France. An alternative way to enjoy the scenery is to take a leisurely 90-minute boat trip through the lock from a wharf near the bridge (Apr–Oct).

Environs
Cahors makes a good base from which to explore the sights of the Lot. Visit the historic towns of Figeac,

birthplace of Jean-François Champollion who first deciphered Egyptian hieroglyphs, and the **Grotte de Pech-Merle** with its extra-ordinary painted walls.

Grotte de Pech-Merle
Cabrerets. **Tel** 05 65 31 27 05.
☐ Apr–Oct daily. 🖼
www.pechmerle.com

arcilhac-sur-Célé ②
is ancient village
s a ruined 10th-
ntury Benedictine
bey. Just outside is
e Grotte de Bellevue,
th its stalagmites and
her weird under-
ound rock
mations.

Espagnac-Ste-Eulalie ③
The 12th-century Priory of
Notre-Dame-Ste-Eulalie has
an elaborate belltower.

D802

Célé

D19

D41

D17

St Pierre-Toirac

D822

D86

D127

D662

Lot

D8

alvignac

Figeac ④
Excellent hotels and restaurants
are located here, as well as the
Musée Champollion, with its cast
of the Rosetta stone.

Cajarc ⑤
Medieval houses still survive
in this tiny village. A short
drive away is the Renaissance
Château de Cénevières.

kilometres   5

miles   5

KEY

▬▬ Tour route

══ Other roads

Orchards and vineyards outside Agen

Agen ⑰

Lot-et-Garonne. 🏠 35,000. ✈ 🚆
🚌 ℹ 38 rue Garonne (05 53 47 36
09). 🏛 Tue–Sun. www.ot-agen.org

Vast orchards of regimented
plum trees – producing the
celebrated *pruneaux d'Agen* –
characterize the landscape
around this small provincial
city. Crusaders returning from
the Middle East brought the
fruit to France in the 11th
century, and monks in the
Lot valley nearby were the
first to dry plums for prunes
in commercial quantities.

Agen's **Musée Municipal des
Beaux-Arts** contains paintings
by Goya, including his *Ascent
in a Hot-Air Balloon*, Sisley's
September Morning, Corot's
landscape *L'étang de Ville
d'Avray* and works by
Picabia. Undisputed jewel of
the collection is the *Vénus du
Mas*, a beautifully proportioned marble statue dating

from the 1st century BC,
discovered nearby in 1876.

🏛 **Musée Municipal des
Beaux-Arts**
Pl du Docteur Esquirol. **Tel** 05 53 69
47 23. ⬜ Wed–Mon. ⬤ 1 Jan, 1
May, 1 Nov, 25 Dec. 🎫

Environs
The fortified village of Moirax,
8 km (5 miles) south of Agen,
has a 12th-century Roman-
esque church of great beauty
and symmetry. Two of the
appealing sculpted capitals
depict biblical accounts of
Daniel in the lions' den, and
Original Sin.

The bastide town *(see p445)*
of Villeneuve-sur-Lot, 34 km
(21 miles) south of Agen
stands astride the River Lot.
It has a tall 14th-century
tower that once formed a
defensive gateway. The red-
brick Romano-Byzantine
church of Ste-Catherine was
built in 1909 but contains

restored 15th-century stained-
glass windows. Just to the
east of Villeneuve is the pretty
medieval hill-top village of
Penne D'Agenais.

Larressingle ⑱

Gers. 🏠 200. 🚌 to Condom.
ℹ Condom (05 62 28 00 80).

With its ramparts, ruined
donjon (defence tower) and
fortress gate, Larressingle is a
tiny fortified village in the
middle of the Gascon countryside. It dates from the 13th
century, and is one of the last
remaining Gascon villages
with its walls still intact. The
state of preservation is unique,
and gives an idea of what life
must have been like for the
small, embattled local communities who had to live for
decades under conditions of
perpetual warfare.

Condom ⑲

Gers. 🏠 7,500. 🚌 ℹ 50 bd de la
Libération (05 62 28 00 80). 🏛 Wed,
Sat am. www.tourisme-tenareze.com

Long a centre for the
Armagnac trade, Condom is a
market town built around the
late-Gothic **Cathédrale St-
Pierre**. In 1569 during
the Wars of Religion, the
Huguenot (French Protestant)
army threatened to demolish
the cathedral, but Condom's
citizens averted this by paying
a huge ransom.

The river Baïse skirts the
town centre. Notable among
Condom's fine 17th–18th-
century mansions is the **Hôtel
de Cugnac** on rue Jean-Jaurès,
with its ancient *chai* (wine
and spirit storehouse) and
distillery. On the other side of
the town centre, the **Musée
de l'Armagnac** is the place to
find out, finally, what the
difference between the
brandy of Armagnac and
Cognac really is.

🏛 **Musée de
l'Armagnac**
2 rue Jules Ferry. **Tel** 05
62 28 47 17. ⬜ Apr–Oct:
Wed–Mon; Nov–Mar:
Wed–Sun pms. ⬤ Jan,
public hols. 🎫 ♿

ARMAGNAC

Armagnac is one of the world's most expensive brandies. It is also one of the leading
products of southwest France: approximately
6 million bottles are produced annually,
45 per cent of which are exported to
132 countries. The vineyards of Armagnac
roughly straddle the border between the
Gers and the Lot-et-Garonne regions
and the Landes. Similar in style to
Cognac, its more famous neighbour,
Armagnac's single distillation leaves
more individual flavours in the spirit.
The majority of small, independent
producers offer direct sale to the
public: look out for the battered,
often half-hidden farm signs
advertising *Vente Directe*.

A Tenarèze Armagnac

D'ARTAGNAN

Gascons call their domain the "Pays d'Artagnan" after Alexandre Dumas' rollicking hero from *The Three Musketeers* (1844). The character of d'Artagnan was based on Charles de Batz, a typical Gascon whose chivalry, passion and impetuousness made him ideal as a musketeer, or royal bodyguard. De Batz's life was as fast and furious as that of the fictional hero, and he performed a feat of courtliness by arresting Louis XIV's most formidable minister without causing the slightest offence. The French have other opinions on the Gascon nature too: a *promesse de Gascon,* for example, means an empty promise.

Statue of Dumas' musketeer d'Artagnan in Auch

windows show a mix of prophets, patriarchs and apostles, with 360 individually characterized figures and exceptional colours. Three depict the key biblical events of Creation, the Crucifixion and the Resurrection.

Auch went through an urbanization programme in the 18th century, when the allées d'Etigny, flanked by the grand Hôtel de Ville and Palais de Justice, were built. Some fine houses from this period line the pedestrianized rue Dessoles. Auch's restaurants are known for their hearty dishes, including *foie gras de canard* (fattened duck liver).

Auch ⑳

Gers. 🏛 *23,500.* 🚉 🚌 🛈 *1 rue Dessoles (05 62 05 22 89).* 🛍 *Thu & Sat.* www.auch-tourisme.com

The ancient capital of the Gers department, Auch (pronounced "Ohsh") has long been a sleepy place which comes alive on market days. The new town by the station is not a place which encourages you to linger. Head instead for the Old Town on the outcrop

Medallion from Cathédrale Ste-Marie

overlooking the river Gers. If you climb the 234 stone steps from the river, you arrive directly in front of the restored late-Gothic **Cathédrale Ste-Marie,** begun in 1489. The furnishings of the cathedral are remarkable: highlights are the carved wooden choir stalls depicting more than 1,500 biblical, historical and mythological characters, and the equally magnificent 15th-century stained glass, attributed to Arnaud de Moles. The

Auvillar ㉑

Tarn-et-Garonne. 🏛 *1,000.* 🛈 *pl de la Halle (05 63 39 89 82).*

A perfect complement to the high emotion of Moissac *(see pp442–3),* Auvillar is one of the loveliest hilltop villages in France. It has a triangular marketplace lined with half-timbered arcades at its centre, and extensive views from the promenade overlooking the river Garonne. There are picnic spots along this panoramic path plus an orientation map. This includes all but the chimneys visible in the distance, belonging to the nuclear plant at Golfech.

Sunflowers, a popular crop in southwest France grown for their seeds and oil

Moissac ㉒

At the core of this otherwise unremarkable riverside town is the abbey of St-Pierre, one of the undisputed masterpieces of French Romanesque art. Founded in the 7th century by a Benedictine monk, the abbey was subsequently ransacked by Arabs, Normans and Hungarians. In 1047, Moissac abbey was united with the rich foundation at Cluny and prospered

Abbot Durand under the direction of Abbot Durand de Bredon. By the 12th century it had become the pre-eminent monastery in southwest France. The superb south portal was created during this period.

Abbey of St-Pierre
The church's exterior belongs to two periods: one part, in stone, is Romanesque, the other, in brick, is Gothic.

Christ in Majesty
The figure of Christ sits in judgment at the centre of the scene. He holds the Book of Life in His left hand and raises His right in benediction.

Tympanum
The lower register of the balanced, compact tympanum shows the expressive "24 Elders with crowns of gold" from St John's vision.

★ **South Portal**
The carved south portal (1100–1130) is a masterful translation into stone of St John's dramatic vision of the Apocalypse (Book of Revelation, Chapters 4 and 5). The Evangelists Matthew, Mark, Luke and John appear as "four beasts full of eyes". Moorish details on the door jambs reflect the contemporary cultural exchange between France and Spain.

VISITORS' CHECKLIST

Tarn-et-Garonne. 13,000.
🚉 🚌 👤 6 pl Durand de Bredon
(05 63 04 01 85). 🛍 Sat, Sun
ams. **Abbey** ⬭ daily. **Cloisters**
⬭ daily (phone for details).
✝ 6:30pm Mon–Fri, 7:30pm Sat,
10.30am Sun. 📷 📹
http://tourisme.moissac.fr

★ **Cloister**
*The late 11th-century
cloister is lined with
alternate double and single
columns in white, pink,
green and grey marble.
In all, there are 76 richly
decorated arches.*

FLOORPLAN: CHURCH AND CLOISTER

Ancienne Salle Capitulaire
Chapelle du St Sacrement
Choir
Musée Claustral
Sacristy
Cloister
Nave
South Portal
Narthex

Cloister Capitals
*Flowers, beasts and
scenes from both the Old
and New Testaments are
featured in these superbly
sculptured 11th-century
Romanesque capitals.*

STAR FEATURES

★ South Portal

★ Cloister

Montauban ㉓

Tarn-et-Garonne. 🏘 58,000. 🚉 🚌
👤 4 rue du Collège (05 63 63
60 60). 🛍 Sat, Wed.
www.montauban-tourisme.com

Montauban deserves more
attention than it usually gets,
as Toulouse's little pink-brick
sister and the capital of the
17th-century "Protestant
Republic" of southern France.
The painter Ingres was born
here in 1780, and the town's
great treasure is the **Musée
Ingres**, a 17th-century palace
with an exceptional bequest of
paintings and 4,000 drawings,
plus works by Van Dyck, Tintoretto, Courbet and sculptor
Emile Bourdelle, an associate
of Rodin, also from here.
    Above all, Montauban is a
civilized shopping centre, with
a double-arcaded main square
(place Nationale) built in the
17th and 18th centuries. A few
streets away lies the stark
white **Cathédrale Notre-Dame**,
built on the orders of Louis
XIV in 1692, in the backlash
against Protestant heresy.

🏛 **Musée Ingres**
Palais Episcopal, 13 rue de l'Hôtel
de Ville. *Tel* 05 63 22 12 91. ⬭
Tue–Sun (Jul–Aug: daily). ⬤ 1 Jan,
14 Jul, 1 Nov, 11 Nov, 25 Dec. 📹

Gorges de l'Aveyron ㉔

Tarn-et-Garonne. ✈ Toulouse. 🚉
Montauban, Lexos. 🚌 Montauban.
👤 Mairie, St-Antonin-Noble-Val
(05 63 30 63 47). www.tourisme-
saint-antonin-noble-val.com

At the Gorges de l'Aveyron,
the sweltering plains of
Montauban change abruptly
to cool, chestnut-wooded hills.
Here the villages are of a
different stamp from those of
Périgord and Quercy, displaying an obsession with defence.
    The château at Bruniquel,
founded in the 6th century, is
built over the lip of a preci-
pice. Further along the D115,
the village of Penne's position
on the tip of a giant rock fang
is even more extreme. The
gorge narrows and darkens;
from St-Antonin-Noble-Val,
beside the river, the valley
turns towards Cordes.

Cordes ㉕

Tarn. 🏘 *1,050.* �''🚌 🛈 *pl Jeane Ramel-Cals (05 63 56 00 52).* 🛒 *Sat.*
www.cordessurciel.fr

Sometimes known as Cordes-sur-Ciel, this is a fitting description as the town seems suspended against the skyline. During the 13th-century Cathar wars the entire town was excommunicated. Devastating epidemics of plague later sent it into decline, and the town was in an advanced state of decay at the beginning of the 20th century.

Restoration work began in the 1940s and the ramparts and many of the gates built in 1222 have been well preserved. Also intact are Gothic houses like the 14th-century **Maison du Grand Fauconnier**.

Today, Cordes still exudes a sense of loss. The town of which Albert Camus wrote "Everything is beautiful there, even regret", is now dependent on tourism. "Medieval" crafts aimed at visitors abound and a collection at the **Musée d'Art Moderne et Contemporain** evokes Cordes' former embroidery industry. The museum also houses works of modern art by such artists as Picasso and Miro. The **Jardin des Paradis** offers a corner of beauty and hope to reflect in.

🏛 Musée d'Art Moderne et Contemporain

Maison du Grand Fauconnier. **Tel** *05 63 56 14 79.*
⭘ *mid-Mar–mid-Nov: daily.*
⬤ *Jan.* 🌀 🛇

Cathédrale Ste-Cécile perched above the town of Albi

Albi ㉖

Tarn. 🏘 *51,275.* 🚏 🚌
🛈 *pl Ste-Cécile (05 63 36 36 00).*
🛒 *Tue–Sun.* www.albi-tourisme.fr

Like many another large town in this region, Albi is not only red, but also red hot, and not ideal for afternoon visits in summer. You need to get up in the cool early morning to walk the streets around the market and the cathedral.

Then make for the **Musée Henri de Toulouse-Lautrec** in the Palais de la Berbie ahead of the crowds. The museum contains the most complete permanent collection of the artist's work in existence, including paintings, drawings and his famous posters for the Moulin-Rouge. There are also canvases by Matisse, Dufy and Yves Brayer. After a stroll around the beautiful terraced gardens, step next door to the vast red-brick **Cathédrale Ste-Cécile**, built in the aftermath of the Albigensian crusade in 1265. It was intended as a reminder to potential heretics that the Church meant business. From a distance, its

semi-circular towers and narrow windows give it the appearance more of a fortress than a place of worship. Every feature, from the huge bell-tower to the apocalyptic fresco of the *Last Judgement*, is on a giant scale, built deliberately to dwarf the average person. The effect is breathtaking.

🏛 Musée Toulouse-Lautrec

Palais de la Berbie.
Tel *05 63 49 58 97.*
⭘ *Apr–Sep: daily; Oct–Mar: Wed–Mon.* ⬤ *1 Jan, 1 May, 1 Nov, 25 Dec.*
🌀 🛗 🛇 🎧
www.musee-toulouse-lautrec.com

Castres ㉗

Tarn. 🏘 *45,000.* ✈ 🚏 🚌
🛈 *2 pl de la République (05 63 62 63 62).* 🛒 *Tue–Sun.*
www.tourisme-castres.fr

Castres has been a centre for the cloth industry since the 14th century. Today it is also the headquarters of one of France's biggest pharmaceutical companies. In the large collection of Spanish art in the **Musée Goya**, the artist himself is well represented by a large, misty council scene and by a series of powerful prints, *Los Caprichos*. Outside, the formal gardens between the town hall and the river Agout were designed in the 17th century by Le Nôtre *(see p179)*, the landscape architect of Vaux-le-Vicomte and Versailles.

🏛 Musée Goya

Hôtel de Ville. **Tel** *05 63 71 59 30 or 05 63 71 59 27.* ⭘ *Jul–Aug: daily; Sep–Jun: Tue–Sun.* ⬤ *1 Jan, 1 May, 1 Nov, 25 Dec.* 🌀

TOULOUSE-LAUTREC

Comte Henri de Toulouse-Lautrec was born in Albi in 1864. Crippled at 15 as a result of two falls, he moved to Paris in 1882, recording the life of the city's cabarets, brothels, racecourses and circuses. A dedicated craftsman, his bold, vivid posters did much to establish lithography as a major art form. Alcoholism and syphilis led to his early death at the age of 36.

Lautrec's *La Modiste* (1900)

Bastide Towns

Bastide towns were hurriedly built in the 13th century by both the English and the French, to encourage settlement of empty areas before the Hundred Years' War. They are the medieval equivalent of "new towns", with their planned grid of streets and fortified perimeters. Over 300 bastide towns and villages still survive between Périgord and the Pyrenees.

A broad arcaded marketplace *is the central feature of most bastides. Montauban's arcades still shelter a variety of shops.*

The central square is surrounded by a grid of interconnecting streets and alleys. This differs markedly from the usual jumble of medieval houses and lanes.

Lauzerte, *founded in 1241 by the Count of Toulouse, is a typical bastide town of grey stone houses. The town, long an English outpost, is perched for security on the brow of a hill.*

The church could be used as a keep when the bastide's outer fortifications had been breached.

Stone houses protected the perimeter.

MONFLANQUIN

This military bastide town was built by the French in 1256 on a strategic north–south route. It changed hands several times during the Hundred Years' War.

Today, the bastides *form a convenient network of market towns, known as the* route des bastides. *The best time to visit them is on market day, when the central squares are crammed with stalls.*

Porte de la Jane *in Cordes is a typical bastide feature. These narrow gateways were easily barred by portcullises.*

Toulouse ㉘

Toulouse, the most important town in southwest France, is the country's fourth largest metropolis, and a major industrial and university city. The area is also famous for its aerospace industry (Concorde, Airbus, the Ariane space rocket all originated here), as shown by the Cité de l'Espace just outside the city.

Best seen on foot, Toulouse has fine cuisine, one of France's most striking churches, lively street life and a rose-brick Old Town, which is described as "pink at dawn, red at noon and mauve at dusk".

The river Garonne, crossed by the Pont Neuf

Houseboats at their moorings on the Canal du Midi

Exploring Toulouse

This warm southern city has steadily expanded, crescent-like, from its original Roman site on the Garonne. First it was a flourishing Visigoth city, then a Renaissance town of towered brick palaces built with the wealth generated by the *pastel* (blue pigment) and grain trades. The grandest of these palaces still survive in the Old Town, centred around Place du Capitole and the huge 18th-century **Hôtel de Ville**. Here, and in place St-Georges and rue Alsace-Lorraine, is the main concentration of shops, bars and cafés. The city's large student population keeps prices down in the numerous cafés, oyster bars and bookstores, and in the fleamarket, held on Sundays in place St-Sernin.

A ring of 18th- and 19th-century boulevards encircles the city, surrounded in turn by a tangle of autoroutes. The left bank of the Garonne is under development (St-Cyprien) and is linked by Toulouse's driverless metro. The former abattoir has been superbly converted into a centre for modern and contemporary art, **Les Abattoirs** (Wed–Sun), the highlight of which is Picasso's theatre backdrop *Minotaur disguised as Harlequin.*

🅐 Les Jacobins

This church was begun in 1229 and completed over the next two centuries. It was the first Dominican convent, founded to combat dissent. The Jacobins' convent became the founding institution of Toulouse University. Its church, a Gothic masterpiece, features a soaring, 22-branched palm tree vault in the apse. The delicate Gothic Chapelle St-Antonin (1337) contains frescoes of the Apocalypse dating from 1341.

🏛 Musée des Augustins

21 rue de Metz. **Tel** 05 61 22 21 82.
⬤ daily. ⬤ 1 Jan, 1 May, 25 Dec.
🖼 ♿ ☕ www.augustins.org

Palm vaulting in the apse of Les Jacobins

Toulouse became a centre of Romanesque art owing to its position on the route to Santiago de Compostela (see p400). The museum has sculpture from the period and 12th-century Romanesque capitals, as well as cloisters from a 14th-century Augustinian priory. There are also 16th–19th-century French, Italian and Flemish paintings here, including work by Ingres, Delacroix, Constant and Laurens.

Façade of Musée des Augustins

♠ Fondation Bemberg
Hôtel d'Assézat, 7 pl d'Assézat. **Tel** 05 61 12 06 89. ◯ Tue–Sun. ● 1 Jan, 25 Dec. 🎫 🐾 📷
This 16th-century palace houses the collection of local art lover Georges Bemberg, and covers Renaissance paintings, 19th–20th-century French paintings, *objets d'art* and bronzes.

⚑ Basilique St-Sernin
Pl St-Sernin. **Tel** 05 61 21 80 45. ◯ daily.
This is the largest Romanesque basilica in Europe, built in the 11th–12th centuries to accommodate pilgrims. Highlights are the octagonal brick belfry, with rows of decorative brick arches topped by an enormously tall spire. Beautiful 11th-century marble bas-reliefs of Christ and the symbols of the Evangelists by Bernard Gilduin are in the ambulatory.

🏛 Cité de l'Espace
Av Jean Gonord. **Tel** 08 20 37 72 23. ◯ daily in summer. ● Jan. 🎫 🐾 🅿 📷 www.cite-espace.com
Southeast of the city centre, this vast "space park" includes two planetariums, interactive exhibits related to space exploration, the Terradome "film-experience" on the history of the earth, an IMAX cinema, and a lifesize replica of the Ariane 5 rocket, where visitors can learn how, in theory at least, to launch rockets and satellites.

The tiered, 12th-century tower of Basilique St-Sernin

SIGHTS AT A GLANCE

Basilique St-Sernin ①
Fondation Bemberg ④
Le Capitole ②
Les Jacobins ③
Musée des Augustins ⑤

0 metres 250
0 yards 250

Key to Symbols see back flap

THE PYRENEES

PYRENEES-ATLANTIQUES · HAUTES-PYRENEES
ARIEGE · HAUTE-GARONNE

The mountains of the Pyrenees form a conspicuous frontier across southwestern France. Over centuries this remote terrain has fostered tenacious people, many descended from Spanish emigrants and refugees. Today it is the last remaining wilderness in southern Europe and a habitat for rare animal species.

Heading east from the Atlantic coast, the hills are wonderfully lush after the plains of Aquitaine. The deeper the Pyrenees are penetrated, the steeper the valley sides and the more gigantic the snow-clad peaks become. This is magnificent, empty, dangerous country, to be approached with caution and respect. In summer the region offers over 1,600 km (1,000 miles) of walking trails, as well as camping, fishing and climbing. In winter there is both cross-country and downhill skiing at the busy resorts along the border, much livelier than their Spanish counterparts.

Historically, the Pyrenees are known as the birthplace of Henri IV, who put an end to the Wars of Religion in 1593 and united France, though the region has been character-ized more often by inde-pendent fiefdoms. The region's oldest inhabitants, the Basque people *(see p455)* have maintained their own language and culture, and their resorts of Bayonne, Biarritz and St-Jean-de-Luz reflect this, looking to the sea and to summer visitors for their livelihood.

Inland, Pau, Tarbes and Foix rely on tourism and medium-scale industry, while Lourdes receives four million pilgrims every year. For the rest, life has been regulated by agriculture, though economic constraints today are causing an exodus from the land.

Countryside around St-Lizier, in the heart of the Pyrenean countryside

◁ Barèges, a ski resort and spa town in the Hautes-Pyrénées

Exploring the Pyrenees

The towering Pyrenees cut across southwest France from the Mediterranean to the Atlantic coast, encompassing the craggy citadel of Montségur, the pilgrimage centre of Lourdes, Pau, capital of the hilly Béarn country, and the Basque port of Bayonne. This formidable range, an unspoiled paradise for walkers, fishermen and skiers, is as lush on its French side as it is arid in Spain, and contains the wild and beautiful Parc National des Pyrénées. Throughout the region, visitors can expect cool temperatures and grandiose scenery. Lovers of history and architecture will be richly rewarded by St-Bertrand-de-Comminges and St-Jean-de-Luz, among the region's important sights.

Marzipan sweets, a speciality of southwest France

The galleried church in the Basque village of Espelette

GETTING AROUND

Access to the Basque coast in the western Pyrenees is via the A63/N10 from Bordeaux. The length of the Pyrenees, including the mountain valleys, is served by the A64, which runs from Bayonne to Toulouse, via Orthez, Pau, Tarbes and St-Gaudens. Once you are high up, expect narrow, twisting roads and slow driving. The scenic but demanding D918/D618 road crosses 18 high passes between the Atlantic and the Mediterranean.

There are airports at Biarritz, Pau and Lourdes. Both Pau and Lourdes, together with Orthez and Tarbes, are on the rail route which loops south between Bordeaux and Toulouse.

SIGHTS AT A GLANCE

Aïnhoa ❹
Arreau ❻
Bayonne ❶
Biarritz ❷
Foix ❽
Forêt d'Iraty ❽
Lourdes ❿
Luz-St-Sauveur ⓮
Mirepoix ⓴
Montségur ⓳
Oloron-Ste-Marie ❾
Orthez ❺
Parc National des Pyrénées ⓭
Pau ❿
St-Bertrand-de-Comminges ⓰
St-Jean-de-Luz ❸
St-Jean-Pied-de-Port ❼
St-Lizier ⓱
Sauveterre-de-Béarn ❻
Tarbes ⓫

Wild pottock ponies on moorland in the Forêt d'Iraty

St-Jean-de-Luz seen from Ciboure, across the Nivelle estuary

KEY

▬	Motorway
▬	Major road
▬	Secondary road
▭	Minor road
▬	Scenic route
▬	Main railway
---	Minor railway
▬	International border
▬	Regional border
△	Summit

Bayonne ❶

Pyrénées-Atlantiques. 🏠 46,000.
🚊 🚌 ▮ pl des Basques (08 20 42
64 64). 🔄 daily. www.bayonne-
tourisme.com

Bayonne, capital of the French Basque country, lies between two rivers – the turbulent Nive which arrives straight from the mountains, and the wide, languid Adour. An important town since Roman times because of its command of one of the few easily passable roads to Spain, Bayonne prospered as a free port under English rule from 1154 to 1451. Since then it has successfully withstood 14 sieges, including a particularly bloody one directed by Wellington in 1813.

Grand Bayonne, the district around the cathedral, can be easily explored on foot. The 13th-century **Cathédrale Ste-Marie** was begun under English rule and is northern Gothic in style. Look for the handsome cloister and the 15th-century knocker on the north door – if a fugitive could put a hand to this, he was entitled to sanctuary. The pedestrianized streets around form a lively shopping area, especially the arcaded rue du Port Neuf, with cafés serving hot chocolate, a Bayonne speciality. (Fine-quality chocolate-making was introduced by the Jews who fled Spain at the end of the 15th century, and it has remained a

Grand Bayonne, clustered around the twin-spired cathedral

Lighthouse at Biarritz

speciality of the town.) Bayonne is also famous for its ham.

Petit Bayonne lies on the opposite side of the quay-lined river Nive. The **Musée Basque** gives an excellent introduction to the customs and traditions of the Basque nation, with reconstructed house interiors and exhibits on seafaring. Nearby, the **Musée Bonnat** has a superb art gallery. The first floor here is a must for art lovers, with sketches by Leonardo, Van Dyck, Rubens and Rembrandt and paintings by Goya, Corot, Ingres and Constable.

🏛 Musée Basque
37 quai des Corsaires. **Tel** 05 59
59 08 98. ◯ Tue–Sun (Jul–Aug:
daily). ⬤ public hols. 📷 🔄 ▮
www.musee-basque.com

🏛 Musée Bonnat
5 rue Jacques Lafitte. **Tel** 05 59 59
08 52. ◯ Wed–Mon. ⬤ public hols.
📷 🔄 www.musee-bonnat.com

Biarritz ❷

Pyrénées-Atlantiques. 🏠 27,000.
✈ 🚊 ▮ Javalquinto, square
d'Ixelles (05 59 22 37 00). 🔄 daily.
www.biarritz.fr

Biarritz, west of Bayonne, has a grandiose centre, but has been developed along the coast by residential suburbs. The resort began as a whaling port but was transformed into a playground for the European rich in the 19th century. Its popularity was assured when Empress Eugénie discovered its mild winter climate during the reign of her husband, Napoleon III. The town has

three good beaches, with the best surfing in Europe, two casinos, and one of the last great luxury hotels in Europe, the Palais (see p586), formerly the residence of Eugénie.

In the port des Pêcheurs, the **Musée de la Mer** aquarium is home to specimens of some of the marine life found in the Bay of Biscay. Below it, a narrow causeway leads across to the Rocher de la Vierge, offering far-reaching views along the whole of the Basque coast. The Musée du Chocolat is fine compensation for a rainy day.

🏛 Musée de la Mer
Esplanade du Rocher-de-la-Vierge,
14 plateau de l'Atalaye. **Tel** 05 59
22 75 40. ◯ Apr–Oct: daily; Nov–
Mar: Tue–Sun. ⬤ 1 Jan, 2nd–3rd wk
Jan, 25 Dec. 📷 🔄 ▮ ▯
www.museedelamer.com

Altar in Eglise St-Jean-Baptiste

St-Jean-de-Luz ❸

Pyrénées-Atlantiques. 🏠 14,500.
✈ Biarritz. 🚊 🚌 ▮ 20 bd Victor
Hugo (05 59 26 03 16). 🔄 Tue & Fri.
www.saint-jean-de-luz.com

St-Jean is a quiet fishing town out of season and a scorching tourist resort in August, with shops to rival the chic rue du Faubourg St-Honoré in Paris. In the 11th century whale carcasses were towed here to feed the whole village. The natural harbour protects the shoreline, making it one of the few beaches safe for swimming along this stretch of coast.

An important historical event took place in St-Jean: the wedding of Louis XIV and the Infanta Maria Teresa

St-Jean-de-Luz, a fishing village that explodes into life in summer

of Spain in 1660, a union that had the effect of sealing the long-awaited alliance between France and Spain, only to embroil the two countries ultimately in the War of the Spanish Succession. This wedding took place at the **Eglise St-Jean-Baptiste**, still the biggest and best of the great Basque churches, a triple-galleried marvel with a glittering 17th-century altarpiece and an atmosphere of gaiety and fervour. The gate through which the Sun King led his bride was immediately walled up by masons: a plaque now marks the place. The **Maison Louis XIV**, with its contemporary furnishings, is where the king stayed in 1660, and is worth a look.

The port is busy in summer, while the restaurants behind the covered markets serve sizzling bowls full of *chipirons* – squid cooked in their own ink – a local speciality. Place Louis XIV is a lovely place to sit and watch the world go by.

🏛 **Maison Louis XIV**
Place Louis XIV. **Tel** 05 59 26 27 58.
⬜ Apr–Oct: daily. 🎫 ☑
www.maison-louis-xiv.fr

Environs
On the other side of the river Nivelle, Ciboure was the birth-place of composer Maurice Ravel. It is characterized by 18th-century merchants' houses, steep narrow streets

and seafood restaurants. A 2-hour coastal walk leads to the neighbouring village of **Socoa**, where the lighthouse on the clifftop offers a fine view of the coast all the way to Biarritz.

Basque men in traditional berets

Aïnhoa ❹

Pyrénées-Atlantiques. 🏠 680.
🚌 ℹ La Mairie (05 59 29 92 60).
www.ainhoa.fr

A tiny township on the road to the Spanish border, Aïnhoa was founded in the 12th century as a waystation on

the road to Santiago de Compostela *(see pp400–1)*. The main street of 17th-century whitewashed Basque houses and a galleried church from the same period survive.

Environs
There is a similar church in the village of Espelette nearby. Typically Basque in style, the galleries boosted the seating capacity and separated the men from the women and children. Espelette is the trading centre for *pottocks*, an ancient local breed of pony, auctioned here at the end of January. It is also the shrine of the local crop, the red pimento pepper, especially in October when a pepper festival is held here.

At the foot of the St-Ignace pass lies the mountain village of **Sare**. From the pass you can reach the summit of la Rhune by cog railway. This provides the best vantage point in the entire Pays Basque. The descent on foot is worthwhile.

11th-century château, Espelette

Sauveterre-de-Béarn and the remains of the fortified bridge over the Gave d'Oloron, the Pont de la Légende

Orthez ❺

Pyrénées-Atlantiques. 🏠 *11,000.* 🚉
🚌 ℹ *Maison Jeanne d'Albret, rue Bourg Vieux (05 59 38 32 84).* 🛒
Tue; Nov–Mar: foie gras market Sat.
www.tourisme-bearn-gaves.com

Orthez is an important Béarn market town, its 13th–14th-century fortified bridge a vital river-crossing point over the Gave de Pau in the Middle Ages. It has a spectacular Saturday morning market held from November to February, selling *foie gras*, smoked and air-cured Bayonne hams, and all kinds of fresh produce. Fine buildings line the rue Bourg Vieux, especially the house of Jeanne d'Albret, mother of Henry IV, on the corner of rue Roarie. Jeanne's enthusiasm for the Protestant faith alienated both her own subjects and Charles X, and ultimately caused the Béarn region to be drawn into the Wars of Religion (1562–93).

Sauveterre-de-Béarn ❻

Pyrénées-Atlantiques. 🏠 *1,400.*
🚌 ℹ *pl Royale (05 59 38 50 17).*
🛒 *Sat.* **www**.tourisme-bearn-gaves.com

An attractive market town, Sauveterre is well worth a night's stay. It has stunning

views southward over the Gave d'Oloron, the graceful single arch of the river's fortified bridge, and the 16th-century **Château de Nays**. Fishermen gather here for the annual world salmon-fishing championships, in the fast-flowing Oloron (April to July).

Be sure to visit the **Château de Laàs**, 9 km (5.5 miles) along the D27 from Sauveterre, which has an excellent collection of 18th-century decorative art and furniture – notably the bed Napoleon slept in on the night after his defeat at Waterloo. There is also a pretty park with a maze.

♣ **Château de Laàs**
Tel *05 59 38 91 53.* ⬜ *Apr–Oct: Wed–Mon (Apr: pm only; Jul–Aug: daily).* 🔲

The Château de Nays at Sauveterre in the Béarn region

St-Jean-Pied-de-Port ❼

Pyrénées-Atlantiques. 🏠 *1,700.*
🚌 🚉 ℹ *14 pl du Général de Gaulle (0810 75 36 71).* 🛒 *Mon.*
www.pyrenees-basques.com

The old capital of Basse-Navarre lies at the foot of the Roncesvalles Pass. Here the Basques crushed the rearguard of Charlemagne's army in 778 and killed its commander, Roland, later glorified in the *Chanson de Roland*.

Throughout the Middle Ages this red sandstone fortress-town was famous as the last rallying point before entering Spain on the pilgrim road to Santiago de Compostela *(see pp400–1)*. As soon as a group of pilgrims was spotted, the townsfolk would ring the church bells to show them the way, and the pilgrims would sing in response.

Visitors and pilgrims in all seasons still provide St-Jean with its income. They enter the narrow streets of the upper town on foot from the Porte d'Espagne, and pass cafés, hotels and restaurants on the way up. The ramparts are worth the steep climb, as is the citadel with panoramic views.

On Mondays the town hosts a craft market, Basque *pelote* matches and, in summer, shows with bulls.

Forêt d'Iraty ❽

Pyrénées-Aquitaine. ⊟ St-Jean-
Pied-de-Port. ⊟ ⓘ St-Jean-Pied-de-
Port (0810 75 36 71), Larrau (05 59
28 62 80).

A plateau of beech woods
and moorland, the Forêt
d'Iraty is famous for its cross-
country skiing and walking.
Here the ancient breed of
Basque ponies, the *pottocks*,
run half-wild. These creatures
have not changed since the
prehistoric inhabitants of the
region traced their silhouettes
on the walls of local caves.

The tourist office at St-Jean-
Pied-de-Port publishes maps
of local walks. The best begins
at the Chalet Pedro car park,
south of the lake on the Iraty
plateau, and takes you along
the GR10 to 3,000-year-old
standing stones on the western
side of the Sommet d'Occabé.

Oloron-Ste-Marie ❾

Pyrénées-Atlantiques. 👥 12,000.
⊟ ⊟ ⓘ allées du Compte de
Tréville (05 59 39 98 00). ⊟ Fri.
www.tourisme-oloron.com

Oloron, a small town at the
junction of the Aspe and the
Ossau valleys, has grown
from a Celtiberian settlement.
There are huge agricultural
fairs here in May and
September, and the town is
famed for producing the

BASQUE CULTURE

Most of Basque country is in
Spain, but around 10 per cent
lies within France. The Basque
people have their own
complex language, isolated
from other European tongues,
and their music, games and folklore are equally distinct. French
Basques are less fiercely separatist than their Spanish counterparts, but both are still deeply attached to
their unique way of life.

***Pelote*, the traditional Basque game**

Cathédrale Ste-Marie

famous classic French berets.
The town's great glory is the
doorway of the Romanesque
Cathédrale Ste-Marie, with its
biblical and Pyrenean scenes.
Spain lies just on the other
side of the Somport pass at

the head of the mountainous
Aspe valley, and the influence
of Spanish stonemasons is
evident in Oloron's **Eglise
Sainte-Croix** with its Moorish-
style vaulting.

Environs
Head up the Aspe valley to
try one of the area's famous
ewe's cheeses, or mixed cow
and goat's cheeses. A side
road leads to Lescun, huddled
around its church, beyond
which is a spectacular range
of saw-toothed peaks topped
by the **Pic d'Anie** at 2,504 m
(8,215 ft), one of the most
beautiful sights in the
Pyrenees. This is also one
of the last refuges of the
Pyrenean brown bear, whose
numbers have been drastically
diminished by human activity,
particularly hunting and the
building of roads and houses.

High moorland above the Forêt d'Iraty, long denuded of timber for use by the French and Spanish navies

Gobelin tapestry in the Château de Pau

Pau ⑩

Pyrénées-Atlantiques. 🏠 86,000.
⊠ 🚌 🚄 ⓘ pl Royale (05 59 27
27 08). 🛒 Mon–Sat.
www.pau-pyrenees.com

A lively university town, with elegant Belle Epoque architecture and shady parks, Pau is the capital of the Béarn region, and the most interesting big town in the central Pyrenees. The weather in autumn and winter is mild, so this has been a favourite resort of affluent foreigners, especially the English, since the early 19th century.

Pau is chiefly famous as the birthplace of King Henry IV. His mother, Jeanne d'Albret, travelled for 19 days from Picardy, in the eighth month of her pregnancy, just to have her baby here. She sang during her labour, convinced that if she did so, Henry would grow up as tough as she was. As soon as the infant was born, his lips were smeared with garlic and local Jurançon wine, in keeping with the traditional custom.

The town's principal sight is the **Château de Pau**, first re-modelled in the 14th century for the ruler of Béarn, Gaston Phoebus (see p463). It was heavily restored 400 years later. Marguerite d'Angoulême, sister of the King of France, resided here in the late 16th century, and transformed the town into a centre for the arts and free thinking.

The château's 16th-century Gobelin tapestries, made by Flemish weavers working in Paris, are fabulous. (The Maison Carrée in Nay – 18 km (11 miles) towards Lourdes – exhibits the former Musée Béarnais' collection of artifacts retracing the history, traditions and culture of the Béarn.)

Outside, the boulevard des Pyrénées affords glorious views of some of the highest Pyrenean peaks, often snow-capped year round. Continue from here to the eclectic **Musée des Beaux-Arts**, where there is a splendid Degas, the *Cotton Exchange, New Orleans*; Rubens' *Last Judgment,* and a work by El Greco.

♠ Château de Pau
Rue du Château. **Tel** 05 59 82 38 02.
◯ daily. ◯ 1 Jan, 1 May, 25 Dec.
🎫 🚫 ⬛
www.musee-chateau-pau.fr

🏛 Musée des Beaux-Arts
Rue Mathieu Lalanne. **Tel** 05 59 27
33 02. ◯ Wed–Mon. ⬤ some
public hols. 🎫 🚫 restricted.

Tarbes ⑪

Hautes-Pyrénées. 🏠 46,500. ✈ 🚄
🚌 🚄 ⓘ 3 cours Gambetta
(05 62 51 30 31). 🛒 Thu.
www.tarbes.com

Tarbes is the capital of the Bigorre region and hosts a major agricultural fair. The **Jardin Massey** in the middle of town was designed at the turn of the 19th century and is one of the loveliest parks in the southwest, with many rare plants, including the North American sassafras, and a 14th-century cloister with finely carved capitals.

The **Maison du Cheval** and the **Haras National** (National Stud), with its thoroughbred stallions, should not be missed.

🏛 La Maison du Cheval
Chemin du Mauhourat.
Tel 05 62 56 30 80. ◯ dailys pms.
⬤ public hols. 🎫 🚫 Jul–Aug &
school hols.

Lourdes ⑫

Hautes-Pyrénées. 🏠 16,000. 🚄 🚌
🚄 ⓘ pl Peyramale (05 62 42 77
40). 🛒 Mon–Sat. **www**.lourdes-
infotourisme.com

Lourdes, one of the great shrines of Europe, owes its celebrity to visions of the Virgin experienced by 14-year-old Bernadette Soubirous in 1858. Five

Château de Pau, birthplace of Henry IV in 1553

◁ St-Lizier in the foothills of the Pyrenees

million people annually visit **Grotte Massabielle**, where the visions occurred, and rue des Petits-Fossés where Bernadette lived, in search of a miracle cure. The **Musée de Lourdes** gives information about Bernadette and the shrine.

Visit the **Grottes de Bétharram** for underground rides by boat and train, or the **Musée Pyrénéen**, about the pioneers who opened up these ranges.

🏛 **Musée de Lourdes**
Parking de l'Egalité. *Tel 05 62 94 28 00*. ◯ *Apr–Oct: daily; Nov–Mar: Mon–Sat.* 🖼 🔥

💥 **Grottes de Bétharram**
St-Pé-de-Bigorre. *Tel 05 62 41 80 04.* ◯ *Feb–late Mar: Mon–Fri pms; late Mar–Oct: daily.* 🖼 🔥 www.betharram.com

Pilgrims participating in open-air mass at Lourdes

Spectacular limestone formations at the Grottes de Bétharram

🏛 **Musée Pyrénéen**
Château Fort, rue du Fort. *Tel 05 62 42 37 37.* ◯ *daily.* ⬤ *1 Jan, 1 & 11 Nov, 25 Dec.* 🖼

Parc National des Pyrénées ⑬

See pp460–61.

Luz-St-Sauveur ⑭

Hautes-Pyrénées. 👥 *1,200.* 🚇 to Lourdes. 🚌 ℹ *pl du 8 mai (05 62 92 30 30).* 🎉 *Mon am.* www.luz.org

Luz-St-Sauveur is an attractive spa town, with an unusual church built in the 14th century by the Hospitaliers de Saint Jean de Jérusalem (later the Knights of Malta), an order established to protect pilgrims. The church is fortified with gun slits that provided protection for pilgrims on the way to Santiago de Compostela.

Environs
The elegant spa town of **Cauterets** makes a good base for climbing, skiing and walking in the rugged mountains of the Bigorre region.

Gavarnie is a former way-station on the Santiago de Compostela pilgrim route. A good track, accessible on foot or by donkey, leads from the village to the spectacular natural rock amphitheatre known as the **Cirque de Gavarnie**. Here the longest waterfall in Europe, at 240 m (787 ft), cascades off the mountain into space, encircled by eleven 3,000-m (9,800-ft) peaks.

Tourists can now share much of the **Observatoire Pic du Midi de Bigorre** with scientists. Access is by cable-car from La Mongie to Le Taoulet and then up to the summit. Alternatively there are a number of walks up to the Pic (4 hours minimum).

The French are justly proud of the Observatory, which has supplied the clearest images of Venus and other planets so far obtained from Earth. The 1-m (3.2-ft) telescope mapped out the moon for NASA's Apollo missions.

🏛 **Observatoire Pic du Midi de Bigorre**
Tel 08 25 00 28 77. ◯ *Jan, Apr, May, Dec: Wed–Mon; Feb, Mar, Jun–Sep: daily.* ⬤ *Oct–Nov.* 🖼 🖥 🍴 www.picdumidi.com

THE MIRACLE OF LOURDES

In 1858 a young girl named Bernadette Soubirous experienced 18 visions of the Virgin at the Grotte Massabielle near the town. Despite being told to keep away from the cave by her mother – and the local magistrate – she was guided to a spring with miraculous healing powers. The church endorsed the miracles in the 1860s, and since then, many people claim to have been cured by the holy water. A religious city of shrines, churches and hospices has since grown up around the spring, with a dynamic tourist industry to match.

Bernadette's vision

Parc National des Pyrénées ⑬

Pyrenean ibex

The Pyrenees National Park, designated in 1967, extends 100 km (62 miles) along the French and Spanish frontier. It boasts some of the most spectacular scenery in Europe, ranging from meadows glimmering with butterflies to high peaks, snow-capped even in summer. Variations in altitude and climate make the park rich in flora and fauna. One of the most enjoyable ways to see it is on foot: within the park are 350 km (217 miles) of well-marked footpaths.

Vallée d'Aspe
Jagged peaks tower above the Vallée d'Aspe and the Cirque de Lescun. An access road to Somport Tunnel has been built here (see p455).

OLORON-STE-MARIE

PIC D'ANIE
2,504 m
(8,215 ft)

PAU

Laruns

PIC DE LA
SAGETTE
2,301 m
(7,550 ft)

PIC DU
MIDI D'OSSAU
2,884 m
(9,462 ft)

Col du Somport, the Somport pass (1,632 m/5,354 ft), is a rugged route into Spain that is now by-passed by a tunnel.

Pic d'Anie
The limestone-flanked 2,504-m (8,215-ft) Pic d'Anie overlooks rich upland pastures watered by melting snow. In spring, the ground is ablaze with Pyrenean varieties of gentian and columbine, found nowhere else.

Pic du Midi d'Ossau
A tough trail leads from the Bious-Artigues lake to the base of the Pic du Midi d'Ossau and encircles the formidable tooth-shaped summit (2,884 m/9,462 ft).

PYRENEAN WILDLIFE

The Pyrenees are home to a rich variety of wild creatures, many of them unique to the range. The ibex, a member of the antelope family, is still numerous in the valleys of Ossau and Cauterets. Birds of prey include the Egyptian, griffon and bearded vultures. Ground predators range from the rare Pyrenean lynx, to civet, pine marten and stoat. The desman, a tiny aquatic mammal related to the mole, is found in many of the mountain streams.

Pyrenean fritillary *flowers through late spring and early summer in mountain pastures.*

The Turk's Cap Lily *flowers June–August on rocky slopes at up to 2,200 m (7,218 ft).*

rèche de Roland
be famous breach in the sheer
est of the Cirque de Gavarnie
rms a gateway for climbers
etween France and Spain.

TIPS FOR WALKERS

The park is crossed by a network of numbered trails. Each is well signposted and shows the length of time needed. Mountain huts offer a meal and a bed for the night. For maps and information, visit the Park Office at Cauterets (05 62 92 50 50) or at Luz-St-Sauveur (05 62 92 30 30), both open year round or visit www.parc-pyrenees.com.

Walking the trail in high summer

The **GR10 long-distance trail** is one of the great walks of France, linking the Atlantic with the Mediterranean.

↑LOURDES

Argelès-Gazost

D'AUBISQUE

COL DU SOULOR

D918

Arrens

D921

D105

PIC DU MIDI DE BIGORRE
2,865 m (9,400 ft) ▲ LA MONGIE
COL DU TOURMALET
BAGNERES-DE-BIGORRE→

Cauterets

D918

Luz-St-Sauveur

M A S S I F   D E
N E O U V I E L L E

BALAITOUS
3,146 m (10,322 ft)

PONT D'ESPAGNE

PIC DE NEOUVIELLE
3,094 m (10,151 ft)

kilometres 5
miles 5

KEY
— National park boundary
─── French/Spanish border
• — GR10 walking route

VIGNEMALE
3,296 m (10,814 ft)

D921

D922

Gavarnie

CIRQUE DE TROUMOUSE

CIRQUE DE GAVARNIE

Brèche de Roland

e Egyptian vulture is seen
l over the Pyrenees, especially
r rocky cliff faces.

Pyrenean bears *are close to extinction but a few still live in the Ossau and Aspe valleys.*

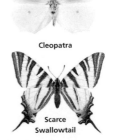

Cleopatra

Scarce Swallowtail

These butterflies *are among several colourful species found at high altitudes.*

Arreau ⑮

Hautes-Pyrénées. 🏠 *865.* 🚌
🛈 *Château des Nestes (05 62 98 63 15).* 🚍 *Thu.* **www**.vallee-aure.com

Arreau stands at the junction of the rivers Aure and Louron. A small, bustling half-timbered town with good shops and restaurants, this is the place to buy the basics for hiking or fishing in the mountains. The town surrounds a handsome town hall with a covered market place beneath it. Next door is a 16th-century house, the Maison de Lys, which has a façade ornamented with the fleur-de-lis motifs.

Environs

St-Lary Soulan is a nearby ski resort and a good base for exploring the entire Massif du Néouvielle. Head for the village of Fabian and the smattering of lakes above it, where the GR10 *(see p461)* and other well-marked trails criss-cross the peaks. Here you may see golden eagles or an enormous lammergeier.

St-Bertrand-de-Comminges ⑯

Haute-Garonne. 🏠 *260.*
🚌 *Montrejeau, then taxi.* 🚌
🛈 *Les Olivetains, parvis de la Cathédrale (05 61 95 44 44).*
🎵 *music festival (mid-Jul–end Aug).*

The pretty hilltop town of St-Bertrand is the most remarkable artistic and historic site in the Central Pyrenees and the venue for an acclaimed music festival

Cloisters in the Cathédrale Ste-Marie, St-Bertrand-de-Comminges

in summer *(see p37).* Some of the best sculpture in the region adorns the portal of the **Cathédrale Ste-Marie**. The adjoining Romanesque and Gothic cloisters contain sarcophagi, carved capitals and statues of the four Evangelists.

St-Bertrand's origins lie on the plain below, in the city founded by the great Roman statesman Pompey in 72 BC. At that time it consisted of two thermal baths, a theatre, a temple, a market and a Christian basilica. All were destroyed by Gontran, the grandson of Clovis *(see p212)* in 585, and six centuries were to pass before the Bishop of Comminges, Bertrand de l'Isle, saw the site as a potential location for a new cathedral and monastery. The town, which was relatively unimportant in political terms, became a major religious centre.

Inside the cathedral, look out for the 66 magnificent carved choirstalls and the 16th-century organ case. The tomb of Bertrand de l'Isle is situated at the far end of the choir, with

an altar beside it; the beautiful marble tomb in the Virgin's chapel just off the nave is that of Hugues de Châtillon, a bishop who provided funds for the completion of the cathedral in the 14th century.

🛈 **Cathédrale Ste-Marie**
Tel 05 61 89 04 91. ◯ *daily.*
◯ *Sun am.* 🚫 📷 *cloisters.*

Fresco in the Cathédrale St-Lizier

St-Lizier ⑰

Ariège. 🏠 *1,500.* 🚌 🛈 *pl de l'Eglise (05 61 96 77 77).*
www.ariege.com/st-lizier

St-Lizier is located in the Ariège, a region famous for its steep-sided valleys and wild mountain scenery. The village dates back to Roman times, and by the Middle Ages was an important religious centre. St-Lizier has two cathedrals; the finer is the 12th–14th-century **Cathédrale St-Lizier** in the lower town. It boasts Romanesque frescoes and a cloister with carved columns. The **Cathédrale de la Sède** in the upper town has the best view.

The imposing 12th-century Cathédrale Ste-Marie in St-Bertrand

St-Lizier, with snow-capped mountains in the distance

Foix ⑱

Ariège. 🔼 10,000. 🚆 🚌 🏛 29 rue Delcassé (05 61 65 12 12). 🖪 Fri & 1st, 3rd & 5th Mon of each month. **www**.tourisme-foix-varilhes.fr

With its battlements and towers, Foix stands four-square at the junction of the rivers Arget and Ariège. In the Middle Ages, Foix's dynasty of counts ruled the whole of the Béarn area. Count Gaston Phoebus (1331–91) was the most flamboyant, a poet who wrote a famous treatise on hunting. He was a ruthless politician, who had his brother and his son put to death.

Some of the pleasures of the medieval court are re-created in the local summer fair, the largest in the southwest. At any time, the 15th-century keep of the **Château de Foix** is worth climbing just for the view. The restored 14th-century **Eglise de St-Volusien** is delightful in its simplicity and grace.

🏰 **Château de Foix**
Tel 05 34 09 83 83. ⬜ Wed–Mon & daily in sch hols. ⬤ 1 Jan, 25 Dec. 🈂
www.sesta.fr/chateau-de-foix.html

Environs
The **Grotte de Niaux**, 15 km (9 miles) south of Foix, has prehistoric cave paintings.

🕳 **Grotte de Niaux**
Tel 05 61 05 10 10. ⬜ by appt only. 🈂 🎟 oblig.

Montségur ⑲

Ariège. 🔼 100. 🏛 05 61 03 03 03. 🈂 🎟 for the château (summer only). **www**.montsegur.fr

Montségur is famous as the last stronghold of the Cathars (see p491). From the car park at the foot of the mount, a path leads up to the small castle above, occupied in the 13th century by *faidits* (dispossessed aristocrats) and a Cathar community. The Cathars themselves lived outside the fortress, in houses clinging to the rock. Opposed to Catholic authority, Cathar troops marched on Avignonnet in 1243 and massacred members of the Inquisitional tribunal. In retaliation, an army of 10,000 laid siege to Montségur for 10 months. When captured, 205 Cathars refused to convert and were burnt alive.

Mirepoix ⑳

Ariège. 🔼 3,300. 🚌 🏛 pl du Maréchal Leclerc (05 61 68 83 76). 🖪 Mon & Thu. **www**.tourisme-mirepoix.com

Mirepoix is a solid country bastide town (see p445) with a huge main square – one of the loveliest in the southwest – surrounded by beamed 13th–15th-century arcades and half-timbered houses.

The **cathedral**, begun in 1317 with the last additions made in 1867, boasts the widest Gothic nave (22 m/72 ft) in France.

The best times to visit the town are on market days, when stalls in the square sell a mass of local produce.

The arcaded main square at Mirepoix

THE SOUTH
OF FRANCE

Introducing the South of France

The South is France's most popular holiday region, drawing millions of visitors each year to the Riviera resorts, and modern beach cities to the west. Agriculture is a mainstay of the economy, producing early fruits and an abundance of affordable wine. The new high-tech industries of Nice and Montpellier reflect the region's key role in the developing south coast sunbelt, while Corsica still preserves much of its natural beauty. The map shows the major sights of this sun-blessed region.

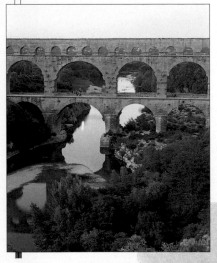

Pont du Gard, *a 2,000-year-old bridge* (see p495), *is a major feat of Roman engineering. It was a key link in the 17-km (10.5-mile) aqueduct, parts of which were underground, carrying fresh water from a spring at Uzès to Nîmes.*

Pont du Gard

St-Guilbem-le-Désert

LANGUEDOC-ROUSSILLON
(See pp476–97)

Carcassonne

Peyrepertuse

The Camargue *lies at the mouth of the Rhône delta, where marshland and inland seas support a rich selection of wildlife. Three visitors' centres give a good introduction to this fragile area and its population of pink flamingoes and white horses* (see pp510–11).

St-Martin-de-Canigou

| 0 kilometres | 50 |
| 0 miles | 50 |

Avignon, *enclosed by massive ramparts, became papal territory when popes decamped from Rome (see p503) in the 14th century, taking up residence in the Palais des Papes which towers over the town. In the summer the town is the scene of the popular Avignon Festival.*

is des Papes, Avignon

PROVENCE AND THE COTE D'AZUR
(See pp498–531)

Musée Matisse, Nice

*Giacometti statue,
St-Paul-de-Vence*

margue

CORSICA
(see pp532–43)

*Statue of Napoleon,
Ajaccio*

0 kilometres   50

0 miles   50

The Côte d'Azur *has attracted sunworshippers and celebrities since the 1920s (see pp474–5). The coast also offers some prize collections of 20th-century art (pp472–3) and yearly events such as the Cannes Film Festival and Antibes Jazz Festival.*

The Flavours of the South of France

Mediterranean France has a fresh, sunny cuisine, with ripe and flavourful fruit and vegetables, fresh fish and seafood, and lean meat from mountain pastures. Good dishes are enhanced by key ingredients: olive oil, garlic and aromatic herbs. Markets are a colourful feast of seasonal produce all year round. Whether you opt for a picnic choice of local hams, sausage, bread and cheese to eat on the beach, share a simple lunch of tomato salad and grilled fish or lamb in a village bistro, or indulge in the sophisticated cuisine of one of France's top chefs, you can be sure of food that is not only authentic and delicious, but healthy too.

Local olives and olive oil

Preserving anchovies in seasoned olive oil in Languedoc-Roussillon

LANGUEDOC-ROUSSILLON

There is a robust Catalan flavour to the food of this region bordering Spain. Spices and almonds add an exotic touch to the fruit and vegetables produced in abundance on the Roussillon plain, and the grass-fed beef and lamb of the Mediterranean Pyrenees. Fish is plentiful: Sète is the largest fishing port on the French Mediterranean, huge oyster and mussel beds thrive in the saltwater lagoons of the coast and the little fishing port of Collioure is famous for its anchovies. Local dishes include *brandade de morue*, a speciality of Nîmes, squid stuffed with anchovies and snails with garlic and ham. Roussillon is famous for its peaches and apricots, and the cherries of Ceret are always the first to be harvested in France. Goat's milk is the main source of cheese, with round, orange-rinded Pélardon the most common.

PROVENCE

This is the land of the olive and of rich green olive oil. These are evident in a wide range of dishes, such as *aioli*, a rich mayonnaise of olive oil and garlic, served with vegetables or fish;

Lobster Prawns (shrimp) Monkfish Squid
Mussels Sea bass Clams
Selection of Mediterranean seafood available in the south of France

REGIONAL DISHES AND SPECIALITIES

The *cuisine du soleil*, "cuisine of the sun", has produced several classic dishes. *Bouillabaisse* is the most famous. The ingredients of this fish stew vary from place to place, though Marseille claims the original recipe. A variety of local seafood (always including *rascasse*, or scorpion fish) is cooked in stock with tomatoes and saffron. The fish liquor is traditionally served first, with croûtons spread with *rouille*, a spicy mayonnaise, and the fish served afterwards. Once a fishermen's supper, it is now a luxury item you may need to order 24 hours in advance. A simpler version is *bourride*, a garlicky fish soup. Rich red wine stews, known as *daubes*, are another speciality, usually made with beef, but sometimes tuna or calamari. Other classics include *ratatouille* and *salade niçoise*.

Fresh figs

Artichauts à la barigoule
Small violet artichokes are stuffed with bacon and vegetables, cooked in wine.

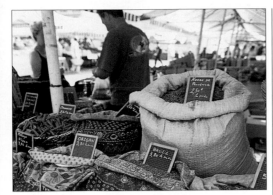
Dried spices and herbs on sale at the market in Nice

huge variety of *charcuterie*, including flavoursome hams and sausages, smoked, cured or air-dried in the traditional way. Wild boar is a delicacy, stewed with chestnuts in red wine. Roast goat *(cabri roti)* is served as a festive meal, spiked with garlic and rosemary. Game, from rabbit to pigeon and partridge, is also very popular. On the coast there is locally caught fish and seafood, including monkfish, squid, sea urchins and sardines, the latter most delicious stuffed with herbs and Brocciu, a ricotta-style soft cheese. Local honey is redolent of mountain herbs, and jams are made from a huge variety of ingredients.

tapenade, a purée of olives, anchovies and capers; and *pissaladière*, a type of pizza made with onions, olives and anchovies, with a distinct Italian accent. Vegetables play a leading role: courgettes (zucchini) or tomatoes stuffed in the Niçois style with meat, rice and herbs; baby artichokes sautéed with bacon; or aromatic *pistou*, a bean and vegetable soup laced with a sauce of basil and garlic. Mediterranean fish is highly prized, and is often best appreciated simply grilled. Meat includes game and rabbit, Sisteron lamb, grazed on high mountain pastures, and the bull's meat stew of the Camargue, served with nutty local red rice. There is also ripe fruit aplenty, from juicy figs to fragrant Cavaillon melons to the vivid lemons of Menton.

CORSICA

The cuisine of Corsica is a robust version of the Mediterranean diet. Chestnuts were once the staple food of the island, and the flour is still widely used. There is a

Ripe chestnuts on the tree in a Corsican forest

ON THE MENU

Beignets des fleurs de courgette Courgette (zucchini) flower fritters.

Estoficada Salt cod stewed with tomatoes, potatoes, garlic and olives.

Fougasse Flat olive oil bread often studded with olives.

Ratatouille Stew of aubergine (eggplant), tomatoes, courgettes (zucchini) and peppers.

Salade Niçoise Lettuce with hard-boiled egg, olives, green beans, tomatoes and anchovies.

Socca Chickpea (garbanzo) pancakes, a speciality of Nice.

Tourte des blettes Pie of chard, raisins and pine kernels.

Brandade de morue *Dried salted cod is cooked in water, then beaten with olive oil and milk to make a purée.*

Bœuf en daube *Beef is marinated in red wine, onions and garlic, then stewed with orange peel and tomato.*

Crème catalane *Originating in Spain, this dessert is an eggy custard topped with a flambéed sugar crust.*

France's Wine Regions: the South

A massive arc stretching from Banyuls, in the extreme southern corner of France, to Nice, close to the Italian border, encompasses the Mediterranean vineyards of Languedoc-Roussillon and Provence. This was for a century an area of mass-produced wine, and much is still of *vin de France* quality. Today, however, the more dynamic producers are applying new technology to traditional and classic grape varieties to revive southern France's nobler heritage of generous, warm, aromatic wines, redolent of sun-baked stone, the scent of wild herbs, and the shimmering waters of the Mediterranean.

Cellar sign, Banyuls

LOCATOR MAP

Languedoc-Roussillon & Provence

Coteaux du Languedoc *is a large and varied appellation stretching from Narbonne towards Nîmes.*

TUCADE

The quality *wines produced by Mass de Daumas Gassac have earnt this vineyard its reputation as the Grand Cru of Languedoc.*

Stop here *to try the wines of Côtes du Roussillon – idiosyncratic yet characterful, dry white wines, dry rosés and medium reds.*

0 kilometres   25

0 miles   25

KEY

Collioure & Banyuls	Costières du Gard
Côtes de Roussillon	Coteaux d'Aix en Provence
Côtes de Roussillon Villages	Côtes de Provence
Fitou	Cassis
Corbières	Bandol & Côtes de Provence
Minervois	Coteaux Varois
Coteaux du Languedoc	Bellet

Rugged valley slopes in Corbières

Hand-picking grapes for Côtes de Provence red wine

WINE REGIONS

Both in the Provence wine region, east of Aix and
Marseille, and in the larger Languedoc-Roussillon
area to the west, new quality wine *appellations* such
as Cabardès (north of Carcassonne), are
joining the more familiar names.

Bandol *is a small* appellation
*that uses a traditional southern
French red grape, the* Mourvèdre,
to produce its quality reds.

La Courtade *reds, whites
and rosés are produced
by the Domaine de la
Courtade, one of three
vineyards located on the
Ile de Porquerolles off
the coast of Provence.*

KEY FACTS ABOUT WINES OF THE SOUTH

Location and Climate
A warm and sunny climate helps
to create generously alcoholic
wines. The flat coastal plains
support acres of vines, but generally the best
sites are on the schist and limestone hillsides.

Grape Varieties
Mass-production grapes such as
Aramon are giving way to quality
varieties such as **Syrah**,
Mourvèdre and **Grenache**. **Cabernet
Sauvignon, Merlot** and **Syrah**, and the
whites **Chardonnay, Sauvignon Blanc** and
Viognier, are increasingly used for
IGPs. Rich, sweet whites are made from
the aromatic, honeyed **Muscat** grape.

Good Producers
Corbières & Minervois: La Voulte
Gasparets, Saint Auriol, Lastours,
Villerambert-Julien.
Faugères: Château des Estanilles,
Châeau de la Liquiere.
St Chinian: Château Cazal-Viel, Domaine
Navarre, Cave de Roquebrun.
Coteaux du Languedoc and IGPs:
Mas Jullien, Château de Capitoul, Domaine
de la Garance, Mas de Daumas Gassac,
Pech-Celeyran. *Roussillon*: Domaine Gauby,
Domaine Sarda Malet. *Provence*: Domaine
Tempier, Château Pibarnon, Domaine de
Trévallon, Mas de la Dame, Domaine
Richeaume, La Courtade, Château Simone,
Château Pradeaux, Château de Bellet.

Artists and Writers in the South of France

Monet's palette

Artists and writers have helped create our image of the South of France – the poet Stephen Liégeard even gave the Côte d'Azur its name in 1887. Many writers, French and foreign, found a haven in the warmth of the south. From Cézanne to Van Gogh, Monet to Picasso, artists have been inspired by the special light and brilliant colours of this seductive region. Today it is rich in art museums, some devoted to single artists like Matisse, Picasso and Chagall, others with varied collections such as those in Céret, Nîmes, Montpellier, St-Tropez, St-Paul-de-Vence and Nice *(see pp482–527)*.

Picasso and Françoise Gilot on the Golfe Juan, 1948

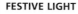

Paul Cézanne's studio in Aix-en-Provence *(see p511)*

FESTIVE LIGHT

The Impressionists were fascinated by the effects of light, and Monet was entranced by "the glaring festive light" of the south which made colours so intense he said no one would believe they were real if painted accurately. In 1883 Renoir came with him to the south, returning often to paint his voluptuous nudes in the filtered golden light. Bonnard too settled here, painting endless views of the red tiled roofs and palm trees.

Post-Impressionists Van Gogh and Gauguin arrived in 1888, attracted by the region's rich colours. Cézanne, who was born in Aix in 1839, analysed and painted the structure of nature, above all the landscape of Provence and his beloved Mont-Ste-Victoire. Pointillist Paul Signac came to St-Tropez to paint sea and sky in a rainbow palette of dots.

THE WILD BEASTS

The Fauves, dubbed "Wild Beasts" for their unnaturally bright and wild colours, led one of the first 20th-century avant-garde movements, founded by Matisse in Collioure in 1905 *(see p29)*. Other Fauves included Derain, Vlaminck, Marquet, Van Dongen and Dufy. Matisse visited Corsica in 1898, and then St-Tropez, and was inspired by the sensuality of Provence to paint the celebrated *Luxe, Calme et Volupté*. Eventually he settled in Nice, where he painted his great series of Odalisques. He wrote, "What made me stay are the great coloured reflections of January, the luminosity of daylight." The exquisite blue-and-white chapel he designed in Vence is one of the most moving of his later works *(see p523)*.

Vincent Van Gogh's *Sunflowers* (1888)

PICASSO COUNTRY

The South of France is, without question, Picasso country. His nymphs and sea urchins, his monumental women running on the beach, his shapes and colours, ceramics and sculpture are all derived from the hard shadows and bright colours of the south.

Pablo Picasso was born in Malaga in Spain in 1881, but he spent much of his life on the French Mediterranean, developing Cubism with Braque in Céret in 1911, and arriving in Juan-les-Pins in 1920. He was in Antibes when war broke out in 1939, where he painted *Night Fishing at Antibes*, a luminous nocturnal seascape. He returned in 1946 and was given the Grimaldi Palace to use as a studio. It is now a Picasso Museum *(see p521)*. He also worked in Vallauris, producing ceramics and sculptures *(see p522)*.

Deux Femmes Courant sur la Plage (1933) by Pablo Picasso

LOST CAVIAR DAYS

Just as F Scott Fitzgerald wrote the Jazz Age into existence, he created the glittering image of life on the Riviera with *Tender is the Night*. He and Zelda arrived in 1924 attracted, like many expatriate writers, by the warm climate and the cheap, easy living. "One could get away with more on the summer Riviera, and whatever happened seemed to have something to do with art," he wrote. They passed their villa on to another American, Ernest Hemingway. Many other writers flocked there including Katherine Mansfield, DH Lawrence, Aldous Huxley, Friedrich Nietzsche, Lawrence Durrell and Graham Greene. Some, like Somerset Maugham, led a glamorous lifestyle surrounded by exotic guests. Colette was an early visitor to St-Tropez, and in 1954, Françoise Sagan captured the youthful hedonism of the time in her novel, *Bonjour Tristesse*.

Scott and Zelda Fitzgerald with daughter

NEW REALISM

In the 1950s Nice produced its own school of artists, the *Nouveaux Réalistes*, including Yves Klein, Arman, Martial Raysse, Tinguely, César, Niki de Saint Phalle and Daniel Spoerri *(see pp526–7)*. They explored the possibilities of everyday objects – Arman sliced violins, packaged and displayed trash; Tinguely exploded TV sets and cars. They had a light-hearted approach, "We live in a land of vacations, which gives us the spirit of nonsense," said Klein. He painted solid blue canvases of his personal colour, International Klein Blue, taking the inspiration of the Mediterranean to its limit.

PROVENÇAL WRITERS

The regions of Provence and Languedoc have always had a distinct literary identity, ever since the troubadours in the 12th–13th centuries composed their love poetry in the *langue d'oc* Provençal, a Latin-based language. In the last century, many regional writers have been inspired by the landscape and local traditions. They were influenced by the 19th-century Felibrige movement to revive the language, led by Nobel prize-winning poet Frédéric Mistral. Some, like Daudet and film-maker turned writer Marcel Pagnol, celebrate the Provençal character; others, such as Jean Giono, explore the connection between nature and humanity.

Frédéric Mistral in the *Petit Journal*

L'HOMMAGE DE LA PROVENCE A MISTRAL

Beaches in the South of France

The glamorous Mediterranean coast is France's foremost holiday playground. To the east lie the Riviera's big, traditional resorts such as Menton, Nice, Cannes and Monte-Carlo. To the west are smaller resorts in coves and bays like St-Tropez and Cassis. Further on is the Camargue reserve at the mouth of the Rhône. West of the Rhône, making a majestic curve reaching almost to the Spanish border, is the long, sandy shore of Languedoc-Roussillon, where a string of purpose-built resorts range from modernistic beach cities to replicas of fishing villages.

The Carlton Hotel logo

The beaches are sandy west of Antibes; eastwards, they are naturally shingly, so any sand is imported. Anti-pollution drives mean that most beaches are now clean, except in a few spots west of Marseille and around Nice. Beaches around towns often charge fees but are usually well equipped.

A rail poster by Domergue advertising the Côte d'Azur

Sète (*p492*) is a seaport with a network of canals. Stretching southwards are 15 km (9.5 miles) of unspoiled, sandy beaches with lots of room, even in high season.

Stes-Maries-de-la-Mer (*p510*), set among the sand dunes of the Camargue, offers white sandy beaches and a naturist beach 6 km (4 miles) to the east. Horse-riding is available.

Cap d'Agde (p487) *is a vast modern resort with long, golden sandy beaches and sports facilities of all kinds. It has Europe's largest naturist resort, accommodating 20,000 visitors.*

La Grande-Motte (p495) *is a huge purpose-built beach resort with excellent sports facilities, famous for its bizarre ziggurat architecture.*

0 kilometres   25

0 miles   25

In Victorian times *the Côte d'Azur, or Riviera, was the fashionable holiday venue of Europe's royalty and rich. They came to gamble and escape northern winters. Summer bathing did not come into vogue until the 1920s. Today the Riviera is busy all year round with the glamorous beaches and nightlife still a major attraction.*

Menton

Monaco

Nice — Cap Ferrat

Antibes

Cannes

Juan-les-Pins

St-Raphaël

St-Tropez

Cassis

La Ciotat

Toulon

Hyères

Menton *(p529)* has a warm climate in winter, giving beach weather all year. Its sheltered, shingly beaches are backed by beautiful villas.

Cannes *(p520)* takes great pride in its golden beaches, keeping them scrupulously clean: most are private with entrance fees.

Cassis *(p513)* is a charming fishing village with a popular casino, white cliffs and some lovely hidden creeks nearby.

St-Tropez *(p516) is flanked by golden beaches mostly occupied by stylish "clubs" offering amenities at a price.*

Nice (p526), *has a visually dramatic waterfront with a wide, handsome promenade, but the beach itself is stony and has a busy highway alongside.*

Cap Ferrat (p528) *is a wooded peninsula which has a 10-km (6-mile) craggy cliff walk offering glimpses of grand villas and private beaches.*

LANGUEDOC-ROUSSILLON

AUDE · GARD · HERAULT · PYRENEES-ORIENTALES

The two distinct provinces of Languedoc and Roussillon stretch from the foothills of the Pyrenees on the Spanish border to the mouth of the Rhône. The flat beaches and lagoons of the coast form a purpose-built sunbelt accommodating millions of holidaymakers every year. In between is a dry, sunburned land producing half of France's table wine and the season's first peaches and cherries.

Beyond such sensuous pleasures are many layers of history, not least the unification of the two provinces. The formerly independent Languedoc once spoke Occitan, the tongue of the troubadours, and still cherishes its separate identity. Roussillon was a Spanish possession until the treaty of the Pyrenees in 1659. Its Catalan heritage is displayed everywhere from the road signs to the Sardana dance, and the flavour of Spain is evident in the popularity of bullfights, paella, and gaudily painted façades.

This stretch of coastline was the first place in Gaul to be settled by the Romans, their enduring legacy evident in the great amphitheatre at Nîmes and the magnificent engineering of the Pont du Gard. The abbeys of St-Martin-du-Canigou, St-Michel-de-Cuxa and St-Guilhem-le-Désert are superb examples of early Romanesque architecture, unaffected by Northern Gothic. The great craggy Cathar castles and the perfectly restored medieval Cité of Carcassonne bear witness to the bloody battles of the Middle Ages.

In parts, the region remains wild and untamed: from the high plateaux of the Cerdagne, to the wild hills of the Corbières or the remote uplands of Haut Languedoc. But it also has the most youthful and progressive cities in France: Montpellier, the ancient university city and capital of the region, and Nîmes with its exuberant *feria* and bullfights. The whole area is typified by an insouciant mixture of ancient and modern, from Roman temples and postmodern architecture in its cities to solar power and ancient abbeys in the mountains.

A sunny stretch of coastline at Cap d'Agde

◁ The abbey of Saint-Martin-du-Canigou perched on Mount Canigou

Exploring Languedoc-Roussillon

Languedoc-Roussillon combines miles of gentle coastline with a rugged hinterland. Its clean, sandy beaches are perfect for family holidays, with resorts ranging from traditional fishing villages to new purpose-built resorts. Inland is quieter, with acres of vineyards in the Corbières and Minervois and mountain walks in the Haut Languedoc and Cerdagne. A rich architectural heritage ranges from Roman to Romanesque, contrasting with the modern, vibrant atmosphere of the main cities.

Jousting on the canal, a regular summer event in Sète

SIGHTS AT A GLANCE

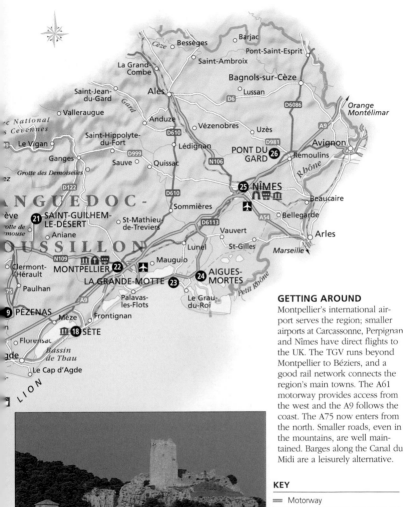

Bessèges
Cèze
Barjac
Pont-Saint-Esprit
Saint-Ambroix
La Grand-Combe
Bagnols-sur-Cèze
Saint-Jean-du-Gard
Alès
Lussan
D6
D6086
Orange
Montélimar
A9
Parc National des Cévennes
Valleraugue
Anduze
Vézenobres
Uzès
Le Vigan
Saint-Hippolyte-du-Fort
D610
Lédignan
D981
Avignon
PONT DU GARD 26
Rémoulins
Ganges
Sauve
Quissac
N106
Rhône
Grotte des Demoiselles
D999
D122
D610
25 NÎMES
Beaucaire
ANGUEDOC-
Sommières
ève
21 SAINT-GUILHEM-LE-DÉSERT
St-Mathieu-de-Treviers
D6113
Bellegarde
otte de mouse
Aniane
Vauvert
A54
Arles
OUSSILLON
Lunel
St-Gilles
Marseille
Clermont-Hérault
N109
Mauguio
MONTPELLIER 22
24 AIGUES-MORTES
Paulhan
LA GRANDE-MOTTE 23
9 PÉZENAS
A9
Palavas-les-Flots
Le Grau-du-Roi
Petit Rhône
Mèze
Frontignan
Florensac
18 SÈTE
Bassin de Thau
de
Le Cap d'Agde
LION

GETTING AROUND

Montpellier's international airport serves the region; smaller airports at Carcassonne, Perpignan and Nîmes have direct flights to the UK. The TGV runs beyond Montpellier to Béziers, and a good rail network connects the region's main towns. The A61 motorway provides access from the west and the A9 follows the coast. The A75 now enters from the north. Smaller roads, even in the mountains, are well maintained. Barges along the Canal du Midi are a leisurely alternative.

KEY

▬▬	Motorway
▬▬	Major road
▬▬	Secondary road
▭▭	Minor road
▬▬	Scenic route
▬▪▬	Main railway
▬▬	Minor railway
▬▬	International border
▬▬	Regional border
△	Summit

0 kilometres	25
0 miles	25

The ruined Barbarossa tower at Gruissan on the Golfe du Lion

Cerdagne ❶

Pyrénées-Orientales. ✈ Perpignan.
🚊 🚌 Mont Louis, Bourg Madame.
ℹ️ Mont Louis (04 68 04 21 97).
www.mont-louis.net

The remote Cerdagne, an
independent state in the
Middle Ages, is today divided
between Spain and France. Its
high plateaux offer skiing and
walking among clear mountain
lakes and pine and chestnut
forests. The Little Yellow Train
is an excellent way to sample
it in a day. Stops include **Mont
Louis**, a town fortified by
Vauban, Louis XIV's military
architect, which still accom-
modates French troops; the
huge ski resort of **Font-Romeu;
Latour-de-Carol** and the tiny
village of **Yravals** below it.
Nearby **Odeillo** is the site of a
huge solar furnace, 45 m
(150 ft) tall and 50 m
(165 ft) wide. Established
in 1969, its giant curved
mirrors create a remarkable
sight in the valley.

Villefranche-de-Conflent ❷

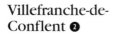

Pyrénées-Orientales. 🏘 240. 🚊 🚌
ℹ️ pl de l'Eglise (04 68 96 22 96).

In medieval times Villefranche's
position at the narrowest point
of the Têt valley made it an
eminently defensible fortress
against Moorish invasion.
Today, fragments of 11th-
century walls remain, along
with massive ramparts, gates
and Fort Liberia high above
the gorge, all built by Vauban

Abbey cloisters of St-Michel-de-Cuxa

in the 17th century. The 12th-
century **Eglise de St-Jacques**
has fine carved capitals from
the workshops of St-Michel-
de-Cuxa, and Catalan painted
wooden statues, including a
14th-century *Virgin and
Child*. The 13th-century oak
door is embellished with
intricate local wrought ironwork, a craft which still
features on many of the shop
signs in town. From the streets

Statue in St-Jacques, Villefranche

of locally quarried pink marble
you can make the climb up
to the **Grottes des Canalettes**,
a superb underground setting
for concerts. The Little Yellow
Train will take you to the
magnificent mountain plain
of the Cerdagne (phone 0806
886 091 to book).

St-Michel-de-Cuxa ❸

Prades, Pyrénées-Orientales. **Tel** 04
68 96 15 35. ⬜ daily. ⬤ Sun am,
religious hols. 🈸

Prades, a small, pink marble
town in the Têt valley, is
typical of the local style. The
Eglise St-Pierre has a southern
Gothic wrought iron belfry
and a Baroque Catalan
interior. But the town is distinguished by the beautiful
pre-Romanesque abbey of
St-Michel-de-Cuxa which lies
3 km (2 miles) further up
the valley, and by the legacy
of the Spanish cellist Pablo
Casals. Casals spent many
years here in exile from
Franco's Spain; every August
the abbey provides the setting
for the Prades music festival
held in his memory.
    An early example of
monastic architecture, St-Michel-
de-Cuxa abbey was founded
by Benedictine monks in
878 and rapidly became
renowned throughout France
and Spain. Distinctive
keyhole arches showing
Moorish influence pierce the
massive walls of the abbey
church, which was consecrated
in 974. The mottled pink
marble cloisters, with their
superbly carved capitals, were
added later, in the 12th century.
    After the Revolution the
building was abandoned, and

THE LITTLE YELLOW TRAIN

Arrive early for the best seats in the carriages of *Le Petit
Train Jaune*, which winds its way on narrow-gauge tracks
through gorges and across towering viaducts up into the
Cerdagne, stopping at small mountain stations along the
way. Built in 1910 to improve access to the mountains, it
now operates mainly for tourists, beginning at Villefranche-
de-Conflent and terminating at Latour-de-Carol.

The Little Yellow Train, with open carriages for summer visitors

For hotels and restaurants in this region see pp588–90 and pp643–6

its famous carvings looted. From 1913, George Grey Bernard, a visiting American artist, began to discover some of the capitals incorporated in local buildings. He sold the carvings to the Metropolitan Museum of Art in New York in 1925, where they formed the basis of the Cloisters Museum – a faithful re-creation of a Romanesque abbey in the unlikely setting of Manhattan.

St-Martin-du-Canigou 4

Casteil. **Tel** 04 68 05 50 03.
⬜ (guided tours only: tours last an hour; times vary with seasons) Jun–Sep: daily; Oct–May: Tue–Sun. ◼ Jan. ▨

Saint-Martin-du-Canigou is situated in a spectacularly remote site a third of the way up Pic du Canigou, on a jagged spur of rock approached only by jeep or a 40-minute climb on foot from Casteil or by hiring a jeep from Vernet-les-Bains. The abbey was built between 1001 and 1026, and financed by Guifred, Count of Cerdagne, who abandoned his family and entered the monastery in 1035. He was buried there 14 years later in a tomb he carved from the rock himself, which can still be seen. The church is early

Nun at St-Martin

Romanesque, based on a simple basilican plan. Two churches are built, quite literally one on top of the other, making the lower church the crypt for the upper building.

The abbey complex is best viewed from above by continuing up the path. From there, its irregular design clinging to the rock is framed by the dramatic mountain setting – the ensemble a tribute to the ingenuity and vitality of its early builders.

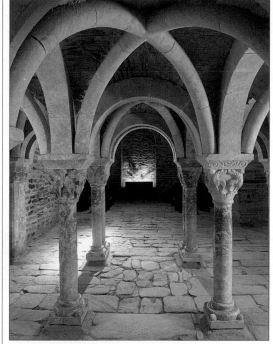
Serrabone priory's chapel tribune, with columns of local marble

Prieuré de Serrabone 5

Boule d'Amont. **Tel** 04 68 84 09 30 (tourist office). ⬜ daily. ◼ 1 Jan, 1 May, 1 Nov, 25 Dec. ▨

Perched high up on the northern flanks of Pic du Canigou, the sacred mountain of the Catalans, is the priory of Serrabone. A final lap of hairpin bends on the approach road (the D618) reveals the simple square tower and round apse of this remote Romanesque abbey, surrounded by a botanical garden of local herbs and woodland plants clinging to the mountain side.

Inside the cool, austere 12th-century building is a surprisingly elaborate chapel tribune, its columns and arches glowing from the local red-veined marble, carved by the anonymous Master of Cuxa, whose work appears throughout the region. Note the strange beasts and verdant flora featured in the capital carvings, especially the rose of Roussillon.

The 11th-century cloister of St-Martin-du-Canigou

Céret ❻

Pyrénées-Orientales. 🏠 8,000. 📧
ℹ️ av Clémenceau (04 68 87 00 53).
🗓 Sat, Tue eve Jul–Aug. 🎪 Fête des
Cerises (May/Jun). www.ot-ceret.fr

Céret is a cherry town,
surrounded by a cloud of
pink blossom in the early
spring, and producing the
very first fruits of the year.
The tiled and painted façades
and loggias of the buildings
have a Spanish feel and the
town was popular with
Picasso, Braque and Matisse.
Today Céret is distinguished
by the **Musée d'Art Moderne**,
its sophisticated modern
architecture housing a
remarkable collection which
includes Catalan artists Tapiès
and Capdeville, 50 works
donated by Picasso, including
a series of bowls painted with
bullfighting scenes, and
works by Matisse, Chagall,
Juan Gris and Salvador Dalí.

The town's Catalan heritage
is evident in regular bullfights
held in the arena, and in its
Sardana dance festivals in July.

Statue by Aristide Maillol, Banyuls

town of **Amélie-les-Bains**,
where fragments of Roman
baths have been discovered.
Beyond, in **Arles-sur-Tech**, the
Eglise de Ste-Marie contains
12th-century frescoes, and a
sarcophagus be-
side the church
door which, ac-
cording to local
legend, produces
drops of unac-
countably pure
water every year.

Catalan flag

and rocky outcrops. The
vermeille (vermilion-tinted)
rock of the headlands gives
this stretch of coast, the loveliest in the region, its name.

The Côte Vermeille extends
all the way to the Costa Brava
in northern Spain. With its
Catalan character, it is as redolent of Spain as of France.
Argelès-Plage has three
sandy beaches and a palm-
fringed promenade, and is
the largest camping centre in
Europe. The small resort of
Cerbère is the last French
town before the border, flying
the red and gold Catalan flag
to signal its true allegiance.
All along the coast, terraced
vineyards cling to the rocky
hillsides, producing
strong, sweet wines
like Banyuls and
Muscat. The difficult
terrain makes harvest-
ing a laborious
process. Vines were
first cultivated here by
Greek settlers in the 7th
century BC, and Banyuls itself
has wine cellars dating back
to the Middle Ages.

Banyuls is also famous as
the birthplace of Aristide
Maillol, the 19th-century
sculptor, whose work can be
seen all over the region. **Port
Vendres**, with fortifications
built by the indefatigable
Vauban (architect to Louis XIV)
is a fishing port, renowned for
its anchovies and sardines.

🏛 **Musée d'Art Moderne**
8 bd Maréchal Joffre. **Tel** 04 68 87 27
76. ◯ Apr–Sep: daily; Oct–Mar: Wed–
Mon. ● some public hols. 🎫 ♿
www.musee-ceret.com

Environs
From Céret the D115 follows
the Tech valley to the spa

Côte Vermeille ❼

Pyrénées-Orientales. ✈ Perpignan.
🚆 Collioure, Cerbère. 🚌 Collioure,
Banyuls-sur-Mer. ℹ️ Collioure (04 68
82 15 47), Cerbère (04 68 88 42 36).
www.collioure.com

Here the Pyrenees meet the
Mediterranean, the coast
road twisting and turning
around secluded pebbly coves

The spectacular Côte Vermeille, seen from the coast road south of Banyuls

Collioure harbour, with one of its beaches and the Eglise Notre-Dame-des-Anges

Collioure ❽

Pyrénées-Orientales. 🏠 *3,000.*
�] 🚃 🛈 *pl du 18 juin
(04 68 82 15 47).* 🛒 *Wed & Sun.*
www.collioure.com

The colours of Collioure first
attracted Matisse here in 1905:
brightly stuccoed houses
sheltered by cypresses and
gaily painted fishing boats,
all bathed in the famous
luminous light, and washed
by a gentle sea. Other artists
including André Derain
worked here under Matisse's
influence and were dubbed
fauves (wild beasts) for their
wild experiments with colour.
Art galleries and souvenir
shops fill the cobbled
streets, but this small fishing
port has changed little since
then, with anchovies still its
main business. Two salting
houses, which can be visited,
are evidence of this tradition.

Three sheltered beaches,
both pebble and sand, nestle
round the harbour, dominated
by the bulk of the **Château
Royal**, which forms part of the
harbour wall. It was first built
by the Knights Templar in the
13th century, and Collioure
became the main port of entry
for Perpignan, remaining
under the rule of Spanish
Aragon until France took
over in 1659. The outer
fortifications were reinforced
ten years later by Vauban,
who demolished much of the

original town in the process.
Today the château can be
toured, or visited for its
exhibitions of modern art.

The **Eglise Notre-Dame-
des-Anges** on Collioure's
quayside was rebuilt in the
17th century to replace the
church which was destroyed
by Vauban. A former lighthouse
was incorporated as a belltower.
Inside the church are no fewer
than five Baroque altarpieces
by Joseph Sunyer and other
Catalan masters of the genre.

Be warned that Collioure
is extremely popular in July
and August, with visitors cram-
ming the tiny streets. Long
queues of traffic are possible,
too, though the building of
another route, the D86, has
helped to ease congestion.

♠ **Château Royal**
Tel *04 68 82 06 43.* ◻ *daily.*
⬤ *1 Jan, 1 May & 25 Dec.* 🎫

Elne ❾

Pyrénées-Orientales. 🏠 *8,000.* 🚃 🛒
🛈 *pl Sant-Jordi (04 68 22 05 07).*
🛒 *Mon, Wed, Fri.* **www**.ot-elne.fr

The ancient town of Elne
accommodated Hannibal and
his elephants in 218 BC on his
epic journey to Rome, and was
one of the most important
towns in Roussillon until the
16th century. Today it is
famed for the 11th-century
**Cathédrale de Ste-Eulalie et
Ste-Julie**, with its superb cloister. Milky blue-veined marble
has been carved into exquisite
capitals, embellished with a
riot of flowers, figures and
arabesques. The side nearest
the cathedral dates from the
1100s; the remaining three
are 13th–14th-century. From
the front of the cathedral are
views of the vines and orchards of the surrounding plain.

Carved capital at Elne, showing "The Dream of the Magi"

Entrance to the Palais des Rois de Majorque, Perpignan

Perpignan ➓

Pyrénées-Orientales. 🏠 120,000.
✈ 🚉 🚌 ℹ Palais des Congrès
(04 68 66 30 30). ● daily.
www.perpignantourisme.com

Catalan Perpignan has a distinctly southern feel, with palm trees lining the Têt river promenade, house and shop façades painted vibrant turquoise and pink, and the streets of the Arab quarter selling aromatic spices, couscous and paella.

Today Perpignan is the vibrant capital of Roussillon, and has an important position on the developing Mediterranean sunbelt. But it reached its zenith in the 13th and 14th centuries under the kings of Majorca and the kings of Aragón, who controlled great swathes of northern Spain and southern France. Their vast **Palais des Rois de Majorque** still straddles a substantial area in the southern part of the city.

Perpignan's strong Catalan identity is evident during the twice-weekly summer celebrations when the Sardana is danced in the place de la Loge. It is a key Catalan symbol. Arms raised, concentric circles of dancers keep step to the accompaniment of a Catalan woodwind band.

One of Perpignan's finest buildings, the **Loge de Mer**, lies at the head of the square. Built in 1397 to house the Maritime Exchange, only the eastern section retains the original Gothic design. The rest of the building was rebuilt in Renaissance style in 1540 with sumptuous carved wooden ceilings and sculpted window frames. While visitors are sometimes offended by the sight of a fast-food restaurant inside, the result is that the Loge de Mer has avoided becoming a hushed museum piece. Instead, it remains the centre of Perpignan life – elegant cafés cluster round it, producing a constant buzz of activity.

Next door is the **Hôtel de Ville** with its pebble stone façade and wrought iron gates. Inside, parts of the arcaded courtyard date back to 1315; at the centre is Aristide Maillol's allegorical sculpture, *The Mediterranean* (1950).

To the east is the labyrinthine cathedral quarter of St-Jean, made up of small streets and squares containing some fine 14th- and 15th-century buildings.

Devout Christ in St-Jean

THE ANNUAL PROCESSION DE LA SANCH

There is a very Catalan atmosphere in Perpignan during the annual Good Friday procession of the Confraternity of La Sanch (Brotherhood of the Holy Blood). Originally dedicated to the comfort of condemned prisoners in the 15th century, members of the brotherhood still wear macabre red or black robes as they carry sacred relics and the crucifix from the Chapel of the Devout Christ to the cathedral.

⛪ Cathédrale St-Jean
Pl de Gambetta. ☐ daily.
Topped by a wrought iron belfry, this cathedral was begun in 1324 and was finally ready for use in 1509. It is constructed almost entirely from river pebbles layered with red brick, a style common throughout the region due to the scarcity of other building materials.

Inside the gloomy interior the nave is flanked by gilded altarpieces and painted wooden statues, with a massive pre-Romanesque marble font. A cloistered cemetery adjoins the church and the Chapel of the Devout Christ with its precious, poignantly realistic medieval wooden Crucifixion. The cathedral replaced the 11th-century church of St-Jean-le-Vieux, whose superb Romanesque doorway can be glimpsed to the left of the main entrance. Some areas may be restricted due to ongoing restoration work.

♛ Palais des Rois de Majorque

2 rue des Archers. *Tel 04 68 34 48 29*. ○ *daily*. ● *1 Jan, 1 May, 1 Nov, 25 Dec.*

Access to the vast 13th-century fortified palace of the Kings of Majorca is as circuitous today as it was intended to be for invading soldiers. Flights of steps zigzag within the sheer red-brick ramparts, begun in the 15th century and added to successively over the next two centuries. Eventually, the elegant gardens and substantial castle within are revealed, entered by way of the Tour de l'Hommage, from the top of which is a panoramic view of city, mountains and sea.

The palace itself is built around a central arcaded courtyard, flanked on one side by the Salle de Majorque, a great hall with a triple fireplace and giant Gothic arched windows. Adjacent, two royal chapels built one above the other show southern Gothic style at its best: pointed arches, patterned frescoes and elaborate tilework demonstrating a distinct Moorish influence. The fine rose marble doorway of the upper King's Chapel is typical of the Roussillon Romanesque

Courtyard in the Hôtel de Ville

style, although the sculpted capitals are Gothic. Today the great courtyard is sometimes used for concerts.

🏛 Musée Josep Deloncle de l'Histoire de la Catalogue Nord

Le Castillet. *Tel 04 68 35 42 05.* ○ *Tue–Sun.* ● *1 Jan, 1 May, 1 Nov.*

The red-brick tower and pink belfry of the Castillet, built as the town gate in 1368, was at one time a prison and is all that remains of the town walls. It now houses a collection of Catalan craft objects, agricultural implements, kitchen furniture, looms, and terracotta pots for storing water and oil. It also holds art exhibitions.

🏛 Musée Rigaud

16 rue de l'Ange. *Tel 04 68 35 43 40.* ○ *Tue–Sun.* ● *public hols.*

This magnificent 18th-century mansion has an eclectic art collection dominated by the work of Hyacinthe Rigaud (1659–1743), who was born in Perpignan and was court painter to Louis XIV and Louis XV.

The first floor has a room of portraits, including works by David, Greuze and Ingres; the Dufy, Picasso and Maillol room; and the Primitifs Catalan, 14th–16th-century Catalan and Spanish paintings, among them the *Retable de la Trinité* (1489) by the Master of Canapost.

The museum also represents the 20th century: Alechinsky, Appel and others from the late 1940s European Cobra movement; the Catalan artist Pierre Daura; and modern Roussillon painters like Brune, Terrus and Violet.

Fortress tower and ramparts, Salses

Salses ⓫

Pyrénées-Orientales. 🏠 *3,000*. 🚉 🚌 🛈 *pl de la République (04 68 38 66 13)*. 🚋 *Wed*. **www**.salses. monuments-nationaux.fr

Looking like a giant sand-castle against the ochre earth of the Corbières vineyards, the **Forteresse de Salses** stands at the old frontier of Spain and France. It guards the narrow defile between the Mediterranean lagoons and the mountains, and was built by King Ferdinand of Aragon between 1497 and 1506 to defend Spain's possession of Roussillon. Its massive walls and rounded towers are a classic example of Spanish military architecture, designed to deflect the new threat posed by gunpowder.

Inside were underground stables for 300 horses and a subterranean passageway.

There is a wonderful view from the keep over the lagoons and surrounding coastline.

The pebble and red-brick Cathédrale de St-Jean in Perpignan

Vineyards covering the hilly terrain of the Corbières

Corbières ⑫

Aude. ✈ Perpignan. 🚍 Narbonne, Carcassonne, Lézignan-Corbières. 🚍 Narbonne, Carcassonne, Lézignan-Corbières. 🛈 Lézignan-Corbières (04 68 27 05 42). **www**.lezignan-corbieres.fr/tourisme

Still one of the wildest parts of France with few roads, let alone villages, the Corbières is best known for its wine and the great craggy hulks of the Cathar castles *(see p491)*. Much of the land is untamed *garrigue* (scrubland) fragrant with honeysuckle and broom; south-facing slopes have been cleared and planted with vines.

To the south are the spectacular medieval castles of **Peyrepertuse** and **Quéribus**, the latter one of the last Cathar strongholds. The guided visits around the remarkable Cathar château at **Villerouge-Termenes** reveal some of its turbulent past. To the west is the barren, uninhabited Razès area in the upper Aude valley. Its best-kept secret is the village of **Alet-les-Bains**, with beautifully preserved half-timbered houses and the remains of a Benedictine abbey, battle-scarred from the Wars of Religion.

Narbonne ⑬

Aude. 🏃 52,000. 🚍 🚍 🚍 pl Roger Salengro (04 68 65 15 60). 🗓 Thu & Sun. **www**.mairie-narbonne.fr

Narbonne is a medium-sized, cheerful town profiting from the booming wine region that surrounds it. The town is bisected by the tree-shaded Canal de la Robine; to the north is the restored medieval quarter with many elegant shops and good restaurants. Located here is one of Narbonne's most intriguing tourist attractions, the **Horreum**. This underground warren of granaries and grain chutes dates from the 1st century BC, when Narbonne was a major port and capital of the largest Roman province in Gaul.

The town prospered through the Middle Ages until the 15th century when the harbour silted up and the course of the river Aude altered, taking Narbonne's fortunes with it. By then, an important bishopric had been established and an ambitious cathedral project, modelled on the great Gothic cathedrals of the North, was

underway. However, the full grandiose design was abandoned and just the chancel, begun in 1272, became the **Cathédrale St-Just et St-Pasteur** we see today.

It is still enormous, enhanced by 14th-century sculptures, fine stained-glass windows and an 18th-century carved organ. Aubusson and Gobelin tapestries adorn the walls, and the Chapel of the Anonciade houses a treasury of manuscripts, jewelled reliquaries and tapestries.

The unfinished transept now forms a courtyard, and between the cathedral and the **Palais des Archevêques** (Archbishops' Palace), lie cloisters with four galleries of 14th-century vaulting.

This huge palace and cathedral complex dominates the centre of Narbonne. Between the Palais des Archevêques' massive 14th-century towers is the town hall, with a 19th-century Neo-Gothic façade by Viollet-le-Duc *(see p200)*, the architect who so determinedly

The vaulted chancel of Cathédrale St-Just et St-Pasteur in Narbonne

CANAL DU MIDI

From Sète to Toulouse the 240-km (149-mile) Canal du Midi flows between plane trees, vineyards and villages. The complex system of locks, aqueducts and bridges is a remarkable feat of engineering, built by the Béziers salt-tax baron Paul Riquet. Completed in 1681, it encouraged Languedoc trade and created a vital link, via the Garonne river, between the Atlantic and the Mediterranean. Today it is plied by holiday barges (www.canal-du-midi.org).

Tranquil waterway of the Canal du Midi

The Cistercian Abbaye de Fontfroide (1093), southwest of Narbonne

restored medieval France. The palace itself is divided into the Palais Vieux (Old Palace) and the Palais Neuf (New Palace). Narbonne's most important museums are in the Palais Neuf, on the left as you enter through the low medieval arches of the passage de l'Ancre. The **Musée d'Archéologie et de Préhistoire** collection includes fragments of Narbonne's Roman heritage, from milestones and parts of the original walls to an assemblage of domestic objects, coins, tools and glassware. The **Chapelle de la Madeleine** is decorated with a 14th-century wall painting and houses a collection of Greek vases, sarcophagi and mosaics.

In the archbishops' former apartments is the **Musée d'Art et d'Histoire**, which is interesting for its luxurious furnishings and richly decorated ceilings as for its art collection. This includes some fine paintings by Canaletto, Brueghel, Boucher and Veronese as well as a large selection of local earthenware.

South of the Canal de la Robine are a number of fine mansions, including the Renaissance **Maison des Trois Nourrices** on the corner of rue des Trois-Nourrices and

rue Edgard-Quinet. Nearby is the **Musée Lapidaire**, with architectural fragments from Gallo-Roman Narbonne, and the 13th-century Gothic **Basilique St-Paul-Serge**. The present building retains the crypt and some sarcophagi of an earlier church on this site.

🏛 **Horreum**
Rue Rouget-de-l'Isle. *Tel 04 68 32 45 30.* ⭘ *mid-Jul–mid-Oct: daily; Nov–mid-Jul: Wed–Mon.* ⬤ *1 Jan, 1 May, 1 & 11 Nov, 25 Dec.* 🈂

🏛 **Musée d'Archéologie et de Préhistoire/Musée d'Art et d'Histoire**
Palais des Archevêques. *Tel 04 68 90 30 65.* ⭘ *mid-Jul–mid-Oct: daily; Nov–mid-Jul: Wed–Mon.* ⬤ *1 Jan, 1 May, 1 & 11 Nov, 25 Dec.* 🈂

🏛 **Musee Lapidaire**
Eglise Notre-Dame de Lamourguié. *Tel 04 68 90 30 65.* ⭘ *mid-Jul–mid-Oct: daily; Nov–mid-Jul: Wed–Mon.* ⬤ *1 Jan, 1 May, 1 Nov, 11 Nov, 25 Dec.* 🈂 ♿

Environs
Southwest (13 km/8 miles), the Cistercian **Abbaye de Fontfroide** has an elegant cloister. The abbey is tucked away in a quiet valley, surrounded by cypress trees.

Golfe du Lion ⑭

Aude, Hérault. 🚶 🚆
🚍 Montpellier. ⛴ Sète. 🛈 *La Grande Motte (04 67 56 42 00).* **www**.ot-lagrandemotte.fr

Languedoc-Roussillon's shoreline (100 km/65 miles) forms an almost unbroken sweep of sandy beach. Only at its southern limits does it break into the rocky inlets of the Côte Vermeille. Purpose-built resorts created since the 1960s emphasize eco-friendly, low-rise family accommodation, some in local styles, others with imaginative architecture.

La Grande Motte marina has distinctive ziggurat-style buildings *(see p495)*. **Cap d'Agde** has Europe's largest naturist quarter. Inland **Agde**, founded by ancient Greek traders, is built of black basalt and has a fortified cathedral. **Port Leucate** and **Port Bacarès** are ideal for watersports. An older town is **Sète** *(see p492)*. A feature of the flat Languedoc coast is its étangs – large shallow lagoons. Those nearest the Camargue are the haunt of thousands of wading birds.

A wide, sandy beach on the Cap d'Agde

Carcassonne ⓯

The citadel of Carcassonne is a perfectly restored medieval town, and protected by UNESCO. It crowns a steep bank above the river Aude, a fairy-tale sight of turrets and ramparts overlooking the Basse Ville below. The strategic position of the citadel between the Atlantic and the Mediterranean and on the corridor between the Iberian peninsula and the rest of Europe led to its original settlement, consolidated by the Romans in the 2nd century BC. It became a key element in medieval military conflicts. At its zenith in the 12th century, it was ruled by the Trencavels who built the château and cathedral. Military advances and the Treaty of the Pyrenees in 1659, which relocated the French–Spanish border, hastened its decline. The attentions of architectural historian Viollet-le-Duc *(see p200)* led to its restoration in the 19th century.

The Restored Citadel
Restoration of La Cité has always been controversial. Critics complain it looks too new, favouring a more romantic ruin.

★ Le Château
A fortress within a fortress, the château has a moat, five towers and defensive wooden galleries on the walls.

Bishop's Tower

Porte d'Aude

R PORTE D'AU

RUE ST LOUIS

R DAME CARCAS

RUE TRENCAVEL

LICES HAUTES

The ramparts were built by Kings Louis VIII, Louis IX and Philip the Bold, in the 13th century.

STAR SIGHTS

★ Le Château

★ Basilique St-Nazaire

★ Basilique St-Nazaire
Within the Romanesque and Gothic cathedral is the famous Siege Stone, said to depict the 1209 Siege of Carcassonne by crusaders.

0 metres	50
0 yards	50

KEY

– – – Suggested route

RELIGIOUS PERSECUTION

Carcassonne's strategic position meant it was often at the centre of religious conflict. The Cathars *(see p491)* were given sanctuary here in 1209 by Raymond-Roger Trencavel when besieged by Simon de Montfort in his crusade against heresy. In the 14th century the Inquisition continued to root out the Cathars. This painting depicts intended victims in the Inquisition Tower.

***Les Emmurés de Carcassonne**, JP Laurens*

VISITORS' CHECKLIST

Aude. 49,000. 4 km
(2 miles) W Carcassonne.
Port du Canal du Midi.
bd de Varsovie.
28 rue Verdun
(04 68 10 24 30).
Tue, Thu & Sat.
Festival de Carcassonne
(Jul–Aug); l'Embrasement de la
Cité (14 Jul); Fête le Sud (Aug).
Le Château daily. 1 Jan,
1 May, 1 & 11 Nov, 25 Dec.
www.carcassonne-tourisme.com

Gallo-Roman walls

Musée Lapidaire

The collection includes Roman amphorae and terracotta, Romanesque murals and fragments from the cathedral, a set of Gothic windows and these medieval stone missiles.

Porte Narbonnaise

Flanked by two sandstone towers, built in 1280, the defences included two portcullises, two iron doors, a moat and a drawbridge.

Old City Entrance

Entering La Cité is still a step back in time, although it is one of France's top tourist destinations, filled with souvenir shops.

The Great Well

Main entrance to La Cité

The *lices*, the easily defended spaces between the inner and outer ramparts, were also used for jousting, crossbow practice and for storage of timber and other materials.

Béziers with its medieval cathedral, seen from Pont Vieux in the southwest

Minerve **⑯**

Hérault. 🏠 120. 🚹 rue des Martyrs
(04 68 91 81 43).
www.minerve-tourisme.fr

In the parched, arid hills of
the Minervois, surrounded
by vines and not much else,
Minerve appears defiant on
its rocky outcrop at the
confluence of the rivers Cesse
and Briant. It is defended by
what the Minervois call the
"Candela" (Candle), an
octagonal tower which is all
that remains of the medieval
château. In 1210, the small
town resisted the vengeful
Simon de Montfort, scourge
of the Cathars, in a siege
lasting seven weeks. This
culminated in the execution
of 140 Cathars, who were
burned at the stake.

Today visitors enter Minerve
by a high bridge spanning the
gorge. Turn right and follow
the route of the Cathars past
the Romanesque arch of the
Porte des Templiers to the
12th-century **Eglise St-
Etienne**. Outside the church
is a crudely carved dove,
symbol of the Cathars, and
within is a 5th-century white
marble altar table, one of the
oldest artifacts in the region.

A rocky path follows the
riverbed below the town,
where the water has cut out
caves and two bridges – the
Grand Pont and the Petit Pont –
from the soft limestone.

Béziers **⑰**

Hérault. 🏠 73,000. ✈ 🚉 🚌
🚹 29 av Saint Saëns (04 67 76 84
00). 🛒 Fri. **www**.beziers-tourisme.fr

Famous for its bullfights and
rugby, and the wine of the
surrounding region, Béziers
has several other points of
interest. The town seems
turned in on itself, its roads
leading up to the massive
14th-century **Cathédrale
St-Nazaire**, with its fine sculpture, stained glass and frescoes.
In 1209, several thousand
citizens were massacred in
the crusade against the Cathars.
The papal legate's troops were
ordered not to discriminate
between Catholics and Cathars,
but to "Kill them all. God will
recognize his own!"

**Statue of the engineer Paul Riquet
in the allées Paul Riquet, Béziers**

The **Musée du Biterrois**
holds exhibitions on local
history, wine and the Canal
du Midi, engineered in the
late 17th century by Paul
Riquet, Béziers' most famous
son (see p486). His statue
presides over the Allées
Paul Riquet, which is lined
by rows of plane trees and
large canopied restaurants,
a civilized focus to this
otherwise business-like town.

🏛 **Musée du Biterrois**
Caserne St-Jacques. **Tel** 04 67 36
71 01. ◻ Tue–Sun. ● 1 Jan,
Easter, 1 May, 25 Dec. 🏷 ♿

Environs

Overlooking the Béziers plain
and the mountains to the north
is Oppidum d'Ensérune, a
superb Roman site. The **Musée
de l'Oppidum d'Ensérune**
has a good archaeological
collection, from Celtic, Greek
and Roman vases to jewellery
and weapons.

The **Château de Raissac**
(between Béziers and Lignan)
houses an unusual 19th-century
faïence museum in its stables.

🏛 **Musée de l'Oppidum
d'Ensérune**
Nissan-lez-Ensérune. **Tel** 04 67 37
01 23. ◻ daily (Sep–Apr: Tue–Sun).
● public hols. 🏷 ♿ limited.
http://enserune.monuments-
nationaux.fr

🏛 **Château de Raissac**
Rte de Lignan sur Orr. **Tel** 04 67 49
17 60. ◻ by appt. **www**.raissac.com

The Cathars

The Cathars (from Greek *katharos*, meaning pure) were a 13th-century Christian sect critical of corruption in the established church. Cathar dissent flourished in independent Languedoc as an expression of separatism, but the rebellion was rapidly exploited for political purposes. Peter II of Aragon was keen to annex Languedoc, and Philippe II of France joined forces with the pope to crush the Cathar heretics in a crusade led by Simon de Montfort in 1209. This heralded the start of over a century of ruthless killing and torture.

CATHAR CASTLES
The Cathars took refuge in the defensive castles of the Corbières and Ariège. Peyrepertuse is one of the most remote, difficult to get to even today: a long, narrow stone citadel hacked from a high, craggy peak over 609 m (2,000 ft) high.

Cathars *(also known as Albigensians) believed in the duality of good and evil. They considered the material world entirely evil. To be truly pure they had to renounce the world, and be non-violent, vegetarian and sexually abstinent.*

The crusade *against the Cathars was vicious. Heretics' land was promised to the crusaders by the pope, who assured forgiveness in advance of their crimes. In 1209, 20,000 citizens were massacred in Béziers and, the following year, 140 were burned to death in Minerve. In 1244, 225 Cathars died defending one of their last fortresses at Montségur.*

CATHAR COUNTRY
Castles and towns with a Cathar association, some of them spectacular sites, are concentrated in Languedoc-Roussillon, the centre of Catharism in the Middle Ages.

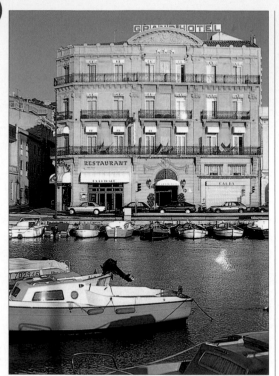

The impressive Grand Hôtel *(see p590)* on quai de la Résistance, Sète

Sète ⑱

Hérault. 👥 *43,500.* 🚉 🚌 ⛴
🛈 *60 grand' rue Mario Roustan
(04 99 04 71 71).* 📅 *Wed & Fri.*
www.ot-sete.fr

Sète is a major fishing and
industrial port. It has a
gutsier, more raffish air than
much of the leisure-oriented
Mediterranean, with its shops

Cimetière Marin in Sète, burial
place of the poet Paul Valéry

selling ships' lamps and
propellers, and its quayside
restaurants full of hungry
sailors demolishing vast
platters of mussels, oysters
and sea snails straight off the
boat. Most of Sète's restaurants can be found in a stroll
along the Grand Canal, with
its Italianate houses painted
in pastel colours and with
wrought iron balconies overlooking Sète's network of
canals and bridges. Boisterous
water jousting tournaments,
dating back to 1666, form part
of the patron saint's festival in
August *(see p37)*.

The **Musée International
des Arts Modestes** displays
everyday objects (including
some by well-known contemporary designers) in amusing
new contexts, within a renovated canalside warehouse.

Above the town is the
Cimetière Marin, where Sète's
most famous son, poet Paul
Valéry (1871–1945), is buried.
There is a small museum and
breathtaking views of the
coast and the mountains.

🏛 **Musée International des
Arts Modestes**
23 quai du Maréchal de Lattre
de Tassigny. **Tel** *04 99 04 76 44.*
⏱ *Apr–Sep: daily; Oct–Mar:
Tue–Sun.* ⬤ *public hols.* 🎟 ♿
www.miam.org

Pézenas ⑲

Hérault. 👥 *9,000.* 🚌 🛈 *Pl des
Etats de Languedoc (04 67 98
36 40).* 📅 *Sat.*
www.pezenas-tourisme.fr

Pézenas is a charming little
town, easily appreciated in a
gentle stroll of its main sights,
and abounding in revealing
details, fragmentary evidence
of its past brilliance as the
seat of local government in
the 16th–17th centuries. Then
the town also played host to
many troupes of musicians
and actors, including Molière.

Best of all are the glimpses
of fine houses through courtyard doorways, such as the
Hôtel des Barons de Lacoste,
at 8 rue François-Oustrin, with
its beautiful stone staircase,
and the **Maison des Pauvres** at
12 rue Alfred Sabatier, with its
three galleries and staircase.

Look out for the medieval
shop window on rue Triperie-
Vieille, and just within the
14th-century **Porte Faugères**,
the narrow streets of the
Jewish ghetto, with its chilling
feeling of enclosure. Shops
selling antiques, second-hand
goods and books abound. All
around the town, vines stretch
as far as the eye can see.

The stone foyer of the Hôtel des
Barons de Lacoste in Pézenas

Parc Régional du Haut Languedoc ㉘

Hérault, Tarn. ✈ Béziers.
🚌 Béziers, Bédarieux. 🚍 St-Pons-
de-Thomières, Mazamet, Lamalou-les-
Bains 🚏 St-Pons-de-Thomières
(04 67 97 38 22).
www.parc-haut-languedoc.fr

The high limestone plateaux
and wooded slopes of upper
Languedoc are a world away
from the coast. From the
Montagne Noire, a mountainous region between Béziers
and Castres, up into the
Cévennes is a landscape of
remote sheep farms, eroded
rock formations and deep
river gorges. Much of this
area has been designated the
Parc Régional du Haut
Languedoc, the second largest
of the French national parks
after Ecrins.

St-Pons-de-Thomières is the
entrance, with access to forest
and mountain trails for walking and riding, plus a wildlife
research centre, where one
can glimpse the mouflons
(wild mountain sheep),
eagles and wild boar which
were once a common sight in
the region.

If you take the D908 from
St-Pons through the park you
pass the village of **Olargues**
with its 12th-century bridge
over the river Jaur. **Lamalou-
les-Bains**, on the park's eastern edge, is a small spa town
with a restored Belle Epoque
spa building and theatre, and
a soporifically slow pace.

Outside the park boundaries
to the northeast there are spectacular natural phenomena. At
the **Cirque de Navacelles**, the
river Vis has joined up with
itself cutting out an entire
island. On it sits the peaceful
village of Navacelles, visible
from the road higher up. The
Grotte des Demoiselles is one
of the most magnificent in an
area full of caves, where you
walk through a calcified
world. A funicular train takes
visitors from the foot of the
mountain to the top.

The **Grotte de Clamouse** is
also an extraordinary experience, the reflections from
underground rivers and pools
flickering on the cavern roofs,
with stalagmites resembling
dripping candles.

🦇 **Grotte des Demoiselles**
St-Bauzille-de-Putois. **Tel** 04 67 73 70
02. ⬤ daily. ⬤ Jan, 25 Dec. 📷
www.demoiselles.com

🦇 **Grotte de Clamouse**
Rte de St-Guilhem-le-Désert, St-Jean-
de-Fos. **Tel** 04 67 57 71 05.
⬤ Feb–mid-Nov: daily. 📷
www.clamouse.com

Apse of St-Guilhem-le-Désert

St-Guilhem-le-Désert ㉑

Hérault. 🏠 250. 🚌 🚏 Maison
Communale (04 67 57 44 33).
www.saintguilhem-valleeherault.fr

Tucked away in the Celette
mountains, St-Guilhem-le-
Désert is no longer as remote
as when Guillaume of Aquitaine retired here as a hermit
in the 9th century. After a lifetime as a soldier, Guillaume
received a fragment of the
True Cross from Emperor
Charlemagne and established
a monastery in this ravine
above the river Hérault.

Vestiges of the first 10th-
century church have been
discovered but most of the
building is a superb example
of 11th–12th-century Romanesque architecture. Its lovely
apsidal chapels dominate the
heights of the village, behind
which the carved doorway
opens on to a central square.

Within the church is a
sombre barrel-vaulted central
aisle leading to the sunlit
central apse. Only two galleries of the cloisters remain:
the rest are in New York,
along with carvings from St-
Michel-de-Cuxa (see p481).

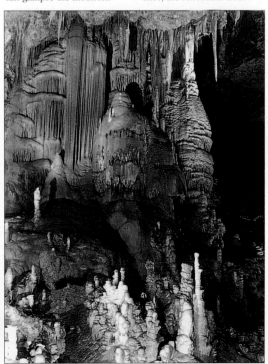

Extraordinary limestone formations at the Grotte de Clamouse

MONTPELLIER CITY CENTRE

Cathédrale de St-Pierre ⑤
Château d'Eau ①
CORUM ⑫
Hôtel de Manse ⑧
Hôtel de Mirman ⑨
Hôtel des Trésoriers
  de la Bourse ⑥
Jardin des Plantes ③
Musée Fabre ⑩
Musée
  Languedocien ⑦
Notre-Dame
  des Tables ⑪
Place de
  la Comédie ⑬
Promenade de Peyrou ②
Tour de la Babote ⑭
Tours des Pins ④

0 metres   250
0 yards   100

Key to Symbols *see back flap*

**Open-air café in the place de la
Comédie, Montpellier**

Montpellier ㉒

Hérault. 🏠 256,000. ✈ 🚆 🚌
ℹ 30 allée Jean de Lattré de Tassigny
(04 67 60 60 60). 🛒 daily. 🎭 Festival
International Montpellier Danse
(Jun–Jul). **www**.ot-montpellier.fr

Montpellier is one of the
liveliest and most forward-
looking cities in the south, with
a quarter of its population
under 25. Sometimes on a
summer evening in university
term time it resembles more a
rock festival than the capital
of Languedoc-Roussillon.

Centre of the action is the egg-
shaped **place de la Comédie**,
known as "l'Oeuf" ("the egg"),
with its 19th-century opera
house fronted by the Fontaine
des Trois Graces and
surrounded by buzzing cafés.
An esplanade of plane trees
and fountains leads to the
CORUM, an opera and conference centre typical of the
city's brave new architectural
projects. The best of these is
Ricardo Bofill's Postmodern
housing complex known as
Antigone, which is modelled
on St Peter's in Rome.
  Montpellier was founded
relatively late for this region
of ancient Roman towns, developing in the 10th century
as a result of the spice trade
with the Middle East. The city's
medical school was founded
in 1220, partly as a result of
this cross-fertilization of
knowledge between the two
cultures, and remains one of
the most respected in France.
  Most of Montpellier was
ravaged by the Wars of Religion in the 16th century. Only
the **Tour de la Babote** and the
Tours des Pins remain of the
12th-century fortifications.
There are few fine churches,

the exceptions being the
Cathédrale de St-Pierre and
the 18th-century **Notre-Dame
des Tables**.
  Reconstruction in the 17th
century saw the building of
mansions with elegant courtyards, stone staircases and
balconies. Examples open to
the public include **Hôtel de
Manse** on rue Embouque-
d'Or, **Hôtel de Mirman** near
place des Martyrs de la
Resistance and **Hôtel des
Trésoriers de la Bourse**. The
Hôtel des Lunaret houses the
Musée Languedocien which
exhibits Romanesque and
prehistoric artifacts.
  Another 17th-century building houses the renovated
Musée Fabre with a collection

PONT DU GARD   ← To Uzès

Left bank

The bridge comprises
three tiers of
continuous arches.

For hotels and restaurants in this region see pp588–90 and pp643–6

of mainly French paintings. Highlights include Courbet's famous *Bonjour M. Courbet*, Berthe Morisot's *L'Eté*, and some evocative paintings of the region by Raoul Dufy.

To view the city's position between mountains and sea go to the **Promenade de Peyrou**, a grand 18th-century square dominated by the **Château d'Eau** and the aqueduct which used to serve the city. North of here is the **Jardin des Plantes**, France's oldest botanical gardens (1593). Not to be missed is **Mare Nostrum**, the new aquarium in the Odysseum leisure zone, which has over 300 marine species.

🏛 **Musée Languedocien**
7 rue Jacques Coeur. **Tel** 04 67 52 93 03. ⬜ *Mon–Sat: pm only.* ⬤ *public hols.* 📷

🏛 **Musée Fabre**
39 bd Bonne Nouvelle. **Tel** 04 67 14 83 00. ⬜ *Tue–Sun.* 📷 🔲 🔟 🔁

Château d'Eau, Montpellier

La Grande-Motte ㉓

Hérault. 🏘 *8,500.* 🚉 🛈 *pl du 1er Octobre 1974 (04 67 56 42 00).* 🛒 *Sun (& Thu: mid-Jun–mid-Sep).* **www**.ot-lagrandemotte.fr

The bizarre white ziggurats of this modern marina exemplify the development of the Languedoc-Roussillon coast.

La Grande-Motte

One of several on the lagoons south of Montpellier, there are marinas and facilities for every kind of sport from tennis and golf to watersports, all flanked by golden beaches and pine forests. To the east are Le Grau-du-Roi, once a tiny fishing village, and Port-Camargue, with its big marina.

Aigues-Mortes ㉔

Gard. 🏘 *8,000.* 🚉 🚌 🛈 *pl St Louis (04 66 53 73 00).* 🛒 *Wed & Sun.* **www**.ot-aiguesmortes.fr

The best approach to this perfectly preserved walled town is across the salt marshes of the Petite Camargue. Now marooned 5 km (3 miles) from the sea, the imposing defences of this once important port have become a tourist experience, worth visiting more for the effect of the ensemble than the tacky shops within. Aigues-Mortes ("Place of Dead Waters") was established by Louis XI in the 13th century to consolidate his power on the Mediterranean, and built according to a strict grid pattern. By climbing up the **Tour de Constance** you can walk out onto the rectangular walls, which afford a superb view over the Camargue.

Environs
To the northeast is **St-Gilles-du-Gard**, also once an important medieval port. Today it is worth a detour to see the superbly sculpted 12th-century façade of its abbey church. This was originally established by the monks of Cluny abbey as a shrine to St Gilles, and a resting place on the famous pilgrimage route to Santiago de Compostela (*see pp400–1*).

Nîmes ㉕

See pp496-7.

Pont du Gard ㉖

Gard. 🛈 *08 20 90 33 30.* 🚉 *from Nîmes.* **www**.pontdugard.fr

No amount of fame can diminish the first sight of the 2,000-year-old Pont du Gard. The Romans considered it the best testimony to the greatness of their Empire, and at 49 m (160 ft) it was the highest bridge they ever built.

It is made from blocks of stone, hauled into place by slaves using an ingenious system of pulleys. The huge build-up of calcium in the water channels suggests the aqueduct was in continuous use for 400–500 years, carrying water to Nîmes along a 50-km (31-mile) route from the springs at **Uzès**. This charming town has an arcaded marketplace and several fine medieval towers.

Water channel | **To Nîmes →**

Right bank

Roman inscriptions include a damaged phallus carving as a good luck symbol.

Some stones weighed up to six tonnes.

Nîmes ㉕

Listed number one on the tourist map of Nîmes is the bus stop designed by Philippe Starck, who is also credited with reworking the city's pedestrian zone. Such innovations are part of the city's current design renaissance. Architectural projects range from imaginative housing to a glittering arts complex, under the guidance of a dynamic mayor. An important crossroads in the ancient world, Nîmes is equally well known for its Roman antiquities such as the amphitheatre, the best preserved of its kind. The city is also famous for its festivals and bullfights (*feria*). These are good times to see the rest of Nîmes with its museums, archaeological collections and Old Town of narrow streets and intimate squares.

Arches of the Roman amphitheatre

Historic Nîmes
Nîmes has had a turbulent history, suffering particularly during the 16th-century Wars of Religion when the Romanesque **Cathédrale Notre-Dame et St-Castor** was badly damaged. During the 17th and 18th centuries the town prospered from textile manufacturing, one of the most enduring products being denim or "de Nîmes". Many of the fine houses of this period have been restored and elegant examples can be seen on rue de l'Aspic, rue des Marchands and rue du Chapitre in the Old Town. Just outside the town centre is the futuristic apartment building, **Nemausus I**.

The Roman gate, the **Porte Auguste**, built 20 years before

Jug from Musée Archéologique

the temple of **Maison Carrée**, was once part of one of the longest city walls in Gaul. Of the original arches still standing, two (large) were for carts and chariots and two (smaller) ones for pedestrians. The other major Roman remnant is the **Castellum**, where water used to arrive from the Pont du Gard (*see p495*). From the Castellum it was distributed around the city through thick pipes.

🌿 Jardin de la Fontaine
Quai de la Fontaine. ⬜ *daily*. ♿
When the Romans arrived in Nîmes, they found a town established by

Jardin de la Fontaine, with a view over the city

For hotels and restaurants in this region see pp588–90 and pp643–6

SIGHTS AT A GLANCE

the Gauls, centred on the source of a spring. They named the town Nemausus, after their river god. In the 18th century, formal gardens were constructed, and a network of limpid pools and cool stone terraces remains. High above the garden on **Mont Cavalier** is the octagonal **Tour Magne**, once a key part of the Roman walls, offering a great view of the city.

Arms of the city in a sculpture by Martial Raysse

The Maison Carrée

🏛 Maison Carrée
Pl de la Maison Carrée. **Tel** 04 66
21 82 56. ☐ daily.
Square House is a very prosaic name for this elegant Roman temple, the pride of Nîmes. Built around AD 2, it is one of the best preserved in the world, with finely fluted Corinthian columns and a sculpted frieze.

🏛 Musée des Beaux Arts
Rue Cité Foulc.
Tel 04 66 67 38 21.
☐ Tue–Sun.
● 1 Jan, 1 May,
1 Nov, 25 Dec. 🕮 🕮
This fine arts museum houses an eclectic collection of Dutch, French, Italian and Flemish works, notably Jacopo Bassano's *Susanna and the Elders*, and the *Mystic Marriage of St Catherine* by Michele Giambono. The Gallo-Roman mosaic of *The Marriage of Admetus*, discovered in 1882, is on the main floor.

🏛 Musée Archéologique
Musée d'Histoire Naturelle, 13 bis
bd Amiral Courbet. **Tel** 04 66 76
74 80. ☐ Tue–Sun. ● 1 Jan,
1 May, 1 Nov, 25 Dec.
The museum's collection of Roman statues, ceramics, glass, coins and mosaics is housed in Nîmes' natural history museum. The exhibits include important Iron Age menhir statues.

venue for concerts, sporting events and bullfights.

🏛 Carré d'Art/ Musée d'Art Contemporain
Pl de la Maison Carrée. **Tel** 04 66 76
35 35. ☐ Tue–Sun. ● 1 Jan, 1 May,
1 Nov, 25 Dec. 🕮 🕮
Nîmes' arts complex, by the British architect Sir Norman Foster, opened in 1993. Five floors of this glass and steel temple, which was built in tribute to the Maison Carrée opposite, lie underground. The complex has a library, a roof-terrace restaurant around a huge glass atrium, and the Musée d'Art Contemporain. Works cover the main European art movements from the 1960s on, and include works by Raysse, Boltanski and Lavier for France.

🏛 Les Arènes
Bd des Arènes. **Tel** 04 66 21 82 56.
☐ daily. ● performance days.
🕮 🕮

All roads lead to the amphitheatre, Les Arènes. Built at the end of the 1st century AD, the design of the oval arena and tiers of stone seats accommodated huge crowds of up to 20,000 spectators. Today it is in use again, a perfect

Key to Symbols *see back flap*

**Bullfight at
Les Arènes in Nîmes**

[Map of Nîmes with streets including: Castellum, RUE GRAVEREL, RUE RANGUEIL, RUE BACHALAS, RUE BAUDIN, RUE CLERISSEAU, PLACE ST CHARLES, BOULEVARD GAMBETTA, RUE NATIONALE, RUE DES ORANGERS, RUE DU MERIER D'ESPAGNE, RUE GENERAL, PERRIER, RUE GUIOT, DE L'HORLOGE, PL AUX HERBES, RUE DE LA MADELEINE, RUE DE L'ASPIC, RUE FRESQUE, PLACE DE LA DELAINE, BD VICTOR-HUGO, PLACE DU MARCHÉ, RUE REGALE, RUE DORÉE, RUE DES GREFFES, BD AMIRAL COURRET, RUE ROUSSY, PORTE DE FRANCE, RUE JEAN-REBOUL, BD DES ARÈNES, PLACE DES ARÈNES, RUE DE LA REPUBLIQUE, RUE BIGONNET, RUE DE LA CITÉ, RUE BOURDALOUE, BD DE LA LIBERATION, Esplanade Charles de Gaulle. Numbered sites: ⑦ Porte Auguste, Grand Temple, Cathédrale Notre-Dame et St Castor ⑧, Musée du Vieux Nîmes, Musée Archéologique ⑨, Hôtel de Ville, Palais de Justice, Les Arènes ⑩, Gare SNCF/Gare Routière 200 m (420 yards), Musée des Beaux-Arts ⑪, Aéroport 12 km (7.5 miles). Directions: AVIGNON, ARLES/MONTPELIER Nemausus I]

PROVENCE AND THE COTE D'AZUR

BOUCHES-DU-RHONE · VAUCLUSE · VAR
ALPES-DE-HAUTE-PROVENCE · ALPES-MARITIMES

From its herb-scented hills to its yacht-filled harbours, no other region of France fires the imagination as strongly as Provence. The vivid landscape and luminous light have inspired artists and writers from Van Gogh to Picasso, Scott Fitzgerald to Pagnol.

The borders of Provence are defined by nature: to the west, the Rhône; south, the Mediterranean; and north, where the olive trees end. To the east are the Alps and a border which has shifted over the centuries between France and Italy. Within is a contrasting terrain of plummeting gorges, Camargue saltflats, lavender fields and sun-drenched beaches.

Past visitors have left their mark. In Orange and Arles, the buildings of Roman *Provincia* are still in use. Fortified villages like Èze were built to withstand the Saracen pirates who plagued the coast in the 6th century.

In the 19th century, rich Europeans sought winter warmth on the Riviera; by the 1920s, high society was in residence all year, and their elegant villas remain. The warm sunlight nurtures intense flavours and colours. Peppers, garlic and olives transform a netful of Mediterranean fish into that vibrant epitome of Provençal cuisine, *bouillabaisse*.

The image of Provence bathed in sunshine is marred only when the bitter Mistral wind scours the land. It has shaped a people as hardy as the olive tree, yet quick to embrace life to the full the moment the sun returns.

Cap Martin, seen from the village of Roquebrune

◁ Lavender fields near the Gorges du Verdon

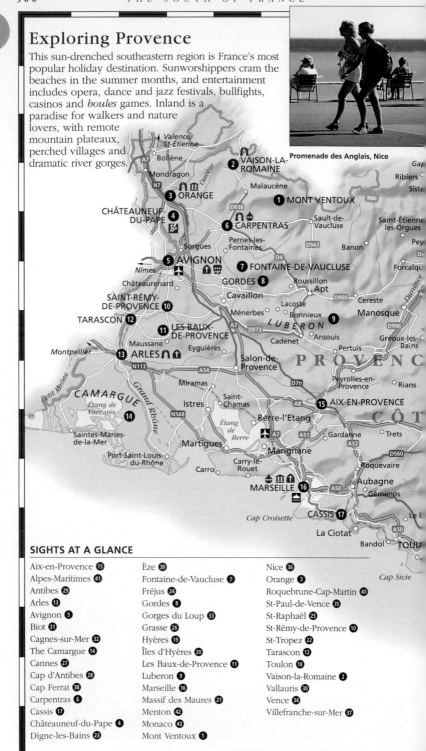

Exploring Provence

This sun-drenched southeastern region is France's most popular holiday destination. Sunworshippers cram the beaches in the summer months, and entertainment includes opera, dance and jazz festivals, bullfights, casinos and *boules* games. Inland is a paradise for walkers and nature lovers, with remote mountain plateaux, perched villages and dramatic river gorges.

Promenade des Anglais, Nice

SIGHTS AT A GLANCE

For additional map symbols *see back flap*

GETTING AROUND

The largest airport in the region, and second busiest in France, is Nice. Fly-drive packages are popular, although mainly recommended for touring inland. Traffic jams on coastal roads in high season can usually be avoided by using the autoroutes. Main coastal towns have good bus and rail links, and bikes can be hired at most rail stations. The Chemin de Fer de Provence railway line runs from Nice to Digne-les-Bains through spectacular mountain scenery. Mountain roads, though tortuous, are good.

KEY

—	Motorway
—	Major road
—	Secondary road
—	Minor road
—	Scenic route
—	Main railway
—	Minor railway
—	International border
—	Regional border
△	Summit

0 kilometres 25

0 miles 25

Spectacular scenery near the quiet market town of Forcalquier

Mont Ventoux ❶

Vaucluse. ✈ Avignon. 🚄 Avignon. 🚌 Carpentras. 🚏 Av de la Prom Saulten Provence (04 90 64 01 21).

The name means "Windy Mountain" in Provençal. A variety of flora and fauna may be found on the lower slopes but only moss survives at the peak, where the temperature can drop to −27°C (−17° F). The bare white seree at the summit makes it look snow-capped even during summer.

Ventoux is the mountain on which the legendary British cyclist Tommy Simpson died during 1967's Tour de France. Today, a road leads to the radio beacon pinnacle, but the trip should not be attempted in bad weather. At other times, spectacular views from the top make the effort worthwhile.

Roman mosaic from the Villa du Paon in Vaison-la-Romaine

Vaison-la-Romaine ❷

Vaucluse. 🏠 6,100. 🚄 🚏 pl du Chanoine Sautel (04 90 36 02 11). 🛒 Tue. **www**.vaison-en-provence.com

This site has been settled since the Bronze Age, but its name stems from five centuries as a Roman town.

Although the upper town, dominated by the ruins of a 12th-century castle, has some charming narrow streets, stone houses and fountains, Vaison's main attractions lie on the opposite side of the river.

The **Roman City** is split into two districts: Puymin and La Villasse. At Puymin, an opulent mansion, the Villa du Paon, and a Roman theatre have been uncovered.

In 1992, the river Ouvèze burst its banks, taking many

lives in Vaison and the nearby area. Damage to some ruins, such as the Roman bridge, has since been repaired. Also at Vaison is the fine Romanesque **Cathédrale Notre-Dame-de-Nazareth**, with medieval cloisters.

🏛 Roman City
Fouilles de Puymin & Musée Théo Desplans, pl du Chanoine Sautel. **Tel** 04 90 36 0211. ⭕ daily. ● Jan–mid-Feb, 25 Dec. 🎫 🎥 ♿ restr. 📷

Orange ❸

Vaucluse. 🏠 30,000. 🚄 🚌 🚏 5 cours Aristide Briand (04 90 34 70 88). 🛒 Thu. **www**.otorange.fr

Orange is a thriving regional centre. The fields, orchards and great vineyards of the Rhône Valley make it an important marketplace for produce such as grapes, olives, honey and truffles. Visitors should explore the area around the 17th-century Hôtel de Ville, where attractive streets open on to quiet, shady squares. Orange has two of the greatest Roman monuments in Europe.

🏛 Roman Theatre
Rue Madeleine-Roch. **Tel** 04 90 51 17 60. ⭕ daily. 🎥 🎫 entrance also valid for Musée d'Orange. ♿ restricted. 📷 📹
Dating from the 1st-century AD reign of Augustus, the well-preserved theatre has perfect acoustics. It is still used for theatre performances and concerts. The back wall rises to a height of 36 m (120 ft) and is 103 m (338 ft) wide. In 2006 an immense glass roof, built high above the theatre so as not to affect the acoustics, replaced the original roof, which was destroyed in a fire.

Statue of Augustus Caesar in the Roman Theatre at Orange

🏛 Triumphal Arch
Av de l'Arc de Triomphe.
The triple-arched monument was built about AD 20. It is elaborately decorated with battle scenes, military trophies and inscriptions to the glory of Tiberius.

🏛 Musée d'Orange
Rue Madeleine-Roch. **Tel** 04 90 51 17 60. ⭕ daily. 🎥
Relics here reflect the Roman presence in Orange, including 400 marble fragments, the earliest of which dates to Emperor Vespasian's reign in the 1st century BC.

Châteauneuf-du-Pape ❹

Vaucluse. 🏠 2,100. 🚄 Sorgues, then taxi. 🚏 pl du Portail (04 90 83 71 08). 🛒 Fri. **www**.paysprovence.fr

Here, in the 14th century, the popes of Avignon chose to build a new castle (château neuf) and plant the vineyards from which one of the finest

View across the vineyards of Châteauneuf-du-Pape

wines of the Côtes du Rhône is produced. Now almost every doorway in this attractive little town seems to open into a *vigneron*'s cellar.

After the Wars of Religion *(see pp54–55)*, all that remained of the papal fortress were a few fragments of walls and tower, but the ruins look spectacular and offer magnificent views across to Avignon and the Vaucluse uplands beyond.

Wine festivals punctuate the year, including the Fête de la Véraison in August *(see p38)*, when the grapes start to ripen, and the Ban des Vendages in September, when the grapes are ready to be harvested.

Avignon ❺

Vaucluse. 🏔 *90,000.* ✕ 🚌 🚆
🛈 *41 cours Jean Jaurès (04 32 74
32 74).* 🛒 *Tue–Sun.* 🎭 *Festival
d'Avignon (3 wks Jul).*
www.avignon-tourisme.com

Massive ramparts enclose one of the most fascinating towns in southern France. The **Palais des Papes** *(see pp504-5)* dominates, but there are also other riches. North of the Palais is the 13th-century **Musée du Petit Palais**, once the Archbishop of Avignon's residence. Now a museum, it displays Romanesque and Gothic sculpture and medieval paintings, with works by Botticelli and Carpaccio.

Rue Joseph-Vernet and rue du Roi-René are lined with 17th- and 18th-century houses. There are also fine churches, such as the **Cathédrale de Notre-Dame-des-Doms**, and the 14th-century **Eglise St-Didier**. The **Musée Lapidaire** contains statues, mosaics and carvings from pre-Roman Provence. The **Musée Calvet** features a superb array of exhibits, such as wrought-iron works and Roman finds. It also gives an overview of French art during the past 500 years, with works by Rodin, Utrillo and Dufy.

Two major modern and contemporary art collections, the **Musée Angladon** and the **Collection Lambert**, have been added to the city's cultural repertoire. The former has works by Van Gogh, Cézanne

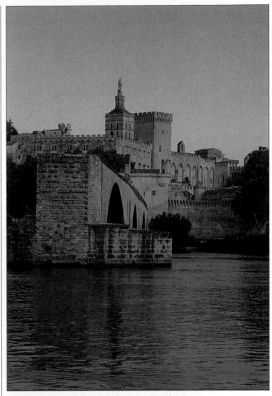

Pont St-Bénézet and the Palais des Papes in Avignon

and Modigliani, while the latter features minimalist and conceptual art.

The place de l'Horloge is the centre of Avignon's social life, with pavement cafés and a merry-go-round from 1900. One of the prettiest streets is the rue des Teinturiers. Until the 19th century, brightly patterned calico called *indiennes* was printed here – inspiration for today's Provençal patterns.

Open-air performance at the Avignon Festival

Avignon's renowned 12th-century bridge, the **Pont St-Bénézet**, was largely destroyed by floods in 1668. People danced on an island below the bridge but over the years, as the famous song testifies, *sous* has become *sur*.

Avignon hosts France's largest festival, which includes ballet, drama and classical concerts. The "Off" festival features 600 companies from all areas of show business.

🏛 **Musée du Petit Palais**
Pl du Palais. **Tel** 04 90 86 44 58.
◯ *Wed–Mon.* ● *1 Jan, 1 May, 25
Dec.* 🎫 🛈 **www**.petit-palais.org

🏛 **Musée Lapidaire**
27 rue de la République. **Tel** 04 90
86 33 84. ◯ *Wed–Mon.* ● *1 Jan,
1 May, 25 Dec.* 🎫 🛈

🏛 **Musée Calvet**
65 rue Joseph Vernet. **Tel** 04 90 86
33 84. ◯ *Wed–Mon.* ● *1 Jan,
1 May, 25 Dec.* 🎫 🛈 ♿ *restricted.*
www.musee-calvet.org

Palais des Papes

Confronted with factional strife in Rome and encouraged by the scheming of Philippe IV of France, Pope Clement V moved the papal court to Avignon in 1309. Here it remained until 1377, during which time his successors transformed the modest episcopal building into the present magnificent palace. Its heavy fortification was vital to defend against rogue bands of mercenaries. Today it is empty of the luxurious trappings of 14th-century court life, as virtually all the furnishings and works of art were destroyed or looted in the course of the centuries.

Pope Clement VI (1342–52)

Benedict XII's cloister incorporates the guest and staff wings, and the Benedictine chapel.

Trouillas tower

Belltower

Military Architecture
The palace and its ten towers were designed as an impregnable fortress. It eventually covered an area of 15,000 sq m (148,000 sq ft).

La Gache tower

Corner tower

Champeaux gate

THE AVIGNON POPES

Seven "official" popes reigned in Avignon until 1376. They were followed by two "anti-popes", the last of whom, Benedict XIII, fled in 1403. Popes or anti-popes, few were known for their sanctity. Clement V died eating powdered emeralds, prescribed as an indigestion cure; Clement VI (1342–52) thought that the best way to honour God was through luxury. Petrarch was shocked by "the filth of the universe" at court. In 1367, Urban V tried to return the Curia (papal court) to Rome, a move that became permanent in 1377.

Benedict XII (1334–42)

★ **Consistory Hall**
Simone Martini's frescoes (1340) were taken from the cathedral to replace works destroyed by fire in the papal reception hall in 1413.

VISITORS' CHECKLIST

Pl du Palais, Avignon. **Tel** 04 90 27 50 00. ◯ Nov–mid-Mar: 9.30am–5.45pm; mid-Mar–Oct: 9am–6.30pm (Jul–Sep: 9am–8pm). Last adm: 1 hr before closing. 🖼 ▥ 🖿 🖿
www.palais-des-papes.com

Papal Power
More like a warlord's citadel than a papal palace, the building's heavy fortification reflects the insecure climate of 14th-century religious life.

★ **Stag Room**
Fourteenth-century hunting frescoes and ceramic tiles adorn Clement VI's study, making it the palace's most lovely room.

Angels' tower

Pope's chamber

Great courtyard

The Great Chapel is 20 m (66 ft) high and covers an area of 780 sq m (8,400 sq ft).

The Great Audience Hall is divided into two naves by five columns with bestiary sculpture on their capitals.

BUILDING THE PALACE

The palace comprises Pope Benedict XII's simple Palais Vieux (1334–42) and Clement VI's flamboyant Palais Neuf (1342–52). Ten towers, some of which are more than 50 m (164 ft) high, are set in the walls to protect its four wings.

STAR FEATURES

★ Consistory Hall

★ Stag Room

KEY

☐ By Benedict XII (1334–42)

☐ By Clement VI (1342–52)

Carpentras

Vaucluse. 🏘 29,000. 🚌 🛈 *Maison de Pays, 97 pl du 25 Août 1944 (04 90 63 00 78).* 🛒 *Fri.*
www.carpentras-ventoux.com

In 1320, Carpentras became capital of the papal county of Venaissin, and remained so until 1791. Modern boulevards trace the former ramparts, with only one original gate, the Porte d'Orange, surviving.

In the Middle Ages the town was home to a large Jewish community. The 1367 **Synagogue** is the oldest in France. The Sanctuary has been restored.

While not openly persecuted under papal rule, many Jews changed faith, entering **Cathédrale St-Siffrein** by the Porte Juive (Jews' Door).

The Law Courts were built in 1640 as the episcopal palace. The Criminal Court has 17th-century carved tablets of the local towns. In the pharmacy of the Hôtel-Dieu, the 18th-century cupboards are painted with quaint figures of monkey "doctors". More regional art and history is on show at the **Musée Sobirats**.

🕎 Synagogue
Pl de la Mairie. *Tel 04 90 63 39 97.* ◻ *Mon–Fri.* ● *Jewish feast days.*

🏛 Musée Sobirats
112 rue du Collège. *Tel 04 90 63 04 92.* ◻ *Wed–Mon.* ● *Oct–Mar & public hols.* 🏷

Riverfront and watermill at Fontaine-de-Vaucluse

Fontaine-de-Vaucluse

Vaucluse. 🏘 650. 🚌 🛈 *chemin du Gouffre (04 90 20 32 22).*
www.oti-delasorgue.fr

The main attraction here is the source of the river Sorgue. It is the most powerful spring in France, gushing at up to 90,000 litres (19,800 gallons) per second from an underground river at the foot of a cliff. It powers the Moulin à Papier Vallis Clausa (papermill), which produces handmade paper using the same methods as in the 15th century, and now sells maps, prints and lampshades. There are also several museums. One is devoted to the poet Petrarch, who lived and wrote here, and another to the French Resistance of World War II.

Gordes

Vaucluse. 🏘 2,100. 🛈 *pl du Château (04 90 72 02 75).* 🛒 *Tue.*
www.gordes-village.com

Perched villages abound in Provence but Gordes is said to attract the most visitors. Dominated by a 16th-century château, the town forms such a harmonious whole that it might have been designed by an architect. The arcaded medieval lanes add to the attractive hilltop position.

Just south lies the **Village des Bories**, a bizarre, primitive habitat. Bories are tiny beehive-shaped huts built of overlapping dry stones. The construction techniques are thought to date back to Neolithic times. This group was inhabited from the 16th to the early 20th century.

The **Abbaye de Sénanque**, to the north, is a fine Romanesque Cistercian monastery.

⛪ Château de Gordes
Tel 04 90 72 02 75. ◻ *daily.* ● *1 Jan, 25 Dec.* 🏷

🏠 Village des Bories
Rte de Gorde. *Tel 04 90 72 03 48.* ◻ *daily.* ● *1 Jan, 25, 31 Dec.* 🏷

Luberon

Vaucluse. ✈ *Avignon.* 🚉 *Cavaillon, Avignon.* 🚌 *Apt.* 🛈 *Cavaillon (04 90 71 32 01).* **www**.cavaillon-luberon.fr

A huge limestone range, the Montagne du Luberon is one of the most appealing areas of Provence. Rising to 1,125 m (3,690 ft), it combines wild

Perched village of Gordes

areas with picturesque villages. Almost the entire area is designated a regional nature park. Within it are more than 1,000 plant species and cedar and oak forests. The wildlife is varied, with eagles, vultures, snakes, beavers, wild boar and the largest European lizards. The park headquarters are in **Apt**, the capital of the Luberon.

Once notorious as the haunt of highwaymen, the Luberon hills now hide sumptuous holiday homes. The major village is **Bonnieux**, with its 12th-century church and 13th-century walls. Also popular are **Roussillon**, with red ochre buildings, **Lacoste**, the site of the ruins of the Marquis de Sade's castle, and **Ansouis**, with its 14th-century Eglise St-Martin and 17th-century castle. **Ménerbes** drew to it the writer Peter Mayle, whose tales of life here brought this quiet region a worldwide audience.

Herb stall at St-Rémy-de-Provence

St-Rémy-de-Provence ❿

Bouches-du-Rhône. 🚺 10,700. 🚃
🚶 pl Jean Jaurès (04 90 92 05 22).
🗓 Wed. **www**.saintremy-de-provence.com

For centuries St-Rémy, with its boulevards, fountains and narrow streets, had two claims to fame. One was that Vincent Van Gogh spent a year here, in 1889–90, at the St-Paul-de-Mausole hospital. *Wheat Field with Cypress* and *Ravine* are among the 150 works he produced here. St-Rémy-de-Provence was also, in 1503,

the birthplace of Nostradamus, known for his prophecies. But, in 1921, St-Rémy found new fame when archaeologists unearthed the Roman ruins at **Glanum**. Little remains of the ancient city, sacked in AD 480 by the Goths, but the site impresses. Around the ruins of a Roman arch is a mausoleum, decorated with scenes such as the death of Adonis.

🏛 Glanum
Tel 04 90 92 23 79. 🕙 Apr–Aug: daily; Sep–Mar: Tue–Sun. ● 1 Jan, 1 May, 1 & 11 Nov, 25 Dec. 🌐 🕭
🖥 🎞 **www**.glanum.monuments-nationaux.fr

Les Baux-de-Provence ⓫

Bouches-du-Rhône. 🚺 480. 🚃 Arles.
🚶 La Maison du Roy (04 90 54 34 39). **www**.lesbauxdeprovence.com

One of the strangest places in Provence, the deserted citadel of Les Baux stands like a natural extension of a huge rocky plateau. The ruined castle and old houses overlook the Val d'Enfer (Infernal Valley), with its weird rocks.

In the Middle Ages Les Baux was home to powerful feudal lords, who claimed descent from the Magus Balthazar. It was the most famous of the Provençal Cours d'Amour, at which troubadours sang the praises of high-born ladies. The ideal of everlasting but unrequited courtly love contrasts with the war-like nature of the citadel's lords.

The glory of Les Baux ended in 1632. It had become a Protestant stronghold and Louis XIII ordered its destruction. The ruins of **Château de Baux de Provence** are a reminder

Deserted medieval citadel of Les Baux-de-Provence

of a turbulent past and offer spectacular views. The living village below has a pleasant little square, the 12th-century **Eglise St-Vincent** and the **Chapelle des Pénitents Blancs**, decorated by local artist Yves Brayer, whose work can be seen in the **Musée Yves Brayer**.

In 1821 bauxite, a deep red mineral, was discovered here and named after the town. Deposits were intensely exploited until they ran out at the end of the 20th century.

To the southwest are the ruins of the **Abbaye de Montmajour** with its 12th-century Romanesque church.

Parading the Tarasque, 1850

Tarascon ⓬

Bouches-du-Rhône. 🚺 14,000.
🚃 🚌 🚶 Les Panaromiques, Av de la République (04 90 91 03 52).
🛒 Tue & Fri. **www**.tarascon.org

According to legend, the town takes its name from the Tarasque, a monster, half-animal and half-fish, which terrorized the countryside. It was tamed by Sainte Marthe, who is buried in the church here. An effigy of the Tarasque is still paraded through the streets each June *(see p37)*.

The striking 15th-century **Château du Roi René** on the banks of the Rhône is one of the finest examples of Gothic military architecture in Provence. Its sombre exterior gives no hint of the beauties within: the Flemish-Gothic courtyard; the spiral staircase; and painted ceilings of the banqueting hall.

Opposite is Beaucaire, a ruined castle and gardens.

🏰 Château du Roi René
Bd du Roi René. **Tel** 04 90 91 01 93. 🕙 daily. ● some public hols. 🌐 🎞

Arles ⑬

Few other towns in Provence combine all the region's charms so well as Arles. Its position on the Rhône makes it a natural, historic gateway to the Camargue (see pp510–11). Its Roman remains, such as the arena and Constantine's baths, are complemented by the ochre walls and Roman-tiled roofs of later buildings. A bastion of Provençal tradition and culture, its museums are among the best in the region. Van Gogh spent time here in 1888–9, but Arles is no longer the industrial town he painted. Visitors are now its main business, and entertainment ranges from the Arles Festival to bullfights.

Emperor Constantine

Palais Constantine was once a grand imperial palace. Now only its vast Roman baths remain, dating from the 4th century AD. They are remarkably well-preserved and give an idea of the luxury that bathers enjoyed.

Musée Réattu
This museum, in the old Commandery of the Knights of Malta, houses witty Picasso sketches, paintings by the local artist Jacques Réattu (1760–1833) and sculptures by Ossip Zadkine, including La Grande Odalisque (1932), above.

Museon Arlaten
In 1904 the poet Frédéric Mistral used his Nobel Prize money to establish this museum devoted to his beloved native Provence. Parts of the collection are arranged in room settings, and even the museum attendants wear traditional Arles costume.

Hotel de ville & entrance to Cryptoportiques

Espace Van Gogh, in a former hospital where the artist was treated in 1889, is a cultural centre devoted to his life and work.

★ Eglise St-Trophime
This church combines a noble 12th-century Romanesque exterior with superb Romanesque and Gothic cloisters. The ornate main portal is carved with saints and apostles.

Tourist information

| 0 metres | 100 |
| 0 yards | 100 |

For hotels and restaurants in this region see pp590–4 and pp646–50

LES ALYSCAMPS

A tree-lined avenue of broken medieval tombs is the focal point of these "Elysian Fields" to the southeast of Arles. It became Christian in the 4th century and was a prestigious burial ground until the 12th century. Some sarcophagi were sold to museums; others have been neglected. Mentioned in Dante's *Inferno*, painted by Van Gogh and Gauguin, it is a place for thought and inspiration.

Les Alyscamps by Paul Gauguin

VISITORS' CHECKLIST

Bouches-du-Rhône. 53,000. 25 km (15 miles) NW Arles. av Paulin Talabot. bd des Lices (04 90 18 41 20). Wed, Sat. Arles Festival (Jul); Prémice du Riz (Sep). **Musée Réattu** Tue–Sun. 1 Jan, 1 May, 1 Nov, 25 Dec. **Museon Arlaten** closed for renovation until 2014. www.museonarlaten.fr

★ Roman Amphitheatre
This is one of the best-preserved monuments of Roman Provence. Each arch is supported by Doric and Corinthian columns. In summer there are bull contests in the 21,000-seat arena. The top tier provides a panoramic view of Arles.

Notre-Dame-de-la-Major
is the church in which the *gardians* (cowboys) of the Camargue celebrate the feast day of their patron saint, St George. Although the building dates from the 12th to 17th centuries, a Roman temple existed on this spot hundreds of years earlier.

★ Roman Theatre
Once a fortress, its stones were later used for other buildings. Today, the theatre stages the Arles Festival. Its remaining columns are called the "two widows".

STAR SIGHTS

★ Roman Amphitheatre

★ Roman Theatre

★ Eglise St-Trophime

KEY

– – – Suggested route

(map labels) RUE DE GRILLE · TEMBRE · RUE BARBES · SSES · R ARISTIDE BRIAND · R. TARDIEU · ROND-POINT DES ARENES · R. DE LA BASTILLE · RUE DIDEROT · CALADE · CLOITRE · R PORTE DE LAURE · R GRAND COUVENT · R. DE LA MADELEINE · MONTEE VAUBAN · ULEVARD DES LICES · To train and bus stations

The Camargue ⑭

The Rhône delta was responsible for the formation of more than 1,120 sq km (424 sq miles) of wetlands, pastures, dunes and salt flats that make up the Camargue, but human efforts are needed to preserve it. The region now maintains a fragile ecological balance, in which a unique collection of flora flourishes, including tamarisk and narcissi, and fauna such as egrets and ibises. The pastures provide grazing for sheep, cattle and small white Arab-type horses, ridden by the *gardians* or cowboys, a hardy community who traditionally lived in thatched huts *(cabanes)* and still play their part in keeping Camargue traditions alive.

Sunset over the Camargue

Camargue gardian

Black Bulls
In a Provençal bull contest (known as a course), the animals are not killed. Instead, red rosettes are plucked from between their horns with a small hook.

0 kilometres   5

0 miles   5

Mas du Pont de R

D570

D572

D570

Méjanes ●

PLAINE DE LA CAMARGUE

Etang de Vacc

D37

PARC REGIONAL DE

PETITE CAMARGUE

Centre de Ginès

Stes-Maries-de-la-Mer

MEDITERRANEE

Les Stes-Maries-de-la-Mer
The May gypsy pilgrimage to this fortified church marks the legendary arrival by boat in AD 18 of Mary Magdalene, St Martha and the sister of the Virgin Mary. Statues in the church depict the event.

Flamingoes
These striking birds are always associated with the Camargue, but the region supports many other breeds, including herons, kingfishers, owls and birds of prey. The area around Ginès is the best place to see them.

For hotels and restaurants in this region see pp590–4 and pp646–50

KEY

—— Nature reserve boundary

– – Walking routes

– – Walking and cycling routes

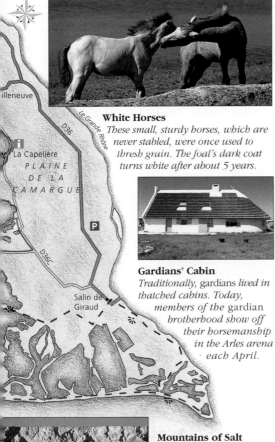

White Horses
*These small, sturdy horses, which are
never stabled, were once used to
thresh grain. The foal's dark coat
turns white after about 5 years.*

Gardians' Cabin
*Traditionally, gardians lived in
thatched cabins. Today,
members of the gardian
brotherhood show off
their horsemanship
in the Arles arena
each April.*

Mountains of Salt
*Sea salt is by far the largest
"harvest" of the Camargue.
Throughout the summer,
vast brine pans evaporate
and the crystals are heaped
into shimmering camelles
up to 8 m (26 ft) high.*

Aix-en-Provence ⑮

Bouches du Rhône. 🏘 *135,000.*
🚉 🚌 ℹ *2 place du Général-de-
Gaulle (04 42 16 11 61).* 🛒 *daily.*
www.aixenprovencetourism.com

Founded by the Romans in
103 BC, Aix was frequently
attacked, first by the Visigoths
in AD 477, later by Lombards,
Franks and Saracens. Despite
this, the city prospered. By the
end of the 12th century it was
capital of Provence. A centre
of art and learning, it reached
its peak in the 15th century
during the reign of "Good
King" René. He is shown in
Nicolas Froment's *Triptych of
the Burning Bush* in the
13th-century Gothic **Cathédrale
de St-Sauveur,** also noted for
its 16th-century walnut doors,
Merovingian baptistry and
Romanesque cloisters.

Aix is still a centre of art
and learning, and its many
museums include the **Musée
Granet** of fine arts and archaeology, and the **Musée des
Tapisseries** (tapestries), in the
Palais de l'Archevêché.

Aix has been called "the
city of a thousand fountains".
Three of the best are situated
on cours Mirabeau. On one
side are 17th- and 18th-century
buildings with wrought-iron
balconies; on the other are
cafés. The Old Town centres
on place de l'Hôtel de Ville,
with its colourful flower
market. In the northwest of
town is the **Pavillon de
Vendôme,** housing furniture
and works of art by Van Loo.

Aix's most famous son is
Paul Cézanne. The **Atelier
Cézanne** is kept as it was when
he died in 1906. Montagne Ste-
Victoire, inspiration for many
of his paintings, is 15 km (9
miles) east of Aix.

🏛 **Musée Granet**
Pl St-Jean de Malte. **Tel** *04 42 52 88
32.* ⏺ *Tue–Sun.* ⏺ *1 Jan, 1 May,
25 Dec.* 📷 🚻 ♿

🏛 **Musée des Tapisseries**
28 pl des Martyrs de la Résistance.
Tel *04 42 23 09 91.* ⏺ *Wed–Mon.*
⏺ *Jan.* 📷 🚻

🏠 **Atelier Cézanne**
9 av Paul Cézanne. **Tel** *04 42 21 06
53.* ⏺ *daily.* ⏺ *Dec–Feb: Sun;
some public hols.* 📷 🚻
www.atelier-cezanne.com

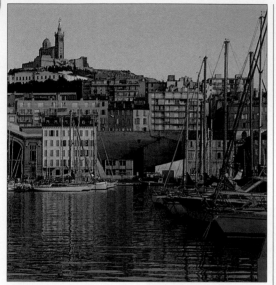

Old harbour of Marseille, looking towards the quai de Rive Neuve

Marseille ⑯

Bouches-du-Rhône. 🏙 *900,000.*
✈ 🚍 🚌 🚢 ⓘ *4 La Canebière*
(0826 500 500). 🗓 *daily.*
www.marseille-tourisme.com

A Greek settlement, founded
in the 7th century BC, then
called Massilia, Marseille was
seized by the Romans in 49 BC.
It became the "Gateway to
the West" for most Oriental
trade. France's largest port and
lively second-largest city has
close links with the Middle
East and North Africa.

Narrow stepped streets,
quiet squares and fine 18th-
century façades contrast with
the bustle of boulevard Canebière and the Cité Radieuse,
Le Corbusier's post-war
radical housing complex.

The old harbour now only
handles small boats, but its
daily fish market is renowned.

Marseille has many excellent
museums. Those in the old
harbour area include the
Musée des Docks Romains,
the **Musée d'Histoire de
Marseille**, the **Musée du
Vieux Marseille**, and the
upbeat **Musée de la Mode**.

The **Musée Cantini**, to the
south, houses the 20th-century
art collection of sculptor Jules
Cantini. It includes Surrealist,
Cubist and Fauve paintings.

On the other side of the city
is the **Musée Grobet- Labadié**,
with its fine furniture, tapestries
and rare musical instruments.

Marseille has an extensive
tramway system and has introduced a bike rental scheme
that allows people to rent a
bike in one part of town and
deposit it in another.

🏛 Musée des Beaux-Arts

Palais Longchamp, pl Aile Gauche.
Tel *04 91 14 59 30.* 🗓 *Tue–Sun.*
⬤ *until late 2012.* 🗓 ♿
This museum is housed in the
handsome 19th-century Palais
Longchamp. Works include
Michel Serre's graphic views
of Marseille's plague of 1721,
Pierre Puget's town plans for
the city and murals depicting
it in Greek and Roman times.

⚓ Château d'If

Tel *04 91 59 02 30.* 🗓 *Apr–Aug:
daily; Sep–Mar: Tue–Sun.* 🗓 💻

The Château d'If (Castle of
Yew) stands on a tiny island 2
km (1 mile) southwest of the
port. A formidable fortress, it
was built in 1529 to house
artillery, but never put to
military use and later became
a prison. Alexandre Dumas'
fictional "Count of Monte
Cristo" was supposed to have
been imprisoned here, and
visitors can see a special cell,
complete with escape hole.
Most real-life inmates were
either common criminals or
political prisoners.

⛪ Notre-Dame-de-la-Garde

Built between 1853 and 1864,
this Neo-Byzantine basilica
dominates the city. Its belfry,
46 m (151 ft) high, is capped
by a huge gilded statue of the
Virgin. The lavishly decorated
interior has coloured marble
and mosaic facings.

⛪ Abbaye de St-Victor

Similar to a fortress in
appearance, the abbey was
rebuilt in the 11th century
after destruction by the
Saracens. In the French
Revolution, the rebels used
it as a barracks and prison.

There is an intriguing crypt
in the abbey's church, with
an original catacomb chapel
and a number of pagan and
Christian sarcophagi.

On 2 February each year, St-
Victor becomes a place of
pilgrimage. Boat-shaped cakes
are sold to commemorate the
legendary arrival of St Mary
Magdalene, Lazarus and St
Martha nearly 2,000 years ago.

⛪ Cathédrale de la Major

Built in Neo-Byzantine style,
this is the largest 19th-century
church in France, 141 m (463
ft) long and 70 m (230 ft) high.
In the crypt are the tombs of
the bishops of Marseille. By it

Le Corbusier's innovative Cité Radieuse in Marseille

For hotels and restaurants in this region see pp590–4 and pp646–50

Cassis

Bouches-du-Rhône. 👥 8,000. 🚋
🚌 ℹ quai Moulins, Le Port (08 92
25 98 92). � Wed & Fri.
www.ot-cassis.com

Toulon ⑱

Var. 👥 170,000. ✕ 🚌 🚋 ⛴
ℹ pl Louis-Blanc (04 94 18 53
00). 🚢 Tue–Sun.
www.toulontourisme.com

Fish market at Marseille

is the small and beautiful Ancienne Cathédrale de la Major.

🏛 Vieille Charité
Rue de la Charité. **Tel** 04 91 14 58 80.
⭕ Tue–Sun. ⬤ pub hols. 🎫 ♿ 🍴
In 1640, the construction of a
shelter "for the poor and beg-
gars" of Marseille was begun
by royal decree. 100 years
later, Pierre Puget's hospital
and domed church were
opened. Now, the restored
building houses the Musée
d'Archéologie Egyptienne, with
its fine collection of Egyptian
artifacts; the Musée des Arts
Africains is on the second floor.

Many villages along this coast
have been built up and have
all but lost their original
charm, but Cassis is still much
the same little fishing port
that attracted artists such as
Dufy, Signac and Derain. This
is a place in which to relax at
a waterside café, watching
the fishermen or street
performers, while enjoying
the seafood and a bottle of
the local dry white wine for
which Cassis is noted.

From Marseille to Cassis the
coastline forms narrow inlets,
the **Calanques**, their jagged
white cliffs (some as much as
400 m/1,312 ft high) reflected
in dazzling turquoise water.
Wildlife abounds here, with
countless seabirds, foxes, stone
martens, bats, large snakes
and lizards. The flora is no less
impressive, with more than
900 plant species, of which 50
are classified as rare. The En-
Vau and Sormiou Calanques
are especially lovely.

In 1793 this naval base was
captured by an Anglo-Spanish
fleet, but was retaken by the
young Napoleon Bonaparte.
The **Musée National de la
Marine** is a focus for history.
The **Musée d'Art de Toulon**,
housed in an Italian Renaissance building, has a collection
representing Fauvism,
Minimalism and Realism. The
tower of the former town hall
is all that remains of pre-war
Quai Cronstadt (rebuilt and
renamed Quai Stalingrad). The
war-damaged Old Town has a
few original buildings, and the
fish market is worth a visit.

🏛 Musée National de la Marine
Pl Monsenergue. **Tel** 04 94 02 02 01.
⭕ daily. ⬤ Tue (Sep–Jun), 1 May, 25
Dec. 🎫 ♿ restr. 🍴 **www**.musee-
marine.fr

🏛 Musée d'Art de Toulon
113 bd Mar Leclerc. **Tel** 04 94 36
81 00. ⭕ Tue–Sun. ⬤ Jan, public
hols. 🎫

Paul Signac's *Cap Canaille*, painted at Cassis in 1889

Tour of the Gorges du Verdon

The Verdon Gorges constitute one of the most dramatic natural sights in Europe. The dark green river Verdon flows through a deeply cut valley with twisted rocks and cone-shaped peaks. In places, the Gorges reach depths of 700 m (2,297 ft), passing through largely uninhabited country between the vast natural amphitheatre of Moustiers-Ste-Marie and the narrow streets of Castellane. Dramatic viewpoints include the Balcons de la Mescla, beyond the Pont de l'Artuby, and the Point Sublime. A detour southwest of Moutiers to Quinson's Musée de Préhistoire is worthwhile.

Aiguines ③
This village has an atttractive 17th-century château with four pepper-pot towers. There is a fine view of the artificial Lac de Sainte-Croix from here.

Verdon Gorges from the Castellane road

Hyères ⑲

Var. 🏠 54,000. ✈ 🚊 🚌 ⛴
ℹ Av Ambroise Thomas (04 94 01 84 50). www.hyeres-tourisme.com
🗓 Tue–Sun.

Towards the end of the 18th century, Hyères became one of the first health resorts of the Côte d'Azur. Among its subsequent visitors were Queen Victoria and writers Robert Louis Stevenson and Edith Wharton.

The main sights are found in the medieval streets of the Vieille Ville, which lead past the spacious, flagstoned place Massillon to a ruined castle and views over the coast.

Modern Hyères is imbued with a lingering Belle Epoque charm which has become popular with experimental film-makers. It continues to attract a health-conscious crowd and is a major centre for aquatic sports.

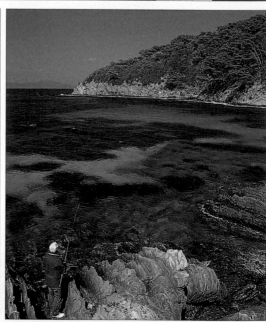

Fishing off Porquerolles, the largest of the Iles d'Hyères

Moustiers-Ste-Marie ④
Set in a deep ravine, this village is famous for pottery. Suspended across the twin peaks above it is an iron chain with a star, first placed here after the Crusades.

Point Sublime ⑥
From this superb viewpoint 180 m (591 ft) high, two walking routes lead to the bottom.

CANNES →

D952 Verdon

La Palud-sur-Verdon ⑤
This village is on the Route des Crêtes, one of the most wild and beautiful walks.

Rougon

D952

D955

ROUTE DES CRÊTES

D23

Verdon

Trigance

D90

LIME

D71

FREJUS →

Castellane ①
This town has a 14th-century clock tower and a lion fountain. On a cliff high above it, once used as a look-out, is the tiny chapel of Notre-Dame du Roc.

KEY

▬ Tour route

═ Other roads

🔆 Viewpoint

Pont de l'Artuby ②
From this boldly curved bridge there is a breathtaking view of the gorge 250 m (820 ft) below.

0 kilometres   2

0 miles   2

Îles d'Hyères ⑳

Var. ✈ Toulon-Hyères. 🚃 🚌 ⛴
Hyères. ℹ Hyères (04 94 01 84 50).
www.hyeres-tourisme.com

Locally known as the Îles d'Or, after the gold colour of their cliffs, this glamorous trio of islands can be reached by boat from Hyères, Le Lavandou and, in summer, Cavalaire and Port-de-Miramar.

Porquerolles, the largest of the three, measures 7 km (4.5 miles) by 3 km (2 miles). It is covered in rich vegetation, much of which, for instance the Mexican bellombra tree, was introduced from a variety of exotic foreign climes.

The island's main town, also known as Porquerolles, looks more like a north African colonial settlement than a Provençal village. It was established in 1820 as a retirement town for Napoleon's most honoured troops. All the

island's beaches lie along the northern coastline. The best, the long, sandy Plage Notre-Dame, one of the finest beaches in Provence, sits in a sheltered bay about an hour's walk from Porquerolles.

A stroll around lush, hilly **Port-Cros**, covering just 2.5 sq km (1 sq mile), takes the best part of a day. It rises to 195 m (640 ft), the highest point on any of the islands.

Port-Cros has been a national park since 1963. A unique reserve of flora and fauna, its waters are also protected. There is even a 300-m (984-ft) scenic swimming route. You can buy a waterproof guide to the underwater wildlife.

The wild, virtually treeless **Île du Levant** is reached by boat from Port-Cros. Its main draw is the oldest naturist resort in France, Héliopolis, founded in 1931. The eastern half of the island, controlled by the French navy, is permanently closed to the public.

Massif des Maures ㉑

Var. ✈ Toulon-Hyères. 🚃 Hyères,
Toulon or Fréjus. 🚌 Bormes-les-
Mimosas. ⛴ Toulon. ℹ 1 pl
Gambetta, Bormes-les-Mimosas
(04 94 01 38 38). **www**.
bormeslesmimosas.com

The dense wilderness of pine, oak and chestnut, covering the Maures mountains probably gave rise to its name, meaning dark or gloomy. It extends nearly 65 km (40 miles) between Hyères and Fréjus. The D558 north of Cogolin leads to the heart of the Maures. Along the way is La Garde-Freinet, well known for its bottle-cork industry.

Northwest of Cannet-des-Maures lies the Abbaye de Thoronet. With the abbeys at Sénanque, in Vaucluse, and Silvacane, in the Bouches-du-Rhône, it is known as one of the "Three Sisters" of Provence.

Harbourside at St-Tropez

St-Tropez ❷

Var. 🏔 6,000. 🚌 ℹ️ quai Jean
Jaurès (04 94 97 45 21). 🛒 Tue & Sat.
www.ot-saint-tropez.com

The geography of St-Tropez kept it untouched by the earliest development of the Côte d'Azur. Tucked away at the tip of a peninsula, it is the only north-facing town on the coast and so did not appeal to those seeking a warm and sheltered winter resort. In 1892 the painter Paul Signac was among the first outsiders to respond to its unspoiled charm, encouraging friends, such as the painters Matisse and Bonnard, to join him. In the 1920s the Parisian writer Colette also made her home here. St-Tropez also began to attract star-spotters, hoping for a glimpse of celebrities such as the Prince of Wales.

During World War II the beaches around St-Tropez were the scene of Allied landings, and part of the town was heavily bombed. Then, in the 1950s, young Parisians began to arrive, and the Bardot-Vadim film helped to create the reputation of modern St-Tropez as a playground for gilded youth. The wild public behaviour and turbulent love affairs of Roger Vadim, Brigitte Bardot, Sacha Distel and others left fiction far behind. Mass tourism followed, with visitors once again more interested in spotting a celebrity than in visiting the **Musée de l'Annonciade** with its out-standing collection of works by Signac, Derain, Rouault,

Bonnard and others. Bardot had a villa at La Madrague, but tourists invaded her privacy, so she left.

Today, there are far more luxury yachts than fishing boats moored in St-Tropez harbour. Its cafés make ideal bases for people- and yacht-watching. Another centre of the action is place des Lices, both for the Harley-Davidson set and the morning market. The tiny **Maison des Papillons** (Butterfly House), with its collection of more than 20,000 species, is an increasingly popular attraction.

The best beaches are found outside the town, including the golden curve of Pampelonne, with its beach clubs and restaurants. This is the beach on which to see and be seen. St-Tropez has no train station, so driving and parking can be a nightmare in summer.

It is said that St-Tropez takes its name from a Roman soldier martyred as a Christian

by the Emperor Nero. Each year in May a *bravade* in his honour takes place when an effigy of the saint is carried through the town to the ac-companiment of musket fire.

Nearby are two small towns of differing character but equal charm. **Port-Grimaud** was only built in 1966 but the sensitive use of traditional architecture makes it seem older. Most of its "streets" are canals. Up in the hills, the winding streets of **Ramatuelle** have been restored to perfection by the largely celebrity population.

🏛 **Maison des Papillons**
9 rue Etienne Berny. *Tel* 04 94 97
63 45. 🕐 Apr–Oct, public & school
hols: Mon–Sat. 🎫

🏛 **Musée de l'Annonciade**
Pl Grammont. *Tel* 04 94 17 84 10.
🕐 Wed–Mon. 🔴 1 Jan, 8 May,
1 Nov. 🎫 📷 🚻

Stylish solution to the traffic problems in St-Tropez

BRIGITTE BARDOT

In 1956, Brigitte Bardot's film, *And God Created Woman*, was shot in St-Tropez by her new husband, Roger Vadim. By settling in St Tropez, "BB" the sex-goddess changed the fortunes of the sleepy little fishing village and ultimately the Côte d'Azur, making it the centre of her hedonistic lifestyle. In 1974, on her 40th birthday, she celebrated her retirement from films at Club 55 on Pampelonne Beach, and now devotes her time to her animal sanctuary.

Brigitte Bardot in 1956

Digne-les-Bains ㉓

Alpes-de-Haute-Provence.
🏛 17,500. 🚉 🚌 ℹ pl de
Tampinet (04 92 36 62 62). 🛒 Wed,
Sat. www.ot-dignelesbains.fr

This charming spa town in
the foothills of the Alps
features in Victor Hugo's *Les
Misérables*. A trip on the *Train
des Pignes* from Nice offers
superb views. Apart from
the spa, Digne also offers a
lavender festival *(see p38)*
and **Le Jardin des Papillons**,
France's only butterfly garden.

🌱 **Le Jardin des Papillons**
St Benoît. *Tel 04 92 31 83 34.*
◯ Apr–Sep (appt only). 🚫 📷 ♿ 🚻 in
summer. 🚻 www.proserpine.org

Fréjus ㉔

Var. 🏛 53,000. 🚉 🚌 ℹ 249 rue
Jean Jaurès (04 94 51 83 83).
🛒 Wed, Fri–Sun. www.frejus.fr

The modern town of Fréjus is
dwarfed in importance by two
impressive historic sites. The
remains of the Roman port of
Amphithéâtre (founded by
Julius Caesar in 49 BC) may
not be as complete as those at
Orange or Arles but they are
of exceptional variety. A great
amphitheatre, fragments of an
aqueduct, a theatre and part of
a rampart gateway remain.
The sea has receded over the
centuries and there are few
traces of the original harbour.
  The cathedral on place
Formigé marks the entrance
to the **Cité Episcopale**. The
fortified enclave includes the
5th-century baptistry, one of
the oldest in France, and the
cathedral cloister, its coffered
medieval roof decorated with
scenes from the Apocalypse.
  In 1959 Fréjus was hit by a
wall of water as the Malpasset
Barrage burst. To the north the
ruined dam can still be seen.

🏛 **Amphithéâtre**
Rue Henri Vadon. *Tel 04 94 51 34 31.*
◯ Tue–Sun. 🔴 1 Jan, 1 May,
25 Dec. 🚫 📷 🎥

🏛 **Cité Episcopale**
58 rue de Fleury. *Tel 04 94 51 26
30.* ◯ Jun–Sep: daily. 🔴 1 Jan,
1 May, 1 & 11 Nov, 25 Dec.
🚫 cloisters. ♿ 🚻 🎥

THE CREATION OF A PERFUME

The best perfumes begin as a formula of essential
oils extracted from natural sources. The blend of
aromas is created by a perfumer called a "nose" because of his or her exceptional sense of smell. A
perfume may use as many as 300 essences, all
painstakingly extracted from plants by various
methods: steam distillation, extraction by
volatile solvents and *enfluerage a froid* (for
costly or potent essences). With this process,
pungent blossoms are placed onto layers of fats
for several days until the fats are saturated.

Lavender water

The oils are then
"washed" out
with alcohol, and
when this evaporates,
it leaves the "pure"
perfume essence behind.

Grasse flowers

St-Raphaël ㉕

Var. 🏛 40,000. 🚉 🚌 ℹ 99 quai
Albert 1er (04 94 19 52 52).
www.saint-raphael.com

Delightfully situated, St-
Raphaël is a charming, old-
style Côte d'Azur resort with
Art Nouveau architecture and
a palm-fronded promenade.
Aside from its beaches,
it offers a marina, a casino,
Roman ruins, a 12th-century
church and a museum with
treasures from a Roman wreck
found by Jacques Cousteau.
  It was here that Napoleon
Bonaparte landed in 1799 on
his return from Egypt.

Grasse ㉖

Alpes-Maritimes. 🏛 50,000. 🚌
ℹ Palais des Congrès, 22 cours
Honoré Cresp (04 93 36 66 66).
www.grasse.fr

Cradled by hills, with
views out to sea,
Grasse is surrounded
by fields of lavender,
mimosa, jasmine
and roses. Grasse
has been the centre
of the world's
perfume industry
since the 16th
century, when
Catherine de'
Médici set the
fashion for
scented leather
gloves. At that
time, Grasse
was also known

---

as the for leather tanning. The
tanneries have gone, but the
perfume houses founded in
the 18th and 19th centuries
are still in business, although
today Grasse perfumes are
made from imported flowers
or chemicals. Fragonard and
Molinard have museums, but
the best place to learn is at
the **Musée Internationale de
la Parfumerie**, which has a
garden of fragrant plants.
  Grasse was the birthplace
of Jean-Honoré Fragonard,
the artist. The **Villa-Musée
Fragonard** is decorated
with murals by his son.
Fragonard's only religious
work is in the **Cathédrale
de Notre-Dame-du-Puy** in
the Old Town, with three
paintings by Rubens. The
place aux Aires and the place
du Cours typify Grasse's
charm, surrounded by streets
with Renaissance staircases
and balconies.

🏛 **Musée International
de la Parfumerie**
2 bd de Jeu du Ballon.
Tel 04 97 05 58 00.
◯ Mon, Wed–Sun.
🔴 Nov; public hols. 🚫
♿ 📷 🚻 www.
museesdegrasse.com

🏛 **Villa-Musée
Fragonard**
23 bd Fragonard.
Tel 04 93 36 80 20.
◯ Wed–Mon. 🔴 Nov;
public hols. 🚫 🚻

**Statue honouring
Jean-Honoré
Fragonard in Grasse**

Lavender fields near Puimoisson, Alpes-de-Haute-Provence ▷

High summer on the beach at Cannes, overlooked by the Carlton Hotel

Cannes ②

Alpes-Maritimes. 🏘 70,000. 🚉 🚌
⛴ 🛈 *Palais des Festivals, 1 La
Croisette (04 92 99 84 22).* 🛒 *Tue–
Sun.* www.palaisdesfestivals.com

Just as Grasse is synonymous
with the perfume industry,
the first thing that most people
associate with Cannes is its
many festivals, especially the
International Film Festival.
There is much more to the

city than these glittering events.
It was Lord Brougham, the
British Lord Chancellor, who
put Cannes on the map,
although Prosper Mérimée,
Inspector of Historic Monuments, allegedly visited Cannes
two months before him. Lord
Brougham stopped here in
1834, unable to reach Nice
due to a cholera outbreak
there. Struck by the beauty
and mild climate of what was
then just a small fishing port,

he built a villa here. Other
foreigners followed and Cannes
became established as a top
Mediterranean resort.

The Old Town which Lord
Brougham knew is centred in
the Le Suquet district, on the
slopes of Mont Chevalier. Part
of the old city wall can still be
seen on place de la Castre,
which is dominated by the
Notre-Dame de l'Espérance,
built in the 16th and 17th centuries in the Provençal Gothic
style. An 11th-century watch
tower is another attractive
feature of the quarter, and the
castle keep houses the **Musée
de la Castre**, the eclectic finds
of a 19th-century Dutch
explorer, Baron Lycklama.

The famed **boulevard de la
Croisette** is lined with gardens
and palm trees. One side is
occupied by luxury boutiques
and hotels such as the
Carlton, built in Belle Epoque
style, whose twin cupolas
were modelled on the breasts
of La Belle Otero, a famous
member of the 19th-century
demi-monde. Opposite are
some of the finest sandy
beaches on this coast. The
glamour of the Croisette, once
one of the world's grandest
thoroughfares, seems faded in
the noise and fumes of summer.

🏝 Îles de Lérins
🚢 *depart from: le Quai des Îles.*
🛈 *Horizon (04 92 98 71 36 for Île
Ste-Marguerite), Planaria (04 92 98
71 38 for Île St-Honorat).*
Just off the coast from Cannes
are the Îles de Lérins. The fort
on **Île Sainte-Marguerite** is
where the mysterious Man in
the Iron Mask was imprisoned
in the late 17th century. A

CANNES FILM FESTIVAL

The first Cannes Film Festival took place in 1946 and,
for almost 20 years, it remained a small and exclusive
affair, attended by the artists and celebrities who lived
or were staying on the coast. The arrival of the "starlet",
especially Brigitte Bardot, in the mid-1950s marked the
change from artistic event to media circus, but Cannes
remains the international marketplace for film-makers
and distributors, with the *Palme d'Or* award conferring
high status on its winner. The annual film festival is
held in the huge Palais des Festivals, opened in 1982.
It has three auditoriums, two exhibition halls,
conference rooms, a casino, night-club and restaurant.

Gérard Depardieu and family arriving at the festival

For hotels and restaurants in this region see pp590–4 and pp646–50

popular theory is that his face had to be hidden because he resembled someone very important indeed – possibly even Louis XIV. Visitors can see the tiny cell that held him for over ten years.

Ile Saint-Honorat has an 11th-century tower in which the resident monks took refuge during raids by the Saracens. There are also five ancient chapels. Both islands offer peaceful woodland walks, fine views and quiet coves for swimming.

Beside the Boulevard de la Croisette

Cap d'Antibes ㉘

Alpes-Maritimes. 🚉 *Nice.* 🚌 🚉
Antibes. 🚢 *Nice.* ℹ *11 pl du Gén de Gaulle, Antibes (04 97 23 11 11).*
www.antibesjuanlespins.com

With its sumptuous villas in their lush grounds, this rocky, wooded peninsula, known as "the Cap" to its regular visitors, has been a symbol of luxury life on the Riviera since it was frequented by Scott Fitzgerald and the rich American set in the 1920s. One of the wealthiest of all, magnate Frank Jay Gould, invested in the resort of Juan-les-Pins and it became the focus of high life on the Cap. Today, memories of the Jazz Age live on at the Jazz Festival, when international stars perform *(see p37).*

At the highest point of the peninsula, the sailors' chapel of **La Garoupe** has a collection of votive offerings and a 14th-century Russian icon. Nearby is the **Jardin Thuret**, created in 1856 to acclimatize

tropical plants. Much of the exotic flora of the region began its naturalization here.

🌿 **Jardin Thuret**
90 chemin Raymond. **Tel** 04 97 21 25 03. ⬜ Mon–Fri. ⬛ public hols.

Antibes ㉙

Alpes-Maritimes. 🏘 *70,000.* 🚌 🚉
🚢 ℹ *11 pl du Général de Gaulle (04 97 23 11 11).* 🚢 *Tue–Sun.*
www.antibesjuanlespins.com

The lively town of Antibes was founded by the Greeks as Antipolis and settled by the Romans. In the 14th century, Savoy's possession of the town was contended by France until it fell to them in 1481, after which **Fort Carré** was built and the port, now a centre of Mediterranean yachting, was remodelled by Vauban.

The Château Grimaldi, formerly a residence of Monaco's ruling family, was built in the 12th century. It now houses the **Musée Picasso**. In 1946 the artist used part of the castle as a studio and, in gratitude, donated all 150 works completed during his

The Goat **(1946) by Pablo Picasso**

stay, including *The Goat*. Most are inspired by his love of the sea, including *La Joie de Vivre*.

The pottery in the **Musée d'Histoire et d'Archéologie** includes objects salvaged from shipwrecks from the Middle Ages to the 18th century.

🏛 **Musée Picasso**
Château Grimaldi. **Tel** 04 92 90 54 20. ⬜ Tue–Sun. 📷 ♿ 🚻 📹
🏛 **Musée d'Histoire et d'Archéologie**
1 Bastion St-André. **Tel** 04 92 90 56 87. ⬜ Tue–Sun. ⬛ public hols. 📷 ♿ 🚻

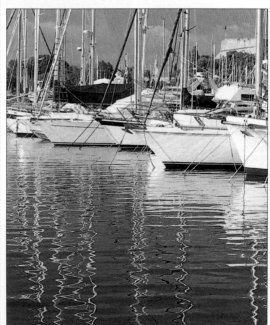
Sailing boats in the harbour at Antibes

Vallauris

Alpes-Maritimes. 🏛 31,000. 🚇 🚌
ℹ️ *square 8 mai 1945 (04 93 63 82 58)*. **www**.vallauris-golfe-juan.fr
🛎 *Tue–Sun*.

Vallauris owes its fame to the influence of Pablo Picasso, who rescued the town's pottery industry. In 1951, the village authorities commissioned Picasso to paint a mural in the deconsecrated chapel next to the castle, and his *War and Peace* (1952) is the chief exhibit of the **Musée National Picasso**. In the main square is a bronze statue, *Man with a Sheep*, donated by Picasso.

🏛 **Musée National Picasso**
Place de la Libération. **Tel** 04 93 64 71 83. ⭕ *Wed–Mon*. ⚫ *1 Jan, 1 May, 1 Nov, 11 Nov, 25 Dec.*
🖼 ♿ *ground floor only.* 🏠
www.musee-picasso.vallauris.fr

Biot ❸

Alpes-Maritimes. 🏛 9,000. 🚇 🚌
ℹ️ *46 rue St-Sebastien (04 93 65 78 00)*. 🛎 *Tue*. **www**.biot.fr

A typical little hill village, Biot has retained its charm and has always attracted artists and artisans. The best known is Fernand Léger who made his first ceramics here in 1949. Some of these and other work by him are in the **Musée Fernand Léger** outside town.
    The town is also famous for its bubble-flecked glassware. The craft of the glassblowers can be seen (and purchased) at the **Verrerie de Biot**.

🏛 **Musée Fernand Léger**
255 chemin du Val-de-Pome.
Tel 04 92 91 50 20. ⭕ *Wed–Mon.*
⚫ *1 Jan, 1 May, 25 Dec.* 🖼 ♿ 🏠
🖥 **www**.musee-fernandleger.fr

🏠 **La Verrerie de Biot**
5 ch des Combes. **Tel** 04 93 65 03 00.
⭕ *daily.* ⚫ *1 Jan, 25 Dec.* ♿ 🏠 🍴

Exterior of the Musée Fernand Léger in Biot, with a mural by the artist

Renoir's studio at the Musée Renoir, Les Collettes in Cagnes-sur-Mer

Cagnes-sur-Mer ❸

Alpes-Maritimes. 🏛 50,000. 🚇 🚌
ℹ️ *6 bd Maréchal Juin (04 93 20 61 64)*. 🛎 *Tue–Fri.* **www**.cagnes-tourisme.com

Cagnes-sur-Mer is divided into three districts. The oldest and most interesting is Haut-de-Cagnes, with its steep streets, covered passageways and ancient buildings, including a number of Renaissance arcaded houses. The other districts are Cagnes-Ville, the modern town where hotels and shops are concentrated, and Cros-de-Cagnes, a seaside fishing resort and yachting harbour. The **Château Grimaldi** in Haut-de-Cagnes was built in the 14th century and reworked in the 17th by Henri Grimaldi. Behind the fortress walls is a shady courtyard. The surrounding marble columns conceal a museum devoted to the olive tree and a small collection of modern Mediterranean art. There is also a group of paintings bequeathed by *chanteuse* Suzy Solidor. The 40 works, all portraits of her, are by artists such as Marie Laurencin and Cocteau. On the ceiling of the banqueting hall is a vast illusionistic fresco of the *Fall of Phaeton* attributed to Carlone in the 1620s.
    The last 12 years of Pierre Auguste Renoir's life were spent in Cagnes, at the **Musée Renoir, Les Collettes**. The house has been kept almost exactly as it was when he died in 1919 and

contains ten of his paintings. It is set in an olive grove, along with his great bronze *Venus Victrix*.

⚜ Château Grimaldi
Tel *04 92 02 47 30.* ⬜ *Dec–mid-Nov: Wed–Mon.* ⬛ *mid-Nov–2 Dec, 1 Jan, 1 May, 25 Dec.* 🎫

�🏛 Musée Renoir, Les Collettes
Tel *04 93 20 61 07.* ⬜ *Wed–Mon.* ⬛ *1 Nov.* 🎫 🅿

La Ferme des Collettes (1915) by Renoir, in Cagnes-sur-Mer

Gorges du Loup ❸❸

Alpes-Maritimes. 🚆 *Nice.* 🚌 *Cagnes-sur-Mer.* 🚌 *Grasse.* 🚌 *Nice.* 🛈 *Tourrettes-sur-Loup (04 93 24 18 93).* **www**.tourrettessurloup.com

The river Loup rises in the Pre-Alps behind Grasse and cuts a deep path down to the Mediterranean. Along its route are dramatic cascades and spectacular views. The superb countryside is crowned by the perched villages for which the region is famous.

Gourdon owes much of its appeal to its ancient houses, grouped round a 12th-century **Château** built on the site of a Saracen stronghold and perched high on the cliffside. Its terraced gardens were laid out by Le Nôtre *(see p179)*.

Tourrettes-sur-Loup is a fortified village in which the ramparts are formed by the outer houses. It is famous for its fields of violets, grown for use in perfume and candied sweets. The **Bastide aux Violettes** museum explores the role of the flower in the village's history and economy.

🏛 Bastide aux Violettes
Tel *04 93 59 06 97.* ⬜ *Tue–Sat & Sun pm.* 🎫 ♿ 🅿
www.tourrettessurloup.com

Vence ❸❹

Alpes-Maritimes. 🚹 *20,000.* 🚌 🛈 *pl du Grand Jardin (04 93 58 06 38).* 🗓 *Tue & Fri.* **www**.vence.fr

Vence's gentle climate has always been its main attraction; today it is surrounded by holiday villas. It was an important religious centre in the Middle Ages. The **Cathédrale** was restored by Vence's most famous bishop, Antoine Godeau. A 5th-century Roman sarcophagus serves as its altar and there are Carolingian wall carvings. Note, too, the 15th-century carved choir stalls and Godeau's tomb.

Just within the ramparts of the Old Town, which retains its 13th–14th-century town gates, is place du Peyra, once a Roman forum. Its urn-shaped fountain, built in 1822, still provides fresh water. On the edge of town, the **Chapelle du Rosaire** was built from 1947–51 and decorated by Henri Matisse,

Domed roof in Vence

in gratitude to the nuns who nursed him during an illness. On its white walls, biblical scenes are reduced to simple black lines tinted by splashes of light from the blue and yellow stained-glass windows.

⛪ Chapelle du Rosaire
466 av Henri Matisse. ***Tel*** *04 93 58 03 26.* ⬜ *Mon–Thu (Mon–Sat school hols).* ⬛ *mid-Nov– mid-Dec, public hols.* 🎫 🅿

Market day in the Old Town of Vence

Street-by-Street: St-Paul-de-Vence ③⑤

**Restaurant sign,
St-Paul-de-Vence**

One of the most famous and visited hill villages of the Nice hinterland, St-Paul-de-Vence was once a French frontier post facing Savoy. Its 16th-century ramparts offer views over a landscape of cypress trees, and red-roofed villas with palm trees and swimming pools. The village has been heavily restored but its winding streets and medieval buildings are authentic. It has proved a magnet for artists, both established and aspiring, throughout the 20th century. Today galleries and studios dominate the village.

View of St-Paul-de-Vence
The local landscape is a favourite subject for artists. Neo-Impressionist Paul Signac (1863–1935) painted this view of St-Paul.

The Chapelle des Pénitents Blancs is 16th century.

Ramparts provide a walk which encircles the village.

To Fondation Maeght

Auberge de la Colombe d'Or

The Boules court and adjacent café are the village social centre.

R DE LA POURTOUNE

RUE DES DORIERS

RUE DES BAUQUES

R DE LA CAS

RUE GRANDE

COURTINE ST PAUL

BASTION ST REMY

FONDATION MAEGHT

Built in 1964 by Paris art dealers Aimé and Marguerite Maeght, this is one of Europe's finest museums of modern art. The striking pink and white building, set outside St-Paul, was designed by Catalan architect José-Luis Sert, who worked on it directly with artists such as Miró and Chagall. Inside are paintings by Bonnard, Braque, Kandinsky, Chagall and others. There are also summer concerts, exhibitions, a library and lectures. In the terraced gardens, sculptures, mobiles and mosaics by Arp, Calder, Miró, Giacometti and Hepworth are set amid the pine trees.

L'Homme qui Marche
by Giacometti

The Colombe d'Or
This famous auberge includes a Léger mural (above) on the terrace; a Braque dove by the pool; a Picasso and a Matisse in the dining room.

The Musée d'Histoire de Saint-Paul has local waxwork scenes from the town's past.

Le Donjon, a grim medieval building, was used as a prison until the 19th century.

Eglise Collégiale
Begun in the 12th century, the church's treasures include a painting of St Catherine, attributed to Tintoretto.

Grand Fountain
This charming cobble-stoned place has a pretty urn-shaped fountain.

VISITORS' CHECKLIST

Alpes-Maritimes. 2,900.
840 ave Emile Hugues, Vence (04 93 58 37 60). 2 rue Grande (04 93 32 86 95). **www**.saint-pauldevence.com **Fondation Maeght Tel** 04 93 32 81 63. **www**.fondation-maeght.com

Rue Grande
The doors of the 16th- and 17th-century houses bear coats of arms.

CELEBRITY VILLAGE

The Colombe d'Or (Golden Dove) auberge *(see p574)* was popular with many of the artists and writers who flocked to the Riviera in the 1920s. Early patrons included Picasso, Soutine, Modigliani, Signac, Colette and Cocteau. They often paid for their rooms and meals with paintings, resulting in the priceless collection that can be seen by diners today. The rich and famous have continued to come to St-Paul: Zelda and F Scott Fitzgerald had a dramatic fight over Isadora Duncan at dinner here one night, and Yves Montand married Simone Signoret on the terrace. A photo display of celebrity visitors in St-Paul museum features Sartre and de Beauvoir, Greta Garbo, Sophia Loren, Burt Lancaster and Catherine Deneuve.

Artist Marc Chagall (1887–1985), who moved to St-Paul-de-Vence in 1950

Nice ㊱

The largest resort on the Mediterranean coast and the fifth biggest city in France, with its second busiest airport, Nice was founded by the Greeks and colonized by the Romans. Its temperate winter climate and verdant subtropical vegetation have long attracted visitors. Until World War II it was favoured by aristocrats, including Tsar Nicholas I's widow who visited in 1856 and Queen Victoria who stayed in 1895. This glittering past has contributed to Nice becoming capital of the Côte d'Azur, and today it is also a centre for business conferences and package holidays. Nice has worthy museums, good beaches and an atmospheric street life. Best of all is Carnival: 18 days of celebrations finishing on Shrove Tuesday in a fireworks display and the Battle of the Flowers *(see p39)*.

Nice's Old Quarter

Yachts at anchor in Nice harbour

🏛 Palais Lascaris
15 rue Droite. *Tel* 04 93 62 72 40.
🕐 *Wed–Mon.* ⬤ *some public hols.*
This stuccoed 17th-century palace is decorated with ornate woodwork, Flemish tapestries and illusionistic ceilings thought to be by Carlone. Its small but delightful collection includes a reconstruction of an 18th-century apothecary's shop.

🏛 Musée d'Art Moderne et d'Art Contemporain
Promenade des Arts. *Tel* 04 97 13 42 01. 🕐 *Tue–Sun.* ⬤ *1 Jan, Easter, 1 May, 25 Dec.* 🚻 🔲
www.mamac-nice.org
The museum occupies a strikingly original complex of four marble-faced towers linked by glass passageways. The collection is particularly strong in Neo-Realism and Pop Art, with works by Andy Warhol, Jean Tinguely and Niki de Saint-Phalle. Also well-represented are such Ecole de Nice artists as César, Arman and Yves Klein.

Exploring Nice
The promenade des Anglais, running right along the seafront, was built in the 1830s with funds raised by the English colony. Today it is an eight-lane, 8-km (5-mile) highway, with galleries, shops and grand hotels like the **Negresco**, reflecting Nice's prosperity.

Nice was Italian until 1860, and the pastel façades and balconies of the Old Town have a distinctly Italianate feel. It lies at the foot of a hill still known as the Château for the castle which once stood there. The district is largely restored and its tall, narrow buildings house artists and galleries, boutiques and restaurants. The daily flower market in the cours Saleya should not be missed. The **Cimiez** district, on the hills overlooking the town, is the fashionable quarter of Nice. The old monastery of Notre-Dame-de-Cimiez is well worth a visit. Lower down the hillside are Les Arènes, remains of a Roman settlement with

vestiges of the great baths and an amphitheatre. Excavated artifacts are on show at the archaeological museum, next to the Musée Matisse. At the foot of the Cimiez hill is the **Musée Chagall**.

Discover Nice by night on a guided tramway tour. The circuit takes in 14 works of art by some of the most celebrated creators of the contemporary art scene. Tickets can be booked in advance at the tourist office.

🏛 Musée Matisse
164 av des Arènes de Cimiez. *Tel* 04 93 81 08 08. 🕐 *Wed–Mon.* ⬤ *some public hols.* 🚻 🔲
www.musee-matisse-nice.org
Inspired by the Mediterranean light, Matisse spent many years in Nice. The museum, housed in and below the 17th-century Arena Villa, displays drawings, paintings, bronzes, fabrics and artifacts. Highlights include *Still Life With Pomegranates* and his last completed work, *Flowers and Fruits*.

***Blue Nude IV* (1952) by Henri Matisse**

An azure view – relaxing on the promenade des Anglais

VISITORS' CHECKLIST

Alpes-Maritimes. 349,000.
7 km (4.5 miles) SW. av
Thiers (36 35). 5 bd Jean
Jaurès (04 93 85 61 81). quai
du Commerce (3260). 5 prom
des Anglais (08 92 70 74 07).
Tue–Sun. Carnival.
www.nicetourism.com

Masséna exhibits trace the
history of Nice from 1800
to the 1930s.

⛪ Cathédrale Ste-Réparate
This 17th-century Baroque
building is surmounted by a
handsome tiled dome. Its
interior is lavishly decorated
with plasterwork, marble and
original panelling.

🏛 Musée Chagall
36 av du Docteur Ménard. **Tel** 04 93
53 87 20. ◯ Wed–Mon. ● 1 Jan,
1 May, 25 Dec. ♿ 🖼 ▭ ⛪
This is the largest collection of
works by Marc Chagall, with
paintings, drawings, sculpture,
stained glass and mosaics. Best
of all are the 17 canvases of
the artist's *Biblical Message*.

🏛 Musée des Beaux-Arts
33 av des Baumettes. **Tel** 04 92 15 28
28. ◯ Tue–Sun. ● 1 Jan, Easter,
1 May, 25 Dec. ♿ restr. 🖼 Thu. ⛪
www.musee-beaux-arts.org
The 19th-century home of a
Ukrainian princess displays
works sent to Nice by Napoleon III after Italy ceded
the city to France in 1860,
as well as paintings by
Renoir, Monet and Dufy.

🏛 Palais Masséna
65 rue de France. **Tel** 04 93 91 19
10. ◯ Wed–Mon. ♿ ⛪
Housed in a 19th-century
Italianate villa, the Palais

⛪ Cathédrale Orthodoxe Russe St-Nicolas
Completed in 1912, the
cathedral was built in memory
of a young Tsarevitch who
died here in 1865. The
exterior is of pink brick and
grey marble with elaborate
mosaics. The interior is
resplendent with icons.

🏛 Musée des Arts Asiatiques
405 prom des Anglais. **Tel** 04 92 29
37 00. ◯ Wed–Mon. ● 1 Jan,
1 May, 25 Dec. ♿ ▭ ⛪
⛪ **www**.arts-asiatiques.com
Exhibits of ancient and contemporary art from across Asia,
in Kenzo Tange's uncluttered
white marble and glass setting.

NICE

Cathédrale Ste-Réparate ④
Hôtel Negresco ②
Musée d'Art Moderne
    et d'Art
    Contemporain ⑥
Musée Chagall ①
Palais Lascaris ⑤
Palais Masséna ③

Chapelle de St-Pierre, Villefranche

Villefranche-sur-Mer ㊲

Alpes-Maritimes. 6,649.
Jardin François Binon (04 93 01
73 68). Sat & Sun.
www.villefranche-sur-mer.com

One of the most perfectly
situated towns on the coast,
Villefranche lies at the foot of
hills forming a sheltered
amphitheatre. The town
overlooks a beautiful natural
harbour, which is deep enough
to be a naval port of call.

The bright and animated
waterfront is lined by Italianate
façades, with cafés and bars
from which to watch the
fishermen. Here, too, is the
medieval **Chapelle de St-Pierre**,
which, after years of service
storing fishing nets, was
restored in 1957 and decorated
by Jean Cocteau. His frescoes
depict non-religious images
and the life of St Peter.

Also worth a visit is the
16th-century **Citadelle St-Elme**,
incorporating the town hall
and two art galleries.

Behind the harbour, the
streets are narrow, winding,
and often stepped. Walking
through them, you get the
odd glimpse of the harbour.
The vaulted 13th-century rue
Obscure has always provided
shelter from bombardment,
right up to World War II.

Chapelle de St-Pierre
Quai Amiral Courbet. **Tel** 04 93 76
90 70. mid-Dec–mid-Nov:
Tue–Sun. 25 Dec.

Cap Ferrat ㊳

Alpes-Maritimes. 2,000. Nice.
Nice. Beaulieu-sur-Mer.
59 av Denis Femeria (04 93 76 08
90). www.saintjeancapferrat.fr

The peninsula of Cap Ferrat
boasts some of the most
sumptuous villas found on the
Riviera. From 1926 until the
author's death, the best-known
was Somerset Maugham's Villa
Mauresque, where he received
celebrities from Noël Coward
to Winston Churchill.

High walls shield most of
the exclusive villas, but possibly the best one is open to
the public. The **Villa Ephrussi
de Rothschild** is a terracotta
and marble mansion set in
themed gardens on the crest
of the cape. It belonged to
the Baroness Ephrussi de
Rothschild, who bequeathed
it to the Institut de France in
1934. It is furnished as she
left it, with her collections of

priceless porcelain, items that
belonged to Marie Antoinette
and a unique collection of
drawings by Fragonard.

The town of **Beaulieu** lies
where the cape joins the mainland. A pleasant marina with
an exceptionally mild climate
and very fine hotels, it is the
site of another unique house,
the extraordinary **Villa
Kerylos**. Built between 1902
and 1908 for archaeologist
Theodore Reinach in imitation
of an ancient Greek residence,
it contains lovingly reproduced
mosaics, frescoes and furniture.

**Villa Ephrussi de
Rothschild**
Cap Ferrat. **Tel** 04 93 01 33 09.
Feb–Oct: daily; Nov–Jan:
Mon–Fri pms, w/e & school & public
hols: daily.
www.villa-ephrussi.com

Villa Kerylos
Imp Gustave Eiffel, Beaulieu. **Tel** 04
93 01 01 44. as above.
www.villa-kerylos.com

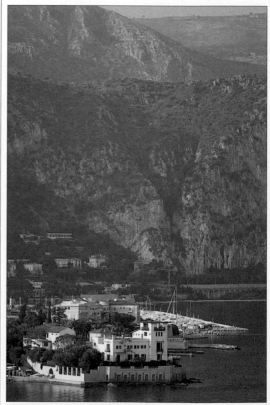

Greek-style Villa Kerylos at Beaulieu on Cap Ferrat

Louis XV salon at the Villa Ephrussi de Rothschild, Cap Ferrat

Eze ㊴

Alpes-Maritimes. 👥 3,100. 🚉 🚌
ℹ️ pl Général de Gaulle (04 93 41 26 00). **www**.eze-riviera.com

For many, Eze is the ultimate perched village, balancing on a rocky pinnacle high above the Mediterranean. Every summer, thousands of visitors stream through the 14th-century fortified gate. The flower-decked buildings are almost all shops, galleries and craft workshops. At the top of the village, the château is surrounded by the lush tropical plants of the **Jardin Exotique**. The view from here is superb.

Further along the Upper Corniche is the Roman Alpine Trophy **La Turbie** (see pp46–7). This vast 6 BC structure dominates the surrounding village, with magnificent views towards Monaco and Italy.

🌸 **Jardin Exotique**
Rue du Château. **Tel** 04 93 41 10 30. 🔲 daily. 🔴 25 Dec. 🖼️

🏛 **La Turbie**
🔲 Apr–mid-Sep: daily; mid-Sep–Mar: Tue–Sun. 🔴 public hols. 🖼️ 📷 📋
www.ville-la-turbie.fr

Roquebrune-Cap-Martin ㊵

Alpes-Maritimes. 👥 12,000.
🚉 Nice. 🚌 🚌 ℹ️ 218 av Aristide Briand (04 93 35 62 87). 🌐 Wed.
www.roquebrune-cap-martin.com

The medieval village of Roquebrune overlooks the wooded cape where the villas of the rich and famous still abound. Visitors here have

included Coco Chanel and Greta Garbo. The cape has not always been kind – poet WB Yeats died here in 1939 and architect Le Corbusier was drowned off the coast in 1965.

In 1467 Roquebrune believed that by performing scenes from the Passion it escaped the plague, and every August it continues this tradition.

View from Roquebrune

Alpes-Maritimes ㊶

Alpes-Maritimes. 🛫 Nice. 🚉 Nice. 🚌 Peille. 🚌 Nice. ℹ️ La Mairie, Peille (04 93 91 71 71). **www**.peille.fr

In the hinterland of the Côte d'Azur, it is still possible to find quiet, unspoiled villages off the tourist track. The tiny twin villages of **Peille** and **Peillon** are typical. Both have changed little since the Middle Ages, perched on outcrops over the Paillon river, their streets a mass of steps and arches. Peille, the more remote, even has its own dialect. The Alpes-Maritimes countryside is also unspoiled, its

craggy gorges, tumbling rivers and windswept plateaux just a few hours from the coast. Of note are the ancient rock carvings of the **Vallée des Merveilles** and rare wildlife in the **Parc National du Mercantour**.

Menton ㊷

Alpes-Maritimes. 👥 30,000. 🚉 🚌
ℹ️ Palais de l'Europe, 8 av Boyer (04 92 41 76 76). 🌐 daily.
www.menton.fr

Menton's beaches, with the Alps and the golden buildings and Belle Epoque villas of the Old Town as a backdrop, would be enough to lure most visitors. In the 19th century, Queen Victoria and famous writers and poets often holidayed here. Tropical gardens and citrus fruits thrive in the town's perfect climate, mild even in February for the lemon festival (see p39).

The **Basilica St-Michel** is a superb example of Baroque architecture in yellow and pink stone. The square before it is paved with a mosaic of the Grimaldi coat of arms. The **Salle des Mariages** in the Hôtel de Ville was decorated in 1957 by Jean Cocteau. Drawings, paintings, ceramics and stage designs by the renowned artist are displayed in the **Musée Jean Cocteau**, housed in a 17th-century fort. Inside the Palais Carnolès, the **Musée des Beaux-Arts** features works from the Middle Ages to the 20th century.

🎭 **Salle des Mariages**
Hôtel de Ville. **Tel** 04 92 10 50 00.
🔲 Mon–Fri. 🔴 public hols. 🖼️
🏛 **Musée Jean Cocteau**
Vieux Port. **Tel** 04 93 57 72 30.
🔲 Wed–Mon. 🔴 public hols. 🖼️
🏛 **Musée des Beaux-Arts**
3 av de la Madone. **Tel** 04 93 35 49 71. 🔲 Wed–Mon. 🔴 public hols.

Mosaic at the Musée Jean Cocteau in Menton

Monaco

Travellers to Monaco by car would do well to take the Moyenne Corniche, one of the most beautiful highways in the world, with incomparable views of the Mediterranean coastline. Arriving among the skyscrapers of Monaco today, it is hard to envisage the turbulence of its history. At first a Greek settlement, later taken by the Romans, it was bought from the Genoese in 1297 by the Grimaldis who, in spite of bitter family feuds and at least one political assassination, still rule as the world's oldest ruling dynasty. Monaco covers 1.9 sq km (0.74 sq miles) and, although its size has increased by one-third in the form of landfills, it still occupies an area smaller than that of New York's Central Park.

Aerial view of Monaco

Grand Casino

Exploring Monaco

Monaco owes its renown principally to its Grand Casino. Source of countless legends, it was instituted in 1878 by Charles III to save himself from bankruptcy. The first casino was opened in 1865 on a barren promontory (later named Monte-Carlo in his honour) across the harbour from ancient Monaco-Ville. So successful was Charles's money-making venture that, by 1870, he was able to abolish taxation for his people. Today, Monaco is a tax haven for thousands, and its residents have the highest per capita income in the world.

Visitors come from all over the world for the Grand Prix de Monaco in May and the Monte-Carlo Rally in January (see p39). Many of the greatest singers perform in the opera season. There is a fireworks festival (July–August), and an international circus festival at the end of January as well as world-class ballet and concerts. Facilities exist for every sort of leisure activity, and there is much else to enjoy without breaking the bank, including **Fort Antoine** and the neo-Romanesque **Cathédrale**.

♖ Grand Casino
Place du Casino. **Tel** 00 377 98 06 76 76. ☐ daily, from noon. ♿ www.montecarloresort.com
Designed in 1878 by Charles Garnier, architect of the Paris Opéra (see p97), and set in formal gardens, the Casino gives a splendid view over Monaco. The lavish interior is still decorated in Belle Epoque style, recalling an era when this was the rendezvous of Russian Grand Dukes. Anyone can play the odds on the one-armed bandits of the Salon Blanc or the roulette wheels of the Salons Européens. Even the most exclusive of the gaming rooms can be visited at a price, but their tables are for the big spenders only.

♟ Palais Princier
Place du Palais. **Tel** 00 377 93 25 18 31. ☐ Apr–Nov: daily. ▓
Monaco-Ville, the seat of government, is the site of the 13th-century Palais Princier. The interior, with its priceless furniture and carpets and its

Skyscrapers and apartment blocks of modern Monte-Carlo

MONACO'S ROYAL FAMILY

Prince Albert II officially assumed the Monaco throne in July 2005, three months after his father died, aged 81, ending a reign of over 55 years. Prince Rainier III was an effective ruler, descended from a Grimaldi who entered the Monaco fortress in 1297. His wife, former film star Grace Kelly, died tragically in 1982. Prince Albert and his sisters, Caroline and Stephanie, remain a focus of media attention.

Prince Rainier III, Princess Grace and Princess Caroline

magnificent frescoes, is only open to the public in the summer. The changing of the guard is at 11:55am.

🏛 Musée des Souvenirs Napoléoniens et Archives Historiques du Palais

Pl du Palais. *Tel 00 377 93 25 18 31.* 🏛 daily. 🔴 1 Jan, 1 May, Grand Prix, Nov, 25 Dec. 🖼

A genealogical tree on the wall traces the family links between the Grimaldis and Bonapartes. Also on

show are Napoleon's personal effects and numerous portraits.

🐟 Musée Océanographique

Av Saint-Martin. *Tel 00 377 93 15 36 00.* 🏛 daily. 🖼 🚻 🛗 🛈 **www**.oceano.mc

This museum was founded in 1910 by Prince Albert I. Its aquarium, fed with sea water, holds rare species of marine plants and animals. The museum houses an important scientific collection, diving equipment and model ships. Marine explorer Jacques

Guard outside the Palais Princier

Cousteau established his research centre here.

♣ Jardin Exotique

62 bd du Jardin Exotique. *Tel 00 377 93 15 29 80.* 🏛 daily. 🔴 19 Nov, 25 Dec. 🖼 🛈 **www**.jardin-exotique.mc

These gardens are considered to be the finest in Europe, with a huge range of tropical and subtropical plants. A museum of anthropology offers evidence of mammoths once living on the coast here.

🏛 Nouveau Musée National de Monaco

17 av Princesse Grace. *Tel 00 377 98 98 91 26.* 🏛 daily. 🔴 1 Jan, 1 May, Grand Prix, 19 Nov, 25 Dec. 🖼 🎫 🛈

This museum, housed in two adjoining villas and surrounded by lush gardens, hosts temporary exhibitions. There are usually two a year, on themes of photography and nature.

MONACO

Cathédrale ④
Grand Casino ⑥
Jardin Exotique ①
Musée Océanographique ⑤
Musée des Souvenirs Napoléoniens et Archives Historiques du Palais ②
Palais Princier ③

KEY

— Grand Prix route

0 metres 250
0 yards 250

Key to Symbols *see back flap*

CORSICA

HAUTE-CORSE · CORSE-DU-SUD

*C*orsica, where the people speak their own language, has all the attributes of a mini-continent. There are tropical palm trees, vineyards, olive and orange groves, forests of chestnut and indigenous pine, alpine lakes and cool mountain torrents filled with trout. Most distinctive of all is the parched maquis (scrub), heavy with the scent of myrtle, which Napoleon swore he could smell from Elba.

The fourth largest island in the Mediterranean after Sicily, Sardinia and Cyprus, Corsica has been a problem and a bafflement to mainland France ever since 1769, when it was "sold" to Louis XV by the Genoese for 40 million francs. Before that, following years of struggle, the Corsican people had enjoyed 14 years of independence under the revered leadership of Pasquale Paoli. They understandably felt cheated by the deal with the French, and have resented them ever since. To holiday-makers visiting the island – in July and August tourists outnumber the inhabitants six to one – the Corsican–French relationship may be a matter of indifference. However, there is a strong (and sometimes quite violent) separatist movement, which does deter some tourists. As a result, Corsica's wild beauty has been preserved to an extent not seen in the rest of the Mediterranean.

For 200 years, from the 11th to the 13th century, Corsica was a colony of the old Tuscan republic of Pisa, whose builders founded beautifully proportioned Romanesque churches. These buildings are, along with the megalithic stone warriors in Filitosa, the noblest monuments to be seen here. For the rest, the birthplace of Napoleon is a place of wild seacoasts and mountain peaks, one of the last unspoiled corners of the Mediterranean: poor, depopulated, beautiful, old-fashioned and doggedly aloof.

The village of Oletta in the Nebbio region around St-Florent

◁ A fisherman with feline friends in Bastia

Exploring Corsica

Corsica's main appeal is its scenery: a wildly beautiful landscape of mountains, forests, myrtle-scented maquis and countless miles of sandy beaches. Late spring (when the wild flowers are in bloom) and early autumn are the best times to visit – the temperature is moderate and there aren't too many visitors. The island is renowned for its superb hiking trails, some of which become cross-country skiing trails during the winter. Downhill skiing is also possible in February and March.

Calvi's port and 15th-century citadel

KEY

═══ Major road
─── Secondary road
╌╌╌ Minor road
─── Scenic route
△ Summit

WINDS OF CORSICA

The island is affected by winds from every direction. The two not shown here are the Mezzo-giorno, which blows at noon, and the Terrana, strongest at midnight.

Tramontane (cold wind blowing from the north)

Maestrale (can be very strong)

Grecale (bringing rain in autumn and spring)

Ponente (milder west wind)

Levante (warm)

Libeccio (dry in summer and bringing rain in winter)

Sirocco (dusty wind from Africa)

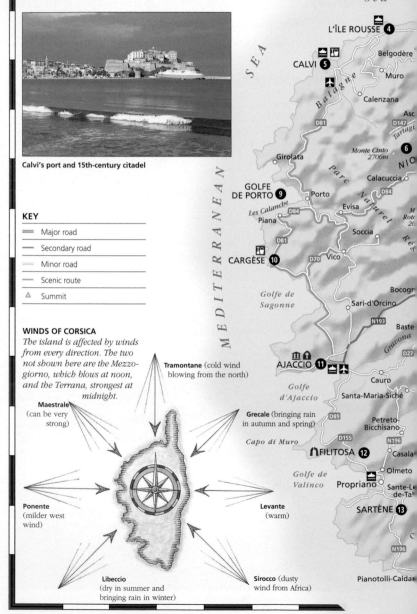

Ligurian Sea

L'ÎLE ROUSSE 4
Belgodère
CALVI 5
Muro
Calenzana
Monte Cinto 2706m 6
Girolata
Calacuccia
GOLFE DE PORTO 9
Porto
Evisa
Les Calanche
Piana
Soccia
CARGÈSE 10
Vico
Bocogn
Sari-d'Orcino
Baste
AJACCIO 11
Cauro
Golfe d'Ajaccio
Santa-Maria-Siché
Capo di Muro
Petreto-Bicchisano
FILITOSA 12
Casala
Olmeto
Golfe di Valinco
Propriano
SARTÈNE 13
Pianotolli-Calda

CAP CORSE ①
Rogliano
Centuri-Port
Macinaggio
Pino
Luri
D80
Canari
D80
Golfe de
t-Florent
Monte Stello
△ 1307m
Nonza
Erbalunga
Lavasina
i des
ates
Patrimoniog
-FLORENT ③
② BASTIA
Oletta
D81
Casatorra
-Pietro-
-Tenda
D82
Murato
Borgo
Casamozza
Golo
nte-Nuovo
Vescovato
Ponte-Leccia
N198
N193
Morosaglia
Figareto
Francardo
CASTAGNICCIA
⑧
Moriani-Plage
Piedicroce
Cervione
D71
CORTE
Prunete
Phare-d'Alistro
ca
Venaco
N200
Bravone
Vezzani
Tavignano
Vivario
zzavona
Aléria
D344
ORIENTALE
Ghisonaccia
⑮
Mignataja
Travo
CÔTE
avo
Solenzara
nte Incudine
2136m
D268
N198
Zonza
Conca
Lecci
D368
Porto-Vecchio
ari
N198
BONIFACIO

The Calanche cliffs in the Golfe de Porto

GETTING AROUND

Car ferries (which should be booked well in advance) depart from Marseille, Nice and Toulon, arriving at Bastia, L'Île Rousse, Calvi, Ajaccio, Propriano and Porto-Vecchio. There are also ferries from Sardinia to Bonifacio, and from Genoa, Livorno and La Spezia to Bastia. Small airports are at Ajaccio, Bastia, Calvi and Figari. Corsica's roads are narrow, twisting and often tortuously slow, though breathtaking views reward the effort. A car is a must for exploring the island, as public transport is limited. Carry spare petrol – filling stations are few and far between.

0 kilometres   20

0 miles   10

Corte's Old Town, with its citadel high up on a rocky outcrop

Cap Corse ❶

Haute-Corse. 🚉 Bastia. 🚌 Bastia.
🚢 Bastia. 🛈 pl St-Nicolas, Bastia
(04 95 54 20 40).
www.bastia-tourisme.com

Cap Corse is the northern tip of Corsica, 40 km (25 miles) in length but seldom more than 12 km (7.5 miles) wide, pointing like an accusatory finger towards Genoa.

There are two roads out of Bastia to the cape: the D81 leading west across the mountains and joining up with the D80 after the wine village of Patrimonio; and the D80 travelling north along the eastern shore to **Erbalunga** and **Macinaggio**. The road is narrow and twisting, a taste of what awaits you in Corsica.

From the coastal village of **Lavasina**, the D54 leads left off the D80 to Pozzo; from here it is a 5-hour round trip on foot to the 1,307-m (4,300-ft) summit of **Monte Stello**, the highest peak on the cape. The 360-degree view from the top takes in St-Florent to the west, the massif of central Corsica to the south and the Italian island of Elba to the east.

Further up the coast, the restored **Tour de Losse** is one of many 16th-century Genoese towers along the coast – part of an elaborate system which enabled all Corsican towns to be warned within 2 hours of impending barbarian raids.

The charming 18th-century fishing port of **Centuri**, near the tip of the peninsula on the west coast, is an ideal spot for a delicious seafood feast. **Pino**, a pretty little village

The village of Erbalunga on the east coast of Cap Corse

straggling down the green mountainside further to the south, has no hotel, only a lovely little church dedicated to the Virgin, full of model ships placed there by mariners grateful for her protection.

On the way south along the vertiginous lower corniche, be sure to turn left up the hill to **Canari**. One of the larger villages in this area, Canari has a jewel of a 12th-century Pisan church, Santa Maria Assunta, a magnificent view across the sea, and a thoroughly convivial hotel-restaurant. All the by-roads in this thickly wooded area seem to lead somewhere interesting. There are dozens of picturesque hamlets in the vicinity, and it should be borne in mind that from this point onwards the landscape becomes steadily less attractive as the road winds on past the old asbestos workings and beaches of black sand below the village of **Nonza**.

Bastia ❷

Haute-Corse. 👥 39,000. 🚉 🚌
🚢 🚢 🛈 pl St-Nicolas (04 95 54 20
40). 🛒 Tue–Sun.
www.bastia-tourisme.com

A thriving port and the administrative capital of Upper Corsica, Bastia is utterly different in style from its sedate west coast rival, Ajaccio. The Genoese citadel and colourful 19th-century Italianate buildings around the old port are for many people their first taste of the authentic Mediterranean – as it was half a century ago, and as it stubbornly remains in our imagination.

The centre of Bastia's life is the **place St-Nicolas**, facing the wharf where ferries from the mainland and Italy arrive. Heading south along the waterfront you come to the **place de l'Hôtel de Ville**, site of a daily food market. Bordering the square are the early 17th-century **Chapelle de l'Immaculée Conception**, with its ornate 18th-century interior, and the mid-17th-century **Eglise de St-Jean-Baptiste**, whose façade dominates the Vieux Port.

From here it is a short walk up to the 16th-century **citadel**, where there are two more churches worth seeing: the Rococo **Chapelle Sainte-Croix**, with its striking *Black Christ*, fished out of the sea by Bastiais fishermen in 1428; and the 15th-century **Sainte-Marie**, which has a *Virgin* made of a tonne of solid silver.

Bastia's Vieux Port seen from the Jetée du Dragon

For hotels and restaurants in this region see pp594–5 and pp650–1

St-Florent ❸

Haute-Corse. 🏠 *1,500.* 🚗
ℹ️ *Bâtiment Administratif (04 95 37 06 04).* 🎫 *first Wed of month.*
www.corsica-saintflorent.com

St-Florent is almost a Corsican St-Tropez – chic, affluent, and packed with yachts. Its citadel, which houses photography exhibitions, dates from 1439, and is a fine example of Genoese military architecture. The town itself is pleasant to wander around; its main attraction, the 12th-century Pisan **Cathédrale de Santa Maria Assunta**, lies just inland on the road to Poggio-d'Oletta.

Environs

A leisurely 4-hour circuit by car of the **Nebbio** region, which extends in an amphitheatre around St-Florent, might take in the following: **Santo Pietro di Tenda; Murato**, famous for its magnificent **Eglise de San Michele de Murato**, a 12th-century Pisan Romanesque construction built of white and green stone; the **San Stefano** pass, with the sea on either side; **Oletta**, which produces a special blue cheese made from ewes' milk; the **Teghime** pass; and finally the wine village of **Patrimonio**, where there is a strange, big-eared menhir dating from 900–800 BC.

Along the coast to the west of St-Florent lies the barren, uninhabited **Désert des Agriates**. If you can face the 10-km (6-mile) haul to the sea – on foot, by bike or by motorbike – the Saleccia beach is the most beautiful on the island.

San Michele de Murato

L'Île Rousse ❹

Haute-Corse. 🏠 *2,400.* 🚗 🚌 🚢
ℹ️ *av Calizzi (04 95 60 04 35).*
🎫 *summer: daily; winter: Tue & Fri.*
www.balagne-corsica.com

Founded in 1758 by Pasquale Paoli, leader of independent Corsica, L'Île Rousse is today a major holiday resort and ferry terminal. The centre of town is dominated by a marble statue of Corsica's national hero, Paoli. On the north side of the square is the covered market, with the Old Town just beyond.

In summer, L'Île Rousse becomes overcrowded, its beaches a mass of bodies. It is worth travelling 10 km (6 miles) up the coast to **Lozari**, which offers a magnificent, virtually unspoiled stretch of sand.

Environs

One very pleasant way to discover the **Balagne** region is to take the tram-train from L'Île Rousse to Calvi and back. This odd little service runs all year (more frequent in summer), roughly keeping to the coastline and stopping at Algajola, Lumio and various villages along the way.

Calvi ❺

Haute-Corse. 🏠 *5,500.* 🚗 🚌 🚢
ℹ️ *Port de Plaisance (04 95 65 16 67).*
🎫 *daily.* **www**.balagne-corsica.com

Calvi, where Nelson lost his eye in an "explosion of stones" in 1794, is today half military town, half cheap holiday resort. Its 15th-century citadel is garrisoned by a crack French regiment of the foreign legion; while beyond the ferry port is a seedy, apparently endless campsite and trailer park.

The town makes a half-hearted case for being the birthplace of Christopher Columbus, but there is no real evidence to support this. A much better claim to fame is the food, which is very good and reasonably priced by Corsican standards. There is also a very respectable jazz festival at Calvi towards the end of June.

Outside town, the 19th-century **Chapelle de Notre-Dame de la Serra** is gloriously sited on a hilltop commanding extensive views in all directions.

French foreign legionnaire

The Chapelle de Notre-Dame de la Serra, 6 km (3.5 miles) southwest of Calvi

Corte's 15th-century citadel seen at dawn

The Niolo ❻

Haute-Corse. 🚍 Corte. 🛈 route de Cuccia (04 95 48 05 22).

The Niolo, west of Corte, extends westward to the Vergio pass and the upper Golo basin, and to the east as far as the Scala di Santa Regina. It includes Corsica's highest mountain, the 2,700-m (8,859-ft) **Monte Cinto**, and its biggest river, the **Golo**, which meets the sea south of Bastia.

Alone of the various regions of Corsica, the Niolo persists in the cultivation of livestock as its economic mainstay.

The main town, **Calacuccia**, is suitable for excursions to Monte Cinto. The nearby ski resort of **Haut Asco** is best reached by the D147 from **Asco**, but enthusiasts can walk from Calacuccia (8–9 hours). To the south is the huge forest of **Valdu Niello**.

Corte ❼

Haute-Corse. 🏠 6,700. 🚍 🚍 🛈 la Citadelle (04 95 46 26 70). 🚲 Fri. www.centru-corsica.com

In the geographical centre of Corsica, Corte was the chosen capital of the independence leader Pasqual Paoli from 1755–69, and today is the seat of the island's university. In the Old Town is the 15th-

century citadel, housing the **Museu di a Corsica**. Its exhibits relate to traditional Corsican life and anthropology.

Corte is the best base for exploring nearby mountain areas, especially as it stands exactly halfway along the GR20, the legendary 220-km (137-mile) trail from Calenzana to Conca.

🏛 **Museu di a Corsica**
La Citadelle. **Tel** 04 95 45 25 45. ◐ Apr–Jun & Oct: Tue–Sun; Jul–Sep: daily; Nov–Mar: Tue–Sat. ◑ public hols. 🈺 ♿ 📷 🎒 📷
www.musee-corse.com

Environs

Don't miss the wildly beautiful **Gorges de la Restonica**, about 12 km (7.5 miles) out of town via the D623. Above these gorges adventurous walkers may wish to make the well-marked climb to the snow-fed **Lac de Melo** (allow 60–90 minutes); or the **Lac de Capitello**, 30 minutes further on, where the snow stays as late as early June. The path – in winter a cross-country ski trail – follows the river.

South of Corte, the **Forêt de Vizzavona** features beech and pine woodland crisscrossed by trout-filled streams and walking trails (notably the GR20). It is a perfect refuge from the summer heat and is also an excuse to take the small-gauge train up from Ajaccio or Bastia, which stops at Vizzavona.

The Castagniccia ❽

Haute-Corse. 🚁 Bastia. 🚍 Corte, Ponte Leccia. 🚍 Piedicroce, La Porta, Valle-d'Alesani. 🛈 Folelli (04 95 35 82 54). www.castagniccia.fr

East of Corte is the hilly, chestnut-covered region of Castagniccia (literally "small chestnut grove"), which most Corsicans agree is the very heart and kernel of the island. It was here that independence leader Pasquale Paoli was born in 1725, and that the revolts against Genoa and later France began in earnest in 1729. Alas, many of the villages in this beautiful, remote area are nearly empty, their inhabitants having joined the 800,000 or so Corsicans (almost three times the present population) who live and work in mainland France or Italy. It seems hard to believe that in the 17th century, when the great chestnut forests introduced here by the Genoese were at the height of their production, this was the most prosperous and populated region in Corsica.

The D71 from Ponte Leccia (north of Corte) to the east coast winds through the centre of the Castagniccia region, and to see it at a leisurely pace will take the best part of a day. Arm yourself with a picnic before you start, as there is little to be had in the way of supplies en route.

◁ Limestone cliffs of Bonifacio *(see p543)*

Golfe de Porto ❾

Corse-du-Sud. 🚶 🚌 🚓 *Ajaccio.*
🚌 *Porto.* ℹ *Porto (04 95 26 10
55).* www.porto-tourisme.com

Porto is sited at the head of
the Golfe de Porto, one of
the most beautiful bays in the
Mediterranean, which for the
sake of its fauna and flora has
been included in UNESCO's list
of the world's common cultural
heritage sites. The town has a
magnificent Genoese watchtower – the perfect spot for
admiring the sunset – and
regular boat excursions
(Apr–Oct) to the Calanche,
Scandola and Girolata.

The **Calanche** begin 2 km
(1.2 miles) out of Porto, on the
road to Piana. These 300-m
(1,000-ft) red granite cliffs
plunge sheer to the sea, and
are quite simply breathtaking.
They are accessible only by
boat or on foot: well-defined
trails start from the Tête du
Chien and the Pont de Mezanu,
while boat tickets are available
at Porto's Hôtel Le Cyrnée.

East of Porto are the Gorges
de la Spelunca, accessed by
a mule route punctuated by
Genoese bridges.

Just south of Porto along a
spectacular corniche drive
passing under granite archways, lies the pretty village
of **Piana**, a good base for
visiting this whole area, with
information on recommended
walks. One particularly
worthwhile destination is the
cove at **Ficajola** just below
Piana – a truly delightful beach.

Porto's marina and Genoese watchtower

Environs

The road over the mountains
from Porto to Calvi offers no
more than a taste of this
grandiose corner of
Corsica – you have to take
to the sea to view it
properly (ferries from Porto
and Galéria). **Girolata**, a tiny
hamlet north of Porto, can be
reached only by sea or via a
mule track (4 hours round
trip on foot) from a clearly
marked point 23 km (14 miles)
north of Porto on the D81.

At the mouth of the Golfe
de Girolata, the **Réserve
Naturelle de Scandola**, instituted in 1975, is the first land-
and-sea reserve in France,
covering over 10 sq km (4 sq
miles) of sea, and a similar
area of cliffs, caves and
maquis. Marine life is abundant in these clear, protected
waters; the birds include
ospreys, puffins and falcons.

CORSICAN FLOWERS

For lovers of wild
flowers, Corsica is a
Mediterranean
jewel. Much of the
island is covered
with maquis, a
tangle of aromatic
shrubs and low
trees which
flowers from late
winter onwards.
Among its dense
variety are the
showy rockroses,
which shower the
ground with short-
lived pink or white petals,
and brilliant yellow
broom. Grassy and rocky
slopes are good places to
spot the widespread tassel
hyacinth and the Illyrian
sea lily which grows only
in Corsica and Sardinia.

**Rock-
rose**

The town of Piana with the Calanche in the background

**Spanish
broom**

Illyrian sea lily

Tassel hyacinth

For hotels and restaurants in this region see pp594–5 and pp650–1

Cargèse's Greek rite church

Cargèse ⑩

Corse-du-Sud. 👥 1,000. 🚌 ℹ️ *rue du Docteur Dragacci (04 95 26 41 31).* **www**.cargese.net

Cargèse overlooks the sea from a promontory between the bays of Sagone and Pero. It is a small town with an odd history: many of the people who live here are the descendants of 17th-century Greek refugees from Turkish rule, given asylum in Corsica.

A few Cargèsiens still speak Greek, and their icon-filled Eastern (Greek) rite church faces its Catholic counterpart in an attitude that must once have seemed confrontational. Nowadays the old rivalries have vanished, and the Orthodox priest and Catholic *curé* often stand in for one another.

There are many splendid beaches in the vicinity, notably at **Pero** and **Chiuni** just to the north, and at **Ménasina** and **Stagnoli** to the south.

Ajaccio ⑪

Corse-du-Sud. 👥 60,000. ✈️ 🚢 🚌 📷 ⛴️ ℹ️ *3 bd du Roi Jérôme (04 95 51 53 03).* 🔄 *Tue–Sun.* **www**.ajaccio-tourisme.com

Ajaccio, a noisy, busy town by Corsican standards, was the birthplace of Napoleon Bonaparte in 1769. Napoleon never returned to Corsica after crowning himself emperor of the French in 1804, but the town – modern capital of nationalist Corsica – celebrates his birthday every 15 August.

The 16th-century **Cathédrale Notre-Dame de la Miséricorde**, where Napoleon was baptized in 1771, houses Delacroix's painting *Vierge du Sacré-Coeur*.

A few streets away, the **Maison Bonaparte**, where Napoleon was born and spent his childhood, contains family portraits, period furniture and assorted memorabilia.

Much more interesting is the art collection assembled by Napoleon's unscrupulous uncle, Cardinal Fesch, who merrily looted churches, palaces and museums during the Italian campaign and brought the swag home to Ajaccio. Housed in the 19th-century Palais Fesch, the **Musée Palais Fesch** contains the finest collection of Italian primitive art in France after the Louvre. Among its masterpieces are works by Bellini, Botticelli, Titian and Veronese, Bernini and Poussin. Next to the Palais Fesch stands the **Chapelle Impériale**, built in 1855 by Napoleon III to accommodate the tombs of the Bonapartes. From here, walk back along the quay to the Jetée de la Citadelle, which offers superb views of the town, the marina and the Golfe d'Ajaccio. The adjacent 16th-century **citadel** is occupied by the army.

🏛️ **Maison Bonaparte**
Rue St-Charles. *Tel 04 95 26 26 26.* 🔄 *Tue–Sun.* 🎫 🚫 **www**.musee-maisonbonaparte.fr

🏛️ **Musée Palais Fesch**
50 rue Cardinal Fesch. *Tel 04 95 21 48 17.* 🔄 *Wed–Mon.* 🎫 ♿ **www**.musee-fesch.com

Environs
From the Quai de la Citadelle there are daily excursions to the **Îles Sanguinaires** at the mouth of the Golfe d'Ajaccio.

At Vero, 21 km (13 miles) northeast on the N193, is an unusual park, **A Cupulatta**, with over 150 species of tortoises and turtles (Apr–Oct).

A statue-menhir at Filitosa

Filitosa ⑫

Centre Préhistorique de Filitosa, Corse-du-Sud. *Tel 04 95 74 00 91.* 🔄 *Apr–Oct: daily.* 🎫 🚫 📷 **www**.filitosa.fr

The 4,000-year-old, life-size stone warriors of Filitosa are the most spectacular relics of megalithic man in Corsica. Discovered in 1946, these phallus-like granite menhirs represent an interesting progression from mere silhouettes to more detailed sculpture, etched with human features.

The five most recent and most sophisticated figures (about 1500 BC) stand around a thousand-year-old olive

Statue of Napoleon by Laboureur in place Maréchal Foch, Ajaccio

For hotels and restaurants in this region see pp594–5 and pp650–1

The fortified Old Town of Bonifacio, with the harbour in the foreground

tree, in the field below a tumulus. Other finds, which include a heavily armed warrior with shield, helmet and sword, can be seen in the site's archaeological museum.

Sartène ⓭

Corse-du-Sud. 🏠 3,600. 🚌
ℹ️ cours Soeur Amélie (04 95 77 15 40). 🚘 summer: daily; winter: Sat.
www.oti-sartenevalenco.com

Sartene is a medieval fortified town of narrow cobbled streets and grey granite houses rising above the Rizzanese valley. Founded by the Genoese in the early 16th century, it has survived attacks by Barbary pirates and centuries of bloody feuding among the town's leading families.

Despite all this, Sartène has a reputation for deep piety, reinforced each year by the oldest and most intense Christian ceremony in Corsica, the Good Friday Catenacciu (literally, the "chained one"). A red-hooded penitent, barefoot and in chains, drags a wooden cross through the Old Town in a re-enactment of Christ's ascent to Golgotha.

Environs

In the town centre, the **Musée de la Préhistoire Corse** has a collection of Neolithic, Bronze and Iron Age artifacts.

🏛 **Musée de la Préhistoire Corse**
Bd Jaques Nicolai. **Tel** 04 95 77 01 09. ☐ May–Sep: daily; Oct–Apr: Mon–Fri. 🈂 🕭
www.prehistoire-corse.org

Bonifacio ⓮

Corse-du-Sud. 🏠 2,700. 🚍 🚢
ℹ️ rue Fred Scamaroni (04 95 73 11 88).
🚘 Wed. www.bonifacio.fr

Bonifacio is the southern-most town in Corsica, dramatically sited on a limestone and granite cliff peninsula with stunning views (see pp538–9). Its handsome harbour at the foot of the cliffs is the focus of life: cafés, restaurants and boutiques abound and boats depart regularly for neighbouring Sardinia and the uninhabited island of Lavezzi.

From the harbour, steps lead up to Bonifacio's fortified Old Town. The citadel, which was built by the conquering Genoese at the end of the 12th century, has long been the town's main defensive post, and from 1963–83 was the headquarters of the French foreign legion. From here, wander down to the tip of the promontory to see the three old windmills and the ruins of a Franciscan monastery.

Côte Orientale ⓯

Haute-Corse & Corse-du-Sud.
✈️ Bastia. ℹ️ Aléria, Salenzara, Porto-Vecchio. 🚢 Bastia, Porto-Vecchio. ℹ️ Aléria (04 95 57 01 51), Porto-Vecchio (04 95 70 09 58).

The flat, rather dreary alluvial plain stretching from Bastia to Solenzara has been rich farmland since 1945, the year it was finally drained and rid of malaria. More recently, holiday resorts and even high-rise hotels have mushroomed along the coast, cashing in on its long, sandy beaches.

The best sight in **Mariana**, which is otherwise uncomfortably close to the Bastia-Poretta airport, is the early 12th-century cathedral of Mariana known as **La Canonica**. A short distance away is the slightly older **Eglise de San Perteo**, surrounded by meadows.

About halfway down the coast, the port of **Aléria**, originally a Greek colony and the base for Rome's conquest of Corsica in 259 BC, is interesting for its rich archaeological heritage. Just outside town, a museum housed in the 16th-century Fort de Matra chronicles daily life in Roman Aléria.

Towards the southern tip of the island, the fortified town of **Porto-Vecchio**, built by Corsica's Genoese conquerors, is now an extremely popular seaside resort. The setting is perfect for the conventional seaside holiday, with umbrella pines, cork oak forests and glorious white sandy beaches within easy reach of the town, especially at **Palombaggia** and **Pinarello**.

The Golfe de Porto-Vecchio

TRAVELLERS' NEEDS

WHERE TO STAY

Many of France's 22,000 registered hotels are charming, idiosyncratic and good value. On these four pages, the types of hotel on offer are summarized and tips provided on what to expect from French hotels. The hotel listings pages *(see pp550–95)* describe some of the best hotels around the country in every price category and style, from slick, modern chain hotels to small, classic, family-run establishments. Also included are *chambres d'hôte* (a sort of French bed and breakfast), which range from simple farms to grandiose châteaux, as well as the best hostels. France is one of the most popular countries in the world for self-catering holidays and information is given on renting a rural home or *gîte*, and how to get the most out of a camping holiday.

The Hôtel Euzkadi at Espelette in the Pyrenees *(see p586)*

THE CLASSIC FAMILY HOTEL

If you're touring on a budget, the small, family-run, family-orientated hotel lurking in virtually every village and town is for you. It's likely to be the focal point of the village, with the bar and dining-room (if the food is up to standard) full of locals. The atmosphere is entirely informal, with children, cats and dogs happily at home. In the hotel's dozen or so bedrooms, old-fashioned charm will make up for a lack of sprightliness and, perhaps, the mere trickle of hot water from the shower.

The annual *Logis de France* guide details over 4,000 of these family-run, mainly one- and two-star hotel-restaurants. They tend to be located in small towns or rural locations; there are none in Paris. Most are no more than roadside inns, but off the beaten track you will discover many converted farmhouses and inexpensive seaside hotels. While the *Logis* is a useful reference source, the quality of places listed can be uneven.

THE CHATEAU HOTEL

Many of France's châteaux and mansions have been converted into luxury hotels. They include everything from Renaissance piles with sweeping lawns to medieval castles with battlements and keeps. Grand hotels can be found all over France, with rich pickings in the Loire, the Savoie, the Haute-Savoie and the Rhône delta. The properties included in the **Relais et Châteaux** brochure are recommended.

Typically, rooms are beautifully designed and the food is *haute cuisine*. Bedrooms range from grand suites to more simple abodes, often in converted farm-buildings, making it possible, if you're willing to forgo four-poster beds and antiques, to live in luxury without breaking the bank.

THE CITY HOTEL

Every big city has a clutch of hotels close to the train station or port. They range from cheap accommodation to a grand hotel or two. The most famous city hotels are the palace hotels in Paris and the Riviera resorts such as Nice and Cannes. Note that many city hotels do not have a restaurant or a salon and it is always worth checking the quality of the bedroom before you book it.

THE MODERN CHAIN HOTEL

Outlets of modern hotel chains are useful for inexpensive pitstops if you're travelling through France. Many are situated on the outskirts of towns by motorways or main roads. The cheapest are the one-star, no-frills **Formule 1** motels, offering bedrooms with a double and single bed and no en suite facilities.

Two-star chains include **Ibis/Campanile, Hotels Première Classe** and **Etap**. Three-star chains include **Novotel** and **Mercure**; both offer en suite accommodation and usually allow one child to stay with no charge, provided the

Le Négresco in Nice on the Côte d'Azur *(see p593)*

The Meurice hotel in the Tuileries Quarter of Paris *(see p555)*

whole family sleeps in one room (Novotel has free accommodation for two under-16s).

THE RESTAURANT-WITH-ROOMS

Throughout France, many upmarket restaurants also offer accommodation. Usually, the bedrooms match the restaurant's smartness and are priced accordingly. Sometimes, though, gourmet restaurants have simple bedrooms hidden away upstairs – great finds for those who like to splash out on food while saving on lodging. Refer to the restaurant listings on pages 600–51.

MEALS AND FACILITIES

In high season, many resort hotels insist on half board or *demi-pension* (a per person rate for the room, dinner and breakfast). There is also full board or *pension*, which covers lunch too. While it is cheaper to opt for inclusive rates, meals come from set or limited-choice menus, which often omit the more interesting dishes.

Many smaller family-run hotels do not provide meals on Sunday evenings and often stop serving dinner as early as 9pm on other days.

Rooms usually have double beds; twin or single beds must be requested when booking. All mid-range hotels have a choice of bathroom facilities. A short walk down the corridor to a separate bathroom can reduce the room rate considerably. A bathroom with a bath *(un bain)* is usually more expensive than one with a shower *(une douche); un cabinet de toilette* has a basin and bidet, without a bath, shower or a WC. If you do not have *pension* or *demi-pension* accommodation, breakfast is often charged as an extra. Go instead to the local café, as it tends to be cheaper and more filling.

Hôtel de l'Abbaye at Talloires in the French Alps *(see p580)*

GRADINGS

French hotels are graded from one star to five stars (the top five-star hotels are labelled "palace"). Hotels with two or more stars must have a lift where appropriate, a phone in every room and at least 40 per cent of their bedrooms en suite. Three-star hotels must offer breakfast in the room and have 80 per cent en suite rooms. Four- and five-star hotels must have room service, air conditioning and all of their rooms en suite.

PRICES

Rates, inclusive of tax and service, are quoted per room (apart from *pension* and *demi-pension* arrangements). There is usually a small supplement for a third person in a room for two, and little reduction for single travellers.

As a rule, the higher the star rating the more you pay. Rates for a double room start from about €40 per night for a one-star hotel and go up to €100 or more for a four-star hotel. Costs also vary geographically with remote rural areas like Brittany being the cheapest. For equivalent accommodation in fashionable areas like the Dordogne and Provence expect to pay 20 per cent more, and a further 20 per cent again for Paris and the Côte d'Azur. Prices vary seasonally too, with coastal and alpine areas putting up their tariffs by up to 50 per cent in peak periods.

BOOKING

Always book well in advance for Paris, and for hotels in popular tourist areas in July and August.

In seaside resorts, most hotels shut down from October to March and ski resort hotels often close in April, so phone ahead when travelling out of season to make sure a place open.

Reservations can normally be held with a credit card. If you want to make a booking while you are in France, there are tourist offices in all main cities, offering reservations up to 8 days in advance.

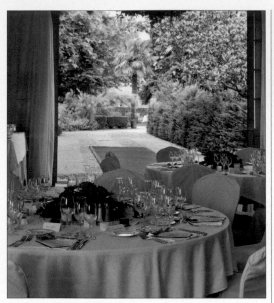

The dining room of the Hôtel de la Cité, Carcassonne *(see p589)*

BED AND BREAKFAST

French bed and breakfasts, called *chambres d'hôte,* come in all shapes and sizes, from tiny cottages to elaborate châteaux full of family portraits and antiques, plus some *fermes-auberges (see p597).* In all cases you will stay in a private home, and should not expect hotel services or amenities. Many offer dinner – *table d'hôte* – on request, where you usually dine *en famille.* Over 25,000 rural *chambres d'hôte* are registered and inspected by **Gîtes de France**. Look out for the yellow and green *chambres d'hôte* signs on the roadside.

Roadside signs also lead to many B&Bs that are not registered. Information on these is available from local tourist offices.

The Gîtes de France logo

SELF-CATERING

The *gîte* is a rural holiday home, often converted from a farmhouse or its outbuildings. A *gîte* holiday is a popular and relatively cheap way to see France, particularly out of season, but you must book many months in advance for the best *gîtes.*

Gîtes de France registers some 45,000 *gîtes*, all inspected and graded to indicate the level of facilities. You can book from a selection of 2,500 in the company's main brochure (available from the London office), or direct. Each of its 95 regional offices produces a booklet with all the *gîtes* in its *département*. These are also available through the head office in Paris, **Maison des Gîtes de France**, which itself publishes a series of listings catering for those with more specialised requirements.

Clévacances, another reliable organization, has listings of good quality *gîtes* throughout France.

France has plenty of other kinds of self-catering accommodation: expensive south-coast villas; ski resort chalets; city and coastal apartments. The *Allo Vacances* website (www.allovacances.com) provides a booking service for holiday lets throughout the different regions.

CAMPING

Eleven thousand official sites are spread around France's diverse countryside. The **Fédération Française de Camping et de Caravaning (FFCC)** publishes a comprehensive list, updated every year. Gîtes de France's *Camping à la Ferme* guide covers some simpler sites on farm land.

Campsites are graded from one to four stars. Three- and four-star sites are usually impressively spacious with plenty of amenities and electricity connections for a percentage of tents and caravans. One- and two-star sites always have toilets, a public phone and running water (though in one-star sites sometimes only cold water). What they lack in facilities they often make up for in peacefulness and rural charm.

Note, some sites only accept visitors with a **camping carnet**. *Carnets* are available from the RAC and the clubs listed on the facing page.

HOSTELS

Hostels are a money-saving option for single travellers, though cheap hotels are often no more expensive for those travelling with a partner.

The IYHF's Hostelling guide details the **FUAJ**'s (Fédération Unie des Auberges de Jeunesse) 220 hostels around France, open to all ages and offering dormitory accommodation. If you are not a member of the **YHA** (Youth Hostel Association) in your home

Holidaymakers enjoying the pool at a campsite in high season

country, you have to pay a small surcharge each time you stay in a French youth hostel. **UCRIF** (Union des Centres de Rencontres Internationales de France) has 50 centres with a cultural bent scattered around France. All have single, shared and dormitory accommodation and a restaurant.

In summer, you can stay in university rooms. Contact **CROUS** (Centre Régional des Oeuvres Universitaires et Scolaires) for more details. *Gîtes d'étape* are usually large farmhouses with dormitories close to walking, cycling and horse-riding routes. Gîtes de France's *Gîtes d'Etape et de Séjour* guide details 1,600 sites.

DISABLED TRAVELLERS

A number of associations publish information on accommodation throughout France with wheelchair access: the **Association des Paralysés de France (APF)**, the **Groupement pour l'Insertion des Personnes Handicapées Physiques (GIHP)**, and Gîtes de France's guide

The Carlton Intercontinental in Cannes *(see p592)*

Accessibles. APF have their own travel company, APF Evasion, to help organise a holiday. **Les Compagnons du Voyage** (part of SNCF/ RATP), can organise transport, escorted or not, on all public transport networks throughout France. There is also a useful website, www.guide-accessible.com, which lists, region by region, transport companies adapted for wheelchair access.

FURTHER INFORMATION

A selection of brochures can be obtained from **Maison de la France**, including *City Breaks in France* and *France's Cultural Sites*, as well as the magazine *Traveller in France*. The French Government Tourist Office distributes *Logis de France* guides, and all the booklets for château-hotels and château-B&Bs. However, it only distributes the *Relais et Châteaux* guide over the counter.

The first port of call for all non-hotel accommodation in the French countryside should be Gîtes de France, including for B&B (brochures available from their Paris shop).

When in France, local tourist offices are the best source of information for B&Bs and self-catering accommodation.

Loisirs Accueil are special booking agencies which deal with queries for hotels, campsites, *gîtes* and B&Bs in their area. A list of all 53 offices in France is available from the UK French Tourist Office.

DIRECTORY

CHAIN HOTELS

Campanile
Tel 0825 00 30 03 France.
www.campanile.com

Etap
Tel 0892 68 89 00 France.
www.etaphotel.com

Formule 1
Tel 0892 68 56 85 France.
www.hotelformule1.com

Hotel Première Classe
Tel 0892 68 81 23 France.
www.premiereclasse.com

Ibis
Tel 0870 609 0963 UK.
Tel 0892 68 66 86 France.
www.ibishotel.com

Novotel
Tel 0870 609 0962 UK.
Tel 0825 88 44 44 France.
www.novotel.com

Relais et Châteaux
Tel 0825 82 51 80 France.
www.relaischateaux.com

SELF-CATERING & B&B

Clévacances
Tel 02 51 47 71 07.
www.clevacances.com

Gîtes de France
59 St-Lazare, 75009 Paris.
Tel 01 49 70 75 85 or 0891 16 22 22 (chambre d'hôte). www.gites-de-france.com

CAMPING

Fédération Française de Camping et de Caravaning (FFCC)
78 rue de Rivoli, 75004 Paris. *Tel 01 42 72 84 08.*
Fax 01 42 72 70 21.
www.ffcc.fr

HOSTELS

CROUS
39 av G-Bernanos, 75231 Paris Cedex 05.
Tel 01 40 51 36 00.
www.crous-paris.fr

FUAJ (Fédération Unie des Auberges de Jeunesse)
27 rue Pajol, 75018 Paris.
Tel 01 44 89 87 27.
www.fuaj.fr

UCRIF
27 rue de Turbigo, 75002 Paris. *Tel 01 40 26 57 64.*
www.ethic-etapes.fr

YHA (Youth Hostel Association)
Trevelyan House, Matlock Derbyshire DE4 3YH.
Tel 0800 019 1700.
www.yha.org.uk

American Youth Hostel Association
8401 Colesville Road, Suite 60, Silver Spring, MD 20910. *Tel (301) 495 1240.* www.hiusa.org

DISABLED TRAVELLERS

APF
17 bd August Blanqui, 75013 Paris.

Tel 01 40 78 69 00.
Fax 01 45 89 40 57.
www.apf.asso.fr

GIHP
32 rue de Paradis, 75010 Paris.
Tel 01 43 95 66 36.
Fax 01 45 40 40 26.
www.gihpnational.org

Les Compagnons du Voyage
34 rue Championnet, LAC CG25, 75018 Paris.
Tel 01 58 76 08 33.
www.compagnons.com

FURTHER INFORMATION

Loisirs Accueil
www.loisirs-accueil.fr

Maison de la France Office
Lincoln House, 300 High Holborn, London W1V 7JH. *Tel 090 6824 4123* (within UK only). www.uk.franceguide.com

Choosing a Hotel

Hotels have been selected across a wide price range for facilities, good value, and location. All rooms have private bath, TV, air conditioning, and are wheelchair accessible unless otherwise indicated. Most have Internet access, and in some cases, fitness facilities may be offsite. The hotels are listed by area. For map references, *see pp154-169.*

PRICE CATEGORIES
The following price ranges are for a standard double room and taxes per night during the high season. Breakfast is not included, unless specified:
€ under €80
€€ €80–€130
€€€ €130–€180
€€€€ €180–€250
€€€€€ over €250

PARIS

BEAUBOURG AND LES HALLES Hôtel Britannique
€€€€   Map 13 A3
20 av Victoria, 75001 **Tel** *01 42 33 74 59* **Fax** *01 42 33 82 65* **Rooms** *40*

The Britannique has many repeat visitors, who return for the central location beside Châtelet, as well as the Grand Tour atmosphere and helpful staff. A real *hôtel de charme*, with beautiful, characterful rooms and an abundance of old-fashioned charm. **www.hotel-brittanique.fr**

CHAILLOT QUARTER Hameau de Paswsy
€€€   Map 5 B3
48 rue de Passy, 75016 **Tel** *01 42 88 47 55* **Fax** *01 42 30 83 72* **Rooms** *32*

In the heart of the residential quarter of Passy, a stone's throw from the Eiffel Tower and the Trocadero, Hameau de Passy lies in a private lane, which is an oasis of green. Guest rooms overlook the garden. Breakfast is included and can be served in your room, upon request. Wi-Fi access available. **www.paris-hotel-hameaudepassy.com**

CHAILLOT QUARTER Concorde La Fayette
€€€€   Map 1 C2
3 pl du Général Koenig, 75017 **Tel** *01 40 68 50 68* **Fax** *01 40 68 50 43* **Rooms** *1000*

The formulaic Concorde La Fayette with its fascinating tower (one of the few in Paris) is thoroughly high-tech. Its facilities include a fitness club, a bar on the 33rd floor, restaurants and a shopping gallery. The guest rooms afford truly splendid views over Paris and the Bois de Boulogne. **www.concorde-lafayette.com**

CHAILLOT QUARTER Hôtel du Bois
€€€€   Map 2 D5
11 rue du Dôme, 75016 **Tel** *01 45 00 31 96* **Fax** *01 45 00 90 05* **Rooms** *41*

Two minutes from the Arc de Triomphe and the Champs Elysées, Hôtel du Bois is ideal for haute-couture boutique-lovers. Behind a typically Parisian façade lies an interior rejuvenated by the designer Michel Jouannet. The decor is light and airy, with bold fabrics and bright art on the walls. **www.hoteldubois.com**

CHAILLOT QUARTER Costes K
€€€€   Map 2 D5
81 av Kléber, 75016 **Tel** *01 44 05 75 75* **Fax** *01 44 05 74 74* **Rooms** *83*

Not to be confused with the more expensive Hôtel Costes, this hotel is located just steps from the Eiffel Tower. It was designed and decorated by Spanish architect Ricardo Bofill, who used sycamore, stucco, marble and stainless steel to create a feel of luxury. Cool Asian-style guest rooms.

CHAILLOT QUARTER Hôtel Elysées Regencia
€€€€€   Map 2 E4
41 av Marceau, 75016 **Tel** *01 47 20 42 65* **Fax** *01 49 52 03 42* **Rooms** *43*

Colour is the central theme at this modishly decorated hotel right in the heart of the designer shopping district. Choose your room from a palette of blue, fuschia, aniseed (lime green) or lavender. The hotel also boasts a grand piano in the reception area, a panelled bar and a massage room. **www.regencia.com**

CHAILLOT QUARTER Hôtel Keppler
€€€€€   Map 2 E5
10 rue Kepler, 75016 **Tel** *01 47 20 65 05* **Fax** *01 47 23 02 29* **Rooms** *39*

After extensive renovations, the Keppler is a chic and refined four-star hotel. High ceilings throughout add to the sense of space, while the facilities in the guest rooms, such as plasma screens, satellite TV and allergy-free pillows, are welcome innovations. **www.keppler.fr**

CHAMPS-ELYSEES Royal Magda Etoile
€€€   Map 2 D3
7 rue Troyon, 75017 **Tel** *01 47 64 10 19* **Fax** *01 47 64 02 12* **Rooms** *37*

Just minutes' walk from the Etoile, in a quiet cobbled street, the Royal Magda Etoile is smartly decorated in varying tones of cream. Rooms are on the small side, but the staff are exceptionally helpful and friendly and will go out of their way to help guests, especially families. **www.paris-hotel-magda.com**

CHAMPS-ELYSEES Claridge-Bellman
€€€€€   Map 2 F5
37 rue François 1er, 75008 **Tel** *01 47 23 54 42* **Fax** *01 47 23 08 84* **Rooms** *42*

The Claridge-Bellman is a miniature version of the old Claridge Hotel and is managed by its former directors. The hotel has a truly traditional feel. It is quiet, sober and efficiently run, and is furnished throughout with tapestries and antiques. **www.hotelclaridgebellman.com**

Key to Symbols *see back cover flap*

CHAMPS-ELYSEES Four Seasons George V
31 av George V, 75008 **Tel** *01 49 52 70 00* **Fax** *01 49 52 71 10* **Rooms** *245* **Map** *2 E5*

This legendary hotel, dotted with salons, old furniture and art, lost a little of its charm when it was renovated. But it gained a stunning restaurant, Le Cinq, which boasts an award-winning chef and sommelier. There is also a great spa. Sheer opulence. **www.fourseasons.com/paris**

CHAMPS-ELYSEES Hotel Chambiges
8 rue Chambiges, 75008 **Tel** *01 44 31 83 83* **Fax** *01 40 70 95 51* **Rooms** *34* **Map** *6 F1*

An elegant, cosy hotel on a quiet street just 5 minutes' walk from the Champs-Elysées. Warm colours and a classically Parisian atmosphere suffuse the whole place. In warm weather, enjoy breakfast on the flowery patio. **www.hotelchambiges.com**

CHAMPS-ELYSEES Hôtel Vernet
25 rue Vernet, 75008 **Tel** *01 44 31 98 00* **Fax** *01 44 31 85 69* **Rooms** *50* **Map** *2 E4*

Gustave Eiffel (architect of the Eiffel Tower) created the dazzling glass roof of the dining room here. The impressive lobby has white and gold panelling, sumptuous red velvet curtains, antiques and marble flooring. The rooms are large and quiet with flat screen TVs and Wi-Fi access. **www.hotelvernet.com**

CHAMPS-ELYSEES Le Bristol
112 rue du Faubourg-St-Honoré, 75008 **Tel** *01 53 43 43 00* **Fax** *01 53 43 43 01* **Rooms** *187* **Map** *3 A4*

One of Paris's finest hotels. First opened in 1925, the Bristol's large rooms are sumptuously decorated with antiques and have magnificent marble bathrooms. The restaurant offers outstanding cuisine by chef Eric Frechon, winner of three Michelin stars. **www.lebristolparis.com**

CHAMPS-ELYSEES Plaza Athénée
25 av Montaigne, 75008 **Tel** *01 53 67 66 65* **Fax** *01 53 67 66 66* **Rooms** *191* **Map** *6 F1*

The last word in luxury, the legendary Plaza Athénée is popular with honeymooners, aristocracy and haute couture shoppers. The restaurant by Alain Ducasse is wonderfully romantic, while Le Bar du Plaza is now the hottest address in Paris for cocktails. **www.plaza-athenee-paris.fr**

CHAMPS-ELYSEES San Régis
12 rue Jean-Goujon, 75008 **Tel** *01 44 95 16 16* **Fax** *01 45 61 05 48* **Rooms** *44* **Map** *7 A1*

Since it opened in 1923 the opulent San Régis has been popular with the jet set, who are drawn to its quiet, central location. A particularly welcoming, intimate luxury hotel, it is full of antiques and overstuffed sofas. Some rooms have wonderful balcony views over the rooftops. **www.hotel-sanregis.com**

INVALIDES AND EIFFEL TOWER QUARTER Grand Hôtel Levêque
29 rue Cler, 75007 **Tel** *01 47 05 49 15* **Fax** *01 45 50 49 36* **Rooms** *50* **Map** *6 F3*

The Levêque lies between the Eiffel Tower and the Invalides on a pedestrianized street with a quaint fruit-and-vegetable market. The great location isn't the only attraction – guest rooms are well kept and the hotel also provides Internet access. **www.hotel-leveque.com**

INVALIDES AND EIFFEL TOWER QUARTER Hôtel Bourgogne et Montana
3 rue de Bourgogne, 75007 **Tel** *01 45 51 20 22* **Fax** *01 45 56 11 98* **Rooms** *32* **Map** *7 B2*

Situated in front of the Assemblée Nationale, this hotel has an air of sobriety. Its features include an old-fashioned elevator and an all-white circular hall with brightly coloured sofas. The guest rooms are decorated in a classical, aristocratic style. Extremely stylish. **www.bourgogne-montana.com**

INVALIDES AND EIFFEL TOWER QUARTER Hôtel de Suède St-Germain
31 rue Vaneau, 75007 **Tel** *01 47 05 00 08* **Fax** *01 47 05 69 27* **Rooms** *39* **Map** *7 B4*

Located near the Orsay and Rodin museums, Hôtel de Suède St-Germain offers elegant rooms, decorated in late 18th-century style with pale colours. Guests receive an exceptionally warm welcome. The deluxe rooms offer a view over the park. A lovely little garden to breakfast in completes the picture. **www.hoteldesuede.com**

INVALIDES AND EIFFEL TOWER QUARTER Hôtel de Varenne
44 rue de Bourgogne, 75007 **Tel** *01 45 51 45 55* **Fax** *01 45 51 86 63* **Rooms** *25* **Map** *7 B2*

Hidden beyond the hotel's severe façade is a narrow courtyard garden where guests breakfast in the summer. The bedrooms, furnished in elegant Louis XVI or Empire style, are impeccable. The hotel is popular with French government officials. **www.varenne-hotel-paris.com**

INVALIDES AND EIFFEL TOWER QUARTER Duc de St-Simon
14 rue de St-Simon, 75007 **Tel** *01 44 39 20 20* **Fax** *01 45 48 68 25* **Rooms** *34* **Map** *7 C3*

The Hôtel Duc de St-Simon is justifiably one of the most sought-after hotels on the south side of the Seine. This is a charming 18th-century mansion furnished with antiques, which lives up to its aristocratic pretensions. **www.hotelducdesaintsimon.com**

LATIN QUARTER Hôtel des Grandes Ecoles
75 rue Cardinal Lemoine, 75005 **Tel** *01 43 26 79 23* **Fax** *01 43 25 28 15* **Rooms** *51* **Map** *9 B5*

This hotel is a cluster of three small houses around a beautiful garden, where you can breakfast in good weather. The rooms are all comfortable and furnished with traditional 18th-century-style floral wallpaper; some open on to the courtyard. Internet and Wi-Fi access are available. **www.hotel-grandes-ecoles.com**

LATIN QUARTER Hôtel Esmeralda €€

4 rue St-Julien-le-Pauvre, 75005 **Tel** *01 43 54 19 20* **Fax** *01 40 51 00 68* **Rooms** *19* **Map** *9 A4*

The much-loved bohemian Hôtel Esmeralda lies in the heart of the Latin Quarter. With old stone walls and beamed ceilings, its charm has seduced the likes of Terence Stamp and Serge Gainsbourg. The best rooms overlook Notre-Dame cathedral. Breakfast is not provided here. **www.hotel-esmeralda.fr**

LATIN QUARTER Hôtel des Grands Hommes €€€

17 pl du Panthéon, 75005 **Tel** *01 46 34 19 60* **Fax** *01 43 26 67 32* **Rooms** *31* **Map** *13 A1*

Teachers at the Sorbonne frequent this quiet family hotel close to the Jardin du Luxembourg. It boasts a great view of the Panthéon from the attic rooms on the upper floor. The guest rooms are comfortable. Wi-Fi service is available. **www.hoteldesgrandshommes.com**

LATIN QUARTER Hôtel les Degrès de Notre Dame €€€

10 rue des Grands Degrès, 75005 **Tel** *01 55 42 88 88* **Fax** *01 40 46 95 34* **Rooms** *10* **Map** *9 B4*

An exceptionally friendly place to stay. The staff are genuinely welcoming and the wood-panelling and oak beams around the building make it even more special. Lovely, clean bedrooms with Internet access available. The Bar Restaurant and Tea Room serves great food at a low price. **www.lesdegreshotel.monsite-orange.fr**

LATIN QUARTER Hôtel de Notre-Dame €€€€

19 rue Maître Albert, 75006 **Tel** *01 43 26 79 00* **Fax** *01 46 33 50 11* **Rooms** *34* **Map** *9 B5*

The picturesque Hôtel de Notre-Dame overlooks Notre-Dame cathedral and the Seine on one side, and the Panthéon on the other. The furnishings are functional, but some rooms have beams or an old stone wall. The main appeal here is the location. The hotel has its own sauna and Wi-Fi access. **www.hotel-paris-notredame.com**

LATIN QUARTER Hôtel du Panthéon €€€€

19 pl du Panthéon, 75005 **Tel** *01 43 54 32 95* **Fax** *01 43 26 64 65* **Rooms** *36* **Map** *13 A1*

This hotel is managed by the same family as the Hôtel des Grands Hommes: the welcome is equally warm and the decor similarly Classical. Extra romance and luxury can be found in room 34 with its divine four-poster bed. Wi-Fi is available throughout the hotel. **www.hoteldupantheon.com**

LUXEMBOURG QUARTER Hôtel du Globe €€€

15 rue des Quatre-Vents, 75006 **Tel** *01 43 26 35 50* **Fax** *01 46 33 62 69* **Rooms** *14* **Map** *8 F4*

Occupying a 17th-century building by the Jardin du Luxembourg, the popular Hôtel du Globe provides excellent accommodation. The guest rooms are decorated with antique furniture and colourful fabrics. Breakfast is brought to your room. Reserve in advance. **www.hotelduglobeparis.com**

LUXEMBOURG QUARTER Aviatic €€€€

105 rue de Vaugirard, 75006 **Tel** *01 53 63 25 50* **Fax** *01 53 63 25 55* **Rooms** *43* **Map** *8 E5*

True to its Parisian past and long-standing family hotel tradition, the much-loved Aviatic combines bohemian style with modern comforts. The rooms are individually decorated with charming pieces found at local flea markets and warm, bright textiles. Parking is available for an additional fee. **www.aviatic.fr**

LUXEMBOURG QUARTER Hôtel Louis II €€€€

2 rue St-Sulpice, 75006 **Tel** *01 46 33 13 80* **Fax** *01 46 33 17 29* **Rooms** *22* **Map** *8 E4*

The charming, light-filled rooms of the Louis II are all individually styled. Each is characterized by exposed wooden beams, tasteful decor and great attention to detail. Rooms overlook rue St-Sulpice or rue de Condé. The suites in the roof are particularly appealing. **www.hotel-louis2.com**

MONTMARTRE Regyn's Montmartre €€

18 pl des Abbesses, 75018 **Tel** *01 42 54 45 21* **Fax** *01 42 23 76 69* **Rooms** *22* **Map** *4 E1*

Near Sacré-Cœur, this is an impeccably kept budget hotel. All the rooms are decorated with pastoral *toile de Jouy* patterns, and those on the top floor have views of the Eiffel Tower. Around the corner is Café des Deux Moulins at 15 rue Lepic, where Amélie worked in the film *Amélie*. **www.paris-hotels-montmartre.com/regyns**

MONTMARTRE Relais Montmartre €€€

6 rue Constance, 75018 **Tel** *01 70 64 25 25* **Fax** *01 70 64 25 00* **Rooms** *26* **Map** *4 E1*

In the heart of Montmartre's network of steep winding streets, this charming hotel is all femininity with delicate floral fabrics, antique furniture and painted beams. Quiet, intimate and romantic with the added bonus of being well situated for neighbourhood restaurants. **www.hotel-relais-montmartre.com**

MONTMARTRE Terrass Hôtel €€€€€

12-14 rue Joseph-de-Maistre, 75018 **Tel** *01 46 06 72 85* **Fax** *01 42 92 34 30* **Rooms** *98* **Map** *4 E1*

Montmartre's most luxurious hotel, the rooms here are comfortable and airy with neo Art-Deco touches and, in some classic rooms, bold stripes. The big draw is the restaurant, where in the summer fashionable Parisians take in a world-class view over the city. **www.terrass-hotel.com**

MONTPARNASSE Hôtel Apollon Montparnasse €€

91 rue Ouest, 75014 **Tel** *01 43 95 62 00* **Fax** *01 43 95 62 10* **Rooms** *33* **Map** *11 C3*

Close to the Parc des Expositions of the Porte de Versailles, the Apollon Montparnasse is decorated with Grecian statues and fine furnishings. The guest rooms are simple, but well equipped. Parking is available for an additional fee. The hotel also provides Wi-Fi facilities. **www.paris-hotel-paris.net**

MONTPARNASSE Hôtel Delambre Montparnasse   €€€   Map 12 D2

35 rue Delambre, 75014 **Tel** *01 43 20 66 31* **Fax** *01 45 38 91 76* **Rooms** *30*

Located a few steps from Montparnasse cemetery, and close to the Jardin de Luxembourg and the Latin Quarter, this hotel mixes modern and classical styles. Guest rooms are simply furnished, with all modern conveniences. **www.delambre-paris-hotel.com**

MONTPARNASSE Hôtel Le Ste Beuve   €€€€   Map 12 D1

9 rue Ste Beuve, 75006 **Tel** *01 45 48 20 07* **Fax** *01 45 48 67 52* **Rooms** *22*

The Ste-Beuve is a small, carefully restored hotel for aesthetes and habitués of the Rive Gauche galleries. There is a fireplace in the hall, the rooms are pleasantly decorated in pastel shades and several modern paintings add to the atmosphere. **www.hotel-sainte-beuve.fr**

MONTPARNASSE Villa des Artistes   €€€€   Map 12 D2

9 rue de la Grande Chaumière, 75006 **Tel** *01 43 26 60 86* **Fax** *01 43 54 73 70* **Rooms** *55*

The Villa des Artistes aims to recreate Montparnasse's artistic heyday when Modigliani, Beckett and Fitzgerald were all visitors here. The guest rooms are clean, but the main draw is the large patio garden and fountain, where you can breakfast in peace. **www.villa-artistes.com**

MONTPARNASSE Le St-Grégoire   €€€€€   Map 7 C5

43 rue de l'Abbé Grégoire, 75006 **Tel** *01 45 48 23 23* **Fax** *01 45 48 33 95* **Rooms** *20*

Le St-Grégoire is a fashionable townhouse hotel with immaculately decorated guest rooms with 19th-century furnishings. Book a room with a delightful private terrace. At the centre of the drawing room is a charming fireplace. Parking is available for an additional fee. **www.paris-hotel-saintgregoire.com**

OPERA QUARTER Ambassador   €€€€€   Map 4 E4

16 bd Haussmann, 75009 **Tel** *01 44 83 40 40* **Fax** *01 42 46 19 84* **Rooms** *297*

One of Paris's best Art Deco hotels, the Ambassador has been restored to its former glory with plush carpeting and antique furniture. The ground floor has pink marble columns, Baccarat crystal chandeliers and Aubusson tapestries. The restaurant, 16 Haussmann, is popular with Parisian gourmets. **www.ambassador.paris.radissonsas.com**

OPERA QUARTER Edouard VII Hotel   €€€€€   Map 4 E5

39 av de l'Opéra, 75002 **Tel** *01 42 61 56 90* **Fax** *01 42 61 47 73* **Rooms** *70*

The only hotel on the impressive Avenue de l'Opéra, the Edouard VII is centrally located between the Louvre and the Opéra Garnier, which makes it perfect for sightseeing. Request a room at the front for a breathtaking view over the Opéra House. **www.edouard7hotel.com**

OPERA QUARTER Le Grand Hôtel Intercontinental   €€€€€   Map 4 D5

2 rue Scribe, 75009 **Tel** *01 40 07 32 32* **Fax** *01 42 66 12 51* **Rooms** *470*

Directly next to the Opéra Garnier, this hotel is a sumptuous example of good taste. The rooms all have pictures with a musical theme reflecting the hotel's location. The opulent restaurant, the Café de La Paix, is renowned in the Opéra Quarter. **www.IHG.com**

ST-GERMAIN-DES-PRES Grand Hôtel des Balcons   €€   Map 8 F5

3 rue Casimir Delavigne, 75006 **Tel** *01 46 34 78 50* **Fax** *01 46 34 06 27* **Rooms** *50*

Embellished with Art Nouveau features, this hotel has a beautiful hall with stained-glass windows and striking 19th-century-style lamps and wood panelling. Most guest rooms, quiet and well-decorated, enjoy a balcony. High-speed Internet access with Wi-Fi is available. **www.hotelgrandsbalcons.com**

ST-GERMAIN-DES-PRES Hôtel des Marronniers   €€€   Map 8 E3

21 rue Jacob, 75006 **Tel** *01 43 25 30 60* **Fax** *01 40 46 83 56* **Rooms** *37*

Situated between a courtyard and a garden, this hotel provides perfect tranquillity. The cosy rooms are decorated with country fabrics. Those on the fourth floor garden side provide memorable views over the Parisian rooftops and the St-Germain-des-Prés church steeple. **www.hotel-marronniers.com**

ST-GERMAIN-DES-PRES Hôtel du Quai Voltaire   €€€   Map 8 D2

19 quai Voltaire, 75007 **Tel** *01 42 61 50 91* **Fax** *01 42 61 62 26* **Rooms** *33*

Overlooking the river, this hotel was once the favourite of Blondin, Baudelaire and Pissarro, and has featured in several films. It is best to avoid the rooms facing the quay, as they suffer from traffic noise. Higher floors are quieter, though, and the views are superb. **www.quaivoltaire.fr**

ST-GERMAIN-DES-PRES Hôtel d'Angleterre   €€€€   Map 8 E3

44 rue Jacob, 75006 **Tel** *01 42 60 34 72* **Fax** *01 42 60 16 93* **Rooms** *27*

Once the British Embassy, the Hôtel d'Angleterre has retained many of the original features, including the fine old staircase, the exquisite garden and the salon mantelpiece. The guest rooms are individually decorated; many have exposed beams and wonderful four-poster beds. **www.hotel-dangleterre.com**

ST-GERMAIN-DES-PRES Hôtel des Sts-Pères   €€€€   Map 8 E3

65 rue des Sts-Pères, 75006 **Tel** *01 45 44 50 00* **Fax** *01 45 44 90 83* **Rooms** *39*

Situated in one of the old aristocratic mansions of St-Germain-des-Prés, this hotel has quiet, large rooms – the best has an outstanding fresco on the ceiling. The lounge bar is popular with authors from the nearby publishing houses. **www.paris-hotel-saints-peres.com**

ST-GERMAIN-DES-PRES Hôtel de l'Abbaye St-Germain   🖼️📧   €€€€€
10 rue Cassette, 75006 **Tel** *01 45 44 38 11* **Fax** *01 45 48 07 86* **Rooms** *44*   **Map** *8 D5*

A 17th-century abbey, just steps from the Jardin du Luxembourg, this charming hotel has a history as a preferred hideout for artists and writers. Its finely furnished guest rooms and apartments have been tastefully done up and provided with modern facilities. For a real splurge, there are four duplex apartments. **www.hotelabbayeparis.com**

ST-GERMAIN-DES-PRES L'Hôtel   🖼️📶🏊📧   €€€€€
13 rue des Beaux-Arts, 75006 **Tel** *01 44 41 99 00* **Fax** *01 43 25 64 81* **Rooms** *20*   **Map** *8 E3*

A riot of exuberance and opulence, this Jacques Garcia-designed hotel is gloriously decadent. Each room is unique; the Oscar Wilde suite, where the Irish author died and which boasts period furnishings, is the most famous. There's also a beautiful spa and a restaurant with one Michelin star. **www.l-hotel.com**

ST-GERMAIN-DES-PRES Lutétia   🖼️🅿️📶🏊📺📧   €€€€€
45 bd Raspail, 75006 **Tel** *01 49 54 46 46* **Fax** *01 49 54 46 00* **Rooms** *230*   **Map** *8 D4*

The Lutétia is a mainstay of glamour on the south side of the river. The building's style is partly Art Nouveau and partly Art Deco, and has been restored throughout. Publishers and chic shoppers are regular customers in the restaurant. The location is convenient. **www.lutetia-paris.com**

ST-GERMAIN-DES-PRES Relais Christine   🖼️🅿️📶📺📧   €€€€€
3 rue Christine, 75006 **Tel** *01 40 51 60 80* **Fax** *01 40 51 60 81* **Rooms** *51*   **Map** *8 F4*

Always full, the Relais Christine is the epitome of the *hôtel de charme*. Part of a cloister from a 16th-century abbey, the hotel is a romantic, peaceful haven. The guest rooms, especially the deluxe rooms, are bright and spacious. Wi-Fi facilities are available. Reserve in advance. **www.relais-christine.com**

THE MARAIS Hôtel Caron de Beaumarchais   🖼️📧   €€€
12 rue Vieille du Temple, 75004 **Tel** *01 42 78 14 15* **Fax** *01 40 29 06 82* **Rooms** *19*   **Map** *9 C3*

Pretty 18th-century-style fabrics and crystal chandeliers adorn this elegant boutique hotel. The rooms are cosy, yet not too small, with wooden beams and oodles of character. There are also 21st-century touches, such as Internet access and air conditioning. **www.carondebeaumarchais.com**

THE MARAIS Hôtel de la Bretonnerie   🖼️   €€€
22 rue Ste-Croix de la Bretonnerie, 75004 **Tel** *01 48 87 77 63* **Fax** *01 42 77 26 78* **Rooms** *29*   **Map** *9 C3*

Carved stone walls and an arched dining room in the basement are some of the charming features of Hôtel de la Bretonnerie, housed in a 17th-century mansion. Its spacious rooms, with beams and antique furniture, are each decorated differently. Service is warm and friendly. **www.hotelbretonnerie.com**

THE MARAIS Hôtel des Deux-Iles   🖼️📧   €€€€
59 rue St-Louis-en-l'Ile, 75004 **Tel** *01 43 26 13 35* **Fax** *01 43 29 60 25* **Rooms** *17*   **Map** *9 C4*

It's a privilege to be able to stay on the Ile St-Louis, and this converted 17th-century mansion offers an affordable way to do so. Here the atmosphere is peaceful, the small bedrooms are attractive and the lounge has a real fire. **www.deuxiles-paris-hotel.com**

THE MARAIS Hôtel du Bourg Tibourg   🖼️📧   €€€€
19 rue du Bourg-Tibourg, 75004 **Tel** *01 42 78 47 39* **Fax** *01 40 29 07 00* **Rooms** *30*   **Map** *9 C3*

This stylish spot was decorated by top interior designer Jacques Garcia and is extremely popular with fashionable visitors to Paris. The rooms are opulent and all bathrooms are fully clad in black marble. The beautiful interior courtyard is a pleasant feature. **www.bourgtibourg.com**

THE MARAIS Hôtel Duo   🖼️🏊📺📧♿   €€€€
11 rue du Temple, 75004 **Tel** *01 42 72 72 22* **Fax** *01 42 72 03 53* **Rooms** *58*   **Map** *9 B3*

A family-run hotel for three generations, the former Axial Beaubourg is still in the same hands, but has been given a trendy makeover. The stylish, contemporary decor features teal and brown, and there is a bijou bar and Japanese garden – all just steps from the Pompidou Centre. **www.duo-paris.com**

THE MARAIS St-Paul-le-Marais   🖼️📧   €€€€
8 rue de Sévigné, 75004 **Tel** *01 48 04 97 27* **Fax** *01 48 87 37 04* **Rooms** *28*   **Map** *10 D3*

Close to the historic place des Vosges, this hotel has wooden beams and old stone, with simple and modern furniture. Request a room facing the courtyard to avoid the noise of traffic coming from the rue de Sévigné. **www.hotelparissaintpaullemarais.com**

THE MARAIS Murano Urban Resort   🖼️🅿️📶🏊📺📧♿   €€€€€
13 bd du Temple, 75003 **Tel** *01 42 71 20 00* **Fax** *01 42 71 21 01* **Rooms** *52*   **Map** *10 D1*

The über-hip and sleek Murano is the Marais' most luxurious hotel. Rooms feature huge Pop Art representations of 20th-century idols and have coloured lighting that changes to suit your every mood. An equally cool bar and restaurant complete the glamorous scene. **www.muranoresort.com**

THE MARAIS Pavillon de la Reine   🖼️🅿️📺📧   €€€€€
28 pl des Vosges, 75003 **Tel** *01 40 29 19 19* **Fax** *01 40 29 19 20* **Rooms** *56*   **Map** *10 D3*

Set back from the marvellous place des Vosges, the Pavillon de la Reine is the best hotel in the Marais. Incredibly romantic, the hotel has a peaceful courtyard and sumptuous guest rooms, furnished with excellent reproduction antiques. **www.pavillon-de-la-reine.com**

Key to Price Guide *see p550* **Key to Symbols** *see back cover flap*

TUILERIES QUARTER Hôtel Louvre Ste Anne

€€€ Map 8 E1

32 rue Ste Anne, 75001 **Tel** *01 40 20 02 35* **Fax** *01 40 15 91 13* **Rooms** *20*

A small pleasant hotel located 5 minutes' walk from the Louvre and Opéra. The hotel may be due for a makeover, but the rooms are clean, the staff are helpful and there is a splendid reception area with a *trompe l'oeil* painting. A popular hotel with Japanese guests who frequent the nearby sushi restaurants. **www.paris-hotel-louvre.com**

TUILERIES QUARTER Brighton

€€€€ Map 8 D1

218 rue de Rivoli, 75001 **Tel** *01 47 03 61 61* **Fax** *01 42 60 41 78* **Rooms** *65*

A real insiders' location, the Brighton provides a much-sought-after Rivoli address without the sky-high prices. The guest rooms have beautiful, high ceilings and large windows that look out either over the Jardin des Tuileries or over the courtyard. **www.espritdefrance.com**

TUILERIES QUARTER Hôtel du Louvre

€€€€ Map 8 E1

Pl André Malraux, 75001 **Tel** *01 44 58 38 38* **Fax** *01 44 58 38 01* **Rooms** *177*

This, the first luxury hotel in France, was built in 1855 by order of Napoleon III. The lavish rooms have spectacular views: the Pissarro Suite is where the artist painted his view of the place du Théâtre Français. Parisians regularly pop into the buzzing brasserie for lunch. **www.hoteldulouvre.com**

TUILERIES QUARTER Hôtel de Crillon

€€€€€ Map 7 C1

10 pl de la Concorde, 75008 **Tel** *01 44 71 15 00* **Fax** *01 44 71 15 02* **Rooms** *147*

With its magnificent location on the glittering place de la Concorde, the Crillon offers unsurpassed elegance. The hotel has a fine Royal Suite and terrace, a sublime dining room and a fashionable bar designed by French fashion designer, Sonia Rykiel. **www.crillon.com**

TUILERIES QUARTER Meurice

€€€€€ Map 8 D1

228 rue de Rivoli, 75001 **Tel** *01 44 58 10 10* **Fax** *01 44 58 10 15* **Rooms** *150*

The Meurice is a perfect example of successful restoration, with excellent replicas of the original plasterwork and furnishings. The staff here are unfailingly helpful and the hotel offers personalized shopping and art-buying tours. The hotel's spa is first rate and the only place in Paris to offer Valmont products. **www.lemeurice.com**

TUILERIES QUARTER Ritz

€€€€€ Map 4 D5

15 pl Vendôme, 75001 **Tel** *01 43 16 30 70* **Fax** *01 43 16 45 38* **Rooms** *162*

A legendary address, the Ritz still lives up to its reputation, combining elegance and decadence. The Louis XVI furniture and chandeliers are all original, and the floral arrangements are works of art. The Hemingway Bar is home to the glitterati. **www.ritzparis.com**

ILE DE FRANCE

BARBIZON Hostellerie La Dague

€

5 grande rue, 77630 **Tel** *01 60 66 40 49* **Fax** *01 60 69 24 59* **Rooms** *25*

Located in an artists' village in the heart of the forest, this rustic ivy-clad manor house has a romantic setting. It is popular with Parisians, so book early. The bright rooms have pretty floral furnishings; there is also a modern annex. The traditional French restaurant is charming. **www.inter-hotel.fr**

BELLEVILLE MamaShelter

€

109 rue de Bagnolet, 75020 **Tel** *01 43 48 48 48* **Fax** *01 43 48 49 49* **Rooms** *170*

This concept hotel designed by Philippe Starck offers exceptionally low prices for non-refundable reservations; if you require flexibility, the prices increase. The contemporary rooms all have iMacs, satin-cotton sheets, and microwaves. There is a trendy lounge bar and restaurant too. **www.mamashelter.com**

ENGHIEN-LES-BAINS Grand Hôtel Barrière

€€€€€

85 rue Général de Gaulle, 95880 **Tel** *01 39 34 10 00* **Fax** *01 39 34 10 01* **Rooms** *43*

In the heart of this bustling spa town overlooking a lake, the Grand Hôtel lives up to its name. The interior was designed by Jacques Garcia. The rooms are luxurious, some in Louis XV style. The hotel has a traditional gourmet restaurant, a theatre and a casino. **www.lucienbarriere.com**

FONTAINEBLEAU Grand Hôtel de l'Aigle Noir

€€€€

27 pl de Napoléon Bonaparte, 77300 **Tel** *01 60 74 60 00* **Fax** *01 60 74 60 01* **Rooms** *18*

This prestigious mansion overlooks Fontainebleau château and its vast park. The elegant rooms are decorated in styles ranging from Louis XIII to Napoleon III. The conciergerie can organize a host of activities in the area and the bar serves snacks all day. **www.hotelaiglenoir.com**

MAFFLIERS Château de Maffliers

€€

Allée des Marronniers, 95560 **Tel** *01 34 08 35 35* **Fax** *01 34 08 35 00* **Rooms** *99*

This 19th-century château lies in the heart of the L'Isle d'Adam forest, surrounded by a huge private park. The contemporary guest rooms have all modern conveniences including WiFi. Some non-smoking and wheelchair-accessible rooms. Bikes available to explore the forest. **www.accorhotels.com**

ROISSY-CHARLES-DE-GAULLE Sheraton Paris Airport €€€€

Terminal 2, Charles de Gaulle airport, Roissy, 95716 **Tel** *01 49 19 70 70* **Fax** *01 49 19 70 71* **Rooms** *252*

This state-of-the-art Sheraton is actually built in to Terminal 2 and guarantees the longest lie-in to anyone with a morning flight. Its neat and comfortable rooms have plenty of amenities and triple glazing, which means you can watch the planes taxiing by without hearing a thing. **www.sheratonparisairport.fr**

ST-GERMAIN-EN-LAYE Pavillon Henri IV €€€

19-21 rue Thiers, 78100 **Tel** *01 39 10 15 15* **Fax** *01 39 73 93 73* **Rooms** *42*

This sumptuous hotel is housed in a historic lodge built by Henri IV. It was here in 1638 that Louis XIV was born, and later where Dumas wrote *The Three Musketeers*. There is a wonderful panorama of Paris, and a gourmet restaurant. The rooms are stylish. **www.pavillon-henri-4.com**

ST PRIX Hostellerie du Prieuré €€€

74 rue Auguste Rey, 95390 **Tel** *01 34 27 51 51* **Fax** *01 39 59 21 21* **Rooms** *8*

Located just 15 minutes by train from the Gare du Nord, this former *bistrot* now houses 8 spacious bedrooms, all individually furnished. The "Pompadour" is particularly grand and has a view of Paris in the distance. A copious breakfast is served, and there are restaurants nearby. Friendly, helpful staff. **www.hostelduprieure.com**

ST-SYMPHORIEN LE CHATEAU Château d'Esclimont €€€€

28700 **Tel** *02 37 31 15 15* **Fax** *02 37 31 57 91* **Rooms** *53*

This magnificent 16th-century fairytale château has a private forest, tennis courts, a golf course and a fitness circuit. This turreted building offers meticulously kept, comfortable rooms. The gourmet restaurant provides impeccable service. Dogs are welcome. **www.grandesetapes.fr**

VERSAILLES Hôtel de Clagny €€

6 impasse de Clagny, 78000 **Tel** *01 39 50 18 09* **Fax** *01 39 50 85 17* **Rooms** *18*

The welcome in this quiet hotel near the train station is genuinely friendly. The rooms are simply furnished and clean, but unremarkable. There are numerous restaurants in the vicinity, and the owners of the Hôtel de Clagny are only too pleased to offer guidance.

VERSAILLES Trianon Palace €€€€€

1 bd de la Reine, 78000 **Tel** *01 30 84 50 00* **Fax** *01 30 84 50 01* **Rooms** *199*

This is undoubtably the most splendid hotel in the region. Built in Regency style, the hotel offers gorgeous, luxury guest rooms. The gourmet restaurant, run by Brit chef Gordon Ramsey, is the jewel in the crown. There is also a spa and a hammam (Turkish bath) for guests. **www.trianonpalace.fr**

LE NORD & PICARDY

AMIENS Hôtel de Normandie €

1bis rue Lamartine, 80000 **Tel** *03 22 91 74 99* **Fax** *03 22 92 06 56* **Rooms** *28*

This pleasant hotel with a red brick and stucco façade stands in a quiet street near the cathedral and railway station. The rooms are spacious, with modern furnishings. The hotel has an arrangement with Le T'Chiot Zinc, an inexpensive traditional restaurant where meals can be taken. Parking is extra. **www.hotelnormandie-80.com**

AMIENS Victor Hugo €

2 rue de l'Oratoire, 80000 **Tel** *03 22 91 57 91* **Rooms** *10*

This friendly family hotel near the famous Gothic cathedral has a stone Bible carved into the façade. An old wooden staircase leads to the guest rooms. It makes an ideal base for exploring the city and is within easy walking distance of shops, restaurants and bars. **www.hotel-a-amiens.com**

BERCK-SUR-MER Hôtel Neptune €

Esplanade Parmentier, 62600 **Tel** *03 21 09 21 21* **Fax** *03 21 09 29 29* **Rooms** *63*

This excellent, ultra modern hotel is right on the seafront. The guest rooms are airy, many with a view. The rooms are fully adapted for disabled guests. The restaurant, with its impressive view, serves traditional local food, including seafood and steak. **www.hotelneptuneberck.com**

BOULOGNE-SUR-MER Hôtel Hamiot €€

1 rue Faidherbe, 62200 **Tel** *03 21 31 44 20* **Fax** *03 21 83 71 56* **Rooms** *12*

This lively portside hotel-restaurant has refurbished but somewhat old-fashioned rooms with plain walls, coloured bedspreads and dark furniture. The soundproofing is good. The Grand Restaurant has an excellent menu and a view; the less expensive Brasserie has a busy terrace. **www.hotelhamiot.com**

CALAIS Kyriad €

Digue G Berthe, 62100 **Tel** *03 21 34 64 64* **Fax** *03 21 34 35 39* **Rooms** *45*

Right on the beach, behind lines of old-fashioned bathing huts, is this modern hotel-restaurant. The guest rooms accommodate up to three people, and are wheelchair-accessible. The restaurant has a changing menu. **www.hotel-plage-calais.com**

Key to Price Guide *see p550* **Key to Symbols** *see back cover flap*

CAMBRAI Château de la Motte Fénélon

Square Château, 59400 **Tel** *03 27 83 61 38* **Fax** *03 27 83 71 61* **Rooms** *40*

Set in its own gardens, this 1850s château is handsomely decorated with grand guest rooms in the main building, and more modest rooms in the annexes. There is also a tennis court. The restaurant serves excellent traditional cuisine in a brick-vaulted cellar. **www.cambrai-chateau-motte-fenelon.com**

CHANTILLY-GOUVIEUX Château de la Tour

Chemin de la Chaussée, 60270 **Tel** *03 44 62 38 38* **Fax** *03 44 57 31 97* **Rooms** *41*

Just 20 minutes' drive from Charles de Gaulle airport, this imposing *fin-de-siècle* residence and its matching extension is a haven of luxury set in 5 ha (12 acres) of grounds. The dining room has beautiful wood flooring. There is a pleasant terrace, and facilities for disabled guests. **www.lechateaudelatour.fr**

DOUAI La Terrasse

36 Terrasse St Pierre, 59500 **Tel** *03 22 85 04 43* **Fax** *03 22 8506 69* **Rooms** *24*

This charming hotel has a sophisticated low-key interior and the owners' passion for painting is evident in the many canvases that grace the walls. The excellent restaurant offers a wide range of fish dishes according to the catch of the day and the cellar is stocked with a fine selection of vintage wines. **www.laterrasse.fr**

DUNKIRK Hôtel La Réserve

82 quai des Hollandais, 59140 **Tel** *03 28 66 50 21* **Fax** *03 28 66 74 44* **Rooms** *7*

This small, reliable hotel in the centre of the town provides a good base from which to explore the area. The attractive rooms overlook the Yacht basin, and on the ground floor there is a popular, reasonably priced restaurant serving a wide range of fish dishes.

FERE-EN-TARDENOIS Château de Fère

Rte de Fismes, 02130 **Tel** *03 23 82 21 13* **Fax** *03 23 82 37 81* **Rooms** *19 (plus 7 suites)*

In the background of this 16th-century hotel, set in vast grounds, are the ruins of the medieval castle of Anne de Montmorency. Each guest room here is unique, and the two dining rooms are splendid – with an amazing wine cellar, which can be visited. There are full facilities for disabled visitors. **www.chateaudefere.com**

GOSNAY La Chartreuse du Val de St Esprit

1 rue de Fouquières, 62199 **Tel** *03 21 62 80 00* **Fax** *03 21 62 42 50* **Rooms** *63*

On the outskirts of Béthune, this hotel is housed in an elegant château dating from 1764. Spacious guest rooms overlook the tree-filled park. There are three restaurants: the Chartreuse for the gourmet, Robert II for traditional cuisine and Le Vasco for trendier guests. **www.lachartreuse.com**

HARDELOT PLAGE Hôtel du Parc

111 av François Ier, 62152 **Tel** *03 21 33 22 11* **Fax** *03 21 83 29 71* **Rooms** *81*

A bright, airy and contemporary hotel with rooms that have balconies or terraces overlooking extensive grounds. The hotel is located less than 30 minutes' drive from fashionable Le Touquet and within easy reach of the coast and 2 neighbouring golf courses. There is also a good restaurant. **www.hotelduparc-hardelot.com**

LAON-VILLE HAUTE Hôtel La Bannière de France

11 rue Franklin Roosevelt, 02000 **Tel** *03 23 23 21 44* **Fax** *03 23 23 31 56* **Rooms** *18*

Housed in a coaching inn dating from 1685, this hotel provides a good base for exploring the ancient city of Laon. The excellent guest rooms have been fitted with all the modern conveniences. The dining room combines classic cuisine with Old World charm. **www.hoteldelabannieredefrance.com**

LE TOUQUET Hôtel Be Cottage

41 rue Jean Monnet, 62520 **Tel** *03 21 05 15 33* **Fax** *03 21 05 41 60* **Rooms** *25*

This contemporary hotel stands in the centre of town, near the beach. It is close to the covered market and the lively rue St Jean. The rooms are spacious and modern; non-smoking rooms are also available. The restaurant rotates its menu daily, with a buffet in the evenings. **www.hotelbecottage.com**

LILLE Hôtel Kanai

10 rue de Bethune, 59000 **Tel** *03 20 57 14 78* **Fax** *03 20 57 06 01* **Rooms** *31*

An elegant arcaded front marks the entrance to this entirely refurbished hotel situated next to the excellent Christmas market. The moderately-priced rooms are decorated in a pleasingly modern style. A library offers the day's newspapers. Children under 13 stay free. **www.hotelkanai.com**

LILLE Alliance Couvent des Minimes

17 quai du Wault, 59000 **Tel** *03 20 30 62 62* **Fax** *03 20 42 94 25* **Rooms** *83*

This converted 17th-century convent combines ancient and modern elements. Traditional Flemish brick arches surround the dining room with its sensational roof, while the guest rooms have benefited from the best of modern design. Some rooms are equipped for the disabled. **www.alliance-lille.com**

LONGPONT Hôtel de l'Abbaye

8 rue des Tourelles, 02600 **Tel** *03 23 96 02 44* **Rooms** *11*

Located between Soissons and Villers-Cotterets, this hotel is named after the 12th-century abbey opposite, and is nearly as old. The guest rooms are old-fashioned and comfortable. The popular restaurant serves *cuisine du terroir*, grillades and game in winter. **www.hotel-abbaye-longpont.fr**

LUMBRES Moulin de Mombreux   **P** **†↑**   €€€
Chemin de Mombreux, 62380 **Tel** *03 21 39 62 44* **Fax** *03 21 93 61 34* **Rooms** *24*

This romantic 18th-century mill, hidden in its own grounds on the banks of the river Bléquin, works its charm on all who visit. Guests fall asleep to the sound of a waterfall. The restaurant is furnished with antiques and fine exposed beams. **www.moulindemombreux.com**

MAUBEUGE Hôtel Shakespeare   **P** **†↑**   €
3 rue du Commerce, 59600 **Tel** *03 27 65 14 14* **Fax** *03 27 64 04 66* **Rooms** *35*

This is a functional and efficiently run hotel with friendly staff where you can stay without breaking the bank. It has an old-style frontage with a covered terrace for the bistro restaurant, which features a selection of grilled food. **www.shakespearemaubeuge.fr**

MONTREUIL Le Darnétal   **†↑**   €
Pl Poissonerie, 62170 **Tel** *03 21 06 04 87* **Fax** *03 21 86 64 67* **Rooms** *4*

A small hotel in the upper town of Montreuil, the rooms here are old-fashioned. The auberge is decorated with a host of pictures, knick knacks and copper ornaments. It also has a popular traditional restaurant, which specialises in fresh fish; book ahead. **www.darnetal-montreuil.com**

MONTREUIL Château de Montreuil   **P**   €€€€€
4 chaussée des Capucins, 62170 **Tel** *03 21 81 53 04* **Fax** *03 21 81 36 43* **Rooms** *18*

The only relais château in Nord Pas de Calais, this elegant manor house is located inside the ramparts of the Montreuil that was once on the sea, before the sea retreated. There are lovely gardens, and a fine restaurant with an excellent wine list. **www.chateaudemontreuil.com**

REUILLY-SAUVIGNY L'Auberge le Relais   **P** **†↑**   €€
2 rue de Paris, 02850 **Tel** *03 23 70 35 36* **Fax** *03 23 70 27 76* **Rooms** *7*

A good base for visiting the champagne cellars just over the border, as well as in Epernay and Reims, this hotel-restaurant has pretty, brightly coloured rooms and a pleasant conservatory overlooking a lovely garden. There is also an excellent gourmet restaurant. **www.relaisreuilly.com**

SARS-POTERIE Hôtel du Marquais   **P** **†↑**   €
65 rue Général de Gaulle, 59216 **Tel** *03 27 61 62 72* **Fax** *03 27 57 47 35* **Rooms** *11*

Originally part of a series of farm buildings, this is now a friendly, family-run hotel. The modern colour scheme complements the antique furniture and photographs. On sunny days, breakfast is served in the garden. There is also a private tennis court. **www.hoteldumarquais.com**

ST OMER Hôtel St-Louis   **P** **†↑**   €
25 rue d'Arras, 62500 **Tel** *03 21 38 35 21* **Fax** *03 21 38 57 26* **Rooms** *30*

At this stone-built former coaching inn you can see the arches where horses and carriages were led through to the stables. The hotel, which is well placed to visit St Omer, has disabled access, and the rooms in the annex have been refurbished. There is also a brasserie. **www.hotel-saintlouis.com**

ST QUENTIN Hôtel des Canonniers   **P**   €€
15 rue des Canonniers, 02100 **Tel** *03 23 62 87 87* **Fax** *03 23 62 87 86* **Rooms** *7*

An old town house has been elegantly converted into a comfortable, family hotel. It is surprisingly quiet despite being in the centre of St Quentin. Large spacious individual rooms with period features and some suites for families. Breakfast is served in a courtyard garden on fine days. **www.hotel-canonniers.com**

VERVINS La Tour du Roy   **P** **†↑**   €€€
45 rue du Général Leclerc, 02140 **Tel** *03 23 98 00 11* **Fax** *03 23 98 00 72* **Rooms** *22*

Steeped in history, this prestigious 17th-century château with its three towers was the site of German army headquarters in 1870, 1914 and 1940. General de Gaulle stayed here in 1956. The château has stately bedrooms, and a fine restaurant. **www.latourduroy.com**

WIMEREUX Hôtel St Jean   **P**   €€
1 rue Georges Romain, 62930 **Tel** *03 21 83 57 40* **Rooms** *24*

Located in the city centre, this hotel is situated within an attractive old building. Rooms are well decorated and brightly coloured. There is a spa and sauna for hotel guests and a golf course 3 km (1.5 miles) away. The bar is available 24 hours a day to residents. Space for parking is limited, so book in advance. **www.hotel-saint-jean.fr**

CHAMPAGNE

BAZEILLES L'Auberge du Port   **P** **†↑**   €
Rue de la Gare, 08140 **Tel** *03 24 27 13 89* **Fax** *03 24 29 35 58* **Rooms** *20*

This quiet country hotel just outside the historic city of Sedan has pleasing flower-filled gardens by the river Meuse, a theme reflected by the flowery fabrics in the guest rooms. The restaurant overlooks the river and surrounding countryside, and there is a lovely veranda. Closed 30 Jul–29 Aug. **www.auberge-du-port.fr**

CHALONS-EN-CHAMPAGNE Hôtel du Pot d'Etain   🔲 P   €€

18 pl de la République, 51000 **Tel** *03 26 68 09 09* **Fax** *03 26 68 58 18* **Rooms** *30*

Right in the centre of Châlons-en-Champagne in the heart of the champagne vineyards, this hotel is housed in an attractive building dating from the 15th century. The pleasant, renovated bedrooms are furnished with antiques. Enjoy homemade pastries and croissants for breakfast. **www.hotel-lepotdetain.com**

CHAMPILLON Royal Champagne   P 🔢 🏃 🗐 🔣   €€€€€

Bellevue, 51160 **Tel** *03 26 52 87 11* **Fax** *03 26 52 89 69* **Rooms** *25*

The ideal retreat for Champagne enthusiasts, this former coaching inn is now a relais château with a first-class reputation as a hotel and restaurant. The elegant bedrooms offer superb views over the vineyards and the Valley of the Marne. The wine list is outstanding. **www.royalchampagne.com**

CHARLEVILLE-MEZIERES Hôtel de Paris   P   €

24 av Georges Corneau, 08000 **Tel** *03 24 33 34 38* **Fax** *03 24 59 11 21* **Rooms** *27*

Le Paris is just 5 minutes' walk from the centre of the capital of the French Ardennes and its fine main square – the place Ducale. Fronted by a bourgeois residence, the hotel occupies three separate buildings. The modern rooms have been insulated for sound. Nearby are restaurants. **www.hoteldeparis08.fr**

COLOMBEY-LES-DEUX-EGLISES La Grange du Relais   P 🔢 🔣 🔣   €

26 route Nationale 19, 52330 **Tel** *03 25 02 03 89* **Fax** *03 25 01 51 81* **Rooms** *10*

Excellent refurbished country auberge, located just a short walk from the home of Charles de Gaulle and the memorial in his honour. This is a good base to visit Clairvaux abbey and the General's favourite champagne house, Drappier, in Urville. The quiet, spacious rooms are housed in the ancient stables. **www.lagrangedurelais.fr**

COURCELLES-SUR-VESLE Château de Courcelles   P 🔢 🔣 🏃 🔣 🗐   €€€€

8 rue du Château, 02220 **Tel** *03 23 74 13 53* **Fax** *03 23 74 06 41* **Rooms** *18*

A very special hotel, this perfect Louis XIV château was built in the 1690s. The buildings have been splendidly restored, with a fine restaurant, a special wine list, 20 ha (50 acres) of parkland, good sports facilities and disabled access. The trees still display shrapnel from World War I. **www.chateau-de-courcelles.fr**

EPERNAY Hôtel de la Cloche   🔢   €

3 pl Mendès-France, 51200 **Tel** *03 26 55 15 15* **Fax** *03 26 55 64 88* **Rooms** *19*

The best value inexpensive hotel in Epernay, the Hôtel de la Cloche is just a few metres from the church of Notre Dame and a short walk to the avenue de Champagne, where the famous names have their establishments. Guest rooms are bright with modern furnishings. **www.hotel-la-cloche.com**

EPERNAY Hôtel Villa Eugène   🔲 P 🔣 🏃 🗐   €€€

82–84 av de Champagne, 51200 **Tel** *03 26 32 44 76* **Fax** *03 26 32 44 98* **Rooms** *15*

This elegant 19th-century residence lies close to the famous Epernay champagne houses. The hotel has been sensitively refurbished with individually styled rooms; all are handsome, spacious and luxurious. Breakfast can be enjoyed in the luminous conservatory. **www.villa-eugene.com**

ETOGES Château d'Etoges   P 🔢 🏃 🗐 🔣   €€€

4 rue Richebourg, 51270 **Tel** *03 26 59 30 08* **Fax** *03 26 59 35 57* **Rooms** *28*

Now a grand private hotel (*chambre d'hôte*), the original medieval fortress was converted to a fairytale castle in the 17th century with fountains, much admired by Louis XIV. The building is protected by the *monuments historiques*. There is an excellent restaurant, and guests may use a boat on the moat. **www.etoges.com**

FAGNON Abbaye des Sept Fontaines   P 🔢 🏃   €€€

Fagnon, 08090 **Tel** *03 24 37 38 24* **Fax** *03 24 37 58 75* **Rooms** *23*

Originally a 12th-century monastery, rebuilt in 1693, this château hotel has the distinction of having hosted Marshal Foch, Emperor William II of Germany and General de Gaulle. There is a huge lawn and a childrens' play area, an 18-hole golf course, a restaurant and a quiet terrace. **www.abbayeseptfontaines.fr**

GIVET Les Reflets Jaunes   🔲 P 🏃 🗐   €

2 rue Général de Gaulle, 08600 **Tel** *03 24 42 85 85* **Fax** *03 24 42 85 86* **Rooms** *17*

Located near a forest in the Meuse Valley, Les Reflets Jaunes stands in the centre of this frontier town near Belgium. The city was fortified by Vauban and was the birthplace of Etienne Méhul, composer of the revolutionary song *Le Chant du Départ*. Restaurants are nearby. **www.les-reflets-jaunes.com**

HAYBES SUR MEUSE l'Ermitage Moulin Labotte   P 🔢   €

52 rue Edmond Dromart, 08170 **Tel** *03 24 41 13 44* **Fax** *03 24 40 46 72* **Rooms** *10*

In the heart of the Ardennes forest, this mill dating from the end of the 18th century houses a hotel and restaurant. The great cogs from the mill still adorn the dining room. Comfortable guest rooms are furnished in traditional style. The restaurant serves local cuisine. **www.moulin-labotte.com**

LANGRES Grand Hôtel de l'Europe   P 🔢   €€

23 rue Diderot, 52200 **Tel** *03 25 87 10 88* **Fax** *03 25 87 60 65* **Rooms** *26*

An old coaching inn on the main street of this attractive town, the Grand Hôtel de l'Europe has simple refurbished guest rooms, which are quieter at the back. The restaurant serves typical country food. Langres was the birthplace of Diderot, editor of the famous encyclopedia. **www.grand-hotel-europe-langres.federal-hotel.com**

MAGNANT Le Val Moret

P ⑪ ⚑ ⬥   €

Rue Maréchal Leclerc, 10110 **Tel** *03 25 29 85 12* **Fax** *03 25 29 70 81* **Rooms** *42*

This pretty, flower bedecked modern motel on the A5 from Troyes to Dijon is ideally placed to explore the Champagne route in Aube and Nigloland entertainment park for children. There is secure parking. The restaurant is good, with a recognized chef and quality wine list. **www.le-val-moret.com**

MESNIL-ST-PERE Auberge du Lac - Au Vieux Pressoir

P ⑪ 目 ⬥   €€

5 rue du 28 Août 1944, 10140 **Tel** *03 25 41 27 16* **Fax** *03 25 41 57 59* **Rooms** *21*

A typical half-timbered Champagne house in a village on the edge of the Lac d'Orient, Europe's biggest manmade lake, this hotel provides fantastic bird-watching opportunities, especially in April and September. The hotel is accessible for disabled guests, with a good restaurant. **www.auberge-du-lac.fr**

MOUSSEY Domaine de la Creuse

P   €€€

10800 **Tel** *03 25 41 74 01* **Rooms** *5*

Stunning rural *chambre d'hôte* in a beautifully modernized 18th-century courtyard-style farm, typical of this part of the Aube-en-Champagne. It is a 10-minute drive from the Michelin-starred restaurant, La Parentale. The combination is hard to beat as a base to explore this attractive area. **www.domainedelacreuse.com**

REIMS Hôtel Crystal

⌧ P   €€

86 place Drouet d'Erlon, 51100 **Tel** *03 26 88 44 44* **Fax** *03 26 47 49 28* **Rooms** *31*

This 1920s hotel in the busiest part of Reims is surprisingly quiet, with pleasantly decorated rooms. The lobby and elevator retain their Art Deco style, and there is a garden, where breakfast is served in summer. The nearby place Drouet Derlon has a choice of restaurants. **www.hotel-crystal.fr**

REIMS Hôtel de la Paix

⌧ P ⚏ ⚑ ⑪ 目 ⬥   €€€

9 rue de Buirette, 51100 **Tel** *03 26 40 04 08* **Fax** *03 26 47 75 04* **Rooms** *169*

This fine hotel is in the heart the city, within walking distance of the cathedral, the best restaurants and the high-speed rail station. The elegant central courtyard blends 15th-century architecture with modern touches, and is ideal for a drink or breakfast in fine weather. Spacious lounge and Champagne bar. **www.bestwestern-lapaix-reims.com**

REIMS Château Les Crayères

⌧ P ⑪ ⚑ 目 ⬥   €€€€€

64 bd Henry Vasnier, 51100 **Tel** *03 26 82 80 80* **Fax** *03 26 82 65 52* **Rooms** *20*

Superbly aristocratic château with every luxury set in an English-style park next to the Roman *crayères* – the wine cellars of the Champagne houses which have been cut into the chalk. There is a superb restaurant, one of the best in France. **www.lescrayeres.com**

SEDAN Le Château Fort

⌧ P ⑪   €€

Port des Princes, 08200 **Tel** *03 24 26 11 00* **Fax** *03 24 27 19 00* **Rooms** *54*

For years no one knew what to do with Europe's largest fortress. Now it hosts an exceptional hotel, under the banner of France Patrimoine, restored to the highest standards of the *monuments historiques*. Some rooms have disabled access, and there is a good restaurant. **www.hotelfp-sedan.com**

SEPT SAULX Le Cheval Blanc

P ⑪   €€

2 rue Moulin, 51400 **Tel** *03 26 03 90 27* **Fax** *03 26 03 97 09* **Rooms** *24*

Between Reims and Chalons en Champagne in the middle of prestigious vineyards, this excellent hotel is attractively furnished. The rooms open on to the delightful gardens on the river Vesle. The beautifully presented restaurant has a terrace with flowers. Hotel is closed 14–28 Feb, & Mon–Tue from Jan-Apr. **www.chevalblanc-sept-saulx.com**

ST-DIZIER Hôtel de Champagne

⌧ P ⑪ ⬥   €

19 av Jean-Pierre Timbaud Marnaval, 52100 **Tel** *03 25 04 49 61* **Fax** *03 25 07 11 91* **Rooms** *30*

This welcoming hotel, located in the outskirts of the town, has a cheerful breakfast room with a grand piano. Bedrooms are simply furnished but are clean, peaceful and have Wi-Fi access. Special rates apply at weekends. Facilities include a bar and a restaurant. **www.hotel-de-champagne.fr**

TROYES Champs des Oiseaux

P   €€€

20 rue Linard Gonthier, 10000 **Tel** *03 25 80 58 50* **Fax** *03 25 80 98 34* **Rooms** *12*

The finest hotel in Troyes, this is located by the cathedral in the town centre. The sheer charm of the restored 15th- and 16th-century buildings as well as top service never fail to impress. The planted courtyards and brick half-timbered walls make for a memorable stay. Snacks are served. **www.champdesoiseaux.com**

TROYES La Maison de Rhodes

P ⬥   €€€€

18 rue Linard Gonthier, 10000 **Tel** *03 25 43 11 11* **Fax** *03 25 43 10 43* **Rooms** *11*

A sister hotel to the Champ des Oiseaux, this is almost as grand, with stunningly restored 16th-century architecture, including brick and timber galleries and stairways. Though a newer hotel, it is just as popular. The hotel has disabled access, and an organic restaurant for guests who book a table. **www.maisonderhodes.com**

VIGNORY Le Relais Verdoyant

P ⑪ ⚑   €

Quartier de la Gare, 52320 **Tel** *03 25 02 44 49* **Fax** *03 25 01 96 89* **Rooms** *7*

Just outside the village of Vignory, this converted farm in a peaceful hamlet makes for a relaxing stay. It is a few kilometres from Colombey les Deux Eglises, where the great cross of Lorraine marks the resting place of Général de Gaulle. Excellent, reasonably priced restaurant. **www.le-relais-verdoyant.fr**

Key to Price Guide *see p550* **Key to Symbols** *see back cover flap*

WILLIERS Chez Odette   `P` `🍴`   €€€€
Rue Principale, 08110 **Tel** *03 24 55 49 55* **Fax** *03 24 55 49 59* **Rooms** *9*

Right by the Belgian border, this hotel is an exercise in contrasts – on the outside it looks like a country family hotel and bistro, but inside it is startlingly elegant, with ultra modern decor and furnishings. There is a gastronomic restaurant, a bistro and a bar. **www.chez-odette.com**

ALSACE & LORRAINE

COLMAR Hôtel St Martin   `🔲` `▤`   €€
38 grand' rue, 68000 **Tel** *03 89 24 11 51* **Fax** *03 89 23 47 78* **Rooms** *40*

Near the Schwendi fountain in the middle of Alsace's most picturesque town, this hotel comprises three houses dating from the 14th and 17th centuries and an inner courtyard with a Renaissance stair turret. There are a number of good restaurants on the doorstep. **www.hotel-saint-martin.com**

COLMAR Hostellerie Le Marechal   `🔲` `🍴` `▤`   €€€€
4 pl Six Montagnes Noires, 68000 **Tel** *03 89 41 60 32* **Fax** *03 89 24 59 40* **Rooms** *30*

This luxurious 16th- and 17th-century house, by the river Lauch in the old part of the city, is home to the Hostellerie Le Marechal. Some of the guest rooms have four-poster beds and views of the canal. The candlelit restaurant, A L'Echevin, faces the canal. **www.le-marechal.com**

DIEVE Hostellerie du Château des Monthairons   `🔲` `P` `🍴` `🏃`   €€€
26 rte de Verdun, Les Monthairons, 55320 **Tel** *03 29 87 78 55* **Fax** *03 29 87 73 49* **Rooms** *25*

This grand 19th-century château is in its own walled grounds, south of Verdun. Its features include two chapels, a heronry and a private beach on the Meuse. First-floor rooms are furnished with antiques; the others are modern. The restaurant has a terrace overlooking the countryside. **www.chateaudesmonthairons.com**

DRACHENBRONN Auberge du Moulin des 7 Fontaines   `P` `🍴`   €
1 sept Fontaines, 67160 **Tel** *03 88 94 50 90* **Fax** *03 88 94 54 57* **Rooms** *10*

Hidden in the forest, this auberge is run by the Finck family in typical rural Alsace style. The old-style bedrooms are situated in the converted 18th-century mill. There are exceptional-value meals on the terrace in summer. It is a great favourite with hikers. **www.auberge7fontaines.com**

EGUISHEIM Hostellerie du Pape   `🔲` `🍴`   €€
10 grand rue, 68420 **Tel** *03 89 41 41 21* **Fax** *03 89 41 41 31* **Rooms** *44*

This hotel is a former *maison de vigneron*, a wine-grower's house with vine-covered balconies. It is named in honour of Pope Leon IX, who was born in the village in 1002. His statue is nearby. The restaurant serves traditional local dishes. **www.hostellerie-pape.com**

GERARDMER Le Grand Hôtel   `🔲` `P` `🍴` `♒` `🔟` `🚻` `♿`   €€
Place du Tilleul, 88400 **Tel** *03 29 63 06 31* **Fax** *03 29 63 46 81* **Rooms** *90*

This may be the oldest hotel in Gerardmer but it has a thoroughly modern luxury feel. The charming decor chimes perfectly with the traditional Vosges setting. There is a relaxing garden, two pools and three restaurants. Nearby you'll find the famous lake, mountain scenery and low-land skiing. **www.grandhotel-gerardmer.com**

GUNDERSHOFFEN Le Moulin   `P` `🍴` `🏃` `▤` `♿`   €€€
7 rue du Moulin, 67110 **Tel** *03 88 07 33 30* **Fax** *03 88 72 86 47* **Rooms** *12*

A really beautiful conversion of a picturesque water mill has resulted in this unexpected *hotel de charme* on the edge of the northern Vosges. Rooms are authentic and comfortable and the hotel also has a very popular Michelin-starred restaurant, Le Cygne. Convenient for Strasbourg and the Maginot Line. **www.hotellemoulin.com**

JUNGHOLZ Les Violettes   `🔲` `P` `🍴` `♒` `🏃` `🔟` `▤` `♿`   €€€€
Route de Thierenbach, 68500 **Tel** *03 89 76 91 19* **Fax** *03 89 74 29 12* **Rooms** *22*

This is an imaginative and luxurious reconstruction of a charming sandstone Alsacien hotel. It has the feel and welcome of a large family home. A conservatory overlooks the surrounding countryside and there is a huge spa with saunas, hammams, two pools and a Jacuzzi. The restaurant is highly recommended. **www.les-violettes.com**

KAYSERSBERG Hôtel Constantin   `🔲` `P`   €
10 rue Père Kohlman, 68240 **Tel** *03 89 47 19 90* **Fax** *03 89 47 37 82* **Rooms** *20*

A beautifully restored 17th-century house in the centre of the old town conceals a hotel that has been modernized to create stylish rooms. Breakfast is served in the conservatory; other meals are available next door at the Relais du Château, owned by the same family. **www.hotel-constantin.com**

LA PETITE PIERRE Aux Trois Roses   `🔲` `P` `🍴` `♒` `🏃` `🔟`   €€
19 rue Principale, 67290 **Tel** *03 88 89 89 00* **Fax** *03 88 70 41 28* **Rooms** *40*

This hotel is in an 18th-century house in the middle of this attractive hilltop village. Some of the pleasant rooms have balconies, and there is a guest lounge with an open fire. Excellent value for money. The dining room serves traditional Vosgien dishes. The village is home to the Maison du Parc. **www.aux-trois-roses.com**

LAPOUTROIE Les Alisiers
P **11**   €€
5 rue du Faudé, 68650 **Tel** *03 89 47 52 82* **Fax** *03 89 47 22 38* **Rooms** *16*

This attractive hotel has grown out of a pretty converted farm dating from 1819. The refurbished guest rooms are decorated in country style. The terrace has fabulous views of the hills and valleys. From the dining room you can enjoy the excellent food and the view at the same time. **www.alisiers.com**

LUNEVILLE Château d'Adoménil
P **11** **≋** **大** **目**   €€€€
54300 **Tel** *03 83 74 04 81* **Fax** *03 83 74 21 78* **Rooms** *14*

This imposing Relais Château in an extensive park on the river Meurthe is not far from the 18th-century splendours of Nancy. The guest rooms are splendidly bourgeois in the château itself or Provençal in theme in the beautiful outbuildings. The restaurant is a gourmet rendezvous. **www.adomenil.com**

METZ Grand Hôtel de Metz
⌨ **P**   €€
3 rue des Clercs, 57000 **Tel** *03 87 36 16 33* **Fax** *03 87 74 17 04* **Rooms** *62*

A stylish hotel on a pedestrianized street in the centre of this fine, underrated city, with French and Prussian architecture. The hotel is an interesting combination of Baroque entrance hall and rustic rooms, near the cathedral and the covered market. Good restaurants are nearby. **www.hotel-metz.com**

NANCY Grand Hôtel de la Reine
⌨ **P** **11** **目**   €€€
2 pl Stanislas, 54000 **Tel** *03 83 35 03 01* **Fax** *03 83 32 86 04* **Rooms** *43*

Experience the Ancien Régime in Europe's finest Neo-Classical square – the stunningly restored place Stanislas. The hotel occupies the house originally built in 1752 for the steward to Stanislas, Duke of Lorraine, the last king of Poland. A host of famous visitors includes Tsar Alexander I of Russia. **www.hoteldelareine.com**

OBERNAI Hôtel Restaurant des Vosges
⌨ **11**   €
5 pl de la Gare, 67210 **Tel** *03 88 95 53 78* **Fax** *03 88 49 92 65* **Rooms** *20*

A cheerful and welcoming small hotel by the train station, this is a mixture of old and modern buildings with a pleasant, traditional atmosphere. The rooms are exceptionally well kept. The restaurant is a cross between traditional Alsace and bistro style. **www.hotel-obernai.com**

REMIREMONT Hôtel du Cheval de Bronze
大   €
59 rue Charles de Gaulle, 88200 **Tel** *03 29 62 52 24* **Fax** *03 29 62 34 90* **Rooms** *35*

A former coaching inn, set behind the 17th-century arcades of this attractive town in the foothills of the Vosges, this simple provincial hotel is ideal for visiting the Vosges mountains. The Ballon d'Alsace is an easy drive, as is the World War I mountain battlefield Hartmannswillerkopf.**www.hotelchevalbronze.com**

SAVERNE Chez Jean
⌨ **P** **11**   €€
3 rue Gare, 67700 **Tel** *03 88 91 10 19* **Fax** *03 88 91 27 45* **Rooms** *25*

A four-storey traditional Alsace house in the centre of town, this was once a convent. The rooms are tastefully decorated in local style. There are good views of the surrounding hills. There is a sauna for guests' use. The Winstubs' Rosestiebele restaurant is on the ground floor. **www.chez-jean.com**

SELESTAT Auberge des Alliés
11   €
39 rue des Chevaliers, 67600 **Tel** *03 88 92 09 34* **Fax** *03 88 92 12 88* **Rooms** *17*

Set in the old town, part of this hotel-restaurant occupies a house dating from 1537. The city contained one of the finest schools in Europe; its unique library holds the *Cosmographiae Introductio*, with the first reference to America in print. Rooms are small and simple, with old-fashioned decor.

SELESTAT Hostellerie Abbaye de la Pommeraie
⌨ **P** **11** **目**   €€€
8 av Maréchal Foch, 67600 **Tel** *03 88 92 07 84* **Fax** *03 88 92 08 71* **Rooms** *13*

In the old city of Selestat, famous for its centuries-old library, this fine 17th-century building was once part of the medieval Baumgarten Abbey. The guest rooms are everything you would expect of a Relais Château, and there are two very good restaurants. **www.pommeraie.fr**

STRASBOURG Au Cerf d'Or
⌨ **11** **≋** **大** **目**   €€
6 pl de l'Hôpital, 67000 **Tel** *03 88 36 20 05* **Fax** *03 88 36 68 67* **Rooms** *43*

An inexpensive base for visiting the sights of old Strasbourg, this old-style, half-timbered Alsace family hotel has refurbished rooms throughout. The main hotel has more charming rooms, but the annex has a small pool and a sauna. There are several restaurants on the nearby waterfront. **www.cerf-dor.com**

STRASBOURG Hôtel Chut
11 **&**   €€€
4 rue du Bain aux Plantes, 67000 **Tel** *03 88 32 05 06* **Fax** *03 88 32 05 50* **Rooms** *8*

Two picturesque 16th-century half-timbered houses make up this hotel in the historic Petite France quarter of old Strasbourg. Within, old and contemporary have been successfully blended and a Zen ambience pervades. There is a good restaurant, and parking is possible by arrangement. One room has wheelchair access. **www.hote-strasbourg.fr**

VENTRON Les Buttes - L'Ermitage
⌨ **P** **11** **大** **&**   €€
L'Ermitage Frère Joseph, 88310 **Tel** *03 29 24 18 09* **Fax** *03 29 24 21 96* **Rooms** *62*

Two hotels in one in the Parc Naturel Régionale des Ballons des Vosges, a protected part of the Vosges at the foot of the mountains. Les Buttes has a gastronomic restaurant, while simpler, traditional food is served at the Ermitage. These hotels make an ideal base for skiing in winter or mountain walking in summer. **www.frerejo.com**

Key to Price Guide *see p550* **Key to Symbols** *see back cover flap*

NORMANDY

AGNEAUX Château d'Agneaux

Av Ste Marie, 50180 **Tel** *02 33 57 65 88* **Fax** *02 33 56 59 21* **Rooms** *13*

A 13th-century château hotel nestled in the intensely rural Vire Valley. Individual rooms preserve the character of the hotel with period furniture, parquet flooring and wooden panelling. Two restaurants are housed in the medieval farm buildings. Equidistant from Mont-St-Michel, the Cotentin Peninsula and the Normandy beaches. **www.chateau-agneaux.fr**

ALENÇON Hôtel des Ducs

50 av Wilson, 61000 **Tel** *02 33 29 03 93* **Fax** *02 33 29 28 59* **Rooms** *24*

Centrally located opposite the train station, this hotel is comfortable and well maintained. The bedrooms are modern in style and have simple, unfussy furnishings. Bathrooms are clean and functional. The pretty garden is a nice place to have breakfast in fine weather. **http://hotel-centre-ville.hoteldesducs-alencon.fr**

AUDRIEU Château d'Audrieu

Le Château, 14250 **Tel** *02 31 80 21 52* **Fax** *02 31 80 24 73* **Rooms** *25*

This 18th-century château was transformed into a luxurious hotel in 1976. A short distance from Bayeux, it has an immense park, providing wonderful views. The stunning guest rooms are elegantly furnished with period pieces. There is an excellent gourmet restaurant. The hotel is closed mid-Dec–mid-Feb. **www.chateaudaudrieu.com**

BAGNOLES-DE-L'ORNE Le Manoir du Lys

Route de Juvigny, 61140 **Tel** *02 33 37 80 69* **Fax** *02 33 30 05 80* **Rooms** *30*

A family *hotel de charme* offering childrens' breakfast, baby-sitting services (48 hours' notice) and a transport service to the station at Bagnoles sur Orne. There is plenty to do for the active – bike riding, climbing and tennis; and for the not so active there's billiards, ping pong, golf, cookery weekends and a local casino. **www.manoir-du-lys.fr**

BAYEUX Hôtel Bellefontaine

49 rue de Bellefontaine, 14400 **Tel** *02 31 22 00 10* **Fax** *02 31 22 19 09* **Rooms** *20*

Situated a few minutes' walk from the city centre, and within sight of the town's magnificent cathedral, this lovely 18th-century château is surrounded by a vast park. The rooms are spacious, and those in the converted stables are particularly suitable for families. **www.hotel-bellefontaine.com**

CABOURG Castel Fleuri

4 av Alfred Piat, 14390 **Tel** *02 31 91 27 57* **Fax** *02 31 24 03 48* **Rooms** *22*

A welcoming, unsophisticated *hotel de charme* with smallish but nicely decorated rooms and some family suites. Well placed in the town centre just 200 metres (650 ft) from the beach in this fashionable seaside resort. The pleasant garden is an added bonus. **www.castel-fleuri.com**

CAEN Best Western Le Dauphin

29 rue Gémare, 14000 **Tel** *02 31 86 22 26* **Fax** *02 31 86 35 14* **Rooms** *37*

In a quiet but central location, this old priory has been tastefully renovated, retaining original features such as the arched windows and stone walls. The rooms are comfortable; non-smoking and family rooms are available. There is a breakfast buffet, and a gourmet restaurant. **www.le-dauphin-normandie.com**

CAEN Hôtel Mercure Porte de Plaisance

1 rue Courtonne, 14000 **Tel** *02 31 47 24 24* **Fax** *02 31 47 43 88* **Rooms** *126*

An atmosphere of quiet elegance pervades, with every attention paid to the guests' comfort. The rooms of this chain hotel, centrally located opposite the harbour, are cosy and tastefully furnished. Disabled guests are catered for, and there is parking for an additional charge. **www.accorhotels.com**

CAMBREMER Château les Bruyères

Route du Cadran, 14340 **Tel** *02 31 32 22 45* **Fax** *02 31 32 22 58* **Rooms** *13*

This beautiful château, set in a large tree-filled park, is a prime example of First Empire architecture. Rooms – some housed in a neighbouring 18th-century house – are individually-styled. Marcel Proust is among the guests to have stayed here. The excellent restaurant serves a varied menu and specializes in local cider. **www.chateaulesbruyeres.com**

CEAUX Le Relais du Mont

La Buvette, 50220 **Tel** *02 33 70 92 55* **Fax** *02 33 70 94 57* **Rooms** *28*

South of Avranches, this hotel faces west and enjoys splendid sunsets over the bay of Mont-St-Michel. Le Relais du Mont offers decent-sized, well-maintained rooms. There are good facilities, family rooms and an excellent restaurant. **www.relais-du-mont.fr**

CHERBOURG Hôtel Renaissance

4 rue de l'Eglise, 50100 **Tel** *02 33 43 23 90* **Fax** *02 33 43 96 10* **Rooms** *12*

Good-value, well-maintained hotel with attractive rooms, each named after different flowers. The hotel is well located overlooking the harbour, and conveniently placed for the cross-Channel ferries and for the Cité de la Mer museum. The staff are very friendly. Limited parking is available. **www.hotel-renaissance-cherbourg.com**

CREPON La Ferme de la Rançonnière

Route d'Arromanches, 14480 **Tel** *02 31 22 21 73* **Fax** *02 31 22 98 39* **Rooms** *35*

An attractive fortified stone farm dating from the 13th century, featuring a typical closed courtyard with arched gateways. The rooms and the restaurant have been decorated in the same historic style. Only 3 km (1.5 miles) from the sea with golf courses all around and plenty of opportunities for sailing and bike riding. **www.ranconniere.fr**

DEAUVILLE Hôtel Normandy Barrière

38 rue J Mermoz, 14800 **Tel** *02 31 98 66 22* **Fax** *02 31 98 66 23* **Rooms** *290*

Deauville's landmark, this Anglo-Normandy manor house is a luxury hotel with beautiful, spacious rooms and fitness facilities. The large Belle Epoque dining room serves classic, traditional Normandy fare. Although it has been modernized, the hotel retains its 1920s charm. **www.lucienbarriere.com**

DOUAINS-PACY-SUR-EURE L'Etape de la Vallée

1 rue Edouard Isambard, 27120 **Tel** *02 32 36 12 77* **Fax** *02 32 36 22 74* **Rooms** *15*

A lovely villa set on the banks of the Eure river, this makes an ideal stopover for visiting nearby Giverny. Choose from cosy rooms with river views in the main building, or from the more modern and spacious rooms at the back. A pretty terrace overlooks the ornamental gardens. Restaurant serves good, classic dishes. **www.etapedelavallee.com**

ETRETAT Domaine St Clair

Chemin de St Clair, 76790 **Tel** *02 35 27 08 23* **Fax** *02 35 29 92 24* **Rooms** *21*

Stunningly situated with panoramic views of the village and cliffs of Etretat, this 19th-century Anglo-Norman château has comfortable rooms, some with private spa baths. The rooms are individually decorated with four-poster beds and period furniture. **www.hoteletretat.com**

FECAMP Le Grand Pavois

15 quai Vicomté, 76400 **Tel** *02 35 10 01 01* **Fax** *02 35 29 31 67* **Rooms** *35*

Built on the quay, this modern hotel has an attractive, marine-themed interior. The bedrooms are bright and spacious, and those at the front have balconies overlooking the port. There is a piano bar with live music on some nights. Good choice of restaurants within easy walking distance. **www.hotel-grand-pavois.com**

FONTENAI-SUR-ORNE Le Faisan Doré

Rte Paris, 61200 **Tel** *02 33 67 18 11* **Rooms** *16*

This decent-sized hotel is located in the Suisse Normande region, close to Argentan. The quieter rooms overlook the pretty garden. There is a well-stocked bar with over 140 different wines. Meals can be taken in the brightly decorated restaurant, or outside in summer. **www.lefaisandore.com**

GRANDCHAMP MAISY Hôtel Duguesclin

4 quai Henri Crampon, 14450 **Tel** *02 31 22 64 22* **Fax** *02 31 22 34 79* **Rooms** *25*

This friendly, modern hotel is located on the seafront promenade. The rooms are simply furnished and well maintained. The excellent restaurant specializes in seafood. Parking is available. This fishing port is a good base for visiting the D-Day landing beaches at Pointe du Hoc. **www.leduguesclin.eu**

GRANVILLE Hôtel Michelet

5 rue Jules Michelet, 50400 **Tel** *02 33 50 06 55* **Fax** *02 33 50 12 25* **Rooms** *19*

The hotel is close to the shops, restaurants and the casino in this charming historic port. An attractive Colonial-style building, tastefully renovated, with simply furnished, well-kept rooms, some with a view. Convenient for the beach and thalasso centre. Free parking. **www.hotel-michelet-granville.com**

HONFLEUR La Ferme Siméon

Rue Adolphe Marais, 14600 **Tel** *02 31 81 78 00* **Fax** *02 31 89 48 48* **Rooms** *34*

Ancient farmhouse mansion that was the haunt of the Impressionist artists from the Honfleur school. Now a luxury hotel, restaurant and spa centre. Beautifully converted guest rooms; spacious and charmingly furnished. The oak-beamed restaurant serves excellent food. **www.fermesaintsimeon.fr**

L'AIGLE Hôtel du Dauphin

Pl de la Halle, 61300 **Tel** *02 33 84 18 00* **Fax** *02 33 34 09 28* **Rooms** *30*

This fine stone-built inn has a lot of history, as it was established in 1618 and the original stables were razed during the bombardment of L'Aigle in 1944. Now a hotel that has been in the same family for over 60 years, it has a restaurant, a brasserie and a shop. The rooms are functional, and there is a comfy lounge. **www.hotel-dauphin.fr**

MACE Hôtel Île de Sées

Vandel, 61500 **Tel** *02 33 27 98 65* **Fax** *02 33 28 41 22* **Rooms** *16*

A rural hotel surrounded by a large park set in the heart of Normandy studfarm country. This traditional half-timbered former dairy is a friendly hotel with pleasant, cosy rooms in soft pastel tones. An ideal place to unwind and relax. Delicious food served in the comfortable restaurant. **www.ile-sees.fr**

MESNIL-VAL Hostellerie de la Vieille Ferme

23 rue de la Mer, 76910 **Tel** *02 35 86 72 18* **Fax** *02 35 86 12 67* **Rooms** *34*

An 18th-century farmhouse with several attractively converted outbuildings make up this Anglo-Norman hotel complex set in its own park near the beach. The guest rooms are romantically old-fashioned, with oak beams and great views. Rustic-style seafood restaurant. **www.vielle-ferme.net**

Key to Price Guide *see p550* **Key to Symbols** *see back cover flap*

MONT-ST-MICHEL Terrasses Poulard

BP 18, 50170 **Tel** *02 33 89 02 02* **Fax** *02 33 60 37 31* **Rooms** *29*

An old stone building at the heart of Mont-St-Michel with magnificent views over the bay, as well as the abbey and the gardens. The rooms are small but clean and comfortable. The hotel is under the same ownership as the famous omelette restaurant La Mère Poulard. **www.terrasses-poulard.fr**

MORTAGNE AU PERCHE Le Tribunal

4 pl Palais, 61400 **Tel** *02 33 25 04 77* **Fax** *02 33 83 60 83* **Rooms** *21*

Some rooms in this pretty hotel date back to the 13th century. It is a well-kept establishment with plush guest rooms and great baths. A stay here gives an experience of pleasant simplicity. The restaurant serves local dishes, on an outside terrace in summer. **www.hotel-tribunal.fr**

MORTAIN Hôtel de la Poste

1 pl des Arcades, 50140 **Tel** *02 33 59 00 05* **Fax** *02 33 69 53 89* **Rooms** *25*

On the spectacular Cherbourg peninsula, this attractive 19th-century house overlooks the lovely river in Mortain. A pleasant family-run hotel with comfortable, quiet rooms and good service. Fine restaurant with an excellent wine list. Disabled facilities and a private garage. **www.hoteldelaposte.fr**

OUISTREHAM Hôtel de la Plage

39–41 av Pasteur, 14150 **Tel** *02 31 96 85 16* **Fax** *02 31 97 37 46* **Rooms** *16*

The owners have refreshed this pleasing family hotel, which lies a short walk from the expansive beach. The rooms are large and comfortable, and there's an in-house sauna. To the west you'll find wartime sites like Pegasus Bridge; to the east the beaches with family activities such as kite surfing, sand yachting and sailing. **www.hotel-ouistreham.com**

PONT AUDEMER Belle-Île-sur-Risle

112 rte de Rouen, 27500 **Tel** *02 32 56 96 22* **Fax** *02 32 42 88 96* **Rooms** *24*

Set on an island in its own large garden of ancient trees and roses, the hotel has a fitness centre, sauna, and two pools (outdoor and indoor). The rooms are comfortable and elegant, ideal for a relaxing stay. Superb cuisine in the 19th-century rotunda. Closed mid-Nov–mid-Mar. **www.bellile.com**

PONT DE L'ARCHE Hôtel de la Tour

41 quai Foch, 27340 **Tel** *02 35 23 00 99* **Fax** *02 35 23 46 22* **Rooms** *18*

This attractive 18th-century Norman house sits at the river's edge, backing on to the village's ramparts. The interior reveals typical Normandy architecture with timber and brick walls. The good-sized rooms are individually decorated. Patio garden. Restaurants nearby. **www.hoteldelatour.org**

ROUEN Hôtel Notre-Dame

4 rue de la Savonnerie, 76000 **Tel** *02 35 71 87 73* **Fax** *02 35 89 31 52* **Rooms** *28*

This was the home of Bishop Cauchon, Joan of Arc's accuser, until his death in 1442. This hotel located between the cathedral and the Seine has spacious rooms decorated in contemporary colours. The staff are friendly. Good buffet breakfast. Choice of restaurants nearby. **www.hotelnotredame.com**

ROUEN Le Vieux Carré

34 rue Ganterie, 76000 **Tel** *02 35 71 67 70* **Fax** *02 35 71 19 17* **Rooms** *14*

City-centre hotel near the Musée des Beaux Arts and a short walk from the cathedral. This charming timbered 18th-century building hides prettily decorated, intimate guest rooms. Cosy atmosphere and attentive service. There is a shaded cobbled courtyard and tearoom. **www.vieux-carre.fr**

ST-LO Hôtel Mercure

5–7 av de Briovère, 50000 **Tel** *02 33 05 08 63* **Fax** *02 33 05 15 15* **Rooms** *67*

Opposite the town's ramparts, this modern hotel is attractive and quiet and has comfortable and well-proportioned guest rooms. The restaurant "Le Tocqueville" is in a large room with lovely views of the Vire river and serves regional specialities. There is also a cosy bar. **www.mercure.com**

ST-PATERNE Château de St-Paterne

Le Château, 72610 **Tel** *02 33 27 54 71* **Rooms** *10*

Henry IV's 15th-century love-nest is set in a private park just on the outskirts of Alençon. This is not so much a hotel as a family château, where a fixed menu is served *en famille* to guests in the candlelit dining room. Magnificent rooms with stately furnishings Closed mid-Dec–mid-Mar. **www.chateau-saintpaterne.com**

ST-VAAST-LA-HOUGUE Hôtel de France et Fuchsias

20 rue de Maréchal Foch, 50550 **Tel** *02 33 54 40 41* **Fax** *02 33 43 46 79* **Rooms** *35*

A lovely country house hotel near the fishing harbour of St-Vaast, renowned for its oysters. Country-style cosy rooms, most overlooking the exotic garden. The restaurant "Des Fuchsias" is set in a conservatory and serves delicious warm oyster dishes. Good buffet breakfast, too. Closed Jan–Feb. **www.france-fuchsias.com**

ST-VALERY-EN-CAUX La Maison des Galets

22 cour Le Perrey, 76460 **Tel** *02 35 97 11 22* **Fax** *02 35 97 05 83* **Rooms** *14*

Situated between the port and the cliffs, some of the rooms in this comfortable hotel overlook the harbour. Inside, old and new combine to create a pretty, relaxed ambience. The "chambre bleu" has a glorious view of the sea from the bathroom, and there are panoramic views of the waterfront from the restaurant. **www.lamaisondesgalets.com**

VERNON Hôtel d'Evreux
11 pl d'Evreux, 27200 **Tel** *02 32 21 16 12* **Fax** *02 32 21 32 73* **Rooms** *12*

This typical Norman building in the centre of Vernon, behind magnificent lime trees, is a former coaching inn with bright, sunny rooms and old-fashioned furniture. The restaurant, with its giant fireplace, serves innovative traditional fare. Parking is available. **www.hoteldevreux.fr**

BRITTANY

AUDIERNE Hôtel de la Plage
21 bd Emmanuel Brusq, 29770 **Tel** *02 98 70 01 07* **Fax** *02 98 75 04 69* **Rooms** *22*

Agreeable modern, good-value, family hotel situated on the beach. The rooms are characterized by cheerful marine decor and great views of the Bay of Audierne. Billiards can be played in the bar. Excellent seafood restaurant. Well placed for a tour of the sites of Finistère. **www.hotel-finistere.com**

BENODET Domaine de Kereven
Bénodet, 29950 **Tel** *02 98 57 02 46* **Fax** *02 98 66 22 61* **Rooms** *12*

A number of buildings attractively built in traditional style on the site of an 18th-century cider farm. Pleasantly furnished, characterful rooms overlook the expansive grounds. Just 1.5 km (1 mile) from the popular beaches at Bénodet and not far from the cathedral city of Quimper. Closed Dec–Mar.

BREST Hôtel de la Corniche
1 rue Amiral-Nicol, 29200 **Tel** *02 98 45 12 42* **Fax** *02 98 49 01 53* **Rooms** *16*

This modern hotel, built of local stone in the Breton style, is on the west side of the city near the naval base. It is conveniently located for walks along the scenic coastline. The rooms are simply furnished. The hotel restaurant offers a set evening menu four nights per week; reservations required. **www.hotel-la-corniche.com**

CARNAC Hôtel Tumulus
Route du Tumulus, 56340 **Tel** *02 97 52 08 21* **Fax** *02 97 52 81 88* **Rooms** *23*

This hotel is located near the pre-historic sights that make Carnac world famous. Refurbished, elegant rooms mix a Gustavian style with a touch of the Orient. There are fine views across the grounds onto Quiberon Bay. The pool, lush gardens, wellness centre and restaurant add to this hotel's appeal. Closed Dec–Feb. **www.hotel-tumulus.com**

CHATEAUBOURG Moulin Ar Milin
30 rue due Paris, 35221 **Tel** *02 99 00 30 91* **Fax** *02 99 00 37 56* **Rooms** *32*

Attractive water mill converted into a *hotel de charme* with two parts: the Hôtel de Moulin in the original mill and the more recent Hôtel du Parc. There are 100 different types of tree in the park, which has a river running through it and a tennis court. The first-class restaurant has a noted wine list. Closed 25 Dec–early Jan. **www.armilin.com**

DINAN Moulin de la Fontaine des Eaux
Vallée de la Fontaine des Eaux, 22100 **Tel** *02 96 87 92 09* **Fax** *02 96 87 92 09* **Rooms** *5*

Set in a wooded valley 5 minutes' drive from the port of Dinan, this converted 18th-century watermill overlooks its own lake and grounds. This is a *chambre d'hôte* only; there is no restaurant, but breakfast is provided. Simply furnished rooms, with disabled access. Private parking. **www.dinanbandb.com**

DINARD Hôtel de la Vallée
6 av Georges V, 35801 **Tel** *02 99 46 94 00* **Fax** *02 99 88 22 47* **Rooms** *24*

A completely refurbished and modernized hotel centrally located on the harbour front but away from the hustle and bustle of the resort. Choose one of the front rooms, as they have lovely views. The restaurant is the rising star of Dinard cuisine; excellent sea food as well as a choice of beef or duck. Closed Jan. **www.hoteldelavallee.com**

DOL DE BRETAGNE Domaine des Ormes
35120 **Tel** *02 99 73 53 00* **Fax** *02 99 73 53 55* **Rooms** *45*

This is part of a privately owned holiday resort with an 18-hole golf course, aquaparc, horse-riding school and adventure park. The guest rooms are charming – there are even 18 cosy tree-houses with rooms, accessible by rope ladder! The restaurant serves classic French food. **www.lesormes.com**

FOUESNANT Hôtel l'Orée du Bois
4 rue Kergoadig, 29170 **Tel** *02 98 56 00 06* **Fax** *02 98 56 14 17* **Rooms** *15*

Simple, well-furnished rooms with ensuite showers are excellent value; the rooms with just a wash basin are a bargain. A cheerful breakfast room is decked out in bright marine decor and there's a terrace for breakfast on fine days. The hotel is just a few minutes' walk from the beach at Cape Coz and the coast paths. **www.hotel-oreedubois.com**

ILE DE GROIX Hôtel de la Marine
7 rue du Général de Gaulle, 56590 **Tel** *02 97 86 80 05* **Fax** *02 97 86 56 37* **Rooms** *22*

Expect a warm welcome at this hotel in the middle of the beautiful island of Groix. This relaxing hideaway has charming guest rooms, which overlook either the sea or the garden terrace. At the restaurant, great care is taken in the preparation of fine fish dishes. **www.hoteldelamarine.com**

Key to Price Guide *see p550* **Key to Symbols** *see back cover flap*

LOCQUIREC Le Grand Hôtel des Bains　　🈂️ P 🍴 ≋ 🛖　　€€€

15 rue de L'Eglise, 29241 **Tel** *02 98 67 41 02* **Fax** *02 98 67 44 60* **Rooms** *36*

Convenient for visiting the Armorique Regional Park, this Belle Epoque spa hotel has gardens that lead to a sandy beach. Rooms have stylish contemporary furnishings, most with balconies. Beauty and health treatments are available. Restaurant open evenings only. The chef uses fresh, local produce. **www.grand-hotel-des-bains.com**

MORLAIX Hôtel de l'Europe　　🈂️ 🍴　　€€

1 rue d'Aiguillon, 29600 **Tel** *02 98 62 11 99* **Fax** *02 98 88 83 38* **Rooms** *60*

This Second Empire hotel, located in the city centre, has an elegant and richly decorated interior. The guest rooms are well equipped and soundproofed. Each room is different, from traditional to modern. Service is attentive. Buffet breakfast. The brasserie is good value. **www.hotel-europe-com.fr**

PENESTIN SUR MER Hôtel Loscolo　　P 🍴　　€€

La Pointe de Loscolo, 56760 **Tel** *02 99 90 31 90* **Fax** *02 99 90 32 14* **Rooms** *13*

A traditional building with slate roof, on a cape with magnificent sea views to both sides and good walking nearby. The rooms are comfortable; some have a private terrace. The breakfast is copious; half-board rates are good value. The restaurant serves rich cuisine. Closed Dec–Mar. **www.hotelloscolo.com**

PLEVEN Manoir du Vaumadeuc　　P 🛖　　€€

Le Vaumadeuc, 22130 **Tel** *02 96 84 46 17* **Fax** *02 96 84 40 16* **Rooms** *13*

This grand old manor house nestles in the Fôret de la Hunaudaye. The building dates from the 15th century, and inside the magnificent granite staircase leads you to the first-floor guest rooms. The wooded park around it has a beautiful rose garden and lake. Heliport and parking. **www.vaumadeuc.com**

PLOUBAZLANEC Les Agapanthes　　P 🍴 🛖　　€

1 rue Adrien Rebours, 22620 **Tel** *02 96 55 89 06* **Fax** *02 96 55 79 79* **Rooms** *21*

On the village square, this 18th-century hotel reveals a bright, modern interior. The rooms are clean and comfortable and prettily decorated in a maritime theme. There is an extension with more spacious rooms that are ideal for families. Most rooms have a view of Paimpol Bay, as does the terrace. **www.hotel-les-agapanthes.com**

PLOUGONVELIN Hostellerie de la Pointe de St-Mathieu　　🈂️ P 🍴 ≋ 🛖　　€€

Pointe de St-Mathieu, 29217 **Tel** *02 98 89 00 19* **Fax** *02 98 89 15 68* **Rooms** *23*

Situated near a lighthouse and ancient abbey ruins, this hotel was once a traditional farm but has grown into a modern hotel. The farmhouse now houses a restaurant serving sophisticated seafood dishes. The hotel makes a great base from which to explore the dramatic Atlantic coastline. **www.pointe-saint-mathieu.com**

QUIBERON Hôtel Bellevue　　P 🍴 ≋ 🛖　　€

Rue de Tiviec, 56173 **Tel** *02 97 50 16 28* **Fax** *02 97 30 44 34* **Rooms** *38*

Located near the seafront, casino and thalassotherapy centre, this modern hotel forms an L-shape around the heated swimming pool. The guest rooms are comfortable; the restaurant is airy and bright. Poolside buffet breakfast or Continental breakfast in your room. Demi-*pension* only. Private parking. **www.bellevuequiberon.com**

QUIMPER Hôtel Gradlon　　P 🛖　　€€

30 rue de Brest, 29000 **Tel** *02 98 95 04 39* **Fax** *02 98 95 61 25* **Rooms** *20*

Just 2 minutes' walk from the historic city centre, this hotel has charming, peaceful rooms – a few overlooking the enclosed flower garden and fountain. Some disabled access. Continental breakfast is served on the pretty veranda. Cosy salon bar with open fire. **www.hotel-gradlon.com**

RENNES Le Coq-Gadby　　🈂️ P 🍴 🛖　　€€€€

156 rue d'Antrain, 35700 **Tel** *02 99 38 05 55* **Fax** *02 99 38 53 40* **Rooms** *24*

An elegant 17th-century building just 5 minutes' drive from the city centre. Calm and intimate with classic period furnishings, polished parquet floors and ornate mirrors. The guest rooms "Olympe", "Louis XV", "Louis XVI" and "Anglaise" are vast and elegant. Spa and sauna next door to hotel. **www.lecoq-gadby.fr**

ROSCOFF Hôtel Bellevue　　P 🛖　　€

Bd Ste Barbe, 29681 **Tel** *02 98 61 23 38* **Fax** *02 98 61 11 80* **Rooms** *18*

This old Breton house, just a few minutes from the ferry terminal, enjoys fine views of the sea and old port. The guest rooms are a little cramped, but bright and quiet. At the back of the building is a pleasant patio garden where Continental breakfast is served on warm days. **www.hotel-bellevue-roscoff.fr**

ST MALO Hôtel Elizabeth　　P 🛖　　€€

2 rue des Cordiers, 35400 **Tel** *02 99 56 24 98* **Fax** *02 99 56 39 24* **Rooms** *17*

This hotel is located within the ramparts of the old town, just 2 minutes' drive from the ferry terminal. The building has a 16th-century stone façade. The interior is classic in style, if a little sombre. Rooms are comfortable and well equipped. Friendly owners, and private garage. Closed Jan. **www.hotel-elizabeth.fr**

ST THEGONNEC Ar Presbital Koz　　P 🍴　　€

18 rue de Gividic, 29410 **Tel** *02 98 79 45 62* **Fax** *02 98 79 48 47* **Rooms** *6*

Rustic, comfortable bed and breakfast. This 18th-century building, once a presbytery, has six spacious guest rooms. No television. Breakfast can be taken outside on the terrace. Mme Prigent, the owner, will prepare a three-course dinner if you reserve before midday. Large garden with parking. **http://ar.presbital.koz.free.fr**

VANNES Villa Kerasy ⬛📋♿ €€

20 av Favrel et Lincy, 56000 **Tel** *02 97 68 36 83* **Fax** *02 97 68 36 84* **Rooms** *15*

A hotel with plenty of charm, the Asian-inspired Villa Kerasy takes the French East India Company and the spice route as its theme. Each room represents a different port. The spa specializes in Ayurvedic treatments, which promise revitalization, an end to stress and a spiritual awakening. Closed mid-Nov–mid-Dec & Jan. **www.villakerasy.com**

THE LOIRE

AMBOISE Le Choiseul ⬛🍽♨🎾🛏📋 €€€

36 quai Charles-Guinot, 37400 **Tel** *02 47 30 45 45* **Fax** *02 47 30 46 10* **Rooms** *32*

An ivy-covered 18th-century manor house set in elegant grounds, with views of the Loire. The comfortably sized guest rooms are traditionally decorated. The airy restaurant serves sophisticated cuisine. There are pretty flower-filled walks and tennis courts. **www.grandesetapes.fr**

ANGERS Hôtel Mail ⬛ €

8 rue des Ursules, 49100 **Tel** *02 41 25 05 25* **Fax** *02 41 86 91 20* **Rooms** *26*

A charming hotel in a quiet corner of the city centre, this 17th-century building was once part of a convent. The bedrooms are tastefully decorated. A particularly good breakfast is served in the dining room. There is also a shaded courtyard with tables. Friendly owners. **www.hotel-du-mail.com**

ANGERS Hôtel Anjou 📺⬛🍽🛏📋 €€

1 bd de Maréchal Foch, 49100 **Tel** *02 41 21 12 11* **Fax** *02 41 87 22 21* **Rooms** *53*

The interior of this city-centre hotel has eclectic decoration, with Art Deco mosaics, 17th- and 18th-century fixtures, ornate ceilings and stained-glass windows. The rooms are spacious and elegantly furnished. "Le Salamandre" restaurant is recommended. Parking available. **www.hoteldanjou.fr**

AZAY LE RIDEAU Le Grand Monarque ⬛🍽 €

3 pl de la République, 37190 **Tel** *02 47 45 40 08* **Fax** *02 47 45 46 25* **Rooms** *24*

In a peaceful setting, this hotel comprises two buildings, one an ancient staging post, the other a *hôtel particulier*, separated by a tree-lined courtyard. The rooms are traditionally furnished and the bathrooms functional. There's a rustic dining room and an attractive terrace overlooking the park. Closed Dec–Feb. **www.legrandmonarque.com**

AZAY LE RIDEAU Manoir de la Rémonière 📋⬛♨🛏🎾 €€

La Chapelle Ste Blaise, 37190 **Tel** *02 47 45 24 88* **Fax** *02 47 45 45 69* **Rooms** *6*

A 15th-century château built on the sight of a Roman villa by the River Indre not far from the Château d'Azay-le-Rideau. The stately bedrooms have an old-world feel and views onto the grounds and the Gallo-Roman ruins. There is a large pool and ample sporting possibilities, including archery and fishing. **www.manoirdelaremoniere.com**

BEAUGENCY Hôtel de la Sologne ⬛🛏 €

6 pl St Firmin, 45190 **Tel** *02 38 44 50 27* **Fax** *02 38 44 90 19* **Rooms** *16*

This typical Sologne stone building on the main square overlooks the ruined castle keep of St Firmin. The bedrooms are small, but cosy and bright, simply furnished. There is a pretty flower-decked patio where breakfast can be taken. Private parking available. **www.hoteldelasologne.com**

BOURGES Le Bourbon 📺⬛🍽🛏📋 €€€

Bd République, 18000 **Tel** *02 48 70 70 00* **Fax** *02 48 70 21 22* **Rooms** *58*

An ancient 17th-century abbey building in the centre of Bourges now houses this comfortable hotel. The bright spacious rooms are furnished in a modern, elegant style. Impressive salon bar and gastronomic restaurant in the former chapel St Ambroix. Parking available. **www.alpha-hotellerie.com**

CHAMPIGNE Château des Briottières ⬛🍽♨🛏 €€€

Rte Marigné, 49330 **Tel** *02 41 42 00 02* **Fax** *02 41 42 01 55* **Rooms** *14*

Family-run 18th-century château set in the 50-ha (124-acre) park à l'Anglaise. The rooms have luxurious furnishings with canopied beds and rich fabrics. There is also a charming cottage with double rooms for families. Romantic dinners as well as cooking classes for groups are on offer; reservations required. **www.briottieres.com**

CHARTRES Le Grand Monarque 📺⬛🍽📋 €

22 place des Epars, 28005 **Tel** *02 37 18 15 15* **Fax** *02 37 36 34 18* **Rooms** *55*

This converted 16th-century staging post, with massively thick stone walls, has been managed by the same family since the 1960s. The hotel is part of the Best Western network. The rooms are simple. There is a pleasant bistro, and a gastronomic restaurant, "Le Georges". Spa for guests. **www.bw-grand-monarque.com**

CHÊNEHUTTE-LES-TUFFEAUX Le Prieuré ⬛🍽♨🛏 €€€

Le Prieuré, 49350 **Tel** *02 41 67 90 14* **Fax** *02 41 67 92 24* **Rooms** *36*

This former priory, dating from the 12th century, has magnificent views over the Loire. The bedrooms in the priory have a romantic, refined decor, two with fireplaces. More modern bedrooms are found in the bungalows scattered in the park.The elegant restaurant serves gourmet cuisine with the best regional produce. **www.grandesetapes.fr**

Key to Price Guide *see p550* **Key to Symbols** *see back cover flap*

CHENONCEAUX Hostel du Roy
9 rue du Dr Bretonneau, 37150 **Tel** *02 47 23 90 17* **Fax** *02 47 23 89 81* **Rooms** *30*

A sprawling hotel-restaurant, with a 16th-century fireplace and a dining room hung with hunting trophies. The well-equipped rooms are simple and appealing, and the atmosphere relaxing. There is a garden and pretty terrace. The restaurant serves classic dishes, including game in season. **www.hostelduroy.com**

CHENONCEAUX Hôtel du Bon Laboureur
6 rue de Dr Bretonneau, 37150 **Tel** *02 47 23 90 02* **Fax** *02 47 23 82 01* **Rooms** *25*

Near the famous château, this inn is set in its own park. The bedrooms are located in the collection of 18th-century stone dwellings. They are small but well equipped and have designer bathrooms. Some are suitable for disabled guests. The oak-beamed restaurant is good. Closed Jan–mid-Feb. **www.bonlaboureur.com**

CHINON Hostellerie Gargantua
73 rue Voltaire, 37500 **Tel** *02 47 93 04 71* **Fax** *02 47 93 08 02* **Rooms** *8*

This hotel, in the ancient Palais du Boulliage with its pointed roof and turret, is a local landmark. The guest rooms are comfortable, if cramped. Each has a theme, from Jeanne d'Arc and Richelieu to the Empire period. Pleasant dining room and terrace. Modern and classic cuisine. Closed Dec. **www.hotel-gargantua.com**

CHINON Hôtel Diderot
4 rue Buffon, 37500 **Tel** *02 47 93 18 87* **Rooms** *26*

The palm and olive trees that grow around the 18th-century building testify to the mild climate. This elegant creeper-clad hotel is found on a quiet street near Chinon city centre. The rooms are calm, simple and well-maintained. Breakfast served in a rustic dining room. Free municipal parking nearby. **www.hoteldiderot.com**

CHINON Château de Marçay
Le Château, 37500 **Tel** *02 47 93 03 47* **Fax** *02 47 93 45 33* **Rooms** *39*

Elegant hotel in this restored 15th-century fortified château. Enjoy the lovely views over the surrounding parkland and vineyards from the well-appointed bedrooms. Refined and aristocratic atmosphere, impeccable service and cuisine. Closed mid-Jan–mid-Mar. **www.chateaudemarcay.com**

COUR-CHEVERNY Hôtels des Trois Marchands
Pl de l'Eglise, 41700 **Tel** *02 54 79 96 44* **Fax** *02 54 79 25 60* **Rooms** *24*

Just a kilometer (0.6 mile) from the château, this ancient coaching inn with a garden has been in the same family since 1865. The bedrooms are comfortably furnished in a rustic style. Take breakfast in one of the three Louis XIII dining rooms. Excellent restaurant. Parking available.

FONTEVRAUD-L'ABBAYE Le Prieuré St-Lazare
38 rte St Jean de l'Habit, 49590 **Tel** *02 41 51 73 16* **Fax** *02 41 51 75 50* **Rooms** *52*

The surroundings of this hotel, housed in the former St Lazare priory within the famous royal abbey complex, are stunning. The rooms are elegantly decorated in a modern, contemporary style. The restaurant, in the ancient cloister, is a gourmet's delight. Closed mid-Nov–Mar. **www.hotels-francepatrimoine.com**

GENNES Aux Naulets d'Anjou
18 rue Croix de la Mission, 49350 **Tel** *02 41 51 81 88* **Fax** *02 41 38 00 78* **Rooms** *19*

At the edge of the village in private grounds, this hotel is quiet and comfortable. The warm welcome compensates for the lack of architectural interest. The rooms are simple and bright. The restaurant serves traditional cuisine with no frills. Reading room and lounge. Closed mid-Dec–Jan. **www.hotel-lesnauletsdanjou.com**

GIEN La Poularde
13 quai de Nice, 45500 **Tel** *02 38 67 36 05* **Fax** *02 38 38 18 78* **Rooms** *9*

On the banks of the river Loire, just steps away from the Musée de la Faïencerie, this hotel is functional and somewhat lacking in charm. The 19th-century bourgeois house has pleasant rooms simply furnished with Louis-Philippe furniture. The restaurant serves excellent food. **www.lapoularde.fr**

LA CHARTRE SUR LE LOIR Hôtel de France
20 pl de la République, 72340 **Tel** *02 43 44 40 16* **Fax** *02 43 79 62 20* **Rooms** *21*

This ivy-clad hotel in the city centre has a delightful garden bordering the river. Good value standard-sized bedrooms. Simply furnished, but comfortable. The bar and the brasserie are basic, but the dining room is pleasant. Generous portions of good food. Pretty garden terrace. Closed 25 Dec–end Jan. **www.hoteldefrance-72.fr**

LA FERTE ST AUBIN Orée des Chênes
Rte de Marchily, 45240 **Tel** *02 38 64 84 00* **Fax** *02 38 64 84 20* **Rooms** *26*

This hotel-restaurant complex was built to reflect the local Solange architecture. Situated in a vast park, a peaceful stay is ensured. The comfortable rooms are furnished with style. Regional dishes are served in the excellent restaurant. Good base for fishing and walking holidays. **www.chateaux-france.com/plessisbeauregard/**

LE CROISIC Fort de l'Océan
Pointe du Croisic, 44490 **Tel** *02 40 15 77 77* **Fax** *02 40 15 77 80* **Rooms** *9*

A Vauban construction, 17th-century ramparts enclose this former fortress facing the sea. Nothing remains of the harsh military lifestyle. The guest rooms are stylish and comfortable, with some equipped for disabled visitors. The restaurant serves wonderful seafood. **www.hotelfortocean.com**

LE MANS Auberge de la Foresterie   €

Route de Laval, 72000 **Tel** *02 43 51 25 12* **Fax** *02 43 28 54 58* **Rooms** *40*

Elegant and welcoming hotel with pleasant gardens and a pool-side terrace for meals when the weather is fine. Easy access by tram to the historic centre of Le Mans and the cathedral. One child under 13 stays free, in the same room. **www.aubergedelaforesterie.com**

LOCHES Hôtel de France   €

6 rue Picois, 37600 **Tel** *02 47 59 00 32* **Fax** *02 47 59 28 66* **Rooms** *19*

In an elegant former staging post built of local tuffeau stone with a traditional slate roof, this hotel is situated near the historic medieval gate. The rooms are simply furnished, comfortable and well maintained. Restaurant serves good regional dishes such as home-smoked salmon. **http://h.france.loches.free.fr**

LOUE Hôtel Ricordeau   €€

13 rue de la Libération, 72540 **Tel** *02 43 88 40 03* **Fax** *02 43 88 62 08* **Rooms** *13*

A former coaching inn, this lovely stone building has comfortable rooms, each decorated in a different style. Some bedrooms overlook the pretty garden that leads down to the river, where boats are moored for guests' use. Copious breakfasts with cold meats, cheese, cake, fruit and home-made jams are available. **www.hotel-ricordeau.fr**

LUYNES Domaine de Beauvois   €€

Rte de Cléré-les-Pins, 37230 **Tel** *02 47 55 50 11* **Fax** *02 47 55 59 62* **Rooms** *36*

This Renaissance manor house built around a 15th-century tower overlooks its own lake. The park is so vast that the pathways are signposted. Rooms are large and comfortable, with luxurious marble bathrooms. Enjoy a candlelit dinner in the acclaimed restaurant. **www.grandesetapes.fr**

MONTBAZON Château d'Artigny   €€€€€

Rte de Monts, 37250 **Tel** *02 47 34 30 30* **Fax** *02 47 34 30 39* **Rooms** *65*

This 20th-century château has grounds overlooking the River Indre. The grandiose classical exterior is matched by a formal Empire-style interior. The Baroque-style guest rooms are sumptuous. The splendid rotunda restaurant serves gourmet regional specialities. Superb wine list. **www.grandesetapes.fr**

MONTLOUIS SUR LOIRE Château de la Bourdaisière   €€€

25 rue de la Bourdaisière, 37270 **Tel** *02 47 45 16 31* **Fax** *02 47 45 09 11* **Rooms** *22*

A magnificent château refurbished as luxury accommodation. Gabrielle d'Estrées, mistress of Henri IV, was born here in 1565. Some of the elegant, luxurious guest rooms have period furniture. The pavilion in the grounds houses six bedrooms. The gardens are open to the public. Closed Jan–Feb. **www.chateaulabourdaisiere.com**

MONTREUIL-BELLAY Relais du Bellay   €

96 rue Nationale, 49260 **Tel** *02 41 53 10 10* **Fax** *02 41 38 70 61* **Rooms** *43*

The 17th-century main building and stylishly furnished annex house the guest rooms. All are calm and quiet, some with disabled access. Heated pool, sauna, Turkish bath, Jacuzzi and gym available. The Splendid hotel, which shares the hotel grounds, has a restaurant. **www.hotelrelaisdubellay.fr**

MUIDES SUR LOIRE Château de Colliers   €€€€

41500 **Tel** *02 54 87 50 75* **Fax** *02 54 87 03 64* **Rooms** *6*

This château, a short drive east of Blois in the woods, is both rustic and grand. In the 18th century it belonged to a governor of Louisiana. There is a delightfully romantic room, at the top of the building, with Empire period furniture and a roof terrace. Dinner is by reservation only. **www.chateau-colliers.com**

NANTES All Seasons   €

3 rue de Couëdic, 44000 **Tel** *02 40 35 74 50* **Fax** *02 40 20 09 35* **Rooms** *65*

Part of the Accor group, this modern hotel is functional rather than attractive. It stands in a busy pedestrian square in the city centre, well placed for visiting the sights. Reasonably sized, comfortable rooms, some with disabled access. Good buffet breakfast. Parking for a fee. **www.accorhotels.com**

NANTES Amiral   €

26 bis rue Scribe, 44000 **Tel** *02 40 69 20 21* **Fax** *02 40 73 98 13* **Rooms** *49*

Cinemas, theatre, restaurants and Passage Pommeraye are on the doorstep of this city centre hotel. The sound-proofing in the bedrooms is good. The façade is modern and bright, and the guest rooms are fully equipped and comfortable. Continental breakfast. **www.hotel-nantes.fr**

NANTES Hôtel La Pérouse   €€

3 allée Duquesne, 44000 **Tel** *02 40 89 75 00* **Fax** *02 40 89 76 00* **Rooms** *46*

Named after a French navigator, this chic hotel with its zen atmosphere opened in 1993. The rooms have glossy wooden flooring and crisp contempory furniture. Reasonably quiet. The breakfast buffet is good. Free access to nearby gym for guests. **www.hotel-laperouse.fr**

NOIRMOUTIER EN L'ILE Hotel Fleur de Sel   €€

Rue des Saulniers, 85330 **Tel** *02 51 39 09 07* **Fax** *02 51 39 09 76* **Rooms** *35*

This hotel stands in the heart of a vast landscaped Mediterranean-style garden with a swimming pool. Some guest rooms are decorated with English-style pine and face the pool; others have a marine theme and private terrace. The chef serves the best cuisine in the Vendée. Closed Nov–mid-Mar. **www.fleurdesel.fr**

Key to Price Guide *see p550* **Key to Symbols** *see back cover flap*

ONZAIN Domaine des Hauts de Loire

Rte d'Herbault, 41150 **Tel** *02 54 20 72 57* **Fax** *02 54 20 77 32* **Rooms** *32*

This former hunting lodge with large grounds retains its grandeur, with richly furnished, bright, comfortable guest rooms. This is an unashamedly expensive place to relax. The chef prepares cutting-edge and classic food, served with superb local wines. There is a tennis court. Closed Dec–Feb. **www.domainehautsloire.com**

ORLEANS Hôtel de l'Abeille

64 rue Alsace Lorraine, 45000 **Tel** *02 38 53 54 87* **Fax** *02 38 62 65 84* **Rooms** *31*

Named in honour of Napoleon and his emblem the bee, this hotel has been run by the same family since 1920. It is something of a shrine to Joan of Arc. The grand Neo-Classical building houses well-decorated, old-style rooms and a good library. There is a terrace looking onto the cathedral. **www.hoteldelabeille.com**

RESTIGNE Manoir de Restigné

15 rte de Tours, 37140 **Tel** *02 47 97 00 06* **Fax** *02 47 97 01 43* **Rooms** *10*

Sitting among vineyards near Bourgueil is this tastefully restored 17th-century manor house, offering spacious, elegantly furnished bedrooms named after grape varieties. Meals are served in the former wine cellar and there is a lovely 18th-century orangerie in the grounds. Closed Jan–mid-Feb. **www.manoirderestigne.com**

ROCHECORBON Domaine des Hautes Roches

86 quai de la Loire, 37210 **Tel** *02 47 52 88 88* **Fax** *02 47 52 81 30* **Rooms** *14*

Surrounded by Vouvray vineyards, near Tours, this was once a monks' residence. Fully restored, it has all modern comforts. The underground rooms, hewn into the tuffeau chalk in this "troglodyte" hotel, are spacious and characterful. Dine in the château or on the terrace. Closed Feb–Mar. **www.leshautesroches.com**

ROMORANTIN-LANTHENAY Grand Hôtel du Lion d'Or

69 rue Georges Clémenceau, 41200 **Tel** *02 54 94 15 15* **Fax** *02 54 88 24 87* **Rooms** *16*

This former Renaissance mansion house is now a gastronomic halt in an historic town. From the outside the building is unimpressive, but the interior has instant charm. The luxury bedrooms lead off from a cobbled courtyard. The decor is authentic Napoléon III. Formal gardens. **www.hotel-liondor.fr**

SALBRIS Domaine de Valaudran

Route de Romorantin, 41300 **Tel** *02 54 97 20 00* **Fax** *02 54 97 12 22* **Rooms** *32*

This big family house set in 2 ha (5 acres) of gardens in the heart of the Sologne has been transformed into a pleasant country-house hotel. The stylish, contemporary rooms contrast with the stately home exterior. A billiard table is available. The good, traditional restaurant uses home-grown vegetables. **www.hotelvalaudran.com**

SAUMUR La Croix de la Voulte

Rte de Boumois, 49400 **Tel** *02 41 38 46 66* **Fax** *02 41 38 46 66* **Rooms** *4*

This manor house, outside Saumur, dates from the 15th century. Built at a crossroads or *croix*, it was the turning point for the royal huntsmen. The bedrooms are all different, two with original Louis XIV fireplaces, and classic furnishings. Breakfast served at poolside in fine weather. **www.lacroixdelavoulte.com**

SAUMUR Hôtel Anne d'Anjou

32-34 quai Mayaud, 49400 **Tel** *02 41 67 30 30* **Fax** *02 41 67 51 00* **Rooms** *44*

The decor in this elegant mansion, sitting between the river Loire and the château, is sophisticated and romantic. This fine building with its impressive façade, grand staircase and painted ceiling has guest rooms decorated in Empire or contemporary style. Breakfast in the courtyard. **www.hotel-anneanjou.com**

SILLE-LE-GUILLAUME Relais des Etangs de Guibert

Neufchâtel-en-Saosnois, 72600 **Tel** *02 43 97 15 38* **Fax** *02 43 33 22 99* **Rooms** *15*

North of Le Mans, this beautiful stone-built country house is situated at the edge of the forest in a charming and romantic setting, with a turret overlooking the flower-filled grounds and lake. Individually decorated rooms in warm tones, some with original beamed ceilings. Friendly. **www.lesetangsdeguibert.com**

SOUVIGNY-EN-SOLOGNE Ferme des Foucault

Ménestreau-en-Villette, 45240 **Tel** *02 38 76 94 41* **Fax** *02 38 76 94 41* **Rooms** *3*

Deep in the forest in the Sologne countryside is this attractive redbrick and timber farmhouse. The immense bedrooms are cosy, with superb bathrooms. One even has a fireplace. The other rooms are decorated with paintings by the owner's daughter. Friendly, relaxed atmosphere. **www.ferme-des-foucault.com**

ST LAURENT NOUAN Hôtel Le Verger

14 rue du Port-Pichard, 41220 **Tel** *02 54 87 22 22* **Fax** *02 54 87 22 82* **Rooms** *14*

Ideally placed for visiting the famous Loire châteaux, and only 8 km (5 miles) from Chambord, this 19th-century bourgeois house has an interior courtyard and fountain. The rooms are well maintained, spacious and calm. The wooded park ensures a peaceful stay. **www.hotel-le-verger.com**

ST NAZAIRE Au Bon Acceuil

39 rue Marceau, 44600 **Tel** *02 40 22 07 05* **Fax** *02 40 19 01 58* **Rooms** *17*

This enchanting hotel in a peaceful corner of the city centre had the fortune to escape the destruction of World War II. The guest rooms are simple, modern and functional. The dining room is a little gloomy, but serves good seafood. Friendly and welcoming atmosphere. Closed last 2 weeks Jul. **www.au-bon-accueil44.com**

ST PATRICE Château de Rochecotte

St Patrice, Langeais, 37130 **Tel** *02 47 96 16 16* **Fax** *02 47 96 90 59* **Rooms** *35*

Situated a short way from Langeais, Prince Talleyrand's château was completely renovated and opened as an elegant hotel in 1986. It is set in a charming, tranquil 8-ha (19-acre) park and woodland. The guest rooms are large, each with a view. The interior is decorated sumptuously. Closed mid-Feb–mid-Mar. **www.chateau-de-rochecotte.fr**

TOURS Hôtel L'Adresse

12 rue de la Rôtisserie, 37000 **Tel** *02 47 20 85 76* **Rooms** *17*

A completely refurbished hotel concealed behind a discreet but elegant façade of an 18th-century town house. The rooms offer an appealing blend of minimalist modern and 18th-century architecture. Located right in the city centre, it is ideal location for restaurants, the conference centre and the train station. **www.hotel-ladresse.com**

VOUVRAY Château de Jallanges

9 Jallange, Vernou sur Brenne, 37210 **Tel** *02 47 52 06 66* **Fax** *02 47 52 11 18* **Rooms** *7*

An imposing Renaissance brick château, and now a family home, the comfortable guest rooms are furnished with style. Guests are taken on a guided tour from the private chapel to the top of the turrets from where there is a superb view. A good base for exploring Touraine. **www.jallanges.com**

BURGUNDY & FRANCHE-COMTE

ALOXE-CORTON Hôtel Villa Louise

9 rue Franche, 21420 **Tel** *03 80 26 46 70* **Fax** *03 80 26 47 16* **Rooms** *11*

The finest Corton-Charlemagne vines provide a magnificent backdrop to this 17th-century wine-makers' domaine. Cosy bedrooms have well-equipped bathrooms. The rustic interior includes a homely sitting room with open fireplace. Wine-tasting evenings for guests. There are Turkish baths, a solarium and a pool. Closed Jan–Feb. **www.hotel-villa-louise.fr**

ARC-ET-SENANS La Saline Royale

Arc-et-Senans, 25610 **Tel** *03 81 54 45 00* **Rooms** *30*

To stay in this World Heritage site and architectural museum is a unique experience combining high-class dormitory accommodation with Louis XVI magnificence. The breathtaking saltworks, an 18th-century masterpiece by Nicolas Ledoux, takes in guests, but you must book well in advance. Closed Nov–Feb. **www.salineroyale.com**

AUXERRE Le Parc des Maréchaux

6 av Foch, 89000 **Tel** *03 86 51 43 77* **Fax** *03 86 51 31 72* **Rooms** *25*

Close to the town centre, is this elegant, renovated Napoleon III building. The pretty bedrooms, each named after a famous French *maréchal*, are decorated in soft golden tones and furnished in the Empire style. The quietest rooms overlook the lovely park planted with century-old trees. Cosy bar for guests. **www.hotel-parcmarechaux.com**

BEAUNE Hôtel Grillon

21 rte de Seurre, 21200 **Tel** *03 80 22 44 25* **Fax** *03 80 24 94 89* **Rooms** *20*

Charming hotel sitting in a walled garden, just 15 minutes' walk from Beaune town centre. The rooms in the main building are cosy, with traditional furnishings. There are more spacious, modern-style rooms in the extension. Breakfast is served in the conservatory, or on the garden terrace in summer. **www.hotel-grillon.fr**

BEAUNE Hôtel Le Cep

27 rue Maufoux, 21200 **Tel** *03 80 22 35 48* **Fax** *03 80 22 76 80* **Rooms** *64*

In the heart of the Old Town is this elegant hotel, renovated in a Renaissance style. Legend has it that Louis XIV preferred to stay here rather than at the hospice. The rooms, some with Baroque decor, are ornately furnished with antiques. Each is named after local wine. **www.hotel-cep-beaune.com**

BESANÇON Hôtel Charles Quint

3 rue du Chapitre, 25000 **Tel** *03 81 82 05 49* **Fax** *03 81 82 61 45* **Rooms** *9*

A charming hotel situated in the historic centre. The tastefully decorated interior combines 18th-century architecture with modern amenities. The rooms are elegant without being ostentatious, the best are those with a small terrace overlooking the garden. Breakfast is served in a wood-panelled salon, or outside in fine weather. **www.hotel-charlesquint.com**

BOUILLAND Le Vieux Moulin

Le Village, 21420 **Tel** *03 80 21 51 16* **Fax** *03 80 21 59 90* **Rooms** *26*

A renovated watermill set in this spectacular Burgundy village in the Rhône valley. Modern, comfortable rooms with simple, stylish furnishings. Views of either the river or the surrounding countryside. Sauna, Jacuzzi and fitness centre. Renowned contemporary restaurant. Closed Jan–mid-Mar. **www.le-moulin-de-bouilland.com**

CHABLIS Le Bergerand's

4 rue des Moulins, 89800 **Tel** *03 86 18 96 08* **Fax** *03 86 18 96 09* **Rooms** *18*

This popular bed & breakfast on the edge of the River Serein is the perfect place to stop over and sample the local wines. The rooms are bright and gaily decorated and there is a comfortable lounge bar, a tea room, a hamman and a Jacuzzi. A buffet breakfast is available, and picnic baskets are prepared on request. **www.chabils-france.fr**

Key to Price Guide *see p550* **Key to Symbols** *see back cover flap*

CHABLIS Hostellerie des Clos ⌧ ℗ ⑪ ⒱ ☰ ⛨ €€

Rue Jules-Rathier, 89800 **Tel** *03 86 42 10 63* **Fax** *03 86 42 17 11* **Rooms** *36*

The owner has renovated a medieval convent in this famed wine village. There are comfortable, modern rooms and one of the best restaurants in the region (Michelin starred). The terrace overlooks a delightful garden and vineyards. Three rooms have wheelchair access. Closed mid-Dec–mid-Jan. **www.hostellerie-des-clos.fr**

CHAGNY Lameloise ⌧ ℗ ⑪ ⛫ ☰ €€€

36 pl d'Armes, 71150 **Tel** *03 85 87 65 65* **Fax** *03 85 87 03 57* **Rooms** *16*

Luxury hotel and gastronomic restaurant situated in an elegant Burgundian house, which has stood for nearly a century in the small town square. Ample rooms have impeccable bathrooms. The refined classic decor includes oak beamed ceilings and period furniture. The restaurant is excellent. Closed mid-Dec–end-Jan. **www.lameloise.fr**

CHAILLY-SUR-ARMANÇON Château de Chailly ⌧ ℗ ⑪ ≋ ⛫ ⒱ ☰ €€€€€

Rue Dessous, 21320 **Tel** *03 80 90 30 30* **Fax** *03 80 90 30 00* **Rooms** *45*

One façade of this beautifully restored château is ornately Renaissance, while another recalls the building's medieval heritage. Luxury accommodation with spacious, meticulously maintained rooms. Facilities include a golf course, tennis, Jacuzzi, Turkish bath and four eateries. **www.chailly.com**

DIJON Le Jacquemart €

32 rue Verrerie, 21000 **Tel** *03 80 60 09 60* **Fax** *03 80 60 09 69* **Rooms** *31*

In the heart of the city, near the Palais des Ducs, the Musée des Beaux Arts, and the lucky owl. An attractive 18th-century bourgeois house with decent-sized rooms and antique-style furniture. The decor is sombre, but characterful. Quiet and comfortable. Continental breakfast. **www.hotel-lejacquemart.fr**

DIJON Hostellerie du Chapeau Rouge ⌧ ℗ ⑪ ⛫ ☰ €€€

5 rue Michelet, 21000 **Tel** *03 80 50 88 88* **Fax** *03 80 50 88 89* **Rooms** *30*

Charming 16th-century hotel located in the heart of the city. The well-worn floorboards and period fireplaces still exist, but the decor is contemporary. Chic, individually decorated rooms vary in style from Asiatic to Baroque, romantic to feng shui. Creative gastronomic cuisine is served in the glass-domed dining room. **www.chapeau-rouge.fr**

DOLE La Chaumière ℗ ⑪ ≋ €

346 av du Maréchal-Juin, 39100 **Tel** *03 84 70 72 40* **Fax** *03 84 79 25 60* **Rooms** *19*

This ancient farmhouse, outside the city centre of the charming former capital of Comté, has authentic furniture that matches the ambience. Elegant and comfortable, well-maintained and soundproofed rooms ensure a tranquil night. Exceptional restaurant with Michelin-starred creative cuisine. **www.la-chaumiere.info**

GEVREY-CHAMBERTIN Hôtel les Grands Crus ℗ ☰ €€

Rte des Grands Crus, 21220 **Tel** *03 80 34 34 15* **Fax** *03 80 51 89 07* **Rooms** *24*

A light, airy hotel with wonderful views over the grands crus vineyards. Located in the heart of the Côte de Nuits, this country house built in a typical Burgundian style has traditionally furnished rooms that overlook the garden. The comfy lounge centres around an open fireplace. **www.hoteldesgrandscrus.com**

JOIGNY La Côte St Jacques ⌧ ℗ ⑪ ≋ ⛫ ⒱ ☰ ⛨ €€€

14 faubourg de Paris, 89300 **Tel** *03 86 62 09 70* **Fax** *03 86 91 49 70* **Rooms** *31*

Smartly renovated hotel overlooking the River Yonne, with a delightful garden leading to the water's edge. Soft, harmonious colours and contemporary furniture create a pleasing ambience. Superb facilities: spa, private boat for guests, winter lounge with open fire and summer lounge with terrace. The restaurant is outstanding. **www.cotesaintjacques.com**

LA BUSSIERE-SUR-OUCHE Abbaye de la Bussière ℗ ⑪ ⛨ €€€€

La Bussière-sur-Ouche, 21360 **Tel** *03 80 49 02 49* **Fax** *03 80 49 05 23* **Rooms** *15*

A superb conversion of a 12th-century abbey surrounded by a tranquil park. Each room has a view of the grounds with its 52 types of tree and ornamental lake. Two fine Michelin-starred restaurants are presided over by award-winning chef Olivier Elzer. A perfect base for visiting the Burgundy vineyards. **www.abbaye-dela-buissiere.com**

LEVERNOIS Hostellerie de Levernois ℗ ⑪ ⛫ ⒱ ☰ ⛨ €€€

Rue du Golf, 21200 **Tel** *03 80 24 73 58* **Fax** *03 80 22 78 00* **Rooms** *26*

Not far from Beaune, in the heart of the Burgundy countryside nestles this classic 19th-century manor house. Set in a park with a small river running through it, a relaxing stay is guaranteed. The rooms retain traces of the era, with parquet floors and Burgundy tiles, yet the facilities are up to date. A converted barn houses an authentic bistro. **www.levernois.com**

MALBUISSON Hôtel Le Lac ⌧ ℗ ⑪ ≋ €

31 Grand Rue, 25160 **Tel** *03 81 69 34 80* **Fax** *03 81 69 35 44* **Rooms** *54*

Perched above the lake of St-Point in the Jura mountains, this imposing, elegant 1930s building has prettily decorated rooms, some with a lake view. The atmosphere is comfortable and pleasant, although service is abrupt – but that's normal for the region. Great buffet breakfast. **www.hotel-le-lac.fr**

MALBUISSON Le Bon Acceuil ℗ ⑪ €

Rue de la Source, 25160 **Tel** *03 81 69 30 58* **Fax** *03 81 69 37 60* **Rooms** *12*

Situated between the forest and the shores of Lac St Point is this friendly hotel. Rooms are spacious and comfortable, with simple pinewood furniture and homely fabrics. The restaurant serves outstanding contemporary cuisine, remaining faithful to the local produce. Closed mid-Dec–mid-Jan & 2 wks Mar. **www.le-bon-accueil.fr**

MARTAILLY-LES-BRANCION La Montagne de Brancion   P ⅰ 🏊   €€
Col de Brancion, 71700 **Tel** *03 85 51 12 40* **Fax** *03 85 51 18 64* **Rooms** *19*

East of Tournus, perched on a hillside a few steps away from the medieval village, this hotel has a panoramic view of the surrounding countryside. All rooms face east looking out over the Mâconnais mountains and the vineyards. The bright, prettily-decorated rooms have modern furnishings. The restaurant is highly recommended. **www.brancion.com**

NANS-SOUS-STE-ANNE A l'Ombre du Château   🏊 P 🏃   €€
6 rue du Château, 25330 **Tel** *03 81 86 54 72* **Fax** *03 81 86 43 29* **Rooms** *4*

Located southwest of Ornans, this converted 18th-century stone outbuilding of a château is set in a vast wooded park. Well-kept rooms have been carefully and tastefully restored. There is a generous breakfast with home-made pastries. The American owners aim to please. Closed Nov–Apr. **www.frenchcountryretreat.com**

NANTOUX Domaine de la Combotte   P 🏊 🏃   €€
2 La Combotte, 21190 **Tel** *03 80 26 02 66* **Fax** *03 80 26 07 84* **Rooms** *5*

Near Beaune, this family-run wine estate offers *chambres d'hôte*. Large comfortable rooms, one with wheelchair access and one family room. Well-equipped, with modern decor. The owners delight in sharing their passion for wine and truffles. **www.lacombotte.com**

NEVERS Clos Ste Marie   P   €
25 rue du Petit-Mouësse, 58000 **Tel** *03 86 71 94 50* **Fax** *03 86 71 94 69* **Rooms** *17*

After visiting the sights of Nevers, unwind in this attractive, calm hotel just 5 minutes from the pedestrianized centre. Pretty, bright and well-proportioned rooms are furnished with quaint fabrics and antique furniture. The flower-filled garden can be enjoyed whilst having breakfast on the shady terrace. **www.clos-sainte-marie.fr**

NITRY Auberge de la Beursaudière   P ⅰ &   €
5 & 7 rue Hyacinthe-Gautherin, 89310 **Tel** *03 86 33 69 70* **Fax** *03 86 33 69 60* **Rooms** *11*

Midway between Auxerre, Chablis and Vézelay, this hotel stands in a 12th-century former priory. The attractive bedrooms are each named after ancient trades: *Le Sabotier, La Dentellière, La Repasseuse*. The best, *Le Vigneron* and *L'Ecrivain*, are spacious and elegant. Buffet breakfast served in a former wine cellar. Closed Jan. **www.beursaudiere.com**

NUITS-ST-GEORGES Hôtel la Gentilhommière   P ⅰ 🏊 📺 ▤   €€
13 vallée de la Serrée, 21700 **Tel** *03 80 61 12 06* **Fax** *03 80 61 30 33* **Rooms** *41*

This former 16th-century hunting lodge with its typical Burgundy tiled roof is now a beautiful hotel and renowned restaurant. The bedrooms are classically furnished, and the suites are decorated in styles from colonial to zen. Well-mastered cuisine. Terrace overlooks the river. Closed Jan. **www.lagentilhommiere.fr**

POLIGNY Hostellerie des Monts de Vaux   P ⅰ ▤   €€€
Monts Vaux, 39800 **Tel** *03 84 37 12 50* **Fax** *03 84 37 09 07* **Rooms** *10*

Run by the Carrion family since 1967, this hotel occupies an elegant coaching inn on the outskirts of Poligny, in lovely gardens. The rooms are decorated in a bourgeois style with antique furniture. Refined atmosphere. Good Jura cuisine and wine in the restaurant. Tennis. **www.hostellerie.com**

PORT-LESNEY Château de Germigney   🏊 P ⅰ 🏊 ▤   €€€
Le Parc, 39600 **Tel** *03 84 73 85 85* **Fax** *03 84 73 88 88* **Rooms** *19*

This hotel is located just 6 km (4 miles) from Arc-et-Senans in its own grounds bordering the Loue river. This exquisite château has tastefully decorated rooms with modern facilities. Smaller, less expensive rooms are in the annex. Exceptional restaurant and natural water pool. Relaxed and unstuffy service. **www.chateaudegermigney.com**

SAULIEU Le Relais Bernard Loiseau   P ⅰ 🏊 🏃 📺 ▤   €€€€€
2 rue d'Argentine, 21210 **Tel** *03 80 90 53 53* **Fax** *03 80 64 08 92* **Rooms** *33*

A renowned hotel and acclaimed restaurant established by the late Bernard Loiseau. Modern comfort and traditional Burgundy furnishings – wooden panelled walls, red floor tiles. The refined rooms have either a fireplace, or balcony overlooking the gardens à l'Anglaise. Fine service. Closed Jan. **www.bernard-loiseau.com**

ST-AMOUR-BELLEVUE L'Auberge du Paradis   P ⅰ 🏊 ▤   €€
Le Plâtre-Durand, 71570 **Tel** *03 85 37 10 26* **Rooms** *8*

A young dynamic couple have tastefully renovated this auberge. The bedrooms take their names from different spices and are decorated with style and originality. Chic, contemporary decor with open plan bathrooms. Some rooms have balconies overlooking the garden. Breakfast is copious. Good restaurant. Closed Jan. **www.aubergeduparadis.fr**

ST-GERVAIS-EN-VALLIERE Moulin d'Hauterive   P ⅰ 🏊 🏃 📺 ▤   €
Hameau de Chaublanc, 71350 **Tel** *03 85 91 55 56* **Fax** *03 85 91 89 65* **Rooms** *20*

Not far from Beaune, in a secluded setting on the bank of the Dheune river, this converted watermill was built in the 12th century by the monks of Citeaux abbey. Each room is unique, tastefully furnished with antiques. The owner-chef serves inventive home-cooking. One room has wheelchair access. **www.moulinhauterive.com**

VALLÉE DE COUSIN Hostellerie du Moulin des Ruats   P ⅰ 🏃   €€
9 rue des Isles Labaumes, 89200 **Tel** *03 86 34 97 00* **Fax** *03 86 31 65 47* **Rooms** *25*

A few kilometres from the old fortified town of Avallon, in the valley formed by the River Cousin, lies this former flour mill, now a classic hotel-restaurant. Comfortable, charming rooms with traditional furnishings have views over the garden or the river; some with a terrace. Restaurant serves classic cuisine. Closed mid-Nov–mid-Feb. **www.moulindesruats.com**

VEZELAY L'Espérance
St-Père-sous-Vézelay, 89450 **Tel** *03 86 33 39 10* **Fax** *03 86 33 26 15* **Rooms** *34*

The guest rooms here are in three buildings: the main building has classic furnishings, Moulin has rustic charm, and Pré des Marguerites is contemporary, with terraces overlooking the garden. Wonderful restaurant, excellent but expensive wines, and impeccable service. Closed mid-Jan–mid-Mar. **www.marc-meneau-esperance.com**

VILLENEUVE-SUR-YONNE La Lucarne aux Chouettes
7 quai Bretoche, 89500 **Tel** *03 86 87 18 26* **Fax** *03 86 87 18 26* **Rooms** *4*

On the banks of the river, four typical Burgundian 17th-century houses have been converted into sophisticated *chambres d'hôtes* all with a river view. The individually decorated rooms have oak beams, four-poster beds, *toile de Jouy* fabric, antique furniture and hand-painted bathroom tiles. Charming dining room and terrace. **www.lalucarneauxchouettes.fr**

VONNAS Georges Blanc
Pl Marché, 01540 **Tel** *04 74 50 90 90* **Fax** *04 74 50 08 80* **Rooms** *41*

Sumptuous hotel-restaurant in an ancient timbered and brick mansion, surrounded by a garden. The luxurious rooms were decorated by Pierre Chaduc. The atmosphere sways between refinement and opulence; the decor mixes Louis XIII and rustic styles. Most bathrooms have Jacuzzis. Spa with sauna. **www.georgesblanc.com**

YONNE Hôtel d'Avallon Vauban
53 rue de Paris, 89200 **Tel** *03 86 34 36 99* **Fax** *03 86 31 66 31* **Rooms** *26*

This charming ivy-clad house, on the main road into Yonne, is a great base for exploring the area. The bedrooms are simply furnished, those at the back being quieter and having views directly over the pretty garden. The shady courtyard is a great place to enjoy breakfast in fine weather. **www.avallonvaubanhotel.com**

THE MASSIF CENTRAL

BEAULIEU-SUR-DORDOGNE Manoir de Beaulieu
4 pl Champ de Mars, 19120 **Tel** *05 55 91 01 34* **Fax** *05 55 91 23 57* **Rooms** *25*

Situated in the main square of this pretty village, this traditional hotel was founded in 1913. The rooms have been nicely renovated and are decorated in different styles; whether rustic or modern each one is comfortably sized with a well-maintained bathroom. The lounge bar has comfy leather chairs. **www.manoirdebeaulieu.com**

BELCASTEL Du Vieux Pont
Le Bourg, 12390 **Tel** *05 65 64 52 29* **Fax** *05 65 64 44 32* **Rooms** *7*

Being lulled to sleep by the murmuring of the river is just one of the attractions of this unpretentious hotel. Rooms are spacious, light and airy, and all have river views. Across the medieval cobbled bridge, the same family also run an imaginative but affordable restaurant. Closed Jan–mid-Mar. **www.hotelbelcastel.com**

BÉNÉVENT L'ABBAYE Le Cèdre
Rue de l'Oiseau, 23210 **Tel** *05 55 81 59 99* **Fax** *05 55 81 59 98* **Rooms** *16*

In the lush countryside northwest of Aubusson lies this classic hotel and restaurant. Behind the 18th-century granite façade hides a contemporary interior. Rooms range from romantic, with four-poster beds, to plainly furnished. The beautiful garden has a terrace shaded by a monumental cedar tree. Closed Jan–Feb. **www.hotelducedre.fr**

CHAMALIERES Hôtel Radio
43 av Pierre et Marie Curie, 63400 **Tel** *04 73 30 87 83* **Fax** *04 73 36 42 44* **Rooms** *26*

Built in the 1930s, this Art Deco hotel on a hill overlooking Clermont-Ferrand retains its original mosaics, mirrors and decorative ironwork, alongside radio memorabilia. Spacious rooms have period furnishings, some with balconies. First-class restaurant and attentive service. **www.hotel-radio.fr**

CONQUES Hôtel Ste Foy
Le Bourg, 12320 **Tel** *05 65 69 84 03* **Fax** *05 65 72 81 04* **Rooms** *17*

Facing the much-visited abbey in one of the most charming Aveyron villages, this ancient 17th-century inn retains traces of its rustic past. Old stone walls, low ceilings and oak beams are complemented by elegant furniture and modern amenities. Idyllic interior courtyard, and shady terrace. Restaurant recommended. Closed Nov–Easter. **www.hotelsaintefoy.fr**

LAGUIOLE Michel Bras
Route de l'Aubrac, 12210 **Tel** *05 65 51 18 20* **Fax** *05 65 48 47 02* **Rooms** *15*

Built on a hillside with a spectacular view of the Aubrac plain houses, this futuristic construction is one of France's most acclaimed hotel-restaurants. The amply-sized rooms, with floor-to-ceiling windows, are contemporary and minimalist with modern facilities. The restaurant is a gourmet's paradise. Closed Nov–Easter. **www.michel-bras.fr**

LIMOGES Hôtel Jeanne d'Arc
17 av du Général-de-Gaulle, 87000 **Tel** *05 55 77 67 77* **Fax** *05 55 79 86 75* **Rooms** *50*

A surprisingly atmospheric hotel near Limoges train station and within walking distance of the centre. The building has been tastefully renovated without losing its 19th-century feel. The rooms are stylish and equipped with all the three-star comforts you'd expect. **www.hoteljeannedarc-limoges.fr**

LIMOGES Domaine de Faugeras

Allée de Faugeras, 87000 **Tel** *05 55 34 66 22* **Fax** *555341805* **Rooms** *9*

Located in its own park on the edge of the city centre, this 18th-century manor house is a peaceful place to stay. Cultural heritage blends successfully with modernity. The rooms are contemporary in style, and well-equipped. The pleasant lounge has an open fireplace and there is a spa and brasserie. **www.domainedefaugeras.com**

MENDE Hôtel de France

9 bd Lucien-Arnault, 48000 **Tel** *04 66 65 00 04* **Fax** *04 66 49 30 47* **Rooms** *27*

This entirely renovated staging post, dating from 1856, offers rooms that are cosy, comfortable and stylish; the quietest ones overlook the gardens. Relax in front of a roaring fire in winter, or enjoy breakfast on the pretty terrece in summer. A friendly family-run hotel. **www.hoteldefrance-mende.com**

MILLAU Château de Creissels

Rte de St-Afrique, 12100 **Tel** *05 65 60 16 59* **Fax** *05 65 61 24 63* **Rooms** *30*

A short distance from Millau is this 12th-century château with stunning views over the Tarn valley and the Millau viaduct. Rooms in the 1970s extension are comfortable and quiet, with balconies overlooking the gardens. Enjoy local dishes in the stone-vaulted restaurant. Closed Jan–Feb. **www.chateau-de-creissels.com**

MONTSALVY Auberge Fleurie

Pl du Barry, 15120 **Tel** *04 71 49 20 02* **Fax** *04 71 49 29 65* **Rooms** *7*

This ivy-clad village inn situated in the south of Auvergne, offers excellent value for money. The rustic charm of the original building is complemented by pretty, colourful fabrics in the individually decorated rooms. The largest rooms have canopied beds. Creative cuisine is served in the restaurant. Closed mid-Jan–mid-Feb. **www.auberge-fleurie.com**

MOUDEYRES Le Pré Bossu

43150 **Tel** *04 71 05 10 70* **Fax** *04 71 05 10 21* **Rooms** *6*

Authentic low, stone cottage with a thatched roof in the heart of the Auvergne countryside. The bedrooms, named after birds, are modern and comfortable with relaxing decor and furniture imported from Asia. There are home-made jams for breakfast and home-grown vegetables for dinner. Closed Nov–Easter. **www.auberge-pre-bossu.com**

PAILHEROLS Auberge des Montagnes

Le Bourg, 15800 **Tel** *04 71 47 57 01* **Fax** *04 71 49 63 83* **Rooms** *23*

On the flanks of the Monts du Cantal, it's worth seeking out this cosy mountain auberge. In winter there are log fires; in summer head for the large garden with a children's play area. The restaurant attracts locals from miles around with its good-value country cooking. Treatments available in the spa. **www.auberge-des-montagnes.com**

PERIGNAT-LES-SARLIEVE Hostellerie St Martin

Allée de Bonneval, 63170 **Tel** *04 73 79 81 00* **Fax** *04 73 79 81 01* **Rooms** *32*

Located a few kilometres south of Clermont-Ferrand, this splendid Cistercian abbey dates from the 14th century. It now houses a comfortable hotel surrounded by a peaceful park. There are three styles of rooms: standard (in the modern annex), and superior and deluxe in the ancient building. **www.hostelleriestmartin.com**

PEYRELEAU Grand Hôtel de la Muse et du Rozier

Rue des Gorges du Tarn, 12720 **Tel** *05 65 62 60 01* **Fax** *05 65 62 63 88* **Rooms** *38*

This century-old hotel sits in an idyllic spot amongst the trees at the water's edge. The quaint exterior contrasts with the contemporary design inside; natural materials, white walls and light create a purist atmosphere. The rooms all have river views. There is a mini-beach at the riverside, and a good restaurant. Closed mid-Nov–Apr. **www.hotel-delamuse.fr**

PONTGIBAUD Hôtel Saluces

Rue de la Martille, 15140 **Tel** *04 71 40 70 82* **Fax** *04 71 40 71 70* **Rooms** *8*

Located in the centre of this beautiful Renaissance town, this 15th–16th-century house looks like a small château. It is family-run and offers a warm welcome. The rooms are large, attractively decorated, and each has its own bath/ shower. There is a bar and afternoon teas are served in the salon. **www.hotel-salers.fr**

RODEZ La Ferme de Bourran

Quartier de Bourran, 12000 **Tel** *05 65 73 62 62* **Fax** *05 65 72 14 15* **Rooms** *7*

This small hotel with modern bedrooms occupies a renovated farmhouse, which sits on a hillock in a secluded spot near Rodez. Bright contemporary and comfortable rooms are painted in white, grey and ivory tones. The relaxing lounge has a lovely open fireplace, and there is a large terrace for breakfast in summer. **www.fermedebourran.com**

SALERS Le Bailliage

Rue Notre-Dame, 15410 **Tel** *04 71 40 71 95* **Fax** *04 71 40 74 90* **Rooms** *27*

The Bailliage is one of the nicest places to stay in this attractive mountain town. Cheaper rooms occupy a separate annex, but all are comfortable and some positively jolly. There's a garden and a restaurant in which to sample Salers cheese. Closed mid-Nov–mid-Mar. **www.salers-hotel-bailliage.com**

ST-ALBAN-SUR-LIMAGNOLE Relais St Roch

Château de la Chastre, chemin du Carreirou, 48120 **Tel** *04 66 31 55 48* **Fax** *04 66 31 53 26* **Rooms** *9*

The pretty granite pink stone building contrasts with the lush green of the surrounding countryside. The rooms in this 18th-century mansion are classically decorated and elegantly furnished with antiques and tapestries. Cosy lounge bar with over 300 whiskies. The owners have a delightful restaurant nearby. Closed Nov–Easter. **www.relais-saint-roch.fr**

Key to Price Guide *see p550* **Key to Symbols** *see back cover flap*

ST-ARCONS-D'ALLIER Les Deux Abbesses

Le Château, 43300 **Tel** *04 71 74 03 08* **Fax** *04 71 74 05 30* **Rooms** *6*

An entire tiny hamlet has been restored to form this outstanding hotel. Four cottages house the rooms, cobbled streets serve as corridors and the château houses a reception and dining room. Romantic rooms, and fantasy-style bathrooms: an old wine *cuve* serves as a bathtub, an animal's trough as a handbasin. Closed Nov–Easter. **www.lesdeuxabbesses.com**

ST-BONNET-LE-FROID Le Clos des Cimes

Le Bourg, 43290 **Tel** *04 71 59 93 72* **Fax** *04 71 59 93 40* **Rooms** *12*

Gourmet pilgrims compete for rooms at this fabulous auberge deep in the countryside. The prize is a luxurious room with original artworks and stunning views over the valley. The Marcon family run the place with tremendous attention to detail. Prepare to be pampered. Cooking lessons available. Closed Jan–Easter. **www.regismarcon.fr**

ST GERVAIS D'AUVERGNE Castel-Hôtel 1904

Rue de Castel, 63390 **Tel** *04 73 85 70 42* **Fax** *04 73 85 84 39* **Rooms** *15*

Rooms are surprisingly affordable in this turreted château where period furniture, oak beams and highly polished floors ensure a homely atmosphere. Guest rooms are set round an attractive courtyard. There are two good restaurants: one rustic, the other grand. Closed Nov–Easter. **www.castel-hotel-1904.com**

ST-MARTIN-VALMEROUX Hostellerie de la Maronne

Le Theil, 15140 **Tel** *04 71 69 20 33* **Fax** *04 71 69 28 22* **Rooms** *21*

Not far from Salers, encircled by the Auvergne volcanoes, is this 19th-century manor house. Renovated with taste it houses sunny, prettily decorated rooms with stylish classic furnishings. Discover the park by following one of the suggested walks, or take a siesta in the treehouse. The restaurant is one of the best in the region. **www.maronne.com**

ST-PRIEST-BRAMEFANT Château de Maulmont

Maulmont, 63310 **Tel** *04 70 59 14 95* **Fax** *04 70 59 11 88* **Rooms** *18*

Superb 19th-century château surrounded by parkland and lovely gardens. Well-equipped spacious bedrooms feature elegant, classic decor and period furniture. The oak panelled dining room serves delicious traditional fare. Boating and golf are nearby. Closed mid-Nov–Apr. **www.château-maulmont.com**

VICHY Aletti Palace Hotel

3 pl Joseph-Aletti, 03200 **Tel** *04 70 30 20 20* **Fax** *04 70 98 13 82* **Rooms** *129*

Vichy's top hotel oozes Belle-Epoque grandeur from its stately reception hall to the crystal chandeliers. Guest rooms have been modernized but are tranquil and well proportioned. Fine restaurant and a terraced pool. In World War II, the Aletti was home to Vichy's Minister of War. **www.hotel-aletti.fr**

VITRAC Auberge de la Tomette

Le Bourg, 15220 **Tel** *04 71 64 70 94* **Fax** *04 71 64 77 11* **Rooms** *16*

A lovely country retreat set in huge gardens with a games area for children. Recent enhancements include a heated pool, sauna and *hammam*. The rooms are restful and spacious; six designed for families. Equal thought and attention goes into the cooking. Closed Nov–Easter. **www.auberge-la-tomette.com**

YGRANDE Château d'Ygrande

Le Mont, 3320 **Tel** *04 70 66 33 11* **Fax** *04 70 66 33 63* **Rooms** *19*

A meticulously renovated, quality hotel is housed in this grand 19th-century building. The rooms are beautiful, bright and elegant. A vast park offers walking, cycling, horse riding and boating. Inside there is a hamman, fitness centre, sauna and billiards. Good restaurant serving local produce. Closed Jan–Mar. **www.chateauygrande.fr**

THE RHONE VALLEY & FRENCH ALPS

ANNECY Hôtel Palais de l'Isle

13 rue Perrière, 74000 **Tel** *04 50 45 86 87* **Rooms** *33*

Opposite the Palais de l'Isle, this hotel sits like a Venetian *palazzo* on the edge of the Thouin canal. The renovated rooms in the 18th-century house are comfortable and well-equipped, with modern decor using neutral colours. The best rooms are found on the canal side. **www.hoteldupalaisdelisle.com**

BAGNOLS Château de Bagnols

Le Bourg, 69620 **Tel** *04 74 71 40 00* **Fax** *04 74 71 40 49* **Rooms** *21*

In 1987 Lady Hamlyn restored this château north of Lyon, surrounded by Beaujolais vineyards, and created a luxury hotel. The 13th-century building has turrets, moat and drawbridge. The rooms are richly decorated in velvet, silk and antiques. Michelin-starred restaurant. **www.chateaudebagnols.com**

BRIANÇON Hôtel Cristol

6 rte d'Italie, 05100 **Tel** *04 92 20 20 11* **Fax** *04 92 21 02 58* **Rooms** *24*

Well-kept, traditional hotel. The attractive bedrooms are modern, airy and bright; some have balconies with a view of the Vauban fortifications. Friendly service, and children are well catered for here. Charming dining room serves interesting themed menus. **www.hotel-cristol-briancon.fr**

CHALMAZEL Château de Marcilly Talaru 　　　　　🅿 €€
42920 **Tel** *04 77 24 88 09* **Fax** *04 77 24 87 07* **Rooms** *5*

Situated at an altitude of 900 m (3,000 ft), Chalmazel becomes a small ski resort in winter. The bedrooms at this hotel reflect the overall grandeur of the magnificent fortified medieval château, with four-poster beds and classic furnishings. There are well-equipped bathrooms too. Breakfast included. *Table d'hôte* on request. **www.chateaudechalmazel.com**

CHAMBERY Hôtel des Princes 　　　　　 €€
4 rue de Boigne, 73000 **Tel** *04 79 33 45 36* **Fax** *04 79 70 31 47* **Rooms** *45*

Situated in the grandest section of the Old Town, near La Fontaine des Elephants, this charmingly old-fashioned hotel has quiet, comfortable rooms, though not very spacious. The service is welcoming and friendly. There are several restaurants nearby to choose from. **www.hoteldesprinces.eu**

CHAMBERY Château de Candie 　　　　　 €€€
Rue du Bois de Candie, 73000 **Tel** *04 79 96 63 00* **Fax** *04 79 96 63 10* **Rooms** *35*

Dominating the valley of Chambèry, this splendid hotel has a panoramic view of the mountains. A 14th-century Savoyard house has been beautifully transformed and offers sumptuous bedrooms decorated with refinement. A tranquil spot surrounded by its own park. Excellent restaurant serving classic gourmet cuisine. **www.chateaudecandie.com**

CHAMONIX MONT BLANC Le Hameau Albert 1er 　　　　 €€€€
119 impasse du Montenvers, 74402 **Tel** *04 50 53 05 09* **Fax** *04 50 55 95 48* **Rooms** *36*

Part of a hotel complex including the traditional hotel Albert 1er, the authentic and unusual Chalet Soli and the chic La Ferme. The large chalet-hotel has stunning views of Mont Blanc. The well-proportioned rooms have elegant designer furniture. Two good restaurants, one with two Michelin stars. There is also a sauna. **www.hameaualbert.fr**

CHANTERMERLE-LES-GRIGNAN Le Parfum Bleu 　　　　 €€
26230 **Tel** *04 75 98 54 21* **Fax** *04 75 98 54 21* **Rooms** *5*

The sound of cicadas and aroma of lavender – this is quintessential Drôme-Provençale. A beautifully restored stone farm-house with bright blue shutters offers comfortable *chambres d'hôtes*, each with a private entrance. The rooms have original stone floors and simple, modern furnishings. Buffet breakfast. *Table d'hôte* on request. **www.parfum-bleu.com**

CHONAS L'AMBALLAN Domaine de Clairefontaine 　　　　 €€
Chemin des Fontanettes, 38121 **Tel** *04 74 58 81 52* **Fax** *04 74 58 80 93* **Rooms** *28*

Set in a magnificent park in a small village south of Vienne, among ancient trees, this former manor house has impeccably furnished rooms. The modern annex has more chic rooms with balconies. The restaurant has a good reputation but can be inconsistent. **www.domaine-de-clairefontaine.fr**

CLIOUSCLAT La Treille Muscate 　　　　 €
Le Village, 26270 **Tel** *04 75 63 13 10* **Rooms** *12*

A pleasant Provençale inn in a village renowned for its pottery. The bedrooms are individually decorated: choose from Basque red, pastel blue or African. Some rooms have south-facing balconies. The vaulted dining room serves local cuisine. Breakfast is served in the garden on sunny days. Closed Jan–mid-Feb. **www.latreillemuscate.com**

CORDON Le Cordonant 　　　　 €
Les Darbaillets, 74700 **Tel** *04 50 58 34 56* **Fax** *04 50 47 95 57* **Rooms** *16*

A friendly family-run hotel at this ski resort west of Chamonix, the trim, well-kept chalet has a garden. The rooms are comfortable, with pretty rustic furniture. The best rooms have great views of Mont Blanc. The restaurant serves hearty alpine cuisine. Good value. **www.lecordonant.fr**

DIVONNE-LES-BAINS Château de Divonne 　　　　 €€€
115 rue des Bains, 01220 **Tel** *04 50 20 00 32* **Fax** *04 50 20 03 73* **Rooms** *34*

From this charming 19th-century mansion set in a large park, not far from Geneva, there are panoramic views of Mont Blanc and Lake Geneva. Inside is a monumental staircase. The rooms are richly furnished. Tennis courts on site, and golf course nearby. Classic cuisine. **www.chateau-divonne.com**

EVIAN-LES-BAINS Hôtel Royal Palace 　　　　 €€€€€
Rive Sud du Lac de Genève, 74500 **Tel** *04 50 26 85 00* **Fax** *04 50 75 38 40* **Rooms** *144*

An imposing hotel situated on the water's edge by Lake Geneva. Four restaurants, jogging trails, spa treatments, a private garden and a children's club are all on offer. Rooms and suites are tastefully decorated and most have impressive views over the lake. **www.evianroyalresort.com**

GRENOBLE Splendid Hôtel 　　　　 €
22 rue Thiers, 38000 **Tel** *04 76 46 33 12* **Fax** *04 76 46 35 24* **Rooms** *45*

Smart centrally located hotel in a quiet location, with a walled garden. The guest rooms range from classical to modern, with gaily painted frescoes. Efficient service and amenities. Continental and *à la carte* breakfast served in the dining room, or garden terrace. **www.splendid-hotel.com**

GRESY-SUR-ISÈRE La Tour de Pacoret 　　　　 €
Montailleur, 73460 **Tel** *04 79 37 91 59* **Fax** *04 79 37 93 84* **Rooms** *11*

The tower has been here since 1283 when it was erected to guard the Combe de Savoie. Beside it, this quality hotel with stylish rooms has developed. The bedrooms, each named after a flower, are decorated in warm tones. The mountain scenery can be enjoyed from the terrace. Traditional dishes served. **www.hotel-pacoret-savoie.com**

Key to Price Guide *see p550* **Key to Symbols** *see back cover flap*

LE POET LAVAL Les Hospitaliers

€€

Vieux Village, 26160 **Tel** *04 75 46 22 32* **Fax** *04 75 46 49 99* **Rooms** *20*

A beautifully restored hotel in the centre of a tiny hilltop medieval village east of Montélimar. The elegantly furnished bedrooms, in the old stone buildings, are spacious and quiet. The restaurant offers first-class service, excellent cuisine and a wide range of good Rhône valley wines. **www.hotel-les-hospitaliers.com**

LES DEUX ALPES Chalet Hôtel Mounier

€€

2 rue de la Chapelle, 38860 **Tel** *04 76 80 56 90* **Fax** *04 76 79 56 51* **Rooms** *46*

Now a quality hotel, this former alpine farm has plenty of character. Contemporary, yet ultra cosy rooms have a chic authentic chalet atmosphere. Well-equipped with up to date amenities, the hotel is constantly being upgraded. The lounge features an open fireplace. Good restaurant. Closed May–Jun & Sep–mid-Dec. **www.chalet-mounier.com**

LYON Hôtel des Artistes

€€

8 rue Gaspard-André, 69002 **Tel** *04 78 42 04 88* **Fax** *04 78 42 93 76* **Rooms** *45*

Close to the place Bellecour, the Saône River and next door to the Theâtre des Célestins, this delightful hotel is a favourite haunt of actors. Pleasant, bright, airy rooms. Breakfast is served in an attractive room that is decorated with a Jean Cocteau-style fresco. **www.hotel-des-artistes.fr**

LYON La Maison du Greillon

€€

12 Montée du Greillon, 69009 **Tel** *04 72 29 10 97* **Rooms** *5*

This large building was once home to Lyon sculptor Joseph Chinard. Now a small and tranquil bed and breakfast with its own garden, fountain and terrace, and great views of the Croix-Rousse and the Saône. The well-kept rooms have elegant classical furnishings. There is a roomy dining room and a kitchen for guests to use. **www.legreillon.com**

LYON Cour des Loges

€€€€

6 rue du Bœuf, 69005 **Tel** *04 72 77 44 44* **Fax** *04 72 40 93 61* **Rooms** *62*

This luxury hotel occupies four renovated Renaissance mansions around a central galleried courtyard in Vieux Lyon. The reception area has a stunning glass roof. The elegant rooms blend Renaissance and contemporary decor. The restaurant serves classic cuisine. **www.courdesloges.com**

MANIGOD Hôtel-Chalets de la Croix-Fry

€€€

Rte du Col de la Croix-Fry, 74230 **Tel** *04 50 44 90 16* **Fax** *04 50 44 94 87* **Rooms** *10*

High on a mountain pass east of Annecy, this delightful chalet-style hotel combines Alpine rustic with comfort in a friendly atmosphere. The wooden interior is charming, decorated with Savoyard furniture. The guest rooms are cosy. Closed May and October–November. **www.hotelchaletcroixfry.com**

MEGÈVE Les Fermes de Marie

€€€€€

163 chemin de Riante Colline, 74120 **Tel** *04 50 93 03 10* **Fax** *04 50 93 09 84* **Rooms** *71*

Lovingly restored chalets with chic country-style rooms. The bedrooms reflect Savoyard charm with rustic furniture and decor in natural colours. The ambience is professional, yet relaxed and friendly. The facilities are superb: spa, sauna, Jacuzzi, hairdresser, games room, fitness centre and a good restaurant. Closed May–Jun. **www.fermesdemarie.com**

MONTELIMAR Sphinx

€

19 bd Desmarais, 26200 **Tel** *04 75 01 86 64* **Fax** *04 75 52 34 21* **Rooms** *24*

Old-fashioned charm greets visitors to this former 17th-century *hôtel particulier*. Situated in the historic city centre, it is surprisingly calm, with a private courtyard and delightful shady terrace. Relax and enjoy the restful atmosphere of the comfortable, homely ambience. **www.sphinx-hotel.fr**

PEROUGES Hostellerie du Vieux Pérouges

€€€€

Pl du Tilleul, 01800 **Tel** *04 74 61 00 88* **Fax** *04 74 34 77 90* **Rooms** *28*

This historic inn is a filmmaker's dream, converted from 13th-century buildings and set in a medieval hilltop village. The four ancient houses are clustered around the main square. The decor is different in each house. Ultra-classic cuisine serving regional dishes with precision. **www.hostelleriedeperouges.com**

ROMANS SUR ISERE Hôtel l'Orée du Parc

€€

6 av Gambetta, 26100 **Tel** *04 75 70 26 12* **Fax** *04 75 05 08 23* **Rooms** *10*

After visiting le Palais Idéal du Facteur Cheval, head 25 km (16 miles) south to Romans, and relax in this charming hotel. A tastefully renovated 20th-century manor house in its own park, all the rooms are non-smoking and filled with modern, elegant furnishings. **www.hotel-oreeparc.com**

SERVAS Le Nid à Bibi

€€

Lalleyriat, 1960 **Tel** *04 74 21 11 47* **Fax** *04 74 21 02 83* **Rooms** *5*

A peaceful night's sleep awaits at this adorable *chambre d'hôtes* next to Bourg. Cosy, comfortable and well-equipped rooms each have a private bathroom. Guests enjoy a homely atmosphere and have use of the living area and garden. Hearty breakfast with home-made jams, pastries, and cold meats. *Table d'hôte* on request. **http://lenidabibi.com**

ST-CYR-AU-MONT-D'OR L'Ermitage Hôtel

€€€

Chemin de l'Ermitage Mont Cindre, 69450 **Tel** *04 72 19 69 69* **Fax** *04 72 19 69 71* **Rooms** *29*

Just 15-minutes drive from Lyon city centre, this design establishment harmonizes different materials with success: concrete, wood, glass, aluminium and stone. The rooms are luminous with quirky accessories, ultra-modern equipment and a view of Fourvière. Lyon specialities are served in the terrace restaurant. **www.ermitage-college-hotel.com**

ST-ETIENNE Mercure Parc de l'Europe
Rue Wuppertal, 42000 **Tel** *04 77 42 81 81* **Fax** *04 77 42 81 89* **Rooms** *120*

This large, practical, modern building lacks charm, but is conveniently situated for the city centre. The bedrooms are bright and well maintained, with fully-equipped bathrooms. The interior has a theatrical theme. There is also a cosy bar and a contemporary restaurant serving local produce. **www.mercure.com**

TALLOIRES Hôtel l'Abbaye
Chemin des Moines, 74290 **Tel** *04 50 60 77 33* **Fax** *04 50 60 78 81* **Rooms** *33*

This elegant hotel occupying a former 17th-century Benedictine abbey is beautifully situated on the shores of Lac d'Annecy. Cézanne used to be a regular guest. The large rooms have wonderfully decorated period ceilings and antique furniture. Attractive garden and good restaurant. Closed Jan–mid-Feb. **www.abbaye-talloires.com**

VAL D'ISERE Christiania
Chef Lieu, 73152 **Tel** *04 79 06 08 25* **Fax** *04 79 41 11 10* **Rooms** *70*

Splendid modern chalet with a magnificent view of the ski slopes at this popular resort for the rich and famous. Luxurious fully equipped rooms, all with balconies, are decorated in an elegant Alpine theme. Pamper yourself in the health and fitness centre. Superb buffet breakfast. **www.hotel-christiania.com**

VALLON PONT D'ARC Le Clos des Bruyères
Rte des Gorges, 07150 **Tel** *04 75 37 18 85* **Fax** *04 75 37 14 89* **Rooms** *32*

Situated in the Gorges d'Ardèche, this modern hotel, built in a Provençal style, has bedrooms that open on to the pool via a balcony or terrace. Family rooms are available. Hire a canoe or quad and take a picnic to explore the river and countryside. Nautical-themed restaurant. **www.closdesbruyeres.net**

POITOU & AQUITAINE

ARCACHON Hôtel Le Dauphin
7 av Gounod, 33120 **Tel** *05 56 83 02 89* **Fax** *05 56 54 84 90* **Rooms** *50*

This well-run hotel dating from the late 19th century is instantly recognizable from its red-and-white brickwork. It's located a few blocks back from the sea in a quiet residential district. Spick-and-span rooms have simple pine furnishings and white walls. **www.dauphin-arcachon.com**

BONNEUIL-MATOURS L'Olivier
11 rue du petit Bornais, 86210 **Tel** *05 49 02 73 53* **Rooms** *4*

This delightful bed and breakfast is on the edge of the Forêt de Moulière, close to Futuroscope, Chauvigny, Châtellerault and Poitiers. The four bedrooms are homely and individually styled. One is in the attic and two have canopied beds. There is a sitting room and dining room for communal use and a delightful garden. **www.vienne-hotes-lolivier.com**

BORDEAUX La Maison du Lierre
57 rue Huguerie, 33000 **Tel** *05 56 51 92 71* **Fax** *05 56 79 15 16* **Rooms** *12*

Close to Bordeaux's chic Golden Triangle, this small hotel – its homely atmosphere more like a *chambre d'hôte* - has been renovated with flair. Rooms are stylish. Generous homemade breakfasts may be served in the interior courtyard. It is wise to book ahead. **www.maisondulierre.com**

BORDEAUX La Maison Bord'Eaux
113 rue Docteur Albert Barraud, 33000 **Tel** *05 56 44 00 45* **Fax** *05 56 44 17 31* **Rooms** *6*

Wine lovers will enjoy this small boutique hotel where a large range of wines is available by the glass or bottle. The owners can also arrange wine-tasting visits to châteaux. Rooms look on to a garden where breakfast and meals are often served. Parking is available which is rare for a city hotel. **www.lamaisonbord-eaux.com**

CAP-FERRET La Maison du Bassin
5 rue des Pionniers, 33950 **Tel** *05 56 60 60 63* **Fax** *05 56 03 71 47* **Rooms** *7 (plus 4 annex rooms)*

Ultra-chic and highly sought-after address at the end of the Cap-Ferret peninsula. A colonial ambience is achieved with highly polished wood, cane chairs and arty knick-knacks. Try one of the tasty tropical rums as an aperitif, before dining on the tropical veranda. Reservations by phone only. **www.lamasiondubassin.com**

CARSAC La Villa Romaine
Saint Rome, 24200 **Tel** *05 53 28 52 07* **Fax** *05 53 28 58 10* **Rooms** *17*

This plush hotel occupies a group of beautifully restored stone buildings that stand on the site of a Gallo-Roman villa, next to some magnificent water gardens and in the heart of the Périgord Noir. Rooms are equipped with all the luxury modern comforts and are all spacious and peaceful. **www.lavillaromaine.com**

CIERZAC Le Moulin de Cierzac
Rte de Cognac, 17520 **Tel** *05 45 83 01 32* **Fax** *05 45 83 03 59* **Rooms** *7*

A short drive south of Cognac is this hotel-restaurant in a 17th-century mansion set in extensive grounds. Pleasant rooms contain exposed beams; some have river views. The restaurant serves local specialities. Afterwards, choose your *digestif* from a vast array of cognacs. **www.moulindecierzac.com**

Key to Price Guide *see p550* **Key to Symbols** *see back cover flap*

COGNAC Les Pigeons Blancs 🅿️ 🍴 ⛲ €€

110 rue Jules-Brisson, 16100 **Tel** *05 45 82 16 36* **Rooms** *6*

In the heart of the cognac vineyards, this 17th-century auberge offers a warm welcome and a handful of elegantly decorated rooms decked out with period furniture. Two are non-smoking. Other facilities include an excellent restaurant and a garden. Baby-sitting available. **www.pigeons-blancs.com**

COULON Le Central 🅿️ 🍴 📖 €

4 rue d'Autremont, 79510 **Tel** *05 49 35 90 20* **Fax** *05 49 35 81 07* **Rooms** *13*

Situated in the mysterious fens of the Marais Poitevin, this traditional village hotel has been in the same family for three generations. The guest rooms are bright, clean and tasteful. Downstairs is a deservedly popular restaurant. You'll need to book well ahead. Disabled access. **www.hotel-lecentral-coulon.com**

EUGENIE-LES-BAINS La Maison Rose 🅿️ 🍴 ♨️ 📺 €€€€

334 rue René Vielle, 40320 **Tel** *05 58 05 06 07* **Fax** *05 58 51 10 10* **Rooms** *31*

The illustrious chef Michel Guérard draws worshippers to Eugénie, a thermal spa dating back to the 18th century. This, the most modest of his five hotels, feels like a country house, from the rose-filled garden to the pretty guest rooms – not lavish but absolutely immaculate. Closed Dec–Jan. **www.michelguerard.com**

EUGENIE LES BAINS Les Prés d'Eugénie 🅿️ 🍴 ♨️ 📺 📖 €€€€€

334 rue René Vielle, 40320 **Tel** *05 58 05 06 07* **Fax** *05 58 51 10 10* **Rooms** *32*

Michel Guérard's highly acclaimed hotel has six gorgeous suites in addition to its simple but luxurious bedrooms. The 19th-century manor is famed for its *cuisine minceur* restaurants which offer residents the option of losing weight while revelling in some of France's finest cooking. **www.michelguerard.com**

GRENADE-SUR-L'ADOUR Pain Adour et Fantaisie 🍴 ⛲ 📖 ♿ €€

14-16 pl des Tilleuls, 40270 **Tel** *05 58 45 18 80* **Fax** *05 58 45 16 57* **Rooms** *11*

This elegant hotel overlooking Grenade's arcaded central square on one side, and the river on the other, is home to one of the region's best restaurants. In keeping with the hotel's 17th-century architecture, antiques, oak panelling and parquet predominate. Spacious rooms. **www.chateauxhotels.com/fantaisie**

HOSSEGOR Les Hortensias du Lac 🅿️ ♨️ €€€

1578 av du Tour du Lac, 40150 **Tel** *05 58 43 99 00* **Fax** *05 58 43 42 81* **Rooms** *24*

This hotel, set in pine forests not far from the ocean and overlooking Hossegor lake, provides a peaceful retreat. Guest rooms in the 1930s villa are tranquil, with their neutral tones offset against dark wood, all with a terrace or balcony. Splendid champagne buffet breakfast. Closed mid-Nov–Easter. **www.hortensias-du-lac.com**

LA ROCHELLE Les Brises 🍴 🅿️ €€

Chemin de la Digue-Richelieu, rue Philippe Vincent 17000 **Tel** *05 46 43 89 37* **Fax** *05 46 43 27 97* **Rooms** *48*

A comfortable and popular hotel within walking distance of the vieux port and the bustling city centre. It's worth paying extra for a seafront room. Not only are they more spacious, but they also benefit from balconies with wonderful views out to sea and the offshore islands. **www.hotellesbrises.eu**

LE BOIS-PLAGE-EN-RE Hôtel L'Océan 🅿️ 🍴 ♨️ €€€

172 rue St-Martin, 17580 **Tel** *05 46 09 23 07* **Fax** *05 46 09 05 40* **Rooms** *29*

There's a real seaside feel to this hotel on the southern coast of the Île de Ré. Potted palms, giant parasols and sun-bleached wooden decking outside; inside, pretty pastels and marine motifs for the rooms. Not surprisingly, ultra-fresh fish dominates the restaurant menu. Massage and beauty treatments are available. **www.re-hotel-ocean.com**

MAGESCQ Relais de la Poste 🅿️ 🍴 ♨️ ⛲ 📺 📖 €€€€

24, av de Maremne, 40140 **Tel** *05 58 47 70 25* **Fax** *05 58 47 76 17* **Rooms** *24*

This small and wonderfully relaxed hotel set in a 19th-century coaching inn has a garden and nicely landscaped pools. It combines comfort, celebrated cuisine, fine wines and family tradition. You're not far from the sea here, with Bayonne and Biarritz within easy striking distance. Closed mid-Nov–Christmas. **www.relaisposte.com**

MARGAUX Le Pavillon de Margaux 🅿️ 🍴 ♨️ €€

3 rue Georges-Mandel, 33460 **Tel** *05 57 88 77 54* **Fax** *05 57 88 77 73* **Rooms** *14*

In the centre of Margaux village, this handsome hotel provides a comfortable base for exploring the Médoc vineyards. Guest rooms, which are "sponsored" by local wine châteaux, are individually styled. Some have antiques and four-posters, others rattan and floral fabrics. **www.pavillonmargaux.com**

MARTHON Château de la Couronne 🅿️ ♨️ €€€€

Château de la Couronne, 16380 **Tel** *05 45 62 29 96* **Rooms** *5*

A boutique château hotel and sometime film and TV location offering five suites decorated in a bold, contemporary style with original artworks. Everything is supplied for relaxation: three sitting rooms, a private cinema, a billiard room, a music room and a large extent of private parkland. **www.chateaudelacouronne.com**

NIEUIL Château de Nieuil 🅿️ 🍴 ♨️ ⛲ 📖 €€€

16270 **Tel** *05 45 71 36 38* **Fax** *05 45 71 46 45* **Rooms** *14*

King François I hunted in the extensive park surrounding this superb Renaissance château with its pepper-pot towers and sweeping staircase. A quiet night is assured in the elegant, comfortable rooms. The stables now house an excellent restaurant. **www.chateaunieuilhotel.com**

POITIERS Château du Clos de la Ribaudière 🏨🍴 €€
Chasseneuil Centre, Chasseneuil du Poitou, 86360 **Tel** *05 49 52 86 66* **Fax** *05 49 52 86 32* **Rooms** *39*

Close to Poitiers, this magnificent hotel and restaurant is housed in a château dating back to the 18th century. The bedrooms are spacious and sophisticated. Special-price breaks are available for two people including a night's stay, meals and either a game of golf or a visit to nearby Futuroscope. **www.ribaudiere.com**

ROCHEFORT-SUR-MER La Corderie Royale 🅿🍴🛏🍴📋 €€€
Rue Audebert, 17300 **Tel** *05 46 99 35 35* **Fax** *05 46 99 78 72* **Rooms** *50*

The best place to stay in Rochefort, both for comfort and convenience, this hotel-restaurant stands on the leafy banks of the River Charente between the yacht harbour and the royal rope-making factory (after which the hotel is named). The restaurant is a good place for lunch. **www.corderieroyale.com**

ROYAN Domaine de St Palais 🅿 €€
50 rue du Logis, St Palais sur Mer, 17420 **Tel** *05 46 39 85 26* **Rooms** *4*

This elegant haven is discreetly set back from the bustling coast near Royan. It occupies a building that is largely 18th century but has a history dating back even earlier. Two of the stylish rooms overlook the garden and two look on to woods. There are also eight apartments and one suite. **www.domainedesaintpalais.eu**

SABRES Auberge des Pins 🅿🍴🏃 €€
Rte de la Piscine, 40630 **Tel** *05 58 08 30 00* **Fax** *05 58 07 56 74* **Rooms** *25*

From the moment you enter this attractive farmhouse, deep in the forests of the Landes Regional Park, you know you're in for a treat. This is country living at its best: old-style hospitality, homely rooms, open fires in winter and quiet corners to curl up in with a book. Fine restaurant. **www.aubergedespins.fr**

SEIGNOSSE La Villa de l'Etang Blanc 🅿🍴 €€€
2265 rte de l'Etang Blanc, 40510 **Tel** *05 58 72 80 15* **Fax** *05 58 72 83 67* **Rooms** *10*

This charming hotel is set in a park with direct access to the Etang Blanc. The elegant rooms are individually decorated in a romantic style. There's a good restaurant with a wonderful view of the lake. It serves traditional seasonal dishes with discreet, professional service. Closed mid-Nov–Apr. **www.villaetangblanc.fr**

ST-EMILION Au Logis des Remparts 🅿🛏📋 €€€
18 rue Guadet, 33330 **Tel** *05 57 24 70 43* **Fax** *05 57 74 47 44* **Rooms** *17*

Outside peak season, when prices drop, this modest hotel provides a comfortable overnight stop. Its main draws are the sizeable terraced garden and swimming pool. The rooms lack character, but those on the back benefit from views over the vineyards. **www.logisdesremparts.com**

ST-EMILION Hostellerie de Plaisance 🛗🅿🍴📋 €€€€€
Pl du Clocher, 33330 **Tel** *05 57 55 07 55* **Fax** *05 57 74 41 11* **Rooms** *17 (plus 4 suites)*

Upscale hotel in an exceptional location overlooking St-Emilion and its famous vineyards. Luxurious rooms boast the full range of amenities, including magnificent bathrooms. Some have private terraces. The service is top-notch and the restaurant one of the region's best. **www.hostelleriedeplaisance.com**

ST-LOUP-LAMAIRE Château de St Loup sur Thouet - The Keep 🅿 €€€€
Château de St-Loup, 79600 **Tel** *05 49 64 81 73* **Fax** *05 49 64 82 06* **Rooms** *13*

This moated medieval château is owned by a count. The keep houses bed and breakfast rooms, many with four-poster beds; the best is the Suite of the Black Prince. There are other stately rooms in the main château, which is open to visitors during the day. The extensive grounds include parkland and an orangery. **www.chateaudesaint-loup.com**

ST-SEURIN-D'UZET Blue Sturgeon 🅿🍴🛏 €€
3 rue de la Cave, 17120 **Tel** *05 46 74 17 18* **Rooms** *4*

A calm, chic, eclectically-furnished bed and breakfast in the small village of St-Seurin-d'Uzet, which is alleged to be the first place in Europe to have produced caviar in the 1920s (hence the hotel's name). Good beaches nearby and the famous vineyards of the Médoc are just across the Gironde estuary. Dinner is served on request. **www.bluesturgeon.com**

TRIZAY Les Jardins du Lac 🅿🍴🛏🏃 €€
3 chemin de Fontchaude, 17250 **Tel** *05 46 82 03 56* **Fax** *05 46 82 03 55* **Rooms** *8*

A well-run hotel midway between Rochefort and Saintes. The modern buildings are surrounded by landscaped gardens with a trout lake and woodland. Airy and well-maintained rooms all offer lake views. Meals are served outside in fine weather. A lovely, relaxing place to stay. **www.jardins-du-lac.com**

PERIGORD, QUERCY & GASCONY

AGEN Hôtel Château des Jacobins 🅿📋 €€€
1 pl des Jacobins, 47000 **Tel** *05 53 47 03 31* **Fax** *05 53 47 02 80* **Rooms** *15*

Built in the early 19th century, this small, ivy-clad château with a walled garden is an oasis of calm in the city centre. The rooms are elegantly decorated with period furniture and chandeliers. There's secure parking and you'll find plenty of fine restaurants within easy walking distance. **www.chateau-des-jacobins.com**

Key to Price Guide *see p550* **Key to Symbols** *see back cover flap*

ALBI La Regence George V €

27–29 av Maréchal Joffre, 81000 **Tel** *05 63 54 24 16* **Fax** *05 63 49 90 78* **Rooms** *20*

This comfortable, inexpensive hotel near the train station and not far from the city centre offers a choice of standard rooms or larger junior suites. All are decorated in warm and bright colours. Outside there is a terrace and a small garden. Breakfast only but there are plenty of restaurants nearby. **www.laregence-georgev.fr**

ALBI Hostellerie du Grand St Antoine €€€

17 rue St-Antoine, 81000 **Tel** *05 63 54 04 04* **Fax** *05 63 47 10 47* **Rooms** *44*

Owned by the same family for five generations, the Grand St Antoine claims to be one of the oldest hotels in France. Guests have the use of a swimming pool and a tennis court 3-km (2-miles) away. Parking is available for an extra charge. The restaurant serves traditional southwestern cuisine. **www.hotel-saint-antoine-albi.com**

BEYNAC-ET-CAZENAC Café de la Rivière €

Bourg, 24220 **Tel** *05 53 28 35 49* **Rooms** *3*

This renowned restaurant situated above the River Dordogne has three simple bed and breakfast rooms. There is one double and two twins; all have wooden floors, white linen bedspreads and en-suite bathrooms. Free Wi-Fi Internet access is also available. Closed Nov–Apr. **www.cafedelariviere.com**

BOURDEILLES Hostellerie Les Griffons €€

24310 **Tel** *05 53 45 45 35* **Fax** *05 53 45 45 20* **Rooms** *10*

All of the rooms in this 16th-century mansion have plenty of character, with exposed beams, and vividly coloured paints and fabrics. Some rooms are in the attic and others have views over the river. The restaurant serves dinner plus Sunday lunch. Closed Nov–mid-Apr. **www.griffons.fr**

BRANTOME Le Moulin de l'Abbaye €€€€€

1 rte de Bourdeilles, 24310 **Tel** *05 53 05 80 22* **Fax** *05 53 05 75 27* **Rooms** *19*

Treat yourself to a night of luxury in this romantic, creeper-covered mill on the River Dronne. Rooms are in the mill and in two handsome old houses nearby, but all share the same fresh yet sophisticated decor. Terraced waterside gardens proivde the perfect breakfast spot. Closed mid-Nov–Apr. **www.moulinabbaye.com**

CHAMPAGNAC-DE-BELAIR Le Moulin du Roc €€€€

Av Eugène le Roy, 24530 **Tel** *05 53 02 86 00* **Fax** *05 53 54 21 31* **Rooms** *13*

In a magical setting on the river Dronne, just outside Brantôme, is this luxury hotel hidden under swathes of greenery in a converted 17th-century watermill. In addition to the sumptuous, individually styled rooms, there is a superb restaurant, an indoor pool and tennis court. Closed Dec–Mar. **www.moulinduroc.com**

CHANCELADE Château des Reynats €€€

Av des Reynats, 24650 **Tel** *05 53 03 53 59* **Fax** *05 53 03 44 84* **Rooms** *50*

Just west of Périgueux, this charming 19th-century château makes for an agreeable night's stay. Standard rooms in the "Orangerie" annex are bright and breezy, but for real atmosphere upgrade to the château rooms. There's a top-notch resturant, too, and spacious grounds. **www.chateau-hotel-perigord.com**

COLY Manoir d'Hautegente €€€€

Haute Gente, 24120 **Tel** *05 53 51 68 03* **Fax** *05 53 50 38 52* **Rooms** *17*

Not far from Sarlat and the Lascaux caves is this picturesque manor house, once the mill and forge of an abbey. It is now a family-run, friendly hotel with log fires, private fishing and well-tended riverside gardens. Half-board mandatory in high-season; the food is excellent. Closed Nov–Apr. **www.manoir-hautegente.com**

CONDOM Le Logis des Cordeliers €

Rue de la Paix, 32100 **Tel** *05 62 28 03 68* **Fax** *05 62 68 29 03* **Rooms** *21*

Modern hotel offering modest but well priced rooms in the centre of Condom. Picture windows lend space and light and many rooms have balconies overlooking the pool. There is no in-house restaurant, but you can eat in the highly rated Table des Cordeliers next door. Closed Jan. **www.logisdescordeliers.com**

CORDES SUR CIEL Hostellerie du Vieux Cordes €€

21 rue St-Michel, 81170 **Tel** *05 63 53 79 20* **Fax** *05 63 56 02 47* **Rooms** *21*

At the top of the medieval town, with lovely views over the valley, this hotel occupies a three-storey stone building with vaulted ceilings. Prices of the rooms vary according to their size and style. Some are quite elaborately decorated, while others, labelled "eco", are simpler. The restaurant serves dishes based on local produce. **www.vieuxcordes.fr**

CUQ-TOULZA Cuq en Terrasses €€€

Cuq le Château, 81470 **Tel** *05 63 82 54 00* **Fax** *05 63 82 54 11* **Rooms** *7*

A renovated 18th-century hill-top house in the Cocagne region, midway between Toulouse and Castres. The rooms have overhead beams and varnished flagstone floors. Nestling in the lovely gardens is an inviting pool. The restaurant menu draws on the produce of local farms. **www.cuqenterrasses.com**

DOMME L'Esplanade €€

Rue du Pont Carrel, 24250 **Tel** *05 53 28 31 41* **Fax** *05 53 28 49 92* **Rooms** *15*

Perched on the edge of a cliff, the best rooms in this elegant hotel offer panoramic views of the Dordogne valley. Some have canopied four-poster beds to match the refined, opulent decor. Less dramatic but very comfortable rooms are among the streets of the medieval bastide. Closed mid-Nov–Mar. **www.esplanade-perigord.com**

FIGEAC Château du Vigier du Roy
52 rue Emile Zola, 46100 **Tel** *05 65 50 05 05* **Fax** *05 65 50 06 06* **Rooms** *9*

Centuries ago, this mansion with its 14th-century tower was once the residence of a judge, the King's representative in Figeac. The rooms all have a medieval flavour, with four-poster or canopied beds. The restaurant is in the former guards' room. **www.chateau-viguier-figeac.com**

GOUDOURVILLE Château de Goudourville
82400 **Tel** *05 63 29 09 06* **Fax** *05 63 39 7 5 22* **Rooms** *6*

This château betweeen Agen and Moissac dates back to the 11th century and the guest rooms are redolent with history. The rooms – some of them enormous – are decorated with 18th-century furniture and tapestries and have views over the valley, the village or the battlements. **www.chateau-goudourville.fr**

LACAVE Le Pont de l'Ouysse
Le Pont de l'Ouysse, 46200 **Tel** *05 65 37 87 04* **Fax** *05 65 32 77 41* **Rooms** *14*

There's a Provençal air to this chic restaurant-with-rooms in riverside gardens not far from Rocamadour. Inside, cool creams blend with ochre hues, and the rooms and two apartments are fabulously quiet. In their fourth generation, the Chambon family have created a real hideaway. Inventive cuisine. **www.lepontdelouysse.fr**

LE BUGUE SUR VEZERE Domaine de la Barde
Route de Périgueux, 24260 **Tel** *05 53 07 16 54* **Fax** *05 53 54 76 19* **Rooms** *18*

Elegant guest rooms are housed within an 18th-century manor house (9 rooms), an old mill (8 rooms) and the forge (1 room). The large grounds include classical gardens and a jet-stream swimming pool. If you want to get away from it all there are riverside paths and meadow walks nearby. **www.domainedelabarde.com**

LECTOURE Hôtel de Bastard
Rue Lagrange, 32700 **Tel** *05 62 68 82 44* **Fax** *05 62 68 76 81* **Rooms** *31*

Despite its name, this elegant hotel is one of the best in the Gers. Antique furnishings are coupled with modern comforts in an 18th-century townhouse. Facilities include a small garden, sun deck and swimming pool. Refined regional cuisine makes the restaurant perennially popular. Closed 22 Dec–1 Feb. **www.hotel-de-bastard.com**

LES-EYZIES-DE-TAYAC Les Glycines
24620 **Tel** *05 53 06 97 07* **Fax** *05 53 06 92 19* **Rooms** *24*

A charming and luxurious small hotel in Périgord Noir, which is particularly convenient for visiting the prehistoric painted caves nearby. The best rooms (junior suites) have their own private terraces and direct access to the garden. A choice of picnics can be ordered from the reception. **www.les-glycines-dordogne.com**

MARTEL Relais Ste-Anne
Rue du Pourtanel, 46600 **Tel** *05 65 37 40 56* **Fax** *05 65 37 42 82* **Rooms** *21*

Behind the discreet entrance hides a lovely old building, once a girls' boarding school complete with chapel, in spacious grounds. Everything is designed for a relaxing stay, from the beautifully appointed rooms – some with private terrace – to the heated pool. Hearty breakfasts. Closed mid-Nov–Mar. **www.relais-sainte-anne.com**

MAUROUX Hostellerie Le Vert
46700 **Tel** *05 65 36 51 36* **Fax** *05 65 36 56 84* **Rooms** *6*

Ancient cedar trees shade the grounds of this 17th-century house, part of a former wine estate at the heart of the Cahors wine region. The rooms are spacious and exposed stone walls give them great character. Reserve for dinner in the cool dining room or on the flower-filled terrace. Closed Nov–Mar. **www.hotellevert.com**

MERCUES Château de Mercuès
46090 **Tel** *05 65 20 00 01* **Fax** *05 65 20 05 72* **Rooms** *30*

Dominating the Lot valley is this turreted 13th-century château where the bishops of nearby Cahors once lived. It is now a luxury hotel offering rooms on a suitably grand scale, gourmet dining among chandeliers or in the courtyard, tennis courts and extensive parkland. **www.chateaudemercues.com**

MOISSAC Le Moulin de Moissac
Esplanade du Moulin, 82200 **Tel** *05 63 32 88 88* **Fax** *05 63 32 02 08* **Rooms** *36*

Though not the most attractive building, this hotel in a former mill more than compensates with its quiet, riverside location, efficient service and well-equipped rooms. All come with DVD/CD player, Wi-Fi Internet and coffee machine. Central Moissac is a stroll away. **www.lemoulindemoissac.com**

MONTCUQ EN QUERCY Domaine de St Géry
46800 **Tel** *05 65 31 82 51* **Fax** *05 65 22 92 89* **Rooms** *5*

The carefully-maintained grounds of this hotel yield costly truffles, which have pride of place on the dining room menu. All the rooms are different, the most unusual is a vaulted cellar with two terraces. The others have either a private terrace or direct access to the garden. **www.saint-gery.com**

NONTRON La Maison des Beaux Arts
7 av du Général Leclerc, 24300 **Tel** *05 53 56 39 77* **Rooms** *5*

The "House of Fine Arts" is a restored 19th-century town house in pleasant Nontron. Inside, it is light and brightly decorated and there are magnificent views from the windows. Drawing and painting courses are sometimes held here. There is also a self-contained apartment available for rent. **www.la-maison-des-beaux-arts.com**

Key to Price Guide *see p550* **Key to Symbols** *see back cover flap*

ROCAMADOUR Domaine de la Rhue   P 🏊   €€€

46500 **Tel** *05 65 33 71 50* **Fax** *05 65 33 72 48* **Rooms** *14*

A short drive from Rocamadour is this peaceful hotel in beautifully converted 19th-century stables. Exposed beams and stonework give the spacious rooms an upscale rustic charm. Some come with a terrace, others with a kitchenette. The nearest restaurants are in Rocamadour. **www.domainedelarhue.com**

SARLAT Le Moulin Pointu   🍽 🏊   €

Ste Nathalene, 24200 **Tel** *05 53 28 15 54* **Fax** *05 53 28 15 54* **Rooms** *5*

Conveniently located on the outskirts of Sarlat, this bed and breakfast has cosy rooms with direct access to the garden, which has a pond and a small river. Breakfast can be enjoyed on the terrace near the swimming pool. Dinner (available on request) is shared with the family and other guests. **www.moulinpointu.com**

SEGUENVILLE Château de Seguenville   €€

Cabanac Seguenville, 31480 **Tel** *05 62 13 42 67* **Fax** *05 62 13 42 68* **Rooms** *5*

Perched on a hill near Toulouse, this château has great views of the surrounding countryside. A monumental staircase leads to the bedrooms, which are decorated with warm and bright colours; some have antique baths and basins. The panoramic terrace doubles as a dining room for breakfast and dinner in summer. **www.chateau-de-seguenville.com**

ST-AFFRIQUE-LES-MONTAGNES Domaine de Rasigous   P 🍽 🏊   €€

Domaine de Rasigous, 81290 **Tel** *05 63 73 30 50* **Rooms** *8*

This genteel estate offers a peaceful spot within easy reach of Albi, Castres, Toulouse and Carcassonne. Three of the spacious rooms are suites and there is a large warm lounge where you can enjoy tea by the fireside. Outside, the park is shaded by ancient trees. Free bike hire is available. Closed mid–Nov–mid–Mar. **www.domainederasigous.com**

ST-CIRQ-LAPOPIE Le Château de St-Cirq Lapopie   🏊   €€€

Le Bourg, 46330 **Tel** *05 65 31 27 48* **Rooms** *4*

An exquisitely restored château in the middle of one of the prettiest villages in France. The most original feature is the heated indoor swimming pool carved out of the rock on which the village stands. Rooms are beautifully decorated. Meals are not available. Closed Oct–May. **www.longitudehotels.com/chateau-st-cirq-lapopie/en**

ST-JEAN DE CORNAC Le Manoir de Saint Jean   P 🍽 🏊 🚹   €€€

82200 **Tel** *05 63 05 02 34* **Fax** *05 63 05 07 50* **Rooms** *10*

A 19th-century manor house in the Quercy Blanc has been converted into Le Manoir de Saint Jean. The hotel is surrounded by orchards, vineyards and ancient parkland, and has a pretty terrace giving onto the garden. The restaurant is noted for its fine cuisine. Each room is allocated its own covered parking space. **www.manoirsaintjean.com**

ST-VIVIEN Auberge du Moulin de Labique   P 🍽 🏊   €€

St Eutrope de Born, Villeréal, 47210 **Tel** *05 53 01 63 90* **Fax** *05 53 01 73 17* **Rooms** *6*

This welcoming 18th-century country residence is decorated with antique furniture, paintings and patterned wallpaper. Enjoy breakfast or a glass of local wine on the terrace while listening to the babbling mill stream. The excellent dinners are created with home-grown food and local produce. **www.moulin-de-labique.fr**

TEYSSODE Domaine d'en Naudet   P 🏊 🍸   €€

81220 **Tel** *05 63 70 50 59* **Rooms** *4*

One singular room here is in a converted watchtower; the others are in the old barn and stables facing south over the garden and a nearby Roman road. Breakfast can be enjoyed on the upper terrace with views of the countryside. There are tennis courts and a golf course nearby. Wi-Fi Internet access is also available. **www.domainenaudet.com**

TOULOUSE Les Loges de St Sernin   📺 📋   €€

12 rue St Bernard, 31000 **Tel** *05 61 24 44 44* **Rooms** *4*

This renovated private city house with guest bedrooms on the upper floors offers superb comfort. On a street near Toulouse's principal monument, Basilique St-Sernin, and within easy walking distance from the main square, it could not be more conveniently located. The owner is welcoming and obliging. **www.dormiratoulouse.net**

TOULOUSE Hôtel des Beaux Arts   📺 P 🍽 📋   €€€€

1 pl du Pont Neuf, 31000 **Tel** *05 34 45 42 42* **Fax** *05 34 45 42 43* **Rooms** *19*

Behind a beautiful Belle Epoque façade, beside the Pont Neuf, lies a chic hotel with modern comforts. The less expensive rooms are on the small side – better to upgrade for river views and more space. For a special occasion, opt for room 42 with its own tiny terrace among the roof tiles. **www.hoteldesbeauxarts.com**

THE PYRENEES

AINHOA Ithurria   P 🍽 🏊 📋   €€€

Pl du Fronton, 64250 **Tel** *05 59 29 92 11* **Fax** *05 59 29 81 28* **Rooms** *28*

This pretty 17th-century Basque inn was a stop on the pilgrimage route to Compostela. Opposite is the village's *pelota* court. Rooms are comfortable and prettily decorated, and the cosy dining room has an open fireplace, oak beams, and a menu with local specialities. Closed Dec–mid-Apr. **www.ithurria.com**

ANGLET Château de Brindos   `P ⑪ ☲ 〒 🗐`   €€€€€

1 allée du Château, 64600 **Tel** *05 59 23 89 80* **Fax** *05 59 23 89 81* **Rooms** *29*

Set in extensive, wooded grounds, this luxurious country house hotel offers gracious living beside a peaceful lake. Modern facilities include a weight room, sauna and *hammam*, with the beach and a golf course a short drive away. Enjoy breakfast on the jetty over the lake. **www.chateaudebrindos.com**

ARBONNE Laminak   `P ☲`   €€

Route de St Pée, 64210 **Tel** *05 59 41 95 40* **Fax** *05 59 41 87 65* **Rooms** *12*

A cosy hotel in a big, beautifully furnished Basque house with countryside and mountain views from the windows. Three of the rooms have private terraces, and outside there is a large garden. Light evening meals are available on request. Within reach of eight golf courses. **www.hotel-laminak.com**

ARGELES GAZOST Hôtel le Miramont   `❄ P ⑪ 🗐`   €€€

44 av des Pyrénées, 65400 **Tel** *05 62 97 01 26* **Fax** *05 62 97 56 67* **Rooms** *27*

This stylish hotel harking back to the 1930s is set amid manicured gardens in an attractive spa town. Eight rooms, furnished with antiques, are in a separate villa in the gardens, sharing the facilities of the main wing. Chef Pierre Pucheu serves Atlantic-Pyrenees delicacies. **www.hotelmiramont.com**

ARREAU Hôtel d'Angleterre   `❄ P ⑪ ☲ 🧍`   €€

Rte Luchon, 65240 **Tel** *05 62 98 63 30* **Fax** *05 62 98 69 66* **Rooms** *17*

This 17th-century inn, set in a pretty village of slate-roofed houses in the foothills of the Pyrenees, offers a good restaurant, plainly furnished but comfortable rooms, a garden, swimming pool, terrace and children's games area. A great base for exploring the stunning countryside. **www.hotel-angleterre-arreau.com**

AURIGNAC Le Moulin   `P`   €

Samouillan, 31420 **Tel** *05 61 98 86 92* **Rooms** *2*

A restored mill in a quiet tributary valley of the Garonne. Choose your room by theme: Zen, elephants or French country house. There is a minimum two-night stay and discounts are available for longer stays. Meditation and other spiritual workshops are often held here, or you can relax in the large garden. **www.moulin-vert.net**

BEAUCENS Eth Berye Petit   `🗐 P 🧍`   €

15 route de Vielle, 65400 **Tel** *05 62 97 90 02* **Rooms** *3*

Family-run bed and breakfast in an 18th-century farmhouse situated in a quiet hamlet south of Lourdes. Two of the rooms are cosy spaces in the attic; the third room is larger and has its own balcony with mountain views. *Table d'hôte* dinner on Friday and Saturday evenings by prior arrangement. **www.beryepetit.com**

BIARRITZ Villa Le Goëland   €€€€

12 plateau d'Atalaye, 64200 **Tel** *05 59 24 25 76* **Rooms** *4*

This grand old villa is close to both the town centre and the beach. There are magnificent views over the Port Vieux, the Rocher de la Vierge and the distant coast of Spain. One room has its own large private terrace. As it is a family home, no meals are available, but there are a number of good restaurants nearby. **www.villagoeland-biarritz.com**

BIARRITZ Hôtel du Palais   `P ⑪ ☲ 🧍 〒 🗐`   €€€€€

1 av de l'Impératrice, 64200 **Tel** *05 59 41 64 00* **Fax** *05 59 41 67 99* **Rooms** *132*

The grande dame of Biarritz's hotel scene, with an ambience harking back to the resort's Belle Epoque heyday. A magnificent heated seawater pool, direct beach access, a putting green, a playground and kids' pool complement the lovely rooms and outstanding restaurants. **www.hotel-du-palais.com**

CAMON Château de Camon   `P ⑪ ☲`   €€€

Camon, 9500 **Tel** *05 61 60 31 23* **Rooms** *9*

This massive abbey, dating back to the 10th century, dominates a pretty, fortified village within easy reach of Mirepoix and Montségur. Classically French rooms are sumptuous and spacious. The restaurant (dinner only) draws on local and seasonal ingredients. In summer tables are set in the abbey cloister. Closed Nov–mid-Mar. **www.chateaudecamon.com**

ESPELETTE Hôtel Euzkadi   `P ⑪ ☲ 〒`   €

285 rte Karrika Nagusia, 64250 **Tel** *05 59 93 91 88* **Fax** *05 59 93 90 19* **Rooms** *27*

Set in quiet countryside not far from the Atlantic beaches, this small and friendly family-run hotel has a pretty terrace, well-appointed rooms, a large swimming pool, tennis courts and secure parking. Owners Michèle and André Darriadou's restaurant serves Basque-influenced dishes. **www.hotel-restaurant-euzkadi.com**

ISSOR Les 3 Baudets   `🗐 P ☲`   €

64570 **Tel** *05 59 34 41 98* **Rooms** *5*

An 18th-century former farmhouse in a peaceful location surrounded by woods and meadows between Arette and Oloron-Ste-Marie. A good base from which to explore the central-western Pyrenees. It has five spacious rooms and a restaurant in the old sheep barn where grilled meats and home-made desserts are served. **www.3baudets-pyrenees.com**

LASSEUBE Maison Rancésamy   `P ⑪`   €€

Quartier Rey, 64290 **Tel** *05 59 04 26 37* **Rooms** *5*

This delightful rural retreat in the undulating countryside northwest of Oloron-Ste-Marie is run by charming and hospitable owners. The rooms are cosy and meals (*table d'hôte* dinner only) are exquisitely prepared. A place to unwind and enjoy the peace, or to use as a base while exploring the Pyrenees. **www.missbrowne.com**

Key to Price Guide *see p550* **Key to Symbols** *see back cover flap*

LOUHOSSOA Domaine de Silencenia
64250 **Tel** *05 59 93 35 60* **Rooms** *5*

Just off the road between St-Jean-Pied-de-Port and Cambo-les-Bains lies this bed and breakfast in its own grounds with a swimming pool and small lake. The cosy bedrooms are individually decorated and equipped with four-poster beds. Breakfast and an excellent *table d'hôte* dinner are available. **www.domaine-silencenia.com**

LOURDES Grand Hôtel de la Grotte
66 rue de la Grotte, 65100 **Tel** *05 62 94 58 87* **Fax** *05 62 94 20 50* **Rooms** *83*

One of the grandest hotels in the historic pilgrimage town of Lourdes, close to the famous grotto and fortress, with large rooms furnished opulently in Louis XVI style – some with views of the cathedral. The restaurants offer a choice of buffet or brasserie dining. Closed Nov–mid-Apr. **www.hotel-grotte.com**

MAUBOURGUET La Maison at Maubourguet
40 rue de l'hotel de ville, 65700 **Tel** *05 62 31 71 19* **Fax** *05 62 31 71 19* **Rooms** *3*

This small English-run bed and breakfast in an untouristy town north of Tarbes is an ideal base for exploring western Gascony. The owners couldn't be more welcoming and obliging. The rooms are decorated with warmth and charm. Private, secluded garden with swimming pool. Parking in the square nearby. **www.maisonatmaubourguet.com**

MIREPOIX La Maison des Consuls
6 pl Maréchal Leclerc, 09500 **Tel** *05 61 68 81 81* **Fax** *05 61 68 81 15* **Rooms** *8*

Housed in a charming 14th-century building that was once the district's courtroom, this hotel is located on a renowned medieval square in the heart of this picturesque little town. The rooms are filled with an eclectic array of antiques. The café-bar serves breakfast and snacks. **www.maisondesconsuls.com**

MONEIN Maison Canterou
Quartier Laquidée, 64360 **Tel** *05 59 21 41 38* **Rooms** *5*

A traditional farmhouse with inner courtyard on a wine estate producing Jurançon wines, sitting on the rolling Béarn hills. All the rooms are prettily decorated. "Palombière" under the eaves is spacious, while "Mansengou" has a balcony opening out to face the Pyrenees. "Cupidon" is for romantics. *Table d'hôte* is available on request.

ORTHEZ Reine Jeanne
44 rue Bourg Vieux, 64300 **Tel** *05 59 67 00 76* **Fax** *05 59 69 09 63* **Rooms** *30*

Occupying an 18th-century building in this historic Béarnaise town straddling the Gave de Pau river, this pleasant hotel has small guest rooms around a sheltered courtyard, as well as a modern wing with larger rooms. Country-style restaurant with traditional cooking. **www.reine-jeanne.fr**

PAU Bristol
3 rue Gambetta, 64000 **Tel** *05 59 27 72 98* **Fax** *05 59 27 87 80* **Rooms** *22*

This long-standing hotel (founded in 1903) is centrally located making it ideal for exploring Pau on foot. The rooms are tastefully decorated and varied, some have a balcony while others have a view of the Pyrenees. The bathrooms are equipped with large baths and showers. Free Wi-Fi is available. **www.hotelbristol-pau.com**

PAU Hôtel du Parc Beaumont
1 av Edouard VII, 64000 **Tel** *05 59 11 84 00* **Fax** *05 59 11 85 00* **Rooms** *80*

This luxurious modern hotel, part of the Concorde group, stands in beautiful grounds next to Pau's casino and palm-lined boulevard with great views of the Pyrenees. Rooms are lavishly furnished, and there is a heated pool, whirlpool, sauna and *hammam* (Turkish bath). **www.hotel-parc-beaumont.com**

SARE Ttakoinenborda
Maison Ttakoinenborda, 64310 **Tel** *05 59 47 51 42* **Rooms** *4*

A traditional 17th-century farmhouse near the beautiful town of Sare, surrounded by fields and woods. *Table d'hôte* dinner includes Basque specialities and home-made bread. A useful base from which to explore the inland Basque Country and the coast or to hop over the border into Spain. **http://guesthouse.sare.france.com**

SARE Hôtel Arraya
Pl du Village, 64310 **Tel** *05 59 54 20 46* **Fax** *05 59 54 27 04* **Rooms** *20*

Modern facilities blend with old-world character at this half-timbered hotel on the pilgrimage route to Compostela. Whitewashed stone walls are half-covered in foliage, bedrooms are rustic, decorated in Basque colours, and the restaurant serves regional specialities. Closed Nov–Mar. **www.arraya.com**

SAUVETERRE DE BEARN La Maison de Navarre
Quartier St Marc, 64390 **Tel** *05 59 38 55 28* **Fax** *05 59 38 55 71* **Rooms** *7*

This pink mansion house in a beautiful medieval village has bright, airy guest rooms. Comfortable, good value for money, and child-friendly. The family donkey, Zebulon, lives in the garden, and the beaches of the Atlantic coast are not too far away. Excellent restaurant. Closed Nov–Apr. **www.lamaisondenavarre.com**

ST-ETIENNE DE BAÏGORRY Hôtel Arcé
Rte Col d'Ispeguy, 64430 **Tel** *05 59 37 40 14* **Fax** *05 59 37 40 27* **Rooms** *20*

This welcoming Basque inn is set in the Aldudes valley, in the foothills of the Pyrenees, ideal for exploring the Basque country. The pool is on the opposite bank of the river, along with a tennis court. There is a pleasant restaurant terrace, and guest rooms with modern styling. Closed mid-Nov to mid-Mar. **www.hotel-arce.com**

ST GIRONS Hôtel Eychenne   🅿 ⅓ 🏛   €€€
8 av Paul Laffont, 09200 **Tel** *05 61 04 04 50* **Fax** *05 61 96 07 20* **Rooms** *35*

The former coaching inn has been run by the same family for seven generations, and the light, airy bedrooms and gracious public areas are filled with antiques and heirlooms. The facilities are modern, however, and there is a pretty garden where you can lunch in the open air. **www.ariege.com/hotel-eychenne/**

ST JEAN-DE-LUZ La Devinière   🅿   €€€
5 rue Loquin, 64500 **Tel** *05 59 26 05 51* **Fax** *05 59 51 26 38* **Rooms** *10*

The bedrooms in this charming 18th-century building are all different, prettily decorated and furnished with antiques, artworks and rare books. There is a cosy lounge-library with an open fireplace and a grand piano, and a breakfast-tea room. There is also a tiny garden, but no restaurant. **www.hotel-la-deviniere.com**

ST JEAN-PIED-DE-PORT Hôtel les Pyrénées   🖥🅿⅓🏛🎴🖥🏛   €€€
19 pl du Général-de-Gaulle, 64220 **Tel** *05 59 37 01 01* **Fax** *05 59 37 18 97* **Rooms** *20*

This 18th-century coaching inn stands at the French end of the Roncevaux pass, where the pilgrims' route to Santiago de Compostela crosses the Pyrenees. Immaculate rooms, health club with heated outdoor pool, and a restaurant offering both gastronomic and budget menus. **www.hotel-les-pyrenees.com**

ST-LIZIER Villa Belisama   ⅓ 🏛   €€
Rue Notre Dame, 09190 **Tel** *05 61 02 83 24* **Rooms** *3*

In a historic village above St-Girons lies this charming bed and breakfast in a restored house (parts of which date to the 12th century). Guest rooms are large and there is a garden, a small pool and a library with an esoteric collection of books. Breakfast as well as *table d'hôte* dinner on request. **www.ariege.com/belisama**

LANGUEDOC-ROUSSILLON

AIGUES-MORTES Hôtel des Croisades   🅿⅓🏛   €
2 rue du Port, 30220 **Tel** *04 66 53 67 85* **Fax** *04 66 53 72 95* **Rooms** *15*

Just outside the ramparts, beside the canal, this appealing hotel has a pretty garden, modern and well-equipped rooms, and helpful staff. The sights of historic Aigues Mortes are a short walk away, and the wetlands and beaches of the Camargue are nearby. Parking for a fee. **www.lescroisades.fr**

AIGUES-MORTES Hôtel St Louis   🅿⅓   €€
10 rue Amiral Courbet, 30220 **Tel** *04 66 53 72 68* **Fax** *04 66 53 75 92* **Rooms** *22*

Spacious rooms with modern comforts and a location next to the famous Constance Tower make this friendly hotel in an 18th-century building one of the better places to stay in Aigues-Mortes. Good restaurant, pretty patio, and garage parking available for a fee. Closed mid-Oct–Easter. **www.lesaintlouis.fr**

BARJAC Hôtel Le Mas du Terme   🅿⅓🏛🎴🏛   €€
Rte de Bagnoles sur Ceze, 30430 **Tel** *04 66 24 56 31* **Fax** *04 66 24 58 54* **Rooms** *23*

Set among its own vineyards and lavender fields, this sturdy old stone farmhouse-hotel in the heart of the Ardèche has plenty of character, lovely surroundings, charming bedrooms and public areas, and a fine restaurant. Activities for children include riding, ping-pong and *boules*. **www.masduterme.com**

BEZIERS Hôtel le Champ-de-Mars   🅿   €
17 rue de Metz, 34500 **Tel** *04 67 28 35 53* **Fax** *04 67 28 61 42* **Rooms** *10*

This family-run establishment offers comfortable, good-sized bedrooms. Located in a quiet side street, it is close to the sights, restaurants and cafés of historic Béziers. Baskets filled with geraniums adorn the front, while most rooms overlook the small, flower-filled back garden. **www.hotel-champdemars.com**

BEZIERS Clos de Moussanne   🅿🏛   €€
Route de Pezenas, 34500 **Tel** *04 67 39 31 81* **Rooms** *4*

The imposing entrance to this *chambre d'hôtes*, sheltered by two plane trees, is at the end of a leafy alley. The sophisticated bedrooms in this former convent have parquet floors, contemporary furnishings and modern bathrooms. The best also have a terrace overlooking the pool. Table d'hôte on request. **www.leclosdemoussanne.com**

BIZE-MINERVOIS La Bastide Cabezac   🅿⅓🏛🏛🔧   €€
18–20 Hameau Cabezac, 11120 **Tel** *04 68 46 66 10* **Fax** *04 68 46 66 29* **Rooms** *12*

A relaxing stay awaits at this charming bastide, which nestles among olive trees and vines. Outside there are typical ochre-coloured walls and shuttered windows; inside, the rooms are modern and comfortable with warm, sunny colours and regional furniture. The restaurant is excellent, and wine tastings can be organized. **www.la-bastide-cabezac.com**

BOUZIGUES La Côte Bleue   🅿⅓🏛   €€
Av Louis Tudesq, 34140 **Tel** *04 67 78 31 42* **Fax** *04 67 78 35 49* **Rooms** *31*

This modern hotel close to the charming fishing village of Meze, on the inner shore of the calm Thau lagoon, has somewhat bland rooms but fantastic sea views from the balconies. Its highly regarded restaurant specializes in plump, tasty oysters, shellfish and crustaceans. **www.la-cote-bleu.fr**

Key to Price Guide *see p550* **Key to Symbols** *see back cover flap*

BRIGNAC La Missare

9 rue de Clermont, 34800 **Tel** *04 67 96 07 67* **Rooms** *4*

Sculptured balconies and carved stone walls contrast with the original role of this 19th-century farmhouse. The former outhouses have been converted into delightful *chambres d'hôtes*; each room individually decorated with Louis XV beds and eclectic *objets d'art* collected by the owners. **www.la.missare.free.fr**

CARCASSONNE Des Trois Couronnes

2 rue Trois Couronnes, 11000 **Tel** *04 68 25 36 10* **Fax** *04 68 25 92 92* **Rooms** *69*

This business-like hotel looks across the river Aude towards the battlements of medieval Carcassonne, and its fourth-floor restaurant has unbeatable views of the floodlit ramparts at night. Very good value, with much better facilities than most local hotels in its price bracket. **www.hotel-destroiscouronnes.com**

CARCASSONNE Hôtel de la Cité

Pl August-Pierre Pont, 11000 **Tel** *04 68 71 98 71* **Fax** *04 68 71 50 15* **Rooms** *61*

The finest hotel in the Languedoc-Roussillon region, with immaculate service, opulent rooms, a glorious pool, formal gardens, superb restaurants and an unbeatable location within Carcassonne's medieval town, La Cité. Golf, canoeing and white-water rafting are available nearby. **www.hoteldelacite.com**

CASTILLON DU GARD Le Vieux Castillon

Rue Turion Sabatier, 30210 **Tel** *04 66 37 61 61* **Fax** *04 66 37 28 17* **Rooms** *32*

Restored buildings in a medieval village have been converted into a stylish, discreet and prestigious hotel with fine facilities and wonderful food. Le Vieux Castillon is part of the prestigious Relais et Châteaux consortium, living up to demanding standards. Book well in advance. **www.vieuxcastillon.com**

CERET La Terrasse au Soleil

1500 rte de Fontfrede, 66400 **Tel** *04 68 87 01 94* **Fax** *04 68 87 39 24* **Rooms** *41*

This hotel is perched on the slopes above the village of Céret (where Picasso lived and worked) and has great views of Mt Canigou and the Pyrenees. The restaurant is renowned for its regional cuisine. This is a great place for an active family, with pretty rooms and good facilities. Closed Dec–Mar. **www.terrasse-au-soleil.com**

COLLIOURE Relais des Trois Mas

Rte de Port-Vendres, 66190 **Tel** *04 68 82 05 07* **Fax** *04 68 82 38 08* **Rooms** *23*

This lovely hotel comprises several restored old buildings in pine-shaded gardens, with superb views of the Côte du Vermeille and the port and town of Collioure. Most rooms have terraces or verandas, and all have sea views. La Balette restaurant has a fine traditional menu. **www.relaisdestroismas.com**

FERRIERES-LES-VERRERIES Mas de Baumes

34190 **Tel** *04 66 80 88 80* **Fax** *04 66 80 88 82* **Rooms** *7*

This converted glassworks hides in an isolated location. Bedrooms each reveal a different theme – Barbara Cartland, Oriental or 18th century – with contemporary decor that blends elegantly with the ancient stone building. Refined, yet relaxed ambience. Original cuisine served in the restaurant. Closed Nov–Easter. **www.oustaldebaumes.com**

MOLITG-LES-BAINS Château de Riell

66500 **Tel** *04 68 05 04 40* **Fax** *04 68 05 04 37* **Rooms** *22*

Exuberant Baroque-style château rising out of the pine trees. The interior is very contemporary with stone floors, ochre tones and a flamboyant jungle-lounge. Stylish, comfortable rooms, some located in maisonettes in the park. Generous, creative cuisine is served in the *bodega*-type restaurant. Closed Nov–Easter. **www.chateauderiell.com**

MONTPELLIER Hôtel du Palais

3 rue Palais des Guilhem, 34000 **Tel** *04 67 60 47 38* **Fax** *04 67 60 40 23* **Rooms** *26*

The Hôtel du Palais is in an attractive, century-old building in the heart of the old quarter of Montpellier. Bedrooms are on the small side, but with welcoming personal touches such as fresh flowers. A good choice for a budget short break. Plenty of restaurants nearby. **www.hoteldupalais-montpellier.fr**

MONTPELLIER New Hotel du Midi

22 bd Victor Hugo, 34000 **Tel** *04 67 92 69 61* **Fax** *04 67 92 73 63* **Rooms** *44*

A Hausmann-style building, with *belle époque* touches, situated on the bustling Place de la Comédie. The refurbished and spacious rooms have modern amenities and are decorated in warm tones such as chocolate and caramel, raspberry and *pistache*. Centrally located with a choice of restaurants nearby. **www.new-hotel.com**

NARBONNE Grand Hôtel du Languedoc

22 bd Gambetta, 11100 **Tel** *04 68 65 14 74* **Fax** *04 68 65 81 48* **Rooms** *40*

This stylish hotel in a 19th-century building is a short walk from Narbonne's cathedral, city-centre shopping, markets and museums. The popular restaurant retains traces of its Belle Epoque elegance. Spacious rooms with high ceilings, air-conditioning and soundproofing. **www.hoteldulanguedoc.com**

NIMES Imperator-Concorde

Quai de la Fontaine, 30000 **Tel** *04 66 21 90 30* **Fax** *04 66 67 70 25* **Rooms** *60*

Built in 1929, this hotel has been frequented by the rich and famous including Ava Gardner and Hemingway. The well-equipped rooms, some with a 1930s decor others more modern, overlook an enchanting garden planted with cedars and palm trees. The restaurant is recommended for its imaginative regional dishes. **www.hotel-imperator.com**

NIMES New Hôtel la Baume
🖼️📧 €€€
21 rue Nationale, 30000 **Tel** *04 66 76 28 42* **Fax** *04 66 76 28 45* **Rooms** *34*

Housed in an elegant 17th-century townhouse, la Baume is one of the most pleasant places to stay in Nîmes. A short step from the sights, it blends old-world charm with modern facilities. Some rooms are even listed as historic monuments. No restaurant, but a welcoming café-bar. **www.new-hotel.com**

PERPIGNAN Hôtel de la Loge
📧 €
1 rue des Fabriques d'en Nabot, 66000 **Tel** *04 68 34 41 02* **Fax** *04 68 34 25 13* **Rooms** *22*

This affordable hotel in the heart of Perpignan's medieval quarter is housed within the walls of a 16th-century Catalan mansion with a mosaic forecourt and fountain. Its comfortable rooms all have en-suite facilities. Unassuming and cosy, ideal for a short break. **www.hoteldelaloge.fr**

PERPIGNAN Villa Duflot
🅿️🍴♒🏃📧🛗 €€€
Rond point Albert Donnezan, 66000 **Tel** *04 68 56 67 67* **Fax** *04 68 56 54 05* **Rooms** *25*

An Italian villa enclosed in its own vast park at the edge of a busy urban area. The elegant interior, bathed in light from large bay windows has Art-Deco touches and contemporary sculptures. Well-sized, renovated rooms are smart and comfortable. The pleasant restaurant opens out onto the pool and serves regional cuisine. **www.villa-duflot.com**

PRADES Castell Rose
📧🅿️♒🏃 €€
Chemin de la Litera, 66500 **Tel** *04 68 96 07 57* **Rooms** *5*

A charismatic hacienda-style *chambre d'hôtes* ideally situated for visiting the abbey of St-Martin-du-Canigou. The imposing pink marble building has a grand arcaded gallery and tower overlooking Spanish gardens and an immense park. The pleasant rooms are furnished with period furniture. Stylish and refined. **www.castellrose-prades.com**

QUILLAN Hôtel Cartier
📶🅿️🍴📧 €
31 bd Charles de Gaulle, 11500 **Tel** *04 68 20 05 14* **Fax** *04 68 20 22 57* **Rooms** *28*

The family-run Hôtel Cartier is housed in a 1950s Art Deco building in the centre of Quillan. The clean, comfortable rooms are simple, almost Spartan, with neutral colours. The restaurant is similarly unassuming, but friendly, affordable and as popular with locals as it is with visitors. **www.hotelcartier.com**

SAILLAGOUSE L'Atalaya
🅿️🍴♒ €€
Llo, 66800 **Tel** *04 68 04 70 04* **Fax** *04 68 04 01 29* **Rooms** *13*

Clinging to a hillside in the Cerdagne region, this pretty stone auberge has a spectacular view towards Spain – which is most impressive from the edge of the pool. Comfortable, well-maintained bedrooms are individually, tastefully decorated. Quality fabrics and stylish furniture create a luxury feel. Closed Nov & Jan–Mar. **www.atalaya66.com**

SETE Grand Hôtel
📶🅿️🍴🏃📧 €
17 quai de Tassigny, 34200 **Tel** *04 67 74 71 77* **Fax** *04 67 74 29 27* **Rooms** *43*

Set beside Sète's famous canal, this 19th-century building has been restored to its former grandeur, and its conservatory-restaurant is one of the finest in Sète. Rooms are freshly decorated and well equipped – the best have balconies overlooking the canal. Service is extremely professional. **www.legrandhotelsete.com**

SOMMIERES Hôtel de l'Orange
🅿️♒ €€€
7 rue des Beaumes, 30250 **Tel** *04 66 77 79 94* **Rooms** *7*

Located in the Cévennes region, this charming *hôtel particulier* dating from the 17th century is situated on the terraces looking down to the village. Well-proportioned bedrooms vary in style, from traditional to modern with colourful furnishings. Carefully-tended ornamental gardens are pleasant to stroll in. **www.hotel.delorange.free.fr**

ST CYPRIEN L'Ile de La Lagune
📶🅿️🍴♒🏃📺📧🛗 €€€€
Bd de l'Almandin, Les Capellans, 66750 **Tel** *04 68 21 01 02* **Fax** *04 68 21 06 28* **Rooms** *22*

One of the most luxurious hotels in the region, this building was constructed in the 1990s on an island in the middle of a lagoon. The impressive white structure, reminiscent of Spanish architecture, houses smart, airy, contemporary rooms with balconies. The excellent restaurant has a pleasant terrace. Private beach. **www.hotel-ile-lagune.com**

UZES Hostellerie Provençale
📶🅿️🍴📧 €€
1–3 rue Grande Bourgade, 30700 **Tel** *04 66 22 11 06* **Fax** *04 66 75 01 03* **Rooms** *9*

A small friendly hotel ideally situated for exploring this lovely old town, especially on market day. While the old stone building with its *tommette* tiled floors and rustic furniture recalls the past, amenities are up to date. Some rooms have Jacuzzis. The dining room is gaily decorated and serves typical Provençale fare. **www.hostellerieprovencale.com**

PROVENCE AND THE COTE D'AZUR

AIX EN PROVENCE Hôtel St Christophe
🅿️🍴📶📧🏃🛗 €€
2 av Victor Hugo, 13100 **Tel** *04 42 26 01 24* **Fax** *04 42 38 53 17* **Rooms** *67*

This superb townhouse hotel has bedrooms with all modern facilities – book in advance to secure a room with a tiny balcony. Decorated in Art Deco style, the ground floor is a bustling old-fashioned brasserie of the best kind, with tables indoors and out. Very central location. **www.hotel-saintchristophe.com**

Key to Price Guide *see p550* **Key to Symbols** *see back cover flap*

AIX EN PROVENCE Hôtel des Augustins

3 rue de la Masse, 13100 **Tel** *04 42 27 28 59* **Fax** *04 42 26 74 87* **Rooms** *29*

In a converted 12th century convent, with the reception housed in a 15th-century chapel, the Hôtel des Augustins offers a haven of peace in the heart of bustling Aix. The rooms are large and comfortable in traditional Provençal style. No restaurant, but places to eat nearby. **www.hotel-augustins.com**

ANTIBES La Bastide de la Brague

55 av No.6 La Brague, 06600 **Tel** *04 93 65 73 78* **Rooms** *5*

A welcoming, family-run bed and breakfast, serving meals on request. This large Provençal house offers five comfortable, well-decorated and spacious bedrooms, some with their own private patios. Breakfast can be taken outside, under the olive trees, on the terrace in fine weather. **www.bbchambreantibes.com**

ANTIBES Mas Djoliba

29 av Provence, 06600 **Tel** *04 93 34 02 48* **Fax** *04 93 34 05 81* **Rooms** *13*

Mas Djoliba is a big, old-fashioned farmhouse set among lots of greenery, with palm trees surrounding the pool terrace. Convenient for old Antibes and the beaches nearby, it is perfect for a romantic weekend or a longer stay. Closed end Oct–Mar. Half-board obligatory May–Sep. **www.hotel-djoliba.com**

ARLES Hotel de Amphithéâtre

5–7 rue Diderot, 16200 **Tel** *04 90 96 10 30* **Fax** *04 90 93 98 69* **Rooms** *33*

This bargain hotel has plenty of character and a perfect location next to Arles' amphitheatre. Some of the rooms are on the small side, but the decor is charmingly Provençal. The public areas are pleasant, the service is helpful and there is discounted parking available nearby. A good choice for families. **www.hotelamphitheatre.fr**

ARLES Hôtel Calendal

5 rue Porte de Laure, 13200 **Tel** *04 90 96 11 89* **Fax** *04 90 96 05 84* **Rooms** *38*

This relaxing hotel in the historic centre of Arles, near the Roman arena, has charmingly decorated and air-conditioned rooms, a few with balconies overlooking the arena or the Roman theatre. Breakfast is served in the garden, which is shaded by palm trees. **www.lecalendal.com**

ARLES Hôtel d'Arlatan

26 rue du Sauvage, 13200 **Tel** *04 90 93 56 66* **Fax** *04 90 49 68 45* **Rooms** *47*

The former 15th-century town residence of the Comtes d'Arlatan, this is one of the most beautiful historic hotels in the region. The rooms are furnished with antiques. Glass panels in the salon floor reveal 4th-century Roman foundations. Walled garden and stone terrace. **www.hotel-arlatan.fr**

BEAULIEU SUR MER La Réserve de Beaulieu

5 bd du Général Leclerc, 06310 **Tel** *04 93 01 00 01* **Fax** *04 93 01 28 99* **Rooms** *39*

A luxury hotel right on the seafront, in the heart of Beaulieu near the sailing harbour. The elegant rooms are decorated in warm pastel tones, and there is a magnificent pool next to the sea. The gastronomic restaurant has two Michelin stars. Closed mid-Oct–mid-Dec. **www.reservebeaulieu.com**

BIOT Hôtel les Arcades

16 pl des Arcades, 06410 **Tel** *04 93 65 01 04* **Fax** *04 93 65 01 05* **Rooms** *12*

This 15th-century inn is a quirky haven of tranquillity. The rooms are small (even poky) but undeniably atmospheric. Top-floor rooms have terraces with views to the sea. The bar serves as breakfast room and restaurant, which you share with the local bohemian set and their dogs. **www.hotel-restaurant-les-arcades.com**

BORMES-LES-MIMOSAS Domaine du Mirage

38 rue de la Vue des Iles, 83230 **Tel** *04 94 05 32 60* **Fax** *04 94 64 93 03* **Rooms** *33*

Perched above the bay of Le Lavandou and a 10-minute drive from one of the Riviera's best beaches, this Victorian-style hotel has spectacular views from its balconies and a beautiful pool. Light dishes are served by the pool at lunch, while in the evening you can choose from a short seasonal menu. Attentive staff. **www.domainedumirage.com**

CANNES La Villa Tosca

11, rue Hoche, 06400 **Tel** *04 93 38 34 40* **Fax** *04 93 38 73 34* **Rooms** *22*

A large Beaux-Art-style hotel, ideally located for the beach, train station and the Palais des Festivals. In the rooms, there's a mix of contemporary and antique furniture with plenty of original features. It is well worth paying a little extra for one of the larger rooms, some of which have balconies. **www.villa-tosca.com**

CANNES Hôtel Molière

5 rue Molière, 06400 **Tel** *04 93 38 16 16* **Fax** *04 93 68 29 57* **Rooms** *24*

This 19th-century building is very close to la Croisette, Cannes' sea-front esplananade, with bright and comfortable rooms and balconies overlooking an attractive garden where breakfast is served. Good value and very much in demand – book well in advance. **www.hotel-moliere.com**

CANNES Hôtel Splendid

4 av Felix Faure, 06400 **Tel** *04 97 06 22 22* **Fax** *04 93 99 55 02* **Rooms** *62*

This white wedding-cake of a hotel with its Belle Epoque frontage right in the centre of Cannes has fantastic views of the yacht harbour from the rooftop restaurant, and some sea-facing rooms have great balconies. Very good service, and a warm, friendly atmosphere. **www.splendid-hotel-cannes.fr**

CANNES Eden Hôtel

€€€€

133 rue d'Antibes, 06400 **Tel** *04 93 68 78 00* **Fax** *04 93 68 78 01* **Rooms** *115*

This boutique hotel is bright, colourful and trendy, with a hint of 1960s retro complementing the modern feel. Close to the town's fashionable shopping streets, its facilities are being enhanced with the addition of a heated pool, whirlpool, massage room and fitness centre. **www.eden-hotel-cannes.com**

CANNES Carlton Inter-Continental

€€€€€

58 la Croisette, 06414 **Tel** *04 93 06 40 06* **Fax** *04 93 06 40 25* **Rooms** *341*

The grandest of the grand, this is where the stars come to stay. During the film festival, there is a long waiting list for reservations. Art Deco surroundings, with discreetly luxurious facilities in the rooms and public areas, and a private beach with loungers and parasols. **www.intercontinental.com/cannes**

CAP D'ANTIBES La Garoupe et Gardiole

€€

60–74 chemin de la Garoupe, 06160 **Tel** *04 92 93 33 33* **Fax** *04 92 67 61 87* **Rooms** *37*

Pines and cypresses surround the pink 1920s buildings of this delightful (and delightfully affordable, by Cap d'Antibes standards) hotel. Tiled floors, beamed ceilings and whitewashed walls perpetuate the rural image. Bedrooms are light and airy. Shady terrace and pretty pool. **www.hotel-lagaroupe-gardiole.com**

CAP D'ANTIBES La Jabotte

€€

13, av Max Maurey, 06160 **Tel** *04 93 61 45 89* **Rooms** *10*

A small hotel with a bed-and-breakfast feel, La Jabotte is fully booked weeks ahead in summer thanks to the tastefully decorated rooms, warm welcome and incredibly reasonable prices. A house *apéritif* is served every evening in the courtyard. The beach is just steps away. Closed Nov. **www.jabotte.com**

CAP D'ANTIBES Hôtel du Cap (Eden Roc)

€€€€€

Bd Kennedy, 06600 **Tel** *04 93 61 39 01* **Fax** *04 93 67 76 04* **Rooms** *120*

Built in 1870, this is the ultimate Antibes palace, and a hideaway for the rich and famous. Most accommodation is in luxury suites or apartments. Seaside cabanas are available and there is a huge heated seawater pool. Superb food, obsequious service and state-of-the-art facilities. **www.hotel-du-cap-eden-roc.com**

CASSIS Les Jardins de Cassis

€€€

Rue Auguste Favier, 13260 **Tel** *04 42 01 84 85* **Fax** *04 42 01 32 38* **Rooms** *34*

The most pleasant place to stay in the picturesque port of Cassis, this hotel is much in demand, so book early. The guest rooms, in a cluster of buildings painted in pastel shades, are small but well planned. Good facilities include a Jacuzzi and a pool in a garden of lemon trees and bougainvillea. Closed Dec–Mar. **www.lesjardinsdecassis.com**

CASTELLANE Nouvel Hôtel du Commerce

€€

Pl de l'Eglise, 04120 **Tel** *04 92 83 61 00* **Fax** *04 92 83 72 82* **Rooms** *34*

This hotel, in the picturesque small town of Castellane, makes a good base for exploring the surrounding area. The pretty, well equipped and immaculate rooms overlook the market square or the crag that surmounts Castellane. The dining room veranda is a lovely, airy spot. Closed Nov–1 Mar. **www.hotel-fradet.com**

EZE Château Eza

€€€€€

Rue de la Pise, 06360 **Tel** *04 93 41 12 24* **Fax** *04 93 41 16 64* **Rooms** *11*

This remarkable building is a collection of medieval houses perched at the summit of Eze's "eagle's nest". Once home to Prince William of Sweden, it has been converted into a tiny jewel of a luxury hotel with elegant rooms and utterly breathtaking views from its terraces. Closed Nov–mid-Dec. **www.chateaueza.com**

FONTVIEILLE Hôtel La Peiriero

€€

36 av des Baux, 13990 **Tel** *04 90 54 76 10* **Fax** *04 90 54 62 60* **Rooms** *42*

This welcoming family hotel has been created in a traditional Provençal farm, known as a *mas*. The food, the colours and the atmosphere are all typically Provençal. In summer it is cool and relaxing and in winter warm and cosy. Children are well catered for with a specially designed play area. **www.hotel-peiriero.com**

JUAN LES PINS Hôtel des Mimosas

€€€

Rue Pauline, 06160 **Tel** *04 93 61 04 16* **Fax** *04 92 93 06 46* **Rooms** *34*

Palm trees surround this gracious hotel, built at the turn of the 19th century and offering character and style at a reasonable rate. The hotel is beautifully presented, with comfortable, cool, simply furnished rooms. Request a quieter room overlooking the swimming pool. Closed Sep–May. **www.hotelmimosas.com**

LES ARCS SUR ARGENS Logis du Guetteur

€€€

Pl du Château, 83460 **Tel** *04 94 99 51 10* **Fax** *04 94 99 51 29* **Rooms** *13*

Within the tower of an 11th-century castle – a prominent landmark overlooking the small village – this cosy hotel is a fine place to stay in summer or winter, almost equidistant between Mediterranean beaches and Alpine ski slopes. Views from the ramparts are epic. **www.logisduguetteur.com**

LES BAUX DE PROVENCE L'Hostellerie de la Reine Jeanne

€

Grande rue, 13520 **Tel** *04 90 54 32 06* **Fax** *04 90 54 32 33* **Rooms** *10*

This old house in the centre of one of Provence's most charming – and most-visited – villages has a dozen rooms, each different and attractively decorated and simply furnished. Not ideal for small children, and parking nearby is always a challenge. **www.la-reinejeanne.com**

Key to Price Guide *see p550* **Key to Symbols** *see back cover flap*

LES BAUX DE PROVENCE Auberge de la Benvengudo

Vallon de l'Arcoule, 13520 **Tel** *04 90 54 32 54* **Fax** *04 90 54 42 58* **Rooms** *28*

With comfortable, lavishly decorated bedrooms, a large garden and tennis court, this attractive country house near the hilltop village of Les Baux is one of the most charming places to stay on the fringes of the Bouches du Rhône. It is a good base for exploring the region. Closed Nov–Mar. **www.benvengudo.fr**

MARSEILLE Sofitel Marseille Vieux Port

36, bd Charles Livon, 13007 **Tel** *04 91 15 59 00* **Fax** *04 91 15 59 50* **Rooms** *134*

Decorated in minimalist style with dark wood and streamlined furniture, this luxury hotel is most remarkable for its spectacular views of the Vieux Port. Opt for one of the 28 rooms with terraces. The major sights are all nearby and the top-floor restaurant has panoramic views. **www.accorhotels.com**

MENTON Hôtel Aiglon

7 av de la Madone, 06500 **Tel** *04 93 57 55 55* **Fax** *04 93 35 92 39* **Rooms** *28*

Not far from the seafront, the Aiglon offers every comfort, including a heated swimming pool and a luxuriant garden. Housed in a charming 19th-century townhouse, it is nicely decorated and has a good restaurant with tables on a terrace shaded by palms. **www.hotelaiglon.net**

MOUSTIERS STE MARIE La Bastide de Moustiers

Chemin de Quinson, 04360 **Tel** *04 92 70 47 47* **Fax** *04 92 70 47 48* **Rooms** *12*

Outside one of the region's prettiest villages, La Bastide de Moustiers is housed in a 17th-century building, but contains the latest facilities. Surrounded by a gorgeous garden, the hotel has sweeping views of the surrounding mountains and a good restaurant. There is a room with disabled access. **www.bastide-moustiers.com**

NICE Hôtel Windsor

11 rue Dalpozzo, 06000 **Tel** *04 93 88 59 35* **Fax** *04 93 88 94 57* **Rooms** *57*

The Hôtel Windsor provides a wide array of services and facilities, including a pool in an exotic palm garden, a children's play area, and a health and beauty centre offering massage and a sauna. Some rooms are individually decorated by local artists. Snack bar and restaurant. **www.hotelwindsornice.com**

NICE Hôtel Suisse

15, Quai Rauba Capéu, 06300 **Tel** *04 92 17 39 00* **Fax** *04 93 85 30 70* **Rooms** *42*

When it comes to value for money in Nice, it is hard to beat this sleek hotel a few steps from the food market in the cour Saleya. There is no swimming pool, but the beach is just across the street and there are balconies with views of the Baie des Anges. The staff are friendly and helpful. **www.hotel-nice-suisse.com**

NICE La Pérouse

11 quai Rauba-Capeu, 06300 **Tel** *04 93 62 34 63* **Fax** *04 93 62 59 41* **Rooms** *60*

La Pérouse has the best view in Nice. At the eastern end of the Baie des Anges, it perches on a clifftop site between the Promenade des Anglais and the port. Sea-facing rooms have small terraces, which are very peaceful. In summer the restaurant has tables beneath lemon trees. **www.hotel-la-perouse.com**

NICE Le Negresco

37 promenade des Anglais, 06000 **Tel** *04 93 16 64 00* **Fax** *04 93 88 35 68* **Rooms** *120*

The Negresco is the grande dame of Riviera hotels and has been a landmark on the promenade des Anglais since it opened in 1913, with a seemingly endless list of rich and famous guests. Superbly decorated and furnished with works of art, flawless service and modern facilities. **www.hotel-negresco-nice.com**

SEILLANS Hôtel des Deux Rocs

Place Font d'Amont, 83440 **Tel** *04 94 76 87 32* **Fax** *04 94 76 88 68* **Rooms** *13*

This 17th-century Provençal mansion on the village square has a strong family atmosphere, decorated with antiques and traditional fabrics. Rooms at the front are the biggest and brightest. Mediterranean cuisine is served beside the square's fountain in summer. Closed Jan–mid-Feb. **www.hoteldeuxrocs.com**

ST-JEAN-CAP-FERRAT Hôtel Brise Marine

58 av Jean-Mermoz, 06230 **Tel** *04 93 76 04 36* **Fax** *04 93 76 11 49* **Rooms** *16*

If you are looking for a calm place to relax, this small hotel is ideal. Facing the sea on one side and the Alpes-Maritime on the other, the views are magnificent. The lack of a swimming pool is made up for by the fact that the beach is 50-metres (160-ft) away. Closed Nov–Feb. **www.hote-brisemarine.com**

ST-JEAN-CAP-FERRAT Royal Riviera

3 av Jean Monnet, 06230 **Tel** *04 93 76 31 00* **Fax** *04 93 01 23 07* **Rooms** *96*

This luxury hotel in the glitzy resort of St-Jean-Cap-Ferrat has an enviable asset – its own private sandy beach. Some of the rooms seem small for the price, but service aims to satisfy every whim. The L'Orangerie, a smaller building facing the swimming pool, houses 16 pleasant rooms. **www.royal-riviera.com**

ST PAUL DE VENCE Hostellerie des Remparts

72 rue grande, 06570 **Tel** *04 93 32 09 88* **Fax** *04 93 24 10 47* **Rooms** *9*

In the heart of this picturesque village, the Hostellerie des Remparts offers modern comforts in a medieval setting. Its rooms are furnished with antiques, and have marvellous views. There is a small garden terrace. The village is car-free and parking is some distance away. Closed Mondays out of season. **www.hostellerielesremparts.com**

ST PAUL DE VENCE La Colombe d'Or   🅿 🍽 ♨ 👥 🗐 ♿   €€€€€

Pl de Gaulle, 06570 **Tel** *04 93 32 80 02* **Fax** *04 93 32 77 78* **Rooms** *25*

The most luxurious place to stay in St Paul, this former farmhouse in a fabulous setting once hosted Impressionist painters, and originals by Picasso and Matisse grace its walls. The guest list is still impressive, and early reservations are necessary. The restaurant is highly rated. **www.la-colombe-dor.com**

ST TROPEZ Lou Cagnard   🅿   €€

Av Paul Roussel, 83990 **Tel** *04 94 97 04 24* **Fax** *04 94 97 09 44* **Rooms** *19*

Occupying an old town house, this small hotel is only a minute's walk away from St Tropez's lively square, the place des Lices. Request a room overlooking the small garden with its shady mulberry trees; there is no air conditioning, and rooms in the front are noisy with open windows. Closed Jan & Dec. **www.hotel-lou-cagnard.com**

ST TROPEZ Pastis Hôtel St Tropez   🅿 ♨ 🛉 🗐 ♿   €€€€

61 av du Général Leclerc, 83990 **Tel** *04 98 12 56 50* **Fax** *04 94 96 99 82* **Rooms** *9*

St-Tropez attracts more than its share of ostentation, but this nine-room inn decorated with contemporary art and a judicious mix of modern and antique furniture is for those who prefer a more discreet charm. The heated pool is surrounded by centuries-old palm trees. There is a strict "no dress code" policy. **www.pastis-st-tropez.com**

ST TROPEZ La Ponche   🅿 🍽 👥 🗐   €€€€€

Port des Pêcheurs, 83990 **Tel** *04 94 97 02 53* **Fax** *04 94 97 78 61* **Rooms** *18*

For those looking for a boutique hideaway in St Tropez, this cluster of one-time fishermen's cottages may fit the bill. The bedrooms are large and artfully chic, and include two family-size rooms. Among the famous guests have been Pablo Picasso and 1950s film star Romy Schneider. Closed Nov–mid-Feb. **www.laponche.com**

VENCE Mas de Vence   🏊 🅿 🍽 ♨ 👥 🗐 ♿   €€

539 av Emile Hugues, 06140 **Tel** *04 93 58 06 16* **Fax** *04 93 24 04 21* **Rooms** *41*

This modern establishment may not appeal to those looking for somewhere quaint, but its architecture and colours are in keeping with Provençal tradition and it has excellent facilities including air-conditioned, insulated rooms, a small garden, and a terrace restaurant. **www.azurline.com**

VILLEFRANCHE-SUR-MER Hôtel La Flore   🏊 🅿 ♨ 👥 🗐 ♿   €€€

5 bd Princess Grace de Monaco, 06230 **Tel** *04 93 76 30 30* **Fax** *04 93 76 99 99* **Rooms** *31*

This traditional hotel dating from the beginning of the 20th century has been completely renovated in a Provençal style. The rooms are calm and overlook the sea and Villefranche's famous port. The Citadelle and a myriad of different restaurants are a few minutes' walk away. **www.hotel-la-flore.fr**

VILLEFRANCHE-SUR-MER Hôtel Versailles   🏊 🅿 🍽 ♨ 🗐   €€€€

7 bd Princesse Grace, 06230 **Tel** *04 93 76 52 52* **Fax** *04 93 01 97 48* **Rooms** *46*

This modern hotel has enough facilities for a longer stay, including a swimming pool, a restaurant specializing in Provençal cuisine, a large terrace and bedrooms with great views. Perhaps its only (slight) drawback is its location on a busy thoroughfare. Secure parking. Closed Nov–mid-Mar. **www.hotelversailles.com**

CORSICA

AJACCIO Hôtel Kallisté   🅿 🗐 ♿   €€

51 cours Napoléon, 20000 **Tel** *04 95 51 34 45* **Fax** *04 95 21 79 00* **Rooms** *48*

Right in the middle of the busy Cours Napoléon, the rooms are surprisingly quiet in this well-run, clean hotel. Wrought-iron banisters and exposed stone walls add a rustic touch to the building, which dates back to 1864. Just a few minutes' walk to the train and bus stations. **www.cyrnos.net**

AJACCIO Hôtel Les Mouettes   🅿 ♨ 👥 🗐 ♿   €€€€

9, cours Lucien Bonaparte, 20000 **Tel** *04 95 50 40 40* **Fax** *04 95 21 71 80* **Rooms** *28*

This hotel, not far from the centre of town, has its own stretch of sandy beach – and a pool. The spacious rooms are decorated in classic style, reflecting the building's 19th-century façade. There's no restaurant, but a hearty breakfast and snack plates are served. Closed mid-Nov–mid-Mar. **www.hotellesmouettes.fr**

BASTIA Hôtel Posta Vecchia   👥 🗐   €€

Quai des Martyrs de la Libération, 20200 **Tel** *04 95 32 32 38* **Fax** *04 95 32 14 05* **Rooms** *50*

Conveniently situated in the heart of the city, this busy hotel is next to the bustling, colourful, old port with its lively restaurants. Ask for a room in the front so that you can watch the evening promenade along the tree-lined quay. Public parking in front. **www.hotel-postavecchia.com**

BASTIA Hôtel Pietracap   🅿 ♨ 🗐   €€€€

Rte San Martino, San Martino di Lota, 20200 **Tel** *04 95 31 64 63* **Fax** *04 95 31 39 00* **Rooms** *39*

Supremely comfortable hotel in a beautiful setting along the coast road from Bastia. A large park, with olive trees that are over 100 years old, separates the hotel from the sea. Large outdoor swimming pool. Private car park. Closed Dec–Apr. **www.hotel-pietracap.com**

Key to Price Guide *see p550* **Key to Symbols** *see back cover flap*

BONIFACIO Hôtel le Royal

8 rue Fred Scamaroni, 20169 **Tel** *04 95 73 00 51* **Fax** *04 95 73 04 68* **Rooms** *14*

Busy hotel in the old town with views over the cliffs and sea. Freshly painted, pastel-coloured rooms. The cathedral is a few minutes' walk away, and steps lead down to the lively quayside. The little tourist train stops just outside. The restaurant serves mainly local dishes. **www.hotel-leroyal.com**

BONIFACIO Hôtel Résidence du Centre Nautique

Quai Nord, Port de Plaisanc, 20169 **Tel** *04 95 73 02 11* **Fax** *04 95 73 17 47* **Rooms** *11*

With its nautical-theme decor, this is the only hotel in Bonifacio that overlooks the harbour. Duplex rooms – some facing the port – are spacious and comfortable. The restaurant serves delicious food, though the service can be abrupt. The private parking is a bonus for the centre of town. Closed Oct–Mar. **www.centre-nautique.com**

CALVI Hostellerie l'Abbaye

Rte Santore, 20260 **Tel** *04 95 65 04 27* **Fax** *04 95 65 30 23* **Rooms** *43*

This pretty ivy-covered hotel was built on the walls of a 16th-century abbey. Ideally positioned on a slight incline, just above the port, it is set back from the road and is surrounded by an immaculate garden. A 5-minute walk takes you to the town centre. Closed Nov–Apr. **www.hostellerie-abbaye.com**

CORTE Hôtel Dominique Colonna

Vallée de la Restonica, 20250 **Tel** *04 95 45 25 65* **Fax** *04 95 61 03 91* **Rooms** *29*

It would be hard to imagine a more idyllic location than this lush green valley, with a small waterfall. Rooms are tastefully decorated in contemporary style and the service is impeccable. There is an excellent traditional restaurant next door, or the village restaurants are just 20-minutes' walk away. **www.dominique-colonna.com**

ÎLE ROUSSE Best Western Hôtel Santa Maria

Rte du Port, 20220 **Tel** *04 95 63 05 05* **Fax** *04 95 60 32 48* **Rooms** *56*

Superbly situated on the road to the islet of Île Rousse, this charming hotel has its own little beach and is just a short walk to the main square, with its shops and restaurants. All rooms have a terrace with sea views. Restaurant serves lunch in July and August. **www.hotelsantamaria.com**

PIANA Les Roches Rouges

Rte Porto, 20115 **Tel** *04 95 27 81 81* **Fax** *04 95 27 81 76* **Rooms** *30*

Built in 1912, this splendid hotel retains all the charm of that era. Large, simply furnished rooms look out onto the bay of Porto, nominated by UNESCO as one of the world's five most beautiful bays. Excellent dining room with terrace and garden. Closed Nov–Mar **www.lesrochesrouges.com**

PORTO Le Maquis

Porto, 20150 **Tel** *04 95 26 12 19* **Fax** *04 95 26 18 55* **Rooms** *6*

Quiet family-run hotel on the outskirts of town, on the coast road to Calvi. Surprisingly sophisticated menu in the charming restaurant. Dramatic views over the mountains. Comfortable rooms, pretty garden, and parking available. Closed Dec–Jan. **www.hotel-lemaquis.com**

PORTO-VECCHIO Chez Franca

Rte de Bonifacio, 20137 **Tel** *04 95 70 15 56* **Fax** *04 95 72 18 41* **Rooms** *14*

This modern hotel is conveniently situated between the town and the port. A lot of care has gone into the renovation of the rooms. The superb beaches of Guilia and Palombaggia are a few kilometres away. Good base for excursions to Zonza and Bavella. Closed Dec. **www.francahotel.com**

PROPRIANO Le Lido

Av Napoléon, 20110 **Tel** *04 95 76 06 37* **Fax** *04 95 76 31 18* **Rooms** *11*

Le Lido has a unique location on a rocky peninsula with a beach. The simple decor doesn't aim to compete with the setting, but terracotta tiles, mosaics and wood beams lend charm. Opt for a main floor room opening onto the beach. The very good restaurant specializes in oven-baked lobster. Closed Nov–mid-Apr. **www.le-lido.com**

SARTENE Hôtel St Damianu

Quartier San Damien, 20100 **Tel** *04 95 70 55 41* **Fax** *04 95 70 55 78* **Rooms** *28*

A cracker of a hotel. Large airy rooms have terraces with fabulous views of the gulf of Valinco or the mountains. Facilities include a huge swimming pool surrounded with teak decking, a garden, *hammam*, disabled access, secure parking, and an excellent dining room. Closed Nov–Apr. **www.sandamianu.fr**

ST FLORENT Hôtel Maxime

Rte La Cathédrale, 20217 **Tel** *04 95 37 05 30* **Fax** *04 95 37 13 07* **Rooms** *19*

Set back from the street on the way to the 12th-century cathedral of Santa Maria Assunta, this modern hotel is an oasis of calm only a minute's walk from the hurly-burly of the fashionable port. Pleasant, airy rooms with sea views from the top floor.

VIZZAVONA Hôtel du Monte D'Oro

Col de Vizzavona RN 193, 20219 **Tel** *04 95 47 21 06* **Fax** *04 95 47 22 05* **Rooms** *24*

You'll feel as though you are in an Agatha Christie novel the moment you walk into this charming hotel, built in 1880 and set in the forest on the road between Ajaccio and Bastia. Wood-panelled corridors, large living room and elegant dining room serving organic food. A *gite* is also available for rent. Closed Nov–Apr. **www.monte-oro.com**

WHERE TO EAT

The French consider eating well an essential part of their national birthright. There are few other places where people are as passionately knowledgeable about their cuisine and their wine. Restaurant reviews, as well as cooking and food shows on television, are avidly followed and the general quality of both fresh food and restaurant offerings is vastly better in France than it is in most other European countries.

This introduction to the restaurant listings, which are arranged by region and town *(see pp600–51)*, looks at the different types of restaurant in France and gives practical tips on eating out, reading menus, ordering and service – everything you need to know to enjoy your meal. At the front of the book is a guide to a typical menu and an introduction to French wine *(see pp24–7)*. The main food and wine features are at the beginning of each of the five regional sections.

FRENCH EATING HABITS

The traditional large meal at noon survives mainly in rural regions. In cities, lunch is increasingly likely to consist of a sandwich, salad or a steak in a café, while dinner is the main meal of the day. Usually, lunch is from noon to 2pm and dinner is from 8 to 10pm, with last orders taken 30 minutes before closing time.

Some family-owned places are closed at weekends, so it may be difficult to find a meal anywhere outside your hotel on Sundays, except in large cities. Off the beaten track and in resort towns, restaurants and hotels are often closed out of season, so it is advisable to ring ahead.

Over the past few decades, French eating habits have changed dramatically. The growing popularity of the cuisine of former French colonies means that North African and Vietnamese places are now easy to find, as are Chinese restaurants. Burger and Tex-Mex joints are also popular with young people. As city-dwellers and suburbanites in France have become almost as health-conscious as other Europeans, there has been an explosion of "light" foods; and the rise of the *hypermarchés* (hypermarkets) has resulted in less fresh produce on the menu as more frozen and prepared food is eaten.

REGIONAL COOKING

One of the great pleasures of travelling in France is sampling the country's regional

Typical elegant terrace restaurant in Provence

cuisine. In every *département* of France, menus will nearly always include local specialities, which reflect predominant local products and agriculture. A good way to divide France gastronomically is the butter/olive oil divide. In the north, butter is generally used in cooking; in the south, olive oil; and in the southwest, goose and duck fat predominate.

Each region takes great pride in its own cuisine. Nationally, the best-known dishes come from four regions: Alsace, a province with close German ties; the southwest, where *cassoulet*, a rich stew of white beans, tomatoes, sausage and duck is a well-loved dish; the Alps, which gave *fondue* to the nation; and Provence, famed for *bouillabaisse*, a rich fish soup from Marseille.

The gastronomic capital of France is, however, considered to be Lyon, which boasts a significant proportion of France's best restaurants and many superb no-nonsense bistros known as *bouchons*.

La Cigale, a Belle Epoque brasserie in Nantes *(see p623)*

RESTAURANTS

Encompassing the whole alphabet of French cuisine, restaurants in France range from tiny whitewashed places with rush-bottomed chairs to stately, wood-panelled château dining rooms and the top kitchens of famous chefs. Many hotels have fine restaurants open to non-residents, a selection of which can be found in the hotel listings *(see pp550–95)*.

Prices for restaurants of the same rating are more or less consistent throughout France except in large cities, where they can be more expensive. The quality of the food and service, though, is the most significant price factor and you can easily spend over 150€ per head to eat at one of the top establishments.

There are several different kinds of French cuisine that you may come across. *Haute cuisine* is the traditional cooking method, where the flavour of the food is enhanced with rich sauces. *Nouvelle cuisine* challenged this method, especially for the diet-conscious, in using light rather than creamy sauces which bring out the texture and colour of the ingredients. *Cuisine bourgeoise* is French home cooking. *Cuisine des Provinces* uses high-quality ingredients to prepare traditional rural dishes. *Jeune Cuisine Française* is the latest trend, where young chefs have rebelled against Michelin traditions to create their own cooking style.

BISTROS

When the French go out to eat, they are most likely to visit the broadest class of restaurant, the bistro. Bistros vary enormously – some urban bistros are formally decorated, while those in smaller cities and in the country tend to be more casual. Generally they offer a good, moderately

The restaurant L'Excelsior at Nancy in Lorraine *(see p614)*

priced meal from a traditional menu of an *entrée* or *hors d'oeuvre* (starter), *plats mijotés* (simmered dishes) and *grillades* (grilled fish and meats), followed by cheese and dessert.

BRASSERIES

Brasseries have their origin in Alsace and were originally attached to breweries; the name brasserie actually means brewery. Usually found in larger cities, they are big, bustling places, many with fresh shellfish stands outside. They serve beer on tap as well as a *vin de la maison* (house wine) and a variety of regional wines. Menus include simple fish and grilled meat dishes along with Alsatian specialities like *choucroute garnie* (sauerkraut with sausage and pork). Prices are very much on a par with those you would pay at bistros. Like cafés, brasseries are usually open from morning until night and serve food all day long.

Camembert

FERME-AUBERGES

In the country you may eat at a simple "farm inn", where good, inexpensive meals, often made with fresh farm produce, are taken with your host's family as part of your room and board. For more details on *ferme-auberges*, see under Bed and Breakfast on page 548.

CAFES

Cafés represent the soul of France. Every place but the tiniest hamlet can be counted on to have a café, open as a rule from early in the morning until 10pm or so. They serve drinks, coffee, tea, simple meals and snacks such as salads, omelettes and sandwiches throughout the day, and usually provide a cheaper breakfast than most hotels.

As well as serving refreshments, cafés are a good source of information and provide the traveller with endless opportunities to observe the French at their most relaxed.

In villages, almost the entire population might drift in and out of the single café during the course of a day, while large cities have cafés that cater for a specific clientele, such as workers or students. Paris's most famous cafés were traditional meeting places for intellectuals and artists to exchange ideas *(see p152)*.

Auberge du XII Siècle at Saché in the Loire Valley *(see p624)*

Tables outside a café in the Old Town of Nice on the Côte d'Azur

BISTRO ANNEXES

Over the past few years, baby-bistros or bistro annexes have appeared in larger cities, especially Paris and Lyon, as a new category of restaurant. They are lower-priced sister eateries of famous – and much more expensive – restaurants run by well-known chefs. Many of them offer *formule prix-fixe* (fixed-price) menus and the chance to sample the cooking of a celebrated kitchen in relaxed surroundings.

FAST FOOD

If you want to avoid the American fast food chains, wine bars and *salons du thé* are also good value for light meals. Cafeterias, found in some shopping centres, serve tasty food at reasonable prices.

RESERVATIONS

In cities and larger towns it is always best to make a reservation, especially from May to September. This rarely applies to cafés or in the country, where you can walk into most places without a reservation. However, if you are travelling in remote rural and resort areas off season, it is worth checking first that the restaurant is open all year.

If you have a reservation and your plans change, then you should call and cancel. Smaller restaurants, in particular, must fill all their tables to make a profit, and "no-shows" threaten their livelihood.

READING THE MENU AND ORDERING

When the menu is presented, you'll usually be asked if you'd like an aperitif. Since many French people do not drink spirits before a meal, this could be Kir (white wine mixed with a dash of black-currant liqueur), vermouth, light port (drunk in France as a cocktail) or a soft drink.

Opening the menu, *les entrées* or *hors d'oeuvre* are starters. *Les plats* are the main courses, and most restaurants will offer a *plat du jour*, or daily special; these are often seasonal or local dishes of particular interest. A selection of dishes from a classic French menu is given on pages 24–5.

Cheese is served as a separate course between the main course and dessert. Coffee is served black, unless you specify *"crème"*. Alternatively, you can ask for a *tisane*, or herbal tea.

WINE

As restaurants put a large mark-up on wine, it is better to further your connoisseurship with bottles purchased in shops, rather than when dining out. Local wine, however, is often served in carafes. Ordering a *demi* (50 cl) or *quart* (25 cl) carafe is a cheap way to try out a region's wines.

French law divides the country's wines into three classes, in ascending order of quality: Vin de France, Indication Géographique Protégée (IGP) and Appellation d'Origine Contrôlée (AOC). The Vin de France wines are rarely found in restaurants, but for help in choosing a regional wine (IGP upwards), refer to the wine features in the regional sections of this book. For an introduction to French wine, see pages 26–7.

When in doubt, order the house wine. Few restaurants will risk their reputation on an inferior house wine, and they often provide value for money.

WATER

Tap water is supplied on request free of charge, and is perfectly safe to drink. The French also pride themselves on their wide range of mineral waters. Favourite mealtime brands include Evian and the slightly fizzy Badoit.

Le Moulin de Mougins *(see p650)*

HOW TO PAY

Visa/Carte Bleue (V) is the most widely accepted credit card in France. Master-card/Access (MC) is also commonly accepted, while American Express (AE) and Diners Club (DC) tend to be accepted only in upmarket establishments. However, you should always carry plenty of

La Tour d'Argent in the Latin Quarter of Paris *(see p603)*

cash, especially when touring the countryside, as many smaller restaurants still do not take any credit cards. If in doubt, ask when you make a reservation.

SERVICE AND TIPPING

The pace of a French meal is generally leisurely. People think nothing of spending 4 hours at the table, so if you are pressed for time, go to a café or brasserie. A service charge of 12.5 to 15 per cent is almost always included in the price of your meal, but most French people leave a few euro cents behind in a café, and an additional 5 per cent or so of the total bill in other restaurants. In the grander restaurants, which pride themselves on their service, an additional tip of 5 to 10 per cent is correct.

Thirty euro cents is sufficient for toilet attendants, and 50 or 70 euro cents an item is appropriate for a cloakroom attendant.

DRESS CODE

Even when dressed casually, the French are generally well turned out; visitors should aim for the same level of presentable comfort. Running shoes, shorts, beach clothes or active sportswear are unacceptable everywhere except cafés or beachside places.

The restaurant listings indicate which restaurants require men to wear a jacket and tie (see pp600-51).

CHILDREN

French children are introduced early to restaurants and as a rule are well behaved. Consequently, children are well received almost everywhere in France. However, few restaurants provide special facilities like high-chairs or baby seats, as children are expected to behave sensibly, and there is often not much room for push-chairs.

PETS

Dogs are usually accepted at all but the most elegant restaurants. As the French are great

The Eychenne hotel-restaurant at St-Girons in the Pyrenees *(see p588)*

dog lovers, do not be surprised to see your neighbour's lapdog sitting on the next door *banquette*.

SMOKING

Despite all attempts to circumvent the no-smoking laws, especially in restaurants and cafés, the French have had to bow to the inevitable and should now adhere to government regulations about smoking in public.

Therefore, in line with other European countries, since 2007 smoking has been banned in all public places throughout France.

An elegant dining room in a hotel in Evian-les-Bains

WHEELCHAIR ACCESS

Though the restaurants of newer hotels usually provide wheelchair access, it is often restricted elsewhere. A word when you are booking your table should ensure that you are given a conveniently located table and assistance, if needed, when you arrive.

The listings show restaurants with wheelchair access.

Refer also to page 549 of this book, which gives the names and addresses of some organizations which provide advice to disabled travellers in France.

VEGETARIAN FOOD

France remains difficult for vegetarians, although some progress has been made in recent years. In most non-vegetarian restaurants the main courses are firmly orientated towards meat and fish. However, you can often fare well by ordering from the *entrées* and should never be timid about asking for a dish to be served without its meat content. Provided you make your request in advance, most smart restaurants will prepare a special vegetarian dish.

Only larger cities and university towns are likely to have fully fledged vegetarian restaurants. Otherwise cafés, pizzerias, crêperies and Oriental restaurants are good places to find vegetarian meals.

PICNICS

Picnicking is the best way to enjoy the wonderful fresh produce, local bread, cheeses and *charcuterie* from the markets and enticing shops to be found all over France. For more details see pages 652–5.

Picnics are also a good way to eat cheaply and enjoy the French countryside. Picnicking areas along major roads are well marked and furnished with tables and chairs, but country lanes are better still.

Choosing a Restaurant

The restaurants in this guide have been selected across a wide range of price categories for their good value, exceptional food and interesting location. This chart lists the restaurants by region, in chapter order. Map references for Paris restaurants correspond with the Paris Street Finder, see pp154–69.

PRICE CATEGORIES
The following price ranges are for a three-course meal for one, including a half-bottle of house wine, tax and service:
€ under €30
€€ €30–€45
€€€ €45–€60
€€€€ €60–€90
€€€€€ over €90

PARIS

BASTILLE Bistrot du Peintre   €€
116 ave Ledru Rollin, 75011 **Tel** *01 47 00 34 39*   **Map** *10 F5*

This laid-back bistro, in a turn-of-the-century building with Art Deco mouldings, is popular with local artists and media types who come for the decent prices and the busy terrace. The food is simple but decent, such as steak and excellent fish dishes, all served with *frites* and vegetables.

BASTILLE Le Bistrot Paul Bert   €€
18 rue Paul Bert, 75011 **Tel** *01 43 72 24 01*

This bistro's popularity is not surprising, given its combination of vintage decor – complete with zinc bar – and classic bistro cooking. Staff are welcoming, the *steak-frites* is one of the best in town, and the dining room is always buzzing with a mix of Parisians and international gourmets. The wine list is exceptional.

BASTILLE Le Repaire de Cartouche   €€€€
8 bd Filles du Calvaire, 75011 **Tel** *01 47 00 25 86*   **Map** *10 D2*

Rodolphe Paquin might not get as much press as some other Parisian chefs, but his two-level, country-style restaurant continues to offer some of the best value for money in town. There's a bargain lunch menu and sophisticated *à la carte* offerings such as *lièvre à la royale* (hare in wine sauce) and "crispy pig's head".

BEAUBOURG AND LES HALLES Le Tambour   €
41 rue Montmartre, 75002 **Tel** *01 42 33 06 90*   **Map** *9 A1*

This Les Halles institution, decorated with wacky Parisian memorabilia, serves food until 3:30am (until 1am Sun and Mon), making it a prized destination for Paris's night-hawks. Its late night hours do not reduce the quality of the fare, which is consistently restorative, hearty bistro food along the *steak-frites* line.

BEAUBOURG AND LES HALLES Au Pied du Cochon   €€
6 rue Coquillière, 75004 **Tel** *01 40 13 77 00*   **Map** *8 F1*

This colourfully restored brasserie was once popular with high society, who came to observe the workers in the old market and to savour the onion soup. Although touristy, this huge place is fun, and its menu has something for everyone (including excellent shellfish). Still one of the best places after a night out.

BEAUBOURG AND LES HALLES Aux Tonneaux des Halles   €€
28 rue Montorgueil, 75001 **Tel** *01 42 33 36 19*   **Map** *9 A1*

A genuine Parisian bistro, Aux Tonneaux des Halles is one of the last surviving bistros of its kind, with its real zinc bar and one of the tiniest kitchens in Paris. Service is not particularly quick, but when the food is this good, who cares! The wine list offers good value.

BEAUBOURG AND LES HALLES Café Beaubourg   €€
43 rue Saint-Merri, 75004 **Tel** *01 48 87 63 96*   **Map** *9 B2*

With views of the animated piazza of the Beaubourg museum, Café Beaubourg has elegant and contemporary decor. Simple and reliable, if slightly overpriced, fare is guaranteed – a variety of tartares, grilled meats and fish. The menu even offers a light and tasty Thai salad.

BEAUBOURG AND LES HALLES Le Hangar   €€
12 impasse Berthaud, 75003 **Tel** *01 42 74 55 44*   **Map** *9 B2*

Anyone who has found this locals' favourite in its quiet spot next door to the doll museum is sure to go back for the simple yet seductive cooking. Two trademark dishes are the pan-fried *foie gras* on olive oil mash and the runny chocolate cake. There isn't much in the way of decor, but the food more than makes up for it.

BEAUBOURG AND LES HALLES Chez la Vieille   €€€
1 rue de Bailleul, 75001 **Tel** *01 42 60 15 78*   **Map** *8 F2*

Portions are getting smaller in Paris restaurants, but not in this old-fashioned bistro where diners are encouraged to help themselves to pâtés, salads and desserts such as chocolate mousse and home-made tarts. Main dishes are equally hearty; think tripe stew or *blanquette de veau* (veal in white sauce).

Key to Symbols *see back cover flap*

BEAUBOURG AND LES HALLES Georges

€€€€

19 rue Beaubourg, 75004 **Tel** *01 44 78 47 99* **Map** *9 B2*

On the top floor of the Pompidou Centre, the Georges offers stunning views from its immense terrace. This trendy restaurant serves light and inspired cuisine, such as *mille-feuilles* of crab and mushrooms. Minimalist decor, with lots of steel and aluminium.

CHAILLOT AND PORTE MAILLOT Bistro le Goupil

€€

4 rue Claude Debussy, 75017 **Tel** *01 45 74 83 25* **Map** *1 C1*

This vintage bistro on the edge of Paris has a loyal following among locals, who come for the perfectly cooked entrecôte or more sophisticated dishes such as monkfish with artichokes and wild mushrooms. The young chef surveys the lively scene from his open kitchen. Reservations are essential.

CHAILLOT AND PORTE MAILLOT La Plage

€€

Port Javel, 75015 **Tel** *01 40 59 41 00* **Map** *5 B5*

A spectacular site facing the Statue of Liberty on the Ile aux Cignes, the French and Mediterranean cuisine here is as good as the view. The huge terrace is the place to be seen at lunchtime, as well as an idyllic spot for a summer candlelit dinner. The decor is an attractive mix of wood and pastel tones. Service can be slow.

CHAILLOT AND PORTE MAILLOT Chez Géraud

€€€

31 rue Vital, 75016 **Tel** *01 45 20 33 00* **Map** *5 B3*

Géraud Rongier, the jovial owner, is a scrupulous observer of *cuisine du marché*, using what's fresh at the market each day to create dishes like shoulder of lamb cooked on a spit, *sabodet* sausage in red wine sauce, skate with mustard or roast pigeon with port sauce. The mural was specially created for the restaurant.

CHAILLOT AND PORTE MAILLOT Oum El Banine

€€€

16 bis rue Dufrenoy, 75016 **Tel** *01 45 04 91 22* **Map** *5 A1*

The owner of this small, Moroccan restaurant in the chic residential quarter learned her art from her mother. Good *harira* (a thick, spicy soup), flavourful tagines, *pastilla* (a savoury puff-pastry tart) and *brik* (stuffed pastry triangle). Couscous is served with five choices of *ragoût*.

CHAILLOT AND PORTE MAILLOT Le Timgad

€€€€

21 rue Brunel, 75017 **Tel** *01 45 74 23 70* **Map** *1 C3*

As this has been Paris's best-known, most elegant Maghrebian restaurant for years it's essential to book ahead. The menu has many different *briks*, *tagines* and couscous dishes, as well as specialities like grilled pigeon, *pastilla* and *méchoui* (whole roast lamb), which needs to be ordered in advance.

CHAILLOT AND PORTE MAILLOT Zébra Square

€€€€

3 pl Clément Ader, 75016 **Tel** *01 44 14 91 91* **Map** *5 B4*

Part of the Hotel Square complex, this modern building has stylish, minimalist decor that has been spiced up by splashes of zebra print. The equally innovative, modern cuisine is also served in great style. Brunch on Sundays is especially popular. A hit with the fashion and media crowd.

CHAMPS-ELYSEES Granterroirs

€€

30 rue Miromesnil, 75008 **Tel** *01 47 42 18 18* **Map** *2 B4*

In the modish Champs-Elysées area it is a surprise to come across this *épicerie*-restaurant decorated like a country kitchen, with long, shared wooden tables. More than 800 products line the shelves, many of which can be tasted in salad and open sandwich plates; a different hot dish is served every day. Lunch only.

CHAMPS-ELYSEES Le Bœuf sur le Toit

€€

34 rue du Colisée, 75008 **Tel** *01 53 93 65 55* **Map** *3 A4*

This Art Deco brasserie run by the Flo group, which owns many historic brasseries in Paris, is one of the more reliable places to eat around the Champs-Elysées. Alongside classic *steak-frites*, sole *meunière* and seafood platters, you will find more adventurous specials such as lobster soup and monkfish cooked with Sauterne.

CHAMPS-ELYSEES Savy

€€

23 rue Bayard, 75008 **Tel** *01 47 23 46 98* **Map** *2 F1*

Opened in 1923, this Art-Deco restaurant with cosy booths in the front room is dedicated to the hearty cooking of the Aveyron region in central France. Order a marbled steak or the lamb shoulder for two, served with crisp shoestring *frites*, with one of the excellent wines from the cellar, perhaps a Mercury from Burgundy.

CHAMPS-ELYSEES Sens

€€

23 rue Ponthieu, 75008 **Tel** *01 42 25 95 00* **Map** *3 A5*

This concept restaurant, clad in soft greys and silvers, makes clever use of lighting to create the urban-chic feel that attracts the trendy crowd. Plastic, trunk-like pillars prop up the mezzanine. The menu features interesting Asian-influenced dishes such as grilled sea bream with wok-fried vegetables.

CHAMPS-ELYSEES Mini Palais

€€€

Grand Palais, 1 av Winston Churchill, 75008 **Tel** *01 42 56 42 42* **Map** *3 A5*

Michelin-starred chef Eric Fréchon presides over the kitchen at this brasserie, housed in the Grand Palais. The cuisine focuses on well-sourced, top-quality seasonal produce. Be sure not to miss the special house dessert of a giant rum baba, served with vanilla cream.

CHAMPS-ELYSEES La Fermette Marbeuf 1900 👥 ♿ 🍷 €€€€
5 rue Marbeuf, 75008 **Tel** *01 53 23 08 00*   **Map** *2 F5*

Fabulous Belle Epoque mosaics, tiles and ironwork were discovered beneath the formica walls of this Champs Elysées bistro. La Fermette Marbeuf also serves good classic food, including a tasting menu with a wide range of *appellations contrôlées* wines.

CHAMPS-ELYSEES Lasserre 🅿 🍴 🍷 €€€€€
17 av Franklin Roosevelt, 75008 **Tel** *01 43 59 02 13*   **Map** *7 A1*

Built for the 1937 World Fair to imitate the interior of a luxury liner, this restaurant, once favoured by Marc Chagall and Dalí, combines opulent decor with exceptional wines and deliciously refined cuisine by chef Christophe Moret. His dishes are inspired by 19th-century recipes such as macaroni with black truffles. Service is faultless.

CHAMPS-ELYSEES Le Cinq 🅿 👥 ♿ 🍴 🍷 €€€€€
31 av George V, 75008 **Tel** *01 49 52 70 00*   **Map** *2 E5*

For a rare splurge, it's hard to do better than this sumptuous Michelin-starred restaurant in the George V. The technically stunning food is not stuck in a time warp; ingredients such as wasabi and harissa make their way into some dishes. The €85 lunch menu is something of a bargain, given the quality of the food.

CHAMPS-ELYSEES Pavillon Ledoyen 🅿 👥 🍽 ♿ 🍴 🍷 €€€€€
1 av Dutuit, 75008 **Tel** *01 53 05 10 01*   **Map** *7 B1*

The cuisine at Pavillon Ledoyen is refined. Delicacies are skillfully prepared with meticulous care and innovation, and include many fish and seafood specialities. Ask for a table in the dining room – a re-creation of a 1950s grill room – or one on the terrace.

ILE DE LA CITE AND ILE SAINT-LOUIS Isami 🍽 €€€
4 quai Orléans, 75004 **Tel** *01 40 46 06 97*   **Map** *9 C4*

As you walk through the door of this little Seine-side restaurant the hostess will warn you that they "serve only raw fish here", which is why this restaurant is so popular with Japanese expats and locals who come here for sushi of a quality rarely found in Paris. There is also a carefully chosen selection of fine sakes.

ILE DE LA CITE AND ILE SAINT-LOUIS Mon Vieil Ami 👥 🍷 €€€
69 rue St Louis en l'Ile, 75004 **Tel** *01 40 46 01 35*   **Map** *9 B4*

Star Alsatian chef Antoine Westermann runs this modern bistro with stone walls, frosted glass partitions and a long shared table on one side. Vegetables from market gardener Joël Thiébault feature in inventive dishes, which occasionally draw on North African ingredients such as preserved lemon or couscous.

INVALIDES AND EIFFEL TOWER QUARTER Le Troquet 👥 🍷 🍴 €€
21 rue François Bonvin, 75015 **Tel** *01 45 66 89 00*

This is a jewel in an unlikely residential street with a view of the Eiffel Tower. Locals soak up the friendly atmosphere and devour Basque chef Christian Etchebest's fabulous cooking. The menu is chalked up on a blackboard each day in the retro-style dining room.

INVALIDES AND EIFFEL TOWER QUARTER Au Bon Accueil 👥 🍷 €€€
14 rue Monttessuy, 75007 **Tel** *01 47 05 46 11*   **Map** *6 E2*

Au Bon Accueil looks like a bistro from the outside with its terrace overlooking the Eiffel Tower but, once inside, the quality of the food and chic contemporary decor make it feel like a mini *haute cuisine* restaurant. If you are on a budget try the amazing value *prix-fixe* menus at lunch and dinner, which don't skimp on ingredients.

INVALIDES AND EIFFEL TOWER QUARTER La Villa Corse 🅿 👥 🍽 ♿ 🍷 €€€
164 bd de Grenelle, 75015 **Tel** *01 53 86 70 81*   **Map** *6 E5*

In a pleasant neighbourhood, La Villa Corse is one of the city's best restaurants for fresh and strongly flavoured Corsican-Mediterranean cuisine. The menu features wild boar stew, olive veal, Brocciu cheese and chestnut bread – a speciality from the city of Bonifacio. Good choice of Corsican wines.

INVALIDES AND EIFFEL TOWER QUARTER L'Arpège 👥 🍽 🍷 €€€€€
84 rue de Varenne, 75007 **Tel** *01 47 05 09 06*   **Map** *7 B3*

Alain Passard's three-star restaurant near the Musée Rodin is one of the most highly regarded in Paris. It has striking pale-wood decor, sprightly service and excellent food. The menu is based on the very best seasonal produce, with creative and harmonious pairings of ingredients. Don't miss the apple tart.

INVALIDES AND EIFFEL TOWER QUARTER Le Jules Verne 👥 🍽 🍴 🍷 €€€€€
2nd platform, Eiffel Tower, 75007 **Tel** *01 45 55 61 44*   **Map** *6 D3*

This is no tourist trap: reservations at the Jules Verne on the second platform of the Eiffel Tower are among the hardest to obtain in Paris. The sleek, all-black decor suits the monument perfectly and the pretty, flavourful cuisine is very good indeed.

JARDIN DES PLANTES QUARTER Marty Restaurant 🅿 👥 ♿ 🍴 €€€
20 av des Gobelins, 75005 **Tel** *01 43 31 39 51*   **Map** *13 B3*

The Marty was established by E Marty in 1913 and is still family-run. The interior is authentic Art Deco in style, but the cuisine steals the show. The menu features hearty fare, such as roast duck or rabbit casserole, and seasonal dishes, such as gazpacho. Excellent *crème brûlée*.

Key to Price Guide *see p600* **Key to Symbols** *see back cover flap*

LATIN QUARTER Le Grenier de Notre Dame

18 rue de la Bûcherie, 75005 **Tel** *01 43 29 98 29*

€

Map *9 A4*

Le Grenier de Notre Dame opened in the 1970s and still exudes its original hippie atmosphere. Mostly organic ingredients go into the filling, predominantly macrobiotic meals such as vegetarian casserole or vegetarian escalope in breadcrumbs. Good choice of reasonably priced wines, including some vintage Bordeaux wines.

LATIN QUARTER Le Balzar

49 rue des Ecoles, 75005 **Tel** *01 43 54 13 67*

€€

Map *9 A5*

There's a fair choice of brasserie food here but the main attraction is the Left Bank ambience. Traditionally dressed waiters weave their way among the hustle and bustle, providing express service, with archetypal brasserie decor to match: there are large mirrors and comfortable leather seats.

LATIN QUARTER Perraudin

157 rue St-Jacques, 75005 **Tel** *01 46 33 15 75*

€€

Map *12 F1*

From the red-and-white tablecloths to the zinc-topped bar and the cuisine, everything at Perraudin looks and feels like a genuine 1900s bistro. On the menu are staples like *carré* of lamb and *frites*, carpaccio of beef with Parmesan, and creamy *riz au lait* (rice pudding). Reservations for 7–8pm only – or wait at the bar (tables turn over quickly).

LATIN QUARTER Le Petit Pontoise

9 rue Pontoise, 75005 **Tel** *01 43 29 25 20*

€€

Map *9 B5*

This is a popular neighbourhood venue, where herbs and spices are used inventively on the daily changing menu. A typical menu will probably be composed of *foie gras* with figs, followed by a whole vanilla roasted sea-bass and, finally, pineapple roasted in ginger. Reservations recommended.

LATIN QUARTER Le Pré Verre

8 rue Thénard, 75005 **Tel** *01 43 54 59 47*

€€

Map *9 A5*

The brothers Marc and Philippe Delacourcelle run this plum-walled bistro whose cooking draws liberally on Asian ingredients – a signature dish is salt cod roasted with cassia bark and served with smoked potato purée. Wines come from small producers and the dining room is always lively.

LATIN QUARTER La Tour d'Argent

15–17 quai de la Tournelle, 75005 **Tel** *01 43 54 23 31*

€€€€€

Map *9 B5*

Established in 1582, originally in a stone tower, the Tour appears to be eternal. The young chefs hired by patrician owner Claude Terrail have rejuvenated the classic menu at this luxurious panoramic restaurant, with one of the finest wine cellars. The ground-floor bar is also a gastronomic museum. There's a cheaper set menu at lunchtime

MONTMARTRE Au Grain de Folie

24 rue la Vieuville, 75018 **Tel** *01 42 58 15 57*

€

Map *4 F1*

Paris has few vegetarian restaurants, and this one has a truly cosy feel. The main courses consist of salads with interesting combinations of vegetables and grains (most of which are organic). Au Grain de Folie's apple crumble is highly recommended, so be sure to leave room.

MONTMARTRE Hotel Amour

8 rue de Navarin, 75009 **Tel** *01 48 78 31 80*

€

Map *4 F2*

Food at this low-key but trendy bistro with vintage decor, below Montmartre in the fashionable 9th *arrondissement*, is a cross between all things French and Anglo Saxon. Think macaroni cheese, burgers and *crème brulée*. In summer request a table in the pretty courtyard.

MONTMARTRE La Famille

41 rue des Trois Frères, 75009 **Tel** *01 42 52 11 12*

€€

Map *4 F1*

The contemporary French cuisine at La Famille is as delicious as it is avant-garde. Don't be surprised if your meal is presented with a smiley face drawn in the sauce! Dishes such as marinated salmon in a thyme and rosemary crust are excellent. The decor borders on minimalist.

MONTMARTRE Le Wepler

14 pl de Clichy, 75018 **Tel** *01 45 22 53 24*

€€

Map *6 D1*

Established in 1892, this retro-style brasserie is open until late into the night. Good for afternoon tea, early evening cocktails and pre- or post-show suppers. Le Wepler serves appetizing large shellfish platters as well as *sauerkraut*, *andouillette* (sausage) and *confit de canard*.

MONTMARTRE Table d'Eugène

18 rue Eugène Sue, 75018 **Tel** *01 42 55 61 64*

€€€

Map *6 D1*

Slightly off the beaten track, this tiny restaurant is considered by many locals to be one of the best in Montmartre. Chef Geoffroy Maillard proves his worth, with innovative cuisine based around high-quality, carefully sourced seasonal produce. There is also an excellent selection of wines from independent producers. Book ahead.

MONTPARNASSE Port Manech

52 rue du Montparnasse, 75014 **Tel** *01 43 21 96 98*

€

Map *12 D2*

Port Manech is just like a little piece of Brittany right here in Paris. Try the tasty pancakes such as Provençal (mushrooms and snail butter), washed down perfectly with a cup of cider. There is a large choice of flambéed pancake varieties for dessert.

MONTPARNASSE La Régalade
49 av Jean Moulin, 75014 **Tel** *01 45 45 68 58*   €€
    Map 11 C5

Gourmet fare for a bargain at this traditional bistro. Try dishes such as duck *foie gras* casserole or pan-fried cod with leek vinaigrette for a main course, and the chef's speciality Grand Marnier soufflé for dessert. The seasonal menu is based on a *cuisine du marché*. Reservations essential.

MONTPARNASSE Le Timbre
3 rue Sainte Beuve, 75006 **Tel** *01 45 49 10 40*   €€
    Map 12 D1

Manchester native Chris Wright runs this postage-stamp-sized bistro with an open kitchen near the Luxembourg gardens. If the blackboard menu is resolutely French with neo-bistro dishes such as lentil salad with pork cheek or sea bream with olives, the plate of British cheese does pay tribute to his origins.

MONTPARNASSE Restaurant l'Assiette
181 rue du Château, 75014 **Tel** *01 43 22 64 86*   €€€
    Map 11 C4

Long run by cigar-smoking chef Lulu and frequented by socialist politicians, this insider's bistro was taken over by the young, Alain Ducasse-trained David Rathgeber in 2008. His menu of bistro classics such as marinated herrings with warm potato salad and crème caramel "revisited" is attracting a younger set of celebrities.

MONTPARNASSE La Cagouille
10–12 pl Constantin Brancusi, 75014 **Tel** *01 43 22 09 01*   €€€
    Map 11 C3

This large venue, on the stark new place Brancusi in the rebuilt Montparnasse district, is one of Paris's best fish restaurants. Fish is served simply with few sauces or adornments. Unusual seasonal delicacies might include black bay scallops and *vendangeurs* (tiny red mullet).

MONTPARNASSE La Coupole
102 bd du Montparnasse, 75014 **Tel** *01 43 20 14 20*   €€€
    Map 12 D2

This famous brasserie has been popular with the fashionistas, artists and thinkers since its creation in 1927. Under the same ownership as Brasserie Flo, it has a similar menu: shellfish, smoked salmon and good desserts. Flambéed beef is a speciality. Open from breakfast until 2am.

OPERA QUARTER Chartier
7 rue du Faubourg Montmartre, 75009 **Tel** *01 47 70 86 29*   €
    Map 4 F4

Despite its impressive 1900s decor, Chartier caters to people on a budget, mostly students and tourists, though some of the old *habitués* still come back for the basic cuisine (hard-boiled eggs with mayonnaise, house pâté, roast chicken and pepper steak). Expect no-frills service; the waiters are very busy.

OPERA QUARTER La Bourse ou la Vie
12 rue Vivienne, 75002 **Tel** *01 42 60 08 83*   €€
    Map 10 F5

Looking for the best steak-*frites* in Paris? You may well find it at this restaurant with a red-and-yellow, 1940s decor near the old stock exchange. The secret here is top-quality meat and the animal fat that is used to cook the *frites*; order it doused in creamy cracked-peppercorn sauce. A soundtrack of French chanson adds to the atmosphere.

OPERA QUARTER La Vaudeville
29 rue Vivienne, 75002 **Tel** *01 40 20 04 62*   €€
    Map 4 F5

This is one of seven brasseries owned by Paris's reigning brasserie king, Jean-Paul Bucher. Good shellfish, Bucher's famous smoked salmon, many fish dishes as well as classic brasserie standbys like pig's trotters and *andouillette* (tripe sausage). Quick, friendly service and a noisy ambience make it fun.

OPERA QUARTER Willi's Wine Bar
13 rue des Petits-Champs, 75001 **Tel** *01 42 61 05 09*   €€
    Map 8 F1

This charming, cosy wine bar has been offering a range of over 250 kinds of wine since 1980. The menu includes cream of asparagus soup with tarragon, salt-roasted lamb and, of course, an excellent wine list. The bar also sells an array of examples of "wine art".

OPERA QUARTER Un Jour à Peyrassol
13 rue Vivienne, 75002 **Tel** *01 42 60 12 92*   €€€
    Map 10 F5

The Commanderie de Peyrassol, one of the best vineyards in Provence, runs this restaurant dedicated to truffles, wine and other products from the area. The two rustic-meets-modern dining rooms have a warm Provençal atmosphere, reinforced by the earthy aroma of dishes such as truffle-laced scrambled eggs.

OPERA QUARTER Drouant
16–18 pl Gaillon, 75002 **Tel** *01 42 65 15 16*   €€€€
    Map 4 E5

This former Alsatian brasserie founded in 1880 is now a contemporary restaurant run by Antoine Westermann, who is also behind the bistro Mon Vieil Ami *(see p602)*. Order *à la carte* to sample his generous *hors d'oeuvres*, which fill the table with little bowls and plates. Upstairs are several private salons for groups.

OPERA QUARTER La Fontaine Gaillon
1 rue de la Michodière, 75002 **Tel** *01 47 42 63 22*   €€€€
    Map 4 E5

Housed in a 17th-century mansion, Fontaine Gaillon is partly owned by legendary film actor Gérard Depardieu. The menu changes daily and might include *confit de canard* or lamb chops, and strawberries in Anjou wine. The interiors are comfortable, and there is a good wine list.

Key to Price Guide *see p600* **Key to Symbols** *see back cover flap*

SAINT-GERMAIN-DES-PRES Chez les Filles €

64 rue du Cherche Midi, 75006 **Tel** *01 45 48 61 54* **Map** *7 C5*

Moroccan sisters run this small, lively restaurant, with exotic afternoon tea breaks. Tagines, salads and couscous are on the lunch menu, while teatime treats include great pastries washed down with lots of mint tea. The interior features wrought-iron work and kilims bearing Moroccan accents. Closed Sun.

SAINT-GERMAIN-DES-PRES La Crèmerie €

9 rue Quatre Vents, 75006 **Tel** *01 43 54 99 30* **Map** *8 E4*

A former dairy store dating from 1880, this little shop with a painted glass ceiling has been a wine bar since the 1950s. The current owners, a pair of former architects, focus on "natural" wines served with bread and butter from Brittany, hams from Spain, sausage from the Ardèche and burrata cheese from Puglia in Italy.

SAINT-GERMAIN-DES-PRES J'Go €€

Rue Clement, 75006 **Tel** *01 43 26 19 02* **Map** *8 E4*

This lively Toulousian wine bar doubles as a *rotisserie* serving juicy spit-roasted lamb from Quercy, whole-roasted chicken and black pig from Bigorre. The set menu is excellent value, offering pâté, a giant salad and delicious lamb with creamy white beans. Tapas are also served and the wine (by the bottle or the glass) is consistently excellent.

SAINT-GERMAIN-DES-PRES L'Epigramme €€

9 rue de l'Eperon, 75006 **Tel** *01 44 41 00 09* **Map** *8 F4*

With terracotta tiles, wood beams and windows looking onto a leafy courtyard, L'Epigramme has plenty of Left Bank charm. The glassed-in kitchen turns out impeccable modern bistro food such as Basque farmer's pork on a bed of turnip choucroute; also look out for game in season. Service is equally polished.

SAINT-GERMAIN-DES-PRES Polidor €€

41 rue Monsieur le Prince, 75006 **Tel** *01 43 26 95 34* **Map** *8 F5*

Once frequented by Verlaine and Rimbaud, this is bohemian Paris incarnate. The place has kept its reputation by sticking to traditional cuisine at rock-bottom prices. Grilled steak, *daube de bœuf*, veal and various dessert tarts feature on the menu.

ST-GERMAIN-DES-PRES Joséphine Chez Dumonet €€€

117 rue du Cherche-Midi, 75006 **Tel** *01 45 48 52 40* **Map** *11 C1*

Pre-World War II bistros with old-fashioned menus have become a rarity in Paris, which explains the popularity of Joséphine. Start with the help-yourself marinated herrings before superb steak tartare or perhaps a rib-sticking cassoulet; desserts are equally gargantuan. The wine list is lengthy and expensive.

SAINT-GERMAIN-DES-PRES Le Procope €€€

13 rue de l'Ancienne Comédie, 75006 **Tel** *01 40 46 79 00* **Map** *8 F4*

Opened in 1686, Paris's oldest café welcomed literary and political figures such as Voltaire and Diderot. Nowadays, it's still a hub for the intelligentsia, who sit alongside those curious about this historical place. *Coq au vin* (chicken cooked in wine) is the speciality. Shellfish platters are also popular.

THE MARAIS Chez Hannah €

54 rue des Rosiers, 75004 **Tel** *01 42 74 74 99* **Map** *9 C3*

L'As du Fallafel may be better known, but Chez Hannah serves falafel sandwiches to rival any in this street filled with Jewish delis. They come packed with crunchy chickpea balls, tahini sauce, melting aubergine and chilli, to be eaten in the lively dining room or standing in the street. A locals' favourite.

THE MARAIS Bistrot de L'Oulette €€

38 rue des Tournelles, 75004 **Tel** *01 42 71 43 33* **Map** *10 E3*

A tiny restaurant with good-quality food at reasonable prices. The fixed-price menu is particularly good value. Southwestern cuisine includes delicious *confit de carnard* and *cassoulet*, followed by white chocolate soup for dessert. There is also superb home-made chestnut bread.

THE MARAIS Chez Jenny €€

39 bd du Temple, 75003 **Tel** *01 44 54 39 00* **Map** *10 D1*

This huge brasserie on the place de la République, with waitresses in traditional dress, has been a bastion of Alsatian cooking since it was founded over 60 years ago. The *choucroute* (sauerkraut) *spéciale Jenny* makes a hearty meal, followed by a sorbet and a fruit liqueur.

THE MARAIS Le Colimaçon €€

44 rue Vieille du Temple, 75004 **Tel** *01 48 87 12 01* **Map** *9 C3*

Le Colimaçon (snail) refers to the restaurant's centrepiece: a corkscrew staircase. A listed building dating from 1732, it has period wooden beams in the ceiling. Snails are also on the menu, along with frogs' legs in parsley and tomato sauce and *blanquette* of veal, the house specialty.

THE MARAIS Les Philosophes €€

28 rue Vieille du Temple, 75003 **Tel** *01 48 87 49 64* **Map** *9 C3*

Among the many cafés run by Xavier Denamour in this street, Les Philosophes is the most popular at meal times for its above-average bistro fare: the *steak-frites* are just as they should be, and tomato *tarte tatin* is a speciality. The terrace is perfect for people-watching, and service is jovial if rushed.

THE MARAIS Le 404

€€€

69 rue des Gravilliers, 75003 **Tel** *01 42 74 57 81*   **Map** *9 B1*

It's a party every night at this North African restaurant lined with low tables and poufs (there is also seating in the mezzanine). The later the hour, the higher the volume, and by the end of the night everyone is on their feet. The food is good, too: try one of the tagines, or the house speciality, couscous.

THE MARAIS Le Gaigne

€€€

12 rue Pecquay, 75004 **Tel** *01 44 59 86 72*   **Map** *9 C2*

Chef Mickaël Gaignon had years of *haute cuisine* training under his belt before opening this intimate ivory-and-plum dining room with paintings of food on the walls. His inventive, seasonal cooking focuses on the quality of the ingredients, such as scallop tartare flavoured with lemon and served with red chicory.

THE MARAIS L'Ambroisie

€€€€€

9 pl des Vosges, 75004 **Tel** *01 42 78 51 45*   **Map** *10 D3*

In a former jewellery shop restored by Chef Bernard Pacaud, this is one of only a handful of Parisian restaurants with three Michelin stars. The cuisine includes a langoustine *feuillantine* (langoustines wrapped in very thin pastry) flavoured with sesame seeds, and veal escalope served with minced artichokes. Reservations accepted one month in advance.

TUILERIES Le Fumoir

€€

6 rue de l'Amiral Coligny, 75001 **Tel** *01 42 92 00 24*   **Map** *4 F2*

A café by day and a rather sultry restaurant-bar at night, Le Fumoir serves remarkably good food with a Scandinavian touch that often appears in condiments such as cranberries or horseradish. Cocktails are good and there is an intimate library at the back with big leather armchairs.

TUILERIES QUARTER Café Marly

€€€

93 rue de Rivoli, 75001 **Tel** *01 49 26 06 60*   **Map** *8 E2*

In a wing of the Louvre, this is a handy restaurant when feet ache and bellies rumble after trekking round the galleries. You'll find everything from salads and burgers to traditional and contemporary French cuisine. It's also in a top spot for a coffee on the terrace overlooking the Louvre's main thoroughfare.

TUILERIES QUARTER Le Grand Véfour

€€€€€

17 rue de Beaujolais, 75001 **Tel** *01 42 96 56 27*   **Map** *12 F1*

This 18th-century restaurant has two Michelin stars and is considered by many to be Paris's most attractive. Chef Guy Martin's creative dishes include *foie gras* ravioli with a truffle sauce, and hazelnuts and chocolate with caramel ice cream and sea salt.

ILE DE FRANCE

BARBIZON Hôtellerie du Bas-bréau

€€€€

22 Grande Rue, 77630 **Tel** *01 60 66 40 05*

Author Robert Louis Stevenson has been among the celebrated guests at this hotel-restaurant with its classic menu and enormous wine list. The much-praised cooking includes sole with caviar, wild boar and venison in season and for dessert, Grand Marnier soufflé.

BOULOGNE-BILLANCOURT Le Pré Catelan

€€€€€

Bois de Boulogne, rte de Suresnes, 75016 **Tel** *01 44 14 41 14*

Housed in a chic Napoleon III villa, in a charming setting by the Bois de Boulogne, this Michelin-starred restaurant serves *haute cuisine* fit for a king. Chef Frédéric Aton strives for perfection, with dishes such as *foie gras* in port, fried with lentils and served in a cream of *foie gras* and black truffle sauce.

DAMPIERRE Auberge Saint-Pierre

€€

1 rue de Chevreuse, 78720 **Tel** *01 30 52 53 53*

This half-timbered inn facing the grand château de Dampierre has a rustic, convivial dining room. The gourmet menu has fine dishes such as tartare of potatoes with *foie gras*, salad of baby scallops with white radish, stuffed quail with lentils and chicken leg with *foie gras* stuffing.

ISSY-LES-MOULINEAUX Les Symples de l'Os à Moelle

€€

18 av de la République, 92130 **Tel** *01 41 08 02 52*

This restaurant replicates the winning formula of La Cave de l'Os à Moelle, an annex of the gourmet bistro L'Os à Moelle in the 15th arrondissement. Seated at long tables, diners help themselves to a multitude of pâtés, soups and salads which are followed by a hearty main course and a buffet of cheeses and desserts... all for €25.

ISSY-LES-MOULINEAUX L'Ile

€€€

Parc Ile Saint-Germain, 170 quai Stalingrad, 92130 **Tel** *01 41 09 99 99*

Set in the heart of the Ile St-Germain Park, with its vast terrace shaded by chestnut trees, this restaurant is a great place for outdoor dining in the warmer months. The setting can also be admired from the conservatory in cooler weather. Fine traditional cuisine includes revisited classics such as salmon and scallop tartare with mango and ginger.

Key to Price Guide *see p600* **Key to Symbols** *see back cover flap*

LE-PERREUX-SUR-MARNE Les Magnolias
48 av de Bry, 94170 **Tel** *01 48 72 47 43*

After working in a series of *haute-cuisine* restaurants, young chef Jean Chauvel went out on a limb and opened this wildly creative restaurant in a little-known suburb of Paris. The risk has paid off: food-lovers come from far and wide for his graphically presented dishes, each of which comes with a whimsical menu description.

MAISONS LAFFITTE Les Jardins de la Vieille Fontaine
8 av Grétry, 78600 **Tel** *01 39 62 01 78*

An elegant setting inside a beautiful white mansion near the Maisons-Laffitte Park. Seasonal menus offer gastronomic cuisine in an unpretentious manner. Delicious, well-presented dishes like a *mille-feuille* of goat's cheese and aubergine or caramelized, pan-fried cod. Irresistible desserts. Reasonably priced wine.

NEUILLY-SUR-SEINE Le Zinc Zinc
209 ter av du Général-de-Gaulle, 92200 **Tel** *01 40 88 36 06*

Le Zinc Zinc has reinvented the bistro for the 21st century, serving breakfast, lunch, tapas and dinner with a huge choice of dishes for every appetite. You can sit at the bar for a simple meal of *steak-frites* or Spanish ham, or have a three-course dinner of contemporary bistro fare in the bordeaux-and-cream dining room.

PROVINS Aux Vieux Remparts
3 rue Couverte, 77160 **Tel** *01 64 08 94 00*

In the medieval part of town, this timbered building boasts a restaurant and a hotel. The Aux Vieux Remparts is a gastronomic restaurant serving creative fare such as prawns with aubergine caviar, carpaccio of monkfish, and chocolate cake made with salt and served with caramelized lemon.

RAMBOUILLET Le Cheval Rouge
78 rue du Général de Gaulle, 78120 **Tel** *01 30 88 80 61*

This intimate restaurant is close to the Château de Rambouillet. The good-humoured chef serves up an array of delicious traditional fare such as *foie gras*, snails and steak tartare. A great-value buffet is on offer at lunchtimes. Some of the tables are in the conservatory.

RUEIL-MALMAISON Relais de St-Cucufa
114 rue Générale-de-Miribel, 92500 **Tel** *01 47 49 79 05*

Combining Breton and Italian flair, the chefs present a traditional menu that includes *morille fricassée* with poached egg; lobster, grapefruit and avocado salad; platter of grilled shellfish; fillet of beef and roast lamb. Enjoy lunch in the attractive garden or dinner in front of the fire. Classic wine selection.

ST-GERMAIN-EN-LAYE Le Saint Exupéry
11 av des Loges, 78100 **Tel** *01 39 21 50 90*

In an elegant setting in the Ermitage des Loges hotel, near the château, this restaurant is frequented by locals. The young chef enlivens classic dishes, such as entrecôte steak with pan-fried Jerusalem artichokes, gratin of scallops and braised chicory and stuffed-squid risotto. The children's menu is excellent value.

ST-OUEN Le Soleil
109 av Michelet, 93400 **Tel** *01 40 10 08 08*

Steps away from the St-Ouen flea market and a short drive from the Stade de France, this charming bistro has a vibrant interior. The menu includes duck confit with spicy aubergine or more classic dishes such as a Charolais entrecôte. Superb Rum baba for dessert. Good, slightly expensive wine. Book ahead.

VERSAILLES La Terrasse
11 rue St-Honoré, 78000 **Tel** *01 39 50 76 00*

A fun restaurant specializing in southwestern cuisine. On a warm day the large, shaded terrace is a godsend. The decor inside is bright and kitsch. Specialities include some intriguing *foie gras* combinations, such as *foie gras* with gingerbread, as well as duck with honeyed peaches.

VERSAILLES Le Valmont
20 rue au Pain, 78000 **Tel** *01 39 51 39 00*

Refined cuisine at this yellow-and-blue bistro tucked behind the market hall. Chef Philippe Mathieu presents an ambitious menu with dishes such as escalope of veal deglazed with *Banyuls* vinegar, John Dory with fennel and ginger, and *fondant au chocolat* for dessert. Good wines by the glass.

LE NORD & PICARDY

AIRE-SUR-LA-LYS Hostellerie des Trois Mousquetaires
Château de la Redoute, rte de Béthune, 62120 **Tel** *03 21 39 01 11*

Rural peace and the charm of a 19th-century mansion in its own grounds with a lake. Unusually, the kitchens are visible, and serve imaginative classic cuisine. The varied menu includes regional dishes. A popular destination with visitors from the UK; book ahead.

AMIENS Le Pré Porus
95 rue de Voyelle, 80000 **Tel** *03 22 46 25 03*

Attractive and popular riverside restaurant by the Somme. The very varied menu specializes in all sorts of fish dishes as well as grilled meat according to the season and pan-fried *foie gras* with mango. A good place to stop for lunch while visiting the nearby historic Roman waterways and market gardens.

AMIENS L'Aubergade
78 rte Nationale, 80480 **Tel** *03 22 89 51 41* **Fax** *03 22 95 44 05*

Mediterranean-looking restaurant run by Eric Boutte, a young chef who won his first star and is making a name for himself. After working in top Paris restaurants, he returned to his native Amiens with a vision for his restaurant. His favourite ingredient is duck. Other dishes include pan-fried scallops with *foie gras* and lime soufflé with prunes.

ARRAS La Faisanderie
45 grand place, 62000 **Tel** *03 21 48 20 76*

Also on the magnificent Grand Place, with its splendid scrolled gable façades, this restaurant is housed in a 17th-century building with a splendid brick vaulted dining room. The cuisine is dictated by what the chef finds at the market. The best of several restaurants on the square, by far.

BEAUVAIS La Table de Céline
6 bis rue Antoine Caron, 60000 **Tel** *03 44 45 79 79*

This traditional restaurant is decorated in soothing tones, and has an open fire in winter, with an agreeable terrace for outdoor dining in the warmer months. Choice dishes include ingredients such as scallops, prawns, duck *foie gras*, salmon and local lamb. Closed Mon, and Tue, Thu, Fri and Sat lunch.

BERGUES Le Bruegel
1 rue du Marché aux Fromages, 59380 **Tel** *03 28 68 19 19* **Fax** *03 28 68 67 12*

Bergues is just outside Dunkirk and is a pleasant surprise. This is a very popular restaurant for families, with long tables and waiters in medieval dress. The picturesque building by the canal dates from 1597, when Spain ruled Flanders. Pork cheeks and lentils and other Flemish dishes with beer are the order of the day.

BOULOGNE-SUR-MER La Matelote
80 bd Ste Beuve, 62200 **Tel** *03 21 30 17 97* **Fax** *03 21 83 29 24*

One of the rising gastronomic stars, this is a top-notch seafood restaurant on the seafront, opposite the National Marine centre. The interior is smart, with sea-going ornaments and a red-and-gold Louis XVI motif. Try the warm lobster with artichoke hearts and basil or monkfish in Parmesan.

CALAIS Histoire Ancienne
20 rue Royale, 62100 **Tel** *03 21 34 11 20* **Fax** *03 21 96 19 58*

This is a modernized restaurant that has managed to preserve its image as an old-fashioned bistro, with a zinc counter and the old-style bench seating. It is located opposite the Parc Richelieu. The well prepared menu is split between grilled meats and traditional local dishes.

CALAIS Le Channel
3 bd de la Résistance, 62100 **Tel** *03 21 34 42 30* **Fax** *03 21 97 42 43*

A good fish restaurant right next to the harbour, the yacht club and the Bassin du Paradis, with a fine view of the boats coming and going. The restaurant is bright and nicely decorated with painted woodwork. It has a wine list to be proud of. An ideal spot to wait for the ferry.

CAMBRAI Le Jolly Sailor
11 rue de Douai, 59400 **Tel** *03 27 81 29 66*

Simple, good-value traditional cuisine is on offer at this restaurant housed in a bright-yellow building, with a terrace overlooking a canal. The menu draws on market availability and changes daily. The atmosphere is warm and welcoming, and there is often live music.

CASSEL Estaminet T'Kasteel Hof
Rue St-Nicolas, 59670 **Tel** *03 28 40 59 29*

There are sweeping views of the flat countryside from this Flemish-style *estaminet* (no-frills café) which serves local dishes, often with local cheeses, accompanied by beer. It was at Cassel that the "Grand Old Duke of York", son of George III, marched his 10,000 men up to the top of the hill (as popularized in a song).

COMPIEGNE Bistro des Arts
35 cours Guynemer, 60200 **Tel** *03 44 20 10 10*

A lively bistro serving sophisticated, good-value fare. Located in the centre of town, with an artistic atmosphere. Chairs and red leather benches, but no tablecloths. Each day's menu is put up on the slate according to the market. The cuisine is traditional French, and usually includes a meat and a fish dish.

COMPIEGNE Alain Blot
21 rue Maréchal Foch, Rethondes, 60153 **Tel** *03 44 85 60 24* **Fax** *03 44 85 92 35*

The proprietor's motto is that seafood should be "a simple expression of the sea". This starred restaurant, with a delightful dining room and veranda opening onto an immaculate garden, is known for its range of classic dishes, such as grilled bass with caramelized red onion. Book ahead.

Key to Price Guide *see p600* **Key to Symbols** *see back cover flap*

DOUAI La Terrasse

36 terrasse St-Pierre, 59500 **Tel** *03 27 88 70 04* **Fax** *03 27 88 36 05*

An excellent hotel and restaurant in a lane next to the Collégiale St Pierre, with an extensive wine list of over 1,000 references. The opulent restaurant is decorated with paintings. Try the chef's inspiration – smoked salmon stuffed with asparagus and grilled scallops with black pudding.

DUNKIRK Estaminet Flamand

6 rue des Fusiliers-Marins, 59140 **Tel** *03 28 66 98 35*

Having suffered from many wars, Dunkirk is not a scenic tourist destination. It has, however, retained its culinary traditions, exemplified here in this pleasant *estaminet* (simple café). Delicious and authentic Flemish cuisine including marrow bones, Maroilles cheese, beer tart and sugar tart.

DUNKIRK L'Estouffade

2 quai de la Citadelle, 59140 **Tel** *03 28 63 92 78* **Fax** *03 28 63 92 78*

A small, popular restaurant specializing in seafood, with views of the port. In summer there is a quiet terrace onto the quay that runs alongside the commercial basin. Turbot is a speciality here. Desserts include chocolate and fruit delights.

LAON La Petite Auberge

45 bd Brossolette, 02000 **Tel** *03 23 23 02 38*

Chef Willy Marc Zorn serves a creative and exotic menu, with distinct Oriental influences. His specialities include hot *foie gras de canard* and local pork with polenta and Espelette peppers. The extensive wine list has more than 200 prestige vintages, and each dish is complemented by a selected bottle.

LILLE Au Bout des Doigts

5 rue St-Joseph, 59000 **Tel** *03 20 74 55 95*

A different concept for the French in dining out, meals at this restaurant comprise a selection of eight to ten small dishes. There are no knives and you can eat with your fingers. The cooking is based on mixing flavours, and the wine is drawn from all over the world. The decor is contemporary.

LILLE La Ducasse

95 rue de Solferino, 59000 **Tel** *03 20 57 34 10*

This traditional brasserie in the lively Halles district is something of an institution in Lille. Regional cuisine and beer from a local micro brewery are the highlights, but there is also a mechanical musical box and an accordionist who plays on Friday evenings for the diners who like to sing. Choose a table on the terrace in fine weather.

LILLE Le Compostelle

4 rue Saint-Etienne, 59800 **Tel** *03 28 38 08 30* **Fax** *03 28 38 08 39*

Just off the Grand Place is this former 16th-century hostel on the route to the shrine of St-Jacques de Compostelle (Santiago de Compostela) in northwest Spain. Today the hostel combines old-fashioned charm with contemporary decor. The chef provides a nice blend of regional and traditional cuisine.

MONTREUIL-SUR-MER Auberge de la Grenouillère

Rue de la Grenouillère, La Madeleine-sous-Montreuil **Tel** *03 21 06 07 22* **Fax** *03 21 86 36 36*

Three kilometres from Montreuil, this Picardy farm on the banks of the Canche is furnished traditionally with copper, antique sideboards and wall paintings of frogs enjoying a good meal. The modern menu is backed up by a good wine list. Tasty crayfish and frogs' legs. The restaurant gained its first Michelin star in 2008.

POIX DE PICARDIE L'Auberge de la Forge

14 rue du 49ème Régiment BCA, Caulières, 80290 **Tel** *03 22 38 00 91* **Fax** *03 22 38 08 48*

A former staging post on the way from Amiens to Neufchatel, this half-timbered Picardy inn serves old-fashioned hearty fare. The restaurant is smart and attractive. The chef's speciality is duck, in various forms. The *endives gratinées*, ham with Maroilles cheese, and endives and scallops are also good.

RECQUES-SUR-HEM Château de Cocove

Av de Cocove **Tel** *03 21 82 68 29* **Fax** *03 21 82 72 59*

This fine 18th-century château, halfway between Calais and St-Omer, is a real rural retreat. Napoleon had parties here while waiting to invade England. The restaurant is in the beautifully restored old stone stables. Trays of shellfish can be specially prepared if ordered in advance.

ROEUX Le Grand Bleu

41 rue Henri-Robert, 62118 **Tel** *03 21 55 41 74*

A wooden chalet houses this popular establishment where fish dishes, such as turbot with aubergine chips, are the speciality. Wine is served either by the glass or by the bottle. Choose a window table and enjoy the view of Le Grand Bleu lake, which turns a beautiful shade of blue in the sunshine.

ROYE La Flamiche

20 pl de l'Hôtel de Ville, 80700 **Tel** *03 22 87 00 56* **Fax** *03 22 78 46 77*

Known as a prestige gastronomic restaurant throughout the area (with a Michelin star since 1964), Madame Klopp has run this impeccable establishment for many years. Try the pan-fried scallops, the tajine of Somme eels or local *flamiche* with leeks. The dining room is filled with an exhibition of sculpture and paintings.

SANGATTE Les Dunes   🅿️🚶   €€
Rte Nationale 48, Blériot Plage, 62231 **Tel** *03 21 34 54 30* **Fax** *03 21 97 17 63*

This hotel and restaurant is located at Blériot Plage where, in 1909, an intrepid Frenchman set out on his successful attempt to be the first man to cross the Channel in powered flight. Today this establishment is very handy for the Channel Tunnel. Great seafood: try the cassoulet of mussels.

SARS-POTERIES L'Auberge Fleurie   🅿️🚶🍽️   €€€€
67 rue Général de Gaulle, 59216 **Tel** *03 27 67 38 22* **Fax** *03 27 65 88 73*

This grand farmhouse with pretty gardens has been converted into a restaurant serving classic French cooking at its best. The pike-perch on a bed of cabbage and bacon is good, as is the shellfish. In winter, venison, wild boar and partridge feature regularly on the menu.

STEENVOORDE Auprès de mon Arbre   🚶🍽️   €€
932 rte d'Ecke, 59114 **Tel** *03 28 49 79 49*

In this town, famous for its carnival giants which parade each year through the centre, and for its church steeple with its high belfry, this restaurant is well regarded. The owner was the chef at a well-known Lille restaurant before settling here in the late 1990s. Classic French as well as traditional Flemish cuisine.

WIMEREUX Hôtel Atlantique   🅿️🚶🍷   €€€€
Digue de mer, 1st floor, 62930 **Tel** *03 21 32 41 01* **Fax** *03 21 87 46 17*

Right on the promenade, with a great view of the sea, as you would expect. The chef Alain Delpierre comes as something of a surprise in this old-fashioned setting. Red mullet in a salad with balsamic vinegar is one speciality. There are also 18 refurbished guest rooms – ask for one facing the Channel.

CHAMPAGNE

AIX-EN-OTHE Auberge de la Scierie   🅿️🚶♿🍽️🍷   €€€
La Vove, 10160 **Tel** *03 25 46 71 26.* **Fax** *03 25 46 65 69*

Auberge de la Scierie is run by a Franco-Australian-British couple, who worked together at the Savoy in London, and together speak five languages. They specialize in shellfish with a distinctly Oriental flavour. This auberge, set in 3 ha (8 acres) of grounds with a swimming pool, also has guest rooms, and cookery courses are offered.

ARSONVAL Hostellerie de la Chaumière   🅿️🚶♿🍽️   €€€
Arsonval, 10200 **Tel** *03 25 27 91 02* **Fax** *03 25 27 90 26*

For many years now this hospitable Anglo-French couple have been welcoming guests to their restaurant and hotel overlooking the Aube. It is close to the route de Champagne. Dishes include home-made *foie gras*, and some of the best kidneys and bacon in France. Rustic dining room, with wooden beams.

BAR-SUR-AUBE Le Cellier aux Moines   🚶   €€
Rue Général Vouillemont, 10200 **Tel** *03 25 27 08 01* **Fax** *03 25 01 56 22*

As the name implies, this huge 12th-century cellar in the centre of this pleasant old town (once the main route to Switzerland) has been converted into a restaurant with a vineyard theme. The staff wear *vignerons'* outfits for groups. Try the *andouillette* (tripe sausage) with excellent local Chaource cheese.

BREVONNES Au Vieux Logis   🅿️🚶♿🍽️   €€
1 rue de Piney, 10220 **Tel** *03 25 46 30 17*

This first-class restaurant is part of a completely refurbished traditional hotel. The menu features classic French cuisine, including dishes such as snails in garlic cream with local Chaource cheese. This is a good choice for those visiting the artificial lakes nearby as well as the Fôret de L'Orient.

CHALONS-EN-CHAMPAGNE Les Temps Changent   🅿️🚶📋♿   €€
1 rue Garinet, 51000 **Tel** *03 26 66 41 09*

Head to the Hôtel d'Angleterre in the town centre to dine at this popular bistro. There is a different menu every day that focuses on seasonal produce. Try the roast shoulder of lamb with basil or the delicious passion fruit soufflé accompanied by wine served either by the glass or bottle.

CHALONS-EN-CHAMPAGNE Au Carillon Gourmand   🚶📋🍽️   €€€
15 bis pl Monseigneur Tissier, 51000 **Tel** *03 26 64 45 07*

In the centre of the old town in the Notre-Dame-de-Vaux quarter, this welcoming restaurant has a pleasant covered terrace that opens onto the street. The *plat du jour* (dish of the day) is chosen according to what is best at the market. Try carpaccio of salmon or spiced duck pâté.

CHAUMONT Les Remparts   🅿️🚶📋♿🍽️   €€€
72 rue de Verdun, 52000 **Tel** *03 25 32 64 40*

This coaching inn has a restaurant, brasserie and hotel, all on-site. The restaurant specializes in dishes that include truffles and the local Langres cheese. Much cheaper meals are available in the Brasserie 1-2-3, located in the same building. Both restaurants look out over the attractive grounds.

Key to Price Guide *see p600* **Key to Symbols** *see back cover flap*

COMBEAUFONTAINE Le Balcon
1 pl 15 Juin 1940, 70120 **Tel** *03 84 92 11 13* **Fax** *03 84 92 15 89*

This good old-fashioned provincial restaurant, half an hour from Langres, deserves recognition. Try the chef's recommendation – the *menu gourmand* – and you will come away more than satisfied in body and wallet. The brasserie offers good weekday lunches. Rooms are also available.

EPERNAY La Table Kobus
3 rue Dr Rousseau, 51200 **Tel** *03 26 51 53 53* **Fax** *03 26 58 42 68*

An excellent brasserie near the centre of this town that is all about champagne. Uniquely, you can bring your own bottle of champagne to drink with your meal. The menu is classic French cuisine. The home-made terrine of *foie gras fait maison* is particularly recommended.

FOUCHERES Auberge de la Seine
1 faubourg de Bourgogne, 10260 **Tel** *03 25 40 71 11* **Fax** *03 25 40 84 09*

A picturebook posting inn halfway between the Côte des Bar and the Champagne vineyards. The restaurant in Louis XIII-style opens onto a pretty riverside terrace. The chef, who has run the kitchens of other starred restaurants in the area, specializes in lobster.

JOINVILLE Le Soleil d'Or
9 rue Capucins, 52300 **Tel** *03 25 94 15 66* **Fax** *03 25 94 39 02*

This 17th-century house, with elegant guest rooms and a restaurant, was the home of the Guise family. The dining room is decorated with statues from a 14th-century convent, and there is an agreeable covered terrace. An original menu that changes every day.

LANGRES La Pignata
59 rue Diderot, 52200 **Tel** *03 25 87 63 70*

Italian restaurant serving pizzas and other tasty dishes, such as veal with Milanese sauce or seafood tagliatelle, with house wine. It is located in the centre of this historic fortress town. Wander the old cramped streets and try to spot the first barracks allocated to the Foreign Legion, in 1832.

LANGRES L'Auberge des Voiliers
Lac de la Liez, 52000 **Tel** *03 25 87 05 74*

Hidden away from the historic city of Langres this auberge overlooks a good-sized lake with views of the city walls. The main restaurant serves "modernized" traditional dishes – *foie gras* with rhubarb or fillet of pike with nettle soufflé. There is also a cheaper brasserie if you prefer more simple cuisine.

LE MESNIL-SUR-OGER Le Mesnil
2 rue Pasteur, 51190 **Tel** *03 26 57 95 57* **Fax** *03 26 57 78 57*

In a pretty wine-growing village in the heart of the Champagne vineyards is this gourmet restaurant, set in an attractive old house. The restaurant owner is happy to show clients round his fine wine cellars. The village is the home of the museum of the vine and wine in the Maison Launois.

L'EPINE Aux Armes de Champagne
31 av de Luxembourg, 51460 **Tel** *03 26 69 30 30* **Fax** *03 26 69 30 26*

A top-class establishment, with a restaurant and hotel rooms, next to the majestic 15th-century basilique Notre Dame. Classic French cuisine is prepared with vegetables from the restaurant's garden, such as asparagus with truffle sauce and flakes of *foie gras,* or lobster with apricots. Good vegetarian selection.

NOGENT-SUR-SEINE Au Beau Rivage
20 rue Villiers-aux-Choux, 10400 **Tel** *03 25 39 84 22* **Fax** *03 25 39 18 32*

This riverside hotel and restaurant comes highly recommended, particularly since the bedrooms have been refurbished. An attractive terrace looks out from the dining room onto the Seine. French traditional *cuisine gastronomique*, with *foie gras* and rabbit on a menu that will make your mouth water.

REIMS La Brasserie Boulingrin
48 rue Mars, 51100 **Tel** *03 26 40 96 22* **Fax** *03 26 40 03 92*

This famous Reims brasserie and a regular meeting place for locals has kept its Art Deco mosaics of jolly grape harvesters *vendangeurs en Champagne*. Good value and a lively place to dine, near the covered market. Oysters and steak tartare are specialities. There is also a large selection of champagnes.

REIMS Le Café du Palais
14 pl Myron Herrick, 51100 **Tel** *03 26 47 52 54*

An Aladdin's cave of paintings, photos and a famous Art-Deco, stained-glass roof by Jacques Simon, have been assembled over the years by owner Jean-Louis Vogt. This is a much-loved family run brasserie in the heart of Reims, which has been in existence since 1930. Excellent main dishes, great desserts and a fine selection of champagne.

REIMS L'Assiette Champenoise
40 av Paul Vaillant-Couturier, Tinqueux, 51430 **Tel** *03 26 84 64 64* **Fax** *03 26 04 15 69*

A well-established gastronomic star, which is reflected in the price. Lobster dishes are a speciality, and pigeon and lamb are other favourites of chef Arnaud Lallement. Housed in an elegant *maison de maitre*, the restaurant has two rosettes. Attractions include a beautiful flower garden and terrace.

ROCROI Hôtel-Restaurant le Commerce

5 pl d'Armes, 08230 **Tel** *03 24 54 11 15*

This pleasantly old-fashioned, good-value restaurant set in the central square of an amazingly well-preserved and unique star-shaped fortress rebuilt by Vauban in 1675. It serves traditional and local dishes such as *escargots*, *coq au vin* or rabbit in cider, and for dessert *île flottante* (poached meringues), chocolate mousse or profiteroles.

SEDAN Le Saint-Michel

3 rue Saint-Michel, 08200 **Tel** *03 24 29 04 61*

Situated beneath the Château Fort de Sedan, this restaurant is combined with a hotel and a gift shop stocked with local crafts and culinary produce. The traditional menu includes Ardennes specialities, such as wild boar, pork kidneys and a variety of cured meats and hams.

SIGNY LE PETIT Au Lion d'Or

Pl de l'Eglise, 08380 **Tel** *03 24 53 51 76* **Fax** *03 24 53 36 96*

On the circuit of fortified churches, this restaurant and hotel is housed behind an 18th-century red-brick façade. The non-smoking Louis XIII restaurant serves a delicious *foie gras* with a wild rose jam. Skilfully prepared fish is another speciality of this well-run dining establishment.

ST IMOGES La Maison du Vigneron

Rte Départamentale 951, 51160 **Tel** *03 26 52 88 00* **Fax** *03 26 52 86 03*

Between Reims and Epernay, in a village in the heart of the Parc Régionale de la Montagne Noire et de Reims, is this good restaurant and champagne house. Excellent regional dishes imaginatively prepared and, if you wish, accompanied by the owner's champagne vintages.

STE MENEHOULD Le Cheval Rouge

1 rue Chanzy, 51800 **Tel** *03 26 60 81 04* **Fax** *03 26 60 93 11*

There are two places to eat in this establishment: the restaurant, with its distinctive fireplace, or in the much cheaper brasserie, which specializes in pigs' trotters. Monsieur Fourreau, the owner of the establishment, sends pigs' trotters all over Europe.

TROYES Les Crieurs de Vin

4 pl Jean Jaurès, 10000 **Tel** *03 25 40 01 01*

An inexpensive wine bar with an agreeably raffish air run by two wine fanatics. In the front they sell wine to take away, and in the back they sell it to accompany their bistro-style menu. Lots of exposed beams and bare wooden tables. The traditional French menu is on a blackboard.

TROYES Tartines et Bulles

31 rue de la Cité, 10000 **Tel** *03 25 80 58 23*

In attractive premises, this restaurant uses local produce to turn out good, cheap dishes. The speciality is *tartines gratinées* (toasted sandwiches) made with local Chaource cheese. There are copious salads, as well delicious desserts. Wine is served by the glass or jug, and there's a choice of two champagnes by the glass.

TROYES Au Jardin Gourmand

31 rue Paillot de Montabert, 10000 **Tel** *03 25 73 36 13* **Fax** *03 25 73 36 13*

In the heart of the old town, with its forest of half-timbered houses, this charming restaurant quietly pleases all who come here. The speciality is the local delicacy, *andouillette* (tripe sausage). Pleasant small panelled dining room and delightful terrace for eating out in summer. Try the lavender ice cream.

VILLEMOYENNE La Parentele

32 rue Marcelin Lévêque, 10260 **Tel** *03 25 43 68 68* **Fax** *03 25 43 68 69*

This restaurant has made a name for itself with crayfish cooked in coconut cream and ravioli *au foie gras*. In a short time the owners, two brothers who took over the family business, won their first Michelin star. Experts say the champagne wine list is perfect.

ALSACE & LORRAINE

BAERENTHAL L'Arnsbourg

18 Untermuhlthal, 57230 **Tel** *03 87 06 50 85* **Fax** *03 87 06 57 67*

One of the few three-rosette restaurants in France, hidden in a pretty glade in the forest of the northern Vosges. Brother and sister team Jean-Georges and Cathy Klein conjure up light imaginative dishes, such as *grillade de foie gras* of duck with crystalized lemon, accompanied by great wines.

BITCHE Le Strasbourg

24 rue Col. Teyssier, 57230 **Tel** *03 87 96 00 44* **Fax** *03 87 96 11 57*

Excellent hotel restaurant in the shadow of Vauban's fascinating citadelle, which contains a memorial to the American infantry that liberated the town. Le Strasbourg has a big traditional dining room, with a beautiful white moulded fireplace. The cuisine here is traditional, with *foie gras* and a range of fish dishes.

Key to Price Guide *see p600* **Key to Symbols** *see back cover flap*

COLMAR La Table de Louise
2 rue Edouard-Richard, 68000 **Tel** *03 89 24 00 00*

Austere but fashionable decor in this attractive brasserie brings a touch of 1900s Parisian style to comfortable, old-fashioned Colmar. The wide ranging traditional menu includes terrine of goose *foie gras* with pumpkin chutney. Situated just 2 minutes from the very beautiful half-timbered Renaissance town centre.

COLMAR Le Caveau de St Pierre
24 rue de la Herse, 68000 **Tel** *03 89 41 99 33*

Built in 1568 into the medieval fortifications, this restaurant stands in the Little Venice quarter, reached by a boardwalk along the canal. Warm traditional decor with painted beams. Specialities include fillet of beef cooked in a sauce of local Munster cheese, fish dishes and *choucroute* (pickled cabbage served with sausage and bacon).

ILLHAEUSERN L'Auberge de l'Ill
2 rue de Collonges, 68970 **Tel** *03 89 71 89 00* **Fax** *03 89 71 82 83*

The Mecca of Alsacien cuisine, and still a Haeberlin family affair, this restaurant has held three rosettes for over 40 years! Set on the banks of the river Ill in the heart of the village, with gardens and storks nesting. Lobster with quinoa and Oriental spices, salmon soufflé, terrine of goose *foie gras* with truffles is available.

KAYSERSBERG Restaurant Saint Alexis
Restaurant Saint Alexis, 68240 **Tel** *03 89 73 90 38*

Hidden in the hills above the vineyards of Kaysersberg and Riquewihr, this old farm, set in cherry orchards by a chapel dating in part from the 5th century, houses a popular restaurant. Every menu starts with soup, followed by meat pie or stewed cockerel or game and omelette. Book ahead.

KAYSERSBERG Au Lion d'Or
66 rue Général de Gaulle, 68240 **Tel** *03 89 47 11 16* **Fax** *03 89 47 19 02*

Right in the old town, a lot of history surrounds this excellent, unpretentious institution, built in 1521 and run by the same family since 1724. A carved lion's head decorates the door into the restaurant. The characterful dining room has a big open fire in winter. Traditional dishes include wild game, *foie gras* and *sauerkraut*.

LEMBACH Gimbelhof
Rte Forestière, 67510 **Tel** *03 88 94 43 58*

Upgraded Alsacien farm lost in the hills right on the German frontier, 10 km (6 miles) north of Lembach and only an hour from Strasbourg. Across the valley is the magnificent ruined château de Fleckenstein. Excellent local dishes. This very professional and modestly priced establishment is well supported by both Germans and locals. Book ahead.

LEMBACH Auberge du Cheval Blanc
4 rue de Wissembourg, 67510 **Tel** *03 88 94 41 86* **Fax** *03 88 94 20 74*

In an 18th-century coaching inn, this restaurant in the village of Lembach is the best in the north of Alsace. The owner was the Gault Millau's most promising chef 2009 and serves truly excellent traditional regional dishes as well as the best French *haute cuisine*. Cheaper set menus are also available.

LES THONS Le Couvent des Cordeliers
Les Thons, 88410 **Tel** *03 29 07 90 84*

A fine ramshackle collection of 15th-century monastery buildings north of Renaissance Châtillon-sur-Saône is home to this unusual restaurant. The owner roasts slices of gammon over an open fire. Very popular; book ahead and ask to be seated downstairs, *"en bas"*. There is a free museum.

MARLENHEIM Le Cerf
30 rue Général de Gaulle, 67520 **Tel** *03 88 87 73 73* **Fax** *03 88 87 68 08*

At the northern end of the Route des Vins, this old coaching inn, owned by the same family since 1930, serves modernized traditional Alsace dishes. It has a reputation for serving a good square meal, even second helpings. *Choucroute* with suckling pig and pan-fried *foie gras*. Rooms available.

METZ Le Bistrot des Sommeliers
10 rue Pasteur, 57000 **Tel** *03 87 63 40 20* **Fax** *03 87 63 54 46*

A gastronomic experience wrapped up in brasserie clothing. The chef was formerly second in one of France's top restaurants. The wine list is outstanding, with 400 different labels covering the whole country. Excellent bistro-style food, with a mostly business clientele. Crayfish *vol au vent* is a speciality.

METZ Restaurant des Roches
29 rue Roches, 57000 **Tel** *03 87 74 06 51* **Fax** *03 87 75 40 04*

Set on the ground floor of an 18th-century building opposite France's oldest theatre, this restaurant specializes in fish – bass, daurade and turbot – and shellfish. You can pick your own live lobster from the glass tank. In summer there is a terrace for dining alongside the Moselle.

NANCY Chez Tanesy
223 Grande Rue, 54000 **Tel** *03 83 35 51 94*

A discrete 18th-century façade conceals what is reputed to be the best restaurant in Nancy and certainly the most reasonably priced. The restaurant is named after the well-known local chef who owns and runs the establishment. *Coquilles St Jacques* with truffle sauce is recommended. Close to Place Stanislas.

NANCY L'Excelsior

50 rue Henri Poincaré, 54000 **Tel** *03 83 35 24 57*

This classic Nancy brasserie with Belle Epoque decor and stained-glass windows is a famous rendezvous spot for artists. In continuous use since 1911, it has excellent service, and you can also reserve your table over the Internet. L'Excelsior serves refined dishes with *foie gras* and *choucroute garnie*.

OBERNAI La Cloche

90 rue Général Gouraud, 67210 **Tel** *03 88 49 90 43*

In a 14th-century house with original panelling and windows is this tavern-style restaurant. Located in the heart of the old town, it offers traditional Alsace cuisine with Munster cheese in the sauces. Always two different fish on the menu, and *tarte flambée* in the evenings. Excellent service. Book ahead.

RIEDISHEIM Restaurant de la Poste

7 rue Général de Gaulle, Riedisheim, 68400 **Tel** *03 89 44 07 71* **Fax** *03 89 64 32 79*

A coaching inn since 1850, six generations of the Kieny family have maintained this restaurant with its elegant dining rooms. You will find traditional Alsace cooking with suckling pig a speciality, according to the season. They are also great experts in cooking with chocolate.

RIQUEWIHR Le Sarment d'Or

4 rue du Cerf, 68340 **Tel** *03 89 86 02 86* **Fax** *03 89 47 99 23*

In a beautiful 16th-century house, tucked away in a quiet Renaissance street of this wonderfully preserved village, this restaurant's beamed dining room is elegantly decorated. The cooking combines invention and tradition. Warm *kugelhopf* cake for breakfast from the family shop just nearby. Rooms available.

SAVERNE Taverne Katz

80 grand rue, 67700 **Tel** *03 88 71 16 56*

In the centre of the town opposite the huge château, this taverne was built in 1605 and is still beautifully preserved inside and out with a traditonal flowered terrace and polished wood in the dining room. The food is French with a regional slant, and includes duck with *foie gras* and medallions of rabbit.

STRASBOURG Pâtisserie Winter

25 rue du 22 Novembre, 67000 **Tel** *03 88 32 85 40* **Fax** *03 88 22 04 28*

This is a good place for the ordinary visitor to Strasbourg, who does not have the expense account of a Member of the European Parliament. Simple meals at reasonable prices at this location in the city centre. Good salads and *pâtisseries* with beer or wine.

STRASBOURG Au Crocodile

10 rue Outre, 67000 **Tel** *03 88 32 13 02* **Fax** *03 88 75 72 01*

One of the finest restaurants in France's other capital. Splendid polished woodwork, elegant decor and the famous crocodile brought back from a campaign in Egypt by an Alsatian Captain in the French army. Super service and light original cuisine. A truly great wine list that covers the world.

VERDUN Hostellerie le Coq Hardi

Av de la Victoire, 55100 **Tel** *03 29 86 36 36* **Fax** *03 29 86 09 21*

This traditional, classic French provincial hotel and restaurant has good food, a great wine list and an elegant dining room. Try the langoustine lasagne and snails. The bistro option provides cheaper, quick meals, such as steak and chips. There is a pleasant summer terrace.

WINDSTEIN Auberge des Deux Châteaux

33 rue des Châteaux, 67110 **Tel** *03 88 09 24 41*

An exceptional little hotel-restaurant between two ruined medieval castles in the regional park. On the D53 between Jaegerthal and Dambach, turn up the valley of the Windstein and keep going until you get to the top. The food is traditional Alsatian, and specialities are game and *tarte flambée*. There are great views. Closed Dec–Jan.

WISSEMBOURG Daniel Rebert

7 pl du Marché aux Choux, 67100 **Tel** *03 88 94 01 66* **Fax** *03 88 54 38 78*

Daniel Rebert is one of the best chocolatiers and pâtissiers in France. In the shadow of his luxury production of cakes and chocolates there is a discreet *salon de thé*, serving light lunches. Afterwards, you can choose the cakes and chocolates from the dizzying display to take home.

NORMANDY

ACQUIGNY Hostellerie d'Acquigny

1 rue d'Evreux, 27400 **Tel** *02 32 50 20 05*

This former coaching inn houses a charming restaurant. The regulars appreciate the inexpensive set menus, but it is worth choosing *à la carte*: pan-fried *foie gras* with dried fruit or roast cod steak served with chorizo and a creamy garlic sauce are both good choices. Expect an eclectic wine list and animated service.

Key to Price Guide *see p600* **Key to Symbols** *see back cover flap*

ALENCON Le Bistrot ⬛⬛⬛⬛ €
21 rue de Sarthe, 61000 **Tel** *02 33 26 51 69*

Classic French bistro with the distinctive old-fashioned, green-painted front, red-chequered tablecloths and old film posters. The regularly changing menu includes black pudding and *filet mignon* of pork in cream, which are local favourites. A well-stocked, sensibly priced wine list complements the food.

AUMALE La Villa des Houx ⬛⬛⬛⬛ €€€
6 av Général de Gaulle, 76390 **Tel** *02 35 93 93 30* **Fax** *02 35 93 03 94*

A former *gendarmerie* (police station), this is an ideal place to stop along the route from Rouen to Amiens. The menu offers the refined taste of real Normandy cuisine, with a modern twist. Try the *foie gras* with fruit crumble as a starter, followed by stuffed, boned quail and Calvados soufflé.

BARNEVILLE-CARTERET Marine ⬛⬛⬛⬛ €€€€
11 rue de Paris, 50270 **Tel** *02 33 53 83 31* **Fax** *02 33 53 39 60*

At this restaurant near the port, chef Laurent Cesne prepares inventive dishes such as tartare of scallops perfumed with fresh ginger, and roast lamb served with tomatoes, olives, rocket and Parmesan cheese. Modern, comfortable dining room; precise and attentive service. Wine list matches food.

BAYEUX La Coline d'Enzo ⬛⬛ €€€
4 rue des Bouchers, 14400 **Tel** *02 31 92 03 01*

The focus here is on fish: sea bass cooked in clay is a speciality. The dishes are creative and delicious. At lunch time opt for the *suggestion du jour* (daily special), which is particularly good value. The restaurant has a modern feel with bright decor that successfully combines the old with the new. Book ahead.

BEUVRON EN AUGE Le Pavé d'Auge ⬛⬛⬛ €€€
Les Halles, 14430 **Tel** *02 31 79 26 71* **Fax** *02 31 39 04 45*

The talented chef serves food made from locally sourced produce. The dining room, in the renovated ancient village market hall, has lots of charm. The menus focus on fish, with a small choice of meat and poultry. Choose from Isigny oysters or grilled langoustines, and then braised hake or *rascasse*.

BRIQUEVILLE-SUR-MER Couleurs Saveurs ⬛ €€
2 rte de Bretonnière, 50290 **Tel** *02 33 61 65 62*

This coastal restaurant, north of Granville, serves a menu of surprising flavour combinations in its bright, modern dining room. Expect to find dishes such as fillet of fish roasted with *demi-sel* butter and served with citrus fruits and wasabi, or spicy local lamb with tumeric sauce, and sponge cake with grapefruit marmalade for dessert.

CAEN Le Pressoir ⬛⬛⬛⬛ €€€€€
3 ave Henri-Chéron, 14000 **Tel** *02 31 73 32 71* **Fax** *02 31 26 76 64*

Award-winning chef Ivan Vautier and his wife Sandrine run this excellent, contemporary restaurant which uses the best local ingredients in an innovative take on Norman cuisine. The *à la carte* menu offers a wide range of dishes and there are sensibly priced set menus too. Closed Mon, Sun dinner, Feb school hols & 23 Jul–21 Aug.

CHERBOURG Le Faitout ⬛ €€
25 rue Tour-Carrée, 50100 **Tel** *02 33 04 25 04* **Fax** *02 33 04 60 36*

A bastion of tradition, Le Faitout is located in an old quarter of the city. This animated bistro-style restaurant serves family-style dishes *par excellence*. Sample the delicious red mullet, fresh Barfleur mussels, grilled sardines and a wonderfully crispy confit of duck.

COSQUEVILLE Au Bouquet de Cosqueville ⬛⬛⬛⬛ €€
Hameau Remond, 50330 **Tel** *02 33 54 32 81* **Fax** *02 33 54 63 38*

Good portions of fresh seafood, such as lobster cooked in cider, local fish and shellfish, served at this elegantly rustic restaurant in an ivy-clad house in the village centre. Freshest local produce chosen with care. Tasty crêpes and *crème brulée* for dessert. Impressive wine list.

COURSEULLES SUR MER Paris ⬛⬛⬛ €€€
Pl 6-Juin, 14470 **Tel** *02 31 37 45 07* **Fax** *02 31 37 51 63*

A good-value-for-money restaurant in this relaxed seaside resort, north of Caen, on the Côte Nacre. Friendly service in the simply furnished dining room, where simple seafood and meat dishes are prepared with care. The terrace and veranda outside are protected from the gusty sea breezes.

DEAUVILLE Le Spinnaker ⬛⬛ €€€€
52 rue Mirabeau, 14800 **Tel** *02 31 88 24 40* **Fax** *02 31 88 43 58*

After a stroll along the seafront promenade, make your way to one of Normandy's finest fish restaurants. An attractive modern dining room specializes in fish and seafood, and also grilled meat dishes. Delicious cannelloni of langoustine and chestnut is a innovative choice. Friendly, attentive service. Closed Jan.

DIEPPE Bistrot de Pollet ⬛ €€
23 rue Tête de Bœuf, 76200 **Tel** *02 35 84 68 57*

Small, friendly bistro-style restaurant with chef's daily suggestions, depending on the catch of the day, in the old fishing quarter of the port. Simple unfussy fish dishes: haddock salad, grilled sardines, poached sole and bass. Limited selection of wines. Packed with locals and regulars; book ahead.

DOMFRONT Auberge Grand Gousier
1 pl Liberté, 61700 **Tel** *02 33 38 37 25*

Domfront escaped destruction during the bombardments of 1944, and this family-run auberge is testimony to this, standing in the medieval town centre with its authentic fireplace. The speciality is warm oysters with a creamy Camembert sauce. The portions are generous and the welcome genuine.

DRUBEC La Haie Tondue
La Haie Tondue RN175, 14130 **Tel** *02 31 64 85 00*

This handsome old, vine-clad restaurant out in the countryside has an attractive terrace and plenty of Norman beams and half timbering. Authentic, traditional cuisine includes pan-fried crayfish with aubergine "caviar" and veal with a cheese sauce. Good value for money.

EVREUX La Croix d'Or
3 rue Joséphine, 27000 **Tel** *02 32 33 06 07*

A lively and popular brasserie in this pleasant cathedral town. The locals say that the Empress Josephine used to eat here. The menu today focuses on huge platters of oysters and other seafood, as well as a range of simply prepared, delicious fresh fish dishes.

FALAISE l'Attache
Rte de Caen, 14700 **Tel** *02 31 90 05 38* **Fax** *02 31 90 57 19*

Reservations recommended for this restaurant in the heart of Calvados. A beautifully renovated former staging post, with the dining room decorated in relaxing tones. The classic repertoire has an added dimension – the chef uses long-forgotten plants and aromatic herbs to flavour his cuisine. Impeccable service. Reservation recommended.

FECAMP La Marée
77 quai Bérigny, 76400 **Tel** *02 35 29 39 15*

This lively restaurant on the harbour is frequented by both locals and tourists, who come to feast on the wonderfully fresh seafood and fish dishes. The entire menu is dedicated to fish, and specialities include home-made fish soup, smoked fish and huge seafood platters. There is a small, sunny terrace and a good range of wines.

FOURGES Moulin de Fourges
38 rue du Moulin, 27630 **Tel** *02 32 52 12 12* **Fax** *02 32 52 92 56*

A beautiful riverside watermill that would no doubt have pleased Monet, who lived at nearby Giverny. Local produce innovatively used to achieve astonishing results. During the winter months the Moulin is transformed into a mountain chalet-style restaurant serving mainly *fondue*. Pleasant dining area, and decent wines. Closed Jan.

GISORS Le Cappeville
17 rue Cappeville, 27410 **Tel** *02 32 55 11 08* **Fax** *02 32 55 93 92*

Rustic restaurant in the oldest part of town, serving traditional Normandy cuisine. The chef Pierre Potel shows his skill in creating tasty dishes using local produce. Try the succulent veal, or the ravioli with snails. Impressive cheeseboard is on offer. La Cappeville has a friendly, relaxed atmosphere.

GRANVILLE La Citadelle
34 rue du Port, 50406 **Tel** *02 33 50 34 10* **Fax** *02 33 50 15 36*

Overlooking the bay of St-Michel, the reliable cooking and the view over the fishing port from the terrace is enough to draw anyone over the bridge. Elegant, modern dining room serves generous portions. The freshest seafood platter in town, the biggest portion of sole, and Norman scallops. Closed Jan.

HONFLEUR Côte Resto
8 pl Saint-Catherine, 14600 **Tel** *02 31 89 31 33* **Fax** *02 31 89 90 17*

Attractive traditional timber-and-brick building with a terrace opposite the church. Wonderfully fresh seafood dishes. Simplicity is the key, using the best produce. Savour the *millefeuille* of beetroot and sardines, or the *choucroute* of haddock with saffron cream sauce. You can also compose your own seafood platter. Good white wine selection.

HONFLEUR La Ferme St Siméon
Rue A.Marais, 14600 **Tel** *02 31 81 78 00* **Fax** *02 31 89 48 48*

A luxurious place to eat in this pretty fishing port. The restaurant of this spa hotel is known for elaborate fish dishes such as stuffed red mullet with jellied cauliflower consommé and *croque en bouche bouillabaisse*. The elegant dining room has an Old-World charm and a wonderful beamed ceiling. There is also an excellent wine list.

LA FERRIERE AUX ETANGS Auberge de la Mine
Le Gué-Plat, 61450 **Tel** *02 33 66 91 10* **Fax** *02 33 96 73 90*

At this former mine-workers' cantine, traditional Norman dishes are produced with originality, such as veal sweet-breads with Vire *andouille*, and roast pollack with herbs. Delicious desserts include *savarin* (alcohol-soaked yeast cake) with Calvados, and caramelized apples on a skewer, plus an excellent cheese board. Closed Jan.

LES ANDELYS La Chaine d'Or
27 rue Grande, 27700 **Tel** *02 32 54 00 31* **Fax** *02 32 54 05 68*

Book a table in this restaurant to taste such delicacies as langoustines accompanied by citrus fruit chutney, a *foie gras* trio, roast sole with black olive risotto or a confit of Limousin lamb. Romantic setting on the banks of the Seine in an 18th-century auberge. Rooms available. Closed Jan.

Key to Price Guide *see p600* **Key to Symbols** *see back cover flap*

LYONS LA FORET Restaurant de la Halle
*Pl Benserade, 27480 **Tel** 02 32 49 49 92*

An attractive, traditional Norman village surrounded by the largest beech forest in Europe merits this good local restaurant, located opposite the ancient market hall. Simple, straightforward, delicious cuisine, especially the lamb cooked with rosemary. Starchy service.

MONT-ST-MICHEL Auberge St Pierre
*Grande rue, 50170 **Tel** 02 33 60 14 03 **Fax** 02 33 48 59 82*

Lamb grazed on the surrounding salt marshes, known as *agneau pré salé*, features on the menu in this charming timbered 15th-century building. Seafood is also a house speciality. Try the favourites such as crab or salmon. Fresh local produce is used in the preparation of traditional dishes.

MONT-ST-MICHEL La Mère Poulard
*Grande rue, 50170 **Tel** 02 33 89 68 68*

A deluxe brasserie on the famous Mont St-Michel, where visitors come from all over the world to sample the famous omelette Mère Poulard, cooked in a long-handled pan over a fire. Also delicious are the *pré-salé* lamb (lamb fed on the surrounding salt marshes), and spit-roasted pig.

PONT AUDEMER Belle Isle sur Risle
*Belle Isle sur Risle, 27500 **Tel** 02 32 56 96 22*

Part of the Relais du Silence chain, this gracious hotel and restaurant is housed in an elegant, ivy-covered 19th-century gentleman's residence. The menu balances fish and meat dishes and demonstrates an original use of spices. On Saturdays and public holidays a pianist plays while you dine.

PONT L'EVEQUE Auberge de l'Aigle d'Or
*68 rue de Vaucelles, 14130 **Tel** 02 31 65 05 25 **Fax** 02 31 65 12 03*

A well-maintained 16th-century coaching inn with a pretty courtyard provides an attractive setting for a good-value meal of *escargots Pays d'Auge*, and free-range chicken cooked in a cider sauce. The menu changes seasonally and ensures the best local produce. Attentive service.

PONT SAINT-PIERRE Hostellerie La Bonne Marmite
*10 rue René Raban 27300 **Tel** 02 32 49 70 24 **Fax** 02 32 48 12 41*

A top Logis de France not too far from Rouen in an old coaching inn. The dining room is as elegant as the building, with a *caisson* ceiling. Try the *foie gras de canard à l'ancienne* and the warm lobster salad. This is Norman cooking at its best. The wine cellar boasts some fine old Bordeaux.

PUTANGES PONT ECREPIN Hôtel du Lion Verd
*Pl de l'Hôtel de Ville, 61210 **Tel** 02 33 35 01 86 **Fax** 02 33 39 53 32*

This welcoming hotel-restaurant sits on the riverside of the Orme. The menu offers local Normandy produce with pride and a refreshing approach. The result is wonderful hearty terrines, Auge Valley *cochon de lait* (suckling pig) and home-made desserts such as strawberry tart. Good-value lunch menu.

ROUEN Le 37
*37 rue St-Etienne-des-Tonneliers, 76000 **Tel** 02 35 70 56 65*

Attractive city centre bistro, chic and zen, presents a cuisine that is a touch more modern than its celebrated parent, Restaurant Gill. Enjoy savoury dishes such as crab tortilla with rocket salad, and duck leg served with vegetables seasoned with Thai spices. For dessert try the citrus fruit gratin with mandarin sorbet. Reservations recommended.

ROUEN La Couronne
*31 pl Vieux Marché, 76000 **Tel** 02 35 71 40 90 **Fax** 02 35 71 05 78*

In the oldest auberge in France, dating from 1345, the experienced, talented chef ensures that you pass a memorable moment here with classic gourmet dishes such as pan-fried escalope of *foie gras*, lobster with champagne sauce, and duck à la Rouennaise. Great Normandy cheeses.

ROUEN Restaurant Gill
*8-9 quai de la Bourse, 76000 **Tel** 02 35 71 16 14 **Fax** 02 35 71 96 91*

A highly recommended restaurant on the Seine quays. For over 20 years chef Gilles Tournadre has been creating sophisticated dishes in this elegant dining room. Specialities include langoustines served with fresh tomato chutney, pigeon *à la rouennaise* and fillet of bass with onion marmalade. Remarkable wine list.

STE CECILE Le Manoir de l'Acherie
*Acherie, 50800 **Tel** 02 33 51 13 87 **Fax** 02 33 51 33 69*

In this old-fashioned manor house, with rooms in a converted chapel, the produce of Normandy features highly, such as cream, apples, calvados and cider. Expect to find ham and lamb either braised in calvados, or served in a cider-flavoured sauce. Even the apple tart is flambéed in this apple brandy. Good cheeseboard.

TROUVILLE SUR MER Régence
*132 bd Fernand Moureaux, 14360 **Tel** 02 31 88 10 71 **Fax** 02 31 88 10 71*

Beautiful interior with mirrors and 19th-century wood panelling decorated by hungry Impressionist painters. The charming service and refined ambience lend to the feeling of elegance and good value. Not far from the shore, the seafood and shellfish are the house specialities. Well-presented dishes.

VEULES LES ROSES Les Galets

3 rue Victor Hugo, 76980 **Tel** *02 35 97 61 33* **Fax** *02 35 57 06 23*

Traditional brick-built restaurant close to the pebbly beach, which is typical of the Côte d'Albâtre. Comfortable dining area inside, and lovely terrace outside. If you want to have a meal by the sea, this is just the place, but book ahead. Classic dishes prepared with care.

VILLERS BOCAGE Les Trois Rois

2 pl Jeanne d'Arc, 14310 **Tel** *02 31 77 00 32* **Fax** *02 31 77 93 25*

In a vast square surrounded by a garden and vegetable patch, this restaurant flaunts all the characteristics of a traditional Norman restaurant. Spacious, elegant dining area serving generous portions of well-prepared local dishes, such as tripe and fresh fish dishes. Efficient service.

BRITTANY

AUDIERNE Le Goyen

Pl Jean-Simon, 29770 **Tel** *02 98 70 08 88* **Fax** *02 98 70 18 77*

Classic seafood is served at this hotel-restaurant facing the sea. Deliciously fresh oysters and seafood platters are a good choice. The menu also includes pollack accompanied by a vegetable risotto and green pea sauce, and pan-fried *coquille St-Jacques* (scallops) in an Arabica bean crust, accompanied by *endive à l'orange*.

AURAY L'Eglantine

17 place St-Saveur, 56400 **Tel** *02 97 56 46 55*

Sitting on the quay of the pretty Saint-Goustan port, this restaurant offers a selection of both fish and meat options. Freshly caught sole and turbot are simply prepared and seafood platters are excellent, while other fish dishes are accompanied by elaborate sauces. Meat-lovers will appreciate the succulent pigeon and steak.

BELLE ILE EN MER La Désirade

Le Petit Cosquet, 56360 **Tel** *02 97 31 70 70*

This family hotel and restaurant is in an attractive, traditional Brittany farmhouse only a few minutes from the beach. The chef specializes in fresh ingredients, with fish and seafood to the fore. Picnics can be ordered for a day's outing on the shore of this wonderful island. Closed Jan–Apr.

BREST Da Vinci

6 rue Louis Pasteur, 29200 **Tel** *02 98 46 90 90*

This Italian restaurant offers a pleasant alternative to the many local seafood restaurants. It is run in tandem with an Italian grocery shop by the Halles food market. Ravioli, pasta and risotto are prepared on the premises and there is a selection of Italian wine to accompany it. A popular local spot so book in advance.

BREST La Fleur de Sel

15 bis rue de Lyon, 29200 **Tel** *02 98 44 38 65* **Fax** *02 98 44 38 53*

A modern, bright city centre restaurant, with simple, comfortable furnishings. The dishes are prepared with precision. Try the skate fish with black olive *tapenade* and pesto, or a *parmentier* of lamb. Good value for money, especially the *fomule* at midday. Service can sometimes be a little stuffy.

CARANTEC Restaurant Patrick Jeffroy

20 rue Kélénn, 29660 **Tel** *02 98 67 00 47* **Fax** *Q2 98 67 08 25*

A magnificent view over Kélénn beach from the restaurant in this fabulous 1930s manor house hotel. Shellfish in abundance. Classic and modern cuisine combine to perfection. Terrine of crab is served with artichoke and accompanied by a vinaigrette of shallots, coconut milk and Thai curry. Extensive choice of Loire valley wines.

CARNAC La Calypso

158 rte du Pô, 56340 **Tel** *02 97 52 06 14*

Overlooking the oyster beds of the Anse du Pô, this popular seafood restaurant is all the more charming for the colourful character that runs it. The house speciality is lobster or steak cooked over a wood fire in the hearth. A choice of fish of the day is offered as well as the usual seafood platters. Booking is essential.

CONCARNEAU Le Petit Chaperon Rouge

7 pl Duguesclin, 29900 **Tel** *02 98 60 53 32*

Following the "Little Red Riding Hood" theme with its wicker baskets and red tablecloths, this crêperie near the harbour has a delicious choice of savoury and sweet fillings, such as La Blandette (goat's cheese, spinach, ham and cream) and Mère Grande (banana and honey flambéed with rum).

DINAN La Mère Pourcel

3 pl des Merciers, 22100 **Tel** *02 96 39 03 80* **Fax** *02 96 39 49 91*

This restaurant in a stunning timbered Gothic building is a Dinan landmark, serving generous portions of seasonal gourmet cuisine. Locally reared lamb is on offer, along with a variety of innovative fish dishes. There is a good selection of fine wines. The tables are on the cobbled street. Closed Jan.

Key to Price Guide *see p600* **Key to Symbols** *see back cover flap*

GUIMILIAU Ar Chupen

43 rue de Calvaire, 29400 **Tel** *02 98 68 73 63*

After admiring the richly decorated church, step down the road to this restaurant in a renovated Breton farmhouse. Traditional lacy galettes, made with sarrazin flour, and crêpes are prepared to order. The choice of fillings seems endless. Good place for children, and vegetarians. Friendly staff.

HEDE L'Hostellerie du Vieux Moulin

Ancienne rte de St Malo, 35630 **Tel** *02 99 45 45 70* **Fax** *02 99 45 44 86*

Built in the 19th century as part of a complex to supply water power, the restaurant overlooks the Hédé castle, with the ruins of the old watermill in the grounds. Good-value lunchtime menus, including pan-fried scallops, lightly grilled langoustines, and succulent duck. Rooms available.

LE CONQUET Le Relais de Vieux Port

1 quai Drellach, 29217 **Tel** *02 98 89 15 91*

You can almost dangle your feet in the water as you sit to choose the fillings for your crêpe. Seafood is the house speciality. Try a crêpe filled with fresh scallops or prawns accompanied by a green salad. Leave room for dessert, especially the Bonne Maman with caramelized apples and whipped cream.

LORIENT Le Neptune

15 av de la Perrière, 56100 **Tel** *02 97 37 04 56* **Fax** *02 97 87 07 54*

The haul at the nearby fishing port of Keroman determines the dish of the day at this restaurant. Modern interior, with some tables in a pretty conservatory at the rear of the dining room. The menu includes flambéed lobster, and fricassée of monkfish. Generous portions and friendly service.

MORLAIX Brasserie de l'Europe

1 rue d'Aiguillon, 29600 **Tel** *02 98 88 81 15*

An authentic brasserie in the town centre next to the hotel of the same name. Everything from breakfast to sandwiches and cooked dishes is served right through the day from 8am until 9:30pm. There is a conservatory for winter and a pleasant terrace for summer.

NOYAL-SUR-VILAINE Auberge du Pont d'Acigné

Le Pont d'Acigné, 35530 **Tel** *02 99 62 52 55*

Not far from Rennes, overlooking the Vilaine river and an attractive water mill, is this delightful gourmet restaurant. The creative menu is based on seasonal market produce; dishes include roast veal flavoured with liquorice, and a warm lobster, beetroot and tarragon starter. There is also a fine selection of desserts.

PAIMPOL L'Islandais

19 quai Morand, 22500 **Tel** *02 96 20 93 80* **Fax** *02 96 20 72 68*

A popular crêperie overlooking the lively Paimpol harbour. The chef presents a good selection of traditional Breton galettes, always a favourite with children and a good option for vegetarians. Shellfish is abundant, with fresh oysters, mussels, lobsters and langoustines. Expect to pay more for seafood.

PERROS-GUIREC Le Gulf Stream

26 rue des Sept-Iles 22700 **Tel** *02 96 23 21 86* **Fax** *02 96 49 06 61*

An excellent and reasonably priced hotel-restaurant with a warm, family feel. There are fine views of the coast from the dining room. As well as the expected fish and other seafood, the restaurant serves traditional French food according to the season. There is also a good wine list.

PLOUBALAY Le Gare

4 rue des Ormelet, 22650 **Tel** *02 96 27 25 16*

Thomas Mureau, the former owner of the renowned Fleur de Sel at St Malo, concocts dishes with a touch of personality in this rustic restaurant. Of particular note are the brochettes of St-Jacques accompanied by a truffle-flavoured vinaigrette, and the Breton *sablé* served with pineapple and coriander. The best tables overlook the garden.

QUIBERON Le Relax

27 bd Castéro, 56170 **Tel** *02 97 50 12 84*

With lovely sea views and a pretty garden, this restaurant is guaranteed to make you relax. A wide selection of superbly cooked seasonal fish, as well as mussels, langoustines, crabs and oysters. Tasty seafood sauerkraut. Good wine cellar and a sommelier who knows his stuff, but is not stuffy.

QUIMPER L'Ambroisie

49 rue Elie Fréron, 29000 **Tel** *02 98 95 00 02*

Located just at the end of one of the tiny streets in the centre of Quimper, a short walk from the cathedral. L'Ambroisie offers good, simple cuisine using quality produce. Try the roast monkfish in a spicy crust, smoked salmon roulade with asparagus and poached eggs, and the tartare of fresh fruit with ice cream.

RENNES Léon le Cochon

1 rue du Maréchal Joffre, 35000 **Tel** *02 99 79 37 54*

A popular restaurant with a pig theme that has mellowed somewhat over time. Pork sausage from Morteau and pig's trotters are still on the menu, but you can also try terrine de *foie gras* marinated in Jurançon, beef, duck, prawns and fish. It is possible to order take-away of most dishes, including the *foie gras*.

RENNES Le Tire-Bouchon
2 rue du Chapitre, 35000 **Tel** *02 99 79 43 43*

This relaxed friendly restaurant offers unpretentious home cooking. Mackerel pâté, braised beef and carrots, and rice pudding are just some of the dishes on offer. The wines are selected by the owner, who has a preference for "*vins naturels*". Ideally located just around the corner from the tourist office.

ROSCOFF Le Surcouf
14 rue Amiral Révellière, 29680 **Tel** *02 98 69 71 89* **Fax** *02 98 69 71 89*

Near the church, this brasserie-style restaurant serves regional cuisine. The fixed-price menus have a wide choice of local coastal produce. Start with a plate of mussels, sea snails, whelks and a half-dozen oysters. For the main course, choose a lobster from the tank, or the delicious seafood casserole.

ROSCOFF Le Temps de Vivre
17-19 pl Lacaze-Douthiers, 29680 **Tel** *02 98 61 27 28* **Fax** *02 98 61 19 46*

The acclaimed chef Jean-Yves Crenn does wonderful things with vegetables in this restaurant facing the sea. Seafood is the speciality: pan-fried scallops served with braised chicory, fruit chutney and lemon, ginger and coconut milk sauce. Good selection of wines. Friendly staff.

ST-BRIEUC Amadeus
22 rue de Gouët, 22000 **Tel** *02 96 33 92 44* **Fax** *02 96 33 92 44*

In one of this historic town's oldest buildings, this elegant gourmet restaurant specializes in fish – a carpaccio of scallops with vanilla olive oil dressing, and fillet of sole are outstanding. The wide range of tempting desserts includes Amaretto chocolate cake, and Breton butter biscuits with fruit.

ST-BRIEUC L'Air du Temps
4 rue du Gouët, 22000 **Tel** *02 96 68 58 40*

A welcome addition to the local culinary scene, this pleasant bistro-style restaurant is fast establishing a good reputation. The interior combines 200-year-old stone walls with modern decor. Dishes are served in cast-iron Staub ware. *Coquille St Jacques* are cooked at your table.

ST-MALO La Corderie
9 chemin de la Corderie, 35400 **Tel** *02 99 81 62 38*

A fish restaurant in an attractive old house. The menu changes according to whatever the fishing boats bring in. *Coquilles St Jacques* are served with a seaweed flavoured cream sauce. Meat dishes such as duck breast in honey are also on offer. A quiet spot with fine views over the moorings and the Tour Solidor.

ST-MALO Le Chalut
8 rue de la Corne de Cerf, 35400 **Tel** *02 99 56 71 58* **Fax** *02 99 56 71 58*

One of St Malo's best restaurants, the chef excels in fish dishes and well-chosen produce simply prepared. A platter of fish served with a saffron-flavoured sauce, and St-Pierre with coriander are examples of the delicious dishes on offer. Good selection of cheese, too. Reservations recommended.

VANNES Les Remparts
6 rue Alexandre-le-Pontois, 56000 **Tel** *02 97 47 52 44*

Tasty meals at reasonable prices are served in this restaurant opposite the ramparts. The chef uses regional ingredients with originality. Try the gravlax of organic salmon with horseradish or one of the vegetarian options. Good selection of wines by the glass, many from organic producers.

VITRE La Taverne de l'Ecu
12 rue Baudairie, 35500 **Tel** *02 99 75 11 09* **Fax** *02 99 75 82 97*

This half-timbered Renaissance house provides a historic ambience for a meal in one of two dining rooms. Menu changes seasonally. Try the venison served with a chestnut flan, fish with sorrel sauce or roast leg of rabbit. Home-made bread accompanies your meal.

THE LOIRE VALLEY

AMBOISE Le Choiseul
36 quai C.Guinot, 37400 **Tel** *02 47 30 45 45* **Fax** *02 47 30 46 10*

Elegant 18th-century hotel with a pretty garden and views of the Loire from the airy dining room. The sophisticated menu changes seasonally; in spring a meal might include spicy roast pig, and in summer roast pollack served with *gnocchi*. Good Touraine wines and many other regional wines.

ANGERS Ma Campagne
14 promenade de la Reculée, 49000 **Tel** *02 41 48 38 06*

A traditional, country-style auberge just a few minutes' walk along the river from the centre of town. The terrace has great views overlooking the River Maine. The cheaper menus are particularly good value for money. For dessert, the pear coated in chocolate is recommended.

Key to Price Guide *see p600* **Key to Symbols** *see back cover flap*

ANGERS Le Lucullus
5 rue Hoche, 49000 **Tel** *02 41 87 00 44* **Fax** *02 41 87 00 44*

This pretty restaurant carved into the tuffeau rock has two lovely vaulted dining rooms. Classic dishes and regional specialities served with an added touch from the chef. Try the tasty lobster flan with basil sorbet, accompanied by a lobster *velouté*, and the classic fillet of beef with *morille* mushrooms.

BEAUGENCY Le P'tit Bateau
54 rue du Pont, 45190 **Tel** *02 38 44 56 38* **Fax** *02 38 46 44 37*

Near the château, the P'tit Bateau is the most appealing restaurant in town. Popular with locals, it offers traditional cuisine in a rustic dining room with exposed beams and open fireplace. Fresh fish, game in season and wild mushrooms feature on the menu. There is a courtyard terrace for sunny days.

BLOIS Hôtel Restaurant Coté Loire
2 pl de la Grève, 41000 **Tel** *02 54 78 07 86*

A good old-fashioned 16th-century restaurant and hotel overlooking the River Loire. The simple but reasonably-priced menu changes regularly and there is sometimes a *menu unique* at lunch time. The Coté Loire is a good place to break while visiting the château and neighbouring sites on the Loire.

BLOIS L'Orangerie du Château
1 av Jean Laigret, 41000 **Tel** *02 54 78 05 36* **Fax** *02 54 78 22 78*

Housed in the 15th-century château's former winter garden, the fine setting is matched by the food and wine here. The menu features regional favourites with an innovative approach, such as pan-fried scallops with goat's cheese *gnocchi*, or escalope of *foie gras* served with beetroot sauce. A dependable wine list with good Touraine producers.

BOUCHEMAINE La Terrasse
4 pl Rouzebouc, 49080 **Tel** *02 41 77 11 96* **Fax** *02 41 77 25 71*

Located in a hamlet on the confluence of the rivers Loire and Maine, this restaurant has a panoramic view. The menu features freshly caught eels, pike-perch, salmon and other freshwater fish. Classic dishes are excellently prepared, such as *sandre au beurre blanc* (pike-perch in butter). Ironically, there is no terrace.

BOURGES La Courcillière
Rue de Babylone, 18000 **Tel** *02 48 24 41 91*

By the marshes overlooking the river Yèvre, it's worth the 20-minute walk from the city centre for freshwater fish and local cooking – classic dishes such as pike-perch fillet, eel in red wine or delicious salmon. Traditional dining area with modern bright decor, and delightful terrace. Attentive service.

BOURGES Le Jacques Coeur
3 pl Jacques Coeur, 18000 **Tel** *02 48 26 53 01*

This restaurant, with its small dining room, offers a menu of classic dishes based on the very best local produce. Choices include fillet of salmon served with saffron-infused chicory and a creamy langoustine sauce, and pigeon *en croute* with *foie gras* accompanied by artichoke purée. There is a good selection of local cheeses.

BOURGUEIL Le Moulin Bleu
7 rue du Moulin-Bleu, 37140 **Tel** *02 47 97 73 13* **Fax** *02 47 97 79 66*

The house at the foot of this pretty blue mill has two vaulted dining rooms serving traditional dishes in a friendly atmosphere. The cuisine remains faithful to the region, with Touraine-reared veal served with a Vouvray butter sauce. Good Bourgeuil producers on the wine list. In the off-season only open Friday and Saturday evenings.

BRACIEUX Le Rendez-vous des Gourmets
20 rue Roger Brun, 41250 **Tel** *02 54 46 03 87*

This auberge was taken over and completely renovated by Didier Doreau, the former second chef from the nearby luxury Relais. He has successfully created his own place offering traditional and regional cuisine at an affordable price. The restaurant has become very popular so it is best to book ahead.

CHARTRES Le Grand Monarque – Le Georges
22 pl des Epars, 28000 **Tel** *02 37 18 15 15* **Fax** *02 37 36 34 18*

Within this magnificent 17th-century staging post are both a gourmet "Le Georges" restaurant, and a brasserie serving traditional food. The cuisine is ambitious and flavourful, with dishes such as crayfish served with beetroot and girolles, and sea bass with onion confit and ceps. Excellent desserts. First-rate wine cellar.

CHENONCEAUX Hôtel Restaurant la Roseraie
7 rue du Docteur Bretonneau, 37150 **Tel** *02 47 23 90 09*

A pleasant 18th-century *hotel de charme* close to the château. The traditional restaurant serves classic French cuisine. The "dégustation" menu offers particularly good value for money and includes dishes such as fish terrine with garden vegetables, rissolé of lamb with mushrooms and a delicious crème caramel.

CHINON Les Années 30
78 rue Haute St-Maurice, 37500 **Tel** *02 47 93 37 18* **Fax** *02 47 93 33 72*

This elegant little eatery on the way up to the château has a chef who has brought back the spark to this menu. Stéphane Charles presents dishes such as poached langoustines with Mexican spices, and sea bass served with an exotic fruit sauce, roast pineapple and sweet potato. Good local wines.

CLISSON La Bonne Auberge   🚶🔥   €€€€
1 rue Olivier de Clisson, 44190 **Tel** *02 40 54 01 90* **Fax** *02 40 54 08 48*

A comfortable auberge in the city centre with three attractive dining rooms, one set in a conservatory with garden views. The specialities here include lobster gratin, *paupiettes* of sea bass, scallops with truffles and pigeon breast in red Chinon sauce. The desserts are delicate, and the selection of Muscadets is good.

CONTRES La Botte d'Asperges   🚶☰🧑‍🦽🍷   €€
52 rue Pierre-Henri Mauger, 41700 **Tel** *02 54 79 50 49* **Fax** *02 54 79 08 74*

Locally grown asparagus features prominently on the menu, in season. Behind the rustic atmosphere is an inspirational chef who prepares such delights as leg of rabbit stuffed with mushrooms and cured ham, and for dessert crème brûlée perfumed with basil and thyme. Small, well-chosen wine list. You can also take food away.

DOUE-LA-FONTAINE Auberge de la Bienvenue   🅿️🚶🔥   €€€
104 rte de Cholet, 49700 **Tel** *02 41 59 22 44* **Fax** *02 41 59 93 49*

A pretty inn situated in this town of roses. The menu offers elaborate, savoury preparations using welcome favourites, such as calf's liver in port and pepper sauce, terrine of *foie gras* flavoured with local Coteaux du Layon wine and saddle of Aveyron lamb. Other dishes include local products such as pike-perch, crayfish and wild mushrooms.

FONTEVRAUD-L'ABBAYE La Licorne   🚶🧑‍🦽🔥🍴🍷   €€€€
Allée Sainte-Catherine, 49590 **Tel** *02 41 51 72 49* **Fax** *02 41 51 70 40*

Next to the splendid abbey, this popular restaurant has a pretty courtyard terrace and elegant dining room. The menu includes creations such as langoustine ravioli in morel sauce and, for dessert, strawberries flavoured with roses. Good Saumur wines. Book ahead.

GENNES Auberge du Moulin de Sarré   🍽️🅿️🚶🧑‍🦽🔥   €
Rte de Louerre, 49350 **Tel** *02 41 51 81 32*

After taking a tour of the 16th-century watermill (the only working one in the region), try either the menu of *fouées* (warm bread puffs, made from flour ground at the mill) with fillings such as goat's cheese or *rillettes* (duck pâté), or the fresh trout menu (fished on the spot). Reservations are required.

GIEN Restaurant la Poularde   🚶☰🧑‍🦽   €€€€
13 quai de Nice, 45500 **Tel** *02 38 67 36 05* **Fax** *02 38 38 18 78*

A classic restaurant on the banks of the Loire, serving traditional cuisine in an elegant dining room, with Gien tableware. The menu includes roast pike-perch served with a Chinon wine sauce, or eel accompanied by a saffron-infused sauce, and seasonal red fruit with mango cream. Game appears on the menu in season.

LA FERTE IMBAULT Auberge à la Tête de Lard   🅿️🚶☰🔥   €€
13 pl des Tilleuls, 41300 **Tel** *02 54 96 22 32*

An authentic, completely refurbished country hotel in the heart of the Sologne houses a delightful restaurant, which offers a traditional menu with choices such as wild boar and other seasonal country dishes. This is a good place to stop when visiting the Loire Châteaux. Closed Sun dinner; Tue lunch; Mon.

LAMOTTE BEUVRON Hôtel Tatin   🚶☰🔥🍷   €€€
5 av de Vierzon, 41600 **Tel** *02 54 88 00 03* **Fax** *02 54 88 96 73*

This elegant hotel-restaurant serves traditional fare made with fresh local produce. The menu includes *foie gras*, salad of home-made pâté and warm goat's cheese, pike-perch, pigeon, steak and the famous *tarte Tatin*. There is a good selection of quality Sancerre and Cheverny wines.

LANGEAIS Au Coin des Halles   🅿️🚶🧑‍🦽🔥   €€
9 rue Gambetta, 37120 **Tel** *02 47 96 37 25*

This restaurant is the venture of Pascal Bouvier, former chef of the illustrious Choiseul at Amboise. It successfully combines a Zen interior with excellent cuisine and affordable prices. The menu is varied – mullet and sandre (pike-perch) from the Loire, shoulder of lamb, duck, Brittany sardines and *foie gras*. Next to the Château de Langeais.

LE MANS Le Bistrot du Mans   🚶☰🧑‍🦽🔥   €
12 rue Hippolyte Lecornué, 72000 **Tel** *02 43 87 51 00*

Cheerful, busy, traditional brasserie, beautifully decorated in early 20th-century style. The wide ranging menu features such classic dishes as fresh asparagus wrapped in smoked salmon and served with Hollandaise sauce, or steak with blue cheese sauce. Breakfast is served until midday. Great value.

LE MANS Le Nez Rouge   🚶🔥   €€
107 grande rue, 72000 **Tel** *02 43 24 27 26*

A charming timbered restaurant in the medieval part of Le Mans. The young chef has trained in some of the best restaurants in France. His dishes are based on the freshest produce, such as lobster and veal sweetbreads. The dining room is cosy and intimate, and there is a terrrace across the road. Book ahead.

LEMERE L'Auberge de Jable   🅿️🚶🧑‍🦽🔥   €€
le Clos de Jable, 37120 **Tel** *02 47 95 47 95*

A delightful country restaurant in a huge 15th-century farm, set in 20 ha (50 acres) of fields and vineyards. The auberge is run by a Franco-American couple who have plans for *chambres d'hôtes*. The chic decor is matched by the elegant food. Sweetbreads and pan-fried *foie gras* are served outside in fine weather and by an open fire in winter.

LES SABLES D'OLONNE L'Affiche
21 Quai Giné, 85100 **Tel** *02 51 95 34 74*

Diners crowd in to this intimate little fish restaurant: the food is excellent, the menu is varied and the wine is good. Make sure you get the right restaurant on the busy Quai – there are several but this one serves the best seafood platters, which is why it is so popular with the locals. Booking essential.

MALICORNE-SUR-SARTHE La Petite Auberge
5 pl du Guesclin, 72270 **Tel** *02 43 94 80 52* **Fax** *02 43 94 31 37*

In summer dine on the riverside terrace and watch the boats go by; in winter take refuge around the magnificent medieval fireplace. Enjoy classic cuisine with an innovative twist, such as a delicious tartare of scallops accompanied by beetroot, or perfectly cooked venison with blueberry jam.

MONTBAZON La Chancelière Jeu de Cartes
1 pl des Marronniers, 37250 **Tel** *02 47 26 00 67* **Fax** *02 47 73 14 82*

Modern, sophisticated cuisine prepared with precision. This restaurant proposes savoury but uncomplicated dishes such as creamy Richelieu truffle risotto, or escalope of *foie gras* served with polenta flavoured with figs and lemon. Well-selected wine list with good Vouvray and Bourgeuil producers.

MONTOIRE-SUR-LE-LOIR Le Cheval Rouge
Pl Foch, 41800 **Tel** *02 54 85 07 05* **Fax** *02 54 85 17 42*

After visiting the chapel and prior's lodging where Ronsard (16th-century French poet) spent his last years, stop off and dine on classic cuisine in this antiquated staging post. Enjoy well-prepared regional dishes in the attractive dining room or outside on the shady terrace with its ancient plane trees.

MONTSOREAU Diane de Méridor
12 quai Philippe de Commines, 49730 **Tel** *02 41 51 71 76* **Fax** *02 41 51 17 17*

While dining you have a view of the château which was the film setting for the interpretation of la Dame de Montsoreau by Alexandre Dumas. Carved out of tuffeau rock, in this town perched above the Loire, this restaurant is rustic with exposed beams and an open fireplace. It specializes in freshwater fish dishes cooked to perfection.

NANTES La Cigale
4 pl Graslin, 44000 **Tel** *02 51 84 94 94* **Fax** *02 51 84 94 95*

This ornate Belle Epoque brasserie dates from 1895 when it was frequented by celebrated writers and Nantes elite. The quality of the cuisine matches the exceptional interior. Oysters, carpaccio of salmon and beef *à la plancha* (cooked on a hot plate). Open all day. Extensive wine list.

NANTES Les Temps Changent
1 pl Aristide-Briand, 44000 **Tel** *02 51 72 18 01*

Excellent chef with a vision of modern cuisine. This welcoming venue provides quality French dishes that combine classic produce and inventive cooking. Menu includes sea bream served with a green pea sorbet, and confit of lamb accompanied by aubergine and curry sauce. Interesting wines.

NANTES Le Pressoir
11 quai de Turenne, 44000 **Tel** *02 40 35 31 10*

More than a simple bistro, this restaurant is a newcomer on the quays. The young chef presents interesting dishes such as *foie gras* and oxtail terrine, *pot au feu* of goose, and wild duck served with shallots. The wine list is extensive, many available by the glass. Book ahead.

NANTES L'Océanide
2 rue Paul Bellamy, 44000 **Tel** *02 40 20 32 28*

A first-class seafood restaurant and one of the best in Nantes. It was designed in World War II – when it was impossible to travel – to resemble the interior of an ocean liner. Being next to the Talensac market with its 14 fishmongers, 10 butchers and 16 *charcutiers* means the fresh ingredients change daily.

NOUAN-LE-FUZELIER Le Dahu
14 rue Henri Chapron, 41600 **Tel** *02 54 88 72 88*

This rustic dining room in a converted barn is set in a lovely garden in the heart of the Solange countryside. This is prime hunting territory, and the menu features not only game in season, but also a selection of fish dishes, such as brill served with local asparagus. Well-chosen wine list, with organic vintages from Quenioux.

ONZAIN Domaine des Hauts de Loire
Rte de Herbault, 41150 **Tel** *02 54 20 72 57* **Fax** *02 54 20 77 32*

Gastronomic cuisine is served in this former hunting lodge, set within its own park. Superb dishes are presented by chef Rémy Giraud, such as potatoes stuffed with caviar d'Aquitaine, guinea fowl accompanied by chestnut ravioli and a coffee-flavoured sauce, and lobster served with rum and cinnamon sauce. Classic wine list.

ORLEANS La Chancellerie
27 pl du Martroi, 45000 **Tel** *02 38 53 57 54*

This lively brasserie-restaurant is located on the town's main square. Built by order of the Duke of Orléans in 1754, it was used to keep the carriages, and later became the omnibus station. The interior has high ceilings, a marble bar, leather banquettes and brass trimmings. Staple fare enlivened by good wines. Snacks and salads are also available.

ORLEANS La Dariole
25 rue Etienne Dolet, 45000 **Tel** *02 38 77 26 67*

A surprising little restaurant and tearoom in a 15th-century, half-timbered building in the narrow streets of the city centre. Open during the day and on Friday and Tuesday evenings, the menu includes meat and seafood and changes fortnightly with dishes like *Coquilles St Jacques* with rosemary on a skewer. Excellent value.

ORLEANS La Terrasse du Parc
Av du Parc Floral, 45100 **Tel** *02 38 25 92 24*

When the prestigious Les Antiquaires was closed for redevelopment work in the city centre, owner Philippe Bardau opened this elegant establishment in the park. A super-modern conservatory with huge bay windows overlooks the park and a terrace. Refined gourmet menu. Ideally book 48 hours ahead.

ROCHECORBON Les Hautes Roches
86 quai Loire, 37210 **Tel** *02 47 52 88 88* **Fax** *02 47 52 81 30*

The dining room in this château is decorated in contemporary tones and serves meticulously prepared classic cuisine. The chef concocts irresistible dishes, such as salad of warm *foie gras* and figs, Racan pigeon, Charolais beef, and fillet of John Dory with a classic Béarnaise sauce. The cellar has wonderful wines from the best local producers.

SACHE Auberge du XII siècle
1 rue du Château, 37190 **Tel** *02 47 26 88 77* **Fax** *02 47 26 88 21*

In a historic building, a stone's throw from the Balzac museum, the dining room of this restaurant has a rustic atmosphere, with exposed beams. There is a good choice of fixed-price menus with classic dishes, such as pigeon, roast scallops and poached turbot, and raspberry *feuillantine* for dessert.

SANCERRE Auberge la Pomme d'Or
Pl de la Mairie, 18300 **Tel** *02 48 54 13 30* **Fax** *02 48 54 19 22*

This small restaurant in a former coaching inn serves classic dishes. The savoury cuisine uses seasonal produce from the region. Enjoy the simplicity of the Chavignol goat's cheese, breast of guinea fowl with asparagus or pike-perch, complemented by a glass of Sancerre.

SAUMUR Auberge St Pierre
6 pl St Pierre, 49400 **Tel** *02 41 51 26 25* **Fax** *02 41 59 89 28*

On a square near the château in a former 15th-century monastery, this convivial restaurant serves regional specialities prepared with care. Dishes include pike-perch fillet and chicken cooked in Loire wine. Accompany a regional cheese with a glass of fruity red wine, such as St Nicolas de Bourgueil.

ST-OUEN LES VIGNES L'Aubinière
29 rue Jules Gautier, 37530 **Tel** *02 47 30 15 29* **Fax** *02 47 30 02 44*

North of Amboise, this small rustic restaurant opens onto a pretty garden that leads down to the river. Enjoy the creations of chef Jacques Arrayet, who serves outstanding dishes including steamed pollack on a fennel purée, and breast of guinea fowl stuffed with chorizo and served with a gratin of Jerusalem artichokes.

THOUARCE Le Relais de Bonnezeaux
Rte Angers, 49380 **Tel** *02 41 54 08 33* **Fax** *02 41 54 00 63*

This large, pleasant dining room is located in a converted railway station overlooking the vineyards – this is sweet wine country. Imaginative cuisine with regional produce in dishes such as pigeon with an Anjou sauce and the speciality, eel braised in Coteaux du Layon wine.

TOURS L'Atelier Gourmand
37 rue Etienne Marcel, 37000 **Tel** *02 47 38 59 87* **Fax** *02 47 50 14 23*

A charming, small restaurant in a 15th-century building in the old part of Tours. Fabrice Bironneau presents a competitively priced, interesting menu. Dishes include braised beef and lamb *cassoulet*. Warm, homely ambience. Good wine selection. Book ahead.

TOURS L'Odéon
10 pl de la Gare, 37000 **Tel** *02 47 20 12 65*

Just a short walk from Tours' station, this Art Deco-style restaurant provides high-quality French regional dishes such as smoked salmon, duck, or pigeon, and a special all-lobster menu. There is a good selection of classic French desserts, and the wine list is particularly extensive.

TOURS L'Arche de Meslay
14 rue Ailes in Parçay Meslay, 37210 **Tel** *02 47 29 00 07* **Fax** *02 47 29 04 04*

Worth the 9-km (6-mile) detour from the city centre, this refined, contemporary restaurant has a sunny terrace and a kitchen in full view. Watch the chef prepare a delicious roast langoustine, or *bouillabaisse tourangelle* (regional fish stew). A good selection of wines is available by the half bottle.

TOURS La Rive Gauche
23 rue du Commerce, 37000 **Tel** *02 47 05 71 21*

This restaurant has gained national recognition within a very short space of time. A varied menu features dishes with imaginative combinations such as Racan pigeon cooked with Lapsang Souchong tea. Prices remain reasonable, with a lunchtime discovery menu for just €35. Themed cookery workshops are also held here.

Key to Price Guide *see p600* **Key to Symbols** *see back cover flap*

TOURS La Roche Le Roy   Ⓟ🚹🗐Ⓣ🖥Ⓟ   €€€€
55 rte de St-Avertin, 37000 **Tel** *02 47 27 22 00* **Fax** *02 47 28 08 39*

On the edge of the city centre, in an elegant 18th-century manor, is this Michelin-starred restaurant serving classic quality French cuisine. Specialities include creamed lentils with *foie gras* and a distinctive version of steak *Rossini*. There is a good selection of wines from the Loire and Bordeaux.

VALAIRE L'Herbe Rouge   Ⓟ🚹🖥   €
le Bourg, 41120 **Tel** *02 54 44 98 14*

Hidden away in tiny Valaire, a few kilometres from Chaumont-sur-Loire, is this excellent country bistro. The decor is somewhat stuck in the 1950s with plastic stools and other kitsch touches, but there is a pleasant terrace for fine days. Simple traditional cooking includes chicken liver pâté, *paupiette de veau* (stuffed veal) and *clafouti*. Good local wines.

VENDOME La Vallée   Ⓟ🚹♿🖥Ⓟ   €€
34 rue Barré-de-St-Venant, 41100 **Tel** *02 54 77 29 93*

This restaurant serves well-prepared traditional dishes by chef Marc Georget, who is respectful of the quality of the produce. Offerings include Loire valley asparagus in season, fish from Brittany and well-sourced veal. Classic, rustic dining room. Good regional wines too.

VIGNOUX SUR BARANGEON Le Prieuré   Ⓟ🚹♿🖥   €€€
2 rte de St Laurent, 18500 **Tel** *02 48 51 58 80* **Fax** *02 48 54 56 01*

Near to Vierzon, this lovely hotel-restaurant was built in 1862 to serve as the village presbytery. High-quality gourmet cuisine is served in the elegant dining room or on the covered terrace by the pool. Expect to find dishes such as duck confit with sautéed potatoes and pan-fried monkfish with a lobster sauce.

VOUVRAY La Cave Martin   🚹🖥Ⓟ   €
66 vallée Coquette, 37210 **Tel** *02 47 52 62 18*

In this wine village, this restaurant carved into the tuffeau rock has a rustic menu with *andouillettes* (tripe sausages), duck breast and confit, and a decent choice of salads. Start with a glass of local fizzy wine, and finish with an unctuous sweet Vouvray with dessert. Book ahead.

BURGUNDY & FRANCHE-COMTE

ARBOIS Jean-Paul Jeanet   Ⓟ🗐🖥ⓉⓅ   €€€€
9 rue de l'Hôtel de Ville, 39600 **Tel** *03 84 66 05 67*

In the centre of picturesque Arbois, this ancient convent houses an impressive hotel and restaurant. The dining room is elegant and rustic with a pretty terrace. Staff are attentive and enthusiastic. The cuisine of Jean-Paul Jeanet constantly evolves, and his dishes are created with passion and harmony. Exciting desserts too.

ARNAY LE DUC Chez Camille   Ⓟ🚹♿   €€€€
1 pl Edouard Herriot, 21230 **Tel** *03 80 90 01 38*

This former holiday residence of a Marechal de France has a modern dining room serving traditional Burgundy fare, where game takes pride of place. Hearty, rustic dishes that eschew contemporary trends. Specialities include a marvellous rabbit pâté, guinea fowl with pheasant, and confit of cabbage.

AUTUN Les Ursulines   🖥   €€€€
14 rue de Rivault, 71400 **Tel** *03 85 86 58 58*

Situated above the ramparts of the old town, with superb views of the Morvan countryside, this elegant, gastronomic restaurant serves up classic gourmet cuisine. Dishes include turbot served with a squid sauce, duck fillet with honey, and a melt-in-the-mouth chocolate fondant. The vast courtyard is good for outdoor dining in summer.

AUXERRE Le Jardin Gourmand   Ⓟ🚹🖥   €€€€€
56 bd Vauban, 89000 **Tel** *03 86 51 53 52* **Fax** *03 86 52 33 82*

Adventurous and inventive dishes are on offer at this attractive dining room in a former wine-grower's house. Try the puff pastry parcel of green asparagus with poached egg and white Alba truffles. The menu changes with the season, and with the chef's vegetable garden. Wonderful cheeses. Pleasant patio. Book ahead.

AVALLON Relais des Gourmets   Ⓟ🚹♿🖥   €€
45–47 rue de Paris, 89200 **Tel** *03 86 34 18 90*

A traditional auberge with two dining rooms in the fine fortified town of Avallon. The glass-domed, light and airy Salle des Oliviers does indeed have olive trees planted in it. The set menus offer a good selection of both fish and meat dishes, and a vegetarian choice. The bistro, La Salle Bourguignonne, has simple good-value fixed-priced menus.

BEAUNE La Ciboulette   🚹🗐♿Ⓟ   €
69 rue Lorraine, 21200 **Tel** *03 80 24 70 72* **Fax** *03 80 22 79 71*

A delightful little bistro frequented by locals; always a good sign. The basic decor is in contrast with the high standard of cooking. Hearty dishes, such as steak with pungent Epoisses cheese. The best value in town. Local wine merchants come here to choose from the excellent wine list.

BEAUNE Le Bistro de L'Hôtel
3 rue Samuel Legay, 21200 **Tel** *03 80 25 94 10*

Expect a friendly welcome at this restaurant and the adjacent L'Hôtel de Beaune, both within the city walls. High quality ingredients are sourced from local suppliers. The menu varies depending on the season, but most dishes are French with Italian influences. Excellent wine list and lovely terrace. Cooking courses and *domaine* visits are available.

BEAUNE L'Ecusson
Pl Malmedy, 21200 **Tel** *03 80 24 03 82*

Wooden floors and oak beams give a rustic look to this restaurant. The cuisine is daring and stamped with the chef's personality. Trademark dishes include fillet of Charolais beef with cannelloni stuffed with Bourgogne truffles. To finish, why not try the Epoisse-flavoured ice cream? There are several good Burgundies on the wine list.

BEAUNE Hostellerie de Levernois
Rte de Cobertault, Levernois, 21200 **Tel** *03 80 24 73 58* **Fax** *03 80 22 78 00*

This beautiful old mansion with formal gardens occupies an idyllic country setting. The classic restaurant serves up "serious" cuisine, such as snail and frogs' leg risotto, Charolais beef with a Pinot Noir sauce, and shoulder of lamb *de sept heures*, or salmon smoked over vine cuttings. Vast wine list. Faultless service.

BELFORT Le Pot au Feu
27 bis grand' rue, 90000 **Tel** *03 84 28 57 84* **Fax** *03 84 58 17 65*

This bustling restaurant in a 17th-century vaulted cellar serves homely dishes alongside modern, innovative cuisine. Opt for the *pot au feu*, which is a braised beef and vegetable stew, or pan-fried veal kidneys with *morille* mushrooms, or salmon sushi with wasabi and horseradish sauce.

BONLIEU La Poutre
25 Grande Rue, 39130 **Tel** *03 84 25 57 77*

A charming farmhouse dating from 1740 houses this rustic dining room with stone walls and oak beams. Relax in the friendly atmosphere, and delight in the good home cooking based on regional specialities. Well-presented dishes include pan-fried *foie gras* and crayfish *ragoût*. Ideally situated for visits to the spectacular Cascades du Hérisson.

CHABLIS La Cuisine au Vin
16 rue Auxerroise, 89800 **Tel** *03 86 18 98 52*

Proprietor Daniel Etienne Defaix, largely responsible for the development of Chablis, has also launched this attractive restaurant. Traditional Burgundy recipes are given a contemporary make-over. An interesting range of well-prepared dishes are on the menu and include ham on the bone and parsley-imbibed snails.

CHAGNY Lameloise
36 pl d'Armes, 71150 **Tel** *03 85 87 65 65* **Fax** *03 85 87 03 57*

Family owned for more than a century, Lameloise is known for its reassuringly classic French dishes. Well-mastered Burgundian cooking: guinea fowl and *foie gras*, poached in a *consommé* and served with caramelized salsify and quince, and vanilla macaroon with pistachio cream. Pure, powerful flavours done to perfection.

CHAINTRE La Table de Chaintré
Le Bourg, 71570 **Tel** *03 85 32 90 95* **Fax** *03 83 32 91 04*

Not far from Mâcon, this well-established restaurant comes highly recommended, with a menu that changes weekly. Try the *menu découverte*, with four small main dishes, cheese and dessert, or order *à la carte* favourites like sea bass, Bresse chicken, or Erquy scallops. Great desserts are also on offer.

CHALON-SUR-SAONE L'Air du Temps
7 rue de Strasbourg, 71100 **Tel** *03 85 93 39 01* **Fax** *03 85 93 39 01*

Plainly furnished restaurant, with flavours and colours that explode on the palate. The regional menu changes every 15 days and uses seasonal ingredients. The chef simplifies classic dishes, and delicacies include *escargots* and roasted veal fillet. Friendly service.

CHAROLLES Restaurant Fédéric Doucet
2 av de la Libération, 71120 **Tel** *03 85 24 11 32*

Where better to enjoy a Charolais steak than at Charolles? This beautiful, chic, provincial restaurant, near to the village church, serves modern cuisine with a nod to the traditional. The chef's talent shines in dishes such as the sole with Collioure anchovies, and beef with goat's cheese. Desserts also reveal careful preparation. Good Mâcon wines.

CHASSAGNE-MONTRACHET Le Chassagne
4 impasse Chenevottes, 21180 **Tel** *03 80 21 94 94* **Fax** *03 80 21 97 77*

Definitely the right place to enjoy a glass of Chassagne – at the Chassagne restaurant. Try the deliciously fresh lobster, or John Dory with anchovies served with Paimpol beans, accompanied by the local Chardonnay, or the venison with pumpkin and a good red Pinot. The quality outweighs the price.

DIJON D'Zenvies
12 rue Odebert, 21000 **Tel** *03 80 50 09 26*

A contemporary bistro situated near Les Halles serving simple gourmet cuisine. The chef is part of the new generation who remain faithful to quality produce and present unfussy dishes. Specialities include *foie gras* served with a chutney, steak with a "real" Béarnaise, cod with crushed potatoes and a rich chocolate tart. Good choice of wines by the glass.

DIJON Le Bistrot des Halles

10 rue Bannelier, 21000 **Tel** *03 80 49 94 15*

At lunch time, this 1900s-style bistro is roaring. Located next to the market, it attracts food merchants and local business people with its meat pie, *jambon persillé* and *bœuf bourguignon*. Well-known Dijon chef Jean-Pierre Billoux, who has an upmarket restaurant in Dijon centre, oversees this bistro.

DIJON Le Chabrot

36 rue Monge, 21000 **Tel** *03 80 30 69 61* **Fax** *03 80 50 02 35*

The cosy interior, chatty owner and regional specialities make this restaurant very popular. Le Chabrot presents traditional dishes with an innovative twist, such as the snail ravioli. There is a good selection of Burgundy wines; some of them are sold by the glass.

DIJON Hostellerie du Chapeau Rouge

5 rue Michelet, 21000 **Tel** *03 80 50 88 88*

Simply the best place to eat in town. The methodical and determined chef invites diners to travel the world with compositions like monkfish in a sesame crust. Many of the dishes reflect an Asiatic note. The quality of the meat is also impressive: black pig from Bigorre and Bresse chicken. Luscious desserts.

DOLE La Chaumière

346 mal-Juin, 39100 **Tel** *03 84 70 72 40* **Fax** *03 84 79 25 60*

You need an open mind and a curious nature to enjoy the cuisine at this delightful, elegant restaurant. There are creative, unusual dishes such as fillets of whiting with Jerusalem artichokes, spinach, lemon and coriander, or turnips flavoured with Campari and seared duck breast, and olive sorbet. Take the plunge. Rooms available.

FONTANGY Ferme Auberge de la Morvandelle

Précy-sous-Thil, 21390 **Tel** *03 80 84 33 32*

This is a working farm, open to guests only at the weekend. The dining area is in a converted barn, providing an authentic countryside experience. The farm supplies many of the ingredients for its home-made dishes such as chicken liver salad, roast guinea fowl and fruit tarts. Book ahead.

GEVREY-CHAMBERTIN Chez Guy

3 pl de la Mairie, 21220 **Tel** *03 80 58 51 51* **Fax** *03 80 58 50 39*

A charming little restaurant with exposed oak beams, and a terrace for fine days. Simple local cuisine such as *coq au vin* and hearty *joue de bœuf*, both cooked slowly in red wine. More contemporary dishes include bream with a parsnip and hazelnut purée and lobster sauce. A fine selection of fairly priced wines. Good service.

IGUERANDE La Colline du Colombier

Colombier, 71340 **Tel** *03 85 84 07 24*

Michel and Marie-Pierre Troisgros have renovated this ancient farmhouse, which looks down over the surrounding countryside and village. The cuisine focuses on local beef and veal and organic produce. Simple, modern dishes are prepared with care and served in a charmingly rustic dining room.

LONS-LE-SAUNIER Le Relais des Salines

26 rue des Salines, 39000 **Tel** *03 84 43 01 57*

In the heart of the Jura lies this lively brasserie dishing up hearty mountain favourites in a friendly animated dining room. Satisfying dishes focus on meat, cheese and potatoes. There is a good selection of salads too. The Jura Chardonnays, Poulsards and Savagnins make a welcome appearance, sold by the pitcher or glass.

MAGNY-COURS Absolue Renaissance

2 rue de Paris, 58470 **Tel** *03 86 58 10 40*

Paces away from the Formula One circuit, this restaurant sits in a vast garden, with its own vegetable patch. Menus consist of classic dishes that have been revived with a contemporary flourish. Expect to find tasty options such as a *trilogie* of salmon – marinated, tartare and smoked.

MALBUISSON Le Bon Acceuil

Rue de la Source, 25160 **Tel** *03 81 69 30 58*

This colourful restaurant is one of the most inventive kitchens in the Haut-Doubs, and very reasonably priced too. The menus change seasonally, but expect to find creative dishes like oyster tempura with a beetroot emulsion, and roast lamb with potato *gnocchi*. The sommelière is knowledgeable about Jura wines. Reservation recommended.

MONTFAUCON La Cheminée

3 rue de la Vue des Alpes, 25660 **Tel** *03 81 81 17 48*

As the address suggests, the Alpine scenery around the restaurant is spectacular. Located just a few kilometres from Besançon, this auberge, with its comfortable rustic dining room, is full of charm. Tasty dishes are based on local produce. Specialities include pan-fried lamb and a *fricassée* of lobster.

NEVERS Jean-Michel Couron

21 rue St-Etienne, 58000 **Tel** *03 86 61 19 28* **Fax** *03 86 36 02 96*

Intimate, elegant restaurant, attentive service and remarkable cuisine. Well-mastered dishes using the best produce to create perfectly balanced flavours in dishes such as fillet of Charolais beef on lentils, accompanied by hazelnut pasta and Parmesan. Inventive desserts and good wines by the glass too.

NITRY Auberge de la Beursaudière
Chemin de Ronde, 89310 **Tel** *03 86 33 69 69* **Fax** *03 86 33 69 60*

A typical Morvan welcome awaits here, where the staff wear peasant costume. The portions are generous. The menu includes *andouillette de Clamecy* (tripe sausage), veal hock, *corniotte Morvandelle* (cheese filled pastry), *côte de bœuf* and *tournedos* (thick medallion of beef). Rooms available.

NUITS-ST-GEORGES L'Alambic
Rue de Général de Gaulle, 21700 **Tel** *03 80 61 35 00*

In this celebrated wine village lies L'Alambic, with a menu of 450 different wines, 75 of which are Nuits-St-Georges. On the culinary front no real surprises; classic Burgundy dishes are on offer in the attractive vaulted Cisterian dining room. The menu includes *fricassée* of snails, *oeuf en meurette* and quails with prunes and polenta.

PORT LESNEY Le Bistro Pontarlier
Port Lesney, 39600 **Tel** *03 84 37 83 27* **Fax** *03 84 73 88 88*

One of the best-value restaurants in the region, this bistro is well established in the old school house of a pretty wine-growing village in the Arbois area. It is associated with the luxury hotel, Château de Germigny, in the same village, with the same chefs and cuisine – but simpler and less expensive. Excellent bistro atmosphere.

PULIGNY-MONTRACHET La Table d'Olivier Leflaive
Pl du Monument, 21190 **Tel** *03 80 21 37 65* **Fax** *03 80 21 33 94*

Located in a famous wine village, this rustic restaurant is named after its founder, who makes all the wines himself. The restaurant specializes in wine-tasting lunches in which cold meats, Bresse chicken and Burgundy cheeses are offered alongside wines to taste, such as St-Aubin, Bourgogne Blanc and Puligny-Montrachet. Reservations required.

QUARRE LES TOMBES Auberge de l'Atre
Les Lavaults, 89630 **Tel** *03 86 32 20 79* **Fax** *03 86 32 28 25*

The decorative interior of this restaurant in the Morvan region contrasts with the rustic simplicity of the building. The dining room has an authentic hearth, or *âtre*, and there is an attractive terrace. There are classic dishes, such as roast lamb with rosemary and soufflé flavoured with *marc de bourgogne*.

SAULIEU Le Relais Bernard Loiseau
2 rue d'Argentine, 21210 **Tel** *03 80 90 53 53* **Fax** *03 80 64 08 92*

This restaurant remains one of France's best. The chef Patrick Bertron has successfully taken on the challenge, motivated by Mme Loiseau. There are well-mastered, imaginative interpretations of traditional dishes such as pan-fried scallops served with a *palet* of pumpkin and cockles. Delicious desserts. Extensive wine list.

SENS La Madeleine
1 rue Alsace-Lorraine, 89100 **Tel** *03 86 65 09 31* **Fax** *03 86 95 37 41*

With the two-Michelin-star rating, here you will find elegant, refined cuisine with great attention to the ingredients. Seasonal menus offer specialities such as *foie gras* with apple and saffron compôte, sea bass and a gorgeously gooey chocolate mousse with raspberry sauce. Good Chablis and local Irancy wines. Book ahead.

ST-AMOUR BELLEVUE L'Auberge du Paradis
Le Plâtre Durand, 71570 **Tel** *03 85 37 10 26*

Once a bakery, then a grocer's, now one of the most dynamic restaurants in Burgundy. The chef here oozes enthusiasm and personality. Daring combinations of spices result in exciting dishes, including bold desserts such as spicy *crème au chocolat* with apple cream. The pretty dining room is decorated with bright, chequered fabrics and Moroccan rugs.

ST PERE SOUS VEZELAY L'Espérance
St Père sous Vézelay, 89450 **Tel** *03 86 33 39 10* **Fax** *03 86 33 26 15*

L'Espérance serves perhaps the greatest food in Burgundy, in an elegant dining room that opens out onto a terrace with superb views. Marc Meneau, one of France's finest chefs, presents modern classics, such as scallops with lemon or fresh truffles, and tender, succulent Quercy lamb. Classic wine list.

ST-ROMAIN Les Roches
Pl de la Mairie, 21190 **Tel** *03 80 21 21 63*

Small hotel-restaurant sitting on the main square of this village well known to wine connoisseurs. Plain, no-frills cooking in a dining room to match. Relax with a chilled glass of St Romain Blanc accompanied with home-made nibbles, then tuck into hearty, homely dishes such as the veritable *haché parmentier*. One of the best value places in the region.

TOURNUS Le Restaurant Greuze
1 rue A Thibaudet, 71700 **Tel** *03 85 51 13 52* **Fax** *03 85 51 75 42*

Ultra-classic cuisine and decor, the restaurant itself is a monument to a bygone era. Here's the place to enjoy some of the best classic cooking in France, such as scallops with vegetable *pot au feu* perfumed with citronelle, Bresse chicken, or a succulent steak of Salers-Charolais beef. Good Mâcon and Beaujolais wines.

VERDUN-SUR-LE-DOUBS L'Hostellerie Bourguignonne – Didier Denis
2 av Pdt-Borgeot, 71350 **Tel** *03 85 91 51 45* **Fax** *03 85 91 53 81*

On the riverbank, in the heart of the countryside, this rustic establishment serves unpretentious, straightforward cooking with local ingredients. They do a very good local Charolais beef fillet, and a seafood couscous with lobster, scallops and king prawns, flavoured with star anise and peppery mint. Excellent wine list.

VENOY Le Moulin de la Coudre   🅿 🚶 ♿ 🖼   €€€
2 rue des Gravottes, La Coudre, 89290 **Tel** *03 86 40 23 79*

Near to Auxerre in the heart of the Yonne lies this restored water mill housing a hotel and restaurant. Classic cuisine is prepared with touches of originality; menus change weekly according to seasonal produce and the whim of the chef. In winter relax with coffee in front of the open fireplace, in summer enjoy the flower-filled garden.

VILLENEUVE SUR YONNE Auberge La Lucarne aux Chouettes   🚶 ♿ 🖼   €€€€
7 quai Bretoche, 89500 **Tel** *03 86 87 18 26* **Fax** *03 86 87 22 63*

Renovated by actress Leslie Caron, this 17th-century inn has a lovely setting by the river Yonne. Dining outside on the terrace is delightful in summer. The dining room is cosy with exposed beams. The menu presents traditional dishes, such as snails and wild mushroom salad.

VILLERS-LE-LAC Le France   🅿 🚶 🍴   €€€€
8 pl Cupillard, 25130 **Tel** *03 81 68 00 06* **Fax** *03 81 68 09 22*

The cuisine here is fine and inventive, full of contrasts but still simple. The chef has his own herb garden outside and an expansive selection of spices collected during his travels. The dining room is airy and bright. Try the pigeon breast accompanied by a chocolate sauce and served with liquorice salsify. Refreshing sorbets.

VINCELOTTE Auberge des Tilleuils   🅿 🚶 🖼 🍴   €€€
12 quai de l'Yonne, 82290 **Tel** *03 86 42 22 13*

This attractive auberge on the banks of the river serves cuisine that is packed with flavours, not only from Burgundy, but from other French regions too. Dishes include garlic from Arleux, lentils from Puy and *andouille* from Vire. Try succulent entrecôte steak, pan-fried in Bordier butter. Good selection of Burgundy wines, especially Irancy.

VONNAS Georges Blanc   🅿 🚶 📋 🍴 🍴   €€€€€
Pl Marché, 01540 **Tel** *04 74 50 90 90* **Fax** *04 74 50 08 80*

A popular shrine of cooking with smooth service in a dining room crammed with antiques. The ambience wavers between the refined and the rustic. Inventive cuisine is prepared by M Blanc's two sons, including Bresse chicken with *foie gras* and lobster ravioli with sorrel. Excellent wines.

THE MASSIF CENTRAL

ALLEYRAS Le Haut Allier   🅿 🚶 📋 🖼 🍴   €€€€€
Pont d'Alleyras, 43580 **Tel** *04 71 57 57 63* **Fax** *04 71 57 59 99*

This hotel-restaurant nestled in the Allier gorge is well worth seeking out for its warm welcome and inventive cuisine. Local produce features in traditional dishes such as saddle of Saugues lamb, or more imaginative dishes such as a crumble of Auvergne ham. The set menus represent excellent value.

AUMONT-AUBRAC Restaurant Prouhèze   🅿 🚶 🖼 🍴 🍴   €€€€
2 rte du Languedoc, 48130 **Tel** *04 66 42 80 07* **Fax** *04 66 42 87 78*

The award-winning chef uses only the freshest ingredients to create elegant and unusual flavours. Menu highlights include an *aligot* (potatoes with cheese) casserole and pan-fried fillet of Aubrac beef with *vin jaune*. Good selection of Languedoc wines. Its sister restaurant, Le Compostelle, serves less expensive country fare.

BELCASTEL Vieux Pont   🅿 🚶 📋   €€€€€
Le Bourg, 12390 **Tel** *05 65 64 52 29*

This imaginative restaurant lies across a medieval cobbled bridge: the air is fresh, and the river burbles beside the stylishly rustic dining room. Dishes are prepared with talent and modernism. Quality produce is used to create dishes such as Mont Royal pigeon with *cèpes* and Aveyron veal. Reservation recommended.

BOUDES La Vigne   🚶 📋 🖼   €€
Pl de la Mairie, 63340 **Tel** *04 73 96 55 66*

In the main square of this small wine-making village lies one of the few truly creative restaurants in the region. The chef is constantly seeking out new ideas. Menus change regularly; expect to find dishes such as cod and scallop mousse. The cheeses and desserts are treated with the same attention. Good-value set menus.

BOUSSAC Le Relais Creusois   🚶 🍴   €€€
40 Maison Dieu, rte de la Châtre, 23600 **Tel** *05 55 65 02 20* **Fax** *05 55 65 13 60*

Do not be put off by the incongruous exterior or the downbeat decor – this is award-winning cuisine. The chef seeks inspiration from far and wide to deliver original dishes, such as pike-perch with parsnip purée, and duck with elderberries. Some tables afford views over the beautiful Petite Creuse valley. Phone to make sure it is open. Closed Jan–mid-Mar.

BRIVE-LA-GAILLARDE Chez Francis   🚶 ♿ 🍴   €€
61 av de Paris, 19100 **Tel** *05 55 74 41 72*

Reminiscent of an authentic Parisian bistro, this retro pub has become an institution in Brive. The cuisine is generous and well prepared. Regional favourites are revisited such as baby squid, Jerusalem artichokes, or veal *pot au feu*. Good selection of southern French wines. Reservation recommended.

CLERMONT-FERRAND Le Caveau　　　　　　📋🕐　　€€

9 rue Philippe Marcombes, 63000 **Tel** *04 73 14 07 03*

Don't be deterred by the uninviting entrance; at the bottom of the simple staircase is a delightful vaulted dining room. Dishes are rustic and traditional. Huge chunks of Salers or Aubrac beef and *coq au vin* make this a meat eater's paradise. Luckily the desserts are not of the same gargantuan proportions. Book ahead.

CLERMONT-FERRAND Amphitryon Capucine　　　　📋　　€€€€

50 rue Fontgiève, 63000 **Tel** *04 73 31 38 39*

In this small, wooden-fronted restaurant guests can enjoy the best seasonal local ingredients in a dining room complete with a fireplace and oak beams. Simple dishes, well prepared without pretention, include *gnocchi* with roast langoustine and truffles, and potted chocolate pudding. Good wines from Languedoc and Auvergne.

CLERMONT-FERRAND Goûts et Couleurs　　　　🖐🕐　　€€€€

6 pl Champgil, 63000 **Tel** *04 73 19 37 82*

The geometric 1980s decor is softened by an ancient vaulted ceiling in this former mirror workshop. Modern, inventive cuisine using quality ingredients offers the best value in town. Good choice of both meat and fish dishes. Leave room for delicious desserts such as warm lemon madeleines with citrus fruit jelly and margarita sorbet.

COLLONGES-LA-ROUGE Auberge Le Prieuré　　　P🚶🖐🕐　　€€

Pl de l'Eglise, 19500 **Tel** *05 55 25 41 00*

Typical 18th-century auberge built in the local red stone, with a pretty terrace. Simple, well-prepared classic dishes such as the *foie gras* with onion confit, pan-fried duck breast, and pike-perch with lemon butter sauce. If you are in a rush, there is a *casse croûte* menu, where the starter and main course are served at the same time.

FLORAC La Source du Pêcher　　　　🍽P🚶🕐🍷　　€€€

Rue Remuret, 48400 **Tel** *04 66 45 03 01* **Fax** *04 66 45 28 82*

Charming little restaurant in a converted mill where you can watch the fish jumping while you eat. Regional produce takes pride of place – duck with bilberries, local lamb, Lozère trout and chestnut-flower honey, depending on the season. Excellent choice of Languedoc wines. Closed from November to Easter.

LAGUIOLE Michel Bras　　　　P🚶📋🖐🍷🍷　€€€€€

Rte de l'Aubrac, 12210 **Tel** *05 65 51 18 20* **Fax** *05 65 48 47 02*

A wall of glass overlooks the Aubrac countryside from this three-star hilltop restaurant. Michel and Sebastien Bras are renowned for their cutting-edge cuisine. The pan-fried pigeon breast, flavoured with asafoetida and served with Cévenne onions and a juniper and orange sauce, is out of this world. Closed Nov–Easter.

LE PUY-EN-VELAY Tournayre　　　　　　📋　　€€€

12 rue Chênebouterie, 43000 **Tel** *04 71 09 58 94*

This delightful restaurant is located in one of the oldest *hôtels particuliers* in Le Puy-en-Velay, which dates from the 12th century. The dining room has vaulted ceilings and stone walls. The chef prepares typical Auvergne cuisine, as well as more elaborate dishes like warm lobster tart, and langoustine crumble with *morille* mushrooms.

LE PUY-EN-VELAY François Gagnaire　　　P📋🖐🍷🍷　€€€€

4 av Clément Charbonnier, 43000 **Tel** *04 71 02 75 55*

Sophisticated restaurant housed in the Hôtel du Parc. The dining room is simply furnished, with colourful Raoul Dufy prints lining the walls. The chef is an old master who knows exactly where he's going. He creatively treats local ingredients with a modern twist. Dishes include pan-fried *foie gras* on a bed of artichokes, and turbot with wild mushrooms.

LE ROUGET Hôtel des Voyageurs　　　　　　🕐　　€€

20 av de 15 septembre 1945, 15290 **Tel** *04 71 46 10 14* **Fax** *04 71 46 93 89*

Situated 25 km (16 miles) southwest of Aurillac is this stone-built Cantal hotel-restaurant serving well-prepared traditional dishes. The reasonably priced *menu du terroir* includes choices such as the risotto with prawns, and pan-fried sea bream served with citrus-fruit-flavoured quinoa. Good selection of wines.

LIMOGES Chez Alphonse　　　　　　　　📋　　€

5 pl de la Motte, 87000 **Tel** *05 55 34 34 14* **Fax** *05 55 34 34 14*

This lively bistro serves regional cuisine made with fresh ingredients that the chef himself sources daily from the local market. The traditional Limousin dishes are usually meat or fish based; the *prix-fixe* menus are great value. Generous cheese platter and good chocolate mousse. Reservations recommended. Closed 27 Jul–10 Aug; 29 Dec–12 Jan; Sun.

LIMOGES Chez François　　　　　　　📋🖐　　€

Pl de la Motte, 87000 **Tel** *05 55 32 32 79* **Fax** *05 55 32 87 39*

Unbeatable value and a convivial atmosphere at this restaurant inside Limoges' covered market hall. It is only open at lunchtime. Be sure to get here early for a place at the communal tables – or prepare to queue. The food is nothing fancy, but well cooked and tasty. The single, three-course menu changes daily.

LIMOGES L'Amphitryon　　　　　　🚶🕐🍷🍷　€€€€

26 rue de la Boucherie, 87000 **Tel** *05 55 33 36 39* **Fax** *05 55 32 98 50*

Chic contemporary dining space in the heart of old Limoges. The food is sophisticated and the flavours delicate, in keeping with the Limoges porcelain on which it is served. A regular favourite is the fillet of Limousin beef, while desserts centre around seasonal fruits.

Key to Price Guide *see p600* **Key to Symbols** *see back cover flap*

MILLAU La Braconne

7 pl Maréchal Foch, 12100 **Tel** *05 65 60 30 93*

Under the arcades of a picturesque square is this friendly restaurant with an authentic 13th-century vaulted dining room. The terrace is also attractive with comfy wicker chairs. Classic savoury cuisine with specialities like succulent flambéed leg of lamb. The homely atmosphere makes this a relaxing place to stop for a meal.

MONTLUCON Le Grenier à Sel

10 rue Ste-Anne, 03100 **Tel** *04 70 05 53 79* **Fax** *04 70 05 87 91*

This ivy-covered 16th-century mansion has huge fireplaces and an elegant dining room decked out in restful pastel tones. In fine weather, meals may be served on the enchanting terrace. Try cannelloni filled with whiting and crayfish and served with seasonal vegetables. Good-value set menus.

MONTSALVY L'Auberge Fleurie

Pl du Barry, 15120 **Tel** *04 71 49 20 02*

A charming ivy-clad auberge with oak beams, an open fireplace and a rustic feel. The chef places emphasis on the presentation of his creative dishes. The menus change according to seasonal produce with specialities such as a carpaccio of hare served with fennel and basil-flavoured butter. Delicious desserts include chocolate meringue pudding.

MOUDEYRES Le Pré Bossu

Le Bourg, 43150 **Tel** *04 71 05 10 70* **Fax** *04 71 05 10 21*

Restaurant-with-rooms that is well worth seeking out for the peaceful location and expertly executed cuisine. Many of the herbs and vegetables – including old-fashioned varieties – come from the garden. There is even a vegetarian menu – a rare treat in this corner of France. Dinner only. Closed Nov–Apr.

MOULINS Le Trait d'Union

16 rue Gambette, 3000 **Tel** *04 70 34 24 61*

Upmarket contemporary bistro in the city centre serving cuisine that balances classicism and modernism. The chef, who has worked with some of the country's best, pays homage to the region with dishes such as *Monts du Forez* veal and classic steak *Rossini*. There is a selection of local goat's cheeses.

MURAT Le Jarrousset

Rte de Clermont-Ferrand, 15300 **Tel** *04 71 20 10 69* **Fax** *04 71 20 15 26*

Surrounded by attractive gardens, just east of Murat, is this discreet restaurant. The chef seeks inspiration from top-quality ingredients, most of them sourced locally. The gastronomic menu changes every season, allowing for lots of creativity.

RODEZ Goûts en Couleurs

38 rue Bonald, 12000 **Tel** *05 65 42 75 10*

Situated in the old town, looking out onto Embergues Square, this charming dining room is decorated with the owner's colourful paintings. Dishes such as an *île flottante* of truffles with liquorice, and Brill with Nadaillac snails bear witness to the imaginative cuisine of the chef. Good wine selection and friendly service.

ST-BONNET-LE-FROID Auberge des Cimes

Le Bourg, 43290 **Tel** *04 71 59 93 72* **Fax** *04 71 59 93 40*

The restaurant at the Clos des Cimes hotel has been awarded its third Michelin star. Depending on the season, you'll feast on roast lamb, suckling pig perfumed with sage, or fragrant mushrooms. Wonderful selection of Auvergne and Ardeche cheeses, matured on the premises. Delicious desserts, too. Closed Jan–mid-Mar.

ST-JULIEN-CHAPTEUIL Vidal

Pl du Marché, 43260 **Tel** *04 71 08 70 50* **Fax** *04 71 08 40 14*

In a sleepy village surrounded by mountain peaks, the Vidal family run a convivial restaurant decorated with murals depicting local scenery. Dishes include *foie gras* served with toasted blueberry gingerbread, stuffed fillet of beef, and Velay lamb. Closed mid-Jan–Feb.

UZERCHE Restaurant Jean Teyssier

Rue du Pont-Turgot, 19140 **Tel** *05 55 73 10 05* **Fax** *05 55 98 43 31*

A taste of the Mediterranean has come to the Corrèze with dishes such as *vol-au-vent* with Roquefort sauce, braised lamb with parsnip purée and trout with courgette gratin. Wonderful panoramic restaurant with views of the Vezère. Closed mid-Feb–mid-Mar.

VICHY Brasserie du Casino

4 rue du Casino, 03200 **Tel** *04 70 98 23 06* **Fax** *04 70 98 53 17*

A veritable institution on the Vichy restaurant scene, across the road from the Grand Casino. Dine in stylish Art Deco surroundings – all wood and mirrors and big bench-seats – on upscale brasserie fare. *Foie gras* served warm with balsamic vinegar and raspberry charlotte are among the classics on offer.

VICHY Jacques Decoret

15 rue du Parc, 3200 **Tel** *04 70 97 65 06*

This restaurant is continuously improving. Imaginative dishes are prepared with precision. Pan-fried *foie gras* with *Bonite bouillon* and langoustines cooked with dill and horseradish are just some of the dishes that testify to the chef's creativity and culinary talent.

THE RHONE VALLEY AND FRENCH ALPS

ANNECY Le Belvédère   P ♿ ⌂ 🍴 🍷   €€€€€

7 chemin Belvédère, 74000 **Tel** *04 50 45 04 90*

This dining room has comfy leather chairs, a wonderful view of the lake and a pretty terrace. Appetizing contemporary recipes are prepared with finesse. Dishes such as *foie gras* perfumed with vanilla and served with fig compote explode with flavours. Divine desserts too, such as creamed apple with saffron and home-made sorbet.

BOURG-EN-BRESSE Les Quatres Saisons   🍴 🍷   €€

6 rue de le République, 1000 **Tel** *04 74 22 01 86*

Friendly, convivial restaurant serving traditional dishes, which have been jazzed up with a modern touch. The chef, passionate about both wines and local produce, livens up old favourites: tartare of scallops, crab and prawns with a wasabi coulis, or fillet of pork with honey, Szechuan pepper and kumquat. Good Rhône and Burgundy wine selection.

CHAMBERY Château de Candie – L'Orangerie   P ⌂ 🍴 🍷   €€€€€

Rue de Bois de Candie, Chambéry le Vieux, 73000 **Tel** *04 79 96 63 00* **Fax** *04 79 96 63 10*

A 14th-century château in its own grounds is the beautiful setting for this elegant restaurant. Classic produce is prepared with a contemporary touch in such dishes as tartare of scallops with crushed cashew nuts, or more rustic hare with lemon confit. Closed 2 weeks Apr & 2 weeks Nov.

CHAMONIX La Calèche   🍴   €

Rue Dr Paccard, 74400 **Tel** *04 50 55 94 68*

A traditional Chamonix mountain restaurant that has been run by the same family since 1946. Enjoy typical Savoyard specialities such as *tartiflette*, fondue and *raclette*, as well as grilled meat, in the dining room crammed with old skis, Swiss clocks, copper pans and a bobsleigh from the 1924 Winter Olympics. Good Savoie wines.

CHAMONIX Les Jardins du Mont Blanc   P ♿ ⌂ 🍴 🍷   €€

62 Allée du Majestic, 74400 **Tel** *04 50 55 35 42*

A mountain hotel offering savoury modern Alpine cuisine using the best produce the region can offer. The chef revisits classic dishes, such as salt cod, and prepares them with subtlety and faultless precision. Magnificent desserts too. Tendency to be noisy when there are large groups. Good-value menu at lunchtime.

CHAMONIX Le Hameau Albert 1er   P 🍴 ♿ ⌂ 🍴 🍷   €€€€€

119 impasse Montenvers, 74402 **Tel** *04 50 53 05 09* **Fax** *04 50 55 95 48*

Luxury Savoyard hotel-restaurant in the mountains, with a view of Italy. The superb cooking of Pierre Carrier tempts the palate. The vegetable patch next door provides him with seasonal inspiration for dishes such as fish accompanied by *ratte* potatoes and violet artichokes with a Château Chalon sauce, or a gratin of salsify. Good cheeseboard.

COLLONGES AU MONT D'OR Paul Bocuse   P 🍴 ▤ ♿ 🍴 🍷   €€€€€

40 quai de la Plage, 69660 **Tel** *04 72 42 90 90* **Fax** *04 72 27 85 87*

Paul Bocuse has become an institution for French cooking and is simply irreplaceable. Try delicacies such as black truffle soup with pastry, the cooked-to-perfection turbot with its *beurre blanc* sauce, or the legendary gratin of crayfish. The wines are also superb. Reserve a table well in advance.

COURCHEVEL Le Genépi   🍴   €€€

Courchevel 1850, 73120 **Tel** *04 79 08 08 63*

This restaurant is one of the best value-for-money places at the luxury ski resort of Courchevel 1850. Both traditional mountain fare and classic dishes are prepared with finesse, such as carpaccio of duck with basil, lobster ravioli and stuffed rabbit, and are served in the elegant, rustic dining room.

COURCHEVEL Le Chabichou   P 🍴 ♿ ⌂ 🍴 🍷   €€€€€

Quartier des Chenus, 73120 **Tel** *04 79 08 00 55* **Fax** *04 79 08 33 58*

Reserve a table by the huge windows to enjoy views of the mountains. With two Michelin stars, Le Chabichou offers exotic and creative cuisine at one of the most popular restaurants in this extensive resort. Refined ambience and old-school favourites with an elaborate touch, such as Bresse pigeon stuffed with *foie gras*, pear and cloves.

EVIAN LES BAINS Histoire de Goût   🍴 ▤ ⌂   €

1 av Général Dupas, 74500 **Tel** *04 50 70 09 98*

Restaurant and wine bar serving gourmet bistro food. Perch at the zinc-topped bar and choose from over 200 wines, or settle in the elegant vaulted dining room adorned with wrought-iron chandeliers. Good-value menus include a vegetarian option – the *découverte* menu is particularly recommended.

GRENOBLE Le Mas Bottero   🍴 ⌂   €€

168 Cours Berriat, 38000 **Tel** *04 76 21 95 33*

Dishes here reflect the Provençal roots of the young chef, as well as his devotion to organic produce. Tasty offerings include artichokes served with rocket *pistou*, pigeon in a hazelnut crust and organic salmon with celery and green apple. In summer, tables are set up outside, under the ancient wisteria.

Key to Price Guide *see p600* **Key to Symbols** *see back cover flap*

GRENOBLE A Ma Table ▣ €€€
92 cours Jean-Jaurès, 38000 **Tel** *04 76 96 77 04* **Fax** *04 76 96 77 04*

There are regular changes to the menu, depending on seasonal local produce, at this small, prettily decorated restaurant. Well-mastered classic cuisine includes dishes such as caramelized pear and gorgonzola tart with smoked duck breast, Vercors trout in mustard sauce and a duck *cassoulet* with almonds and coconut. Book ahead.

GRENOBLE Le Fantin Latour ▣▤▥▦▧▨ €€€€€
1 rue Général Beylié, 38000 **Tel** *04 76 01 00 97*

The presentation at this chic restaurant is extravagant: apéritifs are presented on a bed of wild plants, and the dessert comes decorated with pebbles. The cuisine also breaks down traditional boundaries in using creative combinations of herbs and spices, as in pigeon served with a lichen and sage sauce. Dynamic staff too.

LA CLUSAZ La Scierie ▦ €€
321–331 rte du Col des Aravis, 74220 **Tel** *04 50 63 34 68*

This restaurant is located in a former saw mill in the bustling centre of the popular ski resort. The chef has created an extensive menu at reasonable prices, with dishes ranging from local mountain *charcuterie* and salad to more elaborate affairs such as John Dory fillet served with a sage and Parmesan risotto.

LAMASTRE Restaurant Barattéro ▣▥▦ €€€€
Pl Seignobos, 07270 **Tel** *04 75 06 41 50* **Fax** *04 75 06 49 75*

This is an elegant restaurant with an attractive garden, at the Hotel Midi in the lovely Ardèche town of Lamastre. Classic cuisine such as pan-fried *foie gras* salad, Bresse chicken, crayfish with a richly flavoured sauce and Ardèche chestnut soufflé. The wine list focuses on St-Joseph and St-Péray. Book ahead.

LARGENTIÈRE Le Chêne Vert ▣▥▦ €€
Rocher, 7110 **Tel** *04 75 88 34 02*

Traditional Ardèchois hotel and restaurant situated in the countryside, near Aubenas. Choose from well-prepared regional classics such as *foie gras* served with a fig confit or roast rabbit flavoured with thyme accompanied by a *tartiflette* Ardèchoise. To finish, a fruit salad topped by a frothy cream infused with Bourbon vanilla.

LE BOURGET-LE-LAC Beaurivage ▣▥▧▦ €€€€
Boulevard du Lac, 73370 **Tel** *04 79 25 00 38*

Superbly situated on the banks of the lake, this typical auberge has a dining room opening out onto a lovely terrace overhung with plantain trees. Take in the view while you enjoy classic Savoyard cuisine, grilled lobster and a risotto flavoured with *bouillabaisse*, or the chicken breast stuffed with *foie gras* and served with risotto.

LYON Brasserie Georges ▤▧▥▦ €€
30 cour Verdun, 69002 **Tel** *04 72 56 54 54* **Fax** *04 78 42 51 65*

Huge, bustling city centre bistro with fast service and a splendid Art Deco interior. The extensive menu includes a choice of Lyonnais specialities such as *andouillette* (tripe sausage) and Dauphinoise potatoes, but also a variety of seafood dishes, sauerkraut and omelette. Good choice for children and vegetarians.

LYON La Gargotte d'Ivan ▣▧▦ €€
15 rue Royale, 69001 **Tel** *04 78 28 79 20*

Just north of the Grand Théâtre lies "Ivan's Canteen", a friendly restaurant with retro decor, Rococo gilding and mirror-lined walls. The young and talented chef prepares semi-gastronomic dishes at bistro prices. The menus include dishes based on grand classics enlivened with a touch of originality. Small selection of good wines at reasonable prices too.

LYON 33 Cité ▣▤▧▦ €€€
33 quai Charles de Gaulle, 69006 **Tel** *04 37 45 45 45*

Modern city-centre brasserie facing the Cité Internationale. This stylish dining room offers classic and contemporary cuisine prepared with care; dishes include a *millefeuille* of crab, lightly cooked tuna with sesame seeds and Dombe duck breast "Rossini". Wines can be ordered by the glass or bottle.

LYON L'Alexandrin ▤▨ €€€€
83 rue Moncey, 69003 **Tel** *04 72 61 15 69*

The young chef here creates gourmet Lyonnais dishes. Faultless preparation results in cooked-to-perfection dishes with personality. These include pike mousse with a creamy crayfish sauce, and Bresse chicken cooked in vinegar. The same care is taken with the vegetables, including the *cocotte* of vegetables with chestnuts.

LYON Nicolas le Bec et Taka ▧▨▥ €€€€
14 rue Grolée, 69002 **Tel** *04 78 42 15 35* **Fax** *04 72 40 98 97*

Cutting edge, inventive cuisine with audacious touches shows in dishes such as caramelized Bresse pigeon with a pomegranate reduction. The setting is elegant and contemporary, and there's an excellent wine list with a particularly good range of Burgundies, but at a price. Closed 2 weeks Jan & 2 weeks Aug.

MEGEVE La Petite Ravine ▣▧▦ €
743 chemin de la Ravine, Demi Quartier Combloux, 74120 **Tel** *04 50 21 38 67*

Typical alpine chalet restaurant with a homely, convivial ambience. In winter, skiers stop off to relax and have a bite, in summer hikers settle back to admire the view. The selection of dishes is limited but tasty regional favourites are included; cheese fondue, *croûte au* Beaufort cheese and salads. Ideal for all the family.

MEGEVE La Taverne du Mont d'Arbois   P 🖥   €€€€

3001 rte Edmond de Rothschild, 74120 **Tel** *04 50 21 03 53*

Once a tavern frequented by locals, this authentic chalet now attracts a chic Megève crowd. The chef prepares dishes based on traditional recipes. Carpaccio of bream and crayfish gratin are on the menu, alongside old favourites such as *raclette* and fondue. The desserts are excellent.

MORZINE La Chamade   🏃 ⛓ 🖥   €€

Morzine, 74110 **Tel** *04 50 79 13 91* **Fax** *04 50 79 27 48*

Traditional Alpine family-run restaurant with a wide menu. Pizzas cooked in wood-fired ovens, cheese platters and regional fare such as piglet and *charcuterie* (cold meats). Other options include Morzinoise *tomme* salad, rabbit with lentils and a hearty mixed grill. Vegetarian dishes are also available.

ROANNE La Troisgros   P 🏃 ▤ ⛓ 🍴 🍷   €€€€€

Pl Jean Troisgros, 42300 **Tel** *04 77 71 66 97* **Fax** *04 77 70 39 77*

La Troisgros is one of the most prestigious restaurants in France, with elegant contemporary decor. Sit in the dining room with its pure lines and zen atmosphere and feast on delights such as duck fillet with cherries. There is also a specialized food library.

ST-AGREVE Domaine de Rilhac   P 🏃 ⛓   €€€€

Rilhac, 07320 **Tel** *04 75 30 20 20* **Fax** *04 75 30 20 00*

Located in a peaceful corner of the Ardèche, in this renovated farmhouse, chef Ludovic Sinz creates classic dishes with an innovative approach. On the menu, there is a choice of dishes such as pumpkin soup with snails, pan-fried chicory with scallops and chestnut sauce and, to finish, a warm chocolate tart.

ST-ETIENNE Le Bistrot de Paris   🖥   €

7 pl Jean Jaurès, 42000 **Tel** *04 77 32 21 50*

This convivial bistro is located on an attractive square in the city centre. The menu changes daily, according to whatever is available and freshest at the local market. Dishes here are all excellent value for money, and there is a pleasant terrace for summer dining and watching the rest of world pass by.

ST-MARTIN-DE-BELLEVILLE La Bouitte   P 🏃 🖥 🍴   €€€€€

St Marcel, 73440 **Tel** *04 79 08 96 77* **Fax** *04 79 08 96 03*

In a charming Alpine chalet, this restaurant serves inventive dishes using regional Alpine herbs. Try the local fish, such as the tantalizing *féra du lac Léman* served with artichoke-filled cannelloni. There is also a very good selection of cheese and desserts. Cookery courses are available.

TAIN L'HERMITAGE Lycée Hotelier de l'Hermitage   🖥 P   €

Rue Jean Monnet, 26600 **Tel** *04 75 07 57 14*

On the outskirts of this famous wine-making town lies this training college for aspiring chefs, waiters and sommeliers. The students run two restaurants serving classic gourmet dishes. Each Thursday, the evenings have a chosen theme. The menu changes constantly and the prices include an apéritif and wine. Only open during term time.

TALLOIRES La Villa des Fleurs   P 🏃 🖥   €€€

Rte du Port, 74290 **Tel** *04 50 60 71 14* **Fax** *04 50 60 74 06*

The cuisine at this charming stone-built house set in its own grounds focuses on fish caught in Lake d'Annecy, a stone's throw away. Try the succulent local *féra* fish, or the poached trout. Traditional regional dishes are also served. Dine outside with a view of the lake in fine weather. Pleasant service. Rooms available.

TOURNON Le Tournesol   🏃 🖥 🍷   €€

44 av Maréchal Foch, 07300 **Tel** *04 75 07 08 26* **Fax** *04 75 07 08 26*

Smart restaurant near the riverside with a panoramic view of the Hermitage vineyards. The interior is smart and contemporary, and the young chef shows his originality in dishes such as *foie gras* with apple coulis, or salmon cooked in maple syrup and flavoured with fresh ginger. Home-made desserts. Well-chosen wines.

URIAGE-LES-BAINS Les Terrasses d'Uriage   P ▤ 🍴 🍷   €€€€

Pl de la Déesse-Hygie, 38410 **Tel** *04 76 89 10 80*

Located in a typical thermal resort is this dynamic restaurant offering interesting, innovative dishes with a touch of eccentricity. The elegant dining room in a Napoleon III building opens out onto a lovely park. Savour dishes such as guinea fowl with sorrel and dill *fromage blanc*. Desserts are wonderful too, and there's a vast choice of wines.

VALENCE Restaurant Pic   P 🏃 ▤ ⛓ 🖥 🍴 🍷   €€€€€

285 av Victor Hugo, 26000 **Tel** *04 75 44 15 32* **Fax** *04 75 40 96 03*

Refined restaurant with inspirational cuisine in a luxurious hotel. Lobster with red fruit and berries, celery and green pepper have enhanced the reputation of this constantly evolving, non-conventional establishment. Great Rhône wines. The restaurant runs cookery courses.

VIENNE La Pyramide   P ▤ ⛓ 🖥 🍴 🍷   €€€€

14 bd Fernand Point, 38200 **Tel** *04 74 53 01 96*

One of France's classic Michelin-starred hotel-restaurant establishments. Professionalism reigns supreme. Gastronomic creations are based on regional produce; choices include pan-fried *foie gras* flavoured with Madagascar pepper and *féra du lac* fish with a pea purée and emulsion of Shimeji mushrooms. Superb selection of Rhône wines.

Key to Price Guide *see p600* **Key to Symbols** *see back cover flap*

POITOU & AQUITAINE

ANGOULEME Le Terminus   €€€€
3 pl de la Gare, 16000 **Tel** *05 45 95 27 13*

Chic, modern restaurant where good food, prompt service and well-priced menus make up for the location on a busy main road. Ultra-fresh seafood takes pride of place, with particular mention of the mixed fish grill and Spanish *fricassée* of monkfish. Leave room for one of the wicked desserts.

ARCACHON Chez Yvette   €€
59 bd du Général Leclerc, 33120 **Tel** *05 56 83 05 11*

Seafood doesn't come much fresher than at this venerable Arcachon restaurant run by former oyster farmers. Success stories include lamprey *à la bordelaise* (eel-like fish cooked in wine) and roast turbot, but it is hard to resist the spectacular seafood platters. It's wise to book ahead.

ARCINS Le Lion d'Or   €€
11 rte de Pauillac, 33460 **Tel** *05 56 58 96 79*

A small and welcoming village auberge in the heart of the Médoc vineyards north of Margaux. Loved by locals who appreciate the traditional seasonal cooking. Local Pauillac lamb is a springtime favourite, while in autumn the accent is on game. No fixed menus, but prices remain reasonable.

BORDEAUX Bistrot d'Edouard   €€
16 pl du Parlement, 33000 **Tel** *05 56 81 48 87*

On one of Bordeaux's prettiest squares, this fuss-free bistro offers a broad range of inexpensive fixed-price menus. Don't expect gourmet dining, but the food is reliable, covering everything from salads, omelettes, vegetarian dishes and fish to regional specialities. Outside dining in summer.

BORDEAUX Le Café du Musée   €€
Musée d'Art Contemporain, 7 rue Ferrère, 33000 **Tel** *05 56 44 71 61*

Splendid lunch spot on top of the contemporary art museum. Modern decor complements stylish dishes ranging from *foie gras* and oysters to duck spring rolls and sashimi. The Sunday buffet is a must on the Bordeaux scene. Also serves coffee, desserts and light meals until 6pm.

BORDEAUX La Tupina   €€€
6 rue Porte de la Monnaie, 33800 **Tel** *05 56 91 56 37* **Fax** *05 56 31 92 11*

The heart of La Tupina is the open fire over which succulent meats are grilled and in winter a cauldron of soup bubbles away. This is an excellent place to try bordelais specialities such as lamprey in wine, grilled shad or baby eels cooked in olive oil with garlic and hot pepper. Simple, old-fashioned desserts.

COGNAC Les Pigeons Blancs   €€€€
110 rue Jules-Brisson, 16100 **Tel** *05 45 82 16 36*

Owned by the same family since the 17th century, this former post house is renowned for its excellent service, wine and food. The popular daily menu really does change every day. Veal sweetbreads with an aged red Pineau sauce and a glass of VSOP cognac is a sure-fire winner. Fabulous dessert trolley.

COULON Le Central   €€€
4 rue d'Autremont, 79510 **Tel** *05 49 35 90 20* **Fax** *05 49 35 81 07*

A deservedly popular hotel-restaurant in the Marais. Indulge yourself with original dishes such as snail *cassoulet* or rabbit lasagne. More traditional fare includes *foie gras* and lamb with lashings of herbs and garlic – an absolute classic. Portions are generous. Book ahead. Closed Feb.

EUGENIE-LES-BAINS La Ferme aux Grives   €€€€
111 rue Thermes, 40320 **Tel** *05 58 05 05 06* **Fax** *05 58 51 10 10*

The more "rustic" of Michel Guérard's much acclaimed restaurants still serves sublime food. Normally heavy southwestern dishes are reinvented for a modern palate, such as oysters served with ginger shavings and fresh coriander leaves accompanied by a "chantilly" of green tea.

GRENADE-SUR-L'ADOUR Pain Adour et Fantaisie   €€€€
14–16 pl des Tilleuls, 40270 **Tel** *05 58 45 18 80* **Fax** *05 58 45 16 57*

Elegant, Michelin-starred restaurant run by a former pupil of Michel Guérard. Trademark dishes include duck *foie gras* flavoured with local *jurançon* wine and juniper. Fish and seafood changes with the seasons. Good-value lunch menu, and a romantic riverside terrace for summer dining.

ILE D'OLORON L'Ecailler   €€
65 rue du Port, La Cotiniere, 17310 **Tel** *05 46 47 10 31*

On the west coast of the island, looking on to La Cotinière harbour is this hotel and restaurant, which inevitably specialises in seafood, including lobster from its own tank. Other choices on the menu include grilled fish and meat dishes such as the rib steak with coarse sea salt. A terrace and patio-garden allow for outdoor dining.

JARNAC Restaurant du Château

15 pl du Château, 16200 **Tel** *05 45 81 07 17* **Fax** *05 45 35 35 71*

This restaurant near Château Courvoisier is renowned throughout the Cognac region for producing quality regional cuisine. Highlights are the tartare of langoustines and scallops with a mango vinaigrette, guinea fowl with a *morille* stuffing served with aubergine caviar, and a Cognac-laced soufflé for dessert with a Cognac digestif to round things off.

LA ROCHELLE Le Boute en Train

7 rue des Bonnes Femmes, 17000 **Tel** *05 46 41 73 74* **Fax** *05 46 45 90 76*

You are assured a warm welcome at this lively French bistro where all the fresh foodstuffs come from the nearby market. This means a great choice of daily dishes and a menu which changes with the seasons. Fortunately, the chocolate mousse is a standard. Book ahead.

LA ROCHELLE Le Comptoir des Voyages

22 rue St-Jean du Perot, 17000 **Tel** *05 46 50 62 60* **Fax** *05 46 41 90 80*

Another addition to the Coutanceau stable, this time with a colonial theme – potted palms, rattan chairs and flavours from around the world. From the single menu you might start with a carpaccio of red tuna with a tartare of vegetables, followed by saddle of lamb cooked in Guinness and for dessert, chocolate pizza. Simply sublime.

LANGON Claude Darroze

95 cours du Général-Leclerc, 33210 **Tel** *05 56 63 00 48* **Fax** *05 56 63 41 15*

Inside this unassuming hotel-restaurant you'll find wonderfully over-the-top decor and some of the region's best food and wine. Depending on the season, you might be regaled with a hearty stew of lamprey eels served with leeks and a stunning Grand Marnier soufflé, light as air. There's an extensive wine list with a choice of more than 600 wines.

MARGAUX Le Pavillon de Margaux

3 rue Georges Mandel, 33460 **Tel** *05 57 88 77 54*

This wine bar (serving cheeses, *charcuterie* and other tapas) is located in a hotel in one of the principal towns of the Médoc wine-producing region. Full meals *table d'hôte*-style are also served, strictly by reservation only, in the elegant surroundings of the nearby Château Marojallia.

MIMIZAN Hôtel Atlantique

38 av de la Côte d'Argent, 40200 **Tel** *05 58 09 09 42* **Fax** *05 58 82 42 63*

Very popular, modestly priced restaurant in a hotel on the seafront at the north end of the beach. Seafood is a speciality, with good *soupe de poisson* as well as regional gastronomic favourites such as *magret de canard, confit de canard* and wild boar with prunes.

MONT-DE-MARSAN Didier Garbage

RN 134, Uchacq-et-Parentis, 40090 **Tel** *05 58 75 33 66* **Fax** *05 58 75 22 77*

One of France's up-and-coming chefs turns out authentic landaise cuisine in his convivial, slightly rustic restaurant outside Mont-de-Marsan. Look forward to lamprey, elvers (freshwater eels) and expertly crafted fish dishes, in addition to meats and luscious desserts. There's also a bistro for casual dining.

MONTMORILLON Le Lucullus

4 bd de Strasbourg, 86500 **Tel** *05 49 84 09 09* **Fax** *05 49 84 58 68*

A traditional country auberge where the food takes precedence. The set menus change frequently and present plenty of choice, including a vegetarian option. Sample crab and asparagus flan or pork with *foie gras* sauce. The attached brasserie offers cheaper, less formal dining.

NIORT La Table des Saveurs

9 rue Thiers, 79000 **Tel** *05 49 77 44 35* **Fax** *05 49 16 06 29*

Despite its town-centre location and classy cuisine, this popular restaurant offers excellent value for money. Even the cheapest menu includes three courses. This is regional cooking, which means plenty of fish dishes, such as a langoustine crumble or duo of pike-perch and red mullet.

PAULLIAC Château Cordeillan-Bages

Rte des Châteaux, 33250 **Tel** *05 56 59 24 24* **Fax** *05 56 59 01 89*

This popular restaurant in the heart of Bordeaux's vineyards is aspiring to its third Michelin star. The Pauillac lamb is a signature dish, representing traditional cuisine; the molecular cuisine proposes dishes such as hot oyster soufflé and crispy sea water. Well worth a splurge.

POITIERS Le Pince Oreille

11 rue des trois rois, 8600 **Tel** *05 49 60 25 99*

Live music – including jazz, blues and swing – is as much of an attraction as the food and drink in this city-centre "café-concert-restaurant". The menu concentrates on straightforward specialities, notably meat, fish and vegetables grilled *à la plancha,* Brazilian-style to make them crusty and caramelized. Wine tasting events are also held here.

POITIERS Les Bons Enfants

11 bis rue Cloche-Perse, 86000 **Tel** *05 49 41 49 82* **Fax** *05 49 46 05 38*

A charming restaurant decorated with souvenirs from the classroom and old school photographs. The cuisine is traditional with favourites such as veal with girolle mushrooms and shallots, and chocolate mousse. The portions are generous and service is cheerful, but the tables are packed close together in the small dining room. Book ahead.

Key to Price Guide *see p600* **Key to Symbols** *see back cover flap*

ROCHEFORT La Belle Poule
102 av du 11 Novembre, 17300 **Tel** *05 46 99 71 87* **Fax** *05 46 83 99 77*

A modern building made more agreeable thanks to a massive fireplace and lots of greenery. The chef uses herbs and spices to splendid effect in his regionally inspired dishes. Favourites include roast pigeon with stuffed cabbage, and roast scallops perfumed with vanilla.

ROYAN La Jabotière
Esplanade de Pontaillac, 17200 **Tel** *05 46 39 91 29* **Fax** *05 46 38 39 93*

Modern cuisine in a renovated beachfront restaurant. Sample carpaccio of scallops marinated in lime juice and orange confit or fricassée of veal sweetbreads served with a sweet potato gratin, finishing with an apple and apricot soufflé. In summer, the terrace is packed with customers enjoying the excellent lunch deals. Closed Jan.

SABRES Auberge des Pins
Rte de la Piscine, 40630 **Tel** *05 58 08 30 00*

Gorgeous landaise farmhouse run by an adorable family. The oak-lined dining room provides the perfect setting for typical landaise cuisine, ranging from flavourful asparagus and fresh fish to duck in all its guises. Best of all, though, is the boned pigeon stuffed with *foie gras*. Good selection of local wines and armagnac.

SAINTES Relais du Bois St-Georges
Parc Atlantique, 132 Cours Genet, 17100 **Tel** *05 46 93 50 99* **Fax** *05 46 93 34 93*

Two first-class restaurants, part of a hotel on the outskirts of Saintes in big, beautiful grounds with lawns, a tennis court, an indoor pool, a lake, a croquet lawn and piano bar. The gastronomic restaurant serves excellent seafood. The bistro, La Table du Bois, is much cheaper, serving good local dishes.

ST-EMILION L'Envers du Décor
11 rue du Clocher, 33330 **Tel** *05 57 74 48 31* **Fax** *05 57 24 68 90*

Local vignerons rub shoulders with tourists in this delightful little bistro-cum-wine bar. The menu runs the gamut from omelettes and salads to more elaborate regional dishes, or you can choose from daily specials on the chalkboard. Winner of the award for the best wine list in France in its class.

ST-MARTIN-DE-RE La Baleine Bleue
Quai Launay Razilly, Ilot du Port, 17410 **Tel** *05 46 09 03 30* **Fax** *05 56 09 30 86*

The fish couldn't be much fresher at this celebrated portside restaurant. Menus change daily depending on the catch, but typical offerings are scallop carpaccio, home-smoked salmon and cod with lemon confit. For dessert, try the roast figs with spicy ice cream. Closed Jan.

TALMONT L'Estuaire
1 av de L'Estuaire, 17120 **Tel** *05 46 90 43 85*

Situated beside the Gironde estuary (as the name suggests), this restaurant is a short way from the preserved old village of Talmont and its remarkable clifftop church. The menu is particularly strong on traditional fish and seafood dishes. It is also a bar, tearoom and seven-room hotel.

PERIGORD, QUERCY & GASCONY

AGEN Mariottat
25 rue Louis-Vivent, 47000 **Tel** *05 53 77 99 77* **Fax** *05 53 77 99 79*

It comes as a surprise to find this elegant restaurant tucked down a very ordinary backstreet, but inside the 19th-century mansion, with its chandeliers and high ceilings, you're in for a treat. Duck reigns supreme – *assiette tout canard* is the signature dish, alongside succulent Agen prunes and summer fruits.

ALBI Le Jardin des Quatre Saisons
19 bd de Strasbourg, 81000 **Tel** *05 63 60 77 76* **Fax** *05 63 60 77 76*

A gourmet restaurant that won't break the bank, here there are just three menus at lunchtime, each with a wide selection of dishes. At Le Jardin des Quatre Saisons, the cooking is very much seasonal, but among the regular favourites you'll find *foie gras* in various guises, seafood *pot au feu* and roast pigeon.

ALBI Le Vieil Alby
23–25 rue Toulouse-Lautrec, 81000 **Tel** *05 63 38 28 23*

This welcoming and well-priced hotel-restaurant is a good place to try typical local dishes, such as a raddish and pork liver salad, followed by *cassoulet* or perhaps tripe cooked Albi-style. All desserts are home-made. In warm weather, dine in the lovely interior courtyard with its retractable roof.

AUCH Le Papillon
Carrefour de l'Arçon "Au Petit Guilhem", Montaut-les-Creneaux, 32810 **Tel** *05 52 65 51 29*

There are some lovely after lunch walks to be had from this restaurant, which sits in a small village northeast of Auch. Choose from four set menus or *à la carte*, which offers home-made cassoulet, *foie gras* and good fish and seafood options. A small garden has swings for children.

BERGERAC La Flambée

Rte de Périgeux, 49 av Marceau-Fevry, 24100 **Tel** *05 53 57 52 23*

Depending on which of the three set menus you choose, you could opt for smoked herring, smoked salmon, oysters, *foie gras, escargots* or frog's legs as a starter. A good main course to select is the *magret de canard*. Desserts include apple crumble. Also a very relaxing hotel with swimming pool.

BRANTOME Les Frères Charbonnel

57 rue Gambetta, 24310 **Tel** *05 53 05 70 15* **Fax** *05 53 05 71 85*

The restaurant of the Hôtel Chabrol has a well deserved reputation for its upscale regional cuisine and excellent service. Black périgord truffles add style to omelettes and to the house special, pike-perch *vol-au-vent*. These can be enjoyed in the dining room, or on the riverside terrrace. Closed Feb.

BRANTOME Le Moulin de l'Abbaye

1 rte de Bourdeilles, 24310 **Tel** *05 53 05 80 22* **Fax** *05 53 05 75 27*

Dine in luxury on innovative dishes, such as duck *foie gras* poached in walnut liqueur, in this converted mill in a romantic setting on the bank of the Dronne river. Luscious desserts might include a gratin of strawberries with white chocolate. A magical setting and impeccable service. Closed Nov–Apr.

CAHORS Auberge du Vieux Cahors

144 rue St Urcisse, 46000 **Tel** *05 65 35 06 05*

Regional cuisine is the focus of the menu in this 15th-century auberge in the historical town centre of Cahors. Specialities include duck *foie gras*, beef carpaccio flavoured with truffle, Burgundy snails and a wide choice of fish dishes. There are a few terrace tables for outdoor dining.

CAHORS Le Balandre

5 av Charles-de-Freycinet, 46000 **Tel** *05 65 53 32 00* **Fax** *05 65 53 32 26*

For fine dining in Cahors, head for the restaurant in the Hôtel Terminus, where 1930s decor complements refined Quercy cuisine. Rustic dishes, such as roast Quercy lamb laced with juniper juice, are given a modern twist. Or try duck cannelloni served with walnut *rillette*. Cahors wines feature strongly.

CASTRES Café du Pont

Les Salvages, 81100 **Tel** *05 63 35 08 21*

Les Salvages lies about 6-km (4-miles) northeast of Castres en route to the scenic rock formations of the Sidobre. This restaurant has a shady terrace on the bank of the River Agout. Seasonal ingredients and local produce predominate on the menu. Upstairs there are five guest bedrooms.

CHAMPAGNAC-DE-BELAIR Le Moulin du Roc

Champagnac-de-Belair, 24530 **Tel** *05 53 02 86 00* **Fax** *05 53 54 21 31*

A romantic waterside setting plus top-notch cuisine make this gourmet restaurant stand out. The lunch menu (not served on Sundays) offers particularly good value. Iced garden herb soup and roast breast of guinea fowl with *foie gras* are just two of the treats in store.

CONDOM La Table des Cordeliers

1 rue des Cordeliers, 32100 **Tel** *05 62 68 43 82* **Fax** *05 62 28 15 92*

Modern cuisine using top-quality local produce is prepared with talent at this contemporary restaurant housed in the cloisters of a 13th-century convent. Depending on the season, enjoy *cèpe* mushroom *tartelette*, succulent duck and an apple dessert accompanied by iced nougat with prunes. Good choice of regional wines and armagnacs.

CORDES-SUR-CIEL Bistrot Tonin'ty

Hostellerie du Vieux Cordes, Haut de la Cité, 81170 **Tel** *05 63 53 79 20*

One of several restaurants and hotels in the medieval town of Cordes which are owned by master *pâtissier* Yves Thuries. There is an enchanting courtyard shaded by an ancient wisteria and, in summer, tables are also set out on the terrace overlooking the valley. The menu focuses on salmon and duck.

DOMME L'Esplanade

Le Bourg, 24250 **Tel** *05 53 28 31 41* **Fax** *05 53 28 49 92*

Welcoming and efficient service, well-presented dishes and an unbeatable panorama of the Dordogne valley keep customers coming back to this hotel-restaurant. Ask for a window or terrace table. Signature dishes include *foie gras de canard* with truffles in season, and the delectable chocolate gâteau.

FIGEAC La Cuisine du Marché

15 rue Clermont, 46100 **Tel** *05 65 50 18 55* **Fax** *05 65 50 18 55*

In a former wine cellar in the heart of Figeac's medieval core, this attractive restaurant takes pride in using only the freshest ingredients. Star billing goes to its wide range of fish dishes, though you'll also find plenty of local classics, all prepared in the open kitchen. The set menus represent good value.

FOURCES Château de Fources

Fources, 32250 **Tel** *05 62 29 49 53*

Fources is one of Gascony's most delightful villages. Its Renaissance château, beside the river, is now a hotel-restaurant where you can dine in a magnificent dining room with broad stone walls or at shaded tables outside. The hotel boasts palatial rooms, some with four-poster beds. Reservations essential.

Key to Price Guide *see p600* **Key to Symbols** *see back cover flap*

FRANCESCAS Le Relais de la Hire

11 rue Porte-Neuve, 47600 **Tel** *05 53 65 41 59* **Fax** *05 53 65 86 42*

The chef of this upmarket village restaurant near Nérac makes full use of his herb garden and edible flowers to create dishes that are a feast for all the senses. Try the temping artichoke soufflé with *foie gras* or oriental-flavoured roast turbot with caramelized onions, followed by desserts that look almost too good to eat.

GAILLAC Les Sarments

27 rue Cabrol, 81600 **Tel** *05 63 57 62 61* **Fax** *05 63 57 62 61*

The brick arches and exposed beams of this 14th-century wine vault in the heart of old Gaillac provide a striking setting for the beautifully presented food that tends towards the traditional, but with imaginative touches. Particularly fine desserts. Good opportunity to sample Gaillac wines at reasonable prices.

ISSIGEAC La Brucelière

Place de la Capelle, 24560 **Tel** *05 53 73 89 61*

In a charming village 15 km (9 miles) from Bergerac is this former coaching inn with a traditional dining room. The menu includes regional produce, with a particular emphasis on seafood such as lobster and crayfish. The dishes are creative, with a touch of exoticism and the atmosphere is relaxed. A spacious, shady terrace overlooks the garden.

LACAVE Le Pont de l'Ouysse

Le Pont de l'Ouysse, 46200 **Tel** *05 65 37 87 04* **Fax** *05 65 32 77 41*

A chic restaurant-with-rooms not far from Rocamadour. It's in a lovely riverside setting, sheltered under an imposing cliff. Inventive variations on local dishes include hot pot of duck liver with Paimpol beans. There are good-value lunch menus, but it is magical dining under the trees at night.

LES EYZIES-DE-TAYAC Au Vieux Moulin

2 rue du Moulin-Bas, 24620 **Tel** *05 53 06 94 33* **Fax** *05 53 06 98 06*

Dine on well-priced regional cuisine in a 17th-century mill with its rustic interior, or beside the river in peaceful, flower-filled gardens. Among the simple but beautifully prepared dishes, choose from *escalope* of *foie gras* with truffle sauce or truffle risotto, with pigeon casserole to follow. Closed Nov–Apr.

MANCIET La Bonne Auberge

Pl du Pesquerot, 32370 **Tel** *05 62 08 50 04* **Fax** *05 62 08 58 84*

The same family has been running this small hotel-restaurant for over 40 years, and it shows in the quality of the creative southwestern cuisine. The platter of local specialities is a great introduction to Gascon fare, and menus change regularly. Fabulous Armagnac list – some over 100 years old.

MARMANDE Le Moulin d'Ane

Virazeil, 47200 **Tel** *05 53 20 18 25*

Consistently excellent seasonal cuisine in this restored 18th-century water mill near Marmande. Typical southwestern dishes include succulent blonde d'Aquitaine beef, tender fillets of duck breast, and apple tart laced with armagnac. Be sure to try the exceptionally plump and juicy Marmande tomatoes.

MONBAZILLAC La Tour des Vents

Moulin de Malfourat, 24240 **Tel** *05 53 58 30 10* **Fax** *05 53 58 89 55*

Book a window or terrace table to enjoy the wonderful views over the Dordogne valley to Bergerac. Good-value menus offer local specialities, including *foie gras* and duck, but also fish and seafood. There is even a vegetarian option. Treat yourself to a glass of sweet Monbazillac with *foie gras* or dessert. Closed Jan.

MONTAUBAN Au Fil de l'Eau

14 quai de Dr Lafforgue, 82000 **Tel** *05 63 66 11 85* **Fax** *05 63 91 97 56*

An ancient building housing a spacious modern restaurant on the banks of the river. The menu is composed of traditional dishes such as pan-fried *foie gras* accompanied by gingerbread, *omelette aux truffes* and duckling served with a rich red wine sauce. Good regional wines.

PERIGUEUX Le Clos Saint-Front

5 rue de la Vertu, 24000 **Tel** *05 53 46 78 58* **Fax** *05 53 46 78 20*

Reservations are recommended at this restaurant near Périgueux's prehistory museum, with its inventive, inexpensive cuisine and peaceful courtyard garden. According to the season, you could opt for lamb flavoured with spices and rosemary, or sole served with an onion, thyme and lemon compote. Reservations recommended.

PERIGUEUX L'Essentiel

8 rue de la Clarté, 24000 **Tel** *05 53 35 15 15* **Fax** *05 53 35 15 15*

Another city-centre restaurant where it's wise to reserve. The dining room's sunny southern colours complement dishes such as roast *foie gras* with gnocchi. There's also a pretty, pocket-sized garden. The wine list offers more than 100 wines to choose from.

PUJAUDRAN Le Puits St-Jacques

Pl de la Mairie, 32600 **Tel** *05 62 07 41 11* **Fax** *05 62 07 44 09*

Michelin-starred restaurant where you can feast on pan-fried *foie gras* with gingerbread, or Limousin beef with shallot confit. Neither pretentious nor too pricey if you opt for a set menu. Rustic chic ambience, with lots of red Toulousain brick work and a pleasant patio.

PUJOLS La Toque Blanche

⬛⬛⬛⬛⬛   €€€€

Pujols, 47300 **Tel** *05 53 49 00 30*

A renowned gourmet restaurant in a medieval village between Agen and Villeneuve-sur-Lot. The best place to eat is in the air-conditioned conservatory, which has panoramic views. The menu changes with the seasons but is always based on local products. Dessert choices include home-made ice creams and sorbets. A hotel adjoins the restaurant.

PUYMIROL Les Loges de l'Aubergade

⬛⬛⬛⬛⬛⬛⬛   €€€€€

52 rue Royale, 47270 **Tel** *05 53 95 31 46* **Fax** *05 53 95 33 80*

One of the southwest's great restaurants is set in a beautiful medieval lodge on a hilltop. Here Michel Trama creates sublime dishes such as *foie gras*, pan fried and served with toasted hazelnuts. Equally theatrical setting with Baroque drapes and exposed stone, and a gorgeous Italianate courtyard.

ROCAMADOUR Sainte Marie

⬛⬛   €€

Pl des Senhals, 46500 **Tel** *05 65 33 63 07*

There is a splendid view over the Alzou valley from the terrace of this hotel-restaurant, which clings to the rock in the middle of Rocamadour. Local Quercy and southwestern dishes using fresh produce make up the menu – home-made cassoulet and *confit de canard* – with options for children available. Inexpensive "express" menu at lunchtimes.

SARLAT La Couleurvrine

€

1 pl de la Bouquerie, 24200 **Tel** *05 53 59 27 80*

A hotel and restaurant housed in one of the towers of the town's old ramparts. Starters include duck *foie gras* and pâté of hare. Main courses include scallops, pan-fried monkfish, stuffed mushrooms, and venison. For less formal dining there is a bistro serving an inexpensive dish of the day and staging jazz recitals in the evening.

SORGES Auberge de la Truffe

⬛⬛⬛⬛   €€€

Le Bourg, 24420 **Tel** *05 53 05 02 05* **Fax** *05 53 05 39 27*

Sorges is the self-proclaimed truffle "capital" of France, and this auberge is the perfect place to sample Périgord's "black diamond". The top-price menu features truffles with every course. Less expensive fare is on offer, too, and the set menus start at a reasonable price. Truffle-hunting weekends are offered.

ST-MEDARD Le Gindreau

⬛⬛⬛⬛⬛⬛   €€€€

Le Bourg, 46150 **Tel** *05 65 36 22 27* **Fax** *05 65 36 24 54*

In a hamlet northwest of Cahors, Alexis Pélissou has created one of the region's finest restaurants. Using top-quality local produce, he reinvents traditional standards for modern tastes. Meals are served in the former schoolhouse or on the terrace shaded by chestnut trees. Big choice of local wines. Closed 18–26 Oct & 20 Dec–12 Jan.

TOULOUSE Brasserie Flo Les Beaux Arts

⬛⬛⬛   €€€€

1 quai de la Daurade, 31000 **Tel** *05 61 21 12 12* **Fax** *05 61 21 14 80*

An authentic and bustling brasserie serving a broad range of dishes, from salads and seafood to southwestern favourites. To start, you could opt for a flavoursome dish of scallops baked with chanterelle mushrooms, followed by a seafood *pot-au-feu*, and prune-and-armagnac ice cream. The menu changes regularly.

TOULOUSE Les Jardins de l'Opéra

⬛⬛⬛⬛   €€€€

1 pl du Capitole, 31000 **Tel** *05 61 23 07 76* **Fax** *05 61 23 63 00*

Gourmet dining at its most refined in the restaurant of the Grand Hôtel de l'Opéra. Hushed tones and widely spaced tables create a suitably reverent atmosphere for dishes such as whole lobster garnished with a seaweed crust, or figs cooked in Banyuls wine and filled with vanilla ice cream. Impeccable service.

TURSAC La Source

⬛⬛   €€

Le Bourg, 24620 **Tel** *05 53 06 98 00*

If you're looking for somewhere to eat while exploring the Vézère valley, try this friendly little village restaurant. Simple, tasty dishes include wild mushroom soup and walnut pie. There's a vegetarian menu, using produce fresh from the garden, and some international options, for a change. Closed Tue & Wed.

VAREN Le Moulin de Varen

⬛⬛⬛⬛   €€

Le Bourg, 82330 **Tel** *05 63 65 45 10*

A converted mill in the Aveyron gorges, near the lovely town of St-Antonin-de-Noble-Val. There's no carte, but plenty of choice on the set menus, all of which offer excellent value for money. The food is beautifully presented and the atmosphere relaxed. Closed Sun dinner & Mon.

THE PYRENEES

AINHOA La Maison Oppoca

⬛   €€€

Le Bourg, 64250 **Tel** *05 59 29 90 72*

This hotel and restaurant is situated in the centre of one ot the most beautiful villages in the French Basque country. *Foie gras* and suckling pig are on the menu with, of course, gâteau basque for dessert. Upstairs there are ten light and comfortable guest rooms with large beds.

Key to Price Guide *see p600* **Key to Symbols** *see back cover flap*

ASCAIN Atelier Gourmand
Place de Fronton, 64310 **Tel** *05 59 54 46 82*

Sitting at the foot of a church in the picturesque Pyrenean village of Ascain is this lively, trendy restaurant. The menu includes Basque favourites. Take your pick from finger-licking tapas, *pipérade* and *axoa* (a spicy Basque stew) or fillet of sea bream.

AUDRESSEIN L'Auberge d'Audressein
Castillon, 09800 **Tel** *05 61 96 11 80*

This restaurant-with-rooms in a former blacksmith's forge has various set menus named after the local valleys. Dishes include typical Ariège recipes. There are seven guestrooms looking on to the river, the valley or the village. A great place to come if you are in search of quiet countryside and the simple life.

AX-LES-THERMES L'Auzeraie
1 av Théophile Delcassé, 09110 **Tel** *05 61 64 20 70*

A restaurant and 33-room hotel in a pleasant spa town, which makes a handy stop on the way from the Ariège to Andorra or Spain. At lunchtime from Monday to Friday you can take pot luck with an inexpensive menu of *entrée du jour* and *plat du jour*. A children's menu is also available.

BAGNERES DE LUCHON Les Caprices d'Etigny
30 bis allées d'Etigny, 31110 **Tel** *05 61 94 31 05*

Fine mountain views from the tables in the conservatory-style dining room. The menu stresses local lamb and beef grilled over a wood fire, and trout from the nearby Lac d'Oo presented in a number of different styles. The good wine list emphasizes the finer wines of southwestern France.

BAREGES Auberge du Lienz (Chez Louisette)
Rte Lienz, 65120 **Tel** *05 62 67 17* **Fax** *05 62 92 65 15*

A good choice for an *après-ski* meal, at the foot of the local pistes, with stunning views of the Pic du Midi de Bigorre. Menu mainstays include mutton stewed in Madeira wine, trout and sumptuous soufflés. The *pièce de résistance* is the ham *garbure* – a hefty dish of ham, bacon and cabbage.

BAYONNE Le Bayonnais
38 quai des Corsaires, 64100 **Tel** *05 59 25 61 19* **Fax** *05 59 59 00 64*

With a handful of tables on the terrace and more inside, this small restaurant has a well-deserved reputation for imaginative dishes, such as baby lamb, sole with lentils, chestnut soup with *foie gras*, and pastilla with figs. Well-chosen wine list emphasizes regional wines and major names from elsewhere in France.

BAYONNE Auberge du Cheval Blanc
68 rue Bourgneuf, 64100 **Tel** *05 59 59 01 33*

Stray from the set menu at this well-regarded hotel in the riverside Petit Bayonne quarter. The menu changes with the seasons, with local dishes such as *xamano* (ham and mashed potatoes), fine Atlantic seafood, interesting soups and casseroles and delicious desserts. Respectable wine list. Closed Feb, 2nd wk Jul, 1st wk Aug & 2nd wk Nov.

BIARRITZ Chez Albert
Port des Pêcheurs, 64200 **Tel** *05 59 24 43 84* **Fax** *05 59 24 20 13*

From the terrace there are superb views of Biarritz's picturesque fishing harbour and surrounding cliffs and beaches, making this fine seafood restaurant popular. Arrive early for the best tables. Piled platters of seafood, freshly caught lobster, sole, sea bream, tuna and sardines are among the treats here. Closed Jan.

BIARRITZ Le Sissinou
5 av Maréchal Foch, 64200 **Tel** *05 61 65 10 50 42*

Managed by chef Michel Cassou-Debat – a veteran of some of France's top establishments – Sissinou is one of Biarritz's most talked-about restaurants. Elegant in a minimalist way. Wonderful food such as tuna carpaccio and a fricassée of veal sweetbreads served with carrots flavoured with balsamic vinegar and desserts that invite indulgence.

FOIX Le Phoebus
3 rue Irénée Cros, 09000 **Tel** *05 61 02 87 87*

This restaurant on the banks of the Ariège river has big windows overlooking the water towards the castle, which is floodlit at night. Roast pigeon, and iced tomato and raspberry soup are two of the specialities here. Closed Mon, Sat lunch, Sun dinner & 23 Jul–23 Aug.

LARRAU Etchemaïté
Larrau, 64560 **Tel** *05 59 28 61 45* **Fax** *05 59 28 72 71*

This family-run mountain inn and restaurant has a spectacular location and a cosy dining room with open fireplace and great views. Favourites are lamb and duck dishes garnished with apples, *cèpes*, or *foie gras* and there is usually a good choice of Atlantic seafood, too. Varied wine list.

LOURDES Le Magret
10 rue des 4 Freres Soulas, 65100 **Tel** *05 62 94 20 55*

One of the better places to eat in Lourdes city centre. The menu varies according to the season with Gascon black pork, Pyrenean lamb, *magret de canard* (duck breast), veal, lamb and duck as reliable specialities. Regional wines from the nearby Jurancon and Madiran regions accompany the meal. Vegetarians are catered for.

MIREPOIX Les Remparts
6 cours Louis Pons Tande, 09500 **Tel** *05 61 68 12 15*

Chef Nicolas Coutand serves inventive dishes, inspired by traditional Pyrenean and Mediterranean cuisine. The restaurant has two dining rooms: one in a cosily converted cellar, the other with a wide, wood-beamed ceiling and colourful paintwork. Robust classic dishes of the region. Children's menu is available.

MONTSEGUR Costes
Le Village, 09300 **Tel** *05 61 01 10 24*

This simple café-restaurant is part of a hotel beneath the crag that is home to Montségur's ruined castle. Organic ingredients are used in tasty local dishes, mostly prepared on the open wood fire – game, duck, wild mushrooms, pork and, of course, *cassoulet*. Just the thing after the steep clamber to the castle. Phone to check winter opening.

ORTHEZ Au Temps de la Reine Jeanne
44 rue Bourg-Vieux, 64300 **Tel** *05 59 67 00 76* **Fax** *05 59 69 09 63*

This rustic eating-place is attached to a comfortable country inn. The menu is equally rustic, with plenty of local dishes, including offal and rich meaty dishes. Liver, black pudding, suckling pig, *foie gras*, *cassoulet* and monkfish all make an appearance. Good value.

PAU Chez Pierre
16 rue Louis Barthou, 64000 **Tel** *05 59 27 76 86* **Fax** *05 59 27 08 14*

Chez Pierre exudes 19th-century elegance and prides itself on the old-fashioned, club-like atmosphere that harks back to Pau's heyday as a British expatriate's hideaway. Classic French regional cooking along with some surprises, such as cod with Espelette peppers, and an extensive wine list.

ST-BERTRAND-DE-COMMINGES L'Oppidum
Rue de la Poste, 31510 **Tel** *05 61 88 33 50*

Located in the old town just below St-Bertrand's celebrated cathedral, is this small, friendly hotel and restaurant serving good, unpretentious food. Featuring on the menu are the local stew, *garbure*, *foie gras* and trout. All accompanied by local wines. There are 15 simple guest bedrooms upstairs.

ST GAUDENS La Connivence
Chemin Ample, Valentine, 31800 **Tel** *05 61 95 29 31*

The outdoor terrace with its fine views is one of the main attractions of La Connivence. The bill of fare is traditional, as is the atmosphere, but helpings are generous and the wine list, though limited, is well chosen. Service is prompt and friendly. An unpretentious spot for lunch or dinner. Closed Mon, Sat lunch & Sun dinner.

ST-JEAN-DE-LUZ Chez Pablo
5 rue Mlle Etcheto, 64500 **Tel** *05 59 26 37 81*

One of the resort's oldest restaurants and run by the same family since 1932. It serves traditional Basque cuisine prepared with seasonal ingredients, specializing in fish and seafood. Good dishes to opt for are cod croquettes, cod-stuffed peppers, prawns with rice and *chipirones* in their own ink. Home-made desserts. Closed Wed.

ST-JEAN-DE-LUZ Restaurant Txalupa
Pl Corsaires, 64500 **Tel** *05 59 51 85 52*

Txalupa is a favourite local restaurant. Expect the best catches of the Atlantic coast prepared in dishes such as king prawns in a hot vinegar dressing, sardines in tomato salsa, oysters and lots of other shellfish, tuna, cod and monkfish. Extensive wine list, and imaginative desserts. Book ahead.

ST-JEAN-DE-PIED-DE-PORT Relais de la Nive
4 pl Charles de Gaulle, 64220 **Tel** *05 59 37 04 22*

The most conspicuous place to eat in St-Jean-de-Pied-de-Port, and as a result always busy with passing pilgrim traffic, is this *brasserie-crêperie*, which picturesquely overhangs the river between the new bridge and the old. It serves inexpensive meals as well as snacks such as pancakes, sandwiches and ice cream.

ST-LARY SOULAN La Grange
13 rte Autun, 65170 **Tel** *05 62 40 07 14*

This old-fashioned farm building at St-Lary-Soulan in the high Pyrenees is a delightful place to stop for lunch. A well-appointed and attractively decorated restaurant, it exudes rustic charm. The traditional bill of fare includes robust meaty main dishes, with game, beef and lamb grilled over a wood fire. Closed Nov–Apr.

ST-LIZIER De la Tour
Rue du Pont, 09190 **Tel** *05 61 66 38 01*

This place overhanging the River Salat is the most convenient place to eat while visiting the historic village of St-Lizier. On the menu is trout from the Couserans region, lamb, duck and home-made pâtés and terrines. A good, inexpensive midday meal is served on weekdays and there is also a children's menu.

ST-SULPICE-SUR-LEZE La Commanderie
Pl de l'Hôtel de Ville, 31410 **Tel** *05 61 97 33 61* **Fax** *05 61 97 32 60*

In a fortified *bastide* village famous for its medieval architecture, La Commanderie has fans all over the world for its innovative cooking. Chef Jean Pierre Crouzet creates dishes such as vegetable ragoût with *morille* mushrooms and ewe's cheese, and roast pigeon with garlic and juniper. Lovely, spacious dining room. Closed 2 weeks in Dec.

Key to Price Guide *see p600* **Key to Symbols** *see back cover flap*

SARE Baratxartea
J.B. Fagoaga, 64310 **Tel** *05 59 54 20 48*

An ancient Basque house is the setting for this hotel and restaurant in the exceptionally pretty town of Sare. The menu is rich in home produce: vegetables are from the garden, *charcuterie* is prepared over the winter months, hams are cured in the barn and jams are home-made.

TARBES L'Ambroisie
48 rue Abbé Torné, 65000 **Tel** *05 62 93 09 34* **Fax** *05 62 93 09 24*

The top restaurant in Tarbes attracts plaudits for dishes ranging from roast pigeon to *foie gras* in peach compote. Housed in a 19th-century church building, the restaurant offers a changing menu, brisk service and food worth lingering over. Wine list features the finer Madiran domains. Book ahead.

LANGUEDOC-ROUSSILLON

AIGUES-MORTES Le Café des Bouzigues
7 rue Pasteur, 30220 **Tel** *04 66 53 93 95*

It is usually easy to find a table in this large traditional bistro. The menu is strongly Mediterranean, with plenty of regional seafood, Provençal dishes and reasonably priced wines from Provence and Languedoc. Lamb with thyme and garlic and peach salad are among the outstanding dishes.

AIGUES-MORTES Marie Rosé
13 rue Pasteur, 30220 **Tel** *04 66 53 79 84*

A delightful restaurant located in an ancient presbytery with a kitchen garden. The chef prepares Provençale dishes with a delicate touch. Talent and accomplishment shine through in dishes such as the violet flan, sea bream and *calamars à la plancha,* and baby lamb with artichokes. There is also a small selection of well-chosen wines.

ANDUZE Auberge Les Trois Barbus
Rte de Mialet, Generargargues, 20140 **Tel** *04 66 61 72 12*

Deep in the Cevennes above the Camisards valley, with spectacular views, this rustic hotel-restaurant has the added attraction of a pool that diners may use for an after-lunch dip. Traditional Cevennes and Languedoc dishes as well as more adventurous offerings. Delicious *foie gras* and truffles. Closed Feb–mid-Mar.

ARLES SUR TECH Les Glycines
Rue du Jeu de Paume, 66150 **Tel** *04 68 39 10 09* **Fax** *04 68 39 83 02*

Arles sur Tech is a place that beckons you to pause for a while, and this hotel-restaurant is an excellent place for a lunch stop. It is very good value for money, with a lovely wisteria-covered patio and a menu that emphasizes regional cuisine and local produce, with plenty of ham, pork and sausage dishes. Closed Jan.

BEZIERS Octopus
12 rue Boieldieu, 34500 **Tel** *04 67 49 90 00* **Fax** *04 67 28 06 73*

Béziers has no shortage of quality places to eat, but Octopus stands out from the crowd. With fresh, chic decor, this restaurant feels very welcoming. The modern menu is balanced by a well-chosen list of wines from the Languedoc-Roussillon vineyards.

BIZE MINERVOIS La Bastide Cabezac
18–20 hameau Cabezac, 11120 **Tel** *04 68 46 66 10*

Attractive 18th-century staging post with an elegant restaurant. The chef is motivated and dynamic, producing outstanding dishes such as delicate crayfish tart, and monkfish roasted in a pinenut crust flavoured with curry and served with Camargue rice and a light lemongrass sauce.

CAP D'AGDE Le Brasero
Port Richelieu, rue Richelieu, 34300 **Tel** *04 67 26 24 75* **Fax** *04 67 26 24 75*

Overlooking the port with its yachts and fishing boats, Le Brasero has a well-earned reputation for good-value seafood. Its seafood platters are generous and varied, and other marine delights include grilled fish of all kinds, fresh anchovies, squid, tuna and swordfish. Grilled meat dishes also available. Book ahead.

CARCASSONNE Le Languedoc
32 allée d'Iéna, 11000 **Tel** *04 68 25 22 17* **Fax** *04 68 25 04 14*

This restaurant appeals to people who like their surroundings and cuisine to be traditionally French, even a little staid. The menu features all the regional classics, and Le Languedoc is one of the best places for *cassoulet* – the hearty bean and sausage casserole that is the Languedoc's most typical dish. Closed Jan.

CARCASSONNE Les Bergers d'Arcadie
70 rue Trivalle, 11000 **Tel** *04 68 72 46 01*

A friendly unpretentious little restaurant close to the ramparts of the magnificent citadel. Cuisine is based on Languedoc produce and combines old and new influences to create an interesting menu. Specialities include poached *foie gras,* and *cochon de lait* glazed with caramelized honey and served with seasonal mushrooms. Delicious desserts.

CARCASSONNE Le Parc Franck Putelat
80 chemin des Anglais, 11000 **Tel** *04 68 71 80 80*

The chef, with the help of his young kitchen team, has stamped his personality on this gastronomic restaurant in a comparatively short time. Contemporary food is served in a relaxed yet refined atmosphere. Expect spectacular fish dishes such as spider crab, sea urchin and caviar prepared with simplicity. Gourmet desserts. Good-value set menus.

COLLIOURE La Balette
114 rte de Port-Vendres, 66190 **Tel** *04 68 82 05 07* **Fax** *04 68 82 38 08*

Specialities at this cheerful restaurant, part of the Relais des Trois Mas, include soused Collioure anchovies marinaded in Banjul wine vinegar, terrine of *foie gras* and chestnuts, sea bass served with chicory crumble, and pigeon cooked in honey. Set above the picturesque bay of Collioure. Book ahead in summer.

COLLIOURE Le 5e Péché
18 rue Fraternité, 66190 **Tel** *04 68 98 09 76*

The best produce Catalogne has to offer combined with the skill of the Japanese chef make this small restaurant a great success. An original range of Japanese-inspired dishes include carpaccio of freshly caught fish, stir-fried tuna with a Banyuls-flavoured sauce and a *crème Catalane* of caramelized artichokes. Book ahead.

CUCUGNAN Auberge du Vigneron
2 rue Achille Mir, 11350 **Tel** *04 68 45 03 00* **Fax** *04 68 45 03 08*

The dining room is in the cool wine cellar of a charming inn in the heart of an attractive Corbières village. The menu is Catalan-influenced, with fresh seafood and duck prepared in a variety of ways, even with figs or peaches. The wine list is unpretentious, with a good choice of the muscular reds of the Corbières domains.

FONTJONCOUSE L'Auberge du Vieux Puits
Av St Victor, 11360 **Tel** *04 68 44 07 37*

The small village of Fontjoncouse in the Corbière countryside has been made famous by this superb restaurant. Chef Gilles Goujon is both energetic and ambitious. The menu ranges from a simple, *salade niçoise* to more complex dishes such as lobster-stuffed cannelloni. Game also features when in season. Excellent wines.

GIGNAC Restaurant Matthieu de Lauzun
3 bd de l'Esplanade, 34150 **Tel** *04 67 57 50 83*

At this restaurant, west of Montpellier, chef Matthieu de Lauzon prepares inventive Mediterranean cuisine. Dishes are carefully prepared and harmonious. Vegetables with prawn tempura and cucumber gazpacho is a sweet success. Desserts are delicious. Good wines from up-and-coming producers.

LE BOULOU L'Hostalet de Vivès
Rue de la Mairie, Vivès, 66490 **Tel** *04 68 83 05 52*

Not far from the artist town of Céret lies this lovely auberge serving authentic Catalan cuisine. A favourite with the locals, it has a good choice of well-prepared dishes at reasonable prices – a real bonus in this region popular with tourists. Discover Catalan dishes such as *cargolade* (grilled snails), and rabbit served with *aioli*.

MARAUSSON Parfums de Garrigues
37 rue de l'Ancienne Poste, 34370 **Tel** *04 67 90 33 76*

Comfortable dining room with sunny tones and a pretty shady courtyard in the centre of a sleepy village, near to Beziers. The fine southwest cuisine includes the best regional produce and reflects the scents of the Garrigue. The menu includes a refreshing goat's milk *crème* with Bouzigues oysters, and veal served with grilled vegetables.

MINERVE Relais Chantovent
17 Grande Rue, 34210 **Tel** *04 68 91 14 18*

The terrace of this restaurant offers diners stunning panoramic views over the Gorges du Brian. There is a choice of menus, each with a different emphasis: regional menu, duck menu, aromatic herb menu and truffle menu. The wine list is extensive and contains many high-quality vintages. Reservations are advised.

MONTPELLIER Petit Jardin
20 rue Jean-Jacques Rousseau, 34000 **Tel** *04 67 60 78 78*

The menu is locally-inspired in this pretty restaurant in Montpellier's historic quarter. The "Little Garden" is tucked away from the street, and diners may eat indoors, looking out at its greenery, or in the garden among the flowers, fruit trees and potted herbs. Dishes include fish soup and lamb with garlic and rosemary.

MONTPELLIER Chez Boris
20 rue de l'Aiguillerie, 34000 **Tel** *04 67 02 13 22*

The most talked about bistro in town, and rightly so. Located near the Musée Fabre in the centre of the city, the atmosphere here is friendly and relaxed. Classic dishes have been reinvented: think *cochon au lait* (pork in milk) is cooked with spices. The portions are generous, and wine can be ordered by the glass.

MONTPELLIER La Diligence
2 pl Pétrarque, 34000 **Tel** *04 67 66 12 21*

A sophisticated restaurant in the city centre, located on a historic square between the place de la Comédie and the place de la Préfecture. La Diligence occupies a 14th-century listed building with graceful stone vaulting. There is a choice of set menus: lunch, taster or gourmet. Good wine list.

Key to Price Guide *see p600* **Key to Symbols** *see back cover flap*

MONTPELLIER Jardin des Sens

11 av St Lazarre, 34000 **Tel** *04 99 58 38 38* **Fax** *04 99 58 38 39*

Probably the best restaurant in town. Continuously innovative, with regional specialities given a new twist, such as terrine of lobster with mango and melon, and some delicious juxtapositions such as pigeon with a cacao sauce. The wine list features finer wines of the Corbiéres slopes and the domaines of the Languedoc.

NARBONNE Le Table de St-Crescent

Domaine St-Crescent, 68 ave Général Leclerc, 11100 **Tel** *04 68 41 37 37*

An address to impress, with a superb, seasonally influenced menu that combines the best produce of the Mediterranean with that of the Languedoc hinterland, with wines to match. Ravioli of Leucate oysters, roast duck with Collioure anchovies and more. Perfect for a special evening.

NARBONNE Restaurant Le H

Rte de Narbonne Plage, 11100 **Tel** *04 68 45 28 50*

Heading out of the town centre towards the beach, you will come across this lovely restaurant. Surrounded by rows and rows of La Clape vines sits Gérard Bertrand's wine domaine. The room is rustic yet chic with stone walls and thick wooden beams, which provides the perfect setting for a carpaccio of duck or a chunk of beef.

NIMES Le Cheval Blanc

1 pl des Arènes, 30000 **Tel** *04 66 76 19 59*

A lively wine bar with a classic brasserie-style interior, comfy banquet seating and some Art-Deco features in the historic centre of Nîmes. The wine list is extensive, featuring established names as well as lesser known southern Rhône and Languedoc wines. Typical fare – *brandade* (smoked fish with cream), pig's trotters and *côte de boeuf* – is well-prepared.

NIMES L'Orée du Parc

755 rue Tour de l'Evèque, 30000 **Tel** *04 66 84 50 57*

The restaurant of the L'Orangerie hotel stands in the middle of a park filled with ancient trees, about a 15-minute stroll from Nîmes' historic town centre. A relaxed and comfortable setting, there is a conservatory with a cosy atmosphere and a terrace for summer dining. Dishes are traditional but sophisticated. Good wine list.

NIMES Aux Plaisirs des Halles

4 rue Littré, 30000 **Tel** *04 66 36 01 02* **Fax** *04 66 36 08 00*

With a particularly good regional wine list from the Languedoc, Corbières, Minervois, Provence and Hérault, Aux Plaisirs des Halles is decorated with clean, modern lines. French cuisine with a Provençal influence by chef Sébastien Granier. Closed Sun, Mon; 2 wks Oct–Nov & some public hols.

NIMES Le Lisita

2 bd des Arènes, 30000 **Tel** *04 66 67 29 15* **Fax** *04 66 67 25 32*

Le Lisita is not to be missed. This is one of the most popular restaurants in Nîmes, serving cutting-edge food and an outstanding wine list. The surroundings are attractive too, with modern design set off by old stone walls in two rooms, plus an attractive terrace facing Les Arènes. Closed Sun, Mon.

PERPIGNAN La Galinette

23 rue Jean Payra, 66000 **Tel** *04 68 35 00 90*

The spacious, refined, modern dining room has a formal air. By contrast, in the kitchen is a chef passionate about food and prepared to take risks. Seafood is a speciality: prawns with coriander, red mullet tart and fillet of fish *à la plancha*. An expert sommelier is on hand to help you choose from an impressive selection of regional wines.

PERPIGNAN Le Chap'

18 bd Jean Bourrat, 66000 **Tel** *04 68 35 14 14*

Gourmet restaurant in one of Perpignan's smart hotels. The decor in the dining room is contemporary and the menu is equally chic and modern. Technically superb dishes include risotto *à la chlorophyll*, and fish crumble flavoured with ginger and lemongrass. Some old favourites still feature for those feeling less adventurous.

PEZENAS L'Entre Pots

8 av Louis-Montagne, 34120 **Tel** *04 67 30 00 00*

Frequented by locals, this trendy restaurant housed in a former wine warehouse has a convivial, intimate atmosphere. Unpretentious gourmet cuisine is based on the regional produce and flavours of the Garrigue. The wine list is deliberately short with an emphasis on the best Languedocs. Book ahead.

PORT CAMARGUE Le Carré des Gourmets

Pointe de la presqu'ile, 30240 **Tel** *04 66 53 36 37*

This gourmet restaurant forms part of the Le Spinaker hotel complex. A contemporary dining room boasts a lovely terrace facing out over the marina. The chef successfully combines Camargue and Catalan influences with dishes like *pata negra* cured ham, and pigeon stuffed with pine nuts. Great Languedoc wines.

PORT-VENDRES La Cote Vermeille

Quai Fanal, 66660 **Tel** *04 68 82 05 71* **Fax** *04 68 82 05 71*

This super seafood restaurant has a great quayside location with views of the fishing harbour and coastline. Fishing nets, lobster pots and stuffed fish adorn the walls, and fresh fish, shellfish, squid and lobster adorn the menus. Closed Thu dinner, Sun dinner & Mon.

PRADES Le Jardin d'Aymeric   ⬛📘♿   €€
3 av Général de Gaulle, 66500 **Tel** *04 68 96 53 38*

Refined Catalan cuisine prepared using fresh regional produce and perfumed with local mountain herbs. The menu revisits traditional dishes such as saddle of lamb with thyme accompanied by a light parsley-flavoured sauce, and seasonal fruit gratin. Good selection of regional Roussillon wines at reasonable prices.

QUILLAN Cartier   🅿🧍🍷   €€
31 bd Charles de Gaulle, 11500 **Tel** *04 68 20 05 14*

A family-run restaurant and hotel in a town that serves as the crossroads for routes across the eastern Pyrenees. The menu concentrates on traditional dishes and ingredients of the region, including duck, *foie gras*, *cassoulet*, wild mushrooms and truffles. Limoux, Fitou and Corbières vintages dominate the wine list.

SAILLAGOUSE La Vielle Maison Cerdane   🧍🍽   €€€
Pl de la Cerdagne, 66800 **Tel** *04 68 04 72 08*

This venerable restaurant and hotel, in an old coaching inn, has been run by the Planes family since 1895. The chef serves up Catalan specialities, including *caneton aux raisin* (duck casserole), *ollada* (rustic meat and vegetable stew), and *crème catalane* for dessert. There is also a good selection of tapas. Closed Sun dinner & Mon in winter.

SETE La Palangrotte   🧍📘   €€€
Quai de la Marine, 34200 **Tel** *04 67 74 80 35* **Fax** *04 67 74 97 20*

In Sète there is nowhere more pleasant to sample the famous oysters and other shellfish of the Etang de Thau lagoon than this cheerful marine-themed restaurant. Some of the best seafood on the coast, better for lunch than dinner. Closed Mon, Sun dinner (except Jul, Aug).

SOURNIA Auberge de Sournia   🧍🍴   €€
4 rte de Prades, 66730 **Tel** *04 68 97 72 82*

In the heart of the Pyrénées-Orientales is this quaint auberge run by an enthusiastic young couple. The food has regional flourishes, enlivened with a modern touch. Duck in all its guises is the speciality; try the savoury duck breast stuffed with goat's cheese. Other dishes include scallops, red mullet and king prawns.

ST MARTIN DE LONDRES Les Muscardins   🅿🧍📘🍷   €€€€
19 rte Cevennes, 34380 **Tel** *04 67 55 75 90* **Fax** *04 67 55 70 28*

Surprising to find such a sophisticated dining experience in a little country town, but Les Muscardins is worth a special expedition for monkfish accompanied by risotto perfumed with yucca flowers, and carpaccio of smoked Aubrac veal. The surroundings are elegant. Good selection of regional wines.

UZES La Taverne   🧍🍴🍷   €€
Rue Sigalon, 30700 **Tel** *04 66 22 47 08*

Located in the pedestrian area in the centre of the town, this atmospheric restaurant has a vaulted ceiling and a pretty terrace that is perfect for summer dining. It serves local specialities, such as *brandade de Nîmes* (salt-cod dip), and *filet de taureau de Camargue* (Camargue steak). There is an extensive wine list.

VILLEFRANCHE DE CONFLENT Auberge St-Paul   🧍♿🍴🍷   €€€€€
7 pl Eglise, 66500 **Tel** *04 68 96 30 95* **Fax** *04 68 96 05 60 30*

Originally a 13th-century chapel, this village restaurant has an attractive terrace and a charming, rustic dining room. The menu is cosmopolitan, with fresh local produce and a sophisticated wine list, with fine Burgundy and Roussillon vintages. Closed Sun dinner, Mon, Tue.

PROVENCE AND THE COTE D'AZUR

AIX-EN-PROVENCE Brasserie Léopold   🧍📘♿🍴🍷   €€€
2 av Victor Hugo, 13090 **Tel** *04 42 26 01 24* **Fax** *04 42 38 53 17*

Classic French brasserie with dozens of tables and bustling waiters, on the ground floor of the comfortable Hôtel Saint-Christophe in the centre of Aix. A great place for a full-scale meal, a snack or just a drink at any time of day or year. Strong on regional cuisine and traditional brasserie fare.

AIX-EN-PROVENCE Mas d'Entremont   🅿🧍♿🍴🍷   €€€€
Quartier des Platrières, 13090 **Tel** *04 42 17 42 42* **Fax** *04 42 21 15 83*

The food is imaginative, the list of Provençal wines is good, and the setting in a lush park above Aix at Célony is delightful. Plenty of regional meat and fish. In summer, dine on a lovely terrace overlooking the gardens, with fine views. The dining room has huge picture windows overlooking the park. Closed Sun dinner, Mon lunch, Nov–Apr.

AIX-EN-PROVENCE Yamato   🅿📘♿🍴🍵🍷 €€€€
21 av des Belges **Tel** *04 42 38 00 20*

Run by Koji and Yuriko Somaya, this is arguably the most authentic Japanese restaurant in Aix-en-Provence. Whether you dine in the Zen garden or in the airy dining room, you'll be transported far from France to the Orient. The sushi is superb, as are the less predictable dishes such as *chawanmushi* (grilled eel). Closed Mon–Tue lunch.

AIX-EN-PROVENCE Le Clos de la Violette

10 av Violette, 13100 **Tel** *04 42 23 30 71* **Fax** *04 42 21 93 03*

This is an elegant address in a chic mansion standing in its own gardens: tranquil, intimate and perfect for a romantic evening. People do dress up a little to eat here. The wine list is extensive (and very strong on local and Provençal wines) and the menu is Provençal with a modern edge. Closed Sun, Mon.

ARLES La Gueule du Loup

39 rue des Arènes, 13200 **Tel** *04 90 96 96 69* **Fax** *04 90 96 96 69*

La Gueule du Loup ("the Wolf's Maw") is more welcoming than its ferocious name implies, with a menu that changes virtually daily and serves up exquisite Provençal cuisine in charmingly rustic surroundings. Prompt service and a good choice of wines. Not cutting-edge cuisine, but good at what it does. Closed Sun, Mon lunch & Jan.

ARLES Lou Marques

Bd Lices, 13631 **Tel** *04 90 52 52 52* **Fax** *04 90 52 52 53*

Lou Marques – the restaurant of the venerable Hôtel Jules César – is one of the best places to eat in Arles, with a central location, pleasant terrace with tables under white umbrellas, and a bill of fare that concentrates on classic Provençal dishes. Dignified surroundings. Closed Mon, Sat lunch, Sun dinner.

ARLES L'Atelier de Jean-Luc Rabanel

7 rue des Carmes, 13200 **Tel** *04 90 91 07 69*

Arrive with a large appetite at this small restaurant in the centre of Arles; there is a minimum of seven courses at lunch and 13 at dinner. Jean-Luc Rabanel works almost exclusively with organic produce from his own vegetable garden and each dish is a miniature work of art. Reserve ahead or drop into the casual bistro next door. Closed Mon–Tue.

AVIGNON La Fourchette

17 rue Racine, 84000 **Tel** *04 90 85 20 93* **Fax** *04 90 85 57 60*

Much loved locally, La Fourchette is a quirky little place with walls adorned by antique forks and festival posters. The menu is traditional Provençal, with a modern take on dishes such as duck breast in garlic and vegetable crêpes. Excellent choice of cheeses. Closed Sat, Sun, Aug. Reservations required.

AVIGNON Le Petit Bedon

70 rue Joseph-Vernet, 84000 **Tel** *04 90 82 33 98* **Fax** *04 90 85 58 64*

Le Petit Bedon, just inside the walls of Avignon's old quarter, has a good reputation for tasty dishes such as poached vegetables with tapenade and *pistou*, *bourride de loup* (monkfish stew), and courgette purée with garlic. Amiable atmosphere. Provençal wines. Closed Sun lunch (all year), Mon lunch Nov–Apr.

AVIGNON Christian Etienne

10 rue Mons, 84000 **Tel** *04 90 86 16 50* **Fax** *04 90 86 67 09*

The wine list is strong on Provençal and Rhône Valley vintages, the location in the medieval heart of Avignon near the Papal Palace is hard to beat, and the food is equally unbeatable in this highly regarded restaurant, with menus that emphasize imaginatively treated local produce. Closed Sun, Mon (except in Jul).

AVIGNON La Mirande

4 pl de la Mirande, 84000 **Tel** *04 90 14 20 20* **Fax** *04 90 86 26 85*

One of the most delicious places to eat in Avignon, with tables outside beneath olive trees and the floodlit walls of the Palais des Papes or indoors in a grand dining room in what was once a cardinal's palace. Extensive, dazzling menu and wine list. Friendly service. Book ahead. Closed Tue, Wed; mid-Jan–mid-Feb.

BIOT Les Terraillers

11 rte Chemin Neuf, 06410 **Tel** *04 93 65 01 59*

Sophisticated restaurant serving dishes that are rich in every sense of the word, flavoured with truffles and the herbs of surrounding hills. The *foie gras escalope* is not to be missed, and the lamb is a culinary triumph. The wine list highlights some of the better *vins de France* of Provence. Closed Wed, Thu, Nov.

BONNIEUX La Bastide de Capelongue Restaurant Edward Loubet

84480 **Tel** *04 90 75 89 78* **Fax** *04 90 75 93 03*

Two Michelin stars keep this fine restaurant ahead of the local competition. Reservations essential, especially during the Cannes Film Festival. The menu changes with the seasons and celebrates the produce and flavours of the Luberon hills and the Mediterranean coast such as truffles *en croûte* and roasted venison. Closed Wed; Nov–Mar.

CAGNES Fleur de Sel

85 Montée de la Bourgade, 06800 **Tel** *04 93 20 33 33*

Delightful small restaurant serving unpretentious cooking at affordable prices – especially the set menus. Attractively rustic surroundings – the restaurant is in the heart of the village of Haut de Cagnes, next to the medieval church. Adequate choice of inexpensive wines. Closed Wed.

CAGNES Entre Cour et Jardin

102 Montée de la Bourgade, 06800 **Tel** *04 93 20 72 27*

At this small, charming restaurant in the medieval centre of Cagnes, the chef/owner serves classic local dishes, which follow the seasons. The food is very tasty and portions are generous. Service is friendly. Changing exhibitions of paintings by local artists adorn the whitewashed walls.

CANNES Le Pastis

28 rue du Commandandement André, 06400 **Tel** *04 92 98 95 40*

With an interior that feels like a cross between an American diner and a French bistro, Le Pastis is perfect for a casual meal at any time of day. The menu is mostly Mediterranean with dishes such as *daube à la niçoise* (beef stew), but you will also find Caesar salad and steak tartare. Near the main shopping street and beach. Closed Sun lunch.

CANNES Ondine

15 bd de la Croisette, 06400 **Tel** *04 93 94 23 15*

Beach restaurants usually have modest gastronomic aspirations, but Ondine is an exception. Chef Jean-Pierre Silva visits the market every day to hand-select the freshest ingredients. The focus is on fish, with dishes such as crab salad and turbot with spring vegetables. Excellent wine list. Closed Wed.

CANNES La Cave

9 bd de la République, 06400 **Tel** *04 93 99 79 87*

La Cave has been running since 1989 and is popular with both locals and tourists. Its large choice of traditional, Provençal dishes is made from fresh, locally sourced ingredients. The wine list has over 350 references, including an excellent selection from local producers. Closed Sat lunch, Sun.

CANNES Le 38

38 rue des Serbes, 06400 **Tel** *04 92 99 79 60* **Fax** *04 93 99 26 10*

It is difficult to eat more lavishly than in the posh surroundings of the Royal Gray, where diners can expect some of the finest cooking in Cannes – but at a surprisingly affordable price, and with courteous service. The accent is on Provençal flavours and Mediterranean seafood. Extensive wine list. Closed Sun, Mon.

CANNES La Palme d'Or

73 la Croisette, 06400 **Tel** *04 92 98 74 14*

Children are not actually barred from this restaurant of the stars, nor is it essential to wear a tie – but diners who are not dressed to impress may feel self-conscious here. The food is imaginative and superb, with an impressive, costly wine list. Reservations required. Closed Sun, Mon, Jan–Mar.

CARPENTRAS Chez Serge

90 rue Cottier, 84200 **Tel** *04 90 63 21 24* **Fax** *04 90 60 30 71*

Chez Serge is a surprising discovery in sleepy Carpentras – a mix of old and new that is reflected in its style and menu. There's inventive, refined international cooking and evening wine tastings. Fresh fish is cooked in imaginative ways and wild mushrooms feature often on the menu.

CASTELLANE Auberge du Teillon

Rte Napoléon - La Garde, 04120 **Tel** *04 92 83 60 88* **Fax** *04 92 83 74 08*

Pleasant country inn 6 km (4 miles) from the busy tourist hot-spot of Castellane. The bill of fare is unprententious and changes according to the seasons, emphasizing traditional Provençal dishes, simply prepared including home-smoked salmon. Rooms available. Closed Nov–Mar; Sun dinner, Mon (except Jul & Aug).

CAVAILLON Restaurant Prévôt

353 av de Verdun, 84300 **Tel** *04 90 71 32 43*

A gastronomic treat in the heart of the pretty market town of Cavaillon, where chef Jean-Jacques Prévôt is mad about melons – his restaurant has them as a decorative motif and there is even a set menu dedicated to the gourd family. Melon and scallops are recommended. Good portfolio of wines. Closed Sun.

CHATEAU-ARNOUX La Bonne Etape

Chemin du Lac, 04160 **Tel** *04 92 64 00 09* **Fax** *04 92 64 37 36*

This charming inn, located in a nondescript market town, has an outstanding array of dishes and emphasizes fresh local produce, especially lamb. The wine list is lengthy, featuring vintages from almost every French region. The dining room is decorated with paintings and tapestries. Closed Mon, Tue in Sep–Jun, Jan–mid-Feb.

CHATEAUNEUF DU PAPE La Mère Germaine

3 rue Commandant Lemaitre, 84230 **Tel** *04 90 83 54 37* **Fax** *04 90 83 50 27*

Surrounded by vineyards, this restaurant has an outstanding list of local and regional wines. The cooking is classic Provençal, servings are generous and La Mère Germaine offers good value and friendly service. Go for lunch to enjoy the view.

COLLOBRIERES La Petite Fontaine

1 pl de la Republique, 83610 **Tel** *04 94 48 00 12* **Fax** *04 94 48 03 03*

This simple restaurant is in the centre of Collobrières, a sleepy hill village in the heart of the Massif des Moaures. Specialities include chicken and garlic *fricassée*, rabbit with fresh herbs and duck with wild mushrooms, complemented by wines from the local wine co-operative. Closed Sun dinner, Mon, last two weeks Sep.

DIGNE-LES-BAINS La Chauvinière

52 rue Hubac, 04000 **Tel** *04 92 31 40 03*

This small, traditional restaurant is situated in the old part of the town. The chef uses the very best seasonal ingredients, and the menu includes freshly prepared *foie gras* dishes and a range of home-made *pâtisserie*. The atmosphere is welcoming, and there is a pretty terrace for outdoor dining.

Key to Price Guide *see p600* **Key to Symbols** *see back cover flap*

DIGNE-LES-BAINS Le Grand Paris

19 bd Thiers, 04000 **Tel** *04 92 31 11 15* **Fax** *04 92 32 32 82*

This rather grand hotel-restaurant has an air of bourgeois respectability that may be a little off-putting to some – for a more relaxed atmosphere, sit outside on the terrace. Classic food, such as *brandade* (mashed potatoes) with peppers, lamb *mignonette*, and pigeon. Good choice of Rhône and Provençal wines. Closed lunch Mon–Thu, Dec–Mar.

EZE Troubadour

4 rue du Brec, 06360 **Tel** *04 93 41 19 03*

Pleasant, traditional restaurant in the centre of Eze's labyrinth of stone buildings that can only be reached on foot. The Troubadour has three small dining rooms, tucked inside medieval walls and offering a respite from the summer sun. Set menus and *à la carte* options feature classic Provençal cooking. Closed Sun, Mon, mid-Nov–mid-Dec.

FAYENCE Le Moulin de la Camandoule

Chemin de Notre Dame, 83440 **Tel** *04 94 76 00 84* **Fax** *04 94 76 10 40*

In an ancient olive mill, this hotel-restaurant benefits from a peaceful and idyllic setting. Chef Philippe Choisy offers several menus and *à la carte* dishes of high quality; the flavours are Provençal and the ingredients all fresh and seasonal. Lunch is often served on the terrace. Closed Wed, Thu.

FAYENCE Le Castellaras

Rte de Seillans, 83440 **Tel** *04 94 76 13 80* **Fax** *04 94 84 17 50*

Le Castellaras serves dishes that balance tradition with innovation: lamb fillet with tarragon sauce; scampi marinated in olive oil, lemon and tarragon; polenta in truffle oil. The wine list draws mainly from the Côtes de Provence vineyards. Closed Mon, Tue (except Jul–Aug). Book ahead. Closed Jan.

GIGONDAS Les Florets

Rte des Dentelles, 84190 **Tel** *04 90 65 85 01* **Fax** *04 90 65 83 80*

The terrace of this hotel-restaurant has fine views of the Dentelles de Montmirail. Well-presented regional cooking is complemented by the fine wines of the Gigondas region. The restaurant is popular, so arrive early or book ahead. Closed Wed, Jan–mid-Mar.

GRASSE Bastide St Antoine

48 av H. Dunant, 06130 **Tel** *04 93 70 94 94* **Fax** *04 93 70 94 95*

Jacques Chibois's superb restaurant is attached to his delightful boutique-hotel in Grasse's quartier St-Antoine, with a menu that will excite gourmets and lovers of inventive French cuisine – duckling, truffles, and an inventive approach to vegetables. There is also an excellent, mainly Provençal wine list.

JUAN LES PINS Les Pêcheurs

10 bd Maréchal Juin, Cap d'Antibes, 06160 **Tel** *04 92 93 13 30* **Fax** *04 92 93 15 04*

The Hotel Juana has recently exchanged its celebrated rooftop restaurant for this luxurious restaurant on the beach with high-tech touches and a vast terrace. Chef Francis Chauveau's cuisine is delicious and creative. Indulge in the grilled sea bass with lemons and marinated vegetables. Closed Tues, Wed (except Jul–Aug).

LA CADIERE D'AZUR Hostellerie Bérard

Av Gabriel Peri, 83740 **Tel** *04 94 90 11 43* **Fax** *04 94 90 01 94*

This renowned hotel-restaurant in the converted buildings of an 11th-century convent has a fine view over the Bandol vineyards. Owners and chefs Rene and Jean François Bérard do marvellous things with fish and shellfish, including a sublime mussel soup flavoured with saffron. Local Bandol wines. Closed Mon, Tue, Jan.

MARSEILLE Chez Madie (Les Galinettes)

138 quai du Port, 13002 **Tel** *04 91 90 40 87* **Fax** *04 91 31 44 74*

A Marseillais institution for generations (it is now in the hands of the granddaughter of the eponymous founder). Legendary *bouillabaisse*, *bourride* and other fish dishes are complemented by tripe and pigs' trotters. Definitely not for vegetarians, nor for picky children. Closed Sun.

MARSEILLE Toinou

3 cours Saint-Louis, 13001 **Tel** *04 91 33 14 94*

This is the place for seafood platters in Marseille. Set on a lively square, Toinou started over 40 years ago as a takeaway counter. It still does a roaring takeaway trade, though many people now opt to enjoy a meal in the simple dining room. For a taste of everything, try the Toinou Spécial for two people.

MARSEILLE Les Arcenaulx

25 cours d'Estienne d'Orves, 13000 **Tel** *04 91 59 80 30* **Fax** *04 91 54 76 33*

In the old warehouse district north of the Vieux Port, Les Arcenaulx is housed in the former premises of a 17th-century publisher. A great place to start or end an evening's bar-hopping in nearby streets. Dishes include scallops with grilled almonds, and steak tartare. Closed Sun.

MARSEILLE Restaurant Michel

6 rue des Catalans, 13007 **Tel** *04 91 52 30 63* **Fax** *04 91 59 24 05*

Bouillabaisse is the speciality of the house at this fine, busy brasserie. Other fish dishes include *bourride*, sardines, and the always reliable catch of the day, fresh and simply grilled. Popular with locals – get there early to be sure of a table. Wine list includes names from Bandol and Cassis.

MARTIGUES Le Miroir 🚶🖼 €€€
4 rue Marcel Galdy, 13500 **Tel** *04 42 80 50 45*

Facing the fishing port of Martigues, with its colourful wooden boats, this restaurant specializes in fish. There is plenty of space, with six dining rooms and two terraces – choose an outside table for maximum charm. Cooking is simple yet tasty, with dishes such as mussels with fennel and saffron. Closed Sat lunch; Sun, Mon & Wed dinner & Jan.

MENTON Le Mirazur 🅿🗎♿🖼🍴 €€€€€
30 av Aristide Briand, 06500 **Tel** *04 92 41 86 86*

Argentinian-born Mauro Colagreco is a promising chef who has settled in Menton, where his contemporary restaurant boasts its own tropical garden. Like a painter, he decorates his plates with dabs and flourishes, often using wild herbs and flowers picked from the mountains. There is a good-value lunch menu. Closed Mon–Tue; Dec–Feb.

MONACO Maya Bay 🅿🗎♿🖼🍴 €€€€
24 av Princesse Grace, 98000 **Tel** *00 37 7 97 70 74 67* **Fax** *00 37 7 97 77 58 10*

Chef Olivier Streiff's punk haircut and black eyeliner is a tribute to the Doors, and his cooking has an equally rock 'n' roll style. A typical dish is duckling with banana, dried fruits, confit apple and roasted juniper berries. The dining room has a lush, tropical feel and the restaurant has a separate sushi bar. Closed Mon–Sun; Nov.

MOUGINS Le Moulin de Mougins 🗎🖼🍴 €€€€€
Notre-Dame-de-Vie, rte départementale 3, 06250 **Tel** *04 93 75 78 24* **Fax** *04 93 90 18 55*

Alain Llorca's two-Michelin-star restaurant is the place for a special treat, with superb, imaginative cuisine that leans towards seafood prepared in new ways. The wines include some of the very best of Provence. The garden terrace is adorned by modern sculptures. Reservations are essential. Closed Mon & Tue lunch, Sun dinner.

MOUSTIERS La Treille Muscate 🖼🍴 €€€
Pl de l'Eglise, 04360 **Tel** *04 92 74 64 31* **Fax** *04 92 74 63 75*

Excellent food such as *pistou* of vegetables in this lovely little Provençal bistro, with a great location on the main square of one of the region's prettiest villages. Good value, with a choice of set menus and a decent wine list, La Treille Muscate is especially pleasant for a relaxed al fresco lunch. Closed Wed; Dec–Feb.

NICE Bistrot d'Antoine 🗎🖼 €€€
27 rue de la Préfecture, 06300 **Tel** *04 93 85 29 57*

Armand Crespo, formerly of Lou Cigalon in Valbonne, is the man behind the revival of this Niçoise bistro. He can often be seen buying produce at the nearby market. Meat off the grill is the main event: try the duck *magret* or the veal kidneys, which could make an offal-lover out of anyone. Well-chosen wines. Closed Sun–Mon; Aug.

VENCE Le Pigeonnier 🚶🗎🖼 €€€
3 pl du Peyra, 06140 **Tel** *04 93 58 03 00*

At this traditional restaurant serving local cuisine the menu includes a large selection of fish, seafood and meat dishes. In summer diners can enjoy the sunny terrace, while in winter the dining room is warmed by a large open fire. Closed Mon, Sun dinner (except Jul & Aug); Jan, Nov.

VENCE Les Bacchanales 🚶♿🖼 €€€
247 av de Provence **Tel** *04 93 24 19 19*

Christophe Dufau made his name in Tourrettes-sur-Loup before moving his restaurant into this slightly-hard-to-find villa on the edge of Vence. His cooking is original without resorting to unnecessary flourishes. Typical of his style is a starter of caramelized melon with crumbled ricotta and spicy *soubressade* sauce. Closed Tue–Wed.

VILLEFRANCHE-SUR-MER L'Oursin Bleu 🗎♿🖼🍴 €€€
11 quai Courbet, 06230 **Tel** *04 93 01 90 12* **Fax** *04 93 01 80 45*

A bubbling aquarium in the foyer hints that this cheerful little eating place puts the accent on fresh fish. The location is delightful, on the quayside, with tables under umbrellas on the terrace and a dining room decorated with seafaring memorabilia. The ideal place for a long, lazy, summer lunch. Closed Tue; Nov–Mar.

CORSICA

AJACCIO Pampasgiolu 🗎🖼 €€
15 rue de la Porta, 20000 **Tel** *04 95 50 71 52.*

Book ahead at this popular eating place in the old city, with its attractive, rustic dining rooms and small terrace. Try the *spuntini* (snack) platters of fish or meat local specialities or go for the veal with olives. Good desserts including chestnut fondant. Closed lunch, Sun.

AJACCIO Le 20123 🚶🗎🖼 €€€
2 rue su Roi du Rome, 2000 **Tel** *04 95 21 50 05*

Named for the tiny Corsican town of Pila-Canale, this restaurant aims to bring an authentic taste of the village to the city. You can eat on the lantern-lit terrace, in the dining room filled with bric-a-brac or at a long shared table in the cellar. Try the *charcuterie* and hearty meat stews. Closed lunch; Mon.

Key to Price Guide *see p600* **Key to Symbols** *see back cover flap*

BASTIA Brasserie La Réserve
Port de Toga, 20600 **Tel** *04 95 31 05 35*

Overlooking the port, this modern brasserie is popular with locals, and is the ideal spot for a simple, leisurely lunch, while watching the fishing boats drift in and out of the harbour. The chef and staff are very friendly, the food is good, and the portions are generous. Closed Sun.

BASTIA A Casarella
6 rue Ste Croix, 20600 **Tel** *04 95 32 02 32*

Hidden in the maze of streets in the citadel area, this is a reliable place to try Corsican cuisine with the occasional luxury touch, as in *brocciu* (the local fresh cheese) cooked with *foie gras*. Among the chef's other specialities are stuffed sardines, veal roasted with herbs and Corsican *crème brûlée*. Closed Sat lunch; Sun; Oct–Apr.

BONIFACIO Le Goeland Beach
Plage de la Tonnara **Tel** *04 95 73 02 51*

In the middle of a nature reserve, Tonnara beach creates a breathtaking setting for this waterfront restaurant. The speciality is fish grilled over the wood fire (priced by weight), but you can also try typically Corsican dishes such as aubergines baked with tomato sauce. Drop into the snack bar at any time of day. Closed Nov–Apr.

CALVI Le Bout du Monde
Plage du Calvi, 20260 **Tel** *04 95 65 15 41*

Excellent food at this friendly but classy beach spot. You'll be spoiled for choice between seafood platters, langoustine ravioli, scallops in orange butter, grilled rib of beef or huge salads, followed by caramelized apple tart or chestnut cream. Closed dinner in winter.

CORTE U Museu
13 Quart Quatre Fountains, 20250 **Tel** *04 95 61 08 36*

At the foot of the citadelle in the old town, this large restaurant has several dining rooms, including a tree-shaded terrace. There is a wide choice of dishes ranging from pizzas, pastas and salads to traditional Corsican dishes of white beans and lamb, *brocciu*-stuffed lasagne (stuffed with a Corsican cheese) and grilled meats with herbs. Closed Nov–Apr.

ILE ROUSSE A Siesta
Promenade à Marinella, 20220 **Tel** *04 95 60 28 74* **Fax** *04 95 60 27 03*

Fresh seafood is the pride of this trendy beach restaurant. On hot nights they'll move the tables directly onto the beach so you can dine under the stars on spidercrabs, lobsters or *bouillabaisse*. Other choices include seafood ravioli and carpaccio of fish. Excellent desserts and wine list. Closed Nov–Mar.

PORTO VECCHIO Le Lodge
Quai Pascal Paoli, Port de Plaisance, 20137 **Tel** *04 95 22 47 93*

This trendy restaurant next to the harbour attracts a young crowd, especially in the evenings, when the atmosphere is very lively. The cooking is traditional and of good quality, with generous portions. Service is relaxed and friendly. Great cocktails are served at the bar. Closed Feb.

PORTO VECCHIO Le Bistro
4 Quai Pascal Paoli, Port de Plaisance, 20137 **Tel** *04 95 70 22 96*

Lively eating spot situated in the yachting harbour in the lower town. Pretty dining room and large terrace. Fresh seafood with a choice of red mullet with anchovies and tomatoes, sea bream or grilled spiny lobster. Excellent *tartare* of beef or civet of wild boar. There's a new tapas bar and a good choice of *crêpes suzettes*. Closed Feb & Sun.

PORTO VECCHIO Casadelmar
Rte de Palombaggia **Tel** *04 95 72 34 34*

In a contemporary luxury hotel a few minutes from the centre of Porto Vecchio, this restaurant makes luxurious use of seasonal, mostly local ingredients. Dishes often have an Italian slant, as in raviolini of beef tartare with aged pecorino and 25-year-old balsamic vinegar. The hotel also has a more casual restaurant. Closed Nov–Apr.

PROPRIANO Chez Parenti
10 av Napoléon **Tel** *04 95 76 12 14* **Fax** *04 95 76 27 11*

Run since 1935 by the Parenti family, this restaurant was originally a fisherman's shack – it still has a modest façade, but the terrace overlooking the sea will soon make you forget it. The speciality is freshly caught seafood, though you will also find delicious meat dishes. Save room for the Corsican cheeses. Closed Mon lunch & Sun dinner; Nov–Apr.

SARTENE Auberge Santa Barbara
Alzone (3 km [2miles] out of Sartène on the road to Propriano), 20100 **Tel** *04 95 77 09 06* **Fax** *04 95 77 09 09*

Outdoor eatery in lovely gardens, owned by Corsica's foremost female chef, Gisèle Lovichi. Choose between home-made *charcuterie* or country soup with its vegetable salad, and stuffed leg of lamb or saddle of lamb with herb crust. Finish with *fiadone*, a dessert made with Corsican cheese, lemons and eggs. Closed mid-Oct–Mar; Mon.

ST-FLORENT La Rascasse
Quai d'Honneur, 20217 **Tel** *04 95 37 06 99* **Fax** *04 95 35 00 08*

Inventive cooking in this smart fish restaurant in a prime position on the port. Ensconce yourself on the terrace and study the yachts as you wait for your order of fish soup, seafood risotto or grilled squid. Try the classic *bouillabaisse* or a grilled lobster, and leave room for one of the sublime desserts. Closed Wed (except Jul & Aug).

Shopping in France

Shopping in France is a delight. Whether you go to the hypermarkets and department stores, or seek out the small specialist stores and markets, you will be tempted by stylish French presentation and the quality of goods on offer. Renowned for its food and wine, France also offers world-famous fashion, perfume, pottery, porcelain and crystal. This section provides guidelines on opening hours, and the range of goods stocked by the different types of stores. There are also details of quintessentially French products which are worth hunting down and a size conversion chart to aid clothes shopping.

Olive Oil from Baux

Fresh nectarines and melons on sale at a market stall

OPENING HOURS

Food shops open anywhere between 7–8am and close around noon for lunch. In the north, the lunch break generally lasts for 2 hours; in the south, it is 3–4 hours (except in resorts, where it is shorter). After lunch, most food shops re-open until 7pm or later.

Bakeries open early and close early, although many stay open until 1pm or later, to catch the late baguette buyers and to serve a range of lunchtime snacks.

Supermarkets, department stores and most hypermarkets remain open all day, with no lunchtime closure.

General opening hours for non-food shops are 9am–6pm Monday through Saturday, often with a break for lunch. Many of these shops are closed on Monday mornings, and the smaller shops may stay closed all day. In the tourist regions, however, shops usually open every day in high season.

Sunday is by far the quietest shopping day, although most food shops (and newsagents) are open in the morning. Virtually every shop in France is closed on Sunday afternoon.

HYPERMARKETS AND DEPARTMENT STORES

Hypermarkets (*hypermarchés* or *grandes surfaces*) can be found on the outskirts of every sizeable town: look for signs indicating *centre commercial*. Much bigger than supermarkets, they sell mainly groceries, but their other lines include clothing, home accessories and electronic equipment. They also sell discount petrol (gasoline). **Carrefour**, **Casino**, **Auchan**, **Leclerc** and **Intermarché** are the biggest.

Department stores (*grands magasins*), such as **Monoprix** and **Franprix** are usually found in town centres. The more upmarket **Printemps** and **Galeries Lafayette** also have out-of-town locations.

A local bakery, which often sells pastries as well as bread

SPECIALIST SHOPS

One of the pleasures of shopping in France is that specialist food shops continue to flourish, despite the influx of supermarkets and hypermarkets. The *boulangerie* (bakery) is frequently combined with a *pâtisserie* selling cakes and pastries. The *traiteur* sells prepared foods. *Fromagers* (cheese shops) and other shops specializing in dairy products (*produits laitiers*) may be combined, but the *boucherie* (butcher) and *charcuterie* (pork butcher-delicatessen) are often separate shops. For general groceries go to an *épicerie* or *alimentation*, but don't confuse this with an *épicerie fine*– a delicatessen.

Cleaning and household products are available from a *droguerie*, while hardware is bought from a *quincaillerie*. The term *papeterie* (stationer) covers both the expensive, specialist retailers and their hypermarket equivalents.

MARKETS

This guide lists the market day for every town featured in the Area by Area section. To find out where the market is, ask a passerby for *le marché*. Markets are held in the morning and usually finish promptly at noon. Look for local producers, including those with only one or two special items to sell, as their goods are often more reasonably priced and of better quality than stalls with multiple items. By law, price tags include the origin of all produce: *pays* means local. Chickens from Bresse are marketed wearing a red, white and blue badge with the name of the producer. If you are visiting markets over several weeks, look for items just coming into season, such as fresh walnuts, the first wild asparagus, early artichokes or wild strawberries. At the market, you can also buy spices and herbs, some offbeat peculiarities (such as decorative cabbages), shoes and clothing.

The year is full of seasonal regional markets in France, specializing in such things as truffles, hams, garlic, *foie gras* and livestock. *Foires artisanales* may be held at the same time as the seasonal markets, selling local produce and crafts.

Sausages and cheeses, regional specialities on offer in a Lyon market

REGIONAL PRODUCE

French regional specialities are available outside their area of origin, but it is more interesting to buy them locally as their creation and flavour reflect the traditions, tastes and climate of the region.

Provence, in the south, prides itself on the quality of its olive oil, the best of which is made from the first cold pressing, lovingly decanted every day for a week. If you cannot get to a niche olive oil producer in Provence, head to **Oliviers et Co** which has branches throughout the country, and sells an excellent selection of oils. Be sure to indulge in a tasting session to sample the flavours. In the temperate north, the delicious Camembert cheese is the product of fresh Norman milk that has been cured for at least 3 weeks.

Popular drinks are also associated with particular regions. Pastis, made from aniseed, is popular in the south. Calvados, made in Normandy from apples, is popular in the north. Crème

Pastis 51, drunk in the south

de Fruit de Dijon, the secret ingredient to many a good cocktail or dessert, comes in many flavours (from peach to wild strawberry) in addition to the well-known black-currant – **Crème de Cassis**. Visit local producers to buy good versions of this thick, alcoholic syrup.

To a large extent, location determines the quality of regional produce. For example, the culinary tradition of Lyon *(see pp380–1)*, France's premier gastronomic city, stems from the proximity of Charolais cattle, Bresse chickens and pork, wild game from La Dombes, and the finest Rhône Valley wines.

Alongside sachets of dried herbs from Provence and plaited strings of garlic and onions, be sure to buy the seasoning loved by all self-respecting francophile cooks – salt from the Ile de Ré *(see p416)* or Guerande. If you happen to be visiting the area, check out the salt flats and pick up the crumbly coarse grains at a local market. The Fleur de Sel is a delicate flaky variety and the Sel Marin is a grey, coarser type of salt.

BEAUTY PRODUCTS

French women are renowned for their beauty, and there is a plethora of good beauty products in France. The major French labels, such as **Chanel** and **Guerlain**, are available overseas, but

die-hard cosmetics fans should scour the local beauty counters to find special products that are only on sale in France.

While in Paris, beauty junkies must visit the Chanel store on the rue Cambon and the Guerlain store on the Champs Elysées to buy scent that is only available in those particular stores. Throughout the rest of the country, supermarket brands such as Evian, Eau Thermale d'Avene and Barbara Gould are huge hits with magazine beauty editors. In particular, the cold cream by Eau Thermale d'Avène, the foaming cleanser by Barbara Gould and Evian's facial toning gel can be found in many a fashionista's make-up bag. Similarly, many a groomed Parisian swears by Nuxe's cult body oil *Huile Prodigeuse*, Caudalie's *Vinotherapary Cabernet* body scrub (with grape extracts) and Elancyl's anti-cellulite toning cream.

Oenobiol tanning supplement capsules and Phytomer's hair care range are considered absolutely necessary by St-Tropez beach lovers looking to lessen sun damage to hair and skin.

A more traditional approach to French grooming can be found by buying *savon de marseilles* – good-quality traditional soap made with plenty of olive oil.

True scent aficionados should head for Grasse *(see p517)*, the perfume capital of the world. Be sure to visit the three largest scent factories, **Fragonard**, **Molinard** and **Galimard**, all of which have scent available for purchase.

Provençal dried herbs for culinary use and for making teas

ACCESSORIES

French fashion is rightfully famous, but aside from the main couture labels and stores *(see pp142–4)*, the best way to get the French look is to accessorize *à la Français*. In keeping with the French tradition of specialist local trades, there are certain regions that excel in producing accessories.

For a start, a hand-made umbrella from Aurillac *(see p364)* is guaranteed to chase away rainy-day blues in style. The best-known umbrella manufacturers are **L'Ondée au Parapluie d'Aurillac**, **Piganiol** and **Delos**, who will customize one for you with a photograph of whomever you choose to chase away the storms.

Beautiful hands are easily available courtesy of the glove trade in Millau. Visit **L'Atelier Gantier** (the Glove Workshop) to pick up a stunning pair of expertly hand-stiched leather gloves in one of a seemingly endless array of colours.

More casual chic can be found with brightly coloured wicker baskets from local markets and hardware stores. These quickly turn a casual ensemble into boho-chic outfit. Beachside boutiques are great places for picking up stylish sarongs, beads and bracelets for any trip to *la plage* (the beach). **K Jacques** sandals from St-Tropez have long been must-have items among the fashion set.

When it is time to hit the slopes rather than the beach, French skiwear labels such as Rossignol can be a good buy, but only at the end of the season. At the height of *piste* time, ski resort shops are expensive. Once the snow starts to melt, however, ex-rental gear including skis and boots can be picked up relatively cheaply, while ski jackets, hats and *après* ski wear tends to be gloriously cut-price.

HOUSEHOLD GOODS

If you are in the market for housewares, the best stores are **Ikea**, **Alinea** and **Habitat**. **Truffaut** sells garden furniture, and **Leroy Merlin** is the hypermarket of the DIY, home improvement world.

It is surprisingly rare to see the whole range of kitchen goods in a specialist shop. Instead, try the kitchen section of department stores. General hardware shops stock cast-iron cooking equipment. White china is sold in specialist shops.

Travelling through Normandy provides the perfect excuse for sampling many wonderful products, not least the *crème de chantilly*, but for tableware fans or lingerie lovers, the lace industry here is also guaranteed to please. While the **Alençon** lace is extremely expensive and mainly finds its way onto couture sold in top Parisian stores, hitting the shops in Argentan, Chantilly *(see pp204–5)* and Bayeux *(see pp252–3)* is likely to yield exquisite yet affordable pieces. It is worth hunting around for lace pieces which can be used to liven up an outfit: lace has made a fashion comeback in recent times and a customized delicate flower on a bag or blouse is *à la mode*.

Lace curtains are easy to come by, as are lovely table-cloths. The easiest way to be sure not to miss anything, is to take "the lace road" and tour the lace museums and boutiques of Alençon, Argentan, Caen *(see pp253–4)*, Courseulles, Villedieu-les-Poêles and La Perrière.

With a beautiful tablecloth in place, you can proceed to pick up stunning crystal from which to sniff, swirl and sip great French wine. The most famous French crystal maker, **Baccarat**, has a museum where you can take in some of their amazing creations and a store where you can buy a little Baccarat bauble to take home with you. A cheaper French crystal maker which is still elegant for every-day wear is **Crystal d'Arques**. You can tour the small museum in the factory and buy stemware at discount prices in the factory store.

Pottery is available at reasonable prices, especially near centres of production, such as Quimper *(see p274)* in Brittany, Aubagne near Marseille and Vallauris *(see p522)* near Grasse.

Porcelain from Limoges *(see p356)* sets off any meal beautifully: a dinner set from the **Royal Limoges** factory store can be a great investment.

Similarly, stunning **Aubusson** tapestries are seriously expensive and unlikely to be an impulse holiday purchase. However, interior design fanatics could do worse than plan their tapestry or rug purchase

SIZE CHART

Women's dresses, coats and skirts

French	36	38	40	42	44	46	48	
British	8	10	12	14	16	18	20	
American	4	6	8	10	12	14	16	

Women's shoes

French	36	37	38	39	40	41		
British	3	4	5	6	7	8		
American	5	6	7	8	9	10		

Men's suits

French	44	46	48	50	52	54	56	58
British	34	36	38	40	42	44	46	48
American	34	36	38	40	42	44	46	48

Men's shirts

French	36	38	39	41	42	43	44	45
British	14	15	15$\frac{1}{2}$	16	16$\frac{1}{2}$	17	17$\frac{1}{2}$	18
American	14	15	15$\frac{1}{2}$	16	16$\frac{1}{2}$	17	17$\frac{1}{2}$	18

Men's shoes

French	39	40	41	42	43	44	45	46
British	6	7	7$\frac{1}{2}$	8	9	10	11	12
American	7	7$\frac{1}{2}$	8	8$\frac{1}{2}$	9$\frac{1}{2}$	10$\frac{1}{2}$	11	11$\frac{1}{2}$

around a trip to the home of weaving in Aubusson (see pp356–7).

Finishing touches are fun to shop for and can certainly be more frivolous. Be sure to visit the local markets for gingham cotton napkins, linen cleaning cloths and seafood accoutrements (such as lobster crackers and oyster forks). In Provence be sure to stock up on cheap, brightly coloured cookware – tagines, terracotta bowls and painted plates are all in abundance.

WINE

To buy wine straight from the vineyards (domaines) and wine co-operatives, follow the tasting (dégustation) signs.

You may be expected to buy at least one bottle, except where a small fee is charged for wine-tasting. Wine co-operatives make and sell the wine of small producers. Here you can buy wine in 5- and 10- litre containers (en tonneau), as well as in bottles. Wine sold en tonneau, once opened, needs to be consumed fairly quickly, as it will deteriorate within a few days. Wine sold in bottles travels better.

Nicolas is France's main off-licence, with many branches.

FACTORY OUTLETS

The French sales system is very rigid (see p140) but true bargain hunters know that

factory shops have some items on sale all year round. The biggest factory outlets in France can be found in and around Troyes in outlet malls called **Marques Avenue** (Brands Avenue), **Marques City** (Brands City) and **McArthur Glen**, a large American outlet. They sell everything from Yves Saint Laurent suits to Black and Decker drills, Cristofle silverware and Bonpoint babygros. As different an experience as you can get from browsing around French markets and local specialist stores, what factory outlets lack in charm they make up for in bargains. If a whole new wardrobe is in order, it is definitely worth a trip.

DIRECTORY

HYPERMARKETS AND DEPARTMENT STORES

For details of addresses, visit the following websites

Auchan
www.auchan.fr

Carrefour
www.carrefour.fr

Casino
www.supercasino.fr

Franprix
www.franprix.fr

Galeries Lafayette
www.galerieslafayette.com

Intermarché
www.intermarche.com

Leclerc
www.e-leclerc.com

Monoprix
www.monoprix.fr

Printemps
www.printemps.com

REGIONAL PRODUCE

Crème de Cassis
Gabriel Boudier
14 rue de Cluj
21007 Dijon.
Tel 03 80 74 33 33.

Oliviers et Co
For details of addresses,
visit www.oliviers-co.com

BEAUTY PRODUCTS

Chanel
31 rue Cambon 75008
Paris.
Tel 01 42 86 26 00.
www.chanel.com

Fragonard
20 bd Fragonard 06130
Grasse.
Tel 04 93 36 44 65.
www.fragonard.com

Galimard
73 route de Cannes
06130 Grasse.
Tel 04 93 09 20 00.
www.galimard.com

Guerlain
68 av des Champs Elysées
75008 Paris.
Tel 01 45 62 52 57.
www.guerlain.fr

Molinard
60 bd Victor Hugo 06130
Grasse.
Tel 04 93 36 01 62.
www.molinard.com

ACCESSORIES

L'Atelier Gantier
21 rue Droite 12100
Millau. Tel 05 65 60 81 50.

Delos
14 rue Rocher
15000 Aurillac.
Tel 04 71 48 86 85.
www.delos-france.com

K Jacques
32 rte Plages
83990 St Tropez.
Tel 04 94 9/ 41 50.
www.kjacques.com

L'Ondée au Parapluie d'Aurillac
27 rue Victor Hugo
15000 Aurillac.
Tel 04 71 48 29 53.

Piganiol
9 rue Ampère
15000 Aurillac.
Tel 04 71 63 42 60.

HOUSEHOLD GOODS

Alençon Lace Museum
Cour carrée de la Dentelle
61000 Alençon.
Tel 02 33 32 40 07.

Alinea
www.alinea.fr

Aubusson
Manufacture Saint-Jean
3 rue Saint-Jean
23200 Aubusson.
Tel 05 55 66 10 08.

Baccarat
20 rue des Cristalleries
54120 Baccarat.
Tel 03 83 76 60 06.
www.baccarat.com

Cristal d'Arques
Zone industrielle 62510
Arques. Tel 03 21 95 46 96.

Habitat
www.habitat.net

Ikea
www.ikea.com

Leroy Merlin
www.leroymerlin.fr

Royal Limoges
28 rue Donzelot
Accès par le quai
du Port du Naveix
87000 Limoges.
Tel 05 55 33 27 37.
www.royal-limoges.fr

Truffaut
www.truffaut.com

WINE

Nicolas
www.nicolas.com

FACTORY OUTLETS

Marques Avenue
Av de la Maille 10800
Saint Julien les Villas.
Tel 03 25 82 80 80.
www.marquesavenue.com

Marques City
35 rue Danton 10150
Pont Sainte Marie.
Tel 03 25 46 37 48.
www.marquescity.fr

McArthur Glen
ZI des magasin d'usines du
Nord 10150 Pont Sainte
Marie. Tel 03 25 70 47 10.
www.mcarthurglen.fr

Entertainment in France

Paris is one of the world's great entertainment cities, but France's reputation as a centre of excellence in the arts extends well beyond the capital. Whether you prefer to attend theatre or catch a film, listen to jazz or techno, or watch modern dance, the country has a wide array of choices. The regional chapters in this guide will give you an insight into local gems, while these pages provide an overview of entertainment trends and events. Major festivals, such as Avignon and Cannes, occupy an important place in French hearts, so book well ahead if you plan to attend. For small festivals and local happenings, tourist office websites have up-to-the-minute listings.

The spectacular setting of Avignon Theatre at night

THEATRE

Going to the theatre in France can be as formal or intimate as you choose. A trip to a major theatre can involve dressing up, making special *souper* (late dinner) reservations at a nearby restaurant specializing in theatre-goers and quaffing exorbitantly priced champagne during the interval. On the other hand, a trip to a small-scale theatre can be about casual dress, cheap tickets and an intimate experience.

French movie stars frequently return to the stage, including Gérard Depardieu and Ardant in *The Beast in the Jungle*, reflecting the popularity of the theatre. Whatever the genre, the French love an evening *au théâtre*, be it a French farce or a festival of street theatre.

France's biggest theatre festival is at **Avignon** *(see p503)* which is held during three weeks in July and is mainly open air. It also includes ballets, drama and classical concerts. Many outdoor theatres operate in summer and are often free – contact the town's tourist office for a programme.

Circus is also dear to the French. In small towns, summertime is often heralded by the circus loudspeaker strapped to the top of a car cruising the streets and inviting adults and children alike to flock to the big top.

Large-scale *spectacles* or shows are another popular form of theatre, be they massive musicals or *son et lumières* performances. Marionettes are also given due respect in France, where puppet shows go beyond traditional Punch and Judy territory.

FILM

La Septième Art, as the French refer to film, reveals the respect with which the genre is held. From the Lumière brothers and their innovative technology to contemporary critical smashes, such as *The Chorus* and *Amélie*, and the *Nouvelle Vague*, France's influence on film is undeniable. The French are supportive of local, independent cinemas, and small towns are often fiercely protective of their screening centre. So when visiting the cinema, try to avoid the behemoths of UGC and Gaumont and instead head to a tiny *salle de cinéma*. If your language skills won't stretch to seeing a French film while in France, be sure to catch the VO *(Version Originale)* of any other language films, which will be screened in the film's original language. VF *(Version Française)* denotes a dubbed screening in French. As any expatriate in France knows, hearing a strange French voice coming out of a Hollywood A-lister's mouth is likely to dull any enjoyment of a major blockbuster movie.

Another thing to bear in mind is the French attitude to snacking. Essentially it is only acceptable for children, and even then only at a designated time after school. While French cinemas do have concession stands selling popcorn and sweets, it is only the foreigners who can be heard munching throughout the tense parts of the film. On the other hand, some French cinemas have bars and restaurants attached, so that film goers can dissect the movie over a meal. Many cinemas run mini directors' festivals with several films shown back to back, attracting serious film buffs and those curious to learn more.

As the fame of **Cannes** *(see p520)* reflects, film festivals are taken seriously by the French. Cannes itself is a maelstrom of media hype, old-school glamour and shiny new cash. It is an amazing experience if you can get tickets to any of the films or parties, but these are notoriously difficult to get as they are by invitation only.

Poster promoting La Rochelle international film festival

Red carpet and razzmatazz at the Cannes film festival

An easier way to experience the fabulous side of film is to attend the lower-key American and Asian film festivals in **Deauville** *(see p255)*. The former is seen as a major launch pad for US independent films looking for European release, and attracts big stars and cult directors alike. The competition section of the festival has ten films in the running each year. The chic town of Deauville is small and accessible and, while the chance of bumping into a huge star is slim, it feels possible.

The film festival in **La Rochelle** *(see p416)*, the second largest in France, does not attract big actors, but film fans will not be disappointed with the selection of movies.

A truly great way to catch a film in France is at an open-air festival. There are many such events throughout the country; check local listings so as not to miss out. And if you are lucky enough to be in Arles *(see pp508–9)*, an epic experience can be had at their annual showing of historical Roman blockbusters, screened against the backdrop of a magnificent Roman amphitheatre. Contact **Théâtre Antique** for details.

DANCE

Dancing is a way of life in France. From formal lessons to spontaneous outbreaks of grooving in the village square, moving to music is central to all types of celebration. Most foreigners' first experience with French dancers occurs in a nightclub and is, more often than not, accompanied by an expression of surprise. In even the most upscale nightclub, it is not unusual to see trendy twentysomethings jiving away to *le rock*, a formal form of rock and roll dancing. French teens are taught *le rock* before being unleashed on the party scene, and a basic understanding of its signature twirls and twists is considered vital to being a good dancer.

The love affair with formal dance sessions starts young, but lasts until late in life: tea dances are a major fixture of most older people's social calendars. Community centres, sports halls, restaurants and chic nightclubs often host *thé dansants* (tea dances), normally in the late afternoon or early evening.

Another way to experience French dance culture is to head to a *guingette*, a moored party boat with a convivial, old-fashioned atmosphere. People here dance the *quadrille* or the *musette* to accordion music, spinning around on the banks of the river. While the guingettes were traditionally clustered around the Marne river, they have now spread throughout France and are definitely worth seeking out if your travels take you close to a major tributary.

In general, lots of dancing takes place near to water in France. Those looking to get into the groove in the south should take their dancing shoes to the quays in Bordeaux and Marseille.

Of course, once a year, on 13 and 14 July, a most unusual impromptu dancing venue springs up around the country with the *Bals des Pompiers*. The "Firemen's Balls" are a national institution when the French of all ages head down to their local fire station to celebrate Bastille day by dancing to everything from Piaf to hip hop until the early hours of the morning.

If you would prefer to watch rather than participate, there are several major dance festivals that celebrate the dance traditions of different regions. The **Gannat festival** held in the Auvergne *(see p353)* is a fine example of a regional dance extravaganza, as is the **Festival Interceltique de Lorient** *(see p270)* which celebrates Celtic music and dance. The main international dance festivals are held in **Montpellier** *(see pp494–5)* and **Lyon** *(see pp378–81)*. These provide a wonderful opportunity to enjoy major contemporary dance talent from around the world.

Wonderful costumes and choreography at the Montpellier dance festival

MUSIC

The French music scene is about far more than Johnny Hallyday, although it must be said that the ageing rocker still manages to sell stacks of records, concert tickets and gossip magazines. It should also be pointed out that he is actually Belgian, but the French have taken him to their hearts anyway. Neither is the scene just about Bob Sinclair, Daft Punk, Air and "Le French Touch". However, the fact that both dance music and rock happily coexist in the French charts reflects a truism of the music scene over here, which is that there is space for all kinds of tunes. *Chanson* has made a huge comeback over recent years as the success of the movement's poster boy Benjamin Biolay reveals. The new French *chanson* scene is dominated by Biolay, although other well-known artists in this genre include Vincent Delerm and Benabar.

Female crooners are also all the rage; listen to Lara Fabian or reality TV pop star Chimène Badi for confirmation of this.

The other recent musical phenomenon in France came off the back of a hit film *The Chorus* (*Les Choristes*, 2004) which has seen impressive soundtrack sales, and one can at least speculate on the impact it might have had on attendance at evensong.

The event which best symbolizes this musical cornucopia is the Fête de la Musique. Every year on 21 June, France resonates to the sound of this national music festival. Amateur and professional musicians alike set up their stages throughout villages and towns and peform. The best way to enjoy this is to walk around and try and take in as many different "concerts" as possible, but be aware that for some wannabe rock stars this is their only chance to shine, regardless of whether or not they can sing. Musical quality aside, what is most impressive about the Fête de la Musique is the sheer

number of genres that one can hear in a few streets. Ranging from full orchestras to one-man rap artists, you can expect to hear everything from accordion music to panpipes, *chanson*, hip hop and electro.

If you prefer your festivals a little more specialized, visit one of the events focusing on the very best of everything from chamber music to jazz. The July **Festival of Francofolies** in La Rochelle (*see p416*) brings together French music enthusiasts from around the world just as **Jazz in Antibes** draws top performers to this chic seaside town (*see p521*). The **Chorégies d'Orange**, France's oldest opera festival, takes place throughout July and August in the well-preserved Roman amphitheatre, which retains perfect acoustics. The organ festival in **Aubusson** (*see pp356–7*) focuses around the amazing organ in the Sainte Croix church and **La Roque d'Anthéron** looks set to continue to pull in piano-loving crowds. The **Colmar international festival** (*see p227*) is a major draw for classical music buffs, and the **Aix festival** (*see p511*) is a must for any serious fan, while the **Montpellier** (*see pp494–5*) **and Radio France** event appeals to music lovers throughout the world.

CLUBS

Cool clubs and artful partying most definitely exist outside the capital city, despite what Parisians may believe. There are, of course, bars, clubs and discos throughout the country, and night owls looking to dance are unlikely to be disappointed by the range of options on offer. Small local venues can be great fun, and community events such as open-air parties and festivals are almost always worth a look-in. In general, nightclubs open late and even in small towns, don't really get going till after midnight. The French are more likely to nurse a few drinks rather than dash around buying multiple

rounds, and shots are almost unheard of over here. It is considered uncouth to drink wine outside of mealtimes, although champagne is always a good thing! The prevailing custom is to club together with friends and buy a bottle of spirits between you. The nightclub will present you with plenty of mixers and – the big benefit of going for this option – you will usually get a table all to yourselves. Tables are generally reserved for those in possession of a full bottle of spirits; a single gin and tonic does not warrant a seat. As extravagant as this may seem, it is generally cheaper than buying individual drinks for four or more people.

In terms of dress code, trainers are almost always forbidden, and the smarter the better could be seen as the rule. In house or hip-hop clubs strict dress codes tend to be relaxed. However, in more traditional *boites de nuit* (night clubs) getting glammed-up is the way to go. Clubs with difficult door policies can often be out-foxed by late diners. If you are worried about getting in, call ahead and make a dinner reservation. Alternatively flaunt designer labels at the doormen.

To experience one of France's most glamorous clubs head to **Les Planches** – an uber-chic spot outside Deauville (*see p255*). Aside from its swimming pool in which starlets frolic at 3am, vintage cars tear around town rounding up party goers with a generally hedonistic atmosphere, Les Planches offers a friendly, fun vibe.

Up in the mountains **Le Privilege** in Chamonix (*see p322*) and **Le Loft** in Méribel are jumping Alpine party places.

The Cote d'Azur (*see pp499–531*) is, of course, renowned for its hedonistic nightlife. **Les Caves du Roy** in the Hotel Byblos and **Nikki Beach** in St Tropez (*see p516*) are perfect for the jet set, while **Jimmy'z** in Monaco (*see pp530–1*) is the place to hang out with highrollers.

SPECTATOR SPORTS

Sporting enthusiasts are spoiled for choice in France, with opportunities to indulge in spectator sport throughout the country. If you don't want to wait to see the *grande finale* of the **Tour de France** in Paris, why not see it start in Brittany *(see pp268–85)*. Alternatively, taking in the spectacle from a tiny village en route is a great experience (drivers beware: the Tour takes precedence and the traffic will be stopped for a very, very long time).

If football is more your thing, then head to the Olympic stadia to catch huge teams, such as **Lyon** and **Marseille**, in action.

Surfing fans should make for Biarritz *(see p452)*, Lacanau *(see p424)* and Hossegor *(see p424)* to watch the tournaments there, while ski aficionados might want to watch the European Cup in Les Trois Vallées *(see p322)*.

Golfers flock to the **PGA Open** held outside Paris and to the **LPGA in Evian**, which is the world's second most valuable tournament after the US Open.

Riders will be drawn to one of France's national studs at the **Haras National de Pompadour** for dressage, show-jumping and other competitions throughout the year. Similarly, equine enthusiasts should not miss out on exciting horse racing at the renowned **Chantilly Racecourse**.

The **Le Mans** 24-hour car race is an institution, as is the famous **Grand Prix** in Monaco *(see pp530–1)*. The **French Grand Prix** at Magny Cours, south of Nevers *(see pp339–40)* is also well worth a visit.

No visitor to France in the summer should miss out on one of the greatest spectator sports of them all: head to the village square and take in a game of *petanque* (also known as *boules*).

DIRECTORY

THEATRE

Avignon Theatre Festival
www.festival-avignon.com
Tel 04 90 14 14 14.

FILM

Cannes Film Festival
www.festival-cannes.fr

Deauville Film Festival
www.festival-deauville.com

La Rochelle Film Festival
www.festival-larochelle.org

Théâtre Antique d'Arles
Association Peplum.
Tel 04 90 93 19 55.
www.festivalpeplum-arles.com

DANCE

Festival Interceltique de Lorient
Tel 02 97 64 03 20.
www.festival-interceltique.com

Gannat Festival
Tel 04 70 90 12 67.
www.gannat.com

Lyon Festival
Tel 04 72 07 41 41.
www.biennaledelyon.org

Montpellier Festival
Tel 08 00 60 07 40.
www.montpellierdanse.com

MUSIC

Aix Festival
Tel 04 42 17 34 00.
www.festival-aix.com

Aubusson Festival
Tel 05 55 66 32 12.
www.orgue-aubusson.org

Choregies d'Orange
Tel 04 90 34 24 24.
www.choregies.asso.fr

Colmar International Festival
Tel 03 89 20 68 97.
www.festival-colmar.com

Festival of Francofolies
Tel 05 46 28 28 28.
www.francofolies.fr

Jazz in Antibes
Tel 04 97 23 11 10.
www.antibesjuanlespins.com

Radio France and Montpellier Festival
Tel 04 67 02 02 01.
www.festivalradiofrancemontpellier.com

La Roque d'Antheron
Tel 04 42 50 51 15.
www.festival-piano.com

CLUBS

Les Caves du Roy
Av Paul Signac
83990 St-Tropez.
Tel 04 94 56 68 00.

Jimmy'z
Le Sporting Club
Av Princesse Grace
Monte Carlo.
Tel 00 377 98 06 73 73.

Le Loft
Parc Olympique
La Chaudanne
73550 Méribel.
Tel 04 79 00 36 58.
www.leloftmeribel.com

Nikki Beach
Route de Epi
Ramatuelle
83350 St-Tropez.
Tel 04 94 79 82 04.
www.nikkibeach.com

Les Planches
Les Longs Champs
14910 Blonville
sur Mer.
Tel 02 31 87 58 09.

Le Privilege
Rue des Moulins
74400 Chamonix.
Tel 04 50 53 29 10.
www.barleprivilege.com

SPECTATOR SPORTS

Chantilly Racecourse
Rue Plaine des Aigles,
Chantilly, Oise.
Tel 03 44 62 44 00.
www.france-galop.com

French Grand Prix
Magny Cours 58170.
Tel 03 86 21 80 00.
www.fia.com

Grand Prix
Automobile Club de Monaco.
Tel 00 377 93 15 26 00.
www.fia.com

Haras National de Pompadour
Tel 08 11 90 21 31.
www.haras-nationaux.fr

LPGA in Evian
www.evianmasters.com

Le Mans
Tel 02 43 40 24 24.
www.lemans.org

Olympique Lyon
350 av Jean Jaurès 69007
Lyon. www.olweb.fr

Olympique de Marseille
3 bd Michelet 13008
Marseille. www.om.net

PGA Open
www.pgafrance.net

Tour de France
www.letour.fr

Specialist Holidays and Outdoor Activities

France offers an amazing variety of leisure and sport activities, making it a wonderful choice for a specialist holiday. The French take great pride in the *art de vivre*, which entails not only eating and drinking well, but also pursuing special interests and hobbies. For the best in entertainment and spectator sports, festivals and annual events, see *France through the Year* on pages 36–9. Information on leisure and sporting activities in a particular region is available from the tourist offices listed for each town in this guide. The suggestions below cover the most popular, and also the more unusual, pursuits.

Students honing their culinary skills on a Hostellerie Bérard cookery course

SPECIALIST HOLIDAYS

French government tourist offices *(see p669)* have an extensive range of information on travel companies that offer special interest holidays. and can send you a copy of *The Traveller in France Reference Guide*.

If you want to improve your French, many language courses are available. These are very often combined with other activities, such as cooking or painting. For more information, request *Cours de français pour étudiants étrangers* (French courses for foreign students) from the **French Institute** in London.

Young people can enjoy a French-speaking holiday by working part time on the restoration of historic sites with **Union REMPART** *(Union pour la Réhabilitation et Entretien des Monuments et du Patrimoine Artistique)*.

A tantalizing array of gastronomic courses is on offer, to introduce you to classical French cuisine or the cooking of a particular region. For experienced cooks, more advanced and specialist courses are available too. Wine-appreciation courses can also be found and are always very popular.

There are numerous art and crafts courses throughout the country, catering to everyone from the absolute beginner to the most accomplished artist.

Nature lovers can enjoy the national parks *(parcs nationaux)* and join organized bird-watching and botanical trips in many areas, including the Camargue, the Cévennes and Corsica.

Le Guide des Jardins en France, published by Actes

Painting the picturesque French landscape

Sud, is a useful reference guide when visiting France's many beautiful gardens.

GOLF

There are golf courses all over France, especially along the north and south coasts and in Aquitaine. Players have to reach a minimum standard and obtain a licence in order to play, so be sure to take your handicap certificate with you. Top courses offer weekend or longer tutored breaks geared to all levels of experience. The **Fédération Française de Golf** will provide a list of all the courses throughout France.

Specialist golf packages, including deluxe hotel accommodation, can be ideal for serious golfers and their non-golfing partners alike. The spectacular Hotel Royal and its renowned **Evian Masters** golf course is a very exclusive, pampering option. The 18-hole course is guaranteed to appeal to fans. There is also a spa and five swimming pools, perfect for lazing. The climbing wall, squash and tennis courts will appeal to more active visitors.

In the south, the **American Golf Academy** offers a team of golf pros who are adept at coaching children, beginners and also experts through their eight different courses and private lessons. Their summer schools and master classes are highly sought after.

The **Hotel de Mougins**, with a lovely address on the "avenue du Golf", is situated near to ten prestigious golf courses, including the Golf Country Club Cannes, the Royal Mougins Golf Club and the Golf d'Opio-Valbonne. The hotel can arrange rounds at the different clubs, and offers packages which include extras, such as lunch in the clubhouse.

The **Golf Hotel Grenoble Charmeil** can organize green fees for three courses, including the Grenoble International course. In Brittany, the **St-Malo Golf and Country Club** has a

19th-century manor house interior and an impressive 27-hole golf course, surrounded by the Mesnil forest.

TENNIS

Tennis is a very popular sport in France, and courts for hourly hire can be found in almost every town. It is a good idea to bring your own equipment with you, as hire facilities may not be available.

HIKING

In France, more than 60,000 km (38,000 miles) of long-distance tracks, known as *Grandes Randonnées* (GR), are clearly marked. There are also 80,000 km (50,000 miles) of the shorter *Petites Randonnées* (PR).

The routes vary in difficulty and include long pilgrim routes, alpine crossings and tracks through national parks. Some *Grandes* and *Petites Randonnees* are open for mountain biking as well as horse riding.

Topo Guides, published by **Fédération Française de la Randonnée Pédestre**, describe the tracks, providing details of transport, places for overnight stops and food shops. A series geared specifically toward families is *Promenades et Randonnées*.

CYCLING

For advice on cycling in France, contact the British **CTC** (Cyclists' Touring Club) or the **Fédération Française de Cyclisme**.

Escaping into the forest at Fontainebleau *(see pp180–1)*

Serious cyclists could live their dreams by joining up for a Tour de France stage vacation with the **Velo Echappe** *Etape du Tour* team. The company organizes two types of adventure – a fully guided programme or a self-guided option. They handle all the registration forms and paperwork, and on the guided option they will put you up in a hotel a block away from the end of the stage. Applications to the tour company must be received by the end of March every year to have a chance to ride along with the Tour de France professionals.

At the other end of the scale, people who enjoy a gentle bike ride could opt for a wine cycling tour through the vineyards of France. Freewheeling down the Route des Grands Crus in Burgundy may be more than enough holiday exercise for some.

Duvine Adventures organize tours that take in famed vineyards such as La Tache, Romanée-Conti and Nuit-St-Georges. The riding includes flat spells and hills, and there are excellent lunches.

Local tourist offices provide details about riding facilities in their areas. **Voies Vertes** offers information on "greenways", easy rides through some of France's loveliest countryside. *Gîtes de France (see p549)* offer dormitory accommodation in the vicinity of well-known tracks.

Mountain biking – a great way to explore

HORSE RIDING

There are many reputable companies that offer riding breaks from one-hour treks to long weekends or holidays of a week or more. The best way to choose is to decide which type of countryside you would prefer to see from the saddle. If the Mont St Michel *(see pp256–61)* and the beaches of Brittany appeal, then **A La Carte Sportive** offer stables with horses trained in trekking for beginners and intermediates. For more experienced riders, riding a Camargue mount through the countryside of Provence *(see pp510–11)* is a wonderful treat. **Ride in France** organizes rides through beautiful scenery, vineyards and picturesque villages,

Hiking along the Gorges du Verdon in Provence (see pp514–15)

allowing riders to experience the flora and fauna of the area. Horse lovers with a taste for the historical, or those hankering after a little luxury, could do worse than to sign up for a break with the **Cheval et Chateaux** company which organizes horse-riding tours around chateaux in the Loire. Not only do riders get to take in the majesty of the chateaux of the region, the overnight accommodation also comes courtesy of a castle. It makes an ideal way to play lord or lady of the manor while indulging in a passion for trekking.

MOUNTAIN SPORTS

The French mountains, especially the Alps and the Pyrenees, provide a wide range of sporting opportunities. In addition to winter downhill skiing and *ski de fond* (cross-country), the mountains are enjoyed in the summer by rock-climbers and mountaineers, and by those skiers who can't wait for winter and so indulge in some of Europe's best glacier skiing.

Climbers should contact the **Fédération Française de la Montagne et de l'Escalade** for more information on the best climbing locations and other useful tips.

Winter sports fans should join the serious skiers and snowboarders who head to the French hills in droves every season. The mountains here have terrain to satisfy all levels of expertise from toddlers in the kids' club through to death-defying off-piste athletes, adrenalin junkie snowboarders, kite-surfers and middle-of-the-road snow fans who are happiest cruising blue runs and eating in slope-side restaurants.

SKIING

Undoubtedly, France has some of the best ski resorts anywhere in the world. The sheer scale of some of the larger areas can be quite daunting if you're on a week-long trip – especially to those who insist on covering all the trails on the map. The Trois Vallées ski area (*see p322*), for example, is made up of three valleys which include the resorts of Courchevel, Méribel, Val Thorens and Les Ménuires. Added together, they comprise a staggering 600 km (375 miles) worth of pistes.

The Trois Vallées is an excellent example of how French ski resorts differ wildly in style. Super-chic stations such as Courchevel and Méribel draw skiers from around the world, often dressed in cutting-edge ski fashion and using the latest high-tech equipment. In these resorts the hotels – especially those dubbed to be "in" are expensive, and eating and drinking in the "see and be seen spots" here puts a significant dent in the most generous of holiday budgets. On the other hand, resorts which are considered less glamorous, such as Vals Thorens and Les Menuires, can be enjoyed without designer labels and huge credit card limits.

The main consideration when choosing a resort should be the percentage of terrain to suit your ability. For example, a beginner might be miserable in a resort aimed at experts and offering only a few green runs. Similarly, a confident intermediate looking to improve will be frustrated by a ski area full of easy cruising slopes over-run with beginners.

It is also important to think about whether or not it matters to you if the village is picturesque. Die-hard ski fans can overlook ugly concrete architecture in towns such as Flaine, while those looking for the bigger picture would be best off heading to somewhere pretty, such as La Clusaz or Megève (*see p322*).

The proximity of accommodation to piste is also very important; most people find it is worth paying a premium for accommodation near the slopes and lifts, rather than having to stagger back in heavy boots carrying your skis after a long day's schussing.

Aside from obvious concerns such as nightlife, children's crèches and the efficiency of lift networks, it can also be useful to look at historic snow reports for the last few years for the time you are planning your trip. The weather can be unpredictable though so be sure to also check the resorts' snow-making capabilities. Armed with these details you should be in a good position to pick the right resort for you but remember, while the Alps get most of the attention, the Pyrenees can offer some seriously good skiing, too.

AERONAUTICAL SPORTS

Learning to fly in France can be relatively inexpensive. Information on the different flying schools is available from the **Fédération Nationale Aéronautique**. There are also plenty of opportunities to learn the exhilarating skills of gliding, paragliding and hang gliding. For more information, contact the **Fédération Française de Vol Libre**.

If piloting a plane is a little too much, you can opt for ballooning instead. France has an illustrious ballooning history, being the birthplace of the Montgolfier brothers who pioneered the art in 1783. **Ballon de Paris** provide a tethered taste of adventure in Paris with a trip into the air in the **Parc André-Citroën**, but floating unfettered over the countryside can be arranged by several companies around the country. **France Balloons** can organize trips over Fontainebleau (*see pp180–1*) outside Paris or over the Burgundian vineyards. Alternatively, they offer the opportunity to appreciate the spectacular chateaux of the Loire from a balloon. In Provence **Hot Air Balloon Provence** can float you over the picturesque villages, cornfields and vines of the Lubéron (*see pp506–7*).

WATER SPORTS

Whitewater rafting, kayaking and canoeing all take place on many French rivers, especially in the Massif Central. More information on these sports and the best places to take part can be obtained from the **Fédération Française de Canoë-Kayak**.

The Atlantic coast around Biarritz (*see p452*) offers some of the best surfing and windsurfing in Europe. Excellent windsurfing can also be found in Brittany, with **Wissant** in particular being a big draw. A charming small fishing village, Wissant is considered a decent stop on any windsurf tour.

Surfers who prefer to do it without the sail head to **Hossegor** outside Biarritz (*see p452*) for fantastic waves. The surfing here is world-class and perhaps not ideal for beginners, but the after-surf scene is great fun for anyone who is more interested in lying on the beach or paddling at the shore than carving up the water.

Similarly the town of **Lacanau** (*see p424*) plays host to international surf competitions, drawing wave fans from all over the world.

Sailing and waterskiing are also very popular in France. Contact the **Fédération Française de Voile** for more details. Training schools and equipment hire are found at places along the coast and on lakes.

If cruising on a boat is your kind of thing, there are many outlets that can help. One of the swankier options is to take a **Sunsail** bareboat tour around the Côte d'Azur, although this option is only available to those who have reached a certain level of boatmanship. The company also offers a range of skippered tours around the beautiful coastline.

Swimming facilities throughout the country are generally good, although beaches in the South of France can become very crowded in high season (*see pp474–5*).

HUNTING & FISHING

Although hunting is a popular sport in France, a *permis de chasse* is required, for which there is a fee. You will need a copy of your own national hunting licence and to pass an exam in French, which makes it difficult for visitors. There are regional variations on the season, depending on the type of hunting. Since the hunting ban came into force in England, many French hunts have found English hunters a welcome boost to their numbers.

All kinds of fishing, for both fresh and seawater fish, are available, depending on the individual area. Local fishing shops sell the *carte de pêche*, which gives details of regulations.

NATURISM

There are nearly 90 naturism centres in France. These are mostly located in the south and southwest of the country, as well as in Corsica. Information in English can be obtained from French Government Tourist Offices (*see p669*), or from the **Fédération Française de Naturisme**.

PUBLIC EVENTS

To join the French as they enjoy their spare time, look out for local football and rugby matches, cycling races or other sporting events suited to spectators.

Special seasonal markets and local *fêtes* often combine antiques fairs and *boules* tournaments with rock and pop concerts, making an enjoyable day out.

SPA HOLIDAYS

France is renowned for its sea-water based thalasso-therapy spa techniques, with many centres, salons and hotels offering "thalasso" treatments. The seaside towns and resorts seem to be the most logical place to head for ocean-based treatments, and not surprisingly there are some excellent spots dotted around the coastline.

Chic seaside town Deauville (*see p255*) plays host to upscale spa seekers in the **Algotherm Thalassotherapy Spa**. Similarly the **Sofitel Thalassa** in Quiberon (*see p278*) offers top-class water therapy. More water therapy can be found near the springs at Vichy (*see pp358–9*) at the **Les Celestins** spa and at the **Evian Royal Resort** (*see p391*).

Wine in France is considered to be almost as important as water, so it is not surprising that a spa specialising in "vinotherapy" or wine therapy has hordes of loyal fans. Head to **Les Sources de Caudalie** spa among the vines near Bordeaux and indulge in a vinosource grape facial and cabernet scrub.

If big name treatments are your thing, you should head to **Le Mas Candille** which

hosts the first Shiseido spa in continental Europe. The products used are as exceptional as one would expect from such a swanky brand, and the techniques are Oriental-based.

Finally, if a thoroughly indulgent approach to a spa session is your idea of holiday heaven, then splurge at the new **Four Seasons Terre Blanche** in Provence. The half-day retreat of total indulgence involves a salt and oil scrub, an aromatherapy massage, an acupressure facial and an oriental head massage. If you want to go *à la carte*, you can choose from a wide range of delights, such as an eye-lifting facial, a body-toning massage or an Oshadi clay wrap.

If you can't escape from the city, the Valmont spa at the **Hotel Meurice** and the **Four Seasons** spa at the George V can provide the ultimate escape and spa break right in the centre of Paris.

YOGA

The beautiful countryside in France provides the perfect backdrop for a restorative yoga retreat holiday. The **Manoloya Yoga Centre** offers relaxing and fun hatha yoga holidays throughout Provence and at its Avignon-based centre. For the more dynamic style of ashtanga yoga, try **The Shala** retreats held in the beautiful foothills of the Cevennes.

Another excellent option is a break at the **Domaine de la Grausse** in the foothills of the Pyrenees, where walking and visiting local waterfalls, chateaux, medieval villages and even taking in some cave paintings are all on the agenda. Those with any energy left over can take advantage of options to go mountain biking, riding, playing golf and fishing.

Beginners and experienced yoga fans alike are welcome at the **Europe Yoga Centre**, which specializes in hatha and also astanga yoga. Both individual retreats and group holidays can be arranged at the centre.

GOURMET

For gourmets looking to learn how to recreate some of the stunning meals enjoyed in French restaurants, or wine buffs seeking to increase their knowledge and cellar at the same time, there are many excellent options. The sheer number of cookery classes available throughout the country may seem over-whelming, so the first step in choosing an activity holiday of this kind is to consider your initial skill level and what you wish to achieve from the break. From die-hard kitchen disasters to budding restaurateurs, there is a gourmet break in France which will suit.

Two options for beginner chefs are the "cookery holiday" from **Cook in France**, which emphasizes fun rather than serious hard work in the kitchen; and Rosa Jackson's cooking school, **Les Petits Farcis**, in Nice (see pp526–7), where she guides food-lovers around the town's glorious fresh produce stalls explaining how to spot the best melon, or how to cook the intimidating artichoke. The Cook in France team offers many specialized

courses (such as matching wine to food) alongside their standard culinary classes, while Rosa Jackson's cooking school offers the opportunity to rustle up a menu based on whatever looks great in the market on that particular day.

Budding culinary stars might want to head to Alain Ducasse's **Ecole de Cuisine** in Paris, which organizes both cooking and wine courses. It offers day and evening courses, held in an ultra-modern, professionally equipped kitchen. Also in Paris is the **Ecole Ritz Escoffier**, which holds workshops, for both adults and children, at the Ritz Hotel. Lessons last from an hour to half a day and cover themes such as chocolate or making the perfect pastry.

Oenophiles, on the other hand, might like to join with the **French Wine Explorers** who offer tours around vineyards. Alternatively, arranging wine classes via the French tourist office can be an excellent idea. **Wine Travel Guides** has an informative website for independent travellers, listing vineyards that are recommended by regional wine experts.

ARTS AND CRAFTS

France is a top choice for creative people looking to get away from it all and to express themselves in beautiful surroundings. Whether your preferred method of expression is scribbling in a notebook by yourself on the banks of a river, or perfecting your pastel technique in an art master class, there is an outlet for you somewhere in France.

Mas Saurine offers residential and non-residential painting holidays in the Pyrenees, 30 minutes from Perpignan. Small group classes, geared to different levels of ability, are taught in an old stone barn by exhibiting artists.

Courses in stone and bronze sculpture are on offer in Normandy, near Honfleur, with experienced sculptor **Sally Hersh**. Some of the artist's pieces are also available for purchase.

Those with a passion for seeing life through a lens are well catered for with photography courses by **Graham and Belinda Berry** at their farmhouse in Lot, southwest France. Courses suitable for all ages and abilities are offered here.

DIRECTORY

SPECIALIST HOLIDAYS

French Institute
17 Queensberry Place, London SW7 2DT United Kingdom.
Tel 020 7073 1350.
www.institut-francais.org.uk

Union REMPART
1 rue des Guillemites, 75004 Paris.
Tel 01 42 71 96 55.
www.rempart.com

GOLF

American Golf Academy
Tel 06 81 54 96 42.
www.american-golf-academy.com

Fédération Française de Golf
68 rue Anatole France, 92300 Levallois Perret.
Tel 01 41 49 77 00.
www.ffgolf.org

Golf Hotel Grenoble Charmeil
38210 Saint Quentin sur Isère. *Tel 04 76 93 67 28.*
www.golfhotelgrenoble.com

Hotel de Mougins
205 av du Golf 06250 Mougins.
Tel 04 92 92 17 07.
www.hotel-de-mougins.com

Hotel Royal and Evian Masters
South Shore Lake Geneva, 74500 Evian.
Tel 04 50 26 85 00.
www.evianroyalresort.com

St Malo Golf and Country Club
Domaine de St-Yvieux, 35540 Le Tronchet.
Tel 02 99 58 96 69.
www.saintmalogolf.com

HIKING

Fédération Française de Randonnée Pédestre
64 rue du Dessous des Berges, 75013 Paris.
Tel 01 44 89 93 90.
www.ffrandonnee.fr

CYCLING

CTC
Parklands, Railton Rd, Guildford, Surrey GU2 9JX, United Kingdom.
Tel 0844 736 8450.
www.ctc.org.uk

Duvine Adventures
www.duvine.com

Fédération Française de Cyclisme
5 rue de Rome, 93561 Rosny-sous-Bois.
www.ffc.fr

Velo Echappe
www.veloechappe.com

Voies Vertes
www.voiesvertes.com

HORSE RIDING

A La Carte Sportive
www.carte-sportive-com
www.iowners.net

Cheval et Châteaux
www.cheval-et-chateaux.com

Ride in France
www.rideinfrance.com

DIRECTORY

MOUNTAIN SPORTS

Féderation Française de la Montagne et de l'Escalade
8–10 quai de la Marne, 75019 Paris.
Tel 01 40 18 75 50.
www.ffme.fr

SKIING

For information on the different resorts, visit the following websites:
www.flaine.com
www.laclusaz.com
www.megeve.com
www.les3vallees.com
www.courchevel.com
www.meribel.net
www.valthorens.com
www.lesmenuires.com

AERONAUTICAL SPORTS

Ballon de Paris
Parc André-Citroën, 75015 Paris.
Tel 01 44 26 20 00.
www.ballondeparis.com

Fédération Française de Vol Libre
4 rue de Suisse, 06000 Nice.
Tel 04 97 03 82 82.
www.federation.ffvl.fr

Fédération Nationale Aéronautique
155 av Wagram, 75017 Paris.
Tel 01 44 29 92 00.
www.ff-aero.fr

France Balloons
Tel 08 10 60 01 53.
www.franceballoons.com

Hot Air Balloon Provence
www.montgolfiere-provence-ballooning.com

WATER SPORTS

Fédération Française de Canoë-Kayak
87 quai de la Marne, 94340 Joinville-le-Pont.
Tel 01 45 11 08 50.
www.ffck.org

Fédération Française de Voile
17 rue Henri Bocquillon, 75015 Paris.
Tel 01 40 60 37 00.
www.ffvoile.fr

Hossegor Tourist Office
Pl des Halles – B.P. 6, 40150 Hossegor.
Tel 05 58 41 79 00.
www.hossegor.fr

Lacanau Tourist Office
Pl de l'Europe, 33680 Lacanau.
Tel 05 56 03 21 01.
www.medococean.com

Sunsail
www.sunsail.com

Wissant Tourist Office
Pl de la Mairie, 62179 Wissant.
Tel 08 20 20 76 00.
www.ville-wissant.fr

NATURISM

Fédération Française de Naturisme
www.ffn-naturisme.com

SPA HOLIDAYS

Algotherm
10 rue Alexander Fleming 14200 Herouville-Saint-Clair.
Tel 02 31 06 16 26.
www.algotherm.fr

Evian Royal Resort
Rive Sud du Lac de Génève 74501 Evian-les-Bains.
Tel 04 50 26 85 00.
www.evianroyal resort.com

Four Seasons Provence
Domaine de Terre Blanche, 83440 Tourrettes, Var.
Tel 04 94 39 90 00.
www.fourseasons.com

Hotel Four Seasons George V
31 av George V, 75008 Paris.
Tel 01 49 52 70 00.
www.fourseasons.com

Hotel Meurice
228 rue de Rivoli, 75001 Paris.
Tel 01 44 58 10 10.
www.lemeurice.com

Le Mas Candille
Bd Clément Rebuffel, 06250 Mougins.
Tel 04 92 28 43 43.
www.lemascandille.com

Les Celestins Vichy
111 bd des Etats-Unis, 03200 Vichy.
Tel 04 70 30 82 00.
www.vichy-spa-hotel.fr

Sofitel Thalassa Quiberon
Pointe de Goulvars, BP 10802 Quiberon Cedex, 56178 Quiberon.
Tel 02 97 50 20 00.
www.thalassa.com

Les Sources de Caudalie
Chemin de Smith Haut Lafitte 33650 Bordeaux–Martillac.
Tel 05 57 83 83 83.
www.sources–caudalie.com

YOGA

Domaine de la Grausse
09420 Clermont la Grausse, Ariège.
Tel 05 61 66 30 53.
www.yoga-in-france.com

Europe Yoga Centre
46800 St Matre, Lot.
Tel 05 65 21 76 20.
www.europeyoga.com

Manolaya Yoga Centre
FFPY 39 rue de la Bonneterie, 84000 Avignon.
Tel 04 90 82 10 52.
www.manolaya.org

The Shala
Les Pauses, St André de Majencoules, Gard 30570. www.theshala.co.uk

GOURMET

Cook in France
Tel 05 53 30 24 05.
www.cookinfrance.com

Ecole de Cuisine
64 rue du Ranelagh, 75016 Paris.
Tel 01 44 90 91 00.
www.ecolecuisine-alainducasse.com

Ecole Ritz Escoffier
Tel 01 44 16 30 50.
www.ritzescoffier.com

French Wine Explorers
www.wine-tours-france.com

Les Petits Farcis
7 rue du Jésus, 06300 Nice.
Tel 06 81 67 41 22.
www.petitsfarcis.com

Wine Travel Guides
www.winetravel guides.com

ARTS AND CRAFTS

Graham and Belinda Berry
46800 Montcuq.
Tel 05 65 31 49 72.
www.imagefrance.co.uk

Mas Saurine
Comi de l'Estrada, 66320 Joch.
Tel 04 68 05 85 66.
http://mas-saurine.com

Sally Hersh
UK *Tel* 01798 861 248.
www.sallyhersh.com

SURVIVAL
GUIDE

PRACTICAL INFORMATION

France is justifiably proud of its many attractions, for which it has excellent tourist information facilities. Both in France and abroad, French government tourist offices are an invaluable source of reference for practical aspects of your stay. Most towns and large villages have a tourist information office; the relevant address, telephone

FNOTSI
Tourist information logo

number and website (if available) are provided for each town and area listed in this guide. Domestic tourism in France creates peak holiday migration periods, especially between 14 July and 31 August. Consequently, the hotel and restaurant trades are seasonal. A little forward planning will allow you to avoid the pitfalls of seasonal closure.

VISAS AND PASSPORTS

Citizens of EU countries, apart from the UK and Ireland, can enter France with a national identity card. Visitors from the UK, Ireland, the US, Canada, Australia and New Zealand need a full passport. Tourist trips may last up to 3 months, after this a *carte de séjour* (residency permit) is required. Like most EU countries (but not the UK and Ireland) France is part of the Schengen agreement for shared border controls. If you enter the Schengen area through a member country, you are free to cross into all member countries within your 90-day stay.

Non-EU nationals who wish to work or study in France, or stay longer than three months, should obtain a visa from a French consulate in their home country. For more information, check the website of your French embassy and your own country's foreign office.

CUSTOMS INFORMATION

EU residents are allowed to carry any amount of goods between EU countries without paying customs duties, as long as the goods are for personal use. Among the limits generally accepted as being for personal use are 800 cigarettes, 90 litres of wine and 110 litres of beer.

Visitors from outside the EU can reclaim sales tax *(TVA)* on many French goods if more than €175 is spent in one shop in one day. To claim the tax back you must get a *détaxe* form from the store and take your goods out of the EU within three months. Present the receipt at customs when

leaving the country, and mail the stamped receipt as instructed. The refund will then be sent to you or credited to your bank card. There are *détaxe* desks at all main airports and in big stores. Full information is available from **Direction Générale des Douanes**.

Office de Tourisme in the Vence region of France

TOURIST INFORMATION

All cities, towns and many villages have *offices de tourisme*, which provide invaluable free maps and information on local attractions and accommodation. Tourist offices often produce useful guides covering walking and cycling routes, bike-hire, local gastronomy, traditional farm produce and more. Some regional and *département* offices also offer well-priced hotel and tour packages, and many city offices have organized imaginative guided tours and themed routes.

Before travelling to France, you can get basic orientation information and advice from France's official tourist website

FranceGuide or from the French government tourist office (usually called **Atout France**) in your country. For in-depth regional planning it is best to use the websites of the relevant Regional Tourist Boards *(Comité Régional du Tourisme)* or those of the many *départements (Comités Départementaux du Tourisme)*. The latter provide a valuable range of detailed information. Nearly all websites are available in English. Links to these sites can be found on the FranceGuide website.

ADMISSION CHARGES

Most museums and monuments in France charge an entry fee, usually from €2 to €10. There are often family discounts, and those under 26 years old with an EU passport have free access to permanent exhibitions at state-owned sights.

Several multi-entry schemes are available that reduce costs if you plan to visit a number of sights. Foremost, the Paris Museum Pass gives unlimited entry to over 60 museums and monuments in and around Paris for either 2, 4 or 6 days. It can be bought in advance online (www.paris museumpass.com). Other places have local schemes, which often include unlimited use of local transport. Check local tourism websites to see what is available.

Colonne de la Grande Armée

Sign to monument of cultural importance

◁ Menton, Côte d'Azur with backdrop of the Alps

The Arc de Triomphe du Carrousel and the Musée du Louvre in Paris

OPENING HOURS

This guide lists which days of the week sights are open. National museums and sights normally close on Tuesdays, with a few exceptions that close on Mondays. Generally, the larger museums and sights are open from 9 or 10am–6pm, sometimes with one late evening a week, often Thursday. Note that smaller museums and churches may close from 12:30–2pm.

Opening times can also vary considerably by season, especially for country châteaux, estates and gardens. Many are open daily in the peak July to August holiday season and then close completely from November to March, or are only open at weekends. Most sights are closed on Christmas day and New Year's day.

See page 652 for details on opening hours for shops; page 674 for banks; and pages 596–7 for restaurants.

TAXES AND TIPPING

A service charge of 12.5 to 15 per cent is included on all restaurant bills and it is customary to round up the bill by a few euros in a restaurant, or a few cents in a café, especially if the service has been good. In grander restaurants, an extra tip of 5–10 per cent is the norm.

For taxi drivers, the usual tipping rate is around 10 per cent. For hotel porters, it is common to tip around 75 cents to €1.

TRAVELLERS WITH SPECIAL NEEDS

France is working hard to improve access to all its services. There are disabled parking spaces in many streets and all public car parks. These can be used free of charge with a European Blue Badge. SNCF (French railways) has introduced the *Accès Plus* scheme, through which wheelchair users and others with mobility problems can book ahead to guarantee a space and free assistance. For information go to the "Everyday Life" *(Vie Pratique)* section on the SNCF website and look under *Services + (see p682).*

In Paris, some buses, some RER lines and one Métro line (no. 14) are wheelchair accessible *(see pp688–9).* By law, all taxis must carry wheelchair-users for no extra charge *(see p688).*

Much has been done to improve access to attractions, but access to smaller historic houses and country châteaux can be difficult at times. The blue *Tourisme & Handicap* label indicates attractions, hotels, restaurants and other facilities that meet full disabled access criteria. Many hotels and *chambres-d'hôtes* (bed and breakfasts) have adapted rooms, and major booking agencies such as *Logis de France* or *Gîtes de France* indicate this on their websites.

For information on disabled facilities in France, the best resource is the **Association des Paralysés de France** *(APF),*

which produces an annual *Guide Vacances* holiday booklet. The **Infomobi** website also has comprehensive information on transport services for the disabled in and around Paris. Both these resources are in French only. Further information in English can be found on the FranceGuide website.

TRAVELLING WITH CHILDREN

Families travelling in France benefit from a range of cost-cutting discounts including reduced or free admission to attractions for children. Children under 4 travel free on most public transport and children aged 4 to 11 (4 to 9, in Paris) travel half price.

Some of the big French hotel chains (notably Novotel) specialize in catering for families, while many small country hotels and *chambres-d'hôtes* have cost-efficient family rooms *(chambres familiales).* If you base yourself in one area for two days or more, a self-contained *gîte,* with several rooms and a kitchen, can offer exceptional value for money *(see pp548–9).*

Virtually all French restaurants welcome children, and many have a children's menu *(menu d'enfants)* for €5–€8.

The FranceGuide website has information on attractions throughout France, while local tourism websites list regional-specific family attractions and activities. For more ideas, consult websites such as **France for Families** and **Kids in Tow**.

The Château de Versailles has excellent disabled access

SENIOR TRAVELLERS

Senior visitors to France do
not enjoy reduced admission
fees at national museums and
monuments although some
privately-owned châteaux and
attractions do offer lower
prices for older people.
Discounted travel on public
transport is only available with
multi-journey passes issued
by some cities, and the SNCF
Carte Senior for the over 60s
(see p682). However, these
cards are not much use for
short visits, as you'll only
notice the discount if you
make several journeys on each
system. Railpasses (see p682)
bought in advance outside
France can be better value.

STUDENT INFORMATION

Students aged under 26 with
a valid **International Student
Identity Card** (ISIC) benefit
from many discounts, as well
as those available to everyone
in France aged 25 or under.
The Centre d'Information et
de Documentation Jeunesse
will provide you with further
information (www.cidj.com).

GAY AND LESBIAN TRAVELLERS

France has prominent gay and
lesbian communities that are
becoming ever more part of

the cultural mainstream. The
Marais district of Paris is the
country's foremost "gay
village", but there are gay
clubs and services all over
the capital. There are gay
communities in many other
cities, especially in Toulouse,
Nantes, Montpellier and Nice.
Tune into Radio FG (98.2 MHz)
or consult listings in *Têtu* and
Lesbia magazines for a wide
range of gay-friendly information. For further help,
contact **Centre Gai et Lesbien**
in Paris.

TRAVELLING ON A BUDGET

How much you spend on a
holiday in France will vary
enormously depending on
what you do. However, in
general, two people staying
at a basic hotel (an average
of €60 for a double room),
eating both lunch and dinner
in restaurants, visiting a few
attractions and using public
transport can roughly expect
to spend €160 per day in most
parts of France, or €80 each.
Staying in Paris, the Côte
d'Azur and other fashionable
resorts is expensive but less-
visited rural regions such as
Normandy, inland Brittany
and Lorraine can be more
affordable. Travelling in peak
season (July–mid-September)
will also be costly with high

**International Student
Identity Card**

hotel rates, particularly in
the most popular regions.
December and March, the
winter sports season, can also
be pricey, particularly in the
Alps. If you want to keep
costs down it is best to travel
during the low season when
hotel prices are much
cheaper. City hotels, however,
can be more reasonable
between July and August
when most French people
head for the country.
Staying in a *chambre-
d'hôtes* (bed and breakfast) is
a good alternative to costly
hotels. Traditionally, these are
located in the countryside but
they are now popping up in
towns and the average price
for a comfortable double
room is around €40 including
breakfast. Another option is a
gîte, which offers self-catering
facilities, though these usually
require a minimum stay of
a weekend or a week.
When dining, opt for a set
menu – ordering from the à la
carte menu will be far more
expensive. Taking your main

Waiting to travel at Marseille Gare St-Charles train station meal at midday rather than in the evening will mean you can make the most of the best-value set menus or *formules*. To keep costs down when sightseeing, opt for a City Pass that gives unlimited travel on local transport as well as entry to local monuments *(see p689)*. If you intend to rent a car, book it in advance through an Internet rental agency to get the best rates.

FRENCH TIME

France is one hour ahead of Greenwich Mean Time (GMT) in both winter and summer.

ELECTRICAL ADAPTORS

The voltage in France is 220 volts. Plugs are the standard

Queueing for the Eiffel Tower

type used in most of Europe with two round pins, or three for applications that need to be earthed. Many hotels offer built-in adaptors for shavers.

CONVERSION CHART

Imperial to metric
1 inch = 2.54 centimetres
1 foot = 30 centimetres
1 mile = 1.6 kilometres
1 ounce = 28 grams
1 pound = 454 grams
1 pint = 0.6 litre
1 gallon = 4.6 litres

Metric to imperial
1 millimetre = 0.04 inch
1 centimetre = 0.4 inch
1 metre = 3 feet 3 inches
1 kilometre = 0.6 mile
1 gram = 0.04 ounce
1 kilogram = 2.2 pounds
1 litre = 1.8 pints

RESPONSIBLE TRAVEL

In France, as in many other countries, there has been a rapid growth in environmental awareness. **Echoway** is one of the leading French ecotourism organizations, encouraging heightened awareness of responsible travel. **Mountain**

Riders promotes sustainable winter tourism in the Alps, providing information on how to get to the mountains by public transport and arranging group walks to clean up mountain pistes each spring.

France has a long-running rural tourism network, with farmhouse accommodation available through the central Gîtes de France agency *(see p549)*. There are also smaller organizations with a more defined ecological stance such as **Accueil Paysan**, which is a network of small-scale farmers practising low-impact, sustainable agriculture. Another alternative to staying in a hotel is camping, and there are over 9,000 fully-equipped campsites across the country to choose from *(see p548)*.

Information on local green tourism *(tourisme vert or eco)* initiatives and activities can be found through local tourist offices. Many towns have weekly markets selling only organic and traditional produce (usually called a *marché bio*), which allow visitors to give back to the local community. Market days have been provided throughout the guide.

DIRECTORY

EMBASSIES

Australia
4 Rue Jean Rey, 75015 Paris. **Map** 6 D3. *Tel 01 40 59 33 06*. **www.**france.embassy.gov.au

Canada
35 Ave Montaigne, 75008 Paris. **Map** 6 F1. *Tel 01 44 43 29 00*. **www.**canadainternational.gc.ca

United Kingdom
35 Rue du Faubourg St-Honoré, 75383 Paris. **Map** 3 C5. *Tel 01 44 51 31 00*. **http://**ukinfrance.fco.gov.uk/fr

United States
2 Ave Gabriel, 75008 Paris. **Map** 3 A5. *Tel 01 43 12 22 22*. **http://**france.usembassy.gov

FRENCH TOURIST OFFICES

Australia
Level 13, 25 Bligh St, Sydney NSW 2000. *Tel (2) 9231 52 44*. **www.**au.franceguide.com

Paris Convention and Visitors Bureau
25 Rue des Pyramides, 75001 Paris. *Tel 01 49 52 42 63*. **www.**parisinfo.com

United Kingdom
Lincoln House, 300 High Holborn, London WC1V 7JH. *Tel 0906 824 4123*. **www.**uk.franceguide.com

United States
444 Madison Ave, New York, NY 10022. *Tel (1) 212 838 7800*. **www.**us.franceguide.com

CUSTOMS INFORMATION

Direction Générales des Douanes
Tel 08 11 20 44 44. **www.**douane.gouv.fr

GAY AND LESBIAN TRAVELLERS

Centre Gai et Lesbien
63 Rue Beaubourg, 75003 Paris. *Tel 01 43 57 21 47*.

SPECIAL NEEDS

APF
www.apf.asso.fr

Infomobi
www.infomobi.com

Tourisme & Handicaps
www.tourisme-handicaps.org

FAMILIES AND STUDENTS

France for Families
www.france4families.com

International Student Identity Card (ISIC)
www.isic.org
www.isiccard.com

Kids in Tow
www.kidsintow.co.uk

RESPONSIBLE TRAVEL

Accueil Paysan
Tel 04 76 43 44 83.
www.accueil-paysan.com

Echoway
www.echoway.org

FranceGuide
www.franceguide.com

Mountain Riders
www.mountain-riders.org

Personal Security and Health

On the whole France is a safe place for visitors, but it is always a good idea to take the normal precautions of looking after your possessions and avoiding unfamiliar or unfrequented residential urban areas after dark. If you fall ill during your stay, pharmacies generally offer good advice while the emergency services can be contacted for any serious medical problems. Consulates and consular departments *(see p671)* at your embassy can also provide assistance in an emergency.

French pharmacy sign

Gendarmes

POLICE

Violent crime is not a major problem in France, but as in any country it is advisable to be on your guard against petty theft, especially in cities. If you are robbed, lose any property or are the victim of any other type of crime, report the incident as soon as possible at the nearest *commissariat de police* (police station). In an emergency, dialling 17 will also connect you to the police department, but you will still have to go to a station to make a statement. In small towns and villages, crime is reported to the *gendarmerie*, the force mainly responsible for rural policing. The *mairie* (town hall) is also a good place to go for help but this will only be open during office hours.

At all police stations you will be required to make a statement, called a *PV* or *procès verbal*, listing any lost or stolen items. You will need your passport, and, if relevant, your vehicle papers. It is important to keep a copy of your police statement for your insurance claim.

LOST AND STOLEN PROPERTY

The likelihood, and impact, of street theft can be considerably reduced by a few simple precautions. In the first instance, ensure that all possessions are covered by a comprehensive travel insurance policy before arrival. Once in France, avoid risky city neighbourhoods, and beware of pickpockets, especially on the Paris Métro during rush hour (particularly just as the carriage doors are closing). When you sit at a pavement café table, always keep your bag within reach and in sight, preferably on your lap or on the table, and never leave it on the ground or hanging on the back of a chair. Keep bags zipped up and held close to you when walking along, and never leave luggage unattended at train stations or other travel centres. Keep valuables securely concealed and only carry with you as much cash as you think you will need for the day.

For lost or stolen property, it may be worth returning to the station where you reported the incident to check if the police have retrieved some of the items. In addition, all French town halls have a *Bureau d'Objets Trouvés* (lost property office), although they are often inefficient and finding items can take time. Lost property offices can also be found at larger train stations, which will be open during office hours.

If your passport is lost or stolen, notify your consulate immediately *(see p671)*. The loss of credit or debit cards should also be reported as soon as possible to your bank to avoid fraudulent use.

TRAVEL INSURANCE

All travellers in France should have a comprehensive travel insurance policy providing adequate cover for any eventuality, including potential medical and legal expenses, theft, lost luggage and other personal property, accidents, travel delays and the option of immediate repatriation by air in the event of a major medical emergency. Winter sports are not covered by standard travel policies so if you are planning to ski or to undertake any other adventure sports in France you will need to pay an additional premium to ensure you are protected. All insurance policies should come with a 24-hour emergency number in case of need.

IN AN EMERGENCY

The phone number for all emergency services is 112, but in practice it is often quicker to call the relevant authority direct on their traditional two-digit numbers. In a medical emergency call the **Service d'Aide Médicale Urgence** (SAMU), who will send an ambulance. However, it can sometimes be faster to call

DIRECTORY

EMERGENCY NUMBERS

All Emergency Services
Tel 112.

Ambulance (SAMU)
Tel 15.

Fire (Sapeurs Pompiers)
Tel 18.

Police and Gendarmerie
Tel 17.

the **Sapeurs Pompiers** (fire service) who also offer first aid and can take you to the nearest hospital. This is particularly true in rural areas, where the fire station is likely to be much closer than the ambulance service based in town. The paramedics are called *secouristes*.

HOSPITALS AND PHARMACIES

All European Union nationals holding a European Health Insurance Card (EHIC) are entitled to use the French national health service. However, under the French system patients must pay for all treatments and then reclaim most of the cost from the health authorities. Therefore, non-French EU nationals who use health services in France will need to ensure they keep the statement of costs (*feuille de soins*) that is provided by the doctor or hospital. This should include stickers for any prescription drugs, which must be stuck onto the statement by the pharmacist once you have made your purchase. Around 80 per cent of the cost can be claimed back by following the instructions provided with your EHIC card. This can be a time-consuming process, and it can often be simpler to use private travel insurance. Non-EU nationals must have full private medical insurance while in France and pay for services in the same way, claiming their costs back in full from their insurance company.

Well-equipped public hospitals can be found throughout France. In all towns and cities there are hospitals with general casualty/emergency departments (called *urgences* or *service des urgences*) that can deal with immediate medical problems. If your hotel cannot direct you to one, call the SAMU or fire service. Should you require an English-speaking doctor, your consulate should be able to recommend one in the area, and in Paris and some other cities in France, there are both American and British private hospitals.

Pharmacies, identified by an illuminated green cross sign, are plentiful and easy to find. French pharmacists are highly trained and can diagnose minor health problems and suggest appropriate treatments. When one is closed, a card in the window will give details of the nearest *pharmacie de garde* that is open on Sundays or during the night.

NATURAL HAZARDS

Forest fires are a major risk in many parts of France. High winds can mean fires spread rapidly in winter as well as in summer, so be vigilant about putting out all campfires and cigarette butts. Keep well away from any area where there is a fire, as its direction can change quickly.

Before exploring any of the country's seven national parks or its regional nature parks (*parcs naturels*), visit the relevant park information centre to check the regulations and recommendations that apply within the area, and take care to observe them. When walking in mountains or sailing, inform the relevant authority – such as a park information centre or a harbourmaster – of your intended route and when you expect to return. Never try to

Police car

Fire engine

Ambulance

walk in remote mountain areas or across tidal marshes without an experienced guide, or against local advice.

During the hunting season (Sep–Feb and especially Sundays) dress in visible colours when out walking and avoid areas where hunters are staked out in hides (*see p663*).

SAFETY ON BEACHES

There are many good family beaches throughout France where bathing is rarely dangerous. Many beaches are guarded in summer by lifeguards (*sauveteurs*) – always heed their instructions and only swim in supervised areas. Also look out for the system of coloured flags, indicating whether it is safe to swim. Green flags mean bathing is safe; orange flags warn that bathing may be dangerous and that only the part of the beach marked out by flags is guarded. Swimming outside this area is therefore not recommended. Red flags indicate dangerous conditions (high waves, shifting sands, strong undercurrents), so all bathing is forbidden. Many beaches also display blue flags, which are used throughout the European Union as a sign of cleanliness.

Fire hazard poster

ATTENTION AU FEU

Banking and Local Currency

You may bring any amount of currency into France, but anything over €7,500 (cash and cheques) must be declared on arrival. The same applies when you leave. Travellers' cheques are the safest way to carry money abroad, but credit or debit cards, which can be used to withdraw local currency, are by far the most convenient. Bureaux de change are located at airports, large railway stations and in some hotels and shops, although banks usually offer the best rates of exchange.

ATM machine in Paris

USING BANKS

Most banks will exchange foreign currency and travellers' cheques, but the commission rates vary, so it is worth looking around to make sure you get the best deal. Virtually all bank branches have ATMs (automatic teller machines), which accept major credit and debit cards. Most ATMs can give instructions in English.

Travellers' cheques can be obtained from **American Express** (AmEx), **Travelex** or your bank. American Express cheques are widely accepted and no commission is charged if they are exchanged at their offices. In the case of theft, cheques are replaced at once.

BANKING HOURS

In Paris, and many other cities, banks are generally open from 9 or 10am–5pm Mon–Fri, with some branches open on Saturdays. Elsewhere banks are usually closed on Mondays and generally open from 8 or 9am–12:30pm and 2–5pm Tue–Fri and 8 or 9am–12:30pm on Saturday. There are, however, many variations between banks, and individual

Credit and debit card readers require you to enter your PIN number

branches. All banks close on Sundays and public holidays, and many also close at noon on the working day before the holiday.

BUREAUX DE CHANGE

Outside Paris, independent bureaux de change are rare except in major railway stations and high-density tourist areas. Privately owned bureaux de change can have variable rates: check commission and minimum charges first.

CREDIT AND DEBIT CARDS

Major credit cards such as **Visa** or **MasterCard** and debit cards such as Switch, Maestro or Cirrus are widely used, and are essential for most large transactions such as renting a car. Many French businesses do not accept American Express credit cards.

French credit and debit cards operate on a chip-and-PIN system so you will need to know your PIN *(code personnel)*. If you have a North American card that does not use chip-and-PIN technology you must ask that your card be swiped.

Given the high commission rates often charged for exchanging travellers' cheques, the most economical and convenient way to get local currency is just to withdraw it from an ATM with a debit card. Bear in mind, however, that ATMs may run out of notes during weekends. If an ATM is not working, you can also withdraw up to €300 per day on major credit cards at the foreign counter of a bank. The bank may need to obtain telephone authorization for such withdrawals first.

THE EURO

France was one of the twelve countries taking the euro (€) in 2002, with the original currency, the franc, phased out on the 17 February 2002.

EU members using the euro as sole official currency are known as the Eurozone. Several EU members have either opted out or have not met the conditions for adopting the single currency.

Euro notes are identical throughout the Eurozone countries, each one including designs of fictional monuments and architectural structures, and the 12 stars of the EU. The coins, however, have one side identical (the value side), and one side with an image unique to each country. Both notes and coins are exchangeable in any of the participating Euro countries.

Bank Notes

Euro bank notes have seven denominations. The €5 note (grey in colour) is the smallest, followed by the €10 note (pink), €20 note (blue), €50 note (orange), €100 note (green), €200 note (yellow) and €500 note (purple). All notes show the stars of the European Union.

€5 note

€10 note

€20 note

€50 note

€100 note

€200 note

€500 note

€2 coin   €1 coin   50 cents   20 cents   10 cents

Coins

The euro has eight coin denominations: €1 and €2; 50 cents, 20 cents, 10 cents, 5 cents, 2 cents and 1 cent. The €2 and €1 coins are both silver and gold in colour. The 50-, 20- and 10-cent coins are gold. The 5-, 2- and 1-cent coins are bronze.

5 cents   2 cents   1 cent

Communications and Media

French telecommunications are very efficient. Most landline telephones are provided by France Télécom, which also owns Orange, the international mobile phone group. Public telephones can be found in most public places and usually require a phone card *(télécarte)*. Post offices *(bureaux des postes)* are identified by the blue-on-yellow La Poste sign; the postal service was previously known as PTT and this is often still indicated on road signs. Foreign-language newspapers are available in most large towns, and some TV channels and radio stations broadcast foreign-language programmes.

A distinctive yellow French mail box

LOCAL AND INTERNATIONAL PHONE CALLS

All French telephone numbers have ten digits, and you must key in all the digits even if you are in the same area. In landline numbers the first two digits indicate the region: 01 is for Paris and the Ile de France; 02, the northwest; 03, the northeast; 04, the southeast; and 05, the southwest. French mobile phone numbers begin with 06, and 08 indicates a special rate number. All 0800 numbers are free. For landline numbers, cheap rates operate on evenings, weekends and public holidays. It is best to avoid making calls from hotels as most add hefty surcharges.

To call France from abroad, dial 00 33 and omit the initial zero from the 10-digit French number. You cannot call French 08 numbers from outside the country.

To call abroad from France, dial 00 and then the country code (Australia 61, USA and Canada 1, Irish Republic 353, New Zealand 64 and UK 44).

France Télécom public telephone

MOBILE PHONES

Mobile phone coverage is generally good throughout France, although signals may be weak in some mountain areas. French mobiles use the European-standard 900 and 1900 MHz frequencies, so UK mobiles work if they have a roaming facility enabled. North American mobile phones will only operate in France if they are tri- or quad-band. Always check roaming charges with your service provider before travelling, as making and receiving calls can be very expensive. Some companies offer "packages" for foreign calls which can work out cheaper.

If you expect to use your phone frequently it can be more economical to get a cheap pay-as-you-go French mobile from one of the main local providers such as **Orange France**, **Bouygues Télécom** or **SFR**. All three companies have shops in most towns. You can also insert a local SIM card into your own phone, but this will only work if your phone has not been blocked by your service provider.

PUBLIC TELEPHONES

Few pay phones *(cabine téléphonique)* now accept coins, so to use one you will need a phone card *(télécarte)*. Sold in *tabacs*, post offices, train stations and some news-agents, cards are available for 50 or 120 telephone units, and are simple to use. When you enter a phone box, the phone display will say "*Decrochez*", your signal to pick up the phone, followed

by "*Introduisez votre carte*", for you to insert your card. The display will then say "*Patientez SVP*", followed by "*Numéro-tez*", at which point you dial the number you wish to call. For local calls, one unit lasts up to 6 minutes. Don't forget to take your card with you when you finish the call.

Many phones also accept credit cards (with a PIN number), and Travelex bureaux de change *(see p674)* also sell an International Telephone Card that can be used in several countries and provides good value for money. There are still a few coin and token-operated pay phones left in some cafés. At some large train stations and post offices there are staffed telephone booths *(cabines)* where you pay after you have made your call. This can be a cheaper option when making long-distance calls.

INTERNET ACCESS

The Internet is widely used in France, but surprisingly, Internet cafés are a lot less common than in much of Europe. They are plentiful in Paris, and there are usually a few in most cities and resorts, but in small towns and rural areas, they can be hard to find. It is often much easier to get online if you travel with a laptop. In Paris there are free Wi-Fi hotspots in many Métro stations, public libraries and other locations, and similar projects are being introduced in other major cities. Many hotels and even *chambres-d'hôtes* now offer Wi-Fi connections, but check that these are free. Most hotels use one of several subscription services such as Orange France and **Meteor**, with which you buy a certain amount of time-credit and are then given an access code. Any time-credit remaining can be used anywhere that uses the same service.

French Wi-Fi servers often use different frequencies to those in the UK and North America, so you may need to manually search for the network (for more details, see the Orange Wi-Fi website). If you need to use a cable connection, note that the French modem socket is incompatible with US and UK plugs. Adaptors are available, but it is often cheaper and easier to buy a French modem lead.

POSTAL SERVICES

The postal service in France is fast and usually reliable. There are post offices in most towns, and there are large main offices in all cities. Postage stamps *(timbres)* can be bought at post offices individually or in a *carnet* of seven or ten, although the most convenient place to buy stamps is often at a *tabac*, where phonecards can also be purchased.

Post offices usually open from 9am–5pm Mon–Fri, often with a break for lunch, and 9am–noon on Saturdays. Post offices in towns and cities are best avoided when they first open as this is when they are at their busiest.

Letters are posted in yellow mail boxes which often have separate slots for post within the town you are in, within the *département* and for other destinations *(autres destinations)*. There are eight different price zones for international mail. Information on all mail services is provided on the **La Poste** website.

NEWSPAPERS AND MAGAZINES

Newspapers and magazines can be bought at newsagents *(maisons de la presse)* or newsstands *(kiosques)*. Regional newspapers tend to be more popular than the Paris-based national papers, such as the conservative *Le Figaro*, weighty *Le Monde* or leftist *Libération*. The daily *International Herald Tribune* can be found in Paris and throughout France. Other foreign newspapers are also often available on the day of publication in resorts and large cities.

The weekly listings magazines *Pariscope* (Thursday) and *L'Officiel des Spectacles* (Wednesday) give the latest on entertainment news in Paris. *Les Inrockuptibles* magazine has information on current music, film and the other arts from all over France. Many smaller cities have their own listings magazines, usually in French and often free, which can generally be found at tourist offices.

TV AND RADIO

All French television networks use Digital Video Broadcasting (DVB). There are 18 free channels, including the major national channels *TF1* and *France 2*. *Canal Plus* (or *Canal +*), a subscription-only channel, offers a broad mix of programmes including live sports and films in English with French subtitles. A film shown in its original language is listed as *VO (Version Originale)*; a film dubbed into French is indicated as *VF (Version Française)*. Most hotels subscribe to *Canal +*, and many also have cable and satellite TV, including English-language stations such as CNN, MTV, Sky and BBC World.

It is easy to pick up UK radio stations, including *Radio 4* (198 long wave). *BBC World Service* broadcasts through the night on the same wavelength. *Voice of America* can be found at 90.5, 98.8 and 102.4 FM. *Radio France International* (738 AM) gives daily news in English from 3–4pm.

Newspapers sold in France

La Poste road sign

TRAVEL INFORMATION

France enjoys sophisticated air, road and rail travel. Direct flights from all over the world serve Paris and some regional airports. Paris is the hub of a vast internal rail network and of Europe's high-speed train network, with the Euro-star to London, Thalys to Brussels and TGVs to Geneva and other destinations. Motorways cross into all surrounding countries including, via the Eurotunnel, the UK. France is also served by frequent Channel and Mediterranean ferries.

Getting to or from France on the national carrier, Air France

ARRIVING BY AIR

France is served by nearly all international airlines. Most long-haul flights arrive at Paris Charles de Gaulle airport, but there are flights from Europe and North Africa to many other airports around the country.

Airlines with regular flights between the UK and France include **British Airways**, **Air France** and low-cost airlines such as **bmibaby**, **Flybe**, **Jet2**, **Ryanair** and **easyJet**. From North America there are direct flights to Paris from about 20 cities, mainly on **Air Canada**, **American Airlines**, **Delta**, **United** and Air France. **Qantas** provides connecting flights from Australia and New Zealand.

PARIS AIRPORTS

Paris's Charles-de-Gaulle airport (CDG), about 30 km from the city, is the main hub airport in France. Access to central Paris is by RER line B from CDG2, which takes 40 minutes to Gare du Nord and 45 minutes to Châtelet-Les Halles. Regular bus services run from the airport to different parts of Paris, and to Disneyland Paris theme park. Air France buses run to the Arc de Triomphe and western Paris, and to Montparnasse;

each journey takes about 45 minutes. RATP buses (Roissybus) depart every 20 minutes for L'Opéra and take about 50 minutes. Taxis into central Paris cost around €30–€45 and can take up to an hour depending on traffic.

Paris's other main airport, Orly, in the south of the city, serves primarily domestic and short-haul international flights. Shuttle buses link the airport with RER line C at Pont de Rungis and an automatic train, Orlyval, links the airport with RER line B at Antony, from where trains run to Châtelet-Les Halles in 35 minutes. Air France buses for central Paris depart every 30 minutes; RATP Orlybus runs to Denfert-Rochereau Métro; and the

Jetbus connects Orly to Châtelet-Les Halles, departing every 15–20 minutes. Taxis take 25–45 minutes to the city centre, and cost about €25.

ARRIVING BY SEA

Several regular ferry services operate between the UK and Ireland and France. Dover–Calais is the fastest route: **P&O Ferries** has up to 25 crossings daily, with a journey time of 90 minutes or less. **Seafrance** also offers several crossings a day. **Norfolkline** runs from Dover to Dunkerque in about two hours and has some of the lowest fares. Further west, French operator **Transmanche Ferries/LD Lines** has crossings between Newhaven and Dieppe (about 4 hrs) and Portsmouth and Le Havre (8 hrs overnight). The biggest operator in the western Channel is **Brittany Ferries**, which sails from Portsmouth to Caen (7 hrs overnight), Poole to Cherbourg (6 hrs overnight), Portsmouth to St Malo (10 hrs overnight), Plymouth to Roscoff (8 hrs overnight), and between Cork and Roscoff (14 hrs). From April/May to September/October, Brittany Ferries also runs high-speed services on the Poole–Cherbourg and

Plying the Mediterranean with SNCM Ferryterranée

Portsmouth–Cherbourg routes (4 hrs 30 mins). **Condor Ferries** sail from Portsmouth to Cherbourg in 5 hours (July–September only) and from Poole and Weymouth to St Malo via Jersey or Guernsey (May–September only).

Irish Ferries runs between Rosslare and Cherbourg (17 hrs overnight) from January to December, and to Roscoff (15 hrs 30 mins overnight) from mid-May to September. SNCM run ferries from a range of European ports (see p683).

ARRIVING BY TRAIN

There are at least 20 **Eurostar** trains daily between London St Pancras and the Gare du Nord in Paris. The journey via the Channel Tunnel takes 2 hrs 15 mins. Several trains also stop at Ebbsfleet or Ashford in Kent, Calais–Frethun, Lille (1 hr 30 mins from London) and Disneyland® Paris.

Paris and its six main stations are the great hub of the French rail network. Travelling from Belgium, Holland and north Germany, you arrive at the Gare du Nord; from other parts of Germany you come into the Gare de l'Est. Trains from Switzerland and Italy arrive at the Gare de Lyons. From Spain you come into the Gare d'Austerlitz. Outside Paris, other major rail hubs include Lille, Tours, Bordeaux and Lyon. For more information on French rail services and travelling to France by train (see pp680–82).

Eurotunnel logo

ARRIVING BY ROAD

Passengers from the UK can travel to France with their vehicle either by ferry or on the **Eurotunnel** shuttle through the Channel Tunnel. Eurotunnel runs at least four trains an hour during the day, and the trip takes about 35 minutes. Fares compete with those of the ferry companies, and similarly vary by season, day and time of travel. For Eurotunnel crossings, it is possible to turn up and wait for the next available space.

Coach travel is a good-value alternative, and **Eurolines** runs three to five departures daily from Victoria Coach Station in London to Bagnolet in eastern Paris. Coaches also run from London and other parts of the UK to Lille, Lyon, Marseille and several other French towns and cities.

GREEN TRAVEL

Travelling in France without flying or driving is easier than in many countries thanks to the high quality of public transport, particularly the SNCF rail network. There are daily train services from across Europe, ferries to the UK, Ireland and Mediterranean destinations, and the Eurostar connection with London (see pp680–85).

The French government has introduced an "Ecomobility" programme, which aims to make it easier to transfer from trains to local buses, bicycles or other non-car forms of transport. This includes free cycle schemes like the *Vélib'*, now in use in Paris and other cities (see p689). Many regions have also developed **Voies Vertes**, long distance paths for cycling or walking, such as the one along the Loire from Orléans to St-Nazaire.

DIRECTORY

AIRLINES

Air Canada
Tel 01 888 247 2262
(Canada), 0825 880 881
(France).
www.aircanada.com

Air France
Tel 0820 320 820 (France).
www.airfrance.com

American Airlines
Tel 01 800 433 7300
(USA), 0826 460 950
(France). www.aa.com

British Airways
Tel 0844 490 0787 (UK),
0825 825 400 (France).
www.britishairways.com

bmibaby
www.bmibaby.com

Delta
Tel 01 800 221 1212
(USA), 08 11 64 00 05
(France). www.delta.com

easyJet
Tel 0871 244 2366 (UK),
0826 103 320 (France).
www.easyjet.com

Flybe
www.flybe.com

Jet2
Tel 0871 226 1737 (UK),
0821 230 203 (France).
www.jet2.com

Qantas
Tel 13 13 13 (Australia),
08 11 98 00 02 (France).
www.qantas.com

Ryanair
Tel 0871 246 000
(UK), 0892 780 270
(France).
www.ryanair.com

United
Tel 01 800 864 8331
(USA), 0810 72 72 72
(France).
www.united.com

FERRY SERVICES

Brittany Ferries
www.brittany-ferries.com

Condor Ferries
www.condorferries.co.uk

Irish Ferries
www.irishferries.com

Norfolkline
www.norfolkline.com

P&O Ferries
www.poferries.com

Seafrance
www.seafrance.com

**Transmanche
Ferries/LD Lines**
www.transmanche
ferries.com

RAIL TRAVEL

See also p682

Eurostar
Tel 08705 186 186 (UK),
0892 35 35 39 (France).
www.eurostar.com

ROAD TRAVEL

Eurolines
Tel 0871 781 8181 (UK),
0892 899 091 (France).
www.eurolines.com

Eurotunnel
Tel 08705 35 35 35 (UK),
0810 630 304 (France).
www.eurotunnel.com

GREEN TRAVEL

Train+Bicycle Travel
www.velo.sncf.com

Voies Vertes
www.voiesvertes.com

Travelling by Train

SNCF logo

The French state railway, Société Nationale des Chemins de Fer (**SNCF**), runs Europe's most comprehensive national rail network. Its services include high-speed long-distance TGVs and mainline expresses, overnight sleepers, Motorail and rural branch lines that reach every corner of the country. Lines closed for economic reasons are replaced by SNCF's modern buses, free to railpass holders. Travel off the main lines can be slow, though some cross-country journeys are quicker if you change trains in Paris.

TRAVELLING AROUND FRANCE BY TRAIN

France has always been known for the punctuality of its trains, and has maintained a high level of investment in the state-owned rail system, SNCF. The pride of the SNCF is its TGV high-speed trains, with journey times such as Lille–Lyon or Paris–Marseille in just 3 hours. In addition, frequent, fast and comfortable main-line express trains provide a comprehensive city-to-city service, while regional lines provide connections to smaller towns and villages. SNCF is also the largest bus operator in France, filling in the gaps where railway lines have been closed.

Sleeper trains are a convenient way to travel long distances at night, and motorists can travel with their cars on **AutoTrain** trains. Most (but not all) long-distance trains have restaurant cars.

Further information on French railways is provided on the main SNCF website (*see p682*) where reservations can also be made. To book

a long-distance train from abroad, visit www.voyages-sncf.com. **Rail Europe** also offers a comprehensive information and booking service for travel throughout Europe. For useful links and an invaluable guide to every aspect of using French and other European railways, visit **The Man in Seat 61** website.

LOCAL AND SCENIC RAILWAYS

Alongside the national rail network there are several special railways that operate around France. On Corsica, the **Chemins de Fer de la Corse** has narrow-gauge lines between Calvi, Bastia and Ajaccio. Particularly spectacular is the rail trip along the north-west coast between L'Ile-Rousse and Calvi. In summer, old-style *trains touristiques* run on this and other lines. In Provence, the privately run **Chemins de Fer de Provence** runs the *Train*

des Pignes over a magnificent 150-km (90-mile) mountain route from Nice to Digne-les-Bains. SNCF also runs many more *trains touristiques* on particularly scenic sections of its regional network. These are usually in mountainous areas during the winter months and in summer on the coast and in the countryside. *Gentiane Bleu* trains run from Dijon to the winter snows in the Jura, and the *Train des Merveilles* runs from Nice into the Alps at Tende. For a guide to all these routes visit www.trainstouristiques-ter.com.

Several privately or locally owned rail lines around France are kept going by enthusiasts who offer excursions for part of the year, often using steam trains. The *Chemin de Fer de la Baie de la Somme* travels around the Somme Bay in Picardy and the *Chemin de Fer Touristique du Tarn* operates in the Tarn hills near Albi. Nearly all of these companies are members of the **UNECTO** association.

Symbol for Paris suburban trains

RER

TYPES OF TRAIN

SNCF trains are divided into several types. TGV (*Train à Grande Vitesse*) trains are the flagships of the network, travelling on specially built track at around 300 kph (186 mph). There are four main TGV route networks; to the north, west, east and south-east from Paris, with additional hubs at Lille, Lyon, Bordeaux and Marseille. In some places, TGVs have separate stations built outside town centres. The trains have first- and second-class carriages, and some of them offer Internet access. Seat reservations are obligatory for all TGV trains: tickets can be bought at stations until shortly before departure time, or booked ahead online.

Within the TGV network there are several international services including Eurostar, linking France with the UK;

The train to Le Montenvers is a particularly scenic route

Thalys, which runs between Paris and Belgium, and Holland and Germany; Lyria, serving Switzerland and Artesia, which runs a TGV service to Turin and Milan, and a conventional train from Paris to Rome. Non-TGV international trains also operate, notably the nightly Elipsos from Paris to Madrid and Barcelona.

Corail trains are conventional long-distance express trains with modern carriages; Corail Téoz trains run by day; Corail Lunéa trains are overnight with sleepers. Corail Intercités trains are slightly faster with fewer stops. Reservations are obligatory for all Corail trains and can be made through Rail Europe or SNCF.

Motorail trains allow drivers to cut out long distances by travelling overnight with their car on the same train. Routes

The TGV, with its distinctive-looking "nose"

run from Calais to Nice via Avignon, and Calais to Narbonne. AutoTrains run from Paris to Nice, Narbonne and Bordeaux. Reservations are essential.

TER trains are regional services that usually stop at every station. Reservations are not required and tickets can generally not be bought in

advance. Route maps and information (in French only) for each region are available at stations and on the TER website *(see p682)*. Transilien is the TER network for the Ile-de-France around Paris, which is integrated with the RER suburban trains and the Métro.

TGV RAIL SERVICE

Trains à Grande Vitesse, or high-speed trains, travel at speeds up to 300 kph (186 mph). There are four routes: TGV Nord from Paris Gare du Nord, TGV Atlantique from Paris Gare Montparnasse, TGV Sud-Est from Paris Gare de Lyon and TGV Est from Paris Gare de l'Est.

KEY

▬	Nord
▬	Atlantique
▬	Sud-Est
▬	Est

The automatic ticket machines at the Gare de Lyon in Paris

FARES AND PASSES

Fare rates vary according to the type of train. For all trains that can be booked online (TGV, Corail, Motorail), there are two or three basic fare rates for each class. The cheapest tickets are called Prem's, which must be booked well in advance and cannot be altered after payment. On most TER and some Corail trains, fares are cheaper at off-peak times *(périodes bleus)*; peak times *(périodes blanches)* are 5–10am Monday and 3–8pm Friday and Sunday.

SNCF sells several travel cards that give fare reductions of around 50 per cent. Examples are the *Carte 12–25* for young people, *Carte Senior* for over-60s, *Carte Escapades* for frequent travellers and *Carte Enfant +* for parents with small children. Further details are available on the SNCF website.

For visitors intending to make several train journeys around France it is worth investing in a multi-journey rail pass, which can only be bought outside the country. The **Inter-Rail** pass, for UK and other European residents, is valid for several European countries, giving unlimited travel for 3, 4, 6 or 8 days (not necessarily consecutively) within one month. Visitors from outside Europe can buy a France Railpass, permitting 3 to 9 days of unlimited travel within one month, or a **Eurail** Select Pass that covers France and neighbouring countries. Be aware that some trains, including the TGV, charge additional supplements, which are usually included in the price. For more information visit the Rail Europe website.

BOOKING TICKETS

Train tickets can be bought at any SNCF station and by phone or online. At most stations, there are both staffed counters and automatic ticket machines *(billetterie automatique),* which accept cash or credit cards and have instructions in English. Tickets for trains that require a reservation (TGV, Corail) can be bought up to 90 days in advance and up until 5 minutes before departure. Tickets bought in advance can be collected from the station, or sent to your address.

From outside France, you can book TGV and Corail tickets through www.voyages-sncf. com, the English arm of the SNCF website, although it can be easier to use Rail Europe. Travellers with mobility problems can arrange assistance through the *Accès Plus* programme; more information is available online or from FranceGuide *(see pp668–71).*

Note that before any train journey in France, you must validate your ticket in a *composteur* machine.

TIMETABLES

French railway timetables change twice a year, in May and September, and all of them can be consulted on the SNCF website. Stations have free regional TER timetables available and information on the TGV network. Other free leaflets provide information on topics such as travelling with children, reduced fares and travel for the disabled.

Composteur Machine
Yellow composteur *machines (left) are located in station halls and at the head of each platform. You must validate passes by inserting tickets and reservations separately, printed side up. The* composteur *will punch your ticket and print the time and date on the back. A penalty may be imposed by the inspector on the train if you fail to do this.*

Travelling by Boat

With both Mediterranean and Atlantic coastlines, France offers excellent opportunities for sailing and has very good facilities. Inland, there is an extensive network of rivers, canals and other waterways. Cruising through them is an ideal way to discover some of the country's most charming countryside. Frequent scheduled ferries also connect mainland France to Corsica and other parts of the Mediterranean as well as to the British Channel Islands off Normandy.

Boats moored along the Canal du Midi, Roussillon

TRAVELLING BY FERRY

Car ferries sail to Corsica from Marseille, Nice and Toulon, the main operators being **SNCM** and **Corsica Ferries**. **La Méridionale** sails between Corsica and Sardinia, and **Moby Lines** also connects Corsica with Livorno and Genoa in mainland Italy. **Grimaldi Ferries** sails from France to Morocco, and Italy. Regular ferries also connect France and North Africa; SNCM runs to Algeria and Tunisia, while **Comanav** has a luxury service from Sète to Morocco.

In the Atlantic, **Manche-Iles Express** and **Compagnie Corsaire** sail from St-Malo and the Normandy ports of Granville, Barneville-Carteret and Diélette to the British Channel Islands. For a guide to all European ferry services visit www.ferrylines.com.

SAILING IN FRANCE

France has excellent sailing facilities, with marinas all around its coast. On the Atlantic coast, well-equipped ports include Honfleur and St-Vaast-la-Hougue in Normandy, St-Malo and Pleneuf-St-André in Brittany and La Rochelle and Arcachon on the west

coast. Among the best in the Mediterranean are St-Cyprien near the Spanish border, Antibes on the Cote d'Azur and the small harbours of Corsica. Boats for charter or short-term hire are available at most marinas and information on rules and permits is available from the **Ministère de l'Ecologie**. The **Fédération Française de Voile** provides updates on sailing conditions.

CANAL AND RIVER TRIPS

There are many options for exploring French waterways, from short boat trips to cruises of several days. The official guide to the system is provided by **Voies Navigables de France**. Many companies offer cruises around France, among the best of which are **En Peniche**, which uses traditional barges or *peniches*; **Locaboat** and **Crown Blue Line**. For narrow boats on the Canal du Midi, try **Minervois Cruisers**.

Short excursions are popular around the Marais Poitevin wetlands between La Rochelle and Poitiers, and along the Canal de Bourgogne from Dijon. **Les Caminades** runs trips along the Dordogne in traditional *gabarre* boats. For rides on the River Seine in Paris *see p689*.

see p689

DIRECTORY

FERRY SERVICES

Comanav
Tel 04 67 46 68 00.
www.aferry.fr

Compagnie Corsaire
Tel 0825 138 100.
www.compagniecorsaire.com

Corsica Ferries
Tel 0825 095 095.
www.corsica-ferries.fr

Grimaldi Ferries
Tel 04 94 87 11 45 (in France).
www.grimaldi-lines.com

Manche-Iles Express
*Tel 0825 133 050 (in France),
01418 7013 (in Jersey).*
www.manche-iles-express.com

La Méridionale
Tel 0810 201 320.
www.lameridionale.fr

Moby Lines
Tel 00 49 (0)611 14020.
www.mobylines.com

SNCM
Tel 3260 (24-hrs for all ports).
www.sncm.fr

SAILING INFORMATION

Fédération Française de Voile
www.ffvoile.fr

Ministère de l'Ecologie
www.developpement-durable.gouv.fr

CANAL AND RIVER TRIPS

Les Caminades
Tel 05 53 29 40 95.
www.best-of-perigord.tm.fr

Crown Blue Line
Tel 04 68 94 52 72.
www.crownblueline.com

En-Peniche
Tel 04 67 13 19 62.
www.en-peniche.com

Locaboat
Tel 03 86 91 72 72.
www.locaboat.com

Minervois Cruisers
Tel 01926 811842 (in UK).
www.minervoiscruisers.com

Voies Navigables de France
www.vnf.fr

On the Road

France's network of modern motorways (autoroutes) allow quick and easy access to all parts of the country. However, you can save money on tolls and explore France in a more leisurely way by using some of the other high-quality roads that dissect the country. This section outlines both alternatives and gives instructions on how to use motorway toll booths (*péage*) and French parking meters (*horodateurs*), as well as some of the rules governing driving in France. There are also tips on how to get weather and traffic forecasts, where to hire a car and how to get the best road maps.

Motorway and main road signs

WHAT TO TAKE

Effective insurance is essential when taking a car to France. All car insurance policies in the EU automatically include minimum third-party insurance cover, which is valid in any EU country. However, the extent of cover provided beyond the legal minimum varies between insurance companies, so it is best to check your policy before you travel, and, if necessary, procure additional cover. For holders of fully-comprehensive car insurance, most companies provide full European cover for a small extra premium; some do not charge for this, but still require you to notify them before travelling. It is also advisable to have breakdown cover with one of the Europe-wide networks with English-speaking phonelines.

While driving in France you must carry in the car your driving licence, passport, the vehicle registration document and a certificate of insurance. You must also have a set of spare light bulbs, at least one red warning triangle and a luminous reflecting jacket to be worn if you ever have to stop on a motorway because of a breakdown or other emergency. You can be fined if you are stopped by the

police and do not have this equipment. The car's country of registration should be displayed on a sticker or as part of the registration plate, and right-hand drive cars need headlamp deflectors for driving on the right – kits are available at most ports.

BUYING PETROL

All fuel stations have unleaded petrol and diesel fuel (*gazole* or *gas-oil*, or a high-grade *gas-oil* +). Many stations also have LPG (*GPL*). The cheapest are attached to big supermarkets, and many major service stations have 24-hr pumps, with payment by credit card.

RULES OF THE ROAD

Wearing seat belts, in the front and back of the car, is compulsory in France, as is the use of booster seats for children under 10. It is illegal to use a mobile phone while driving, even if it's on hands-free mode. Dipped headlights must be used in poor visibility, and motorcyclists must have dipped headlights lit at all times. Unless road signs

indicate otherwise, *Priorité à droite* means that you must give way to any vehicle joining the road from the right except on roundabouts. Flashing headlights mean that the driver is claiming the right of way. For further details consult AA or RAC websites (*see p687*).

SPEED LIMITS AND FINES

Speed limits in France are as follows:
• On autoroutes: 130 kph (80 mph); 110 kph (68 mph) when it rains.
• On dual carriageways: 110 kph (68 mph); 90–100 kph (56–62 mph) when it rains.
• On other roads: 90 kph (56 mph); 80 kph (49 mph) when it rains.
• In towns and villages: 50 kph (31 mph).

There are also lower speed limits on all roads for vehicles towing a trailer or caravan.

On-the-spot fines are levied for speeding, not stopping at a Stop sign, for overtaking where forbidden and exceeding the speed limit by over 40 kph (25 mph). Driving with over 0.05 per cent alcohol in the blood is illegal.

MOTORWAYS

Most motorways in France are toll roads (*autoroutes à péage*). The **Société d'Autoroutes** website (*see p687*) lists the rates charged for each journey. There are also toll-free autoroutes, notably those around big cities like Paris (A3 and A86) and Lille, and some cross-country stretches such as the A84 from Caen to

A sign at a gas pump points to *GPL* (LPG) or *gazole* (petrol)

The scenic route around Mont Cenis Lake

Rennes, and the A75 south of Clermont-Ferrand.

Much of the autoroute network includes rest areas, petrol stations every 40 km (25 miles) and emergency phones every 2 km (1 mile).

OTHER ROADS

RN (*Route Nationale*) roads are the main alternative to motorways for long-distance trips. They are often far more attractive, but can be more congested. To get really off the beaten track, travel by D (*départementale*) roads, which snake around the countryside.

Look out for *Bis/Bison Futée* signs, which indicate quieter, alternative routes.

Try to avoid travelling at the French holiday rush periods known as *grands départs*. The worst times are weekends in mid-July, and the beginning and end of August.

Certain signs are particularly useful to know when driving in and out of towns. Follow *Centre Ville* signs for the town centre and *Toutes Directions* (all routes) to take you out of the centre to where you can find ongoing routes. If your destination is not signposted, follow *Autres Directions*.

SCENIC ROUTES

France's dense web of *Routes Nationales* and D–roads weave through some of the country's most gorgeous scenery. The most celebrated roads are in mountain regions, such as the Col du Galibier road over the Alps east of Grenoble (N91, then D902) but there are many others throughout the country. Some hug the coast, such as the roads along the Côte d'Azur or the rugged coasts of Brittany and Normandy. Information on these *routes touristiques* is available from tourist offices (*see p669*).

ROAD CONDITIONS

The French Highway Authorities' *Bison Futé* website (*see p687*) provides essential information for driving in France, with details of weather conditions, winter driving requirements and road works. Check also www.autoroutes.fr for motorway driving.

Motoring organizations like the **AA** and **RAC** sell tailor-made route-planning services, giving scenic options and road conditions (*see p687*).

USING THE AUTOROUTE TOLL

Collect a ticket from the toll booth and keep it safe until you reach an exit toll where you will be charged according to the distance travelled and type of vehicle used. To pay at small tolls, just throw your coins into the large receptacle.

Gare de Péage de Fresnes

2000 m

Motorway Sign
These signs (left) indicate the name and distance to the next toll booth. They are usually blue and white; some show the tariff rates for cars, motorbikes, trucks and caravans.

Toll Booth with Attendant
When you hand in your ticket at a manned toll booth, the attendant will tell you the cost of your journey on the autoroute and the price will be displayed. You can pay with coins, notes, credit cards or with a cheque in Euros. A receipt is issued on request.

Automatic Machine
On reaching the exit toll, insert your ticket into the machine and the price of your journey is displayed in Euros. You can pay either with coins or by credit card. The machine will give change and can issue a receipt.

USING AN HORODATEUR MACHINE

1 If using coins, insert according to the tariff shown.

2 If using a card, insert and press the blue button for each 15 minutes required.

3 To obtain the ticket, press the green button.

4 Remove ticket when it emerges and place inside the car windscreen.

Horodateurs

These parking meters operate from 9am–7pm Mon–Fri. Unless otherwise indicated, parking is free Sat–Sun, public holidays and in August.

PARKING

Parking regulations vary from town to town, but most cities have street pay-and-display machines *(horodateurs)*, with spaces marked out in blue. Some machines accept a parking payment card sold at *tabacs*. Parking is normally limited to 2 hours. Charges are relatively low, and in most provincial towns parking is free between noon and 1:30pm. In narrow streets, parking may be confined to one side of the street and this can alternate at different times of the month.

Finding a parking space in larger cities, especially in Paris, can be difficult and it is often easier to use a car park. These are well indicated by a large "P" sign accompanied by the word *libre* to indicate that there are spaces available.

CAR HIRE

All the main international car-hire companies operate in France, as well as local French-based companies like **ADA** and **Rentacar**, which often have very competitive prices. You will nearly always get the best rates by booking a car in advance through one of the Internet car rental booking services like **Auto**

Europe or **Autos Abroad**. Requirements for car hire vary, but in general you must be over 21 and have held a driving licence for at least a year. You will need to present your licence, passport and a credit card against a deposit.

The price quoted should include all taxes and unlimited mileage. All rental contracts include basic third-party insurance, and some companies also include comprehensive insurance. Extras such as car seats, snow chains or an automatic car, should be indicated when booking.

Before you drive away check the general condition of the car and also ensure it has a set of spare bulbs, a warning triangle and a luminous jacket, which are all legal requirements in France *(see p684)*.

MAPS

Each chapter in this guide begins with a map of the region showing all the sights and information on getting around. As additional maps, the excellent **Michelin** Tourist and Motoring Atlas at a scale of 1:200,000 is the most comprehensive driving map available. The red-cover Michelin maps of the whole of France (scale 1:1,000,000) are useful for planning trips,

as are the regional maps with orange covers (scale 1:200,000). Larger scale Michelin maps with green covers are only for certain parts of France such as Paris and the French Riviera.

The **Institut Géographique National** (IGN), the equivalent of the British Ordnance Survey, produces high-quality maps in different scales. Particularly useful are their *Cartes de Randonnée* (scale 1:25,000), an excellent series of walking maps covering every part of the country. Also recommended, are the **Blay Foldex** town maps.

In France, all newsstands and petrol stations stock maps and most tourist offices provide good free maps. In the UK, **Stanfords** is one of the best places to look for a full selection of French maps.

TRAVELLING BY COACH

The French railway is so fast and reliable that there is not much demand for long-distance coaches and they tend to only operate in areas with poor train services.

Eurolines offers a wide range of low-priced international services, many of which make stops within France. These services are centred on the Porte de Bagnolet bus station in Paris (Métro Galliéni).

Veolia Transport runs an extensive network of coaches that cover the Ile de France, and **Lignes d'Azur** provides a good service along the Côte d'Azur.

Local buses are definitely an important means of transport, particularly in rural areas. These run in and out of villages from the *gare routière* (bus station), which is often located next to the SNCF train station of the main town of each *département* or area. Buses run mostly at peak times to take people to and from work and school.

TAXIS

There are taxi services in every part of France, although in rural areas you will normally have to book a car

Mountain cyclists in the Alps

by phone. Hotels, bars and restaurants will have the numbers of local taxis. Otherwise, in towns look for a taxi rank *(station de taxi)* outside railway stations, airports or in the town centre.

All taxis must use meters *(compteurs)*, but prices do vary from one region to another. In general, the pick-up charge should be about €2 plus €0.5 or more per km. It is often possible to agree a fixed price for a long journey. For city taxis *see pp688–9*.

CYCLING

Cycling is extremely popular in France and facilities are steadily improving as part of the government-backed "Eco-mobility" scheme *(see p679)*. Several long-distance **Voies Vertes** footpaths and cycle tracks have been created, and more are being established. Every local tourist office has a leaflet on nearby *véloroutes*, and many have developed their own schemes, such as the network of cycle routes

around the main Loire Valley châteaux *(La Loire à Vélo)*. Details are available from local tourist offices and *département* websites.

Bicycles can be taken on nearly all **SNCF** trains and on some routes you can reserve a rental bike at your destination station when booking a train ticket. There are also cycle hire shops in nearly every town with standard and mountain bikes *(VTT)* for rent at reason-able prices. Tourist offices can advise on local companies.

More information on cycling in France can be found on the Maisons de la France websites and through the **Fédération Française de Cyclisme** (in French only). Most cities offer rental cycling schemes *(see p689)*.

HITCH-HIKING

It is not easy to get around France by hitch-hiking, and it is not advisable to try either. There is, however, a safe car-sharing *(covoiturage)* scheme called Allostop (www.allostop. net), which has branches in many towns and through which you can set up lifts at reasonable rates.

DIRECTORY

GENERAL MOTORING INFORMATION

AA
Tel 0800 085 7253.
www.theaa.com

RAC
Tel 0844 891 3111.
www.rac.co.uk

Societé d'Autoroutes
www.autoroutes.fr

Zagaz
www.zagaz.com (for fuel price guide in French).

CAR HIRE

ADA
Tel 0825 169 169.
www.ada.fr

Autos Abroad
Tel 0844 826 6536 (UK).
www.autosabroad.com

Auto Europe
Tel 1 888 223 5555 (USA & Canada).
www.autoeurope.com

Avis
Tel 0820 050 505 (France), 0844 581 8181 (UK). www.avis.com

Budget
Tel 0825 003 564 (France), 0844 544 3455 (UK). www.budget.com

Europecar
Tel 0825 358 358 (France), 0871 384 0235 (UK). www.europcar.com

Hertz
Tel 0825 861 861 (France), 0845 191 536 (UK). www.hertz.com

National/Citer
Tel 0800 131 211 (France), 0871 384 1140 (UK).
www.nationalcar.com

Rentacar
Tel 0891 700 200.
www.rentacar.fr

MAPS

Blay Foldex
www.blayfoldex.com

Institut Géographique National
www.ign.fr

Michelin
www.viamichelin.fr

Stanfords
12–14 Long Acre, London WC2E 9LP.
Tel 020 7836 1321.
www.stanfords.co.uk

COACH TRAVEL

Eurolines
Tel 0892 899 091.
www.eurolines.fr

Lignes d'Azur
www.lignesdazur.com

Veolia Transport
www.veolia-transport.com

CYCLING

Fédération Française de Cyclisme
Tel 01 49 35 69 00.
www.ffc.fr

SNCF
www.velo.sncf.com
(for train and bicycle travel – in French only).

Voies Vertes
www.voiesvertes.com

Travelling within Cities

The charming centres of France's cities are best enjoyed on foot. If, however, you need to cover a fair amount of ground in a day, it is best to use the excellent range of public transport available. Paris and many other cities have tram and underground rail networks, often integrated with local train and bus services, and efforts have been made to create user-friendly ticketing systems. France has led the world in encouraging urban cycle use as an alternative to the car, with easy-access bike-hire schemes. In each city, local tourist offices will provide full information on services, including free maps.

Marseille tram travelling along the Boulevard Longchamp

PARIS METRO, RER AND TRAM

The **RATP** operates 14 Métro underground train lines. The Métro is the most convenient way to get around the city, and you are never far away from a station in central Paris. Each line can be identified by its colour and number. The direction the train is travelling in is indicated by the name of the station on the front of the train – this is always the last station on the route, so it's worth checking the Métro map before boarding. Trains run frequently on each line from 5:20am–1:20am daily (to 2:20am Sat).

The newer RER lines complement the Métro and run across Paris and the suburbs. There are five lines (A–E), each with branches. The most useful for visitors are B3, from Charles-de-Gaulle airport; A4, to Disneyland Paris Resort; and C5, to Versailles.

Paris also has three tramway lines: from Gare de St-Denis to Noisy-le-Sec; La Défense to Porte de Versailles; and Pont du Garigliano to Porte d'Ivry.

OTHER METRO AND TRAM SYSTEMS

The cities of Lyon, Marseille, Toulouse, Lille and Rennes all have Métro systems. The Lille Métro serves the whole conurbation known as Lille-Métropole, including towns such as Roubaix and Tourcoing. All Métros connect with SNCF railways at main stations.

Rouen's two-line Métro is actually made up of overground trams (light rail lines) that connect the city to the outer suburbs. Some 22 other cities around France use trams as well as local buses, and Paris too has some suburban tram lines that connect with the Métro and RER.

BUSES

Every city has local buses. In Paris, RATP buses provide cheap opportunities for sightseeing. Throughout France, most routes operate from around 6am to midnight; routes and times are indicated at bus stops. Most French cities also have several night bus routes, and in Paris and

the Ile-de-France, 42 Noctilien bus routes operate throughout the night, passing the main railway stations. A fast-growing number of buses in Paris and other cities have wheelchair ramps. On all French city buses, you must board at the front of the bus, and get off through the middle or rear doors. Tickets can be bought from the driver or in advance from a range of outlets, which saves time when boarding.

LOCAL TRAINS

Regional TER lines *(see p681)* are operated by SNCF and are well integrated with local transport around cities. In some cases, tickets are interchangeable. Around Paris the SNCF Transilien lines form a third level of rail services with the Métro and RER.

TAXIS

In Paris and most other cities taxis have a light on top of the car which is white when the taxi is free, and orange, or just switched off, when it is taken. Paris taxi fares are more expensive between 5pm and 10am, Monday–Saturday, and all day Sunday and holidays, and cost more for any journey outside central Paris (limited by but including the Boulevard Périphérique). Many taxis take credit cards, but often only for fares over €15. At busy times the best places to find taxis in Paris are taxi ranks *(station de taxis)* marked with a blue T sign. Ranks are found at major road junctions and train stations. Though operated by several companies, there is now a single number to phone for taxis in Paris. All taxis in France are required to carry wheelchair users for no extra charge, but in the Paris region **Taxis G7** provide a specialized service for passengers with mobility problems.

In other cities taxis are similarly operated by several companies. Taxi ranks are found at airports, most train stations and around city centres. Otherwise tourist offices and hotels can provide you with local firm numbers.

Taking a bicycle from one of the Vélib' stands in Paris

CYCLING

Great efforts are underway in French cities to encourage town cycling. On Sundays, some major streets are closed to traffic to make way for cyclists and rollerbladers. Paris city council has a world-leading pro-cycling programme, and expects to have 600 km of cycle routes by 2013. The centrepiece of the programme is the **Vélib'** scheme, where you can pick up a basic bike at any one of hundreds of Vélib' stations around Paris and leave it at another. To do this you must purchase a Vélib' card, which are available for a day (€1) or a week and can be bought from machines at the Vélib' bike racks, or by annual subscription. Other cities run similar bike-sharing schemes under different names (the **Vélo'V** in Lyon, **Le Vélo** in Marseille). Tourist offices will have full information on them.

TICKETS

In Paris, RATP T-tickets are valid for city buses, the Métro and the RER. Tickets are available singly or for lower prices in carnets of 10 and can be bought at Métro and RER stations, the airports, tourist offices and *tabacs*. Single tickets can also be bought on board buses but are not valid for other forms of transport. Don't forget to validate your ticket.

An alternative aimed at tourists is the ParisVisite card, which gives unlimited travel on all systems for 1, 2, 3 or 5 days, as well as discounted admission fees to sights. The card is sold at Métro, RER and train stations, as well as at tourist offices or online.

Nearly all larger cities offer some kind of city pass for visitors, giving unlimited travel and other advantages for one or more days. Enquire at tourist offices for local schemes.

Cruise boats plying the river Seine

SEINE CRUISES

A boat trip on the Seine is one of the classic ways to see Paris. The long-running **Bateaux-Mouches**, **Bateaux Parisiens** and **Vedettes du Pont-Neuf** offer traditional cruises along the river with multi-lingual commentary. The **Batobus** is a more flexible alternative, allowing you to hop on and off as many times as you want during the day. Another option is to see a more intimate side of Paris with a cruise along the St-Martin canal. Full information is available from tourist offices.

General Index

Acknowledgments

Dorling Kindersley would like to thank the
following people whose contributions and
assistance have made the preparation of this book
possible.

Main Contributors
John Ardagh, Rosemary Bailey, Judith Fayard, Lisa
Gerard-Sharp, Robert Harneis, Alister Kershaw,
Alec Lobrano, Anthony Roberts, Alan Tillier, Nigel
Tisdall.

Contributors and Consultants
John Ardagh is a writer and broadcaster, and
author of many books on France, among them
France Today and *Writers' France*.

Rosemary Bailey has written and edited several
guides to regional France, including *Burgundy,*
the *Loire Valley* and the *Côte d'Azur*.

Alexandra Boyle is a writer and editor who has
worked in publishing in England and France for
20 years.

Elsie Burch Donald, editor and writer, is the
author of *The French Farmhouse*.

David Burnie B.Sc. has written over 30 books on
natural sciences, including *How Nature Works*.

Judith Fayard, an American based in Paris, was
Paris bureau chief for *Life* magazine for 10 years,
and is now European editor of *Town & Country*.
She contributes to various publications, including
the *Wall Street Journal*.

Lisa Gerard-Sharp is a broadcaster and author of
several regional guides to France and Italy.

Robert Harneis is editorial correspondent for the
English language newspaper *French News*.

Colin Jones is Professor of History at Exeter
University. His books include *The Longman
Companion to the French Revolution* and *The
Cambridge Illustrated History of France*.

Alister Kershaw is an Australian writer and broadcaster who has lived in the Loire Valley for 30 years.

Alec Lobrano is an American writer, based in
Paris. He is the European editor of *Departures*
magazine and contributes to *International Herald
Tribune, Los Angeles Times* and *The Independent*.

Anthony Roberts is a writer and translator who
has lived in Gascony for 15 years, contributing to
various publications including *The Times, World
of Interiors* and *Architectural Digest*.

Anthony Rose is the wine correspondent of *The
Independent* and co-author of *The Grapevine*.

Jane Sigal is the author of two books on French
food, *Normandy Gastronomique* and *Backroom
Bistros, Farmhouse Fare*.

Alan Tillier is the main contributor to the
Eyewitness Guide to Paris. He has lived in Paris
for more than 20 years as correspondent for
various journals, including the *International
Herald Tribune, Newsweek* and *The Times*.

Nigel Tisdall is a travel writer and author of
guides to Brittany and Normandy.

Patricia Wells is food critic of the *International
Herald Tribune* and author of the *Food Lovers'
Guide to Paris* and the *Food Lovers' Guide to France*.

Additional Contributors
Nathalie Boyer, Caroline Bugler, Ann Cremin, Jan
Dodd, Bill Echikson, Robin Gauldie, Adrian
Gilbert, Peter Graham, Marion Kaplan, Jim
Keeble, Alexandra Kennedy, Rolli Lucarotti, Fred
Mawer, Lyn Parry, Andrew Sanger, Katherine
Spenley, Clive Unger-Hamilton, Roger Williams.

Additional Photography
Jo Craig, Andy Crawford, Michael Crockett, Mike
Dunning, Philip Enticknap, Philippe Giraud, Steve
Gorton, Alison Harris, John Heseltine, Roger Hilton,
Andrew Holligan, Paul Kenwood, Oliver Knight,
Eric Meacher, Neil Mersh, Roger Moss, Robert
O'Dea, Ian O'Leary, Tony Souter, Alan Williams,
Peter Wilson.

Additional Illustrations
Dinwiddie Maclaren, John Fox, Nick Gibbard,
Paul Guest, Stephen Gyapay, Kevin Jones
Associates, Chris Orr, Robbie Polley, Sue Sharples.

Additional Cartography
Colourmap Scanning Limited; Contour Publishing;
Cosmographics; European Map Graphics; Meteo-
France. Street Finder maps: ERAMaptec Ltd
(Dublin), adapted with permission from original
survey and mapping by Shobunsha (Japan).

Cartographic Research
Jennifer Skelley, Rachel Hawtin (Lovell Johns);
James Mills-Hicks, Peter Winfield, Claudine Zarte
(Dorling Kindersley Cartography).

Design and Editorial Assistance
Peter Adams, Azeem Alam, Elizabeth Ayre,
Laetitia Benloulou, Steve Bere, Sonal Bhatt,
Uma Bhattacharya, Hilary Bird, Anna Brooke,
Arwen Burnett, Cate Craker, Maggie Crowley,
Alison Culliford, Lisa Davidson, Simon Davis,
Emer FitzGerald, Helen Foulkes, Fay Franklin,
Tom Fraser, Anna Freiberger, Rhiannon Furbear,
Catherine Gauthier, Camilla Gersh, Eric Gibory,
Emily Green, Vinod Harish, Robert Harneis,
Elaine Harries, Victoria Heyworth-Dunne, Paul
Hines, Nicholas Inman, Rosa Jackson, Sarah
Jackson-Lambert, Stuart James, Laura Jones,
Nancy Jones, Kim Laidlaw Adrey, Cécile Landau,
Maite Lantaron, Delphine Lawrance, Jude Ledger,
Siri Lowe, Francesca Machiavelli, Carly Madden,
Hayley Maher, Nicola Malone, Lesley McCave,
Ella Milroy, Malcolm Parchment, Lyn Parry,
Helen Partington, Shirin Patel, Alice Peebles,
Alice Pennington-Mellor, Marianne Petrou,
Pollyanna Poulter, Pete Quinlan, Salim Qurashi,
Marisa Renzullo, Philippa Richmond, Nick Rider,
Ellen Root, Baishakhee Sengupta, Shailesh
Sharma, Kunal Singh, Shruti Singhi, Cathy
Skipper, Andrew Szudek, Helen Townsend, Dora
Whitaker, Fiona Wild, Nicholas Wood, Irina Zarb.

Special Assistance
Mme Jassinger, French Embassy Press Department; Peter Mills, Christine Lagardère, French Railways Ltd.

Photographic Reference
Altitude, Paris; Sea and See, Paris; Editions Combier, Maçon; Thomas d'Hoste, Paris.

Photography Permissions
Dorling Kindersley would like to thank the following for their assistance and kind permission to photograph at their establishments: The Caisse Nationale des Monuments Historiques et des Sites; M. A. Leonetti, the Abbey of Mont St-Michel; Chartres Cathedral; M. Voisin, Château de Chenonceau; M. P Mistral, Cité de Carcassonne, M. D. Vingtain, Palais des Papes, Avignon; Château de Fontainebleau; Amiens Cathedral; Conques Abbey; Fontenay Abbey; Moissac Abbey; Vézelay Abbey, Reims Cathedral and all the other churches, museums, hotels, restaurants, shops, galleries and sights too numerous to thank individually.

Picture Credits
a = above; b = below/bottom; c = centre; f = far; l = left; r = right; t = top.

Works of art have been reproduced with the permission of the following copyright holders; ©ADAGP, Paris and DACS, London 2011: 29c, 29crb, 30bl, 63tl, 64–65, 65tl (d), 90t, 93cra, 93cb, 93bl, 93br, 99t, 213b, 351t, 335br, 482t, 508ca, 522b, 524bc, 524br, 529br; ©ARS, NY and DACS, London 2011: 92c; ©DACS, London 2011: 93t, 381br, 422t; © Succession H. Matisse/DACS, London 2011: 29bl, 92bl, 526br; © Succession Picasso/DACS, London 2011: 88cl, 90b, 473t, 521t.

Photos achieved with the assistance of the EPPV and the CSI: 136–7; Photo of Euro Disneyland ¯ Park and the Euro Disneyland Paris ® 178cr; The characters, architectural works and trademarks are the property of The Walt Disney Company. All rights reserved; Courtesy of the Maison Victor Hugo, Ville de Paris: 91t; Musée National des Châteaux de Malmaison et Bois-Preau: 173b, Musée de Montmartre, Paris: 133t; Musée National de la Legion d'Honneur: 60t; © Sundancer: 142bl.

The publisher would like to thank the following individuals, companies and picture libraries for permission to reproduce their photographs:

AIR FRANCE: D Toulorge 678tl; ALAMY IMAGES: Andy Arthur 420bc, Sébastien Baussais 674tr, Directphoto.org 669br, David R. Frazier Photolibrary, Inc 672cl, Glenn Harper 96tl, Philippe Hays 675cb, Hemis/Camille Moirenc 18, Neil Juggins 682tl, Michael Juno 239c, Justin Kase Zfivez 673tr, a la poste 676tr, 670b, Jack Sullivan 673cr, vario images GmbH & Co.KG/Rainer Unkel 676bl; ALPINE GARDEN SOCIETY/CHRISTOPHER GREY-WILSON: 460bl, 460br; AGENCE PHOTO AQUITAINE: D. Lelann 421tl; ANCIENT ART AND ARCHITECTURE COLLECTION: 47 crb, 50c, 50cb, 52br, 57bl, 252–3b, 335bl, 382t, 434t, 438b; PHOTO AKG, BERLIN: 45cra, 46bl, 58bc, 55crb, 402t, 403b; ARCHIVES PHOTOGRAPHIQUES, PARIS/DACS: 422t; by kind

permission of WWW.ARTINSWFRANCE.COM: 660b; ATELIER BRANCUSI/CENTRE GEORGES POMPIDOU, PARIS: Bernard Prerost 93br; ATELIER DU REGARD/A ALLEMAND: 442cl, 442cr, 442b.
HOSTELLERIE BERARD: 660cl; BIBLIOTHÈQUE NATIONALE, DIJON: 49cb; F. BLACKBURN: 461bl; GERARD BOULLAY/PHOTOLA: 87bl, 87cra; BRIDGEMAN ART LIBRARY: Albright Knox Art Gallery, Buffalo, New York 275br; Anthony Crane Collection 211br; Bibliothèque Nationale, Paris 50cr–51cl, 52t, 53cr, 69bl; British Library, London 52bl, 68br, 292c, 293br, 293tl; Bonhams, London 59tc, 62tl; Château de Versailles, France 69tr; Christies, London 29c, 513b; Giraudon 28tr, 28tl, 56cr–57cl, 57tl, 59tl, 69bc, 181b, 334c, 343c, 365t; Guildhall Library, Corporation of London 417b; Hermitage, St Petersburg 29bl; Index 472b; Kress Collection, Washington DC 293bl; Lauros-Giraudon 46t, 69br; Musée des Beaux Arts, Quimper 243c; Musée Condé, Chantilly 50tl, 57tr, 68bl, 69tc, 69tcl, 69cb, 204t, 293c; Musée d'Orsay, Paris 28cb; Musée du Quai Branly, Paris 112cb; Paul Bremen Collection 255t; Sotheby's New York 55tl; V&A Museum, London 338b; Walters Art Gallery, Baltimore, Maryland 356t; JOHN BRUNTON: 514b; MICHAEL BUSSELLE: 182–3.
CAMPAGNE, CAMPAGNE: 350t; C. Guy 325t; Lara 191cr; B. Lichtstein 217b, 324cl; Pyszel 190bl; CNMHS, PARIS/DACS: Longchamps Delehaye 213tl; CASTELET/GROTTE DE CLAMOUSE: 493b; CEPHAS: Stuart Boreham 260–1; Hervé Champollion 322tr, 334t, 350b; Mick Rock 38c, 398tl, 398cl, 471t, 518–9; JEAN LOUP CHARMET: 47b, 50br, 52clb, 58t, 62cl, 62clb, 63tl, 63tc, 64bl, 64br, 65crb, 214b, 243b, 265br, 269b, 274t, 281b, 300br, 343br, 358b, 359t, 361c, 401cr, 401br, 421b, 475t, 507t, CHATEAU DE LA LIQUIERE: 470ca; CHATEAU MARGAUX: 26cb, 26bc; CITÉ DES SCIENCES ET L'INDUSTRIE: Michel Lamoureux 136ca; NASA/ESA 136tr, 137br; Sylvain Sonnet 136clb; BRUCE COLEMAN: Udo Hirsch 371br; Flip de Nooyer 387br; Hans Reinhard 323tl, 323tr; COLLECTION CDT GARD: 325bl; CDT LOT: 439b; PHOTOS EDITIONS COMBIER, MÂCON: 203t; CORBIS: Gary Braasch 469c; Michael Busselle 13cl; Ray Juno 10cl, Patrice Latron 684br, Reuters 657tl, Robert Harding World Imagery/Charles Bowman 685tl; JOE CORNISH: 116, 234–5, 370br, 448.
DANSMUSEET, STOCKHOLM/PETER STENWALL: 64cr–65cl; E. Donard; 35tr, 35c, 35cl, 35bc; EDITIONS D'ART DANIEL DERVEAUX: 400cr–401cl; PHOTO DASPET, AVIGNON: 504bl; DOHERTY: 245tc; DOMAINE DE LA COURTADE: 471cr; DOMAINE SARDA MALET: 470cb; DOMAINE TEMPIER: 471cl.
ET ARCHIVE: 300bl; Cathedral Treasury, Aachen 4t; 48cl; Musée Carnavalet, Paris 61tl; Museum of Fine Arts, Lausanne 55br; Musée d'Orsay, Paris 61cra; Musée de Versailles 56b; 299bl; National Gallery, Scotland 58br; Victoria and Albert Museum, London 53tl; 343bl; EUROPEAN COMMISSION: 675; MARY EVANS PICTURE LIBRARY: 9c, 46br, 50bl, 51c, 53b, 54tl, 56cla, 58c, 62b, 63cr, 63br, 65br, 113cl, 177b, 183c, 191t, 197b, 235c, 279t, 291b, 293tr, 301bl, 315c, 366b, 393c, 455t, 465c, 473b, 508tl, 545c, 667c; Explorer 31b, 54clb.
FESTIVAL D'AVIGNON: Marc Chaumeil 656cl; FESTIVAL INTERNATIONAL DU FILM DE LA ROCHELLE: 656br; PHOTO FLANDRE, AMIENS: 193b; FNOTSI: 668tc.
GETTY IMAGES: Axiom Photographic Agency/Ian Cumming 283tl, AFP/Jean Ayissi 689tl, De Agostini

Picture Library 484t, Manfred Mehlig 680bl, National Geographic/Ed George 683, Panoramic Images 151br, Sergio Pitamitz 689bl, Peter Scholey 669tl, WireImage/Tony Barson 67bc; GIRAUDON, PARIS: 8–9, 15t, 29cra, 29br, 46ca, 48tl, 48clb, 49tl, 50cl, 52cr–53cl, 56tl, 56clb, 58cl, 60cl, 60cr–61cl, 333br, 347br, 369b, 491clb MS Nero EII pt.2 fol. 20V0; Lauros-Giraudon 44tl, 44bc, 45t, 45crb, 45cb, 45br, 47tc, 49tr, 51crb, 55cr, 60clb, 60br, 351b, 491cl; Musée d'Art Moderne, Paris 29tr; Musée de Beaux Arts, Quimper 28cl; GÎTES DE FRANCE: 548cb; RONALD GRANT ARCHIVE: 21b, 66clb. LA HALLE SAINT PIERRE: *Untitled* Stavroula Feleggakis 133br; SONIA HALLIDAY PHOTOGRAPHS: Laura Lushington 309tr; ROBERT HARDING PICTURE LIBRARY: 30bl, 37tr, 39tr, 39cl, 43b, 112br, 240tl, 243tr, 322bl, 322br, 323br, 349t, 400cla, 437cr, 461tr, 489b, C. Bowman 452t; Explorer, Paris 39cr, 67br, 101br, 179b, 362t, 371tr, 460cb, 461tl, 484b, 497br, 660b, 671cl; R. Francis 86clb; D.Hughes 392–3; W.Rawlings 49br, 67tl, 237tl, 256b; A.Wolfitt 26tr, 170; HEMISPHERES IMAGES: Hervé Hughes 259br; JOHN HESELTINE: 139c; Honfleur, Musée BOUDIN: 262b; DAVID HUGHES: 367t, 367b; THE HULTON DEUTSCH COLLECTION: 191br, 301br, 473c, 516b; FJ Mortimer 190tl. THE IMAGE BANK: Peter Miller 372; IMAGES: 323c, 460cl, 460tr. JACANA: F Gohier 460tl; JM Labat 461bc; TREVOR JONES: 204b. MAGNUM PHOTOS LTD: Bruno Barbey 20b, 31tr, 36bl; R Capa 472tr; P Halsman 525b; THE MANSELL COLLECTION: 31tl, 282t, 295b, 459b, 504tl; MAS DAUMAS GASSAC: 470cr; JOHN MILLER: 224b, 336tr, 407b; MONTPELLIER DANSE FESTIVAL: 657br; MUSÉE DE L'ANNONCIADE, ST-TROPEZ: 524tr; MUSÉE D'ART MODERNE ET CONTEMPORAIN DE STRASBOURG: Edith Rodeghiero 231t; MUSÉE DES BEAUX ARTS, CARCASSONNE: 489tl; MUSÉE DES BEAUX ARTS, DIJON: 343tl; MUSÉE DES BEAUX ARTS DE LYON: 381tr, 381bl, 381br; MUSÉE DE LA CIVILISATION GALLO-ROMAINE, LYON: 47cr, 378cl; MUSÉE DEPARTMENTAL BRETON, QUIMPER: 274bl; MUSÉE FLAUBERT, ROUEN: 265bl; MUSEUM NATIONAL D'HISTOIRE NATURELLE, PARIS: 138c; COURTESY OF THE MUSÉE MATISSE, NICE: 526b; MUSÉE NATIONAL D'ART MODERNE, PARIS: 92clb, 93t, 93cr, 93cb, 335br; Succession Henri Matisse 92bl; MUSÉE RÉATTU, ARLES: M Lacanaud 508ca; CLICHÉ MUSÉE DE SENS/J.P. ELIE: 330tl; MUSÉE TOULOUSE-LAUTREC, ALBI: 444b. NETWORK PHOTOGRAPHERS: Barry Lewis 338t; Rapho/ Mark Buscail 661tl; Rapho/De Sazo 661tr. OFFICE DE TOURISME DE VENCE: 668c; ORIENT-EXPRESS HOTELS TRAINS & CRUISES: 548tl; OTC MARSEILLE: 688cla. PHOTOLIBRARY: Duncan Maxwell 2–3; Jean-Marc Romain 673crb, Widmann Widmann/F1 Online 674bl; PICTURES COLOUR LIBRARY: 402b, 426, 544,

666–7; MICHEL LE POER TRENCH: 30br; CENTRE GEORGES POMPIDOU: Bernard Prerost 93b; POPPERFOTO: 251c; LA POSTE: 677bl; PYRENEES MAGAZINE/DR: 400bl. REDFERNS: William Gottlieb: 64clb; RESTAURANT DE LA TOUR D'ARGENT: 598br; RETROGRAPH ARCHIVE: M. Breese 474tl, 474tr; RÉUNION DES MUSÉES NATIONAUX: Musée des Antiquités Nationales 403c; Musée Guimet 111t; Musée du Louvre 57ca, 101bl, 102t, 102bl, 102br, 103tl, 103c, 103b; Musée Picasso 88cl, 90b, 473t; Musée de Versailles 179t; RF REYNOLDS: 245bc. M REYNARD 674B; REX FEATURES: Sipa 22t; ROCAMADOUR: 437t; ROGER-VIOLLET: 113tc; FOUNDATION ROYAUMONT: J Johnson 172t; RÉUNION DES MUSÉES NATIONAUX: *Le Duo* (1937) by Georges Braque, Collections du Centre Pompidou, Musée Nationaux d'Art Moderne, 93ra. SIPA PRESS: 132bl; PHOTO SNCM/SOUTHERN FERRIES: 678br; SNCF – SOCIETE NATIONAL DES CHEMINS DE FER: 680tl, 682bc, Fabro & Leveque 683tr; SPECTRUM COLOUR LIBRARY: P Thompson 249el; FRANK SPOONER PICTURES: Bolcina 37b; Uzan 66br; Simon 67ca; Gamma Press 39b, 67crb; STA TRAVEL GROUP: 670tr; JEAN MARIE STEINLEN: 404; TONY STONE IMAGES: 322c, 326; SYGMA: 531t; C de Bare 36t; Walter Carone 150t; P Forestier 314–5; Frederic de la Fosse 520b; D Goldberg 21c; L'Illustration 108tl; T Prat 436c; L de Raemy 66br. EDITIONS TALLANDIER: 42, 44cb, 47tl, 48br, 48br–49bl, 51t, 51b, 52cl, 53tr, 54br, 58clb, 58bl, 58cr–59cl, 59crb, 59bl, 61tr, 61crb, 61br, 63bl, 63bc, 64cla, 64crb, 65tc, 65tr; TELARCI 49cr; TOURIST OFFICE SEMUR-EN-AUXOIS: 335t; COLLECTION L. TREILLARD: © Man Ray Trust/ADAGP, Paris and DACS, London 2011 65tl(d). JEAN VERTUT: 44br–45bl; VISUAL ARTS LIBRARY: 28b; VIEW PICTURES: Paul Rafferty 135b. WORLD PICTURES: 323bl. ZEFA: 178c, 351t; O. ZIMMERMAN/MUSÉE D'UNTERLINDEN 6800 COLMAR: 227t.

Front Endpaper: All special photography except THE IMAGE BANK rcb; PICTURES COLOUR LIBRARY lcr; JEAN MARIE STEINLEN lcl; TONY STONE IMAGES rca. Back Endpaper: All special photography except JOE CORNISH lbl.

Jacket
Front - CORBIS: Robert Harding World Imagery. Back - DORLING KINDERSLEY: May Alexander clb; John Hesletine bl; Rough Guides/David Abram cla; GETTY IMAGES: Taxi/Shaun Egan tl. Spine - CORBIS: Robert Harding World Imagery t.

All other images © Dorling Kindersley. For more information see www.dkimages.com

Phrase Book

In Emergency

Help!	Au secours!	oh se**koor**
Stop!	Arrêtez!	aret-**ay**
Call a doctor!	Appelez un médecin!	apuh-**lay** uñ med**sañ**
Call an ambulance!	Appelez une ambulance!	apuh-**lay** oon oñboo-**loñs**
Call the police!	Appelez la police!	apuh-**lay lah** poh-**lees**
Call the fire department!	Appelez les pompiers!	apuh-**lay** leh poñ-**peeyay**
Where is the nearest telephone?	Où est le téléphone le plus proche?	oo ay luh tehleh**fon** luh ploo prosh
Where is the nearest hospital?	Où est l'hôpital le plus proche?	oo ay l'**o**peetal luh ploo prosh

Communication Essentials

Yes	Oui	wee
No	Non	noñ
Please	S'il vous plaît	seel voo play
Thank you	Merci	mer-see
Excuse me	Excusez-moi	exkoo-**zay** mwah
Hello	Bonjour	boñ**zhoor**
Goodbye	Au revoir	oh ruh-**vwar**
Good night	Bonsoir	boñ-**swar**
Morning	Le matin	ma**tañ**
Afternoon	L'après-midi	l'apreh-**meedee**
Evening	Le soir	swar
Yesterday	Hier	ee**yehr**
Today	Aujourd'hui	oh-zhoor-**dwee**
Tomorrow	Demain	duh**mañ**
Here	Ici	ee-**see**
There	Là	lah
What?	Quel, quelle?	kel, kel
When?	Quand?	koñ
Why?	Pourquoi?	poor-**kwah**
Where?	Où?	oo

Useful Phrases

How are you?	Comment allez-vous?	kom-moñ tal**ay voo**
Very well, thank you.	Très bien, merci.	treh byañ, mer-**see**
Pleased to meet you.	Enchanté de faire votre connaissance.	oñshoñ-**tay** duh fehr votr kon-ay-**sans**
See you soon.	A bientôt.	byañ-**toh**
That's fine	Voilà qui est parfait	vwalah kee ay par**fay**
Where is/are…?	Où est/sont…?	oo ay/soñ
How far is it to…?	Combien de kilomètres d'ici à…?	kom-**byañ** duh keelo-metr d'ee-see ah
Which way to…?	Quelle est la direction pour…?	kel ay lah deer-ek-**syoñ** poor
Do you speak English?	Parlez-vous anglais?	par-lay voo oñg-**lay**
I don't understand.	Je ne comprends pas.	zhuh nuh kom-proñ pah
Could you speak slowly please?	Pouvez-vous parler moins vite s'il vous plaît?	poo-**vay** voo par-**lay** mwañ veet seel voo play
I'm sorry.	Excusez-moi.	exkoo-**zay** mwah

Useful Words

big	grand	groñ
small	petit	puh-**tee**
hot	chaud	show
cold	froid	frwah
good	bon	boñ
bad	mauvais	moh-**veh**
enough	assez	as**say**
well	bien	byañ
open	ouvert	oo-**ver**
closed	fermé	fer-**meh**
left	gauche	gohsh
right	droit	drwah
straight ahead	tout droit	too drwah
near	près	preh
far	loin	lwañ
up	en haut	oñ oh
down	en bas	oñ bah
early	de bonne heure	duh bon urr
late	en retard	oñ ruh-**tar**
entrance	l'entrée	l'on-**tray**
exit	la sortie	sor-**tee**
toilet	les toilettes, les WC	twah-**let**, vay-**see**
free, unoccupied	libre	leebr
free, no charge	gratuit	grah-**twee**

Making a Telephone Call

I'd like to place a long-distance call.	Je voudrais faire un interurbain.	zhuh voo-**dreh** fehr uñ añter-oorbañ
I'd like to make a collect call.	Je voudrais faire une communication PCV.	zhuh voo**dreh** fehr oon komoonikah-syoñ peh-seh-veh
I'll try again later.	Je rappelerai plus tard.	zhuh rapel-**eray**ploo tar
Can I leave a message?	Est-ce que je peux laisser un message?	es-**keh** zhuh puh leh-**say** uñ meh**sazh**
Hold on.	Ne quittez pas, s'il vous plaît.	nuh kee-**tay** pah seel voo play
Could you speak up a little please?	Pouvez-vous parler un peu plus fort?	poo-**vay** voo par-**lay** uñ puh ploo for
local call	la communication locale	komoonikah-syoñ low-kal

Shopping

How much does this cost?	C'est combien s'il vous plaît?	say kom-**byañ** seel voo play
I would like …	je voudrais…	zhuh voo-**dray**
Do you have?	Est-ce que vous avez?	es-**kuh** voo zav**ay**
I'm just looking.	Je regarde seulement.	zhuh ruh**gar** suhl**moñ**
Do you take credit cards?	Est-ce que vous acceptez les cartes de crédit?	es-**kuh** voo zaksept-**ay** leh kart duh kreh-**dee**
Do you take traveller's cheques?	Est-ce que vous acceptez les chèques de voyage?	es-**kuh** voo zaksept-**ay** leh shek duh vwa**yazh**
What time do you open?	A quelle heure vous êtes ouvert?	ah kel urr voo zet oo-**ver**
What time do you close?	A quelle heure vous êtes fermé?	ah kel urr voo zet fer-**may**
This one.	Celui-ci.	suhl-wee-**see**
That one.	Celui-là.	suhl-wee-**lah**
expensive	cher	shehr
cheap	pas cher, bon marché	pah shehr, boñ mar-**shay**
size, clothes	la taille	tye
size, shoes	la pointure	pwañ-**tur**
white	blanc	bloñ
black	noir	nwahr
red	rouge	roozh
yellow	jaune	zhohwn
green	vert	vehr
blue	bleu	bluh

Types of Shops

antiques shop	le magasin d'antiquités	maga-**zañ** d'oñteekee-**tay**
bakery	la boulangerie	booloñ-**zhuree**
bank	la banque	boñk
book store	la librairie	lee-**brehree**
butcher	la boucherie	boo-**shehree**
cake shop	la pâtisserie	patee-**sree**
cheese shop	la fromagerie	fromazh-**ree**
chemist	la pharmacie	farmah-**see**
dairy	la crémerie	krem-**ree**
department store	le grand magasin	groñ maga-**zañ**
delicatessen	la charcuterie	sharkoot-**ree**
fish seller	la poissonnerie	pwasson-**ree**
gift shop	le magasin de cadeaux	maga-**zañ** duh kad**oh**
greengrocer	le marchand de légumes	mar-**shoñ** duh lay-**goom**
grocery	l'alimentation	alee-moñta-**syoñ**
hairdresser	le coiffeur	kwafuhr
market	le marché	marsh-**ay**
news-stand	le magasin de journaux	maga-**zañ** duh zhoor-**no**
post office	la poste, le bureau de poste, le PTT	pohst, booroh duh pohst, peh-teh-teh
shoe shop	le magasin de chaussures	maga-**zañ** duh show-**soor**
supermarket	le supermarché	soo pehr-**marshay**
tobacconist	le tabac	tabah
travel agent	l'agence de voyages	l'azhoñs duh vwayazh

Sightseeing

abbey	l'abbaye	l'abay-**ee**
art gallery	la galerie d'art	galer-**ree** dart
bus station	la gare routière	gahr roo-tee-**yehr**

Central Paris

AVENUE DE WAGRAM
AVENUE DE LA GRANDE ARMÉE
AVENUE CARNOT
AVENUE MACMAHON
RUE DU FAUBOURG ST HONORE
BD HAUSSMANN
RUE DE COURCELLES
RUE DE MIROMESNIL
RUE TRONCHET

Arc de Triomphe
PL CHARLES DE GAULLE
AV DE FRIEDLAND
AVENUE HOCHE
BD

AVENUE FOCH
AVE BUGEAUD
AVENUE
VICTOR HUGO
AVENUE D'IENA
AVENUE DES CHAMPS ELYSEES
RUE WASHINGTON
RUE LA BOETIE
AV F.D
AVENUE DE MARIGNY
RUE ROYALE
RUE
RUE DE RIV

PLACE VICTOR HUGO
R COPERNIC
RUE BOISSIERE
RUE LAURISTON
RUE KLEBER
AVENUE MARCEAU
RUE DE SERBIE
RUE FRANCOIS PREMIER
ROND POINT DES CHAMPS ELYSEES
PLACE DE LA CONCORDE
JARD DES TUILERI

AVENUE RAYMOND POINCARE
PLACE AMIRAL DE GRASSE
AVE PIERRE 1ER
AVENUE GEORGE V
PREM DE SERBIE
PLACE FRANCOIS PREMIER
COURS LA REINE
QUAI DES TUILERI

CHAILLOT
AVENUE D'EYLAU
PRES WILSON
AV DU
AVENUE DE NEW YORK
La Seine
QUAI
D'ORSAY
QUAI D'ANAT

AVENUE G MANDEL
CIMETIERE DE PASSY
PLACE DU TROCADERO ET DU 11 NOVEMBRE
JARDINS DU TROCADERO
BRANLY
L'UNIVERSITE
RUE SAINT DOMINIQUE
INVALIDES
RUE ST
BOULEVARD
RUE D'UNIVERS

RUE B FRANKLIN
QUAI
AVENUE DE
AVENUE RAPP
AVENUE DE LA BOURDONNAIS
AVENUE BOSQUET
RUE SAINT DOMINIQUE
BD DE LA TOUR MAUBOURG
AV DU MARECHAL GALLIENI
PLACE DES INVALIDES
RUE SAINT DOMINIQUE
RUE DE BELLECHASSE

Tour Eiffel
PARC DU CHAMP DE MARS
RUE DE GRENELLE
MOTTE PICQUET
AVE DES INVALIDES
RUE DE GRENELLE
BD RASPAIL

PLACE JOFFRE
AVENUE DE LA
AV DE TOURVILLE
JARDIN DE L'INTENDANT
BOULEVARD DES INVALIDES
RUE DE VARENNE
RUE VANEAU

Port de Bir Hakeim
AVENUE DE SUFFREN
AVENUE DE LOWENDAL
AVENUE DE SEGUR
PRESIDENCE DU CONSEIL
PLACE DE FONTENOY
RUE DE BABYLONE

CHAMPS-ELYSÉES AND INVALIDES
Pages 104–115
Street Finder maps 1–3, 6, 7

THE LEFT BANK
Pages 116–127
Street Finder maps 7–9, 12, 13

KEY

■	Major sight
M	Metro station
RER	RER station
🚌	Main bus stop
P	Main car park
✚	Hospital with casualty unit

0 metres   500

0 yards   500